SANTAG
Arbeiten und Untersuchungen zur Keilschriftkunde

Herausgegeben von
Karl Hecker und Walter Sommerfeld

Band 5

2000
Harrassowitz Verlag · Wiesbaden

A Concise Dictionary of Akkadian

edited by

Jeremy Black · Andrew George · Nicholas Postgate

with the assistance of
Tina Breckwoldt, Graham Cunningham,
Marie-Christine Ludwig, Clemens Reichel,
Jonathan Blanchard Smith, Junko Taniguchi
and Cornelia Wunsch

2nd (corrected) printing

2000
Harrassowitz Verlag · Wiesbaden

Users of the dictionary are recommended to consult the web page http://www.soas.ac.uk/cda-archive/ for a list of addenda, corrigenda, and supplementary information about individual entries

Bibliografische Information der Deutschen Nationalbibliothek:
Die Deutsche Nationalbibliothek verzeichnet diese Publikation in der Deutschen Nationalbibliografie; detaillierte bibliografische Daten sind im Internet über http://dnb.d-nb.de abrufbar.

Bibliographic information published by the Deutsche Nationalbibliothek:
The Deutsche Nationalbibliothek lists this publication in the Deutsche Nationalbibliografie; detailed bibliographic data is available in the internet at http://dnb.d-nb.de

For further information about our publishing program have a look at our website http://www.harrassowitz.de/verlag

Printed on permanent/durable paper.
Printing and binding: Memminger MedienCentrum AG
Printed in Germany

ISSN 0179-6365
ISBN 978-3-447-04264-2

Contents

Preface	vii-viii
Introduction	ix-xiv
Key to abbreviations	xv-xvi
Index of verbal roots	xvii-xxiv
Concise dictionary of Akkadian	1-450

Preface

The idea of creating a concise and relatively inexpensive Akkadian-English dictionary was conceived in 1989 by Nicholas Postgate. It was plain from the start that it would need to be based on the *Akkadisches Handwörterbuch* (AHw) of W. von Soden, who gave the scheme his blessing in the autumn of that year. From the start Jeremy Black and Andrew George agreed to collaborate in the venture, and in the course of the work we received considerable assistance from other colleagues with Assyriological experience. Although the three Editors have undertaken different proportions of the work, decisions on the dictionary's content and presentation were made collectively. Our procedure was first to produce a drastically abbreviated English translation of AHw, letter by letter. This was then checked against AHw by a second collaborator. To reduce the risk of misunderstandings of AHw's intentions either the first or the second stage was done in each case by a native German-speaker (Tina Breckwoldt, Marie-Christine Ludwig or Cornelia Wunsch). Each letter has been processed at some stage by at least one of the principal Editors. During or after the first stage the provisional text of each letter was word-processed, and the next major stage was the inclusion of corrections and additions. These came from various sources, including the addenda and corrigenda of AHw itself. The principal concern was to take full advantage of the material in the encyclopaedic Chicago *Assyrian Dictionary* (CAD), now almost complete, wherever this amplified or corrected AHw. Further to this the reviews of both dictionaries in the Assyriological literature were initially harvested by Clemens Reichel, but for each letter responsibility for the difficult task of harmonizing or adjudicating between AHw and CAD where they diverged rested with one of the Editors. There followed a long period during which the complete text was subjected to various editorial and typographical refinements, as well as philological revision and correction.

Acknowledgements

It will be evident that our principal debt by far is to Professor von Soden himself. The production of CDA has taken all of ten years, and this serves to emphasize the single-minded dedication with which the AHw was achieved. Of the collaborators named on the title page Tina Breckwoldt carried out a large part of the initial stage of abbreviation and translation, as well as establishing some of the word-processing guidelines. At the other end of the line Graham Cunningham has had a major role in converting a rather ragged text into a coherent whole, single-handedly re-ordering and re-numbering the lemmata, checking all cross-references, standardizing abbreviations and punctuation, proof-reading, etc. etc. Both these collaborators put their own time and expertise into the project far beyond the call of duty. Our thanks go likewise to Clemens Reichel, to Marie-Christine Ludwig for her considerable input at the first and second stages, and to Cornelia Wunsch for her timely assistance with the last of the second-stage checking. Jonathan Blanchard Smith toiled indefatigably deciphering the handwriting of much of the first draft and committing it to disk. Junko Taniguchi prepared with great thoroughness the necessary documentation for the standardization of the logograms with R. Borger's *Assyrisch-babylonische*

Zeichenliste. To all these collaborators, who often contributed independent philological improvements of their own, we are much indebted, but we must stress that none of them can be held responsible for the inadequacies and especially the inconsistencies which doubtless still exist.

At the very beginning Professor von Soden alerted us to the fact that a *Rückläufiges Wörterbuch des Akkadischen* (SANTAG 1; Harrassowitz 1990) was being produced by his colleague and successor at Münster, Karl Hecker. He has supported our project since that time, and at the final stages of the work, in 1998, he reviewed the manuscript for us and sent a long list of improvements and additions, particularly for the Old Assyrian material. We are grateful to him and Walter Sommerfeld for accepting the CDA in the SANTAG series. Several other scholars have given us assistance with particular words and issues. Alphabetically, we would like to thank David Brown, Stephanie Dalley, John Emerton, John MacGinnis, Alasdair Livingstone, Eleanor Robson, Christopher Walker, and Martin West, as well as the authors of anonymous corrections inscribed in earlier drafts of the dictionary used in our respective libraries. We would like to say a special word of thanks to Michael Jursa and his colleagues for his unwitting contribution in the shape of the lists of words which regularly appear in the *Archiv für Orientforschung*.

Given that our intention has been to create a work tool for students, we have striven to keep the cost of the volume as low as possible, and the text has been supplied to the printers in camera-ready form. For the first nine years of our work, which was done on a series of Macintosh machines, we used a font called "Raydia", designed and given to us by Roy Norman. We are very grateful for this: although with the passage of time it has been overhauled for technical reasons, his font made a substantial contribution to the dictionary. For the final camera-ready version we converted the font to "Assyrian Dictionary", originally generated for the Oriental Institute in Chicago. Guy Deutscher gave unstintingly of his time and computing expertise in the final stages of producing the printout. For ever-present help with computing resources in Trinity College, Cambridge, our thanks are due to Laura Cordy and Peter Thompson. Nicholas Postgate would also like to include a special word of thanks to Neil Mitchison, on whose verandah in Brebbia large sections of the first draft were transcribed.

Over the years we have had a great deal of financial assistance for the support of our collaborators. Our thanks are due to the British Academy, to the C.H.W. Johns Memorial Fund and to the Master and Fellows of Trinity College in Cambridge, to the Shillito Fund and the Faculty of Oriental Studies in the University of Oxford, and to the School of Oriental and African Studies in the University of London.

Jeremy Black
Faculty of Oriental Studies
University of Oxford

Andrew George
School of Oriental and African Studies
University of London

Nicholas Postgate
Faculty of Oriental Studies
University of Cambridge

July 1999

Introduction

The purpose of the dictionary

The demand for a relatively short and inexpensive dictionary of Akkadian is undeniable, especially in the English-speaking world. The only complete and sufficiently modern dictionary of Akkadian available hitherto is Wolfram von Soden's *Akkadisches Handwörterbuch* (AHw). While anyone working seriously on the textual riches of the ancient Near East will end up reading German, it is not encouraging for beginners in Akkadian to be told that they must learn German first. The Chicago *Assyrian Dictionary* (CAD) still lacks several volumes (at the time of writing, P, R, T, Ṭ and U), and even more than AHw it is far too expensive for a beginner or for those with a non-specialist interest in the language. Moreover, there is the purely physical consideration that neither dictionary can be conveniently transported in even the most capacious briefcase.

Our experience in our respective universities suggests that for these reasons *A Concise Dictionary of Akkadian* (CDA) will be much used by students, and in their first year or two this is perfectly appropriate. Nevertheless, we must stress here that it is in no way a substitute for the two fundamental Akkadian dictionaries. Far more than in modern or even Classical languages, these are essential research tools, which need to be constantly consulted by anyone working on the original texts. There are several reasons for this. The CDA does not give textual references, so that the contexts in which a word is used cannot be controlled, which is essential as soon as finer nuances of meaning require to be established. Nor can our succinct presentation convey the relative rarity of many words, or indeed the degree of uncertainty surrounding their normalization, meaning, or even their very existence. In AHw and CAD the writing of the word is given sign by sign for each textual passage. The normalized transcription of each Akkadian word is derived from an interactive process drawing on the attested writings and our perceptions of the morphophonemic structure of Akkadian. Especially with infrequent words the attested writings can often admit of more than one defensible normalization, an ambiguity to which the format of CDA cannot do full justice. The actual writing of a word may also include a determinative which can help to define the area of meaning (e.g. giš for wooden and kuš for leather items), and this too is not usually given in CDA. Further, CDA does not list the lexical equivalences, whether with Sumerian or synonyms in Akkadian, and these too can play a major role in establishing a word's meaning.

CAD, AHw and new material

As explained in the Preface, the CDA is based on Professor von Soden's AHw. This means that unless there was a compelling reason to the contrary, we have accepted the normalization and translation of a word as given in AHw. We have however used different principles for determining the alphabetical order of the entries, and adopted a simplified numbering system for words normalized identically. The publication of AHw was spread over more than twenty years, from 1958 to 1981. There are inevitably changes and inconsistencies in its format and content. Some of these will be reflected in the CDA, though we have of course noted the detailed addenda and corrigenda at the end of the third volume of AHw. In preparing these, Professor von Soden took account of relevant volumes of the CAD, when these existed; for the CDA we have checked our first draft against all published volumes of the CAD. In the Nachwort to AHw (in Band III) Professor von Soden explains that the pressure of time did not allow him always to take account of newly emerging philological commentaries or all of the reviews devoted to both the AHw and the CAD in journals. We have consulted such reviews, as also the lists of words treated in Assyriological literature published in the *Archiv für Orientforschung*, and some of the principal textual editions which have appeared since the completion of the AHw itself. Consequently there are additions and occasional corrections to AHw incorporated in the CDA. The style of the dictionary does not permit us to provide chapter and verse in justification of such changes, and the Editors are considering how best to make such justification available to colleagues. We must stress that there are certainly many more improvements which could have been made on the basis of the Assyriological literature published since 1982 but which we have not taken on board, and significant fresh material appears every year. We would be grateful to receive suggestions from colleagues for addenda and corrigenda for an eventual revised edition.

Principles for ordering of lemmata

The words ("lemmata") are arranged in the order of the English alphabet, ignoring any internal brackets and using the generally accepted conventions that dotted letters (*ṣ* and *ṭ*) follow the undotted letter, and *š* follows *ṣ*. We have not used the symbol *ś* in our dictionary, although this is found occasionally in AHw in some Old Akkadian contexts, nor have we used the vowel *o*, nor a symbol for the velar nasal in some loanwords from Sumerian. In our transcriptions and in the alphabetical ordering we use the letter *y* instead of the *j* of AHw (and of CAD, which follows German practice). This means that I and Y entries are separated from each other, but in a single volume this should not cause inconvenience.

Those familiar with other Semitic languages should note that neither /h/ nor /ḥ/ is recognized in transcriptions of Akkadian, although there is good reason to think that the difference between the two phonemes is reflected in the realization of an underlying adjacent /a/ vowel as *a* or *e* respectively. A glottal stop indicated in the cuneiform script is often represented in our transcription by an aleph ('); this need not always have been an aleph in origin, and again the difference between a Semitic aleph and 'ayin is reflected in the realization of an underlying adjacent /a/ vowel as *a* or *e*. This is not the place to discuss the realization of other phonemes surviving in Arabic such as the ghayin.

The only other problem with the alphabetization concerns letters with a macron, for long vowels, or a circumflex, for contracted vowels, and words transcribed with an aleph ('). The principle by which these are ordered is relatively unimportant to the user, since all words displaying the same basic letters are placed together. AHw and CAD have quite different practices, and ours is different again. To satisfy the curious our practice is as follows: words are first ordered alphabetically ignoring macrons and circumflexes, so that all words containing the same letters in the same order are found together. Within the resulting groups of words, starting from the beginning of each word, words containing unmarked vowels are placed before those containing vowels with macrons, and both are placed before vowels with circumflexes. As for aleph, it does not count as a "letter" for alphabetization purposes, and does not have a position in the alphabetical sequence. A word containing an aleph will be placed immediately after the same sequence of letters without an aleph, or in the place where that word would be if it existed.

Following AHw the head-words are presented in their notional Old Babylonian forms, in contrast to the CAD which adopts a Standard Babylonian version. This has certain consequences for the order of the lemmata, most significantly that words with an initial /w/ are found under W, and verbs with /ī/ as middle radical are to be sought under their uncontracted form (e.g. *diānum*). There are inevitably difficulties with words whose root has /w/ as a first radical. In some cases one derivative from the root (e.g. the verb) may be attested in Old Babylonian and listed under W, while another derivative (e.g. an adjective) may only be known from later dialects, in which case it will probably be found in A. In these cases the derivations and derivatives listed at the end of the entries should make the position clear.

Mimation (that is, the final *-m* of the nominative case ending) is ignored in the alphabetic ordering of the entries; this usually makes very little difference to the order, but note that the final *-m* of dative or loc.-adv. forms *is* observed, and this can have a significant effect on the position of some entries, such as *-kum* or *aḫum*.

Words with identical transcriptions, or differing only by the presence or absence of mimation, are differentiated by Roman numerals (e.g. *kibsu(m)* I, *kibsu* II). In CDA only the substantive entries (shown in a **bold** font) are numbered thus; where we also list an identically transcribed word or words as a variant of a word or words whose substantive entry is elsewhere (shown in *italics*), a cross-reference to that entry is given, but unlike AHw further Roman numerals are not assigned to the variant(s).

The lemma

Nouns are listed in the nominative singular, as are adjectives in their masculine form. A few nouns are cited in nominative plural form where a singular is not attested. Verbs are listed in the nominative infinitive of the G stem, where that stem is attested (or has been reconstructed for the convenience of the dictionary, in which case the reconstructed form may be marked with an asterisk, e.g. **aḫû(m)*). In most instances where a verb is not attested in the G stem it will be listed under the D, Š or N form, whichever is attested. Note that such forms can be tracked down by use of the index of roots (pp. xvii-xxiv). Quadriliteral verbs are listed under their N stem, if this is attested, where the Š stem will also be found; if only the Š stem is known, seek it under Š.

As in AHw the lemmata are presented in their Old Babylonian or Old Assyrian form, where attested. In these cases, as with the occasional word attested only in Old Akkadian, the form will normally retain its mimation. If the word is also attested in later dialects the mimation is bracketed, e.g. *eleppu(m)*, and if it is not attested in any of the earlier dialects, no mimation is shown. As mentioned above, the mimation is ignored in the alphabetization. There are special problems with Assyrian forms, and the following guidelines, which were adopted late in the day, may not have been applied fully consistently. Where a Babylonian form exists it is used as the head-word, and Assyrian forms which differ in accordance with regular changes between the two dialects are not separately specified: thus, for instance, the Assyrian *emādu(m)* is not specified in the entry *emēdu(m)* since this is an entirely predictable change, and the same applies to short syllables subject to vowel assimilation, such as *nēmudu* for the Babylonian *nēmedu*. Nonetheless, in some cases such forms have been mentioned for the user's convenience. Where, on the other hand, no Babylonian form is attested, the word is cited in its Assyrian form. Thus the verb *etāku* is known only from Assyrian texts and we have refrained from inventing its Babylonian equivalent, so that it is listed as *etāku* (not *etēku*). Similar considerations apply e.g. to *wazzunum* and nouns such as *utḫurum*. Again the list of roots (pp. xvii-xxiv) should assist the user in tracking down some of these less predictable entries.

After the first form of the lemma, shown in bold type, other forms may be listed, in italics. These may be contemporary variants, or the forms attested in other dialects either as a result of predictable dialectal differences or less regular changes. The different dialects are often specified, but the caveats applying to the dialectal distribution of the word as a whole (see below) also apply here. In many cases we are at present unable to determine the correct normalization of a word, because of ambiguities in the way it is written in cuneiform: in such cases the format is **x** (or *y*), implying that one or other of the forms is possible (but not both).

Difficulties tracking down a word

The ambiguities of the cuneiform script frequently make it difficult to track a word down, especially for the student starting out. Apart from problems caused by incorrect grammatical analysis of verbal forms, most elusive words will be located by trying one of three strategies. The first is to look under *e* instead of *i*, or vice versa: many cuneiform signs do not distinguish the two vowels (such as *li* = *le*), and even signs which can (such as *mi* and *me*) are often used "wrongly" for each other. In general, AHw and hence CDA normalize to *e* (rather than *i*) more frequently than CAD, and in particular the rule is usually observed that /i/ followed by /r/ or /ḫ/ in a closed syllable is realized as /e/ (see GAG §9b). Hence the /pirsum/ form of *parāsum* has to be sought under *persum*. A second frequent difficulty is posed by the inability of many cuneiform signs to differentiate voiced from unvoiced and emphatic from unemphatic consonants. Thus the sign DA may be read as *da* or *ṭa*, AD as *ad*, *at* or *aṭ*, BU can be *bu* and *pu*, and UB can be *ub* or *up*; etc. etc. This is in most cases purely a graphic uncertainty caused by the multivalence of the sign, and it is not the duty of the dictionary to alert the user to all these options. (One particular problem of Old Babylonian texts is posed by cases where a word with a written *ḫ* may alternate with forms showing no consonant in that position (e.g. *(ḫ)alālu*). The real nature of the phoneme is difficult to determine, and it is not assisted by the use of the AḪ sign, which in OB may also be used for a glottal stop, and only after 1500 was differentiated from the new sign A'). Thirdly, especially in earlier texts the scribes often did not indicate double consonants. Hence those reading cuneiform texts need to bear in mind the possibility that where they see only a single written consonant it may be shown by us as doubled.

Further details of the lemma

Where desirable to avoid uncertainty, a word may be followed by a statement identifying its part of speech (e.g. adv.) or by f. for feminine nouns not instantly recognizable as such, pl. for nouns cited in their plural form, or pl. tant. for nouns cited and thought to occur solely in the plural. There may also follow, introduced by f. or pl., feminine or plural forms of the word; these are usually only given where they diverge from the expected.

The principal meaning(s)

The meaning of a word is normally presented between inverted commas, thus "elephant". For verbs, the English infinitive is used at first, thus "to cut off", but the "to" is not repeated further on in the article. Alternative English renderings of the same area of meaning are separated by commas, "to gain control of, acquire", while distinct meanings may be separated by semicolons, "to restore; have success". When the meaning of a word is not known or unclear, the dictionary states mng. unkn., mng. uncl. or mng. uncert., categories which obviously overlap. Following AHw practice, single inverted commas are sometimes used to convey the "original" or "etymological" meaning of a word, a concept which may overlap with "literally". The symbol ~ before a meaning signifies "approximately". In many cases, especially with nouns, the broad area of meaning is certain but the precise translation impossible to determine; with these generic meanings the broad area is indicated between parentheses, e.g. (a plant) or (a disease). If a precise but tentative identification can be suggested we have tended to use the formulation: (a plant, phps.) "parsley".

The periods of attestation

After the principal meaning(s) are shown the dialects in which the word is attested, unless it is encountered generally throughout the Babylonian and Assyrian dialects of Akkadian, in which case in keeping with AHw practice no dialectal distribution is given. After Old Akkadian in the 3rd millennium

BC, we distinguish the two main dialects of the vernacular, each of which is divided chronologically into Old, Middle or Neo-Babylonian (OB, MB and NB) and Old, Middle or Neo-Assyrian (OA, MA and NA). These main periods may be be further refined by geographical qualifications, such as (N.Mes.), (Bogh.) or (Urar.). After about 1500 BC, in a parallel development, a more or less degraded version of Old Babylonian was preserved by the scribal tradition in Babylonia, in Assyria, and in the various surrounding centres where Akkadian was used as a legal or scholarly medium. This is called "jungbabylonisch" by German philologists, which corresponds broadly to the term "Standard Babylonian" introduced for the CAD. However, the two terms do not coincide exactly and we have elected to retain the abbreviation "jB", partly because it is very familiar to Assyriologists, and partly to emphasize that the period attribution is that of AHw. It is probably not necessary to underline that there was always a degree of cross-fertilization between the "jB" literary dialect and the contemporary vernaculars, especially Middle and Neo-Babylonian.

There is only one important respect in which our period designations diverge from AHw, and that is in our abandonment of the category "spätbabylonisch" (spB). The CAD uses the equivalent term "Late Babylonian", but differently at different stages of the dictionary's compilation. The task of establishing our own criteria and applying them to each entry consistently was too daunting, and we decided that for our purposes the simplest solution was to include all spB (and CAD LB) references under Neo-Babylonian. Users of CDA should therefore be aware that NB now includes both the later vernacular (after 625 BC on) and other texts of the Persian and Seleucid periods not written in jB or Standard Babylonian.

It is important to emphasize that these chronological and geographical categories cannot reflect the real distribution of each word's usage, only its **attestations**. The periods listed refer only to the texts from which the word is known to us, not to the periods in which the word may really have been used. In the course of preparing the CDA one of the commonest changes from AHw has been the addition of new period attestations, and we can be confident that as new texts are found many of our words will turn up outside their presently known range of dialect and time.

While mentioning dialectal distribution we should refer to the limits of our textual catchment area. Generally the dictionary includes words in Akkadian texts from the earliest Old Akkadian in the 24th century BC to the latest cuneiform texts of the 1st century AD. Akkadian, like 20th century English, was a broad church, and under "Akkadian texts" we include even the most divergent products of Hurrian or Canaanite scribes. This means that the dictionary does include loan words from other languages (such as Hurrian, Sumerian and West Semitic languages) provided they have been incorporated into an Akkadian text; however such words are not included when they are listed as equivalents of Akkadian words in bilingual or multilingual texts. In general, Akkadian words attested solely in texts in other languages are not included, but where a known Akkadian word is encountered, for instance, in a Hittite or Elamite text, this may be recorded.

Amplified meanings

After the statement of dialectal attestation there follows amplification of the meaning(s), which differs in its arrangement from entry to entry. In the case of verbs the entry is arranged according to the verbal stems attested (G, D, Š and N, with tn and t forms of each where appropriate; and the occasional ŠD and R stems). The vowel of class (*a/a*, *i/i*, *u/u*, *a/u* etc.) is usually stated for the G stem, together with other details of the conjugation which are not to be predicted. In longer entries where the further meanings can be divided into significant groups they may be numbered (1., 2., etc.). These groups are not intended to correspond to similar subdivisions in the corresponding AHw entries. Such numbering is also used in cases, mostly nouns, where quite distinct meanings are given under a single entry.

Logograms

Logographic writings of a word, usually borrowed from Sumerian, are shown in small Roman capitals between square brackets, thus [UDU]. They are usually placed after the dialectal distribution, but different logographic writings may apply to parts of an entry only (e.g. to the D stem of a verb, or a specialized usage of a noun), in which case they are shown in the appropriate place. No uniformity prevails among cuneiform specialists in the transcription of logograms. With rare exceptions we have adopted the values given in R. Borger, *Assyrisch-babylonische Zeichenliste* (3. Auflage, with Supplement; Alter Orient und Altes Testament 33/33A, Neukirchen-Vluyn 1986), since it seems best that the work-tools of the Assyriologist should be as consistent with each other as possible. Borger's choice of transcription is intended not merely to indicate the sign in use, but also to reproduce the presumed Sumerian value associated with that meaning. Hence, in contrast to AHw, we write [MÁ.GUR8] rather than [MÁ.TU] as the logogram for *makūru(m)*; this does not imply that AHw was wrong, but is a necessary consequence of our exclusion of the lexical section of the AHw entries, from which the user can usually identify the "correct" Sumerian values.

Derivations and derivatives

Akkadian is unusual among Semitic languages in that our modern dictionaries are arranged alphabetically word by word, instead of by roots. This is a consequence of two considerations: there are too many foreign imports from languages which do not share the Semitic word structures (primarily of course Sumerian), and in too many cases the (usually) triliteral root of an "indigenous" Akkadian word cannot be confidently identified. In this respect we have followed the practice of AHw and CAD, but one can only regret the consequent separation of closely related words from their close relatives, so that, for instance, *kīnu(m)*, *mukinnu(m)* and *takittum* have to be sought in different parts of the dictionary. As a poor mitigation of this separation, at the end of each entry for an "indigenous" Akkadian word are listed words "derived" from it (preceded by the symbol >), and/or a word from which it "derives" (preceded by <). It will hardly need stressing that one form does not always strictly derive from another, but for pure convenience we have adopted the convention that the verbal infinitive is primary, and other forms derive from it. In some cases, where two closely related forms are placed next to each other, we have not felt the need to state their relationship (e.g. *gašīšiš* and *gašīšu(m)*).

When a word is borrowed into Akkadian from elsewhere, the derivation section merely indicates the presumed language of origin (preceded by <), e.g. Sum., Hurr., W.Sem., Ug., Hitt., Elam. etc.

Cross-references

After the derivatives section (and elsewhere) there may also be cross-references introduced by an arrow (→). These often go back to the "rod-and-ring" symbol adopted by AHw, and like it they are intended to draw the user's attention to another entry for a variety of different reasons. Similarly with the many italicized head-words which are followed only by an arrow referring the user to a main entry, the form in question may not always be listed under the main entry since some are forms not acknowledged by CDA but listed solely to assist the user in tracking down the correct entry. There are however many fewer such cross-references than in AHw, partly because the density of entries on the page makes them less necessary. In particular cross-references to an entry have generally not been included where they would have come immediately before or after it.

Key to abbreviations

abbr.	**stands for**
abbr.	abbreviation, abbreviated
absol.	absolute(ly)
abstr.	abstract
acc.	accusative
Achaem.	Achaemenid inscriptions
act.	active
adj.	adjective, adjectival
adv.	adverb(ial)
Akk.	Akkadian
Alal.	Alalakh
Am.	El-Amarna
appos.	apposition
Arab.	Arabic
Aram.	Aramaic
arch.	archaic, archaizing
archit.	architecture, architectural
Ass.	Assyrian
astr.	astrological, astronomical
Bab.	Babylonian
BC	before Christ
Bogh.	Boghazköy
c.	*circa*
caus.	causative
cf.	comparer
cohort.	cohortative
col.	colophon(s)
coll.	collective
comb.	combination(s)
comm.	commentary
condit.	conditional
conj.	(subordinating) conjunction
dat.	dative
denom.	denominative
descr.	description
desig.	designation, designating
det.	determinative
dimin.	diminutive
dir.	direct
distrib.	distributive
DN	divine name
du.	dual
Eg.	Egypt(ian)
e.g.	*exempli gratia*
Elam.	Elamite
ellipt.	elliptical
epith.	epithet
erron.	erroneous(ly)
esp.	especially
Ešn.	Ešnunna
etc.	*et cetera*
etym.	etymology
euph.	euphemism, euphemistic
ext.	extispicy
f.	feminine
fact.	factitive
fDN	female divine name
fig. etym.	*figura etymologica*
fPN	female personal name
freq.	frequent(ly)
GAG	W. von Soden, *Grundriss der akkadischen Grammatik* (3., ergänzte Auflage; Rome 1985)
gen.	genitive
gener.	general(ly)
Gilg.	Epic of Gilgameš
Gk.	Greek
gramm.	grammatical
hendiad.	hendiadys
Hitt.	Hittite
Hurr.	Hurrian
hypocorist.	hypocoristic
i.e.	*id est*
imper.	imperative
incl.	including
indic.	indicative
indir.	indirect
Indo-Iran.	Indo-Iranian
infin.	infinitive
ingress.	ingressive
intens.	intensive
interj.	interjection
interrog.	interrogative
intrans.	intransitive
Iran.	Iranian
irreg.	irregular
iter.	iterative
jB	jungbabylonisch
Kass.	Kassite

leg.	legal
lex.	lexical(ly)
lit.	literature, literary
liter.	literal(ly)
loc.-adv.	locative-adverbial
log.	logogram
lw.	loanword
m.	masculine
MA	Middle Assyrian
mag.	magic(al)
math.	mathematical
MB	Middle Babylonian
med.	medicine, medical(ly)
metath.	metathesis(ed)
meteor.	meteorological
misc.	miscellaneous
Mit.	Mittani
MN	month name
mng.	meaning
myth.	mythological
NA	Neo-Assyrian
NB	Neo-Babylonian
neg.	negative
N.Mes.	North Mesopotamia
nom.	nominative
nom. unit.	*nomen unitatis*
OA	Old Assyrian
OAkk	Old Akkadian
OB	Old Babylonian
obj.	object
obl.	oblique
occas.	occasional(ly)
om.	omen(s)
OPers.	Old Persian
opp.	opposite
orig.	originally
o.'s	one's
o.s.	oneself
p.	page
pass.	passive
perf.	perfect
pers.	person(al)
phps.	perhaps
pl.	plural
PlN	place name
pl. tant.	*plurale tantum* (plural only)
PN	personal name
poet.	poetic
pos.	positive
poss.	possessive
prec.	precative
pred.	predicate, predicative
prep.	preposition(al)
pres.	present
Pre-Sarg.	Pre-Sargonic
pret.	preterite
prob.	probable, probably
prof.	profession(al)
proh.	prohibitive
pron.	pronoun, pronominal
ptcl.	particle
ptcp.	participle
rdg.	reading
recipr.	reciprocal(ly)
ref.	referring
refl.	reflexive
rel.	relative
rit.	ritual
RN	royal name
roy. inscr.	royal inscription(s)
Sanskr.	Sanskrit
Sem.	Semitic
sg.	singular
sim.	similar(ly)
s.o.	someone
sq.	square
st. abs.	status absolutus
stat.	stative
st. constr.	status constructus
s.th.	something
subj.	subject
subjunct.	subjunctive
subord.	subordinate
subst.	substantive(s), substantival
suff.	suffix(es)
Sum.	Sumerian
syll.	syllable, syllabic(ally)
syn.	synonym
term.-adv.	terminative-adverbial
TN	temple name
topog.	topographical(ly)
trans.	transitive
transf.	transferred
Ug.	Ugarit(ic)
uncert.	uncertain
uncl.	unclear
unkn.	unknown
Urar.	Urarṭu, Urarṭian
usu.	usually
var.	variant(s)
vb.	verb(al)
vent.	ventive
voc.	vocative
vol.	volume
W.Sem.	West Semitic
wr.	writing, written

Symbols

~	approximately
<	comes from
>	goes to
→	see
*	unattested form

Index of verbal roots

This index refers the reader to those lemmata which are verbs in which the given root letters occur. It is intended for practical purposes, to assist the user in identifying a particular verb and find its entry in the dictionary, and does not necessarily carry any implications about the history or etymology of the verb. It does not refer to other parts of speech. The aleph sign used here (') stands for all weaknesses, including medial ā, ī, and ū, but excluding initial w.

'''	ḫaḫû II
''d	âdu
''l	âlu; e'ēlu(m)
''r	êru(m)
''ṣ	wiāṣum
''š	âšu
'b'	apû III; ebû II
'bb	ebēbu(m)
'bd	abātu(m) II
'bḫ	ebēḫu
'bk	abāku(m) I.II
'bl	abālu(m); apālu(m) I; ebēlu; wabālu(m)
'br	abāru(m) III; ebēru(m) I.II
'bs	uppusu II
'bt	abātu(m) I.II
'bṭ	ebēṭu(m) I.II; ubbuṭu IV
'd'	edû(m) II
'db	edēpu(m)
'dd	edēdu(m)
'dḫ/k	edēḫu(m)
'dl	edēlu(m)
'dm	adāmum
'dp	edēpu(m)
'dq	edēqu(m)
'dr	adāru(m) I.II; edēru(m)
'dš	edēšu(m)
'g'	egû(m) III
'gg	agāgu(m); ekēku; eqēqu
'gm	agāmu
'gr	agāru(m); egēru(m)
'ḫ'	aḫû(m) II; ḫaḫû II
'ḫr	aḫāru(m)
'ḫz	aḫāzu(m)
'k'	ekû(m) II
'kd	ekēdu(m)
'kk	ekēku
'kl	akālu(m); ekēlu(m)
'km	akāmu II; ekēmu(m)
'kp	ekēpu(m); ukkupu
'kṣ	ekēṣu
'kš	akāšu(m)
'l'	elû(m) III; utlellû(m)
'l''	šutelū'u
'ld	(w)alādu(m)
'lḫ	elēḫu(m)
'lk	alāku(m)
'll	alālu(m) II.III; elēlu(m) II.III
'll'	ne'ellû
'lp	alāpu(m); elēpu(m)
'lṣ	elēṣu(m)
'lt	alātu(m); ḫalātum
'm'	amûm V; ewûm I; itmû
'md	emēdu(m)
'mm	emēmu(m)
'mq	emēqu(m) I.II
'mr	amāru(m) I.II; emēru(m) I.II
'ms	amāṣu
'mṣ	amāṣu; emēṣu(m) I.II
'mš	amāšu; emēšu
'n'	enû(m) III
'nb	enēbu
'nḫ	anāḫu(m) I.II
'nn	enēnu(m) I.II.III.IV; utnēnu(m) II
'nq	enēqu(m)
'nš	enēšu(m)
'nt	enētu
'p'	apû III; epû(m) II
'pl	apālu(m) I.II; uppulu(m) II
'pp	apāpum
'pq	epēqu(m)
'pr	apāru(m); ebēru(m) I; epēru(m)
'ps	epēsum I; uppusu II
'pš	epēšu(m) II
'q'	eqû(m); uqqû(m) II
'qb	ekēpu(m)
'qq	eqēqu
'qr	(w)aqāru(m)
'r'	arû(m) III.IV.VI; erû(m) III; warûm II
'rb	erēbu(m) I; nērubu(m)
'rd	arādu; (w)arādu(m)
'rḫ	arāḫu(m) I.II; erēḫu
'rk.	arāku(m)
'rm	arāmu
'rp	erēpu(m)
'rr	arāru(m) II.III; erēru(m); na'arruru(m)
'rs'	šutērsû(m)
'rš	erēšu(m) I.II; *warāšum
's'	azû(m) I; esû
'sd	ussudu
'sḫ	esēḫu(m) I; ezēḫu(m)
'sk	esēḫu(m) I; esēqu(m)
'sl	esēlu
'sm	(w)asāmu(m)
'sp	esēpu(m)
'sq	esēqu(m)
'sr	esēru(m) II.III
'ṣ'	eṣû; (w)aṣû(m)
'ṣb	waṣābum
'ṣd	eṣēdu(m) II
'ṣl	eṣēlu(m)
'ṣn	eṣēnu(m)
'ṣp	eṣēpu(m); waṣābum
'ṣr	esēru(m) II; eṣēru(m); uṣṣuru(m) II.III

'š'	ešē'u(m); ešû(m) IV.V; išû(m)
'šb	ešēbu; (w)ašābu(m)
'šr	ašāru(m); ešēru(m); (w)ašāru(m)
'šš	ašāšu(m) III.IV; uššušu(m) III
't'	nentû
'tk	atāku; etāku
'tl	itūlu(m)
'tm	etēmu(m)
'tn	etēmu(m)
'tq	etēqu(m)
'tr	(w)atāru(m)
'ṭ'	eṭû II
'ṭl	eṭēlu(m)
'ṭr	eṭēru(m) I.II
'w'	awûm; ewûm I.II
'z'	azû(m) I; ezû(m) I.II
'zb	ezēbu(m)
'zḫ	ezēḫu(m)
'zr	azāru; esēru(m) II; ezēru
'zz	ezēzu(m); izuzzum
b''	bâ'u(m) I.II; bu''û(m) II
b'd	biātum
b'l	ba'ālu(m); bâlu; bêlu(m); bullu I
b'r	bâru(m) I.II.III; bêru(m) I.II
b'š	ba'āšu; bâšu(m) I.II; be'ēšu(m); bêšu(m)
b't	biātum
b'ṭ	bâṭu
bbl	babālu(m); wabālu(m)
bd'	bedûm
bdd	buddudu
bdḫ	badāḫu
bdm	badāmu
bdq	batāqu(m)
bdš	badāšu
bḫ'	baḫû II; bu''û(m) II
bḫr	beḫēru; buḫḫuru
bḫš	buḫḫušu
bk'	bakû(m)
bl'	belû(m) II
blkt	nabalkutu(m) II
bll	balālu(m)
blm	balāmu
blṣ	balāṣu I.II
blṭ	balāṭu(m) II
bn'	banû(m) II.IV
bnn	bunnunu
bql	baqālu
bqm/n	baqāmu(m)
bqr	baqāru(m); buqquru; (w)aqāru(m)
bqš	baqāšu
br'	barû(m) I.III.IV; berû(m) II; bitrû II
brḫ	barāḫu
brm	barāmu(m) I.II
brq	barāqu(m)
brr	barāru
brṣ	barāṣu
brš	barāšu
bsl	basālu
bsm	bussumu(m) II
bsr	bussuru(m)
bṣr	baṣāru(m)
bṣṣ	baṣāṣu
bšl	bašālu(m)
bšm	bašāmu(m) II.III
bšš	bašāšum
bš'	bašû(m)
btq	batāqu(m)
btr	butturu II
bṭl	baṭālu(m)
bṭ'	bedûm
bz'/ḫ	bazā'um
d'b	da'āpu
d'k	dâku(m)
d'l	dâlu(m)
d'm	da'āmu(m) I.II
d'n	diānum
d'p	da'āpu; dêpu
d'r	duārum
d'ṣ	dâṣu(m)
d'š	diāšum
dbb	dabābu(m) II
dbq	dubbuqu
dbr	dabāru I
dgl	dagālu(m)
dḫ'	daḫû(m) II
dḫs	duḫḫusu
dk'	dekû(m) II
dkk	dakāku(m) I.II
dkm	dakāmu
dkš	dakāšu(m)
dl'	dalû II
dlḫ	dalāḫu(m)
dll	dalālu(m) I.II
dlb	dalāpu(m)
dlp	dalāpu(m)
dm'	dawûm; dummû
dmm	damāmu(m)
dmq	damāqu(m)
dmṣ	damāṣu
dmš	damāšu
dn'	danû(m)
dnn	danānu(m) II
dpn	dapānu(m) II
dpr	duppuru(m) I
dqq	daqāqu
dqš	daqāšu(m)
dr'	darû(m); derû; durrû(m)
drg	darākum II
drk	darāku(m) I.II.III
drq	darākum II
drr	darāru(m) I.II
drs	darāsu(m)
drš	darāšu(m) I.II; darāsu(m)
dš'	dešû(m)
dšp	dašāpu(m)
dw'	dawûm
g''	gâ'u; ga'ûm
g'r	giāru(m)
g's	gêsu(m) I; gêšu(m) I
g'š	gâšu(m) I.II; gêšu(m) I.II
gbb	kabābu II
gdd	gadādu
gdm	gadāmu
gḫb	guḫḫubu
gl'	galû II
glb	gullubu(m) II
gld	galātu(m)
gll	galālu II; gullulu(m)
glš	galāšu; gullušu
glt	galātu(m)
glt'	nagaltû
gm'	gamā'u
gml	gamālu(m)
gmm	gamāmu
gmr	gamāru(m) II
gmt	gummutu
gn'	genû
gnḫ	ganāḫu
gnn	ganānu
gnṣ	ganāṣu
gp'	gepû
gpr	gapāru(m)
gpš	gapāšu(m)
gr'	gerû(m)
grd	garādu(m)
grḫ	garāšu
grm	garāmu
grn	qarānu(m)
grr	qarāru(m); šugarruru(m)
grṣ	karāṣu(m)
grš	garāšu(m); qarāšu(m)
grš'	*nagaršû
gsṣ	gazāzu(m); kaṣāṣu(m) I
gš'	gešû
gšr	gašāru(m)
gšš	gašāšu(m)
gz'	gutezzû
gzz	gazāzu(m)
ḫ'b	ḫâbu; ḫiāpum
ḫ'd	ḫiādu; ḫiāṭu(m)
ḫ'l	ḫâlu; ḫiālum
ḫ'p	ḫâpu; ḫiāpum
ḫ'q	ḫâqu; ḫiāqu(m)
ḫ'r	ḫiāru(m)
ḫ's	ḫâsu
ḫ'š	ḫâšu(m) I.II; ḫiāšum
ḫ't	ḫâtum
ḫ'ṭ	ḫiāṭu(m)

ḫb'	ḫabû(m) II.III.IV; kubbû II
ḫbb	ḫabābu(m)
ḫbl	ḫabālu(m) II.III.IV
ḫbr	ḫabāru(m) I.II; kabāru(m)
ḫbṣ	ḫabāṣu(m) I.II
ḫbš	ḫabāšu(m) I.II
ḫbt	ḫabātu(m) I.II.III.IV
ḫd'	ḫadû(m) III.IV
ḫdd	ḫadādu I.II; kadādu
ḫdl	ḫadālu(m) I.II
ḫdq	ḫadāqu
ḫdr	adāru(m) I
ḫdš	ḫadāšu
ḫḫ'	ḫaḫû II
ḫk'	ḫakûm
ḫkm	ḫakāmu(m)
ḫkr	ḫakāru(m)
ḫl'	ḫalûm III; ḫelû(m) II
ḫlb	ḫalābu
ḫll	alālu II; ḫalālu(m) I.II.III
ḫlp	ḫalāpu(m) I.II
ḫlq	ḫalāqu(m)
ḫlṣ	ḫalāṣu(m); ḫarāṣu(m)
ḫlṣ'	neḫelṣû(m)
ḫlš	ḫalāšu(m)
ḫlt	ḫalātum
ḫm'	ḫamā'u; ḫamû I.II; ḫawû
ḫmd	ḫamādu(m)
ḫml	ḫamālu
ḫmm	ḫamāmu(m)
ḫmr	ḫamāru(m); ḫemēru
ḫmṣ	ḫamāṣu(m)
ḫmš	ḫamāšu(m) I.II; kamāsu(m) II
ḫmṭ	ḫamāṭu(m) II.III
ḫn'	ḫanû(m) II; ḫunnû(m)
ḫnb	ḫanābu(m)
ḫnm	ḫanāmum
ḫnn	ḫanānu
ḫnp	ḫanāpu I.II
ḫnq	ḫanāqu(m)
ḫnṣ	ḫanāṣu
ḫnš	kanāšu(m) I
ḫp'	ḫapûm; ḫepû(m) II
ḫpd	ḫuppudum II
ḫpp	ḫapāpu I.II
ḫpr	ḫapāru(m) I.II; ḫepēru
ḫpt	ḫapātum
ḫqm	ḫuqqumum
ḫqr	ḫaqāru
ḫr'	ḫarû IV; ḫerû(m) II
ḫrb	ḫarābu; ḫarāpu(m) I
ḫrbš	naḫarbušu
ḫrd	ḫarādu(m) III.IV
ḫrk	ḫarāku
ḫrm	ḫarāmu(m) I.II
ḫrmm	naḫarmumu
ḫrmṭ	naḫarmuṭu(m)
ḫrp	ḫarāpu(m) I.II
ḫrr	arāru(m) III; ḫarāru(m) I; šuḫarruru(m) II; šuḫruru
ḫrs	ḫarāsu
ḫrṣ	ḫarāṣu(m); karāṣu(m)
ḫrš	ḫarāšu(m) I.II.III
ḫršš	naḫaršušu
ḫrṭ	ḫarāṭum
ḫs'	ḫesû(m)
ḫsp	ḫasāpu(m)
ḫsr	ḫasāru(m)
ḫss	ḫasāsu(m)
ḫṣ'	ḫazûm II
ḫṣb	ḫaṣābu(m) I.II
ḫṣn	ḫaṣānu(m)
ḫṣṣ	*aṣāṣu(m) I.II
ḫš'	ḫašû(m) IV.V.VI
ḫšb	ḫašābu
ḫšḫ	ḫašāḫu(m)
ḫšl	ḫašālu(m)
ḫšr	ḫašāru
ḫšš	ḫašāšu(m) I.II
ḫt'	ḫatû(m) II.III
ḫtk	ḫatākum
ḫtn	ḫatānu
ḫtp	ḫatāpu(m)
ḫtr	ḫatāru
ḫṭ'	ḫaṭû(m) II
ḫṭm	ḫaṭāmu
ḫṭp	ḫaṭāpu(m)
ḫṭṭ	ḫaṭāṭu(m) I.II
ḫw'	ḫawû
ḫz'	azû(m) I
ḫz'	ḫazûm II; ḫutenzû
ḫzm	ḫazāmu
ḫzq	ḫazāqu
k''	gâ'u; ka''û
k'd	kâdu(m) I.II
k'n	kânu(m)
k'l	kullu(m) III
k'p	kâpu
k'r	kâru(m) I.II
k's	kêsu(m)
k'ṣ	kâṣu
k'š	kâšu
kb'	kubbû II; kubbu'u
kbb	kabābu II; kapāpu(m)
kbd	kabātu(m)
kbl	kabālu(m)
kbr	kabāru(m)
kbs	kabāsu(m); kapāṣu(m) II
kbṣ	kapāṣu(m) II
kbš	kabāsu(m); kabāšu
kbt	kabātu(m)
kdd	kadādu
kdn	kuddunu
kdp	kadāpu
kdr	kadāru(m) II.III.IV
kl'	kalû(m) V
kll	kullulu(m) II; šuklulu(m) II
klm	kullumu(m)
klm'	nekelmû(m)
klṣ	kalāṣu(m)
km'	kamû(m) II; kawûm II
kmd	kamādu(m)
kml	kamālu
kmm	kamāmu
kmr	kamāru(m) IV
kms	kamāsu(m) I.II
kmṣ	kamāsu(m) I.II
kmš	kamāsu(m) II
kn'	kanû(m)
knb	kunnupu
knk	kanāku(m)
knn	ganānu; kanānu(m)
knp	kunnupu
knš	kanāšu(m) I.II
knz	kanāzu
kp'	kepû(m)
kpd	kapādu(m)
kpl	kapālu(m)
kpp	kapāpu(m)
kpr	kapāru(m) I.II.III
kps	kapāṣu(m) II
kpṣ	kapāṣu(m) II
kpš	kapāšu(m)
kpt	kapādu(m); kapātu(m)
kr'	ḫerû(m) II; karā'u; karû(m) II
krb	karābu(m) II
krk	karāku
krm	karāmu(m)
krr	karāru I.II
krs	karāsu
krṣ	karāṣu(m)
krt	karātu
krṭ	karāṭu(m)
ks'	kasû(m) III
ksm	kasāmu(m)
ksp	kasāpu(m) I.II
ksr	kasāru(m)
kss	kasāsu(m)
kṣ'	kaṣû(m) III
kṣb	kaṣābu
kṣd	kaṣādum
kṣp	kaṣāpu
kṣr	kaṣāru(m)
kṣṣ	gazāzu(m); kasāsu(m); kaṣāṣu(m) I
kš'	kašû(m) I.II.III
kšd	kašādu(m)
kšḫ	ḫašāḫu(m)
kšp	kašāpu(m)
kšr	kašāru(m)
kšš	kašāšu(m) I.II
kšṭ	kašāṭu(m)
kt'	katā'um
ktm	katāmu(m)

ktr	katāru I.II
ktt	katātu(m)
kṭp	qatāpu(m)
kw'	kawûm II
kzb	kazābu(m) I.II
kzr	kezēru(m) I
kzz	gazāzu(m)
l''	le'û(m); lu''û(m) II
l'b	la'ābu(m)
l'd	lâdu(m)
l'k	lêku(m)
l'm	lêmu(m); luāmum; lummu II
l'p	la''upum II; liāpum
l'š	la'āšu(m); lâšu I.II
l't	la'ātu
l'ṭ	lâṭu(m)
lb'	labû; lawûm II
lbb	labābu(m)
lbt	lapātu(m)
lbk	labāku(m)
lbn	labānu(m)
lbr	labāru(m)
lbš	labāšu(m)
lgg	lagāgu
lḫb	laḫābu
lḫd	laḫātu
lḫm	laḫāmu(m) I.II; leḫēmu
lḫš	laḫāšu(m)
lḫt/ṭ	laḫātu
lk'	lakû(m) II; lekû
lkd	lakādu(m)
lkk	lukkuku
lks/ṣ	lukkusu
ll'	lalû II; lullû II
lm'	lawûm II; lemû(m) I.II
lmd	lamādu(m)
lmm	lamāmu I.II
lmn	lemēnu(m)
lmṣ	lummuṣu
lpn	lapānu(m)
lpp	lapāpu(m)
lpt	lapātu(m)
lq'	laqā'u; lekû; leqû(m) II
lqḫ	laqāḫu
lqt	laqātu(m)
lsm	lasāmu(m)
lt'	letû(m) II
ltk	latāku(m)
lw'	lawûm II
lz'	lezû II
lzn	lezēnu
lzz	lazāzu
m''	mâ'u(m); ma'û(m); muā'um
m'd	mâdu(m)
m'ḫ	mâḫum
m'n	mânu
m'q	muqqu II
m'r	mâru; (w)âru(m)
m's	mêsu; mêšu(m)
m'ṣ	mâṣu(m); wiāṣum
m'š	mêsu; mêšu(m); muāšu
m't	mâtu(m)
m'z	mâzu(m)
md'	medû
mdd	madādu(m) I.II
mdl	madālu
mdr	madāru(m) II
mgg	magāgu
mgr	magāru(m); makāru(m) I; mugguru
mgš	muggušu(m)
mḫ'	maḫû(m)
mḫḫ	maḫāḫu(m)
mḫl	maḫālu
mḫr	maḫāru(m)
mḫṣ	maḫāṣu(m)
mk'	makû(m) III.IV; mekû(m) V
mkk	makāku
mkl	mekēlu
mkr	makāru(m) I.II
mks	makāsu(m)
mkš	makāšu
ml'	malā'u; malû(m) IV
mld	(w)alādu(m)
mlḫ	malāḫu IV
mlk	malāku(m) II.III
mll	malālu(m) I; mēlulu(m)
mls/š	malāsu
mlt	malātu
mn'	manû(m) IV; menû(m)
mqr	(w)aqāru(m)
mqq	magāgu
mqt	maqātu(m)
mr'	marû(m) II.III; murrû I
mrḫ	marāḫu(m)
mrk'	namarkû
mrq	marāqu(m)
mrr	marāru(m) I.II.III
mrs	marāsu
mrṣ	marāṣu(m)
mrš	*warāšum
mrṭ	marāṭu
ms'	mesû(m) II; wussûm
msḫ	masāḫum
msk	masāku(m)
msr	masārum; maṣāru(m)
mṣ'	maṣû(m); (w)uṣṣû(m)
mṣl	šumṣulu(m)
mṣr	masārum; maṣāru(m)
mṣṣ	muzzuzu
mš'	mašā'u(m); mašû(m) II; muššu'u; šumšû(m); wussûm
mšd	mašādu(m)
mšḫ	mašāḫu(m) I.II
mšk	masāku(m)
mšl	mašālu(m)
mšr	mašāru(m); (w)ašāru(m)
mšš	mašāšu(m)
mtḫ	matāḫu
mtq	matāqu(m)
mtr	matāru(m); (w)atāru(m)
mṭ'	maṭû(m) II
mz'	mazā'u(m) II; mazûm II
mzq	mazāqu
mzr	masārum; maṣāru(m); mazāru
mzz	muzzuzu
n''	nâ'u; na'û(m); nê'u(m)
n'd	na'ādu(m); nâdu(m)
n'ḫ	nâḫu(m)
n'k	nâku; niāku(m)
n'l	itūlu(m); na'ālu(m); nâlu(m)
n'm	na'āmu(m)
n'p	na'āpu(m); nâpu I.II
n'q	nâqu(m) I.II
n'r	na'āru(m); nêru(m)
n's	na'āsu(m)
n'ṣ	nâṣu(m)
n'š	na'āšu; nâšu(m); nêšu(m)
n't	nêtu I.II
n'ṭ	nâṭu
nb'	nabā'u(m); nabû(m) II; nebû(m) II
nbb	nabābu
nbḫ	nabāḫu
nbk/q	nabākum
nbṭ	nabāṭu(m)
nbz	nabāzu
nd'	nadû(m) III.IV; naṭû(m) IV
ndd	nadādu(m)
ndk	nadāqu
ndn	nadānu(m) II
ndq	nadāqu
ndr	nadāru(m) I.II
ndš	nadāšum
ngb	nagābum
ngg	nagāgu(m)
ngl	nagālu
ngr	nagāru(m) II
ngš	nagāšu(m)
ng'	nagû(m) II
nḫ'	naḫû; neḫû(m) II
nḫl	naḫālu(m) I.II
nḫr	naḫāru(m) I.II
nḫs	naḫāsu(m)
nḫṣ	nuḫḫuṣu
nḫš	naḫāšu(m)
nḫt	naḫātu(m)
nḫṭ	nuḫḫuṭu
nkd	nakādu(m)
nkl	nakālu(m)

nkm	nakāmu(m)
nkp	nakāpu(m)
nkr	nakāru(m)
nks	nakāsu(m)
nkš	nakāšu(m)
nlš	nalāšu(m)
nm'	itmû; nawûm II
nmr	nawāru(m)
nmš	namāšu(m)
np'	napû(m) II; nepûm; nuppu'um
npd	napādu II
npg	napāgu
npḫ	napāḫu(m)
npk	nabākum
npl	napālu(m) I.II.III
npq	nabākum; napāqu(m); nuppuqu(m)
npr	napāru
npṣ	napāṣu(m)
npš	napāšu(m) I.II
npt	napātu
nq'	naqû(m)
nqb	naqābu(m)
nqd	naqādu(m)
nqr	naqāru(m)
nrb	narābu(m)
nrṭ	narāṭu(m)
ns'	nesû(m) II
nsḫ	nasāḫu(m); našāḫu(m)
nsk	nasāku(m)
nsq	nasāqu(m)
nsr	nasāru
nss	nasāsu(m); našāšu I
nṣb	naṣābu(m) I.II
nṣr	naṣāru(m)
nṣṣ	našû(m) II
nš'	našû(m) II; nešû(m)
nšb	nuššubum
nšḫ	našāḫu(m)
nšk	nasāku(m); našāku(m)
nšp	našāpu(m)
nšq	našāqu(m)
nšr	našāru(m) I.II
nšš	našāšu I.II
nt'	naṭû(m) IV; nentû; nuttûm II
ntk	natāku(m)
ntp	naṭāpu(m)
ntr	natāru
nṭ'	naṭû(m) III.IV
nṭl	naṭālu(m)
nṭp	naṭāpu(m)
nw'	nawû(m) II
nwr	nawāru(m)
nz'	nezû
nzl	nazālu(m)
nzm	nazāmu(m)
nzp	nazāpum
nzq	nazāqu(m)
nzr	nazāru(m)
nzz	našāšu I; nazāzu(m)
p'd	pâdu(m); puādum
p'g	puāgu(m)
p'ḫ	puḫḫu(m)
p'n	pênu
p'q	piāqum; puqqu(m)
p'r	pâru(m) I.II
p'ṣ	pa'āṣu(m)
p'š	pâšu; puāšu(m)
p't/ṭ	puādum
pd'	padû(m)
pg'	pagû(m) II
pgl	pagālu
pḫ'	peḫû(m) II
pḫd	paḫādu
pḫḫ	paḫāḫu
pḫr	paḫāru(m) II
pḫs/ṣ	paḫāsu(m)
pḫz	paḫāsu; paḫāzu
pkl	pagālu
pkr	pakāru; pukkuru
pl'	pelû III
pld	palādu II
plḫ	palāḫu(m)
plk	palāku(m); palāqu(m)
plk'	nepelkû(m)
pll	palālum
plq	palāqu(m)
pls	palāsu(m)
plsḫ	napalsuḫu(m)
plš	palāšu(m)
plṭ'	napalṭû
pn'	panû(m)
png/k	panāku
pnn	bunnunu
pq'	peqûm
pqd	paqādu(m)
pqr	baqāru(m)
pr'	parā'u(m) I.II; parû III.IV; purrûm II
prd	parādu(m) I.II
prd'	napardû II
prḫ	parāḫu; parāku(m); parā'u(m) I
prk	parāku(m)
prk'	naparkû II
prq	parāqu
prqd	naparqudu(m)
prr	parāru(m); šuparruru(m) II
prs	parāsu(m) I.II
prsḫ	napalsuḫu
prṣ	parāṣu(m) I.II
prš	naprušu(m) II; parāšu(m)
pršd	naparšudu(m)
pršm	paršumu
prṭ	parāṭu
przḫ	šuparzuḫu
ps'	pasû; pesû
psḫ	pasāḫu(m)
psk	passuku
psl	pasālu(m)
psm	pasāmu(m)
psn	pesēnu
psq	pasāqu(m)
psr	bussuru(m)
pss	pasāsu(m)
pṣ'	peṣû(m) II
pṣd	paṣādu(m)
pṣm	paṣāmu
pṣn	paṣānu(m)
pṣṣ	paṣāṣu
pš'	pašû(m)
pšḫ	pašāḫu(m)
pšl	bašālu(m); pašālu(m)
pšn	pašānu
pšq	pašāqu(m)
pšr	pašāru(m)
pšš	pašāšu(m); pasāsu
pšṭ	pašāṭu(m)
pt'	petû(m) II
ptḫ	patāḫu(m)
ptl	patālu(m)
ptn	patānu(m) I.II
ptq	patāqu(m) I.II
pṭm	paṭāmum
pṭr	paṭāru(m)
pzr	pazāru(m)
q''	gâ'u; qu''û(m)
q'b	qâpu(m)
q'd	qâdu
q'l	qa'ālum; qâlu(m); qiālu(m)
q'p	qâpu(m); qiāpu(m)
q'š/t	qiāšu(m)
qb'	qabû(m) II; qu''û(m)
qbl	qitbulu; qubbulu
qbr	qebēru(m)
qbt	ḫabātu IV; qubbutu
qd'	qadā'um; qadû II
qdd	qadādu(m)
qdp	qadāpu
qdš	qadāšu(m)
ql'	qalû(m) II
qll	qalālu(m) I.II
qlp	qalāpu(m)
qlt	qullutu
qm'	qamû(m) II; qemûm; qu''û(m)
qmm	qamāmu
qmš	qummušu
qn'	qanû(m) II; qenû
qnn	kanānu(m); qanānu(m)
qnp	qunnupu
qlp'	neqelpû(m)
qp'	qapû
qpl	kapālu(m)

qr'	qerû(m)
qrb	qerēbu(m)
qrd	garādum; qarādu(m)
qrḫ	qarāḫu
qrm	qarāmu
qrn	qarānu(m)
qrr	qarāru(m)
qrš	qarāšu(m)
qšd	qašādu(m)
qt'	qadā'um; qatû(m) II
qtl	qatālum
qtn	qatānu(m)
qtp	qatāpu(m)
qtr	qatāru II
qṭ'	qaṭû
qṭp	qatāpu(m)
qw'	qu''û(m)
r''	râ'u; re'û(m)
r'b	ra'ābu(m); râbu(m); riābu(m)
r'd	râdu(m)
r'ḫ	riāḫu(m)
r'k	râku
r'm	râmu(m) II.III; rêmu(m); ru''umu
r'q	rêqu(m); riāqu(m); ruāqu(m)
r's	râsu(m)
r'ṣ	râṣu(m); rêṣu(m)
r'š	râsu(m); riāšu(m)
r'ṭ	râṭu(m)
r'z	ra'āzu
rb'	rabû(m) II.III; rubbu'um
rbb	rabābu(m)
rbk	rabāku(m)
rbq	rabāqum
rbṣ	rabāṣu(m)
rbš	rabāšum
rd'	redû(m) I.II
rdd	radādu(m)
rdm	radāmu
rdp	radāpu
rg'	ruggû(m)
rgb	ragābu; ruggubu II
rgg	ragāgu(m) I.II
rgm	ragāmu(m)
rgš	ragāšum
rḫ'	reḫû(m)
rḫb	ra'ābu(m)
rḫḫ	raḫāḫu(m)
rḫp	ruḫḫupu
rḫṣ	raḫāṣu(m) I.II.III
rḫš	raḫāšu(m)
rḫt/ṭ	raḫātu
rkb	rakābu(m)
rkk	rakāku
rkn	rakānu(m)
rkp	rakābu(m)
rks/š	rakāsu(m)
rm'	ramû(m) II.III
rmk	ramāku(m)
rmm	ramāmu(m); râmu(m) II
rmṣ	ramāṣu
rp'	rapā'um
rpd	rapādu(m) II
rpq	rapāqu(m)
rps	rapāsu(m)
rpš	rapāšu(m)
rpt/ṭ	rapātu
rq'	raqû(m); ruqqû
rqb	raqābu
rqd	raqādu(m)
rqq	ragāgum II; raqāqu(m)
rs'	russû(m)
rsb	rasābu(m)
rsn	rasānu(m)
rsp	rasābu(m)
rṣ'	raṣûm
rṣd	raṣādu(m)
rṣn	rasānu(m); raṣānu(m)
rṣp	raṣāpu
rš'	rašû(m) I.II.III
ršb	rasābu(m); rašābu(m)
ršd	rašādu
ršk	rašāku(m)
ršš	rašāšu
rt'	retû(m) II
rtḫ	ruttuḫu
rtm	ratāmu
rtt	ratātu
rṭ'	retû(m) II
rṭb	raṭābu(m)
rṭp	raṭāpu(m)
rz'	razû
rw'	re'û(m)
ry'	re'û(m)
s''	sâ'u(m); se'û
s'b	sa'ābu; sâbu(m)
s'd	sâdu(m); sêdu
s'k	sâku(m)
s'l	sa'ālu; sâlu
s'm	siāmu(m)
s'p	sa'ābu; sâbu(m)
s'q	siāqu(m)
s'r	sâru(m); sêru(m)
s's	su''usu
s'ṭ	sâṭu
sb'	sabā'u(m); sabû(m)
sbk	sabāku(m); tabāku(m)
sbl	zabālu(m)
sbs	subbusu II; šabāsu(m)
sbṣ	šapāṣu
sdd	sadādu(m) I.II
sdḫ	sadāḫum
sdr	sadāru(m)
sg'	sagû I; segû
sḫ'	sehû(m)
sḫḫ	saḫāḫu(m)
sḫl	saḫālu(m)
sḫm	saḫāmu(m)
sḫn	saḫānu
sḫp	saḫāpu(m)
sḫr	saḫāru(m)
sḫš	saḫāšu(m)
skd	zaqādum
skk	sakāku(m)
skl	sakālu(m) I.II
skn	sakānu; šakānu(m)
skp	sakāpu(m) I.II
skr	sekēru(m) I.II
skt	sakātu(m)
sl'	salāḫu(m) II; salā'u(m) I.II.III; sullû(m) I; šalû(m) I.II.III
sld	salātu(m) II
slḫ	salāḫu(m) I.II
sll	salālu(m)
slm	salāmu(m) II
sln	sullunu II
slq	salāqu I.II
slt	salātu(m) II
sm'	samû II
smd	samādu(m)
smḫ	samāḫu(m)
smk	samāku(m)
smr	samārum
smš	samāšu(m)
snb	sanāpu(m)
snn	sanānu
snp	sanāpu(m)
snq	sanāqu(m) I.II
sns/š	sanāšu
sp'	sepû(m) II.III; suppû II
spd	sapādu(m)
spḫ	sapāḫu(m)
spk	sapāku
spn	sapānu(m)
spq	sapāqu
spr	sepēru
sqd	zaqādum
sql	saqālu
sqp	zaqāpu(m)
sqr	zakāru(m); zaqāru(m)
sr'	surrûm I; zarû(m) II
srd	sarādu(m); serēdu
srḫ	sarāḫu(m)
srm	sarāmu(m)
srp	sarāpu
srq	sarāqu(m)
srr	sarāru(m); sarruru
ss'	šasû(m)
stl	satālu
stḫ	sadāḫum
sṭr	šaṭāru(m) II
ṣ''	ṣê'u; ṣuā'u
ṣ'd	ṣâdu(m) I.II

ṣ'ḫ	ṣiāḫu(m)
ṣ'l	ṣâlu(m)
ṣ'n	ṣânu; ṣênu(m)
ṣ'p	ṣuppu II
ṣ'r	ṣêru(m); ṣurrum IV
ṣ'y	ṣê'u
ṣb'	ṣabā'um; ṣabû(m) II; ṣapû(m) II; ṣubbû(m)
ṣbb	ṣabābu
ṣbl	zabālu(m)
ṣbr	ṣabāru(m) I.II
ṣbt/ṭ	ṣabātu(m)
ṣd'	ṣadû(m)
ṣdr	ṣadāru
ṣḫr	ṣeḫēru(m)
ṣḫt	ṣaḫātu(m) I.II
ṣl'	ṣalā'u; ṣelû(m) I.II; ṣullû
ṣll	ṣalālu(m); ṣullulu(m) II
ṣlm	ṣalāmu(m)
ṣlp	ṣalāpu(m)
ṣm'	ṣamû(m) II
ṣmd	ṣamādu(m) II
ṣmn	zummunu
ṣmr	ṣamāru(m); ṣemēru(m)
ṣmt	ṣamātu
ṣnḫ	ṣanāḫu
ṣp'	ṣapû(m) II
ṣpḫ	ṣappuḫu
ṣpn	ṣapānu
ṣpp	ṣabābu
ṣpr	ṣapāru(m)
ṣrd	ṣarātu(m)
ṣrḫ	ṣarāḫu(m) I.II.III.IV; ṣurruḫu II
ṣrk	ṣarākum
ṣrm	ṣarāmu(m)
ṣrp	ṣarāpu(m) I.II
ṣrr	sarāru(m); ṣarāru(m) I.II
ṣrš	ṣarāšu(m)
ṣrt	ṣarātu(m)
ṣw'	ṣawwûm
š''	šâ'u(m); šê'u(m) I.II; še'û(m); šuḫḫû III; šuta''ûm
š'b	šâbu(m); šiābum
š'ḫ	šêḫu; šiāḫu(m) I
š'k	šâqum II
š'l	šâlu(m) I.II; šêlu(m); šiālu(m)
š'm	šâmu(m); šiāmu(m); šummu(m) II
š'n	šênu; *šiānum; šunnu(m)
š'p	šêpu
š'q	šâqu(m) I.II.III.IV; šêqu(m)
š'r	ša'āru(m); šâru; še'ēru; šêru(m); šurru(m); šuš'uru
š'ṣ	šiāṣum
š't	šêtu(m) II
š'ṭ	šâṭu I.II; šêṭu(m); šiāṭu
šb'	šapû(m) II.IV; šebû(m) I
šb''	*šube''û(m)
šbb	šabābu(m) I.II
šbḫ	šabāḫu I; šapāḫu(m); šubbuḫu
šbr	šebēru(m)
šbs	šabāsu(m)
šbṣ	šapāṣu(m)
šbš	šabāsu(m); šabāšu(m)
šbt	šapāṭu(m) I; šubbutu
šbṭ	šabāṭu(m) II
šd'	šadû IV; tuddû
šdd	šadādu(m)
šdḫ	šadāḫu(m)
šdl	šadālu(m)
šg'	šegû(m) II
šgg	šagāgu
šgl	šagālu(m)
šgm/n	šagāmu(m) II
šgrr	šugarruru(m)
šgš	šagāšu(m)
šḫ'	šaḫû II.III; šêḫu; šuḫḫû(m) II.III.IV
šḫd	šaḫādum
šḫḫ	šaḫāḫu(m)
šḫl	šaḫālu(m)
šḫn	šaḫānu(m)
šḫq	šeḫēqu
šḫrr	šuḫarruru(m) II; šuḫruru
šḫt	šaḫātu(m) III.IV
šḫṭ	šaḫāṭu(m) III.IV; šaḫāṭu(m) I.II.III
šk'n	šukênu(m)
škk	šakāku(m)
škl	šukkulu(m)
škm	šakāmu(m) I.II; šakānu(m)
škn	šakānu(m)
škr	šakāru
šks	šakāsum
škṣ	šakāṣu(m)
škš	šagāšu(m)
škt	šakātu(m) I.II
šl'	šalā'um; šalû(m) I.II.III; šelû II.III
šlg	šalāgu(m)
šlḫ	salāḫu(m) I.II; šalāḫu(m)
šll	šalālu(m) I.II.III
šlm	šalāmu(m) II
šlp	šalāpu(m)
šlp'	nešalpû
šlq	šalāqu(m)
šlš	šalāšu(m)
šlṭ	šalāṭu(m) I.II
šm'	šawûm II; šemû(m) I
šmd	šamādu
šmḫ	samāḫu(m); šamāḫu(m) I.II
šmk	šamāḫu(m) I
šmm	šamāmu
šmr	šamāru(m) I.II
šmt	šamātu; šamāṭu(m) II
šmṭ	šamāṭu(m) I.II
šn'	šanā'u; šanû(m) III.IV.V.VI; šenû(m)
šnḫ	šanā'u
šnn	šanānu(m)
šnq	sanāqu(m) I; šunnuqu
šnṣ	šanāṣu
šnš	sanāšu
šp'	suppû II; šapû(m) II.III.IV; šepûm
šp'l	šupêlu(m)
špḫ	šapāḫu(m)
špk	šapāku(m)
špl	šapālu(m)
špp	šapāpu(m)
špr	šapāru(m); šitpuru
šps	šapāṣu
špṣ	šapāṣu(m)
špš	šapāšum
špt	šapātu; šapāṭu(m) I.II
špṭ	šapāṭu(m) I.II
šq'	šaqû(m) II.III
šql	šaqālu(m)
šqll	šuqallulu(m)
šqmm	šuqammumu(m) II
šqr	šaqāru
šr'	šarû(m) II; šerû I.II.III.IV; šurrû(m) II.IV
šrb	šarābu
šrbṣ/ṭ	našarbuṭu(m)
šrd	šitrudu
šrḫ	šarāḫu(m) I.II.III
šrk	šarāku(m) I.II
šrm	šarāmu(m)
šrp	šarāpu(m)
šrq	šarāqu(m) I.II.III
šrr	šarāru(m) I.II.III
šrṣ	šarāṣu
šrṭ	šarāṭu(m)
šs'	šasû(m)
št'	šatû(m) II.III
štḫ	šatāḫu
štn	šatānu
štp	šatāpu; šutattupu
štq	šatāqu
šṭ'	šeṭû(m) II
šṭp	šaṭāpu(m)
šṭr	šaṭāru(m) II
šṭṭ	šaṭāṭu
šw'	šawûm II
šwr	šuwwurum
t''	tamû II; ta'û(m); tê'u

t'b	têbum
t'l	têlu(m)
t'm	tu''umu II
t'p	tâpu; têbum
t'r	târu(m)
tb'	tebû(m)
tbk	tabāku(m)
tbl	tabālu(m)
td'	tuddû
tdn	tadānu(m)
tgn	taqānu(m)
tḫḫ	taḫāḫu
tkk	takāku(m)
tkl	takālu(m)
tkp	takāpu(m)
tl'	tullû II
tlk	tullukum
tll	talālu(m); tullulu
tlm	šutlumu(m); tullumum
tm'	tamû(m) II.III
tmḫ/k	tamāḫu(m)
tmm	tamāmum
tmr	temēru(m)
tp'	tappûm II; tapû
tpk	tabāku(m)
tpš	tapāšum
tqm/n	taqānu(m)
tr'	tarû(m) I.II
trḫ	tarāḫu
trk	tarāku(m)
trp	tarāpu
trq	tarāqu(m)
trr	tarāru(m)
trs/ṣ	ṭarāsu
trṣ	tarāṣu(m) I.II
trš	tarāšum
tṣ'	taṣû(m); teṣû(m)
tšb	*tašābu(m)
tw'	tawûm
tz'	teṣû(m)

ṭ'b	ṭiābu(m)
ṭ'm	ṭêmu(m)
ṭ'n	ṭênu(m)
ṭ'p	ṭâpu(m)
ṭb'	ṭebû(m)
ṭbḫ	ṭabāḫu(m)
ṭḫ'	ṭeḫû(m) I.II
ṭḫd	ṭaḫādu(m)
ṭlm	ṭullumum
ṭm'	ṭawûm
ṭmm	ṭummumu II
ṭnp	ṭanāpu
ṭp'	tâpu; ṭepû(m)
ṭpl	ṭapālu(m)
ṭpp	ṭapāpu
ṭpr	ṭapāru(m)
ṭpš	ṭapāšu II
ṭr'	ṭerû(m)
ṭrd	ṭarādu(m)
ṭrr	ṭarāru
ṭrs/ṣ	ṭarāsu
ṭrš	ṭarāšu
ṭw'	ṭawûm

w''	wu''ûm
w'r	(w)âru(m)
w'ṣ	wiāṣum
w'š	wêšum
wb'	(w)abā'u(m)
wbd	wabātum
wbl	wabālu(m)
wbt/ṭ	wabātum
wd'	tuddû; *wadûm
wkl	wakālum
wkm	wakāmu(m)
wl'	alā'u
wld	(w)alādu(m)
wm'	wamā'um
wml	(w)amālu(m)
wn'	wanā'um
wp'	(w)apû(m)
wpd	wabātum
wpš	(w)apāšu(m)
wpt/ṭ	wabātum
wq'	(w)aqû(m)
wqr	(w)aqāru(m)
wr'	warûm II
wrd	(w)arādu(m)
wrḫ	arāḫu(m) I
wrq	(w)arāqu(m)
wrš	(w)arāšu(m)
ws'	wussûm
wsm	(w)asāmu(m)
wsq	asāqu
wṣ'	(w)aṣû(m); (w)uṣṣû(m)
wṣb	waṣābum
wṣṣ	(w)uṣṣuṣu(m)
wš'	mašû(m) II
wšb	(w)ašābu(m)
wšm	wašāmum
wšp	(w)ašāpu(m)
wšr	(w)ašāru(m)
wšṭ	(w)ašāṭu(m)
wt'	(w)atû(m)
wtr	(w)atāru(m)
wzn	wazzunum

z''	ze'û; zu''û
z'b	zâbu(m)
z'k	sâku(m)
z'n	za'ānu(m)
z'p	zu''upu
z'q	ziāqu(m)
z'r	zâru I; zêru(m)
z'z	zâzu(m)
zbl	zabālu(m)
zk'	zakû(m) II
zkd	zaqādum
zkp	sakāpu(m) I; zaqāpu(m)
zkr	zakāru(m)
zm'	zemû; zummû(m) II
zmn	zummunu
zmr	samārum; zamāru(m) II
zn'	zenû(m) II
znd	zanādu
znn	zanānu(m) I.II
znq	zunnuqu
zpr	zapāru
zqd	zaqādum
zqn	zaqānu(m)
zqp	zaqāpu(m)
zqr	zakāru(m); zaqāru(m)
zqt	zaqātu(m) I.II
zr'	zarû(m) I
zrb	zarāpu
zrbb	nazarbubu(m)
zrp	zarāpu
zrq	zarāqu(m)

A

a → *ana* I

-a "my" (1 sg. pron. suff.); → *-ī*

-a → also *-am*

ā "that, those; the afore-mentioned" NB, late NA often wr. *a'*, a_4 (→ GAG §63g); < Aram. emphatic state

-ā "my" (1 sg. pron. suff.) NB for *-ī* (→ GAG §42j-k^1)

â, a-a → *ai* I.II

a-a- → *ayya…, ayyi…, ayyu…*

a'ālu → *e'ēlu*

a''ālu → *e''ēlu*

a'āru → *wârum*

ab → *abu* I

ababdûm (a civil servant) OB; < Sum.

ababim → *abu* I 3

ababu I "forest" jB lex.

ababu II mng. unkn. jB lex.

abādu → *abātu* II N

abaḫšinnu(m), *abaḫsennu*, *ebuḫušinnu*, *ubuḫšinnu* ~ "stalk" Bab. as edible commodity

abaḫu → *appaḫu*

abāku(m) I "to lead away" OA, NA, M/NB **G** (*a/u*) OA "take (commodities) to"; + vent. "fetch" commodities, animals; often with *ippāniya* ("myself in person"); Bab. as OA "take to", + vent. "fetch" objects, animals, also people, NB "hale" witness, debtor; NB *ana kaspi a.* 'take away for silver' = "buy" **Gt** Mari "lead away" **D** Mari "dispatch, forward" goods; jB "push away, displace"; NA "shift" work onto s.o. **Š** jB "have s.o. bring" s.o. **N** pass. of G j/NB; > *abku, abkūtu, abiktu, ābiku*?

abāku(m) II "to overturn, upset" O/jB **G** (*a/u*); also transf., omen, divine verdict, witchcraft **D** ~ G **N** pass. of G; > *ābiku*?

abal "without" NB

aballu (a vessel for water); < Sum.

abalu → *ablu*

abālu(m) "to dry (up)" Bab., NA **G** (*a/a*) [ḪÁD.A] intrans. "become dry, dry up" O/jB of liquid, plant, swamp; of (parts of) body **Gtn** iter. of G **D** trans. "dry" (up) spittle; parts of body; drugs; swamp, field, orchard **Dt** pass. of D **Š** ~ D, esp. stat.; > *ablu*; *nābalu*, *nābališ*, *nūbalum*; *tābalu*, *tābīlu*; *ubbulu*; *šābulu*

abālu → also *apālu* I; *wabālum*

abamātu "sea" jB lex.

abaraḫḫum (an object) OB

abarakkatu(m), *abrakkatu* ~ "stewardess, housekeeper" O/jB, NA [MUNUS.AGRIG] jB also as divine title; < Sum.

abarakku(m) ~ "steward, housekeeper" Bab., M/NA [(LÚ.)AGRIG; NB also IGI.2.DUB] administrator of temple or secular household, later high state official; NA *a. rabû* "Chief Steward"; also as divine title; < Sum.; > *abarakkūtu*; *abarakkatu*; → *abarikkum*; *mašennu*

ab(a)rakkūtu "function of stewardess" jB [MUNUS.AGRIG]; < *abarakku*

abar(a)ša "truly, certainly" jB

abarikkum, *abrikk/qqu*, *agriqqu* = *abarakku* ? O/jB lex.; jB(lit.) also as divine title; < Sum.

abarnīum (a kind of cloth, phps.) "from Abarna" OA

abartu(m) "opposite shore, bank" OAkk, NB (roy. inscr.) for *ebertu* I; < *ebēru* I

abāru(m) I "(the metal) lead" [A.GAR5; 1st millennium roy. inscr. A.BÁR], MA also *annuku abāru*; (at Aššur) *kisal a.* "Lead Courtyard"?; < Sum.?

abāru(m) II, occas. *apāru, ubāru* **1.** Bab.(lit.) (a kind of clamp) **2.** jB transf. "embrace, physical strength" of god, king, in *bēl a., gāmer a.*; *ša a.* "wrestler"; > *abāru* III

abāru(m) III "to embrace" O/jB **G** (pret. *ībir*) **D 1.** of magic "embrace intensely, bind" limbs, person; of stars **2.** leg. "accuse s.o., denounce"; < *abāru* II denom.; > *mubbirtu*; → *ibru*; *itbāru*

abāru → also *ḫabāru* II G

abaruḫ (an object) Nuzi; < Hurr.?

abasigga "receding water" jB lex.; < Sum.

abašlu → *ašlu*

abašmû, *amašpû, amašmû*, lex. also *abašmītu* (a stone) M/jB, NA, often mag.

abat(ti a)gurru → *abattu* 5

abattu MA, M/NB **1.** "river-gravel" **2.** jB "stone of carob(-bean)" **3.** jB "pestle"; MA as PN **4.** MB, NB (a kind of irrigation pipe) **5.** jB lex. *abat(ti a)gurru* "*a.* of baked brick" (a kind of flower)

abatu → *awātu*

abātu(m) I "to destroy" **G** (*a/u*, O/jB also *i'abbat, i'but* (→ GAG §97h)) objects, buildings; living beings; OA "ruin (economically)" **D** "destroy completely" objects, parts of body, living beings; jB occas. + *eli* instead of acc. **Dt** pass. of D [GUL.MEŠ] **Š** caus. of G OB(lit.) **N** pass. of G (forms → GAG §97j); > *abtu*

abātu(m) II "to run away, flee from" **G** (*a/u*) OA, OB "flee from, abandon" **N** (*nābutu, na'butu, nābudu*; *i/i* (→ GAG §97l)) Bab., M/NA [ZÁḪ] "to escape" of slave, conscript; of political refugee; in battle **Ntn** Bogh. iter. of N "run away repeatedly" of servant; > *munnabtu, munnabtuttu, nābutum*

abātu → also *aptu*

abâtu → *abūtu*; *apâtu*

abā'u → *wabā'um*

abaya (a water-fowl) jB lex.

abb... also = *ana b...*

abbālu "very sad" NB; < Aram.

abbāšu (a textile) MA

abbatu → *ammatu* II

abbā'ū → *abu* I

abbu "swamp"? jB; > *abbû*

abbū → *abu* I

abbû "swamp fauna"? jB lex.; < *abbu* + *-ī*

abbunnu (a kind of bird) jB lex.; → *appānum* II

abbuttānû; f. *abbuttānītu* "wearer of *abbuttu* hair-style" MB as fPN; as name of horse

abbuttu(m) (a hair-style) O/jB, Nuzi as mark of slavery; *a. šakānum* "to give (s.o.) an *a.* hair-style", also as punishment; *a. gullubu* "to shear the *a.* hair-style off"; (a part of the head, of the hair) jB om., of baby's abnormality, of dog

abbuttu → also *abbūtu*; *apputtum* II

abbūtu(m), Ass. *abbuttu* "fatherhood", esp. transf. "fatherly attitude, patronage"; *a. X ṣabātu* "to adopt X's cause, intercede for X"; Mari *abbūt bītim* "heads of households"; < *abu* I

abbūtu → also *abu* I

abdu "servant, slave" jB; < W.Sem.

abdû (a prof. desig.) MB

abgallu → *apkallu*

abiḫeri mng. unkn. Nuzi

abiktu, NA *apiktu* "defeat" M/jB, NA [BAD5.BAD5(-) (→ *dabdû, taḫtû*)] *a. šakānu* "to inflict a defeat"; *lipî a.* 'fat of the defeat' (a plant) jB lex.; < *abāku* I; > *abkūtu*

ābiku mng unkn. jB lex.; < *abāku* ?

abīlum → *awīlu*

ābilu → *āgilu*

abi(n)gallu (a priest) jB lex.; < Sum.

Abirtum → *Ebirtum*

ābirû (or *abīrû*) ~ "weak, poor"? jB

abītu → *ebītu*

abiyānum "poor" Mari; < W.Sem.

abiyāru, NA *abiyūru* (a plant) jB/NA lex.

abkigu only in pl. *abkigētu* "cow" jB(lit.); < Sum.

abkininītu (a bird) jB lex.

abku "captive" j/NB; < *abāku* I

abkūtu "defeated state" MB; < *abiktu*

ablu, NB also *abalu* "dry, dried" [ḪÁD.A] of meat; wood; asphalt; pl. *ablūtu* "hay"?; < *abālu*

abnu(m) m. & f.; pl. *abnū* and *abnātu(m)* "stone" [NA4] **1.** "stone, rock" in gener. **2.** "(semi)precious stone" **3.** compounds: *aban alādi* "birth stone"; *a. erê* "pregnancy stone"; *a. išāti* "fire stone, flint" **4.** "stone (vessel)" jB, NA **5.** "stone (bead)"; jB lex. "amulet-stone" **6.** O/MA, OB "stone (weight)"; Nuzi "pebble, counter" for accounting **7.** transf. jB "(hail)stones" also *a. šamê* "hailstones"; lex. "stones, kernels of fruits"; med., lex. "stones" in body **8.** lex. "date panicle" (different word ?); → *gabû*

abrakkatu → *abarakkatu*

abrakkūtu → *abarakkūtu*

abrammu (a bird) jB lex.

abratemum (a bird) OB lex.

abrikku, abriqqu → *abarikkum*

abriš "like a stack of wood" jB; < *abru* III

abru(m) I "strong, robust"? O/jB(lit.) as f. pl. *abrātu(m)* "populace, humanity"

abru(m) II, *apru* **1.** O/jB "wing" (of bird) **2.** O/jB(lit.) "fin" (of fish); > *kittabru*?

abru(m) III "pile of brushwood" OAkk(Ur III), jB [IZI.ḪA.MUN] for fuel; > *abriš*

abru IV, *aplu* (a kind of priest) Bab. lex.; > *abrūtu*

abrummu → *amrummu*

abrūtu "*abru*-priesthood" jB lex.; < *abru* IV

absaḫurakku, absaḫurum → *abšaḫurum*

absinnu(m), *abšennu* "furrow" O/jB [AB.SÍN] also j/NB astr. constellation Spica, eastern part of Virgo [MUL.AB.SÍN; NB also MUL.ABSIN]; < Sum.

abšaḫurum, *absaḫurum, absaḫurakku* (a fish) OB, jB lex.; < Sum.

abšānu(m) "yoke, harness" Bab.(lit.) transf., humans draw/bear (*šâṭu/wabālum*) yoke of gods, i.e. are submissive; → *uppašannu*

Abšarrāni → *abu* I 7

abšennu → *absinnu*

abšu I (a kind of belt)? jB lex.

abšu II, *apšu*; Hurr. pl. *abšena* (a legume) M/NA, Nuzi, jB lex.

abtu "destroyed" j/NB of gods, buildings; f. pl. "ruins" NA, NB(roy. inscr.); < *abātu* I

abu(m) I "father" (st. constr. *abi*, occas. *abu, ab*; nom. with pron. suff. *abī*, M/NB, NA also *abū(y)a*; *abūšu* etc.; pl. *abbū*, O/MA *abbā'ū*, MB(Alal.), Am. *abbūtu*) [AD] **1.** "(natural) father"; rarely pl. *abbū* "parents" **2.** "ancestor, forefather" often in roy. inscr. **3.** *ab(i) abi(m)*, OB lex. *ababim* "grandfather" **4.** jB *abi muti* "father-in-law" of wife **5.** transf. "father" of gods, humans; "(one acting as) father"; OA "principal, boss" of a firm; "expert" craftsman **6.** compounds: *a. Amurrim* (→ *amurru* 3); *a. ašlim* (→ *ašlu* 3); Mari *abu bītim* "household head, superintendent"; *abi ṣābim* (an official); *abu PlN* "(tribal) chief of PlN"; OAkk *a. ālim* "father of the city" **7.** in O/MA month *Ab(u) šarrāni* "Father of the kings"? **8.** in PN, of people, gods **9.** interj. "father!" ~ "think of that; oh dear!" **10.** (part of the seed plough) jB lex. **11.** OA transf. "down-payment'; > *abbūtu*

Abu(m) II (5th Bab. month) OAkk, Bab. [ITI.NE(.NE.GAR)]; OB *isin Abi* "*Abu* festival" also as MN; → *ebūru*

abu → also *apu* I

abû → *apû* I.III

abūbāniš, *abūbiš* "like a flood" M/NB(lit.); < *abūbu*

abūbu(m) "flood, deluge" Bab. [A.MA.RU] **1.** esp. as cosmic event "the Flood"; *ša lām a.* "antediluvian", *til a.* "ruin mound from the Flood"; "violent spate"; as divine title **2.** (name of a monster); > *abūbāniš*

abūdānûm → *abūtānû*

abuḫuru (a kind of flour) MA

abukkatu, *bukkatu* (a kind of rush)? jB lex., med. [LI.DUR; LI.TAR; occas. LI.TUR]; *ḫīl a.* "sap of *a.*" (a drug)

abulīlu, *bulīlu* (the berry of the box-thorn) jB lex.

abullu(m) f.; pl. *abullātu(m)* "gate (of city or large building)" [ABUL] *a. kawītum* "outer gate"; *maṣṣār a.*, *ša a.*, *mār a.*, *bēl a.* "gatekeeper"; OB *a. šūdûm* "to acquaint s.o. with gate", i.e. to forbid exit; *a. edēlu/peḫû* "to shut/seal up gate"; Bab. "gate tax"; at Nuzi, as a public authority; transf. "entrance" to region, nether world, heaven etc.; OB ext., jB lex. (parts of the organs, esp. portal fissure of the liver); > *abulmaḫḫu, abultannu*

abulmaḫḫu "high gate" j/NB; < *abullu* + Sum. maḫ

abultannu "gatekeeper" Nuzi [LÚ.ABUL] alternating with *maṣṣār abulli*; < *abullu* + Hurr. suff.

ābulu → *āgilu*

abunikītu mng. unkn. MB

abunnatu(m) "umbilical cord, navel" Bab. [LI.DUR] also transf. "centre", "central point" of land, army; "socket" of chariot, spade

aburriṣānu, Bogh. *burriṣānu* mng. unkn. M/jB lex.

aburriš "in a green pasture" M/jB(lit.); mostly transf. ref. to human prosperity, *a. rabāṣu/ašābu* "to lie/dwell in a green meadow"; < *aburru*

aburru(m) "water-meadow, pasture" O/jB transf. ref. to situation of contented populace; > *aburriš*

aburru → also *amurru*

abūsātu pl. tant. "forelock" jB; *abūsāt šīri* (a deformity)

abusin → *abušim*

abūsu(m), *abussu(m)*; pl. f., NA also *ubsātu* "storehouse; stable" O/jB; Ug. *bīt a.*; Ass. *bīt abūsāte/u* (also in Aššur temple)

abušim, *abuš/sin* mng. uncl. jB

abūtānû, *abūdānûm, abuttānû* (a fish) O/jB lex.; < *abūtu* + *-ān* + *-ī* *ābuttum* → *apputtum* II

abutu → *awātum*

abūtu(m); pl. *abâtum* (a fish) O/jB; > *abūtānû*

ad → *adi*

adaburtu (a bird) jB lex.

ad(')a(d)du → *ad'attu*

adadu (a loincloth or kilt ?) jB lex.

adagu(r)ru, *adakurru* (a vessel for libations) M/NB, Nuzi [DUG.A.DA.GUR$_5$; DUG.A.DA.GUR$_4$; DUG.A.DA.KUR]; < Sum.

adaḫa (a garment) Am.; < Eg.

adakanni → *akanni*

adakurru → *adagurru*

adallu ~ "strong" jB lex.; < Hurr.?

adamatu I, *adanatu* '(red blood)' (a dark-coloured bodily discharge) jB lex., med. [ADAMA]; < *adammu*

adamatu(m) II, *adamutu*, *adu/imatu* O/jB **1.** (a plant (with red blossoms ?)) **2.** pl. (dark red earth used as dye); < *adammu* ?

adamdunû "Adamdun vessel"; < PlN

ada(m)mu, *adumu* "red" OAkk, M/jB; Bogh. "red (blood)"; "red (garment)"; lex., syn. for "important person"; > *adamatu* I, II?, *adantu*

adammû "conflict, battle" M/jB lex., lit.; mag., desig. of mythical being; < Sum.

adammūmu, *admūmu*; NA pl. f. "wasp" jB, NA

adamtu mng. unkn. jB lex.

adamu → *adammu*

adāmum, Mari *edēmum* "to be engaged in" OA, Mari **G** stat., activity, business matter **D** ~ G ?; > *admūtum*

adamukku → *edamukku*

adamutu → *adamatu* II

adanatu → *adamatu* I

adanniš, *addanniš* "very much, greatly" NA; < *ana* I + *danniš*

adannu → *adānum*

adantu "(reddish? species of) shrew" jB; < *adammu*

adānum, *ḫadānum* (OB often wr. *ḫa/'a$_4$-da-num* etc.), *adannu*, *adiānu*; pl. f. "fixed date, time limit" Bab. (Ass. → *edānu*) [UD.DUG$_4$.GA; U$_4$.SUR] *ūm a.* "fixed day"; jB *ina lā a.* "at the wrong time"; astr. "period"; *eqel a.* "objective"

adappu, *dappu* "horizontal crossbeam" j/NB in buildings, of timber; for door, of metal; also "board"?

adappu → also *atappu*

adapu I **1.** jB lex. (a musical instrument) **2.** jB (a kind of Sum. hymn accompanied by that instrument); < Sum.

adapu II; pl. f. (a type of bandage) jB lex.; → *edappātu*

adapu III "wise" jB lex.

adāqu → *edēqu*

adārānu (a plant) jB lex.

adartu → *atartu*

adaru I (a vessel) NB of silver

adaru II (an animal or insect) jB lex.

adāru(m) I, *ḫadāru* "to be dark, gloomy" **G** (*a/u*) j/NB [KA×GI$_6$]; of day; of gods, people; of heavenly bodies "become obscured"; of plants ? **D** O/jB "darken", esp. stat. with *pānū/ī* "look gloomy" **Dt** jB, NA "become gloomy" **Š** "darken" j/NB, NA **N** "become dark"; astr. "become eclipsed" [KA×GI$_6$] OB, j/NB **Ntn** iter. of N jB; > *adru* I, *adriš*, *adirtu* I; *addiru*; *na'duru*; *tādirtu*; *udduru*

adāru(m) II "to be afraid (of), fear" **G** (*a/u*) NB *ēnē a.* 'fear the eyes' = "with an eye to, in consideration of" **D** "frighten" OA, jB **Štn** iter. of Š O/jB **Št** pass. of Š **N** "become restless, worry about" OA, OB, jB **Ntn** iter. of N OA, OB, jB; > *adirtu* II, *idirtu*; *adīru*, *adīriš*; *ādiru*; *mušādiru*

adāru(m) III (or *aṭāru(m)*?), *atāru* (a tree) Bab., MA [GIŠ.ÍLDAG (→ also *ildakku*)]

adašḫu mng. unkn. jB lex.

ada(š)šu → *adušsu*

adattu "succulent part of reed" jB [GI.ÚR]; → *adnātu*

ad(')a(t)tu (or *at(')a(t)tu*, *ad(')a(d)du*) (an ornament) Qatna of gold, precious stone

adbaru → *atbaru*

add... also = *ana d*...

addâ "daddy"? OB

addaḫšum → *andaḫšu*

addanniš → *adanniš*

addār → *dāru* I

A(d)daru (12th Bab. month) [ITI.ŠE(.KIN.TAR)]; *A. maḫrû* "first *A.*"; *arḫu atru ša A.* [ITI.DIRIG.ŠE(.KIN.TAR)] "intercalary *A.*", NB also *A. arkû*

addāt → *dāt*

addatum (a wooden tool) OB

adda'u (a dwelling) jB lex.

addiru "very dark" jB; < *adāru* I

addu ~ "throwstick" M/jB

addû → *adû* III

addunānum → *andunānu*

addurārum → *andurāru*

adi, OAkk, OA also *adum*, NA often *adu*, also *ad* "until, as far as" [EN] **1.** prep. of time "till", "within", "during, in the course of", also *adi/u* *libbi*; *ad(i) mati*; *adi inanna*; *ad(i/un)akanni*, *adikanna* "until now" (→ *akanna* II); of space "up to, as far as", also *adi maḫar*; of amount of silver, degree of hunger; *adi ulla* "for ever" (→ *ulla* II); *adi šāri* "for all time; everywhere" (→ *šār*); "including, together with" M/NB, NA for *qadum*; before numerals "times, multiplied by" [A.RÁ], *adi šalāšīšu* "three times" (→ GAG §71a; OA → *ana* I 15); OA "concerning, on the subject of"; OAkk *adi danniš* "very much"; jB *adi surriš* "instantly" **2.** conj. (→ GAG §§116c, 173a-g) with pres. "until"; Mari "as soon as"; MA "while"; NB *kī adi* in oath → *kī* 4; with pret. "until; not before, as soon as"; OA "concerning the fact that"; with stat. "as long as, while" **3.** *adi lā* prep. "before, in advance of"; conj. with pres. or pret. "before; as long as ... not" **4.** *adi muḫḫi* NB, occas. NA for *adi*, prep. of time, space; conj.; mostly *adi muḫḫi ša* with pres. or perf. **5.** *adu/i bīt* NA for *adi*, as conj. with pres. "until", with *lā* "before" **6.** Am., Bogh. adv. ~ "indeed, truly" **7.** with pron. suff. only in → *adīni*, *adīšu*

adianni → *adû* I

adiānu → *adānum*

adikanna → *akanni*

adīlu; NB pl. *adīlānu* (part of a ceremonial garment) M/NB

adimatu → *adamatu* II; *mati*

adinakanni → *akanni*

adīni, Mari also *adīnu*, M/jB mostly *adīna*, once *adinnu* 'up to us' = "hitherto, till now" OA, O/jB; of time, OA "so far, till now"; otherwise neg. *a. ul/lā* "not yet" with stat., pres., pret., OB perf.; < *adi* + *-ni*; M/NA → *udīni*

adiptu → *ediptu*

adīriš "fearfully" jB; < *adīru*

adirtu I "gloominess" Bab. transf. "sorrow"; < *adāru* I

adirtu II "fear, apprehension" O/jB esp. pl.; < *adāru* II

adirtu → also *atartu*

adīru "fear" M/jB; < *adāru* II; > *adīriš*

ādiru "full of awe" jB; *lā ā.* "fearless, impudent" j/NB (MB/MA → *lādiru*); < *adāru* II

adiššu (an object) jB mag.

adīšu "till then" OB, Mari; < *adi* + *-šu*

adiu → *adû* I

admanu → *watmanum*

admūmu → *adammūmu*

admūtum "contributed share" OA; < *adāmum*

adnātu pl. tant. "world, people" jB

adnu → *atnu*

adriš "dimly, faintly visible" jB of celestial bodies; "darkly, unhappily" of people; < *adru* I

adru I "dark, gloomy" jB of mood; NA of textile; < *adāru* I

adru(m) II, MA gen. also *idri* , f.; pl. *adrātu* and *adrū* "threshing floor" Ass. as topog. feature; payment *ina adr(āt)i* "at threshing time"; NA also "courtyard"?

adrû "ibex-like" jB desig. of sheep; < Sum.

adu → *adi*

adû I, Ass. *adiu*; pl. *adû*, *adê* "(treaty-)oath; supernatural power of an oath" M/NA, M/NB *a. šakānu/tamû/naṣāru* "to establish/swear/keep a treaty"; NA *a. ša šarri* "(loyalty) oath to king"; j/NB, NA *bēl a.* "vassal"

adû II "now" NB; also *enna a.* "now then"

adû(m) III, *addû* "a (day's) work, stint" O/jB *ṣābū a.* "daily workers"; transf. sun's, moon's "tasks"; < Sum.

adû IV (a kind of headgear)? jB lex.

adû V "leader" jB lex.

adû VI mng. unkn. jB lex.

adû → also *aduššu*; *edû* I

âdu "to take notice of" MB **G** (pres. *i'âd*, pret. *i'īd*) **Š** "notify, inform" s.o.; → *na'ādu*

adudi(l)lu, *aduda'ilu* "praying mantis" jB

adūgu, *atūgu* "oven" jB; < Sum.

adugu(l), *aduku(l)* ~ "indeed" Bogh. (in texts from Eg.)

adum → *adi*

adumatu → *adamatu* II

adumu → *adammu*

adunakanni → *akanni*

adūpi mng. unkn. jB lex.

adurtu "village" jB lex.; < *adurû*

aduru "mirror"? jB lex.

adurû(m), *edurû*, *aturu*, *udurû*? "village, farmstead" Bab. [É.DURU5]; < Sum.; > *adurtu*

aduššu, *ada(š)šu(m)*, *adû* ~ "enclosure wall" O/jB

ae'u → *ya'u*

agâ, *agāi(a)* m. & f. sg. & pl.; f. rarely *agāta/i* "this" NB; < Aram.?; → *agannû*; *ingâ*

agabbu → *akabbu*

agadibbu, *gadibbu* "hand seeder-plough" jB lex.; < Sum.

agāgu(m) "to be(come) furious" Bab. **G** (*a/u*; stat. *agug*) of god, human **Gtn** "be steadfastly angry"? **D** stat. only "is very angry" **Š** caus. of G **N** "get angry"; > *aggu*, *aggiš*, *aggāgû*; *uggu*, *uggatu*, *uggugum*

agāi(a) → *agâ*

agakkum "whey" OB lex.; < Sum.

agalapû in *mê a.* (a kind of impure water) jB med.

agālu(m) I, *agallu* "donkey" Bab., NA(lit.) [DÚSU]

agālu II (a temple employee) jB lex.

agāmi "today" Am.; < W.Sem.

agammu "marsh(es), lagoon" jB

agāmu "to be furious" Bab. **G** lex. only **D** MB in stat. "is infuriated"; > *tēgimtu*; *igimtu*

agāmu → also *akāmu* I

agana "well now, come on!" OB, Mari before prec., imper.; < *a* + *gana* (→ GAG §124b)

aganatallû → *agannutillû*

agannu, NB *aggannu*; pl. usu. f. "bowl, cauldron" Qatna, M/NA, M/NB, Am., Nuzi for liquids; of copper, stone, clay

agannû; mostly m. pl. *agannûtu*; f. pl. *agannâ/êti* "these" NB; < *agâ* + *annû* I

aga(n)nutillû, *aganatallû* "dropsy" M/NB [A.GA.NU.TIL-]; < Sum.

agappu(m), NA also *aqappu* "wing" Bab., NA "wing" of bird, also as joint of meat; *a. ēnē* "eye-lashes"; OB lex. "wing" of door; → *kappu* I

agappu → also *akabbu*

agargarītu (a mineral) jB [A.GAR.GAR.^{d}ÍD]

agargarû (kind of fish(-spawn)) Bab.; < Sum.

agargarūtu "fish resources" jB [A.GAR.GAR.KU$_{6}$]; < Sum.

agarimuri (a food) MA

agarinnu(m), *garinnu* O/jB **1.** "womb" or transf. "mother" **2.** in metallurgy "basin, crucible" **3.** "(first) beer mash" [AGARIN$_{4/5}$; AMA.TÙN]; < Sum.

agarrūtu → *agru*

agāru(m) "to hire, rent" **G** (*a/u*) person, animal, ship, cart, house **D** OA = G **N** pass. of G, of person; > *agru*, *agirtum*, *agrūtu*; *āgirum*, *āgirtu*; *igru*; *munnagru*; *nāgurtu*

ag(a)runnu "cella" jB; < Sum.

agasalakku(m), *agasal/ilikku(m)* (a kind of axe) O/jB [AGA.SILIG]; < Sum.; → *agû* I

agašgû "youngest son; junior, novice" jB, NA of scribe, physician etc.

agāšū; f. *agāšiya*; pl. *agāšunu* "that (one), those (ones)" NB; < *agâ* + *šū*, *šī*, *šunu*

agāta/i → *agâ*

agatukullu "butt end of a weapon" jB lex.; < Sum.

agāum → *agû* I

agbaru → *akbaru*

agg... also = *ana g*...

aggāgû "furious" jB; < *agāgu*

aggannu → *agannu*; *akkannu*

aggiš "furiously" Bab., NA; < *aggu*

aggu(m) "furious" Bab. mostly with *libbu* ("heart"); < *agāgu*; > *aggiš*; → *akku*

aggullu → *akkullu*

agiddû → *agittû*

āgilu, *ābi/ulu*, jB also *agillu* ? "towman" of boat O/jB lex.

agirtum "hired maid-servant" O/jB; < *agāru*

āgirtu "(female) hirer, mistress" jB; < *agāru*

āgirum "hirer" OB [LÚ.ḪUN]; < *agāru*

agittû, *agiddû*, *egiddû* "headband; bandage" jB lex.; < Sum.

agīum → *agû* I

agriqqu → *abarikkum*

agru(m); pl. OB *agrū*, NA, NB *agrūtu*, NB also *agarrūtu* "hireling; hired man" [LÚ.ḪUN.GÁ; OB also ÉRIN.ḪUN.GÁ; NB also LÚ.A.GAR]; Bab., NA astr. "Aries" (constellation) [MUL.(LÚ.)ḪUN(.GÁ)]; < *agāru*; > *agrūtu*

agrunnu → *agarunnu; garunnu*

agrūtu "hire (contract)" M/NB; Am. "wages"; < *agru*

agû(m) I, OAkk *agā/īum* "tiara, crown" [AGA] symbol of rule of god, king; transf. jB "corona" of planet, star, sun; OB om. "circle" of oil, incense; jB lex. "ring, band" round axe; < Sum.; → *agasalakku*

agû(m) II, *egû* "wave, flood" Bab. [A.GI$_{6}$.A; A.GU$_{4}$; A.GA] of river etc.; transf. ref. to wrath of gods, demons; < Sum.; → *binûtu*

agû III (a garment) jB lex.

agû → also *egu*

agubbû, *egubbû* "holy water vessel" jB [(DUG.)A.GÚB.BA]; < Sum.

agugillu ~ "sorcerer" jB; < Sum.; > *agugiltu*

agugiltu ~ "sorceress" jB; < *agugillu*

***agūgu** unattested; mng. unkn.

agūgūtu "status of *agūgu*" jB

aguḫḫu(m); OAkk Hurr. pl. *aguḫḫena* "sash, belt" OAkk, O/jB

agūnu "tiara" jB lex.

agurrutu → *gurrutu*

agurrum m. & f. **1.** "baked brick" Bab., M/NA [SIG$_{4}$.AL.ÙR.RA; OB math. SIG$_{4}$.AL.UR$_{5}$.RA]; often coll.; O/MB also as unit of measurement; *a. uqnî elleti* "blue-glazed brick", *a. ešmarê* "yellow-glazed brick"; *a. ša atbari/pēle peṣê/ašnugalli* "building block of basalt/white limestone/alabaster"; *a. kaspi ebbi* "slab of pure silver" **2.** (an impost) NB

agusīgu → *ḫusīgu*

aḫa in *aḫa aḫa* "one by one"? OA; < *aḫu* II

aḫā'iš, *aḫāyiš* "each other, one another" Ass. as obj., NA *a. ṣabātu* "to join forces"; *ištu/itti a.* "together"; *urki a.* "one after the other"; *ana a.* "one another, together"; < *aḫu* I; > *aḫîš*; → *aḫāmiš*

aḫāmiš, Am., Bogh. *ḫa(m)miš*, NB also *aḫame(š)šu* "each other, one another" M/NB, occas. NA as obj.; as gen., NB *pūt a. našû* "they stand security mutually"; *kī a.* "together, at the same time"; *itti a.* "together"; *malla a.* "all together"; *arki a.* "one after the other"; *ana (muḫḫi) a.* "together"; *ana pāni/tarṣi a.* "face to face"; *meḫret a.* "in the same way"; < *aḫu* I; → *aḫā'iš*

aḫamma, jB also *aḫammu* "apart, separately" OA, occas. Bab., NA; < *aḫu* II

aḫannâ "on this bank" j/NB of river, marsh etc.; < *aḫu* II + *annû* I

aḫannumma → *aḫennâ*

aḫānu I "to another place" NB leg., divert property "elsewhere"; < *aḫu* II + *-ānu*

aḫānum II (a type of worker) Mari

aḫarātum "on the far bank" Mari; opp. → *aqdamātum*; < W.Sem.; → *aḫāru*

aḫarriš "in future" jB; < *aḫāru*

aḫarrum "later, thereafter" OB; opp. → *pānānu*; < *aḫāru*

aḫartiš "for the future" MB; < *aḫāru*

aḫāru(m) "to be behind" **G** Am. stat. only "is late, delayed" **D** trans. "hold back, delay" s.th.; intrans. "stay behind, delay, be in default"; stat. "is outstanding, overdue"; OB of days "are left, remain"; OA "set aside" statue ? **Š** OAkk, jB? "make s.o./s.th. late"?; > *aḫrītu, aḫrâ, aḫrûtu, aḫrâtaš, aḫrītiš; aḫartiš, aḫertum; aḫarrum, aḫarriš, ḫaramma; aḫurrû; uḫḫuru, uḫḫurtu; uḫrû; uḫurrā'um; tēḫirtu*; → *aḫarātum*

aḫāta, *aḫāti/u* "in equal shares" NB; < *aḫu* I

aḫātatum "little sister" OB; < *aḫātu* I

aḫātu(m) I, NB *aḫattu*; pl. OA *aḫuātum*, OB *aḫḫātu* "sister" [NIN] "(natural) sister"; transf. OA as complimentary term; OB of f. subst.s *a. ... a.* "the one ... the other"; < *aḫu* I; > *aḫātūtu, aḫḫūtu* II, *aḫātatum*

aḫātu II **1.** "bank" NA(roy. inscr.) of river, sea **2.** MA pl. "sleeves" of garment **3.** jB transf. ref. to moral transgression "limit"?; < *aḫu* II

aḫātu → also *aḫāta*; *aḫu* II 3

aḫâtu → *aḫītu*; *aḫû* I

aḫātūtu "sisterhood" Nuzi; < *aḫātu* I

aḫāzu(m) "to take; marry; learn" **G** (*a/u*) **1.** of demons, diseases "seize, grasp" **2.** of husband, also father-in-law "take (a woman in marriage), marry" **3.** "take notice of, learn" **4.** "make s.th. o.'s own, acquire" **5.** *puzram a.*, *marqītu a.* "take refuge", *ḫarrānam a.* "take to road" **6.** j/NB *dīn PN a.* "take PN to law" **7.** OB "take" troops (into battle), OA *rābiṣam a.* "take on as agent" **8.** occas. ~ D "inlay" with metal **Gt** "be connected with; well versed in" **D** (OA infin. also *eḫḫuzum*) "mount, plate, inlay" with metal, stone (< *iḫzu* denom.) [GAR(.RA)]; "marry" pl. **Dt** pass. of D **Š 1.** "make s.o. take s.th." **2.** "make s.o. marry" **3.** "make s.o. learn", "instruct, incite" s.o., "point out, indicate to" s.o. **4.** OAkk "make s.th. available" **5.** → G 5 with *puzru* etc. "hide" s.th., s.o. **6.** leg., *dīnam š.* "institute proceedings against s.o." **7.** "ignite, set fire to" **8.** stat. "has a right to, is entitled to" real estate **9.** "have an object mounted in precious metal" **Štn** "instruct, inform s.o. repeatedly"; OB of disease "infect repeatedly" **Št^1** OB "be instructed, incited"? **Št^2** lex. "ignite" fire, "make" fire "catch" **N** pass. of G 2 "marry each other"; of fire etc. "catch, spread"; > *aḫiztu, aḫzūtu; iḫzu* I, *iḫzētu; āḫizum, āḫizānu; aḫḫāzu; aḫuzzatu; tāḫāzu, tāḫāziš; tāḫīzu; uḫḫuzu; māḫāzu, māḫāziš; mušāḫizu, muštaḫḫizum; nanḫuzu*

aḫê "separately, by itself" O/jB, Bogh., NA; > *aḫennâ*; → *aḫu* II

aḫē'iš → *aḫîš*

aḫennâ, *aḫennû*, Mari *aḫannumma* "each by it/himself, apart, separately" O/jB of persons, ingredients; jB of hair "in strands"; < *aḫê* + *annû* I

aḫertum, NB *aḫištu* "remainder" OB math., NB; < *aḫāru*

aḫḫ... also = *ana ḫ...*

aḫḫātu → *aḫātu* I

aḫḫāzu 'the seizer' (a demon) jB [^{d}DÌM.ME.LAGAB] **1.** as demon often in incantations after Lamaštu and Labāṣu **2.** "jaundice" (the disease caused by the *a.* demon); < *aḫāzu*

aḫḫu "dry wood" jB lex.

aḫḫū → *aḫu* I

aḫḫur → *ḫurri*

aḫḫūtu(m) I "brotherhood" [ŠEŠ(.MEŠ)-; in PNs PAP.MEŠ] "(adopted) brotherhood"; "brotherly relations"; < *aḫu* I

aḫḫūtu(m) II "sisterhood" OB(Susa); < *aḫātu* I

aḫi → *aḫu* I.II

aḫia "outside" j/NB; *aḫia aḫia* "each side" of; < *aḫu* II

aḫiātum → *aḫītu*; *aḫû* I

aḫirtum → *aḫertum*

aḫiš "on o.'s own" jB "alone"? of planet; < *aḫu* II ?

aḫîš, *aḫē'iš*, *aḫîše*, *aḫiyāši* "each other, one another" NA; *(kī) a.* "together"; *issi a.* → *issaḫîš*; *ana a.* "one another"; *ina muḫḫi a.* "one after the other"; < *aḫā'iš*

aḫištu → *aḫertum*

aḫītu(m) **1.** "side"; also acc. *aḫītam(ma)*, *aḫīta* as adv. "aside, on one side" **2.** "surroundings, environment" NA pl. *aḫītāte*; esp. pl. "entourage, associates" **3.** pl. OB ~ "extra shares"; "(strange, i.e.) unfortunate, adverse" events, omen(s) **4.** sg. jB as subst. "misfortune", "defamation" **5.** OB "additional payment" of dues or perquisites; < *aḫû* I

aḫiu → *aḫû* I

aḫiyāši → *aḫîš*

āḫizānu(m), *āḫiziānu* "(the) one who marries/d" OB, MA; < *āḫizu* + *-ān*

aḫiztu "married woman"? jB; < *aḫāzu*

āḫizum "informed person"? Mari; < *aḫāzu*

aḫlamatti "in Aramaic" NB; < *aḫlamû*

aḫlamû (desig. for Aramaeans) M/NA, MB; OB as PN ?; lex. "Aramaic" language; > *aḫlamatti*

aḫmaḫam, *aḫmaḫim* "one another" OB(Susa); < *aḫam* + *aḫu* I; > *aḫmāmu*

aḫmāmu "one another" OB(Susa); also *aḫmāmiš*; *ana a.* "against each other", also *eli a.*; *mala a.* "together, equally"; < *aḫmaḫam*

aḫnu → *uḫnu*

aḫrâ → *aḫrītu*

aḫrâtaš "for ever after" j/NB(lit.); *a. nišī*, *a. ūmī* "for posterity"; < *aḫrītu*

aḫrâtu, *aḫriātum* → *aḫrītu*

aḫrītiš, *aḫriātiš* "for the future" O/jB in *aḫrītiš ūmī* "in future days"; < *aḫrītu*

aḫrītu f.; mostly pl. OB *aḫriātum*, M/NB *aḫrâtu* "later time" Bab. *aḫrât ūmī* "later days"; *(nišī) aḫrâti* "posterity"; MB *ana aḫrâ(ti)* adv. "for the future"; < *aḫāru*; > *aḫrâtaš*, *aḫrītiš*, *aḫrûtu*

aḫrušḫu (a vessel) O/MB(Alal.), Bogh. for liquids, solids; < Hurr.

aḫrûtu "descendants" jB lex.; < *aḫrītu* abstr.

aḫšad(a)rapannu "satrap (of the Persian empire)" NB; < OPers.

aḫu(m) I "brother" (st. constr. *aḫi*, OA *aḫu/ū*; nom. with pron. suff. *aḫūni/ka*; *aḫī*, *aḫūa* "my brother", M/NB *aḫūya*; acc. *aḫāka*; st. abs. *aḫ* OAkk, OA in PN; du. *aḫā* OB; pl. *aḫḫū*, W.Sem. *aḫāte*, OB after numerals *aḫānu*; st. constr. *aḫḫī* OB all cases; with pron. suff. *aḫḫūka*) [ŠEŠ; OB also ŠEŠ.A.NI; PAP in later PNs, NA] **1.** "(natural) brother"; *a. rabû/ṣeḫru* "older/younger brother"; *a. abim* "father's brother, uncle" **2.** transf. (address for people of equal rank); "colleague"; "fellow tribesman"; *a. rabû* "deputy teacher" **3.** *aḫum aḫam* "one another, mutually", also *a. ana a.*, *a. mala a.*, *a. kīma a.*; > *aḫḫūtu* I; *aḫātu* I etc.; *aḫāta*; *aḫāmiš*, *aḫā'iš*, *aḫîš*, *aḫmaḫam*, *aḫmāmu*; *aḫû* II; → *atḫû*

aḫu(m) II "arm, side" (st. constr. *aḫ(i)*) **1.** "arm", *a. nadû* "to 'drop o.'s arm', i.e. be lazy, negligent", j/NB *nadê a. rašû* "to become negligent"; *uppi a.* "armpit"; *birti a.* "chest"?; transf. "arm, handle" of an instrument; OB du. transf. "strength, ability" **2.** "side"; Bab. [GÚ] "shore" of sea, "bank" of river; "edge" of town, field; "wing" of army; "flank" of animal; of object, part of liver, other parts of body; *a. šattim* "turn, beginning of (financial) year"; *a. ana a.* "side by side"; *(ina) a.* jB as prep. "beside, at" **3.** NB "part, share", "one-half"; pl. f. *aḫātu* "partner, joint proprietor" **4.** pl. m. *aḫānu* "arm fetters"? NB; "wings"? of a building jB **5.** "sleeve (flap)" of garment M/NA, MB, Nuzi; > *aḫû* I, *aḫiš*?, *aḫia*, *aḫa*, *aḫītu*; *aḫamma*; *aḫātu* II, *aḫānu* I, *aḫannâ*, *aḫullâ*; → *aḫê*; *aḫum*; *aḫunê*

aḫû(m) I, Ass. *aḫiu* "outside(r), strange" [BAR] of person, also as subst. "stranger"; (desig. of planet =) Mars; of appearance "abnormal"; of textual passage "non-canonical, extraneous" [pl. also BAR.BAR]; < *aḫu* II + *-ī*; > *aḫītu*

***aḫû(m)** II **G** not attested **Gt** OA, Am. "to fraternize, become brothers" **Št** "pair off with", M/jB of stars, features in extispicy "stand opposite each other"; of enemies "join forces, conspire" **N** MB(Alal.) "fraternize"; < *aḫu* I denom.; > *atḫû*, *atḫûtu*; *šutāḫû*

aḫû → also *ḫaḫû*

aḫula, *aḫūlamma* "alas!" NA, also in PNs

aḫulab → *aḫulap*

aḫulabakku "lamentation with *aḫulap*-exclamations" jB lex.; < *aḫulap* + *-akku*

aḫūlamma → *aḫula*

aḫulap (or *aḫulab*), OB also *aḫulup*, OB lex. *aḫulapum* "(it is) enough!" OAkk, Bab.; as declaration of clemency by god, as petition for clemency by worshipper; jB *šam a.* (a plant name); > *aḫulabakku*

aḫullâ, *aḫullû*, NB *aḫullûa* "on the other bank; on the other side, beyond" j/NB, occas. NA; < *aḫu* II + *ullû* I

aḫulup → *aḫulap*

aḫum "separately, besides" OA; → *aḫu* II

aḫunê "separately, individually" OB; > *aḫunêš*; → *aḫu* II

aḫunêš "individually" Mari; < *aḫunê* + *-iš*

aḫurrû "junior" jB **1.** "social inferior" **2.** "younger child"; < *aḫāru*

aḫussu → *uḫultu*

aḫušḫu (a wooden object) MB(Alal.), Nuzi; < Hurr.

aḫuššu → *amuššu*

aḫuš'u (a poet. epith. of copper) jB lex.

aḫuzzatu "marriage gift; marriage-like protection" MA, MB; < *aḫāzu*

aḫzūtu "mounting(s)" of metal objects M/NB; < *aḫāzu*

ai I, *ē* (before consonant), *â*, *ya* "not" **1.** OAkk, OA, O/jB vetitive ptcl. before pret. "may (you, he etc.) not ..." (→ GAG §§81i, k, 154c); OA before perf., stat.; jB in denial *ai addin* "I certainly did not give" **2.** OA double neg. *ē lā* with 2 pers. pret. = strong pos. exhortation "definitely" **3.** "no!" O/jB usu. before a voc.; Am. before proh.

ai II, *â*, *ayyi*, *ayya/u* "alas!" Bab.

ai III "where?" OAkk in PNs; OB lex.; > *ēm*; → *ayyikīam* etc.

aigalluḫu (a horned animal)? Am., Nuzi

a'īlu → *awīlu*

a'īluttu → *awīlūtum*

ainibu → *yānibu*

aiwa (a cereal foodstuff) Nuzi; < Hurr.

akâ adv. mng. unkn. Bogh.

akabbu (or *akappu*, *agabb/ppu*) (a tree) Nuzi

aka(k)ku in *a. nāri* (a plant name) jB lex.

akalu(m), *aklu(m)* [NINDA; NB also NINDA.ḪI.A, NINDA.MEŠ] **1.** "bread, loaf; food" [→ also *kusāpu* 2]; *a. ḫarrāni* "journey bread", *a. ginê* "offering bread"; *a. tumri* "charcoal baked bread"; jB *bēl a.* "guest" (or read *kusāpu*?) **2.** NB (a small unit of capacity) [for NINDA as length measure → *ginindanakku*?] **3.** MB "expenditure"?; < *akālu*

akālu(m) "to eat" **G** (*a/u*) [GU$_7$] **1.** of men, animals "eat, feed (on)"; of baby *tulâša a.* "feed (from) her breast"; "bite" o.'s lips **2.** transf. of fire, god causing disease, pest, enemy "consume, devastate"; of pain, grief "consume; irritate, hurt" part of body **3.** "soak up" liquid, "absorb" fat **4.** "use up, spend" money **5.** "have usufruct of, enjoy" field, agricultural product, share, booty **6.** in idioms → *asakku* II, *ikkibu*, *karṣu*; OB math. of wall etc. "decrease in width" **Gtn** iter. of G [GU$_7$.GU$_7$] **Gt** of lands "ravage each other"; of stars "cover, absorb each other" **Š** caus. of G [GU$_7$] "make" men, animals, fire "eat, feed on, consume" food, medication, goods, booty, lands; "steep" an object in liquid; OA "satisfy" a claimant; jB stat. "is infected" with a disease **Št** [GU$_7$] OB math. "multiply together", freq. "square" measured lengths **N** pass. of G [GU$_7$]; > *akalu*; *aklu*; *ākilu*, *ākiltum*, *akkilu*; *akiltu*; *iklu* II, *ikiltu*; *akussu*, *ukultu*, *uklu* II; *ukullû* I; *mākalum*, *mākaltu*, *mākālu*; *tākaltu*?; *tākultu*; *šūkulu*, *šūkultu*; *mušākilu*, *mušākilūtum*; → *musakkiltu*

akalūtu(m) ~ "tree" O/jB; → *kalûtu* II

akā(m)mu "granary"? jB lex.

akāmu I, *agāmu* "dust-cloud, mist" jB; < *akāmu* II

akāmu II mng. uncert. jB **G** stat. only, of moon; > *akāmu* I; **D** → *wakāmum*

akāmu → also *akammu*

akanna I, *kanna/â*, *ekannam* "so, thus" MA, M/NB, Am., Bogh., Ug., introducing dir. speech; *k.-ma* "just so, similarly"; < *akī/kī* + *anna*

akanna II, *akannu/i* "here" M/NB, jB; *an(a) a.* "hither"; MB with *adi* → *akanni*; < Aram.; > *akannaka*

akannaka, *akannaku(nu)* "there" NB; < *akanna* II + *-ka/-kunu*

akannama, *kannama* "similarly, likewise" Am., Bogh., Ug.

akanni "now" M/NA; MA *anakanni*, NA also *adi/u(n)akanni*, MB *adikanna* "till now, so far"

akanni → also *akanna* II

akannu → *akanna* II

akānu → *akkannu*

akânu "hither, this way" MB; < *akī* + *-ānu*

akappu → *akabbu*

akaru mng. unkn. jB lex.

akāšu(m) "to walk, go" Bab., O/MA **G** (*u/u*) [DU] of messenger, person, snake **Gt** "go away" **D** "drive away, expel" person, disease, demon; ~ "press, push away" part of liver; OA stat. of tablet "is mislaid"? **Dtn** iter. of D **Dt** pass. of D "be expelled, driven off"; > *ukkušu*

akatu mng. unkn. jB lex.

akāwa "on (this) side" Nuzi; < Hurr.

akayû → *kayyu*

akbaru(m), *akkabaru*, *agbaru* "jerboa"? Bab., NA as food; as fPN, also *Akbartum*

akê → *kē*

akī, *akkī* "as" NA, NB **1.** prep. (alternating with → *kī*) "like, in accordance with; (in substitution) for"; *akī arḫi* "per month" **2.** conj. of

time "as soon as, when"; *akī ša* "just as, in the way that"; < *ana* I + *kī*; > *akânu*; → *akanna* I
akia "in the following way" M/NA, Bogh.; → *kīam*
akiltu "expended goods, consumption" NA; < *akālu*; → *aklu*
ākiltum f. 'that eats' OB om. mng. uncl. of pest; < akālu
ākilu(m) "that eats, eating; eater, devourer" 1. Mari rit. (a cultic performer) **2.** jB of lion, desig. of the jackal **3.** O/jB "caterpillar"; < *akālu*
akītu(m); pl. *akiātu/i*, NB *akâte* (a cultic festival) OAkk, Bab., NA [Á.KI.IT; A.KI.TU; Á.KI.TUM] MB onwards freq. celebrated at the New Year; *ūm/isin akīti* "*akītu* day/festival"; also in PN; jB, NA *(bīt) a.* "*akītu* festival building"; *a. ṣēri* "*a.* in the countryside"; *bāb a.* "*akītu* gate"
akk... also = *ana k...*
akkabaru → *akbaru*
akkadattu "in Akkadian" NB
akkadīya "cock, rooster"; < Akkade (Aram. form)
akkadû(m), OA gen. *akkidīyē*; f. *akkadītu(m)* "from Akkade, made in Akkade, Akkadian" [URI(.KI)] of language; furniture, boats, cloth; jB lex. (a breed of sheep); < Akkade + *-ī*
akkā'i, *akkāya* "how?" (interrog. ptcl.) j/NB; NB *a. kī* (conj.) **1.** "how" **2.** "as soon as, when"
akkā'ikī "how much, how many?" NB; < *akkā'i* + *kī*
akkamdaš, *akkandaš*, *anakandaš* "spoke (of a wheel)" MB; < Kass.
akkannu, *a(k)kānu* **1.** "wild ass" M/jB **2.** (a breed of horses) Nuzi **3.** (a bird) jB
akkāya → *akkā'i*
akkê → *kē*
akkī → *akī*
akkīam → *kīam*
akkidīyē → *akkadû*
akkilu(m) "eater" O/jB of lion "(man) eating"; < *akālu*
akkīma → *kīma* 9
akku "furious" NA; < Aram.; → *aggu*
akkū → *kūm*
akkû, *akû* "owl" jB lex., NA
akkullakku (or *aqqullakku*) (a vegetable) jB lex.; < *akkullu*
akkullānu (or *aqqullānu*) (a copper object)? jB lex.; NA as PN
akkullātu pl. tant. "clods"? of field NB
akkullu (or *aqqullu*), *aggullu*; pl. f., occas. m. "hatchet, pick(axe), adze" Bab., NA [(GIŠ.)NÍG.GUL]; < Sum.; > *akkullakku*

akla "apart from" (prep.) jB erron.?
aklabû (a plant) jB lex.
aklu(m) "eaten, consumed" O/MB; OB *aklam išātim* "consumed by fire"; MB "expended" commodities; < *akālu*; → *akiltu*
aklu → also *akalu*; *waklum*
akmu mng. unkn. jB lex.
aksuppu → *askuppu*
akṣu, *ekṣu*, arch. *wakṣum* ~ "brazen, dangerous" O/jB of enemies, mountains, illness; < *ekēṣu* ?; > *ekṣiš*
aktam, *atkam* (a medicinal plant) jB lex., med.; *zēr a.* "seed of *a.*"
akû I "weak, powerless, humble" M/NB, jB; > *akûtu* I; → *makû* I ?
akû(m) II "cripple" Bab.; > *akûtu* II
akû III ~ "mooring pole"? jB lex.
akû → also *akkû*
akukarumma in *a. epēšu* "to redeem" Nuzi; < Hurr.
akukia in *a. ... a.* "so much ... so much" MA (→ GAG §117e appendix)
akukūtu; jB obl. pl. *akukāti* "firebrand" Bogh., jB; astr. "red glow in sky" (freq. wr. ḪA-ḪA-ḪA-*tum* = *'a₄-ku₆-ku₆-tum*)
akullu in *bīt a.* (part of an elaborate house) NA
akullû → *ukullû* I
akūnu (a vessel for liquids) Am.; < Eg.
akussu → *ukultu*
akuṣīmu, *(a)kuṣīmānu*, *kurṣīmatu* (a plant) O/jB lex., med.
akuttu (a part of a waggon) jB lex.; < Sum.
akûtu I "powerlessness"; < *akû* I abstr.
akûtu II "disablement" jB; *a. alākum* "to become crippled"; < *akû* II abstr.
al → *ali* I; *alla* 1; *eli*
aladiru, *ladiru* (a plant) jB lex., med.
aladlammû "human-headed bull-colossus" M/jB(Ass.), NA [ᵈÀLAD.ᵈLAMMA]; < Sum.
alādu → *walādum*
alaḫḫinu(m), *alḫenu*, NA *laḫḫinu* "miller"? Ass.; NA (an official in temple service); OA *rabi a.* (an official); > *alaḫḫinūtum*; *laḫḫinatu*
alaḫḫinūtum (office of the *a.*) OA
alaḫittu mng. unkn. jB
alaknu (a kind of rush) jB lex.
alaktu(m), *alkatu*; pl. → *alkakātu* "way, course" [A.RÁ] **1.** "gait" of man, animal; "route, journey" of gods, people, *a. parāsu* "to break/interrupt s.o.'s course"; "course" of stars, water; of illness, fire **2.** OA, jB transf. "way of life, behaviour", *a. še'û(m)* "to look after s.o." **3.** Bab., NA "business trip, caravan"; < *alāku*

alāku(m) "to go" **G** (*illak*, *illik*; perf. *ittalak* (→ GAG §97n)) [DU] **1.** of person, animal; + vent. "come", jB imper. *alka* "well, now then!"; + *ana* "go to" somewhere, + dat. pron. suff. "to" s.o.; "move along, walk"; *ana šīmti/šīmāti a.* "go to o.'s destiny, die"; OB *a. epēšum* "travel"; MA (of horses) "trot"?; *warki/ana pī ... a.* "follow, serve" s.o.; → *dinānu*; as ptcp. *ālik maḫri* 'who walks in front' = "predecessor" [IGI.DU]; *ālik pānim* 'who walks before' = "leader, predecessor" (→ *ālik-pānûtu*); *ālik arki* "successor" **2.** of letters, tablets etc. "arrive"; of military campaign, vehicles, celestial bodies "move"; of wind "blow"; of rain "fall"; of incense, radiance "spread"; of skin, flesh etc. "flake off"; of liquids "flow"; of time "pass" **3.** with internal objects: + *idu* "go at s.o.'s side" = "come to s.o.'s aid"; "go on, along" a way, path, road, "pass through" the desert; *šiddam pūtam a.* 'go length and width' of an area = "survey" a field **4.** *ilka a.* "perform (military) service"; *dikûtu a.* "report for call-up"; NB *našpartu a.* "fulfil an order, manage/run a business" **5.** with abstr. noun ending in *-ūtu* and before adv. "become" **6.** misc.: of price "be current, in force", of commodity "be worth, fetch"; of interest "accumulate"; of (ominous) signs "appear"; "be appropriate, possible, available"; of greed "aim at" silver; *ana pānīšu/ša a.* "advance, grow larger"; NB math. *X* GAM/A.RÁ/*ana Y a.* "multiply X by Y" **7.** NA with ellipsis of *qabā'u* freq. before dir. speech **Gtn** [DU.DU] "go, come repeatedly; roam about, wander", *muttallik mūši* [LÚ.GE_6.A.DU.DU; (LÚ.)GE_6.DU.DU] 'who walks around during the night' = "night-watchman"; OB of leg muscles "twitch persistently" **Gt** "go off, away" (→ GAG §92e) differentiation between pret. of Gt and perf. of G difficult **Š** caus. of G [DU] with abstr. noun ending in *-ūtu* or adv. "make s.o./s.th. (become)" s.th.; stat. "is appropriate, suitable" [TÚM.MA]; > *alaktu*, *alkakātu*, *ilkakātu*; *ilku* I, *alku* I; *āliku*, *āliktu*, *ālikūtu*, *ālikānum*, *ālik-pānûtu*; *allaku*, *allāku*; *mālaku* I; *muttalliku*; *muttalliktu*; *šūluku*; *tāluku*; *tallaktu*, *tallakku*

alāla/i → *alālu* I

alallu(m), *elallu* (a stone) Bab. mag., also used in building

alallû I, *elallû* "drain, pipe" O/jB [ÁLAL]; → *alû* IV

alallû II, *alû*, *elû* (device for hoisting water) O/jB; < Sum.

alallû III (a plant) jB

alālu I, *alāla/i*, *alīli* (a work cry), "work song" M/NB, NA esp. *a. š/sasû* "to sing a work song"; > *alālu* III ?

alālu(m) II, *ḫalālum* "to hang up, suspend" Bab. **G** (*a/u*, pres. OB *i'allal*, jB *illal*) "hang (up)" people as punishment, "hang up, suspend" objects; stat. OB ext. "is 'hanging'" (wr. *ḫalil* etc.) **Gt** "be tangled; be allied with" also in PNs OAkk, OB **D** stat. only ext. "is hung (about) with" s.th. **Dt** pass. of D **Š** jB in *qāta šūlulu* "stay o.'s hand" **N** of objects "be hung up"; of lamentation "hang (in the air)"?; > *mālaltu*; *ma'lalum*?

alālu III O/jB **G** not attested **Gt** "to sing a joyful song; boast" **Š** "exult, celebrate" **Štn** iter. of Š; < *alālu* I denom.?; > *elēlu* I, *elēlānû*; *alīlu*; *illatu* II; *mušaḫlilu*

alamattu → *almattu*

alamdimmû → *alandimmû*

alamgātu f. pl. "sculptures" MA; < Sum.?

alamgû "seal-cutter" jB lex.; < Sum.

alamittu, *elamittu*, *ḫulamē/ītu*, MA *alamūtu* (a wild species of date palm) MA, j/NB

alamû (an aquatic plant)? M/NA, jB as drug

alamūtu → *alamittu*

alandimmû (or *alamdimmû*) "physique, form" jB [ALAN.DÍM(.A/MA)] esp. in physiognomic omens; < Sum.

alânu → *aliānu*

ālānû(m); f. *ālānītu* "living in a (foreign) place, abroad, exile" O/jB, Mari, MA in fPN; < *ālu* I + *-ān* + *-ī*

alappānu, *labb/ppānu* **1.** O/jB lex. "sweet pomegranate" **2.** O/jB, Mari, NA (a sweet beer) in *(šikar) l.*; Mari *ša a.* "(female) brewer"

alapû, j/NB, NA also *el(a)pû*, *elappû*, *anapû* (an aquatic plant, phps.) "seaweed; algae" Bab., NA

alāpu(m) **G** mng. uncl. jB **Št** OB "to make immovable, paralyse" part of body; > *alpu* II; *nēlepu*?

alāpu → also *elēpu*

alašû "Cypriot" Mari; < Alašia

alātu(m) (var. of *la'ātu*) "to swallow (up)" Bab. **G** (*u/u*) ext., transf. of parts of the body or foetus "absorb" **D** ~ G, jB also transf. "suppress" revolt; > *ma'lātu*; → *ḫalātum*

alātû (a social class, palace dependant ?) Nuzi

alā'u ~ "to lick" **G** jB lex. **Št** → *šutelū'u*

ālāyû "citizen, (dependent) villager" O/jB, MA; < *ālu* I + *-ay*; > *ālāyûtu*; → *ālīum*

ālāyû → also *alli'ayya*

ālāyûtu "status of dependent villager" MA; < *ālāyû*

aldu → *waldum*

aldû(m) "(grain) quota" O/jB; [AL.DÙ] esp. for sowing; < Sum.

alê → *ali* I

algamišu, *algamešu*, *algamisu* (a kind of stone) jB [NA4.ALGAMES]; → *gamēsu*

algarsurrû "drumstick"? OB lex.; < Sum.

algumes (or *algurit*?) (a piece of jewellery)? jB/NA

alḫenu → *alaḫḫinu*

ali I, *alê*, *al*, NB *alu* "where?" OAkk, Ass., O/jB **1.** "where?" **2.** conj. "where(ever)" OA, OB(lit.) **3.** prep. "at the place of" OA before infin.; > *alumma*

ali II ~ "surely" Mari

aliānu, *alânu* (a tree) O/jB lex.

ālidānu "progenitor" MA; < *walādum*

alidni, *aridni* (a plant) jB lex.

ālidu → *wālidum*

ālidūtu in *lā ālidūtu* "sterility" jB; < *wālidum*

ālikānum "traveller" OB; < *ālikum* + *-ān*

ālik-pānûtu "going in front, leadership" NB; < *ālik pāni* abstr. (→ *alāku* G 1)

āliktum 'going; goer' f. **1.** Mari ~ "flying column" **2.** jB lex. (a kind of bow) **3.** (a kind of metal weapon); < *āliku*

āliku(m) 'going; goer' **1.** adj. jB, NA "moving, walking"; "falling out" of hair; "alight" of stove; Mari "appropriate" **2.** subst. OA, O/jB "traveller; messenger" **3.** Nuzi, jB → *ṣēru* 4; < *alāku* ptcp.

ālikūtu subst. 'going' = "philandering" jB; *ālikūt maḫri* "precedence"; < *āliku* abstr.

alilānu (a tree) jB lex.

alīli → *alālu* I

alīlu(m), *elīlu* (or *ālēlilu*?); f. *a/eliltu* ~ "powerful" Bab., NA as epith. of deities, kings, warriors; < *alālu* III

alimbû (a (mythical?) bovid) jB lex.; < Sum.

alimu ~ "honoured, of high rank" jB; < Sum.

alīq pî → *līqu* I

āli(s)su → *wālidum*

ālišam "village by village" OB, Mari; < *ālu* I + *-išam*

ālittiš in *lā ālittiš* "like a barren woman" jB; < *wālittum*

ālittu → *wālittum*

alītum → *elītu*

alium → *elû* II

ālīum "citizen, local" OA, in pl.; < *ālu* I; → *ālāyû*

alkakātu(m) pl. "ways of life; actions, behaviour" Bab.(lit.) of gods, demons, people; < *alaktu* irreg. pl.; → *ilkakātu* 1

alkanniwe (part of a vehicle) Nuzi; < Hurr.

alkatu → *alaktu*

alku I "state service" NA(lit.); < *alāku*

alku II "course" of canal, "region along the bank" NB; < Aram.

all... also = *ana l...*

alla "beyond; apart from" j/NB **1.** prep. (also wr. *al*) "beyond, past; more than; apart from"; in comparative clauses instead of *eli* **2.** before prep.: *alla ana*, *alla ina* "beyond, past; apart from" **3.** adv. "instead, rather"; < *ana* I + *lā*; → *allânum*

allaḫarum → *annuḫaru*

allak "hub (of a wheel)" M/jB lex.

allakkāniš → *allānu* I

allaku "always moving" M/jB; < *alāku*

allāku "traveller, messenger; agent" j/NB; < *alāku*

allallu I (a kind of bird) jB

allallu II, *allallû* ~ "powerful" j/NB epith. of gods

allalu mng. unkn. jB lex.

allâmi → *allû* II

allân → *allânum*

Allānātum (an Ass. month name) O/MA, jB lex.

allānu(m) I "oak; acorn" [GIŠ/Ú.AL.LA.AN]; jB as drug; OA pl. *allānū* "oak-resin"?; med. [NAGAR(-); GIŠ.LAM.MAR] "(suppository shaped like) acorn"; *a. Kaniš*, *allakkāniš* "Kaniš-oak" (a tree)

allānu II (a garment) MA

allānu III (a prof.)? M/NB also as PN

allānu IV pl.? (a small measured amount) NB

allânum, *allân* adv. "from there" OA, also *allânumma*; as prep. + subst. or, also NB, pron. suff. "beyond, over and above, apart from"; < *allû* I + *-ānum*; → *alla*; *ellān* ?

allapak conj. "when"? jB lex.

allattūrum (a small pipe) OB; < Sum.

allatu → *illatu* I

allêmi → *allû* II

alli'ayya, jB *ālāyû* "driveller" O/jB lex.

allikâmma "somewhere else" Nuzi; < *allû* I

allītiš "the day after tomorrow" OA; < *allû* I; → *līdiš*; *ullītiš*

allu(m) I "hoe, pickaxe" OAkk, OA, Bab. [GIŠ.AL] as agricultural and building tool; *a. našû* "to bear the hoe", *a. šutruku* "to make the hoe ring out"; as symbol of Ninurta, also Eg. royal emblem; *ša a.* "labourer" OB lex.; < Sum.

allum II (a type of coefficient) OB math.

allu(m) → also *ellu* I; *ullumma*

allû(m) I "that (one)" Nuzi, Ug., jB (= *ullû* I); > *allânum, allītiš; allikâmma, allukâ*

allû II, *allûmi, allêmi, allâmi, illûmi* ~ "certainly; furthermore" Am.; < W.Sem.

alludānu (a meteor. phenomenon) jB om.

alluḫappu "(a kind of) hunting net; (a net-like sack)" jB [SA.AL.ḪAB]; ^{d}*a.* (a demon); < Sum.

alluḫarum → *annuḫaru*

allukâ "there" Nuzi; < *allû* I

allûmi → *allû* II

allumza/i → *alluzu*

allunātu → *alluttu*

allūru (a ceremonial dress) MB(Alal.), Nuzi, jB lex.; < Hurr.?

alluttu(m), lex. also *allu'u*; pl. *allunātu(m)* "crab" j/NB; as animal; as figurine etc.; astr. "(constellation) Cancer", also another star [MUL.AL.LUL; MUL.NAGAR]; OA pl. "tongs, pincers"?; < Sum.; → *kušû*

allu'tu, *alūtu* (a plant) jB lex.

allu'u → *alluttu*

alluzu, *allumza/i* (a spiny plant) M/jB lex., med.; root, seed as drug

almānu(m) "widower" Mari; jB ^{d}*A.* as DN (name of star); > *almānūtu, almattu*

almānūtu "widow(er)hood" jB in *a. alāku* "to enter *a.*"; Nuzi "widow's allowance"; < *almattu, almānu* abstr.

almattu(m), NB also *alamattu*; pl. *almanātu(m)* "widow" Bab., MA [NU.MU.SU; MUNUS.NU.KÚŠ.Ù; MA MUNUS.NU.KÚŠ.KU]; astr. (a star); > *almānūtu*

almīn "without number, innumerable" j/NB(lit.); < *al* (→ *eli* ?) + *mīnu* II

almû mng. unkn. jB lex.; epith. of deity

alningu, *alnikkum* (a spice) OAkk, OB; also a mineral ?

alpu(m) I "bull, ox" [GU$_4$; coll. pl. GU$_4$.ḪI.A; NA usu. GU$_4$.(NÍTA.)MEŠ]; *a. mê, a. nāri* "water, river ox"; *a. kīši* "water buffalo"? jB; *a. šadê* (a wild animal) Am.; *a. epinnim* "plough ox"; *a. warkatim* [GU$_4$.(Á.)ÙR.RA] "rear ox (of team)"; math. *pūt alpim* 'ox's forehead', i.e. "trapezoid" [SAG.KI.GU$_4$]; → *rē'i-alpūtu*

alpu II ~ "threatening" jB lex.; < *alāpu*

alsudilû (a primitive farming tool) jB lex.; < Sum.

altalû ~ "forest" jB lex.

altammu → *aštammu*

alta(p)pipu (a box or chest) Am.; < Hurr.?

altapūtu → *iltappu*

altarru I "strong, heroic" jB lex.

alta(r)ru(m) II "assigned work" O/jB; < Sum.

alti "well, now then!" jB; < Sum.

alti → also *aššatu*

altikkarum mng. unkn. OB lex.

alṭu → *waštum*

alu → *ali* I

alû I, *elû* "bull of heaven" jB myth. figure; astr. sign of the zodiac, constellation "Taurus" [MUL.GU$_4$.AN.NA]

alû II (an evil demon) M/jB, Bogh., NA [A.LÁ; occas. U$_{18}$.LU]; < Sum.

alû(m) III (a kind of drum) Bab. [GIŠ.Á.LÁ]; < Sum.

alû IV, *elû* ~ "pipe" Bab. "(clay) pipe, drain?"; lex. "wind-pipe"; < Sum.; → *alallû* I

alû → also *alallû* II; *elû* II.III

ālu(m) I m., Am. occas. f.; pl. *ālū, ālānu*, OB freq. *ālānû* "village, town, city" [URU(.KI); pl. OB occas. URU.DIDLI.BI.KI; later freq. URU.MEŠ; also URU.URU; URU.DIDLI] "city" opp. to country (*ṣēru*); OB *ša libb-ālim* "town-dweller"; *ā. bēlūti, ā. šarrūti* etc. "capital, royal city"; of sectors *ā. elû* "upper city", *(āl) libb(i) āli* "inner city", esp. of Aššur; "municipality, city authorities", *ā. ū rabiānum/šībūtum* "city and mayor/elders"; OA *ālum* "the City" = Aššur; > *ālû, ālīum, ālāyû, ālāyûtu, ālānû, ālišam; ša-muḫḫi-ālūtu*

ālu(m) II, *ēlu* "ram" OAkk, Mari, Qatna, MA, M/jB, Am., Bogh. [(UDU.)A.LU(M)] also as ornament

ālû(m); pl. *āliūtum* "townsman" OA; < *ālu* I

âlu ~ "to cut"? jB lex.

a'lu ~ "tribe, confederation"? jB(Ass.) [GIŠ.DA]; < W.Sem.?

alulūtum, jB *lulūtu* (a kind of mineral)? OB math., jB

alumma "wherever"? jB; < *ali* I

alupatḫi (a topog. desig.) Nuzi; < Hurr.

alūtu (a kind of soup) jB lex.

alūtu → also *allu'tu*

ālūtu → *ša-muḫḫi-ālūtu*

aluzinnu **1.** ~ "buffoon, clown" Bab. **2.** (a plant) Bogh.; > *lezēnu* ?

alzibadar (colour desig. for horses) MB, also name of horse; < Kass.

-am, *-a* **1.** "to me" (1 sg. dat. suff.) **2.** vent. affix (→ GAG p.251); → *-nim*

amadēnum → *amandēnum*

ama'errû ~ "female mourner" jB lex.; < Sum.

amagallu "forest" jB lex.; < Sum.

amaḫḫu, *amuḫḫu* "enceinte, city-wall" jB; < Sum.

amališ "like an *a.* tree"; < *amalu*

amalītu, *amalūtum*, *amalu* (a cultic functionary) desig. of a goddess O/jB; < Sum.

amalu (a conifer) jB; > *amališ*

amalu → also *amalītu*

amālu → *wamālum*

amalubukku (a reed shelter) jB lex.

amaluktu, *maluktu*, *maruktu* (a cultic functionary) desig. of a goddess jB lex.; < Sum.

amalūtum → *amalītu*

amāmû (an eye cosmetic) jB lex.

ama(n)dēnum (a farm tool) OB; *ša a.* "(worker) with *a.*"

amānītu, *amannum* (a vegetable) O/jB, Ug.

amānu in *ṭābat a.* (a reddish salt) j/NB lex., med.; < Mt. Amanus ?

āmânû "talker, chatterbox" jB; < *awûm* ptcp.? + *-ān* + *-ī*

amarātu → *amru*

amar(girim)ḫilibû (a stone); < Sum.; → *ḫilibû*

amaridu (a spiny plant) jB lex.

amāriš (strange) "to look at" O/jB; < *amāru* I + *-iš*

amarsānu → *amursānu*

amartu(m) I, NB also *amaštu* "partition wall" Bab., Am.; between houses; "side" of a bed, chest; "arm-rest" of a chair; < *amaru* II

amartu II; pl. *amrātu* (a measure)? jB glass-making text

amaru(m) I, *emerum*; NB pl. *amarānu* "pile of bricks" Bab., OA [SIG$_4$.ANŠE]; Nuzi in *amarwumma epēšu*; > *amārum* II

amaru II; pl. f. "side wall" jB, NA; of bed; > *amartu* I

amāru(m) I "to see" **G** (*a/u*) [IGI; IGI.DU$_8$] **1.** "see" s.th., s.o.; "dream" a dream; "look at; inspect, examine"; "read" tablet etc.; *pān X a.* "see face of X", "see X in person", NA/NB "get audience"; OAkk, Ass. *ēn(ē) X a.* "visit X"; "experience, get to know"; "examine, inspect, keep an eye on"; "look after, look with favour on" persons; "be shown" brotherhood, patronage; "suffer" punishment, loss; "see", i.e. "make, profit"; *ina qāti(m) a.* "learn from s.o." **2.** ingress. "see, catch sight of"; "find", "locate, discover, trace (out)"; "establish" the results of a calculation **3.** act. stat. "recognizes; comes to know"; NB/NA *ina/ana muḫḫi X a.* "is devoted to X", NB also "is keen on" s.th. **R** Mari **Gtn** iter. of G; Mari stat. "has learnt thoroughly" **Gt** jB "see from now on"?, mng. uncl. **D** rare; OA "examine" metal; → *mummertu* **Š** caus. of G **Št** "make s.o. meet" s.o. **N** pass. of G [IGI; IGI.LÁ] **1.** of animals, tablets etc. "be seen", of heavenly bodies "become visible, appear"; "be found"; "be checked, inspected" **2.** recipr. "meet with (= *itti*), happen upon" s.o.; astr., of heavenly bodies "be opposite" **Ntn** iter. of N 1; > *amāriš*; *amru*; *amertu* I.II; *āmeru*, *āmertu*, *āmerānu*; *ammāru*; *atmartu*?; *imru*; *mummertu*; *nāmaru*, *nāmartu*; *nāmurtu*; *tāmartu*; *nanmurtu*; → *kallâmāre*

amārum II "to pile up bricks" **G** (*i/i*) OA; < *amaru* I denom.

amarwumma → *amaru* I

amāsu → *amāṣu*

amaṣiru mng. unkn. jB

amāṣu (or *amāsu*) mng. unkn. jB **D**; = *ḫamāṣu* ?; > *anṣu*?, *atmāṣu*?

amašmû, *amašpû* → *abašmû*

amaštu → *amartu* I

amāšu ~ "to be paralysed"? jB **G** lex., med., of hands etc.; > *āmišu*?; *anšūtu*; *imšu*; *umšu*; *imištu*

amat-šarrūtu → *amtu*

amatu (desig. of terrain) Nuzi; < Hurr.?

amātu → *amtu*; *amu*; *awātu*

amāyû (an aquatic plant) jB lex.

ambassu, *anba(s)su* "(game-)park"? j/NB, NA; < Hurr.?

ameḫaru → *awiḫaru*

amēliš → *awīliš*

amēltu → *awīltum*

amēlu → *awīlu*

amēlūtu → *awīlūtum*

amerānu → *awirānum*

āmerānu "eye-witness" MA, M/jB; < *āmeru* + *-ān*

amertu(m) I, *ime/irtu(m)*, *iwirtum* "view, opinion" O/jB; esp. "preference, choice" of land; < *amāru* I; → *imirtu*

amertu II, *amеštu* "inspection, review" NB of soldiers, grain etc.; < *amru*

āmertu f. "that sees" jB; < *āmeru*

āmeru(m), *āmirum* "that sees, reads" etc.; of murderer *āmir dami* "shedder of blood"; < *amāru* I ptcp.; > *āmerānu*, *āmertu*

ameštu → *amertu* II

amḫara (a medicinal plant) O/jB

amiḫaru → *awiḫaru*

amikû (a tree)? NA

amīlānu (a medicinal plant) jB [Ú.LÚ.U18/19.LU; LÚ-*a-nu*, NA-*a-nu*]; < *awīlu*

amīliš → *awīliš*

amīltu → *awīltum*

amīlu → *awīlu*

amīlūtu → *awīlūtum*

amīrāniš "like a deaf man"? jB; < *amīru*

amirānu → *awirānum*

amīru "obstruction of the ear (through ear-wax)" jB; also "deaf"?; > *amīrāniš*

āmirum → *āmeru*

āmišu (or *amīšu*) ~ "enemy" jB lex.; < *amāšu* ?

amkamannu (desig. of horses) Nuzi

amm... also = *ana m*...

amma "look!; lo!" OA before nominal and vb. sentence, for emphasis; > *ammāmin*; *ammaka*, *ammânum*, *ammîša; ammiu*

ammaka(m), *ammak*, NA also *ma(k)ka* "there" Ass.; NA *issu (am)ma(k)ka* "from there"; < *amma* + *-ka(m)*

ammaki/u conj. "instead of" jB + subjunct.; < *ana* I + *makû* II ?

ammal "as much, as many as" MB(Ass.); → *ammar*; *mala* I

ammāmin "would that, if only" OA + pret.; < *amma* + *-min*

ammammu I, *ammu* (a large beer jar) jB lex.; < Sum.

ammammu II (a bird) jB lex.

ammannâ "anybody"? MB

ammânum "from there" OA; < *amma* + *-ānum*

ammar, NA also *mar* "as much as" M/NA; prep. *a. ubāni* "a finger's breadth"; rel. pron. + subjunct. *a. imḫurūni* "as much as he received"; < OA *ana* I + *mala* I ?; → *ammal*; *rūṭu*

ammarkarra, *ammari/uakal*, *ḫammarākāra*; pl. *ammariakallānu* "accountant" NB; < OPers.

ammarsigu → *amursiggu*

ammartu "overseer"? of people jB, desig. of goddess; < *ammāru* f.?

ammartû "eaglet" Bogh. lex.; < Sum.

ammaru mng. unkn. Nuzi

ammāru; pl. *ammārāni* "overseer" NB; < *amāru* I; > *ammartu*

ammaruakal → *ammarkarra*

ammašabbû (a container) jB lex.

ammaštakal → *maštakal*

ammati → *mati*

ammatiš → *ammatu* II

ammatu(m) I "forearm; cubit" [KÙŠ]; *kiṣir a.* "elbow"; as linear measure "cubit", st. abs. *ammat* [1.KÙŠ]; NB as area measure, also *a. ṣeḫertu* "small cubit"; NB as vol. measure *a. qaqqari*; *X ina ammati* "X cubits (long)"; *a. rabītu* "big cubit"; *a. šarri* "royal cubit"; NB astr. (a measurement of angle); jB transf. "strength"?; lex. "cubit-measure" of wood?

ammatu II, *abbatu* 'strong, stable', syn. for "earth" jB; also term.-adv. *ammatiš*

ammatu III (syn. for mother) jB lex.

ammatu IV mng. unkn. Ug. leg.

ammi "there" OA; → *ammiu*

ammidakkum "lye"? Mari, in metal treatment

ammînannâ "why now?" M/jB; < *ammīni* + *inanna*

ammīni(m), *ammīn* "why?"; < *ana* I + *mīnu* I; → *miššum*

ammîša(m) "there, thither" OA, NA; < *amma* + *-išam*

ammiu(m); f. *ammītu(m)*; pl. m. NA *ammûte*, f. OA *ammiātum*, M/NA *ammâte* "that" Ass., Am.; > *ammûri*; → *ammi*; *annû* I

ammu(m) I, *ḫammum* "people" OB, jB lex.; < W.Sem.

ammu II (a name of the Tigris) jB lex.

ammu → also *ammammu* I; *emmu*; *ḫammu* II

ammûte → *ammiu*

ammûri ~ "at that time" NA/jB; < *ammiu* + *-ri(g)*; → *annûrig*

ammušmu in *bīt a.* (a storehouse)? jB rit.

amnakku (a kind of white sand) jB/NA for manufacture of glass; < Sum.?; → *immanakku* ?

ampannu (a kind of wood) Nuzi; < Hurr.

ampannuḫlu "an *ampannu*-wood worker" Nuzi; < Hurr.

amrimmum → *amrummu*

amru(m) "seen, chosen" by DN etc.; "inspected" of troops Bab., NA; jB *lā a.*, also pl. *lā am(a)rātu* "'not seen', unseemly"; < *amāru* I

amrû(m) "beam, timber" OB, Nuzi, in construction of house, ship

amrummu(m), *amrimmum*, *abrummu* "outlet, water-gate" O/jB; < Sum.?

amšāli(m), *amšāla*, once *amšat* "yesterday" Bab.; *šamšāli*, *šanšāla* (< *ša a.*) "the day before yesterday"; > *amšālûm*; → *timāli*

amšālûm "of yesterday" OB; < *amšāli* + *-ī*

amšûm "palm fibre" OB

amtu(m), NB also *andu*; pl. *amātu(m)* "maid, female slave" [GÉME; OB freq. SAG.GÉME; Am., Nuzi also MUNUS.GÉME, MUNUS.ÌR] of social class; OA, of Anatolian spouse; also desig. of o.s. in letters addressed to persons of higher rank; *a. DN* "servant of DN"; *a. ēkalli(m)* "slave of the palace", NA "royal concubine"; NB *a. šarri* "royal slave";

a.-šarrūtu "position as a royal slave"; > *amūtu* I; *amtuttu;* → *qinnatu*

amtuttu(m) "status of a female slave" OA, Nuzi for *amūtu* I

amu(m); pl. f. "raft" Bab., usu. of reed; → *ḫāmu*

amû I "one-handed"? OB, jB lex.

amû II (a spiny plant) jB lex.

amû III ~ "palate" jB lex.; < Sum.

amû IV ~ "list of reciprocals" NB

amûm V vb. mng. unkn. OAkk in PNs, e.g. *Īmi-ilum*

amû → also *awûm* Gt; *ḫammu* II

amuaštu → *amumeštu*

amūdāya, *amūdu* (a wooden part of the harness) M/jB; → *mudāyû*

amuḫḫu → *amaḫḫu*

amultu (a plant) jB lex.

amumeštu, *amumištu*, *amuaštu* (a spiny plant) jB lex.

amumiḫḫuri ~ "substitute, proxy" Nuzi; < Hurr.

amūmu (desig. of beer) NA

amumunna "city gate" Nuzi; < Hurr.

amūqu → *emūqu*

amurdinnu, *murdinnu* "bramble"? M/jB [GIŠ.GEŠTIN.GÍR]; also a disease

amurrānu "western" Nuzi; < *amurru* + *-ānu*

amurrānu → also *murrānu* 1

amurriqānu → *awurriqānum*

amurru(m), Nuzi also *aburru* "Amurru" **1.** (divine name) [^{d}MAR.TU] **2.** toponym for Syria and the West **3.** OAkk, OB "Amorite(s)" (→ *amurrû*) [mostly MAR.TU]; OB *abi a.* [AD.DA.MAR.TU] "prince, sheikh"; Mari *rabi a.* (a high-ranking officer), *ṭupšar a.* "Amorite scribe" **4.** Bab., NA "west wind; the West" [IM.MAR.TU; NB also IM.KUR.MAR; also astr., NA, NB IM.4] **5.** jB (western star = Perseus) [MUL.MAR.TU]; > *amurrû*, *amurrānu*

amurrû(m) "of, from Amurru" OA, O/jB [MAR.TU]; "Amorite" people; jB lex. *amurrītu* f. (a kind of wool); < *amurru* + *-ī*

amursānu, *amuršānu*, *amarsānu* "wild pigeon" jB; → *araššannu*; *uršānu* II

amursiggu, *amursikku*, *ammarsigu* (a bird) jB

amuršānu → *amursānu*

amuššu, *aḫuššu*, *a'uššu*, *arūšu* (a bulbous vegetable) M/jB

amuttu → *amūtu* I.III

amūtu(m) I, MA *amuttu* "status of a maid, female slave" M/NB [GÉME-; Nuzi also GÉME.MEŠ]; < *amtu* abstr.

amūtu(m) II; pl. OB *amuwātum* "liver" OAkk, Bab. [BÀ] of a sacrificial sheep; ext. "findings on a sheep's liver, liver omen"

amūtu(m) III, OA *amuttum* (a precious metal, phps.) "meteoric iron" OA, Am. [KUG.AN]

amuzi(n)nu(m) (a plant, drug) Mari, jB

an → *ana* I

-ān (ending) → GAG p.305

ana I, *an* (*aš-š...* etc.) "to, for" (freq. abbr. *an*, with assimilation of *n* to following consonant (OA often wr. *a*)) (prep., governs subst. in gen., pers. pron. in dat.) [from MB onwards DIŠ; O/MB occas. NAM; M/jB ŠÈ] **1.** of space etc.: move, go, come "to, towards", bring, send, give, speak, write "to", also *ana ṣēr(i)*, *ana muḫḫi*; sit down "near, beside"; lay, put, throw down "onto"; substitute, compensate "for"; weigh "for"; sacrifice "to"; wait "for"; look "at"; submit "to"; set "against"; grow angry "at" **2.** of time: "for", *ad-dār* "forever"; "within" **3.** of purpose, intention: "for" marriage, work, journey; give "for" o.'s life; before infin. "(in order) to" **4.** "for, in favour of" s.o. **5.** "towards, against" **6.** "in view of, in the light of" s.th., *ana šuāti* "thereupon" **7.** "by order of, on behalf of" **8.** buy, sell, exchange s.th. "(in return) for" **9.** distrib.: "by", *šatta ana šatti* "year by year", *idi ana idi* "on all sides" **10.** "per, for each" NA, NB *ana ūmu* "per diem" **11.** causal and sim.: "about, concerning" house, field; weep, rejoice "over" s.th. **12.** NB comm., of noun "(derived) from, belonging to" vb. **13.** NB *ana lā* → *alla*, NB *analānuššu* "without him" **14.** NA, NB as nota accusativi (→ GAG §114e) **15.** modal: *ana pī* "according to"; OA, OB *ana gamrim*, jB, NA *ana gimirtīšu* "completely"; → *siḫirtu* 3, *qātu* 11, *zīmu*; OA *ana šalšīšu* "three times" (Bab. → *adi* 1); NA *ana ešrāte* "ten times", "by" one-third, a quarter etc. **16.** pleonastic before term.-adv.: e.g. *ana ma'diš* "to a great degree" **17.** before prep., adv. → *maḫru* II, *pānu* I 8 etc. **18.** "as for, with respect to", OA, OB *ana ša* "with respect to the fact that, with respect to that which"; NB → *ašša*

ana II "I" OB(lit.), by-form of *anāku*

anabu (or *anapu*) (a loincloth or kilt ?) jB lex.

anadaru "bearded" jB lex.

anagmaḫḫu (a drinking vessel) jB lex.; < Sum.

anāḫu(m) I "to be(come) tired" **G** (*a/a*) stat. "becomes tired", "makes an effort, strives"; of buildings etc. "become dilapidated" **Gtn** iter. of G jB med., of limbs, person **D** OA "tire (s.o.), oppress" **Š** Bab. "trouble, exert, strain" s.o.; stat. "is very wearied" **Št** "make an effort", "weary o.s., be depressed"; astr. "endure" **N** OB "become tired", "struggle, suffer hardship, be exhausted"; > *anḫu*; *anīḫu*; *anḫūtu*; *inḫu* I; *mānaḫu*; *mānaḫtu*; *šūnuḫu*, *šūnuḫiš*; *tānēḫu*, *tānēḫtu*; *tānuḫiš*

anāḫu II "to perform an *inḫu* song" O/jB **G** (pres. *inniḫ*) esp. rit., *inḫa a.* **D** ~ G rit., of *assinnu*; < *inḫu* II denom.

ana'īni → *mīnu* I

anaka → *anāku*; *annaka*

anakandaš → *akkamdaš*

anakanni → *akanni*

anakannu → *akanna* II

anakku → *anaqqu*

anāku, NA also *annuku*, NB also *anaka* "I; me" [Bogh. GÁ.E] as pred. freq. *anākuma*; OB *ša anāku* "as for me"; NB also acc. (to stress a pron. suff.), dat.; → *ana* II; *anuki*

analānuššu → *ana* I 13

anāma "as soon as" OA; → *annāma*

anameru (a plant) jB; as drug; *zēr a.* "seed of *a.*"

anamû → *anmû*

ananiḫu, *nana/iḫu* (a garden herb, phps.) "mint" j/NB

ana(n)nu (a syn. of copper) jB lex.

anantu(m); pl. *an(a)nātu* "battle, strife" Bab.(lit.); → *anuntu*

anānu → *enēnu* I

anapu → *anabu*

anapû → *alapû*

anāpum "to rage" OB **G** (i/i)

anāqāte f. pl. "she-camels" NA; < Arab.

anaqqu (or *anakku*) (a drinking vessel) jB lex.; < Sum.

anarḫallum (desig. of child) OA

anatu (a ring) jB lex.

anaummiš → *annummiš*

anba(s)su → *ambassu*

anbû (or *anpû*) mng. unkn. jB lex.

andaḫšu(m), *andāšu*, OA *addaḫšum* (an alliaceous plant)

andakullûm (a corvée worker)? OB; also as PN

andanānu → *andunānu*

andarārum → *andurāru*

andaš "king" jB lex.; < Kass.

andāšu → *andaḫšu*

andēsu "inspection, review" NB; < OPers.

andillu → *andullu*

andu → *amtu*

andugû (a meteor. term)? jB lex.; < Sum.?

anduḫallatu, *antuḫallatu*, *im/nd/tuḫallatu* "(a kind of) lizard" M/jB [KUN.DAR.GURUN.NA; EME.ŠID.ZI.DA; NIR.GAL.BÚR]

andullu(m), M/jB(Ass.) *andillu* "shelter, canopy" Bab. [AN.DÙL; AN.DUL7]; transf. "(royal, divine) protection, aegis", also in PNs; < Sum.; → *ṣulūlu*

andunānu, *addunānum*, *andanānu* "substitute" O/jB; NA → *dunānu*; → also *ardanānu*; *dinānu*

andurāru(m), *addurārum*, *andarārum*, NA, NB *du/arāru* "freedom, exemption" [AMA.AR.GI] of edict; release from (debt) slavery; cancelling debts; *a. šakānu* "promulgate *a.* edict"; < *darāru* I

andurû "(a kind of) door" jB lex.

anēnu → *anīnu*

angallu ~ "wise" M/jB

angāšu, *angāsu*? "plum (tree)" NA

angillu "lament" M/jB; var. of *ikkillu*

angubbû(m) ~ 'standing in the sky' O/jB [AN.GUB.BA] **1.** "tutelary deity" **2.** astr. (desig. of certain stars) **3.** (a class of priests); also as desig. of deities; < Sum.

angurinnu (a metal object) MA, Am.; → *ingurēnu*

anḫu(m) "tired" O/jB of people, animals; M/NB of buildings "dilapidated"; < *anāḫu* I; > *anḫūtu*

anḫullīme → *imḫur-līmi*

anḫullu → *imḫullu*

anḫullû/u? (a plant) jB lex., mag. [wr. Ú.AN.ḪÚL(.LA/LÚ)]; < Sum.?

anḫurašru → *imḫur-ešrā*

anḫūtu "tiredness; dilapidation" j/NB, NA of people; buildings, divine images etc.; < *anḫu*

anīḫu(m) "tired, weary" O/jB; *lā a.*, NB *lânīḫu* "indefatigable"; < *anāḫu* I

ani(m)mû ~ "kindness, peace" jB lex.

anīna **1.** "now" NA, NB also *anīn* **2.** "earlier" Nuzi, Bogh. **3.** "where?" Nuzi **4.** mng uncl. Am.

anīnu, *anīni*, *anēnu* "we" NA, NB; NB also gen. and dat.; < Aram.; → *nīnu*

aniu, *aniteu* (syn.s of copper) jB lex.

ankibītu "of heaven and earth" jB epith. of Ištar; < Sum.

ankinūtu (a plant) jB lex., med. as drug

ankunnu (a heavy bronze object)? MB(Alal.)

anmû, *anamû* "this" O/MB, O/MB(Alal.), Bogh., Ug.

ann... also = *ana n...*

anna, *anni*, *annû* "yes, certainly" O/jB, Nuzi; > *annu*, *annāma*; *inanna*; *annanna*; → *akanna* I; *annû* I; *ēni*

annabu → *arnabu*

annaka(m), Ug. also *annakānu*, NA also *ḫannak(a)*, *nak(a)* "here" Ass., *ana/adi/issu a.* "to/as far as/from here"; < *annû* I + *-kam*

annaku(m) "tin; lead" [AN.NA]; MA *a. paṣiu* 'white lead', i.e. "tin", *a. abāru* "lead"

annāma OA, O/jB "there; thus, in this way"; jB, NA ~ "in the same way"; OB lex. + pron. suff. *annāmašu* "there he is"; < *anna* + *-ma*

annamru; pl. *annamrāni* (a copper object) NA

annania ~ "such-and-such" MA; < *ann(iu)* + *anniu* ?

annanna; f. *annannītu* "NN, so-and-so, such-and-such" O/jB [NENNI; f. (MUNUS.)NENNI (*-tum*) etc.]; Nuzi (a class of women)?; < *anna* + *anna*

annânum "here; from here" OA, O/jB, Am., Bogh.; < *annû* I + *-ānum*

annekīam → *annikīam*

annettān → *annittān*

anni I "now" OAkk, OA; < *annû* I

anni II (a desig. of textiles) Nuzi

anni → also *anna*

annikīam, *annekīam*, *annikê(m)*, *annikâ(m)*, Ug. *annikānu* "here, hither" O/MB; < *anni(u)* + *-kīam*

anni(m)miš "no sooner than" jB (→ GAG §§116c, 174g); < *annimmû*

annimmû(m), *annummû(m)*, *annimmamûm*, OB (Ešn.) *unummīum* "this one here" O/jB (acc. *annammiam*, *annimmiam*; f. OB *annummītum*, *anni(m)mītum*; du. obl. *annim=mūtīn*; pl. m. *annummuttum*, *annummūtum*, jB lex. *annimmamūtum*; f. OB *anniamātum*?); MB, Bogh. "this"; > *annimmiš*, *annummiš*; *annummânum*; → *annû* I; *unummium*

annīnati(m) invariable "this" MB(Alal.); → *annû* I

annīnum "here" OB(N.Mes.); < *annû* I + *-ānum*

annîš "here, hither" O/jB; also *ana a.* "hither", *ištu a.* "hence"; < *annû* I

annîša(m), NA also *ḫannîša* "here, hither" Ass., Mari; < *annû* I + *-išam*

annittān, *annettān* "this then" OB, often interrog.; < *annû* I f. du. as adv.?

annītu, *anniu* → *annû* I

annu(m) "(word of) consent, assent, approval" Bab. of omen, *a. kīnu* "authentic consent", *a. apālu* "to say yes"; < *anna*

annu → also *Anu* I; *arnu*

annû(m) I, *anniu(m)*, NA also *ḫanniu*, *ḫannû*, OB occas. with nunation "this, those" [j/NB NE; ŠEŠ (for m. pl. *annûti*)]; OB f. sg. *annītum* "this matter"; *annītam lā annītam* 'this one, not this one', "one way or another"; *a. ū a.* "various"; NA *a(n)nûte ... a(n)nûte ...* "some ..., others ..."; *(a)kī (ḫ)anni(ma)* "thus, in the same way"; > *anni* I; *annania*?; *annânum*, *annīnum*; *annikīam*, *annaka*; *annîš*, *annîša*, *annittān*, *annûrig*; *anumma*; *agannû*, *aḫannâ*, *aḫennâ*; → *ammiu*; *anna*; *annimmû*; *annīnati*

annû II "look!" Am.; < W.Sem.

annû → also *anna*

annuḫaru(m), *alla/uḫarum*, Mari also *innuḫarum* f. (a mineral) O/jB [IM.SAḪAR. BABBAR.KUR.RA] sim. to alum, as drug

annuka mng. unkn. NB

annukâ, *annukanna* "here" Elam, Nuzi

annuku → *anāku*; *annaku*; *annuqum*

annumma → *anumma*

a(n)nummânum "here" Mari; < *annummû* + *-ānum*

annummiš, *anaummiš* "here, hither" O/jB; < *annummû*

annummû → *annimmû*

A(n)nunītu(m) OAkk, Bab. **1.** (a goddess) **2.** (a constellation, north-east part of Pisces)

annuqum (a type of jewellery, phps.) "ring"? OA; → *unqu* I

annûri(g) "at this moment, now" NA; < *annû* I + *-ri(g)*; → *ammûri*

annuš ~ "look!" Am.

anpatu (a bird) jB

anpû → *anbû*

anqullu, *aqqullu* (an atmospheric phenomenon; a fiery glow) Bab., NA [IZI.AN.NE(=BIR$_9$?)]; jB "feverish heat"; NA *aban a.* "meteor"?

ansammum → *assammu*

ansamullu (a class of person) jB lex.

anṣabtu(m), *inṣabtu(m)*, *iṣṣabtum*; pl. *i/anṣabātu/i*; also du. OA *iṣṣabtān* "ring, earring" Bab., OA

anṣu "obstinate"? jB lex.; < *amāṣu* ?

anšamû mng. unkn. jB f. *anšamītu* as epith. of door

anšanûm 'of Anšan' OB as desig. of a bow

anšu → *enšu*

anšūtu "paralysis" jB; < *amāšu*

anšūtu → also *enšūtu*

anta(l)lû(m), *attalû* "eclipse" Bab., NA [AN.GE$_6$; AN.TA.LÙ] of sun, moon, planet, star; Bogh.

transf. of king, jB of lands; < Sum.; → *namtallûm*

antasurrû (or *antašurrû*) (a precious stone or metal) jB; astr. (a star or constellation); < Sum.

antaṣû (a scribe) jB

antašurrû → *antasurrû*

antu I "ear of barley" jB lex., NA

antu(m) II mng. unkn. O/jB

antuḫallatu → *anduḫallatu*

antupšalli → *antuwašalli*

antušû 'sitting in the sky' (a constellation) jB [(MUL.)AN.TUŠ.A.MEŠ (always pl.)]; < Sum.

antuwašalli, *antupšalli* (a high Hitt. court official) Bogh., Ug.; < Hitt.

Anu(m) I, OB usu. *Annum* "An(um)" (the god of heaven) OAkk, Bab. [AN; NB ᵈ60]; of Ištar *anātima* "you are supreme deity"; < Sum.; > *Anūtu*

anu(m) II (a metal) O/jB lex.; < Sum.

anu III "(the cuneiform sign) AN" M/jB [AN]

anu IV (a syn. for wood or tree) jB lex.

anuki "I" Am.; < W.Sem.; → *anāku*

Anukkū → *Anunnakkū*

anūmīšu "then, at that time" OB *ištu a.*, *warka a.* "since, after that time"; < *ana* I + *ūmu* I + *-šu*

anumma, *annumma*, *anummu*, OB(Ešn.) *unumma* "now", esp. of messages "herewith" OB, Am., Nuzi, Bogh., Ug., jB lex. [Ug. UD-*ma*]; < *annû* I loc.-adv. + *-ma*

anummamê, *anummê* "here is" Ug.; < *anumma*

anummânum → *annummânum*

anummê → *anummamê*

anummīkê "there" Bogh. lex.; < *anumma*

anummu → *anumma*

Anunītu → *Annunītu*

Anunnakkū, occas. *Anukkū*, *Enunnakkū* "(the) gods" [ᵈA.NUN.NA(.KE4.NE)] **1.** OB, M/jB the gods as a whole **2.** M/NB the gods of the earth and netherworld; < Sum.

anuntu; pl. *anunātu* "fight, combat" jB, NA; → *anantu*

anūnu "fear, dread"? jB; < Sum.

anunūtu, *(e)nunūtu* (a plant) M/jB lex., med.; also (an insect)?

anuššannu (a metal object) Qatna; < Hurr.?

anuššu (a leather object) jB lex.

Anūtu "position of An; divinity" j/NB [ᵈ60- ; ᵈAN-]; < *Anu* I

anūtu → also *unūtu*

anzaḫḫu (a kind of glass) Qatna, M/jB, Bogh., NA [AN.ZAḪ]; < Sum.

anzalīlu, jB *anzanīnu*; f. *anzaliltu* "matchmaker; pimp"? M/jB

anzamātum pl. mng. unkn. OAkk; desig. of field

anzananzû → *anzanunzû*

anzanīnu → *anzalīlu*

anzâniš "like Anzû" jB(Ass.); < *Anzû*

anzannu mng. uncl. Nuzi, desig. of commodities, fields; < Hurr.

anzannu → also *arzānu*

anzanu(n)zû, *anzananzû* "water-table, subterranean waters" jB; < Sum.

anzillu(m), *anzullu* "taboo; abomination" O/jB; *a. kabāsu*, *a. kubbusu* "to infringe a taboo"; *anzillašu* "s.th. (to be) avoided by s.o."

Anzû "Anzû; lion-headed eagle" [ANZU.MUŠEN]; also astr., desig. of star(s); > *anzâniš*

anzūzu (a type of spider) jB [ŠÈ.GUR4]

apadu "small" jB lex.

apālu(m) I, OB also *abālum* "to pay; answer" **G** (*a/u*; NB pres. once *iḫappal*?) **1.** "pay" s.o. s.th. (= 2 acc.), "repay" s.th., "settle" claim; "pay off, satisfy" s.o.; M/NA "make in full" sacrificial offering; Bab. math., astr., of solution "give the result" **2.** "answer" s.o. (= acc.); ext. "correspond to" another feature **3.** OA, OB "answer to", "be answerable to" s.o. (= acc.), "justify o.s. before" **4.** with *idu*, *kūm* "stand in for, represent", freq. in PN **Gtn** iter. "pay", "stand in for" on separate occasions **Gt** "answer one another, have discussion", "stand in for permanently" **D** "satisfy" s.o; "pay off" an obligation; "pay" a debt; NA "make answerable" **Dt(t)** "be held responsible" **Š** "make s.o. answer" **N** "be paid off, become satisfied"; > *āpilu*, *āpiltum*, *āpilānu*; *iplū*; *mūtaplu*; *nāpaltu*; *nāpalû*; *tāpalu*; *tāpiltum*, *tāpultum*

apālu(m) II "to be (too) late" **G** jB of star "be late" **D** OA stat. of birth "is retarded"; jB of Adad (= thunderstorm) "come later than expected" **Dt** "be delayed"; > *aplu* I, *apiltu* I; *tāpalātu*; *uplētum*; *uppulu* I, *uppultu*; → *aplu* II and derivatives; *uppulu* II

apalwaliḫurra (a prof. desig.) Nuzi

apāniš "through the window(s)" jB; < *aptu* + *-ān* + *-iš*

apāpu(m) mng. uncl. Mari **G** unattested **N** (or *napāpum*?) ~ "infiltrate"

apara(k)ku mng. unkn. NA lex. in *ṣubāt a.* "*a.* garment"

aparu (a loincloth) jB lex.

apāru(m), occas. *epēru* "to cover the head" Bab., M/NA **G** (*e/e*, OB *a/u*) "put" crown, helmet etc. "on the head of" s.o. (= acc.), stat. "wears";

transf. of moon, star, king "be decked with" halo, radiance etc.; OB stat. of sheep's tongue "be covered, capped" ext. **Gtn** iter. of G, MA "constantly crown" king **Gt** stat. "is decked with" **D** "put headgear (= acc.) on head of" s.o. (= acc.) **N** "be crowned, covered"; > *apru*; *itpuru*; *upru* I; *upurtu*

apāru → also *abāru* II

apāšu → *wapāšum*

apātu → *appatu* II; *aptu*

apâtu, *abâtu*, *epâtu*, OB *a/epiātum*, Bogh. *apiētum* f. pl. "numerous, teeming", epith. of *nišū*, also absol., "humanity"

apâtu → also *apû* I

apellu mng. unkn. Nuzi; desig. of arrows; < Hurr.

apiātum, apiētum → *apâtu*

apiktu → *abiktu*

āpilānu 'the answerer' (a bird) jB; < *apālu* I

apilḫa mng. unkn. jB lex.

apillû (a cultic performer) jB [A.BIL]

apiltu(m) I **1.** M/NB "remainder; remaining debts" **2.** OAkk (a vessel) **3.** jB (a part of the year); < *aplu* I; → *a.* II

apiltu(m) II "heiress" O/jB; < *aplu* II; = *a.* I ?; → *aplatu*

āpilu(m); f. *āpiltum* 'answerer' **1.** Mari, jB, also *aplûm* (a kind of prophet) **2.** MB *āpil bābi* (a doorkeeper) **3.** Nuzi (a prof.); < *apālu* I

apisāmūš (a type of bow)? Am.; < Hurr.

apisasi? (a tree)? NA

apislat (an illness) jB; → *apišalû*

apiš "like reed-beds" jB; < *apu* I

apišalû (a cripple)? jB; < PlN Apišal; → *apislat*

apītaš mng. unkn. jB

apītu(m) (a kind of fallow land) O/jB

apkallatu f. "wise one" jB [ABGAL], also as PN; < *apkallu*

apkallu, *abgallu* "wise man, expert" Bab., NA [ABGAL] epith. of gods; of Adapa etc.; pl. "the (seven) sages"; *a. šamni* "oil (divination) expert"; < Sum.; > *apkallatu*

apkīsu "furrow" jB; < Sum.

aplatu "heiress" jB lex. (= *apiltu* II); < *aplu* II

aplu(m) I; f. *apiltu* "late" OB; < *apālu* II; > *apiltu* I; → *a.* II

aplu(m) II; st. constr. *apil, apal* "heir, son" [IBILA; j/NB, NA freq. A; NB PN occas. EDURU; NA PN also ^{d}IBILA] *a. rēštû, a. ašarēdu* "prime heir", *a. kīnu* "legitimate heir"; *apil erṣeti* 'son of the earth', desig. of date palm; > *apiltu* II, *aplatu*; *aplūtu*; = *a.* I ?

aplu → also *abru* IV

aplûm → *āpilu* 1

apluḫtu(m) "armour" O/jB

aplūtu(m) "status of heir; inheritance, estate" O/jB [IBILA]; < *aplu* II

app... also = *ana p...*

appadān "pillared hall, apadana" NB; < OPers.

appadētu → *uppadētu*

appaḫu, *a(b)baḫu* ~ "branches" jB lex.

appān in PN for *ana pān* (→ *pānu* I)

appanannu (a metal object) Am.(Mit.); < Hurr.

appāni → *appatu* II

appannu (a part of a building, portico) Nuzi; < Hurr.; → *appātu*

appānum I (a pulse, phps.) "chick-pea" Mari

appānum II (a bird) Bogh.; → *abbunnu*

apparrītu; pl. *apparrâtu* "tufted hair, strand of hair" jB; → *apparrû*

apparrû, *ḫapparrû*; f. *apparrītu* "with tufted hair" O/jB; MB as PN; (desig. of pig, sheep); → *apparrītu*

appāru(m), jB also *ippāru*; pl. m. & f. "reed-bed, marsh" [AMBAR], NA also "reed(s)"; *qan a.* "reed"; fish, birds *simat a.* "belonging to the marshes" [ME.TE AMBAR.RA]; NB *rab a.* "marsh overseer"; < Sum.

appatān → *appatu* II

appatiš "as with a bridle" jB; < *appatu* II

appatu(m) I "tip" NB (of metal implements); < *appu*

appatu(m) II; NA pl. once *appāni* "bridle, rein" Bab., M/NA [ṄA (KUŠ.)PA; AB] j/NB, NA *mukīl appāti* 'bridle-holder', "chariot driver"; also jB lex. *appatān* du. (a wooden object)?; > *appatiš*

appātu in *bīt a.* "portico" jB (= *bīt ḫilāni*); < Akkadization of *appannu* ?

appātu → also *appatu* I.II; *appu*

appiš conj. "since, given that" OA, OB, jB lex.; < *appu*

appītā f. du. "nostrils"? jB of ape's snout; < *appu*

appitti "likewise; just as" NB, also *ana appittu*; < *ana* I + *pitti*

appu(m) f. "nose" Bab., M/NA [KIR$_4$] **1.** liter.: "nose", also du., of person, animal; "beak" of bird; *rēš a.* "tip of the nose"; *ḫēḫēn a.*, *nurub a.* "soft parts of the nose"; *naḫīr a.*, *piliš a.* "nostril"; *libbi a.* "nasal cavity"; *birīt a.* "nasal septum"?; *dūr a.* "'wall of the nose', cheek"; *ḫaṣarti a.* "nasal mucus"; *šār a.* "breath" **2.** idioms: *labān a.* (a gesture of prostration); *a. qadādu/quddudu* (a gesture of grief); Mari *a. maḫāṣum* (a gesture of distress); OB *a.-šu* *kašādum* "to defeat" s.o.; *ṣibit a.* "moment" **3.** transf.: "tip" of tongue, finger, penis, beard; "extremity" of shapes, objects etc.; "rim" of vessel; "crown" of tree; "fringe" of garment; "point" of land, "causeway, bund"; MB wooden "stake"; > *appiš*; *appatu* I; *appītā*

appudētu → *uppadētu*

appultu → *uppultu*

appūna, jB also *appunnāma*, Bogh., Am. also *appunāna* "moreover" OAkk, OA, O/jB

apputtu(m) I, *appūtum* ~ "please; it is urgent" (interj.) O/MA, OB, jB lex.; → *a.* II ?

a(p)puttum II (or *abbuttum*, *āb/puttum*) ~ "difficult situation" OA; = *a.* I ?

apru(m) in *aprūssa* "with head covered" OB of woman; < *apāru*

apru → also *abru* II

aprušu (a plant) jB, NA as drug; oil, seed, flour of *a.*

apsammi/akku → *apusammikku*

apsasû(m); f. *apsasā/ītu(m)* **1.** (an exotic bovid) **2.** (a myth. animal with the body of a cow), "sphinx" OAkk, O/jB as figurine; jB(Ass.) of bull-colossus; [(MUNUS.)ÁB.ZA.ZA]; < Sum.

apsû(m) "(cosmic) underground water" Bab., NA [ABZU(=ZU.AB)] **1.** lit., as home of fish, location of foundations; *kār a.* "quay of the *a.*" (a ritual place) **2.** "(deities of) the *apsû*" **3.** (a primeval deity) **4.** NA$^?$, NB (a water tank in temple) **5.** j/NB *bīt a.* (a part of the temple) [É/ÈŠ.ABZU]; < Sum.

apšitûm "agreed allocation" OB of division of land, "contingent" of troops; < Sum.

apšu → *abšu* II

aptu(m); pl. *apātu* "window, window opening" Ass., O/jB [AB] in house, NB in sluice; OB *ina pī a. nadānum, madādum* "to pay in the house of the recipient"; DN ^{d}*Kilili ša apāti, abāti*; "niche of dovecot"?; *a. uzni* "ear-hole" O/jB; < Sum.; > *apāniš*

apu(m) I, *abu* "reed-bed; reeds (coll.)" Ass., O/jB [GIŠ.GI]; *apukka* "to your reed-bed"; *qān a.* "marsh-reed"; *šaḫ a.* "wild boar" (→ *šaḫapu*); *ḫašḫūr a.* (a plant); > *apiš*

apu II "hole, opening" in the ground NA rit.

apu III (a leather object)? jB

apû I, *abû* "veiled" Bab. of eyes; < *apû* III

apû II (a spiny plant) jB

apû III, *abû* "to become veiled, cloudy" jB med. **G** of eyes; > *apû* I; *ipītu*$^?$; *upû* I

apû → also *wapûm*

apuḫḫu ~ "fear" jB

apurugiš mng. unkn. NB

ap(u)sammikku(m), *apsammakku* (a geometrical shape) O/jB [ÁB.ZÀ.MÍ]; < Sum.

āputtum → *apputtum* II

apūtu(m) (a plant) jB

aqappu → *agappu*

aqarḫu (a piece of jewellery) Am.(Mit.) of coloured stones; < Hurr.

aqartu → *waqrum*

aqāru → *waqārum*

aqdamātum "near bank" Mari of a river; < W.Sem.; opp. → *aḫarātum*

aqdamum "former time" OB; < W.Sem.; → *qadmu*

aqqabu; pl. *aqqabāni* "remainder"? NA of textiles; < Aram.

aqqullakku → *akkullakku*

aqqullānu → *akkullānu*

aqqullu → *akkullu*; *anqullu*

aqrabu "scorpion" jB lex.; < W.Sem.

aqru → *waqrum*

aqūpu → *uqūpu*

ār ~ "forest" jB lex.

ārā "earth, land" NB lex.; < Aram.

arabānû, *ar(i)bānû* (a bird) jB; = *arabû* ?

arabû, *arabūa* **1.** (an edible water-fowl) [ARA$_4$.BU.MUŠEN] (→ *arabānû*) **2.** (a plant) jB; < Sum.?

ar'abu (or *ar'ibu*) (a plant) jB lex.

arabūa → *arabû*

araddu, *arant/du* "wild ass" jB; < W.Sem.

ar(a)d-ēkallūtu "palace service" NB [LÚ.ÌR.É.GAL-]; < *wardum* + *ēkallūtu*

arad-šarrūtu "royal service" NB [LÚ.ÌR.LUGAL-]; < *wardum* + *šarrūtu*

aradu → *wardum*

arādu "to serve" Am.(Syria) **G** "be servant of" king **D** ~ G; < *wardum* denom.

arādu → also *warādum*

aragubbû (a mathematical term) OB lex.; < Sum.

araḫḫu(m) I, *arḫu* "storehouse, granary" OB lex., jB; < Sum.

araḫḫu II (a genre of Sum. songs) jB; < Sum.

Araḫsamna/u (8th Bab. month) j/NB [ITI.APIN(.DU$_8$.A)]; < *warḫum* + *samnu* I

Araḫtu (major canal in northern Babylonia) j/NB; < *urḫu* I ?

araḫûm ~ "fixed metrological ratio"? OB math. [A.RÁ.ḪI]; < Sum.

arāḫu(m) I, occas. *warāḫum* "to hasten" O/jB **G** (pret. *īraḫ*; stat. *aruḫ*) "be urgent, hurry"; vent. "come quickly" **D** "speed up, send speedily"; "scare away"; in hendiad. *urruḫu* +

vb. "do X quickly" **Štn** iter. "hurry (s.o./th.) very much"; > *arḫu* I, *arḫiš*; *urruḫiš*; *murriḫu*; → *erēḫu*

arāḫu(m) II ~ "to devour, destroy" O/jB **G** (*a/u*) of fire, dog "consume" opponent, life **Š** caus. of G; → *erēḫu*

arakarûm ~ "factor"? OB math. [A.RÁ.KÁRA]; < Sum.

arāku(m) "to be long" [GÍD(.DA)] **G** (*i/i*) of distance; transf. in PN of arm (*idum*); of time, patience, life, reign "be long, last long; drag on; be too long" **D** of space, time "make long, lengthen; be overdue"; in hendiad. *urruku* + vb. "do X at length" **Dt** "be protracted" **Š** "prolong, extend" time; > *arku*, *ariktu*; *arraku*; *urku*; *mūraku*, *māraku*; *urāku*

aralaš (a plant) jB lex.; < Kass.?

arallû(m), *arallu* "netherworld" O/jB [ARALI(=É.KUR.BAD)] jB *šad a.* "mountain of the netherworld", also desig. of temple; < Sum.

aramanātu f. pl. ~ "lairs"? jB of wild animals

aramanītum; pl. *aramaniātum* ~ "constant in an equation"? OB math.; < Sum.?

arammu(m) ~ "causeway" Bab. "ramp" (for siege); "embankment, bund" of canal; → *armu* III

arāmu, jB also *erēmu* "to cover" Bogh., jB **G** (*i/i*) "cover s.th. with s.th." (= 2 acc.), drum with skin, object with gold; "place (tablet) in a (clay) case"; ext., bodily parts; of cloud "cover" moon, planet; of smoke "veil" face; transf. "cover" s.o.'s face etc. with radiance, gloom etc. **D** "cover up"; > *armu* I; *nāramu*; *ermu*; *erimtu* II, *urindu*; *tārīmu*; OA, OB → *ḫarāmum* I

arandu → *araddu*; *arantu*

arâniš "like eagles" jB [TI$_8$.MUŠEN]; < *erû* I + *-ān* + *-iš*

arannu → *arānu* I

arantu, *arandu* (a kind of grass) jB

arantu → also *araddu*

arānu I, NB also *arannu*, *arranu* f. "chest, cashbox, coffin" j/NB of wood, stone

arānu(m) II "to be guilty" **G** Am. stat. only **D** Mari "blame"; < *arnu* denom.?

arapšannu (a precious object)? Am.(Mit.); < Hurr.?

arāpu → *erēpu*

arāqu → *warāqum*

araraku → *ararû* I

ararathu (a tree) jB lex.; < Hurr.?

arariḫuru (a functionary) Nuzi; < Hurr.

arari(y)ānu (a plant) M/jB med.

ararratu "female miller, grinder" MB [MUNUS.ÀR.ÀR (→ *ṭē'ittu*)]; < *ararru*

ararru(m) "miller, grinder" Bab. [(LÚ.)ÀR.ÀR (→ *ṭē'inu*)]; OB *bīt a.* "mill"; < Sum.; > *ararratu*, *ararrūtu*, *āriru*

ararrūtu "work of a miller" jB; < *ararru*

ararû I, *arāru*, *araraku* (a plant) jB lex., med.

ararû II (a word for granary) jB lex.

ararû III (a male prostitute)? jB lex.

arāru I subst. "curse" jB, NA; < *arāru* II infin.

arāru(m) II "to curse; insult" OAkk, Bab., M/NA **G** (*a/u*) "curse" s.o./s.th., *erretam/ arratam a.* "curse s.o. with a curse"; > *arru* I, *ariru* 1; *arratu*, *erretu* I; *arāru* I; *errerû*

arāru(m) III, *ḫarāru* "to be convulsed" Bab. **G** (*u/u*, pres. also *i'arru/ar*) [UR$_4$] of human beings, demons, animals, earth(quake) "tremble, shake", lit. "suffer cramp, be convulsed"?; med., of parts of body (freq. *ḫarāru*, different word?); of sea, rivers "be rough, muddy" **Gtn** iter. **D** ~ "stir up, frighten"; om., med. in stat. of parts of body "suffers cramp, convulses" **Dt** ~ "be stirred up, convulsed" **N** ingress. "begin to convulse"? **Ntn** iter. of N and G [UR$_4$.UR$_4$]; > *ariru* 3; *arurtu*; *tārūru*?; the verbs *arāru* III, *erēru* and *ḫarāru* cannot yet be differentiated in every case; → also *tarāru*

arāru → also *ararû* I

arasu(m) **1.** OB (a container for salt)? **2.** NA mng. unkn.

arašiyannu (a functionary) Alal.

araššannu (a bird) Am.(Mit.); = *amursānu* ?

arašu → *waršum*

arāšu → *erēšu* I; *warāšum*

arathu (a tree) jB lex.; < Hurr.?

arattû; f. *arattītu* "excellent", liter. '(coming) from Aratta' j/NB of seats, daises, land; of a mark on the exta; < PlN + *-ī*

arazallu → *arzallu*

arazapanatašu (a functionary) NB; < OPers.?

araziqqu (part of a waggon) jB lex.

arbâ → *erbâ*

arballu "sieve" NB; < Aram.

arbānu (a plant) jB lex.

arbānû → *arabānû*

arbašītu (a type of pot) MB

arba'u(m); f. *arbattu* "four" after *kibrātu(m)* "the edges" (of the world) OAkk; also O/jB(lit.) arch. for *erbû*, f. *erbettu* [LIMMU]; → *erbe*

arbe, *arbēt* → *erbe*

arbîšu → *erbêšu*

arbītum, arbium → *arwium*
arbu(m) I, OB phps. *warbum* "waste, uncultivated" Bab., of meadow (*ugāru*); = *ḫarbu* I ?; > *arbūtu* I
arbu II "fugitive, runaway" Nuzi, jB; < *nērubu*; > *arbūtu* II
arbû → *arwium*; *erbû*
arbūtiš "into barren land" jB; < *arbūtu* I
arbūtu I "desolation" M/jB [(MUNUS.)KAR-] in *a. šūluku* "to make desolate, lay waste"; < *arbu* I > *arbūtiš*
arbūtu(m) II "flight, rout" O/jB, of army, person in *a. alāku* "to take flight"; status of a fugitive; < *arbu* II
ardabu (a measure of capacity, ~ 56 litres) NB; < Aram. or OPers.?
ardadillu, *artatillu*, *aštatillu* (a plant) M/jB lex., med. [Ú.AŠ.TÁL.TÁL]
ardadu ~ "thief" jB
ardanānu ~ "phantom, double" of a dead person M/jB med.; → *andunānu*
ardat lilî → *lilium*
ardatu → *wardatum*
ardiš → *arṭiš*
ardu → *wardum*
ardūtu → *wardūtum*
arēbu → *erēbu* II
argabu, *arkabu*, *erkabu* (a bird) jB lex. [ARGAB.MUŠEN]; < Sum.
argamannu "purple" j/NB, NA [SÍK.ZA.GÌN.SA5], of textiles; Bogh. "tribute"
argānum, *argannu*, *ḫargānum* (a conifer; its resin) O/jB esp. med.; → *margānum*
argibillu (a wooden structure)? jB lex.; < Sum.
arginnum (a commodity) OAkk(Susa)
argukkum, *argugu* (an agricultural implement, phps.) "roller" O/jB lex.; < Sum.
arḫā "every month" NB [ITI(.A)(.TA)(.ÀM/A')]; < *warḫum*
arḫālum → *warḫālum*
arḫānû, *erḫānû* 'monthly ...'? jB lex. **1.** "green, unripe date" **2.** (an intestinal disorder); < *warḫum* + *-ān* + *-ī* ?
arḫiš, *urḫiš*, OB occas. *warḫiš* "quickly, hastily" Ass., O/jB; < *arḫu* I
arḫišam(ma) → *warḫišamma*
arḫītum → *warḫītum*
arḫu(m) I; f. *aruḫtu* "fast, quick" O/jB, NA; in OB ext. epith. of *kakkum*; jB(Ass.), NA of copper, bronze; < *arāḫu* I; > *arḫiš*
arḫu(m) II f. "cow" O/jB [(GU4.)ÁB]; → *a.* III
arḫu(m) III f. "half-brick" O/jB [SIG4.ÁB]; = *a.* II ?
arḫu → also *araḫḫu* I; *urḫu* I; *warḫum*
arḫussu "every month, monthly" j/NB [ITI-]; < *warḫum* + *-ūt* + *-šu*
aria → *erium*; *iria*
aribānû → *arabānû*
arībānu (a plant) jB lex.
aribîš → *eribîš*
aribû (a garment) MB
aribû → also *erbû*
ar'ibu → *ar'abu*
aridni → *alidni*
āridu 1. "perpendicular"? of marks on exta jB; < *warādum* **2.** mng. unkn. NB
ariḫu, *aruḫu* (a plant) jB lex., med.
ariktu 1. (a kind of spear) jB [GIŠ.GÍD.DA]; pl. *arkātu* **2.** "length" jB ext., comm. **3.** (a wind instrument) jB; < *arku*
ārimānu (a kind of axe)? jB lex.
arinnu "well" Nuzi; < Hurr.
aripše (an agricultural implement) Nuzi; < Hurr.
ariru (or *āriru*, *arīru*) **1.** (a priest uttering curses)? NB; < *arāru* II **2.** (an epith. of fire) jB **3.** (a weapon) jB; < *arāru* III
āriru "miller" Bogh. lex.; < *ararru*
ārišūtu "agricultural tenancy" NA; < *erēšu* I Ass.
ārittu → *wārittum*
arītu(m) I, *erītu* "pregnant (woman)" Bab., NA [MUNUS.PEŠ4] also of animal; *a. šamni* "pregnant with oil" (a plant); < *arû* IV
arītu(m) II **1.** Ass., M/NB "shield"; of leather, wood, metal; NA LÚ (= *ša* ?) *a.* "shield-bearer"; on chariot **2.** jB (syn. of door) **3.** jB (desig. of planet Venus)
arītu III (a knife, dagger) jB lex.
ariyātu → *eriyātu*
arka → *warka*; *warki*
arkâ ~ "henceforth" MB; < *warkûm* ?
arkabinnu(m) 1. Bab. (kind of door, phps.) "half-door", also *dalat a.* **2.** Nuzi (a festival; a month); < Hurr.?
arkabu (a type of decoration) Nuzi; < Hurr.
arkabu → also *argabu*
arkāna → *warkānum*
arkāniš, *arkānuš* adv. "back; later, subsequently" j/NB *a. târu* "to return"; < *wark(a)* + *-ān* + *-iš*
arkānu → *warkānum*
arkānuš → *arkāniš*
arkat → *warkat*
Arkattu → *Urkītum*
arkalātu → *warkatum*; *ariktu* 1
arkâtu → *warkītum* B

arkâtu → *warkītum* B

Arkayītu → *Urkītum*

arki → *warka*; *warki*

arkillâ (an animal figure)? jB lex.

arkīnišu "afterwards" NB; < *warki*

arkiš adv. "back" jB in *a. târu* "to return"; "behind" in *pāniš u arkiš*; < *warkum*; Ass. → *urkiš*

arkīši "thereafter" NB for *arkīšu*; < *warki*

arkīta → *warkītam*

arkītu → *warkītum*

arku(m), NB also *ašku* "long" [GÍD(.DA)], of objects, time; "tall" of people; *ūmū arkūtu* "long life"; MB *ana a. nadû* "to put off"; < *arāku*; > *arraku, ariktu*

arku → also *warka*; *warki*

arkû → *warkûm*

Arkuzzi (a month) Nuzi; < Hurr.

arma(ḫ)ḫu → *marmaḫḫu*

arma(n)niš "like an apricot?" jB(lit.); < *armannu*

armannu(m), *armanû, ramannu*, OB also *arwānum* "apricot? (tree)" O/jB [GIŠ.ḪAŠḪUR. KUR.RA]; jB, branch used as drug, kernel used as perfume

armarrû → *azmarû*

armašītu (a pottery vessel) MB

armatum (metal sheeting or plating) of copper on door OAkk(Sum.); of gold, as decoration MB

armaya, *armû; f. *armītu* "Aramaic" NA of scribe, document etc.

armēdu (a plant) jB lex.

armītu → *armaya*; *arwium*

armu I "covered" jB of weapon; of tablet "enclosed" in envelope (→ *ḫarāmum* I); < *arāmu*

armu II ~ "mountain goat" M/NA, M/jB hunted; as decoration; NA *kaqqad a.* "goat's head (situla)"

armu III jB lex. = *arammu* ?

armû → *armaya*; *arwium*

armūtu "desolation" jB lex.

arnabtu(m) "female hare" O/jB; OB *Arnabatum* as fPN; < *arnabu*

arnabu(m), *annabu*; pl. f. "hare" OAkk, O/jB; NA as PN; > *arnabtu*

arnu(m), O/jB also *annu* "guilt, fault; penalty" [NAM.TAG.GA] **1.** (secular) "fault", (religious) "sin"; *a. paṭāru, a. pašāru* "to undo, forgive sins"; *bēl a., ša a.* "culprit, sinner"; Am. *awīl a.* "evil-doer" **2.** "penalty, punishment", *a. emēdu/našû* "to impose/suffer punishment"; OA *ana a. n/tadānum* "to subject s.o. to

punishment" **3.** Mari *a. turrum* "transfer responsibility" onto s.o.; > *arānu* II

arnurḫēli (a prof.) Nuzi; < Hurr.

arpa(n)nu (a kind of house)? Nuzi; < Hurr.?

arpu → *erpu*

arqu → *warqum*

arqūtu "greenness, freshness" Bogh., M/jB [SIG₇]; < *warqum*

arr... also = *ana r...*

arrabu(m), *arrabû?, arrapu*; f. *arrabtu* ~ "dormouse"? Bab. [PÉŠ.(GIŠ.)ÙR.RA]; rit., skin of dormouse

arraku(m) "very long, tall" Bab., O/MA; used as pl. of → *arku*

arrānu → *arānu* I

arrapšātum f. pl. (a social class of women)? Mari

arrapu → *arrabu*

arraqu "very green" jB; < *warāqum*

arraṣabattu → *arṣabu*

arrāšum → *errēšu*

arratu(m) "curse" OAkk, OA, M/jB [ÁŠ] *a. arāru* "to curse s.o. (with a curse)"; *a. lā napšuri* "unliftable curse"; NB *a. ilāni* "one cursed by the gods"; < *arāru* II; → *erretu* I

arrātu pl. tant. "brand mark" on the hands of temple slaves NB

arrā'u "on the ground"? NB of goose

arriātum in *ša a.* mng. unkn. OB lex.

arriš (a bird) jB om.

arru I "cursed" jB lex.; < *arāru* II

arru II (desig. of sheep) jB lex.

arru(m) III "decoy bird" M/NB; > *arrūtu*

arru(m) IV (a weapon) OB, jB lex.

arrūrum (a textile or garment) OB; → *ḫarīru* ?

arrūtu "role as decoy" NB; < *arru* III

arsannu, arsānu → *arzānu*

arsasû(m) (a mountain bird) OB

arsikku (a kind of millet)? jB lex.; < Sum.?

arsu ~ *arzānu* NA lex.

arsuppu, *ersuppu* **1.** "carp" M/jB [GU₄.UD.KU₆]; *qulipti a.* "carp scales"; *mīli a.* "carp flood" **2.** (a cereal, phps.) "einkorn" M/jB, NA [ŠE.EŠTUB]; *miris a.* "einkorn broth" **3.** (a kind of apple)? jB lex.

arṣabu, *arraṣabattu*; pl. f. (an agricultural implement)? NB

arṣatum → *erṣetu*

aršammaya (a group or organization) NB

aršātum f. pl. 'what is cultivated', "barley" OA [GIG]; < *arāšum* II Ass.

aršu → *aršātum*; *eršu* II; *waršum*

aršuzuzil (a drug) MB; → *zuzillu*

artāma (or *artāwa*) "blessed state" NB; < OPers.

artamašše mng. unkn. Nuzi; < Hurr.

artartena (a type of textile) Nuzi; < Hurr.

artartennūtu (a special treatment of textiles) Nuzi; < Hurr.

artatillu → *ardadillu*

artāwa → *artāma*

artītu → *ḫartītum*

artu, *aštu* "branches, foliage" j/NB; < *aru* I

artu → also *uptu*

arṭiš (or *ardiš*) adv. mng. unkn. jB lex.

aru(m) I, *eru(m)*, *ḫarum* "branch, frond" O/jB [PA] of date palm, tamarisk, trees; "stalk" of plant; > *artu*

aru II (a type of wool) jB lex.

aru III "hide" of ox OA

arû(m) I "result" Bab. math. [A.RÁ] **1.** "product" of multiplication **2.** "factor, multiplier" (→ *alāku* G 6) **3.** "ready reckoner, numerical table, astronomical ephemeris"; < Sum.

arû II "granary, storehouse" OA, jB lex.

arû(m) III "to vomit" O/jB **G** (pres. *i'arru*) [BURU$_8$(=ḪAL)] **Gtn** iter. of G **Š** med. "make vomit" with feather

arû(m) IV, *erû* "to be(come) pregnant, conceive" Bab., NA **G** (*i/i*) [PEŠ$_4$] of animal, human; with child (= acc.) **D** "make pregnant" jB **Š** caus. of G "impregnate" **N** Ug. = G ?; > *arītu* I; *mērû*; *erûtu* II; *urû* VI; *āru* I

arû V "hungry" jB lex.

arû VI, *erû* "to cut off" Bab. **G** (*u/u* ?) NB "prune, lop" date palm **D** (*urrû(m)*, j/NB *murrû*) **1.** OB of goddess "sever" (the umbilical cord)? of king **2.** jB of meteor "cut short, stop" luminous display **3.** jB of enemy, flood "ruin" harvest **4.** NB ~ G **Dt** pass. of D 4; > *urrû* I, *urû* II, *muwarrītum*; *tārītu* II

arû → also *erru* II 2; *erû* I-III; *warûm* II

āru I, *māru* "fish spawn" jB lex.; < *arû* IV

āru(m) II "warrior" jB lex.; → *ayyaru* II

âru → *wârum*

arugimānum "legal claim" OAkk, OB usu. pl.; < *ragāmu*

aruḫu → *ariḫu*

arullu (an ornament) Qatna, in necklace

arullu → also *urullu* I.II

arūnu (a plant) jB lex.

aruppu "armpit" jB; → *uruppum*

arūratu → *yarūru*

arurtu, jB also *aruštu* ~ "famine, hunger" O/jB of land, of individuals; < *arāru* III

arūru ~ "outlet of a canal" jB

arūrūtu → *yarūrūtu*

aruštu → *arurtu*; *waršum*

arūšu → *amuššu*

aruthu → *uruthu*

arutû ~ "mountain" jB lex.

arūtu(m), *erūtu* "(clay) pipe" O/jB for libations, over grave

arûtu → *erûtu* I

arwānum → *armannu*

arwium, *arwûm*, *armû* "male gazelle" OAkk, O/jB; OAkk, OB as PN; OB also fPN *Arw/mītum*; OAkk also *Arbium*, *Arbûm*, *Arbītum*

arzallu(m), *arazallu* **1.** jB (a plant) **2.** j/NB (a stone) as jewellery; in mag. **3.** OA (an implement)

arzanikkatu (a plant) jB

arzānu, later *arsānu*, NB *arsannu*, Nuzi *ar/nzannu* "barley-groats" [AR.ZA.NA]; → *arsu*

arzatu I (a container) Nuzi

arzatu II, **arzazu** (a plant) jB lex.

asa'ītu, *asa'ittu*, NA *a/isītu*; pl. *asāyātu*, NA *asi'ātu*, *asâtu*, *esāyātu*, *a/isitāte* "tower" M/NA of fortification wall; "pyramid" of bodies or heads on the battlefield; → *išittu* I

asakkiš, *ašakkiš* "like s.th. tabooed" jB; < *asakku* II

asakku(m) I, *ašakku* (an evil demon) O/jB [ÁZAG(=Á.PA)]; (also disease caused by *a.* demon); < Sum.

asakku(m) II "taboo" OA, O/jB [AZAG(=KÙ.AN)] esp. *a. akālu* "to break a taboo"; (s.th. reserved for a god or king); M/jB *bīt a.* "forbidden building, sanctum"; < Sum.; > *asakkiš*

asallu(m) f. **1.** (a copper vessel) O/jB, M/NA **2.** (a stone) jB lex.

asāmu → *wasāmum*

asanītu; pl. *asaniātu* (an oleiferous plant) MA in perfume recipes

asānum "bear-like"? OA, OB as PN; < *asu* II

asāqu ~ "to strengthen" or "raise up"? jB **G** (*i/i*)

asarru I (an archit. feature) NB, bearing inscription; → *a.* II

asarru II, *ašarru* (a type of lit. document) NA; = *a.* I ?

asarum (a class of person) Mari

asāru → *eseru* II

asatum → *asu* II

asâtu(m) "female doctor" O/jB [Mari MUNUS.A.ZU]; < *asû* I; → *asītu*

asâtu → also *ašâtu*

asḫar, *ašḫar* (a kind of stone) jB lex., med. [ŠIM.BI.SIG$_7$.SIG$_7$] as drug; Bogh. → *išḫar*

asīdu "heel" jB of human, also du.; "heel" of shoe; astr. 'heel' (lowest part) of constellation

asikilla "holy water" jB lex.; < Sum.

asiqatu mng. uncl. NB lex.

asirtu "female captive" jB, also OB fPN *Asīratum*; < *asīru* I

asīru(m) I; pl. *asīrū* "captive, prisoner of war" O/MB, MB(Alal.), Am., Ug.; as PN, also MA; OB *bīt a.* "prison"; < *esēru* II; > *asirtu*; *asīrūtu*

asīrum II (or *azīrum*) (an object) OA

asīrūtu "captivity" j/NB in *a. alāku* "to go into captivity"; < *asīru* I

asisû (a word for copper) jB lex.

asītu "female physician" NB in PN; → *asâtu*

asītu → also *asa'ītu*

askāru → *uskāru*

askuppu(m), *askuppatu(m)*, NA *aksuppu*; pl. m. & f. "(threshold) slab" Bab., NA [NA$_4$.I.DIB] usu. of stone; transf. part of a chariot; part of irrigation device; part of the lung

askuttu → *aškuttu*

asliš "like sheep" jB; < *aslu* I

aslu I "ram; sheep" jB as sacrifice; > *asliš*

aslu II f. (a special cubit measure) jB, NA; *ubān a.* "finger (i.e. subdivision) of *a.* cubit"

asmātu pl. tant. (a type of horse trappings)? jB

asmīdu (a garden plant) j/NB

asmiš "in a fitting manner" j/NB, *a. šūluku* "to make suitable, adorn"; < *wasmum*

asmu → *wasmum*

asnan → *ašnan*

asnû, *assa(n)nû*, NB also *issanu* "(date) from Dilmun" j/NB [TILMUN(=NI.TUK).KI]; lex. also "(copper) from Dilmun"

aspastu; pl. *asupasātu* ? "lucerne" NB; < Iran.

aspastūa "fodderer" NB; < Iran.

aspatu in *bīt a.* mng. unkn. NB

aspu → *waspum*

asqāru → *uskāru*

asqiqu (a bird) jB lex.

asqiqû → *ašgigû*

asqubbītu(m), *asqumbittu*, *asqubbittu*, *is/šqubbītu* "hump" Bab., of cattle, camels; jB om. of deformed foetus

asqūdu, *ašqūdu(m)* OAkk, O/jB, NA [PÉŠ.TÚM.TÚM.ME] **1.** (a rodent); as PN **2.** (a kind of snake); > *ašqūdānum*

asqumbittu → *asqubbītu*

asru mng. uncert. NB

ass... also = *ana s...*

assammu(m), *ansammum*, *assammû*; pl. m. & f. "goblet, drinking vessel" OAkk, Bab. [AN.ZA.AM] of copper, silver, cedarwood; < Sum.

assannû → *asnû*; *assinnu*

assanû → *asnû*

assaru ~ "charioteer" jB

assaštaranni (cloth streamers on fly-whisk) Am.; < Hurr.

assinnu(m), *isinnu/û*, Bogh. *assannû*?, lex. also *assinnatu* ~ (male cultic prostitute) O/jB, Alal., Nuzi, NA [(LÚ.)UR.MUNUS; SAG.UR.SAG]

assinnūtum (rôle of *assinnum*) OB in *a. epēšum* "to act as an *assinnum*"

assu → *asu* I

assukku "sling-stone" Susa, jB

assurri, OB also *ussurre(ma)*, *assurrē*, Am. *aṣṣurri* "(if) perchance" (of undesirable eventuality), "hopefully ... not ..." OA, OB, Am.; before neg. or proh. "on no account should ..."; < *ana* I + *surri*

asu(m) I, OA also *ašum*, Bogh. *assu* "myrtle" [(GIŠ/ŠIM.)AZ; Mari also GIŠ.A.AZ, GIŠ.A.ZU; j/NB, NA ŠIM.GÍR] for incense; *šaman a.* "oil of myrtle" as drug

asu(m) II; pl. f. "bear" O/jB [AZ]; as PN, also f. *Asatum*; < Sum.; > *asānum*

asû(m) I "physician" [(LÚ.)A.ZU; OAkk in PN also A.ZU$_5$] of humans, animals; for eyes; MA *a. ša bētānu* (a kind of superintendent); NB ~ "expert"; < Sum.; > *asâtu*; *asûtu*; → *azugallatu*; *azugallu*; *azugallūtu*

asû(m) II, *esû* **1.** (a wooden part of the loom) OAkk, O/jB, Nuzi **2.** (part of a door) jB lex.

asû → also *azû* I

asumatānu (a bird) jB; < *asumatu* + *-ān* ?

asumatu (a part of the plough) jB lex.; > *asumatānu*?

asumittu(m), NA also *usumittu*, *ušmittu*; pl. *asuminētu(m)* "inscribed slab" Bab., NA of stone, metal; carved relief; as boundary stone, stele, foundation document

asūmû(m) "stele"? NA; Mari as DN ?

asupasātu → *aspastu*

asuppu; pl. f. ~ "out-building, annexe" M/NB; also *bīt a.*; → *asuptu*

asuptu = *asuppu* ? NB

asurrakku "subterranean waters" jB; transf. of deeply laid water conduit; < Sum.

asurrû(m) "lower course, footing" of wall Bab.; plastered, lined with slabs, repaired; transf. (a part of the exta); < Sum.

asūtum (a kind of cloth)? OB

asûtu(m) "profession of physician; medical skill" Bab., NA; < *asû* I

aṣābu → *waṣābum*

aṣappu "pack animal" NA

aṣāpu → *waṣābum*

aṣarru(m) (or *azarru(m)*) (a kind of clock)? jB lex.

aṣāru → *uṣāru*

āṣītu → *wāṣītum*

aṣpu → *waṣpum*

aṣṣ... also = *ana ṣ...*

aṣṣēr → *ṣēru* 2

aṣṣurri → *assurri*

aṣû → *waṣûm*

āṣû → *wāṣûm*

aṣūdu; pl. f. (a dish of food) NA; < Aram.?; → *kallaṣudi*

aṣulimtu (a kind of bitumen)? jB lex.

aṣupātu pl. ~ (reed mats) NB; < Aram.; → *ṣuppatu* II

aṣūru → *azūru*

aṣuṣi(m)tu, *aṣuṣētu*, *aṣuṣu(m)tu*, *ṣuṣimtu* (a medicinal plant) jB; = *ṣaṣumtu*

a/āṣûtu → *wāṣûtum*

ašābu → *wašābum*

ašāgu(m), *ešēgu* (a common spiny plant, phps.) "camelthorn" Bab., Bogh. [(GIŠ.)KIŠI$_{16}$]; *iṣṣur a.* (a small bird)

ašaḫḫu(m) "granary, storehouse" O/jB; also *bīt a.*, pl. f.

ašakkiš → *asakkiš*

ašakku → *asakku* I

ašalallû → *ašilalûm*

ašamšāniš "like a dust storm" jB; < *ašamš(ūtu)* + *-ān* + *-iš*

ašamšūtu(m), OB also *ašamtūtum*; pl. also *ašanšātu* "dust storm" O/jB [DAL.ḪA.MUN; DALḪAMUN]; transf. jB medical condition, "storm" in the abdomen; > *ašamšāniš*

ašannu → *šanannu*

ašāpu → *wašāpum*

ašar, *a/išarma* "straightaway" OB lex.

ašar → also *ašru* III

ašarānum → *ašrānu*

ašarēdu; f. *ašarettu*, NA also *(a)šaressu* "first and foremost, pre-eminent" OAkk, Bab., NA [SAG.KAL; once SAG.ZI; in PN also SAG, MAŠ] of god, king, official, warrior; NA of objects "first-class"; < *ašar* + *wēdum*; > *ašarēdūtu*, *ašarettu*

ašarēdūtu "pre-eminence" O/jB, NA [SAG.KAL-] *a. alāku* "to take first place"; < *ašarēdu*

ašarettu, *(a)šaressu* "crack troops" NA [SAG (.KAL)-]; < *ašarēdu*

ašari "at the same place" OB, also *ašarima*; < *ašru* III

ašarikīam → *ašrakīam*

ašarima → *ašari*

ašariš, jB also *ašriš* "there, thither" O/jB; OB *ištu a.* "from there"; < *ašru* III

ašarma → *ašar*

ašarmadu → *šarmadu*

ašarru → *asarru* II

ašaršani, *ašaršana*, *ašaršani/umma*, MB also *ataršani* "elsewhere, to another place" Bab., OA; < *ašru* III + *šanû* II

ašartu "waste land" jB; also *atartu* in *ṣēr a.* (a type of snake); < *ašru* III

ašarū → *ašru* III

ašāru(m) "to muster, review" **G** (*a/u*) "check, take stock of" animals, equipment etc.; "take care of; check up on" people **Gtn** iter. of G jB **Št** jB ~ "be gathered, mustered"; > *aširtu* I; *āširu*, *āširtu*; *ašru* I; *aššaru*; *māšartu*; *tāšertum*

ašāru → also *wašārum*

ašāšu(m) I (a type of nest made by water fowl) O/jB lex.

ašāšu II (a kind of moth) jB lex.

ašāšu(m) III "to be distressed" OA, O/jB **G** (*u/u*; stat. also *ašuš*) [ZI.IR] "be aggrieved, angry"; jB once trans. "distress" s.o. **Gtn** iter. of G O/jB **Gt** ~ G OA **D** "grieve, distress" s.o., "torture, maltreat" s.o. **Dtn** iter. of D **Dt** "become distressed" **Št** ~ "grieve about s.th., pine away" **Ntn** "constantly become distressed"; > *aššišu*?; *ašuštu*; *uššatu*; *uššušu* I, *uššušiš*

ašāšu IV, *ešēšu*, *ḫašāšu* "to catch" jB **G** (*a/u*) esp. birds; "encompass" learning ?; of flood "engulf"? **Gtn** iter. of G; > *āšišu*

ašâtu, NA also *asâtu* pl. tant. **1.** "reins" M/jB, NA of horses; *mukīl a.* "charioteer" NA **2.** jB lex. (a headdress); < *ašītu* II or *ašutu* pl.?

ašâtu → also *ašītu* I; *ešītu*; *ešû* I

ašāṭu → *wašāṭum*

ašbatum (or *ašpatum*) (an object) OAkk(Sum.)

ašbu (a tree or shrub) jB

ašbu → also *wašbum*

ašbutu → *ašubbatu*

ašdānu (a medicinal plant) jB

ašdiḫu → *išdiḫu* II

ašeratum (a type of garment) Mari

ašertu → *aširtu*; *ešertu* I

ašgagu, *ašgugu* "fight" M/jB

ašgigû, *ašg/kikû*, *aš/sqiqû*, *atgigu* j/NB, NA **1.** (a mineral, phps.) "arsenic" **2.** (a plant) *ašgugu* → *ašgagu*

ašḫa(l)lum, NA *ašḫulu* (a container) of metal, wood or reed OAkk(Sum.), OB, MB(Alal.), NA

ašḫappum → *isḫappu*

ašḫar → *asḫar*

ašḫauššuḫḫu → *ašušḫu*

ašḫulu → *ašḫallum*

ašḫušḫu → *ašušḫu*

ašiannu → *aššiyannu*

ašiarra, *ašiarê* (a class of servants) Nuzi; < Hurr.

ašibu → *yašibum*

āšibu → *wāšibum*

aš(i)lalûm, *ašalallû*; pl. *ašalallâtu* ~ "decorative fancy work" as gift O/MB; O/jB lex.

āšiptu "sorceress, female magician" jB of witch, goddess; < *wāšipum*

āšipu → *wāšipum*

āšipūtu "exorcism" M/NB, NA [MAŠ.MAŠ-] **1.** action, ritual of *āšipu* **2.** desig. of prof. literature of *āšipu*; < *wāšipum*

aširi, usu. Ug. pl. *aširi/uma* (persons of a special status) Am., Ug. etc.; < W.Sem.

aširtu(m) I **1.** "check, inspection"; "advice"? jB, NA [NA.RI] **2.** (a type of religious offering) OB; < *ašāru*

aširtum II "tithe" OB(N.Mes.); < *ešer*

aširtu → also *ašru* I; *ešertu* I

āširtu "(female) inspector, organizer" jB; < *āširu*

āširu(m) "inspector, checker" OA, jB; < *ašāru*

aširuma → *aširi*

ašiš (part of a chariot) OA

ašišû ~ "miserable, wretched" jB lex.

āšišu "encompassing, wise; engulfing" jB; < *ašāšu* IV

ašītu I; pl. *ašâtu* "chaos, confusion in battle" jB; < *ešû* I

ašītu(m) II "metal band, strap" O/MB; of door (pl. → *ašâtu*)

ašītu III ~ "midday" jB lex.

ašium "(meteoric) iron"? OA; → *ušû*

aškadu, *maškadu* (a spiny plant) jB lex.

Aška'ītu → *Urkītum*

aškāpu(m) "leatherworker" [(LÚ.)AŠGAB]; < Sum.

aškāpūtu(m) "leatherwork; craft of the leatherworker" Bab. [LÚ.AŠGAB-]; < *aškāpu*

aškāru → *uskāru*

Aškayītu → *Urkītum*

aškikītu, OB *bašgigītum*, Bogh. *mašgikīdu* (a bird) O/jB

aškikû → *ašgigû*

aškirušḫu (a utensil used in pairs) Alal., Am.; < Hurr.

ašku → *arku*

aškuppu → *atkuppu*

aškuttu(m), *askuttu* [(GIŠ.)AŠKUD(=Á.SUḪ)] Bab. **1.** "locking bar" for barring a door; om., math. "wedge-shape" **2.** (an earth structure in fields and houses); < Sum.

ašlaktum "washerwoman" OAkk (presumed rdg. of [MUNUS.LÚ.ÁZLAG]); < *ašlāku*

ašlāku(m), Nuzi also *ašlašku* "washerman; fuller" [OAkk, O/MB, MA LÚ.ÁZLAG; j/NB, NA LÚ.AZLAG]; < Sum.; > *ašlaktum*, *ašlākūtu*

ašlākūtu "craft of the washerman, fuller" O/jB; < *ašlāku*

ašlalûm → *ašilalûm*

ašlašku → *ašlāku*

ašlu(m) "rush; rope" **1.** j/NB [Ú.NINNI$_5$] harvested; as drug; bed of rushes **2.** O/jB, NA; pl. f. "tow rope; mooring rope" of a ship **3.** Bab., MA "measuring line"; OB *abi ašlim*, NB *abašlu* "surveyor"; "survey team (of 8-12 men)" **4.** Bab. (a linear measure of ~ 60 metres), st. abs. *ašal* "1 rope(-length)" **5.** Nuzi ~ "field"

ašlû (a garment) Nuzi

ašluḫḫe; pl. *ašluḫḫena* adj. mng. unkn. Nuzi; < Hurr.

ašlukatu (a kind of rush) jB lex.

ašlu(k)katu(m), *ašru(k)katu* ~ "storeroom" Bab. [É.UŠ.GÍD.DA] for grain; "lobby, hallway" in temple

ašlukku "storeroom" jB

ašmarû → *ešmarû*

ašmetu ~ "dust storm" jB lex.

ašnan, *asnan* "grain, cereals" O/jB [^{d}ŠE.TIR] as generic term; also as DN

ašni adv. mng. unkn. Am.; < Hurr.?

ašnu(m) (a bowl) OB(N.Mes.); jB in *ašni īni* "eye socket"

ašnugallu(m), *išnugallu(m)*, *gišnugallu(m)* ~ "alabaster" Bab., M/NA [NA$_4$.GIŠ.NU$_{11}$(/NU occas.).GAL] as raw material; for building; for sculpted items; in mag.

ašnugallum → also *aššunugallum*

ašpaltu "social inferior" jB; < *šapālu*

ašpatum → *ašbatum*

ašpû → *yašpû*

ašqāru → *uskāru*

ašqiqû → *ašgikû*

ašqūdānum "like an *a.* (rodent)" OB as PN only; < *asqūdu*

ašqūdu → *asqūdu*

ašqulālu(m), *isqulālu* **1.** O/jB (a weapon, phps.) "lasso" **2.** O/jB "whirlwind" **3.** jB (a marine plant) [Ú.AN.KI.NU.SÁ; Ú.LAL]; < *šuqallulu*

ašrā → *ešrā*

ašrakīam, *ašarikīam*, OA *ašrakam* "there, in that very place" OA, OB; < *ašru* III + *-kīam*

ašrānu(m), *ašarānum* "there, that very place" OB, Am., Nuzi, Bogh., Ug., jB also *ana/ištu/ina a.*; < *ašru* III + *-ānum*

ašratu "heaven" jB; < *ašru* III

ašrātu → *ešertu* I

ašriš I "humbly" M/jB; < *wašrum*

ašriš II M/jB **1.** adv. "to that place, there" **2.** prep. "to, towards", *a. dīni* "to the place of judgement"; < *ašru* III

ašriš → also *ašariš*

ašru(m) I; f. *aširtum* "taken care of" OB in PN; < *ašāru*

ašru II (a disease of the head) Bogh., jB; < Sum.?

ašru(m) III; OA gen. with pron. suff. *išri-*; pl. m. & f., OAkk *ašarū*, Am. *ašrāni* "place, site" [KI] **1.** *ana ašrišu târu/turru* "to return (intrans./trans.) to his/its (former) place" = "be restored, restore"; "place, abode"; pl. "(holy) places, (divine) abodes"; "region"; "building site, land"; "the earth"; Bogh. in Hitt. rit. "part" **2.** st. abs. OA, OB *ašar ištēn* "in a single place"; Bab. *ašar ... ašar ...* "here and there, in one place ... in another ..." (→ *ašaršani*) **3.** in st. constr. as prep. with infin. "where it is possible/suitable/necessary" to do s.th.; Nuzi "from, with, to" (s.o.) **4.** as conj. with subjunct. "where, where ... to"; OB also occas. "as soon as"?; OA "provided that" **5.** OB in *šar inanna* "right now"; > *ašari*, *ašariš*, *ašriš* II; *ašrānu*; *ašartu*, *ašratu*; *ašrakīam*; *ašaršani*; *ašarēdu*

ašru → also *wašrum*

ašru(k)katu → *ašlukkatu*

ašš... also = *ana š...*

ašša, *aššu* conj. "because, inasmuch as, seeing that" NB; < *an(a)* I + *ša*; as prep. → *aššum*

aššābu → *waššābum*

aššābūtu → *waššābūtum*

aššalluḫlu (a functionary)? Nuzi; < Hurr.

aššanu → *aššunu*

aššaru ~ "expert" jB, epith. of *ṭēmu*; < *ašāru*

aššatta/i → šatti

aššatu(m); st. constr. O/jB also *ašti*, j/NB freq. *alti* "wife" [DAM]; occas. also of second "wife"; *a. aḫāzu/ezēbu* "to marry/divorce a wife"; > *aššūtu*

aššiāti → *šiāti*

aššišu in *lā a.* ~ "unruly, disordered"? jB lex.; < *ašāšu* III ?

aššiyannu (desig. of garment) MA, Am., Nuzi; < Hurr.; = *maššiyannu* ?

aššu → *ašša*; *aššum*

aššultu (a plant) jB lex., equated with *šulutu*, *uššultu*

aššum, Bab. also *aššu*, OA *aššumi*, NB occas. *ašša*, *aššut* "because (of)" Bab., O/MA **1.** prep.: "because of, for the sake of" s.o., s.th.; OA, O/jB *aššum(i) kīam* "therefore"; O/jB *a. mīni(m)* "why?"; Bab. + infin. "so that, in order to"; "as for, concerning"; in comm. ~ "related to; derived from" [MU]; NB *a. ša* "because of the fact that" **2.** conj. + subjunct.: Bab. "because (of the fact that)"; Mari, OA + pres. "with a view to, in order to"; OB occas. in reported speech "that"; < *ana* I + *šumu*

aššunu, NA *aššanu* "they" (3 m. pl. pron.) MA(Bogh.), NA; → *šunu*

aš(šu)nugallum (desig. of snake) OB mag.

aššurayītu f. adj. "Assyrian" MA desig. of language

aššurû; f. *aššurītu(m)* "Assyrian" Ass., M/jB; in f.: **1.** DN "the Assyrian Ištar" **2.** jB lex. "ship from Aššur" **3.** OA as PN

aššut → *aššum*

aššūtu(m), Ass. *aššuttu* "marriage, status of a wife" Bab., MA [DAM-.] OB *ana a. aḫāzum*, Nuzi *ana a. leqû*, NB *ana a. rašû* "to take as wife"; *ana a. nadānum* "to give (a woman) in marriage"; < *aššatu* abstr.

aštabarru, *aštebarru* "lance-bearer" NB; < Iran.

aštabīru → *aštapīru*

aštakissu, *ašta/ikiss/ṣṣu* (a rodent) jB lex.

aštalû(m), lex. also *eštalû* (a type of singer) O/jB; Mari pl. f. *aštalêtum*; < Sum.

aštammu, *altammu* "tavern, hostel" Bab., MA [ÉŠ.DAM]; < Sum.

aštammûm; f. *aštammītum* "belonging to the tavern" OB of woman

Aštapi (a month)? Alal.; < Hurr.

aštapīru(m), *aštabīru*, OA *aštipīrum* "slaves, servants, domestic staff" Bab., OA [SAG.GÉME.ARAD; OB also GÉME.(SAG.) ARAD]

aštaru "goddess" jB; < W.Sem.

aštatillu → *ardadillu*

ašte → *išti*

aštebarru → *aštabarru*

ašti → *aššatu*; *išti*

aštikissu → *aštakissu*

aštikittišu (desig. of a horse) Nuzi; < Hurr.?

aštipīrum → *aštapīru*

aštu (a word for woman) jB lex.; < Hurr.

aštu → also *artu*; *aššatu*

aštû "throne" jB; < Sum.

ašturru "gnat" jB lex.

aštuzzu, *aštuttu* (desig. of garments) Nuzi; < Hurr.

ašṭu → *wašṭum*

ašṭūtu(m) "obduracy, stiffness" OB, jB lex.; < *wašṭum*

ašum → *asu* I

ašû(m) I (a disease of the head) Bab.; *šam(mī) a.* "plant(s) for *a.* disease" (name of a plant); → *rašašim*

ašû II ~ "living creatures" O/jB

ašû III (a kind of field)? MB

ašû(m) IV ~ "distinguished, noble" OA, jB

ašû → also *ašium*; *ešû* I.IV; *ḫašû* III; *ušû*; *wašā'um*

âšu ~ "to retch" **G** (pres. *i'âš*) **Gtn** (*ītanâš*) iter. jB

ašuātu → *ašutu*

ašubbatu, *ašbutu* "woman, wife" jB lex.

ašubu → *yašibum*

ašuḫḫennu (a prof. desig.) Nuzi; < Hurr.

ašūḫu(m) ~ "pine-tree" Bab., NA [GIŠ.Ù.SUḪ$_5$] as timber; *zēr a.* "pine kernel"

ašukku(m) (a dais)? jB lex.

ašušḫu, *ašḫaušsuḫḫu*, *ašḫušḫu* (a measuring vessel)? Nuzi; < Hurr.

ašuštu(m) "affliction, grief" O/jB [(NÍG.)ZI.IR; ext. SA$_5$-]; < *ašāšu* III

ašutu; pl. *ašuātu* (a leather strap) jB for a door; → *ašâtu*

atā "why?" also as interj. NA, NB(Ass.)

atā'išu, *at'išu* ~ (a plant) M/jB lex., med. [Ú.KUR.KUR]

atāku "to be(come) bent, crooked" M/jB **G** (*a/a*) of parts of body **D** trans. "bend, twist" s.th.; > *itku*; *uttuku* I

atamu → *watmum*

atannu (a piece of jewellery made in pairs) Nuzi; < Hurr.

atānu(m) f. "she-ass" OAkk, Bab., M/NA [M/NB ÈME, EME$_6$; (ANŠE.)EME$_5$; Mari also EME$_5$.ANŠE]; MB, Nuzi also "mare"; jB lex. *a. nāri* (a water fowl); → *biṣṣūru*

atappiš "like a canal" jB; < *atappu*

atappu(m), NA *adappu* f.; pl. f. & m. "(small) canal, ditch" Bab., NA [PA$_5$; OB math. PA$_5$.SIG]; > *atappiš*

atappû (a plant) jB lex.

ataršani → *ašaršani*

atartu, *atirtu*, NA also *ada/irtu* (a type of grass) jB, NA

atartu → also *ašartu*; *watartum*

ataru mng. unkn. jB lex.

ataru → also *watrum*

atāru → *adāru* III; *watārum*

at(')a(t)tu → *ad'attu*

atātum f. pl. "layers (of reed)" Mari

atbaru(m) (or *adbaru*) ~ "basalt" Bab., M/NA [(NA$_4$.)AD.BAR] for statuary, grindstones; < Sum.

atgigu → *ašgigû*

atḫû pl.; OB du. *atḫê* ? "companions, partners" O/jB; OA as pl. of *aḫu* I "brothers"; < *aḫû* II; > *atḫûtu*

atḫusu, *itḫusu* ~ "carrying-pole" (for fruit)? NA

atḫûtu(m) "partnership" OB, Am.; *a. šakānum* "to establish partnership, brotherly relations" with s.o.; *a. râmu* "to wish partnership" with s.o.; *ana a. leqûm* "to accept in partnership (through marriage)"; < *atḫû* abstr.

atirtu → *atartu*

at'išu → *atā'išu*

atkallušše (a functionary) NB

atkam → *aktam*

atkuppu(m), *aškuppu* "craftsman making objects of reeds" Bab. [(LÚ.)AD.KID]; < Sum.; > *atkuppūtu*

atkuppūtu(m) "craft of the reed worker" OB [(LÚ.)AD.KID-]; NB as prebend; < *atkuppu*

atmanu → *watmanum*

atmartu (title of a goddess) jB; < *amāru* I ?

atmāṣu ~ "stubborn" jB lex.; < *amāṣu* ?

atmu mng. unkn. jB lex.

atmu → also *watmum*

atmû; pl. NB *atmânu* ? (a wooden object) Nuzi

atmû → also *atwûm*

atnannu → *uatnannu*

atnannuḫlu → *uatnannuḫlu*

atnu (or *adnu*) "prayer" jB

atriš "very much, copiously" M/jB; < *watrum*

atru → *watrum*

atruk (or *atruq*) (a cut of meat) NB for offerings, wr. ^{uzu}*a.*

-atta → *-atti*

att... also = *ana t...*

attā, *attu* "you" (2 m. sg. pron.); → *attunu*; *attī*, *attina*; *attamannu*

attadû(m) "spillway"? OB, NB?

attalû → *antallû*

attamannu "each one; whoever you (m.) are" MA, M/NB, Nuzi; < *attā* + *mannu* I

attamukarumma in *a. dabābu* "to conspire"? Nuzi; < Hurr.

Attana, *Attannašwe*, *Attannati* (7th month) MB(Alal.), Nuzi; < Hurr.

attanū(ni) → *attunu*

attartu, NA *uttartu* "(military) cart" M/jB, NA; < *watārum*; → *wattarum* 3

attaru → *wattarum*

attaššiḫu "paternal" Nuzi, of estate, property; < Hurr.

atta'u mng. unkn. jB, desig. of monsters in *Enūma eliš*

atteru "companion" Am.(Eg.); < Hurr.; > *atterūtu*

atterūtu "friendship" Am.(Mit.), Nuzi, Bogh.; < *atteru*

-atti, **-atta(m)** (adv. endings) (→ GAG §113l)

attī "you" (2 f. sg. pron.); → *attā*; *attimannu*

attimannu "whoever you (f.) are" jB; < *attī* + *mannu* I

attina "you" (2 f. pl. pron.) O/MA, O/jB; → *attā*

attinaša (desig. of terrain) Nuzi; < Hurr.

attu → *attā*

attū-, Nuzi after *-u* also *uttū-* "belonging to" with poss. pron. suff. M/NB, Am., Nuzi, Bogh., Ug.; *Elamtu attūka* "Elam is yours"; *ayyūtu attūa* "which ones are mine?"

attultu (a substance) Nuzi; < Hurr.?

attunu, NA also *attanū(ni)*, NB also *attun* "you" (2 m. pl. pron.); → *attā*

atû I jB lex. **1.** (a kind of dark wool) **2.** (Sutian word for ~ throwing stick)

atû(m) II, *atu'u*, OB, Alal., Nuzi, Ug. *utû(m)* "gatekeeper, porter" Bab., M/NA [LÚ.NI.DU$_8$, NB wr. .GAB] NB as family name; < Sum.; > *atūtu* II, *atûtu*; → *sukkal-atû*

atû → also *edû* I; *watûm*

atūdu, *dūdu*, OA *etūdum* "wild sheep; ram" OA, M/jB

atūgu → *adūgu*

atuḫlu (a prof. desig.) Nuzi; < Hurr.

atulīmānu, *talīmānu*, *tulīmātu* pl. tant. "both hands" jB; → *šutlumu*; *talīmu*

atūnu → *utūnu*

aturu → *adurû*

atūtu I (a spiny plant) jB lex.; < Sum.?

atūtum II (or *utūtum*) "female doorkeeper" OB [MUNUS.NI.DU$_8$]; < *atû* II

atûtu, *utûtum*, MB(Ass.) *utu'ūtu* "function of gatekeeper" Bab. [LÚ.NI.DU$_8$-] of man, as prebend; of gods in temple; < *atû* II; → *sukkal-atûtu*

atu'u → *atû* II

atwûm, *atmû* "speech, word; manner of speech" O/jB [once KA.KA]; < *awûm* Gt infin.

aṭāru → *adāru* III

a'û "ferryman" O/jB [A.U$_5$]; < Sum.

a'û → also *ḫaḫû* II

a'uššu → *amuššu*

awarrānum → *awirānum*

awatamulušḫe (an object) Am.; < Hurr.

awātu(m), later Bab. (also occas. OB) *amātu*, M/NA, also Ug. *abutu*, gen. *abiti*; pl. *awâtum*, *amâtu*, *abāte* "word; matter" [INIM] **1.** "word" *a. qabû*, *a. dabābu*, poet. *a. zakāru* "to speak (a word), talk"; *a. ṣabātum* "to 'seize the word', begin to speak" Mari; *a. turrum* "to report" OA, OB; OA *a. qabûm* "to state (o.'s last) will"; MA *a. šakānu* "to declare, make a statement"; of deity, king "order, command"; "wording" of tablet; *a. libbim* "thought" **2.** "legal case, lawsuit"; MA *a. amāru* "to settle a case"; *a. gamrat* "the case is completed"; *bēl awātim/amāti* → *bēlu* 5 **3.** "matter, affair", often pl.; *a. amāru* "to investigate a matter"; *a. napištim* "matter of life"; *ul/lā awassu* etc. "it is not his business, he has not the right to" etc.; < *awûm*; → *lâmātu*

awiḫaru, *ami/eḫaru* "plough" Nuzi [GIŠ.APIN]; as area measure (= 1/10 homer); < Hurr.; → *epinnu*

awīlānu (a bird) jB; < *awīlu*

Awīlatum (hypocorist. form of PN *Awīl-DN*) OB; < *awīlu*

awīliš, jB *amīl/ēliš* "like a human being" O/jB; < *awīlu*

awīltum, later *amīl/ēltu* "woman" OA, O/MB, Am., Nuzi, Bogh. [MUNUS]; jB lex. only; NB "dependent woman, slave?"; < *awīlu*

awīlu(m), later *amīl/ēlu*, OAkk *abīlum*, MA *a'īlu* "man" [LÚ; jB om., med. also NA; Bogh. om. ZA] "human being" (also coll.); MA "husband"; "person, one"; jB, Nuzi *a. ana a.* "one another"; O/jB *a. ... a.* "one ... the other"; OA, OB "free citizen", also *mār/mārū a.*; "citizen" of PlN; as term of respect, OA, NA *lā a.* "no gentleman"; OB *a. Ešnunna* "man (i.e. ruler) of Ešnunna"; Nuzi, NB also "slave"; *a. nāri* (an aquatic animal) jB [LÚ.ÍD]; > *awīliš*, *awīlūtum*, *awīltum*; *amīlānu*, *Awīlatum*; → *šaḫamēlu*

awīlūtum, later *amīl/ēlūtu*, OA *awīluttum*, MA *a'īluttu* "humanity" [(NAM.)LÚ.U$_{18/19}$.LU; LÚ-] **1.** "mankind"; O/MB "anyone" **2.** M/NB freq. as coll. pl. of *awīlu* "servants, slaves, personnel" [Nuzi NAM.LÚ.LÚ.MEŠ]; NB also "(single) slave" **3.** MB "status of a retainer"

4. OA, OB "humanity; gentlemanly behaviour"; < *awīlu* abstr.

awirānum, *ame/irānu*, OB also *awarrānum* "standing water" [jB A.NIGIN] after flood; → *lā'iriānu*

awīru "field" Nuzi; < Hurr.

awītum "value (of goods)" OA, expressed in tin, silver

awûm "to speak" **G** (pret. *īwu*; stat. and 2 pers. sg. imper. *awu*) OA only **Gtn** iter. OA **Gt** (*atwûm*, later *atmû*) "speak" OA; O/jB(lit.) "discuss"; *ište/itti X a.* "negotiate with X"; *ana X a.* "tell X, speak to X"; OA "order (to do s.th.)"; jB *itti libbīya* (etc.) *a.* "think about" s.th. **Št 1.** O/jB, MA "reflect on s.th., debate with o.s.", also *itti/ina libbi š.* **2.** stat., in j/NB comm., of words "are used, considered"; > *āmānû*; *atwûm*; *awātu*; *mūtawûm*; *muštāmû*; *tāwītum*

awurriqānum, jB *amurriqānu* **1.** "jaundice" O/jB [jB IGI.SIG$_7$.SIG$_7$]; ^{d}*A.* deified; *šam(mi) a.* "plant for curing jaundice" **2.** (a bird) OB lex.; < *warāqum*

ayarum → *ḫârum*

ayya → *ai* II

ayyābakala, *(ay)yāb akalī* (a plant) jB lex.; < *ayyābu*

ayyabassa (a plant) jB lex.; < *ayyabtu* + *ša* ?

ayyabāš "let me not be put to shame" jB (desig. of shoe-button)?; < *bâšu* I

a(y)yabba "the sea" Mari, Am., jB; < Sum.?; > *ayyabbītu*

a(y)yabbītu, *yabbītu* f. "of the sea" (epith. of Ištar) MA; < *ayyabba*

ayyābiš, *yābiš* "in a hostile manner" O/jB, NA; < *ayyābu*

ayyabtu "(female) enemy" jB, NA; in pl. "evil" gener.; < *ayyābu*; → *ayyabassa*

ayyābu(m), M/jB also *yābu*; pl. *ayyābū*, occas. *ayyābūtu* "enemy" Bab., NA [(LÚ.)ÉRIM] "hostile" spells; usu. as subst.; > *ayyābiš*, *ayyabtu*, *ayyābūtu*; *ayyābakala*

ayyābūtu(m) "hostility" O/jB; < *ayyābu* abstr.

ayyaka(m), *yaka* Ass. **1.** "where?" as interrog. pron.; NA *issu ayyak(a)* "whence?" **2.** OA "somewhere" **3.** in rel. clause "where" **4.** NA "how?"; < *ayyu* + *-kâm* (→ GAG §113b); > *ayyakamēni*

ayyakamma "somewhere" OA; < *ayyakam* + *-ma*

ayya(k)ku(m), *eyakku*, *yāku* (a type of sanctuary) O/jB, M/NA [É.AN.NA] esp. of goddesses; < Sum.?

ayyalatum f. "hind" OB as PN; < *ayyalu* I

ayyalu(m) I, Ass. *ya('a)lu* "stag, deer" Bab., M/NA [DÀRA.MAŠ] jB *qaran a.* "hartshorn" as drug, also name of plant; > *ayyalatum*

ayyalu II ~ "ally" j/NB; > *yalūtum*

ayyāmi "where?" Am.

ayyāna → *ayyānu*

ayyāniš "whither, where?" Bogh. lex.; < *ayyānu* + *-iš*

ayyānu(m), *yānu(m)*, jB also *ayyinna*, *ayyāna*, lex. also *ya'nu* "where?" O/jB; "whence?" OA; for later usage in negation → *yānu*; < *ayyu* + *-ānum*; > *ayyāniš*, *ayyānumma*; *yānummiš*

ayyānumma "anywhere" M/jB; < *ayyānum* + *-ma*

ayyaraḫḫu (a plant) jB lex.

ayyaraḫi "gold" jB lex.; < Hurr.

ayyartu(m), *yartu*, NB *(ay)yaštu*$^?$; NA pl. IA-*e-re-te* "white coral"? Bab, NA [(NA$_4$.)PA]; < *ayyaru* I

ayyaru(m) I, *iyarum*, Ass. *ya('u)ru* "flower; rosette" Bab., M/NA **1.** j/NB$^?$ "(natural) flower" **2.** "rosette" of stone, gold; *a. pāni* (ornament on divine image) **3.** jB *(ay)yar(i) ili* 'flower of god' = "chamaeleon"? **4.** in names of plants: *a. ḫurāṣi/kaspi* "golden/silver flower" etc.; > *ayyartu*, *ayyarû*, *yarītu*

ayyaru II ~ "young man" OAkk, MB in PNs; jB lex.; → *āru* II

ayyaru III mng. uncl. jB; in comparisons

ayyarum → also *ḫârum*

ayyarû "rosette-like" NB; < *ayyaru* I + *-ī*; > *yarītu*

Ayyāru(m) (2nd Bab. month) Bab. [ITI.GU$_4$(.SI.SÁ)]; > *ayyārû*

ayyārû "born in the month *Ayyāru*" MB in fPN *Ayyārītu*; < *Ayyāru*

ayyarūrūtu → *yarūrūtu*

ayyāṣu, *yāṣu* (a small mammal, phps.) "weasel" Bab.; also "(skin of) weasel?" used as container for oil; OB also PN

ayyâši → *yâšim*

ayyaštu → *ayyartu*

ayyātu → *ayyu*

Ayya'ūtu "function of the goddess Ayya" jB; < Ayya (wife of Šamaš) abstr.

ayyekamēni "anywhere" NA; < *ayyaka* + *-me* + *-ni* ?

ayyēma → *ayyišamma*

ayyeša → *ayyiša*

ayyi → *ai* II

ayyigalluḫu, *ḫaigallatḫe* (a horned animal) Am.(Mit.), Nuzi; < Hurr.

ayyikâ "where, where to?" M/jB, Nuzi; < *ayyikīam*; > *ayyikâni*; *ēkâ*

ayyikâni "where to?" jB; < *ayyikâ* + *-ni*

ayyikīam "where?" OB; < *ayyu* + *-kīam* (→ GAG §113b); > *ayyikâ*; *ēkīam*; → *ai* III

ayyinna → *ayyānu*

ayyiš, lex. also *yiš* "where?; whither?" O/jB; < *ayyu* + *iš*; > *êš*; *īš*; → *mêš*

ayyiša(m), *ayyeša* "whither?" Ass., O/jB; NA also *ana a.*; < *ayyu* + *-išam*; > *ayyišamma*; *êšam*; → *miššam*

ayyišamma, OA also *ayyēma*, Ug. *ayyišammê* "to anywhere" OA, OB, Ug.; < *ayyišam* + *-ma*/*-mê* II; > *êšamma*

ayyītu (a leather strap) for a door M/jB

ayyītu → also *ayyu*

ayyītumma → *ayyumma*

ayyu(m), *ayyû(m)*, jB, NA also *ya'u*; f. *ayyītu(m)*; m. pl. *ayyūtu(m)*; f. *ayyātu(m)* "which?" usu. before subst. *adi ayyi ūmi* "till which day?"; after subst. *mê ayyūti* "which water?"; pred. NA *ya'u ḫīṭāya* "what is my crime?"; in subst. use "which (person); what (thing)", interrog. or indefinite; NB rel. pron. "which, that", NA in indir. question (→ GAG §180c); Bab. occas. for *ayyumma*; > *ayyumma*, *ayyummê*; *ayyaka*, *ayyikīam* etc.; *ayyiš* etc.; *ayyānu*, *yānu* etc.

ayyu → also *ai* II

ayyû (a bird) jB lex.

ayyumma, MB, NA also *ya'umma*; f. *ayyītumma*; pl. *ayyūtumma* "any; anyone"; as adj. *šarrum a.* "any king"; as subst. "anyone"; MB *a. ša* "anyone who"; < *ayyu* + *-ma*

ayyummê; pl. *ayyūttimmê* "anyone" Am., Nuzi, Bogh. for *ayyumma*; < *ayyu* + *-mê* II

azabburu (or *azappuru*) (a plant) Nuzi, jB; → *azupīru* ?

aza'illu → *azamillu*

azal mng. unkn. jB lex.

azallû (a medicinal plant) O/jB [Ú.A.ZAL.LÁ/LA]; < Sum.

azālum (or *azānum*) (a tree) OAkk

azalwannu (a precious stone) Qatna; for necklace, seal; < Hurr.

azamillu(m), MA *aza'illu*; pl. f. "sack, net" O/MA, O/jB, Bogh.; for (transport of) straw, OA also du.; MB for flour

azammu (part of a chariot) MB of gold; → *assammu*

azamrītu, *azamrutu*; pl. *azamrâtu* ~ "lance" M/jB held by figurine; → *azmarû* ?

azamru(m), NA *zamru* "fruit" OB(N.Mes.), M/NA

azamrutu → *azamrītu*

azamû → *zamû*

azangunû (a bird) jB lex.; < Sum.?

azannu, *azānu*, *zānu*; pl. f. "quiver" MB, NA(jB) [MB KUŠ.A.ZA.AN]

azannu → also *ḫazannum* I

azānu → *azālum*; *azannu*

azappu → *aṣappu*; *zappu*

azappuru → *azabburu*

azarkiru mng. unkn. OB lex.

azarru → *aṣarru*

azaru(m), *azzaru* ~ "lynx" O/jB [SA.A.RI.RI] living in marshes

azāru ~ "to help" jB; < W.Sem.

azazḫum (a kind of offering) OB(Alal.); < Hurr.?

azāzu, *ḫazāzu* "to buzz" jB **G** (pres. *i'azzaz*) of ears

azibatu ~ "help" jB lex.; < *ezēbu*

azīru "sputum"? jB

azīrum → also *asīrum* II

azmarû, *ismarû*, *armarrû*, *azzamû* "lance" M/NB; → *azamrītu* ?

azû(m) I, *ḫazû*, *asû* "to sigh, gasp" O/jB **G** om., of ghost, dog, lizard; > *ḫāzû*

azû II (a craftsman)? Nuzi

azugallatu, *azungallatu* "chief physician (f.)" M/jB, NA [A.ZU.GAL] as epith. of Gula; < Sum. > *azugallūtu*

azugallu(m) "chief physician" O/jB [A.ZU.GAL]; < Sum.; > *azugallūtu*; → *asû* I

azugallūtu "higher medical art" jB; < *azugall(at)u*

azukarānu → *azupīru*

azukaraštum (desig. of horses) Nuzi; < Hurr.?

azukirānu → *azupīru*

azūmu (a plant) jB lex.

azungallatu → *azugallatu*

azupīrānītu f. "resembling saffron" jB lex.; desig. of spices

azupīru(m), *azupīrānu*, *azuki*/*arānu* "saffron" Bab. [Ú.ḪAR.SAG(.SAR)] freq. *a. arqu* "yellow"; → *azabburu* ?

azūru (or *aṣūru*) in *a. pindi* mng. unkn. jB lex.

Azzalli → *Izalli*

azzamû → *azmarû*

azzaru → *azaru*

azzatu f.; Hurr. pl. also *azzatena* "she-goat" Nuzi; → *ḫazzatum*

azzubūtum "status of divorced woman"? OB(Susa); < *ezēbu*

azzūzâ → *zūzâ*

B

bā "water" jB lex.

bā → also *bā'um*

ba'ālu(m), *bâlu* "to be dominant, exceptionally big, bright" Bab., NA **G** (*i/i*) [GUR4] of decree "be valid, in force"; of part of body "be exceptionally big"; of stars "be abnormally bright" **D** O/jB "make important, exaggerate" **Dtn** OB iter. of D; > *ba'lu*, *ba'ūlu*

ba'ālu → also *bâlu*

ba'āru → *bâru* I

ba'āšu, NB *be'ēšu* "to smell bad, be of bad quality" Ass., j/NB **G** (*i/i*) of dates "be rotten"; transf. of words, day "be bad"; NB *pān(ī) b.* "be angry", of animals "look bad" **Gtn** iter. **D** "make stink"; j/NB transf. "besmirch" name etc.; > *bīšu* I, *bi'iltu*; *bu'šu*, *būšānu*; *tabāštānu*

ba'āšu → also *be'ēšu*

babaltu (a plant) jB lex.

babalu ~ "leader" jB lex.

babālu(m) "to carry, bring" var. of *wabālu(m)*, supplies **G** forms for infin., ptcp., stat., NB pres. **D** all forms (except Am.) **N** all forms; > *babbilu*, *babbilūtum*; *biblu*, *bibiltu*; *bibbulu*; *mubabbilum*, *mubabbilūtum*

bābānu, NB *bābanna* "at the gate, outside" M/NB of building, courtyard; < *bābu* I + *-ānu*; > *bābānû*

bābānû "outer" j/NB, NA of building, courtyard; < *bābānu* + *-ī*

babaru ~ "forest" jB lex.

babbanû; f. *babbanītu* "excellent, very good" NB; < **ban-banû* (→ *banû* I); > *babbanûtu*

babbanûtu ? "excellence, high quality" jB; < *babbanû*

babbilu(m) "bearer, carrier; tenant farmer" O/jB; < *babālu*

babbilūtum "service as bearer" OB; < *babbilu*

babbirru → *banbirru*

babrunnu "brown" Nuzi of horses; < Indo-Iran.

bābtu(m) I "city quarter, district" OAkk?, Bab., MA [DAG.GI/GI4.A; MA, NB KÁ-] as municipal authority; *mār b.* "member of a city quarter"; < *bābu* I; → *b.* II

bābtu(m) II "commercial goods, merchandise outstanding" OA, OB [KÁ-]; OB, NB ~ "loss, deficit", also astr.; < *bābu* I; = *b.* I ?

bābu(m) I; pl. m. & f. "gate, door" [KÁ] **1.** of house, temple, palace, oven etc.; "city gate" as administrative authority; "sluice gate"; *bāb zīqi* "air vent" **2.** transf. "entrance" to marsh, to *apsû*; "opening, outlet" of objects; of parts of body; ext. *bāb ēkalli(m)* (a part of the liver) [ME.NI] **3.** NB "item" of accounts (< Aram.?) **4.** "point of departure", esp. in *pāna(m) u bāba(m) ul īšu* 'have no beginning or end' = "be beyond recording, control"; > *bābānu*, *bābānû*; *bābtu* I.II

bābu II "small child, baby" jB lex.

badāḫu "to kiss" jB lex.

badāmu mng. unkn. jB lex.

badāqu → *batāqu*

badāšu mng. unkn. jB lex.

baddum (or *baṭṭum*) mng. uncl. Mari, desig. of person

badillum (a bird) O/jB

bādu "evening" NA in *ki/ša/ina/ana b.* "at evening"; < *biātum* Ass.

badu'ītu (a garment) NB

badūlu → *batūlu*

bā'ertu "huntress" jB; < *bā'eru*

bā'eru(m), *bā'iru(m)* **1.** "hunter; fisherman" Bab. [(LÚ.)ŠU.ḪA/ḪA$_6$] **2.** OB, Mari (a type of military auxiliary); < *bâru* I; > *bā'ertu*, *bā'erūtu*

ba''erūtu "substantiation (of evidence)"? MA; < *bâru* III

bā'erūtu(m) "activity of fisherman" OB; NB as temple prebend; < *bā'eru*

bagani "under the protection of" NB; < Aram.; → *gannu* II ?

bagarrānu (desig. of a horse) MB

bagurru (a ladle) Qatna, jB

baḫāšu → *be'ēšu*; *buḫḫušu*

Baḫir (a month) OAkk; < *baḫru* st. abs.?

baḫmādu → *barumtu*

baḫrê ? (a stone, phps.) "coral" jB, NA; < Arab.?

baḫru "boiling hot" jB; (a specific hot dish); < *buḫḫuru*; > *baḫrūtu*, *Baḫir*?

baḫrūtu "boiling state" jB med. in *baḫrūssu* "in its boiling condition, when boiling"; < *baḫru*

baḫšum mng. unkn. OAkk as PN

baḫû I "thin" O/jB of onions; MB, NA of people as PN; < *baḫû* II

baḫû II "to be thin; be scarce" jB **G** (pres. *ibaḫḫu/i*) **D** "make emaciated"; > *baḫû* I

baḫūlātu "men, troops" jB(Ass.), artificially differentiated from → *ba'ūlātu*

baḫûtu → *baḫû* I

bā'ilu; f. *bā'iltu* "ruler" M/jB; m. of DN in PNs; f. of goddess; < *bêlu*

bā'iru → *bā'eru*

ba''ītu "thing sought" M/jB(Ass.) in *b. ili/ī* "desire(d) of the god(s)"; < *bu''û* II Ass.

bakā'iš "to weeping" OB; < *bakû*

bākisu "wailing woman" NA; < *bakû* ptcp.?

bakkarū → *bakru* II

bakkā'um "wailer, mourner" OB lex.; < *bakû*

bakkītu "wailing woman, mourner" j/NB, NA; < *bakkû*

bakkû "tearful" jB; < *bakû*; > *bakkītu*

bakkutu → *baktu*

bakru I "(first-)born" MB, in PNs

bakru II, *pakru*; pl. *bakkarū* "foal" of camel or donkey jB; < Arab.

baktu, *bakkutu* (an official) NB

bakû(m) "to weep" **G** (*i/i*) [ÉR] of human; of animal "cry"; also + dat. "weep over; weep for" **Gtn** iter. of G [ÉR.MEŠ] **Š** caus. of G; > *bakā'iš*; *bākisu*; *bakkû*, *bakkītu*; *bakkā'um*; *bikītu*

bakuḫû ~ "bud, shoot" jB lex.

bal(a) → *balu*

balaggu → *balangu*

balālu(m) "to mix (up); alloy" Bab., NA; OAkk? **G** (*a/u*) [ḪE.ḪE] **1.** "mix (up)" food, drink, drug with (= *ina*); "alloy" metal; stat., of colour "is variegated" **2.** OB *qablam b.* "join battle" **3.** "muddle up, upset" heart, text; ext., of good and bad results "be mixed up, confused" **Gt** stat. OB of people "mix with each other" **D 1.** "coat, smear" with (= *ina*) soil, spittle etc.; transf. *ina dumqi* "with prosperity" **2.** "mix (up)" **3.** OB stat. "is numb, deep in sleep" **Dt 1.** pass. of D; jB "be covered" with s.th. **2.** OB "smear" o.s. **Št** OB lex. **N** jB of people "mix"; > *ballu*, *baliltu*?; *ballussu*; *billu* I, *billatu*; *nablālu*, *nablaltum*; *tabliltum*

balamgu → *balangu*

balāmu "to gag" jB **G** (*i/i*); < Aram.

balangu, *balamgu*, *b/palaggu*, *buluggu*, NA *palaqqu*, *palakku*?, *pilaggu*? (a large drum) jB, NA; OAkk in PN ? [BALAG]; < Sum.

balar "on the other bank" NB; < Sum.

balāṣu I "to stare" jB **G** also in worship **D** "fix" the eyes "in a stare"; > *balṣu*

balāṣu II "to thrust, jerk"? with the rump **G** (*i/i*) of animals **D** ~ G; > *ballūṣītu*, *tuballaṣ-qinnassa*

balāt(a) "without" NA; < *balātu*

bala(t)tu (an ornament) Qatna

balātu(m) "without" OA; also *balātu-* with pron. suff. OA, NA; > *balāta*; → *balu*

ba'latu "mistress" jB; < W.Sem.

balāṭu(m) I "life" [TI(.LA); Am. TIL(.LA); NB also TIN] esp. *ana balāṭ X* "for X's life"; "vigour, good health"; OA *balāṭukka* "during your life-time"; O/MB *lā balāṭu* "loss of life"; O/jB(lit.) "(eternal) life"; *šipat/šammi b.* "life(-giving) spell/plant"; OB, Am. "provisions"; NA "food" for the gods; OA "(meagre) livelihood, small profit"; st. abs. Bogh., j/NB *ana balāṭ* 'within a life-time' = "next year"; < *balāṭu* II infin.

balāṭu(m) II "to live" [TI; TI.LA; TIN] **G** (*u/u*, Ass. *a/a*) stat. "is alive", "is healthy", OB "is solvent"; "live, stay alive, (be allowed to) live"; M/jB, Bogh. "be healed"; j/NB *balāṭ napšāti* "preservation of life"; OA of debt etc. "be revived, recognized" **D** of gods, people "bring back to life, revive"; MA "allow to stay alive", OB "let live; support, provide for"; O/jB "restore to health; cure"; OA, OB "recognize, credit" silver, goods to s.o.; OB "enact, validate" a document **Dt** Mari, jB "receive support, be maintained" **Š** Am. "give life to";

> *balṭu*, *balittum*?, *balṭūtu*, *balṭānumma*; *balāṭu* I; *bulṭu*; *muballiṭṭu*; *muballiṭānu*; *tablittum*; *nablaṭu*

baldaḫû (or *balṭaḫû*) mng. unkn. jB

bali → *balu*

baliltu, *balītu* "rubbish tip" or "waste land"?; *ṣēr b.* (a type of snake) jB; < *ballu* f. or *belû* II ?

baliltu → also *šambaliltu*

balittum "(a kind of) reservoir", "fishpond"? Mari; < *balṭu* f.?

balītu → *baliltu*

baliu ~ "lord" jB lex.

ballu "mixed" j/NB, MA of perfumes; of omens "confused"; "mixture" of animal fodder; < *balālu*; > *baliltu*?

ballu → also *bālu*

ballukku(m), Mari *pa(l)luk/gu* (a tree) OAkk, Bab. [GIŠ.BAL]; (an aromatic substance produced by the *b.* tree) [ŠIM.MUG; ŠIM.BAL; ŠIM.BULUG]; < Sum.

ballussu "mixture" of aromatics ? NA; < *balālu*

ballūṣītu, *pallūṣītu* **1.** (a bird) jB (→ *tuballaṣ-qinnassa*) **2.** (a lizard) jB lex.; < *balāṣu* II

balsû → *palsû*

balṣu, *palṣu* in *b/palṣa īni(m)* "staring" O/jB; < *balāṣu* I

baltu(m), *baštu*? (a spiny plant) Bab., NA [GIŠ.DÌḪ]

bāltu → *bāštu*

balṭaḫû → *baldaḫû*

balṭānumma "alive" Am. [TIL.LA-]; < *balāṭu* II

balṭi(t)tu → *bušṭītum*

balṭu(m) "living, alive" [(LÚ.)TI(.LA)] **1.** Bab., NA of people, animals; "healthy", "(financially) solvent" **2.** j/NB, NA "raw, uncooked" of meat, seeds **3.** NA "green" of wood **4.** MA, NB "intact" of vessels **5.** OA *warḫam balṭamma* "for a whole month"; < *balāṭu* II; > *balṭūtu*

balṭūtu(m) "state of being alive" Bab. [TI; NB also TIN] of people, esp. *balṭūssu(nu)* "alive", of plants "fresh", Bogh. of stones; < *balṭu*

balu(m), *bal(a)*, Am. *bali*; with pron. suff. *balū/ī-* "without" [NU.ME(.A)]; also *ina b.*; esp. "without (permission/knowledge of)" s.o.; O/jB also conj. + subjunct. "without ...ing, without having ...ed"; > *bālu*; *balūt*; → *balātu*; *bilânum*

balû → *belû* II

bālu, *ballu* 'the one without'? (desig. of the planet Mars) jB; < *balu*

bâlu, *ba'ālu* "to supplicate" **G** j/NB

bâlu → also *ba'ālu*

ba'lu; f. *ba'iltu* ~ "large, major" jB; < *ba'ālu*

baluḫḫu(m), *buluḫḫum* (an aromatic plant) OAkk, O/jB [ŠIM.BULUḪ]; *ḫīl b.* "*b.* resin"; < Sum.

balūt "without" MA; < *balu*

bāmâ "half and half, in half" OB; < *bāmtu* I

bāmāniš "in halves" jB; < *bāmtu* I + *-ān* + *-iš*

bamātu(m) pl. tant. "open country, plain" Bab.

bāmtu(m) I, lex. also *bāntu*, *pāndu*; pl. *bāmātu* "half" Bab., Susa, OB(Alal.); st. abs. *bāmat ... bāmat ...* "half ... half ..."; > *bāmâ*, *bāmāniš*

bāmtu(m) II, *b/pānd/tu*; lex. also pl. "ribcage, chest; thorax" O/jB; > *Pandānu*

banaikānu (desig. of a group or organization) NB

banbillu (or *panbillu*) (a dwarf cucumber) jB lex.

banbirru, *babbirru* ~ "leather coat" jB lex.

bandillānu "paunchy, fat" jB om.; < *bandillu* + *-ān*

bandillu ~ "belly" jB, NA of animal; > *bandillānu*

bandû(m) "quotient" OB math., jB; *ṭupšar b.* "mathematician"?; < Sum.

bāndu → *bāmtu* II

banduddû(m) "bucket" O/jB [(GIŠ/GI.)BA.AN.DU$_8$.DU$_8$] esp. rit.; < Sum.

banītu → *banû* I

bānītu → *bāntu*; *bānû*

bannu(m), *bānu* (a ewer) OB; < Sum.

bāntiš "like a mother" jB; < *bāntu*

bāntu "mother" jB; < *banû* IV; > *bāntiš*

bāntu → also *bāmtu* I.II

banû(m) I "good, beautiful" of person, animal [in PNs DÙ]; of object, word, deed, omen etc.; as subst. *banītu* "s.th. good"; < *banû* II; > *banûtu*; *babbanû*, *babbanûtu*

banû(m) II "to be(come) good, beautiful" Bab. **G** (*i/i*) [NB in PN DÙ] of person, object, word, deed etc. **D** "make good, beautify" person, animal, object, building etc.; "look after s.o. kindly, respectfully"; NB "produce s.th. well", NB (+ *tabnītu*) "execute well, do a good job"; > *banû* I; *babbanû*, *babbanûtu*; *būnu* II, *bunna*, *bunnû*; *bunnannû*; *mubannû*, *mubannûtu*, *mubannītum*; *tabnītu* I; → *būnzerru*; *buppānī-*

banû III "built"? jB lex.; < *banû* IV

banû(m) IV "to create; build" **G** (*i/i*) [DÙ] of deity "create" person, grain etc.; of person "engender" child, "make" figurine etc.; "build" house, boat; math. "construct"; ext. of feature "form" a shape **D** Am. "erect" city **Š** lit., caus. of G **N** pass.; > *banû* III; *bānû*, *bāntu*, *bāntiš*;

binītu, binûtu; biniannum; nabnītu; tabnītu II; → *Zēr-bānītu*

bānu (a type of crown) jB lex.

bānu → also *bannu*

bānû; f. *bānītu* "creator, begetter"; M/NB "builder" [(LÚ.)DÙ]; < *banû* IV

banûtu "distinction, beauty" M/jB; < *banû* I

bappiru(m), *pappirum* "beer bread" [BAPPIR; ŠIM]; < Sum.

baqālu "to malt; sprout (intrans.)" jB lex.; < *buqlu* denom.?; > *bāqilu; baqlu; biqlum, biqlētu*

baqāmu(m), O/MA, M/NB *baqānu(m)* "to pluck" **G** (*a/u*) "pluck" (wool from) sheep, (feathers from) bird, (hair from) human; "tear out" plants, Am. "harvest"; "pluck" cotton, fringe on garment **D** "pluck out" hair **Dtn** iter. **Š** caus. of G **N** pass., of sheep, wool, grass "be plucked"; > *baqmu; bāqimu; buqqumu; buqūmu; buqāmu; biqnu*

baqartum → *waqrum*

baqāru(m), M/NB usu. *paqāru* "to (lay) claim to" Bab., OA **G** (*a/u*, occas. *u/u, i/i*) "claim s.th. (= acc.) from s.o. (= acc.)"; absol. "make a claim", "contest" **Gt** "claim from each other" **D** ~ G, "claim for o.s.", "contest" **Dt** "be claimed" **Š** caus. of G MB **N** pass. of house, field, slave "be claimed"; > *baqru; bāqirānum, pāqiru; buqurrû; tapqertu; mupaqqirānu; pirqu* I; → *buqquru*

baqāru → also *waqārum*

baqāšu ~ "to be broad, prominent" jB, stat. of parts of body; > *buqāšum; buqqušum*

baqbaqqu (a small gnat) jB; → *baqqu*

bāqilu(m) "maltster" OAkk, O/jB; [MUNU$_4$.SAR]; also as PN; < *baqālu*

baqīmu → *baqmu*

bāqimu "plucker" Mari, of sheep; < *baqāmu*

baqīnu → *baqmu*

baqīqātu pl. tant. (a type of groats)? jB

bāqirānum, M/NB *pāqirānu*, NB also *paqarānu*, Nuzi also *pāriqānu* "claimant" Bab.; < *baqāru* ptcp. + *-ān*

baqlu; f. *baqiltu* "sprouted" jB; < *baqālu*

baqmu(m), *baqnu*, OAkk, Nuzi also *baqīm/nu* "plucked" O/jB of sheep, wool; OAkk, Nuzi as PN "with thinning hair"; < *baqāmu*

baqqu(m), *bāqu* "(small) fly, mosquito?" Bab.; also as PN; → *baqbaqqu; buqāqum*

baqru(m), M/NB *paqru*, OB also *waqrum* "(entitlement to) claim" Bab. usu. pl.; of slave etc. *b/paqrī rašû(m)* "to be claimed"; *b. apālum* "to satisfy a claim"; *ana b. izuzzum* "to take liability for a claim"; < *baqāru*

baqrum → also *waqrum*

bāqu → *baqqu*

barāḫu ~ "to beam, shine"? jB lex. **G** and **D**; > *barḫu; barīḫu?; burāḫu*

barakku (a corridor or outbuilding) Bab. [É.BAR.RA]; < Sum.; → *parakku*

barāmu I "to be variegated, multicoloured" O/jB, NA **G** [GÙN.A] **Gt** stat. of eye, fleece "is multicoloured, speckled" **D** "make multicoloured; weave (coloured cloth)"; > *barmu; burmu; birmu* I; *burūmītu; burūmû; burrumu, burrumtu; burummu; bitrumu, bitrāmu; barumtu; birimmu; burmāmu; mubarrimu; tabrīmu*

barāmu(m) II "to seal (up)" Bab., NA **G** (*a/u*, NA *i/i*) tablet, door; "emboss" inscription on metal **Š** "have s.th. sealed"; > *birmu* II, *birimtu; nabramu?*

bārānû "rebel" jB(NA); < *bâru* II ptcp. + *-ān* + *-ī*

barāqu(m) "to lighten, shine" Bab.(lit.) **G** (*i/i*) [ḪI.ḪI] *berqu* + *b.* "lightning strikes"; of Adad "strike s.th. with lightning"; of eyes "flash" **D** jB stat. of woman "has flashing eyes?" **Š 1.** "cause lightning to strike" **2.** "strike" enemy etc. "by lightning" **Štn** NB iter. of Š 2 **Ntn** jB "flash, light up repeatedly", MB ptcp. ᵈ*Muttabriqu* as name of demon; > *bāriqum; berqu; burruqu; barraqtu*

barāqum → also *warāqum* D

barāri, *barār(a)* adv. "at dusk, evening" O/jB; < *barāru*; > *barārītu*

barārītu(m), *barartu(m)* "dusk, evening watch" O/jB [EN.NUN.(AN.)USAN/USÁN; EN.NUN.AN.TA; EN.NUN.BAR.RA]; also acc. as adv. *barartam*; < *barāri*

barāru "to flicker" or "be dim"? jB **G** (*u/u*) of eyes "flicker, be scintillating"; of star; of word, lex. only **Š** jB mng. unkn.; > *barāri, barārītu; barīru* I, *barīrītu, barīrātu; barrurum; birratu; birbirrū, birbirrānu; nabrarû?, nabrartu?*

barasiggû, *parasiggû, parsigu* "house altar, small shrine" jB [BÁRA.SI/SIG/SIG$_5$.GA]; < Sum.

barāṣu "to light up, shine" jB **G** (*u/u*); > *birṣu; barīṣu?; burṣa?*

barāšu "to pluck out" jB lex.; > *baršu; biršu; burrušum*

barātu → *birītu*

barbartu "she-wolf" jB; < *barbaru*

barbaru(m) "wolf" OAkk, Bab. [UR.BAR.RA], also as PN; (one of the Ellil stars) jB

[MUL.UR.BAR.RA]; jB *b. urši* 'bedroom wolf' = "scorpion"; > *barbartu*

bardibbu (a garment) jB lex.; < Sum.

bardû ~ "crossbar, lintel" Ug., jB lex., for door, window; < Sum.

bargallu (a desig. of sheep) jB lex.; < Sum.

barḫu "shining" NA, NB in PNs; f. *Bariḫtu* as fPN, MB; also Ug., m. & f. (a class of person)?; < *barāḫu*

barḫum → also *warḫum*

bari(-) "between, among" OA for Bab. *biri-*; < *barû* I; → *barītum*

barīḫu (a stone) jB; < *barāḫu* ?

barīkatu "(salt from) Barīku" jB, NA; < PlN

barīlu, *barīlānu* (a plant, phps.) "sagapenum" jB; var. of *barīrātu*

bāriqum "flashing, lightning" OB epith. of Amurru; < *barāqu*

barīrātu(m) (a plant, phps.) "sagapenum" Bab. [GIŠ/Ú.LUM.ḪA]; < *barāru*; → *barīlu*

barīrītu 'the glittering one'? M/jB, name of a female demon; < *barīru* I ?

barīru I ~ "radiance, glitter" jB; < *barāru*; > *barīrītu*?

barīru II mng. unkn. jB

barīṣu mng. unkn. j/NB astr.; < *barāṣu*

barittannu (or *parittannu*) ~ "grey"? Nuzi, colour of old horses

baritu (or *paritu*) (an object) Qatna, of gold

barītum "intervening space" OAkk (= later *birītu* I); *(in) barīti* "between"; < *barû* I; → *bari-*

bārītum "female diviner" OA, jB; < *bārû*

bariu → *berû* I; *birūyum*

barmu(m) "multicoloured, variegated" O/jB [GÙN.A] of eyes, animal's skin, wool; MB, Nuzi as PN, fPN (*Barundu*, *Barmatu*); < *barāmu* I; > *barumtu*

barraqītu, *pa(r)raqītu* (a plant) jB

barraqtu "emerald" NB; < *barāqu*

barrāqu (a court official) NA

barru I mng. uncl. M/NB, of metals, of the mouth

barrum II (or *parrum*) (a head covering) OAkk

barru → also *bāru* I

barrumu → *burrumu*

barruqu → *burruqu*

barrurum "with scintillating eyes"? OA f. as PN; < *barāru*

barsallu (or *baršallu*) (a kind of sheep) jB lex.; < Sum.

barsillu (a garment) jB lex.

barsillû (a vessel) jB lex.; < Sum.

barsûm (or *parsûm*) (wooden part of ship) OB; < Sum.

baršallu → *barsallu*

baršu(m) "patchy" OB of hair; < *barāšu*

baršu → also *burāšu*

bārtu(m) "revolt, rebellion" Bab., NA [ḪI.GAR]; < *bâru* II; > *bārānû*

baru → *bāru* III

barû(m) I "to see, look at" **G** (*i/i*) [IGI.KÁR; IGI; IGI.TAB; col. (BA.AN.)È; ext. MÁŠ] **1.** "see, behold" **2.** "read" a tablet, in col. "read, check through" **3.** of deity "oversee, watch searchingly" **4.** j/NB (+ *bīru*) "perform divination" **Gtn** jB "see repeatedly" **Gt** jB "look at thoroughly" **D** "announce s.th. to s.o., apprise s.o. of s.th." **Dt** OB of battle "be announced" **Š** "make s.o. (= acc.) see s.th.", transf. "cause to experience" misdeeds, anger etc.; "make s.o. see a dream, reveal in a dream to s.o."; jB (+ *bīru*) "make s.o. perform divination"; > *bārû*, *barû* II, *bārītum*, *bārûtu*; *bari-*, *barītum*; *bīru* I; *biri-*, *birâ*, *birūyum*, *birītu*, *birīt*, *birīt birīt*; *birûtu*; *bitrû* I?; *tabrītu*; *mubarrû*, *mubarrītum*; *nabrītum* III; → *b.* III

barû II "seen, checked" jB [È], of text; of poultice; < *barû* I

barûm III "to be on the market, be available"? OA **G** (*i/i*) **D** "put on the market"?; or all = *b.* I ?

barûm IV vb. mng. unkn. OAkk, OB

barû V (having an eye defect) jB lex.

barû → also *berû* II

bāru I, *barru* "tax, tribute" NB; < Iran.

bāru II (a syn. for open country) jB lex.

bāru III (or *baru*) (a cereal) jB lex.

bāru → also *pāru* II

bārû(m) "diviner" Bab., NA [(LÚ.)MÁŠ.ŠU.GÍD.GÍD; LÚ.ḪAL; (LÚ.)AZU; (LÚ.)NUMUN.LUM, occas. MB(Alal.), NB] usu. by extispicy; jB *mār b.* "(prof.) diviner"; OB *wakil b.*, j/NB *rab b.* "overseer of the diviners"; OB also of divination by oil, smoke; *nēpešti b.* "diviner's procedures"; < *barû* I; > *bārûtu*, *bārītum*

bâru(m) I, *ba'āru* "to catch, trap (with a net etc.)" Bab. **G** (*ā*) fish, birds etc.; wicked people, enemies **Gtn** jB iter. of G [DAB.DAB] **D** "hunt, go hunting"; > *bā'eru*, *bā'ertu*, *bayyāru*, *bayyartu*, *bā'erūtu*; *nabāru*, *nabārtu*; *bu''uru* I.II; → *libāru-šūši*; *pâru* I

bâru(m) II "to revolt, rise against" s.o. (= acc.) O/jB om. **G** (*ā*; Bogh. pres. also *iba''alir*) [ḪI.GAR] **Gt** OB "rise against each other" **N** OB "be set against each other"?; > *bārtu*, *bārānû*

bâru(m) III, OAkk, Ass. *buāru(m)* "to appear, turn up; be durable" **G** (*ū*) OAkk in PN e.g. *DN-šumu-li-bur* mng. uncl., "appear, be firm"? (or → *labāru* G); OA, OB of animal, goods ~ "turn up, become available"; M/NB(lit.) ~ "be durable, stay firm" **D** "affirm, convict" **1.** OB, M/NA leg. "declare, specify, establish precisely", also math. **2.** O/jB "convict s.o. (= acc.) of s.th. (= acc.)"; OB, MA "prove s.o. (to be s.th.)"; OB "confirm (s.th.) to s.o." **Dt** OB "be established precisely"; > *bēru* I; *būrtu* III; *ba''erūtu*; *bu'āru*

ba'rum → *bēru* II

barullu → *burullum*

barumtu, jB *barundu* "coloured wool" M/NB, also pl. *barmātu*, *baḫmādu* jB lex.; < *barmu*

bārûtu "work, lore of the diviner" M/NB [NAM.AZU; LÚ.ḪAL-]; *b. epēšu* "to perform divination"; *iškār b.* (desig. of the series of extispicy texts); < *bārû*

basālu mng. unkn. NA of stone; → *bašālu* ?

basi ~ "soon" NA as prep. "soon after"; as adv. "forthwith"; before vb., gen. of infin. "so that, in order to"

baskiltu(m), *maskiltu*, *biskiltu* (a part of the middle 'finger' of the lung) O/jB ext.

basûm "(square or cube) root" OB math. [BA.SI; BA.SI8; ÍB.SI8]; < Sum.

baṣāru(m) ~ "to tear off" O/jB **G** jB grapes **D** "tear apart"; > *biṣru* II; *bāṣiru*

baṣāṣu "to trickle" jB lex., NA **G**; > *biṣṣu*, *biṣû*, *buṣaṣû*; → *bāṣu*

baṣīḫu "inhabitant of the marshes" NB; < Aram.

baṣillatu (a musical instrument) jB lex.; mistake for → *ḫabaṣillatu* 2 ?

baṣiltu (a type of headcloth) jB lex.

bāṣiru mng. uncl. (a class of person) jB lex.; < *baṣāru*

bāṣiš "like sand" jB; < *bāṣu*

bāṣu(m), later *baṣṣu* "sand" Bab., OA; from river; *šipik b.* "sand dune", *qaqqar b.* "sand desert"; Mari "sandbank" in river; > *bāṣiš*; → *baṣāṣu*

bašālu(m), NA also *pašālu* "to be cooked; become ripe" Ass., M/NB **G** (*a/a*, *i/i*) of food, medicine, glass; of dates "ripen"; also trans. "cook" **Š** [ŠEG6(.GÁ); AL.ŠEG6.GÁ] "cook" food, drugs; NA "fire" bricks; jB "solder"? metal; "melt" silver, wax; "dye" textiles, wool; > *bašlu*; *bušlu*; *bušālu*; *šubšulum*; NA → *basālu* ?

bašāmu I, *bešāmu*, also *bašāmatu* "sackcloth; penitential robe" MB(Alal.), jB; jB lex. *ēpiš b.* "maker of penitential robe"

bašāmu II "to create, form" Bab. **G** (*i/i*) (dry) land, shrine, sculpture; human form; plans, cosmic designs **D** ~ G "create" objects, rites, parts of cosmos **N** pass. of G, NB; > *bišimtu*

bašāmu(m) III ~ "to allocate" OB, jB lex. **G** (*a/u*) share of booty, field

bašāšum "to spread" (intrans.) OB **G** om., of plague

bašgigītum → *aškikītu*

bāšītu(m) "what is present" Bab. **1.** Mari, of troops "available, to hand" **2.** "goods, property"; < *bāšû*

bāšiu → *bāšû*

bašlu "cooked; ripe" M/NB, NA [(AL.)ŠEG6.GÁ (→ *ṣarpu*)] "cooked, boiled" of meat, plants, liquids; "heat-treated" of stone, glazes, ivory, metal; Nuzi "dyed" of textiles; "ripe" of fruits; < *bašālu*

bašmu(m) "(mythical poisonous) snake; horned viper (*Cerastes cerastes*)" O/jB [MUŠ.ŠÀ. TUR/TÙR]; as symbol; OB (a constellation); jB lex. (name of a plant)

baššu mng. unkn. jB lex.

baštu → *baltu*

bāštu(m), later *bāltu* ~ "dignity, (source of) pride"? OAkk, Bab., OA, Am. [TÉŠ] of deity, person; esp. in PNs of protective force; of building, orchard as "pride" of city, land etc.; jB *ṣubāt b.* "formal dress"; < *bâšu* I

bašû(m), M/jB N occas. *napšû* "to be (at hand, available); exist" [GÁL] **G** (*i/i*; no perf.) "be in existence, available"; of eyes, ears "be fixed on, attentive"; of task, responsibility "lie with" s.o.; of power, characteristic "be owned" by s.o.; pret. *ibši* "was/were" (emphatic); M/NA pres. *ibašši*, also pl., as adv. ~ "really, in fact; some"; j/NB *mala bašû* "as much as there is available, everything, everybody"; *adi lā bašê* (infin.) 'until non-existence' of destruction, disease **Š** "bring into being" **1.** of gods "create"; "utter" words, incantation **2.** of human beings "produce" crop, "procreate" children; "weave" a plot **3.** OB "make (s.o.'s ears) fix on, call s.o.'s attention to" **4.** "let happen" **N** ingress. of G **1.** of living beings "come into being; emerge, appear" **2.** of crop "grow, be produced", "become ripe" **3.** of event, lawsuit "happen, take place" **4.** OA of goods, tablet "be available, in safekeeping", OB transf. of claim, profit "materialize, be realized" **5.** OB of eyes "get fixed on" **6.** jB med. of spots? "occur, develop" **Ntn** "happen repeatedly"; > *bāšītu*, *bāšû*; *bīšu* II, *bišītu*; *būšum*; *mušabšû*; *nabšium*; *tabšītu*?

bāšû(m), *bāšiu(m)*; f. *bāšītum* "existing, available" O/jB, MA of corn and field; of exchange-rate; MB(Ass.) *ana ūmī bāšûti* "for ('the existing' =) all days"; f. pl. *bāšâti* "what exists", i.e. status quo; < *bašû*; > *bāšītu*

bâšu(m) I "to be ashamed, come to shame" [TÉŠ] **G** (*ā*) before s.o. (= acc.) **D** "put to shame" **Š** OB mng. uncl., "cause shame"?; > *bayyāšu*; *bayyašû*; *ayyabāš*; *bāštu*; *būštu*

bâšu II "to stamp, tamp" jB **G** (*ī*)

batāqu(m), *badāqu* "to cut off, divide, tear off" **G** (*a/u*) **1.** "cut off" parts of body, object, garment, land; "separate" an area; "hew" statues, slabs etc. out of stone **2.** transf. OA "deduct" money, "drop the rate of exchange"?; stat. *batiq* of price "is (too) low"; *awatam b.* "deal with a matter" **3.** "cut through, pierce" dyke etc.; ellipt. of water(course) "break through (intrans.)"; "divert" water into a canal **4.** OB "interrupt" work; OA ellipt. "break off, depart" **5.** MA, NB "denounce", esp. *bitqē b.* "make accusations", also NA *bēl batāqi* "informer" **D** ~ G **1.** "cut off", esp. MA with pl. obj., parts of body, garments, trees; "cut" ropes **2.** "cut up" corpse **3.** "cut through, pierce" dyke, "divert" watercourse → *butuqtu* **Dt** pass. of D, of breach "be opened" **N** pass. of G **Ntn** iter. of N; > *batqu*, *batiqtu*; *bitqu*, *bitiqtu*; *butiqtu*, *butuqtu*; *biduqtum*; *butuqqû*; *bātiqu*, *bātiqānu*

bātar "thereafter, moreover" NB uncert.; < Aram.

batbatti → *battubattu*

bātiqānu "informer" MA; < *bātiqu* + *-ān*

batiqtu "denunciation" jB, NA; NA also "rumour"?; < *batāqu*

bātiqu(m) **1.** OA "express messenger" **2.** NA, NB "informer, denouncer"; < *batāqu*

batqu(m) "cut (off)" etc. **1.** jB of ligament "torn" **2.** OA of price "low, cheap" **3.** OB of work "interrupted" **4.** NA "damaged" **5.** j/NB as subst. "damage", esp. in *b. ṣabātu* "to repair damage"; NB "loss" of cattle **6.** NA, NB "(repair to) damage"; *rab b.* "supervisor of repairs"; < *batāqu*

battabatte → *battubattu*

battatayya in *ina b.* "each of several; individually" NA; < *battu*

battelibatteli → *battubattu*

battu(m) "side, region around" Ass.; OA *i/ana b.* "outside, to one side"; M/NA *ana b.* "aside, to one side, apart"; NA *ina b.* "somewhere; in one place"; MA *batta u batta* "on both sides"; NA "side (of river)"; > *battubattu*; *battatayya*

battubattu/e, *batte/ibatte/i*, *bat(ta)batte/i*, *pattepatte* "all round, on all sides of" M/NA, as prep. + subst./pron. suff.; *ina/issu/ša b.*; also du. *ina battubattēn* "on both sides of" MA; < *battu*

bātu "half" jB lex.; → *bā'um*

bâtu → *biātum*

batultu, NA *batussu* "adolescent, nubile girl" M/NA, Ug., j/NB [MUNUS.KAL.TUR; NB MUNUS.NAR-?]

batūlu, *badūlu* "boy, young man" M/jB, NA [(LÚ.)KAL.TUR]

baturru (a small chisel)? jB lex.; < Sum.

batussu → *batultu*

baṭālu(m) "to cease" Bab., OA, NA **G** (*i/i*) "miss, fail to do, abandon" work, offerings; "be(come) inactive"; stat. of wool, bread "has run out, is exhausted" **Gtn** iter. OA **Š** caus. "discontinue, interrupt" offerings, tribute, "abandon" campaign, song **N** jB "fall into disuse", of border, weapon; NB of worker "cease work"; jB "cease to be effective"; > *baṭlu*, *baṭiltu*; *biṭiltu*

baṭiltu "interruption" jB(Ass.) in *b. išû/rašû* "to cease"; < *baṭālu*

baṭium → *baṭû*

baṭlu "ceased, disused" Bab., NA of offerings etc.; jB *lā baṭlu* "incessantly"; as subst. "cessation, interruption", esp. in *b. šakānu* "to cause cessation" in deliveries etc.; also (a person) "likely to stop work" OB lex.; < *baṭālu*

baṭṭum → *baddum*

baṭû(m), OAkk *baṭium* ?; OB pl. f. *baṭiātum* (a vessel)? OAkk, OB, NB, of silver, copper

bâṭu "to show contempt"? **G** (*ī*) NB

bā'um, *bû(m)* "half" OB lex., math.; *b. ḫepûm* "to halve"; *ana bā* "in half"; < Sum.; → *bātu*

bâ'u(m) I "to go along" Bab., OA **G** (*ā*) [DIB] **1.** with acc. "walk along, across" road, street, field, sky **2.** "pass, overtake, defeat" s.o. **3.** MB(Ass.) "enter" into (= *ana*) **4.** O/jB occas. with dat. pron. suff. "come near, up to s.o."?; OA imper. (*bā'am*, *bā'ānim*) before imper. or cohort. "come on; now then!" **Gtn** "pass repeatedly" **Š** caus. "move along, past", rit. a censer, torch; "cause" water, flood "to flow over" s.th., s.o., "make" evil signs "pass by"

bâ'um II "to come" Mari, Am. **G** (*ū*); < W.Sem.

ba'ūlātu(m), OB *bûlātum* (jB → also *baḫūlātu*) "people, subjects" OAkk, Bab.(lit.), of human population; esp. *b. Ellil*; < *bêlu*

ba'ūlu "great, important" jB lex.; < *ba'ālu*

ba''uru → *bu''uru* I

bayyādu mng. unkn. NA

bayyartu "huntress" jB; < *bâru* I

bayyāru "huntsman" MA(lit.); < *bâru* I

bayyašû, also *bayyāšu* "modest, decent" jB; < *bâšu* I

bayyātu; pl. *bayyātānu* "nocturnal offering ritual" j/NB(Uruk); < *biātum*

baz(a)ḫātum "military post, outpost" Mari; < W.Sem.

bazā'um, *bazāḫum* ~ "to make (unreasonable) demands" **G** OA **D** OB, Mari, Am. "treat harshly; press" person, household for services, payment; > *baziḫtum*

baziḫarzi (a leather object) MB

baziḫtum ~ "claim, need" OB; < *bazā'um*

bazītu (an exotic animal) NA, or error for *pagītu* ? (→ *pagû* I); NA, NB as fPN

be'ālum → *bêlu*

be'āru → *bêru*

bedûm (or *beṭûm*) mng. unkn. OB **G** (*i/i*) phps. "to be slow" **D** "delay" s.o.; > *nabṭû*?

be'ēšu(m), *ba'āšu*, *beḫēšu*, *baḫāšu* "to stir" Ass., jB **G** (*i/i*) **D** ~ G; > *mubeššu*

be'ēšu → also *ba'āšu*

beḫēru "to select" NB **G** (*i/i*) "choose" animals; "levy" troops; < Aram.; > *bēḫiru*; *biḫirtu*

bēḫiru "recruiting officer" NB, as family name; < *beḫēru*

belânum → *bilânum*

bēltu(m), poet. also *bēletu(m)*, O/MA, MB, Am., Bogh. *bēlatu(m)* "lady; mistress, proprietress (of)" [NIN; GAŠAN; EN] **1.** goddesses, absol.: ^{d}*B.* as DN, esp. NA, NB for Ninlil and Ṣarpānītu in PN; "mistress" of person; of heaven, earth, city, temple etc.; ^{d}*Bēltiya* NB **2.** OB (human) "owner" of slaves, field; "lady" (as respectful address in letters); *bēlet bītim* "head of the household, housewife"; jB "queen" **3.** "possessor, controller" of abstr. attributes, e.g. battle, life, fates, incantations, divination **4.** jB in compounds: as *bēlu* 5*b. amāti* etc.; *b. ikki* (→ *ikku* I); *b. rīdi* (→ *rīdu* I 3); *b. ṣerri* (→ *ṣerru* III 1); < *bēlu*

belû(m) I "extinguished" O/jB of brazier, fire, torch; < *belû* II

belû(m) II, *balû* "to be extinguished, come to an end" O/jB, NA **G** (*i/i*) of fire, smoke; of oil-bubble "burst"; transf. of life, disease etc. **Gtn** iter., of brazier, torch **D** "extinguish" fire, disease, fever; "stop" quarrel, fight; "destroy" people, life etc.; > *belû* I; *baliltu*?

bēlu(m) "lord; proprietor (of)" [EN; rarely ^{d}EN, UMUN; MU.LU] **1.** gods, absol.; "master" of person; of heaven, earth, city, temple etc.; ^{d}*Bēl* as DN, from MB on esp. = Marduk, also Ellil **2.** of humans, as address to king, to superior; "master, owner" of slave, field, house, grain etc.; OB *b. aššatim* "husband" **3.** "possessor, controller" of attributes, e.g. strength, decision, divination; OA *b. lā ilim* of s.o. "without a god", jB *lā b. ilāni*; jB *b. pāni* "nouveau riche, parvenu"?; *b. ḫubulli(m)* "creditor"; *b. niqîm* "owner of the sacrificial lamb, sacrificer"; in divine titles "owner" of a tiara, sceptre, lightning etc.; "master" of life, destiny, decisions, wisdom etc. **4.** of one concerned with, responsible for s.th., e.g. *b. gillati* "sinner", *b. ruḫêa* "my bewitcher", *b. dīktiya* "my killer"; jB *b. gimilli* "recipient of a favour"; NB *b. miṣri* "neighbour" **5.** freq. compounds: *b. adê* "s.o. under an oath" jB; *b. āli* (also *ālūtu*) "ruler of a city" jB, NA; *b. awātim* (jB *amāti*) OA, OB, jB "litigant, opposing party (in court)", Mari "enemy"; *b. birki* 'lord of the knees', "runner, constable" OB, jB; *b. bīti* "tribal chief" NB; *b. dabābi* "man of (evil) talk, enemy" M/NB; *b. dāmi* ~ "murderer" Bab., NA; *b. dēqti* "honest"? NA; *b. dīni* "opposing party" (in court) M/NA, j/NB; *b. dumqim* "friend"? OB; *b. egerrê* 'lord of the formula', "sorcerer" jB besides *bēlet e.*; *b. emūqi* ~ "the powerful, vigorous"; *b. ḫīṭi* "evil-doer, criminal" M/NB, NA; *b. ilki* ~ "commissioner for *ilku*-duties" NA; *b. lemutti* (OB *lumnim*) "enemy"; *b. narkabti* "owner of a war-chariot" NA(jB) (→ *berkabtu*); *b. nukurti(m)* "enemy" OA, NB; *b. parṣi* OB "officeholder", jB "s.o. authorized, competent to perform a ritual"; O/MB *b. pīlāḫāti(m)* (MA *pāḫete*) "commissioner", M/NA, M/NB "governor"; *b. piqitti* "commissioner" NA, NB (a class of temple-officials); *b. qašti* "tenant, cultivator of 'bow-land'" NB(Achaem.); *b. qātāte* "guarantor" NA; *b. salāmi* "ally" NA; *b. ṣālti* (NA *ṣāsse*, also *ṣēlti*) "enemy, (personal) opponent" j/NB, NA; *b. têrti(m)* "commissioner" OB, jB lex.; *b. tērēti* as divine title jB, NA; *b. ṭābti* "benefactor, patron, friend" MA(Bogh.), j/NB, NA; *b.-ṭāb(t)ūtu* "friendship" NB; > *bēlūtum*, *bêlu* ?, *bēltu*

bêlu(m), OA *be'ālum*, Ass. also *pe'ālu*, *pêlu* "to rule (over); dispose of" **G** (*ē*; pres. OAkk *ibe''al*; OA pret. also *ib'el*; ptcp. jB *bā'ilu*) [EN]; "rule over, control" countries; M/NA, M/jB "subject to o.'s rule, take possession of"; jB, NA absol. "rule, be ruler"; stat. "is lord/lady" jB, NA; OB "detain" (s.o.); j/NB "be in charge of (= acc.)"; OA "be responsible for" silver, "lay claim to" s.o. **D** OB "keep s.o. in power" **N** pass. OB "be detained"; OA "be claimed"; < *bēlu* denom.?; > *bā'ilu*; *be'ūlātum*; *ba'ūlātu*, *baḫūlātu*

bēlūtu(m) "rule, domination" Bab., NA [EN-] *b. epēšu* "to rule"; *āl b.* "city of government"; < *bēlu*

bennu(m) I ~ "epilepsy" Bab., NA, also abbr. *be*, *bi*

bennu II mng. unkn. jB

bēram adv. "(for) a double hour" OB, Mari; < *bēru* III

berātu, *birātu* pl. tant. ~ "waters, lagoons" jB

beri(-) → *biri-*

berîš "in hunger, hungrily" jB; < *berû* I

berittu → *birītu*

berītu I "treaty" Qatna; < W.Sem.

berītu II (an insect)? jB lex.

berītu → also *birītu* II

berium mng. unkn. OB lex.

berkabtu "charioteer" NB [LÚ.EN.GIŠ.GIGIR]; < *bēl(u)* + *narkabtu*

berqu, *birqu* "lightning (flash)" M/jB, NA [NIM.GÍR]; also "(symbol of) lightning"; < *barāqu*

berte/i → *birti*

bertu → *birītu*

berû(m) I, Ass. *bariu* "hungry"; of people; < *berû* II; > *berîš*, *berûtu*

berû(m) II, *barû(m)* "to be hungry, starve" **G** (*e/e*, OAkk *a/a*) of humans, animals; of field "be starved (of water)"; transf. of silver "be unexploited" **Gt** → *bitrû* II **Gtn** iter. **D** "starve s.o., let s.o. be hungry" **Š** ~ D **Št** → *bitrû* II; > *berû* I, *berîš*, *berûtu*; *bīru* IV; *būru* IV; *nebrītu*

bēru I, *bīru* "distant" j/NB, NA of mountains; < *bâru* III

bēru(m) II, *bīru(m)*, *ba/e/i'rum* "selected" OAkk, Bab., NA **1.** "elite" of soldiers; OA pl. (an administrative body)? **2.** of objects "choice", wool, vegetables, stone, wood etc., building site; < *bêru* I

bēru(m) III, *bīru* "double hour, league" [DANNA(=KASKAL.GÍD)] **1.** linear measure: "double-hour, mile" (= 1,800 ninda ~ 10,800 metres) **2.** angular measurement: $^{1}/_{12}$ of a circle, 30 degrees **3.** measure of time: "$^{1}/_{12}$ of a day, double-hour" only NA, j/NB (after 700 BC); NB *bēr ūmi* "last double-hour of a day"; *bēr mūši* "last double-hour of a night"; *bēr šēr(t)i* ? "double-hour in the morning"; > *bīriš* II; *bēram*

bēru → also *bīru* I-III

bêru(m) I, Ass. *be'āru(m)* "to choose, select" **G** (*ē*) [BAR] people, textiles, ingredients; jB stat., of hair "is thin"; NB in formula *lū nasḫā lū bērā* (whether words of prayer) "are omitted or merely selected"; OA "examine, check" seal **N** "be checked, tested"; > *bēru* II; *bērūtum* II

bêru II mng. unkn. **G** (*ī*) jB

be'rum → *bēru* II

berullum → *burullum*

berûtu(m), *birûtu(m)* "hunger, starvation" O/jB; < *berû* I

bērūtu(m) I, *bīrūtu(m)* ~ "mound" OAkk, j/NB [SUR$_7$] jB, esp. of corpses after battle

bērūtum II (a collegium of officials) OA; < *bêru* I

bešāmu → *bašāmu* I

beškānu → *biškānu*

bēšu "far apart, distant" O/jB; < *bêšu*

bêšu(m) "to go away, withdraw" O/jB, O/MA **G** of living beings, star; transf., of good times; of part of liver "fork, produce a bifurcation" **N** ~ G of person "withdraw"; > *bēšu*; *mubêšu*

bētānu → *bītānu*

bētānû → *bītānû*

betātu pl. tant. (a decoration used on garments and leather objects) Am.; also M/NA (or → *šabattu* ?)

bētu → *bītu*

be'tu (or *til'etu*) (a commodity) MB, measured in gur

beṭûm → *bedûm*

be'u (a bird) NA lex.

be'ūlātum, *bûlātum* pl. tant. "funds available, working capital" OA, also OB in *bûlāt kīsim* "business capital"; < *bêlu*

biādu → *biātum*

bi'āru "spot on the skin" jB med.

biātum, M/NB *bâtu*, Ass. *biādu(m)* "to spend the night, stay overnight" **G** (*ī*) NB of moon; med. of preparation, ointment etc. "stand overnight" **Gtn** iter. of G **D** NB stat., of moon "spends several nights" **Š** OA "have (people and animals) spend the night"; Bogh., jB med. "let" recipe "stand overnight"; < *bītu* denom.; > *bādu*; *bittu*; *bayyātu*; *nubattu*

bibbu(m) f. (a kind of wild sheep) O/jB, NA **1.** "wild sheep" in mountains; Urar. "(image of) wild sheep" **2.** "planet, star; comet ?" [^{d}UDU.IDIM; MUL.UDU.IDIM(.GU$_4$.UD)] **3.** om., desig. of plague

bibbulu(m), M/jB *bub/mbulu* O/jB, Bogh. **1.** "flood, spate" **2.** "day of the disappearance of the moon" [UD.NÁ.ÀM; UD.NÁ.A] (28th or 29th of month); < *babālu*

bibēnu "temple, side of head" jB, left, right; also ~ "septum of the nose"?

bibiḫtu → *bibītu*

bibiltu(m) "carrying off, deportation" O/jB of troops etc.; Mari pl. ~ "lies"?; < *babālu*

bibinakku (a bird) jB lex.

bibi(r)ru(m) (a disease) O/jB med.

bibītu (or *bibittu*), *bibiḫtu* (a demon or disease) jB

biblu(m); pl. m. & f. "the (action of) bringing; things brought" **1.** "(marriage) gift, present" **2.** "yield, produce" of field, mountain **3.** of river, "high water" [NÍG.DÉ.A] **4.** "(state of) being removed, invisibility (of the moon)", *ūm b.* "(day of the) invisibility of the moon"; NA pl. *bib(i)lāni* "(omens concerning) the new moon" **5.** *bibil libbi* "heart's desire", *b. qāti* "stealing, theft"; *b. pāni* DN ~ "reconciliation, appeasement"?; < *babālu*

bibrû (a bird) M/jB [BIBRA.MUŠEN] also "figurine (of bird)"; Am., Bogh. "rhyton" in the shape of a bird or other animals; < Sum.

bibû(m) "baby"? Bab., in (f)PNs

bību → *bi'u*

bidalu; pl. *bidalum/na* "merchant" Ug.; < Ug.

bīdiya "with my (own) hand" NB; < Aram.

biduqtum "sluice channel" OB; < *batāqu*

bidurḫu → *budulḫu*

biḫirtu "levy" j/NB of soldiers; *b. beḫēru* "to raise a levy"; < *beḫēru*

bi'iltu (a container) j/NB for oil, ghee; < *ba'āšu*

bi'iltu → also *bīšu* I

bikītu(m) "weeping, mourning" Bab. [ÉR]; *b. šakānu*, *b. bakû* "to perform a mourning-ritual"; *ša b.* "(prof.) mourner" O/jB; jB *qan b.* ~ "shepherd's pipe"; < *bakû*

bikru (or *pikru*) (a bead or sim.) Am., of gold

bilânum, *belânum* adv., also*ina bilâni* "without (s.o.'s) knowledge"? Mari; → *balu*

billatu(m), *billetu(m)*, NB also *biltu* "mixture" **1.** Bab. (a dry substance used in the preparation of beer) [DIDA(=KAŠ.Ú.SA); DÍDA(=KAŠ.ÚS. SA)]; ~ "beer of second quality" **2.** MA, MB "alloy" of metals **3.** OB, Mari "mixing vat" **4.** NB "admixture"; < *balālu*

billu I "(ad)mixture" **1.** NA "(component of metal) alloy" **2.** MA, Nuzi "mixed beer"? **3.** jB "complexity, intricacy"?; < *balālu*

billu II **1.** MB, NB (a plant) **2.** jB (a stone)

billudû → *pelludû*

bilṣu(m) mng. unkn. jB; also OAkk as PN ?

biltu(m), NA *bissu*, *bīsu* "load; talent; yield; rent; tribute" [GÚ; GUN] **1.** "load", on donkey (also du.); as unit, of sticks etc.; OA *ša biltim*, pl. *ša bilātim* "carrier(s), porter(s)"; *imēr(um) (ša) b.* "pack-ass"; jB transf. "burden, onus" **2.** "talent" (as unit of weight = 60 minas; NA also 30 minas → *qallu* I); st. abs. *bilat* "1 talent" **3.** ~ "yield" of garden, field, land; trees; barley, dates, wool and metal **4.** ~ "rental payment" on field, flock, equipment etc. **5.** "tribute" of foreign countries; *b. maḫāru* "to receive tribute"; *b. našû* "to bring tribute"; *b. eli/ina muḫḫi PN šakānu/kunnu/emēdu* "to impose tribute on s.o."; < *wabālum*

biltu → also *billatu*

bīltu → *bīšu* I

binâtu → *binītu*

bingu(r)ru (a kind of roof)? jB lex.

biniannum ~ "shape, physique" OB; < *banû* IV

binītu(m); pl. *binâtu*, OB *biniātum* "creation; shape, appearance, structure" OAkk, Bab. **1.** "creature" of a god **2.** "form, shape" **3.** in pl. "limbs" [ME.DÍM] **4.** NB in pl. "creation" of river **5.** (an abnormal growth) on the body [ME.DÍM] **6.** "egg; fish roe" **7.** (wooden beam) OAkk(Sum.) of house; jB of boat **8.** (an item of jewellery); < *banû* IV

binna, *ibinna* "give!" (imper.) j/NB usu. vent. *binnam(ma)*; f. *(i)binnī*, *(i)binnimma*; also + dat. pron. suff., e.g. *ibinnannâši* "give us!"

binnu → *bīnu* I

bintu, *bittu(m)* "daughter" O/jB, MA; < *bīnu* I

bīnu(m) I, *binnu* "son" OAkk, jB, NA in PNs; *bīn bīni* "grandson"; jB *b. qiššê* "sprout of a cucumber"?; > *bintu*

bīnu(m) II "tamarisk" OAkk, OA, O/jB [GIŠ.ŠINIG] as tree, timber; med., mag. for purification; Qatna "tamarisk(-shaped gem)" of lapis lazuli etc.

binûtu "creation, creature; product; form" M/NB [DÙ-] of living beings: *binût (qātē) DN* "creation of (the hands of) DN"; of animals, stones *b. tâmd/ti* "creatures of the sea"; *b. šamê*, *b. apsî* "formed in sky, in *apsû*"; of wood *b. Ḫamāni* "grown in the Amanus"; *b. agê* 'product of the current' (a marine plant); jB "form, appearance" of god, of fabrication of bow; *b. nūni* "fish roe" jB om.; < *banû* IV

biqlētu pl. tant. ~ "germinating malt" jB lex.; < *baqālu*

biqlum ~ "sapling" Mari, of box tree

biqnu "(what has been) plucked, pluckings" jB of goose; < *baqāmu*

birâ adv. ~ "(everywhere) in between"? M/NB; *ana b.* "in accordance with, correspondingly; by an equal amount"; < *biri-*

biraḫḫum → *biriḫḫu*
birānātu → *birtu* I
biraqānum → *pirikānum*
birātu → *berātu*; *birtu* I
birbaṣu (a plant) jB lex.
birbirrānu ~ 'the sparkler' jB (a kind of lizard); < *birbirrū*
birbirrū pl. tant. "radiance; sparkle, flash" Bab. of sun, lightning; < *barāru*; > *birbirrānu*
birdu "pockmark"? jB med., om.; also phps. "pockmarked person"; → *perdum*
birḫu mng. unkn. NA
biri-, *biru-*, *beri(-)* "among, between" Bab. [DAL.BA.(AN.)NA] with pron. suff., after *ina* or *ša*; occas. after st. constr.: OB *kasap birīni* "our shared silver"; j/NB also after *ana*, *ultu*; loc.-adv. *(ina) biru(m)-* OB(Susa), occas. M/jB; spatially "between", "(from) among"; of bilateral relations "between", MB *māmīt birīni* "our mutual oath"; Ug. *(ina) beri X u (ina) beri Y* "between X and Y"; jB(Ass.) as adv. *ina beri* "in between"; < *barû* I; > *birītu* I; *birâ*; *birūyum*; OA → *bari-*
biriḫḫu(m), OAkk *biraḫḫum* ~ "string, bundle" OAkk, O/jB of vegetables etc.
birimdu → *birimtu*
birimmu (a colourful bird) Bogh. lex.; < *barāmu* I
birimtu, MB *birimdu* "sealing" M/jB; < *barāmu* II
bīriš I "over, to the other side" M/jB; → *berîš*
bīriš II "for a double-hour"? MB(Ass.); < *bēru* III
birīt "between, among" Bab. [DAL.BA.(AN.)NA] spatially *(ina/ša) b.*; NA, NB also "within"; NA *issu b.* "from inside" PlN, "from among" people; < *birītu* I st. constr.; → *birti*
birīt birīt, OB also *pirīt pirīt* "mutually" O/jB; < *birītu* I
birītu(m) I, *bi/ertu*, NB also *bištu*; pl. *birê/âtu*, OB *biriātum*, NB also *barātu* "space between, distance" [DAL.BA.(AN.)NA] "partition, dividing baulk" (between fields); "alley" between houses; om. "partition wall" as part of liver; NB astr. "elongation, (angular) distance" (freq. abbr. *bi* or *be*); compounds: *b. purīdī* "area between the legs"; *b. appi* "nasal septum?"; *b. šiddī* "area between curtains" in shrine; MB *b. ālāni* "countryside"; *b. nāri(m)* "region enclosed by river(s)"; *igār birītim* "wall shared by two houses"; *bīt b.* "common house"; < *biri-*; > *birīt*; *birīt birīt*; OAkk → *barītum*
birītu II, *berītu*, MA *berittu*; pl. *bi/erêtu* "fetter" M/jB, M/NA; of bronze, iron; freq. pl., *birêtu/i (parzilli) nadû* "to throw s.o. (= acc.) into (iron) fetters"
birīyu → *birūyum*
birkatu error for → *birratu*
birku(m) "knee" Bab. **1.** of humans, animals, usu. du. **2.** "lap"; *birkāšu* "on his lap", *tarbīt birkēya* "raised on my lap" **3.** as euph. desig. for genitals; also transf. "strength" **4.** *bēl b.* "runner, henchman"; → *burku*; *pētân birki*
birmu I "multicoloured cloth" M/NA, M/NB [GÙN]; < *barāmu* I
birmu II in *birim kunukki* "seal impression" M/jB; < *barāmu* II
birqu → *berqu*
birratu mng. uncl. (a disease of the eyes) jB; < *barāru*
birru "grille, lattice" jB, NA
birru → also *bīru* III
birṣu(m) (a luminous phenomenon) O/jB, om. "sheen"? of oil; night-time "glow"; < *barāṣu*
biršu; pl. m. & f. (a coarse fabric, phps.) "felt" M/NA, j/NB; NA "(garment of) felt?"; < *barāšu*
birti, *berte/i*, *birtu-* "between" M/NA, MB; spatially "between, within"; "(from) among"; NA *birti/e ēnē maddudu* 'to measure between the eyes' = "to make s.th. clear to s.o."; jB lex. *b. aḫī* "chest"; → *birīt* etc.
birtu(m) I, NB also *bištu*; pl. NB also *birānātu* "fort, castle" Bab., NA [NA (URU.)ḪAL.ṢU (→ *ḫalṣu* II)]; OB also of citadel in town; NB also of area protected by fortified outposts; NA, NB *rab b.* "commander of a fortress"; > *birtūtu*
birtu(m) II in *ṣiddu/ṣindu (u) b.* "riffraff" OB lex., jB
birtu → also *birītu*; *birti*
birtūtu "function as fort" jB; < *birtu* I
biru- → *biri-*
bīru(m) I, *bēru* "divination" [MÁŠ] *b. barû* "to perform divination"; *ina b. šakānu*, NA *ina b. uddû* "to determine through divination"; of god(s) *bēl(ē) b.* "lord(s) of divination"; MB pl. f. "oil-divination"?; < *barû* I
bīru II, *bēru* "bull calf" M/NB [GU4.NÍNDA]
bīru(m) III, *bēru*, NB *birru* "baulk, ridge" between fields, canals OB(Susa), j/NB; → *birītu*
bīru IV "hunger, thirst" jB; < *berû* II
bīru → also *bēru* I-III; *bīram*
bi'rum → *bēru* II
birûtu "divination" jB lex.; < *barû* I
birûtu → also *berûtu*
bīrūtu → *bērūtu* I

birūyum, jB *birīyu*, OAkk *barium* "median" OAkk, O/jB; OB of standard measure of medium capacity; < *biri-*

bis "then, afterwards" NA

biskiltu → *baskiltu*

bisru, *bišru* "leek" jB

bissatu mng. unkn. jB lex., desig. of door strap (*ya'u*)

bissu, *bīsu* → *biltu*

biṣiltu (a leather container for oil) jB lex.

biṣinnu → *buṣinnu*

biṣru I "bag" jB lex., of physician, diviner

biṣru II mng. uncert. jB lex.; < *baṣāru*

biṣṣirtānu → *biṣṣūru*

biṣṣu(m) "droplet" O/jB of oil, tears; < *baṣāsu*; → *biṣû*

biṣṣūru(m) "female genitals, vulva" [GAL4.LA] of human, animal; "vulva(-shaped amulet)", of lapis lazuli; *b. atāni*, *biṣṣirtānu* [NA4.PEŠ4/ŠÀ.ANŠE] 'jenny-ass vulva' (a type of seashell), as ornament, drug

biṣû "(tear) drop"? jB lex.; var. of *biṣṣu* ?; < *baṣāṣu*

bišbišu "pith" jB lex., inside reed

bišimtu, *bišemtu*, *bišittu* "formation, shape; product" j/NB; *b. šadî* "product(s) of the mountains"; *b. libitti* "formed of brick"; < *bašāmu* II

bišītu(m) **1.** Mari, jB "property, assets" **2.** jB in *bišīt uzni* "intelligence, wisdom", also used as divine title; *ina lā b. u.* "through absence of understanding" **3.** jB *bišīt libbi* mng. uncl., phps. "the whole body"; < *bašû*

biškānu, *beškānu* "pupa of a caterpillar" NA

bišru "small child" jB lex.

bišru → also *bisru*

biššu, *buššu* "rue"? j/NB, a garden plant

bištu → *birītu*; *birtu* I

bīštu → *bīšu* I

bišû → *bīšu* II

bīšu I, *bi'šu*; f. NB *b(i')iltu* "bad; malodorous" Bab., of words, actions; objects (e.g. fruit, corn, pastry, wool, clothing, soil); < *ba'āšu*

bīšu(m) II, *bišû* "possessions, property" O/jB (st. constr. *biši*, OB also *bīš*; acc. with pron. suff. *bīšašu*); < *bašû*

bi'šu → *bīšu* I

bīt, *bīte* "where; when" [É] **1.** conj., M/NA, jB, NB(Ass.) *(ina) bīt* "where, whither"; "when"; *issu b.* (temporal) "since", (spatial) "from (the place) where"; *adi bīt* "until"; *ana bīt* "concerning the fact that"; *ina bīt ... ina bīt ...* "if ... if ..." **2.** occas. as prep. MB, NA "at"; < *bītu* st. constr.

bītānu, Ass. *bētānu* "in the house, inside" M/NA, M/NB [É-] of wall, transaction, ration; j/NB, NA "interior" of palace, temple, mountain valleys; of person, parts of the body; < *bītu* + *-ānu*; > *bītānû*

bītānû, Ass. *bētānû* "inner, interior" M/NB, NA; of archit. features; NA uzu*bītānītu*, uzu*bītāniāte* ~ "viscera"?; < *bītānu* + *-ī*

bītbītiš "from house to house" jB; < *bītu*

bīte → *bīt*

bitiqtu(m); pl. *bitqātu(m)* "damage, loss; deficit" Ass., OB; in agriculture, trade; < *batāqu*

bītītu "inside"? jB of house; < *bītu*

bitkulla (a kind of meat) NB

bitqu(m) **1.** Bab. "break(age); cutting"; of umbilical cord; "opening, sluice" through dam, canal bank **2.** MA "accusation" **3.** M/NB 1/8 of a shekel **4.** NB 1/2 of a seah measure, uncert. **5.** NB *qēm bitqa/u* (a kind of flour) **6.** NA "levy" of horses etc.; < *batāqu*

bitrāmu(m) "multicoloured" O/jB; of eyes; of a stone, of tortoise(shell), jB lex.; < *barāmu* I

bitru mng. uncert. jB med. in prescriptions

bitrû I "enormous, magnificent" j/NB "magnificent" of sun; "prime quality" of pigs, sheep, cattle, fish; "enormous" of heaps of barley; < *barû* I ?

bitrû II "to be continuous, endure" **Gt** of battle, spell **Št** [ZAL(.ZAL)] "persevere, continue", "hold out; see s.th. through"; "stay permanently; do s.th. (= acc.) permanently"; of activities, natural phenomena, star etc. "continue"; jB also trans. "provide" harvest, rains etc. "permanently"; ext. "pass all the way through", of a hole; > *šutebrûm*; *muštabrītu*; → *berû* II

bitrumu "very colourful" MA, jB; of bird; "multicoloured" of yarn; "piebald" of mule; < *barāmu* I

bittu(m) (a kind of wool) OB?, jB lex.; < *biātum*

bittu → also *bintu*

bītu(m), Ass. *bētu(m)* m.; pl. f. *bītātu(m)*, Ass. also m., M/NA *bētānu* "house" [É; pl. É.MEŠ, also É.ḪI.A(.MEŠ); OB(Susa) É.A.NI] **1.** "house", leg. *b. epšu(m)* "built house" [OB(Susa) É.DÙ.A (also for *bītum* alone)]; *b. kiṣri* "house to let" jB; of (nomad's) tent, in pl. "encampment" **2.** of palace, *b. mār šarri* "palace of the crown prince" NA, NB; *rab/ša muḫḫi b.* "palace supervisor"; *b. ridûti* "house of the succession" (= palace of the crown prince) Bab., NA; *b. kutalli* "rear part of house" NA for *ēkal k.* (→ *ēkallu*), NB **3.** of temple: *b. ili(m)* "temple" Bab., NA; *bīt DN* "temple of DN" (→ *ērib bīti*) **4.** jB, as desig. of "tomb"

5. *b. kunukki(m)* "sealed storeroom" O/MB; *b. niṣirti* "treasure-house" jB; *b. pirišti* "house of secrets" (room in a temple) j/NB; *b. makkūri* "treasure-house" j/NB; *b. karê* "granary" NB; *b. urê* "shed" for sheep, cattle, also *b. alpī*; *b. ruqqi* ~ "shed (for the storage of) pots, vessels" M/NB **6.** *b. kīli* "prison" M/NB; *b. ṣibitti* "prison" jB, NA **7.** "wing of building, room", *b. erši* "bedroom" in palace or temple M/NB, NA; *b. mayyāli(m)* "bedroom" Mari, jB, M/NA; *b. simmilti* "(well of a) staircase" M/NB **8.** *b. eleppi*, *b. narkabti* "ship's cabin", "chariot body"; "container" for weapons, liquids, tablets etc.; *b. qēmi* "flour container"; NB *b. riqqī* "spice-box"; NB *b. nūri* "lantern"? **9.** "estate, premises"; NA, NB "plot of land", *b. narkabti/qašti* etc. "chariot/bow etc. fief" (→ *kussû*, *sisû*); jB(Ass.) occas. for *ašru* III **10.** "family, tribe"; "household"; *b. abi(m)* "paternal house, family" O/jB, NA, *b. abūtu* NB **11.** *Bīt-X* in names of cities, parts of cities, countries **12.** freq. compounds: *b. āli(m)* "City House" (as institution) O/MA; *b. dulli* ~ "workroom", "field under the plough" NB; *b. maškani* "pledge" NB; *b. mēseri* "confinement" jB; *b. qāti* 'house of hand(s)' NA, NB, mng. uncl.; *b. rimki* "bath-house" j/NB, NA, "bathing ritual", *b. r. epēšu* "to perform a bathing ritual"; NB *b. ritti* 'house of the hand' (a kind of state or temple fee); *b. sinniš(ā)ti(m)* "women's quarters" (in the palace) O/MB; *b. šanû* "outhouse, annexe" M/NA; *ša b. šanî/ê* "lackey"; *b. šarri* 'house of the king' NB(Achaem.) = "royal exchequer"; NA *b. šarrāni* (royal mausoleum); *b. šibirri* 'house of the sceptre' mng. unkn., jB lex., NB; *b. ṭābti* "salt desert" NA/jB; *b. ṭuppi(m)* 'tablet house' = "archive room, school" O/jB [É.DUB.BA(.A)]; *b. zīlāqīqi* 'house of the wind' = "desert", jB; > *bīt*; *bītītu*, *bītānu*, *bītānû*; *bītbītiš*; *biātum*

biṭiltu ~ "inactivity"? jB, pl. "derelictions"; < *baṭālu*

bī'u, Ass. *bību*; pl. *bībū*, *bībānu* "opening, outlet" M/NA, M/NB; *b. ša dūri* "drainage opening in wall"

bizazû "frog"-shaped ornament jB lex.; < Sum.

bûm (or *pûm*) (a bird) OB

bû → also *bā'um*

buāru → *bâru* III; *bu'āru*

bu(')āru(m) ~ "happiness" Bab.(lit.); < *bâru* III

buati → *puati*

bubātu → *bubūtu* I

bubbulu → *bibbulu*

bubû(m) **1.** (part of an oven) jB/NA lex. **2.** (a topog. feature) OB

bubuatu → *bubūtu* I

bubuḫtu, *bubuttu* → *bubu'tu*

bubūtu(m) I, *bubātu(m)*, MA *bubuatu* "hunger, starvation" [ŠÀ.GAR; SU.GU$_7$] of individuals, "famine" of land; also "sustenance"

bubūtu(m) II "axle" O/jB, of cart, chariot; OB *b. nārim* mng. unkn.

bubu(')tu(m), *buḫbuḫtu*, *bubuḫtu*, *bubuttu*; pl. *bubu(m)ātu* "boil, pustule" O/jB [Ù/U$_4$/U.BU.BU.UL; BU.BU.UL; Ù/U$_4$.BÚ.BÚ.UL]; → *burbu'tu*

buddarḫu → *budulḫu*

buddudu "to waste, dissipate" NA **D**

budduru, *bunduru*, *buṭṭuru*, *butturu* ~ "bundle of reeds" OB, jB lex.

budû (a cake)? NA, NB (or read *giddê* ?)

būdu(m) I, *pūdu(m)*, *bu'du* f. (an implement) OAkk, O/jB, of wood, metal

būdu(m) II, *pūdu(m)* f. "shoulder" OAkk, Bab. [MURGU] of human beings; ext. "shoulder" of parts of liver etc.

būdu(m) III, *pūdu(m)*; pl. f. (a festival)? OB, Mari

būdu IV, *pūdu* ~ (a pest)? jB

būdu → also *pūdu*

bu'du → *būdu* I

budūḫum mng. unkn. Mari

budulḫu, *bidurḫu*, *buddarḫu* "(resin from) bdellium tree" j/NB

budūrum "profusion"? OB(lit.) in *budūri nūni* "profusion? of fish" (jB → *puzru* 3)

budušsu ~ "roller" jB lex. (an agricultural implement)

buggum (or *puggum*) (a bird) OB

buginnu, *buninnu(m)*, OB also *bukīnum* ~ "bucket, trough" O/jB, esp. rit. for (holy) water; "(flour-)chest"; MB (as symbol of Sîn); < Sum.

bugurru (or *b/pug/qurru*) (a cut of meat) M/NA

buḫbuḫtu → *bubu'tu*

buḫḫû → *bu''û* II

buḫḫuru "to heat" jB **D** a liquid **Dtn** "keep hot"; > *baḫru*, *baḫrūtu*, *Baḫir*?; *buḫru*, *buḫrītu*; *buḫratum*?

buḫḫušu "to check" jB(Ass.) lex. **D** text; < Aram.

buḫlalû (or *puḫlalû*) (an Elam. class of priests) jB

buḫratum (an offering) Mari; < *buḫḫuru* ?

buḫrītu (a hot dish) M/jB med.; < *buḫru* + *-ī*

buḫru "cooked state; cooked food" jB *buḫra(m)* "in cooked state, when ready"; (a hot dish made with cereals); *ṭābat b.* "cooking salt"?; < *buḫḫuru*

bu''ītu → *bu''û* I

bukānu(m), *bukannu* "(wooden) pestle" Bab. [GIŠ.GAN.NA] **1.** as tool; O/jB leg. *bukāna(m) šūtuqu(m)* "to make step over the pestle" (symbolic act in sale transaction) **2.** jB lex., med. (a plant) **3.** jB lex. (an insect), usu. *išid b.* 'base of a pestle'

bukāšum "duke" O/MB; < Kass.

bukīnum → *buginnu*

bukkatu → *abukkatu*

bukratu → *bukurtu*

bukru(m) "son, child" Bab.(lit.) of gods, humans; > *bukurtu*

bukum (a bird) OB

būku (or *pūku*) **1.** Qatna (an ornament) **2.** jB mng. unkn.

bukurtu, *bukratu(m)* "daughter" O/jB(lit.), said of goddesses only; < *bukru*

bulālu (a plant) jB

bûlātum → *ba'ūlātu*; *be'ūlātum*

bulā'u → *bulû*

bulīli (a species of crested bird) jB lex.

bulīlu → *abulīlu*

bulīmānu mng. unkn. MB as PN

bullu I "to throw down, cast away" M/NB D hand; work; of fate (*šīmtu*) "strike down"

bullu II subst. ~ "decay"? M/jB; > *bullûm*, *bullûtum*

bullûm ~ "putrid"? OB, of blood; < *bullu* II + *-ī*; > *bullûtum*

bullûtum "state of decay"? OB, of land in *b. alākum* "to go to wrack and ruin"; < *bullûm*

bultu (a quilt or blanket) Am., Nuzi

būltu → *būštu*

bulṭi(t)tu → *bušṭītum*

bulṭu(m) "life; cure, healing" [TI(.LA)] **1.** "lifetime" **2.** "(state of) life" **3.** "subsistence, food" **4.** "cure" of illness, freq. in pl. "medical treatment, prescription" **5.** "health(y state)"; < *balāṭu* II

bulû(m), MA *bulā'u* "dry wood, dry reed" Bab., MA

būlu(m) "animals, livestock" Bab., NA; [MÁŠ.ANŠE] "domestic livestock", NB *rab b.* "overseer of the herds"; jB of wild animals, *b. ṣēri* "animals of the desert", also *b. Šakkan*

buluggu → *balangu*

buluḫḫum → *baluḫḫu*

bumbulu → *bibbulu*

bunānu → *punānu*

būnatu "daughter" jB lex.; < *būnu* I

bunbullu mng. unkn. jB, NA

bunduru → *budduru*

buninnu → *buginnu*

bunna, *bunni* ~ "thanks to"? MB in PNs; *bunnamma* "be so kind as to ..." OB; < *banû* II

bunna(n)nû pl. tant. "physiognomy, (facial) features" Bab.(lit.) of human, god; jB *ṣalam b.-ya* "likeness of my face"; esp. "(pleasant) features" in PNs, NB also fPN *Bunnanītu*; "(representation of) face" in art etc., also "image" of a chariot; of gardens *b. ālīšu* "the characteristic feature of his city"?; < *banû* II

bunni → *bunna*

bunnu → *būnu* II

bunnû "beautified" j/NB, of appearance; NB (desig. of currency)?; < *banû* II

bunnunu (or *punnunu*) mng. unkn. jB lex.

buntum "daughter" OA; < *būnu* I

bunum → *būnum* III

būnu I "son" jB lex.; > *buntum*, *būnatu*

būnu(m) II, *bunnu* "goodness"; pl. "face" Bab. [DÙ in PNs only] **1.** sg., occas. du. "outward appearance" of god, human, tree, day etc., usu. "good looks"; "favour, good intentions"; NB *b. pāni* "friendly face", "prominence, distinction"; NB *b. zēri* "preferential share" of jointly owned land; OB *ana b.* "in view of" **2.** pl., occas. du. "face" of god, human, *b. namrūtum* "shining happy faces"; < *banû* II; → *būnzerru*; *buppānī-*

būnum III (or *bunum*) (a bird) OB

būnzerru ~ "(fowler's) hide" jB, of reeds; transf. "web" of spider; < *būnu* II + *zerru* I

buppānam "face down" Mari, in *b. abākum* "to turn upside down"

buppānī- "face down, flat on the face" O/jB with pron. suff.; *b.- ṣalālu/saḫāpu/maqātu* "to lie/be prostrate/fall on o.'s face"; of bowl *ina b.-ša* "upside down"?; < *būnu* II + *pānu* I pl.; > *buppāniš*

buppāniš "face down" jB

buqāmu; f. *buqamtu* "lamb ready for plucking" jB; < *baqāmu*

buqāqum "little gnat, fly"? OAkk, OB as PN; < *baqqu* dimin.?

buqārum "cattle" Mari; < W.Sem.

buqāšum "broad(-shouldered)" OAkk, as PN; < *baqāšu*

buqlu(m), *buqulu(m)* ; OA pl. f. **1.** "malt" Bab., OA, Nuzi, Bogh. [MUNU4-8; Nuzi also BÙLUG.MEŠ]; in similes *kīma b. ḫašālu/šeṭû* "to crush/spread out like malt"; *qēm b.* "malt flour" **2.** OA, NB "vegetables"; > *baqālu*

buqqumu; f. *buqquntu* "lamb ready for plucking" jB lex.; "curly-haired" person OB lex.; < *baqāmu*

buqquru "to inquire into, investigate" NB **D**; < Aram.; → *baqāru*

buqqušum "very broad" OAkk, OB, as PN; < *baqāšu*

buqrûm → *buqurrû*

buqulu → *buqlu*

buqūmu(m), MA, M/jB also *buqūnu* "plucking" O/jB, MA [ZÚ.SI.GA; ŠID.SI.GA] as event, season, "(sheep) shearing"; *bīt b.* "plucking house" [É.ZÚ.SI.GA]; MA, MB "plucked wool"; < *baqāmu*

buqurru → *bugurru*

buqurrû, *puqurrû*, MA *b/puqurrā'u*, *buqrûm*; MA pl. *b/puqurrānā'u* "legal claim" O/jB, MA; < *baqāru*

burāḫu ~ "shining"? MB as PN; < *barāḫu*

burallu (a stone object) NA

burallum → also *burullum*

burānû → *burû* I

burāšu(m), NB also *baršu* "(species of) juniper" [GIŠ.LI; (GIŠ.)ŠIM.LI] "juniper tree" as timber; "juniper (resin)"; "(pieces of) juniper wood"

burā'um → *burû* I

burbāni mng. unkn. NA

burbillatu (an insect) NA

burbu'tu; pl. *burbu'ātu*, OB *burbuḫātum* "bubble" O/jB, Bogh.; → *bubu'tu*

burdātu → *purdātu*

burdi → *būrtī šamḫat*

burdû → *purdû*

burgû (or *purgû*) (a type of offering) j/NB; < Sum.

burḫiš, *burḫu* ~ "buffalo" MA, Am.; hunted; in art

burkītu → *burkūtu*

burku, *purku* "knee" M/NB, NA **1.** du. "knees" **2.** "lap" of gods and kings, also transf. ref. to control, protection **3.** *ša b.* "loincloth" MB(Alal.), Am., Nuzi; → *birku*; *meburku*

burkūtu, *burkītu* (or *purkū/ītu*) ~ "(hereditary) share" M/NB of fields

burmāḫu (a big libation bowl) jB [BUR.MAḪ]; < Sum.; → *pūru* I

burmāmu(m) (an animal) OAkk$^{?}$, MB, jB lex.; < *barāmu* I

burmu "colour(ed part)" jB, in *b. īnī* "iris"; < *barāmu* I

burrānu → *murrānu*

burrātu mng. unkn. jB

burriṣānu → *aburriṣānu*

burrum (a kind of cereal) Mari

burrû (a temple servant)? jB lex.; also pl. *burrûtu* Bogh., of women; < Sum

burrumtu (a multicoloured bird) jB; < *burrumu*

burrumu, Ass. *barrumu(m)*; f. *burrum/ntu*, NB also *burrundu* "multicoloured, pied, speckled" [GÙN(.GÙN); GÙN.A] of cloth, clothes; metal, stone; birthmark; tree; bird; animals: horse, dog, cow, sheep, goat; < *barāmu* I

burruqu, Ass. *barruqu* "with flashing eyes" M/jB, Bogh., NA, of humans; jB of goat; < *barāqu*

burrušum "bald"? OAkk, OA *Barrušum* as PN; jB lex.; < *barāšu*

bursaggu/û(m) (or *pursaggu/û(m)*) a kind of offering) Bab. [BUR.SAG.GÁ]; < Sum.

bursallû (a stone bowl) jB lex.

bursiktu → *buršiktu*

bursindu, *bursittu* → *pursindu*

burṣa adv. mng. unkn. jB; < *barāṣu* ?

burṣātu → *purdātu*

burṣimtu, *burṣimdu* (or *pur...*); pl. also *burṣimētu* ~ "pivot-stone box"? j/NB for door-post

buršašillu, *buršasillu*, *buršušallû* (or *pur...*) (a stone bowl) jB; also deified as symbol; < Sum.

buršiktu (or *bursiktu*, *purs/šiktu*) (a wooden implement) jB lex.

buršušallû → *buršašillu*

buršuzaggû (a stone bowl) jB lex.

būrtī šamḫat, *būrta/burdi šamḫat*, *būrtī ša(n)ḫat(i)*, NA also *burdi (šaḫi)* "caterpillar" jB, NA

būrtu(m) I "cistern, well; fish pond; source (of river); hole, pit" Bab. [PÚ]; < *būru* I

būrtu(m) II, NB *būštu* "cow" Bab.; also as fPN; < *būru* II

būrtu(m) III "proof, attestation" OB in *ṭuppi b.* "record of attestation"; < *bâru* III

buru "son" NA; < Aram.

burû(m) I, OA *burā'um*, Nuzi, NB also *būru*; pl. NB also *burānû* "(reed) mat" Bab., OA [GI.KID.(MÁ.)MAḪ; GI.KID.MÁ.ŠÚ.A; GI.KID.MÁ.NIGIN.NA] to cover boat; as shelter, in cult; for roofing, irrigation dyke; OA (a type of rug)

burû II (a garden plant) jB lex.

būru(m) I "cistern, well; pool; pit" Bab., MA; of water; also "pit" of white naphtha, bitumen; for trapping animals; > *būrtu* I

būru(m) II "(bull) calf" OAkk, O/MA, O/jB [(GU$_4$.)AMAR] cow *adi b.-ša* "with her calf"; *b. šizbi* "sucking calf"; occas. of young of other animals, e.g. ass; as epith. of gods, e.g. Sîn, Šamaš; of the king etc., in PNs; > *būrtu* II

būru(m) III (a surface measure) "bur" O/jB = 18 *ikû* (~ 64,800 sq. metres) [BÙR(.IKU)]; st. abs. *būr* "1 bur"; < Sum.

būru(m) IV "hunger" O/jB, NA; < *berû* II

būru V (a type of song) jB

būru VI (a word for sky) jB lex.; < Sum.

būru → also *burû* I

bûru → *bu''uru* I

burubalûm I "ruin, (abandoned) building site" OB, Mari, Elam [BUR.BAL]; < Sum.

burubalûm II (desig. of a supernatural snake) OB mag.

buruburu (a children's game) MB

buruḫli → *wuruḫli*

burullum, *be/arullu(m)*, *burallum* (or *pur...*) (a commercial police official) OA, OB(N.Mes.), MB(Alal.); *b. rabûm* "chief *b.*"

burūmītu "sky-blue lapis lazuli" jB lex.; < *burūmû*

burummu (a bird) jB; < *barāmu* I

burūmû, *burummû* pl. tant. "heaven, sky" j/NB(lit.) *bāb b.* (name of a temple gate in Aššur); *kakkab b.* "star of heaven", *šiṭir b.* "celestial writing" i.e. the stars; < *barāmu* I; > *burūmītu*

bururānu mng. unkn. NB

burussu(m) (or *purussu(m)*); pl. f. "bung, plug" O/jB, NA, of a mash tub; OB "plug" of a water-outlet; NA "stopper" of waterskin

buru(t)tum → *puruttum*

burzaggû (a stone bowl) jB lex.

burzaraš, *burzarašû* (desig. of horses) MB

burzibandû (kind of vessel) NA

burziburzi (a leather belt)? jB lex.

burzidunbarakku (a vessel with a lip or spout) jB lex.; < Sum.

burzigallu "big *pursītu* vessel" jB [(DUG.) BUR.ZI.GAL] for fumigation, incense-burning; < Sum.

burzisilabandû (kind of vessel) jB lex.

burzisilagallû (kind of vessel) jB lex.

busārum "announcement" OB; < *bussuru*

busratu → *bussurtu*

bussumu I "pleasant"? Bogh. lex.; jB lex. of beer

bussumu(m) II "to please" OB **D**

bussurtu(m), j/NB also *busratu*, NA *passurtu* "message, report" Bab., M/NA [KA.DÙ.A] *b. ḫadê(m)/dumqi(m)/lumnim* "glad/good/bad tidings"; OB om. *b. nūrim* "message of light"; < *bussuru*

bussuru(m), NA *passuru* "to bring, send a message" O/jB, NA to s.o. (= acc.); "deliver (pleasant) news"; "extol" a god; > *busārum*; *bussurtu*; *mubassiru*; *tabsertum*

busukku (or *pusukku*) ~ "son" jB lex.

buṣallibu, *buṣellibu* (a plant) jB lex.

buṣaṣû pl. tant. "trifles" jB; < *baṣāṣu*

buṣellibu → *buṣallibu*

buṣinnu, *buṣīnum*, OA, Nuzi also *biṣinnu(m)* [(GIŠ.)GI.ZÚ.LUM(.MA)?] **1.** M/jB "mullein, *Verbascum*" **2.** OAkk, O/jB, NA "wick" (made from *Verbascum* leaves); NA also "lamp" **3.** jB, NA *bīt b.* "lamp"

būṣiš "like a *b.* bird" jB; < *būṣu* I

būṣu(m) I "hyaena" O/jB, NA; also (a bird) ~ "rock partridge"; as PN; > *būṣiš*

būṣu II **1.** M/NA, NB "fine linen, byssus" **2.** M/NA, M/jB, Nuzi m. & f., also *būzu* ? (a type of glass); "glass vessel" for oil, salt

bušālu(m) "what has been cooked" **1.** OA, jB lex. ~ "cooked meat" **2.** jB lex. "ripe date"; < *bašālu*

būšānu(m), *bu'šānu* **1.** O/jB "bad smell" (a disease affecting the mouth, nose and skin) [KIR4.ḪAB] **2.** Bogh., jB (a plant) lex., med. [Ú.ḪAB]; < *ba'āšu*

bušiu → *būšum*

bušlu ~ "ripening" of dates jB; "smelting" of ores, "melting" of glass MA, jB; < *bašālu*

buššānītu (or *puššānītu*) (a star) jB

buššu → *biššu*

būštu(m), j/NB also *būltu* "shame" Bab., OA "sense of shame, modesty; dignity", *ina lā b.-šu* "shamelessly", *ša b. lā išû* "who has no shame"; < *bâšu* I

būštu → also *būrtu* II

bušṭītum, j/NB, NA *bu/alṭi(t)tu* "woodworm, termite"? Bab., NA [AN.TI.BAL] in granary; eats walls

būšum, *bušû(m)*, MA *bušiu* "goods, property" Bab., MA [NÍG.ŠU; NÍG.GÁL(.LA)]; OB usu. pl.; < *bašû*

bu'šu, *būšu* "stench" jB; also (a stinking plant); < *ba'āšu*

butinnu (or *putinnu*) "button" Am., jB lex.; on shoe, Am. of stone

butiqtu "(water-flow from) dam breach" jB, NA; < *batāqu*

butturu I ~ "with a mutilated leg" MB as name of a horse; < *butturu* II

butturu II "to mutilate"? jB lex. **D**; > *butturu* I; *mubattiru*

butturu → also *budduru*

butuqqû(m) "loss(es)" O/jB, in trade etc.; OA *butuqqā'ū* pl. tant. "shortfall, deficiency"; < *batāqu*

butuqtu(m); pl. *butuqātu(m)* "breach, cutting" Bab. [A.MAḪ] **1.** "breach" in dyke, bank, house;

b. batāqu "to make a breach"; "(water from) breach"; transf. ref. to Marduk's word, flow of blood **2.** "(new) cutting" for channel **3.** OA (a type of goods) **4.** jB "loss(es)"; < *batāqu*

buṭnānu, *buṭunānu* (a garden plant) Bogh., j/NB, NA; < *buṭnu*

buṭnatu → *buṭumtu*

buṭnu "terebinth, *Pistacia*" M/jB, NA as tree, for timber; "terebinth (nuts)" (coll.); > *buṭumtu*; *buṭnānu*

buṭṭuru → *budduru*

buṭumtu(m), *buṭuttu*, *buṭuntu*, *buṭnatu* "terebinth" Bab., NA [GIŠ.LAM.GAL] as tree, wood; nut(s); as flour; < *buṭnu*

buṭunānu → *buṭnānu*

buṭuntu, *buṭuttu* → *buṭumtu*

bu''û I "sought for" NB in fPN *Bu''ītu*; < *bu''û* II

bu''û(m) II, Bab., Am. occas. *buḫḫû* "to look for" Bab., M/NA **D 1.** "seek for" things, people; life, friendship etc. **2.** j/NB, NA *ina qātī X b.* 'look in X's hands' for s.th. = "call X to account" for s.th. **3.** M/NA leg. "attempt to start" proceedings **4.** M/NA "to demand, claim" **5.** Am., Bogh., Ug. "ask for, aspire to"; "intend" evil **Dtn** jB "keep seeking out" **Dt** (NA **Dtt**) pass. of D; > *bu''û* I; *ba''ītu*; *teb'ītum*; *mube'u*?

bu''uru I, *bûru*, Ass. *ba''uru* subst. "hunting" jB, NA, *b. epēšu* "to go hunting" of king, of falcon; "prey", transf. in love lyrics "quarry, catch"; < *bâru* I D infin.; → *mu'uru*

bu''uru II adj. "captured" jB; < *bâru* I

buwati → *puati*

būzu → *būṣu* II 2

D

da'ābu → *da'āpu*

da'āmu(m) I "to be(come) dark, dim" Bab.(lit.) **G** (*i/i*, *u/u*) [DARA4; MUD] of sun; esp. stat. of celestial bodies, eyes, torch etc. "is dark" **Gtn** OB of day "become dark" **D** "make dark, darken"; esp. stat., of celestial bodies, diseased parts of body **Dt** OB pass. of D; > *da'mu*; *da'īmu* I; *dāmātu*; *da'ummatu*, *da'ummiš*; *du''umu*, *du''umiš*

da'āmu II, *dâmu* ~ "to wander about" jB **G** (pres. *idâm*) **D** ~ "make to fumble"

da'ānatte "by force" NA; < *danānu* I

da'ānu → *danānu* I.II

da''ānu → *dayyānu*

da'āpu, NA also *da'ābu* "to push (away)" jB, NA **G** (*i/i*) "push, knock (against)" part of body; "push away" stool etc.; "knock down" weapon; NA "push ahead" troops **D** NA "repulse" revolt; "injure by pressure" the nasal septum **Dt** pass. of D "be pushed away" **N** of wall "be knocked over"

da'āqu → *damāqu*

da'atu → *di'atum*

da''atu → *dannatu*; *dannu* I

dababābum "idle talk" OB; < *dabābu* II

dababtu "talk; (faculty of) speech" jB, NA; *d. su/arrāti* "false talk"; *d. šapti/pî*; < *dabābu* I

dabābu(m) I "talk" Bab., NA [DU11; NA also DU11.DU11] "(idle) speech"; *d. kitti/kīnu* "honest, straightforward, talk", neg. *lā kitte*; "complaint", leg. "litigation", *bēl(et) d.* "adversary (in court)"; jB of inscription on bed, content of letter, document; < *dabābu* II infin.

dabābu(m) II "to speak, talk" **G** (*u/u*) [DU11.DU11] **1.** "talk" to (= *ana*), with (= *itti*) s.o.; *itti libbišu d.* "talk with o.'s heart, consider" **2.** "speak, tell" truth, lies; "make" impudent "remarks" etc.; "declare, make statement" in front of s.o.; NA "recite" **3.** "litigate"; j/NB *dīnu d.* "bring an action" (against s.o.); NB *itti X d.*, NA *issi X d.* "accuse X, prosecute X" **4.** "plot" s.th. (NA/NB *ina/ana muḫḫi*) **R** Mari **Gtn** "talk repeatedly" **Rtn** Mari **D** "talk much" **1.** OB "call on s.o. for" (= *ana*), "because of" (= *aššum*) services, payments etc.; "call s.o. to account", transf. of disease **2.** "complain" **3.** Bogh. for Š "cause to speak" **4.** jB "talk nonsense" **DR** Mari **Dt** "be called on"; "be claimed" **Š** "make s.o. speak, talk"; jB rit. "make s.o. say" prayer etc.; leg. "make s.o. declare", "make s.o. litigate"; "stir up, incite to gossip" etc.; "make" woman "compliant" **Št** NB "be made to speak"; > *dabābu* I, *dababtu*, *dababābum*; *dabūbum*; *dibbu*, *dibbatum*; *dābibu*, *dabbibu*; *dubbubiš*, *dubbubtum*; *mušadbibu*, *mušadbibūtu*

dabāru I mng. unkn. jB **G** lex. only; > *dabru*?; *mundabru*?

dabāru II subst. mng. unkn. jB lex.

dabašinnu(m), *tubašinnu* (a leather object) OAkk, Bab., Bogh.

dabatum → *tapatum*

dabbānu (a drug)? jB med.

dabbibu; f. *dabbibtu(m)* "slanderer" O/jB; jB also "garrulous"; NB in PNs; < *dabābu* II

dabbu **1.** NB ~ "bolt, pin"? in house construction **2.** jB lex. "bear"

dabdû(m), *dubdû*, Mari etc. *daw(a)dûm* "defeat, bloodshed" O/jB [BAD.BAD; BAD5.BAD5 (→

abiktu)] *d.* *dâku*/*maḫāṣu*/*šakānu* "to inflict a defeat"

dābibu "(legal) advocate"? M/NB in PN; < *dabābu* II

dabiru (a leather object) jB lex.

dabītu, dabium → *dabû*

dabnû (or *ṭ*/*dap*/*bnû*) mng. unkn. NB

dabru(m) ~ "aggressive" O/jB(poet.) of person, storm; < *dabāru* I ?

dabtu (a slab used in glass-making) jB

dabû, OAkk *dabium*; f. *dabītu(m)* "bear" OAkk, Bab.; also as (f)PN; > *dabûiš*

dabūbum "conversation" OB; < *dabābu* II

dabûiš "like a bear" jB; < *dabû*

dadā (a spiny plant) jB lex.

dadānu (a spiny plant) jB [GIŠ.KIŠI$_{16}$.ḪAB ?]

dâdānū, *diadānū*, jB also *daddānū* pl. tant. "tendon of the neck" O/jB

daddāmu → *damdāmu*

daddānū → *dâdānū*

daddariš "like centaury?" jB; < *daddaru*

daddaru(m), *daddiru* (a foetid plant, phps.) "centaury" Bab.

daddu(m); pl. f. ~ "sole" O/jB of shoe

daddu → also *dādu*

dadmū pl. tant. "villages, settlements; the inhabited world" Bab.(lit.)

dādu(m), M/NB also *daddu* **1.** "darling, favourite" of lover, father, son **2.** also pl. "sexual attractiveness" of male, female **3.** (a fish) [ÁB.KU$_6$] as food

dagālu(m) "to see, look" **G** (*a*/*u*) **1.** "look, (be able to) see", *lā dagāl īnī* "blindness" **2.** Bogh. "experience" **3.** stat. NB "has at his disposal, owns" **4.** OA "look upon (as security), reserve to o.s." **5.** "wait" **6.** "obey" **7.** NA *ēnē X d.* "'look at s.o.'s eyes', attend to s.o." **8.** *pān(ī) X d.* "await" s.o.; "obey" s.o.; Am. "show reverence"; *pān X d.* NA, NB of property "belong to s.o." **9.** *ana pān X d.* "wait for X" **Gtn** iter. of G of eyes "look repeatedly"; "aim" a bow "repeatedly"; *pān X d.* "constantly obey" **Gt** "belong to henceforth" **Š** caus. of G "make see, look", esp. in *pān(ī) X š.* "cause to wait for; make subject to"; NA (*ina*/*ana p.*) *š.* "hand over, transfer ownership of s.th. to s.o.; put under s.o.'s command"; "entrust" with a task **N** in jB *ana X iddagil* "attention was on X"; > *diglu*; *dagiltu*; *dāgilu*; *madgaltu*, *madgalu*; *mušadgilannu*; *šudugultu*

dagāru N jB mng. uncl.

dagiltu "observation" jB in *ša d.* "observer, spy"; < *dagālu*

dāgilu "one who sees" **1.** adj. of eyes "seeing", of man "sighted" **2.** in *d.* *iṣṣūr(āt)e* "augur, bird-watcher"; < *dagālu*

daḫru ~ "angry" jB lex.

daḫû I "beaten"? MA, desig. of textile; < *daḫû* II

daḫû(m) II, *deḫû* "to beat, press down"? O/jB, NA **G** OB, NA "push s.o. on"; stat. of part of exta "is depressed"? **Ntn** of kidneys "be always compressed"?; > *daḫû* I, *deḫû*, *deḫûtu*; *dīḫu*?

dā'ikānu(m) "murderer" Bab., MA; < *dā'iku* + *-ān*

dā'iku(m), *dayyiku*; f. *dayyiktu* "killer; murderer" OA, O/jB; OB also "murderous"; jB lex. as desig. of abortifacient stone = *aban lā alādi*; < *dâku*

da'īmu I "gloom" jB lex.; < *da'āmu* I

da'īmu II ~ "lance" jB lex.; → *id'umu*

dā'inūtu → *dayyānūtu*

da'iqtu → *damqu*

dā'išu(m) "thresher" O/jB desig. of worker, ox; < *diāšum*

dakāku I "to crush" jB **G** lex. only **D** "crush, grind up" drugs, in mortar; > *ḍakkukūtum*; *madakku*

dakāku(m) II ~ "to gambol, scamper" O/jB **G** (*u*/*u*) of lamb, donkey etc.; of child

dakāmu ~ "to bow down" jB **G** lex. **Ḍ** "prostrate" s.o., of disease ? lex.

dakāšu(m) ~ "to press in" O/jB **G** (*a*/*u*) om. of parts of body, stat. "are depressed"; jB med. "press on" s.o.; OB math. "press out, enlarge" geometrical figure **Gt** stat. *tidkuš(at)* "is pressed" OB of liver **D** ~ G of disease ? lex. only; > *dakšu*; *dikšu*, *dikištum*

dakirû ~ "tree" jB lex.

dakkannu(m) "doorway"? O/jB [KI.GIŠGAL]; < Sum.

dakkassu → *takkassu*

dakkukūtum (an edible commodity) OAkk(Ur III); < *dakāku* I

dakšu ~ "pressed down" jB; < *dakāšu*

dakûm (a kind of accommodation)? OB

dakû → also *dekû* II

dâku(m), Ass. *duāku(m)* "to kill; beat" **G** (*ū*) [GAZ] **1.** "kill" person; jB/NA "fight" (→ Gt) **2.** "beat" as punishment; "defeat" enemy, city in battle (→ *dabdû*); of disease and sim. "strike"; infin. *bēl(et) d.* "tormentor", of sorcerer **3.** OA "break (and so invalidate)" tablet **4.** "strike down" mountain; "kill" part of date palm by pruning **Gt** jB/NA "fight with each other", stat. pl. *tidūkū* **Š** O/jB "make s.o. kill s.o." **N** [GAZ] pass. "be killed"; *dīktu iddâk* "a massacre will take place"; > *dā'iku*, *dā'ikānu*; *dīku* I; *dīktu*; *madaktu*; *tidūku*

dakûtu → *dikûtu*

dalabānu → *dalbānu*

dalābu → *dalāpu*

dalāḫu(m) "to disturb, stir up" Bab., OA, NA **G** (*a*/*u*) [LÙ] "muddy" water, "blur" eyes(ight); "disturb, trouble" people, land; "disturb, worry" heart, mind; "embarrass, interfere with" s.o.; stat., of omens "are confused, obscure" **D** ~ G "disturb, trouble" people, water; of face "be blurred" with (= acc.) tears; lex., Am. "hurry" **Š** jB "cause disturbance" **N** [LÙ] pass. "be made turbid"; "be stirred up"; OB of fields "get mixed up" **Ntn** [LÙ.LÙ] iter. of N; > *dalḫu*; *dilḫu*, *diliḫtu*, *dulluḫtu*; *dulluḫiš*; *duluḫḫû*; *dulḫānu*; *dalḫāniš*; *mudalliḫu*

dalālu I "to be small, wretched" O/jB **G** OB stat. of part of liver "is stunted" **D** "oppress" s.o.; > *dallu*, *dallalu*?, *dalīlu* II?; *dullu*?; *dullulu*

dalālu(m) II "to praise" **G** (*a*/*u*) absol. "sing praise"; "praise" god, *dalīlī*/*tanatti*/*tanitti DN d.* "sing praises of DN"; jB *qurud DN d.* "praise valour of DN" **Š** caus. of G Bogh.; > *dalīlu* I; *tadlultum*

dalāmu (or *dalamu*) (a desig. of the underworld)? jB lex.

dalāpiš (or *dalapiš*), *dallapiš* adv. "awake" jB; < *dalāpu*

dalāpu(m), NA *dalābu* "to stir up; be sleepless" Bab., NA **G** (*i*/*i*) **1.** trans. "stir up, keep awake" **2.** intrans. jB/NA "stay awake"; stat. of god, human "is sleepless"; astr. "linger on" **Gtn** jB intrans. "stay awake all night; be always sleepless" **D** jB of enemy "disturb, harass" **Dtn** iter. of D **Š** j/NB, NA "stir up" **N** "become restless"; > *dalpu*, *dalpiš*; *dulpu*; *dalāpiš*; *diliptu*; *dullupu*; *šudlupu*

dal(a)qum mng. unkn. OB as PN

dalbānu(m), *dulbānu*, NB also *dalabānu*; pl. f. "intervening space" Bab.; Susa, math.; M/NB "passageway", also *bīt d.*; < Sum.

dalḫāniš "into a distracted state" jB with *ewûm* Š; < *dalḫu*

dalḫu "troubled, disturbed" j/NB, NA [LÙ] "cloudy" of water, beer; "obscure, confused" of illness, omen; of land, people "unstable, chaotic"; f. *daliḫtu* as subst. sg. & pl. "disturbance, (political) troubles"; < *dalāḫu*

dalīlu(m) I, M/NA *dilīlu*, usu. in pl. "praise" Bab., M/NA [KA.TAR] *d. DN dalālu* "to praise DN"; jB/NA *ana dalīlī* "to sing" the king's "praises"; also as PN; < *dalālu* II

dalīlu II 'poor creature' (a type of frog)? jB; < *dalālu* I ?

dalīqātu → *dulīqātu*

dālītum "bucket" OA, for drawing water; < *dālû*

dallalu 'poor creature' (a type of frog)? jB; < *dalālu* I ?

dallapiš → *dalāpiš*

dallu(m) "small, stunted" O/jB, NA of humans, as PN; OB of grain; < *dalālu* I

dallu → also *dalû* I

dalluqu → *dulluqum*

dalmāḫu → *talmāḫu*

dalpiš "restlessly" jB; < *dalpu*

dalpu "sleepless, restless; watchful" jB, of person; f. *daliptu* occas. = *diliptu* "restlessness", also pl.; lex. (desig. of gold); < *dalāpu*; → *dalāpiš*

daltu(m) f. "door" [GIŠ/GI.IG] *d. šamê*/*erṣeti* cosmic "door of heaven/underworld"; OB ext. (feature on breast of foetus); → *edēlu*

dalû(m) I, *dālu*, *dallu* "bucket" Bab., NA for drawing water; of bronze; NB *bīt d.* "land irrigated by bucket", opp. of *bīt mê*; < *dalû* II

dalû II "to draw" water "with bucket" **G** (*u*/*u*) [BAL], NB also "irrigate" field "with buckets"; > *dalû* I, *dalūtum*; *dālû*, *dālītum*, *dālûtu*; *dīlum*, *dilûtu* I.II; *dulû*; *madlā'um*; → *dullû*

dalû III (a needle or pin) jB lex.; < Sum.

dālu → *dalû* I

dālû "water drawer" M/NB [LÚ.A.BAL] as occupation; also 'dipper' (a bird); < *dalû* II; > *dālītum*, *dālûtu*

dâlu(m), Ass. *duālu* "to move, roam around" O/jB, NA **G** (*ū*) "walk, run around" of human, demon, fox, dog, NA of boat; NA "be active in service"; "prowl" of ghosts, demons **D** "disturb, disrupt" s.o. **Š** Mari "make s.o. run around"; > *dayyālu* I, *dayyaltu*, *dayyālītu*

dalūtum; pl. *daluwātum* "bucket-irrigated field" Mari; < *dalû* II

dālûtu "function of a water drawer" NB; < *dālû*

damāmiš "into (a place of) lamentation" OB; < *damāmu*

damāmu(m) "to wail, moan" OA, O/jB(lit.) **G** (*u*/*u*) of person; of animal "howl"; "creak, rustle" of reed-bed, house, bricks **Gtn** (*a*/*a*, *u*/*u*) "moan, howl persistently" of person, animal (or Ntn ?) **Š** caus. of G "make" people "wail", pigeons "coo" **N** ~ G, OB **Ntn** → Gtn ?; > *damāmiš*; *dimmu*, *dimmatu*; *dumāmu* II

damāqu(m), NA also **da'āqu* "to be(come) good" **G** (*i*/*i*; NA stat. *de'iq*, *dêq*) [SIG_5; stat.

also AL.SA6] **1.** absol. of person, god, object, part of body; of proceedings etc. **2.** Mari "be friendly" **3.** of person, household "prosper, have success, have good luck"; om. "be propitious" [also KAL] **4.** *ana/eli/ina maḫri-/ ina pān X d.* "be pleasing to" s.o. **D** [SIG5] **1.** "improve s.th. in quality, embellish, beautify, polish" **2.** "carry out" proceedings, work etc. "well, properly"; of deity "make" s.o.'s dreams, fate "pleasant"; "make" prayer "acceptable" **3.** NA in hendiad., e.g. *dammiqā epšā* "do it well!" **4.** "do good, do a favour" to (= OB *ana*, jB acc.) s.o.; OA, OB "supply, loan" s.th. "as a favour (*tadmiqtum*)" **5.** Bogh. "approve (of)" **Dtn** OB "continually make good" **Š** jB "make" omen etc. "propitious"; > *damqu, damqam-īnam; damqatu; damqiš; dumqu, dumuqtum, dumuqqû; dumāqū; dummuqu, dummuqtum; mudammiqu, mudammiqatu; tadmīqu, tadmiqtum*

damāṣu ~ "to humble o.s." jB **G** (*u/u*) "prostrate o.s." **Gt** ~ G; > *damṣum*

damāšu ~ "to wipe"? jB lex.; > *dumšu*

dāmātu, *da'mātu* pl. tant. (a dark-yellow paste) jB, NA? [IM.SIG7.SIG7] in medical, glazing recipes; in foundation deposit; on clay figurine; < *da'mu*

damdāmu, *damdammu, daddāmu* (a kind of mule) O/jB [ANŠE.NUN.NA]

damgāru → *tamkāru*

damgiru mng. unkn. jB in *binût d.*

damiqtu → *damqu*

damkāru → *tamkāru*

dammuqu → *dummuqu*

damqam-īnam, *daqqam-īnam, damqa-īni* 'good eye' jB desig. of ocular defect; < *damqu* + *īnu* I

damqatu (a plant) jB lex.; < *damāqu*

damqiš "well; kindly" Bab., OA [SIG5]; < *damqu*

damqu(m), NA also *danqu, daqqu*; f. *dami/eqtu*, MA *da'iqtu*, NA *dêqtu* "good" [SIG5] **1.** adj. of animal, goods, object "of good quality"; morally "good" of person; physically "handsome, beautiful"; "capable, qualified" of soldiers etc.; "good, favourable" name, words, deed, price, omen, message; "kind" of deity, eyes, hands; Mari, MB(Alal.), Am., Bogh. "notable, well-to-do" **2.** M/NA, NB *(mār) damqi* [A/DUMU.SIG/SIG5] (a kind of soldier)? **3.** f. *damiqtu(m)* as subst., sg. & pl. [SIG5- ; MUNUS.SIG5] "good fortune"; with *qabû* etc. "to speak well on behalf of, intercede for" s.o.; jB *amāt d.* "good word"; with *epēšu* "to do a good deed, a kindness"; < *damāqu*; > *damqiš, damqam-īnam*

damṣum, *danṣum* "humble" OB; < *damāṣu*

damšillu (a kind of cucumber)? jB as name of one or more plants

damtum I, *tamtu* O/jB mng. uncl.; Mari phps. "blood, lineage"; < *dāmu* ?

damtu II, *dattu* ~ "form, shape"? jB lex.

damû → *dawûm*

dāmu(m) "blood" [ÚŠ] **1.** liter. sg. & pl.; jB, NA *tābik d.* "shedder of blood"; *(aban) dāme* [NA4.ÚŠ] 'blood-stone' (name of a stone) **2.** transf. *bēl d.* "murderer"; pl. "bloodshed; bloodguilt"; OA pl. "blood-money" **3.** jB pl. "blood" = "lineage" **4.** lex. "red wine" **5.** *dām(ū) erēni(m)* 'cedar-blood' = "cedar resin" as aromatic; > *damtum* I?; → *ḫilidāmu*

dāmu → also *da'mu*

dâmu → *da'āmu* II

da'mu(m), *dāmu* "dark" O/jB [MUD; DARA4] blood, weather; lex. "dark (paste)"; f. pl., lex. "dark wool"; < *da'āmu* I; > *dāmātu*

danāniš "by force" jB; < *danānu* I

danānu(m) I, M/NA *da'ānu* "power, strength" O/jB, M/NA [KALAG] of god, king, enemy; *ina d.* "by force"; "severity" of cold weather; ext. ~ 'reinforcement' (part of liver); < *danānu* II infin.; > *danāniš; da'ānatte*

danānu(m) II, M/NA *da'ānu* "to be(come) strong" **G** (*i/i*) [KALAG(.GA)] liter. and transf., of god, king, person, animal etc.; of city, weapon, watch, reed, part of liver; "be heavy" of injury, disease, debt, NB deficit; "be hard, severe" of terrain, road, weather, work; transf. "pressurize" s.o. (= dat.), of words "be tough, threatening"; OA of silver, cloth etc. "be hard to come by"; with *pānu* of attitude "become hard, harden" **D** "make strong; reinforce" person, building, fortress; parts of body, esp. liver; guard, watch; shouting, grief, fire, treaty, bondage; NA/jB "increase" tribute; jB "assign permanently, bequeath s.th. to s.o."; OAkk, OB "make" work "solid"; "make" words, letter "tough, threatening"; OB *pānī- d.* "harden o.'s attitude" **Dt** pass. "be reinforced, strengthened" **R** (*udanannin*) of part of liver "be of even thickness" **Rt** (*uddanannin*) "match o.'s strength"; > *dannu* I, II?, *dannatu, iddanna*?, *dannūtu, danniš, dannišam, adanniš; da'ānatte; danānu* I, *danāniš; dandannu, dandannūtu; dunnu, dunnānu*?; *dunnunu, dunnuniš, dunnuttu*?; *madnanu; tadnintum*

dandannu, NB also *dannudannu* "all-powerful" M/NB, NA(lit.) as divine, royal title; < *danānu* II

dandannūtu "all-powerfulness" jB; < *dandannu*

danene → *dannina*

daništum (a type of service obligation)? OB

danītu (or *dannītu* ?) (a battle garment) jB lex.

**danna* → *iddanna*

dannatu(m), NA also *da''atu* [BAD4; MUNUS.KALAG.GA] **1.** "fortified (place), fortress" [NA É.KALAG] **2.** "foundation, building site" **3.** Ass. "firm, binding (agreement)", also pl.; NA of conveyance document **4.** "distress, famine, difficulty" **5.** *d. šattim* "hard time of year", *d. kuṣṣim*/*ummatim* "depth of winter/height of summer" **6.** also pl. "strict (command), firm (order)", "threatening, harsh (words)" **7.** (a mark on the exta) **8.** (part of the construction of a window); < *dannu* I; → *iddanna*

dannina/u, *danene* "nether world" O/jB

danniš "very; severely"; < *dannu* I; → *adanniš*

dannišam "very much" OA; < *dannu* I

dannītu → *danītu*

dannu(m) I; NA f. also *da''atu* "strong, powerful, mighty, great" [KALAG(.GA)] of god, king, people, country; animal; of city, fortress, building, building material, implement, weapon, cloth; of mountain; "firm" of statement, command; OA *ṭuppum dannum*, MA *dannutu* "binding document"; "strong" of oath; "urgent" of business, message; "hard, difficult, severe" of terrain, weather, disease, distress, onslaught; "high" of prices; NA "big"; < *danānu* II; > *adanniš*, *danniš*, *dannišam*, *dannatu*, *dannūtu*; → *d.* II

dannu II; pl. NB *dannūtu*, NA *dannāni* "(large) vat, barrel" j/NB, NA; for bread, spices, dates, beer etc., usu. wr. ^{dug}*d.*; *d. kaspi* "silver barrel" in cult; < *d.* I ?

dannudannu → *dandannu*

dannūtu(m) "strength, power" Ass., O/jB [KALAG- ; NAM.KALA(.GA)] **1.** divine "power", human "strength" **2.** "fortress", also *āl d.* "fortified city" **3.** OA "strong, harsh (statement)"; < *dannu* I

danqu → *damqu*

dansum → *damṣum*

danû(m) mng. uncl. OA, jB **G** (*i*/*i*) jB of house "to be of inferior quality"?; OA "disparage (without reason)"?; > *dunnâtu*; *dunā'ū*

dāni- → *dinānu*

dânu → *diānum*

dapānu(m) ~ "to bear down on violently, hurtle towards" O/jB(poet.), jB lex. **G** (*a*/*u*) of chariot; transf. of deity; > *dapnu*, *dapniš*; *dapīnu*, *dappānu*, *dappinu*

daparānum → *daprānu*

dapāru → *duppuru* I; *ṭapāru*

dapatum → *tapatum*

dapdappum → *ṭapṭappum*

dapīnu(m) "overbearing, savage" Bab., NA(lit.) epith. of god, king, lion etc.; astr. = Jupiter, also Procyon [$^{d/mul}$UD.AL.TAR]; < *dapānu*

dāpi'u (or *ṭāpi'u*) (a container) NA, of silver

dapniš "aggressively" O/jB; < *dapnu*

dapnu(m) "aggressive" M/jB(lit.) of god, enemy; battle; < *dapānu*; > *dapniš*

dapnû → *ṭabnû*

dappānu "warlike, martial" M/jB(lit.); < *dapānu*

dappastu → *tappaštu*

dappinnum → *tappinnu*

dappinu "very warlike" jB lex.; < *dapānu*

dappu(m) **1.** OB *d. ša dāmim* "blood clot"? **2.** jB astr. mng. unkn.

dappu → also *adappu*

dappurtum "absence" OA in *d. rašûm*/*išûm* "to be(come) absent, default"; < *duppuru* I

daprānu(m), OB also *daparānum*, *duprānu* "juniper" Bab., NA as timber; as drug; *šaman d.* "juniper oil"; jB *qēm d.* "juniper flour"

daqāqu "to be minute, fine" **G** not attested **D** "crush minutely" enemy, wall; like potsherds; > *daqqu*; *diqqum*, *daqqiqu*, *daqqaqu*, *daqqaqīta*; *duqāqu*; *duqququ*; *diqdiqqu*

daqāšu(m) "to bend down" **G** (*u*/*u*) OB; (*i*/*i*) jB, of person

daqqam-īnam → *damqam-īnam*

daqqaqīta adv.? "tinily"; < *daqqaqu*

daqqaqu in pl. *daqqaqūtu* "tiny ones" jB lex.; < *daqāqu*; > *daqqaqīta*

daqqiqu "very tiny" jB lex.; < *daqāqu*

daqqu(m) "minute, fine" OAkk, O/jB of person in PN; of corn, stone, metal "pulverized"; f. pl. "small amounts left over" of silver, food OB; < *daqāqu*

dar → *darāru* II

dār → *dāru* I

dārâ, MB(Alal.) *dāria* "for ever" M/jB; < *dārû*

daraggu "way, track" jB

darāgum → *darākum* II

darāku I "to follow"? **G** not attested **D** lex. only; > *darku*

darākum II (or *darāg*/*qum*) ~ "to pack up" OA, textiles

darāku III **D** "to thresh" NA; < Aram.; > *mudarriktu*

darānu (a plant) jB lex.

dārânu "for ever" jB lex.; < *dārâ* + *-ānu*

darāqum → *darākum* II

darāru(m) I ~ "to move freely" O/jB **G** lex. only **N** (*nadarruru*) of pig "roam free"; OB of silver "become free" of debts; of gods "run together, converge"; > *andurāru*; *šudarāru*?

darāru II "to intercalate" a month NA **G** (*a/u*; stat. *dār*); < *dīru* denom.; → *derû*

darāru → also *andurāru*

darāsu(m), Bogh. *darāšu* "to trample; push back" Bab., NA **G** (*i/i*) people; OB "repulse"; "trample back, clear"? reeds; O/jB of parts of liver "press down"? **Gt** jB "push each other away" **D** OB "push away, repudiate" wife **N** "be pushed aside"; > *darsu*; *dirsum*

darāšum I "to try"? OB **G** (*i/i*)

darāšu II mng. unkn. jB lex. **G** of wound

darāšu → also *darāsu*

dārâtu → *dārītu* 2

dardarah, *tartarah* ~ "buckle"? MB, of gold, copper etc.; on shoe

dargiš ~ "couch" NB of wood

dargu "stair" NB in *bīt d.* "staircase"; < Aram.

dāria → *dārâ*

dāriāta, *dāriātiš*, *dāriātum* → *dārītu* 2

darikum → darku

darīku; pl. *darīkānu* "pressed dates" NB; < Aram.

dāriš "for ever" Bab., NA; also *ana d.*, *ad-d.*; Am., Bogh., Ug. *adi d.*; OB *d. ūmim/ūmī*; < *dāru* I

dārišam "for ever" jB(roy. inscr.); < *dāru* I

dārītu(m) "perpetuity, eternity" Bab., NA **1.** sg. OB(Susa), Mari *ana d.* "for ever"; Am., Bogh. *ištu/ultu d.* "from time immemorial", *adi d.* "for all time" **2.** freq. pl. *šubat d.* "eternal abode"; *kudurri d.* "eternal boundary"; OB *ana d.* "for ever"; Am. *adi dāriāta*, jB *ša dārâti* "for ever"; OB *dāriātiš ūmī* "for ever"; jB *ana dārât šanāti* "for all years"; < *dārû*

dariu → *darrûm*

dāriu → *dārû*

darku, *derku*, OB also *darikum* "following, later" OAkk, OB as PN, also fPN *Darkatum*; Bab.(lit.) *nišē darkāti* "later people", also f. pl. as subst. "successors, posterity"; < *darāku* I

darkullu → *tarkullu*

darrûm, M/NA *dariu*; MA pl. f. "sacrificial sheep" OB(Susa), M/NA [UDU.SIZKUR.MEŠ] M/NA *d. epāšu* "to sacrifice a sheep"; < Sum.

darsu "deposed" M/NA of gods; < *darāsu*

darû(m) "to last (for ever)" OAkk, O/MB, NA, stat. only; in PNs of person; OB *lū dariāta/i* "may you live for ever"; NA *adi ... darûni* "as long as" (heaven and earth) "last"; > *dāru* I, *dāriš*, *dārišam*; *dārû*, *dārâ*, *dārânu*, *dārītu*, *dārûtu*, *dārûtaš*; *dūru* II, *dūriš*

darû → also *derû*

dāru(m) I "era; eternity" OAkk, Bab., NA; OAkk, OB only st. abs., OAkk *ištum dār* "from time immemorial", OB *ana/ad-dār* "for ever", MB *an dār*; j/NB *ana (ūmī) dāri* "for ever"; Ug. *ana dāri dūri* "for ever and ever"; < *darû*; > *dāriš*, *dārišam*; → *dūru* II

dārum II ~ "lifetime, 60 years"? OB; < W.Sem.?

dāru → also *dūru* I

dārû(m), *dāriu(m)* "lasting, eternal" Bab., NA [DA.RÍ] of gods, royal offspring; of life, kingship, days, years, protection, good deeds etc.; of foundation, temple, wood etc.; < *darû*; > *dārâ*, *dārânu*, *dārītu*, *dārûtu*, *dārûtaš*

darūba (an animal) jB (or scribal error ?)

dārûtaš "for ever" jB; < *dārû*

dārûtu "long lasting life" NA; < *dārû*

dāṣtu ~ "treachery, disrespect" M/jB; esp. pl., as omen interpretation; < *dâṣu*

dâṣu(m) "to treat unjustly, with disrespect" O/jB **G** (*ā*) "pressurize"; jB ptcp. *dayyiṣ amātīya* "that treats my words with disrespect" **D** → *mudiṣṣum*; > *dāṣtu*

dašannu (an item of jewellery) NA, NB of silver

dašāpu(m) "to be sweet" O/jB **G** lex. only, of honey (*dišpu*), dates **D** "make sweet"; stat. transf. of song, sexual charms "are very sweet"; < *dišpu* denom.; > *dašpu*; *duššupu*

dašari "(a type of) palace" NB; < OPers.

dāšâtu → *dēšû*

dašgarinnum → *taskarinnu*

dašnu(m) ~ "mighty" O/jB

dašpu(m) "(honey-)sweet" Bab.; of beer, fruit; of person, also as PN; < *dašāpu*

da(š)šiya (a functionary) NB

daššu(m), *taššu* "buck; ram" OAkk, Bab., M/NA, Nuzi [MÁŠ.GAL] **1.** "buck" male of gazelle, goat, also "ram" of sheep **2.** pl. f. (a metal fitment with a leather strap ?), on furniture etc.; → *mašgallu*

dāšû → *dēšû*

dâšu → *diāšum*

daš'um "spring" OA, as time of year; → *dīšu* II

dāšūš → *idāšūš*

dāt, *dāti*, *dātu-* "behind, after; then" NA in comb. with *ina*, *ana* **1.** as prep. spatially: "behind", *iddātukka* "behind you", *iddāt šarri* "behind the king"; occas. *addāt* **2.** temporally: "after", *iddātuššu* "after him", *iddāt annî* "after this", also *addāt*; as conj. *ina dāt ša ... tašpuranni* "after ... you wrote to me" **3.** adv. *iddāti/e* "afterwards"

dātabarra "legal expert" NB; < OPers.; → *dātu*

dāti → *dāt*

datnu ~ "warlike" jB lex.; < W.Sem.

dattu → *damtu* II

datûm "member" of a family ? OB

dātu "law, decree" NB; < OPers.; → *dātabarra*

dātu(m) → also *di'atum*; *ṭātu*

dātu- → *dāt*

da'tu (part of a plough) jB lex.

da'û (or *ṭa'û*) adj. mng. unkn. jB

da'ūdu mng. unkn. jB lex.

da'ummatu(m) "gloom, darkness" O/jB(lit.) as natural phenomenon; med., mag. of physical condition; < *da'āmu* I

da'ummiš "in pitch dark" jB, also astr. [DAR4-*meš*]; < *da'āmu* I

da'umtu (a cup) jB lex.

daw(a)dûm → *dabdû*

dawûm, jB *damû* "to jerk; convulse" O/jB **G** (*u/u*) of person; of limb "jerk", of eyes "move in uncoordinated manner" **Gtn** iter., of body; > *dāwûm*, *dimītu*; → *ṭawûm*

dāwûm ~ "convulsive"? OB lex.; < *dawûm*

dayyālītu f. "prowling" of witch jB; < *dayyālu* I + *-ī*

dayyaltu ~ "(hunting) foray" NA; < *dâlu*

dayyālu I **1.** jB "prowling" of dog **2.** NA ~ "scout", *rab d.* "scout commander" **3.** jB lex. (desig. of gold); < *dâlu*; > *dayyālītu*

dayyālu II "servant" NB; < Aram.

dayyantu, MB also *diyantu* "(female) judge" [MUNUS.DI.KUD-] M/jB, epith. of goddesses; < *dayyānu*

dayyānu(m), *da''ānu*, MB also *diyānu* "judge" [(LÚ.)DI.KUD] of human beings, occas. as royal title; as divine title; NA *ša pān d.* "president of tribunal"; < *diānum*; > *dayyānūtu*, *dayyantu*

dayyānūtu, NA *dā'inūtu* "judicature, judgeship" O/jB, NA [DI.KUD-]; < *dayyānu* abstr.

dayyaštu "threshing sledge" jB/NA in simile; < *diāšum*

dayyāšu adj. "threshing" of ox jB lex.; < *diāšum*

dayye (a plant) jB lex.

dayyik(t)u → *dā'iku*

dayyiqu "siege wall(s)" jB, NA

deḫû "depressed, pressed in"? jB lex.; < *daḫû* II; > *deḫûtu*

deḫûtu "depression"? O/jB lex.; < *deḫû*

dekû I "raised" NB of hands; < *dekû* II

dekû(m) II, *dakû* "to raise, shift" OAkk, Bab. **G** (*e/e*, *i/i*) [ZI] **1.** "call up, levy" troops, land **2.** "wake up" person **3.** "unleash, stir up" battle, slander **4.** "lift" hand in supplication, as threat; from work; "raise" eyes, head, arms (in surrender) **5.** OB "collect" silver, taxes **6.** M/NB "lift, remove" s.o. from throne, seat; stele, crown, commodity etc.; "clear away" earth, beam, monument **7.** NB ~ "break up" or "weed" field **8.** "charter" a ship **D** "get s.o. moving, incite" **Š** OB, NB "have (troops) called up"; "incite" s.o., s.o.'s heart, to action **N** pass. "be called up"; "be disturbed"; NB of hands "be taken off" (ref. to inactivity); > *dekû* I, *dēkû*; *dīku* II, *dikûtu*; *mudekkû*, *mudakkiu*?

dēkû(m) "summoner (for taxes and corvée work)" Bab. [LÚ.ZI.ZI]; lex. also "(night-) watchman"; < *dekû* II

dēlum "unique, single" OB lex.; < Sum.

dēnu → *dīnu*

dēpu I "warp" jB lex., of textile; < *dêpu*

dēpu II (a thrusting weapon)? j/NB [DUN4] of iron; jB ext. (part of liver); < *dêpu* ?

dêpu "to lay" the warp jB lex.; > *dēpu* I, II?

dêq → *damāqu*

dêqtu → *damqu*

derderru ~ "battle" jB lex.

derku(m) (desig. of a priest)? OB lex.

derku → also *darku*

derkullum → *tarkullu*

derû, NA *darû* "to intercalate" a month NA, NB **G** stat. "is intercalated" **Dt** NB pass. "be intercalated"; < *dīru* denom.; → *darāru* II

deššû "exceedingly opulent" jB of offerings?; < *dešû*

dešû(m) "to sprout" Bab.(lit.) **G** jB lex. only **D** "let flourish" greenery, plants; "let prosper" abundance, wealth; "provide (s.th./s.o.) copiously with (s.th.)" (= 2 acc.), "supply copious" offerings **Dt** pass. of D "be allowed to flourish"; of offering bowl "be copiously supplied" **Dtn** jB iter. of D; < *dīšu* II denom.; > *dēšû*; *deššû*; *duššû*; *dūšum* I; *mudeššû*

dēšu → *dīšu* II

dēšû(m), *dāšû* "abundant, flourishing" O/jB of population, vegetables; < *dešû*

diadānū → *dâdānū*

diānum, later *dânu* "to judge" **G** (*ī*) [DI.KUD] **1.** *dīna(m) d.* "administer justice" (to s.o. = acc.) **2.** "give judgement" **3.** "pass judgement on, sentence" s.o. **4.** "litigate, engage in lawsuit" **D** OB *dīnam/dīnātim d.* "initiate litigation" **N** of decision "be pronounced"; > *dīnu, dittum; dayyānu, dayyantu, dayyānūtu; Madānu*

diāšum, later *dâšu* "to tread down; thresh" Bab., NA **G** (*ī*; j/NB also *ū*) of cattle, people "tread out" corn, "thresh"; transf. "trample, tread down" countries, enemies etc. **Gtn** iter. **D** jB "trample down"; > *dīšu* I; *dā'išu, dayyāšu, dayyaštu*

di'(a)tum, *da'atum*, OA, jB lex. *dātu(m)* "knowledge, information" OA, OB, jB lex.; only in *d. šâlum* "to inquire after" s.th., s.o.; usu. neg., e.g. *di'atī ul tašāl* "you took no notice of me"; < *edû* II

di'ātu → *dimtu* II

dibalû → *dipalû*

dibbatum "argument, chatter" OB; < *dabābu* II

dibbu(m); OB pl. f. "words, utterance" Bab., NA; j/NB, NA "talk, rumour; matter"; Nuzi, NB "(legal) claim(s)"; < *dabābu* II

dibdibbu (or *ṣissippu* ?) "clepsydra" jB lex.; < Sum.

dibḫu → *ṭibḫu*

dibiru ~ "calamity" jB lex., om.

diblu → *tublu*

didabû, *didibû* "scribal apprentice, pupil" NA

didakku (a functionary) NB

didallum, *ditallu, didilu* "ash(es)" O/jB lex.; < Sum.; > *ditalliš*

didānu → *ditānu*

didbû (a door) jB lex.; < Sum.

didennūtu → *titennūtu*

didibbû "(court) judgement" jB lex.; < Sum.

didibû → *didabû*

didilu → *didallum*

didiqqum → *diqdiqqu*

didišû (feature on liver) jB ext.; < Sum.?

dīdū pl.; du. *dīdā* (female garment) M/jB, NB(Susa); loosened, torn, of temple attendant, prostitute, goddess, Lamaštu

digalu, digilu → *diglu*

digīmu → *ṭikmēnu*

digirû "god" jB lex.; < Sum.

diglu(m), *diga/ilu* "vision, view" Bab., NA med. "(power of) sight, vision", *d. ēnē* "eyesight"; OB "view, opinion"; "glance, look"; j/NB (a precious stone)?; < *dagālu*

diglû (a metal object, phps.) "mirror" M/jB, NA; < *dagālu* ?

diḫme(n)nu → *ṭikmēnu*

dīḫu ~ "mark" (on the liver)? jB ext. ~ "depression"; < *daḫû* II ?; OB → *ziḫḫum*

dīḫu → also *di'u* I

dikēnu, dikīmu → *ṭikmēnu*

dikištum ~ "extension"? OB math.; < *dakāšu*

dikkuldû "legal opponent"? NB; < Sum.

dikmennu, dikmēnu → *ṭikmēnu*

dikšu(m) "bulge, swelling" O/jB on body, on liver; lex. "diaphragm" of stomach ?; OB math. (part of geometrical figure); < *dakāšu*

diktu(m), lex. also *tiktu* (a type of flour) Bab.; jB lex. (a plant)

dīktu(m) "fighting, slaughter" Bab., NA **1.** O/jB "fight", OB pl. "blows" **2.** j/NB, NA [GAZ(.MEŠ)] in *d. dâku* "to massacre", *d.-šunu ma'atta adūk* "I massacred them in great numbers"; < *dâku*

dīku I **1.** Bogh., jB, NA "killed" **2.** M/jB "killed" by pruning of date palms, reed etc.; < *dâku*

dīku(m) II "lifting, raising" j/NB "awakening"; "levy, raising (of troops)"; *d. bīti* (a temple ceremony); OA (*ina d.* >) *iddīk qātimma* ? 'at the lifting of a hand', i.e. immediately; < *dekû* II

dikuggallu(m), *diqun/ggallu* "chief justice" Bab. [DI.KUD.GAL] **1.** OB(Hana) an official **2.** M/NB of deity, esp. Šamaš; < Sum.

dikurû "judgement, verdict" jB lex.; < Sum.

dikûtu(m), occas. *dakûtu* "levy" of workers, troops Bab.(lit.) **1.** OB ~ "corvée work", *d. alākum* "to report for duty" **2.** M/jB "levy", *d. māti* "country(-wide) call up"; *erib d.* 'levy locusts', i.e. swarm; < *dekû* II

dilbu → *dulbu*

dilḫu(m) "disturbed state" O/jB **1.** of river water "turbidity" **2.** of person "confusion", of country "disruption"; < *dalāḫu*

diliḫtu "disturbed condition" MB(Susa); < *dalāḫu*

dilīlu → *dalīlu* I

diliptu(m) "sleeplessness, anxiety" O/jB; < *dalāpu*

dilīqātu → *dulīqātu*

dilītu (a stringed instrument) jB lex.

dillatu (a cereal) jB lex.

dīlum "(bucket) irrigation" OB; < *dalû* II

dilûtu I "(action of) bucket irrigation" jB *mê d.* "water drawn by bucket"; < *dalû* II

dilûtu II, *dulûtu(m)*; pl. *di/ulâtu* "device for water drawing, shaduf?" O/jB; < *dalû* II

dimānu (an insect) jB

dimātiš I "like towers" jB; < *dimtu* I

dimātiš II "in tears" OB; < *dimtu* II

dimgur, *dimmigirru* (a kind of wood)? NB for furniture; < Sum.?

dimītu jB **1.** (a bird) **2.** (an illness, phps.) "convulsions"; < *dawûm*

dimmaḫḫu (a priest) jB lex.; < Sum.?

dimmatu(m) "wailing, lamentation" O/jB; *ša d.* "mourner"; < *damāmu*; → *dimtu* II; *zimmatu*

dimmerû "god" jB lex.; < Sum.

dimmetu (a vegetable) jB lex.

dimmigirru → *dimgur*

dimmu "wailing" subst. jB of child; < *damāmu*

dimmu → also *timmu*

dimmuššatu (or *timmuššatu*) ~ "reed-thicket" jB lex.

dimtu(m) I, M/jB also *dint/du* "tower" OAkk, O/jB [AN.ZA.GÀR; Ug. É.AN.ZA.GÀR] "watch-tower", also "(garrison of) tower", as part of wall, of quay; fortified dwelling, also as PlN *D.*, *D.-DN*, *D.-ša-PN*; Nuzi "district, estate (centred on stronghold)", also *bēl d.* (an administrative official); Mari ^{giš}*d.* "wooden siege tower"; OB (a feature in oil omens); jB "pyramid" of skulls; > *dimātiš* I

dimtu(m) II, *dintu*, M/jB also *dindu*; oft. du. *dimā-*; pl. NA *di'āte* "tear" Bab., NA [ÉR], freq. + *alāku* "to flow"; NA *di'āt pāni* "tears (on) face, weeping"; > *dummû*, *dimātiš* II; → *dimmatu*

dimurû (a substance) NB

dinānu(m) "substitution", *ana dinān X alāku* "to go as a substitute for X; give o.s. up to X, lay o.'s life down for X" freq. in introduction of letters; jB *ana d. nadānu* "to give as substitute"; *ṣalam d.* "substitute figure"; OB *ana d.*, MB *aššu d.* "for the sake of", NB letters *ana dānika*, *add-* 'for your sake' = "please"; → *andunānu*; *ardanānu*

dindu → *dimtu* I.II

dingiruggû pl. "the dead (primordial) gods" jB [DINGIR.UG$_5$.GA]; < Sum.

dinnamû → *dunnamû*

dinnû, *dinnûtu* (or *tin...*) ~ "bedstead" O/MB, jB lex. [GIŠ.(NÁ.)AŠ.NÁ/NE]

dintu → *dimtu* I.II

dinû (a kind of flour) NB

dīnu(m), Ass. also *dēnu(m)*; pl. m. & f. "legal decision; lawsuit, trial" [DI; DI.KUD] **1.** "judgement, sentence", *d. diānum/dânu* "to pass verdict"; *d. gamāru* "to pronounce final sentence", *d. gamru* "completed case"; OA *d. kārim* "verdict of *kārum*", OB *d. bīt Šamaš* "verdict of temple of Šamaš" **2.** "decision" of deity, *d. šakānu* "to give a decision" (by omen) **3.** "legal provision, statute" **4.** "legal case, issue", OB *d. amārum* "to look into, examine a case"; *d. parāsu* "to settle a case" **5.** "lawsuit, trial", *d. šūḫuzu* "to grant a lawsuit", *d. napištim* "case of life or death"; *d. epēšu* "to institute legal proceedings" against (= *itti*) s.o.; M/NA *dēna dabāba ba''û* "to initiate legal proceedings"; NB *d. dabābu* "to bring an action against"; NB *d. u ragāmu* "lawsuit and claim"; *bēl d.* "adversary" (in court), OB also *ša dīniša* "her adversary"; NB *bīt d.* "law-court"; NA *ša pān dīnāte* "president of court"; < *diānum*; > *dittum*

dipalû (or *dibalû*) "distortion of justice" jB [DI.BALA]

dipāru(m) m. & f. "torch" Bab. [GIŠ/GI.IZI.GAR] *d. našû*, *d. napāḫu/nuppuḫu* "to raise, light a torch"; transf. "torch" as title of astral deities

dippu(m) (a kind of wooden door); < Sum.

diqāru(m); pl. f. "large bowl, tureen" Ass., O/jB [(DUG.)ÚTUL] of clay, stone, copper, bronze; for oil, perfume, water, medicine, food; "trough" for animals

diqārūtu (a small bowl) jB lex.

di(q)diqqu(m), *duqduqqu*, *dugudug* "wren"? O/jB also as PN; < *daqāqu*

diqqum "small, meagre" OB of provisions; as PN; < *daqāqu*

diqungallu → *dikuggallu*

dirigûm "intercalary month" OB [DIRIG ?]; < Sum.; → *dīru*

dirītu → *ṭerītu* II

dirratu(m), *tirratu* "lash (of whip)" O/jB **1.** jB *d. qinnāzi* "whiplash" (an astronomical phenomenon) **2.** OB(Bogh.) ~ "halter" of donkey ?

dirru → *diru'u*

dirsum "trampling back, clearing"? OB, process on reeds; < *darāsu*

dīru **1.** j/NB, NA "intercalation" **2.** NB "intercalary month"; < Sum.; > *darāru* II; *derû*; → *dirigûm*

diru'u, *dir(ru)* (a kind of bread) NA lex.

disḫu → *tišḫu*

diskarinnum → *taskarinnu*

dīṣtum; pl. *dīṣātum* "abuse(s)" Mari; < *dâṣu*

dišarru ~ "oats" jB lex.

dīšā'u, *dīšī'u*, *tīšā'u* "of, born in spring" Nuzi, of animals; < *dīšu* II

dišḫu → *tišḫu*

dišiptuḫḫu, *diziptuḫḫu* ~ "sweet beer" jB lex.; < *dišpu* + *tuḫḫu* ?

dīšī'u → *dīšā'u*

diškû → *tiškû*

dišpu(m) "honey, syrup" [LÀL(.MEŠ)] *d. šadî* "mountain honey" [LÀL.KUR.RA]; *d. suluppi* "date syrup"; > *dašāpu*; *dišiptuḫḫu*

dīšu I "trampled down" of palm tree jB lex.; < *diāšum*

dīšu(m) II, *dēšu* "(spring) growth; spring" Bab. [Ú.BAR8(.SAR)] O/jB *d. ebūri, kuṣṣi* "summer, winter growth", "grass"; as time of year "spring"; NB as PN; MB *dīš mīli* "spring flood"; > *dešû*; *dīšā'u*; → *daš'um*

ditalliš "into ashes" j/NB, usu. *d. ušēmi* "reduced to ashes"; < *didallum*

ditallu → *didallum*

ditānu, *didānu* "bison"? jB; also (a fish)

ditennūtu → *titennūtu*

ditillû "final judgement" OAkk, jB lex.; < Sum.

dittum "lawsuit" OA; < *dīnu* nom. unit.

di'tu → *di'atum*; *dimtu* II

dium → *tium*

di'u(m) I (or *dī'u(m)*), *dīḫu(m)* (a disease affecting the head) Bab., NA [SAG.GIG] also *muruṣ d.* "*d.* illness"; jB as demon; > *dī'ûm*

di'u(m) II, *d/tû*, *d/tu'u* "(deity's) throne-platform" in temple Bab. [DU6]; < Sum.

dī'u → *di'u* I

di'ûm "afflicted by headache" OB; < *di'u* I

diyantu → *dayyantu*

diyānu → *dayyānu*

diziptuḫḫu → *dišiptuḫḫu*

dû → *di'u* II

duāku → *dâku*

duālu → *dâlu*

duārum "to surround, enfold" OAkk **G** stat. only

du(b)bāqu → *tubāqu*

dubbubiš "into incoherent speech" jB; < *dabābu* II D

dubbubtum "(troublesome) negotiation(s), complaint(s)" OB; < *dabābu* II

dubbuqu D "to join together" Ug.; < W.Sem.

dubdû → *dabdû*

dubdubbē adv. mng. unkn. jB lex.

dubdubbu **1.** (a bird) jB lex. **2.** (a drum) jB; < Sum.

dubgallu "big tablet, compendium" jB; < Sum.; → *ṭuppu*

dublu → *tublu*

dubsarmaḫḫu "chief scribe" jB lex.; < Sum.; → *ṭupšarru*

dubur "foundation" jB lex.; < Sum.; → *tublu*

dudittu → *tudittu*

dūdu(m) I (a metal vessel) Bab., Am., Nuzi, Ug., NA

dūdu(m) II (a bird) jB lex.; NA as PN ?

dūdu → also *atūdu*

dugānu → *tugānu*

dugdumu (or *dukdumu*) (a plant) jB lex.

duglum (or *duk/qlum*) (a commodity) OA

dugsānu → *dunsānu*

dugsigakku (a vessel) Bab. lex.; < Sum.

dugudû → *guduttû*

dugudug → *diqdiqqu*

duḫarum → *tuḫarum*

duḫḫusu, also metath. *dussuḫu* **D** "to oppress" s.o. **Dt** pass., of person "be oppressed", of penitent "be depressed, downhearted" M/jB

duḫnu, *tuḫnu* "millet" M/NA, M/NB

duḫpu(r) → *tuḫpu(r)*

duḫšûm → *dušû* I

dukdumu → *dugdumu*

dulāqum mng. unkn. OB as PN

dulbānu → *dalbānu*

dulbu(m), *dilbu*; pl. f. "plane tree (*Platanus orientalis*)" OAkk, M/jB; as tree, as timber; OA pl. as commodity

dulḫānu "meteorological disturbance" jB; < *dalāḫu*

dulīqātu, Ass. also *da/ilīqātu* pl. tant. ~ "roast corn"? M/NA, jB; as offering

dullu(m); pl. m. & f. "trouble; work, service" **1.** "trouble, hardship"; *d. mullû(m)* "to fill with misery, make full of misery" **2.** "work obligation, corvée"; *d. emēdu* "to impose corvée work"; NA *d. šarri* "royal service"; building, manufacturing "labour" etc. **3.** "work", *d. ṣabātu* "to set to work"; *d. epēšu/muššuru* "to do/neglect work"; "(product of) work"; "craft" **4.** religious "ritual"; < *dalālu* I ?

dullû D "to lift out, unload" dates NB; < Aram.

dulluḫiš adv. "in confusion; hurriedly" jB; < *dalāḫu*

du(l)luḫtu **1.** "hurry, despatch" Am., Ug. **2.** "anxiety" NB of person's state; < *dalāḫu*

dullulu "oppressed" jB of citizens; < *dalālu* I

dullupu "very restless" M/NB as PN; < *dalāpu*

dulluqum, MA *dalluqu* mng. unkn. OB, MA as PN

dulpu "sleeplessness" jB; < *dalāpu*

dulû "bucket" jB lex.; < *dalû* II

duluḫḫû "disturbance" M/jB **1.** "turbidity" in river **2.** "confusion" of person's state **3.** political "disorder"; < *dalāḫu*

dulūtu → *dilūtu* II

dumāmu I, *tu(m)māmu* ~ "leopard" jB

dumāmu II "moaning" jB; < *damāmu*

dumāqū pl. tant. "jewellery, gems" Ass.; of women, king, divine statue; < *damāqu*

dumbunātu → *tumbunātu*

dummû D "to bring to tears" jB, esp. stat. "is brought to tears"; < *dimtu* II denom.

dummuqtum "good deed, benevolence" OB; < *damāqu*

dummuqu(m), Ass. *dammuqu(m)* **1.** OA, OB "good quality" of metal **2.** "very good" of sheep, action; also NB as PN; NA pl. *dammaqūte* (a type of soldier)?; < *damāqu*

dumqu(m), *dunqu*, *duqqu* "goodness, good (thing)" [SIG5] **1.** "welfare" of person; pl. *dumqī qabû(m)* "to decree s.o.'s wellbeing" **2.** "good condition; good appearance, beauty" of person, face etc. **3.** "good deed" OB pl. f., *gimil d.* "reward; return favour"; Mari *bēl d.* "favourite, friend" **4.** "favourable, lucky meaning" of dreams, omens etc. **5.** "good results" **6.** "the best" of s.th., "prime" produce etc.; < *damāqu*

dumšu ~ "towel" jB lex.; < *damāšu*

dumugabû(m); f. *dumugabītu(m)* "baby, suckling" O/jB [(MUNUS.)DUMU.GABA]; < Sum.

dumuqqû "sign of gratitude" jB; < *damāqu*

dumuqtum "good deed, favour" OA; < *damāqu*

dunānu → *andunānu*

dunā'ū pl. tant. ~ "deductions"? OA; < *danû*

dunnamû, *dinnamû* "person of lowly status; fool" jB; < Sum.

dunnānu "strong one"? jB mag.; < *dunnu* ?

dunnâtu f. pl. "inferior quality" NB of commodity; < *danû*

dunnu(m) **1.** OAkk, Bab. "power, strength" [KALAG.GA] jB *d. eriyāti* "intense cold"; *d. qaqqari* "solid ground, bedrock"; *d. qišāti* "depth of the woods"; transf. *dunni pānī* "hardness of attitude" **2.** Ass. "(fortified) farm(stead)", also *(bīt) d.*; Bab. in PlNs **3.** Bab. (a type of bed)? **4.** jB "part of lung"; < *danānu* II

dunnuniš "very firmly" jB; < *dunnunu*

dunnunu "very strong" jB; of fortifications; Bogh. adv. *dunnuna* "very securely"; NB of person "highly respected"; < *danānu* II; > *dunnuniš*

dunnuttu "strengthening"? jB lex.; < *danānu* II ?

dunqu → *dumqu*

dunsānu, *dugsānu* (a vessel) OB; < Sum.

duppuru(m) I **D** Bab., OA "to move away, withdraw; stay away" from; OA "absent o.s. from work"; > *dappurtum*; → *ṭapāru*

duppuru II adj.? mng. unkn. jB lex.

duppussû, *tuppussû* "younger brother" j/NB(lit.), also transf. "second in rank"; < Sum.

duprānu → *daprānu*

dupšikku → *tupšikku*

duqāqu(m) "tiny" O/jB lex., as PN; < *daqāqu*

duqdu "almond (tree)" NA; → *šiqdu*

duqduqqu → *diqdiqqu*

duqqu → *dumqu*

duqququ "very tiny" jB; < *daqāqu*

dūrāniš "over the wall" jB; < *dūru* I + *-ān* + *-iš*

durāru → *andurāru*

durā'u "arm" NA, also "foreleg" of sheep; < Aram.

durdû "goddess" jB lex.

durgallu "(reed) rope" jB lex.; < Sum.

durga(r)rû (a stool or chair) jB lex.; < Sum.

durgu, *duruku* ~ "innermost, central part" M/jB(Ass.) of mountain terrain, foundations; of royal origins *ša d.-šu Aššur* "who is of pure Assyrian descent"

durinnum → *turinnum*

dūriš "for ever" Ug.; < *dūru* II

durmāḫiš "to the *durmāḫu*" jB

durmāḫu 'mighty hawser' jB, cosmic reed rope; < Sum.; > *durmāḫiš*

durrû(m) D "to neglect, reject"? Mari, O/jB lex.

dūru(m) I, OB also *dārum* ? "(city) wall, rampart" [BÀD; OA, Mari BÀD.KI; OAkk pl. BÀD.BÀD] **1.** "city wall"; transf. of DN as protection in PNs; jB reed "fence" of shepherds' camp **2.** "fortified place, fortress"; *bīt d.* jB, NA "fortress", NB "(temple) enclosure" **3.** of parts of the body: *d. appi* "cheeks"; *d. naglabim* "pelvis"? of sheep; *d. libbi(m)* "heart wall"; jB *d. šinni* "gums"?; > *dūrāniš*

dūru(m) II "permanence, eternity" Bab., NA **1.** OB "permanent status" of employment, land tenure **2.** NA *issu d.* "since long ago"; Susa st. abs. *ana dūr u pala* "for ever and always"; j/NB *(ana/ša) d. ūmī* "(for) all time, always"; *(ana) d. dār(i)* "for ever"; < *darû*; > *dūriš*; → *dāru* I

dūru III "lance" jB lex.

duruku → *durgu*

durummu (a bird) jB lex., om.; → *turunnu* I

durušsu "foundation (platform)" Bab. of city, temple; "base" of mountains; transf. of dwelling, support

dusinnum (or *d/tus/ṣinnum*) ~ (potential claimant) OA, of purchased slave, house

dussuḫu → *duḫḫusu*

dususu (a plant) jB lex.

duṣinnum → *dusinnum*

dušmû, *duššumû*; f. *dušmītu* "slave born in the house" Bab., also transf. "servant" of deity; MB(Alal.) in PN; > *dušmûtu*

dušmûtu "status of a slave born in the house" jB; < *dušmû*

duššû "abundant, copious" j/NB(lit.) of water, offerings; of tavern, storeroom "well-stocked"; < *dešû*

duššubu → *duššupu*

duššumum mng. unkn. OAkk, OB as PN

duššumû → *dušmû*

duššupu(m), *duššubu*, Ass. *daššupu* "sweetened; very sweet" O/jB, NA(lit.) of beer, wine, dates; < *dašāpu*

dušû(m) I, OB also *duḫšûm* **1.** O/jB, NA ~ "quartz, rock-crystal" [(NA4.)DUḪ.ŠI.A] **2.** ~ "untanned leather"? [(KUŠ.)DUḪ.ŠI(.A)]; M/NA *eleppāt/ša d.* "rafts of (inflated) skins"; NA, NB *ṣārip d.* "tanner of *d.* leather"; < Sum.; → *tuḫšiwe*

dušû II (a well)? jB lex.

dūšum I (a silver object) OAkk; < *dešû*

dūšu II mng. unkn. jB lex.

dūtu(m) "virility, manliness" O/jB; transf. Nuzi "codpiece" of armour, jB "nook, secret place" of house, shrine etc.

du'u → *di'u* II

du''umiš "in great darkness" OB; < *du''umu*

du''umu "very dark" jB; of skin markings; < *da'āmu* I

Du'ūzu, *Dûzu* "Tammuz" (4th Bab. month) j/NB [ITI.ŠU(.NUMUN.A/NA); ITI.ŠU.GAR.NUMUN.NA]; < Sum.

E

ē → *ai* I

e'a → *ya'u*

Eannakkum "(the temple) Eanna" OAkk; < Sum.

e'āṣu → *wiāṣum*

Ea'ūtu "Ea-ship" j/NB [^{d}DIŠ- ; ^{d}IDIM-], i.e. the rôle of the god Ea; < DN Ea

ebaḫu → *ibaḫu*

ebar "beyond, the other side of" OA; < *ebēru* I

ebaruttum → *ibrūtu*

ebberu → *ebbiru*

ebbiāte → *ebû* I

ebbiru, *ebberu* "pacing, travelling purposefully" M/jB; of knees; < *ebēru* I

ebbiš "in a state of (ritual) cleanliness" jB; < *ebbu*

ebbu(m) "bright; pure" Bab., NA [DADAG(.GA)] "bright, shiny" of metal, precious stone; of wood; "clean" of clothes, water; "pure" of offerings, rituals; of mythical beings; OB "reliable"?, also as subst. ~ "trusted agent, colleague"; < *ebēbu*; > *ebbiš*, *ebbūtum*

ebbûm → *ibbû* I

ebbūbu(m), *enbūbum*, *embūbu* "flute, pipe" Bab. [(GIŠ.)GI.GÍD (→ also *malīlu*)]; songs *ša e.* "with the flute"?; *ša e.* "flute-player"; *e. ḫašî* "windpipe"; → *umbūbu*

ebbūtum "position of trusted colleague" OB; Mari ~ "administrative control"; < *ebbu*

ebēbu(m) "to be(come) bright, pure" **G** (*i*/*i*) "be clean" of hands, "clear" of illness, impurity, omen; "be free" of claims **D** [DADAG] "cleanse", "purify (ritually)", "keep pure"; leg. *pūta ubbubu* 'clear the forehead', i.e. "manumit"; "clear" s.o./o.s. of guilt, claims; "free" s.o. from duties; Mari "take census of" **Dt** [DADAG] "be purified, cleared"; Mari "be counted in census" **Š** ~ D NB "purify" **Štn** OB iter. **Št** NB pass. of Š; > *ebbu*, *ebbiš*, *ebbūtum*; *mubbibum*; *tēbibtu*; *ubbubu*

ebēḫu "to gird, belt up" O/jB **G** (*i*/*i*) person with (= acc.) garment; "surround" building with frieze (*nēbeḫu*); stat., of moon "is encircled" **D** stat. "is surrounded with" **N** astr. "be encircled"; > *ebīḫu*; *nēbeḫu*

ebēḫu → also *ebīḫu*

ebēlu "to net, catch with a net" jB **G** (*i*/*i*) birds, Anzû; < *eblu* denom.?; > *ēbilu*

Eber nāri "across the river", i.e. Syria west of Euphrates NA, NB; < *ebēru* I + *nāru* I

eberta(m) "on the opposite bank" O/MB [MB BAL.RI] *ina*, *ana*, *ša e.*; Nuzi also "on (this) bank"; < *ebertu* I

ebertān "on the opposite bank" M/NA, Nuzi, Bogh., jB; *ina*, *ištu*, *ša e.*; as prep. *e. nāri* "on the other side of the river"; < *ebertu* I

ebertu(m) I "bank, esp. opposite bank; other side" Bab., MA [BAL.RI]; as prep. *(ša) eberti* "(land) across" river, canal; < *ebēru* I; > *eberta*, *ebertān*; → *abartu*

ebertu II "pace; step" M/NA; also of staircase; < *ebēru* I

ebēru(m) I, NB occas.*epēru* "to cross over" **G** (*i*/*i*) [BALA] river, sea, sky etc.; ext. "stretch over, lie across" **Gtn** iter. of G **Š** "make to cross, get s.o./s.th. across, bring across"; > *ebar*, *Eber nāri*; *ebertu* I.II; *eberta*, *ebertān*; *ebbiru*; *abartu*; *nēberu*, *nēbertu*; *mušēbiru*, *mušēbirtu*; → *šutēburum*

ebēru II "to paint (the face)" jB lex.; > *ebrum*, *ibāru*

ebēru III "joy, celebration"? jB lex.

ebēṭu(m) I "to swell up" O/jB **G** (*i/i*) of water; of parts of body; stat. "is swollen" **Gt** "be permanently swollen"? **D** "make swollen"; lex. "fill (with joy)"? **Dt** pass. of D lex. "be filled (with joy)"? **N** "swell up, become swollen" **Ntn** iter. of N; > *ebṭum*; *ubbuṭu* I.II

ebēṭu(m) II ~ "to bind"? **G** MB(Bogh.), NA stat. "is bound" **D** (OB *ḫubbuṭum*) OA, OB mng. uncl. **N** jB "be bound"?; > *ubbuṭu* III; *nēbettu*; NB → *ubbuṭu* IV

ebīḫu, *ebēḫu*, *ibīḫu* (a rope or girdle) Bab., M/NA; also transf., of city wall; < *ebēḫu*

ēbilu ~ "hunter" (with a net) jB lex.; < *ebēlu*

Ebirtum, *Ḫe/ibirtum*, *Abirtum* (month at Mari) OAkk, OB

ebissu, *ibissu*; pl. *ebilāte* "(roped-up) bundle"? NA of saplings, reeds; < *eblu*

ebītu, *abītu* (a plant) jB lex.; < W.Sem.

eblu(m) "rope, thong, string"; as surface measure (= 6 iku or $^1/_3$ bur); NB "field of 1 *eblu* area"; "string" (of dried fruit); > *ebēlu*; *ebissu*; → *ḫabalum*

ebrum "painted, made-up" OB lex.; < *ebēru* II

ebru → also *ibru*

ebṭum ~ "swollen" OB lex., of part of body; < *ebēṭu* I

ebû(m) I; f. pl. *ebbiāte* "thick" O/jB, NA of worm, loaves, trees; "dense" of eclipse; < *ebû* II

ebû II "to be thick" M/NA, M/jB **G** of plant "become thick"; stat. of part of body, urine, rim of pot "is thick"; > *ebû* I; *ibītu*; *ūbu*, *ubātum*; *mūbû*; *mumbium*

ebūbatu "wood, thicket" jB lex.

ebuḫušinnu → *abaḫšinnu*

ebūrâtu → *ebūrû*

ebūru(m), *ibūru*; pl. MA, NB *ebūrānu* "harvest; summer" [BURU$_{14}$] "crop, harvest"; "yield" of orchard; "(activity of) harvesting"; "(time of) harvest", *waraḫ E.* "Harvest month" (= *Abu* II ?); NB "(grain for) harvest, seed(-corn)"; > *ebūrû*

ebūrû(m) adj. "summer" Bab. "(born in) summer" as PN; "summer (lamb)" [OB SILA$_4$.BURU$_{14}$], "summer (vegetables)" (f. pl.) of cucumbers; < *ebūru*

ebuṭṭum (or *ebuttum* ?) "interest-free loan" OA

edābu → *edēpu*

edadû (a flour offering) jB; < Sum.

edakku(m) "outhouse, wing (of a building)" O/jB [É.DA]; < Sum.

edakkû "fish-bone" OB lex.; < Sum.

Edammītu (a title of Ištar) jB lex.; < *edammû*

edammû(m) (a dream-interpreter) O/jB; < Sum.

edamukku, *adamukku* jB **1.** "foetal membrane"? **2.** (a membrane) as drum-skin ?; < Sum.

ēdāniš "alone" jB(Ass.); < *ēdēnu*

ēdāniu → *ēdēnû*

edānu(m), *idānu*, Mari(Ass.) *ḫe/idānum* "fixed time" Ass. "time limit, appointment"; "(repayment) date"; Bab. → *adānum*

ēdānu → *ēdēnu*

ēdānû → *ēdēnû*

edappātu, *eduppātu* ~ "fringe of a towel" jB lex.; Nuzi. sg. *edaptu* ?; < Sum.; → *adapu* II

edaqqu ~ "small child" jB lex.

edātu pl. mng. uncert. MB

eddātu → *eddittu*

eddēlu "he who locks" jB; < *edēlu*

eddeššû → *eddēšû*

eddeštum "new town" OB; < *edēšu*

eddešu → *edešu*

eddēšû(m), *eddeššû* "constantly self-renewing" O/jB of deities, esp. heavenly bodies; of life, reign; < *edēšu*

eddidu (a kind of thorn-bush) jB; < *edēdu*

eddittu; pl. *eddētu*, Am. *eddātu* (a kind of thorn-bush) O/jB, Am.; < *edēdu*

eddu(m) "pointed" O/jB of horns; < *edēdu*

edēbu → *edēpu*

edēdu(m) "to be(come) pointed, spiky" Bab., OA **G** (*u/u*; stat. *ēd*, *edud*) [stat. *ēd* SIG] of parts of body, horn; of horns of moon, sun etc. **Gtn** OB uncl. **D** stat. ~ G "is pointed"; OB in hendiad. "look sharp, do s.th. quickly"; OA "pressurize"? s.o. **N** stat. ~ G "becomes pointed"; > *eddu*; *eddidu*, *eddittu*; *iddum*; *mēdedu*; *udittu*

edēḫu(m), *edēkum* "to cover with patches, with a network" O/jB **G** stat. "is spotted" of stone, face, moon; of entrails "are patchily covered" with tissue **D** "cover (objects) with a network" of wool; stat. ~ G stat. "is patchily covered with (= acc.)" tissue, with network of veins; > *ēdiḫum*; *mēdeḫtum*

edēkum → *edēḫu*

edēlu(m) "to shut, bolt" **G** (*i/i*, Am pret. *īdul*) [TAB] door, city gate; house; hand, mouth; "shut (s.o.) off" from (= *ina*) **Gtn** iter. **D** ~ G door, gate **Dt** pass. of D **N** "be shut, bolted"; "shut o.s. up"; > *edlu*; *eddēlu*; *idiltu*; *mēdelu*; → *daltu*

edēmum → *adāmum*

edēnā (a plant) jB lex.

ēdennu → *ēdēnu*

ēdennû → *ēdēnû*

ēdēnu, *ēdānu*, *ēdennu*, *īdīnu* "alone" M/NB + pers. suff. e.g. *ēdēnukka*, *ēdēnuššu* "on his own; alone"; Nuzi "single" [LÚ.DIL], i.e. without family; < *wēdum* + *-ānu*; > *ēdēnû*; *ēdāniš*

ēdēnû, *ēdennû*, Ass. *ēdāniu*, *ēdānû* "single, sole, lone" M/jB, NA of messenger; of things often in pairs, e.g. horses; of village "isolated"; < *ēdēnu* + *-ī*

edēpu(m), *edēbu*, NA *edābu* "to blow (away)" O/jB, M/NA **G** (*i*/*i*) of demons "blow on" s.o. (= acc.); "blow away"; stat. "is inflated" with (= acc.) **D** ~ G of storm; revolts; stat. "is inflated" **N** MA "be blown away" **Ntn** iter.; > *edpu*?; *idiptu*; *uddupu*

edēqu(m), *adāqu* "to dress, clothe" Bab.(lit.) **G** (*i*/*i*) "clothe" body with (= acc.) **D** ~ G divine statue **Dt** pass. of D "be arrayed in" **Št** OB "have o.s. dressed in" **N** "get dressed, arrayed in" (= acc.); > *tēdīqu*

edēru(m) "to embrace, wrap o.s. round" O/jB **G** (*i*/*i*) person, person's neck; of features in exta; astr. of moon's horns **N** "embrace one another" [GÚ.DA.RI] of persons; lizards; heaven and earth; stat. "have conspired"; > *ēdiru*; *nanduru* II

edešu (or *eddešu*) "bud"? jB lex.; < *edēšu* ?

edēšu(m) "to be(come) new" **G** (*i*/*i*) of clothes, building; "be renewed" of person, god; OAkk infin. *edēšumma* "anew" **Gtn** "constantly renew o.s." of Sîn **D** "renew" [GIBIL] building, clothing, dais etc.; "resume" journey; "restore" life, cult; Mari in hendiad. "repeat" action **Dtn** iter. of D **Dt** pass. of D; > *eššu* I, *eššūtu*, *eššiš*; *uššušu* III; *eddeštum*, *eddēšû*; *tēdištu*; *edešu*?

edigu → *udugu*

ēdiḫum, *ēdikum* "basket mender"? OB, also as PN; < *edēḫu*

ediltu → *edlu*

edinu, OA *idīnum* "desert, steppe" jB lex.; OA mng. uncl.; < Sum.

ediptu, *adiptu* mng. unkn. jB lex.

edirtu → *idirtu*

ēdiru (a garment) jB lex.; < *edēru*

ēdiš "alone" jB; < *wēdum*

ēdiššī- → *wēdiššī-*

edištu → *eššu* I

edlu "shut, bolted; inaccessible" M/jB of door, house; bolt; road; "locked up" of prisoner; < *edēlu*

edpu mng. uncl. jB desig. of sheep's hoof; < *edēpu* ?

edû(m) I, occas. *adû*, *atû* "flood, wave" O/jB of river "flood, spate"; "wave(s)" of sea; as epith. of king; < Sum.

edû(m) II, *idû(m)*, OA *idā'um* "to know" (M/NA → *wadûm*) **G** (pret. only, *īde* (→ GAG §106q)) [ZU]; *ina lā idê* "unwittingly"; stat. "is aware of", also "is known" to s.o.; "know" that = *kī(ma)*, how much = *mala*, where = *ēma*, *ašar*; "be acquainted with" s.o., s.th.; "be conscious of" prayer, guilt; "experience" defeat, fear; "know" person sexually; Am. with *ana* "care for" s.o. **D(t)** → *wadûm* **Š** "cause to know", "acquaint s.o. with s.th." (= acc.), *abullam š.* "show s.o. the city gate", i.e. confine to city; "make s.th. known, convey, make pronouncement" **Št** "inform oneself"? **ŠD** → *wadûm* **N** (*ni*/*endû*) "become acquainted"; > *di'atum*; *edûtu*; *mūdû*, *mūdûtu*, *mūdânūtu*; *šūdûtu*; *mušēdû*; *udû* II?

ēdu → *wēdum*

ēdû → *wēdûm*

eduk → *edūtu*

ēdukku → *wēdum* 5

edullānu → *edulnu*

edullû (an administrative building)? j/NB [É.DUL]; < Sum.

edulnu (or *edullānu* ?) (a functionary) NA lex.

ēdumānu "single" NA i.e. without family [AŠ-]; < *wēdum*

eduppātu → *edappātu*

edurû → *adurû*

edūtu "sleeve"? jB lex. (var *eduk* erron.?)

edûtu, *idûtu* "knowledge, awareness" jB lex.; < *edû* II

ēdūtu "isolation" jB in *ēdūtiya* "by myself"; < *wēdum*

e'ēlu(m), *a'ālu* "to bind (on)" **G** (pres. *i''il*, pret. *ī'il*) "tie up", "tie on to"; "bind" with spells, with legal contract **Gt** ~ "tie all round" **D** ~ G NA (with pl. obj.); NB "make" contract "binding" (on s.o.); stat. of water, foam "is attached together, collects together" **Dt** pass. of D, of water "be collected" **Št** "link" hands; stat. of hands "are linked, folded together" **N** pass. of G of rope; of illness "be attached to, infect" s.o.; > *i'lu*; *e'iltu*, *u'iltu*; *e''ēlu*; *mêlu*?

e''ēlu, *ē'ilu*, *a''ālu* "binder" jB lex., mag., desig. of a demon; < *e'ēlu*

egalkurrû "ritual for entering palace" j/NB [É.GAL.KU$_4$/KUR.RA]; < Sum.; → *ēkallu*

egalturrû f. "little palace" jB [É.GAL.TUR.RA]; < Sum.; → *ēkallu*

egāru "to write down"? MA **G** stat. "is written down"; > *egertu; ugurtu*

egēgu → *ekēku*; *eqēqu*

egemgiru, *egengiru*, *gim/ngiru*, *gergirû* (a medicinal plant, phps.) "*Sisymbrium officinale* or *Eruca sativa*" M/NB [Ú/GIŠ.NÍG.GÁN.GÁN]

egerrû, O/jB also *igerrû(m)*, NA *gerrû* "utterance" Bab., NA [INIM.GAR] "ominous utterance" relating to s.o.; "spoken opinion, reputation", *e. dummuqum/lummunum* "to speak well/ill" of s.o.; *bēl(et) e.* "slanderer (m., f.)"; < Sum.

egertu, *igertu* "inscribed tablet" NA, NB of letter, legal document; < *egāru*

egēru(m) "to lie (transversely) across" O/jB **G** (*i/i*) of animal across a person, another animal; transf. of language "be perverse, difficult" **Gtn** Mari, of enemy "continually thwart" s.o. **Gt** "lie across each other, be crossed over" of animals, parts of liver; transf. "be in disagreement" with s.o.; of heart "be perverse, wrong" **D** mag. "twist" feet of a figurine **Š** mng. uncl. **Št** [GIL] "cross" feet "over each other"; stat. of parts of body "are crossed over each other" **N** "limp, go lame"? **Ntn** med. of feet "continually cross over each other"?; transf. of tongue (speech defect); of animal "continually cross (a path)"?; > *egru*; *etguru*; *tēgirtu*?; → *egāru*

eggetu → *ekketu*

egiddû → *agittû*

egiṣītu → *igiṣītu*

egītu, jB also *igītu*? "negligence, omission" M/NB *e. Ellil* "negligence towards Ellil"; "(sin(s) of) omission"; < *egû* I

egizaggû, *igizaggû*, *igizangû* (an ornamental stone) jB/NA [NA4.IGI.ZAG.GA/GÁ; NA4.IGI.ZÀG.GÁ], also in mag.; < Sum.

egru(m) "transverse, crossed" O/jB, NA of birds, in representation; transf. of language "difficult"; of enemy "perverse"; < *egēru*

egu, *igu*, *egû*, *agû* (a kind of camel-thorn) jB lex.

egû I "negligent" OB lex., jB; f. *egītu* (a class of person); < *egû* III

egû II, *eqû* "antimony (paste), kohl" jB

egû(m) III "to be(come) lazy; be negligent" OAkk, Bab.; M/NA in PNs **G** (*u/u*, *i/i*) "be negligent" towards (= *ana*) deity, person; with respect to (= *ana*) work, task; > *egû* I; *egītu*, *egûtu*; *mēgûtu*; *tēgû*?

egû → also *agû* II; *egu*

egubbû → *agubbû*

egumû(m) "hot water" OB lex.; < Sum.

egusu mng. unkn. jB lex.

egûtu "negligence" jB "(act of) negligence" by diviner; < *egû* I

eguzû mng. uncl. OB lex.; < Sum.

eḫē (a cry of lament) jB

eḫele; pl. *eḫelena*, also abbr. *eḫē* (a type of land tenure) MB(Alal.); *mārū e.* (a social class); < Hurr.

eḫlipakku, *eḫla/upakku* "raw glass" Qatna, Am., Nuzi, Bogh.; < Hurr.

eḫrušḫu (or *uḫrušḫu*) (a vessel) Alal.; < Hurr.

eḫzu(m) (a kind of axe) O/jB [URUDU.GÍN.MUNUS] used on fields

e'iltu(m), *i'iltu(m)* "bond, obligation" O/jB "debt, liability"; OA "obligation" of offerings, jB "obligation" to deity (pl. also *ellētu*), esp. with *paṭāru* (to absolve); < *e'ēlu*

ē'ilu → *e''ēlu*

ēkâ, *ēkâma/e* "where?" M/NB; < *ayyikâ*; > *ēkânu*

ēkalliš "into the palace" jB [É.GAL-]; < *ēkallu*

ēkallītu → *ēkallû*

ēkallu(m) f., rarely m.; Mari pl. occas. *ēkallānu* "palace" [É.GAL; NA also KUR] as building; *ē. māšarti* "review p., arsenal"; *ē. kutalli* "rear p."; *ē. tapšuḫti*, *ē. ṣalāli* "p. of rest", i.e. royal tomb; OB(Susa), Nuzi (part of a private house); as administrative authority, i.e. "the government"; *rab(i) ē.* "palace overseer" [GAL.É.GAL]; *ša ē.* "queen" [prob. MUNUS.É.GAL; MUNUS.KUR]; *ša muḫḫi ē.*, *ša pān ē.* "palace supervisor"; < Sum.; > *ēkalliš*, *ēkallû*, *ēkallūtu*; → *egalkurrû*, *egalturrû*; *ērib-ēkalli*

ēkallû(m) "palace official" O/jB [(LÚ.)ŠÀ.É.GAL]; f. *ēkallītu* j/NB, NA [MUNUS.ŠÀ.É.GAL] "queen(-mother)?"

ēkallūtu → *arad-ēkallūtu*

ēkâma/e → *ēkâ*

ekannam → *akanna* I

ēkânu "where?" NB *ana ē.* "whither?"; < *ēkâ* + *-ānu*

ekdiš "furiously" OB; < *ekdu*

ekdu "wild, furious" Bab. of animal, king, warrior; < *ekēdu*; > *ekdiš*

ekēdu(m) **G** mng. uncl. OB **D** ~ "to revile, slander" jB; > *ekdu*, *ekdiš*; *ukkudu*

ekēku, *egēgu(m)* "to scratch" O/jB **G** (*i/i*) **Gtn** iter. of G **D** ~ G **Dt** "scratch o.s." (or → *takāku* ?); > *ekketu*; *ukkum* I?; *mēkeku*

ekēlu(m) "to be(come) dark" **G** (*i/i*) of sun, moon etc.; divine image; transf. of face, situation etc. **Gtn** "repeatedly become dark"

Gt "become permanently dark"; infin. "condition of darkness" **D** "darken" **Dt** pass. of D; > *eklu, ekletu, ekliš; iklu* I; *uklu* I; *ukkulu, ukkuliš*

ekēmu(m) "to take away, deprive" **G** (*i/i*) [KAR] "take s.th. away" from (= acc.) s.o., usu. unjustly; "rescue" (from adversity); "deprive" s.o. of sleep, joy, life, potency; ext., of feature of liver, stat. "is displaced"?; "absorb, lie over" another feature **Gtn** "repeatedly take away" **Gt** ext. "(mutually or fully) absorb, lie over" **D** ~ G MB "carry away" population **N** pass. of G, OB of fields; > *ekmu; ekkimu, ekkēmu; ikimtu; ukkumu; nēkemtu*

ekēpu(m), NA also *eqābu* ~ "to come close, approach" **G** (*i/i*) in space, time; to girl, sexually; Mari "come up with intent to" temple (< W.Sem.) **Gt** "come very close to"?; stat. "is very near" **D** of time "draw near", "be in good time, early", trans. of Adad "bring" rain "early, in good time" **Št** OA of textiles "pack tightly together"; of cedars, hair "grow close together" **Ntn** or **Nt** of animals "come close together" for copulation; > *nēkepum; ukkupu, ukkupiš; tēkuptum*

ekēṣu mng. unkn. jB lex.; > *akṣu* ?, *ekṣiš* ?

ēkīam "where?, whither?" jB; < *ayyikīam*

ekiltu → *eklu*

ekkēmu(m) "robber" O/jB; < *ekēmu*

Ekkena (a month) OB(Alal.); < Hurr.

ekketu(m), *eggetu* "itching, scabies" Bab.; < *ekēku*

ekkimu(m) "rapacious, thieving" O/jB esp. of demons; < *ekēmu*

ekletu(m) (or *iklētu(m)*) "darkness" Bab. [KÚKKU]; *bīt e.* "dark chamber", "underworld"; < *eklu*

ekliš "gloomily" jB; < *eklu*

eklu(m) "dark" Bab. of day, water; transf. jB of person *ekil pānī* "with gloomy face"; f. *ekiltu* "dark (times)"; f. pl. *eklētu* "dark places"; < *ekēlu*

ekmu "taken away, stolen" jB of land, fortress; < *ekēmu*

ekṣiš "insolently" jB; < *akṣu*

ekṣu → *akṣu*

ekû(m) I, *ikû*; f. *ekūtu*; f. pl. *eki'ātum* "impoverished; orphaned, bereaved" Bab.; at Alal., as social class; freq. f. "orphan(s)" [NU.SÍK]; < *ekû* II; > *ekûtu*

ekû(m) II "to starve, deprive (of food, water)" O/jB **D** land, people; infin. *ukkû ša zunni* "shortage of rain"; > *ekû* I; *ekûtu*; *mēkûtu*; *tēkītu*?

ēku → *īku*

Ēkur 1. (temple of Enlil at Nippur) **2.** jB (a name of the underworld, abode of demons); < Sum.; > *ēkurriš; ēkurru*

ēkurriš "into the Ekur (= underworld)" jB; < *Ēkur*

ēkurru f., occas. m. "temple, chapel" M/NA, M/NB [É.KUR(.RA)] as building; as cult place; *akil, šatam ēkurrāte* "inspector of temples"; < *Ēkur*

ekūrum (or *equrum*) (a wooden object) OAkk

ekûtu jB "impoverishment"; Nuzi "orphanhood"; < *ekû* I

el → *eli*

ela "apart from, in the absence of" Ass., O/jB "except (for)", "if it were not for" (→ GAG §114p); in adv. use "exclusively" OB; < *elu* I ?; > *elaman; elat*

elae, *elaya* (desig. of horse, of tool) Nuzi; < Hurr.

elallu "cloud" jB lex.; < Sum.

elallu → also *alallu*

elallû mng. unkn. MB(Ass.)

elallû → also *alallû* I

elaman "apart from" OB lex.; *e. niāti* "were it not for us"; < *ela* + *-man*

Elama(t)tu(m) "(goddess) of Elam" O/jB [ELAM.MA-] name of the Bow star (*qaštu*); also MN at Susa; < *elamû*

elamittu → *alamittu*

elamītu → *elamû*

elamkû (a kind of arrow) jB lex.

elammakku(m), Nuzi *ela/emmaḫḫu* (a tree, valuable wood) OAkk, O/jB (felled in Syria) as timber; as material for furniture; M/jB med. in prescriptions

elammiḫuru (a craftsman) Nuzi; < Hurr.

elamû; f. *ela(m)mītu* "Elamite" jB, NA desig. of fig, cart, wool, carnelian; > *Elamattu*

elamūtu mng. unkn. jB

elān → *elēnu* 2; *ellān*

elāniš "above, in the upper part" jB(Ass.); < *el(i)* + *-ān* + *-iš*

elānu → *elēnu*; *iliānum*

elânum → *iliānum*

ela(p)pû → *alapû*

elāq pî → *līqu* I

elat "beyond, over and above" NB "in addition to, apart from" (prep.); with pron. suff., *ša*; also adv. "additionally"; < *ela*

elatḫipu (a linen garment) jB lex.

elâtu → *elītu*; *elû* I

elaya → *elae*

eldu (a dairy product) jB lex.

eldu → also *eṣdu*

elēḫu(m) "to strew, sprinkle" O/jB **G** (*i/i*) of dry substances, e.g. flour **D** ~ G; also ~ "to adorn" s.th., with (= acc.) wool, clothing; stat. "is decked out" with; transf., with abundance; > *ulluḫum*

elēlānû "carolling merrily" jB; < *elēlu* I

elēlu I "cheerful song" jB *e. sadrūtu* "songs (written down) in sections"; < *alālu* III

elēlu(m) II "to be(come) pure, free" **G** (*i/i*) [KÙ] of ominous sign "be clear"; "be pure" cultically, of person, incantation; OA, OB of person, person's forehead (*pūtum*) "be free" from claims **D** "purify" [KÙ] weapons in sea; body, mouth, hands; of deity "purify" humans, heaven; by magic; "carry out purely" ritual, offering; "dedicate by purification"; OB "manumit" slave(-woman) **Dt** "purify o.s."; "be purified"; > *ellu* I.II ?, *elliš*, *ella-mê*, *ellūtu*; *ēlilu* ?; *ullulu* I; *mullilu*; *tēliltu*; *tullal*

elēlu III mng. uncl. jB lex.

elemmaḫḫu → *elammakku*

elēn → *elēnu* 2

elēnītu I, *eliyānītu* 'the superior one' jB mag. (desig. of witch); NB "deceitful words"? (→ *elītu* 10); < *elēnû*

elēnītu II "upper garment" NB = *elītu* 4; < *elēnû*

elēnu(m), OB also *eliānum*?, O/MA, Bogh., NB, occas. jB also *elānu* "above, over" Bab. [AN.TA(-); UGU-] **1.** adv. "above", topog., in sky; "above (ground)"; after prep. *ana*, *adi*, *ištu e.* "upwards, upstream", "up to the top", "from above"; *elēnumma* "in addition" **2.** prep. (with pron. suff., e.g. *elēnuššu*; M/NB often *elēn*, *elān*) "above, over"; Nuzi also = "to east of"; "upstream of"; OB "besides, apart from", Am. "more than"; *elān ūri* "pudenda"; < *el(u)* I + *-ānum*; > *elēnû*; *elēnītu* I.II

elēnû "upper" M/NB [AN.TA-; NB also UGU-?] of fields, territory, sea; < *elēnu* + *-ī*; > *elēnītu* I.II

eleppatum → *eleppu*

eleppu(m), *ilippum* f., NB also m. "ship, boat" [GIŠ.MÁ; OAkk, OB freq. MÁ; OAkk pl. MÁ.MÁ] OB also nom. unit. *eleppatum* "(single) boat"; *bēl e.* "ship owner"; *e. bā'erī/ī* "fisherman's boat"; *e. ili* "deity's boat"; *e. qarābi* "battleship"; *e. nēberi* [GIŠ.MÁ.DIRI.GA] "ferry boat"; "(model) boat", Am. as toy; jB of gold

elēpu(m), *alāpu* "to sprout, grow" Bab. **G** (*i/i*) astr. of halo (*agû*); NB stat. in PNs "grants growth to" **Gt** "grow into one another", stat. of parts of body, exta; "be interlocked" of combatants, weapons **D** "make grow" trees; MB transf. "increase" daily stint **Dt/Dtn** NB "increase, multiply" of descendants **Š** "cause" stature "to grow" **Št** "(cause to) interlock", "be made to interlock", of vegetation, in combat; "be made to grow, increase" of descendants, regnal years; > *ellipu*; *līpu*, *līp līpi*; *etlupu*; *nēlepu*?

elēṣu(m) "to swell; rejoice" Bab.(lit.) **G** (*i/i*) of heart, liver "rejoice", also ellipt. of person, stars **Gtn** iter. **Gt** "rejoice constantly" **D** "make joyful" heart, liver; stat. "is swollen", of parts of body **Dt** "be made to swell" **Š** "cause to rejoice" heart, liver etc.; door (mng. uncl.); ellipt. of person; > *elṣu*, *elṣiš*; *ilṣu* II; *ulṣu*, *ulṣāniš*; *ulluṣu*; *mēleṣu*

eleštiḫḫuri (a prof. desig.) Nuzi; < Hurr.

elgulla → *elkulla*

eli, *elu*, *el*, *ili*, OAkk *al* "on, over, above; against; more than" OAkk, Bab., rarely NA [UGU] "on; on to" a place, a thing; of obligation etc. "on; on to" a person; of person "over" another, a task; "in addition to"; "more than" in quantity or quality; "against" enemy, person, esp. of anger, shout; "on account, on behalf of" s.o.; "to" s.o. after *ṭiābu(m)*, *marāṣu(m)* "to please, displease"; < *elu* I; > *elāniš*; → *eliya ša sīsê*

eliānum → *elēnu*

eliātum → *elītu*

eligulla → *elkulla*

eliḫuru (a prof. desig.) Nuzi; < Hurr.

elikulla → *elkulla*

elīlu → *alīlu*

ēlilu, *ellilu*, OA *i(l)lilum* (a kind of soapwort)? jB, OA?; < *elēlu* II ?

ēlilu → also *alīlu*

elinu (a plant) jB lex.

eliš "above; in addition" [AN.TA(*-iš*)] **1.** adv. "up above", i.e. in heaven, or on the earth; *e. u šapliš* "above and below"; "upstream"; "upwards", also *ana e.*; NA med. *ana e.* "by mouth"; "aloud"; OA "in addition", "and further" **2.** occas. j/NB prep. "over" the water; "upstream of"; < *elu* I

eliš → also *iliš*

elīta(m), *elītu*, *ellīta* **1.** OB "furthermore, moreover" **2.** Bab. "aloud"; < *elû* I

elītu(m), *ilītu*, OAkk *alītum*; pl. *eliātum*, *elâtu* 'that which is above' [AN.TA] **1.** OA "top(-load)" of donkey **2.** "upper (stone)" for grindstone; "pestle" for mortar **3.** MA, NB "upper room, structure" **4.** "upper (garment)" (→ *elēnītu* II) **5.** "upper part" of moon, plant, sack, wheel **6.** *e. uzni(m), īni, libbi* "upper part of ear, eye, heart"; of parts of liver [AN.TA; NU.UM.ME] **7.** *elât šamê* [AN.PA] "zenith" **8.** pl. *elâtu* "the upper world" (as opp. to underworld), also = "humanity" **9.** OAkk *aliātum* "the upper lands"; OB "high-lying (fields)" **10.** "deception", pl. "lies" (→ *elēnītu* I) **11.** jB lex. "exterior"; OA *e. ṭuppim* "tablet envelope" **12.** gramm. *(ša) elīti* "(Sum.) prefix"; < *elû* II

elītu → also *elīta*

ēlītu(m) "rising (amount)" Bab.; sg. OB "high amount" (opp. to *wārittum*); pl. "additional payments" in inheritance, bride price; NB "extra payments" of dates; < *elû* III f. ptcp.

eliu (a perfume) MA

eliu → also *elû* I.II

eliyānītu → *elēnītu* I

eliyānu (a garment) jB lex.; < *elu* I

eliya "rider" in *e. ša sīsê* NB(Achaem.); < *eli* ?

elkulla, *elgulla, e/ilik/gulla* (a medicinal plant or plants) M/jB lex., med.

ellabbuḫḫu(m), *ellambuḫḫu, illabbuḫu, (e/il)libbuḫu, ilbuḫḫu* f. "bladder" O/jB, MA of bird, fish, sheep etc.; MA as container for oil; < Sum.?

ella(m)-mê, *illa-mê* "pure in divine powers" O/jB title of Sîn, Šamaš; lex. (a deity's garment); < *ellu* I + *mû* II

ellamkušu, *illaggušu* (a leather object, phps.) "bellows" jB; < Sum.

ellāmu-, *illāmu-* "before" (prep.) jB; OB in PN ?; with pron. suff. "before" s.o., in time; "in front of", in place; < *ina* + *lāmu-*

ellān, *ellānu(m)* "over and above" Ass. **1.** OA adv. "additionally" **2.** prep. "in addition to, apart from"; MA "beyond"; Bogh. "more than"; M/NA "on the far side of"; Ug. "away from"; > *ellatān*; → *allânum* ?; *ullânu* ?

ellarūtu mng. unkn. jB lex.

ellatān "on the other side of" OB(N.Mes.); < *ellān*

ellatu → *illatu* I

ellaya → *elleya*

ellemēšum → *elmēšu*

ellēt, *elliat* mng. uncl. OB *ina e. DN* "with the authority of DN"?; Nuzi "beside, next to"?; < *lētu* ?

elletu → *ellu* I; *illatu* I

ellētu → *e'iltu*

elleya, *e/illaya* **1.** O/jB lex. "no! no way!"? **2.** jB (shout of joy)

elliat → *ellēt*

elliātu → *elû* II

ellibbuḫu → *ellabbuḫḫu*

elligu, *illigu* (a stone) jB; < Sum.

Ellil, *Illil*, OAkk *Enlil* [^{d}EN.LÍL; ^{d}50; NA ^{d}BAD] **1.** the god Enlil **2.** Bab.(lit.) desig. of the supreme deity, *E. ilī* "*E.* of the gods", of Marduk, Aššur, Nergal, Ninurta; > *Ellillatu*; *Ellilūtu*

Elli(l)latu, *Elli(l)lītu* (desig. of supreme goddess) jB [^{d}EN.LÍL.LÁ-] of Ištar, Ninlil; < *Ellil*

ellilu → *ēlilu*

Ellilūtu, *Illilūtum* "power of Enlil, divine supremacy" O/jB [^{d}EN.LÍL(.LÁ)- ; M/jB ^{d}BAD-] of Enlil, Marduk, Aššur, Sîn, Ištar, Ninlil; < *Ellil*

ellimēšu → *elmēšu*

ellipu **1.** (a plant) jB lex., med. **2.** mng. unkn. jB lex.; < *elēpu*

elliš "purely" jB; "clearly" of appearance of moon; "in cultic purity"; < *ellu* I

ellīta → *elīta*

elliu → *elû* II

ellu(m) I, *allu* "pure; clear" [KÙ; SIKIL] "pure, clean" of water, oil; "bright, shining" of metal, stone; of mountains, forests, onions; "(cultically, ritually) pure" of deity, person, hands; of incantation, symbol; temple, place; of meal, offering, wine; *e.* as subst., desig. of priest; Bogh., Ug. "free" as social class; < *elēlu* II; > *ella-mê*; *elliš*; *ellūtu*; → *e.* II

ellu(m) II "sesame oil" Bab. of a specific quality [Ì.GIŠ (→ also *šamnu*)]; < *e.* I ?

ellû → *elû* I

ellūku → *illukku*

ellūru → *illūru*

ellutu → *illatu* I

ellūtu "purity" M/jB; < *ellu* I

elmarumma "oath"? Nuzi in *e. epēšu*; < Hurr.

elmeštu, *elmeru*, MA *elmeltu*, NA *elmessu* (a kind of grass) jB, M/NA; < *elmēšu*

elmēšu(m), *elli/emēšum*, Ass. *e/ilmušu, e/ilmiši* (a valuable stone, phps.) "amber" Bab.(lit.), NA [SUD.ÁG] also as (f)PN; freq. in lit.; > *elmeštu*

elpetu, *ilpitu, elpatu* "alfalfa grass" Bab. [Ú.NÚMUN; Ú.A.NÚMUN], med. in prescriptions

elpû → *alapû*

elṣiš "joyfully" Bab.(lit.); < *elṣu*

elṣu "joyful" OB of heart; < *elēṣu*; > *elṣiš*

eltu → *iltu* I.II

eltuḫḫu → *ištuḫḫu*

elu(m) I "top, upper side" O/jB (rare); > *eli*, *elāniš*; *elēnu*, *elēnû*, *elēnītu* I.II; *eliyānu*; *eliš*; *elû* II, *elītu*, *elûtu*?; *ela*?; → *e.* II; *elû* III

elu II (part of a metal object) NB of censer (= *e.* I "top, lid"?)

elu → also *eli*; *ilu*

elû(m) I, *elium*, *ellû* "high" Bab.(lit.); "tall" in stature; of neck, head "(raised) high"; "exalted"; < *elû* III; > *elīta*

elû(m) II, *ilû*, *alûm*, OAkk *alium*, Ass. *eliu(m)*, MA f. pl. also *elliātu* "upper" [AN.TA; AN-; NIM; Am. UGU-] of parts of body and liver; buildings; *mātum elītum* = "Upper Mesopotamia"; of river, sea, fields; of wind (*šāru*) "north"?; "up above, supernal" of Igigi; OB "outer" tablet; gramm. "(Sum.) prefix"; < *elu* I + -*ī*; > *elītu*; *elûtu*?

elû(m) III, OB also *alûm* "to go up, arise; (stat.) is high" G (*i/i*) [E₁₁; jB also AN.TA] **1.** stat. "is (too) high", "is raised up"; transf. of DN etc. "is exalted" **2.** of living beings "move upwards, climb up" into heaven, mountains, upper land; "come up" out of water; on to roof, wall; "ascend" (*ana*) throne; of animal "mount" sexually **3.** of things "come up, arrive"; of ship "go upstream"; of star, cloud, water "rise"; of land "emerge" (from water); "come up" of plant, lot, metal etc. from kiln; of ornament "go on to" s.th. **4.** transf. of prices "rise"; "climb (socially)"; "apply (etc.) higher up", e.g. to king, law court; leg. of claimant, witnesses "come forward"; of person, tablet etc. "turn up, appear"; math. "emerge, be the result"; of harvest, profit "be produced, result"; NB *ana muḫḫi* (X) *e.* "take on liability for (X)"; *ina* X *e.*, *qātu ina* X *e.* "forfeit X" (→ Gt); of person "get away from" s.o.'s control (*qāt-*), of property "be lost" to owner **Gtn** iter. **Gt** "go up and away"; of person, animal, silver, illness; O/jB *ina* X *e.* "forfeit X" **D** "make higher, raise" wall, building, 'head' (*rēšu*) of building; of deity "lift up, elevate" person, kingship (also with *rēšu*); "extol, praise (deity)"; NA "take away, remove" **Dtn** "repeatedly extol" **Dt 1.** = Gt "forfeit" **2.** "be raised high(er)" than (= *ana*) (→ *utlellû*) **Š** [E₁₁] caus. of G; jB *ana zaqīpi š.* "impale"; "post, install" garrison in fort etc.; Susa *mê š.* "have water close over one, be submerged" (in ordeal); "dedicate" to temple; "get out" from storage, kiln; "embark" person, goods; "bring forward" witnesses; "produce" lesion; "bring out, produce" tablet, lost property; "enter" on tablet; "introduce" bees

to a region; "express" anxiety, thought; *šum* X *š.* "swear oath by X"; "disinherit" heir, "turn off, drive from" fields, land; "take" sheep from fold; "remove" boundary stone etc.; math. "subtract" [E₁₁; NIM], "determine" root; Am. *ša dama šūlû* (desig. of gold) **Štn** iter. of Š **Št** jB of features in liver "be raised (as) high" as (= *ana*); Am. transf. of dowry "be made (as) immense as" **N** ~ *ne'ellû*; > *elû* I, *elīta*; *ēlû*, *ēlītu*; *mēlû*, *mēlītu*, *mūlû*; *ullû* II, *ullūtu*; *mullītum*; *tēlītu*; *šūlû*, *šūlûtu* II, *šēlû'utum*; *mušēlû*, *utlellû*; → *elu* I and derivatives

elû → also *alallû* II; *alû* I.IV

ēlu → *ālu* II

ēlû "claimant" MB; < *elû* III

elu'e (a prof. desig.)? Nuzi; < Hurr.

Elūnum, *Elūlu(m)*, j/NB *Ulūlu* (a festival; 6th Bab. month) [ITI.KIN(.ᵈINNIN.NA)]; OAkk, OB "(festival of) E."; "month of E.", also "second (NB *šanû*, NA *urkiu*) E."; PN E/*Ululāyu*

elupatu (an object) Nuzi; < Hurr.

eluri → *illurê*

elûtu, *ilûtu* in *šubāt e.* (a garment) jB; < *elû* II ?

ēm, *ēma* "wherever" Bab. **1.** prep. "in whatever/every part of", *ēm āli* "in whatever/every part of the town"; *ēm qabli* "wherever there be battle"; j/NB temporal "at whatever time", *ēma arḫi* "at each (new) month" **2.** conj. "wherever", *ēma tannamru* "wherever you appear"; j/NB temporal "whenever"; < *ai* III + -*ma* (→ GAG §114i)

ema'e → *mīya*

emāḫu (a word for temple) jB; < Sum.

emammu, *emāmu* → *umāmu*

emanamumma "tenfold" Nuzi; < Hurr.

emantu "group of ten" Nuzi; < Hurr.; → *emantuḫlu*

emantuḫlu, *emattuḫlu* "decurion" Nuzi [GAL.10]; < Hurr.; → *emantu*

emartu (an ornament)? jB lex.

emāru → *imēru*

emarukku "flood dragon" jB; < Sum.

emāšu (a temple inner room) jB

emāšu → also *umāšu*

emattuḫlu → *emantuḫlu*

embâ (or *imbâ*) "baa" jB of sheep

embūbu → *ebbūbu*

emdu I, *endu* "imposed" jB; < *emēdu*

emdu(m) II, *endu* (an aromatic tree) O/jB, M/NA; its wood as fumigant; NA *ša e.-šu* "the *e.* man/supplier"; *šaman e.* "oil of *e.*"; → *suādu*

emēdu(m) "to lean on; impose" G (OA, early OB *a/u*, later *i/i*) [UŠ] **1.** "lean on" (= acc.)

person, thing; ext., math., stat. "is in contact with, touches, reaches to"; of boat "land", of stars "come into contact with"; "rely on, take refuge with" deity, "in" corner, hiding place; *šadâ(šu) e.* "resort to mountain" (= disappear) **2.** "impose, put s.th. on (= acc.) s.o./s.th."; "install" door, beam; "load" captives on boat; "put" yoke, load "on" donkey, neck; "impose" corvée, tribute, tax etc.; penalty, judgement, oath(-taking); illness, woe; O/MB *pūt- e.* "give guarantee" **Gtn** iter. MB "push ever further" into woods **Gt** OAkk "lie on each other" **D** "install" beams etc.; med. "apply" dressing; *qāta(m) u.* "lay hands on", liter. and transf. of legal act; "dock" a ship; "build" quay "onto" bank; "set" fire to s.th.; "hide (intrans.) in" corners; stat. "is in contact with"; OA "assemble, load" goods etc. **Dt** pass. of D with *qātu* **Š** caus. of G OAkk "cause to take refuge"; NB "cause to impose" tax **Št** "bring" troops etc. "together", "put" (o.'s heads) "together"; "add up" amounts; "knit" o.'s eyebrows; of parts of body, of liver; med. "mix", "add" ingredients "to one another" **N 1.** recipr. of persons "get together" with (= *itti*), "confer"; of troops "combine, join up"; "meet" in battle; of parts of liver, stars "converge, meet up"; Nuzi stat. "adjoins" **2.** "betake o.s. to", "seek refuge in" **3.** pass. of G "be propped up"; "be imposed"; "be placed next to" **Ntn** (or **Nt** ?) "continually join together", astr. "continually conjoin"; > *emdu* I; *ēmidu*, *emmēdu*; *imdu*, *imittu* II; *nēmedu*, *nēmettu*; *etmudu*, *etamdu*; *mummidu*?; *šutēmudu*; *muttetendu*; *umdu*?

emegalammû (a Sum. dialect) jB [EME.GALAM.MA]; < Sum.

emēmu(m) "to be(come) hot" O/jB, NA **G** (*i/i*; stat. *ēm*) [KÚM] of person's body "be hot, run a temperature"; of weather, walls of house **Gtn** [KÚM.KÚM] jB med. "continually have temperature" **D** "heat up" water, oil etc.; > *emmu*, *emmū*, *emmūtu*; *ummu* II; *immu*, *immāniš*

emēqu(m) I "to be wise" OAkk, Bab. **G** stat. (*emuq*) of deity, person **Št** "pray devoutly" to (= *ana*), for (= dat. pron. suff.); > *emqu*, *emqiš*, *emqūtu*, *emuqtu*; *nēmequ*; *ummuqu*, *tēmīqu*; *muštēmiqu*; → *emūqu*

emēqu(m) II ~ "to care for" OB **G** only ptcp. → *ēmiqum* **D** "make, appoint s.o. to care"

emerum → *amaru* I

emēru I "to be red" jB **G** → *emru* I **D** "redden", stat. of eyes "are reddened"

emēru(m) II ~ "to swell" O/jB **G** stat. of heart, gall, pregnant woman "is swollen" **N** "become swollen, enlarged" of body, star **Ntn** iter. of N; > *emru* II

emesallu → *mēsallu*

emeṣu(m) I "to be sour" O/jB **G** stat. (*emiṣ*, *emuṣ*) of beer etc.; > *emṣu* I

emēṣu(m) II "to be hungry" OA, O/jB **G** (Bab. *u/u*, Ass. *i/i*) of people, land; OA *aklam e.* "be hungry for bread" **D** OA "allow" s.o. "to go hungry"; > *emṣu* II; *umṣu* I; *emmiṣum*

emēšu "to strive" MB(Ass.) **Gtn** iter.

emētu(m) "mother-in-law" (or other female relative by marriage) Bab.; < *emu*

emetukû "slanderer" jB lex.; < Sum.

ēmidu "tax assessor" NB; < *emēdu*

ēmiqum; f. *ēmiqtum* ~ 'one who cares for, carer' (a household servant) OA, OB; < *emēqu* II; → *emuqtu*

emittam → *imitta*

emittu → *imittu* I.II

emmea, *embâ* "baa" jB of sheep

emmēdu ~ "lodger, tenant"? jB lex.; < *emēdu*

emmertu → *immertu*

emmeru → *immeru*

emmiṣum ~ "in need, short of cash"? OA; < *emēṣu* II

emmu(m), *ammum* "hot" O/jB, M/NA [KÚM] of bitumen, water, dregs; baked brick, oven; as subst. "hot (water)", *ša e.* "servant bringing hot water"; *emmetu* "hot (bread)"; < *emēmu*; > *emmūtu*, *emmū*

emmū pl. tant. ~ "fuel" MA (or "hot cinders"?); < *emmū*

e(m)mû → *imû*

emmūtu "heat" MB in *e. ūmi* "heat of the day"; < *emmu*

emqiš "intelligently" OB; < *emqu*

emqu(m), *enqu*; f. *emuqtu* "wise, clever" Bab. [KÙ.ZU]; "skilled, clever" craftsman, scribe; "wise" god, king etc.; "crafty" fox; < *emēqu* I; > *emqiš*; *emuqtu*; *emqūtu*

emqūtu "wisdom" Am.?; < *emqu*

emru I "red(dish)" jB of otter; < *emēru* I

emru II "swollen" M/jB lex.; < *emēru* II

emṣu(m) I, *enṣu*; f. *emiṣtu* "sour" O/jB, NA [BIL/BÍL.LÁ] of wine, vinegar, beer; fruit; pastry; < *emēṣu* I

emṣum II, *enṣu* "hungry" OB, jB lex.; < *emēṣu* II

emšu(m), *enšu*, *im/nšu* "lower body, abdomen" O/jB [ḪÁŠ] **1.** of human (also du.), horse

2. (part of a harrow; pl. f. of a chair) **3.** (a kind of lapis lazuli bead); > *emšūtu*?

emšūtu mng. unkn. Nuzi; armour *ana e.*; < *emšu* ?

emu(m), *imu* "father-in-law" (or other male relative by marriage) [UŠBAR$_6$]; *bīt e.* "(father-)in-law's house, family"; *mār(at) e.* "brother/sister-in-law"; *e. rabû* "father-in-law", (as opp. to) *e. ṣeḫru* "son-in-law"; > *emētu*; *emumātu*; *emūtu*

emû I "tongue" jB lex. as part of plough; < Sum.

emû II (a strap) jB lex.

emû → also *ewûm* I; *imû*

emumātu pl. tant. "relatives, in-laws" jB lex.; < *emu*; → *emušutu*

emūqa(mma) "forcibly" MA, Nuzi; < *emūqu*

emūqattam "forcibly, violently" OA; < *emūqu*

emuqtu "carer"? jB (for *ēmiqtu* ?); < *emqu*

emūqu(m), NA also *amūqu*, *mūqu*; pl. m. & f. "strength; force" (freq. du.) [Á; USU] **1.** "bodily strength", *e. ramāni* "own strength, resources"; often in PNs; OA transf. "(financial) support; authority" **2.** of groups of men "military/labour force", "forces" **3.** "force (majeure)"; *ina e.* "forcibly", "forceful, violent" deeds, words **4.** "power, ability, capability", *kīma emūq* "commensurately with"; NA *(lā) mūqā-* "(not) within the power of", e.g. *lā mūqāša* "she cannot ..."; > *emūqamma*; *emūqattam*; → *emēqu* I

emušutu error for → *emumātu* ?

emutin (a kind of bandage) jB lex.

emūtu(m) "relatives by marriage; marriage relationship" O/jB *bīt e.* "father-in-law's house(hold)"; Am. "marriage alliance"; < *emu*

enanna → *enenna*

enanu (a plant) jB lex.

ēnātu → *īnu* I

enbu → *inbu*

enbūbum → *ebbūbu*

endippu, *enduppu* (a temple cook) jB lex.; < Sum.

endu → *emdu* I.II; *undu* I

enduppu → *endippu*

enēbu "to fruit" jB **G** not attested **Gtn** (or **Ntn**) jB lex. **D** lex. **Dtn** "repeatedly gather fruit"? **Dt** "be made to bear fruit"; < *inbu* denom.; > *unnubu*; *innabu*; *nannābu*

enen(na), *enanna*, *enin(na)*, *eninni* "now" M/jB var. of *inanna*

enēnu(m) I, jB also *anānu* "to grant favour, be favourable" OAkk, OA, O/jB **G** (*a*/*u*) esp. in PNs; OA "grant leave (of absence)"; Am. "be merciful"; > *ennu*; *ennanātum*

enēnu II "to punish" OAkk, MA, M/jB **G** (*i*/*i*) of deity, esp. in PNs; > *unnunu* ?

enēnu III "to sin" jB **G** (*e*/*u*) of person, PlN; > *ennenu*; *ennettu*

enēnu IV "to pray" jB lex.; → *utnēnu* II

enēqu(m) "to suck" **G** (*i*/*i*) of child, animal; obj. breast, milk **Gtn** iter. **D** lex. "soak, steep" **Dt** jB "be suckled" **Š** "suckle, give suck to"; > *ēniqu*; *unīqu*, *munīqu*; *tēnīqu*; *šūnuqu*, *mušēniqtu*

enerḫi (a plant) jB lex.

enēšu(m) "to be(come) weak" **G** (*i*/*i*) [SIG]; of person, part of body; transf. "be(come) poverty-stricken"; of building "become dilapidated, fall into disrepair" **Gt** stat. OB *etnuš akalam* "he is short of food" **D** "weaken" person, population, land; (part of) body; cattle; stat. of ziggurrat "was allowed to fall into disrepair" **Dt** OA "become poverty-stricken, insolvent"; > *enšu*, *enšūtu*; *unšu*; *etnušu*; *unnušu*, *unnušūtu*, *munnišu*; *mēnešu*, *mēneštu*, *mēnešūtu*; *tānīštum*

enetu → *entu*

enētu "to flatten"? M/jB, NA **G** not attested **D** liter. "flatten"?; astr. stat. of moon, planets "are faint" **Dt** astr. "be faint, become faint"; > *unnutu*

engisû, *engišû* (a stone) jB [NA$_4$.EN.GI/IGI.SA$_6$]; < Sum.

engiṣu, *engû* (a temple cook) Bab. [EN.ME.GI$_4$]; < Sum.

engišû → *engisû*

engû → *engiṣu*

enguratti adv. mng. unkn. NA

engurru(m) "subterranean waters" O/jB lex.; < Sum.

ēni, OB *īni* ~ "indeed" OAkk, OB; = *anna* ?

eniktum → *enkētum*

enimgallûm "(legal) claim"? OB lex.; < Sum.

enimmû → *inimmû* I

enimtarrum "rejection of claim"? OB lex.; < Sum.

enin(na), *eninni* → *enenna*

ēniqu; f. *ēniqtu* "suckling, unweaned child" NB; < *enēqu*

eni(š)šu (a kind of bandage)? jB lex.

enīta, *enītu* "in changed order" jB of incantation; parts of lung; < *enû* I

enītu → *enīta*; *enû* I; *inītu* I

ēnītu → *ēnû*

enkētum (or *enqētum*) pl. (a kind of fish) OB, purchased for consumption

enkummu(m) "temple treasurer" O/jB [ENKUM]; < Sum.

Enlil → *Ellil*

Enli(l)latu → *Ellillatu*

Enlilūtu → *Ellilūtu*

enma "thus, saying" OAkk ptcl. introducing dir. speech; later → *umma*

enna "now" NA, NB, rarely jB; also *e. agâ*, *e. adû*; *adi (ša) e.*, *adi muḫḫi (ša) e.* "up till now"

ennakku mng. unkn. jB lex.; < Sum.

ennānum; pl. f. "supplication, petition" OA; pl. "indulgence, dispensation"; < *enēnu* I; → *unīnu*

ennenu ~ "malicious" jB of Lamaštu; < *enēnu* III

ennēnu(m), *inninnu* (a kind of cereal) O/jB [ŠE.IN.NU.ḪA] sown; ground into flour

ennettu(m), *e/innintu*, also *ennetu* "sin; punishment" O/jB *e. paṭāru* "to absolve sin"; *bēl e.-ya* "one who has sinned against me"; < *enēnu* III

ennettu → also *ernittu*

ennetu → *ennettu*

ennigû (a priest) jB; < Sum.

ennintu → *ennettu*

ennu(m) "favour" OAkk; OA, OB in PNs divine "favour, mercy"; < *enēnu* I

ennu → also *enu*

e(n)nungallu "chief guardian" Bogh., of forest; < Sum.

enqētum → *enkētum*

enqu → *emqu*

ensû(m) **1.** "dream interpreter" OB lex., jB **2.** (a plant) jB lex.; < Sum.

enṣu → *emṣu* I.II

enšu(m), M/jB(Ass.) also *anšu*; f. *eništu* "weak" [SIG] of person, animal, esp. "sick"; militarily "weak"; socially "weak" as opp. to *dannu*; "poor" exchange rate; of building "dilapidated"; < *enēšu*; > *enšūtu*

enšu → also *emšu*

enšūpu (a bird) jB

enšūtu, MB(Ass.) *anšūtu* "weakness" M/NB of person; of building "dilapidation"; < *enšu*

entu(m), *enetu* "high priestess" OAkk, Bab. [NIN.DINGIR(.RA)]; MB(Ass.), jB *bīt e.* "cloister", syn. of *gagû*; < *enu*

entû (technical term in date cultivation) jB lex.; < Sum.

enu(m), *ennu* Bab. **1.** "lord" [EN] **2.** "high priest(ess)" [EN]; < Sum.; > *entu*; *enūtu*

enu → also *inu* I

enû I ~ "overturned" jB lex.; < *enû* III; > *enīta*

enû II (loincloth or kilt) jB lex.

enû(m) III "to change" **G** (*i/i*) [BAL] "alter" place, street, boundary; MA ellipt. "cross (boundary)"; of person *kalīta e.* "change kidney", i.e. lie on the other side; "change" dynasty, statement, order, judgement; ellipt. "renege" (on earlier agreement); "replace" s.o., "substitute for" **Gt** "change places with one another", "relieve each other" **Št** "change s.th. over into s.th. else", "exchange" with s.o.; "have sexual intercourse"; "reassign" omen to s.o. else **N** pass. of G [BAL] M/NB "be altered" of decision, word (usu. negated); of person **Ntn** "be constantly changing" of facial expression; > *enû* I, *enīta*; *ēnû*; *inītu* I, II?; *tēnû*, *tēnânû*, *tēnītum*; *muštennium*?

ēnu → *īnu* I

ēnû; f. *ēnītu* "substitute" O/jB; < *enû* III

enūma → *inūma*

enungallu → *ennungallu*

Enunnakkū → *Anunnakkū*

enunūtu → *anunūtu*

enūšu → *inūšu*

enūtu j/NB **1.** "lordship" of gods, king **2.** "office of high priestess"; < *enu*

enūtu → also *unūtu*

enzu(m), *ezzu(m)*, *inzum*; pl. mostly f. "goat" [ÙZ; ÙZ.ḪI.A] "female goat"; "goat(s)" gener., *rē'i e.* "goatherd"; *šārat e.* "goat-hair"; astr. "(the constellation) Lyra" [MUL.ÙZ]; also (a kind of bird); → *ḫazzum*

epa(p)pu mng. unkn. jB lex.

eparšû (or *etamšû*) (a garment) MB

epartu (a garment) M/jB lex.

epattum; pl. *epadātum* (a garment) OA, from Talḫad

epâtu → *apâtu*

epeqēnu → *epqēnu*

epēqu(m) ~ "to embrace; grow over, round" OA, O/jB **G** (*i/i*) "grow over" of part of liver etc., usu. stat.; O/jB lex. "embrace (in affection)" **Gt** "grow over each other" **D** ~ G ext., stat. "is grown over, round" part of body; of wave, flood "be turned over"?; OA ~ "pack an *upqum* load" **Dt** pass. of D (or **Gt** ?) OB of lung "be grown over"?; > *epqu* I; *ipqum*; *upqu* I?, II; *etpuqu*; *uppuqu*?; *epūqum*?

eperiš, *epriš* "with earth" jB, with *katāmu* ("to cover"); < *eperu*

epertu(m) "(baked) brickwork" OB(Elam), MB(Ass.) material of wall, of temple; < *eperu*

eperu(m), *epru*, j/NB also *ipiru* "earth, soil; dust" [SAḪAR(.ḪI.A)] "(loose) earth, soil" for building work; from excavation or destruction;

as means of concealment; "dust (storm)", "dust" of the feet; mag. "dust" from street etc.; in self-debasement OA "dust" (on the head), MB "dust" (under king's feet) as self-descr.; jB *bīt e.* 'house of dust', i.e. underworld, *kišid e.* 'conquest of the soil', i.e. doomed to be buried; MB(Ass.) "mortar" in masonry (*e. ša kupri* "*e.* of bitumen"); "earth" yielding ores etc.; math. "volume of earth"; Mari, Alal., Bogh. "land, territory"; > *eperiš*; *epertu*

epēru(m) "to feed, provide for" OAkk, Bab., MA **G** (*i/i*) [ŠE.BA] of king, deity (esp. in PNs) **Š** OB "cause s.o. to provide for, feed" **Štn** NB "cause to be fed regularly" **Št** "forage; hurry about" (or → *šutēburum*?); > *ipru*; *ēpiru*; *nēperētum*

epēru → also *apāru*; *ebēru* I

epēsum "to be difficult" OB **G** stat. (*epis*) of decision (for = dat.) **D** "make difficulties" in contractual situation

epēšum I "action, behaviour" OB *e. damqum* "good behaviour"; < *epēšu* II infin.

epēšu(m) II "to do; make; build" **G** (*e/u*, later Bab. *u/u*) [DÙ; occas. AK, GI] **1.** (without obj.) "act, behave"; "work"; of illness "be active, take effect"; math. "proceed" **2.** "do" s.th.; OA, OB *ša epāšim e.* "do what has to be done"; good, evil (towards s.o.) **3.** "do, carry out, exercise" a function, esp. with abstr. obj. (Akk. *-ūtu(m)*, Hurr. *-umma*), e.g. *abbūtam*, *šarrūtam e.* "perform function of father, king"; with infin. OB *alākam e.* "make a journey", NB *nadānu u maḫāru e.* "carry on commerce"; "commit" crime, "make" rebellion, battle, love; "render" help (*usātu*); "carry out" act(ion), command, instruction; "realize" wish; "do" accounts; "effectuate" exchange; "perform" ritual, magic rites, incantation etc.; "try" a legal case **4.** idioms: *kakkī e.* "take up arms"; Mari, Am. *āla(m) e.* "take" or "fortify a city"; Ug. *dāma e.* "spill blood"; jB *ṣēra e.* "go hunting"; "offer up, sacrifice" animal (also absol. "make offering"); Mari *awātam e.* (also absol.) "speak", Bab.(lit.) *pâ(m) e.* "speak (up)", OB "raise objections"; *šipram e.* "do (agricultural) work on" (+ 2nd acc.); *eqlam*, *kiriam e.* "work field, orchard" (+ 2nd acc. for crop); "cultivate" crop; "manage" house, orchard; "process" wool, "work" metal **5.** "(re)build" temple, house, room, wall, bridge, ship; "make" statue, furniture, garment etc.; food, drink; document; statement, contract; music; "put into effect" scheme; *puzra e.* "act secretively"; "cause" earthquake, wound, anxiety; *bītam e.* "form household, family"; "make profit in" gold, silver; stat. "is formed (like)" **6.** "make into, convert"; Am., Nuzi, Bogh. *ana mārutti*, *šarrūti* "into son, king" etc.; jB/NA "convert" fields into (= acc.) own property **Gtn** iter. **Gt** "do thoroughly"? **D** OB "calculate" amount; "do up" hair; "treat, behave towards" s.o.; (in col.) "execute properly" tablet; Ass. often ~ G "practise" sorcery, "exercise" kingship etc., "conclude" agreement, "perform" prayer, "sacrifice" sheep, "operate" ferry, "work" gold; M/NA leg. in sale "carry out procedure"? **Š** caus. of G **Št** "be active, work on" s.th.; of demons "work against" s.o. (= acc. or dat.) **N** (OB mostly *inneppeš*, *ittenpeš*, *innepiš*, later Bab. *u/u*) pass. of G *šiprum (ul) inneppe/uš* "can(not) be done"; of person "be treated"; of document "be drawn up"; > *epšu*; *ipšu*, *ipšiš*; *epēšu I*; *epištu*, *epūšu*, *epuštu*; *ēpišu*, *ēpištu*, *ēpišānu*, *ēpišānūtu*; *eppešu*; *upīšū*, *upšaššû*; *etpušu*, *itpēšu*, *itepšu*; *uppušu*, *uppuštu*, *muppišu*, *muppišūtu*, *muppišānu*; *mušēpišu*, *mušēpišūtu*; *muštēpišu*, *muštēpišūtu*; *nēpešu*, *nēpišum*, *nēpeštu*

epiātum → *apâtu*

epinnu(m) m. & f. "(seed) plough" [(GIŠ.)APIN] OB alap e. "plough ox" [GU4.APIN(.ḪI.A)]; NB bīt e. "ploughed plot"; OAkk SAG *e.*, NB *rab(i) e.* "official in charge of plough(-team)s"; astr. (a constellation) [MUL.APIN]; Nuzi (a surface measure = *awiḫaru*); < Sum.

epiqtu → *epqu* I

epirru (a bead)? jB lex.

ēpiru "provider, feeder" jB lex.; < *epēru*

ēpissu → *ēpištu*

ēpišānu **1.** NA "instigator" of revolt; NB "activist" **2.** NB "confectioner" of sweetmeats **3.** NB of ox, donkey "working"; < *ēpišu* + *-ān*

ēpišānūtu "agency" NB i.e. responsibility for carrying out tasks (house repairs, agriculture, brewing, prebends); < *ēpišānu*

epištu(m), *ipištu(m)*, jB also *epšetu* "deed, action" Bab., NA [DÙ; also NÍG.DÍM.DÍM.MA] "act(s), achievement(s)"; mag. "machinations"; "rites"; "work, (results of) labour"; agricultural "works, operations"; "fabrication, creation" of ice, (artificial) precious stone; quality of "manufacture, workmanship"; "building work, construction"; < *epēšu* II

ēpištu(m), NA *ēpissu* **1.** OB "work team" **2.** jB "sorceress" **3.** NA "she who acts" (of goddess); < *ēpišu*

epišum, *ipišu/a* (a kind of carpet)? OA in wool; also Bogh.?

epīšū → *upīšū*

ēpišu(m) 1. Bab. "doer; maker; builder, artisan" 2. jB "sorcerer" 3. NA *lā ē.* 'do-nothing', "idler"; < *epēšu* II; > *ēpištu, ēpišānu, ēpišānūtu*

epitātu (a plant) jB lex.

epītu(m) "baked product, pastry" O/MB, Ug.; < *epû* II

ēpītum "female baker" OB; < *ēpû*

eplū → *iplū*

eppešu "clever, effective" Bab. [DÙ] jB *e. tāḫāzi* "skilled in battle"; < *epēšu* II

epqēnu, *epeqēnu(m), epqennu* (a skin complaint) O/jB; < *epqu* II

epqu I "grown over" jB f. *epiqtu*, of part of liver; < *epēqu*

epqu(m) II (a skin complaint, phps.) "leprosy" O/jB *epqa(m) malû* "to be afflicted with leprosy"; > *epqēnu*

epriš → *eperiš*

epru → *eperu*

epšetu → *epištu*

epšu(m); f. *epi/uštu*, NB also *ipištu* "made, built" [DÙ.A; NB also DÙ] *bītu(m) e.* "built-on house(-plot)"; "cultivated" field, orchard; "worked, prepared" metal, work, dates etc., NB *lā epšētu* "unworked items"; NB f. "adjusted, adjustment" of measures; < *epēšu* II

epšu → also *ipšu*

epû(m) I "baked" OAkk, jB; < *epû* II

epû(m) II "to bake" Bab. **G** (*i/i*) bread, peaflour **N** pass., of bread; > *epû* I; *ēpû, ēpītum*; *epītu*; *nēpītu*

ēpû(m) "baker" Bab.; < *epû* II; > *ēpītum*

epūqum mng. uncl. Mari (quality/feature of a stone); < *epēqu* ?

epuštu "(magical) procedure, ritual" j/NB [DÙ.DÙ.BI (= *e.-šu*)]; < *epēšu* II

epūšu "execution, carrying out" NB [DÙ] of work, accounts; < *epēšu* II

eqābu → *ekēpu*

eqbu(m), NA *igbu*? "heel" Bab., NA? [MUD; MA.SÌL; SÌL.MUD ?] of human, demon, sheep; NB *ina eqbinni* "in succession to us" (Aram. usage); also NB mng. unkn.

eqēqu, *egēgu* ~ "to paralyse" O/jB **G** (*i/i* ?) stat. of person "is paralysed" **Gtn** iter., "be continuously unable to move" **D** stat. of tongue "is tied"; > *uqqu*; *uqququ*

eqīdu "cheese" jB, NA

eqlu(m) m., OAkk f.; pl. f. "field; terrain" [A.ŠÀ; NA often A.ŠÀ.GA; OAkk, early OB, OA also GÁN] "cultivated field"; OB *e. šukūsim* "glebe, prebendary f.", *e. akālum* "to enjoy usufruct of f."; Mari *ina lā eqlim* "on uncultivated land"; NB *e. ṣēri* "f. in the desert"; "terrain, territory", *e. ṣumāmīti* "waterless terrain", *e. ṭābu* "easy terrain", *e. namraṣi, nukurti, šulmi* "difficult, hostile, friendly terrain"; math. "area; squared total", also administrative; "distance" overland, Ass. *eqla(m)* "overland"; O/MA *eqlam, ina eqlim* "in the countryside" (opp. to *(libbi) āli(m)*); "wild" in names of plants, insects

eqû(m) "to anoint, smear on" OB lex., Bogh., jB **G** [MAR] eyes, with (= acc.) kohl, ointment; other parts of body **Gtn** iter. **D** stat., of part of body (mng. uncl.) **Dt** "smear o.s. with" paste etc.; > *mēqû, mēqītu*; *uqqû* I; *tēqītu*

eqû → also *egû* II

ēqu (a cult object) M/NA, jB(Ass.); M/NA *bīt ē.* (a shrine); DN *Bēlat-ēqi*; > *ēqūtu*

eqūrum → *ekūrum*

ēqūtu (a cultic practice) NA(Urar.) in *ana ē. šāluku*; < *ēqu*

erâ → *iria*

erânu → *iliānum*

eratti(ya)nnu (part of a weapon)? Am.; < Hurr.

erbâ, *arbâ* "forty"; also jB lex. *elep er-ba-a/a'-ia* "40 (gur) boat"; < *erbe*

erbe, OA *arbe*, NA *rabbi*; f. *erbēt*, Ass. *arbēt*; nom. *erbû(m)*; f. *erbettu(m)* "four", esp. *erbūmi, erbē ūmi, erbet(ti) ūmu* "four days"; NA *rabbi urḫi* "four months"; OB *erbinammatim* "four cubits" (→ *ammatu* I); *kibrāt erbêm/erbetti(m)* [LÍMMU(.BA)] "the four edges (of the world)" (→ *arba'u*); *šārī erbetti* "the four winds"; *sūqī erbetti* "four-ways, crossroads"; with pron. suff. *erbettašu(nu)* [LÍMMU.BI/BA]; divide *ana erbēt* "into four"; *epin erbēt* "four(-ox) plough"; > *erbâ*; *erbettum, erbettītum, erbēnētum*; *erbêšu, erbēšerīšu, erbēšerû*; *rebû* etc.; *šurbu'ītum*

erbēnētum → *erbettum*

erbēšerīšu "fourteen times" OB; < *erbe* + *-šerīšu* (→ GAG §71a)

erbēšerû "fourteenth" Am.; < *erbe* + *-šerû*

erbêšu, *erbîšu*, OA *arbîšu* "four times" OA, O/jB; also *ana/adi e.*; < *erbe* (→ GAG §71a)

erbēt → *erbe*

erbette → *erpette*

erbettītum "(cow) from a team of four" OB; < *erbettum*

erbettum; pl. *erbēnētum* "(team of) four" OB of plough oxen; < *erbe*; > *erbettītum*

erbîšu → *erbêšu*

erbu(m) I, *irbu* "income" [KU4] of temple, palace, land, person; also pl., e.g. *erbī še'im* "income (in) grain"; OA (as import-tax)?; NB "entry fee"? to temple; < *erēbu* I; → *urbu* I

erbu(m) II, *erebu* "(sun)set" Bab. in *ereb šamši* [^{d}UTU.ŠÚ.A; ŠÚ.20] of time "sunset"; of place "the west", Mari also without *šamši*; < *erēbu* I

erbû(m), jB also *eribû*, M/NA *ar(i)bû*; st. constr. *e/arib* "locust" [BURU$_5$] *tibût e.* "locust swarm", also *e. tibûti*; *eli e. mād* "more numerous than locusts"; *erib garābi* "leprosy-l." (a plant name); *e. nāri* "river-l." (a water insect)?; *e. tâmti* "sea-l." (a crustacean)?; *e. turbu'ti* "dust storm-l."; > *eribîš*; *ṣinnarabu*

erbû → also *erbe*

erebu → *erbu* II

erēbu(m) I "to enter" **G** (Bab. *u/u*, Ass. *a/u*; OB perf. occas. *īterib*) [KU$_4$(.RA)] **1.** "come in" (vent.), "go in" to (= *ana*) house, to (meet) s.o.; "enter" house (to take up residence; in marriage, adoption, servitude); land, city, heaven, underworld; *e. u (w)aṣû(m)* "go/come in and out" **2.** "enter" new condition, e.g. *ana wardūtim/qāt PN/ilkim/adê e.* "go into slavery/possession of PN/state service/sworn contract" **3.** "report for duty, present o.s." to, before deity, king, lawcourt **4.** of food, drink, incense "enter" the body; of work, lament *ana libbi-/ina karši- e.*, i.e. be painful; of building, feature on liver "encroach, overlap" **5.** of goods, money etc. "come in, arrive"; of water, caravan, month, season; of sun "set" **Gtn** iter. [KU$_4$.KU$_4$(.MEŠ)], e.g. Lamaštu *mūterribtum ša bītāti* "who continually enters houses"; of caravans "arrive at different times, successively"; "get into" garment "repeatedly"; gramm. "occur" **Gt** O/jB "enter permanently"? **D** (rare) OB "enter" s.th. on (= *ana*) a tablet; Am.; NA stat. (pl. subj.) **Š** caus. of G "introduce" into presence; "post, station" troops in town, land; "take into" temple as offering, house as present; "bring in" harvest, "import" goods; "deliver" letter, tablet etc.; "send in" news; "consign" stele etc. to darkness etc.; "insert", stat. of part of liver "is inserted" **Štn** iter. of Š; > *erbu* I.II; *ēribu*, *ēribtum*, *ērib bīti* etc.; *errēbu*, *errebtu*, *errēbūtu*; *erubbātum*; *urbu* I, *urubātu* I; *nērebu*, *nērebtu*, *nērebūtum*; *šūrubtu*, *mušēribtum*; *tērubtu*

erēbu(m) II, OB also *ḫerēbum*, jB usu. *arēbu* "rook, jackdaw; crow, raven" O/jB [UGA.MUŠEN; BURU$_4$.MUŠEN]; jB *a/ereb zēri* (a kind of crow) [jB BURU$_5$ *zēri*]; *šēp(ā) e./a.* "crow's feet" (a plant) [Ú.GÌR.UGA.MUŠEN]; astr. (a star) "Corvus", also code name for Mars and Saturn [MUL.UGA.MUŠEN; MUL.UG$_5$.GA]; occas. hard to distinguish from *erbû* "locust"

erēdu → *warādum*

erēḫu ~ "to act aggressively" M/jB **G** (*i/i*) towards s.o. (= dat.); "attack" s.o. (= acc.) **Š** mng. uncl.; > *erḫu*, *erḫāniš*, *erḫūtu*; *irḫu*; *mēreḫtu*; → *arāḫu* I.II

erēmu → *arāmu*

erēnu(m) I, *erinnu*, Nuzi also *urīnu* "cedar" [(GIŠ.)EREN] OAkk *qišti e.* "cedar forest"; "cedar (logs)" for roof, column, door etc.; as aromatic wood (OA by weight); med. in recipes; *šaman e.* "cedar oil"; *dām e.* "cedar blood" (i.e. resin); ash, powder of c.; *e. peṣû* "white c." (= *tiyāru*); jB *qiššî e.* "cucumber of c." (a stone); *sumkinnu e.* "cedar shavings"?; < Sum.; → *urnu* II

erēnu II "root" jB comm.; < Sum.

erēpu(m), *arāpu* "to cloud over" (intrans.) O/jB, NA **G** (*u/u*) [ŠÚ; ŠÚ.ŠÚ.RU; ŠÚ.UŠ.RU] of day, of light "grow dark"; transf. of face (*pānū*) **D** stat. "is darkened" of demon, face, eyes; > *erpu*, *erpetu*; *urrupu*; *urpu*, *urpatu* I; *urpāniš*

ereqqu(m) f. "cart, waggon" [(GIŠ.)MAR.GÍD.DA] (later only lit.); OA, MB, Nuzi "waggon (-load)"; astr. "Ursa Major", also desig. of Venus; *e. šamê* "Ursa Minor" [MUL.MAR.GÍD.DA.AN.NA]

erēru(m) "to be parched"? O/jB **G** of drugs "be dry" **D** "parch" drugs etc. **N**? jB stat. of star, planet; > *erru* I

ereššānu "naked" jB lex.; < *eriššī-*

ereštum → *erištu* II

erešu "lady, queen" jB lex.; < Sum.

erēšu(m) I, OAkk *e/arāšum*, Ass. *arāšu(m)* "to sow; cultivate" **G** (Bab. *i/i*, OB pres. also *irruš*; OAkk, Ass. *a/u*) [URU$_4$] "cultivate, plough" a field; with plough (*agadibbu*), jB lex.; "plant, grow, cultivate" crop (sesame, wheat, millet etc.) **Gtn** iter., often over X years **D** ~ G jB "carry out cultivation of" **Š** caus. of G **Štn** jB lex. **N** pass. of G [URU$_4$] of field "be tilled"; of crop "be grown"; > *eršu* II, *ārišūtu*, *aršātum*; *erištum* I; *ērišu* I, *ērišānu*; *errēšu*, *errēšūtu*; *mērešu* I, *mēreštu* I; *mušērišu*; *tērušum*

erēšu(m) II, Ass. *erāšu(m)* "to request, wish for" **G** (*i/i*) [URU$_4$; KAM (esp. in PN)] "request, demand" s.th. from s.o. (= 2 acc.); or from = *išti*, *itti*, Bogh. *ana*, Nuzi *ašar*; of deity "desire, request" offering, prayer, temple etc.; stat. *išti/itti ilim e.* "is desired, requested by god"; of heart, person "desire, want" (obj. unexpressed); freq. in PNs **Gtn** iter. [URU$_4$.ME(Š); URU$_4$.URU$_4$], e.g. statue *mūterriš balāṭīya* "constantly requesting (long) life for me" **Dt** MA pass. "be requested, wanted" **N** pass. of G "be demanded"; "be wanted, desired"; > *eršu* III; *erištu* II; *uršu* II; *ērišu* II; *errēšû*; *mērešu* III, *mērEštu* II

erēšu → also *erīšu*

ergididû (a lament accompanied on the flute) jB lex.; < Sum.

ergilu, *ergiṣu* (a type of locust) jB lex.

erginu (a colour of horses, phps.) "brown" NA

ergisû (a flute-accompanied dirge) jB lex.; < Sum.

ergiṣu → *ergilu*

erḫāniš "provocatively" jB; < *erḫu* + -*ān* + -*iš*

erḫānû → *arḫānû*

erḫu ~ "aggressive" M/jB of soldiers, enemy; transf. of mouth "provocative"; OB of bull ?; < *erēḫu*; > *erḫāniš*; *erḫūtu*

erḫūtu "aggressiveness" MB; < *erḫu*

eria mūri → *erium*

eriānum → *iliānum*

eriātu → *eriyātu*

erib → *erbû*

ērib bīti(m) 'temple-enterer' Bab., NA [(LÚ.) KU₄.É] (member of temple personnel); < *ēribu* + *bītu*; > *ērib-bītūtu*

ērib-bīt-piriŠtūtu "office carrying access to *bīt-pirišti*" NB [(LÚ.)KU₄.É-*b.-p.*] as prebend; < *ēribu*; → *bītu* 5

ērib-bītūtu "status of 'temple-enterer'" NB [(LÚ.)KU₄.É-] as prebend; < *ērib bīti*

ērib-ēkalli(m) 'palace-enterer' (a palace official) O/jB; < *ēribu* + *ēkallu*

eribîš, *aribîš* "like locusts" jB(NA); < *erbû*

ēribtum "import tax" OA; < *ēribu*

eribû → *erbû*

ēribu(m) "entering; enterer" Bab., NA **1.** OB *ērib ana šarrim īrubu* "'enterer' who had access to the king"; NA *ēribūte* '(palace-)enterers' **2.** "(in)coming" [KU₄] of day, month, year; < *erēbu* I; > *ērib-...*; *ēribtum*

eridātum pl. (a container for fish)? OB

erim "side, arm-rest" jB lex. of bed, chair; < Sum.; → *erimmum* II ?

erimmatu(m) 1. "(egg-shaped) bead" O/jB; "(stone) bead" [(NA₄.)NUNUZ] of lapis lazuli etc.; in mag.; also of metal, wood; pl. necklace of *e.* beads (→ *irimmu*) **2.** jB lex. (part of a plough), also *dalat e.*; NB boxwood for making *e.* [GIŠ.NUNUZ] (→ *erimtu* II 4) **3.** jB (part of liver); → *rimmatum* ?

erimmu I, *erimu*, *irimmu* **1.** "mole (on skin)" jB on face, body; white, yellow, red; MA, jB

"discoloration" of flesh **2.** jB lex., also *erimtu* (a red berry)

erimmum II mng. unkn. Mari (or = *erim* ?)

erimtu I "baked brick" OB(Susa)

erimtu II "cover(ing)" M/NA, j/NB **1.** "cover, holder" for axe; of stone **2.** jB lex. "(leather) cover" for chair **3.** j/NB, also *urindu* "tablet envelope" **4.** jB lex. (part of a plough) (→ *erimmatu* 2); < *ermu*

erimtu → also *erimmu* I 2

erimu → *erimmu* I

erinakku (part of a building) MB(Ass.)

erinnu "neck-stock, halter" jB for prisoner; transf. *e. māti* held by gods; < Sum.

erinnu → also *erēnu* I

eriptu (a colourful garment) jB lex.; → *erpu*

eripu, *iripu* (a copper object) Nuzi

eriqā'u (a table) jB lex.

erīru (a garment) jB lex.

erîš "like an eagle" jB; < *erû* I

ērišānu "cultivator" MA of field; < *ērišu* I + -*ān*

erišši- "in nakedness" OA, O/jB with pron. suff. *e. alāku(m)* "to go naked", "in destitution"; < *erium* (→ GAG §67f); > *erešŠānu*; *erišŠuttu*; → *mērešŠû*

erišŠuttu, *errišuttu* "destitution" Bogh.; < *erišŠī-*

eriŠtum I "cultivation" OB also "crop"; < *erēšu* I

eriŠtu(m) II, *erēŠtum*, *iriŠtu* "demand, request, need" [KAM; KÁM; MB ŠU.KAM.MA/MI] "request" by s.o. (= gen.); "desire, request" for (= gen.); "desire, urge" for reproduction, in sheep, goat *erišti* "on heat"; "requirement, need"; *e. eqli*, *musarî*, *kasî* etc. (plant names); 'request' (desig. of ominous sign, feature on liver); < *erēšu* II

eriŠtu → also *eršu* I

erīšu(m), *erēšu(m)*, *irīšu* "scent, fragrance" Bab. of person, meal, water, house; esp. of aromatic woods, incense

ērišu(m) I "ploughing" Mari, of oxen; O/jB lex. "cultivator"; < *erēšu* I

ērišu II "bridegroom" jB (liter. 'one who requests'); < *erēšu* II

erītu → *arītu* I

erium "naked" OA, of person "destitute", of hand, house "empty" (OB → *erišŠī-*); O/jB lex. *eria(m) mūri(m)*, *aria mūri* (a disease); < *erû* III

eriu → also *werûm*

eri(y)ātu(m), *ariyātu*, *iriyātu* "cold weather" jB *dunnu/danān(a) e.* "depths of winter"

erkabu → *argabu*

erkallu, *erkalla* "underworld" jB; < Sum.

erkitušû (a lament) jB; < Sum.
erku (a garment) jB lex.
erkû (a kind of tyre) jB lex., of wood; jB(Ass.) pl. f. *erkâti* in desig. of papyrus boats ?
erkulla (a plant) M/jB med.
ermu(m), OB also *ḫermum* "cover(ing)" O/jB; "envelope" of tablet; "case" of tool; jB lex. (a word for cultivated land); *e. Ani* 'Anu's canopy' = "sky", also wooden "baldachin" (^{giš}*e.*); < *arāmu*
ernama mng. unkn. jB
ernamtaggadû (a dirge) jB lex.; < Sum.
ernettu, ernintu → *ernittu*
ernīnum (a drug) OB med.
ernittu(m), *ernettu(m), ernintu*, Bogh. *ennettu* "triumph, battle objective" Bab.(lit.), NB [U/Ù.MA] *e. kašādu* "to achieve victory"
erpette; pl. *erpettena* mng. unkn. Nuzi; grain for *e.*; < Hurr.
erpetu(m) "cloud" Bab. [DUNGU] red, black etc.; thick; floating; transf. ref. to sorceress's activity; *e. mūti* "cloud of death"; < *erēpu*
erpu, *arpu* "clouded over" j/NB, NA [ŠÚ.A] usu. *ūmu e.* "cloudy day" [U4.ŠÚ.ŠÚ.RU]; < *erēpu*; → *eriptu*
erqu → *warqum*
erratum → *erretu* I
errebtu "immigrant (group)" NB/NA; also *ṣābē e.*; < *errēbu*
errēbu(m) "intruder, new arrival" OAkk, jB; of usurper; of new member of household; also jB lex. for *arbu* "fugitive"; < *erēbu* I; > *errebtu, errēbūtu*
errēbūtu "status as new member" jB lex. of family, household; < *errēbu*
errerû(m) "given to cursing" OB lex.; < *arāru* II
errēšu(m), OAkk also *arrāšum* "cultivator" OAkk, Bab. [Bogh. LÚ.APIN.LÁ] esp. of tenant; also as PN; < *erēšu* I
errēšû "(persistently) demanding" jB lex.; < *erēšu* II
errēšūtu(m) "cultivation (contract)" Bab. [NAM.(GIŠ.)APIN.LA/LÁ] OB *ana e. šūṣûm/leqûm* "to rent" a field; *ana e. nadānum* "to lease" etc.; *kanīk e.* "tenancy contract"; < *errēšu*
erretu(m) I, OAkk *erratum* "curse" OAkk, O/jB *e. arāru* "to curse (s.o.)"; < *arāru* II; → *arratu*
erretu(m) II ~ "weir, barrage" O/jB of reeds, stone; also jB, Nuzi "pigsty" of reeds; < *erru* II
errišuttu → *erissuttu*
erru(m) I ~ "parched" O/jB of wood, malt, aromatic; < *erēru*
erru(m) II, *eru* ~ "ring, band" OAkk, Bab. **1.** "ring, washer" for peg **2.** also *arû*, "headband" in metal, cloth (→ *warûm* I); jB also pl. f. *errēt qaqqadē* **3.** Nuzi "(animal) enclosure, pen" **4.** (enclosed plot of land); < Sum.; > *erretu* II
erru(m) III "intestine(s)" Bab, NA [(UZU.)ŠÀ] of human, animal; diviner *mūdê e.* "who knows the entrails"; *e. qatnu/kabru* "small/large intestine"; *e. gamertu* [NB UZU.ŠÀ.TIL] "rectum"; ext. pl. *errū sāḫirūtu* [ŠÀ.NIGIN] "intestines encircling" the liver; transf. "tendrils" of cucumber; *e. nūni, kalbi, tâmti* "intestine of fish, dog, sea" (plant names)
erru → also *erû* II; *werrum*
errû "colocynth"? M/jB [(Ú.)ÚKUŠ.LAGAB (.SAR)] also as drug; *aban e.* = hard kernel of *e.*?; → *merrû*
ersaḫarḫubbû (a lament) jB lex.; < Sum.
ersiskurrû (a sacrificial lament) jB lex.; < Sum.
ersû(m), *eršû* "ready" OA, O/jB "prepared" of animals, goods, flour etc.; of person "trained"; OB *ša ersîm* "(cloth) finisher"; > *šutērsû*; *tērsītu*
ersuppu → *arsuppu*
erṣetu(m), OAkk *arṣatum* "earth, land; underworld" OAkk, Bab., NA [KI (often KI-*tum/tim* etc.)] **1.** "the earth" (as opp. to heaven) **2.** the earth beneath the surface, i.e. "underworld"; DN ^{d}*Bēlet-e.* "Mistress of the Underworld"; also in PNs **3.** "ground", soaked; ploughed; quakes; for burial **4.** politically "land, territory", jB "district", NB "city quarter" **5.** ext. (area of liver); → *urṣu* II
erṣu → *urṣu* I
eršabadarû (a lament) jB lex.; < Sum.
eršaḫungû (an Emesal cultic prayer) M/jB [ÉR.ŠÀ.ḪUN.GÁ] also associated ritual; < Sum.; → *eršemšaḫungû*
eršannešakku, *eršannašakku* (a lament) jB lex.; < Sum.
eršemmakku (or *eršemmû*) (an Emesal cult song) jB [ÉR.ŠÈM/ŠEM4.MA]; < Sum.
eršemšaḫungû (var. of *eršaḫungû*) jB; < Sum.
eršu(m) I; f. *erištu* "wise" OAkk, O/jB of deity, king etc.; > *eršūtu*; *mērešu* II
eršu(m) II, NA *aršu* "tilled; cultivated" OAkk, O/jB, NA of field, "tilled", also subst. "cultivated plot"; of plant "cultivated", jB pl. *eršūtu* "vegetables"; < *erēšu* I
eršu(m) III "demanded, desired" OAkk, O/MB "wanted, requested" of things; Nuzi "claimed" property; in PNs, of persons; < *erēšu* II

eršu(m) IV f. "bed" [GIŠ.NÁ]; of sickbed *e. ṣabātu(m)* "the bed holds" s.o., i.e. person is confined to bed; *bīt e.* "bedroom"; "(marriage) bed"; → *uršu* I

eršû → *ersû*

eršūtu "wisdom" jB; < *eršu* I

ertabadarû (a lament) jB lex.; < Sum.

ertum → *irtu* I

ērtu → *ēru* II

erṭû → *urṭû*

erum mng. unkn. OAkk

eru → also *aru* I; *erru* II

erû(m) I, *arû*, lex. also *rû* "eagle" Bab. [TI8.MUŠEN] also vulture?; Qatna "eagle (figure)" of gold; astr. "constellation Aquila" [MUL.TI8.MUŠEN]; > *arâniš*, *erîš*

erû(m) II, *arû*, *irûm*, jB also *erru*; pl. m. & f. "grindstone" Bab., M/NA [NA4.UR5; NA4.UR5.UR5]; of *atbaru* stone; for grain, cumin etc.; for grinding potsherds (for grog)

erû(m) III, *arû* "to be naked" **G** OA stat. "is destitute" **D** "strip bare" head (of hair); of wind, "strip" trees, ground; OA "empty, clear out" container (*qablītum*); "strip, prepare" mother (for childbirth); > *erium*, *erûtum* III; *erišši-*, *erišsuttu*, *ereššānu*; *rišummāni*?; *ūru* II, *ūrātu*?; *mērênu*, *mērênû*, *mēreššû*; *murrûm* II

erû → also *arû* IV.VI; *iri'u*; *werûm*

ēru(m) I "awake" O/jB; < *êru*; > *ērūtu*

ēru(m) II, Ass. *e'ru*; jB lex. *ērtu* (a tree) Bab., M/NA [GIŠ.MA.NU] in fields, mountain; esp. mag., med., wood for stick, stave; *ṭābat ē.* (a kind of salt); → *manû* III

êru(m) "to be(come) awake" **G** (pret. *i'ēr*) of person; jB med. of s.o.'s heart "be awake", i.e. conscious **D** "waken"; stat. of weapon "is aroused" against s.o.; > *ēru* I, *ērūtu*; *muštērtum*

e'ru → *ēru* II

erubbātum pl. tant. "pledge, security" OA of person, house, tablet; < *erēbu* I

eruḫlu, *uruḫlu* (a prof. desig.) Nuzi; < Hurr.

erullu (a bird) M/jB med. as ingredient

erūtu → *arūtu*

erûtu I, *arûtu* "back" jB lex. (part of body)

erûtu II, *u(r)rûtu*, *uruttu* "fish spawn" jB; < *arû* IV

erûtum III "nakedness" OB lex. in *ša e.* "destitute person"?; < *erium*

ērūtu(m) "wakefulness" O/jB; < *ēru* I

eru'um → *werûm*

erwiššu "royal service" Nuzi with *našû* "to bear (liability for)"; < Hurr.

esādu mng. unkn. jB med.

esallû (an irrigation construction) NB [É.SAL(.A)]; < Sum.?

esāmum (a topog. term) OB

esāyātu → *asa'ītu*

esēḫu(m), Mari, M/NA *esēku(m)* "to assign, allocate" O/jB, M/NA **G** (*i/i*) field, workers, rations **D** ~ G **Š** Mari "have s.o. assign" field **N** pass. of G, of field; > *isḫu* II, *isiḫtu*, *isiktum*; *mēseḫtu*; *ussuḫum*; *ussuktu*, *ussuku* ?; → *esēqu*

esēḫu → also *ezēḫu*

esēku → *esēḫu*; *esēqu*

esēlu ~ "to blow up, inflate" M/jB **G** stat. *libbu/šuburru e.* "inner body/anus is constipated" **D**, **Dt** → *eṣēlu* D, Dt **N** "become inflated; be constipated" **Ntn** iter., of fish "be bloated"?; > *eslu*; *isiltu*

esēpu(m) "to gather together, collect up" OAkk, O/jB, M/NA **G** (*i/i*) earth, dust; OB grain at harvest; burning coals; locusts; "collect up" powder, liquid (into vessel); Ug. of demon "gather up" victim **D** ~ G "scrape up" earth from furrows **Š** "have s.o. scrape, gather up" **Štn** "have s.o. repeatedly scrape up" **N** of beer "be decanted"; > *mussipu*; *nēsepu*, *nēseptu*

esēqu(m), *esēku*, lex. also *ez/šēqu* "to incise, carve" Bab. **G** (*i/i*) images in stone **D** (mostly written with *k*) **1.** < *isqu* denom. "assign, distribute" lots **2.** of bones, stat. "are etched"? in flesh **Dt** pass. of D 1; > *isiqtu*; *ussuku*?

esertu, OB(poet.) *esratum*, jB also *esettu* "confined woman, concubine" O/jB, MA; sons of *e.*; Nuzi *bīt e.* "harem"; < *esru*

esēru(m) I "confinement" O/jB in *bīt e.* "cage"; < *esēru* II infin.

esēru(m) II, *eṣ/zēru*, *asāru* "to enclose, confine" Bab., M/NA **G** (*i/i*) bird; person, enemy, army; Nuzi *eserta e.* "take a concubine"; "hold back" water, disease, shout; of design "frame" **D** ~ G persons, army; stat., of gall bladder "is enclosed" **Dt** pass. of D **N** **1.** "shut o.s. in" **2.** of windpipe "be constricted"; > *esru*, *esertu*; *asīru* I, *asirtu*, *asīrūtu*; *esēru* I; *isirtu* I; *mēseru*, *mēsertu*; *mussiru*?; *usurtu*

esēru(m) III "to exact payment" **G** (*i/i*) from s.o. (= acc.); of silver, grain etc.; "demand" document; Nuzi *awīlū ša eseri* "debt collectors"; OB more gener. "put pressure on", stat. "is under pressure" **D** ~ G **N** of copper "be exacted"; > *isru* II; *isirtu* II; *usertu*, *esirratu*?

esettu → *esertu*

esigu "ebb, low water" jB lex.; < Sum.

esiḫtu → *isiḫtu*

esikillu (a temple building) O/jB lex.; also *ša e.* (a temple official); < Sum.

esiktum → *isiktum*

esiltu → *isiltu*

esirratu ~ "pressing stone"? NB for beer; < *esēru* III ?

esirtu → *esertu*; *isirtu* II

esittu(m) I "pestle" O/jB [GIŠ.GAZ] of wood, stone; for grain, sesame, bitumen etc.

esittu II (a date-palm tax) NB(Uruk) c. 6%

esittu → also *esertu*; *išittu* I

esītu → *ešītu*

eslu "constipated" jB of invalid; *šāru e.* "air (causing) flatulence"; < *esēlu*

esratum → *esertu*

esru(m) "confined" O/jB lex. "captive" bird; of street "enclosed", i.e. cul-de-sac; < *esēru* II; > *esertu*

essēsum → *eššēšu*

essû, *esû* "hole in ground, clay pit" jB [TÚL.LÁ] earth from "pits"; *e. āli* "town pit"; *šam(mi) e.* (kind of plant)

esu → *eššu* II

esû ~ "to effectuate, bring to pass"? jB **G** (*i/i*) word **D** ~ G Gula *mussât kalāma* "who brings everything to pass", also m. ptcp.; > *isītu*?

esû → also *asû* II; *essû*

eṣādu → *eṣēdu* I.II

eṣāduḫlu "harvester" Nuzi; < *eṣēdu* II Ass. + Hurr. *-uḫlu*

***eṣdu**, *eldu* "harvested" jB lex. of grain; < *eṣēdu* II

eṣēdu(m) I, Ass. *eṣādu* "harvest" Bab., NA [ŠE.KIN(GUR$_{10}$?).KU$_5$] "harvest(ed crop)"; "(time of) harvest"; "(activity of) harvest"; < *eṣēdu* II infin.

eṣēdu(m) II, Ass. *eṣādu(m)* "to harvest" **G** (*i/i*) [ŠE.KIN(GUR$_{10}$?).KU$_5$] "reap" grain, field; also reeds, grass; plenty; transf. of battle "mow down" enemy **Gtn** "harvest" each year **Š** caus. of G **N** pass. NB of harvest (*ebūru*) "be harvested"; > *eṣdu*; *eṣēdu* I; *ēṣidu*, *ēṣid pān mê*, *ēṣidānum*; *eṣāduḫlu*

eṣēlu(m) ~ "to paralyse" O/jB **G** (*i/i*) esp. stat. of parts of body; OA *qātum eṣlat* of slowness to pay **D** ~ G (also *uṣṣulu*) of sheep; of parts of body **Dt** pass. (also *utaṣṣulu*) "become paralysed" **N** ~ Dt **Ntn** iter. of N, of hands, feet etc.; > *uṣṣulu*, *tiṣṣulu*?

eṣemṣēru(m), *eṣenṣēru(m)* "backbone" O/jB, NA [GÚ.MUR$_{7/8}$?] of human, animal; OB *idi e.* = ribs; "(area of) spine" on back of animal, human; as cut of meat "chine"; transf. *e. eleppi* "keel of boat"; of battering ram; < *eṣem(t)u* + *ṣēru*

eṣemtu(m), *eṣen/ttu*, poet. *eṣmetu* "bone" Bab., M/NA [GÌR.PAD.DU; occas. GÌR.PAD.DA] of human, animal; *eṣmētum ṣeḫḫerētum* "cartilage"; ^{uzu}*e.* as offering to dead; "bony (structure), skeleton" of dead persons; of wood = "bone" of divine statues; "bodily frame"; M/NA (a linear measure); > *eṣemṣēru*

eṣennû "tube, spout" on vessel jB lex.

eṣenṣēru → *eṣemṣēru*

eṣentu → *eṣemtu*

eṣēnu(m) "to smell" (trans.) O/jB **G** (*i/i*) [IR] scent (*erīša*), incense, wind; OB oil *ana eṣēnim ul naṭu* "unpleasant to smell", transf. of impudence **D** "sniff at" incense, stench; "snuffle" like a mongoose **Š** caus. of G **N** "be smelled" of scent (*erīšu*)

eṣēpu(m) "to double" Bab., NA **G** (*i/i*) [TAB(.BA)] math. often *ana šina e.* "multiply by two"; stat. "is double", of parts of body; in hendiad. *e.* + *šarākum*, NA *e.* + *tadānu* "give/pay twofold"; "twine" thread, two- and also three-ply (*ana 3-šu*); "plait" reed mat; Mari, of message ~ "come in confirmation"; > *eṣpu*

eṣēru(m) "to draw, design" **G** (*i/i*) [ḪUR] freq. with *uṣurtu*; "make (magical) drawing" on wall, of flour etc.; "draw" plan of, "plan" building; "depict" on a bas-relief; stat., "is/are drawn", of stars in sky, markings on liver; "plan, design" favourable schemes for s.o.; "form" (or "plan"?) wall, city; "prescribe" death (as punishment)?; OB ~ "cross out" a tablet **D** (OB also *wuṣṣurum*) ~ G; > *eṣru*; *iṣurtu*, *uṣurtu*, *iṣratu*; *ēṣiru*; *mēṣiru*; *uṣṣuru* I

eṣēru → also *esēru* II

eṣettu → *eṣemtu*

ēṣidānum 'reaper' OB lex., syn. of *ēṣid pān mê*, also as PN; < *ēṣidu*

ēṣidānu → also *ēṣidu*

eṣidītu "provisions" NA; = *ṣidītu* ?

ēṣid pān mê 'reaper of the water's surface', "water-boatman" (an aquatic insect) jB; < *ēṣidu* + *pānu* I + *mû* I

ēṣidu(m); Nuzi pl. *ēṣidānu* "reaper, harvester" [LÚ.ŠE.KIN(GUR$_{10}$?).KU$_5$; Susa also LÚ.ŠE.KU$_5$.KIN]; OAkk as PN; < *eṣēdu* II; > *ēṣid pān mê*, *ēṣidānum*

ēṣiru "(stone) carver" Bogh., jB; < *eṣēru*

ēṣiš "soon, shortly" OA; < *wīṣum*

eṣmetu → *eṣemtu*

eṣpu(m) "doubled" jB "twin" of metal vessels; "twined" of thread; "double" of onions; OB ext. of trachea; < *eṣēpu*

eṣru "drawn" jB i.e. shown in relief carving; < *eṣēru*

eṣṣu → *iṣu*

eṣṣû f. "(small) gecko" jB lex.

eṣu → *iṣu*

eṣû "to slit, cut into" jB **G** (*i/i*) forehead, head; with blade, wheel

ēṣu → *wīṣum*

êṣum → *wiāṣum*

eṣurtu → *iṣurtu*

êš "whither?" OB; < *ayyiš*; → *îš*; *mêš*

êšam "whither?" OB; < *ayyiša*

êšamma "in any direction" jB; < *ayyišamma*

ešar → *ešer*

ešartu(m) "group of ten" Ass. **1.** OA 'a tenner', i.e. ten shekels of silver [10 GÍN-*tum*] **2.** OA "decemvirate" [10-*tum*] **3.** NA in *rab e.* "chief of a group of ten" officials, scribes [LÚ.GAL 10-*ti/e*]; < *ešer*; → *ešertu* II

ešaru → *išaru* I

ešāru → *ešēru*

ešātu → *išātu*

ešâtu → *ešītu*

ešāwa "(on) the other side" Nuzi; < Hurr.

ešbum → *išbum*

ešdu → *išdu*

ešēbu "to flourish" M/jB **G** (*i/i*) of plants; Ug. transf., of house **D** lex. fact. of G ? **N** lex. **Ntn** (**Gtn** ?) lex.; > *uššubu*

ešēgu → *ašāgu*

ešēqu → *esēqu*

ešer, Ass. *ešar*; f. *ešeret* "ten" (before m. subst. *ešeret*, *eše/arti*; before f. subst. *ešer*); -*(e)šeret* "-teen" (→ GAG §69d); > *aširtum* II; *ešertu* II, *ešartu*; *ešrum*, *ešrû* II; *ešrētu*; *ešrīšu*, *ešriātu*; *išrum* III; *ušurtum*; *ušurā*; -*šer*, -*šeret*, -*šerīšu*, -*šerû* etc.; *ešrā* etc.

ešeriš → *išariš*

ešertu(m) I, *iše/irtu(m)*, jB also *aše/irtu*; pl. usu. *ešrētu*, also *ašrātu*, *išrētu*, OB *išrā/ētum* "chapel, shrine" post-OB only lit. [ZAG.GAR.RA] "shrine" within temple; "chapel" of prince, of people, of family deity (*e. bīt ilīšu*, *e. il bīti*); of gods gener. (but not *e.* + DN); on *kudurru*, divine "shrine", i.e. symbol; also "pious donation"

ešertu II "group of ten" Nuzi, NB ? [10(.MEŠ)-*ti*] esp. *rab e.*; < *ešer*; → *ešartu*

ešertu → also *išaru* I f.

ešeru → also *išaru* I

ešēru(m), Ass. *i/ešāru(m)* "to be/go well; be straight, fair; direct o.s. (towards)" **G** (*i/i*) [SI.SÁ; NA, NB also GIŠ] "go well, be successful" of crop, harvest, animal breeding; human reproduction, birth; "be(come) healthy"; of house, city, land, journey "prosper"; of person "be successful"; of divination, omens, wind "be favourable"; "be(come) right, normal"; of gut, i.e. be evacuated; of sceptre; (neg.) of Lamaštu; "direct o.s. towards, make straight for" (+ *ana*/dat.), of demon to person, army to destruction; also + *ana pān/maḫar*, *eli*; "go straight along" street (= acc.); OA of goods "come straight to" s.o. **Š** (pret. *ušēšir*, OAkk, OB(poet.) *ušūšir*) [SI.SÁ; GIŠ] "put in good condition, in order" plough, cart, house; Am. "prepare, get ready"; MA "process" food; "direct" water, canal; "sweep (out)" house, ground; "purge" intestines; "direct aright" feet, person, person's way; "make successful, cause to prosper"; "put right, make straight", stat. of parts of liver; "steer" s.o. (on right way); "make straight" the way, also ellipt. "go straight ahead" **Št¹** pass. of Š [SI.SÁ] "be put in order"; of person "be guided aright"; of cattle "be steered straight"; "have straightforward (childbirth)" **Št²** "put, keep in order", "get ready" weapons; house, road; "flatten out" unevennesses; "give correct decision", "formulate correct" plans; "get right" text, language; "carry out correctly" ritual, work; "cause to go well" animal, human procreation; "guide (o.'s hand) aright"; "lead" person, people "aright", "secure justice for" s.o.; *ḫarrāna* (etc.) *š.* "take to the road"; ellipt. "go off, start out"; of birth "be (born) straightforwardly" **N** ~ G "become prosperous", "become successful"; "make towards, go for" s.o.; > *išaru* I.II, *išariš*, *išartu*, *išarūtu*; *išertum*?; *mīšaru*, *mīšariš*, *mīšartu*, *mīšarūtu*; *mīšertu*; *mūšaru*?; *mušēšeru*, *mušēšertu*, *muštēšertu*; *šūšuru*, *šūšuriš*; *šutēšuru*; *tēšertu*?

ešeštu mng. unkn. jB in *mukkalli e.* (a title of Nabû)

ešēšu → *ašāšu* IV

ešeum → *ešû* I

ešē'u(m) ~ "to muzzle"? OB lex., jB

ešgallu "great shrine" j/NB [ÈŠ.GAL] as cosmic domain; temple of Anu at Uruk; lex. (a name for the underworld); < Sum.

ešigillu → *sikillu*

ešītīn → *ušû*

ešittu → *išittu* I

ešītu(m), *išītu(m)*, NB also *esītu* "confusion" Bab. "(political) disorder(s)" (sg. & pl.);

"blurring" of the vision; "wildness" of terrain; pl. also *ašâtu* (a term for eclipse) astr., lex.; < *ešû* I

ešium → *ušû*

eškāru → *iškāru*

eškūru → *iškūru*

ešmāḫu "great shrine" jB lex.; < Sum.

ešmarû, *i/ašmarû* (a silver alloy) j/NB for casting and overlay [GU.AN.NA ?]

ešmekku, *iš/smekku* (a stone, phps.) "malachite" Qatna, Am., jB

ešpum → *išbum*

ešqarrurtu → *išqarrurtu*

ešqu "solid, massive" jB of building stone

ešqu → also *isqu*

ešrā, *i/ašrā* "twenty"; < *ešer*; > *imḫur-ešrā*; *ešrû* I, *ešru'u*

ešrētu(m), *išrētum*, OA *i/ušrātum*, j/NB also *ušrētu* pl. tant. "one-tenth" **1.** as fraction, OB *išrēt šiddim* "one-tenth of the side", OA *kī išrāt* (st. abs.) "at one-tenth" **2.** "payment of one-tenth, tithe" OA, OB, Ug. [Ug. ZAG.10]; < *ešrum* f. pl.

ešrētu → also *ešertu* I

ešriātu "tenfold" NA in *ana e.* [10(.MEŠ)-*te/i*]; < *ešer*

ešriš → *išariš*

ešrīšu, *išrīšu* "ten times" OB, Ass.; also *ana/adi e.*; < *ešer*

ešrum; f. *ešurtum* "tenth" OA, OB; < *ešer*

ešru → also *išaru* I; *išru* II

ešrû(m) I, *išrû(m)* "20th day (of month)" Bab. [UD.20.KAM] as special day; also in PNs; < *ešrā*

ešrû II "tenth; one-tenth" M/NB, esp. NB "(temple) tithe", "tithe(-land)", *ša muḫḫi e.* "tithe official"; < *ešer*

ešru'u "a twentieth" NB; < *ešrā*

eššanna → *eššēšu*

eššātu "headband; bandage" jB comm.

eššebītu → *eššebû*

eššebu(m), *eššebû(m)*, *iššebu/û(m)* (a kind of owl)? M/jB, NA; OAkk as PN; > *eššebû*?

eššebû(m), *iššebû(m)*; f. *eššebī/ūtu(m)* (an ecstatic) O/jB, *šārat/lubūš e.* "hair/dress of ecstatic"; m. & f. often in mag.; < *eššebu* ?

eššebû → also *eššebu*

eššēšu(m), *iššē(š)šu(m)*, Mari also *essēsum*; NB pl. *eššanna*, *šeššanna/u*, *e/iššeššāni* (a feast day) Bab. [(UD.)ÈŠ.ÈŠ] OB *eššēšam* (acc.) etc. "on the holiday"; jB of Nabû (and Tašmētu); occasion of offerings, ritual; < Sum.

eššetu → *eššu* I

ešše'u, *išše'u*, *eššû* "touchwood, tinder" jB lex.

eššiš "anew" [GIBIL(.BI)]; also *eššišamma*; < *eššu* I

eššu(m) I; f. *edištu(m)*, more freq. *eššetu(m)* "new" [GIBIL; GIBIL4] of building, ship, tool, clothing etc.; of year, month, day; OB *adi/ina eššētim*, *eššetamma*, M/NB *ina/ana ešši* "(up till) recently"; of people "fresh" arrivals, departures; of dates, grain "fresh(ly harvested)"; < *edēšu*; > *eššiš*, *eššūtu*; *uššušu* III

eššu II, *esu* "shrine" jB lex.; < Sum.

eššû I "cold weather"? jB lex.

eššû II (a word for a door) jB lex.

eššû → also *ešše'u*

eššūtu, Ass. *e/iššuttu* in *ana e.* "anew, newly" M/jB(Ass.), Bogh. [GIBIL-] of new building, appointment, settlement, name; *ana e. ṣabātu* "to reorganize"; Bogh. "recently"; < *eššu* I

eštagurrû → *ištagurrû*

eštalû → *aštalû*

eštu → *ištu*

ešṭuḫḫu → *ištuḫḫu*

ešû(m) I, *ešeum*, *ašû*, *išû* "confused" Bab. [SÙḪ in NA PNs] of thread "tangled"; of person, mind, face; of omens; of eyes "blurred"; also NA [SÙḪ]? in PN; < *ešû* IV; > *ašītu* I, *ešītu*

ešûm II "confusion" Mari of political conditions; < *ešû* IV infin.

ešû III (a loincloth or kilt) jB lex.

ešû(m) IV, *ašû* "to confuse, make unclear" Bab., NA **G** [SÙḪ] person, road; eyes, sight; medical diagnosis **D** "confuse, throw into confusion", "make unclear" **Dt** pass. of D **Š** ~ D "confuse, make uncertain" person, understanding **N** "be confused, in state of uncertainty" of person, land; > *ešû* I.II, *ašītu* I, *ešītu*; *nenšûm*; *šāšû*, *šūšâtu*; *tēšû*; → *mīšītum*

ešû V mng. unkn. NA (activity connected with sand, ground)

etāku "to be on guard" NA **G** of soldiers; stat. "is alert"; of king "is aware" of s.th. **D** "alert" s.o.; stat. "is alerted"

etallu → *etellu*

etallūtu → *etellūtu*

etamdu, *etandu* "touching, laid against each other" OA, NA; of presents "piled up"; OA of silver "amassed", of witnesses "in collusion"; lex. of beads *etandētu* "strung together"?; < *emēdu* I Gt; Bab. → *etmudu*

etamšû → *eparšû*

etandu → *etamdu*

etebranni (or *etepranni*) "humanity, mankind" jB lex. "all people"

etēku → *etāku*

etelletu, *etellatu* "pre-eminent; lady" O/jB as title of goddesses, *e. aḫḫēša* "supreme (among) her brothers"; < *etellu*

etelliš "as a lord" O/jB of gods, kings, persons; esp. *e.* + *alāku* Gtn "to proceed, walk in a lordly way"; < *etellu*

etellu(m), Ass. *etallu(m)*, OB also *itellum*, Bogh. *itillu*; OAkk st. constr. *eteal* "pre-eminent; lord" [NIR.GÁL] of gods, kings; of commands, esp. in PNs (*Etel-pū/ī-DN*); OA "independent"; > *etellu*, *etelliš*, *etelletu*, *etellūtu*; *mētellu*, *mētellūtu*

etellūtu(m), Ass. *etallūtu(m)* "supremacy" Bab., OA, NA; OA "independence", *e. epāšum* "to act on own authority", *ana e.-* "on o.'s own authority"; < *etellu*; → *telūtu*

etēmu(m), *etēnu(m)* "to be smitten, affected"? Bab. **G** stat. of person, house, part of lung **D** "bring into contact, mix together"? **Št** "bring against each other" ingredients; of deity "set" enemies "against each other"; > *etimtum*?; *nētentu*

etenniwa mng. unkn. MB(Alal.); < Hurr.

etennu → *itinnu*

etēnu → *etēmu*

etepranni → *etebranni*

etēqu(m) "to go past; go through; cross over" **G** (*i/i*, Mari pret. also *ītuq*) [DIB] **1.** "proceed along, through" street, land; ellipt. of person, letter "move on" from one place to another **2.** "proceed further, move onward" **3.** "pass by, go past" king (in parade), city; of bird "fly past" ship etc.; of demon, causing illness; of time (year, month, day); fixed time (*a/edānu*), offering, eclipse (intrans.); NB (also trans.) "miss" date (for payment etc.), ellipt. "be late in payment" **4.** "cross (over)" mountain, watercourse, boundary; ext., astr. "stretch across, overlie" of part of liver, astronomical feature; transf. "transgress" moral limit, "break" oath, treaty, law etc.; OB "ignore" regulation **Gtn** iter. [DIB.MEŠ], e.g. of sun "constantly pass across" heaven **Gt** OA "proceed further onwards" **Š** caus. of G [DIB] "channel" water-flow; "pass" ship through control; OB stat. of slave "is made to step over" pestle; NA "carry out" ritual (*takpertu*), also ellipt.; "send, carry past" in parade; NB "make s.o. pass on (empty-handed)"; "make" evil, bad luck, illness "pass on, pass by"; "allow" time "to go past", "miss time for" offering, also ellipt. "miss (date)"; of sun "miss" eclipse; "make transcend, exceed" in quality, rank, size etc. **Štn** iter. of Š; or Št ? **N** pass. of G; of word, boundary "be transgressed"; jB "be made to move on, be resettled"; > *ētiqu*, *ētiqtum*; *mētequ*, *mēteqtu*; *mūtaqu*; *mušētiqtu*; *šūtuqu*, *šūtuqtu*, *šūtuqūtu*

etguru "crossed over, intertwined" jB [GIL] of figures, snakes, cuneiform signs etc.; transf. "complicated" of speech, calculations; < *egēru* Gt

etillû "dropsy" jB lex.; < Sum.

etimtum mng. unkn. OAkk, item assoc. with flour; < *etēmu* ?

ētiqtum "delegation in transit" Mari; < *ētiqu*

ētiqu "passer-by" jB; also f. *ētiqtu*; < *etēqu*

etlupu "bound cross-wise" jB lex.; < *elēpu* Gt

etmudu "touching, laid against each other" jB of clouds "massed up"; < *emēdu* Gt; Ass. → *etamdu*

etnakapû (a tree, or timber) Nuzi; < Hurr.

etnu mng. unkn. Nuzi; < Hurr.

etnušu "very weak" jB; < *enēšu* Gt

etpuqu "grown together"? jB mng. uncl.; < *epēqu* Gt

etpušu "effective"? jB of men, women; < *epēšu* II Gt

etqu → *itqu* 2

ettītu → *ettūtu*

ettu → *ittu* II; *wēdum*

ettūtu(m), *ettītu(m)*, *uttūtum*, lex. also *ettūwatum* "spider" O/jB [AŠ5; AŠ-*tú*] *qê e.* "spider web"; compare Uttu (Sum. goddess of textile manufacture; → *utû*)

etû → *itû*

etūdum → *atūdu*

eṭammum → *eṭemmu*

eṭēlu(m) "to be a man, manly" O/jB **G** Mari stat. "is a man"; jB "reach manhood" **D** jB "bring up to manhood" **Dt** jB "become full-grown man"; > *eṭlu*, *eṭliš*, *eṭlūtu*; *meṭlūtu*

eṭemmu(m), *iṭemmum*, OA also *eṭammum* "ghost" (of dead person) [GIDIM$_{1/2/4}$; OB also KI.DÍM; jB also GU4; Bogh. usu. ^{d}GIDIM] receiving libations, offerings; OA treated well/badly, interrogated; OB in PNs, of king; MB *e. kimtišu* "ghost of his family", ^{d}*e. muttaggišu* "wandering ghost"; Nuzi oath by ghost; in *qāt e.* [ŠU.GIDIM(.MA); ŠU.GU4 (.MA)]; *e. šūlû* "to raise a ghost (from underworld)"; *ša e.* "necromancer"; < Sum.

eṭemmūtu "state of ghost" jB in *e. alāku* "to become a ghost"; < *eṭemmu*

eṭēru(m) I "to take away; save" **G** (*i/i*) [KAR; later also SUR] **1.** "take s.th. from (= acc.)" s.o.; "deny" s.o. heir, wisdom; "remove, separate off" in glass recipe **2.** "save, spare" s.o., freq. in

PNs; OA also *napaštam e.* "save s.o.'s life" (financially); life (*napištu*) in battle, war, by medicine; from hardship, death, hand of death etc. **Gtn** iter. **N** pass. "be taken away", "be rescued"; > *eṭru* I; *ēṭiru*; *eṭṭeru*, *eṭṭēru*

eṭēru II "to pay" NB, D also NA **G** (*i/i*) [KAR; SUR] "pay" person, "pay" silver; infin. *eṭēru ša eqli/agurru* "payment for field/bricks"; stat. of person "is paid off", of commodity "is paid for" **D** "pay off" (fully); NA stat. *uṭṭuru issu pān aḫā'iš* "they are mutually paid off, quit" **Dt** pass. of D NB of silver "be fully paid" **N** pass. of G, of person "be paid (off with respect to = acc.)" silver, o.'s credit (*rāšûssu*); by means of (= acc.) field, dates etc. **Ntn** iter. of N "be paid off in instalments"; > *eṭru* II

eṭirtu mng. unkn. jB lex.; → *eṭru* I.II

ēṭiru; f. *ēṭirtu* "saviour" M/NB, NA in PNs [KAR; SUR]; < *eṭēru* I ptcp.

eṭliš "manly" OB; < *eṭlu*

eṭlu(m) "manly; young man" (pl. as adj. and subst.) [(LÚ.)GURUŠ; OB also ŠUL] **1.** (as opp. to woman) **2.** "(mature) young man" (as opp. to old man) **3.** "man" gener.; of king, of god; < *eṭēlu*; > *eṭliš*; *eṭlūtu*

eṭlūtu(m) "manliness" O/jB esp. implying strength, bravery in battle; < *eṭlu*

eṭru I "taken away" jB lex.; < *eṭēru* I

eṭru II "paid (off)" NA of grain debt; NB of promissory note (*u'iltu*); < *eṭēru* II

eṭṭeru "eager to save" jB of fDN; < *eṭēru* I

eṭṭēru "escaper, deserter" jB; < *eṭēru* I

eṭû I "dark" jB of day, house; "extinguished" of hearth; OA *eṭiūtum* of textiles ?; < *eṭû* II; > *eṭûtu*

eṭû II "to be(come) dark, dim" Bab. **G** (pret. *īṭi*; stat. *eṭu*) of day, sun, moon, star; of torch "burn dimly"; of building "be dimly lit"; transf. of face **Gtn** iter. **D** "darken, make obscure" day; transf. face, eyes; "make (situation) unclear" **Dt** "be darkened" of the earth; light; eyes; > *eṭû* I, *eṭûtu*

eṭûtu "darkness" M/NB, NA esp. *ana e.* "into darkness"; < *eṭû* I

e'u → *ya'u*

ewiṣum (or *ewaṣ/sum*, *ewisum*); pl. f. (a tool)? OA

ewûm I, *emû* "to become" Bab., OA **G** (*i/i*, jB usu. *e/e*) with acc., of day "turn into" darkness, of loan into grain; freq. with *-iš*, e.g. *awīliš* "into a man", *kišubbîš* "into waste land"; with *kī(ma)* "become like", with *-iš*, e.g. *kīma iṣṣūriš* "like a bird"; stat. "is (like)" **D** with *-iš* "make s.o./s.th. like"; "falsify"? tablet **Š** with *kī(ma)*, *-iš* "make s.o./s.th. like" or "into"

ewûm II ~ "to impose on" OB **G** (pret. *īwi*) sins on (= acc.) s.o.; > *iwītu*

ewuru "heir" Nuzi; < Hurr.; > *ewurumma*, *ewurūtu*

ewurumma in *e. epēšu* "to inherit" Nuzi; < *ewuru*

ewurūtu "inheritance" Nuzi; < *ewuru*

eyakku → *ayyakku*

ezbu "abandoned" jB of child; also NA in PN ?; < *ezēbu*

ezēbu(m) "to leave, leave behind" **G** (*i/i*; imper. *ezub*, *ezib*) [TAG4] **1.** "leave, go away (from)" house, land; person, esp. spouse = "divorce"; "quit, give up" work; city, property; ext. of feature "be out of" place **2.** "leave behind, abandon" child, boat; "leave, put aside" to reserve s.th.; math. "keep back" a remainder [(ÍB.)TAG4] **3.** "leave (behind one), bequeath" property; OB *kanīkam*, *kunukkam* (etc.) *e.* "draw up" document **4.** "set aside, ignore" command, decision; "give up, cease to do" **5.** "let go, spare" enemy etc. **6.** "allow to remain, hold over", esp. with neg. "leave no ..."; "leave s.th." for, with (= dat./*ana*), "put at s.o.'s disposal" **Gtn** OA ? **Gt** OA "separate from one another, get divorced" **D** ~ G (rare) jB, Nuzi, M/NA **Š** [KAR] **1.** caus. of G *ṭuppam š.* "have a document drawn up" **2.** "save, rescue" people, city; *napišta/napšāti š.* "save life/lives" (of o.s./others); also in PNs **Štn** iter. of Š 2 **Št** pass. of Š 2 **N** pass. of G [TAG4] of land "be left" untilled; of person "be delayed"; "be left over, survive"; of goods "be deposited" (with = dat.); "be divorced"; > *ezib*; *ezbu*; *izbu*; *izibtu*; *azibatu*, *azzubūtum*; *uzību*; *uzubbû*, *uzubbatu*, *uzzubu*; *mušēzibu*, *mušēzibtu*; *šēzubtum*, *šūzubu*, *šūzubtu*; *tēzubtum*

ezēḫu(m), *esēḫu(m)* "to gird on" O/jB, NA **G** (*i/i*) "strap on, tie on" weapon, belt to (= acc.) s.o.; pouch, wings, fish-cloak; "gird" loins **D** ~ G stat. "is girt" with belt **N** "gird o.s." with (= acc.); > *ezḫu*; *izḫu*; *mēzeḫu*; → *isḫu* I

ezennû (a kind of stone) jB; < Sum.

ezēqu → *esēqu*

ezēru "to curse" M/NA, jB **G** (*i/i*) s.o. with (= acc.) a curse (*izru*) **D** ~ G; > *izru*; → *nazāru*

ezēru → also *esēru* II

ezēzu(m) "to be(come) angry, rage" Bab. **G** (*u/u*, later mostly *i/i*; stat. *eziz*, also *ez(i)*) [ŠÚR; ḪUŠ] of god, person; heart, liver etc. **Gt** OB "rage at one another" **D** "make furious", stat. "is infuriated" **Š** jB "make s.o. furious"; > *ezzu, ezzetu, ezziš; uzzu, uzzatu; mēzezu; šēzuzu, šūzuzu*

ezḫu "tied round" jB lex.; < *ezēḫu*

ezib, O/jB also *ezub* "except (that)" Bab., O/MA **1.** as prep. "except", "but for"; "apart from", e.g. *ezub lā šapārīka* "despite your not writing" **2.** as conj., also *e. ša* "apart from the fact that ...", ext. "disregard (the fact) that ..." **3.** as interj. "never mind!"; < *ezēbu* G imper.

ezibtu → *izibtu*

ezizzu(m) (an alliaceous vegetable) OA, O/jB

ezûm I "to defecate" OB lex.; → *teṣû; zû* I

ezû(m) II "to hurry, be hasty" O/jB stat. only; OB *ezi alākam*, jB *ina alākišu ezi* "is quick in going"

ezub → *ezib*

ezzetu "fury" jB; < *ezzu*

ezziš "furiously, fiercely" Bab. [ŠÚR-*iš*] of shouting, frowning (*nekelmû*); < *ezzu*

ezzu(m) "furious, angry" Bab., NA [ŠÚR] of deity, person, animal, fire, wind; battle, weapon, divine attributes; < *ezēzu*; > *ezziš, ezzetu*

ezzu → also *enzu*

ezzuššiḫe mng. unkn. Nuzi desig. of field; < Hurr.

G

gabābu → *kabābu* I.II

gabadibbu(m), *gabandibb(a)û* "parapet, crenellation" M/NA, j/NB [GAB.DIB (mixes with syll. writings)]; < Sum.

gabagallu(m) (part of chariot, phps.) "box" O/jB; < Sum.

gabandibb(a)û → *gabadibbu*

gabaraḫḫu(m), OB also *kabaraḫḫum* 'breast-beating', "panic"? O/jB [GABA.RAḪ; GABA.RA] of communal dismay; *g. ḫalāqīšu* "lamentation for his loss"; < Sum.

gabarû, *gabrû* m. & f. "copy; reply; opponent" M/NB, NA [GABA.RI] **1.** "copy, duplicate" of document; NB pl. *gabarānê* **2.** "reply" to a letter NA, NB, esp. *g. (ša) egirti* **3.** jB med. "equivalent" of herbs (*šammī*) **4.** astr. "epact", "equivalence" between solar and lunar years? **5.** M/jB "opponent" [once GAB.A.RI.A]; < Sum.

gabāṣu "contraction" of eye jB(Ass.) in *g. iššakin* "contraction took place"; < *kapāṣu* II Ass.

gaba'ū → *gab'u*

gabbaṣu (or *qabbaṣu*) mng. unkn. jB in *šēn* ("shoes") *gabbaṣāti*

ga(b)batinnu "female pudenda" jB lex.

gabbu I "the totality, all (of)" M/NA, M/NB (OB(Ešn.) *qabbum*?) [DÙ] (absol.) "all, everything"; (in appos., after subst.) *gabbu/a/i*; (before pron. suff.) MB *gabbašunu* (acc.), otherwise *gabbi-* (all cases); (st. constr. before gen.) usu. *gabbi*; NB f. (in appos.) *gabbutu*

gabbu II ~ "(animal's) brain"? j/NB as meat offering

gabbû → *gabû*

gabbubu "grilled" NA of sheep; < *kabābu* II D Ass.

gabbutu → *gabbu* I

gabdibbu → *gabadibbu*

gabgabu (a thorn bush) jB lex.

gabību (a kind of pastureland) NB

gabīdu, *kabīdu* "liver" M/jB of person, animal; *g./k. barbari* "wolf's liver" (a plant); → *kabātu*

gabiu → *gabû*

gabrû → *gabarû*

gabsīdum → *qapsīdum*

gabû, MA *gabiu*, NB *gabbû* "alum" M/NA, j/NB [IM.SAḪAR.NA4.KUR.RA] in *ab(a)n(a) gabê/iu* used in glass-making, tanning; med. as drug or salve

gab'u "(mountain) peak, hill" (pl. Mari *gaba'ī*, MA/MB *gab'āni*) Mari, M/NA, Emar

gabudu (a food) NA

gadādu ~ "to separate off" jB lex., NA **G** (*a/u*)

gadalallu 'linen wearer' jB lex., a temple functionary; < Sum.

gadalalû "linen fabric" jB [(TÚG.)GADA.LAL], used as curtain in temple; < Sum.

gadamāḫu(m), *gadmāḫu* "superior linen garment" O/jB [GADA.MAḪ] jB used on demon figurines; < Sum.

gadāmu "to cut off" MA **G** (*i/i*) part of body, as punishment

gadaru (a cloth cover) jB lex.; < Sum.?

gaddāya → *gaṭṭa'a*

gadê "I'm going, I'm off!" OB lex.; < Sum.

gadibbu → *agadibbu*

gadmāḫu → *gadamāḫu*

gadû "young goat" NA, NB of 1-2 years' age; < Aram.

gādu → *gattu* II

ga'ešmāḫu (a shrine) jB lex.; < Sum.

ga'eššu → *ka'iššum*

gagadâ → *kaqdâ*

gāgamu → *gayyānu*

gagdâm → *kaqdâ*

gagû(m) "cloister" O/jB [GÁ.GI$_4$/GI.A] for priestesses, esp. *nadītum* at Sippar; *ana g. erēbum* "to enter the cloister"; as institution; transactions *ina bāb g.* "at the cloister gate"; *ša* or *atu bāb g.* "cloister porter"; < Sum.

gāgu ~ "ring, torc" NA of gold, silver

gaḫḫu → *guḫḫu*

ga'iššu → *ka'iššum*

galādu → *galātu*

galālānu "gravelly" NB as PN; < *galālu* I

galālu I "stone(s)" NB building stone (for stele etc.); "gravel"; < Aram.

galālu II "to roll" (trans.) Bab., M/NA **G** infin. in drug preparations **D** ~ G of river water; "roll" eyes (or "blind"?); > *gallu*; *gillu*?

galamāḫu(m), *galmāḫu(m)*, *kalamāḫu(m)* "chief lamentation-priest" Bab. [GALA.MAḪ; j/NB LÚ.GALA.MAḪ, once ŠÚ.MAḪ]; of specific deity (Enlil, Ištar etc.); performing in cult; < Sum.; → *kalû* III

galāšu ~ "to flatten off"? jB **G** stat., of moon **D** mng. unkn. lex.

galātu(m), NA *galādu* "to tremble, be afraid" Bab., NA **G** (*u/u*, rarely *i/i*) [ḪULUḪ] med. of person, part of body, cow "tremble, shiver"; from fear; "be afraid of (= acc.)"; "ejaculate"; stat., of god, sea, sunrise etc. "is frightful, frightening" **Gtn** iter. of G [ḪULUḪ.ḪULUḪ] "be repeatedly scared" **D** "frighten" s.o., of snake, fortification wall **Dtn** iter. of D of demon, ghost **Dt** pass. of D OB "be frightened" **ŠD** ~ D **Š 1.** "make frightening" divine statue; stat. "is very frightening" **2.** "terrify, scare off"; > *galtu*, *galtiš*; *gilittu*; *mugallitu*; *šuglutu*

galaturru "junior lamentation-priest" jB [LÚ. GALA.TUR; LÚ.ŠÚ.TUR]; < Sum.; → *kalû* III

galaussû "second-ranking lamentation-priest" jB lex.; < Sum.; → *kalû* III

galdanibātu → *kalteniwe*

galdu (a vessel) Am.; < Eg.?

galgaltu I, *galgallatu* "hunger" jB lex.

galgaltu II (a plant) jB lex.

galittu → *galtu*

galītu "deportation"; coll. "deportees" NA; < *galû* II

gallabtu(m) "female barber" OAkk, O/jB [(MUNUS.)ŠU.I]; < *gallābu*

gallābu(m) "barber, hairdresser" [(LÚ.)ŠU.I; KINDA] also as family name, as PN; *mār gallābī* "member of the barbers", *wakil g.* "overseer of the barbers"; of the king, of Šamaš, of the market; transf. desig. of north wind *g. šamê*; *naglabu*, *mušṭu* (etc.) *g.* "razor, comb etc. of barber"; < *gullubu* II; > *gallabtu*; *gallābūtu*

gallābūtu "function of barber" Ass., j/NB [(LÚ.)ŠU.I-] *g. epēšu* "to act as barber", also cultically of king; < *gallābu*

gallâniš "like a *gallû*-demon" jB; < *gallû* I

gallittu → *galtu*

gallu ~ "rolling"? j/NB in *tâmtu gallatu*, also ellipt., without *tâmtu*; < *galālu* II

gallû(m) (a demon) Bab. [GAL$_5$.LÁ] also transf., as desig. of enemy; *ḫiriṣ g. lemni* "scion of" or "sliver from an evil demon"; "constable" as divine title; < Sum.; > *gallâniš*

gallû → also *qallû*

galmāḫu → *galamāḫu*

galpurḫu → *kalpurḫu*

galtappu → *gištappu*

galteniwe → *kalteniwe*

galtiš "fearfully" jB; < *galtu*

galtu; f. *galittu* "fearful" jB; "fearsome" of noise, light etc.; of snake; sea; storm-chariot; < *galātu*

galû I "banished, deported" NB; < *galû* II

galû II "to be deported" NA, NB **G** (NA *i/i*) **Š** "take/send into exile" (partly taken as *šgl* D ?); < Aram.; > *galû* I; *galītu*; *šuglû*, *šagalûtu*

gam "also" NB; < W.Sem.

gamagallum (a ring) OB of carnelian; < Sum.

gamālu(m) "to do a favour; spare" **G** (*i/i*, OAkk also *a/u*) "do s.o. a favour, be kind to"; *gimilla g.* "do favour"; NB "give s.th. as a favour"; "consent"; of deity "spare, save", esp. in PN; of king etc.; *napišta g.* "spare life"; OAkk *lā gamāl* of silver/gold payment, mng. uncl. **Gt** "agree to, accommodate each other" **Št** OB "reach agreement about" field (= acc.); > *gāmilu*, *gammalu* I, *gammalû*, *gammilu*; *gimlu*, *gimiltu*, *gimillu*; *gitmālu*, *gitmāliš*, *gitmālūtu*; *ḫumālu*?, *ḫumalītu*?

gamāmu "to cut off" jB lex. **G**

gamarru, NA *kimarru* "infantry" M/NA

gamartu(m) "totality" O/jB **1.** Mari of troops "whole force" **2.** OB *kannū gamartim* "signs of completion"? **3.** jB gramm., of Sum. morphemes, incl. prospective u- [TIL-] (→ *gamertu* 4); < *gamāru* II

gamāru I "completeness" MB **1.** *ana g.* "completely" **2.** Nuzi "end, completion" of month; < *gamāru* II infin.

gamāru(m) II "to bring to conclusion, complete" **G** (*a/u*) [TIL] "destroy, finish off" people, city, land; "use up completely" corn etc.; "pay out all" silver; "finish, get to end of" month, year etc.; stat. of days etc. "are ended, used up"; "complete" work, building, object; *eqlam ina epēšim g.* "finish working field"; "finish, settle" a lawsuit, account(s); stat. of royal command "is final"; "finalize" decision etc.; in hendiad. "(do s.th.) completely", OA "satisfy s.o. entirely"; "control, own s.th. entirely"; "totally occupy" space, time; astr. of halo "be complete" **Gt** OB of persons' hearts, stat. "are entirely (devoted) to each other" **D** ~ G esp. OB "assemble" workers etc. "in their entirety", "include s.o. in a group", "collect" water, "assign" a field "entirely" to s.o., "pay, supply in full" silver, offering; M/jB "be totally in control of" lands etc.; also abstr. obj., wisdom, strength; *libba g.* "give (o.'s) heart entirely to" s.o., "be fully loyal to"; in hendiad. "do completely"; *ina/ana* + infin. + *g.* "finish (doing s.th.)" **Dt** (NA **Dtt**) pass. of D OB of troops "be completely assembled"; "be finished, used up" etc. **Š** **1.** OA "cause to pay out all" silver **2.** in hendiad. "do to the full"; stat. "is in complete control" **3.** NB "cause to encompass" all wisdom **4.** "have s.o. prepare" account "completely" **N** pass. of G **1.** "be annihilated" of people, animals **2.** "be fully used up" **3.** of speech, illness "come to an end" **4.** of dispute etc., of work, oath "be concluded" **5.** of house, family "be fully assembled"; math. of measure "be filled up" **6.** Nuzi, of months "pass, be completed"; > *gamāru* I; *gamru* I.II, *gamertu*, *gamrūtum*; *gimru*, *gimirtu*, *gimratu*, *gamartu*; *gāmiru*, *gāmirūtu*; *gummurtu*; *mugammerum*, *mugammertu*; *nagmaru*, *nagmuru*; *tagmertu*

gamatu (a measure)? jB lex.

gamā'u vb. mng. unkn. jB lex.

gamertu(m), *gamirtu(m)* "completeness" **1.** OA "communal regulation" **2.** "totality, everything", *ana g.* "in full"; NB *kasap g.* "full price"; NB [TIL-] "complete amount"; *erru g.* → *erru* III **3.** OB "destruction" **4.** gramm. = *gamartu* 3; < *gamru* I

gameru → *gamru* I

gamēsu (a stone) NA for → *algamišu* ?

gamgammu (a bird) jB [GÀM.GÀM.MUŠEN]; < Sum.

gamidu → *gammidatu*

gāmilu(m) "merciful, sparing" O/jB in PNs, also fPN *Gāmiltum*; "pardoner"; *lā g.* "merciless" of soldiers, lion; < *gamālu*

gamirtu → *gamertu*

gāmiru(m) **1.** "strong, effective" OAkk, O/jB of king; as PN **2.** OA *gāmir awâtim* "mediator, arbitrator" **3.** (a kind of bolt)? O/jB, NA; < *gamāru* II; → *kamiru* ?

gāmirūtu(m) "strength, efficacy" O/jB of king; jB *g. epēšu* "to act effectively"; *g. alāku* "to be effective"; < *gāmiru*

gamliš "like a bent (throwing-)stick" jB; < *gamlu*

gamlu(m); pl. f. ~ "bent stick (as projectile), throwing-stick" OAkk, Bab. [GIŠ.ZUBI] as weapon, of wood; epith. of gods, attribute of gods; *ᵈg.* "divine *g.* symbol"; om. of features *kīma g.*, i.e. curved, bent; astr. "constellation Auriga" (also code name for Jupiter) [MUL.ZUBI]; > *gamliš*

gammališ "like a camel" jB; < *gammalu* II

gammalu I "very merciful" jB; < *gamālu*

gammalu II "camel" NA [ANŠE.A.AB.BA; ANŠE.GAM.MAL]; < W.Sem.; > *gammališ*

gammalû "very merciful" jB; < *gammalu* I + *-ī*

gammaru → *gamru* I

gammidatu, NA also *ga(m)midu* (a garment) NA, NB; < *kamādu* ?

gammilu "friendly, accommodating" jB; < *gamālu*

gammirtu → *gamru* I

gammiš (a plant) jB lex., NB

gammištu → *gamru* I

gammurtu → *gummurtu*

gamru(m) I, *gameru(m)*, NA, NB also *gammaru*, with f. *gammir/štu* "complete, total" [TIL; NA also PAP ?] of price, commodities etc.; of quantity, number; *ṭēmu(m) g.* "the entire matter", "full report"; with *libbu*, e.g. *ina l.-šu gamrim* "whole-heartedly"; of lawsuit, accounts, work "completed"; OB as subst. "totality", "all (of ...)", *ana/adi gamrišu* "in its entirety", *ana gamrim* "totally, finally"; < *gamāru* II

gamrum II "outlay, expenses" OA heavy (*mādum*), of trip (*ša ḫarrānim*); *g. gamārum*, *g. lamādum* "to incur expenses"; < *gamāru* II; → *gimru* 3

gamrūtum "entirety" Mari *ana g.-šu* "completely"; < *gamru* I

gamuzu mng. unkn. NA of horses

gana "come on; yallah!" O/jB before imper.; before 1 sg. prec.; < Sum.; → *agana*; *ingana*; *magana*

ganaddu → *ganandu*

ganāḫu "to cough" M/jB **G** (*i/i*) **D** "cough and retch"; → *guḫḫu*

ganandu, *ganaddu* (an ornament) MB of gold, lapis lazuli; < Kass.?

ganānu, *kanānu(m)* ~ "to encircle, shut in" O/jB **G** (*a/u*) troops **D** ~ G stat. "is encircled"; > *ginnatu*

ganāṣu "to lift (nose, lip)" jB **G** lex., med. **D** ~ G of sheep, of diviner (obj. KA.MEŠ, *appu*) **Dt** "wrinkle o.'s nose", "sneer"; > *gunnuṣum*, *muganniṣum*; → *ḫanāṣu*

gandarasānu (linen from Gandhara) NB; < OPers.

gangiṭṭu (a type of song) jB in Akkadian; < Sum.?

ganīnu → *ganūnu* I

gannu I (part of insides of a sheep) NB, as cut of meat, left/right

gannu II; pl. *gannātu/i* "garden" NB; < Aram.; → *bagani*

gannu → also *kannu*; *qannu*

ganungurru (a storeroom) jB lex.; < Sum.

ganunmāḫu(m) "principal storeroom" O/jB [GÁ.NUN.MAḪ]; < Sum.

ganūnu(m) I, *ga/inīnu(m)* "storeroom" [GÁ.NUN(.NA)] OAkk, OB in private houses; Ass., O/jB in temple; j/NB "private chamber" in palace, house; < Sum.

ganūnum II (or *k/qanūnum*) (a weight or measure) OAkk

ganzabāru "treasurer" NB; < OPers.

ganzazû "dripper" jB lex.; < Sum.

ganzer "underworld" jB; < Sum.

gapaḫšu (a child's game) MB

gapānu (or *kapānu*) "bulb"? Bogh. of leek etc.; → *gapnu* ?

gapāru(m) "to be superior" O/jB **G** → *gapru* **D** "overcome"? **Dt** "contend, match strengths"? **N** → *mungapru*

gapāšu(m) "to rise up, swell" O/jB **G** (*u/u*) of hero, heart "be(come) proud, swollen"; stat. of demon, part of liver, river "is enlarged, huge" **D** "enlarge", "swell number of" allies; stat. "is enlarged, swollen" **Dt** of army "be enlarged"; "be swollen, proud" **N** of water-table "rise up"; > *gapšu*, *gapšiš*, *gapšūtu*; *gipšu*, *gipšūtu*; *gupšu*; *guppušum*; *gitpāšu*

gapnu "bush" j/NB in wild; in gardens; of figs, pomegranates, apples; *g. ša karāni* "vine"; NB *bīt g.* "vineyard"; → *gapānu*; *gupnu*

gappu "wing" MA, jB of bird, ghost, winged beasts; pl. *ṣēr ga(p)pāni* "winged snake"?; → *agappu*; *kappu* I

gapru "superior" jB; < *gapāru*

gapsīdum → *qapsīdum*

gapšiš "in spate" jB of high water; < *gapšu*

gapšu; f. *gapuštu* "arisen, proud" O/jB [MAḪ] of flood waters "risen in spate"; of troops "numerous"; transf. of heart, person, goddess, animal "proud, swollen"; also as PN; < *gapāšu*; > *gapšiš*, *gapšūtu*

gapšūtu "numerousness" jB in *gapšūssunu* "in their great numbers" of troops; < *gapšu*; → *gipšūtu*

garabānu → *garbānu*

garābu(m) "mange, scab" O/jB med., mag.; *ša g.* "leper"; *šamnu/aban/ereb g.* (kinds of plant/ stone/locust); > *garbu*, *garbānu*; *gurrubu*?

garādu(m), *qarādu* "to pluck, tear out" (hair etc.) O/jB, NA **G** OB lex. "pluck" wool; transf., of pig "root out" bricks; Am. (imper. *qurud*) mng. uncl. **Gt** "pluck beard of" s.o. **D** "pluck out" hair; stat., of hair "is mangy"; > *gardu* I; *gerdu*; *gurrudu*

garāḫu → *garāšu*

garakku, *girakku* (small brick altar) jB

garāmu "to follow course" **G** (*i/i*) jB of planet

garannu → *garunnu*

garānu → *qarānu*

garāru → *qarāru*; *šugarruru*

garāṣum (a skin complaint) OB lex.; > *garṣu*, *gerriṣānu*; *gurruṣu*

garāṣu → also *karāṣu*

garašgaraš → *gurušgaraš*

garāšu(m), jB lex. also *garāḫu* "to move towards" OAkk, O/jB, MA **G** (pret. *igruš*) **1.** OAkk, OB of person, god "go towards" s.o. (= dat.); MA of animal figures "stride" (or G 2 ?) **2.** jB lex., comm. "copulate", as euph. **N** of women "be made love to"; > *guršu* I?; *gurištu*, *gurušgaraš*?; → *nagaršû*

garāšu → also *qarāšu*

garā'um → *gerû*

garbānu, *garabānu* "leprous" j/NB; < *garbu*

garbu "leprous" M/jB; < *garābu*

gardapatu → *gardupatu*

gardu(m) I, *qardu(m)* "mangy"? O/jB; < *garādu*

gardu II ~ "state worker(s)" NB coll. term; < OPers.?; → *gardupatu*

gardumum (or *qardumum*) (a prof. desig.)? OB

gardupatu, *gardapatu* "leader of *gardu*" NB; < OPers.

garīdu "beaver"? jB med., testicle of *g.*

garinnu → *agarinnu*

gariṣ(t)u, *giriṣ(t)u* "loaf (of bread)" NA, NB; < Aram.

garmartu → *kanwartu*

garrānu → *gerrānu*

garru(m) (a box) O/jB for bread; medicines

garṣu(m) "leprous" MB lex.; < *garāṣum*

garûm "cream" OB lex.; < Sum.

garû → also *gerû*

gārû → *gērû*

garunnu, *garannu*, *gurunnu*, *agrunnu* (small cultic vessel) jB [(DUG.)ŠAB.TUR]

Gasur Ṣalul → *Ṣaliltum*

gaṣāṣu → *gazāzu*; *kaṣāṣu* I

gāṣiṣu "gnashing, grinding" jB of teeth; < *kaṣāṣu* I

gaṣṣānu "calcareous" NA of limestone; < *gaṣṣu* III

gaṣṣatu "firewood" NA; *ša gaṣṣātēšu* "firewood man"; < *kaṣāṣu* I ?

gaṣṣu(m) I ~ "cruel, murderous" O/jB of deities, demons

gaṣṣu II ~ "chopped" NB of beams; < *kaṣāṣu* I

gaṣṣu(m) III "gypsum" Bab, NA [IM.BABBAR] as raw material, mineral; as building material; mag., esp. for figurines; *mê g.* "lime wash"; > *gaṣṣānu*

gaṣṣu → also *gazzu*

gašāru(m) "to be(come) strong, powerful" OAkk, Bab., M/NA(lit.) **G** (*i/i*) of deity, king; of command, cult-ordinance **Gtn** infin. *gitaššuru* = Dt *gutaššuru* ? **D** "make" troops "dominant"; stat. "is very powerful, more powerful" than s.o. **Dt** "strike with great force", "bully" of gods, men; NA of trees "vie with each other"?; > *gašru*, *Gašrānu*, *gašrūtu*; *magšaru*; *mugdašru*

gašāšu(m) "to cut off" **G** (pret. *u*) Bogh. (or → *kasāsu* ?); > *gašīšu*, *gašīšiš*

gaširūtu "appurtenances" jB in *g. šarrūti* "royal paraphernalia"

gašīšiš "on stakes" jB

gašīšu(m) "stake, pole" O/jB, NA for military, legal impalement; < *gašāšu*

gašmušḫu → *kašmušḫu*

Gašrānu "strong" M/NA as DN; < *gašru*

gašru(m), M/NA *gešru* "very strong, powerful" Bab., M/NA(lit.) of deity, king, lion; weapon; *ēmūq(ē) g.* "great strength"; < *gašāru*; > *Gašrānu*, *gašrūtu*

gašrūtu, *gešrūtu* "great strength, power" jB, NA of deity, king; < *gašru*

gâšu(m) I, NA *guāšu* ~ "to run, hasten" O/jB, NA(lit.) **G** (*ū*) of deity; > *gūštu*

gâšu II "to vomit" jB **G** not attested **D** absol. "vomit" **Š** "make s.o. vomit"?

gašūru → *gušūru*

gattu(m) I, *kattu* "form, physical build" of deity, divine statue, human; Mari of donkeys *gattam ṣeḫḫērā* "of very small build"

gattu II, *gādu* (name for Euphrates) j/NB

gaṭṭa'a "reed- or wood-cutter"? NA, NB; < Aram.

ga'ûm "to be superior" OB over s.o.; < W.Sem.

gā'um, *gāwum* "people, tribe" Mari; < W.Sem.

gâ'u, *kâ'u*, *qâ'u* "to spit, spew" jB, NA **G**

gāwum → *gā'um*

gayyānu, *gāgamu* mng. unkn. jB lex., archit. term

gayyātu → *qayyātu*

gazamānu(m), *gazimānu* (a pole) O/jB lex.; < Sum.

gazāzu(m), *kazāzu*, *g/kaṣāṣu* "to shear" OAkk, Bab. **G** (*a/u*) sheep **N** pass. of G, NB; > *gazzu*; *kaziztu*, *kizzatu*; *gizzu*, *gizzatu*; *gāzizu*; *kuzāzu*?; *magzazu*; → *kizzu* I

gazimānu → *gazamānu*

gāzizu "shearer" NB pl. *gāzizē*; < *gazāzu*

gazzu(m), OAkk *gezzum* (or *g/kaṣṣu(m)*?) "shorn" OAkk(Elam), Bab. of sheep; < *gazāzu*

gegu(n)nû(m), OB also *kikunnûm*, Elam *kukunnû(m)*; pl. f. "raised temple" OAkk, Bab. often in appos. to *ziqqurratu(m)*; < Sum.

gelduḫlu, *keltuḫlu*, MA *gelzulu* "bowyer, bow-maker" MA, Nuzi

gelletu → *gillatu*

gelzulu → *gelduḫlu*

gennu → *kinnû*

genû ~ "to thrust, butt" M/jB **G**; **D**

gēnû → *ginû* I

gepû mng. unkn. jB lex.

gerdu, *qerdu* "plucked, carded? wool" jB, NA [SU.TAB.BA] eaten as punishment; < *garādu*

gerdudûm mng. unkn. OB silver for *g.*; < Sum.

gergiltu (ring-shaped part of plough) jB lex.

gergīlu(m) (a bird) O/jB; also OAkk (a city name)

gerginakku "library" jB [IM.GÚ.LÁ; IM.LÁ.A] for tablets; < Sum.

gerginnûm (part of liver) OB; < Sum.?

gergirû → *egemgiru*

gergisu/û (a plant) jB lex.

gergi(ṣ)ṣu ~ (a small battering-ram) jB lex.

gergiššu(m) **1.** "strawberry tree" jB lex. **2.** (a red skin complaint) O/jB; *ša g.* "sufferer from *g.*"; → *qerqišu*

gergû → *gerrigû*

geriddakku (a river fish) jB lex.; < Sum.

germadû "floor-timbers (of ship)"? jB [GE.ER.MÁ.DÙ]; < Sum.

germaḫḫu → *kirmaḫḫu*

gerrabbakku(m) (a sea-fish) jB lex.; < Sum.

gerrānu(m), jB also *garrānu* "wailing, lamentation" OAkk, O/jB

gerridir, *kerridir* (a leather item) MB; < Kass.?

gerrigû, *gergû* (a reed rope) jB lex.

gerriṣānu "mangy (sheep)" jB lex.; < *garāṣum*

gerru(m) I, OB also *kerrum* m. & f. "way; caravan; (military) campaign" Bab., M/NA [KASKAL; Mari also KASKAL.A] **1.** topog. "road, path" to (*ša*) PlN; difficult, narrow etc.; jB *g. šarri* "royal road"; transf. "way of life"; *tappi g.* "travelling companion" **2.** Bab. "caravan" **3.** OB "journey"; *paššur g.* "picnic table" **4.** military "march, campaign"; "(troops on) campaign" **5.** "(religious) procession"; NB *g. maṣṣartu* "patrol"; astr. *rikis g.* (an excerpt from series) **6.** jB pl. *kerrētu* "marching-song"?

gerru II "lion cub, puppy" jB

gerrû → *egerrû*

gerseqqû(m) (palace, temple attendant) Bab. [(LÚ.)GÌR.SIG$_{5/6}$/SÈ(.GA); MB also KI.IR.SI.GA]; < Sum.

gerseqqûtu "post of attendant" Bogh., NB; in palace; NB as prebend in temple; < *gerseqqû*

gerṣu → *kerṣu*

geršānu(m), *girišānu* (a kind of leek) O/jB [GA.RAŠ.SAG.SAR]; < Sum.

geršippum (a tame bird) OB

gerû(m), *garû*, OA *garā'um* "to be hostile to, attack" **G** (*i/i*) with acc. "attack" opponent; *ṣalta g.* "start fight with" s.o. (= acc.); leg. "initiate proceedings against" s.o. (= acc.), also *dīna g.*, NA *dēnu dabābu issi PN g.*; NB *bēl gerîšu* (infin.) "legal opponent" **Gtn** iter. of G OA; jB stat. of Lamaštu *gitarrātu* **Gt** OB "start hostilities against each other" **D** ~ G **Dtn** iter. of D **N** "start hostilities, get into a fight", esp. leg.; > *girûtu*; *gērû*; *magrû*, *magrītu*; *tagrītum*?

gērû(m), *gārû* "opponent, enemy" Bab., M/NA in battle; of animals; in law; < *gerû*

gerzizu → *kerzizu*

gêsu(m) "to assign to, confer on" O/jB **G** (pret. *igēs*); > *gīsu*

gêsu → also *gêšu* I

gešru → *gašru*

gešrūtu → *gašrūtu*

geštû "very first, leading" jB epith. of god [IGI.DU-*ú*]; < Sum.; → *igištûm*

gešû "to belch" jB **G** wind, water, bile as obj. **D** ~ G wind, blood; like ox; > *gišûtu*

gêšu(m) I, *gêsu* "to turn over, grub up" O/jB soil

gêšu II "to spend the night" jB lex.

gezzu → *gazzu*; *gizzu*

giammalu ~ "sprout, shoot" jB lex.

giāru(m) mng. uncl. O/jB **G** "to challenge"? person, "demand"? work **D** "demand"? s.th., field; > *magīrtum*

giballum (a kind of reed) OB lex.; < Sum.

gibarrû, *gibarbarrû* "reed fibres" jB lex.; < Sum.

gibbaru, *gibburu* ~ "hired shepherd"? MA, Nuzi; < Hurr.?

gibbum (or *gippum*) (a sacrificial rite) Mari

gibburu → *gibbaru*

gibētum (class of soldier) Mari

gibillu/û ~ "touch-wood, tinder" jB lex.

giddagiddû (an eye complaint)? jB med.; < Sum.

giddê → *budû*

gi(d)dil → *gidlu*

gidimduḫum (an alcoholic drink) Mari; < Sum.

gidimmu I; pl. f. ~ "water scoop" jB, NA

gidimmu II (a bundle of reeds) jB lex.; < Sum.; → *gidmu*

gidlu(m), freq. wr. *gi(d)dil* "plaited string" Bab., NA **1.** Bab. "plait" of onions etc., used as measure **2.** NA (kind of gold ornament)

gidmu, *gidi(m)mu* "bunch, spray of dates" NB as measure; < Aram.; → *gidimmu* II

gīdu(m); NB pl. f. "sinew, gristle" Bab., M/NA [UZU.SA] usu. of sheep; weighed; for chariot manufacture etc.

gigallūtu → *igigallūtu*

gigiruḫḫe adj. mng. uncl. Nuzi; < Hurr.

gigītu (or *gizītu*) mng. unkn. jB lex.

gigunû → *gegunnû*

gigurbalû (kind of basket) jB lex.; < Sum.

gigurdû (a carrying basket) jB lex.; < Sum.; → *maššû* I 1

gigurkigubbû (kind of basket) jB lex.; < Sum.

gigurru(m) (a basket) OAkk, jB?; < Sum.

giguršugubbû (kind of basket) jB lex.; < Sum.

gigurû **1.** "(the cuneiform sign) U" jB [U] **2.** (a kind of torch) jB lex.; < Sum.

gigurzidākum "flour basket" OB; < Sum.

giḫannu(m), *giḫennu(m)* (basket for wool) O/jB [GI.ḪÉ.EN(.ḪI.A); GI.ḪA.AN(.ḪI.A)]; < Sum.

giḫlû(m), *guḫlû* (a mourning ceremony) O/jB [GI.ḪUL]; < Sum.; → *kiḫullû*

giladu → *gildu*

gilammu → *gišlammu*

gilāmu, *kilāmu* (a kind of ivory) Am., Nuzi

gildu, *giladu* "(animal) hide, skin" NB; < Aram.

gilgidānu "bat" (*Fledermaus*) jB lex.

gilimmum mng. unkn. OB lex.; < Sum.?

gilittu(m) "terror" Bab. [ŠÀ.MUD] *g. rašû* "to become terrified"; < *galātu*

gillatu(m), *gelletu* "sin, sacrilege" Bab.; *bēl g.* "sinner"; > *gullulu*

gillu (a piece of reed) jB lex.; < *galālu* II ?

gilšu, *giššu(m)*, m. & f. ~ "hip(-bone)" O/jB, NA [TUGUL] left/right; is broken; child carried *ina muḫḫi g.-ya*; NB *abul g.* (a gate in Babylon)

giltiu, giltû → *gištûm*

gimāḫu → *kimaḫḫu*

gimgiru → *egemgiru*

gimillu(m), OAkk, NA *gimlu(m)*; pl. f. "requital, favour" [ŠU] "friendly deed (for/as reward)"; OA *awīl g.* "one who can do a favour"; jB *bēl g.-šu* "one owing him a favour"; OA, OB *g. šakānum/epēšum/gamālum* "to do a favour" to (= *eli/i(na) ṣēr*) s.o.; freq. in PNs; *g. turru* "to return a favour", also "avenge" s.o.; < *gamālu*

gimiltu "act of friendliness, favour" M/NB(Ass.) *g. šakānu* "to do a favour"; < *gamālu*

gimirtu(m) "totality" OAkk, Ass., NB esp. *ina/ana gimirtišu* etc. "in its totality, all of it"; in appos. "all", "wholly"; Mari "entire body" of army; < *gamāru* II

gimlu(m) "spare (ox)" O/jB to be kept in reserve; < *gamālu*

gimlu → also *gimillu*

gimratu(m) "totality" Bab.(poet.) "all" gods, men etc.; < *gamāru* II

gimru(m), OB also *kimrum* "totality; costs, expenses" Bab., M/NA **1.** "totality", before gen./pron. suff., in appos. **2.** pl. f. "everything, whole world" **3.** m. "outlay, expenses" incurred in business, labour, travel etc. (→ *gamrum* II); < *gamāru* II

gimuššu "reed pole" jB for boat; < Sum.

ginâ, *ginû* adv. "constantly; usually" M/NB [DIŠ-] **1.** "always, permanently", NB *ana g.* "for ever" **2.** "regularly, normally", *kī(ma) ša g.* "as usual"; NB astr. *naṣāru ša ginê* "regular observation"; jB *ṣubāt g.* "everyday clothing"?; < Akk. lw. in Sum.

gingiru → *egemgiru*

giniggiṇakku (a reed) jB lex.; < Sum.

ginindanakku "measuring rod" j/NB for surveying [GI.NÍNDA.NA- ; NINDA ? (for NINDA as capacity measure → *akalu* 2)]; < Sum.

ginindanginakku (a reed) jB lex.; < Sum.

ginīnu → *ganūnu* I

ginnatu "enclosure" MB in *g. ganānu* "to hem in" (troops); < *ganānu*

ginnu (a hallmark for silver) NB in *kaspu ša g.* "stamped silver", also *kaspu ša lā g.*

ginnû → *kinnû*

ginû(m) I, M/NB also *gēnû*; pl. MA *ginā'ē*, NB *ginānê* "regular contribution (to temple)" Bab., M/NA [GI.NA; DIŠ-] of wool, bread, sheep etc.; *g. ša DN*; *sūt g.* "offerings *sūtu*-measure"; in appos. *sattukkē g.*; officials: MA *rab ginā'ē*, NB *rē'ī g.* "shepherd of g. sheep", *ṣāḫit g.* "oil-presser of regular offerings" (→ *ṣāḫit-ginûtu*); < Sum.

ginû II "child" jB in col.; < Sum.

ginû → also *ginâ*

ginûtu → *ṣāḫit-ginûtu*

gipāru, *giparru*, also *mipāru* (< Emesal?) **1.** M/NB "residence of *en(t)u* in temple" [GI$_6$.PÀR] *en(t)u* enters, leaves g.; *g. ša* fDN; also part of dwelling house **2.** jB ~ "pastureland"; < Sum.

gippum → *gibbum*

gipšu(m) "uprising, welling up" Bab., NA of water; transf. *g. ummāni* etc. "massed body of troops", *g. libbi* "pride"; ext. "thickening"? on liver, lung; < *gapāšu*

gipšūtu "fullness, numerousness" jB in *gipšūssun* "in their multitude"; < *gipšu*; → *gapšūtu*

gipû "date basket" j/NB; < Sum.

girakku → *garakku*

gīrāniš → *gīriš*

girberušḫe (a wall ornament)? Nuzi; < Hurr.

giridû(m) "access road"? O/jB; < Sum.?

girigubbu "footboard of chariot, cart" M/jB [GÌR.GUB]; < Sum.

girim ḫilibê → *girimmu* 2

girimmiš mng. uncl. OB

girimmu, *girinnu* **1.** M/jB, NA lex., med. (a kind of fruit) **2.** Nuzi, Bogh. (*g/kirinnu*) (a precious stone), NA/jB *girim ḫilibê* "underworld *g.*" (a precious stone) **3.** OB as PN ?; < Sum.

girisu-akarrānu (a prof. desig.) NB; < OPers.

giriṣtu → *gariṣtu*

girīṣu (a kind of fruit) jB lex.

girīṣu → also *gariṣtu*

gīriš, *gīrāniš* "like Gira, like fire" jB [^{d}GIŠ.BAR-*iš*]; < *gīru*

girišānu → *geršānu*

girītu(m) (a kind of fish, phps.) "muraena" O/jB

girratu → *kirratu*

girru → *gīru*

girtablilu "scorpion-man" jB [GÍR.TAB.LÚ.U$_{18}$.LU]; < Sum.

girû; pl. *girê*, *girêtum* "1/24 shekel" NB; < Aram. "carob-seed"

gīru(m), *girru* "fire(-god)" O/jB [^{d}GIŠ.BAR; ^{d}GIBIL$_6$] as DN; meaning "fire", *g. ittanpaḫ* "fire was ignited", *ina g. aqmu* "I burnt with fire"; < DN Gira; > *gīriš*

girûtu "hostility" NA; < *gerû*

gisallû(m) (part of roof, phps.) "eaves" Bab.; of domestic house; OB transf. *g. mūtim* "*g.* of death"; MB(Ass.) pl. f. *gisallât šadê* "*g.* of the mountains"; < Sum.

gisandassû, *gisandussû* "reed figure" jB lex., mag. [GI.SAG.DA.SÁ-*ú*]; < Sum.

gisappum (a basket) OB; with handle; < Sum.

gisgallu, *gišgallu* "station (of stars)" jB *g. šuršudu* "to fix (their) station"; < Sum.

gisgimmaru → *gišimmaru*

gisītu → *kisītu*

giskimmu(m), *iskimmu(m)*, *iskimbu* "sign, omen" Bab. *g. damiqti* "good sign"; defined by gods; "brought" by heaven and earth; rdg. of initial GIŠ- uncert. (*gis-* or *is-* ?); < Sum.

gissiu → *gištûm*

gisû → *igisû*

gīsu "endowed with" jB; < *gêsu*

giṣīṣu (desig. of enemy) NA; < *kaṣāṣu* I ?

giṣītu → *kisītu*

giṣṣatu → *kiṣṣatu*

giṣṣiš "into thorn-bushes" OB of pasture

giṣṣu(m) "thorn(-bush)" Bab., NA **1.** "thorny bush" in steppe etc. **2.** transf., of word *kī giṣṣi* "like a thorn" **3.** NA *bīt giṣṣi(te)* mng. uncl.; > *giṣṣiš*

gišallu "boat-pole, rudder" O/jB [GISAL]; < Sum.

gišburru 'releasing wood' jB lex. **1.** (part of door) **2.** mag. (a ritual instrument); < Sum.

gišdabtû (a kind of door)? jB lex.; < Sum.

gišdedû (a musical instrument)? jB lex.; < Sum.

gišdilû (or *zagingišdilû*) (a string of beads) jB lex.; < Sum.

gišgallu "throne-base" jB of column "bases"; < Sum.

gišgallu → also *gisgallu*

gišgimmaru → *gišimmaru*

gišginîš "like a clamp?" jB; < *gišginû*

gišginû (a wooden closure, phps.) "clamp" jB as descr. of king *g. dannu*; < Sum.; > *gišginîš*

gišgi(r)ru "(wooden) spill" NA for lighting fire; or *iṣ girri* ?

gišgiššu "yoke" jB lex.; < Sum.

gišḫaššu "wooden mace" jB; < Sum.

gišḫummu "bench" jB in vehicles; < Sum.

gišḫu(r)ru "plan, design, blueprint" M/NB [GIŠ.ḪUR] for building; of cosmic scheme; mag. "design" in flour; < Sum.

gišimmaru(m), lex. var. *gis/šgimmaru*, *gišnimmaru* etc. m. & f. "date palm" [(GIŠ.) GIŠIMMAR] in plantations; *g. sarru* "false d."; products of d.; door, bowl, images of wood of d.; < Sum.

giškallu (a heavy stick) jB lex.; < Sum.

giškanakku (part of doorframe) j/NB; < Sum.

giškurrû (a mountain tree) jB lex.; < Sum.

gišlammu, *gilammu* "mullein" jB lex. used for wicks; < Sum.

gišmaḫḫu "tree-trunk" or "long beam" jB(Ass.) of cedars; < Sum.

gišnimmaru → *gišimmaru*

gišnû "bed" jB lex.; < Sum.

gišnugallu → *ašnugallu*

gišparru, OB *gišperrum* "trap, snare" O/jB, NA transf. esp. of Šamaš; in similes; < Sum.

gišrinnu(m) "scales" OAkk, O/jB [GIŠ.ERÍN] of Šamaš in judgement; also (part of door); OAkk as deified symbol; < Sum.

gišru(m) "(wooden) bar; bridge" Bab., NA **1.** "bar" to close door; "barrier" **2.** NA, NB "bridge" **3.** NB "(bridge) toll"; *rab g.* "toll-collector"

gišṣappum → *gištappu*

giššakanakku (part of doorframe) j/NB; coated with bitumen; < Sum.

giššaškû (a pole) jB lex; < Sum.

giššu mng. unkn. NB in *abul g.* (a gate at Babylon)

giššu → also *gilšu*

gištaggû "offering" NB(roy. inscr.); < Sum.

gištalgiddû "barrier" jB; < Sum.

gištallu ~ "cross-bar" j/NB, NA [GIŠ.DAL] on door; as carrying pole for divine statue ?; ext. → *tallu* I; < Sum.

gištalû "cross-bar"? Mari, of wooden vessel-stand; < Sum.

gištappu(m), OAkk *g/kišṣappum*, *galtappu(m)*, jB *kerṣappu*, *kilzappu* Bogh., Syria also *kiltappu* "footstool" OAkk, Bab. [GÌR.GUB; NB also GÌR.GUB.BU]; also "threshing-sledge"; Qatna, Am. as element of ornament; Am. transf., ref. to pharaoh's subjects; → *kaltappû*

gištelû (a dignitary) jB lex.; < Sum.?

gištûm, *giltû*, MA *giltiu*, NA *gissiu* "cross-bar" O/jB, M/NA of table, throne etc.; < Sum.; → *ḫelta'u* ?

gištuppu(m) "plaque" O/jB [(NA$_4$.)GIŠ.DUB] i.e. flat ornament of precious stone or metal; < Sum.

gišṭû "(writing) board" jB; < Sum.

gišubbû → *kišubbû*

gišûtu "eructation, belch" M/jB; < *gešû*

gitepatu (a Persian official) NB; < OPers.

gitmāliš "perfectly" jB; < *gitmālu*

gitmālu(m), lex. also *gittamlu* "perfect, ideal"? Bab. epith. of gods, warriors; Gilgameš *g. emūqī* "perfect in strength"; of animals, palm-fronds, parts of liver; < *gamālu*

gitmālūtu "perfection" jB in *g. epēšu* "to act perfectly"; < *gitmālu*

gitnu mng. unkn. jB lex.

gitpāšu in *emūqī g.* "fully supplied with troops" jB; < *gapāšu*

gitrunu → *qitrunu*

gittamlu → *gitmālu*

giṭipū "fresh-pulled stems" of leek NB; < Aram.

giṭṭu "oblong tablet" NB [(IM.)GÍD.DA; IM.GÍ.DA] in lit. col. etc.; leg. as receipt; also ref. to parchment document [KUŠ.GÍD.DA]; < Sum.; → *imgiddû*

giwara, *giwarumma* "tanning"? Nuzi, bag of *g.* "tanning? agent"; *giwarumma epēšu* "to tan?" leather; < Hurr.

gizgazû "beater" jB lex. stick for fulling; < Sum.

gizgizû (a prof. desig.)? jB

gizillû "torch, brand" Bab., NA [GI.IZI.LÁ], esp. rit.; < Sum.

gizinakku(m), *kizinû* "offering place for Sîn" O/jB; < Sum.

gizītu → *gigītu*

gizzānû → *kizzānû*

gizzatu "shearing, wool yield" NB of sheep, goat; < *gazāzu*

gizzatu → also *kizzatu*

gizzu(m) "shearing" Bab., NA "(activity, process of) shearing"; *bīt g.* "shearing shed"; Bab. pl. "(product, yield of) shearing"; < *gazāzu*

gizzu → also *kizzu* I

guāšu → *gâšu* I

gubabtu → *ugbabtu*

gubārum, *kubārum* ~ "(metal) bar, ingot" OB

gubāru → also *gupāru* II

gubbu "cistern" NA, NB *g. (ša) mê* "water cistern"; < Aram.?

gubbuḫu, *qubbuḫu* "bald" O/jB, also as PN

gubgubu (a part of the body) jB

gubgubu → also *guggubu*

gubibātu pl. tant. "roasted grain" NA; < *kabābu* II

gubnatu "(a) cheese" NB; < Aram.

gubru(m) (a kind of lance) O/jB lex.; → *gupru*

gudādu → *kudādu*

gu(d)danagadû "ox-herd" jB lex.; < Sum.

gudapsû(m) (a priest) O/jB [GUDU4.ABZU] of Nanna, Nusku etc.; < Sum.

guddanagadû → *gudanagadû*

gudgudu; pl. f. (side-toes of animals)? MA in descr. of animals' feet

gūdu; pl. *gūdānu* "leather bag, waterskin" NB; < Aram.

guduballata'û "off-duty *pašīšu*-priest" jB lex.; < Sum.

guduballaturrû, *guduballû* "(junior) on-duty *pašīšu*-priest" jB lex.; < Sum.

gudūdu "battle troop" NB; < Aram.

gudugu (a kind of door) jB lex.

guduttû, *dugudû* (an offering table) jB lex.; < Sum.?

guennakku (the governor of Nippur) Bab., NA [GÚ.EN.NA]; < Sum.

guennakkūtu "governorship (of Nippur)" MB [GÚ.EN.NA-]; < *guennakku*

gugallu(m) I "irrigation controller" OAkk, Bab., NA [(LÚ.)GÚ.GAL; OAkk KÙ.GÁL; jB once UGU.GAL] as official, also PN; as epith. of king; of god; < Sum.; > *gugallūtu*

gugallu II 'big ox' jB desig. of drum; < Sum.

gugallūtu "post of irrigation controller" Nuzi, NB [LÚ.GÚ.GAL-]; also "payment to irrigation controller"; < *gugallu* I

gugamlu → *kigamlum*

gugāru mng. unkn. jB desig. of stone

guggalīpu → *gungulīpu*

guggubu, *gubgubu* (a precious ornament or gemstone) Qatna, Am., of lapis lazuli

gugguru(m), *gukkurum*; pl. f. (a clay vessel) O/jB, holding lard; sealed; < Sum.

gugittu (a shout)? jB lex.

gugû "shout(ing), cry(ing)" jB lex.

gugudum → *gugutum*

gugupinnu → *gungupinnu*

gugutum (or *gugudum*, *ku(k)kut/dum*) (a fodder plant) OAkk(Ur III)

guḫaššum, *guḫaṣṣu*, *guḫalṣu* "wire; cord; trimming" Bab., MA [GÚ.ḪAS] "wire" of gold, copper etc.; for lyre; mag. "string, cord"; "fringe, trimming" of carpet, garment

guḫḫu, *gaḫḫu* "cough(ing)" jB; → *ganāḫu*

guḫḫubu D "to cough" jB

guḫlu "kohl, antimony paste" j/NB [ŠIM.BI.ZI.DA (→ *šimbizidû*)] as raw material; med.; as eye make-up

guḫlû → *giḫlû*

guḫšû(m), OB, MA also *gušû* (a reed altar) O/jB, MA [OB GI.GÚḪŠU; jB GI.GUḪŠU] loaded with bread; < Sum.

gukallu → *mukkallu*

gukkallānu → *kukkallānu*

gukkallu → *kukkallu*

gukku → *kukku* I

gukkurum → *gugguru*

gulānu → *gulēnu*

gulbūtu, *gulubūtu*; OB pl. *gulbātum* ? (a kind of cereal) O/jB lex.; < *gullubu* II

gulēnu, *gulīnu*, *gulānu*; pl. m. & f. (an over-garment) NA, NB

gulgullu(m), *gulgullatu(m)*; pl. m. & f. "skull" Bab., NA of humans; dog, bird; NB "skull(-shaped vessel)"

gulībātu pl. tant. "hair-trimmings, clippings" jB from armpit; < *gullubu* II

gulinnu mng. unkn. NB

gulīnu → *gulēnu*

gullēnu "man" jB lex.

gullu(m); pl. f. "bowl" Bab., NA of metal; Mari, Qatna "bowl(-shaped ornament)" in gold; NA "(column) bases" in copper; NB (iron part of defensive grating)

gullubu(m) I "shorn, shaved" Bab.; OB as PN; j/NB cultically "shaven" priest, also as subst., pl. *gullubūtu*; f. *gulubtu* (desig. of wool) lex.; < *gullubu* II; > *gullubūtu*

gullubu(m) II **D** "to shear; shave" Bab., M/NA [SAR] *muttata(m) g.* "shave half (head)" as punishment; as sign of slavery, esp. *abbutta(m) g.*; also lips, cheeks, temples etc.; "excise" tattoo ?; animal, plant; j/NB, NA "shave" as part of cultic dedication; Nuzi, NA "clear" crop from field; Nuzi "plunder, clear out" house **Š** OB uncert.; > *gallābu*, *gallabtu*, *gallābūtu*; *gullubu* I, *gullubūtu*; *gulībātu*; *gulbūtu*; *naglabu*

gullubūtu "(cultic) shaving, i.e. ordination" NB; < *gullubu* I

gullultu(m) "sin, sacrilegious act" Bab. *g. epēšu(m)*, *g. rašû(m)* "to commit sin"; < *gullulu*

gullulu(m) **D** "to sin, commit sacrilege" Bab. towards (= *ana*) s.o.; *annī g.* "commit sins" **Dtn** iter. of D; < *gillatu* denom.; > *gullultu*

gullušu **D** mng. unkn. jB lex.

gulubtu → *gullubu* I

gulubūtu → *gulbūtu*

gumāḫu(m), *gummāḫu* "prize bull" Bab. [GU$_4$.MAḪ; NB also GU$_4$.MAḪ.E] for offerings; transf. ref. to king; < Sum.

gumaki(l)lu (a wooden item) NA

gumālu (a kind of tamarisk) jB lex.

gumānu (part of a plant)? jB lex.

gumāru "carbonized wood, charcoal" NA

gumgumšû (an altar) jB lex.; < Sum.

gummāḫu → *gumāḫu*

gummātu "summer" NB; < Aram.

gummurtu(m), Ass. *gammurtu* "totality, completion" O/jB, NA **1.** *ana g.* "at all, altogether" **2.** jB *gummurta* "altogether" **3.** NA in *i/ana g. libbi* "whole-heartedly, i.e. loyally" (also abbr. *gu-um l.*); < *gamāru* II D

gummutu **D** "to anger" NB; stat. "is very angry"; < Aram.

gum'u mng. unkn. NA (part of an ornament)

gumūru (or *kumūru*) "sword-hilt" Am.

gunakku (an animal-skin skirt) NB (= Gk. *kaunakes* ?); < OPers.

gungītu (a net)? jB lex.

gungu → *kungu* II

gungubinnu → *gungupinnu*

gungubu (or *gungupu*) (part of a chariot) Am.

gungulīpu, *gu(g)galīpu* "(camel's) hump" NA

gungupinnu, *gungubinnu*, *gugupinnu* (an ornament) NA, NB [GÚ.GAB(*-in-nu*)?]

gungupu → *gungubu*

gunnu ~ "mass, bulk" M/NA, jB of troops; "main force"? [GÚ ?]

gunnu → also *gurnu*

gunnuṣum adj. "nose-wrinkling, sneering" OB lex., also as PN; < *ganāṣu*

gunte memētu (an object) Am., in large numbers

-gunu → *-kunu*

gunûm (a storeroom) OB [É.GÚ.NA]; < Sum.

-gunūšu → *-kunūši*

gupārum I mng. unkn. Mari

gupāru II, *gupārû*, *gubāru* "neck; mane" jB also of stone/gold ornament; < Sum.

gupnu "tree(-trunk)" jB, NA; → *gapnu*

guppušum "very proud"? OB as PN; < *gapāšu*

gupru(m) "shepherd's hut" OA, O/jB; also lex. (a table)?; → *gubrum*

gupšu "surge, swell (of water)" jB; < *gapāšu*

gūqānu → *qūqānu*

guqqû; pl. *guqqānû* (a monthly offering) j/NB [GUG] of sheep, oxen, beer, dates; for specific day, month; < Sum.

gurābu "sack, wrapping" NB for alum; for large pot; < Aram.

gurartu → *kurartu*

gurāru → *kurāru*

guraṣu → *gurušgaraš*

gurāštu → *kurartu*

gurduppum, *kurduppum* "basket (for fish)" OB; < Sum.

gurgūgu "roller"? jB for moving ship; < Sum.?

gurgurratu → *qurqurratu*

gurgurru (a plant) jB lex.

gurgurru → also *qurqurru*

gurguššû (a big offering-vessel) jB lex.

gurištu, *kurištu* "vulva" M/jB; < *garāšu*; → *gurušgaraš*

gurištu → also *kurartu*

gurnu(m), *gunnu(m)* "of average quality" O/jB of copper, wool, dates etc.

gurpi(s)su → *qurpissu*

gu(r)rutu, NA *agurrutu* "ewe" M/NA [UDU.U8]

gurru(m), *gurrû* (a metal object) O/jB, MA

gurrû → *gurru*

gurrubu mng. uncl. NB in ZA.GÌN.KUR.RA ("blue dye") *gurrubtum*; < *garābu* ?

gurrudu(m), *qurrudu* "mangy" O/jB lex.; of fish; as PN; desig. of clay lump?; < *garādu*

gurruru → *qurruru*

gurruṣu "scabrous"? NB of skull; < *garāṣum*

gursā/ēnum → *gusānu*

gursi(p)pu → *qurpissu*

guršu I, *quršu* ~ "chapel" NA (or "(ritual) sexual congress" < *garāšu* ?); also *bīt g.* (part of a house); or = *ḫuršu* ?

guršu II (or *quršu*) (a peg)? jB lex.

gūru ~ "foliage, leaves (of reed-plants)" jB [GI.GIL ?] *g. (ša) qanî* "*g.* of reed"

gurummaru(m) (a kind of tree) Bab. [GIŠ.GIŠIMMAR.KUR.RA (liter. "foreign date palm")]; MB *terinnāt g.* "cones of *g.*" as drug; < Sum.

gurummû, *gurunnû* (a reed object) jB

gurunniš → *qurunniš*

gurunnu → *garunnu*; *qurunnu*

gurunnû → *gurummû*

gurušgaraš, *garašgaraš*, *guruṣu-guru/aṣu* etc. "vulva" jB lex., comm., of pig; med. as drug; < *garāšu* or Sum.?; → *gurištu*

guruššû → *kuruštû*

gusānu(m), *kušānu(m)*, OA *k/gursā/ēnum*, *kursinnum*, Nuzi *kusannu*; MA pl. f. (a leather sack) O/MA, O/jB often containing wool; < Hitt.?

gusīgu → *ḫusīgu*

gusû mng. uncert. jB as destination of boat ?

guṣṣu mng. unkn. jB (desig. of snake)

guštappu, *kuštappu* mng. unkn. Am. in pairs, part of harness ?

gūštu(m) ~ "whirling dance"? jB with *gâšu*, of Gušea; < *gâšu* I

gušû (a god's garment) jB lex.

gušû → also *guḫšû*

gūšum (a sheep-offering) OB(Elam)

gušubbû → *kišubbû*

gušūru(m), NA *gašūru* "tree-trunk, beam" [GIŠ.ÙR; OB also GIŠ.ÙR.RA, GIŠ.ŠU.ÙR] "tree-trunk, felled log" of cedar etc.; "beams" often for roof; NA transf. *g.*^{meš} *ša libbi* "beams of heart"; < Sum.

gutaku (a high official) MB of PlN (or error for *guennakku* ?)

gutappû(m) (part of donkey harness) O/jB [GÚ.TAB-]; < Sum.

gutarru "back" jB lex.; < Sum.

gutezzû Dt ~ "to take refuge"? jB lex.; → *gūzu*

gutû → *qutû*

guzalītu → *guzalūtu*

guzallu "ruffian, scoundrel" M/jB lex., also as PN; < Sum.

guzalû(m), *kuzzalûm*; OB pl. f. "chair-carrier, throne-bearer" O/jB [GU.ZA.LÁ] OB (an official); later as epith. of deities and demons; < Sum.

guzālum → *kuzallu*

guzalūtu, *guza/ilītu* "female throne-bearer" jB [(MUNUS.)GU.ZA.LÁ] of humans, goddesses; < *guzalû*

guzāzu (a kind of lettuce)? jB lex.

guzguzu (a garment) NB

guzi "stable-lad" Am. as self-debasing desig.; < Eg.

guzilītu → *guzalūtu*

guzippu → *kuṣippum*; *kuzippu*

guzīru mng. unkn. NA

guziu "drinking cup" jB lex.; < Sum.

guzû (a medicinal plant) MB

gūzu "refuge" NB in PNs; < OPers.?; → *gutezzû*

guzullu → *kuzullu*

Ḫ

ḫabābu(m) "to murmur, chirp, twitter" Bab. **G** (*u/u*) of water; flies "buzz"; birds; lovers; lightning "hiss" **D** of snake "hiss at" s.o. (= acc.); of lover ~ "croon at"; absol., of flies **Š** "make" water "gurgle", cow "low"; > *ḫubbu*; *ḫabību*, *ḫābibum*; *ḫibabītu*; *ḫabūbītu*; *ḫabbūbu*?

ḫabad? (part of a chariot) M/jB; < Kass.?

ḫabālātu → *ḫabālu* I

ḫabalginnu, *ḫabalkinnu* (a kind of iron) MA, Am., jB; < proto-Hattic ?

ḫabalum "strap" Mari; < W.Sem.; → *eblu*; *ḫabānum*

ḫabālu I; pl. often f. "act of violence, wrong-doing" M/jB, NA; NA pl. f. also "wrongs, injustices"; < *ḫabālu* II infin.

ḫabālu(m) II "to do wrong, violence to" s.o. **G** (*i/i*, OB mostly *a/u*) "do wrong to, oppress" the weak, the poor; "take s.th. from s.o. (= 2 acc.) by force, wrongly" **D** ~ G "do wrong to" s.o.; *ḫibiltam ḫ.* "do an injustice" (to s.o.) **Dt** NB "be wrongly taken" **N** "be treated unjustly"; of fields "be ruined"; > *ḫablu*, *ḫabiltu*; *ḫibiltu*; *ḫabālu* I; *ḫābilu* I; *muḫabbiltu*

ḫabālu(m) III "to be in debt; borrow" Ass., O/MB **G** (*a/u*) OA "borrow" (silver etc.) from (= *ana*/dat.) s.o.; NA "owe" s.th. "to" s.o. **D** "lend"; stat. "is in debt" to (= dat./*ana*) s.o. **Dt** "be indebted" to s.o. for (= acc.) s.th. **N** OA "be in debt" to s.o. for (= acc.) s.th.; < *ḫubullu* denom.; > *ḫubbulu*, *ḫubbultu*

ḫabālu(m) IV "to bind, harness" O/jB **G** (*a/a*) waggons; > *ḫābilu* II?; *naḫbalu*, *naḫbaltu*; → *ḫabalum*

ḫabālum → also *ḫabānum*

ḫabannānu "water-tub"? jB

ḫabannatu(m), NA *ḫabnutu* (a container) O/jB, Mari, NA of silver, bronze; Am., Bogh. of stone, for oil; jB, NA of clay; < Eg.

ḫabānum (or *ḫabālum*) (a wooden object) OAkk(Ur III); → *ḫabalum*

ḫabaqūku → *ḫabbaqūqu*

ḫabaraḫḫu (a box) NA containing vegetables; → *abaraḫḫum*

ḫabarānu, *ḫabrānu* (a plant) jB, oil of *ḫ.*

ḫabarattu(m) "noise, clamour" OB "clamour" of mankind; jB "noise, rattling" in chest ?; < *ḫabāru* I

ḫabāru(m) I "to make noise, clamour" O/jB, NA **G** (*u/u*) "be noisy; be busy" of people; stat. *ḫabur* "is noisy"; jB of house "creak" **D** lex. only **Dt** jB "(merrily) create a noise"? **Š** jB "cause to make (joyful) clamour"; "instigate disruption"; > *ḫabrum*; *ḫabbiru*; *ḫabarattu*; *ḫubūru* II; *ḫabburtu*?

ḫabāru(m) II "to be thick, solid" O/jB **G** (f. stat. also *abrat*) of part of body; stat. of sky, earth; transf. of command "is weighty, authoritative" **D** "make" (silver X cubits) "thick"; stat. of parts of body; > *ḫabbartu*?; → *kabāru* D

ḫabāru → also *ḫamāru* D

ḫabarzinānum (a bird) OB

ḫabaṣillatu ~ "reed shoot" jB lex. **1.** (part of reed) **2.** ^{urudu}*ḫ.* (desig. of a drum); → *baṣillatu*

ḫabaṣīrānu (a constellation) jB [MUL.EN.TE.NA.BAR.LUM/SIG$_4$]; < *ḫabaṣīru*

ḫabaṣirtu → *ḫumṣirtu*

ḫabaṣīru → *ḫumṣīru*

ḫabāṣu(m) I ~ "to be distended" O/jB **G** (*u/u*) stat. "is distended" through drinking; "be enlarged" with prosperity **Gtn** iter. of G, of body **D** lex. only **Dt** "be dilated (with joy)" **Š** "make rejoice"; "make pleasing" to s.o.; > *ḫabṣu*, *ḫabṣūtu*; *ḫibṣu*; *ḫubāṣu*; *ḫumbiṣūtu*; *ḫubbuṣu*; *ḫitbāṣu*; *taḫbāṣu*?

ḫabāṣu(m) II "to smite down"? O/jB **G** (*u/u*) of god; "pulverize" with (upper) grindstone; > *ḫābiṣu*; *naḫbaṣu*?; *taḫbāṣu*?

ḫabaštum (an object) OA

ḫabašu → *ḫabšu* I

ḫabāšu(m) I "to become hard, swollen" O/jB **G** (*u/u*) stat. of part of body, liver **D** stat. "is swollen" of head; > *ḫabšu* II?; *ḫibšu*; *ḫubbušu*; *ḫabšānû*; *ḫubšašû*?

ḫabāšu(m) II "to crush, comminute" Bab. **G** (*a/u*) straw, pot, malt etc. **D**, **Dt** jB lex. only **N** transf. of breast "be shattered"; > *ḫabšu* I; *ḫibištu*; *ḫubšu* I?; *ḫabbāšu*; *naḫbašu*, *naḫbaštum*

ḫabātu(m) I "to rob, plunder" OAkk, Bab., M/NA **G** (*a/u*, OB pret. occas. *iḫbit*) [NB SAR] "rob (on road, in countryside)" (acc. = thing, person taken); "rustle, steal" cattle etc.; *ḫubta ḫ.* "carry out a robbery" but also "take (as) plunder"; "raid, plunder" a land etc., caravan; OB math. "dig" clay for bricks; OB also "thresh" **Gtn** iter. of G **Dt** ~ N "be taken as plunder" **Š** MB mng. uncl. **N** pass. of G, of people "be carried off, plundered"; of a robbery "be perpetrated"; > *ḫabtu*, *ḫābitu*; *ḫibtu*; *ḫubtu*; *ḫabbātu* I; *naḫbutu* II

ḫabātu(m) II "to loan (interest-free)" OAkk, O/jB **G** (*a/u*) OB grain, bricks **D** OAkk stat., of recipient "is loaned, owes"; < *ḫubuttu* denom.

ḫabātu(m) III ~ "to wander, roam through" O/jB **G** (*a/u*) with *ana*; with acc. "roam through" mountain, darkness, trouble **Š** "make s.o. wander through" **N** ~ G with *ana*; absol. "wander"; > *ḫabbātu* II; *naḫbutum* I

ḫabātu IV, *qabātu* MB(Ass.) **G** (*a/u*) "to clear away" building **Gt** (*i/i*) ~ "decay", of building

ḫabātu → also *abātu* I; *ḫapātu*

ḫabazûm in *ša ḫ.* (an agricultural worker) OB lex.; < Sum.

ḫabazz(at)u (a vessel) NB; < Aram.?

ḫabbaqūqu, *ḫamba/uqūqu*, NA *ḫabaqūku* (a garden herb) j/NB, NA

ḫabbartu (a kind of garment) jB lex.; liter. "thick (garment)"?; < *ḫabāru* II ?

ḫabbāšu "crusher, chopper" NB (a worker); as PN (also *Ḫambāšu*); < *ḫabāšu* II

ḫabbātu(m) I "plunderer, bandit" Bab. [LÚ.SA.GAZ (→ *ḫ.* II)]; astr. also desig. of planet Mars; < *ḫabātu* I

ḫabbātu(m) II "migrant worker" O/jB, NA [LÚ.SA.GAZ (→ *ḫ.* I)]; < *ḫabātu* III

ḫabbilu → *ḫābilu* I

ḫabbiru (part of a loom) jB lex.; < *ḫabāru* I

ḫabbištu → *kāpišum*

ḫabbītu → *ḫāmītu*

ḫabbu (a pit)? Ug., jB

ḫabbūbu ~ "lover"? jB; < *ḫabābu* ?

ḫabbulu → *ḫubbulu*

ḫabburru → *ḫabbūru*

ḫa(b)burtu ~ "roaring"? NA (epith. of Ištar); < *ḫabāru* I ?

ḫabburu (a kind of wine) NA in *karān ḫ.*

ḫabbūru(m), *ḫabburru*, OB lex. *ḫebbūrum* "sprout, shoot" Bab. [ḪÉNBUR] used in beer, growing out of wall; of various plants, reed; transf. of person "scion", as PN; < Sum.?

ḫabḫayû "from Ḫabḫu" MA, desig. of sheep

ḫabību(m) "happy hubbub" O/jB of people, lands; < *ḫabābu*

ḫābibu(m) "murmurer" OB, as PN; NB f. (a clay vessel); < *ḫabābu*

ḫabigalzu (a medicinal plant) jB; < Kass.

ḫabiltu → *ḫablu*; *ḫibiltu*

ḫābilu(m) I, jB *ḫabbilu* "criminal, wrongdoer" O/jB; OB *ṣāb ḫ.* "criminal band"; desig. of demons; < *ḫabālu* II

ḫābilu II ~ "trapper" jB; desig. of hunter, *ḫ. amēlu*; < *ḫabālu* IV ?

ḫabinniš ~ "secretly"? jB

ḫābiru → *ḫāpiru*; *ḫāwirum*

ḫābiṣu "pulverizing" jB, of grindstone; < *ḫabāṣu* II

ḫabītu → *ḫabû* I

ḫābitu "plunderer" NB; < *ḫabātu* I

ḫābītum "(female) drawer of water" Mari in *ḫ. mê*; < *ḫabû* III

ḫablu(m) adj. and subst. "wronged (person)" [f. *ḫabiltum* MUNUS.ŠAGA.RA], esp. *ḫablu(m) u ḫabiltu(m)*; *utuk/dām ḫ.* "ghost/blood of wronged person"; NA *dēnu ša ḫablūte* "judgement for the wronged"; *ḫ. šutēšuru(m)* "to restore rights to the wronged"; < *ḫabālu* II

ḫabnutu → *ḫabannatu*

ḫabrānu → *ḫabarānu*

ḫabrātu → *ḫabrum*

ḫabrum "clamorous, busy" OB of people; < *ḫabāru* I

ḫabsukku → *kilsukku*

ḫabsurukku (kind of offering meat) NB

ḫabṣirtu → *ḫumṣirtu*

ḫabṣīru → *ḫumṣīru*

ḫabṣu "plentiful" M/jB of gifts; "fertile" of fields; < *ḫabāṣu* I; > *ḫabṣūtu*

ḫabṣūtu "luxuriance" O/jB lex.; < *ḫabṣu*

ḫabšallurḫu, *ḫapšallurḫu*, *ḫapšilurgu*, *ḫup(pa)šilurg/ḫu* (an oil plant) jB lex., med.; < Elam.

ḫabšānû (a desig. of wool) jB lex., in f. pl.; < *ḫabāšu* I

ḫabšarru (or *ḫab/pšerru*) mng. unkn. jB lex.

ḫabšitri (or *ḫapšitri*) (a vessel)? Mari, for ice

ḫabšu I, NA *ḫabašu* "chopped, crushed" M/jB, NA esp. of straw; as subst. "chopped (straw)"; < *ḫabāšu* II

ḫabšu(m) II (or *ḫapšu(m)*) (a vessel) MB(Alal.), jB lex.; OB also as emblem ^{d}*ḫabiš*; < *ḫabāšu* I ?

ḫabtu(m) "robbed" O/jB of man; "taken as plunder"; "having suffered robbery"; < *ḫabātu* I

ḫabum → *ḫa'u*

ḫabû I; f. *ḫabītu(m)* "soft" j/NB of garment; (desig. of pottery vessel); NB in *ḫab(i) uḫīni/u* "over-ripe dates"; < *ḫabû* II

ḫabû II "to be soft" O/jB, of season "be mild"; jB of gall; > *ḫabû* I

ḫabû(m) III "to draw (water)" O/jB, NA **G** (*u/u*) obj. usu. *mê*; jB wine; > *ḫebû*; *ḫābītum*; *naḫbû*

ḫabû IV "to give refuge" NA **G** or **D**; > *ḫibûtu*; *ḫābû*; *naḫbātu*; *taḫbâtu*

ḫābum (or *ḫāpum*) (a kind of gazelle)? OAkk(Ur III); also as PN

ḫābu → also *ḫāpu*

ḫābû, *ḫāpû* (a storage jar) M/NB, NA of brewer; < *ḫabû* IV

ḫâbu "to love" jB lex.; > *ḫībum*

ḫâbu → also *ḫiāpum*

ḫabūbītu "bee" NB pl. *ḫabūbēti*, liter. "buzzer"; < *ḫabābu*

ḫabulillu (a stone) Nuzi; → *ḫublillu* ?

ḫabullu → *ḫubullu*

ḫabūnu "fold, flounce" of garment jB, NA esp. transf. as protection

ḫaburatḫu (a tree) jB lex.

ḫabūtum → *ḫapūtum*

ḫadādu I "to rustle, roar" jB **G** (*u/u*) of storm, flood; of camp, gecko

ḫadādu II "to incise deeply" Bab. **G** stat., of weight "is incised" **D** ~ G stat., of gully in mountain "is cut in"; of part of body "is fissured"; > *ḫuddudu*

ḫadādu → also *kadādu*

ḫadālu I ~ "to tie up, knot" M/jB **G** (*a/u*) "attach" oxen ?; of spider "tie up" fly **Gt** stat. "are tied together" **Št** "knot (i.e. plot) together" iniquity; > *ḫādilu*; *maḫdalu*

ḫadālu(m) II ~ "to retreat, go back"? O/jB **G** (*i/i*) math. of projection on bank **D** "hold back"? water **Š** caus. lex. only

ḫadānu (a wooden appliance) jB lex.

ḫadānum → also *adānum*

ḫadāqu "to press together" jB **G** comm., stat. of part of body; < Aram.

ḫadāru → *adāru* I; *ḫatāru*

ḫadaššatu "bride" jB lex.; < *ḫadāšu*

ḫadaššû "bridegroom" jB lex.; < *ḫadāšu*

ḫadaššūtu "marriage (ceremony)" M/jB; < *ḫadāšu*

ḫadāšu D, Dtn "to rejoice (repeatedly)" jB lex.; > *ḫadaššû*, *ḫadaššatu*, *ḫadaššūtu*; *ḫuduššûm*; → *kadāšu*

ḫaddânu, *ḫādiānu* "(malevolent) rejoicer, gloater" NA pl. *ḫaddânū*, *ḫād(i)ānūte*; < *ḫadû* III

ḫaddilu → *ḫādilu*

ḫaddû "very joyful" NA; < *ḫadû* III

ḫādiānu → *ḫaddânu*

ḫādilu, *ḫaddilu* "knotter" jB desig. of spider; *ḫ. appi* desig. of fisherman; < *ḫadālu* I

ḫadîš "happily, joyfully" Bab., NA; < *ḫadû* I

ḫadi-ū'a-amēlu "joy-woe-man" jB i.e. of fickle mood

ḫadqum (topog. desig., phps.) "steppe" OB

ḫadû I "joyful" j/NB of news; of face, person; < *ḫadû* III

ḫadû(m) II "joy" Bab., esp. *bussurat/awāt/ ṭēmam (ša) ḫadêm* ref. to good news; NB *ina ḫ. libbīšu* "voluntarily"; < *ḫadû* III infin.

ḫadû(m) III "to be joyful, rejoice" **G** (*u/u*, jB also *i/i*) [ḪÚL] about = *ana*/dat.; of person; of heart, face etc.; "be willing, wish", "be content with" an action **Gtn** iter. of G **D** "make happy" person, heart etc. **Dt(n)** lex. only **Š** jB "make s.o. rejoice" **N** NB "reach an agreement together"?; > *ḫadû* I.II, *ḫadîš*, *ḫadûtu*; *ḫadi-ū'a-amēlu*; *ḫādû*, *ḫaddû*, *ḫaddânu*; *ḫidûtu*, *ḫidiātum*; *ḫūdu*; *muḫaddûm*; *taḫdītu*

ḫadû IV "to cut off" NB **D** transf. "cut off" crossing-place (*nēberu*); < Aram.

ḫādû; f. *ḫādītu* "(malevolent) rejoicing, gloating" jB, NA, e.g. *ḫādû'a* "those who gloat over me"; < *ḫadû* III

ḫâdu → *ḫiādu*; *ḫiāṭu*

ḫadûtu, NA also *ḫudûtu* "joy, rejoicing" M/NB, NA; < *ḫadû* III

ḫaerušḫu (a wild beast) NA

ḫaḫḫālum; pl. f. mng. unkn. OA; < Hitt.?

ḫaḫḫarum → *ḫarḫarru*

ḫaḫḫašum "hot, burning (with fever)" O/jB of part of body

ḫaḫḫītu(m) "(garment of) Ḫaḫḫum" OA, Bogh.; < Ḫaḫḫum (in Anatolia)

ḫaḫḫu I "phlegm, mucus" M/jB of human; Bogh. of bull ?; > *ḫaḫû* II ?

ḫaḫḫu(m) II (a fruit (tree), phps.) "plum" or "peach" O/jB, NA

ḫaḫḫu III mng. uncl. jB after iron (*parzillu*); < Aram.?

ḫaḫḫūratta "like a raven" jB, i.e. stiff-legged, of gait ?; < *ḫaḫḫūru*

ḫaḫḫūru(m); f. *ḫaḫḫurtu* "raven" Bab. also as PN; OB transf. "spy"; > *ḫaḫḫūratta*

ḫaḫinnu, *ḫaḫīnu*, NA *ḫiḫinnu* (a thorny plant) jB, NA lex., med.; NA also as descr. of god's weapon

ḫaḫû I, *ḫuḫû(m)* "slag, clinker" O/jB, of potter; from oven

ḫaḫû II, *aḫû*, *a'û* "to spew, spit out" M/jB **G** (pres. *iḫaḫḫu*, *i-'a-ḫa*, *i-a-ú*) blood, bile etc. **Gtn** iter.; < *ḫaḫḫu* I denom.?; > *ḫuḫḫītu*

ḫā'idu → *ḫā'iṭu*

ḫaigallatḫe → *ayyigalluḫu*

ḫā'iru → *ḫāwiru*

ḫā'irūtu "status of consort" jB; < *ḫāwiru*

ḫā'iṭānu "the one who weighed out" (silver) NB; < *ḫiāṭu*

ḫā'iṭu(m), *ḫayyiṭu*, *ḫā'idu* "watcher" O/jB **1.** "night-watchman" [(LÚ.)GE6.(A.)LAḪ5], also epith. of gods, demons; *ḫ. ša muṣlāli* "w. of siesta-time" **2.** jB (an official who weighs out); < *ḫiāṭu*

ḫā'iṭūtu "function of night-watchman" jB [GE6.LAḪ5-]; < *ḫā'iṭu*

ḫakammum "expert" Mari, of doctor; < W.Sem.

ḫakāmu(m) "to understand, apprehend" O/jB, NA **G** (*i/i*) of person **D** ~ G **Š** NA "let s.o. know, inform" **Št** NA "be informed, acquainted" **N** pass. "be understood"; of star "be recognized"; → *ḫakammum*

ḫakāru(m) ~ "to comminute" O/jB **G** (*i/i*)

ḫakê adv. ~ "crooked, askew"? jB comm., ref. to birth

ḫakûm ~ "to take thought"? Mari; < W.Sem.

ḫakurratu (a cut of meat) Bogh. in Hitt. rit.

ḫalābu "to milk" NA **G** milk, breast; < Sem.

ḫalaḫlu → *ḫalḫallu* I

ḫalaḫwu → *ḫawalḫu*

ḫalālum I "to confine, shut away" OA, OB **G** (*a/u*) person; silver **Gtn** infin. "continued confinement" **D** OA stat. "is confined" **Štn** OA "have s.o. continuously confined"; > *ḫillu*?

ḫalālu II ~ "to pipe; murmur" j/NB, NA **G** (*u/u*) of flute, birds, human lungs; of spring water **D** "make emit sound, sound" bell **Dtn** iter. of D; > *ḫālilu* I?

ḫalālu(m) III "to creep, slink" O/jB, NA **G** (*a/u*) of person, animal; transf. of death **Gtn** "crawl through, continually" **N** (*naḫallulu*) ~ G lex. only **Ntn** "creep round, continually"; > *ḫālilum* II; *ḫillatu*; *muttaḫallilu*; → *ḫallulāya*

ḫalālum → also *alālu* II

ḫalānu → *ḫulālu*

ḫalāpu(m) I "to slip into, through" Bab., NA **G** (*u/u*) "slip into, through" s.th. (= acc./*ina/-iš*); stat. "is 'slipped into'", i.e. "clad in" garment, transf. radiance, battle etc. **Gtn** "creep, slip repeatedly into" **Gt** stat. "is clad in, mantled with" radiance etc.; "are tangled" of trees, intestines **D** "clothe s.o. with" (= 2 acc.) [GIR6] garments; leprosy; "overlay" with metal **Š** lex. only **N** "clothe o.s. with" (= acc.) armour etc.; > *ḫāliptu*?; *ḫulāpu*, *ḫuluptu*; *ḫallupu*, *ḫalluptu*; *ḫitlāpu*, *ḫitlupātu*; *naḫlaptu*; *taḫlappānu*; *taḫluptu*, *taḫlīpu*

ḫalāpu II "to accuse"? OB **G** not attested **Š** "indict" s.o.; > *ḫalpu* I, *ḫaliptum*, *ḫalpūtum*; *ḫālipu*

ḫalāqiš "into flight" OB; < *ḫalāqu*

ḫalāqu(m), NB *ḫelēqu* "to be lost; be(come) fugitive" **G** (*i/i*) [ZAḪ; ZÁḪ] **1.** "disappear, get lost" of goods, animals; of road "be lost" by s.o. (= acc.); math. "be unknown" of number **2.** "be destroyed" of ship, walls, goods; animals, people **3.** stat. of part of body "is absent" **4.** "escape, flee" of slaves etc. **Gtn** jB of s.o.'s mouth (i.e. words) "repeatedly get lost" **D** fact. of G [ZÁḪ] "lose"; OA "owe a loss"; "allow" slave "to escape"; "banish, abolish" irrigation buckets; "destroy" enemy, land etc.; "ruin" s.o. **Dtn** iter. of D **Dt** pass. of D **Š** "help, allow s.o. to escape" **Št** pass. of Š; of property "become lost" **ŠD** jB "destroy" **N** NA, NB "escape" of workers etc. **Ntn** NA "continually disappear, be lost", of commodity; > *ḫalqu*, *ḫaliqtu*, *ḫalqūtum*, *ḫelgeni*?; *ḫulqu*; *ḫulāqu*; *ḫuluqqā'um*; *ḫalāqiš*, *ḫulluqiš*; *šaḫluqtu*; *muštaḫalqu*

ḫalāṣu(m) "to comb out, filter" O/jB **G** (*a/u*) wool, goat hair; "strain, filter" sesame (oil);

stat. "seeps out"? of bile **Gtn** lex. only **Gt** OB; > *ḫalṣu* I; *ḫilṣu* I; *ḫāliṣtu*; *ḫulāṣum*

ḫalāṣu → also *ḫarāṣu* N; *kalāṣu* Gtn

ḫalāšu(m) "to scrape off, grub up" O/jB **G** (*a/u*) fungus, wall-plaster, door-jamb **D** ~ G ?; > *ḫilšu*, *ḫilištu*; *maḫlašu*

ḫalātum mng. unkn. OA = *alātu* ?

ḫalā'um → *ḫalû* I; *ḫelû* II

Ḫalbatum (a month) OB(Elam)

ḫalbum "forest" O/jB

ḫalbukkatu (or *ḫalpukkatu*) (a plant) jB lex.

ḫaldimmānu (or *ḫaltimmānu*) "master"? jB lex.

ḫalḫallatu(m) "(a kind of) drum" Bab. [MÈN; MEN$_4$] of copper; accompanying song; thunder like *ḫ*.

ḫalḫallu(m) I, NA, NB *ḫalaḫlu* adj. and subst. (a comestible) M/NA, NB; in basket; NB desig. of flour

ḫalḫallu(m) II (a basket) OAkk, jB

ḫaliltu mng. unkn. jB in *ḫ. ša nāri* "*ḫ*. of river"

ḫālilu(m) I (or *ḫalīlu(m)*) mng. uncl. Bab. in desig. of canal, of beer; OB as PN; < *ḫalālu* II ?

ḫālilum II ~ "spy" Mari; < *ḫalālu* III

ḫālilu III, *ḫallilu* (an iron tool) NB for digging; < Aram.?

ḫaliptum "accusation" OA, also *awātum ḫ*. "accusing word(s)"; < *ḫalpu* I

ḫāliptu (an object) NA, NB; < *ḫalāpu* I ?

ḫālipu "prosecutor" Bogh. in Hitt. laws; < *ḫalāpu* II

ḫaliqtu(m) "lost" O/jB **1.** "lost (item), s.th. lost" **2.** "loss, item/amount lost" **3.** (desig. of part of liver); < *ḫalqu*

ḫāliṣtu, *ḫālištu* "(female) wool-comber" jB lex.; < *ḫalāṣu*

ḫalīṣu; pl. *ḫalīṣiānu* "flayed (animal) skin" j/NB

ḫališiknum (a fabric) OB, for bed

ḫālištu → *ḫāliṣtu*

ḫallā "(dung) pellet" NB of bird; *ḫ. iṣṣūr(i)* (a plant name); < Aram.

ḫallā → also *ḫallu* IV

ḫallālāniš, *ḫallālatti* "like a centipede"? O/jB; < *ḫallulāya*

ḫallālītu; pl. *ḫallāliātu* (an object, phps.) "link (of a chain)" MA

ḫallalū'a → *ḫallulāya*

ḫallamaštu (a kind of legume) jB lex.

ḫallamīs/šu → *ḫulamīsu*

ḫallam(u?) (desig. of meat) NA

ḫallāru → *ḫallūru*

ḫallatu I "garden yield tax" NB esp. *kirî ḫ*. (privately owned orchard); < Aram.?

ḫallatu II (a kind of basket) NB for dates, silver; on ship; < Aram.

ḫallatu → also *ḫallu* I

ḫallatuššû(m) "apprentice" O/jB [ḪAL.LA. TUŠ.A]; < Sum.

ḫallilu → *ḫālilu* III

ḫallimu; pl. *ḫallimānu* "raft" NB

ḫallu(m) I, lex also *ḫallatu* ? "(upper) thigh" O/jB, NA [ḪAL] in du.; of men, women; *ṣubāt ḫ*. "loincloth"; *ḫ. petû* "to open thighs", i.e. sit astride horse, ride; of animals; NA ^{uzu}*ḫallānu* (a cut of meat); Mari on chariot, mng. uncl.; </> Sum.; > *ḫallutānû*; *pētḫallu*

ḫallu II (a clay vessel) jB lex.; < Sum.

ḫallu(m) III "(the cuneiform sign) ḪAL" O/jB [ḪAL] as mark on liver etc.

ḫallu IV, *ḫallā* "vinegar" NA, NB; < Aram.

ḫalluḫum mng. unkn. OA **D** action towards girl

ḫallulāya, *ḫallālū'a* etc. "centipede"? jB med., lex.; also as name of demon; > *ḫallālāniš*; → *ḫalālu* III

ḫalluptu "armour" NA of soldiers, horses; *ša ḫallupṭīšunu* "armour suppliers"; < *ḫallupu*

ḫallupu "armoured" NA in *šupālītu ḫ*. "armoured tunic?"; < *ḫalāpu* I D

ḫallūrtu(m) "a (single) pea" O/jB [GÚ.GAL] in similes; < *ḫallūru*

ḫallūru(m), *ḫullūru*, *ḫillūru*, *ḫallāru* "peas" OAkk, Bab. [GÚ.GAL; pl. OAkk GÚ.GÚ.GAL (.GAL)] phps. "chick-pea"; NB = $^{1}/_{10}$ shekel weight; > *ḫallūrtu*

Ḫallūt (a month) OAkk

ḫallutānû (black patch on donkey's leg) jB lex., med.; < *ḫallu* I

ḫalmaḫḫu (big *ḫallu*-container) jB lex.; < Sum.

ḫalmatru, Nuzi *ḫalwat(ar)ru* (a kind of wood) Nuzi, NB used for chariot parts

ḫalpatānû mng. unkn. Bogh. med.; < *ḫalpû* ?

***ḫalpatu**, NA gen. *ḫalpete* mng. unkn. NA, of eunuchs

ḫalpium, *ḫalpû* (a kind of cistern) O/jB lex.; < Sum.

ḫalpu(m) I "accused, prosecuted" OA, OB; OB also "concealed, furtive"?; < *ḫalāpu* II; > *ḫaliptum*, *ḫalpūtum*

ḫalpu II "substitute (person)" NB; < Aram.

ḫalpû(m) "frost, ice" Bab.; < Sum.; > *ḫalpatānû*?

ḫalpû → also *ḫalpium*

ḫalpukkatu → *ḫalbukkatu*

ḫalpūtum "state of being accused" OA; < *ḫalpu* I

ḫalqu(m) "lost; fugitive" Bab., M/NA [ZAḪ; ZÁḪ; Mari also BA.ḪA] "lost" property; math.

"unknown" value; "fled, fugitive", esp. as subst.; j/NB *zēr ḫalqātî* "nomads"; of field "ruined"; < *ḫalāqu*; > *ḫaliqtu*; *ḫalqūtum*; *ḫelgeni*?

ḫalqūtum "loss" OB of grain; < *ḫalqu*

ḫalṣu(m) I, MB occas. *ḫarṣu* "combed, filtered" Bab., M/NA [BÁRA(.GA/GÁ); occas. BÁRA.AG, BÁRA.GÉ] of sesame, sesame oil "filtered"; of perfumes (*riqqū*), flax; < *ḫalāṣu*

ḫalṣu(m) II m., j/NB also f. "fortress; district" Bab., M/NA "fort, fortification"; esp. Mari, Bogh., M/NA (wr. *ḫal-zu/zi*) "district, province"; *rab ḫ.* "fortress commander"; [NA (URU.)ḪAL.ṢU = log. for *birtu* I ?]; > *ḫalṣūtu*; *ḫalzuḫlu*

ḫalṣum → also *ḫarṣu*

ḫalṣūtu "fortified state" NA; < *ḫalṣu* II

ḫaltappānu (a plant) M/jB, NA lex., med.

ḫaltappātu → *katappātu*

ḫaltappû → *ḫultuppû*

ḫaltib, *ḫatib* (a magical formula) jB

ḫaltikku, *ḫaltikkūtu* (a vessel) Bogh., jB lex.

ḫaltimmānu → *ḫaldimmānu*

ḫaltu → *ḫaštu* I.II

ḫalû(m) I, OAkk *ḫalā'um* (a woollen garment) OAkk, O/MB

ḫalûm II "to be(come) ill" Mari **G** stat., of lion; < W.Sem.

ḫalû → also *ḫālu* II

ḫālu(m) I "maternal uncle" also ref. to (protective) deity, esp. in PNs

ḫālu(m) II, *ḫalû* "(black) mole" on skin O/jB

ḫālu III in *karān ḫ.* "vinegar"? NA

ḫâlu, OA *ḫuālum* "to melt (away)" OA, jB **G** usu. with *zâbu*, intrans. of figurines, enemies **D** "dissolve" jB med.

ḫâlu → also *ḫiālum*

ḫalūlu (a fruit) Nuzi

ḫaluppu(m), *ḫuluppu(m)*, NA also *ḫiluppu*? (a tree) OAkk, O/jB, NA [GIŠ.ḪA.LU.ÚB; occas. ḪU.LU.ÚB]; wood for vessel, furniture; mag., med., seed, twig, bark etc. of *ḫ.*

ḫaluqqā'u, ḫaluqqû → *ḫuluqqā'um*

ḫalwat(ar)ru → *ḫalmatru*

ḫalwû, *ḫa(l)wumma* "boundary wall" Nuzi, esp. *ḫa(l)wumma epēšu* "to build boundary wall round" field etc.; < Hurr.

ḫalziqqu (a container) jB, in reed or leather; < Sum.

ḫalzu → *ḫalṣu* II

ḫalzuḫlu, MA *ḫassiḫlu*; Am. pl. *ḫalzuḫlūti* "district governor" MA, MB(Alal.), Am., Nuzi, of PlN; < *ḫalṣu* II + Hurr. *-uḫlu*

ḫamadīru(m), *ḫamadārum* "parched" OAkk, O/jB of grain; "withered" of tree; OAkk as PN

ḫamadīrūtu in *ḫ. šūluku* "to make withered" M/jB; < *ḫamadīru*

ḫamādu(m) "to hide away, hoard" OB, NB **G** (*i/i*) grain, stones **N** OA "excuse o.s."; > *ḫamdum*; *ḫimittum* I

ḫamālu "to plan, plot" MB **G** (*i/i*) wickedness; > *ḫimiltu*

ḫamāmu(m) "to gather, collect" Bab. **G** (*a/u*) grain, reeds; transf., "concentrate (in oneself)" ritual offices (*parṣē*), wisdom etc., battles **D** ~ G **Dt** "be assembled" of building stones; > *ḫāmimu*; *ḫimmatu*, *ḫimmum*?; *ḫumāmātu*

Ḫamannu (a month) Nuzi; also Alal., a copper item ?

ḫamarḫu mng. unkn. Nuzi, grain *ana ḫ.*; < Hurr.

ḫamāru(m) "to become dry" O/jB **G** (stat. *ḫamar*) of field, eyes, vessel "dry out" (intrans.) **D** fact. "dry out" eyes; lex. infin. also *ḫubburu*, of penis **Dt** "be dried out"; > *ḫamru* II; *ḫumīru*; *ḫummuru*?; *ḫammurtu*?

ḫamaṣīru → *ḫumṣīru*

ḫamāṣu(m) "to tear off, away" Bab., O/MA **G** (*a/u*) "tear" clothing "off" s.o. (= 2 acc.); Mari "plunder" (after infin. abs. *ḫamuṣam*); OB stat. of glance, mng. uncl. **D** ~ G, clothing, metal sheeting; "strip" palm tree, "flay" hide; "plunder, ransack" land, temple, house, emblem **Š** NB "(allow to) despoil" person; > *ḫamṣum*; *ḫimṣu* I; *ḫammuṣu*, *ḫummuṣum*; *naḫmaṣu*; → *amāṣu*

ḫamāšiu "fifth" MA; < *ḫamiš*

ḫamāšu(m) I "to snap off" O/jB **G** (*i/i*) reed, tooth, finger **D** ~ G ?; > *ḫamšu* II, *ḫimšu*; *ḫimištu*; *ḫāmišum*; *ḫummušu* II

ḫamāšu II "to be fifth; do as fifth action" O/jB **G** (*u/u*); also "become one-fifth" in size **D** "quintuple"; < *ḫamiš* denom.

ḫamāšu → also *kamāsu* II

ḫamāti → *ḫammu* II

ḫamâtu pl. tant. "help, assistance" M/NB *ana ḫ.-alāku* "to go to aid" of s.o.; < W.Sem.

ḫamāṭum I "haste, urgency" OB esp. Mari *ṭēm ḫ.* "pressing matter"; < *ḫamāṭu* II infin.

ḫamāṭu(m) II "to hasten, be quick" Bab. **G** (*u/u*) [astr. TAB] "go/come in haste"; in hendiad. "(do s.th.) hastily"; "be hasty" while doing s.th.; "be (too) early", also astr. of heavenly bodies **Gtn** Mari "be constantly in haste" **Gt** MB stat. "is very hasty" **D** Am. "hurry" troops etc. "up" **Š** "send" s.th./s.o. "quickly"; "bring" offering etc. "in good time, early"; "hasten, bring forward time of" s.th. **Št** pass. of Š "be brought early, in good time"; > *ḫamṭu*, *ḫamṭiš*, *ḫamṭūtu*, *ḫamuttu*, *ḫamutta*; *ḫamāṭum* I; *ḫumṭum* I; *ḫitmuṭiš*; *ḫummuṭu* I, *ḫummuṭiš*

ḫamāṭu(m) III "to burn (up)" O/jB, MA **G** (*a/u*) [TAB] of fire, Gira, hot weather; transf. of anger "burn" heart; of fever "burn" parts of body; "etch" leather, "cauterize" like saltpetre **Gt** transf. of pain "burn right up" wicked **D** "burn up, make burn" enemy; of fever "burn up" sick person; of fire "burn up" frost; of gods "burn up" land; "fire" pottery; stat. "is roasted", of bird, fish **Dt** pass. "be burnt up" by demons **Š** ~ D "burn up" land, enemy **Štn** jB ptcp. *muštaḫmiṭu* "ever-ignited"? **N** of heart "be burned, seared"; > *ḫimṭu*, *ḫimittu* II; *ḫumṭu* II; *ḫummuṭu* II; *ḫandutu*?

ḫamā'u "to see" jB lex. **G**; < Aram.

ḫambanû "of Ḫamban" NB of leather items; < PlN Ḫamban

ḫambaqūqu → *ḫabbaqūqu*

ḫambaṣūṣu (a garden herb) NB

ḫambāšu → *ḫabbāšu*

ḫambēqū pl. (a child's game) MB

ḫambuqūqu → *ḫabbaqūqu*

ḫamdagar (a high official) OB(Susa)

ḫamdum "hoarded, hidden away" OA transf. of words, matters; < *ḫamādu*

ḫamdûm (a kind of headdress) Mari

ḫamiltu → *ḫamiš*; *ḫamištu*

ḫamiluḫḫu → *ḫawalḫu*

ḫamīmu (an aromatic plant) "*Amomum*" MA, jB med.

ḫāmimu(m) "(grain) gatherer" O/jB phps. "gleaner"; < *ḫamāmu*

ḫāmiru → *ḫāwiru*

ḫamissâti → *ḫamiš*

ḫamiš st. abs.; f. *ḫam/nša/et*, OA also *ḫaššat*; nom. f. *ḫamištu(m)*, *ḫami/ultu* "five"; OB *ḫamiš ubānātim* "five fingers", *ḫamissâti* "five *sūtu*", *ḫamšet qanî* "five reeds"; *ḫamištūmī* "five days"; NB *ḫamiš qātātu* "five-sixths"; > *ḫamāšu* II; *ḫamištu*, *ḫamuštu*; *ḫamšu* I, *ḫamšiš*, *ḫamšūtu*, *ḫamāšiu*, *ḫamšīšu*; *ḫumšu*; *ḫamiššeret*; *ḫummušu* I, *ḫumušû*, *ḫumušā*, *ḫumūšum*; *ḫamšā*

ḫamiš → also *aḫāmiš*

ḫamiššeret "fifteen" jB lex.; < *ḫamiš* + *-šeret*

ḫamištu(m), *ḫamiltu*, OA also *ḫamuštum* "group of five" OA, O/jB [NAM.5] OA (a body of five officials); OB *wakil ḫ.* "overseer of a group of five (merchants)"; MB *rab ḫ.*; < *ḫamiš*

ḫāmišum "(stalk-)snapper"? OB agricultura worker; < *ḫamāšu* I

ḫamittu → *ḫamutta*

ḫāmītu, NA *ḫabbītu* "hummer; sand-wasp" jB NA; < *ḫawû*

ḫammāmu → *ḫammā'u*

ḫammarākāra → *ammarkarra*

ḫammaru (a tree)? jB/NA lex. in *ḫ. ṭīdi*

ḫammatu → *ḫammu* I

ḫammā'u(m), *ḫammû(m)*, *ḫammāmu* "rebel; usurper" Bab. [IM.GI] **1.** *šar ḫ.* "usurper" **2.** of king, "rebel"

ḫammiš → *aḫāmiš*

ḫammu(m) I; f. *ḫammatu* "family head" Bab., NA epith. of deities, usu. in PNs; > *ḫammūtu*

ḫammu II, OB *ammum*, *amûm* O/jB, NA **1.** "pond, puddle"?, Nuzi, NA pl. *ḫamāti* **2.** jB med. (algae on water)? **3.** jB lex. (an aquatic animal, phps.) "jellyfish"

ḫammu → also *ammu* I

ḫammû (a garment) jB

ḫammû → also *ḫammā'u*

ḫammurtu (a kind of beer) NA; < *ḫummuru* ?

ḫammuru → *ḫummuru*

ḫammuṣu (desig. of low grade of copper) Nuzi; < *ḫamāṣu* D Ass. form

ḫammūtu, NA *ḫa''ūtu* "function of family head" j/NB, NA esp. *bīt ḫ.* "family head's room" [NB É.UR4.UR4]; < *ḫammu* I

ḫampatalli (an object) MB(Alal.); < Hurr.

ḫamqum "valley" Mari; < W.Sem.

ḫamru(m) I "holy place (of Adad, Assur)" occas. ^{d}*ḫ.*; M/NB *tāmirti ḫ.* (a type of irrigated field); *bīt ḫ.*; also in PNs

ḫamru II "dry, dried out"? O/jB; < *ḫamāru*

ḫamrušḫum (a metal vessel) Mari; < Hurr.

ḫamsu ~ "maltreated" MA; f. pl. "mistreatments"; → *ḫummusum*

ḫamṣum "bald(-headed)" OB lex.; also as PN; < *ḫamāṣu*

ḫamšā, *ḫanšā*, *ḫaššā* "fifty" st. abs.; before suff. *ḫamšātsunu/sina* etc.; NB *(bīt) 50-e* "plot of land held by (group of) fifty"; NA, NB *rab 50* "captain of fifty"; jB *50-a-a* "fifty each"; < *ḫamiš*

ḫamšat → *ḫamiš*

ḫamšātu → *ḫamšā*; *ḫamšu* I

ḫamšet → *ḫamiš*

ḫamšiš, *ḫaššiš* "fifthly" jB; < *ḫamšu* I

ḫamšīšu "five times" OA, O/MB; OA *adi ḫ.*; OB [A.RÁ *5-šu*]; < *ḫamiš*

ḫamšu(m) I, *ḫanšu*, *ḫaššu*, NB *ḫanzu*; f. *ḫamuš/ltu(m)* "fifth"; f. "one-fifth" [IGI.5.GÁL];

pl. "fifth part(s)" [ZAG.5]; NB *ḫanšu zittu* "fifth part"; NB *ḫamul* "1/5 mina"; m. "fifth" string of lyre; < *ḫamiš*

ḫamšu II, *ḫanšu* "snapped off" jB of stalks etc.; of deformed foot; < *ḫamāšu* I

ḫamšūtu, *ḫanšūtu* in *5-te-šú* "for the fifth time" NA; < *ḫamšu* I

ḫamṭiš, *ḫanṭiš*, *ḫamṭa* "quickly, immediately" Bab.; < *ḫamṭu*

ḫamṭu, *ḫanṭu* "quick, sudden" M/NB of messenger, death, weapon; "fast-acting" of drug; "quickly cooked"; jB gramm., of Sum. vb. forms (opp. → *marû* I); < *ḫamāṭu* II; > *ḫamṭiš*, *ḫamṭūtu*, *ḫamutta*, *ḫamuttu*

ḫamṭūtu, *ḫanṭūtu* in *ḫanṭūssu* "hastily, at once" jB; < *ḫamṭu*

ḫamṭūtu → also *ḫandūtu*

ḫamû I ~ "to paralyse" jB **G** (*i/i*) humans, flesh (*šīrū*); transf. of army **Gt** "thoroughly paralyse" **D** ~ G "render" s.o. "paralysed" **Š** of disease "make" flesh "paralysed" **N** "be paralysed" of flesh

ḫamû II "to trust" j/NB **G** (*i/i*, occas. *u/u*) esp. prec. and stat. "is secure" **D** "make confident, (re)assure"

ḫamû → also *ḫawû*

ḫāmu(m) "raft" O/jB lex. (var. of *amu*)

ḫāmū pl. tant. "chaff, rubbish" O/jB of corn; of wood; esp. *ḫ. u ḫuṣābu* "scourings and shavings", i.e. valueless property

ḫamuḫḫum mng. unkn. Mari, in desig. of chariot

ḫamuk (a garden herb) NB

ḫamul(tu) → *ḫamšu*

ḫamurītu "throat" jB lex.

ḫamussu → *ḫamuštu*

ḫamūṣu → *ḫamāṣu* G

ḫamuštu(m), NA *ḫamussu* subst. "a fifth" **1.** OB (desig. of a container) **2.** OA (a time period, phps.) "one-fifth" of a month, "week"; *ša PN*, as dating mechanism **3.** NA "(payment for) one-fifth period"; < *ḫamšu* I

ḫamuštum → also *ḫamištu*

ḫamutta(m), Am. also *ḫamittu*, *ḫamuttiš* "at once, soon" O/MB; < *ḫamṭu*

ḫamuttu(m) "haste" O/jB of chariot *ša ḫ.* "express"; Am., jB *ana/ina ḫ.* "hastily, quickly"; < *ḫamṭu*

ḫamûtu mng. unkn. jB lex.

ḫanābu(m) "to sprout, flourish" O/jB **G** (*u/u*) of trees, grain etc.; transf. of divine splendour **Gtn** iter. of G of plants, trees **D** "make flourish" **Dt** of hair "grow luxuriantly" **Š** "make grow luxuriantly"; > *ḫanbu*; *ḫānibu*; *ḫunābu*, *ḫunībum*; *ḫannabu*; *ḫunnubu*; *muḫtanbu*

ḫanāmum "to thrive, be luxuriant" OAkk, OB **G** (*i/i*) of sheep; transf. of laughter "flourish" **Dt** "be (made) luxuriant" of clouds, plenty; > *ḫannāmu*

ḫananābum (a sweet fruit)? OB

ḫanānu mng. unkn. **G** lex. only **D** stat. in desig. of part of body; > *ḫunnunu*?

ḫanānu → also *enēnu* I

ḫanāpu I "to act basely, impiously"? Am. **G** (pret. *u*) in *ḫanpa ḫ.*; < W.Sem.; > *ḫanpu*; *ḫannipu*

ḫanāpu II ~ "to flatter, fawn" NA **G** (*i/i*) of fDN

ḫanāqu(m) "to press, throttle" Bab., NA **G** (*a/u*) stat. of part of body "is constricted"; "wind" s.th. "round tightly"; "throttle, kill by throttling"; NB stat. "is angry" **Gtn** lex. only **Gt** "suffocate" **D** ~ G "throttle, suffocate"; stat. "is constricted" **Dt** pass. of D **Š** caus. of G **N** pass. of G; NB "be(come) angry" **Ntn** iter. of N; > *ḫanqu*; *ḫinqu*; *ḫiniqtu*; *ḫannāqu*, *ḫanniqu*; *maḫnaqu*

ḫanāsu "mourning"? jB comm.

ḫanāṣu "to lift lips, bare teeth" M/jB **G** (*i/i*) of ox **Gt** lex. only **D** ~ G "contort" part of face (nose, lip etc.); "scowl"; "grimace"; of animal "bare teeth" **Dt** ~ D of demon "bare teeth"; → *ganāṣu*

ḫanāšu → *kanāšu* I

ḫanâtu → *ḫanû* I

ḫanbara "granary" NB; < OPers.

ḫanbu(m) "luxuriant" Bab. in PNs; *mār* ᵈ*ḫ.* desig. of Pazuzu; < *ḫanābu*

ḫandabillu (a kind of shell) jB lex.

ḫandabtu (a plant) jB lex.

ḫandašpiru, *ḫandašpuru*, Emar *ḫannašpiru* (a thorny plant) Emar, jB lex.

ḫandû, *ḫanz/sû* "reed pith" jB [GI.ŠÀ.GI]

ḫandūḫu, *ḫin/dduḫḫu* f. (part of a lock)? M/NB in metal; transf., astr. *ḫ. šamê*

ḫandūru, *ḫindūru*, *ḫi(d)dāru* "spur"? Bab., of birds; transf. "projection" on wall

ḫanduttu "vulva" jB lex.

ḫandūtu "roasting"? OB(Alal.) in *še'i ša ḫ.* (= **ḫamṭūtu* < *ḫamāṭu* III ?)

ḫangāru ~ "dagger"? NA; < Aram.

ḫaniaḫḫu → *ḫanû* I

ḫānibu "luxuriant" jB lex. of fruit tree; < *ḫanābu*

ḫanigalbatû "(Hanigalbataean =) charioteer" jB lex.; < PlN

ḫanigalbatûtu "status of a Hanigalbataean" MB(Alal.)

ḫāniqu → *ḫanniqu* 1
ḫanizarrum (a functionary) OB(Shemshara); < Hurr.?
ḫannabu "with luxuriant (hair)" MB in PNs; < *ḫanābu*
ḫannaḫuru (a stone) jB lex.
ḫannak(a) → *annaka*
ḫannāmu(m) "very luxuriant" O/jB of women; clouds ?; < *ḫanāmu*
ḫannāqu **1.** jB lex. "strangler" **2.** jB lex. (a kind of clasp) of reed or wood **3.** NB adj. "very angry"; < *ḫanāqu*
ḫannasru mng. unkn. jB lex.
ḫannašpiru → *ḫandašpiru*
ḫannatu mng. unkn. jB
ḫannipu "baseness, impiety"? Am.; < *ḫanāpu* I
ḫanniqu **1.** jB "strangler" (or *ḫāniqu* ?); **2.** jB lex. (part of funnel on seed-plough); < *ḫanāqu*
ḫannîša → *annîša*
ḫanniu → *annû* I
ḫanpu "baseness" Am.; < *ḫanāpu* I
ḫanqu "strangled" M/NB **1.** Bogh. lex. "strangled" **2.** NB "tightly attached" of neck bands ?; < *ḫanāqu*
ḫanqullatu (a kind of oil) jB lex.
ḫansû → *ḫandû*
ḫansupu (an implement) MA
ḫanṣātu "hips" jB lex.; < Aram.
ḫanšā → *ḫamšā*
ḫanšale/et → *ḫamiš*
ḫanšu → *ḫamšu* I.II; *kanšu* I
ḫanšūtu → *ḫamšūtu*
ḫanṭiš → *ḫamṭiš*
ḫanṭu → *ḫamṭu*
ḫanṭūtu → *ḫamṭūtu*
ḫanû(m) I, Alal. *ḫaniaḫḫu* "from Hana" Bab. [ḪA.NA] of tribe; MB(Alal.) of social class; Nuzi (pl. *ḫanâti*); NB of type of soldier; lex. of sheep, wool
ḫanû(m) II "to pressurize, browbeat" O/jB **G** (*i/i*)
ḫanūnu (a box) Am.; < Eg.
ḫānūtu "a shop" NB in *bīt ḫ.*; < Aram.
ḫanzabu (potter's waste product) jB, NA
ḫanzartum → *ḫaṣartu*
ḫanzētu → *ḫanzizītu*
ḫanzibatu → *ḫazzabatu*
ḫanzizītu, *ḫanzētu* (a flying insect) jB
ḫanzu "goat" jB lex.; < W.Sem.; → *enzu*
ḫanzu → also *ḫamšu* I
ḫanzû → *ḫandû*
ḫapādu → *kapādu* Dtn

ḫapālu (or *ḫapallu*); pl. f. (a container) NA
ḫapālu → also *apālu* I G
ḫapāpu I ~ "to break up, smash" jB **G** (*a/u*) "pound" paste **D** ~ G stat. of door "is smashed"; transf. of witch "shatter" s.o.
ḫapāpu II "to wash, clean" NB; < Aram.
ḫapāru(m) I "to surround, encircle" OB, Bogh. **G** stat. of oil round water **D** of army "encircle" enemy etc.; > *ḫaprātu*; *naḫparum*?
ḫapārum II "to decamp, become vagrant" Mari **G** (pret. *iḫpur*) **D** "get" troops "underway"?; > *ḫāpiru*
ḫapāru → also *ḫepēru*
ḫapātum "to triumph, prevail" OB **G** (*i/i*, also *u/u*) esp. in PNs **Gtn** iter (*u/u*) OB; > *ḫuptu* I
ḫapā'u → *ḫepû* II
ḫapḫappu(m) (base of door post) O/jB lex.
ḫāpiru(m) "(class of) vagrant" OA, O/MB [LÚ.SA.GAZ; Am., Ug. also SAG.GAZ]; < *ḫapārum* II
ḫapparrû → *apparrû*
ḫappu ~ "stinking, foetid" jB, NA of plants; of man; < Sum.?
ḫappû → *ḫuppû* I
ḫaprātu "visible surface" of moon, sun j/NB astr. in *ḫ. Sîn/Šamaš*; NB often abbr. *ḫap*; < *ḫapāru* I, orig. pl. tant.
ḫaptara(ma)nnu (desig. of horses) Nuzi; < Indo-Iran.?
ḫapte (desig. of animal's foot) Nuzi "front" or "rear" side ?; < Hurr.?
ḫapûm "to wrap up"? **G** unattested **D** Mari, bows
ḫapû → also *ḫepû* II
ḫāpu, *ḫābu* (a dark earth) M/jB for dyeing; also OAkk ^{im}*ḫa-um* ?
ḫāpum → also *ḫābum*
ḫāpû → *ḫābû*
ḫâpu "to fear" O/jB **G** stat. (*ḫīp*) "is afraid" **D** "terrify"; also in DN *Ḫīp-raggu* "Terrify the wicked"; > *ḫūpu* II
ḫâpu → also *ḫiāpum*
ḫap'um → *ḫepû* I
ḫapūtum, *ḫabūtum* (an agricultural tool) OAkk, OB [URUDU.ḪA.BU.DA]
ḫaqāru "to investigate"? jB; < Aram.?
ḫâqu, *ḫuāqu* mng. unkn. jB lex. **G**, vb. of motion
ḫâqu → also *ḫiāqum*
ḫarābu "to be(come) deserted" M/NB **G** (*u/u*, NB *i/i*) [A.RI.A] of land, settlements, palace, temple **Š** "devastate, lay waste" land, mountain

Št pass. of Š; > *ḫarbu* I, *ḫarbiš*, *ḫarbānu*, *ḫarbānāti*, *ḫarbūtu*; *ḫarībum*, *ḫarībatu*; *ḫuribtu*; *ḫitrubu*; *šaḫrabbūtu*; *šuḫrubtu*

ḫarābu → also *ḫarāpu* I

ḫarādum I "desert place"? OA

ḫarādu(m) II "onager, wild ass" O/jB; < W.Sem.

ḫarādu(m) III ~ "to fit together, fabricate"? O/jB, NA **G** mat, battering ram **D** mng. uncl.; > *ḫurdu* I

ḫarādu IV "to be awake, on guard" NA **G** (*i*/*i*) also trans. "guard" s.o. **D** "place on guard, alert" **N** "be (put) on o.'s guard"; > *ḫardu* I, *ḫarduttu*; *ḫurādu* I?

ḫaragabaš (a container) Am. in stone, metal

ḫarāgu f. (container used in glass-making) NA

ḫarā'iš → *ḫerû* II

ḫarāku "to post" troops NB **G** stat. only **D** lex. only; < Aram.

ḫārali "door" jB lex.; < 'Subartu'

ḫarambi (a plant) jB lex.

ḫaramma, *ḫaramme*, occas. *ḫaremma* "later, thereafter" M/NA often *ḫ.-ma*; also *ina*/*iḫ-ḫ.*, *issu ḫ.*; < **aḫar* + *amma*; → *aḫāru*

ḫarāmum I "to cover, envelop" OA, OB **G** (*i*/*i*) with 2 acc.; parts of liver; tablet, with clay envelope; OA also "write on envelope" **D** OB "cover up, conceal"; OA ~ G "write on envelopes" **N** "be enveloped" OA; > *ḫarmum* I; *ḫermum*; *ḫarrumum*; *naḫramum*; jB etc. → *arāmu*

ḫarāmu II "to separate, cut off" jB lex. **G** and **D**; > *ḫarmu* II, *ḫarimtu*, *ḫarimtūtu*

ḫarānû → *ḫarû* I

ḫaraptum "autumn" Mari; < *ḫarāpu* I

ḫarāpu(m) I, NA *ḫarābu* "to be early" Bab., NA **G** (*u*/*u*) [NIM] of meteor. phenomena; of hair; of lactation? (*ša tulê*); esp. in hendiad. "(do s.th.) early" **D** ~ G NA "(do s.th.) early" **Š** "make" s.o./s.th. "do" s.th. "early", e.g. palm tree ripen; > *ḫarpu*, *ḫarpiš*, *ḫarpūtu*; *ḫarpū*; *ḫaraptum*; *ḫāripānu*; *ḫarīpum* II; *ḫurpū*; *ḫurāpu*; *ḫurrupu*; *mušaḫripu*

ḫarāpu II "to cut away" jB **G** (*i*/*i*) door, with weapon; > *ḫarīpu* I, *ḫariptu*, *ḫurpu*

ḫarāra, *ḫarrara*, *ḫarḫarra* "objection, protest" NB leg.; < Aram.

ḫararnu (surface measure) Nuzi = $^{1}/_{2}$ *awiḫaru*; < Hurr.

ḫarāru(m) "to dig, hollow out" O/jB **G** (*a*/*u*) "dig over" field; ext., stat. of part of body "is hollow" **D** of part of body, stat. "is hollowed out"; "make incisions in" s.th.; > *ḫarru* I; *ḫerru*; *ḫarriru*; *ḫurruru*; → *ḫurru*

ḫarāru → also *arāru* III; *na'arrurum*; *šuḫarruru* II

ḫarasapanu → *ḫarsapnu*

ḫarāsu "to itch, scratch" **G** infin. "an itch, scabies" **D** lex. only; > *ḫarsu*?

ḫarāṣu(m) "to break off, deduct; incise; make clear" **G** (*a*/*u*) **1.** math. "subtract" measured length; in commerce, accounting "deduct"; of furrow "reduce" yield **2.** "snap off" plant **3.** "cut in, excavate" ditch, furrow ?; stat., of part of liver "is incised" **4.** "define precisely, make/become clear"; "fix, define" value; of illness, stat. "is diagnosed"; j/NB, NA "give, issue clear" command, instructions etc., also in hendiad., e.g. with *šapāru* **D** OA, OB "reduce; (wrongly) diminish" amount, size of field etc. **Št** "calculate deduction", "deduct"; jB om. "balance" interpretations against one another **N** "be deducted" (Mari pret. once *iḫḫaliṣ*); > *ḫarṣu*; *ḫarištum* II; *ḫerṣu*, *ḫerṣētum*, *ḫiriṣtu*; *ḫarīṣu*; *ḫurruṣu*; *maḫraṣu*

ḫarāṣu → also *karāṣu*

ḫarāšu I "to be in labour" jB, NA **G** (*i*/*i*) mother *ḫaršassu* "is in confinement with him" **D** "bring to birth, deliver" child **N** ~ G "be in labour"; > *ḫarištu* I; *muḫarrišu*?

ḫarāšu II "to bind (on)" O/jB **G** transf. of part of body "cripple" **D** ~ G lex., ship, forearm?; "bring together, collect"? trees in park; > *ḫaršu* I; *ḫeršu*; *ḫurrušu*; *maḫrašu*; *muḫarrišu*?; *taḫrīšu*?

ḫarāšum III "to be silent" Mari **G** stat. *ḫariš*; < W.Sem.

ḫarašūtum? mng. unkn. OAkk

ḫarāṭum "to feed on"? OB, NA **G** (pret. OB *iḫruṭ*, NA *iḫriṭ*) grass etc., of sheep, locusts; > *ḫerṭu*

ḫarā'u (part of an ornament) Qatna

ḫarā'um → also *ḫerû* II

ḫarauzzuḫlu (an agricultural worker) Nuzi; < Hurr.

ḫaraziaš, *ḫaraziun*/*š* (a plant) jB lex.; < Hitt.

ḫarbakkannu, *ḫarba(q)qannu* (or *ḫurb*...) **1.** M/jB [ŠEN.ŠEN.(BAL.)BAR.ḪUŠ.MUŠEN] (a bird) also as ornament, of gold **2.** NA (desig. of a kind of horse)

ḫarbānāti pl. "ruins" of house NA; < *ḫarbu* I

ḫarbānu "desert dweller" NA in PN; < *ḫarbu* I + *-ān*

ḫarba(q)qannu → *ḫarbakkannu*

ḫarbiš "like a wasteland" jB; < *ḫarbu* I

ḫarbiwu → *ḫarwiu*

ḫarbu(m) I; f. *ḫarubtu(m)* "deserted" Bab., NA of land, city etc.; as subst. "desert, abandoned land" (pl. *ḫarbī*, *ḫarbānu*; f. *ḫarbāti*); < *ḫarābu*; > *ḫarbānu*, *ḫarbūtu*, *ḫarbiš*; *ḫarbānāti*; → *arbu* 1

ḫarbu(m) II "plough" O/jB [(GIŠ.)APIN.TÚG.KIN] for breaking soil; also as name of bird

ḫarbu III (or *ḫarpu*) (a tree) Nuzi; < Hurr.

ḫarbūtu(m) "desolation" O/jB esp. *ḫ. alāku(m)* "to become a wasteland"; < *ḫarbu* I

ḫardu I "watchful, alert" NA; < *ḫarādu* IV

ḫardum II mng. unkn. OB lex. as desig. of day

ḫardū(t)tu "vigilance, surveillance" NA; < *ḫardu* I

ḫaremma → *ḫaramma*

ḫargallu(m), M/NB *ḫargullu* "locking ring" Bab. for door; of copper, silver; *ḫ. nadû* "to apply lock"; < Sum.

ḫargānum → *argānum*

ḫargullu → *ḫargallu*

ḫarḫadû (or *ḫurḫadû*) (a lyre) jB lex.

ḫarḫarra → *ḫarāra*

ḫarḫa(r)ru(m), *ḫaḫḫarum* "chain" Bab., NA for ox, bucket; NB ornamental, of gold; jB also (a musical instrument); < Sum.

ḫarḫaru(m) "villain, rogue" O/jB

ḫarḫasannum, *ḫarḫazinnu* "(outer) ear" O/jB; also "pelvis, pelvic girdle"?

ḫarḫašakku (a stone bead) jB lex.; < Sum.

ḫarḫazinnu → *ḫarḫasannum*

ḫarḫubbānu, *ḫarḫubbāšir* → *ḫarmunu*

ḫaribānum mng. unkn. OB in *kīma ḫ.* in descr. of liver

ḫarībatu(m), *ḫaribtu* "desolate region" O/jB, MA; lex. *ḫaribtum*, desig. of sheep, mng. uncl.; < *ḫarābu*

ḫarībum "ruination"? OA in *bīt ḫ.*; demon *ša ḫ.*; < *ḫarābu*

ḫarimtu(m), *ḫarintu*, *ḫarmatu* "(temple) prostitute" [(MUNUS.)KAR.KID]; *ḫarimāku* (pred.) "I (f.) am a t. p."; *mār ḫ.* "son of a t. p."; < *ḫarāmu* II; > *ḫarimtūtu*

ḫarim(t)ūtu(m), NB *ḫari'ūtu* "status of temple prostitute"; *ana ḫ. alāku(m)* "to become a t. p."; OB also as prebend

ḫarinnu, *ḫirinnu* "(water-)bag, skin" M/NB; Alal., pl. f. of gold

ḫarintu → *ḫarimtu*; *ḫarinnu*

ḫāripānu ~ "early riser"? NA; < *ḫarāpu* I

ḫariptu "shed blood" MA, M/jB; < *ḫarāpu* II

ḫarīpu I "congealed blood patches" NA, pl. *ḫarīpāni*; < *ḫarāpu* II

ḫarīpum II "lamb" Mari; < *ḫarāpu* I

ḫarīru(m), Mari also *ḫarūrum*, *ḫurūrum*; NA pl. f. ~ "bedspread" Mari, NA (= *arrūrum* ?)

ḫariṣ, *ḫariṣtu* → *ḫarṣu*

ḫarīṣu, Ass. *ḫirīṣu* "(city) ditch, moat" M/NA, M/NB esp. *ḫ. ḫerû*, *ḫ. ḫarāṣu* "to dig ditch"; lex. *šam ḫ.* "ditch plant"; NB [íd]*ḫ.* "moat"; < *ḫarāṣu*

ḫarištu(m) I "woman in confinement" OAkk, jB *dām ḫ.* "blood of *ḫ.*"; < *ḫarāšu* I

ḫarištum II "shortfall (in harvest)"? OB; < *ḫarāṣu*

ḫariu → *ḫarû* I

ḫari'ūtu → *ḫarimtūtu*

ḫarmāku (a profession)? NA

ḫarmatu → *ḫarimtu*

ḫarmil ~ "gristle" NB in division of meat offerings; < Aram.

ḫarmištu; pl. *ḫarmišātu* (a bronze object) Ug.

ḫarmum I "enclosed in envelope" OA of tablet; < *ḫarāmum* I

ḫarmu II "(male) lover, consort" jB of Dumuzi; Apsû; < *ḫarāmu* II

ḫarmu → also *ḫurmu*

ḫarmunu, *ḫarḫubbānu* (or *ḫarḫubbāšir*) (a plant) jB [ḪAR.ḪUM.BA.ŠIR ?]; also (a mineral) [NA4.ḪAR.ḪUM/ḪU.BA.ŠIR]

ḫarpiš "early, in good time" O/jB; < *ḫarpu*

ḫarpu(m); f. *ḫaruptu(m)* "early" Bab., MA [NIM] of rains, harvest etc.; "early" in morning; of sheep, bird; journey; < *ḫarāpu* I

ḫarpu → also *ḫarbu* III

ḫarpū pl. tant. "(early) autumn" Ass.; < *ḫarāpu* I

ḫarpūtu "earliness" NA in *i(ḫ)-ḫarpūte* "early"; < *ḫarpu*

ḫarrānu(m) f., later also m. "way, road; journey, caravan" [KASKAL; OAkk KASKAL.KI; NA, NB also KASKAL.2] **1.** "road", built, open(ed), blocked, kept in order; astr. "path" of heavenly body **2.** transf. ref. to behaviour, *ḫ. išartu(m)* "right way"; also deified **3.** "(business) journey"; "caravan", OA *ša ḫarrānātim* "caravan leader", MB *ḫ. ša ḫurāṣi* "gold(-trading) venture"; OA, OB "journey(-money)"; NB "trading capital" **4.** "(military) campaign", "(army on) campaign, expedition"; OB *ḫ. alākum* "to perform military service"; Hitt., NB(Achaem.) "time, go", e.g. *ina šanīti ḫ.* "for second time"; Ug. *ina ḫ. šakānu* "to subject to legal proceedings" (Hitt. usage)

ḫarrara → *ḫarāra*

ḫarratu → *murratum*

ḫarriru ~ "vole" O/jB, NA [PÈŠ.A.ŠÀ.GA] as food; *lišān ḫ.* "tongue of vole" as drug; also as PN; ᵈ*Ḫ.* (a star); < *ḫarāru*

ḫarru(m) I; NB pl. f. "water channel" Bab., NA [SÙR] as city moat; as canal; < *ḫarāru*

ḫarru(m) II (desig. of kind of lyre) jB lex.

ḫarruḫāya "vulture" jB lex.

ḫarrumum "enclosed in envelope" OA = *ḫarmum* I of tablets in pl.; < *ḫarāmum* I D

ḫarrupu → *ḫurrupu*

ḫarsapnu, *ḫarasapanu*, Bogh. *ḫursennu*? "larva, maggot" jB

ḫarsu mng. unkn. jB lex.; < *ḫarāsu* ?

ḫarṣu(m), once *ḫalṣum*; OB f. → *ḫarištum* II **1.** mng. uncl. Ug. of field; jB, NA of beer, alum **2.** Mari "deducted" **3.** NA, NB "precisely defined", *šīm ḫariṣ* (st. abs.) "at fixed price", NA *ḫariṣtu* "precise (report)", as adv. "precisely", *ṭēmu ḫarṣu* "precise instruction"; NB *ḫariṣ* (st. abs.) "precisely"; < *ḫarāṣu*

ḫarṣu → also *ḫalṣu* I

ḫaršanānum (a valuable stone) OB

ḫaršāyu "Ḫaršu(-horse)" NA

ḫaršītum "Ḫarši(-sheep)" OAkk

ḫaršu(m) I; f. *ḫarištu(m)* "bound (on, together)" O/jB of ship, basket; grain; man; part of body; < *ḫarāšu* II

ḫaršu II (a foodstuff) M/NA

ḫaršû "(field) roller"? M/NB

ḫaršultannu (an agricultural worker) Nuzi

ḫartītum, *artītu* (a red flower) OB, jB lex.

ḫartu (or *ḫurtu*) mng. unkn. jB lex.

ḫarṭibi "(Egyptian) diviner" NA; < Eg.

ḫarum → *aru* I

ḫarû I, Ass. *ḫariu(m)* f. (a large container) Ass., M/NB of pottery, copper; for grain, liquids; NA, NB (desig. of an offering ceremony) (NB pl. *ḫarānê*); jB lex. (container on cart)? (→ *namḫarû*), (an ornament); < Sum.?

ḫarû II (a sanctuary) also *bīt ḫarê* j/NB, NA; officials of *b. ḫ.*; *Nabû ša ḫ.*; jB *ḫ. ša Ninlil*

ḫarû III "palm shoot" O/jB

ḫarû IV ~ "to overcome"? Ug.?, jB **G** (*i/i*) mng. uncl., phps. of hand "interfere"

ḫārû → *ḫērû*

ḫârum, *a(y)yarum* "donkey stallion" Mari in *ḫ. qatālum* for treaty solemnization; < W.Sem.

ḫâru → also *ḫiāru*

ḫarūbu(m), *ḫarūpu(m)* "carob (tree)" OAkk, Bab. as (emergency) foodstuff

ḫarūrakku mng. unkn. MA

ḫarurtu "throat" NA

ḫarūru (part of grindstone) jB

ḫarūrum → also *ḫarīru*

ḫarušḫu, *ḫaurušiḫu* (an animal) MB(Alal.), Am., NA; caught in trap; as ornament; < Hurr.

ḫaruttu "date palm frond" NB; < Aram.

ḫarwaraḫḫu; pl. f. "hay-fork"; < Hurr.

ḫarwar(aḫḫ)uzzu; pl. m. & f. "small hay-fork" Nuzi; < Hurr.

ḫarwiu, *ḫa/urbiwu* (a piece of clothing) Nuzi; < Hurr.

ḫarziqqu (a ring with inset stone) jB lex.; < Sum.

ḫarzuḫarza → *murzumurza*

ḫasappum (or *ḫazappum*) (a bronze object) OAkk, OB(Susa)

ḫasāpu(m) "to tear away, off" Ass., M/NB **G** (*i/i*) thorns; hair, garment-hem; courses of bricks **D** ~ G; MA *ša ḫassupi* "tweezers (for depilation)"

ḫasarratu, *ḫasirratu* (a kind of grass) jB lex.

ḫasāru(m), *ḫesēru* "to flake away, chip off" O/jB **G** (*i/i*) usu. stat., "is chipped" of horn, tooth, corner of tablet **D** ~ G grindstone; stat., ext. of features on liver, e.g. *kaskasu* **N** pass. of G, of throne, part of liver; > *ḫasrum*; *ḫesīru*?; *ḫisrum*; *ḫusirtum*; *ḫussuru*

ḫasāsiš "for understanding" jB; < *ḫasāsu*

ḫasāsu(m) "to be conscious; remember" **G** (*a/u*) **1.** "be aware of" (= *ana*/acc.) s.th., "think about" s.th., "think of" s.o. **2.** "remember"; in speech, prayer "mention" (s.o.'s) name etc. **3.** "understand", "conceive, think of" s.th. **4.** "plan, intend" **Gtn** iter. of G, esp. "repeatedly remember", "repeatedly plan, plot" **Gt** "think deeply about" **D** **1.** "remind" (+ 2nd acc.) **2.** "ponder, reflect" **Š** caus. **1.** "make" s.o. "remember" **2.** "remind" s.o. **3.** NB "notify, make" s.o. "aware of" s.th. **Št** Mari "be made to reflect" **N** **1.** "be taken into account, remembered" **2.** "be perceived, noticed" **3.** "be understood"; > *ḫasāsiš*; *ḫassu*, *ḫassūtu*; *ḫissatu*; *ḫasīsu*; *ḫasīsītu*; *taḫsistu*; *šaḫsasuttu*

ḫasā'u → *ḫesû*

ḫasḫaltu, *ḫašḫaltu*, Bogh. *ḫaskaltu*?; pl. *ḫasḫallātu* "leaf, foliage"? M/NB, NA of fig tree; timber trees; reed; in manufactured ornaments

ḫasḫastu (a tree)? jB

ḫasikku → *ḫašikku*

ḫasirratu → *ḫasarratu*

ḫasīsītu (ear-shaped loaf) Bogh., jB; < *ḫasīsu*

ḫasīsu(m) "ear; wisdom" Bab. **1.** "ear" of human, often du.; transf. of part of liver, of lyre

2. "hearing" **3.** "comprehension, wisdom", e.g. *atra(m) ḫasīs* "very wise", also as PN; *pīt ḫ.* "endowed with wisdom"; as DN ᵈ*Ḫ.* (or ᵈ*Ḫāsisu*); < *ḫasāsu*

ḫāsisu → *ḫasīsu* 3; *ḫassu*

ḫaskaltu → *ḫasḫaltu*

ḫaslu (a waterskin) jB lex.

ḫasrum, *ḫesru*; f. *ḫasirtu* "chipped, broken off" O/jB of tooth; < *ḫasāru*

ḫassāyû mng. unkn. OB (desig. of man); < *ḫesû* ?

ḫassiḫlu → *ḫalzuḫlu*

ḫassu(m), *ḫāsisu* "clever, wise" Bab.; *lā ḫ.* "fool"; < *ḫasāsu*

ḫassū pl. tant. "lettuce" Bab. [Ú.ḪI.IS.SAR] cultivated; *zēr ḫ.* "l. seed"

ḫassû(m) "oppressor" OB lex.; < *ḫesû*

ḫassupu → *ḫasāpu* D

ḫassūtu "wisdom" jB in *ḫ. alāku* "to become wise"; < *ḫassu*

ḫasû → *ḫesû*

ḫâsu ~ "to install" j/NB **G** (pret. *iḫīs*) **Dtt** lex. only

ḫaṣabattu → *ḫaṣbattu*

ḫaṣabtu "sherd (of pottery)" jB [ŠIKA]; < *ḫaṣbu* III nom. unit.

ḫaṣābu(m) I "to break off" Bab. **G** (*a/u*) reed, twig (from = acc.); transf. seed, issue **D** ~ G **N** "be broken off"; math.; > *ḫaṣbu* I; *ḫiṣbu* II; *ḫiṣibtu*; *ḫāṣibu*; *taḫṣību*; *naḫṣabum*?; → *kaṣābu*

ḫaṣābu II "to be green" jB **Š** "make" orchard "verdant"; > *ḫaṣbu* II; *ḫiṣbu* I; *ḫuṣābu*

ḫaṣānu(m) "to hug, take under o.'s protection" j/NB, NA **G** (*i/i*) of goddess "protect" man; of humans "look after, maintain" animals, people **D** ~ G NA; > *ḫiṣnu*

ḫaṣartu(m), *ḫaṣertu(m)*, OB *ḫanzartum*, NB *ḫaṣaštu*, Bogh. *ḫašartu*? 'greenness' Bab. **1.** lex. "(nasal) mucus" **2.** "(yellow-)green wool"

ḫaṣāru(m), *ḫaṣīrum*, *ḫiṣārum*; pl. m. & f. "sheepfold" Bab. esp. Mari; DN ᵈ*Bēlet-ḫ.*; NB (a place where dates were delivered); → *uṣārum*

ḫaṣāṣu(m) I "to snap off" O/jB **G** (*a/u*) neck, reed; transf. of death *ḫāṣiṣ amēlūti* "snapping off mankind"; stat., of part of body "is broken away" **D** ~ G + pl. obj.: reeds, mountains, people **Dt** pass. of D, of reed-stems "be snapped off"; > *ḫiṣṣu* I; *ḫuṣṣuṣu*

ḫaṣāṣu II "to erect (reed hut)" NA, NB **G** (*a/u*) with *ḫuṣṣu*; < *ḫuṣṣu* denom.

ḫaṣaštu → *ḫaṣartu*

ḫaṣbattiš "like a pottery bowl" jB; < *ḫaṣbattu*

ḫaṣbattu, NB also *ḫaṣabattu* (a pottery bowl) j/NB as vessel; NB sg. for pl.; also "(crab's) shell"; < *ḫaṣbu* III

ḫaṣbu(m) I "broken off" O/jB of branch, twig etc.; < *ḫaṣābu* I

ḫaṣbu II "dark green" jB of forest shade; < *ḫaṣābu* II

ḫaṣbu(m) III "pottery, terracotta; potsherd" Bab. [(DUG.)ŠIKA] as material of figurine, vessel; NA, NB (small pot), also of metal; "potsherd"; "sherd" of oven, of skull; "shell" of egg, turtle, pomegranate; > *ḫaṣabtu*, *ḫaṣbattu*, *ḫaṣbattiš*

ḫaṣertu → *ḫaṣartu*

ḫaṣibaru(m), *ḫaṣiburu* (a crested bird) jB

ḫāṣibu(m) "(reed) cutter" Bab. (desig. of workman) OB *ḫ. kiššī*, also as PN; NB *ḫ. qanê*; < *ḫaṣābu* I

ḫaṣiburu → *ḫaṣibaru*

ḫaṣīrum → *ḫaṣāru*

ḫaṣṣaṣu → *ḫuṣṣuṣu*

ḫaṣṣinnu(m); Mari, NB pl. f. "axe" [OB URUDU.ḪA.ZI.IN] of copper, silver, gold etc.

ḫaṣṣu (a plant) jB

ḫaṣṣuṣu → *ḫuṣṣuṣu*

ḫa(ṣ)ṣuttu (a garden herb) j/NB

ḫaṣûm → *ḫazûm*

ḫašābu "to count, reckon" **G** NA (pret. *iḫšub*) **D** lex. only **N** ~ G ? NB

ḫašādu, NB also *ḫašdu* "wedding" j/NB, NA of deities, humans; NB also in PN *Ḫaš(a)daya*

ḫašaḫtu(m) "need, requirement" OA; NA in plant name *ḫ. eqli*; < *ḫašāḫu*

ḫašāḫu(m), OA occas. *kašāḫum* "to need, desire" **G** (Bab *i/i*, Ass. *a/a*, *a/u*) "need, require", "want" s.th.; "desire, wish for" esp. stat. in Am., Bogh., Ug., Nuzi; also of heart "yearn for" s.th. **Gt** jB, ellipt. "be in constant need" **D** "make needful of"; stat. "is in great need" **N** pass. of G jB **1.** "be required" of foodstuffs etc. **2.** "fail, be found wanting"; > *ḫašḫu*; *ḫišiḫtu*, *ḫašaḫtu*; *ḫušaḫḫu*

ḫašaḫušennu (an accounting payment) Nuzi, in silver; < Hurr.

ḫašālu(m) "to crush" **G** (*a/u*) [KUM; GAZ] grain; medicaments; earth, animal droppings; "break up" tools; parts of body; transf. of army "destroy" PlN; stat. of person "is crushed" **D** ~ G "crush, pound up" **Dt** pass. of D med. of baby, mng. uncl. **Š** caus. of G "make" s.o. "crush"; > *ḫašlu*; *ḫašīlātu*; *ḫišiltu*; *ḫuššulu*; *maḫšalum*

ḫašânu → *ḫašiānum*

ḫašartennu mng. unkn. Nuzi (desig. of slave woman); < Hurr.

ḫašartu → *ḫaṣartu*

ḫašaru (a prof. desig.) Elam

ḫašāru mng. unkn. **G** unattested **D** jB lex. only; > *ḫišrum*?

ḫašāšu(m) I "to swell; be happy" O/jB **G** (*u/u*) of lungs **Gtn** iter. of G "rejoice repeatedly" **D** "make" s.o. "happy" **Dt** "be made to rejoice"; > *ḫiššatu*; *ḫušāšum*; *ḫaššāšu*

ḫašāšu(m) II **1.** **G** (*a/u*) OB in hendiad. "to gather" people, logs, fields (or rather "hasten"?) **2.** jB **Gt** "apply" oil **D** "plaster" wall with (= acc.) clay; > *ḫuššu*?; *ḫāšišum*?

ḫašāšu → also *ašāšu* IV

ḫašdu → *ḫašādu*

ḫašduk "beloved"? Elam; < Elam.

ḫašeḫtu → *ḫišiḫtu*

ḫašenni (a valuable stone) Nuzi; < Hurr.

ḫašeruḫuli (a craftsman) MB(Alal.); < Hurr.

ḫašḫalla mng. unkn. Nuzi, grain *ana ḫ.*; < Hurr.

ḫašḫaltu → *ḫasḫaltu*

ḫašḫaštum mng. unkn. OB lex.

ḫašḫāšu(m) ~ "lame, hobbling" O/jB; OB as PN

ḫašḫu(m) **1.** OB "one who needs, needy" **2.** Nuzi *ina ḫ.* "at (his) wish, discretion", also *ḫašḫuššu*; < *ḫašāḫu*

ḫašḫūrakku "'apple' bush" Bogh., jB lex., med.; < *ḫašḫūru*

ḫašḫūru(m), Ass. *šaḫšūru* "apple (tree)" Bab., M/NA [GIŠ.ḪAŠḪUR] as tree; as wood, for furniture; as fruit; also as ornament; *šīpāt ḫ.* "apple-coloured wool"; *ḫ. api* [GIŠ.ḪAŠḪUR. GIŠ.GI] "'marsh'-apple", a drug; fruit, ornament; > *ḫašḫurû*, *ḫašḫūrakku*; → *ḫatḫurētu* ?; *ḫinzūru*

ḫašḫūrû "apple-coloured" MB lex., of stone; NB, of wool; NB also "apple-shaped?", desig. of cut of meat; < *ḫašḫūru*

ḫāši (a plant) jB med.

ḫašiānum, *ḫašuānum*, *ḫašânu* (a plant, phps.) "thyme" OAkk, Bab. esp. M/jB med.; < *ḫašû* III

ḫašibbur → *ḫašimbar*

ḫašiḫapû mng. unkn. Nuzi, garments *ana ḫ.*; < Hurr.

ḫašikkiš (or *ḫasikkiš*) "like a deaf man" jB

ḫašikku (or *ḫasikku*) "deaf" jB

ḫašīlātu pl. tant. (a preparation of dates) NB; < *ḫašālu*

ḫašimbar, *ḫašim/n/bbur* etc. (a plant) jB lex.; < Kass.

ḫašīmu "grain heap"? MA esp. in *bīt ḫ.* (pl. *bīt ḫašīmāte*) "granary"

ḫašimur(u), *ḫašmur*, *ḫaši'ur(u)* "caraway" or "cumin" j/NB; *erû ḫ.* "grindstone for c."

ḫašinbar → *ḫašimbar*

ḫāšišum mng. uncl. OB, as PN; < *ḫašāšu* II ?

ḫašītum (a bronze object) Mari

ḫaši'ur(u) → *ḫašimuru*

ḫašlu(m) "crushed" [KUM] Mari esp. of bread (*aklum*); reeds; M/NA, Nuzi, jB(Ass.) (še)*ḫašlātu(m)* "bruised (grain)"; Susa of law suit (*dīnum*) mng. uncl.; < *ḫašālu*

ḫašmānu(m), Ug. also *ḫusmānu* (a colour) O/jB, MA **1.** (a coloured stone) **2.** (coloured wool)

ḫašmānuḫḫe(na) Nuzi pl. form of *ḫašmānu*

ḫašmar (a falcon) jB lex.; < Kass.

ḫašmītu (a metal) NB, material of agricultural tool

ḫašmur → *ḫašimuru*

ḫašrû mng. unkn. jB lex.

ḫašruqu (an aromatic tree) jB lex.

ḫašša (an official) OB(Susa); < Elam.

ḫaššā → *ḫamšā*

ḫaššāšu "bridegroom" jB lex.; < *ḫašāšu* I

ḫaššat → *ḫamiš*

ḫaššā'um (a cripple) OB lex.

ḫaššiš → *ḫamšiš*

ḫaššu (a sweet meat) jB lex.

ḫaššu → also *ḫamšu* I; *kanšu* I

ḫaššûm "of Haššum" OB; < PlN

ḫaštaru, *ḫaštiwušru* (part of feminine apparel) Nuzi; < Hurr.

ḫaštu I, *ḫaltu* "hole, pit" M/NB "pit (in ground), trap"; "hole" in ship, barrel

ḫaštum II, *ḫaltu* (a kind of stone) O/jB, NA mag.

ḫašû I "dark" jB lex., astr. [UD.ŠÚ.UŠ.RU]; < *ḫašû* V

ḫašû(m) II "lung(s)" Bab. [MUR; du. MUR.2(.MEŠ)] of human, animal; also "lung (-shaped ornament)" in metal; > *ḫašûtum* I

ḫašû(m) III, *ašû* "thyme"? [(GIŠ/Ú.)ḪAR.ḪAR (.SAR)] as food; med. in recipes; *akal ḫ.* "thyme bread"; > *ḫašiānum*; *ḫašûtu* II?

ḫašû(m) IV "to crush, chop" O/jB **G** (*u/u*) foodstuffs; OB woman, as penalty (or "bind"?) **D** ~ G onion etc.; > *ḫušû*; *muḫeššû*

ḫašû V "to become dark" M/jB **G** (*i/i*, *u/u*) of hair, eyes; of person "suffer darkness", i.e. be blinded ?; > *ḫašû* I

ḫašûm VI "to pass over in silence" Mari **G** (*i/i*); < W.Sem.

ḫâšu(m) I "to be anxious" O/jB, NA **G** (*ā*); also of ox "ail" **Gtn** iter. of G **D** "worry, make anxious"
ḫâšu II "to give" jB lex. **G** (*ū* ?)
ḫâšu → also *ḫiāšum*
ḫašuānum → *ḫašiānum*
ḫašūrum, *ḫašurru* (a kind of cypress) Bab. [GIŠ.ḪA.ŠUR] as tree, *qišti ḫ.* "forest of cypress trees"; as oil, perfume, also *šaman ḫ.*; as name of mountain
ḫašūtum I "a lung" OB as cut of meat; < *ḫašû* II nom. unit.
ḫašūtu(m) II (a plant) O/jB; < *ḫašû* III ?
ḫatākum "to decide" OB **G** (*a/u*) absol.
ḫatanu(m), *ḫatnu* "in-law, relative by marriage" **1.** "father-in-law" **2.** "son-in-law" **3.** NA/jB pl. f. "in-laws"; > *ḫatnūtu*
ḫatānu "to protect, shelter" j/NB, NA **G** (*i/i*) of god, king; also in PNs; > *ḫutnu*
ḫatanūtum → *ḫatnūtu*
ḫatāpu(m) "to slaughter" Bab., M/NA **G** (*i/i*) animal **D** "make, bring a *ḫitpu*-offering"; also transf. "sacrifice" enemy **Dt** pass. of D **Š** lex. only; > *ḫitpu*; *taḫtiptu*
ḫatarilum (a bird) OB
ḫatarru (an oil container) MB(Alal.); → *ḫatrum*
ḫatartu (desig. of wool) Nuzi
ḫatāru "to flutter, twitch" jB **G** (*i/i*) of bird, "wag" tail; > *ḫattārû*
ḫatēḫi mng. unkn. Nuzi; < Hurr.?
ḫatḫumma, *ḫattumma* in *ḫ. epēšu* "to kill"? Nuzi; < Hurr.
ḫatḫurētu (a dye) NB of wool; → *ḫašḫūru* ?
ḫatib → *ḫaltib*
ḫatītu, *ḫatītān* "lousy, louse ridden" jB lex.; → *ḫuttutu*
ḫati'u (a fruit) jB lex.
ḫatlunum (an object) OA, attached to garment ?
ḫatnu → *ḫatanu*
ḫatnūtu, OB *ḫatanūtum* in *ḫ. epēšum* "to establish marriage relationship" Mari, MB(Ta'annek); < *ḫatanu*
ḫatrum (or *ḫaṭrum*) (an oil container) Mari; → *ḫatarru*
ḫattārû(m) "with twitching gait"? jB lex.; OAkk as PN ?; < *ḫatāru*
ḫattaššu (a prof. desig.) NB
ḫattu → *ḫātu*; *ḫittu* III
ḫattû "Hittite" jB, NA
ḫattumma → *ḫatḫumma*
ḫatû I "decorated" jB of garment; < *ḫatû* III
ḫatû(m) II "to strike down" Bab., NA **G** (*i/i*) enemy; of illness, "strike" person **Gtn** (or **Dtn**) iter. jB of ghost **D** ~ G of word; of illness; MB *būra ḫ.* "dig a well" **N** pass. of G; > *taḫtû*
ḫatû(m) III mng. uncl. Bab. **G** OB "to load" ship ?; NB "apply" rosettes ? **Št** Mari "decant" wine ?; > *ḫatû* I; *maḫtûtum*?
ḫātu(m), *ḫattu(m)* "terror, panic" Bab., esp. falling on (*maqātu(m)*) person, army etc.; > *ḫayyattu*
ḫâtum ~ "to seize prey"? Mari **G**
ḫaṭāmu "to stop up, block" jB **G** (*i/i*) springs; "muzzle" mouth **D** ~ G (pl. obj.) "block" canals
ḫaṭāpu(m) mng. uncl. O/jB **G** lex. (process applied to grain) **D** "to wipe away"? tears; > *muḫaṭṭipum*
ḫaṭaru → *ḫaṭīru*; *ḫaṭru*
ḫaṭāṭu(m) I "to dig out, excavate" Bab., NA **G** (pret. *iḫṭuṭ*) canal, building trench; ext. part of liver **Š** Mari "have" canal "excavated"; > *ḫiṭṭatu*
ḫaṭāṭu(m) II ~ "to ferment" O/jB **G** (*a/u*) mash; fruit; > *ḫaṭṭu* I
ḫaṭīru, *ḫaṭaru*, *ḫaṭru*; pl. *ḫaṭīrānu* "animal pen" NB for sheep; < Aram.; → *ḫaṭru*
ḫaṭītu → *ḫaṭû* I
ḫaṭru, *ḫaṭaru* "military, professional group" NB esp. at Nippur; < OPers. or Aram. (= *ḫaṭīru* ?)
ḫaṭru → also *ḫatrum*; *ḫaṭīru*
ḫaṭṭā'u, *ḫaṭṭi'u*, *ḫaṭṭû* "sinner, criminal" M/NB; < *ḫaṭû* II
ḫaṭṭu I ~ "fermented" jB lex., of mash; < *ḫaṭāṭu* II
ḫaṭṭu(m) II mostly f.; OB pl. *ḫaṭṭātum* "stick, sceptre" [OAkk GIDRU; GIŠ.GIDRU; GIŠ.NÍG. GIDRU] "stick" of wood, for beating; OB in *ša/rabi*? *ḫaṭṭātim* [GIDRU.GIDRU] (a military officer); "(shepherd's) stick, staff", usu. transf. *ḫ. šarrūti* "royal sceptre"; *ḫ. išartu* "just sceptre"; OA, OB *rabi ḫ.* (a court official); *ḫ.* of deity as illness, punishment; also *ḫ. rē'i* "shepherd's staff" (a plant)
ḫaṭṭû → *ḫaṭṭā'u*; *ḫaṭû* I; *paṭû*
ḫaṭû(m) I, *ḫaṭṭû*, OA *ḫaṭ'um* "defective; criminal" Bab., OA; OA of silver "faulty" (or "insufficient"?); of omen etc. "bad, malign"; as subst. "criminal"; f. subst. *ḫaṭītu(m)* "fault, crime"; < *ḫaṭû* II
ḫaṭû(m) II "to do wrong, commit crime" **G** (*i/i*) [LAL] **1.** absol. "do wrong" (towards s.o. = *ana*/dat., NA *ana libbi*, Bogh., NB *itti*); "commit" crime etc. (e.g. *ḫīṭa*) **2.** stat. "is faulty, unsatisfactory, bad", e.g. of dream **3.** "be neglectful" absol.; "neglect" work, field etc.; "omit" line of text **Gtn** iter. of G **D** ~ G; also

NB "spoil, destroy" **Dt** NB, of words "be misspoken" [LAL.MEŠ] **Š** **1.** "cause s.o. to neglect" **2.** "lead into wrongdoing" **N** "be neglected"; > *ḫaṭû* I; *ḫīṭu* I, *ḫiṭīṭu*; *ḫaṭṭā'u*

ḫâṭu "(instalment of) payment" NB; < *ḫiāṭu*

ḫâṭu → also *ḫiāṭu*

ḫaṭ'um → *ḫaṭû* I

ḫa'u(m), *ḫabum* (a throne cover) OAkk, MA, jB; Mari ?

ḫa'um → also *ḫāpu*

ḫaurušiḫu → *ḫarušḫu*

ḫa'uštarum → *ḫawuštarum*

ḫa''ūtu → *ḫammūtu*

ḫawalḫu, *ḫalaḫwu*, *ḫamiluḫḫu* (an enclosed plot of ground) MA, Nuzi; < Hurr.

ḫawir "later" OB(Elam); < Elam.

ḫāwiru(m), *ḫā'iru*, *ḫāmiru*, *ḫayyiru*, NA *ḫābiru* "husband" Bab., NA; of men, also in PNs; of gods; NA ^{d}*Ḫ*. deified; < *ḫiāru* G ptcp.; > *ḫā'irūtu*

ḫawû, *ḫamû* ~ "to howl, whine"? jB **G** (*u/u*) of dog, ghost, storm; > *ḫāmītu*

ḫawumma → *ḫalwû*

ḫawuratum → *ḫūratu*

ḫa(w)uštarum, *ḫa'uštarum* (a pastry) Mari

ḫāya → *ḫēya*

ḫayālu → *ḫi'ālu*

ḫayāni "child" jB lex.; < 'Subartu'

ḫayyaltu "woman in labour" jB, NA; < *ḫiālu*

ḫayyāšu "hastener" jB in *ḫ. tuqmāte* "h. to battles"; also as DN; < *ḫiāšum*

ḫa(y)yattu "(pathological) terror" jB [IGI.LÁ.ŠÚ]; < *ḫātu*

ḫayyāṭu, *ḫayyattu* "surveyor, inspector" M/jB, NA as epith. of deity; desig. of demon; NA "spy, look-out"; NA "inspection hole" in oven; < *ḫiāṭu*

ḫayyiru → *ḫāwiru*

ḫayyiṭu → *ḫā'iṭu*

ḫazallūnu (a plant) jB lex., med.

ḫazāmu ~ "to mutilate" jB **G** stat., of ear **D** ~ **G** stat., of ear **Š** lex. only; > *ḫazmu*; *ḫazīmum*; *ḫuzzumu*

ḫazannum I, jB *azannu* (an alliaceous vegetable) OB, jB lex.

ḫazannu(m) II, MA, Mari occas. *ḫaziānu(m)*, Nuzi also *ḫazinnu*; pl. Am. *ḫazannūte*, jB *ḫazannāti* "mayor, village headman" not OA; also as PN; > *ḫazannūtu*

ḫaza(n)nūtu(m), MA, Mari occas. *ḫaziānū(t)tu* "office of mayor" Mari, M/NA, M/NB; < *ḫazannu* II

ḫazappum → *ḫasappum*

ḫazāqu mng. unkn. **G** unattested **D** jB lex. only; > *ḫazīqatu*?

ḫazāzu → *azāzu*

ḫaziānu → *ḫazannu* II

ḫaziānū(t)tu → *ḫazannūtu*

ḫazīmum "with mutilated ear" OB, as PN; < *ḫazāmu*

ḫazinnu → *ḫazannu* II

ḫazīqatu, *ḫuzīqatu* (a headcloth) jB, NA; also a skin disease; < *ḫazāqu* ?

ḫāzirum "helper" OB, usu. in PNs; < W.Sem.

ḫazmu "with mutilated ear" jB lex.; < *ḫazāmu*

ḫazru ~ "swamp" jB lex.

ḫazûm (or *ḫaṣûm*) ~ "to raise objections"? OB **D** only

ḫazû → also *azû* I

ḫāzû "croaker" (a bird) jB [ŠU.LÚ.MUŠEN]; < *azû* I

ḫazuannum (a kind of onion) OA

ḫazūru (a garment) M/jB

ḫazzabatu, *ḫan/zza/ibatu* (a plant) jB lex.

ḫazzatum "a goat" OB(N.Mes.); < *ḫazzum* nom. unit.; → *azzatu*

ḫazzibatu → *ḫazzabatu*

ḫazzum "goat" Mari (= *enzu*); < W.Sem.; > *ḫazzatum*

ḫebbūrum → *ḫabbūru*

Ḫebirtum → *Ebirtum*

ḫebû "drawn" jB of water; < *ḫabû* III

ḫedānum → *edānu*

ḫedûtu → *ḫidûtu*

ḫegallu → *ḫengallu*

ḫeḫēnu "(nasal) mucus" jB

ḫēla → *ḫelumma*

ḫelēqu → *ḫalāqu*

ḫelgeni (or *ḫelqeni*) "fugitive"? Nuzi; < *ḫalqu* ?

ḫelta'u (a chair, stool) Alal. (= *gištûm* ?)

ḫelû I "light(-coloured)" jB med., of urine; < *ḫelû* II

ḫelû(m) II, OA *ḫalā'um* "to be bright; cheerful" OA, O/jB **G** (stat. *ḫelu*) of light; transf. of person('s mood) **Gt** "shine brightly" **D** "make bright", stat. "are bright" of fingers, toes; "cheer up"; ptcp. as PN **Š** "illuminate"; "make resplendent"; > *ḫelû* I

ḫelumma in *ḫ. epēšu* "to reach agreement" Nuzi, also *ana ḫēla ḫ. epēšu*; < Hurr.

ḫemēru ~ "to shatter" jB **G** stat. "is cracked (up)"? of tongue **D** "shatter", part of body ?; > *ḫummuru*?; *ḫammurtu*?

ḫengallu(m), *ḫegallu(m)* "plenty" [ḪÉ.GÁL] of plants, animals; "(divine dispensation of) plenty", also as DN ^{d}*Ḫ*.; "plenty(-symbol)" in hand of figure; Mari (a vase); < Sum.

ḫenunu "plenty" jB lex.; < Sum.

ḫenzūru → *ḫinzūru*

ḫepēru, *ḫapāru(m)* "to dig" Ass., j/NB **G** (*i/i*) of human, animal "dig" hole in ground; "dig up" s.th., from ground

ḫepîš "in broken state" OB; < *ḫepû* I

ḫepû(m) I, OA *ḫap'um* "broken" Bab., OA [GAZ] of pot, beams, house; *ḫepâ lišallim* "let him restore broken (text)"; astr. of *ḫaprātu*; < *ḫepû* II; > *ḫepîš*

ḫepû(m) II, *ḫapû*, Ass. *ḫapā'u(m)* "to break" **G** (*i/i*) [GAZ] vessel, stele; tablet, line of text, sign; building; "ruin, destroy" city, land, people; "crack, crush, injure" part of body, transf. "break" heart (*libbu* → *ḫīpu* I 2); "split (open)" body etc., math. "divide, halve"; "break through" thicket; of moon, "break through" cloud; transf., "break" word, contract **D** ~ G "break (up)" rock, fetters etc.; inscribed tablets; lands; parts of body; MB "scatter" herd; NA "open up" wells; "make chips" (→ *ḫupû* 1); "beat" s.o. "up"? **Dtn** iter. NB, houses **Dt** pass. of D [AL.GAZ] "be broken up, shattered" etc.; of assembly "be scattered" **N** pass. of G [GAZ], of *libbu* "be broken"; of kor-measure (*kurrum*) "be halved" **Ntn** iter., of *libbu*; > *ḫepû* I, *ḫepîš*; *ḫīpu* I, *ḫipītu*; *ḫēpû*; *ḫupû*; *ḫuppû* I; *naḫpû*

ḫēpû(m) "breaker" O/jB worker breaking clods, stones; < *ḫepû* II

ḫêpum → *ḫiāpum*

ḫeraḫanniwa mng. unkn. MB(Alal.); < Hurr.

ḫerēbum → *erēbu* II

ḫēriānu → *ḫērû*

ḫerīnum "grass-seed" OB in simile, of sharp object; < Sum.; → *lardu*

ḫerizzi (a valuable stone) Am.; < Hurr.

ḫermum → *ermu*

ḫerru(m); pl. f. (a kind of furrow) O/jB; also transf. jB *ina ḫerrēti maqātu* "to get back home", of army; < *ḫarāru*

ḫersu (a vessel) MA, MB of stone

ḫerṣētum pl. (a kind of field) OB; < *ḫarāṣu*; → *ḫiriṣtu*

ḫerṣu(m), *ḫirṣu(m)* "fragment, cutting" O/jB, NA [GIG] "cut piece" of tree, of measuring-vessel; (a cut of meat); "track, imprint", "rut" of wheel; < *ḫarāṣu*

ḫeršu (a furrow or ditch)? jB lex.; < *ḫarāšu* II

ḫerṭu "(insect) bore hole" jB in simile of holes in liver; < *ḫarāṭum*

ḫerû(m) I "excavated" O/jB of canal; < *ḫerû* II

ḫerû(m) II, OAkk *ḫarā'um* "to dig; excavate" **G** (*i/i*) [BAL] canal, ditch etc., Early Mari *ḫarā'iš* "in order to dig"; well, cistern; "dig up" ground, field **D** ~ G pl. obj. "dig up" tree stumps?; "excavate" cisterns **Dtn** iter. **Š** caus. of G **N** pass., of canal etc.; > *ḫerû* I; *ḫērû*; *ḫirītu* I, *ḫirûtu*; *maḫrûm* II

ḫēru ~ "totality" jB lex.

ḫērû, *ḫārû*; NB pl. *ḫēriānu* "digger" M/NB of wells etc.; < *ḫerû* II

ḫerwu (an agricultural implement) Nuzi; < Hurr.

ḫesēru → *ḫasāru*

ḫesīru "scrap (of cloth)"? jB lex., for headcloth; < *ḫasāru* ?

ḫeslu "weaned" NB of calf; < Aram.

ḫesmu(mma) ~ "buckle, clasp"? Nuzi for garment; *ḫesmumma epēšu* "to buckle up"?; < Hurr.

ḫesru → *ḫasrum*

ḫesû(m), *ḫasû(m)*, *ḫasā'u* "to cover up, shroud" Bab., NA **G** (*i/i*) **1.** of bandage "cover over"; of foundations, covering underworld; face, with (= acc.) hair **2.** "(cover with blows =) batter, beat s.o. up", of demons, persons; transf. "pressurize" s.o. **3.** "break up" mountain with pickaxes **4.** transf. "cover up, conceal" decisions, words **D** ~ G, transf. "conceal, keep secret", Nuzi ellipt. "keep silent"; "squeeze out" drugs, with cloth **Dt** pass. "be pressed, pressurized" **Št** NB "be induced, forced" to ?; > *ḫīsum*; *ḫisītu*, *ḫisûtu*; *ḫassû*, *ḫassāyû*?; *ḫusû* II?; *ḫussû*?; *meḫsû*, *maḫsûtu*?

ḫeštaruḫlu "tailor"? MB(Alal.); < Hurr.

ḫeštiri ~ "garrison"? Nuzi, MB(Brak); < Hurr.

ḫetennu, *ḫutennu*, *ḫutnû* (wooden part of chariot) Nuzi, NA/jB, in pairs or sets; < Hurr.

ḫetnu "$^{1}/_{60}$ shekel"? Nuzi; < Hurr.

ḫewatumma in *ḫ*. *epēšu* "to make journey to" Nuzi; < Hurr.

ḫēya, *ḫīlāya* "watch-tower"? Ug. in *bīt ḫ*.; < W.Sem.?

ḫiādu "to say, pronounce" jB **G** lex. only **Gt** "express o.s."?; > *ḫittu* II

ḫiallu mng. unkn. Nuzi; < Hurr.

ḫiālu(m), *ḫâlu* "to be in labour; exude" Bab., NA **G** [ZUM] **1.** "be in labour" of woman, cow; "be in pain" of people, land etc. **2.** of teeth, earth, field "exude" blood, honey, other liquids; > *ḫīlu*, *ḫīlū*; *ḫīltum*; *ḫayyaltu*

ḫi'ālu, *ḫi/ayālu*; pl. *ḫi'alānu* etc. (a kind of military force) j/NB; < Aram.

ḫiāpum, *ḫêpum*, *ḫâbu*, *ḫâpu* "to cleanse, purify" O/jB **G** temple, drum; stat. of person, face "is cleansed"; of star "be bright" **D** ~ G "purify (cultically)" place, object; person, invalid, leg; ox **Dt** pass. of D, of diviner; > *ḫīpu* II, *ḫūbu* II

ḫiāqu(m), *ḫâqu* "to mix (up)" Bab., M/NA **G** "mix, mingle" beer, waters; ellipt. of lands "be embroiled" in war **Št** "be mixed together" of liquids; transf., of lands **N** "be mixed in" of wine; > *ḫīqu*; *taḫīqtum*

ḫiari (a festival; also as MN) OB(Alal.), Nuzi; < Hurr.

ḫiāru(m), *ḫâru* "to choose" **G** "seek in marriage"; of demons etc., "seek out" sufferer; in *pī nīšī ḫ.* "have people's interests at heart"; j/NB "look out, prepare" offering, provisions etc. **Gtn** iter. of G, of demons **Gt** "woo one another"; > *ḫīrtu*; *ḫāwiru*, *ḫā'irūtu*; *taḫīrtum*?; *takirtum*?

ḫiaruḫḫe "gold" MB(Alal.); < Hurr.

ḫiāšum, *ḫâšu* "to hurry, hasten" Bab. **G** of gods, persons; "speed" of arrow **Gtn** iter. **D** Mari mng. uncl.; > *ḫayyāšu*; *mušḫīštum*

ḫiāṭu(m), *ḫâṭ/du* "to supervise, check; weigh (out)" **G** [LAL] **1.** "watch over, supervise, control" field, land, animals, people; "check, inspect, examine" legal case, foundation stone **2.** "seek out, investigate"; of demons "seek out" sufferer **3.** "weigh out, pay" silver, wool etc.; medical dose **Gtn** iter. [LAL.MEŠ] **D** "inspect" entrails **N** pass. "be checked"; "be weighed out"; > *ḫâṭu*; *ḫā'iṭu*, *ḫā'iṭūtu*, *ḫā'iṭānu*; *ḫayyāṭu*; *ḫīṭu* II; *muḫa''idu*; *taḫīṭtu*

ḫibabītu "bride"? jB lex.; < *ḫabābu*

ḫibarītu(m) (a marshy area) O/jB lex.; as PlN

ḫibbum "thicket"? Mari; < W.Sem. (or → *ḫippum* ?)

ḫibiltu(m), OB(Susa) also *ḫabiltu* "wrongdoing; damage(s)" Bab., M/NA **1.** "wrongful action, crime"; *ḫ. turru*, *ḫ. šullumu* "to repay damages" **2.** OB *ḫibilti PN* "PN's losses" **3.** NA "debt(s)" **4.** NB "(payment in substitution for) debt, damages"; < *ḫabālu* II

Ḫibirtum → *Ebirtum*

ḫibištu(m) "crushed pieces (of aromatic wood)" Bab. also *ḫ. riqqē* "crushed pieces of aromatics"; OB *qutrinni ḫ.* "incense from *ḫ.*"; < *ḫabāšu* II

ḫiblum (a garment) OB

ḫibru(m) **1.** Mari (part of tribe) **2.** jB in plant name *ḫ. inbi* "group of fruit"; < W.Sem.

ḫibṣu(m) 'swelling' **1.** O/jB (a type of leavened bread/pastry) **2.** NA "bump, lump"; < *ḫabāṣu* I

ḫibšu **1.** jB lex. (a rough wool) **2.** jB/NA archit. "recess, niche"; < *ḫabāšu* I

ḫibtu "robbery"? jB; < *ḫabātu* I

ḫībum "beloved" OB f. in fPN *Ḫibti-DN*; jB lex.?; < *ḫâbu*

Ḫibur → *Ḫubur*

ḫiburnu, *ḫuburnu* (a grain-container) M/NA, in temple; *bīt ḫ.*, esp. in *sūtu ša b. ḫ.* "*sūtu*-measure of *b. ḫ.*"; < Hurr.

ḫibuššum mng. unkn. OB (an edible commodity)?

ḫibûtu "secrecy" Bogh. in *kī ḫ.* "secretly"; < *ḫabû* IV

ḫidānum → *edānu*

ḫidāru (desig. of wool) Alal., Ug.; < Hurr.

ḫidâtu → *ḫidiātum*

ḫi(d)dāru → *ḫandūru*

ḫiddu(m), *ḫindu(m)*; Am. pl. *ḫintu/ena* (a bead) OAkk, OA, Qatna, Am., in stone, gold, silver etc.

ḫidduḫḫu → *ḫandūḫu*

ḫidiātum, *ḫidâtu* pl. tant. "joy, rejoicings" Bab. [ḪÚL.MEŠ] *ēkal*, *šubat*, *bīt ḫ.* "palace, dwelling, house of celebrations"; < *ḫadû* III

ḫidirtum → *idirtu*

ḫidlum; pl. f. (a vessel) OB

ḫīdu → *ḫīṭu*

ḫidumû, *ḫudumû* (part of a garment) Am., Nuzi

ḫidûtu(m), *ḫedûtu(m)* "joy, rejoicing" OAkk, Bab. [ḪÚL] OAkk in PNs; *ina ḫ.* "joyfully"; "celebration"; < *ḫadû* III

ḫiḫinnu → *ḫaḫinnu*

ḫilabānu, *ḫilapānu* (a plant with milky sap) jB lex.; < *ḫilpu*

ḫilaḫuli "doorkeeper"? Alal.; < Hurr.

ḫilammu, *ḫilimmu* (a grasshopper) jB

ḫilāni, *ḫillāni*, *ḫitlāni*, *ḫilēni* in *bīt ḫ.* "portico(ed building)" (pl. *b. ḫilānāni*, *b. ḫilānāte*) jB, NA, of Syrian origin; < Hitt.; → *appātu*

ḫilapānu → *ḫilabānu*

ḫilaṣu → *ḫilṣu*

ḫildāmu → *ḫilidāmu*

ḫilēni → *ḫilāni*

ḫilēpu(m), *ḫilpum*? "willow" Bab. [GIŠ.KÌM] as tree; "willow-wood"

ḫilibāna (desig. of the underworld) jB; < *ḫilibû*

ḫilibû "the underworld" M/jB, NA [ḪI.LI.BA] as DN; as name of stone; < Sum.; → *girimmu*, *amar(girim)ḫilibû*

ḫilidāmu, *ḫildāmu* (a kind of meat) NB; < *ḫillu* + *dāmu* ?

ḫilimītu (a vegetable)? MB(Alal.)

ḫilimmu → *ḫilammu*

ḫilištu "scrapings, raked-out matter" jB, from oven; < *ḫalāšu*

ḫillāni → *ḫilāni*

ḫillaru (part of an ornament) Qatna, Alal.; < Hurr.

ḫillālētu → *ḫillu*

ḫillu(m) "covering" OAkk, Bab., NA "(egg) shell"; "cortex, hollow stem" of reed, also as quiver; "layer" of cloud, "haze"; pl. f. OA ~ "custody"?, NB *ḫillālētu* "woollen cover"?; < *ḫalālum* I ?; → *ḫilidāmu*; *ḫiltu* II

ḫillūru → *ḫallūru*

ḫillutu "creeping" subst. NA in fig. etym. after *ḫalālu* III

ḫilpu "milk" NA; < W.Sem.; > *ḫilabānu*

ḫilpum → also *ḫilēpu*

ḫilṣu(m) I, NB also *ḫilaṣu*; pl. f. "filtration; combed, filtered materials" Bab. **1.** OB "filtered oil" **2.** NB "filtration process" for sesame **3.** "combed out (wool)"; < *ḫalāṣu*

ḫilṣu II (a fortification)? jB lex.; M/NB in *bīt ḫ.*, part of temple; NB *rab b. ḫ.* "official in charge of *b. ḫ.*"

ḫilšu "scraping(s), raking(s)" jB; < *ḫalāšu*

ḫiltu I ~ "sleep" jB; pl. in *lamṣat ḫilāti* (a kind of insect)

ḫiltu II (a kind of reed) jB lex., var. of *ḫillu* in *appār ḫ.*

ḫīltum ~ "exudation" OA, of silver; < *ḫiālu*

ḫīltu → also *ḫīštu* II

ḫilû → *ḫulû*

ḫīlu(m) "exudation, resin" Bab., NA [ILLU] of trees, plants; *ḫ. erî* "*ḫ.* of copper", a drug; < *ḫiālum*

ḫīlū pl. tant. "labour pains, birth pangs" jB, NA; < *ḫiālum*

ḫilukannum → *ḫulukannum*

ḫiluppu → *ḫaluppu*

ḫimāru "donkey" jB lex.; syn. of *imēru*; < Aram.

ḫimātu → *ḫimētu*

ḫimdātum → *ḫimittum* I

ḫimētu(m), Ass. *ḫimātu(m)* "butter, ghee" [Ì.NUN(.NA)] as food; med., mag.; rit., in offerings

ḫimiltu "plan" MB; < *ḫamālu*

ḫimištu "snapped off piece, trimming" jB of palm tree; < *ḫamāšu* I

ḫimittum I; pl. *ḫimdātum* "excuse(s)" OA; < *ḫamādu*

ḫimittu II "frostiness" jB med. "shivering"; < *ḫamāṭu* III

ḫimmatu(m) "collected materials, collection" O/jB; OB pl. "accumulated possessions"; jB "collection" of laws, divine attributes; "matter blown together" by storm; "(accumulation of) rubbish"; OB mng. uncl. of ship's load; < *ḫamāmu*

ḫimmum mng. uncl. Mari in *ḫ. šaṭer* "*ḫ.* is written"; < *ḫamāmu* ?; → *ḫimû* 2

ḫimrum (a fermented drink) Mari; < W.Sem.

ḫimsātu, *ḫinsātu* pl. tant. "wrongful possessions" M/NA; → *ḫummusum*

ḫimsukkûm mng. unkn. OB(Elam); < Elam.?

ḫimṣu(m) I; usu. pl. f. 'torn away material' O/jB **1.** "(commercial) profit" **2.** "plundered goods"; < *ḫamāṣu*

ḫimṣu(m) II, *ḫinṣu* "fatty tissue" Bab. [UZU.ME.ḪÉ] esp. ext.

ḫimšu "(act of) snapping off" jB in fig. etym. *ḫ. ḫamāšu* "to break off" dates; < *ḫamāšu* I

ḫimtu, *ḫintu*, *ḫindu*; pl. NA *ḫimāte*, NB *ḫindēti* "leather skin, pouch" Ass., j/NB for water; NB "purse" for money, stones etc.

ḫimṭu(m), *ḫinṭu(m)* subst. "burning" O/jB "scorching" of field; "fever", *ḫ. ṣēti* "heat stroke"? [TAB(.BA)]; *ḫ. libbi*; pl. f. *ḫimṭētu(m)* "heartburn"?; < *ḫamāṭu* III

ḫimû **1.** jB (a rush pad for wound) **2.** Qatna (as ornament), with lapis lazuli inlay (or → *ḫimmum* ?)

ḫimudi mng. unkn. MB(Alal.)

ḫina (a stone) Am., material of vessel; < Eg.?

ḫindu(m) (a mythical being)? O/jB

ḫindu → also *ḫiddu*; *ḫimtu*

ḫinduḫḫu → *ḫandūḫu*

ḫindūru → *ḫandūru*

ḫinḫinu (a kind of spice)? M/NA; *qēm ḫ.* "flour of *ḫ.*"

ḫiniqtu "constriction" jB med., of urinary tract; also "(urine) retention"; < *ḫanāqu*

ḫinišannum (a valuable commodity) OA

ḫinnu "ship's cabin" jB lex.

ḫinqu(m) "constriction" **1.** NA "narrows" of river **2.** jB *ḫ. immeri* (a sheep disease) **3.** O/jB of humans *mūt ḫ.* "death by strangulation?"; jB med. "constriction" of duct; < *ḫanāqu*

ḫinsātu → *ḫimsātu*

ḫinṣu → *ḫimṣu* II

ḫinšu (an implement)? j/NB

ḫintena → *ḫiddu*

ḫintu → *ḫimtu*

ḫinṭu → *ḫimṭu*

ḫinziribu, *ḫizzaribu* (blue-green colour) jB, NA lex.; < *ḫinzūru* + Hurr. *-iwwe*

ḫinzu mng. unkn. MB desig. of images

ḫinzūru, *ḫenzūru*, *inzūru* "apple (tree)" M/jB esp. Nuzi as PN, MN (also Ḫizzurru); "apple(-coloured wool)"; > *ḫinziribu*; *inzaḫurētu*; → *ḫašḫūru*

ḫipindû (a stone)? jB lex.

ḫipītu(m) "breach" O/MB in dyke; in house; < *ḫepû* II

ḫippum "injury, damaged place" Mari, on face; in riverbank (or → *ḫibbum*)

ḫīpu(m) I, NA also *ḫippu* "break(age)" Bab., M/NA [GAZ] **1.** "break, broken place" on object, tablet; NB "fissure" in ground ?; jB/NA stones *ḫ. šadî* "quarried in the mountains" **2.** "act of breaking" tablet; *ḫīp libbi* "distress", also med. **3.** math. "diameter"; < *ḫepû* II

ḫīpu II "purified" jB, of deity; < *ḫiāpum*

ḫīqu "mixed, diluted" O/jB, NA of oil; jB, NA of beer, usu. as subst. [KAŠ.A.SUD], pl. f. *ḫīqāti* "diluted beer", also *ḫ. šikāri*; < *ḫiāqu*

ḫirāpu → *ḫurāpu*

ḫīratu → *ḫīrtu*

ḫir(i)galû (a kind of flour) M/NB, NA

ḫirinnu → *ḫarinnu*; *ḫerīnum*

ḫiriṣtu "deduction" jB lex. in pl.; < *ḫarāṣu*; → *ḫerṣētum*

ḫirīṣu → *ḫarīṣu*

ḫirišnānum (a textile)? OA

ḫirītu(m) I "ditch, channel" Bab., NA **1.** "canal" **2.** "city ditch, (dry) moat"; < *ḫerû* II

ḫirītum II (an ornament) OAkk(Ur III)

ḫirṣu → *ḫerṣu*

ḫīrtu(m), *ḫīratu*, NB *ḫīštu* "(equal ranking) wife" Bab. [MUNUS.NITA.DAM] of humans, deities; < *ḫiāru*

ḫīru(m) (a piece of clothing) Mari, NB?

ḫirûtu(m) "(act of) excavation" Bab. of canals, fields etc.; < *ḫerû* II

ḫisannu, *iḫḫisannu* (a craftsman) NB *mār ḫ.*; < OPers.?

ḫisgalû (sufferer from illness) jB

ḫisītu; pl. *ḫisi'āti* "maltreatment" NA; < *ḫesû*

ḫisnanni (a shrub)? jB lex.

ḫispu (a garden plant) NB

ḫisrum "cutting(s)" OB of reeds; < *ḫasāru*

ḫissatu(m), Bogh. *ḫissetum* "understanding; mention" Bab., NA "wisdom, intelligence", esp. *ḫ. uznē*/*libbi*; "mention" of s.o.('s name); "memory, remembrance, thought for s.o."; < *ḫasāsu*

ḫisû(m), *isû(m)* (a fish) O/jB lex.

ḫīsum ~ "(sealed) envelope" OB on document; < *ḫesû*

ḫisûtu "pressure" NB in *ḫ. ḫesû* "to put pressure on" s.o.; < *ḫesû*

ḫiṣārum → *ḫaṣāru*

ḫiṣbu(m) I "luxuriance, plenty" Bab. [MA.DAM] *ḫ. mātim*/*šadî*/*tâmti* "(abundant) yield of land/ mountain/sea"; < *ḫaṣābu* II

ḫiṣbu II "chip(ping)s" jB of wood, stone, e.g. *ḫ. sāmti* "carnelian chippings"; < *ḫaṣābu* I

ḫiṣibtu "chip" jB; < *ḫiṣbu* II nom. unit.

ḫiṣnu(m), *ḫiṣinu* "protection" O/jB of deity, esp. in PNs; < *ḫaṣānu*

ḫiṣpatum ~ "insolence" OB *ḫ. kabittum* "serious insolence"

ḫiṣṣaṣātu (or *ḫizzazātu* ?) pl. (an offering food)? j/NB

ḫiṣṣu I; pl. f. "reed bundle"? M/NB for irrigation banks; < *ḫaṣāṣu* I

ḫiṣṣu(m) II "gravel" NB; Mari, ext. (as feature on liver)

ḫišeḫtu → *ḫišiḫtu*

ḫišelu- (a garment) OAkk, in Hurr. pl. *ḫišeluḫina*; < Hurr.

ḫišiḫtu(m), *ḫišeḫtu(m)*, *ḫašeḫtu*; NB pl. also *ḫišiḫḫēti* "requirement" Bab. "thing needed"; "desire(d)" of god, as descr. of person; < *ḫašāḫu*

ḫišiltu(m) 'crushings' O/jB, desig. of grain, spices; < *ḫašālu*

ḫišrum mng. unkn. OB lex.; < *ḫašāru* ?

ḫiššamû → *ḫiššā'um*

ḫiššānu(m), *ḫiššāmu* "thorn; needle, pin" OA, jB

ḫiššatu "swelling" O/jB med.; < *ḫašāšu* I

ḫiššātu → *ḫiššā'um*; *kiššātum*

ḫiššā'um, *ḫiššamû* ~ "superb, fine" O/jB of god, person, horse; O/MB also as fPN *Ḫiššātu(m)*

ḫiššumaku "balancing payment" Nuzi; < Hurr.; → *išumaka*

ḫīštu I, *ḫīšūtu* "thorn bushes" j/NB

ḫīštu(m) II, *ḫīltu* "sluice" Bab., diverted channel; *bāb ḫ.* "sluice gate"

ḫīštu → also *ḫīrtu*

ḫišû(m), *išûm* "debt-note" O/jB for deferred purchase price; < Sum.

ḫīšu(m) "band, strap" M/jB **1.** as personal ornament on breast **2.** "(carrying) strap" of gardener, fisherman **3.** "(head)band" **4.** "(reed) coil" for bird's nest

ḫīšūtu → *ḫīštu* I

ḫitbāṣu "very joyful"? jB; < *ḫabāṣu* I

ḫitlāni → *ḫilāni*

ḫitlāpu, *ḫitlupātu* (a garment) jB lex.; < *ḫalāpu* I

ḫitmuṭiš "very quickly" jB; < *ḫamāṭu* II

ḫitpu (an animal sacrifice) NA, NB of sheep, oxen, birds etc.; < *ḫatāpu*

ḫitrubu "very desolate" jB(Ass.); < *ḫarābu*

ḫittu I; NB pl. *ḫittānu* "lintel" M/NB [(GIŠ.) GAN.DU7] *ḫ. ša bābi* "lintel of doorway"

ḫittu II (an utterance, phps.) "riddle" jB lex.; < *ḫiādu*

ḫittu III, *ḫattu* (a beer jar) jB lex.

ḫītu(m) (or *ḫīdu(m)*) (a bathing place)? OB lex.

ḫituḫli (a prof. desig.) Nuzi; < Hurr.

ḫiṭītu(m) "shortfall, loss; crime" Bab. *ḫ. rašû(m)* "to become faulty", "become guilty"; *ḫ. epēšu, ḫabālu(m)* "commit crime"; *ḫ. paṭāru(m), pussusu* etc. "forgive, expunge sin(s)"; < *ḫaṭû* II

ḫiṭṭatu "excavation" NB, esp. of building pit; < *ḫaṭāṭu* I

ḫīṭu(m) I, later *ḫiṭṭu*; MA pl. *ḫīṭāni* "error; lack; crime; penalty" Bab., M/NA [ŠE.BI.DA ?] **1.** "failing, defect" of commodity, person **2.** "crime, sin, error"; *bēl ḫ.*, NB also *ša ḫ.* "guilty person" **3.** *ḫ. emēdu/šadādu* "to impose/bear penalty"; < *ḫaṭû* II

ḫīṭu II "payment" NB; < *ḫiāṭu*

ḫi'u(m) (a garment)? OAkk in Hurr. pl. *ḫi'ina*; jB mng. uncl.

ḫiwaru (a copper vessel) Nuzi; < Hurr.

ḫīya → *ḫēya*

ḫiyālu → *ḫi'ālu*

ḫizzaribu → *ḫinziribu*

ḫizzazātu → *ḫiṣṣaṣātu*

Ḫizzurru → *ḫinzūru*

ḫū'a, *ḫū'u* (an owl) jB

ḫuālum → *ḫâlu*

ḫuāqu → *ḫâqu*

ḫū'atum (a meal)? OB lex.

ḫuballu(m), *ḫubullu*, Nuzi *ḫubb/ppalla/u* "pit, trench" O/jB lex., Nuzi

ḫubāṣu(m) "exuberant one" Bab., as PN; < *ḫabāṣu* I

ḫubballu → *ḫuballu*

ḫubbu; NB pl. f. "buzz(ing), whining" j/NB of noise in head, lamentation; < *ḫabābu*

ḫubbû → *kubbû* I.II

ḫubbultu "debt(s)" Nuzi; < *ḫabālu* III

ḫubbulu, Ass. *ḫabbulu(m)* "indebted" O/MA, jB; OA pl. as subst. "debtors" of s.o.; < *ḫabālu* III

ḫubburu → *ḫabāru* I.II D; *ḫamāru* D

ḫubbuṣu(m), *ḫumbuṣu* "very swollen, exuberant" Bab., in PNs; < *ḫabāṣu* I

ḫubbušu(m) "swollen up" O/jB of humans; transf. (pejorative) as PN; MB of horse; < *ḫabāšu* I

ḫubbuttu (or *ḫupputtu*) (a garment)? NB, wool for *ḫ.* of deity

ḫubbuṭum → *ebēṭu* II D

ḫubibītu → *ḫumbabītu*

ḫubīdu, *ḫupidānu* (a plant) jB lex., med.

ḫubiṣītu → *ḫumbiṣūtu*

ḫublillu (a kind of grain) jB lex.; → *ḫabulillu* ?

ḫubrûm → *ḫuprûm*

ḫubšašû(m) (a pottery vessel) OAkk, O/jB; < *ḫabāšu* I ?

ḫubšu I "dust, flotsam" jB on surface of water; < *ḫabāšu* II ?

ḫubšu II, *ḫubušu* (object used in cult) j/NB

ḫubtātu → *ḫubuttu*

ḫubtu(m) "robbery; plunder" Bab., M/NA [NB SAR] **1.** "(act of) robbery" NB *ḫ. āli* "urban robbery", MA *ḫubat ṣēri* "desert robbery" **2.** "robbed (goods, animals)" etc.; "(human) plunder, captives" in war, also lú*ḫ.*; < *ḫabātu* I

ḫubû mng. unkn. j/NB lex.

ḫūbu I (or *ḫūpu*) (a prof. desig.)? NB

ḫūbu II "cleaning" jB; < *ḫiāpum*

ḫubullu(m), NA *ḫabullu* "debt; interest-bearing loan; interest" [UR5.RA] 1. "(interest-bearing) debt"; *ana ḫ.* "on loan"; *bēl ḫ.* "creditor"; jB *bīt ḫ.* "debtor's prison" **2.** OB(Susa), M/NB "interest (on loan)"; > *ḫabālu* III

ḫubullu → also *ḫuballu*

ḫubūnum, *ḫubunnu(m)*; Am., Bogh. pl. f. *ḫubunnētu* (a small vessel) O/jB of 1/3-1 *qû(m)*; → *ḫuburnu* ?

Ḫubur, *Ḫibur* **1.** jB (underworld river) **2.** O/MA (a month), OA *Ḫubur*, MA usu. *Ḫibur* **3.** jB *ḫubur* (a plant name)

ḫuburnu(m); pl. f. (small vessel) Mari, Nuzi for oil; → *ḫubūnum*

ḫuburnu → also *ḫiburnu*

ḫuburru → *ḫubūru* II

ḫuburtanūru (a high royal official) Ug.

ḫuburtu(m) (a reed item) OB, NA?

ḫubūru(m) I (a beer jar) Bab., OA [MÙD ?] OA du. "(twin) jars", *bīt ḫ.*; NB *sūqi ša ḫ.* "street of *ḫ.*"

ḫubūru(m) II, *ḫuburru* "bustle, clamour" O/jB of mankind; < *ḫabāru* I

ḫubūsum (a weapon) Mari

Ḫubuṣītu → *ḫumbiṣūtu*

ḫubušu → *ḫubšu* II

ḫubuttu(m); pl. *ḫubuttātu(m)*, lex. once *ḫubtātu* "interest-free loan" OAkk, O/jB pl. tant., silver, grain etc.; NB also sg.; > *ḫabātu* II; *ḫubuttūtu*

ḫubuttūtu(m) "interest-free loan" Bab. silver, grain; < *ḫubuttu* abstr.?

ḫubūtu ~ "thicket" Am.; < W.Sem.

ḫudātu → *ḫūdu*

ḫuddudu "deeply incised" jB of wadis; < *ḫadādu* II

ḫudḫudum (an object) OB; → *ḫutḫutu*

ḫudḫummu (or *ḫutḫummu*) (a plant) jB lex.

ḫūdu(m), *ḫudû*; OB pl. f. "happiness, pleasure" Bab., NA **1.** "joy"; "satisfaction, contentment" (with s.th., s.o.) **2.** in *ḫūd(u) libbi* "joy, contentment" [ŠÀ.ḪÚL.LA]; leg. *ina ḫ. l.-šu* "of his own free will" **3.** *ḫ. kabatti/pānī* "contentment, happiness"; < *ḫadû* III

ḫudumû → *ḫidumû*

ḫuduššu I (an age group)? jB lex.; < Sum.

ḫuduššu(m) II "frog (figure)" OB, jB lex., of lapis lazuli

ḫudušŝûm (or *ḫudūšum*) ~ "marriage celebration" Mari; < *ḫadāšu*

ḫudûtu → *ḫadûtu*

ḫūgum (a loaf or cake) Mari; < W.Sem.

ḫuḫāriš "as with a bird-snare" jB

ḫuḫāru(m) m. & f. "bird-snare" [ḪAR.MUŠEN.NA]; as weapon of Šamaš; *ša ḫ.* "bird-snarer"

ḫuḫḫarāte → *ḫurḫurātu*; *ḫuruḫuru*

ḫuḫḫītu(m) "expectoration, vomit" O/jB; < *ḫaḫû* II

ḫuḫḫurāte → *ḫurḫurātu*

ḫuḫḫuru → *ḫuruḫuru*

ḫuḫi(n)nu mng. unkn. Emar, desig. of a stone feature in city

ḫuḫpum (a bronze vessel) OB; < Elam.

ḫuḫû → *ḫaḫû* I

ḫuk "wood" jB lex.; < Elam.

ḫukunna mng. unkn. MB(Alal.), desig. of table; < Hurr.

ḫūlalam, *ḫūlalu* **1.** MB (desig. of horse) **2.** Bogh. lex. (a bird); > *ḫūlaluḫlu*

ḫulālu(m), Qatna *ḫalānu* (a valuable stone) [NA4.NÍR] for vases, ornaments; also as PN (also fPN *Ḫulaltum*); jB *ḫ. īni* (part of eye) [NA4.NÍR.IGI]; *ḫ. kappi iṣṣūri* "bird's-wing *ḫ.* stone" [NA4.NÍR.PA.MUŠEN.NA]

ḫulālû "like *ḫ.* stone" NB in fPN *Ḫulālīti*

ḫūlalu → *ḫūlalam*

ḫūlaluḫlu (an official) Nuzi; < *ḫūlalam* + Hurr. *-uḫlu*

ḫulamētu → *alamittu*

ḫulamīsu, *ḫulamīšu*, *ḫallamīs/šu* **1.** jB lex. (a tree) **2.** jB "chamaeleon"?; NB as PN

ḫulamītu → *alamittu*

ḫulampasḫi mng. unkn. Nuzi; < Hurr.

ḫulāpu(m) (a wrapping)? OA, jB; < *ḫalāpu* I

ḫulāqu "worn-out garment" jB lex.; < *ḫalāqu*

ḫulāṣum (a flour) O/jB as food for pigs; < *ḫalāṣu*

ḫulbaqqu → *ḫuluppaqqu*

ḫulbāṭu adj. mng. unkn. jB lex.

ḫuliam, *ḫuliyam* "helmet" Am., jB as armour; as type of vessel, in stone, metal; (name of a plant)

ḫulīlū mng. unkn. Mari, in *ūm ḫ.*

ḫulium → *ḫulû*

ḫuliyam → *ḫuliam*

ḫullānu; Nuzi pl. f. "(cloth) cover, wrap" M/NA, M/NB [TÚG.GÚ.LÁ] garment, in pairs; *ḫ. aḫi* "wrap with sleeves"; woollen, linen; also "cover" for bed

ḫullu(m), *ullu*; jB pl. *ullāni* "neck ring, torc" O/jB as ornament, of metal; for dog; "ring" on a door; "ring" of fortification walls; < Sum.

ḫulluqiš "in order to destroy" jB; < *ḫalāqu* D

ḫullūru → *ḫallūru*

ḫulmāḫu (a kind of snake) jB lex.; < Sum.

ḫulmiṭṭu ~ "dragon; kind of lizard" jB [MUŠ.ḪUL]; < Sum.

ḫulmum; pl. f. mng. unkn. Mari

ḫulmuna ~ "lamp"? MB(Susa); *ḫ. nuwwuru*; < Elam.

ḫulpālu → *ḫuppalû*

ḫulpaqqu → *ḫuluppaqqu*

ḫulqu(m) "lost property" O/jB; < *ḫalāqu*

ḫulqû → *ḫuluqqā'um*

ḫulsu (a garment) NA lex.

ḫultuppu(m), *ḫultuppû(m)*, occas. *ḫuštuppu* liter. "evilly striking" jB (desig. of demon); also O/jB (a month in Elam); < Sum.

ḫultuppû, *ḫaltappû* "(exorcist's) rod" M/jB; < Sum.; → *mašḫulduppû*

ḫultuppû → also *ḫultuppu*

ḫulṭimmu → *ḫuṭṭimmu*

ḫulû, OAkk *ḫulium*, jB once *ḫilû* (a rodent, phps.) "shrew" OAkk PN; jB, NA mag. [PÉŠ.ḪUL; PÉŠ.SÌLA.GAZ]

ḫūlu; pl. *ḫūlāni* "way, road" M/NA, Nuzi [KASKAL(.2)] "(physical) road"; MA "course" for horses; "journey" of ship

ḫuluḫḫu(m) (light(-coloured) slag) O/jB, NA med.; NA from *ušmetu* stone; < Sum.

ḫulukannum, *ḫilukannum* (a kind of vehicle) OA; < Hitt.?

ḫulūlum (a leather object) OB lex.

ḫulūmum (valuable type of earth)? OB, weighed commodity

ḫuluppaqqu, *ḫulp/baqqu* (a vessel) M/jB [NÍG.TAB.TUR.RA] of copper, pottery; usu. for incense-burning

ḫuluppu (a bird) Bogh. lex.

ḫuluppu → also *ḫaluppu*

ḫuluptu (a cloth cover) jB lex.; < *ḫalāpu* I

ḫuluqqā'um, *ḫaluqqā'u(m)*, *ḫu/aluqqû*, *ḫulqû* "(commercial) loss" [ZÁḪ] "lost goods"; "(financial) loss(es)"; < *ḫalāqu*

ḫulūṭu (a mixed? drink) NA, in *massītu* containers for offerings; < Aram.

ḫumalītu "friendly, sympathetic"? jB of goddess; < *ḫumālu*

ḫumālu "sympathy"? Ug.; < *gamālu* ?

ḫumāmātu, *ḫummētu* pl. tant. "detritus, jetsam" jB mag., in fig. etym. with *ḫamāmu*

ḫumaṣīrum → *ḫumṣīru*

ḫumāšum → *umāšu*

ḫumātum (part of body) OB lex.

ḫumbabītu, *ḫumbubītu*, *ḫu(m)bibītu*, NA *ḫumbabarītu*? jB, NA **1.** (a kind of lizard)? **2.** (a figurine); NA also "Humbaba (figurine)"

ḫumbirra(t)tu (a stone) jB med.

ḫumbiṣūtu, *ḫu(m)biṣītu*; jB pl. *ḫumbiṣāte* "lump of dough"? M/NB, NA; as NB fPN also *Ḫu(m)buṣītu*; < *ḫabāṣu* I

ḫumbubītu → *ḫumbabītu*

Ḫumbuṣītu → *ḫumbiṣūtu*

ḫumbuṣu → *ḫubbuṣu*

ḫumīlātu pl. tant.? mng. unkn. NB, field with *ḫ*.; *ḫ*. of *bīt PN*

ḫumīru ~ "lump"? jB lex., of lead; < *ḫamāru*

ḫummānu (a prof. desig.)? NB

ḫummātu → *gummātu*

ḫummētu → *ḫumāmātu*

ḫu(m)mudāyum (a siege instrument) Mari

ḫummuru(m), *Ass. ḫammuru* "crippled" Bab., MA [KUD.KUD(.DU)] of foot; of human, also as PN; "lame" of horse; MA "stumbling"? of gazelles; < *ḫamāru* or *ḫemēru*; > *ḫammurtu*?

ḫummusum D "to pressurize, oppress" OB; → *ḫamsu*; *ḫimsātu*

ḫummuṣum mng. uncl. OB as PN; < *ḫamāṣu* D

ḫummušu I "1/5 (shekel)" NB; < *ḫamiš*

ḫummušu II "snapped off" jB lex., of grain; < *ḫamāšu* I

ḫummuṭiš "very quickly" O/jB; < *ḫummuṭu* I

ḫummuṭu I "quick" NB, "early-bearing" of palm tree; < *ḫamāṭu* II

ḫummuṭu II "very hot" j/NB of fate?; "parched"? of field; < *ḫamāṭu* III

ḫumsīru → *ḫumṣīru*

ḫumṣirtu, *ḫab(a)ṣirtu* "female mouse" j/NB [PÉŠ.MUNUS]; NB as PN; < *ḫumṣīru*

ḫumṣīru, *ḫumsīru*, *ḫumuṣṣīru(m)*, *ḫumunṣ/sīru*, *ḫa/um(a)ṣ/sīrum*, *ḫab/m(a)ṣīru(m)*, *kamaṣīrum* "(large) mouse" OAkk, Bab. [PÉŠ]; often as PN; > *ḫumṣirtu*; *ḫabaṣīrānu*

ḫumšu(m), NB *ḫunzu* "one-fifth" NB wr. syll., else [5-]; < *ḫamiš*

ḫumtu → *ḫutmu*

ḫumṭum I "haste"? OB; < *ḫamāṭu* II

ḫumṭu(m) II, *ḫunṭu* "heat; fever" **1.** OAkk, O/jB "hot season", also as feast and MN **2.** jB, NA "fever"; < *ḫamāṭu* III

ḫumunnašwe mng. unkn. Nuzi, lamp *ša ḫ*.; < Hurr.

ḫumunsīṣīru etc. → *ḫumṣīru*

ḫumušā "five each" OB; < *ḫamiš*

ḫumušû, *ḫumušā'u*, *ḫumušiu* [5-] **1.** Nuzi, NB "five-year-old" **2.** NB family "of five individuals"?; < *ḫamiš*

ḫumūšum "(the number) five" OB; < *ḫamiš*

ḫumūšum → also *umāšu*

ḫunābu(m) "thriving" O/jB lex., of person; as (f)PN; < *ḫanābu*

ḫunībum "shoot, seedling" Mari; < *ḫanābu*

ḫunima (a vessel) Am.; < Eg.

ḫunnum (a kind of table) OB lex.

ḫunnû(m) "to give shelter, lodge"? Mari, sheep (also MB, mng. uncl.); < W.Sem.

ḫunnubu(m) "very thriving" O/MB in (f)PNs; < *ḫanābu*

ḫunnunu(m) (desig. of men, sheep) jB lex.; < *ḫanānu* ?

ḫunnuṭu "(state of) ripening" jB lex. of grain etc.; → *ḫunṭu*

ḫuntu (part of door) jB lex.

ḫunṭu "ripeness, maturity" jB lex.; → *ḫunnuṭu*

ḫunṭu → also *ḫumṭu* II

ḫunzu → *ḫumšu*

ḫunzû, *ḫunzu'u*, *ḫuzzû* ~ "lame" M/NB usu. as PN, family name; → *ḫutenzû*

ḫupā'u → *ḫupû*

ḫupḫuppu (a container) jB lex.; < Sum.

ḫupidānu → *ḫubīdu*

ḫupirririša (a prof. desig.) OB(Susa); < Elam.

ḫuppa, *ḫuppi* (stance of mourner) jB; < Sum.?; → *ḫuppû* II

ḫuppalla/u → *ḫuballu*

ḫuppalû(m), *ḫut(a)palû*, *ḫurpalû*, *ḫulpālu* (a weapon) jB [GIŠ.TUKUL.SAG.NA4] "mace" or "double-axe"?

ḫuppašilurgu → *ḫabšallurḫu*

ḫuppat(a)ru (a vessel) Qatna, Nuzi, for washing; of gold; < Hurr.

ḫuppātu → *ḫuppu* I.II; *ḫuptu* III

ḫuppi → *ḫuppa*

ḫuppu(m) I; NB pl. f. (a kind of basket) Bab., MA [GI.GUR.ḪÚB] as container; OB "guard"?, on lance; MA, of glass; NA *ša ḫu(p)pānīšu* "basket-dealer"?; < Sum.

ḫuppu(m) II, *uppu(m)*; Ug. pl. f. "hole, pit"? O/jB in fields, of snake?; → *ḫuptu* III

ḫuppu → also *ḫuppû* II; *ḫurpu*; *uppu* II

ḫuppû I, Ass. *ḫappû* "broken (up)" MA, M/NB of head; tablets; MA of spices "crushed"; of population "scattered"; < *ḫepû* II D

ḫuppû(m) II, *ḫuppu* [(LÚ.)ḪÚB.BI/BU] **1.** (cultic dancer) O/jB **2.** (a weaver) M/NB; < Sum.; > *ḫuppûtu*; → *ḫuppa*

ḫuppudu(m) I "blind" O/jB of person, puppy; also as PN; < *ḫuppudum* II

ḫuppudum II "to blind" OB; OAkk "delete" words on tablet ?; > *ḫuppudu* I; → *upputu*

ḫupputtu → *ḫubbuttu*

ḫuppûtu "skill of cultic dancer" NB; < *ḫuppû* II

ḫupri (a capacity measure)? Alal.

ḫuprûm (or *ḫubrûm*) mng. unkn. OB

ḫuprušḫu, *ḫurpušḫu* (a vessel) MB(Alal.), Nuzi of pottery?, metal; < Hurr.

ḫupšena → *ḫupšu*

ḫupšilurg/ḫu → *ḫabšallurḫu*

ḫupšiš "as a plebeian" jB; < *ḫupšu*

ḫupšu(m) "(member of) lower class" esp. MA, Alal. (Hurr. pl. *ḫupšena*), Am., jB(Ass.); "rabble" usu. of soldiers; of mutinous gods; > *ḫupšiš*

ḫuptu I "superiority" M/NB of gods; also in PN; < *ḫapātum*

ḫuptum II; pl. *ḫupāti* (field subject to specific form of duty) OB

ḫuptu(m) III; pl. *ḫuppātu* "hole, hollow" jB, NA in ground; in neck, head; *ḫ. īnē/i* "eye-socket"; OB lex. (a metal bowl); → *ḫuppu* II

ḫupû, MA *ḫupā'u* "fragment" MA, jB **1.** pl. "sherds" of pot, tablet; "chips" of wood; lex. "flakes" of fish; "wisps" of cloud **2.** jB lex. (a vessel holding 1/2 *qûm*); < *ḫepû* II

ḫūpu(m) I "(wheel) rim; ring" OAkk, O/jB "rim, tyre" of wheel; jB lex., transf. "assembly"?

ḫūpu II "fear" NA in *ḫ. libbāte* "fear of s.o.'s anger"; < *ḫâpu*

ḫūpu → also *ḫūbu* I

ḫupurtum → *upurtu*

ḫuqqu mng. unkn. Bogh. lex.

ḫuqqumum vb. or adj.? mng. unkn. OB, action applied to flour

ḫūqu "step, rung (of ladder)" Bab., NA; also NA "landing stage"?; jB transf. "(critical) stage" of illness; (a kind of bird), also (a plant)?

ḫur → *ḫurri*

ḫurādu I; MA/MB pl. f. "soldier; army" M/NA, MB, Urar.; MA *rab(i) ḫ.* "military commander"; < *ḫarādu* IV or Hurr.?

ḫurādu II mng. unkn. j/NB ((part of) a plant)?

ḫuralbu, *ḫurallu* "bed" jB lex.

ḫurāpu(m), Nuzi also *ḫirāpu*; f. *ḫurāptu* "spring lamb" O/jB, M/NA [SILA$_4$.NIM, f. KIR$_{11}$.NIM; Ass. (MUNUS.)UDU.NIM; NA also (MUNUS.) NIM] OB also PN; Nuzi in *kalūmu ḫ.*; Nuzi also "kid" of goat; < *ḫarāpu* I

ḫurāṣānum; f. *ḫurāṣānītum* 'goldie' **1.** OA, OB as (f)PN [OA KÙ.GI-] **2.** jB lex. (a bird, phps.) "goldfinch"; < *ḫurāṣu*

ḫurāṣu(m) "gold" [KÙ.GI; OA also KÙ.KI] *nappāḫ ḫ.* "goldsmith", *ēpiš ḫ.* "gold-worker"; as valuable substance; as PN

ḫurātu(m) pl. tant. "ladder" O/MA

ḫûratu(m), Mari also *ḫawuratum*? "madder (*Rubia tinctorum*)" Bab., M/NA [GIŠ.ḪAB] as shrub; as drug; esp. in dyeing wool, leather

ḫura'u mng. unkn. Nuzi, desig. of grain; < Hurr.

ḫurbabillu, *urbabillu* "chamaeleon"? jB [BAR.GÙN.GÙN.NU]; med. fat of *ḫ.*

ḫurbakkannu, ḫurba(q)qannu → *ḫarbakkannu*

ḫurbāšu(m) "frost; terror" O/jB [MIR.SES] "hoar-frost" and sim.; med. "shivering, cold tremors"; "terror, panic"; "fearsomeness"; > *naḫarbušu*

ḫurbiwu → *ḫarwiu*

ḫurbu "desert" NB; < Aram.

ḫurdatānu "like a *ḫurdatu*" NB of date palm; < *ḫurdatu* I

ḫurdatu(m) I "cross-beam" jB of yoke-shaft, house; tamarisk; > *ḫurdatānu*

ḫurdatu(m) II "female pudenda" Bab., NA; learned etym. *ḫurri-dādu* "hole of love"

ḫurdu(m) I; OB pl. f. "door mat" O/jB i.e. door made from mat; < *ḫarādu* III

ḫurdu(m) II "posthumous child" Ass.

ḫurḫadû → *ḫarḫadû*

ḫurḫudum → *ur'udu*

ḫurḫummatu(m) "foam, scum" O/jB, NA on water, beer, oil etc.

ḫurḫuppu, *urruppu*, *urrumbum* (a vessel with knobs)? O/jB lex.

ḫurḫurātu, NA *ḫuḫḫu/arāte* pl. (a red dye) M/jB, NA
ḫurḫutūtu "arrow" Nuzi; < Hurr.?
ḫuriānum → *ḫurium*; *uriyānu*
ḫuribtu; pl. *ḫurbātu* "desert" M/NB, NA often pl.; < *ḫarābu*
ḫurinum mng. unkn. OB(Susa)
ḫurium, *ḫuriānum* (a spice) OAkk(Ur III)
ḫurīzu I; pl. *ḫurīzā/ētu*, *ḫurīzena* "villa, palace" Nuzi; < Hurr.
ḫurīzu(m) II (a stone) OB, Ug.; = *urīzu* ?
ḫurmu (or *ḫarmu*) (a plant) jB lex.
ḫurnûm → *urnû*
ḫurpalû → *ḫuppalû*
ḫurpatum, *ḫuruppatum* ~ "tent" Mari; → *ḫuruppu*
ḫurpu(m), *ḫuppu*; OB pl. f. ~ "blood clot" O/jB; < *ḫarāpu* II
ḫurpū pl. "early crop" OB; also sg.?; < *ḫarāpu* I
ḫurpušḫu → *ḫuprušḫu*
ḫurratu "hole" NA of mongoose; < *ḫurru* nom. unit.
ḫurratu → also *murratum*
ḫurri, *ḫur* "ever (after)" O/jB, NA; OB "for ever"; NA *ana ḫur*, mostly *aḫ-ḫur* "(t)hereafter", "else, furthermore"
ḫurru(m); NA pl. f. "hole" OAkk, Bab., M/NA [ḪABRUD(.DA)] in wall, door etc.; "burrow" of animal; "ravine"; "cave, mine"; *ḫ. pî* "mouth cavity"; > *ḫurratu*; → *ḫarāru*; *ḫurdatu* II; *iṣṣūru*
ḫurrupu, NA *ḫarrupu* "(very) early"? NB; NA of kind of wine; < *ḫarāpu* I
ḫurruru(m) "deeply incised" O/jB of feature on liver; also PN; < *ḫarāru*
ḫurruṣu(m) "furrowed, incised" Bab. as PN; < *ḫarāṣu*
ḫurrušu "bound" M/jB lex.; also as PN; < *ḫarāšu* II
ḫurrutu → *murrutu*
ḫursāniš → *ḫuršāniš*
ḫursānu(m), *ḫuršānu* "river ordeal" Bab., NA [NB ḪUR.SAG] "place of ordeal", *ana ḫ. alāku/šapāru*; "ordeal procedure"; OB as DN; (name of plant)
ḫursānu → also *ḫuršānu*
ḫursennu → *ḫarsapnu*
ḫurṣatu (a plant) jB lex.
ḫuršāniš, *ḫursāniš* "like a mountain" j/NB; < *ḫuršānu*
ḫuršānu, *ḫursānu* "mountain(s)" M/NB often pl. [ḪUR.SAG (earlier = *šadûm* I)]; Bogh. "siege mound"; < Sum.; > *ḫuršāniš*
ḫuršānu → also *ḫursānu*
ḫuršiānum m. & f. "package" OA
ḫuršu(m), *uršu*; OA pl. f. "(kitchen) storeroom, larder" Ass., OB lex., Mari; *bīt ḫ.* in temples "storehouse"; → *guršu* I
Ḫuršub(i)um (a month) OB(Susa)
ḫurtu → *ḫartu*
ḫūru I "son" jB lex.; < Hurr.
Ḫūru II (a month) Nuzi; < Hurr.
ḫūru → also *ūru* III
ḫurūgu (a goose)? jB lex.
ḫuruḫaru, *ḫuruḫuru* mng. unkn. MA, jB
ḫuruḫuru, NA *ḫuḫḫuru*; pl. *ḫuruḫurātu*, NA *ḫuḫḫarāte* (a kind of bread) M/NA
ḫuruḫuru → also *ḫuruḫaru*
ḫuruppatum → *ḫurpatum*
ḫuruppu(m) **1.** "(metal) dish" M/NA pl. f.; for betrothal feast **2.** "pelvic basin" of ox; NB as cut of meat; part of constellation
ḫurūrum → *ḫarīru*
ḫuruššu (a vegetable) jB lex.
ḫurzazātu (a kind of tube)? jB lex.
ḫurzīnum → *urzīnu*
ḫurzuḫurza → *murzumurza*
ḫusarikku → *kusarikku*
ḫusārum, *ḫušārum* "haematite"? OA, traded; material of seal; pl. m. "h. pieces"; also as PN
ḫusā'ū → *ḫušû*
ḫusīgu, Ass. *k/gusīgu*, jB also *agusīgu* (a stone) M/NA, jB
ḫusīnu (a commodity) NA, in *ša-ḫ.-šu* "*ḫ.* man"
ḫusirtum "broken piece" of reed OB math.; < *ḫasāru*
ḫusmānu → *ḫašmānu*
ḫussû (a vessel) NB; < *ḫesû* ?
ḫussuru(m) "broken off" etc. O/jB; OB lex. of person, "with broken teeth"; OB (desig. of copper), "scrap pieces"?; jB lex. "dilapidated" oven; < *ḫasāru*
ḫusû I (a kind of owl) jB lex.
ḫusû II mng. unkn. jB astr.; < *ḫesû* ?
ḫusuḫusu (a child's game) MB
ḫusukû → *ḫušukû*
ḫuṣābu(m) "twig, branch; stick, splinter" Bab., M/NA "twig" of tree, NB "rib" of palm-frond; (wooden) "peg", "stick" for plough, ship etc.; "off-cut", "chip, splinter" of worthless item; NB gener. "(fire)wood"; NB, as PN; < *ḫaṣābu* II
ḫuṣannu; NB pl. also f. "sash, belt" j/NB [TÚG.NÍG.ÍB.LÁ] worn around hips; also for divine statues; → *ḫuzūnu* II
ḫuṣṣu; pl. f. (a kind of reed hut) M/NB, NA; M/NB also as PlN; > *ḫaṣāṣu* II

ḫuṣṣu → also *ḫūṣu*

ḫuṣṣuṣu, Ass. *ḫaṣṣuṣu*, pl. *ḫaṣṣaṣūte* "snapped off" jB, NA of reeds; < *ḫaṣāṣu* I

ḫūṣu, *ḫuṣṣu* ~ "pain" jB in *ḫ. ḫīp(i) libbi* ~ "stomach pains"

ḫušaḫḫu(m), *kušaḫḫum* "need, shortage; famine" [SU.GU$_7$] "shortage" of grain, straw; OA "needs, requirement"; "neediness, famine"; *šanat ḫ.* "famine year"; "starvation" as illness; < *ḫašāḫu*

ḫušakašu "disposal, disposition" of s.o.? Nuzi; < Hurr.

ḫušālum mng. unkn. OA

ḫušānum (part of ship) OB lex.; < Sum.

ḫušārum → *ḫusārum*

ḫušāšum "rejoicer" OB, as PN; < *ḫašāšu* I

ḫušā'ū → *ḫušû*

ḫušauru/û "prisoner" Nuzi; < Hurr.; > *ḫušaurūtu*

ḫušaurūtu "captivity" Nuzi; < *ḫušauru*

ḫušinu "strength" NB of men; < Aram.

ḫušranni "all humanity" jB lex.

ḫušria (a magical formula) jB

ḫuššu "salve" jB in *ḫuš šamni* "salve of oil"; < *ḫašāšu* II ?

ḫuššû(m) "red" [ḪUŠ.A; OA ḪU.SA ?] epith. of gold, copper; of garment; of pig, honey etc.; < Sum.; → *ḫūšu*; *ruššû*

ḫuššulu(m) "crushed, bruised" O/jB of injured, damaged person; OB as PN; jB of newborn child; < *ḫašālu*

ḫuššurannu mng. unkn. Nuzi (desig. of cart-yoke); < Hurr.

ḫuštuppu → *ḫultuppu*

ḫušû(m), O/MA *ḫušā'ū*, *ḫusā'ū* pl. tant. ~ "(metal) scraps"; < *ḫašû* IV

ḫūšu(m) "red (colour)" O/jB of garment; of glowing oven; → *ḫuššû*

ḫušuātu "strength" jB lex.

ḫušuḫḫu (a garment) Nuzi; < Hurr.?

ḫušukû, *ḫusukû* pl. (part of horse harness) MA, NB

ḫušumma in *ḫ. epēšu* "to tie up (to)" Nuzi, animal, hand, wheel; < Hurr.

Ḫutalše (a month name) Nuzi; < Hurr.; → *Ḫutizzi*

ḫutapalû → *ḫuppalû*

ḫutebānu → *ḫutibānu*

ḫutennu → *ḫetennu*

ḫutenzû vb. "to be(come) lame"? jB lex.; → *ḫunzû*

ḫutḫummu → *ḫudḫummu*

ḫutḫutu (a commodity) MB(Alal.); → *ḫudḫudum*

ḫutibānu, *ḫutebānu* (an official) NB; < OPers.?

Ḫutizzi (a month) Alal.; → *Ḫutalše*

ḫutmu, *ḫumtu* (a bird) jB lex., om.

ḫutnu ~ "(legal) guardian" NA; also in PNs; < *ḫatānu*

ḫutnû → *ḫetennu*

ḫutpalû → *ḫuppalû*

ḫutpu(m) "arrowhead" O/jB of bronze, for *šiltāḫu*

ḫuttu (a storage vessel) M/NB for grain, liquid

ḫuttumumma in *ḫ. epēšu* "to enclose" Nuzi; < Hurr.

ḫuttutu "louse ridden" jB lex.; → *ḫatītu*; *kuttutu*

ḫutugu (an implement) NA

ḫutul (a magical formula) jB

ḫutūlu(m); OA pl. f. (an object) OA, jB lex.

ḫuṭartu, NB also *ḫuṭaštu* "stick, staff" M/NB, NA in king's hand; for beating s.o.; NB "staff(-shaped mark)" on slave; < *ḫuṭāru*

ḫuṭāru, NB also *ḫuṭūru* "branch, stick; staff" j/NB, NA [GIŠ.GIDRU] NA in *ša ḫ.* (an official); NB (a type of soldier); NB also ^{d}*Ḫ.*, deified in cult; > *ḫuṭartu*

ḫuṭaštu → *ḫuṭartu*

ḫuṭṭi(m)mānu "snouty" MB, as PN; < *ḫuṭṭimmu*

ḫuṭṭimmu, *ḫulṭimmu* "snout" j/NB of pig, dog, ape; NB as cut of meat; > *ḫuṭṭimmānu*

ḫuṭūru → *ḫuṭāru*

ḫū'u → *ḫū'a*

ḫuzālu(m), *uzālu*; f. *(ḫ)uzālatum*, *uzāltum* "gazelle kid" [AMAR.MAŠ.DÀ]; also as PN

ḫuzīqatu → *ḫazīqatu*

ḫuzīrānum "Piggy" OB, as PN; < *ḫuzīru*

ḫuzirtu "sow, female pig" MA, as fPN; jB/NA lex. in *ḫ. eqli* (a kind of cricket); < *ḫuzīru*

ḫuzīru(m) "pig" Ass.; as PN also OAkk; > *ḫuzīrānum*, *ḫuzirtu*

ḫuzūnu I (an object) Am., in gold

ḫuzūnu II; pl. f. (a garment) NA; → *ḫuṣannu*

ḫuzzi (a linen garment) Am.

ḫuzzû → *ḫunzû*

ḫuzzumu(m) "mutilated" Bab., of person with imperfect physical/facial feature; < *ḫazāmu*

I

i "let's; come on" O/jB cohort. ptcl. before 1 pl. pret., *i nillik* "let's go"; also in question "should we ...?"; occas. before 3 f. pret. (*i ta/tu-*)

i → also *ina*

-ī "my" (1 sg. pron. suff.) (→ GAG §42); → *-a*; *-ā* I; *-ya*

ia'u → *ya'u*

ibaḫu, *ebaḫu* "womb" jB lex.

ibāru (a mark on skin) jB; *aban ibāri* (a stone); < *ebēru* II

ibašši → *bašû* G

ibbaru → *imbaru*

ibbiltu (or *ippiltu*) (a bird) jB lex.

ibbû I, *ebbûm* 'day of wrath', "19th day of month" O/jB; < Sum.

ibbûm II, *imbû* "loss" O/jB of grain, in commerce; < Sum.

ibḫu (or *ipḫu*) (a kind of bug) jB lex.

ibīḫu → *ebīḫu*

ibilu "camel, dromedary" jB, NA [ANŠE.A.AB.BA]

ibinna → *binna*

ibissā'ū → *ibissû*

ibissu → *ebissu*

ibissû(m); OA pl. *ibissā'ū* "(financial) loss" OA, O/jB [I.BÍ.ZA] *i. amāru(m), i. dagālu(m)* "to suffer a loss"; < Sum.

ibītu "pus" jB lex., med.; < *ebû* II

iblakku (a thin beer) jB lex.; < Sum.

ibratu(m), NA gen. *ibriti* "(outdoor) cult niche" Bab., NA [UB.LÍL.LÁ]

ibrētu pl. tant. "radius and ulna" jB lex. (liter. 'friends'); < *ibru*

ibru(m), Ass. *ebru(m)* "friend, colleague" [KU.LI]; > *ibrētu, ibrūtu*; → *abāru* III

ibrûm "sealed document" OB [KIŠIB.ÍB.RA]; < Sum.

ibrūtu, OA *ebaruttum* "friendship"; OA "group of partners"; jB "friendship, partnership"; "alliance"; < *ibru* abstr.

ibšu (or *ipšu*) "mat" jB of palm fronds, reeds; NB *ēpiš i.* "mat-weaver" [LÚ.SU.TAG.GA], as family name; < *epēšu*

ibūru → *ebūru*

Id, *Ittu*? "River(-god)" O/jB, M/NA [^{d}ÍD; ^{d}ÍD.LÚ.RU.GÚ] *ana I. alākum* "to go to the river-ordeal"; also term.-adv. *Idiš* jB; *ša Id* "ferryman" jB lex.; < Sum.

idānu → *edānu*

idāšūš, *dāšūš*, *tāšūš* (a creepy-crawly, liter.) '60 arms'? jB lex.; < *idu* + *šūši* ?

idatu → *ittu* I

idatūtu mng. uncl. NB

idā'um → *edû* II

iddanna, *inadanna* "if necessary, at a pinch; in any case" OB; < *ina* + *dannatu* ?

iddāt etc. → *dāt*

iddum; pl. f. ~ "sharp end, point" OB of tool; < *edēdu*

iddû → *iṭṭû*

idiltu "locking, lock-up" jB; < *edēlu*

idīnum → *edinu*

īdīnu → *ēdēnu*

idiptu "wind, gust" M/jB; also illness of cattle; Am. ^{d}*i.* as demon; < *edēpu*

idirtu(m), *edirtu(m)*, Mari ḪI-... , NB *idištu* "misery, trouble; dismay" Bab.; < *adāru* II

idišam "side by side, in columns" OB of writing on tablet; < *idu*

īdiššī- → *wēdiššī-*

idištu → *idirtu*

idītu (a kind of mash) jB lex.

idrānu(m) (or *itrānu(m)*); pl. f. "potash" Bab. [NIMUR(=KI.NE); MUN.NIMUR.RA] "salt" on saline fields; < *idru* I

idru I (or *itru*) "saltpetre" M/jB "salt" on saline fields, walls; also med.; > *idrānu*

idru II (or *itru*) (a band, belt) Am., Bogh., jB lex.

idru → also *adru* II

idu(m); pl. m. & f. "arm; side; strength; wage" [Á; DA] **1.** "arm" of person; freq. du.; OB PN *Issu-kabit* "His arm is heavy", *idīn šakānum* "to exert pressure"; *šipir idišu* "his handiwork"; "handle" of tool; "wing" of bird **2.** "side" of person, *i.* (acc.) *alāku, izuzzu* "to go, stand at" s.o.'s "side", "help"; → *naparkû* II, *saḫāru*, *târu* D; *idi ana idi* "on each side"; as prep. *idi/ē* (acc.) "by, next to", *ana/ina i.* "to/at" s.o.'s "side", + loc.-adv. e.g. *iduššu* "at his side"; pl. f. *idāt* "round about, all around" (→ *dāt*) **3.** transf. "strength", *ina idika* "according to your ability" **4.** "purpose, reason", *idāt lemuttim* "evil intentions"; *ina lā idim* "groundlessly"; OB *i. rašûm* ~ "to be set aside", *i. šuršûm* "to put s.th. off, give low priority" **5.** "wage, rental" m. pl., NB f.pl.; OB, NB occas. sg. "wages, pay" of craftsman, of hired worker; "rental, payment for hire" of animal; boat, cart; house, store; > *ittu* I; *idāšūš*; *idišam*

idû → *edû* II

idugallu "head doorkeeper" j/NB [(LÚ.)NI.GAB. GAL] of deity "doorkeeper" of the nether world; NB in cult; < Sum.

id'umu (a lance) jB lex.; → *da'īmu* II

idûtu → *edûtu*

igāriš "like a wall" jB; < *igāru*

igartum, OB also *ikartum* "(a single) wall" OA, OB; for pl. → *igāru*; < *igāru* nom. unit.

igāru(m); pl. f. "wall" [É.GAR$_8$; IZ.ZI; OB rarely I.IZ.ZI, É.ZI, SIG$_4$.ZI] of house, garden; "side" of boat; < Sum.; > *igāriš, igartum*

igbu → *eqbu*

igerrû → *egerrû*

igertu → *egertu*

igiarû (a mathematical term) jB lex.; < Sum.

igiballu ~ "orchard"? jB lex.; < Sum.

igibrû "storm" jB lex.; < Sum.

igibû(m) "reciprocal of reciprocal" Bab. [IGI.BI] math.; < Sum.

igidalû, *igidarû* "with a single eye" as birth defect OB; < Sum.?

igidûm (a list) OB; < Sum.

igigallu(m), *kigallu* "wisdom, wise man" Bab. [IGI.GÁL] O/jB "wisdom"; j/NB "wise one", epith. of god, king; MB(Alal.) (an official)?; < Sum.

igigallūtu, *gigallūtu* "wisdom" j/NB [IGI.GÁL-]; < *igigallu*

Igigû "the (ten) great gods" O/jB; "the gods of heaven" M/NB [^{d}NUN.GAL(.MEŠ)]

igigubbû(m) "coefficient" Bab. math. [IGI.GUB(.BA)]; < Sum.

igimtu "anger, rage" jB; < *agāmu*

iginutukû "blind" jB [IGI.NU.TUKU]?; < Sum.; or → *nāṭilu* ?

igirû(m) "heron" O/jB [ÍGIRA.MUŠEN; I$_5$.GAR. MUŠEN]

igisû(m), *gisû* "contribution, gift" Bab. [IGI.SÁ] OB "(annual) dues" from priests, merchants; "gift, present" for god, king; < Sum.

igiṣigallatu (a priestess) jB lex.; < Sum.

igiṣītu, *egiṣītu(m)* (a priestess) O/jB; < Sum.

igišgulû "finest olive-oil" jB lex.; < Sum.

igištûm "the very first" OB lex. [IGI.DU]; < Sum.; → *geštû*

igitennum "fraction; quotient" OB [IGI.TE(.EN)] math.; < Sum.

igītu → *egītu*

igium → *igû* I 2

igizaggû, igizangû → *egizaggû*

igru(m) "hire, wage" Ass., O/jB for worker; OA pl. tant.; for rental of house, boat, store; < *agāru*

igu → *egu*

igû(m) I **1.** "eye" jB **2.** OB also *igium* "reciprocal" Bab. [IGI] math.; < Sum.

igû II "prince, leader" jB lex.; < Sum.

īgu → *īku*

igulû(m) "fine ointment, oil" Bab. [Ì.GU.LA]; < Sum.

iḫenunnakku 'oil of plenty' = "precious oil" jB for door; < Sum.

iḫḫisannu → *ḫisannu*

iḫzētu(m) pl. tant. "decorative inlay, studding" O/jB [U.GÙN] of garment, metal work, stone; < *iḫzu* I

iḫzu(m) I **1.** "learning, education" Bab. [NÍG.ZU] for craftsmen, singers etc.; pl. "instructions, precepts" **2.** freq. pl. "setting, mount" for precious stone; < *aḫāzu*; > *iḫzētu*

iḫzu II "whip" jB lex.

i'iltu → *e'iltu*

ikartum → *igartum*

ikiltu → *iklu* II

ikimtu "atrophied part" jB ext. [KAR ?]; < *ekēmu*

ikīsu → *ikīšu*

īkiš "like a ditch" jB; < *īku*

Ikišītu "Kiš canal" jB lex.; < Sum.

ikīšu, *ikīsu* (a subordinate family-member) jB lex., NA?

ikkānû "your(s)" (pl.) NA; < *ikkû*

ikkaru(m), Nuzi also *inkaru*; pl. usu. f. "farmer, ploughman" [(LÚ.)ENGAR] M/NA, NB *rab ikkarāti* "overseer of farmers"; as epith. of king; as desig. of king during occupation of throne by substitute; as PN; OB, Nuzi "farm-inspector, estate manager", also desig. of plough animal; Bab. also *mār i.* "member of the *i.* class"; < Sum.

ikkarūtu(m) "farming; ploughing, cultivation" OB, Nuzi [ENGAR-]; < *ikkaru*

ikkê → *kē*

ikkêm → *kīam*

ikkibu(m) "taboo" Bab., NA [NÍG.GIG] ref. to object, action; jB *i. ilī/DN* "anathema to gods/DN"; *i. akālu* "to break a taboo"; "(consequence of breaking) taboo, misfortune"; ref. to s.th. preserved, protected by deity; s.th. offensive to, forbidden by deity, king; *lū ikkibkunu* "let it be taboo to you"; < Sum.

ikkillu(m), *killu(m)* "lamentation; clamour, uproar" Bab., NA [AKKIL] of army, child, mourner; of thunder, earthquake; "cry" of animals, birds; < Sum.; → *angillu*

ikkiltu (an object of gold) Qatna

ikku(m) I ~ "mood, temperament" Bab., NA *i. karû/arāku* "to be short-tempered/long-suffering"; usu. "bad temper, malice"; *bēl(et) i.* "ill-tempered (wo)man"

ikku II "door" jB lex.; < Sum.

ikkû "your(s)" (sg.) NA; > *ikkānû*; → *kû*

Ikkukku → *ikūku*

ikkūm → *kūm*

ikkurratu → *iškurratu*

iklallû (a kind of door) jB lex.; < Sum.

iklātu f. pl. (an object) Alal. in list

iklētu → *ekletu*; *eklu*

iklu I "darkness" jB in *i. pānī* "gloominess"?; < *ekēlu*

iklu II, *ikiltu* "victim" (of disease, predator) jB lex. of animals; < *akālu*

iknusum (an object) OA

ikparum (an ornament) OAkk, OB

ikribu(m) "prayer, dedication; blessing" [ŠÙD; SÍSKUR] "prayer", *i. qabû/šemû/leqû* "to say/hear/accept prayer", *ša i.* "supplicant", *bīt i.* "house of prayer, temple"; esp. OA, OB pl. "votive gifts"; "blessing" by person on deity, king; for long life etc.; < *karābu* II

iksû (or *ikzû*) (a door) jB lex.

ikṣum (or *ikzum*) mng. unkn. OAkk

ikû(m) "field"; (a measure of area) Bab., MA [IKU] **1.** OB "cultivated field" **2.** (an area, c. 60×60 metres, = 100 *mūšar*) [NB also AŠ.IKU]; OB math. (a vol. measure, 1 cubit×1 *ikû*); MA also (a linear measure) **3.** the constellation "Pegasus" [MUL.AŠ.IKU]; < Sum.

ikû → also *ekû* I

īku(m), *ēku*, *īgu(m)* "dyke, ditch" OAkk, O/jB [E] "bank of earth"; "ditch, small canal"; also "plot surrounded by a dyke or ditch"; < Sum.; > *īkiš*

ikūku ~ "rancid oil" M/jB [Ì.ḪAB] med., as ointment; also MB *Ikkukku* as PN ?

ikzum → *ikṣum*

ikzû → *iksû*

ilālūtu → *ulālūtu*

ilānû "favoured by god, lucky" jB [DINGIR-]; < *ilu* + *-ān* + *-ī*

ilâtu → *elītu*

ilbuḫḫu → *ellabbuḫḫu*

ildakku ~ (a type of poplar) jB [(GIŠ.)ÍLDAG(=A.AM) (→ also *adāru* III)]; < Sum.

ildu → *išdu*; *ištu*; *wildum*

ilḫu (a garment)? jB lex.

ili → *eli*

iliānum, *iliyannum*, *i/eriānum*, *elânum*, jB *erânu* (a tree) O/jB lex.; → *iriyannu*; *riānum*

ilig/kulla → *elkulla*

ililum → *ēlilu*

ilimtumma in *i. epēšu* "to oblige, bind"? s.o. Nuzi; < Hurr.

ilippum → *eleppu*

iliš, *eliš* "to, on, like a god" OAkk, OA in PN + *takālum* "to trust in god"; jB "to" or "like god"; < *ilu*

ilittu "birth, offspring" M/NB [MB Ù.TU ?] "birth"; "origin" of god, person; *i. TN/PlN/bīti* etc. "born in, scion of TN/PlN/house", also of animals; < *walādum*

ilītu → *elītu*

iliyannum → *iliānum*

ilkakātu(m) **1.** Mari = *alkakātu* "ways, activities" **2.** NA secondary pl. of *ilku* I "(separate) *ilku* payments"; < *alāku*

ilku(m) I "(state) service" Bab., M/NA military or civilian service for state, NA, NB also for temple; *i. alākum* "to perform *ilkum*-service", *ilik šarri* "royal service", *kasap i.* "silver (paid in lieu) of *i.*"; OB, jB "*ilku*(-land)", also OB *bīt i.*; *i. aḫûm* "alien *i.* (performer)"; NA, NB "(contribution, payment in lieu of) *i.*", NA pl. → *ilkakātu* 2; < *alāku*; → *pilku* II

ilku II ~ "hip area" jB

illā "without" NB + gen., also *illânuššu* "without him"; < *ina* + *lā* (+ *-ān*)

illab(a)raya (a bird) jB

illabbuḫu → *ellabbuḫḫu*

illaggušu → *ellamkušu*

illakkunnu (part of a quiver) Nuzi, of silver

illa-mê → *ella-mê*

illāmu- → *ellāmu-*

illânu- → *illā*

illaru (a maltster's tool) jB lex.

illatu(m) I, also *illitu*, *allatu*, Ass. *ellutu(m)*, st. constr. *ella/et* "band, group" [ILLAT] "family group, clan", OAkk also "(god of) clan"; "band" of evildoers, of soldiers, *i. suppuḫu* "to scatter a band"; "team" of draft-animals, "pack" of dogs, lions etc.; OA, OB "trading caravan"; jB lex. *i. eqli* (a weed)

illatu II "rejoicing, celebration" jB; < *alālu* III

illātu pl. tant. "saliva" jB [ÚḪ.MEŠ] *i.-šu illakā* "his saliva flows"

illaya → *elleya*

illibbuḫu → *ellabbuḫḫu*

illīdiš → *līdiš*

illigu → *elligu*

Illil → *Ellil*

illilum → *ēlilu*

Illilūtum → *Ellilūtu*

illitu → *illatu* I

illu(m) I **1.** "partner, comrade" O/jB **2.** (desig. of quality) OB of cattle; NB of wool

illu II "high water, flood" O/jB lex.; < Sum.

illu → also *īlu* I.II

illukku, *i/ellūku* **1.** jB (a precious stone) also transf., as term of esteem **2.** jB lex. (a ceremonial robe); < Sum.

illûmi → *allû* II

Illūrānu, *Illūratum* → *illūru*

illurê, *illuru*, *eluri* (an exclamation) MA, jB; < Sum.

illurgišdilû ~ "throwing stick" jB; < Sum.

illūriš "like a (red) flower" jB; < *illūru*

illurtu "handcuffs" jB

illuru → *illurê*

illūru(m), *ellūru* (a flower) Bab. [Ú.NÍNDA] usu. red; med. as drug; *i. pānī* "rouge" for facial make-up; as PN, also *Illūrānu*, f. *Illūratum*; > *illūriš*

ilmiši → *elmēšu*

ilmu (or *ilmû*) (part of a quiver) Nuzi

ilmušu → *elmēšu*

ilpitu → *elpetu*

ilpum (a garment) Mari

ilqu, *ilqetu* "leech" jB

ilṣu I "loins" jB lex.

ilṣu II "joy" NA in *i. libbi*; < *elēṣu*

ilt... → also *išt...*

iltânu → *ištēn*

iltappu, *iltepītu*, *altapūtu* "loincloth" j/NB

iltât → *ištēn*

ilte(-) → *išti*

ilteltu → *ittiltu*

iltepītu → *iltappu*

iltēt(u) → *ištēn*

ilti → *ištu*

iltiltu → *ittiltu*

ilti(n)nû → *ištēnû*

iltīn(u), *iltīt(u)* → *ištēn*

iltu(m) I, *eltum* "goddess" OAkk, Bab., OA? [DINGIR; jB also DINGIR.MUNUS] also ref. to demon; to statue; < *ilu*

iltu II, Bogh. *eltu* "chaff" M/jB [IN.RI; IN.(NU.)RI] of cereal; "spikelet; awn" of grain

iltu → also *ištu*

iltuḫḫu, *iltuḫlu* → *ištuḫḫu*

ilu(m), *elu(m)*; pl. *ilū*, *ilānu* "god, deity" [DINGIR; jB NI; jB occas. DINGIR.NITA; OA also EL; pl. also DINGIR.DINGIR] "a" or "the god", also du.; personal "god", *i. išû(m)*, *i. rašû(m)* "to be, get lucky"; OA *bēl lā ilim*, jB *lā bēl ili* "luckless person"; ref. to divine statue, of metal, repaired, in ritual, plundered; OB divine symbols; demon, esp. *ilu lemnu*; mythical hero, deified king; *mārat i.* (a priestess) jB; > *iltu* I, *ilūtu*, *iliš*, *ilānû*; → *muštarīlu*; *rāšīlūtu*; *šerki-ilūtu*

ilû → *elû* II

īlum I (or *illum*); pl. m. & f. (a leather bag) OA, Mari; containing copper; sealed

īlu II, *illu* "reed bundle" M/jB

i'lu(m) **1.** OB "contract, bond" **2.** O/jB, MA [TÚG.SIG4.ZA; OB TÚG.GUZ.ZA ?] "band, binding"? for head, foot; of chair, bed; < *e'ēlu*

ilulaya (a camel)? OB lex.

ilūtu(m), *iluttu* "godhead, divinity" Bab., NA [DINGIR-]; in prayers *i.-ka* "your divinity", i.e. "you"; coll. = "the gods"; *bīt/bāb i.* "divine house/gate"; < *ilu*

ilûtu → *elûtu*

imampû (or *imampadû*) (a kind of list) jB lex.; < Sum.

imāru → *imēru*

imātu mng. unkn. jB lex.

imbâ → *embâ*

imbariš "like fog, cloud" jB; < *imbaru*

imbaru(m), *ibbaru(m)*, occas. *inbaru* "fog, mist" O/jB, NA [MURU9] also "fine drizzle"; > *imbariš*

imbu → *inbu*

imbû, *imbu'u* **1.** Bab. lex. "fibre" (of the date palm) **2.** *i. tâmti* [(NA4.)KA.A.AB.BA; occas. KA+GÍR.A.AB.BA] ~ "algae, scum" on sea

imbû → also *ibbûm* II

imbu'u (a small stone bottle) jB lex.

imbu'u → also *imbû*

imdu(m), j/NB also *indu* "support; imposition" **1.** transf. divine "support", esp. in PNs; Am., j/NB "(archit.) support, buttress" **2.** M/NA, j/NB "imposition, impost" **3.** jB (a piece of jewellery)?; < *emēdu*

imduḫallatu → *anduḫallatu*

imdullu "(clay) lid"? jB lex.; < Sum.

imertu → *amertu* I

imēru(m), *imī/āru(m)*, Ass. *emāru(m)* "donkey" [ANŠE; DÙR; Nuzi also ANŠE.NITA] *ša i.*, NA *ša i.-šu* "donkey driver"; jB "donkey" figurine; Ass., N.Mes. 'donkey-load' (a measure of capacity; a measure of area); *i. šamê* 'sky donkey' (a bird); *i. ḫašî(m)* 'lung donkey' (a part of the liver); *i. eleppi/yāšibi* (a part of ship/ram); > *imērūtum*; → *ḫimāru*

imērūtum "donkey stock" Mari [ANŠE.ḪI.A-*ru-*]; < *imēru*

imgarrû (a kind of list) jB lex.; < Sum.

imgiddû (a single-columned tablet) jB lex., comm.; < Sum.; → *giṭṭu*

imgipû (or *imgipadû*) (a kind of list) jB lex.

imgiriašu → *ingirašu*

imgûm adj. mng. unkn. OB, also in PNs

imgurru; pl. f. "clay envelope" M/NB of cuneiform tablet; "mould" for frit; < Sum.

imḫulliš "like a storm" jB

imḫullu(m), *anḫullu* "destructive wind; storm" [IM.ḪUL]; < Sum.

imḫupû (a tablet) jB lex.; < Sum.

imḫur-ešrā, *-ašru/i/a*, *-ašna(n)*, *-ašla*, *anḫurašru* (a climbing plant) M/jB, NA [Ú.IGI.20]; folk etym. 'it withstands twenty (ailments)' < *maḫāru* + *ešrā*

imḫur-līm(i/e), *anḫullīme* (a medicinal plant) M/jB, NA [Ú.IGI.LIM]; folk etym. 'it withstands a thousand (ailments)' < *maḫāru* + *līm*

imigidû (a kind of list) jB lex.

imikānum (female animal that has given birth) OB lex.; < Sum.

imikkarūru(m) (a kind of grass)? O/jB lex.

imirtu "sight, view" jB *imratsunu mūtu* "sight of them is death"; < *amāru*

imirtu → also *amertu* I

imīru → *imēru*

imištu "contraction" jB med., *i. libbi* "contraction of the heart", i.e. appetite ?; < *amāšu*

imitta(m), *emittam* "on the right" OB, less freq. j/NB, NA [ZAG; 15; Á.ZI]; < *imittu* I acc.

imittu(m) I, *emittu(m)* "right side, the right" [ZAG; OB Á.ZI(.DA); j/NB, NA 15] gener. "the right", *i.-šu* "his right", *sippi i.* "the right-hand doorjamb"; "the right hand", also *qāt i.*; *i. ummāni* "right wing of army"; OB "(neighbour on) the right"; < *imnu*; > *imitta*

imittu(m) II, *emittu(m)* "support; imposition" **1.** transf. divine "support", esp. in PNs **2.** "shoulder" of animal [UZU.ZAG(.LU); OB also MURGU; jB also 15]; also as cut of meat **3.** (a kind of lance) [Ug. ZAG.LU] **4.** "imposition" MA of punishment; NB of tenancy dues; < *emēdu*

imītum mng. unkn. OB of cattle, flocks

imlûm (a cone shape)? OB math. [IM.LÁ]; < Sum.

immanakku, *imnanakku* (a kind of stone or sand) jB, NA [(NA4.)IM.MA.(AN.)NA]; < Sum.; → *amnakku*

immāniš "in daytime" OB; < *immu* + *-ān* + *-iš*

immat(i/e) → *mati*

immatī/ēma → *matīma*

immatimê → *matimê*

immertu(m), Ass. *emmertu* "ewe" Bab., NA? [UDU(.NÍTA)(*-tum*); (UDU.)U8; Nuzi UDU.MUNUS]; also as PN; < *immeru*

immeru(m), Ass. *emmeru(m)*; pl. m. & f. "sheep" [UDU; UDU.NÍTA] also specifically "male sheep, wether"; pl. "sheep; sheep and goats" [UDU.MEŠ; UDU.ḪI.A etc.]; *i. šamni* "fat sheep"; *i. marû(m)* "fattened sheep" [(UDU.)NIGA]; *i. šadî(m)* "mountain, wild sheep" [UDU.KUR(.RA); UDU.NÍTA.KUR]; also in PN; > *immertu*

immu(m) "heat (of day), daytime" O/jB opp. to night; *i. muṣlāli* "heat of midday"; < *emēmu*; > *immāniš*

immû "tablet, record" j/NB; < Sum.

immû → also *imû*

immugubbû (or *mugubbû*) "exercise tablet" jB lex.; < Sum.

immunedû (a kind of list) jB lex.

immunusu, *immunušu* 'female clay'? mng. uncl. jB lex.?; < Sum.

imna, *imnu* adv. "on the right" j/NB, NA [ZAG; 15]; < *imnu*

imnanakku → *immanakku*

imniš "on the right" jB [15-*iš*]; < *imnu*

imnitû 'male clay'? mng. uncl. jB lex.; < Sum.

imnītu "she on the right" (desig. of mother) jB lex.; < *imnû*

imnu(m) subst. "right (side, hand)" [ZAG; 15] st. abs. *ana imen* "on the right"; *imnukka* "in your right hand"; "right side", *imnuššu* "at his right"; > *imna*, *imniš*, *imnû*; *imittu* I, *imitta*

imnu → also *imna*

imnû(m); f. *imnītu* "(lying) on the right" O/jB [Á.ZI.DA; 15] of furniture, part of liver; jB lex. of *šubû*-stone; < *imnu*; > *imnītu*

Impurtanni (1st month at Nuzi); < Hurr.

imra/ātu → *imertu*; *imru*

imriqqu "clay sealing, bulla" jB lex.; < Sum.

imru "observation" jB; pl. f., mng. uncl.; < *amāru* I

imrû(m) I "fodder" O/jB [MUR.GUD] for animal-fattening; < *marû* II

imrû II "family, clan" jB lex.; < Sum.

imsarmupadû (a kind of tablet) jB lex.; < Sum.

imsaršubbû → *saršubbbû*

imsuḫḫu "whirlwind" jB lex.; also lit. [IM.SÙḪ]?; < Sum.

imšu ~ "stiffness"? jB in *i. qāti* "*i.* of the hand"; < *amāšu*

imšu → also *emšu*

imšuguppû ~ "list of required materials" OB, jB lex.; < Sum.

imšukku "(bun-shaped?) exercise tablet"? jB [IM.ŠÚ]; < Sum.

imtanû "tuft of black hair" jB lex.; from donkey's rump; → *imû*

imtu(m) "poison" Bab., ref. to poisonous spittle of demons etc.; "venom" of snake, scorpion; *imat marti* "gall"; *imat mūti* "deadly poison"

imtuḫallatu → *anduḫallatu*

imtuḫsum, *intuḫšum* (a container) OAkk(Sum.)

imṭû, *inṭû* **1.** pl. tant. jB "loss(es)" in business etc.; *i. dāmi* "anaemia" **2.** jB (a cutting implement); < *maṭû* II; > *inṭatta*

imum (an implement) OB

imu → also *emu*

imû, *immû*, *e(m)mû* "tuft of black hair" jB lex.; from donkey's head; → *imtanû*

imûtum mng. unkn. OB

imzidû (a kind of list) jB lex.; < Sum.

ina, *in* (*im-m...*, *ip-p...* etc.) "in, on; by; from" (freq. abbr. *in*, with assimilation of *n* to following consonant (OA often wr. *i*)) [AŠ; TA; Bogh. ŠÈ] **1.** of place "in, on"; of time "on, at", "during", *ina PN* "in the reign of PN"; before infin., *ina amārika* "when you see" **2.** of condition, *ina balāṭim* "in health" **3.** "among", *ina šarrāni* "of, among the kings" **4.** "from, out of", *ina qāt PN* "from the hand of PN" **5.** "by means of, with" tool, weapon etc.; word, incantation; "with, out of" material (brick, stone) **6.** "in consequence of, as a result of", *ina maḫāṣim* "because of beating"; *ina qibīt DN* "at DN's command" **7.** "with respect to; according to", "(measured) by" cubit, *sūtu* etc. **8.** *ina lā* (→ *illā*) "in, because of the absence of", *ina lā idê* "unwittingly" **9.** conj. + stat. subjunct. "so long as", *ina balṭu u šalmu* "while alive and well"

inadanna → *iddanna*

inanna, after prep. also *inanni* "now" OAkk, Bab. absol., and after prep., *adi i.* "till now", *kīma i.* "right now", *ištu i.* "henceforth" etc.; < *ina* + *anna*; → *enenna*; *innannu*; *kīnanna*

inannû (a cry to Sîn) jB lex.; < Sum.; → *iutû*

inânû "very busy" jB; < *inû*

inbaru → *imbaru*

inbu(m), *enbu*, *imbu*; NB pl. also f. "fruit, flower; sexual appeal" [GURUN] "fruit, flower" of tree, plant; *inib (pān) šatti(m)* "*i.* of spring"; *i. kirî* "orchard fruits"; "fruit tree"; "fruit, flower(-shaped jewellery)"; ref. to moon-god, *i. bēl arḫi*; transf. of humans "offspring", esp. in PNs; "(sexual) attractiveness"; > *enēbu*; → *šubultinbi*

indu → *imdu*; *undu* I

induḫallatu → *anduḫallatu*

induḫḫatu mng. unkn. jB lex.

indūru (a waterskin) jB lex.

inedukku → *unnedukkum*

ingâ, *innigâ* "right now" NB; < *ina* + *agâ*

ingallu → *niggallu*

ingana "come on!" Am.; → *gana*

ingara/is/šu → *ingirašu*

ingippu mng. unkn. jB

ingirâšu, *inga/irâ/îs/šu*, MA *imgiriāšu*, NA also *ingiriāšu* (a fruit tree) M/NA, j/NB

ingirēnu → *ingurēnu*

ingiriāšu → *ingirašu*

ingu (part of a plough) jB lex.

ingurēnu, *ingirēnu* (an object) NB; of metal; → *angurinnu*

ingūru ~ (an old garment) jB lex.

inḫu(m) I "hardship, trouble" O/jB, also pl.; < *anāḫu* I

inḫu II (a type of cultic song) MA, jB; > *anāḫu* II

īni → *ēni*; in *ana īni* → *mīnu* I

inimma, *inimmu* ~ "oh!" jB in lamentations

inimmû I, *enimmû* "word" jB(lit.); < Sum.

inimmû II "cup, bowl" jB lex.

inītu(m) I, *enītu(m)*, *inittum* "team of plough-oxen" O/jB; *iniāti illak* "he works with the plough-team"; "(cost of hiring) plough-team"; < *enû* III

inītu II (a secret language)? jB; < *enû* III ?

inītu III (a ship)? jB lex.

inkaru → *ikkaru*

innabu "luxuriant" jB lex.; < *enēbu*

inna(n)nu/a/i "now that, as soon as" jB conj. + stat. subjunct.; < *inanna*

innedukku → *unnedukkum*

innigâ → *ingâ*

inninnatu "Innin-goddess" jB as epith.; < Sum.

inninnu → *ennēnu*

innintu → *ennettu*

innu "look!" jB lex.

innû "ours" (poss. pron.) NA; → *niā'um*

innuḫarum → *annuḫaru*

inṣabtu → *anṣabtu*

inšiš ~ "deceitfully" OB in *i. lamniš*

inšu → *emšu*

intuḫšum → *imtuḫsum*

inṭatta "in need" NB in *i. šakin* "is in need"; < *imṭû* + *-atta*

inṭû → *imṭû*

inu I, *enu*, jB, NB(roy. inscr.) also *inum* "when" OAkk, Bab.(lit.) conj. + subjunct.; OAkk also prep., *inu RN* "at the time of RN"; → *inūma*; *inūšu*

inu(m) II (a stringed musical instrument) O/jB [GIŠ.GÙ.DÉ]

inû ~ "job, craft" jB; > *inânû*

īnu(m) I, OAkk, Ass. *ēnu(m)* f. "eye" [IGI(.2); pl. usu. IGI.2.MEŠ; Am. also IGI.ḪI.A] **1.** "eye" of god, human, animal; NA *ī. šakānu* "to pay regard to"; OB *īnka maḫārum* "to please you"; *ī. lemutti* "evil eye" **2.** transf. *īn alpi* lex. (a wine), OB math. (a geometrical figure); transf. "(spy-)hole" in oven, "mesh, interstice" of net, "thole"? of wheel, "bubble" in beer **3.** "spring, well", Ass. *rēš ēni* "source" **4.** "eye-stone" (desig. of ornamental stones), also fish-, bird-, pig-eye stones; → *damqam-īnam*

īnu II "wine" jB lex.

inūma, *enūma* "when" Bab. [UD] **1.** conj. + subjunct. "when" (Mari also + indic.) **2.** Bogh., Alal., Am. "that", *lū tīde i. šalim* "know that he is well" **3.** prep. "at the time of", *i. dawdêm* "at the time of the defeat" **4.** adv. M/NB "at that time" (→ *inūmīšu*); Am. "now" (for *anumma*); < *inu* I + *-ma*

inūmē, *inūmī* "when" OAkk, OA, rarely OB conj. + subjunct.; < *ūmu* I

inūmīšu "in those days; then" OA, OB, NB(roy. inscr.); OB *ištu/warki i.* "since then"; < *ūmu* I

inūmti → *ūmtum*

inunnakku "butter pot" jB lex.; < Sum.

inūšu, *enūšu*, NB also *inūš* "at that time, then" OAkk, Bab. [UD.BI] esp. in main clause after *inu(ma)*, *kī*; < *inu* I + *-šu*

inyānu (a metal object) NB

inzaḫ(u)rētu, lex. also *inzuḫirētu*, *inzurā/ētu* (a red dye) j/NB in pot; for textiles; also "*i.*-coloured (wool)"; < *ḫinzūru*

inzarû, *inzuruḫu* (an aromatic plant) Bogh., jB as drug

inzum → *enzu*

inzuḫirētu, *inzurā/ētu* → *inzaḫurētu*

inzūru → *ḫinzūru*

inzuruḫu → *inzarû*

ipḫu → *ibḫu*

ipiru → *eperu*

ipištu → *epištu*; *epšu*

ipišu/a → *epišum*

ipītu "clouding over" of eyes jB; < *apû* III

iplū, *eplū*, *iplētu* pl. tant. "exchange equivalent" Nuzi; < *apālu* I

ippāru → *appāru*

ippatu (a sea creature) NB *ša tâmti*

ippēru → *ippīru*

ippiltu → *ibbiltu*

ippīru, *ippēru* ~ "conflict, war" M/jB; < Sum.

ippitti → *pittu* I

ipqum "embrace, protection" OAkk, OB; of deity, in PNs; < *epēqu*

iprasakku (a Persian legal official) NB; < OPers.

ipru(m) "ration, subsistence allowance" [ŠE.BA] for person, family, animal; < *epēru*

ipru → also *eperu*

ipšiš → *ipšu*

ipšu(m), *epšu(m)* "deed, action; sorcery" [DÙ]; OA pl. "(building) works"; Mari "manufacture(d item)"; Am., Ug. "behaviour"; jB "(magical) activities; sorceries"; Bab., NA *i. nikkassī* "doing the accounts"; *i. pî(m)* "utterance, command", OB(lit.) *ipšiš pî* = *ana i. pî*; < *epēšu* II

ipšu → also *ibšu*

ipšur-līmu/e (a medicinal plant) jB lex.; folk etym. 'it undoes a thousand (ailments)' < *pašāru* + *līm*

iptennu, *iptē/īnum* "meal(-time)" O/jB; < *patānu* I

iptu(m) f., st. constr. *ipat* "luxuriance" Bab. *i. kibrātim* "the wealth of the world"; jB "luxuriant" (a plant name)

ipṭiru(m), *ipṭeru(m)* "ransom (money)" O/MA, O/jB freq. pl.; for person, for goods; of person as ransom for other person; < *paṭāru*; → *napṭiru*

ipu(m) "membrane; afterbirth" O/jB, MA? [ÙŠ] "film" on oil; "membrane" in intestines; "placenta" of animal; "blinkers" for horse

iqbīnu mng. uncl. jB lex.

iqnû → *uqnû*

iqūpu → *uqūpu*

ir... → also *er...*

irâ → *iria*

irana mng. unkn. Nuzi

irarazakku "lamentation prayer" jB lex.; < Sum.

iratu → *irtu*

irbu → *erbu* I

irdu (a disease of sheep) jB lex.

irdu → also *išdu*

ir'emum "loved one" OAkk; < *râmu* II

irḫu ~ "aggressiveness, insolence" jB in *iriḫ pîšu* "*i.* of his mouth"; < *erēḫu*

iria, *aria*, *e/irâ* adv. "side by side" Bab. usu. of parts of liver

iriānu → *iliānum*; *iriyannu*

irima'u (or *italma'u*) (a copper object) Nuzi; < Hurr.

irimmu(m) "bead (necklace)" OB, Qatna; → *erimmatu*

irimmu → also *erimmu* I

iripu → *eripu*

irištu → *erištu* II

irīšu → *erīšu*

irītu "guidance"? jB; < *warûm* II ?

iri'u, *erû* "dregs, lees" jB of beer

iriya(n)nu/a (a plant) jB lex.; → *iliānum*

iriyātu → *eriyātu*

irpi (an Egyptian official) Am.; < Eg.

irṣiṣu mng. unkn. NA, a precious item

irtānû, *ištānû* "with breasts" jB transf. of date palm; < *irtu* I + *-ān* + *-ī*

irtu(m) I, *iratu(m)*, OAkk *ertum* "breast, chest" [GABA] of human, deity; du. esp. woman's "breasts"; transf. in battle *i. turru*, *i. ne'û* "to turn s.o.'s breast = put to flight", also refl. "to retreat"; of animal; as cut of meat; transf. "breastplate" as protection or ornament; "breast-piece" of animal's harness; "front" of chariot; "edge, frontage" of sea, building, bow; in prep. usages *ina i.* "opposite"; *ana i.* "towards, against"; > *irtānû*

irtu II (a kind of song) jB

iru mng. unkn. jB in *i. ša buqli* "*i.* of malt"

irûm → *erû* II

īru ~ "strong" jB lex.

isārum (or *iṣārum*) ~ "annexe, outbuilding" OA

isḫappu, *isḫabbu*, OB *ašḫappum* "villain, rogue" O/jB; < Sum.

isḫenabe → *išḫenabe*

isḫu(m) I f. "arm" O/jB of human; "fin, flipper" of fish; "wing" of bird; transf. "strength" jB lex.; → *ezēḫu*

isḫu II, MA *išḫu*; pl. f. *isḫā/ētu* "allocation" Bab., MA of offerings etc.

isḫunnatu(m), *išḫunnatu(m)*, *isḫunnu* "bunch of grapes" O/jB, NA [(GIŠ.)KIN.GEŠTIN]; OB, NB as fPN

isiḫtu(m), *esiḫtu(m)* "allocation" O/jB of commodities allocated to s.o.; OB *ṭuppi i.* "allocation document"; < *esēḫu*; → *isiktum*

isikku "hard"? jB lex. of clay; < Sum.

isiktum, *esiktum* "allocation" Mari, OB(Ešn.); < *esēḫu*; → *isiḫtu*

isiltu(m), *esiltu* ~ "swelling, inflation" O/jB med. of parts of body; of land, troops (an epidemic); < *esēlu*

isimmānu(m), *simmānû*, OB also *simannum* "ration (of flour and malt)" Bab. [ZÌ.MUNU3/4] an edible commodity; j/NB also "allocation, allowance" of military or building materials; < Sum.

Isinītu, *Išinītu* "the Isin canal" jB; < PlN

isinnu(m), *issinu(m)*, *iššinnu*; pl. f. "festival" Bab., M/NA [EZEN] *ūm i.* "feast-day"; *i. DN* "DN's festival", *i. MN* "festival of MN"; also transf. as desig. of battle; OB "festival (allocation of food)"; < Sum.

isinnu → also *assinnu*

isinnû → *assinnu*

isippum mng. unkn OB in *bīt i.*

isiqtu(m) "engraving, scratch" O/jB as incised design, mark on water-clock; < *esēqu*

isirtu I "incarceration" Nuzi; < *esēru* II

isirtu(m) II, *esirtu* "(debt-)collection" O/MB of silver, sheep etc.; < *esēru* III

isitātu → *asa'ītu*

isītu ~ "friendly discourse" M/NB of human, god; locust's "chirping"; < *esû* ?

isītu → also *asa'ītu*

iskimbu, iskimmu → *giskimmu*
ismarû → *azmarû*
ismekku → *ešmekku*
ispillurtu → *išpallurtu*
isqarrurtu → *išqarrurtu*
isqātu → *isqu*; *izqātu*
isqillatu → *išqillatu*
isqippu → *išqippu*
isqu(m), *išqu*, *ešqu*; pl. usu. f. "lot; share" Bab., NA [GIŠ.ŠUB.BA] **1.** *i. nadû* "to cast lots", *ina i. leqûm* etc. "to receive by lot", *i.* + *maqātum* "to fall" to (= *ana*) s.o. **2.** "share (assigned by lot)" of land, inheritance; (by divine disposition) of land, people; of temple income, office, esp. NB of prebends; *bēl i.* "prebendary" **3.** of attribute, rôle assigned to s.o. by destiny, deity **4.** (a musical interval sounded by lyre-strings 1+3); > *esēqu*
isqubbītu → *asqubbītu*
isqulālu → *ašqulālu*
isqūqu(m), *is/šquqqu* (a coarse flour or groats) O/jB [ZÌ.KUM] grindstone for *i.*; *akal i.* "*i.* bread"; < Sum.
isru(m) I (a small granary) O/jB lex.
isru II "exacted payment" M/NB; < *esēru* III
isru(m) III m. & f. (a part of the exta) O/jB
isru → also *išru* II
issaḫîš, *issaḫêš*, *issaḫayyiš(i)* "together" NA; < *issi* + *aḫîš*
issanu → *asnû*
issēn → *ištēn*
issēniš → *ištēniš*
issēnû → *ištēnû*
issēt → *ištēn*
issi → *išti*
issillatu → *išqillatu*
issinu → *isinnu*
issu (or *issutu*); pl. *i(s)sāte* "woman, wife" NA [MUNUS(.MEŠ)]; > *issūtu*; → *iššu*; *sinništu*
issu → also *isu*; *išdu*; *ištu*
issūtu (rôle of female) NA [MUNUS-]; < *issu*; jB → *sinnišūtu*
issurri, *issurru* "perhaps" NA; < *ina* + *surri*
istatirru; pl. *istatirrānu* "stater" NB Gk. coin; < Gk.
istuḫḫu → *ištuḫḫu*
isu(m), *issu* "jaw" O/jB [(UZU.)ME.ZÉ; SI] of human, animal; *i. šaplû* "lower jaw"; astr. in *is lê*, also *iš lê* "bull's jaw", the constellation Hyades [MUL.GIŠ.DA; MUL/MÚL.GU4.AN(.NA)]
isû → *ḫisû*
iṣārum → *isārum*

iṣratu, occas. *miṣratu* "plan, ground-plan" O/jB of building, field etc. *i. eṣēru*, *m. muṣṣuru* "to lay out plan"; < *eṣēru*; → *uṣurtu*
iṣṣabtum → *anṣabtu*
iṣṣēr → *ṣēru* 2
iṣṣu → *iṣu*
iṣṣūriš "like a bird" jB; < *iṣṣūru*
iṣṣurtu "female bird" j/NB [MUNUS.MUŠEN; AMA.MUŠEN] also as fPN; < *iṣṣūru*
iṣṣūru(m) occas. f.; pl. occas. f. "bird" [MUŠEN] wild, tame; *bīt i.* "poultry house"; *šammi i.* (a plant); *aban i.* (a stone); Nuzi "bird(-shaped vessel)"; ext. (feature of entrails); *i. rabû* "duck" [MUŠEN.GAL-*u*/*ú*], *i. sāmu*; in compounds: *i. appāri*, *ašāgi*, *badilli*, *ḫurri* ("rock-partridge"? [BURU5.ḪABRUD.DA]), *kirî*, *kīsi* ("swallow"?), *kubši*, *maškani*, *mê*, *mūši*, *šadî*, *še'i*, *šūri*, *šāri* ('wind-bird', i.e. "weather-cock"); > *iṣṣūriš*, *iṣṣurtu*
iṣu(m), *iṣṣu*, Ass. *e(ṣ)ṣu(m)*; pl. m. *iṣṣū*, OA also f. "tree; wood" [GIŠ] **1.** "tree", *i. kirî* "orchard-tree", *i. bilti* "fruit-bearing tree", *i. šadî* "mountain tree(s)"; Nuzi "woodland, grove" **2.** "wood, timber", "(piece of) wood" ref. to house-beam, "(shaft of) weapon, stake", "fetter"; "firewood"; → *izqātu*; *kātimiṣi*
īṣu → *wīṣum*
iṣurtu(m), M/NA *eṣurtu* "drawing, plan"; transf., divine, royal "design(s)"; OA "inscribed document, writing-board"; < *eṣēru*; → *uṣurtu*
iṣu(s)su mng. unkn. jB lex.
iš "to, for" Early Mari, OB(Diyala)
iš → also *isu*
-iš "to; like" term.-adv. suffix on subst.s and adj.s; → GAG §67
îš "where?" NB; < *ayyiš*; → *êš*; *mêš*
iša(ḫ)ḫu → *išḫu*
išānû ~ "important" M/jB lex.; usu. *lā i.* "powerless, poor" jB; < *išû*
išarma → *ašar*
išariš, Ass. *i/eš(e)riš*, jB also *mišariš* "correctly, normally", *i. apālu* "to answer, repay satisfactorily, satisfy" s.o., *i. alāku*, *i. dabābum*, OA *i. atwûm* "to conduct o.s., negotiate properly"; < *išaru* I; → *mišariš*
išartu(m), occas. *ušartu* "prosperity" O/jB; < *išaru* I
išaru(m) I, *išeru*, *eš(e)ru*, Ass. *eš(a)ru*, NB *mišaru* ? "straight; correct, normal" [SI.SÁ; occas. GIŠ] of clay, wool etc.; "right, just, righteous" of ways, sceptre, word; of deity, man; "fair, handsome" of looks; "in order" of

bowels; f. *išartu* (a musical interval sounded by lyre-strings 2+6); < *ešēru*; > *išaru* II; *išartu*, *išariš*, *išarūtu*, *išertum*?; → *mišaru*

išaru(m) II, M/jB also *(m)ušaru* "penis" O/jB [GÌŠ] of man, dog etc.; *appi i.* "glans penis"; < *išaru* I

išāru → *ešēru*

išarūtu(m) "correct state, normality" Bab. [SI.SÁ-] *i. alāku* "to flourish"; NB "righteousness"; < *išaru* I

išātiš "on fire, ablaze"; < *išātu*

išātu(m), Am. also *ešātu* f.; pl. f. *išātātu(m)* "fire" [IZI; M/NA freq. IZI.MEŠ] Am. *ša i.* of metal (a small brazier)?; "(bon)fire beacon" as signal; med. "inflammation"; OB (a disease of date palms)?; > *išātiš*

išbabtu ~ (a grass or weed) jB

išbum, *ešbum* (or *i/ešpum*) (a prof.) OAkk, also as PN

išburna[tu]? (or *išpurna[tu]*?) "pine cone" jB comm.

išdaḫḫum (a plot? of ground) OB

išdiḫu(m) I, *išdiḫḫu* "profit(able business)" O/jB [NÍG.ME.GAR]; < *šadāḫu*

išdiḫu II, *ašdiḫu* (a garment) jB lex.

išdu(m), *e/ušdu(m)*, OB also *ištum*, M/NB also *ildu*, *irdu*, NA *issu*; pl. f. "foundation, base" [SUḪUŠ (→ *šuršu*); OAkk, OB also DU; ÚR; DÚR] freq. du. **1.** "foundation" of building; transf. of throne, reign, land, city etc.; ref. to persons, "discipline" of troops, *bēl išdīn* "disciplined person"; "position, situation" of s.o. in life, esp. in PNs **2.** "base" of vessel, "hull, keel" of boat; "stand" for jars; "central part" of object; "stump, trunk" of tree; *i. šamê* "base of heaven", i.e. "horizon" [AN.ÚR] **3.** "root" of tree, plant, *i. nasāḫu* "to uproot" **4.** "base" of part of body, feature on liver; jB du. "legs" of person; > *išittu* II; *rašādu* ?

išdun mng. unkn. jB lex.

išennu, *išēnu* → *išīnu*

išeriš → *išariš*

išertum "normal quantity"? OA of goods; < *išaru* I ?

išertu → also *ešertu* I

išeru → *išaru* I

išḫanabaš, *išḫanabe* → *išḫenabe*

išḫar "blood" Bogh. in *aban i.* "blood-stone"; < Hitt.; jB → *asḫar*

išḫenabe, *išḫanabe*, *isḫenabe*, *išḫanabaš*; pl. *išḫanabeāte* (a garment) M/NA, M/NB; < Hurr. or Hitt.?

išḫenaše; pl. *išḫenašena* ~ (desig. of a stool or chair) MB(Alal.); < Hurr.

išḫiḫatum (a wound)? Mari; < *šaḫāḫu* ?

išḫilṣiš "into sherds" jB *i. purruru* "to shatter"; < *išḫilṣu*

išḫilṣu "(pot)sherd" jB [ŠIKA.KUD.DA]; > *išḫilṣiš*

išḫiṭum "razzia, raid" Mari; < *šaḫāṭu* I

išḫiuli "contract" OA; < Hitt.

išḫu, *iša(ḫ)ḫu* (a piece of military kit) MB(Alal.), M/NA, NB of leather, textile

išḫu → also *isḫu* II

išḫû "bridegroom, husband" jB lex.; < Hitt.

išḫunnatu → *isḫunnatu*

išḫuppu (a game)? MB

išibgallu (a chief purification priest) jB lex.; < Sum.

išibkigallu (kind of purification priest) jB lex.; < Sum.

išibmaššugallu (kind of purification priest) jB lex.; < Sum.

išiktu "marshland" jB lex.

Išinītu → *Isinītu*

išīnu(m), *išēnu(m)*, *iši/ennu*, *iššēnu* "stalk, stem" Bab. of grain; also *i. eqli* (a kind of weed); < Sum.

išippu(m) (a purification priest) Bab. [IŠIB(=ME)] of temple staff; Ass., desig. of king; *i. Eridu*, desig. of Adapa; < Sum.; > *išippūtu*; → *išibgallu* etc.

išippūtu "rôle, position of a purification priest" j/NB *i. epēšu* "to fulfil function of *išippu*"; < *išippu*

iširtu → *ešertu* I

išištum mng. unkn. OB lex.

išittu(m) I, *ešittu(m)* "storeroom, treasury" Bab., NA [ERÌM] in temple, palace; "treasure, stores" (→ *lāginu*)

išittu(m) II "foundation, base" O/jB; *išitti šamê* "horizon"; < *išdu*

išītu → *ešītu*

išiu → *ušû*

iškarissu (a kind of rodent) OB lex., jB [PÉŠ.GIŠ.GI.KÚ.E]

iškāru(m), *eškāru(m)*; pl. m. & f. "work assignment" [ÉŠ.GÀR; OB also ÁŠ.GÀR; MA GIŠ.GÀR] **1.** "work assignment" for man, animal, for day(s); MB of daily march **2.** "(assignment of) work materials" **3.** "(delivery of) completed work", NA "(payment in lieu of) work assignment" **4.** OAkk, Bab. "(field for) work assignment" **5.** "text series", e.g. of Gilgameš, Etana; *i. mašmaššūti* "incantation series" etc.; NA *lā ša* *i.* "not in the series"; also f. pl. "(sub-)sets" of songs within an *i.*; < Sum.

iškiḫḫuru (a prof. desig., phps.) "ointment-mixer" Nuzi, desig. of woman; < Hurr.

iškikītum (a bird) OB

iškinū pl. tant. "supplementary payment" OAkk [NÍG.KI.GAR]; < *šakānu*

iškiški mng. unkn. Nuzi *ina MN ša i.*; < Hurr.

išku(m) I f. "testicle" [ŠIR] of man, animal; *tukkannāt i.* "scrotum"; *i. alpi* 'ox's testicle' (a kind of cucumber)

išku II "son" jB lex.; NA in PNs ?

iškurratu, *ikkurratu* (a milk product)? NB

iškūru(m), *eškūru(m)* "wax" [DUḪ.LÀL] jB from bee's honey; for making figurines, for writing boards; OB pl. f. *iškūrātum* "wax-candle"?

iškušḫu (woollen chariot cover, rug)? Nuzi; < Hurr.

iš lê → *isu*

išlītum (a festival) Mari

išlu (a plant) jB lex.; MA pl. f.

išmannu → *iššimannu*

išmarû → *ešmarû*

išmekku → *ešmekku*

išnugallu → *ašnugallu*

išpa (desig. of silver) OA

išpallurtu(m), *pa/illurtu(m)*, NA *ispillurtu* "cross" O/jB, NA [BAR] ref. to cross-shaped object; "crossroads"; astr., ext. "cross-shaped feature"; jB adv. *pallurta* "cross-wise"

išpardu, *išperdu*, *išpar* "horse-bit" M/jB

išpartu(m), *ušpartu* "female weaver" [MUNUS.UŠ.BAR; OB GÉME.UŠ.BAR]; < *išparu*

išparu(m), *ušparu(m)*; Nuzi pl. also f. "weaver" Bab., M/NA [(LÚ.)UŠ.BAR] *bīt i.* "weaver's workshop"; *wakil/rabi i.* "overseer of weavers"; *i. birmi/kitê/ṣiprāti* "weaver of multicoloured/ linen/ṣ. cloth"; > *išpartu*; *išparūtu*

išparūtu "weaver's craft; guild" Nuzi, NB [UŠ.BAR-]; < *išparu*

išpattalu "overnight accommodation" OA; < Hitt.

išpatu(m) "quiver" [Am. KUŠ.É.MAR.RU] usu. of leather for arrows, javelins; also "bow case" jB lex.

išperdu → *išpardu*

išpiku(m), *išpikku* "stores (of crops); grain-bin" OAkk, O/jB [Ì.DUB] usu. pl.; *bīt i.* "store-house"; < *šapāku*

išpu (a container) NB

išpum → also *išbum*

išpurnatu → *išburnatu*

išpurusinnum (or *išpuruzinnum*) (an implement)? OA

išqappu → *išqippu*

išqarrurtu(m), *ešqarrurtu*, *isqarrurtu* (an agricultural implement)? O/jB circular or cylindrical ?; astr. as star emblem, also ^{d}*I.*; → *qarāru* ?

išqātu → *izqātu*

išqillatu(m), *isqillatu*, *(is)sillatu* "(a type of) shell" O/jB [NA$_4$.PEŠ$_4$] of river, canal, sea; also OB, Am. (a container for oil); OB as PN

išqippu, *isqippu*, *išqappu* ~ "earthworm" jB [MAR.GAL] as drug; (name of an illness); ^{d}*I.* as DN; also (a bird)

išqu → *isqu*

išqubbītu → *asqubbītu*

išquqqu → *isqūqu*

išrā → *ešrā*

išrātum, *išrētu* → *ešertu* I; *ešrētu*

išri- → *ašru* III

išriš → *išariš*

išrīšu → *ešrīšu*

išrum I f. (a woollen band, sash) OA

išru(m) II, *ešrum*, *isru(m)*; pl. f. "enclosed village"? O/jB

išrum III "tithe" OB, payment of 10%; < *ešer*

išrû → *ešrû* I

iššā "although" Mari; < *ina* + *ša*

iššakku → *iššiakkum*

iššakkūtu → *iššiakkūtum*

iššanû pron. adj. "hers, belonging to her", also "theirs" NA; → *iššunû*

iššaššūme → *šalšūmi*

iššebu → *eššebu*

iššebû → *eššebu*; *eššebû*

iššēnu → *išīnu*

iššērta → *šērtu* II

iššeššāni, *iššē(š)šu* → *eššēšu*

iššeʾu → *eššeʾu*

iššī "she" (3 f. sg. nom. pron.) NB; → *šī*

iššiakkum, *iššakku* "city-ruler, ensi; (a class of farmer)" [ÉNSI(=PA.TE.SI)] **1.** *i. PlN*; as royal title; *i. Aššur*, title of Assyrian king **2.** Bab. (class of tenants of state land); *i. šarri/šakin māti* "tenants of king/governor"; < Sum.

iššiakkūtum, *iššakkūtu* "ensi-ship" [ÉNSI-] "position of city-ruler"; OB "service of tenant-farmer"; < *iššiakkum*

iššiāre → *šiāru*

iššimannu, *išmannu* (a bronze object) MB(Alal.), Nuzi

iššini "they" (3 f. pl. nom. pron.) NB; → *šina* I

iššinnu → *isinnu*
iššu; pl. *iššū* "woman, wife" O/jB lex., lit.; → *issu*
iššū "he" (3 m. sg. nom. pron.) NB; → *šū*
iššuḫru (an object) Nuzi; < Hurr.
iššuḫurriwe mng. unkn. Nuzi; < Hurr.
iššunu "they" (3 m. pl. nom. pron.) NB; → *šunu*
iššunû pron. adj. "theirs" NA; → *šunûm* I
iššuttu → *eššūtu*
ištā- → *išti*
ištagurrû, *eštagurrû* "(offerings) returned from sanctuary" OB; < Sum.
ištānānu, *iltānānu* "north(ern)" Nuzi; *ina i. eqli* "to the north of the field"; < *ištānu* + *-ānu*
ištānu(m), *iltānu(m)* "North" Bab., NA [IM.SI(.SÁ); j/NB, NA also IM.2] as cardinal point, *bīt i.* "north wing" of palace etc.; "north wind"; "the North (lands)" OB(Shemshara); > *ištānānu*
ištānû → *irtānû*
ištânu → *ištēn*
ištarāniš, *ištariš* "to the goddess" jB with vb.s of calling, attending; < *ištaru*
ištarītu 1. O/jB (a priestess, hierodule) [^{d}15-; Ug. NU.GIG.AN.NA] 2. jB (epith. of Ištar); < *ištarīum*
ištarīum; pl. *ištarīūtum* "man dedicated to Ištar" OA; < *ištaru*; > *ištarītu*
ištartu "goddess" jB; < *ištaru*
ištaru(m); pl. *ištarātum*, *ištarū*, *ištarānu* "goddess" Bab. [$^{(d)}$INNIN, NB pl. ^{d}INNIN.NA.MEŠ; $^{(d)}$IŠ$_8$.DAR; ^{d}15] *ilu(m) u i.* "god and goddess"; *i.-šu* "his goddess"; "(statue of) goddess"; < DN Ištar; > *ištarāniš*; *ištarīum*, *ištarītu*; *ištartu*; *ištarūta*
ištarūta adv. (a musical term) jB [^{d}U.DAR-*ú-ta*]; < *ištaru*
ištât → *ištēn*
ištâtan "each one" Nuzi; < *ištēn*
ište → *išti*
ištēn, *ištēnu(m)*, *iš/ltīn(um)*, *ištiānum*, *iš/ltânu*, later *iltēn*, NA *issēn*; f. *išteat*, *ištiat*, *iš/ltē/īt(um)*, *iš/ltât*, NA *issēt* 1. "one" before noun; emphatic after noun; *i. ina ṣuḫārēka* "one of your lads"; *i. u šina/šitta* "one or two"; NB *i. ina pūt šanî našû* "one guarantees the other"; math. "(the number) one" 2. "single" 3. "the first one" 4. OB *ištītu(m)* "once"; > *ištēnšeret* etc.; *ištâtan*; *ištēnâ*; *ištēniš*; *ištēnīšu*; *ištennūtu*; *ištēnû*; *ištiššu*; *ištiyû*; *ittiltu*
ištēnâ, *ištīnâ*, OA *ištēna* 1. "one each, one by one" 2. Mari "all alike, all together"; < *ištēn*
ištēn-ešret → *ištēnšeret*
ištēniš, *ištīniš*, later *iltēniš*, NA *issēniš*, occas. *ištūniš* "together" [UR.BI; OA ŠU.NÍGIN; NA also TA-] of sending items, mixing ingredients; of time, "at the same time"; OB *i. zâzum* "to divide equally"; "altogether, in total"; < *ištēn*
***ištēnīšu**, jB *iltēnīšu* "for the first time" jB; < *ištēn*
ištēnīu → *ištēnû*
ište(n)nūtu, *ilte(n)nūtu* "single entity" Am., Nuzi, Bogh., Ug. 1. "(indivisible) unity" of kings, fields 2. "single set" of plural items, e.g. garments, armour (→ *ištēnû*) 3. Am., Nuzi adv. "for the first time"; < *ištēn* abstr.
ištēnšeret, poet. *ištēn-ešret* "eleven" Bab.; < *ištēn* + *-šeret*; → *ištēnšerīšu*; *ištēnšerû*
***ištēnšerīšu**, *išteššerīšu* "eleven times" OB; < *ištēn* + *-šerīšu*
***ištēnšerû**, MB *iltēnšerû* "eleventh" M/jB; < *ištēn* + *-šerû*
ištēnu → *ištēn*
ištēnû(m), *ištīnû(m)*, later *ilte/i(n)nû*, Ass. *iš/ltēnīu(m)*, NA *issēnû* "single", Ass. with pl. tant. subst. "one (set, pair of)" shoes etc.; "each one"; Nuzi of sheep "once (shorn)"; jB lex. "one year old"?; NB "one each"; Ug. of kings "in accord, united"; < *ištēnu* + *-ī*
išteššerīšu → *ištēnšerīšu*
ištēt(u) → *ištēn*
išti, *ište*, Pre-Sarg. *ašte/i*, OB also *ištā-*, *ištu*, MA *ilte-*, NA *issi(-)* "with" [KI; NA TA] + subst. or pron. suff. in gen. "with" s.o., O/MA also "from" + vb.s of taking, receiving; Ass. also "with, in possession of" things; > *issaḫîš*; → *ištu*
ištiānum, *ištiat*, *ištīn(u)* → *ištēn*
ištīna/â → *ištēnâ*
ištīniš → *ištēniš*
ištīnû → *ištēnû*
ištiššu "once" Bab [1(*-en*)-*šu*] absol. or after *ana*, *ina*, *kīma*; < *ištēn*
ištištu → *ittiltu*
ištīt(um) → *ištēn*
ištiyû "first" jB; < *ištēn*
ištu(m), *ultu*, *e/uštu*, *iltu/a/i*, NA *issu*, NB *ildu* "from, out of; since, after" [TA] A. prep. 1. of space: "from out of" city, land etc.; *i. X adi Y* "from X to Y"; "down from" sky, tower 2. of time: "since, after" a time, an event; *i. X adi Y* "from X till Y"; + infin. "after having ..." 3. misc.: *i. X adi Y*, e.g. from straw to gold, man to woman, NB *ultu ramnikunu* "on your own"; late freq. *i./ultu muḫḫi* B. conj. + subjunct. 1. "since, after" 2. "when, as soon as" 3. "since,

because" Mari, + indic. **4.** Mari *i.-ša*, NA *i. mar*, *i. bīt*, NB *ultu muḫḫi (ša)* "since"; > *ištūma*; → *išti*

ištu → also *išdu*; *išti*

ištuḫḫu(m), *i/eltuḫḫu*, *istuḫḫu*, *eštuḫḫu*, Nuzi also *iltuḫlu*; pl. f. & m. "whip" Bab.; *ša i.* "whip-holder"; *bīt i.* "whip-container" on chariot

ištūma conj. "if indeed" OA, OB; Mari also + indic.; < *ištu*

ištūniš → *ištēniš*

išû(m) "to have" (no pres., pret. *īši*, *īšu*; stat. rare; → GAG §106r) [TUK; Mari also IN.TUK] "possess" object; "have" merchant, witness, relative, opponent; "suffer from" illness, debts, fear; personal characteristic; of loan "bear" interest; of creditor "be owed s.th." by (= *eli*, OAkk also *itti*, OA *iṣṣēr*); Am. "exist" (< W.Sem.); > *išānû*; → *laššu* I

išû → also *ešû* I; *ḫišû*

išuḫḫu (desig. of a garment) Am.

išumaka/i (a kind of payment) Nuzi; → *ḫiššumaku*

išūtu mng. uncl. jB lex.

išuzzu → *izuzzum*

ita "adjacent to" OB [ÚS.SA.DU] in field descr.; < *itû* st. constr.

itaḫlaṣānu "dislocated, slipped" of exta jB; < *neḫelṣû*

itaḫliṣū? (an illness affecting the head) jB lex.; < *neḫelṣû*

italma'u → *irima'u*

itannu "mesh, interstice" of net jB

itānu mng. unkn. jB lex.

itānû → *itû* 5

itaplustu; pl. *itaplusāte* 'looking' NA in *ša i.* [*ša* IGI.DUḪ] (a copper object); < *palāsu* Ntn

itašlulu → *šalālu* II Ntn

itâtu → *itû* 3

itbārānu "companionable" jB of man; < *itbāru* + *-ān*

itbārtu "club, consortium" jB; < *itbāru*

itbāru(m) "friend, colleague" Bab., OA; also "shareholder" in commercial association; > *itbārānu*, *itbārtu*, *itbārūtu*; → *abāru* III

itbārūtu(m) **1.** O/jB "business partnership" **2.** NB(roy. inscr.) "skill"; < *itbāru*

itê → *itû* 2

ite'(el)lû → *ne'ellû* Ntn

itellum → *etellu*

itepšu "expert, competent" jB; < *epēšu* II

itertum "supplementary consignment" OA of tin etc.; < *watārum*

itguru (a bird) jB om.; → *etguru*

itgurūtu mng. uncl. jB comm.

itḫû mng. unkn. jB lex.

itḫuru; pl. *itḫurānu*, *itḫurāte* (a kind of standard, emblem) M/NA, jB

itḫusu → *atḫusu*

itḫuṣu mng. unkn. NA in *bīt itḫiṣi*

itiḫilum (an object) OA

itillu → *etellu*

itinnu(m), Ass. *etennu(m)*; NA pl. f. "builder" [(LÚ.)ŠITIM; NA LÚ.DIN] NB as family name; < Sum.

itinnūtu(m) "builder's craft" Bab. [LÚ.ŠITIM-] NB also "job of builder" as prebend; < *itinnu*

itirtu(m) (a milk product) OAkk(Sum.); jB lex.

itišutu mng. unkn. Nuzi in *šipir i.* "*i.* work"

itītu in NB(roy. inscr.) = *itûtu* I ?

itku "paralysed"? Bogh. lex., of neck; < *atāku*

itkû, *utkû* "(wooden) peg" jB lex.

itmû Gt ~ "to nod the head" jB lex. **Gtn** *ittamû*?

itpēšu(m) "expert, competent" Bab. of god, king etc.; < *epēšu* II

itpuru "wearing tiara"? jB epith. of Ištar; < *apāru*

itqu(m) m. & f. **1.** "fleece" Bab. [SÍK.ÀKA] of sheep; of person's hair; "(woollen) flock, tuft"; (garment made from fleece) **2.** jB mag., also *etqu*, in *e. eper šēpī* "lump of dust from under s.o.'s feet"

itqulu (a garment) jB lex.

itqūru(m), *itqurtu(m)*; pl. f. "spoon" [(GIŠ.)DÍLIM] of metal, wood; "pan" of a balance; "blade" of an oar; med. *i. (abāri)* (an ointment)

itrānu → *idrānu*

itru → *idru* I.II

itta- → *itti*

ittaḫu "next to, by" NB + gen. subst. or pron. suff.; < *ina* + *ṭāḫu*

ittamir, *ittemir*, *ittiyamir* (a stone) jB

ittamû → *itmû*

ittān mng. uncl. jB lex.

itte- → *itti*

itteltu → *ittiltu*

ittemir → *ittamir*

itti, *ittu*, *itte-*, Am. *itta-*, OAkk, OB also *ittum* "with" [KI; NB also TA ?] **1.** prep. + gen. subst. or pron. suff.; be, stand etc., go, send "with" s.o.; speak, fight, be angry "with"; compete "with", be equal "to" s.o.; divide s.th. "with" s.o.; take, buy s.th. "from, *chez*" s.o.; Mari of troops, be "under" s.o.; NB "at" time of day, "per" mina **2.** conj. Mari "while, whereas", Ug. "as soon as"; > *ittī*

ittī "on top of that, in addition" NB; < *itti*

ittidû (a bird, phps.) "francolin" O/jB [DAR.MUŠEN] with distinctive cry

ittīl-imūt 'he lay down and died' (an owl) jB [KU.KU.BA.ÚŠ.MUŠEN] om., mag.; < *itūlu* + *mâtu*

ittiltu, *itteltu*, Nuzi usu. *ilti/eltu*, *ištištu* "one time, once" M/jB; Nuzi also "the first time", (for *ištēt*) "one"; < *ištēn*

ittilu (a tool) jB lex.

ittiyamir → *ittamir*

ittu(m) I, *idatu*; pl. *idātu(m)* ~ "peculiarity"? Bab., NA [Á] **1.** "characteristic, special nature" **2.** pl. [Á.(2.)MEŠ] "(ominous) conditions", *idāt lemuttim*, *dumqi* "signs of evil, good", *šamê u erṣeti* "of heaven and earth" **3.** NB *lū idat*, *idatumma* introducing solemn statement; < *idu* f.; = *i.* II

ittu(m) II, Ass. *ettu(m)*; pl. *ittātu(m)* "sign" [ISKIM] **1.** "signpost, road marker" **2.** math. "diagram"? **3.** "character(istic mark)" of person, deity **4.** "(ominous) sign", esp. good, bad (*damqu*, *lemnu*) **5.** "password, verbal cue" **6.** in commerce etc. *ana ittišu* "at the agreed point, as agreed"; = *i.* I

ittu → also *Id*; *itti*

ittû(m) I "seed-funnel" [GIŠ.NÍNDA] O/jB on seeder-plough; < Sum.

ittû II (a garment) OB(Alal.)

ittû → also *itu-*; *itû*; *iṭṭû*

ittuḫlu ~ "messenger" Nuzi; < Hurr.

ittum → *itti*

ittuš(šu) "clothing" Nuzi; as ration; a specific garment; < Hurr.

itu(-), *ittû-* "with" MB prep. of things, persons "with, *chez*" s.o.; also jB *ana itišun* "with them"; < *itû*

itû(m), *etû*, *ittû(m)*; pl. m. & f. "boundary; neighbour" [ÚS.SA.DU] **1.** "boundary", upper/lower, east/west; "border, side" of river, field; *i. etēqu* "to cross boundary", esp. transf. "to transgress a limit" **2.** st. constr. *itê* + subst. "alongside", *i. aḫāmiš* "bordering one another" **3.** f. pl. *itâtu(m)*, lex. *itiātu* "borders, environs"; st. constr. as prep. "all round, surrounding" **4.** NB "hull" of ship **5.** "neighbour" [(LÚ.)ÚS.SA.DU], NB pl. also *itānû*; > *ita*; *itu-*; *itûtu* II

itūlu(m), *utūlu(m)* "to lie down; sleep" Bab., OA, NA **Gt** (pres. *ittâl*, pret. *ittīl*; perf. *ittatīl*; imper. *itil*; stat. *utul*; (→ GAG §107j) [NÁ] "lie down", "lie" with spouse; transf. of gall "be lying" **Gtn** iter. [NÁ.NÁ] **D** "put to sleep" **Š** caus. [NÁ] "make" s.o. "lie, sleep"; "lay" ingredient in salt; > *ittīl-imūt*; *muttiītu*?; → *nâlu*

itūnum → *utūnu*

itussarra (or *ituzzarra*) (an ornament) Am.

itussu → *izuzzum*

itûtu(m) I, *utûtu*, NB also *itītu*?; jB pl. *utâtu*? "selection" Bab.; esp. *i. kūn libbi* "steadfast choice" (liter. "choice of steadfastness of heart"); OB *ana i.-ya* "by my free choice"; < *watûm*; → *itītu*

itûtu II ~ "cirumference"; < *itû*

ituzzarra → *itussarra*

iṭemmum → *eṭemmu*

iṭṭû(m), *ittû*, *iddû* f. "bitumen" Bab., NA [ESIR; ESÍR; occas. A.BUL; Mari occas. ESIR.RA] for buildings; boats etc.; figurines; *būrū ša i.* "bitumen springs"; in similes, black *kīma i.* "as pitch"; < Sum.

īṭum → *ūṭu*

i'û mng. unkn. jB lex.

iutû (appeal to Šamaš) jB [I.^{d}UTU]; < Sum.; → *inannû*

iwaru (or *iwi/uru*) (a wooden object) Nuzi; < Hurr.

iwirtum → *amertu* I

iwiru → *iwaru*

iwītu(m) ~ "malicious talk" O/jB; < *ewûm* II

iwuru → *iwaru*

iyarum → *ayyaru* I

iyâti → *yâti*

iyaumaš in *šam i.* (a plant) jB rit.; < Hitt.?

Izalli (or *Azzalli*?) rdg. uncl. (a month) OB(Alal.)

izana'u (a plant) jB lex.

izbu(m) "misbirth, foetal anomaly" O/jB of human, animal; *šumma i.* (teratological omen series); < *ezēbu*

izḫu ~ "belt" jB lex.; < *ezēḫu*

izibtu(m), *ezibtu(m)* **1.** OB (+ *ezēbum*) "deposit", a kind of pledge **2.** OA "divorce money"; < *ezēbu*

izikurum (a bird) OB

izirtu "help, reinforcement" Am.; < W.Sem.; → *izzirtu*

izīru "arm; wing" jB, NA

izišubbû "stroke of lightning" jB [IZI.ŠUB.BA]; < Sum.

izizzum → *izuzzum*

izmum (an extispicy technique) Mari

izqātu, *išqātu* "fetters, handcuffs" j/NB, NA; NB *i.* [GIŠ.ŠU.2(.MEŠ)] *nadû* "to cast into fetters"; < *iṣu* + *qātu*?

izru "curse" jB; < *ezēru*

Izubītu, *Izubû* (a canal) jB; < Sum.

izūtu → *zūtu*

izuzušši mng. unkn. Nuzi; < Hurr.

izuzzum, *uzuzzu(m)*, OA *izizzum*, M/NB freq. *ušuzzu*, also *išuzzu*, NA *itussu* "to stand" **G** (pres. *izzaz*, pret. *izziz*; perf. *ittaziz*; imper. *iziz*, M/NB freq. *išiz*; stat. *na(n)zuz*, M/NB *uš/zuz* etc.; other forms → GAG §107a-h) [GUB; MB also GUB.BA] **1.** gener. of person, thing "stand"; "serve (before)" s.o., esp. deity, king; "serve, be present" (as witness); "be available" of person, animal, boat; "remain"; transf. of oath, legal right "be valid"; OB *i. eli* "be engaged on, work at" s.th.; OB *i. ana* "accept liability for"; OA "stand by, belong to" s.o. **2.** (ingress.) "appear, make an appearance"; "take up service"; "side with" (= *išti*, *itti*) s.o., "go to assistance of" (= *ana*, dat.) s.o.; M/NB of god "visit" s.o. in a hostile manner; of part of liver "stand erect" **Gtn** iter. [jB GUB.ME(Š); GUB.GUB] of a number of people "stand around"; of snake, scorpion "repeatedly rear up" **Gt** arch. OB ingress. for G pres. "take up o.'s stand"; *eli nakrim i.* "triumph over enemy"; of flood "come to a standstill" **Š** ($Š^1$ OAkk occas., Bab. pres. *ušzaz*, pret. *ušziz*; imper. *šuziz*; stat. *šuzuz*; infin. *šuzuzzu(m)*; $Š^2$ OAkk, Ass., j/NB pres. *ušazzaz*, pret. *uša/ezziz*; perf. *uštazziz*; imper. *šuzziz*; stat. *šuzzuz*; infin. *šuzzu(z)zu*) caus. "cause to be present", "appoint" witnesses, substitute, pledge; "make s.o. serve"; "cause to triumph" over enemy; "stable" horse; "erect" stele, statue, tower; "re-erect" wall etc.; transf. OA "make" silver "available"; "enter" items in accounts; "establish" justice; "make" hair, furrow "stand upright"; poet. "create, bring into being" **Štn** MB "constantly make to stand" **Št** jB "cause to appear" **N** OB(lit.) (infin. *nazzazum*; stat. *nanzaz*) ingress. of deity "appear, become present"; > *uzuzzatta*; *ušuzzāyu*; *mazzāzu*; *mazzaztu*, *mazzazānum*, *mazzazānūtum*; *muzzazu*; *mazzizu*, *mazziz-pānuttu*; *nanzāzu*; *mušazzizum*; *šazzuztum*

izzidarû "bed with side-rest" jB lex.; < Sum.

izziḫu (a gem)? Qatna

izzimtu(m) "desire, objective" O/jB usu. with *kašādu(m)* "to achieve"; < *nazāmu*

izzirtu "curse" M/NA, M/jB; < *nazāru*

izziru "curse" M/jB; < *nazāru*

K

-k → *-ka*; *-ki*

-ka, *-k* "you" (2 m. sg. acc. suff.) (→ GAG §42)

kâ → *kīam*

ka'ātu → *qayyātu*

kabābu(m) I, *gabābu(m)*; jB pl. f. "shield" O/jB, NA (with KUŠ or GIŠ det.); *nāš(i) k.* "shield-bearer"

kabābu II, *gabābu* "to burn" Bab. **G** (*a*/*u*) intrans., of fire, wood; transf. of illness; Mari, trans. (submit lamb to extispicy)? **D** trans. "burn, scorch" wood; transf. of Lamaštu "burn" s.o.'s body; > *kabbu*; *kibbu* II; *gabbubu*; *gubibātu*

kabābu → also *kapāpu*

kabādu → *kabātu*

kabāku (a topog. feature) NA

kaballu(m) "leggings" O/MB in pairs, freq. attached to shoes

kabaltu (a plant)? jB lex.

kabālu(m) "to be paralysed" O/jB **G** (*a*/*u*) stat., of part of body **D** "constrict, paralyse" part of body; OB transf. "hinder, obstruct" s.o. **Dt** pass. of D, of lips "be paralysed"; > *kubbulu*; → *kibiltu*

kabaraḫḫum → *gabaraḫḫu*

kabartu "thickness" jB comm.; < *kabru*

kabartu → also *kabbartu; kabru*

kabāru(m) "to be(come) thick, solid" **G** (*i*/*i*; stat. *kabar*, NB also *kabir*) of animal, person; part of body; tree-trunk, grain, door; moon; of voice "loud" **D** (jB once *uḫabbir*) "make thick; thicken" **Ntn** jB of snake "constantly become thick"; > *kabru*, *kabartu*, *kabrūtu*; *kubru*, *kubartu*, *kubārum*, *kuburrû*; *kabbaru*, *kabbartu*; *kubburu*; *mukabbirum*, *muktabbirum*; *takbāru*; *nakbartu;* →*ḫahāru* II

kabāru → also *kawārum*

kabar'ū pl. (a festival)? Mari

kabāsu(m), Am. *kabāšu* "to tread" **G** (*a*/*u*) [ZUKUM; KI.UŠ] **1.** on ground, road, boundary; house, palace; "tread down, trample" ramp, fire; "tread on" neck, foot **2.** transf. "tread down, suppress" enemy, criminal, noise, "forgive, remit" crime, debt; *anzilla k.* "infringe taboo" **3.** OA *rama(n)ka k.* "exert yourself" **4.** M/NA, NB "let" time "pass", NA "continue" **D** ~ G "tread, walk over" land etc.; "tread down, on" neck, opposition; *anzilla k.* "infringe taboo"; OA (also **Dtn**) "drop, suppress" claim **Š** caus. **N** NA/NB **1.** of land "be subdued" **2.** "continue" **3.** OB "set foot on"; > *kabsu* I, *kabistum*?; *kibsu* I; *kubāsu*; *kubussû*; *kubbusum*; *nakbasu*; *šukbusu*

kabāsu → also *kapāṣu* II

kabāṣu → *kapāṣu* I.II

kabaštu → *kabru*

kabāšu "to put headgear on" jB **G** in *kubšu kabiš*; < *kubšu* denom.

kabāšu → also *kabāsu*

kabattu(m), poet. also *kabtatu(m)*, later occas. *kabittu* "liver", also "innards"; usu. transf. "mood, temper, humour", joyful, peaceful, unrestful, angry; "mind, intention"; Am. *kabattuma* [once UZU.UR$_5$] "on the stomach"; → *kabātu*

kabātu(m), NA also *kabādu* "to be(come) heavy" **G** (*i*/*i*) [DUGUD] **1.** of animal, objects; transf. of fear, work, orders, domination; "become burdensome, aggravating", of illness "be serious"; of fire "be extinguished"? **2.** "be important, respected" of person, word; *qaqqadum k.* of respected person **D 1.** "make heavy" penalty; "extinguish" fire; "aggravate, exaggerate" **2.** "treat honourably, respectfully", "regale, entertain honorifically"; with *rēšum, qaqqadum* "honour" s.o.; Ug. "honour (s.o.) with" reward **Dt** "be honoured" OB **Dtn** Am. iter. of D; OA, OB "do the honours and ...", "be so complimentary as to ..." **Š** "give importance to" matter OB; "work" sculpture "massively" NB; > *kabtu, kabtūtu; kabbuttu; kabittu; kubtu; kubātu; kubuddā'u, kubuttû; kubbutu, kubbuttu; nakbatu; takbittu;* → *gabīdu; kabattu*

kaba'u, *kapa'u* ~ "reed foliage" jB lex.; → *takba'u*

ka(b)bartu(m) (part of foot) O/jB of human, also du.; of bird; < *kabbaru*

kabbaru(m) "very thick", freq. serves as pl. of *kabru* Bab., M/NA [GUR4.GUR4] of animal; part of body; textile, trunk of tree; of rain "dense"; < *kabāru*; > *kabbartu*; → *kubburu*

kabbā'um "stitcher" OB; < *kubbû* II

kabbillu (wooden part of chariot) jB lex.; < Sum.

kabbu "glowing" jB, NA; of charcoal, incense; of hot wind; < *kabābu* II

kabbuttu; pl. *kabbutāti* "counterweight (for jewellery)"? Am.; < *kabātu*

kabbutu → *kubbutu*

kabduqqû → *kaptukkûm*

kabḫu mng. unkn. Nuzi

kabīdu → *gabīdu*

kabilukku (a dish or fruit) NA

kabistum (part of a cubit) OA st. abs. *kabsat*; < *kabsu* I ?

kabis/ṣtu → *kapṣu*

kabittigalzu (a plant) jB lex.; < Kass.

kabittu(m) 1. also *kibittum*, "main body (of troops)" Mari, OB(N.Mes.) **2.** euph. "left hand" lex. **3.** (a double pot) lex.; < *kabtu*

kabittu → also *kabattu*

kabkūru(m) (or *kapkūru(m)*) (a container) OAkk, for flour; jB lex.

kablītu (or *kaplītu*) mng. uncl. jB

kablu(m); pl. m. & f. "(furniture) foot" [GIŠ.BAD.GU.ZA] of chair, table etc.

kabnu "casing, tyre (of wheel)"? NB comm.; < Aram.

kabru(m); f. *kabartu(m)*, NB also *kabaštu* "thick, solid" [GUR4.RA] of person (in PN), animal; part of body, flesh; of grain, sesame; of textile, garment; "large" of measuring vessel; < *kabāru*; → *kabbaru*

kabrūtu "thickness" jB lex.; < *kabru*

kabsat → *kabistum*

kabsatu → *kabsu* II

kabsu I "continuous" NA of land-tenure; < *kabāsu*

kabsu II; f. *kabsatu* "young sheep" OB, j/NB, NA

kabs/ṣu → *kapṣu*

kabšarru (or *kapšarru*) "stone-carver" M/NA, M/NB [(LÚ.)KAB.SAR] of precious stones, masonry; < Sum.

kabšarrūtu "profession of stone-carver" Bogh. lex.

kabtatu → *kabattu*

kabtu(m); f. *kabittu(m)* "heavy; important" [DUGUD; IDIM in PNs] **1.** of stone, metal "heavy"; of garment; tribute, booty; transf. "grave, serious" of wound, illness; sin, punishment, quarrel; of mist, cloud **2.** "important, honoured"; as subst. "important person, VIP"; *šumu(m) k.* "respected, famous name"; of divine order, pronouncement; < *kabātu*; > *kabittu*; *kabtūtu*

kabtūtu "majesty" jB, of god; < *kabtu*

kabum → *kabūtu*

kabû(m) ~ "plant pod"? Bab.

kabû → also *kabūtu*; *kubbû* I.II

kabullu → *kamullu*

kabūtu(m); pl. m. *kabû*; OA sg. *kabum* "(animal) dung" Bab., OA [ŠURIM] of horse, sheep etc.; snake; *k. Šeriš* "ox-dung" med.; *libitti k.* "dung-cake"

kabzuzû(m) ~ "educated person"? jB lex.; < Sum.

kabzuzuttu "rôle of educated person"? Bogh.

kadabbedû ~ "oral paralysis, aphasia" jB [KA.DAB.BÉ.DA]; < Sum.

kadādu, lex. also *ḫadādu* "to rub in, anoint" jB **G** (*a/u*) with 2 acc. **D** ~ G ?; > *makaddu, makdādu*

kadammu; pl. f. ~ "dungeon"? NA

kadānu (a rush-like plant) jB

kādānu → *kādu*

kadāpu mng. unkn. jB lex.

kadāru I (a reed fence)? jB lex.

kadāru(m) II "to rear up" Bab., NA **G** (*i/i*) of enemy, battle "rise in opposition", "be insubordinate" **Š** "stir up, incite" battle **Ntn** jB med. "jerk repeatedly"?; > *kadru, kadrūtu, kadriš*; *makdaru*?; *takdīru*?

kadāru III "to delimit" M/NA, M/jB **G** (*i/i*) *kudurra k.* "draw a boundary" **D** ~ G "draw" boundary; < *kudurru* II denom.

kadāru IV "to labour"? NA **G**; < *kudurru* I denom.?

kadāšu "celebration" OB (var. of *ḫadāšu*)

kaddarḫu (a tree) jB lex.

Kadduḫḫa → *Ukaduḫḫa*

kadilû → *qadilû*

kadišeru (a plant) M/jB

kadmuru, *kid(i)muru* mng. unkn. M/NA in name of Ištar temple

kadrayītu f. (epith. of Ištar) jB

kadriš "aggressively" jB; < *kadru*

kadru(m), *qadru*; f. sg. *kadirtu, kadratu* "rearing up, aggressive" Bab., NA of bull, king, deity, enemy; < *kadāru* II

kadrû (or *katrû*), OB also *kidrûm* "present, greeting gift" Bab. to deity; to king; also as "bribe"; < Sum.

kadrūtu "aggressiveness" jB lex.; < *kadru*

kādu; NB pl. *kādānu* "guard, watch" j/NB esp. military, *rab kādānu* "commander of the watch"; *k. naṣāru* "to keep guard"; NB "(fee for) guard" on orchard; *ša k.* "watchman"; *(bīt) k.* "guard-house"; < *kâdu* II

kādû(m) mng. unkn. OB lex.

kâdu(m) I mng. uncl. O/jB **G** (*ā*) "to be distressed"?, "cease"?; > *mukiddum*?

kâdu(m) II "to watch, guard" Bab. **G** (*ū*) NB **D** OB "watch out (for)", "be attentive" **Dt** pass. "be observed"; > *kādu*; *mukiddum*?

kaduḫḫû "with gaping mouth" jB lex.; < Sum.; → *Ukaduḫḫa*

kadurru → *kudurru* I

ka'eššu → *ka'iššum*

kagallu(m), *kankallu, kigallu* f. "(a kind of) waste land" O/jB [KI.GÁL]; < Sum.; → *kikallû*

kagiškarakku → *kannaškarakkum*

kagûm mng. unkn. OB lex.

kaḫama adv.? mng. unkn. MB

kaḫaššinna mng. unkn. Nuzi; < Hurr.

kaḫšu "throne" Am.; < W.Sem.

ka'inimmaku "wish, plan"? jB; < Sum.

kā'iṣu "slaughterer" Nuzi of sheep; < *kâṣu*

ka'iššum, *ga'iššu*, jB *g/ka'eššu* ~ "travelling merchant" O/jB lex.; < Sum.

kakammatum (a part of the body) OB

kakaniaššu (part of body armour) Nuzi, of bronze

kakanuzzû (an object) Nuzi, in pairs

kakardinnu, NA *karkadinnu*, NB *kaškadi/annu*, OB(Alal.) *kakatennu* "victualler" [LÚ.SUM. NINDA] a palace employee

kakdâ/û → *kaqdâ*

kakikkum? "recorder" OB [KA.KI], a municipal official concerned with sales

kakilu (a bird) MB

kakkabānu 'starry one' jB **1.** (a bird) **2.** (an ox) **3.** (a kind of lapis lazuli); < *kakkabu*

kakkabiš "like stars" j/NB; < *kakkabu*

kakkabtu "star" M/NB, NA [MUL; MÚL] as ornament, of gold etc.; NB as brand-mark on slaves, beasts; < *kakkabu*

kakkabu(m) "star" [MUL; later also MÚL, UL, TE and ÁB] also ref. to planets; *k. šamê/šamāmī* "stars of heaven"; *ina k. biātum* Š "to leave (a magic potion) outside overnight" O/jB; *k. rabû* "meteor"; "star(-shaped ornament)" of metal, stone; < Sem. *kabkab-*; > *kakkabtu, kakkabiš, kakkabānu*

kakkaltu, *kalkaltu* (an irrigation device) jB

kakkannu → *kankannu*

kakkartum (a round loaf) OAkk, O/MB; OA "bun (ingot)" of copper; < *kakkaru*

kakkaru, Alal. also *kakkuru* (a round loaf)? Mari, Alal., Am., Bogh. **1.** Mari, Bogh. (a loaf) **2.** Am. (a silver disc)? **3.** Alal., Am. (an ingot)? of copper; > *kakkartum*

kakkassu → *kakkūsu*

kakkišatti "like a weasel" NA; < *kakkišu* + *-atti* (→ GAG §113l)

kakkišu f. ~ "weasel" M/jB, NA also as PN; jB *k. nāri* (a diving bird)

kakku(m) "stick; weapon" [GIŠ.TUKUL; occas. GIŠ.ŠÍTA] **1.** rarely "stick" **2.** gener. "weapon" OA *rabi k.* "armourer"; OB *ṣāb k.*[ḫi.a] "armed troops"; *k. epēšu(m)* "to do battle", *ana k. parākum* "confront for battle"; *k. šebēru(m)* "break weapons"; *k. maḫāṣu(m)* "strike with weapon(s)", also = "afflict with illness" **3.** as divine symbol *k. ša ilim* "divine emblem", *ša Šamaš* etc. **4.** (a feature on liver)

kakku → also *kanku*

kakkû(m), *kakku'u* (a small legume, phps.) "lentil" OAkk, Bab. [GÚ.TUR]; > *kakkûtu*

kakkullu(m), *k/qaqqullu*, MA *kukullu*? f. "mash-tub" O/jB, M/NA [GAKKUL] in similes; also (a wooden box); NA (a basket or tray) for fruit, leavings, *rab qaqqullāte* (an official); MA *ša kukulli* (a desig. of young worker); < Sum.; > *kakkultu*

kakkultu "mash-tub" jB; also M/jB *k. īni* "eyeball"; < *kakkullu* *kakkuru* → *kakkaru*

kakkusakku, *kakkušakku* jB **1.** (a plant)? **2.** (a stone); → *kakkūsu, kanku*

kakkūsu(m), O/jB *kakkussu*, NA also *kakkassu* **1.** ~ (leguminous vegetation) **2.** (a stone) M/jB, NA; < Sum.?; → *kakkusakku*

kakkušakku → *kakkusakku*

kakkušu → *kukkušu*

kakkūtu "a lentil?" jB [GÚ.TUR] also "pimple"; < *kakkû* nom. unit.

kakmûm; f. *kakmītu* "of Kakmum" O/jB (an object; a kind of door); < PlN Kakmum

kaksallû (a kind of wooden peg) jB lex.; < Sum.

kaksû (an arrow) jB

kakugallu, *kakugallāku* (an incantation priest) jB; < Sum.

kakugallūtu "profession of incantation priest" jB; < *kakugallu*

kal(a) → *kalû* II

kalabbu → *kalappum*

kalabūnu, kalabuttu → *kallabūnu*

kalakku(m) I; pl. f. ~ "excavation, trench" Bab. [KI.LÁ; TÚL(.LÁ)] "pit" (in canal-bed, field) and its spoil; esp. math. in problems; "underground store" for grain, straw etc.; < Sum.

kalakku II (a kind of box) M/jB, NA; Nuzi in pairs; also (a seat), "box" in chariot (as part of constellation); NA "kelek, raft"

kalakku III (a kind of wall-plaster) MB, jB(Ass.)

kalakkūtu (a kind of earth)? MA

kalāma, *kalām(u/i)* "all (of it)" Bab. [DÙ.A.BI; DÙ; DÙ.DÙ.A] indeclinable as obj. of vb. or gen. after st. constr.; in appos., e.g. *riqqī kalāma* "all sorts of aromatics", *ilī kalāma* "all the gods"; < *kalû* II + *-ma*

kalamāḫu → *galamāḫu*

kalammaru → *karammaru*

kalammu (part of a chariot) MA, of wood

kalappum, *kalabbu*; pl. f. "pickaxe" Ass., NB?, of metal

kalāṣu(m) "to contract o.s., roll up" O/jB **G** (*i/i*) of part of body; of dog **Gtn** (lex. also *ḫitalluṣu*) iter. of sheep's nose **D** fact. lex. only; > *kalṣum*; *kilṣu*

kalā'um → *kalû* V

kalbānātu (or *labbānātu* ?) pl. tant. (a siege instrument) jB

kalbāniš "like a dog" O/jB; < *kalbu*

kalbānu, *ka/ulbannu* (a plant) M/jB [GIŠ/Ú. MAŠ.ḪUŠ]

kalbatu(m) "female dog, bitch" O/jB [NIG] also transf. (a strap on a plough); < *kalbu*

kalbu(m) "dog" [UR.GI7; UR; Mari also UR.GI7.RA] also "(figure of) dog", "dog figurine"; transf. as term of humility; of subject; astr. "(constellation) Hercules" (with det. MUL); lex. (a fish); *k. urṣi* "badger" [UR.KI]; *k. mê* "otter" [UR.(GI7.)A]; *k. Šamaš* mng. unkn.; → also *lišānu* 5, *zubbu*; > *kalbāniš, kalbatu*

kaldu → *kašdu*

kalgukku(m), *kalguqqu* (a red mineral paste) O/jB, M/NA [KAL.KU7.KU7; IM.KAL.GUG] in glass-making, as drug; < Sum.

kalîš "totally" OAkk, Bab. [DÙ-*liš*]; < *kalû* II

kalītu(m) "kidney" [(UZU.)ÉLLAG(=BIR)] of human; ext. of animal, as meat; *k. birkim/burki* "testicle"; astr. (desig. of star) identity uncl. [MUL.ÉLLAG], *k. Ea* (desig. of crescent moon)

kālītu(m) **1.** lex. (wooden part of chariot) **2.** OAkk(Ur III) (ornamental item), of gold; < *kalû* V

kalkallû (a bowl) jB lex.

kalkaltu → *kakkaltu*

kalku (a component of armour) Nuzi

kallābu → *kallāpu*

ka(l)labūnu; f. *ka(l)labuttu* "(kind of) locust" j/NB, NA; NB f. as PN

kallâmāre "in the early morning" NA; < *kallû* + *amāru* I ?

kallammaḫu (a plant) jB lex.

kallānu mng. unkn. NB

kallāpu, *kallābu*; pl. *kallāb/pāni* (a foot-soldier) NA, NB; *k. šipirti* "messenger"; *rab k.* "chief *k.*"

kallaṣūdi (a drug) jB; < *kallu* + *aṣūdu* ?

kallātu(m), Ass. *kalla/utu* "daughter-in-law, bride" [É.GI4(.A); É.GI.A] of human, deities; OB st. abs. *ana kallāt ū mārat* "to be daughter-in-law and daughter"; also "young woman, bride" in gener.; *k. Šamaš* "dragonfly" (→ *kulīlītu*), *k. ṣerri* 'snake's bride', "lizard", both as drugs; > *kallūtu*

kallatūtu → *kallūtu*

kallê, kalliu → *kallû*

kallimum ~ "delivery (of a person)" OB; < *kullumu*

kallu(m); Ass. pl. f., NB *kallānu* "(kind of) bowl" Bab., M/NA [(DUG.)BUR.ZI.GAL] for liquids, food; of metal; *k. šeleppî* "tortoise's shell"; *k. qaqqadi* "cranium"; → *kallaṣūdi*

kallû(m), NA *kalliu* "express messenger, courier" Bab., NA *k. nāri/tābāli* "river/land courier"; NA *rab k.* "chief courier"; *ina/ana/kī kallê* "post-haste"; → *kallâmāre*

kallūmi → *kalû* II

kallumu → *kullumu*

kallutu → *kallātu*

kallūtu(m), Nuzi also *kallatūtu* "rôle of daughter-in-law, of bride" O/MB [Ug. É.GI. A.MEŠ]; MB *šipir k.* "bridal activity"; < *kallātu*

kalmakru(m) (or *kalmaqru(m)*) "(kind of) battle-axe" Bab. [GIŠ.AGA.SILIG] of metal

kalmarḫu (a tree) Nuzi, jB

kalmartu → *kanwartu*

kalmatu(m) "insect(s), bug(s)" etc. [UḪ] usu. coll.; OAkk as PN

kalpurḫu (or *galpurḫu*) (desig. of grain) Nuzi; < Hurr.

kalṣum "contracted, shrivelled" OB lex.; < *kalāṣu*

kaltappû (an object of gold) NB; = *gištappu* ?

kalteniwe(š), *galteniwe*, NA *galdanibātu* (desig. of grain) Nuzi; NA (an official); < Hurr.

kaltum, *keltum* ~ "vassal(-ruler)"? Mari

kalû I "held back, detained" M/NB of persons; < *kalû* V

kalû II, OA also *kulum*, gen. *kili-* "all, totality" [DÙ; DÙ.A.BI] **1.** st. abs. *kala/i* "everything", "everyone", esp. *kala/i/luma* **2.** st. constr. + subst. "all", "the whole of", "everyone of"; *kal(a) ūmi(m)*, *kallūmi* "all day", "every day", M/NA, M/jB "during the daytime" (jB also = late afternoon); NA *kal mūši* "night-time" **3.** with pron. suff., after subst. "all of it", *mātum kaluša* "the whole land", *ešrēti kališina* "every shrine"; lit. also before subst. **4.** OB(poet.) + *-iš-*, *kalîšša* "totally"; > *kalîš*; *kalāma*; *kalummûm*; *kullatu* I, *kullatān*

kalû(m) III "lamentation-priest" Bab., NA [(LÚ.)GALA; NB also (LÚ.)ŠÚ]; < Sum.; > *kalûtu* I; → *galamāḫu*, *galaturru*, *galaussû*

kalû(m) IV (a yellow mineral paste, phps.) "orpiment" Bab. [IM.KAL.LA; IM.GÁ.LI] for figurines, wax writing-boards etc.; < Sum.

kalû(m) V, OA *kalā'um* "to hold (back), detain" **G** (*a/a*; imper. *kila*) [NB GUL] "hold, detain, arrest" person, slave, prisoner; "restrain, pull up" an animal; "stop, block off" crater, diarrhoea; "hold back, withhold" goods, tribute, "withhold, deny" request; "restrain" noise, weeping, prayer, hair (from falling out); "prevent" s.o. "from" doing s.th.; "moor" boat **Gtn** iter. **D** rare ~ G "withhold" **Š** caus. "make (s.o.) hold (s.o.) back"; "make (s.o.) prevent" s.o. from doing s.th.; "make (s.o.) cease" fighting **ŠD** lex. = Š ? **N** pass. of G; "be held back, delayed"; of blood "be staunched"; of hair "be retained" **Ntn** iter. of N; > *kalû* I; *kālû*, *kālītu*; *kīlu* I, *kilītum*; *kilâtu*; *makallû*, *maklûtu*; *šuklû*; *kula'ūtu*?

kālû, NA *kāliu* (2-4 rather *kalû* ?) **1.** M/NB "dam, barrage" [BÀD.DINGIR.RA] in irrigation system **2.** jB, NA (a bird, phps.) "crane" **3.** NB (a fetter)?, of iron **4.** lex. (a plant); < *kalû* V

kalūlu mng. unkn. lex.

kalūmatu f. "lamb" Nuzi as PN; jB lex. of girl; < *kalūmu*

kalumdu → *kalumtum*

kalūmiš "like lambs" jB; < *kalūmu*

kalūmītu "lamb-rearer"? MA f. prof.; < *kalūmu* + *-ī*

kalummûm; Nuzi pl. *kalummānu* "everything" Mari, Nuzi; usu. + pron. suff.; < *kalû* II

kalumtum, *kalum/ndu* "female lamb" O/jB, freq. as PN; < *kalūmu*

kalūmu(m), OA *kulūmum* "lamb" [(UDU.) SILA4]; freq. as PN; > *kalūmatu*, *kalumtum*, *kalūmītu*, *kalūmiš*

kalundu → *kalumtum*

kalūtu → *kalûtu* II

kalûtu(m) I "lamentation-priesthood" Bab. [(LÚ.)GALA- ; jB also NAM.GALA] as prebend; OB of *kalû* priests as group; "craft of the *kalû*"; "textual corpus of *kalû*"; < *kalû* III

kalûtu II, *kalūtu* ~ "tree" jB lex.; → *akalūtu*

kalwašše (type of payment)? Nuzi; < Hurr.

kalzu; pl. *kalzāni* ~ "precinct"? M/NA of palace in *k. ēkalli* etc.

kâm → *kīam*

kamādu(m) "to beat cloth"? O/jB **G**; **D** mng. uncl.; > *kamdum*; *kāmidu*; *kimdu*; *gammidatu*?

kamakissu → *kamkissu*

kamālu "to be(come) angry" M/NB(lit.) **G** (*i/i*) with (= *itti*) s.o. **Gt** stat. recipr. "are angry with one another" **D** fact.; stat. "is angered" **N** "become angry"; > *kamlu*; *kimiltu*; *kammālu*; *kummulu*; *kitmulu*

kamamtum (a vegetable) OAkk(Ur III); → *kammantu*

kamāmu ~ "to nod the head"? jB **G** (*a/u*) **Š** stat., mng. uncl.

kamāmu → also *qamāmu*

kamannu → *kamūnu* I

kamantu → *kammantu*

kamānu f. (a loaf or cake) M/NB, NA [NINDA.2/3.SÌLA] containing honey, figs etc.; *k. tumri* "loaf (baked on) the coals"; NA also honey "comb"

kamāriš "in the trap" jB; < *kamāru* I

kamāru(m) I, *kamarru* "hunting trap" OA, jB; > *kamāriš*

kamāru II, *kammāru* "defeat" jB; *k. šakānu* "to accomplish defeat of" s.o.

kamāru(m) III (a fish) O/jB [KA.MAR.KU$_6$]; < Sum.

kamāru(m) IV "to pile up, accumulate" Bab., NA [GAR] **G** (*a/u*, NA *i/i*) dates, property; math. "add (up)" [UL.GAR; GAR.GAR] **Gt** "pile up permanently" wealth; "secrete" poison **D** ~ G wealth; corpses **Dt** pass. of D; of wealth etc.; of men "come in crowds" **N** pass. of G of ruins, people "be heaped up"; > *kamru*, *kamrūtu*; *kimru*, *kimirtu*; *kumurrû*; *kitmuru*; *nakmaru*, *nakmartu*; *kumāru*?

kamāsu(m) I, MA *kamāṣu* "to gather in" **G** (*i/i*) harvest, animals, population; "pack (s.th.) into" container, space etc.; MB "deposit" tablet, gold; OB "finish up" doing s.th. **D** "gather in" people, animals; "consign" corpse to tomb **Dt** pass. of D **Š** "store s.th. up", transf. "deposit" wisdom in s.o. **N** "be gathered in"; of journey, shearing "be finished, wound up"; > *kamsum* I; *nakmasu*?; *takmīsu*?

kamāsu(m) II, *kamāṣu*, *kamāšu*, once *ḫamāšu* "to kneel, squat down" Bab., M/NA [(DU$_{10}$.)GAM] **G** (*i/i*) "kneel, crouch" before (= esp. *šapal*, *maḫar*) god, king; of invalid; of part of body; of cow **Gtn** iter. **Gt** stat. ~ G stat. "is crouched, kneeling" of person, animal; pret. MA, of cow **D** stat. "is kneeling", NA "resides, lives" **Dt** "kneel down" **Š** "make to kneel, squat" in cult, enemy in submission **N** ~ Dt **Ntn** iter. of N "constantly be submissive"; > *kamsu* II, *kāmisum*; *kitmusu*; *kummusu*; → *kimṣu*

kamaṣīrum → *ḫumṣīru*

kamāṣu "rest period" jB lex.

kamāṣu → also *kamāsu* I.II

kamaššeru → *kamiššaru*

kamāšu → *kamāsu* II

kamašurru → *kamiššaru*

kamâtiš "to outside" jB; < *kawûm* I

kamātu → *kammantu*

kamâtu → *kawûm* I

kam'atum, *ka'matu*, NA *ka'u*? "truffle" O/jB, NA ?

kamdalum → *kandalu*

kamdum, *kandu* (desig. of textile) OA, jB lex.; < *kamādu*

kameššaru → *kamiššaru*

kamēšu (a food) NA

kamešurru → *kamiššaru*

kamgu → *kanku*

kāmidu(m) "fabric-beater" O/MB, Mari [LÚ.TÚG.DU$_8$(.A)]; < *kamādu*

kamiru (a noble) Am.; → *gāmiru* ?

kāmisum "one who kneels" OB lex.; < *kamāsu* II

kamîš "in a bound state" O/jB, NA, esp. *k. šūšubu* "to make live in bondage"; < *kamû* I

kamiššaru(m), *kama/ešša/eru(m)*, occas. *kama/ešurru* "pear (tree)" O/jB, NA

kamītiš "in bondage" jB

kamītu I "bondage" jB, also pl.; < *kamû* I

kamītu II "(kind of) ring" jB lex.; < *kawûm* I

kamītu → also *kawûm* I

kamkadu, *kankadu* (a plant) jB lex., med., growing in rock crevices

kamkammatu(m) "ring" OAkk(Ur III), O/jB of metal; transf. astr., round moon; med., desig. of part of body

kamkissu, *kamakissu* (part of body of animal) jB lex.

kamlu, once *kamru* "angry" jB of god, man; < *kamālu*

kâmma "so, thus" Am., Nuzi, Ug.; < *kīam* + *-ma*

kammakkum (wooden part of chariot) Mari

kammallu (a tree) NB

kammālu(m) "opponent, ill-wisher" O/jB in *k. naṭālu(m)* "to identify an opponent"; < *kamālu*

ka(m)mantu, *kammandu*, *kamâtu* (an edible plant) j/NB [Ú.ÁB.DUḪ]

kammaru (desig. of gold)? Am., jB

kammaru → also *kawārum*

kammāru → *kamāru* II; *kawārum*

kammu(m) I "board, plaque" Bab., M/NA [KÀM] **1.** "(writing) tablet, board?", "(text on) writing tablet" **2.** M/NA pl. m. & f. "plaque" of gold etc. as ornament; NB pl. f. "board" for smoothing bricks, of wood, iron; Mari, of pine; < Sum.

kammu II, NA *ka'u* ? (a plant used in tanning) jB/NA

kammu III (a metal dowel) M/NA, NB

kamru "piled up" j/NB of stored dates; of heaps of rubble; < *kamāru* IV

kamru → also *kamlu*; *kawārum*

kamrūtu "state of rubble" jB; < *kamru*

kamsum I (desig. of garments) OA, jB; < *kamāsu* I

kamsu II, *kamṣu* "squatting, crouching" MA, jB; of animal; < *kamāsu* II

kamû(m) I "bound" O/jB [LAL] of man, prisoner; the "bound" gods; < *kamû* II; > *kamîš*, *kamītu* I, *kamûtu*

kamû(m) II "to bind" OAkk, Bab. **G** (*i/i*, occas. *u/u*) [LAL; OAkk ŠU.DU8.A] enemy, land; god, demon, bird; transf. of spells, diseases; of feature of liver **D** ~ G **N** pass. of G [LAL]; > *kamû* I.III, *kamîš*, *kamītu* I, *kamûtu*; *kimītu*; *kimûtu*

kamûm III (or *kāmûm*) pl. "fetters"? OAkk; < *kamû* II

kamû → also *kawûm* I.II

kāmûm → *kamûm* III

kamullu, *kabullu* (a plant) jB lex.

kamūnu(m) I, NA *kamū'u*, Nuzi also *kamannu* "cumin" [Ú.GAMUN(.SAR); OAkk Ú.TIR] as spice, drug; *k. bīni* (a tamarisk product); → *kamūšu*

kamūnu II (a fungus) jB, NA [UZU.DIR] in steppe, mountain; on wall; in pot

kamūsaš (a bronze component of harness) MB; < Kass.

kamuššakku(m) (a kind of chair or bed) O/jB [KA.MUŠ]; < Sum.

kamuššatu mng. unkn. jB lex.

kamūšu mng. unkn. j/NB; var. of *kamūnu* I ?

kamûtu "bondage" M/NB(lit.) [LAL] in *kamû(s)su(nu)* "in bondage"; < *kamû* I

kamū'u → *kamūnu* I

kamzūzu → *kanzūzu*

kanagurru(m), lex. var. *kuriguru* (a circular threshing-floor path) OB, jB lex.; < Sum.

kanaḫu → *kana'u*

kanakku **1.** Nuzi (a household item) **2.** jB mng. unkn.

kanaktu(m), Am. *kanatku* (an incense-bearing tree) Bab., M/NA [ŠIM.GIG] *šaman/zēr k.* "oil/seed of *k.*"; "aromatic resin (from *k.*)"

kanāku(m) "to seal" **G** (*a/u*) door, container; silver etc.; tablet, letter; NB "transfer s.th./s.o. to s.o. by sealing (document)"; as magical act, with blood; stat. "is cryptic" **D** OA, Nuzi, jB "seal up" **Š** caus. of G "make s.o. seal"; OB "make s.o. draw up sealed document" **N** "be sealed" of grain, textile, tablet; Mari "be attested by sealed document"; < *kunukku* denom.; > *kanku*, *kanīku*, *kaniktu*; *kinkum* I; *kanniku*; *maknakum*, *maknaktu*

kanakurtum (a type of oil) Mari

kanānu(m), *qanānu* "to roll up" Bab., OA [GÚR] **G** (*a/u*) "wrap up" silver, figurine; of part of body "curl up, contract"; "tuck up" garment; of snake, refl. "coil (o.s.) up" **Gtn** iter., of parts of body; of snake **D** ~ G "contract" part of body; stat. "is curled up" like dog; of horns of moon **Štn** MA "repeatedly bow o.s. down" **N** of foot "contract" (itself) **Ntn** iter. of N of parts of body; of invalid; > *qunnunu*

kanānu → *ganānu*

kanasarru(m), *kanazerru(m)*; pl. f., also *kašanšarātum* (wooden part of wheel) O/jB for carts

kanašû(m), *kanaš/suttu* (a red flower) Bab.; < Sum.

kanāšu(m) I, OAkk, NA also *ḫanāšu(m)* "to bow down, submit" **G** (*u/u*, rarely *i/i*) [GÚR] of enemy, worshipper, subject; of features on liver **Gt** stat. "is constantly submissive" **D** "subject" people, land; mountains; *kišāda k.* "bow o.'s neck, submit o.s." **Dt** "be subjected" **ŠD** ~ D **Š** "make s.o. submit"; > *kanšu* I, *kanšiš*, *kanšūtu*; *kinšu*; *mukannišum*; *šuknušu*

kanāšu II "to gather in" NA, NB **D** people, harvest; < Aram.; > *kanšu* II; *kiništu*

kanāšunu → *kunāšunu*

kanašuttu → *kanašû*

kanatku → *kanaktu*

kana'u, *kanaḫu*? (a plant) jB

kanazerru → *kanasarru*

kanāzu "to store away" NB food, tools; < OPers. *kanz* "treasure" denom.

kandaku "(boat's) hold"? NB for dates

kandalu(m), OB also *kamdalum* (a metal item)? Bab.; → *kundulum*

kandara(sānu) (a linen dress)? NB

kandarû → *kandurû*

kandiršu → *kundirāšu*

kandu "jar" NB for tar, wine; < Aram.

kandu → also *kamdum*

kandurû, Nuzi *kandarû* M/NB **1.** (desig. of terrain), also as PlN **2.** (a vessel, phps.) "rhyton" and/or "potstand"; < Sum.

kanerḫu (a plant) jB lex.

kangannu → *kankannu*

kangiškarakku → *kannaškarakkum*

kangu → *kanku*

kaniktu(m) "sealed document" O/MB; also "sealed (consignment)"; < *kanīku*

kanīku(m) NA f.; pl. m. & f. "sealed document" O/jB, M/NA *kanīkāt šīmātim* "purchase documents"; MA *bīt kanīkāte* "tablet-container"; jB also "(clay) sealing" for jar, door; < *kanāku*

kaniniwe mng. unkn. Nuzi; < Hurr.

kanipānu (a plant) jB lex.

kānišu → *kanšu* I

kankadu → *kamkadu*

kankallu → *kagallu*

kankannu, *kakkannu*, NB *kangannu* "(wooden) pot stand" j/NB, NA esp. for large washing vessels

kankiru (or *kankuru*) (an object) NA of copper

kanku(m), *kakku*, j/NB *kan/mgu* "sealed" Bab. of silver, vessel, document; "sealed (document)"; "(clay) sealing", NB "seal"; transf. jB "closed off, banned" of sea-port, "sealed" of womb, "hidden" of mystery, also in *kakku sakku* (a type of text); < *kanāku*

kankuru → *kankiru*

kanna/â → *akanna* I

kannama → *akannama*

kannaškarakkum, *kanniškarakkum*, *kinnaška=rakkum*, *ka(n)giškarakku(m)* (a kind of table) O/jB [(GIŠ.)KA.KARA$_4$]; < Sum.

kannātu → *kannu* II.III

kanniku "sealer, one who seals" j/NB; NB *k. bābi* "gate-sealer" as family name; < *kanāku*

kanniškarakkum → *kannaškarakkum*

kannu(m) I "(vessel-)stand; (a large vessel)" OAkk, Bab., NA **1.** [GIŠ.GAN] "stand" for pot, for metal vessel **2.** [DUG.GAN] "jar" for milk, oil, beer etc.; "(drinking) goblet"?; "bucket" for well; < Sum.; → *kannulatḫu*

kannu(m) II; pl. f. "band, binding" Bab., NA for hair, attached to clothing; wrestler's "loincloth", "(menstrual) cloth"; "binding" for sheaf; (a kind of trap); NB also of leather

kannu III; pl. f. "shoot, seedling" jB, NA of vine, fruit-trees

kannulatḫu (a household utensil) Nuzi; < *kannu* I + Hurr. *-atḫu* ?

kannūtum "accommodation, board"? OA in *kasap k.*; < *kanû* D

kansu → *kanšu* I

kanṣu (a milk product) OB lex.

kanšiš "submissively" j/NB; < *kanšu* I

kanšu I, *kaššu*, *kānišu*, *kansu*, *ḫanšu*, *ḫaššu* "submissive" M/NA, M/NB; < *kanāšu* I; > *kanšiš*, *kanšūtu*

kanšu II "work-team" NB; < *kanāšu* II

kanšūtu "submissiveness" NB; < *kanšu* I

kantappu ~ "fish's tail"? jB, part of a figurine

kantuḫḫum (attachment to a chariot) Mari

-kanū- → *-kunu*

kanû(m) "to care (for)" **G** "dress up, prepare o.s.", stat. "is cherished" **D** of deity "treat kindly"; of human "praise, do honour to" deity; OA "accommodate, put s.o. up"; "attire (for burial)"; "care for, look after" clothes, house, statue etc. **Dt** pass. of D **N** "be (too much) cared for" jB; > *kanūtu*; *kinûtu*; *kunnû*, *kunnūtu*, *kannūtum*; *teknûm*, *teknītu*

kânu(m) OAkk, Ass. *kuānu(m)* "to be(come) permanent, firm, true" [GI.NA; GIN] **G** (*ū*) of house, land, reign, foundation "be permanent", "firmly established"; astr. "remain visible"; of market "be stable"; of person "be reliable"; of statement "be(come) dependable, immutable"; of *libbu* "be loyal"; of a prediction "be realized"; of a sacrificial animal "be in correct state" **Gtn** iter., of planets "repeatedly stay visible" **Gt** "become permanent" **D** **1.** liter., transf. "establish firmly" foundation, kingship etc.; "give permanence to" sceptre, reign, prosperity; "install" building, beam, door etc.; "permanently deposit" tablets in library; "fix" bowstring **2.** "define, fix" law, time (for s.th.), heavenly movements, boundary; "fix, impose" tax, tribute, domination, offering; OB + acc. infin. "impose" duty to do s.th.; "assign" payment etc. to s.o. **3.** OA "make secure" for s.o. **4.** leg. "establish" (s.o.'s guilt), "convict"; "confirm" s.o.('s statement); "prove, confirm" a fact; NB *eli ram(a)nišu k.* "confess" **5.** in cult "set up" offering, furnishing "correctly" **Dtn** iter. of D **Dt** pass. of D **Dtt** NA of person "be confirmed in post" **D^2** (*uka(w)wan*, Aram. formation) NB "define precisely" **Št** OB ~ "cause to indict" person; > *kīnu*, *kīna*, *kittu* I, *kīniš*, *kīnūtu*; *kūnu*; *kayyānu*, *kayyāniš*, *kayyamānu*, *kayyamāniu*, *kayyamānû*; *kunnu*; *mukinnu*, *mukinnūtu*; *makānu*?; *takittum* I

kanūku mng. unkn. jB lex.

kanūnu → *ganūnum* II; *kinūnu*

-kanūšu → *-kunūši*

kanūtu f. "the cherished" jB epith. of goddess; < *kanû*

kanwartu, MA *kalmartu*, NA *garmartu* (a festival; also as MN) Ass.

kanzabu (a musical instrument) jB; < *kazābu* I

kanzû (a plant) jB lex.

kanzūzu, *kamzūzu* jB **1.** [ZAG(.GA)] ~ "gums" of human **2.** (a dung-beetle)

kapad → *kapdu*

kapādu, MA *kapātu* "to plan, scheme" Bab., M/NA **G** (*u/u*, occas. *i/i*) "plan, have plan for" wish, garden, temple, journey; to do s.th. (infin., acc. or *ana*); battle, evil (against s.o. = dat. or *itti/ana/-iš*); Mari, of consulting omens; NB "hasten" to do s.th. **Gt** "plan, devote o.s. to s.th. consistently" **D** ~ G "plan, scheme" **Dtn** OB *liḫtappud* "let him take constant care of"? **Š** caus. of G; jB also "make s.o. hasten"; > *kapdu*; *kāpidu*; *kappidu*?; *kipdu*; *kitpudu*

kapālu(m), *qapālu(m)* "to roll up, wind up" O/jB, NA **G** (*i/i*) reed-mat **Gt** recipr. "intertwine" each other, of snakes, birds etc.; children's game **D** "roll up" corpse in shroud; dung-ball **Dt** "roll o.s. up" of snake; transf. "form a band, conspiracy" of people, land **N** NA of glaze ~ "roll together"; > *kāpilu*; *kitpulu*, *kitpulūtu*; *kiplu*; *kapilu*?; *kapullum*?; *kappultum*; → *muqappil zê*

kapānu → *gapānu*

kapāpu(m), *kabābu* "to curve, bow" O/jB, NA [GILIM; GÚR] **G** (*a/u*) of parts of body, stat. "are curved, bent"; "surround" s.th. with s.th. (= 2 acc.) **D** "bend, twist" part of chariot; stat. of parts of body, foetus "is bent, curved" **Š** caus. jB/NA "make" mankind "bow down" **N** "be bent, twisted" of neck, part of liver; > *kippu*, *kippatu*; *kuppupu*

kaparru(m) I; jB pl. f. *kaparāti*, Nuzi, Hurr. pl. *kaparrašta* "shepherd-boy" OAkk, O/jB [(LÚ.)KA.BAR]; > *kaparrūtu*

kaparru II ~ "spadix" of palm tree? j/NB; < Sum.?

kaparru III (a whip or goad) j/NB; < Sum.?

kaparrūtu(m) "work of shepherd-boy" O/MB; < *kaparru* I

kapartu → *kapru* I

kapāru(m) I "to peel, strip" Bab. **G** (*a/u*) "peel" reed, pole **D** "clear away, strip off" plants from land, horns from ziggurrat **Dt** OB transf., of affair "be cleared away"; > *kapru* III; *kāpiru*?; *takpūru*, *takpurtu*

kapāru(m) II "to wipe (clean)" Bab., M/NA **G** (*a/u*) tears, hands etc.; vessel, stone **Gtn** iter., teeth, mouth **D** [ŠU.GUR.GUR] "(cultically) wipe clean" s.o.; town, house, field; by ritual activity **N** "be wiped clean" jB; > *kāpiru*?; *kupīrātu*, *kupurtum*; *takpertu*

kapāru(m) III "to smear" Mari, OB(Hana), jB, NA **G** (*a/u* ?) esp. stat. with bitumen (*kupru*) etc. **N** "be smeared" with bitumen; < *kupru* denom.

kapāsu → *kapāṣu* II

kapāṣu(m) I, *kabāṣu(m)* (a seashell) O/jB [NA4.KA.BA/PA.ZA]; also imitations in stone or metal

kapāṣu(m) II, *kabāṣu(m)*, *kap/bāsu(m)* "to bend back, distort" O/jB **G** (*i/i*) of part of body, snake, horn of moon, part of liver **D** "make squint" eyes; stat. "is bent" **N** "be bent up" of parts of liver; > *gabāṣu*; *kapṣu*; *kipṣu*; *kāpiṣu*

kapāšu(m) O/jB **G** (stat. *kapuš*) **1.** OB, jB lex. "be abundant" of smoke **2.** Mari mng. uncl., of acrobat; > *kāpišum*

kapātu(m) O/jB **G** (*i/i*) of ear, mng. unkn. **D** "to bring together, collect" troops; ominous signs; stones; "roll into ball" ingredients (into pill); stat. "is rolled up" of lizard, ~ "form ball", of flesh, hair etc. **Dt** pass. of D; > *kupputu*, *kupputtu*; *kupatinnu*?

kapātu → also *kapādu*

kapa'u → *kaba'u*

kapdu, *kapda/i*, *kapad* adv. "urgently, quickly" NB also *ana k.*; < *kapādu*

kāpidu "planner" jB; < *kapādu*

kapilu (a leather strap)? NA; < *kapālu* ?

kāpilu "winder" OB lex., a prof.; < *kapālu*

kāpiru "wiper" or "caulker" jB lex.; < *kapāru* II or III

kāpiṣu (an official)? jB; < *kapāṣu* II

kāpišum; f. *kāpištum*, jB *ḫabbištu* (a cultic performer) O/jB; < *kapāšu*

kāpītum "stony ground" Mari, in *eqel k.* "stony terrain"; < *kāpu* + *-īt*

kapizzuḫḫu (an object) Am. in pairs; of gold; < Hurr.

kapkapu ~ "powerful" M/jB

kapkūru → *kabkūru*

kaplītu → *kablītu*

kappaltu "groin" jB of man

kapparinnu mng. unkn. NB; → *kubarinnu*

kapparnu (a copper can) Nuzi; < Hurr.?

kappatinnu → *kupatinnu*

kappidu mng. unkn. jB; < *kapādu* ?

kappu(m) I "wing" O/jB [PA] of bird, ant, god, statue; on star; transf. of feature on liver; on lung (*ḫašî*), *k. īni(m)* "eyelid, eyelash"; lex. (branch of tree); → *agappu*; *gappu*

kappu(m) II "hand, palm of hand" **1.** [Á(.2)] of humans, du. *kappāya* "my hands"; *išid k.* "base of hand"; NB *ina muḫḫi k.* "in one go"; of animal "paw" **2.** "(small) bowl" of wood, gold, silver; NA pl. *kappāni* **3.** jB "edge, bank" (or = *kāpu* ?)

kappu(m) III (part of harness) O/jB lex.; < Sum.

kappultum "wrapping" OA as purpose of textile; < *kapālu* D

kapru(m) I; pl. m. & f. "village" [NA URU.ŠE]; *šāt k.*, *šāt kaparti* (a kind of bird)

kapru II (a kind of offering)? M/NB desig. of sheep, beer, dates

kapru III ~ "clipped" lex.; < *kapāru* I

kapsu → *kapṣu*

kapsû "buyer" jB lex.; < Sum.

kapṣu, *kabṣu*, *kap/bsu*; f. *kabis/ṣtu* "bent up, distorted" jB of part of liver; < *kapāṣu* II

kapšarru → *kabšarru*

kapšušiḫuru (desig. of a kind of sheep) Nuzi; < Hurr.

kaptaru (a tree) jB lex.

kaptarû; f. *kaptarītum* "Cretan" Mari; < PlN

kaptukkûm, *kabduqqû* "two-*sūtu* container" O/jB, NA [DUG.2BÁN] for liquids, wool; < Sum.

kapû → *kepû*

kāpu(m); NA pl. *kāpāni* "rock, cliff" Emar, jB, NA of river, of mountain (jB → also *kappu* II 3); OB, in PN of man ?; > *kāpītum*

kâpu ~ "to oppress, wrong"? jB **G** (*ā*)

kapullum mng. uncl. OB, feature of wool; < *kapālu* ?

kaqdâ/û, *q/kak/qdâ/û*, *gag(a)dâ(m)* "constantly" Bab.; < *qaqqadu* ?

kaqqadu → *qaqqadu*

kaqqaršu → *qaqqaršu*

kaqqaru → *qaqqaru*

kaqqullu → *kakkullu*

karābu(m) I "prayer; blessing" M/NB, NA [SISKUR; SÍSKUR; A.RA.ZU]; < *karābu* II infin.

karābu(m) II "to pray, bless, greet" **G** (*a/u*) [ŠÙD] **1.** "pray" before (= *maḫar*) deity on behalf of (= *ana*, dat.) s.o., for (= *ana*) s.th.; "make, utter" prayer (*ikribu*, *tamītu*); in PNs "pray to, supplicate" deity (= acc.) **2.** "dedicate" votive offering, animal, funerary offering **3.** of deity etc. "bless, give benediction to" person, object **4.** "greet (with a blessing)" **Gtn** iter. **Gt** "constantly pray to, call blessings on" **D** ~ G Mari "pray" for (= *ana*) s.o. **Š**, **Štn** caus. of G 1 O/jB ? **N** pass. jB "be greeted"; > *karbu*; *kiribtu*; *kurbu*; *karābu* I; *kāribu*; *karūbu*, *kirību*; *ikribu*; → *kurību*

karagaldu → *karimgaldu*

karakku → *kurukku*

karāku "to roll up, collect" M/NB, NA **G** (*i/i*) **1.** "block" water, canal **2.** "wrap, twine" **3.** "gather" troops **4.** NA in hendiad. mng. uncl., phps. "do promptly" or "do again" **D** "wrap up" tongue **Š** NA "have collected" **Št** jB med. "surround" finger with liquid ? **N** "be wound up" of intestines; transf. of people "be assembled"; > *karku*; *kerku* I, *kiriktu*; *makraku*

karalānu etc. → *karānu* 4

karallu I ~ "goad" jB lex.; also as desig. of jewellery item

karallu II ~ "happiness" jB comm.

karammaru, *kalammaru*, *karriammaru* (an administrative register) NB; < Iran.

karammu (part of storage facility)? NB; → *karmu* II 2

karāmu(m), NB also *kerēmu* "to grasp, restrain" Bab., NA **G** (*i/i*) person; "withhold, delay" payment, journey; "stock up" bricks, seed **N** NA of eyes "be hindered" from seeing; > *karmu* I; *nakramu*

karānānû "wine-coloured" jB lex.; < *karānu*

karānatu(m) 'little wine' OB as hypocorist. PN; j/NB (desig. of stone); < *karānu*

karānu(m), OA, NA *kirānu(m)* "vine; wine" **1.** "vine" [GIŠ.GEŠTIN] **2.** "wine" [GEŠTIN(.NA); later also GIŠ.GEŠTIN] good, poor, red, bitter, strong etc.; NA *rab k.* "wine-overseer" **3.** "grapes" **4.** in comb.: *k. lê*, *k. lāni*, also *karalānu* and var., NA *karān la'u* (a kind of vine); *k. šēlebi* 'fox-wine' (a plant); *ṣer k.* 'vine-snake'; > *karānatu*, *karānû*; *karānānû*

karānû "(red) wine-coloured" jB lex., desig. of lapis lazuli; < *karānu* + *-ī*

karapḫu, *karpaḫu* "fallow land, year" Alal., NA

kararatu (a magical word)? jB

kararû "midday heat" jB [AN.BIR9]

karāru I "to put (down), discard" M/NA, Ug. **G** (*a/u*) "put" s.th. "down, on" somewhere; "lay" foundations; stat. of place "is situated, lies"; "throw, cast" person, lot; "drop" sweat, "deposit" corn etc.; "put, impose" work, duty; "cast" o.'s eye on s.th.; "lay low" s.o., with weapon **N** "be set up" of bed

karāru II mng. unkn. jB **G** stat. (condition of eyes); > *karru* I?; *karriru*?; *karurtu*?

karāsu ~ "to tie up" jB lex., NA **G**; **D** → *mukarrisu* ?; > *kurussu*

karāṣu(m), *garāṣu(m)*, *ḫarāṣu* "to break off, pinch off" O/jB **G** (*i/i*, occas. *a/u*) [KÍD] clay, esp. *k/gerṣī k.* "pinch off a lump"; "gnaw" bone **Gt** lex. only **D** **1.** jB ~ G "pinch off" lumps; of pig "gnaw" wall **2.** OB denom. from *karṣu* "slander" s.o.; > *karṣu*; *kerṣu*; *karriṣum*; *takrīṣu*

karašku "funerary chapel"? Am.(Mit.); < Hurr.?

karašu(m), *karšu(m)* "leek" Bab., NA [(Ú.)GA.RAŠ(.SAR); OAkk once RAŠ.GA.SAR] cultivated; wild, in mountains; also (a stone); → *kurissu*

karašu → also *karšu*

karašû → *karāšu* II

karāšu(m) I "military camp" [KARAŠ(=KI.KAL. BAD, KI.KAL×BAD)] Bogh. also "troops, army"; < Sum.?
karāšu(m) II, *karašû* "catastrophe, disaster" O/jB
karāšu → also *mukarrisu*
karatašna (or *karaurna*) (an object) OB(Alal.)
karatnannu, Qatna *qardanānu* (an ornament) Am., Qatna; in pairs, of gold
karattu "like a grain-store"? jB; < *karû* I + *-attu*
karātu "to slice" jB, NA **G** (*i/i*) "cut off" tail; "fracture"? figurine **D** "cut off" hand, horn; "chew up" lip; > *kartu*
karāṭu(m) **G** mng. unkn. OB stat., condition of gall **N** "to be merciful", as infin. "forgiveness" jB; > *nakruṭu*
karā'u "to bow (o.s.) down" NB; < Aram.
karaurna → *karatašna*
karballatu "(pointed) hat" NA, NB
karbānum → *kirbānu*
karbu "blessed" NB in fPN *Karibti* ?; < *karābu* II
kardû (a kind of door) jB lex.
kargullûm ~ "market value" OB; < Sum.
kāribu; f. *kāribtu* "one who blesses" M/NA, M/NB **1.** (a priest), *niqê kāribi* "offerings for the *k.*" **2.** (a supplicant deity or genie), occas. ^{d}*K.*; MA f. "female genie" in wood; < *karābu* II
kariḫuri (an official) Nuzi
karimgaldu, *karimtaldu*, *karagaldu* "quiver"? M/jB on chariot; < Kass.
karintu → *karmu* I
karkadinnu → *kakardinnu*
karkamisûm "of Carchemish" OB desig. of vessel; < PlN
karkarru (a bird) jB lex.; < Sum.?
karkartu (an edible plant) MB, NA
karkarum mng. unkn. OB, desig. of chair
karkasum, *karkaṣu* (a kind of mash) O/jB lex.
karkittu "prostitute" jB lex.; < Sum.
karku "rolled, gathered" j/NB, NA of threads, textiles; of troops, *ina karkāti* "en masse"; of mash "soaked"?; < *karāku*
karmiš "into a ruin" j/NB in *emi/ušēmi k.* "turned into a ruin"; < *karmu* II
karmu I; f. *karintu* "delayed" NA; < *karāmu*
karmu(m) II "heap, mound" **1.** Bab. "ruin mound", esp. *ana tīlī u k.* "into mounds and ruins" **2.** M/NA, Mari? "grain heap"; *bīt k.* "granary"; *rab karmāni* (an official) (→ *karammu*); > *karmiš*; *karmūtu*
karmūtu "ruination" j/NB esp. in *k. alāku* "to go to ruin"; < *karmu* II

karpaḫu → *karapḫu*
karpāniš "like a pot" jB; < *karpatu*
karpassu (a fibre, phps.) "cotton" NB; < Sanskr.
karpaṣu ~ "magnificent" jB lex.
karpatu(m) "(clay) pot" [DUG] also as measure, OA (= 1/4 *naruqqum*), OB for liquids, st. abs. *karpat*; occas. of stone, metal; < *karpu*
karpum "pot" OA; > *karpatu; karpāniš*
karratu mng. unkn. M/jB, desig. of a window
karriammaru → *karammaru*
karriru (desig. of criminal) jB lex.; < *karāru* II ?
karriṣum; f. *karrištum* "slanderer" OB; < *karāṣu*
karru I adj. mng. uncl. MB epith. of mounds; < *karāru* II ?
karru(m) II "knob" Bab., NA [GÀR(.BA)] "pommel" of sword; *sikkat k.* "knob-pegs", i.e. decorative wall pegs; "knob" on throne, also "throne" (same word ?); transf. "peak" of mountain; < Sum.
karru III (a mourning garment) O/jB
karru → also *kāru*; *kerru* I
karsû(m) (a kind of song) jB
karṣillu(m) (or *karzillu(m)*) "knife, scalpel" O/jB [GÍR.ZAL (later wr. DÙ)] of copper, used by surgeon; < Sum.
karṣu(m) "slander" Bab., NA [EME.SIG(.GA)] *k. akālu(m)* "to slander", *ākil k.*, Mari *ša k.* "slanderer"; NB also "(true) accusation"; < *karāṣu*
karšānû/u (desig. of bison) M/jB, Bogh. [MB GU_4.ŠÀ.GU_4]; < *karšu* + *-ān* + *-ī*
karšu(m), *karašu* m. & f. "stomach, interior"; of human "stomach", *pī k.* "epigastrium"; of animal, also as food item; "insides" in gener., also "womb"; transf. "mind, understanding, mood" etc.; "interior" of house, of ear; *k. ubāni* (fleshy side of finger/toenails); > *karšānû*
karšu → also *karašu*
karšû (a deformation on the exta) jB
kartappu(m), *qartappu(m)*, jB *kerdippu* "(animal) driver" [LÚ.KIR_4.DAB (→ also *sakrumaš*)] esp. of horses; M/NB (a high official); < Sum.
kartillû mng. unkn. jB lex.
kartu ~ "shredded" jB of reeds; < *karātu*
kārtum "current price" OB in *kārat ibbaššû* "the existing price"; < *kāru* nom. unit.
karû(m) I, *qarû*; MA acc. *karu'a*, gen. *karu'e* "grain-heap, grain-store" [GUR_7]; *bīt k.* "granary"; OB also as capacity measure (= 3,600 *kur*); j/NB $^{(giš)}$*k.* "hold" on boat; NB, of property held in common; < Sum.; > *karattu*

karû(m) II "to be(come) short" Bab., M/NA **G** (*u/u*, also *i/i*) [LÚGUD(.DA)] of space, of time; of heart, life "be(come) diminished" **Gtn** [LÚGUD.MEŠ] "contract repeatedly" of parts of body; of life "constantly become diminished" **D** "shorten" time, "diminish" s.o.'s life, "put in desperate straits"; stat. "(are) very short", of parts of body etc.; MA "deduct, subtract"? **Š** "shorten" days; > *kurû, kurītu*?; *kurrû*; → *tagrītum*

karûm → also *ḫerû* II D

kāru(m), NB also *karru* "quay, port" [KAR] **1.** "(river) quay, quay-bank, wall"; NB "bank" of ditch **2.** "port" on river, on sea, in PlNs; *rab kāri* "quay, port overseer"; NB "quay, port dues" **3.** OB ~ "chamber of commerce" **4.** OA "trading colony", e.g. *kārum Kaneš*, st. abs. *kār kārma* "colony by colony"; *bīt k.* OA, also NA "customs house", NB "shop" **5.** OB ~ "current price" (set by *kārum*); < Sum.; > *kārtum*

kārum → also *kerru* I

kâru I "to rub" jB med. **G** part of body; "rub on" medicine **Gtn** iter. **D** ~ G "rub" flesh with (= *ina*) s.th.

kâru(m) II "to be dazed" O/jB, NA **G** (pret. *ikūr*) **D** stat. ~ "is incapacitated"?; > *kūru* I; *kīrtu*?

karūbu "reverently greeted" M/jB, epith. of deities; < *karābu* II

karurtu ~ "hunger cramp" jB lex.; < *karāru* II ?

karzillu → *karṣillu*

kasaku → *kašku*

kasal → *kaslu*

kasāmu(m) "to cut up, chop" OA, O/jB **G** (*a/u*, jB *i/i*) [GAZ] body, wood, reed; med. *malmāliš/ištēniš k.* "chop up together"; > *kasmu*; *kismu, kisimtum, kisittu*; *kāsimum*

kasânītu (a red stone) jB [NA4.GUG.GAZI.SAR]; < *kasû* II

kasappum (an object)? OB

kasāpu(m) I "to break (into bits)" O/jB, M/NA **G** (*a/u*) esp. bread, fig. etym. + *kusāpu* "to break bread, have meal"; wood, fingernail etc. **D** ~ G lex. only **Dt** pass. of D; > *kassupu*; *kusāpu, kusīpu* I, *kuspu*; → *kaspu*

kasāpu(m) II "to make funerary offering" OB(Susa), Mari, jB **G** (*i/i*, jB once *takassap*) in *kispu k.* **N** pass., of funerary offering "be offered"; < *kispu* denom.

kasāru(m), Bab. also *kesēru* "to block; pave" O/jB, M/NA **G** (*i/i*) with stone, bitumen; "block" canal **N** NA of air "be blocked off"; > *kisirtu*; *kāsiru*

kasāsu(m), *kaṣāṣu(m)* "to chew, gnaw" Bab. **G** (*a/u*) of human, animal; of fire; of pain "gnaw"; OB om. of oil "encroach on" water **Gtn** (*u/u*) **D** "gnaw, cause pain"; > *kāsistu*; *kissatu* I?, II, *kiṣṣatu*; *kusāsū*; *kussusu*; → *gašāšu* G

kasilaqqu → *kizalāqu*

kasīlūtum mng. unkn. OA

kāsimum "(reed) chopper"? OB; < *kasāmu*

kasīpu → *kusīpu* II

kāsiru(m) "barrage" O/jB in watercourse; < *kasāru*

kāsistu "gnawer" (f.) jB epith. of fire; of demon?; < *kasāsu*

kasîš "in bondage"? jB; < *kasû* I

kasītu "(magical) constraint" jB; < *kasû* I

kasīyā → *kasû* II

kaskasu(m) "gristly extension of breast-bone, ensiform cartilage" Bab. [GAG.ZAG.GA] of sacrificial sheep; NB as cut of meat; OB of part of furniture-leg

kasku → *kašku*

kaslu, *kasal* (a kind of land-plot) NB; < Aram.?

kaslu → also *kislum*

kasmu "chopped" MA, jB of tree, plant; < *kasāmu*

kaspu(m) "silver" [KÙ.BABBAR; OAkk, OA, also OB freq. KÙ; jB also KI.SAG] as raw material; used for objects; as currency; "price; money"; → *kasāpu* I

kassibānu/û, kassibu → *kusīpu* II

kassidakku → *kaṣṣidakku*

kassupu "broken"? NA; < *kasāpu* I D

ka(s)sūsu(m) "(hunting) falcon" O/jB [ŠÚR.MUŠEN]; also as figurine; as desig. of hero, as PN

kasû I "bound" j/NB [LÁ]; as subst. "captive"; < *kasû* III

kasû II pl. tant.; NB Aram. pl. *kasīyā* (a spice plant, phps.) "mustard" Bab., NA [(Ú.)GAZI.SAR (GAZI freq. wr. SILA4)] as food-plant, in med., roasted, crushed etc., *mê k.* "mustard?-water"; *k. ṣerri* 'snake *k.*' (a plant); transf. ~ "granule"; as desig. of semiprecious stone *aban k.* [NA4.GUG.GAZI.SAR (GAZI wr. SILA4)]; > *kasânītu*; *kasûtu* II

kasû(m) III "to bind" **G** (*u/u*, *i/i*) person, animal; foot, hand, of illness "grip" insides; OA transf. "obligate" s.o.; j/NB "bind" stone, bricks and mortar into wall **Gtn** iter. of illness **D** ~ G "bind" person, animal, limb; OB om. stat. of part of body "is grown over by" (= acc.); OA "obligate" **Dt** pass. of D **Š** caus. of G Mari

N pass. of G; > *kasû* I, *kasîš*, *kasûtu* I, *kasītu*; *kīsu* III; *kisītu*?; *kusītu*, *kusīu*; *maksû*, *maksūtu*

kāsu(m) m. & f.; pl. f. "cup, bowl" [GAL; MB on (DUG.)GÚ.ZI] freq. of metal; for oil, wine; MB, NA as measure of capacity

kasulatḫu (a copper item) Nuzi; < Hurr.

kasumma → *kazumma*

kasurru → *kisurrû*

kasūsu → *kassūsu*

kasûtu I "bondage" jB; < *kasû* I

kasûtu II "mustard? plant" NA; < *kasû* II nom. unit.

kaṣābu ~ "to reduce, pare off"? jB, NA **G** (*a/u*) stat. of part of body; of gold **Št²** mng. uncl., phps. "reach fullness" **N** "be reduced"?; > *kāṣibu*; → *ḫaṣābu* I

kaṣādum "to seize hold" OA **G** not attested **D** person, goods **Dt** pass. "be seized" **N** of person, goods "be seized"; > *kuṣṣudu*?

kaṣāpu, *keṣēpu* "to think" NA, NB **G** (*i/i*) "reckon, estimate", stat. of goods "are reckoned at" value **D** "take s.th. into consideration, think out" s.th.; > *kiṣiptu*

kaṣaru → *kaṣru*

kaṣāru(m) "to tie, knot; gather" **G** (*a/u*, Bab. occas. *i/i*) [KEŠDA; KÀD, KÁD in PNs] **1.** "knot, tie up" string, hair, cloth **2.** "gather" troops, animals, goods; "compose" literary work **3.** "organize" work, battle, protection **4.** "gather, form" cloud, smoke, astr. glow; absol. of cloud etc. "form, be concentrated" **5.** "join together, construct" camp, wall, fort **6.** of ice "consolidate", of part of body "contract?, go hard", transf. *lā kāṣir ikki* "not hardening the heart", i.e. merciful **7.** of god "strengthen" man, esp. in PNs **Gt** stat. recipr. "is interwoven"; "is clad in" fear, radiance **D** ~ G "bind round"; "assemble" troops; "organize" battle; "construct" camp, fort; Mari "fortify" town; of illness "paralyse?"; of field, stat. "is hard" **Dt** "gather together" of troops, clouds **DRt** Mari **Š** caus. "cause to organize" battle; stat. "is hardened"? **Št** "gather" troops etc. "together" **N** pass. of G "be gathered"; of work "be organized"; of part of body "be bound" by cramp ?, "paralysed"?; > *kaṣru*; *kiṣru*, *kiṣirtu*; *kaṣṣārum*, *kaṣṣārūtum*; *kāṣiru*, *kāṣirtum* *kāṣirūtu*; *kāṣiranupši*; *kiṣṣuru*; *kuṣīrum*?; *kuṣṣuru*; *takṣīru*; *makṣaru*; *šutakṣuru*

kaṣāṣu(m) I, *gaṣāṣu* "to grind, grate" O/jB, NA **G** (*a/u*) [KA.GUZ] usu. "grind, grate" o.'s teeth, also absol., without obj., as sign of aggression; "rub"? tongue, heart; ext. stat. "is rubbed away" **Gtn** iter. "persistently grind" teeth, also absol. **D** "cut down, cut back" wings, nails, fingers **Dt** pass. of D of fingers **Št** ~ G, of Adad "grind" (teeth) **N** ~ G as sign of aggression ? **Ntn** ~ Gtn; > *gaṣṣu* II, *gaṣṣatu*?; *giṣīṣu*?; *kaṣṣiṣu*; *kuṣṣuṣu*; *takṣiṣītu*

kaṣāṣu II ~ "rain"? jB

kaṣāṣu → also *gazāzu*; *kasāsu*

kaṣâtam → *kaṣâttam*

kaṣâtiš "in early morning" jB; < *kaṣâtu*

kaṣâ(t)tam "in early morning" OB; < *kaṣâtu*

kaṣâtu(m) f. pl. "early morning" O/jB; < *kaṣû* III; > *kaṣâtiš*; *kaṣâttam*; → *mūškaṣât*

kāṣibu ~ "reducing" jB comm.; < *kaṣābu*

kāṣiranupši (a functionary) OB(Alal.); < *kaṣāru*

kaṣirtu → *kiṣirtu* 1; *qaṣirtu*

kāṣirtum "female 'knotter', tailor" OB; < *kāṣiru*

kāṣiru(m) 'knotter', "tailor"? [LÚ.(TÚG.)KA.KEŠDA] alongside weaver; NA, NB *rab k.* "chief tailor", NB of hats; also jB lex. (a kind of mongoose); OA, as var. of *kaṣṣārum*; < *kaṣāru*

kāṣirūtu "craft of tailor?" NB; < *kāṣiru*

kaṣiṣiḫatu (a spice) j/NB

kaṣru(m), jB occas. *kaṣaru* "firmly joined, solid" of troops, clan; OA "well packed" of donkey; "clustered" of skin marks; astr. of halo ~ "concentrated"; < *kaṣāru*

kaṣṣārum ~ "packing-supervisor" OAkk, OA, Mari of goods in boat, in donkey caravan (OA → also *kāṣiru*); < *kaṣāru*; > *kaṣṣārūtum*

kaṣṣārūtum "function as packing-supervisor" OA; < *kaṣṣārum*

kaṣṣidakku(m), *kazzidakku(m)* "miller" Bab. [(LÚ.)KA/GAZ.ZÌ.DA(-)]; NB also *Kassidakku*, as family name; < Sum.

kaṣṣiṣu "habitually grinding teeth" jB of person; < *kaṣāṣu* I

kaṣṣu → *gaṣṣu* II; *gazzu*; *kaṣû* I

kaṣṣūtu uncert. NB

kaṣû(m) I, Bogh. *kaṣṣu*; f. *kaṣītu* "cold" Bab., NA [ŠED₇] of water; place; oven; transf. Bogh. of words; < *kaṣû* III

kaṣûm II, *qaṣûm* "the (Mesopotamian) steppe" Mari; < W.Sem.

kaṣû(m) III "to be(come) cold" Bab., M/NA **G** (*i/i*) [ŠED₇] of water, weather; med. of patient; infin. *kaṣê ūmi* "cool of the day, evening" **Gtn** iter. of patient, part of body "continually become cold" **D** [ŠED₇] "cool down" (trans.) land; horse, after exercise; med. part of body, concoction; glass in kiln; transf.

"calm" heart; > *kaṣû* I, *kaṣâtu*, *kaṣâtiš*, *kaṣâttam*; *kīṣu*; *kūṣu*, *kūṣû*, *kūṣāyu*; *mukarṣītu*?; *takṣâtu*

kâṣu "to skin, flay" M/NB, NA **G** (*ū*, Nuzi also *ī*) "skin" animal, captive; "flay" skin (of captive); "strip" off layer, from eye, plant? **D** ~ G "flay" animal, person **Š** caus. of G Mari **N** pass. of G; > *kīṣu* I; *kā'iṣu*; *makāṣu*; *takāṣu*?

kâša → *kâšim*

kašādu(m) "to reach, arrive; accomplish; conquer" **G** (*a/u*) [KUR; jB occas. SÁ.SÁ] **1.** "reach, arrive at" place, level; person; time, day, season; of time, event "arrive"; also + *ana*, *ana ṣēr/muḫḫi*, *adi* **2.** "stretch as far as", "be contiguous with"; of house "equal" (in value) **3.** "(succeed in) reach(ing)", "locate" s.o., s.th. **4.** "achieve, get" silver, health, offspring, kingship; desire, plan **5.** "conquer" land, city, "defeat" enemy; of demon, curse, ordeal "catch up with, overcome"; freq. *qātum* as subj. **6.** "complete, accomplish" job, field(-work); "master" instructions **7.** of supplies, people "be sufficient, adequate" **Gtn** iter. of G OB **Gt** OB lex., mng. uncl. **D** "drive off, chase away" person, demon, animal; "send away" messenger; Nuzi "disinherit"; OA, Mari, Bogh. "pursue, follow up" s.o., M/NA "chase, catch up with" animal **Dtn** iter. of D "constantly pursue"; Alal. "repeatedly send away" wife **Š** caus. of G **Št** OB "complete (work on)" field **N** pass. of G; NB also of payment, landholding "belong with, pertain to" **Ntn** ~ Gtn of G 5; > *kašdu*, *kašittu*; *kāšidu*; *kišdu*, *kišittu*; *kuššudu*; *mukaššidu*

kašāḫum → *ḫašāḫu*

kašāme → *kīšamma*

kašanšarātum → *kanasarru*

kâšanu- → *kâšunu*

kašāpu(m) "to cast spells (on s.o. = acc.), bewitch" O/jB **G** (*i/i*) **D** ~ G; > *kišpu*; *kušāpu*; *kaššaptu*, *kaššāpu*, *kaššāpūtu*

kašāru(m), *kešēru* "to restore; have success" **G** (OAkk, OB *a/u*, later *i/i*) **1.** "repair" building etc.; "replace" grain etc.; in PNs, of deity "compensate" **2.** of person "accomplish" s.th. "successfully"; of illness "be(come) satisfactory" **D** ~ G "restore" building **N** ingress. of G "be accomplished successfully"; > *kišertum*?; *kušīru*; *kušurrā'um*; *takšīru*; *kiširru*?, *kiširtu*?; *kušāru*?, *kušartu*

kašāšu(m) I "to gain control of, acquire" OA, O/jB **G** (*a/u*, Am. *i/i*) liter., property, leg. "assume control of" s.o., Am. "control" enemy; transf., wisdom **D** OA "make acquisitions" **N** OB, with *kiššātum* "be taken as pledge" **Rtn**? (ptcp. *muktaššaššu*) jB "constantly gain mastery over" s.o.; > *kaššu*, *kaškaššu*; *kāšišum*; *kašūšu*; *kiššū*, *kiššû*; *kiššātum*, *kiššūtu*; → *kiššatu* I

kašāšu II ~ "to become dizzy"? jB **G** (*u/u*) of patient

kašāṭu(m) "to cut off" Bab, NA **G** (*i/i*) "chop down" tree, vine; "cut off" caravan, descendants; "cut down" oil issue

kašā'um → *kašû* II

kašdu(m), NB *kaldu* "achieved, successful" Bab. [KUR] of revolt, attack; desire, plan; "sufficient, adequate" of work etc.; "arrived" of goods; < *kašādu*; > *kašittu*

kašerkāna mng. unkn. NB (a plant)? rdg. uncert.

kâši → *kâšim*

kāšidu "conquering" NA in DN ^{d}*Kāšidūti*; < *kašādu*

kâšim, *kâši*, *kâšu(m)*, *kâša(m)* "to you" (2 sg. pron.) Bab., NA; OB m. & f. dat. "to, for you"; later *kâša* = m. and *kâši* = f., also acc., gen. after *ša lā* "without"; → *kuašim*; *šâka*

***kâšina** "(to) you" (2 f. pl. acc., dat. pron.) not attested (→ GAG §41i)

kāšišum "creditor, pledge-taker" OB, Ug.; < *kašāšu* I

kašittu(m) **1.** OB "recovered (goods)" **2.** jB "success"; < *kašdu*

kašītu f. mng. unkn. jB lex.

kaškada/innu → *kakardinnu*

kaškaššu(m) "all powerful" Bab., as divine epith.; OB (desig. of divine weapon); < *kaššu*

kaškašum "(the cuneiform sign) KASKAL" OB ext. [KASKAL]

kašku, *kaškiniwe*, *kas(a)ku* (a kind of land holding) Nuzi; < Hurr.

kašmaḫḫum, *kašmāḫu* "first class beer" O/jB [KAŠ.MAḪ]; < Sum.

kašmušḫu (or *gašmušḫu*) (an object) OB(Alal.); < Hurr.?

kaššaptu(m) "sorceress" Bab. [MUNUS.UŠ$_{11}$(.ZU)]; < *kašāpu*

kaššāpu "sorcerer" O/jB [LÚ.UŠ$_{11}$(.ZU)]; < *kašāpu*

kaššāpūtu "sorcery" jB *aklē k. mê k.* "bread of sorcery, water of sorcery"; < *kaššāpu*

kaššidu mng. uncert. jB of sign

kaššu "massive, strong" NB of flood-waters; < *kašāšu* I; > *kaškaššu*

kaššu → also *kanšu* I

kaššû "Kassite" Bab. lex., of words; as PN, as gentilic

kašû(m) I "to cover over" O/jB **G** (*i/i*) with (= acc.) dust **N** of person "be mistreated"?

kašû(m) II, OAkk *kašā'um* ~ "to increase" (intrans.) OAkk, OA, O/jB **G** (*i/i*) jB of profit (*takšītu*) **D** "make profit", infin. *kuššû* "profit"; stat. "is plentifully endowed with" hair; "expand" temple **Št** OB mng. uncl.; > *kuššû*?; *takšû*, *takšītu*

kašûm III mng. unkn. OAkk **G** (pret. *ikšu*)

kâšu "to delay, linger" M/NA, M/NB **G** (*ū*) of person; of plant "be late" **D** "hold up, delay" s.o.; NA "tarry" **Št** "be held up, delayed"?

kâšu → also *kâšim*; *kiāšum*

kašudû "informer" jB lex.; < Sum.

kâšunu, NA before stress *kâšanu-* "you" (2 m. pl. pron.) M/NB, NA dat., after *ana*; gen.; acc.; → *kâtunu*

kašurrītu (textile from Gasur) jB lex.

kašu(r)rû(m) "of Gasur" **1.** "basalt" jB in myth, for door-sockets **2.** OA, of person, of textile; < PlN (= Nuzi)

kašūšu(m) (a divine weapon) O/jB of Nergal; om., as desig. of catastrophe; as epith. of deity, king; < *kašāšu* I

kašūtu mng. unkn. jB comm.

kâta → *kâti*

katabbum → *katappum*

kataduggû "saying, utterance" jB [KA.TA. DUG4.GA]; < Sum.

katamlalu → *kutamlalu*

kātamma → *qātamma*

katammu "lid, cover" NB, for kettle, stove; < *katāmu*

katāmu(m) "to cover" **G** (*a/u*) [DUL] **1.** "cover (s.th.) up" with (= acc./*ina*) earth, light etc.; stat. "is covered" with (= acc.) flesh; "close" lips; of dust, sand "cover, shroud" city, sky **2.** of demon etc., fear, radiance "overwhelm" **3.** "hide, secrete", "seize and detain" person, animal **D** ~ G [DUL] "cover" with (= acc./*ina*) earth, garment etc.; "close" eyes, lips; "cover over" vessel, oven; Am. "conceal" **Dtn** "keep constantly secret" words **Dt** pass. of D of mouth "be closed"; of person "be clad" with garment **ŠD** ~ D ? **Š** caus. "make" dust "cover sky"; "close" lips **Štn** iter. "constantly close" mouth **N** "be covered" with (= acc.) garment **Ntn** [DUL.DUL]? iter. "be constantly overwhelmed", also ~ Gtn; > *katmu*, *katammu*; *kitmu*, *kitimtu*; *kutmu*, *kutummu*; *kutumtu*; *kātimtu*; *kuttumu*, *mukattimtu*; *naktamu*, *naktamtu*; *šaktumu*; *taktīmu*; *kātimiṣi*

katappātu, once *ḫaltappātu* (part of animal's breast) jB lex.; < *katappum* or *katappû* ?

katappum (an object) OA, OB of wood, silver, copper; < Sum.?

katappû "bridle, halter" M/jB [Am., Bogh. KUŠ.KA.TAB(.ANŠE)] for donkey, horse; < Sum.

katarru (a kind of fungus) jB, NA [KA.TAR] in house, on wall; < Sum.?

katāru I "to get (as) help" NA/jB **G** (*i/i*) of troops; < *kitru* I denom.?

katāru II ~ "to wait" NA **G** (*i/i*); < Aram.

katātu(m) "to quiver, vibrate"? O/jB **G** (pret. *iktut*) of part of liver ? **D** "shake"? (trans.) lex. only **Štn** of flesh "quiver continually"? **Št** "be disturbed", astr. "descend"

katâtu "needle"? jB lex.

katā'um "to distrain, take as pledge" OA **G** (*a/a*) slave, tool **Gtn** iter. of G **D** ~ G with pl. obj., slaves; > *kātu*; *kattû*; *kutūtum*

kâti, *kâta*, jB also *kâtu* "you" (2 sg. pron.) Bab.; *kâti* m. & f. acc., gen.; *kâta* m. only, acc., gen., Mari also nom., jB only dat.; → *kuāti*; *šâka*

katimattu, *katimuttu* (a bird) jB

kātimiṣi (a climbing plant)? jB lex.; < *kātim* + *iṣu*

katimtu → *katmu*

kātimtu **1.** jB "net" for birds etc. **2.** (desig. of kind of door); < *katāmu*; → *mukattimtu*

katimuttu → *katimattu*

***kâtina** "you" (2 f. pl. acc. pron.) not attested (→ GAG §41i)

katinnu → *kattinnu*

katmu(m) "covered" O/jB of earth; "concealed"; f. *katimtu* "a secret", *k. šadê* "secret places of mountains" etc.; < *katāmu*

katrû → *kadrû*

kattamma → *kayyānu*

kattā'um → *kattû*

kattillu, *kattellu* (a predatory animal) Bogh., jB killing horse; among demons, diseases

ka(t)tinnu (a metal weapon) MB(Alal.), Nuzi, Emar

kattu → *gattu* I; *kû*

kattû(m), *kattā'um*, *kattu'um*? "corroborator" OAkk, OA?, O/jB of judicial statement; < *katā'um*

katum (a tool) OB ?

katû(m) I "weak, needy" O/jB; < *katûm* II; > *katûtu*

katûm II "to become poor" OA; > *katû* I, *katûtu*; → *qadā'um*

kātu "surety, pawn" MA for loan; < *katā'um*

kâtu → *kâti*; *kā'um*; *qayyātu*

kâtunu "you" (2 m. pl. pron.) M/jB acc., gen., after *ana*; → *kâšunu*; *kunūti*

katurû → *kitturru* I

katûtu "poverty" jB; < *katû* I

kaṭāpum → *qatāpu*

ka'u → *kam'atum* or *kammu* II; *kayyu*

ka''û D NA "to wave" frond

kā'um; pl. *kâtum* (a cloth) OA

kâ'u → *gâ'u*

ka''ulu → *kullu* III

kauriyannu mng. unkn. Nuzi in desig. of gold vessel

ka'urrāku "carver of reliefs"? jB lex.; < Sum.?

kawali → *qawali*

kawalzuru (a metal object) Nuzi; < Hurr.; → *qawali*

kawārum, MA *kabāru*, NB *kammalāru*, *kamru* ~ "ramp" Bab., MA; Mari also (a component of jewellery)

kawatumma in *k. epēšu* ~ "to plunder" or "confiscate"? Nuzi; < Hurr.?

kawûm I, *kamû* "outer" Bab. [(AN.)AŠ.A.AN; BAR(.RA)], *bābum k.* "outer gate"; f. *kamītu* "(area) outside", *kamītuš* "to the outside"; f. pl. *kaw/mâtu(m)* "environs" of city, "open country"; > *kamâtiš*; *kamītu* II, *kimâ*, *takwûm*?

kawûm II, *kamû* "to burn" (trans.) Bab. **G** rare **D** "roast, bake" **N** pass. lex. only; > *nakmû*; *takwûm*?

kayyamān(a) → *kayyamānu*

kayyamānīu → *kayyamānû*

kayyamānu(m) "permanent, regular" Bab., NA [SAG.UŠ] "permanent" water etc.; astr., ext. "normal(ly present)" of features; as adv., also *kayyamān(a)* "constantly"; (desig. of planet) "Saturn" [also TUR.DIŠ]; < *kayyānu* (irreg. extended form); > *kayyamānīu*, *kayyamānû*

kayyamānû, NA *kayyamānīu* "reliable" j/NB of words; NA "permanent" [(LÚ.)SAG.UŠ] of soldier, of lion; of offering "regular"; as adv. "constantly"; < *kayyamānu* + *-ī*

kayyān(alu), *kayyānamma* → *kayyānu*

kayyāniš "constantly" OB; < *kayyānu*

kayyānu(m) "constant, regular" OA, Bab. [SAG.UŠ; jB also GUB] of tribute, rain, famine etc.; of person "constantly present"; of part of liver "normal"; OB *kīma kayyantim(ma)* "as normal"; in adv. usages OB *kayyantam*, also *(ana) kattam(ma)*, O/jB *kayyān*, M/NB *kayyāna/u*, *kayyānamma* "regularly, constantly"; jB "in usual meaning"; < *kânu*; > *kayyamānu*; *kayyāniš*

kayyanzu ~ "property"? Emar

kayyipu "criminal" jB lex.

kayyu, *ka'u*, *akayû* "(donkey) stick" jB lex.; also part of loom

kazabu (a plant) jB lex.

kazābu(m) I "to be attractive, alluring" O/jB **G** stat. of cow **D** "flatter, fawn" of man, dog; > *kazbum*; *kuzbu*, *kuzbānu*, *kuzbānītu*, *kuzubtum*; *kuzābum*; *kanzabu*; *kuzzubu*; *mukanzibtu*

kazābu II "to tell lies" Am. **G** (*i/i*); < W.Sem.; > *kazbūtu*

kazallu (a plant) jB [Ú.KA.ZAL] as drug

kazalluḫu (a plant) jB lex.

kazan, *kazanena* → *qazan*

kazāru → *kezēru*

kazazakku mng. unkn. jB lex.; < Sum.?

kazāzu → *gazāzu*

kazbum "charming, alluring" OB as fPN *Kazubtum*; < *kazābu* I

kazbūtu "lies" Am. in *awât k.*; < *kazābu* II

kaziršu mng. uncl. Nuzi

kazirtum (desig. of slavewoman) OB

kazīru "fringe, curl"? M/jB of plant, also med. (a plant); of stone ornament, pl. *kazīrānu*; < *kezēru* ?

kazitaššu mng. unkn. Nuzi; < Hurr.

kaziztu subst. "cutting off" jB ext.; < *gazāzu*

kazratu → *kezretu*

kazû → *kizû*

kazumma (or *kasumma*) in *k. epēšu* of woman ~ "to scratch" s.o.? Nuzi; < Hurr.?

kazurḫu, *kazušḫu* (a garment); < Hurr.

kazzapurušḫu (an implement) Nuzi, of copper; < Hurr.

kazzaurnu ~ "substitute, compensation"? Nuzi; < Hurr.?

kazzidakku → *kaṣṣidakku*

kazzu → *kizzu* I

kē, *a(k)kê*, *ikkê* "how?", "how!" in exclamations before vb., adj. in st. abs.; in rhetorical questions; OA before number, "approximately"; → *kī*

kē'am → *kīam*

kēkē → *kīkī*

kelēṣu → *kalāṣu*

keltum (a disease) OB lex.

keltum → also *kaltum*

keltuḫlu → *geltuḫlu*

kêm → *kīam*

kēna → *kīna*

kēnu → *kīnu*

kēnūtu → *kīnūtu*

kenniwe mng. unkn. Nuzi; < Hurr.

keppû(m) "skipping rope" O/jB; also as an attribute of Ištar; < *kepû*

kepû(m), *kapû* "to bend (back)" O/jB **G** [GAM] stat. of part of liver, of body, horns of moon "are curved" **D** ~ G stat. "is curved" **Dtn** OB mng.? **Št(n?)** of Ištar "make s.th. whirl round"?; > *keppû*

kerdippu → *kartappu*

kerēmu → *karāmu*

kergīlu → *gergīlu*

kerḫu(m) "enclosure wall; enclosed area" Bab., NA of city, temple court

kerku(m) I "blockage"? Bab., of water-flow; NB in *šušānu ša ker(e)k(ēt)i* (an irrigation worker)?; < *karāku*

kerku II "roll" NA, NB of cloth, of papyrus; < Aram.

kerlammu (a small vessel) jB lex.; < Sum.

kerperušḫu (an object on wall) Nuzi; < Hurr.

kerrētu → *gerru* I 6; *kirrētu*; *kirru*; *qerītu*

kerridir → *gerridir*

kerru(m) I, Mari *karrum*, *kārum* "male sheep" OAkk, OA, Mari

kerru(m) II "(area of) collarbone" Bab., of human, left, right; also du.; of bird

kerrum → also *gerru* I

kerṣappu → *gištappu*

kerṣu, *gerṣu* "pinched-off piece, lump" M/jB, OA? of clay; of dough; OA of piece of metal ?; of miscarried foetus?, also ^{uzu}*k.*; < *karāṣu*

kēru → *kīru* I

kerzizu (an object) jB in Marduk *ša k.*; rdg. uncert.

keserū → *kasāru*

kēsu → *kīsu* II

kēsû (a prof.)? jB lex.

kêsu(m) mng. unkn. OB, jB lex. **G**

keṣēpu → *kaṣāpu*

kešēru → *kašāru*

kettu → *kittu* I

kētu → *kittu* I; *kītu*

kezertum → *kezru*

kezēru(m), *kazāru* "to give s.o. a (special kind of) hair-do" O/jB, NA **G** (*i/i*) king, woman, animal; OB *nēbeḫ/parṣī kezērim* (a payment relating to function of a *kezretum*); > *kezru*, *kezretu*, *kezrūtu*; *kizirtu*; *kuzīrum*; *kazīru*?

kezretu(m), *kazratu* "woman with (special kind of) hair-do" O/jB, NA [MUNUS.SUḪUR.LÁ] a type of cultic prostitute; OB *wakil kezrētim* "overseer of the prostitutes"; jB *iṣṣūr kezrēti* (a bird); < *kezēru*

kezru(m); f. *kezertum* "with (special kind of) hair-do" O/MB lex., NA [LÚ.SUḪUR.LÁ] also as PN, fPN; < *kezēru*

kezrūtu "status of a *kezretu*" MB; < *kezretu*

-ki, *-k*, NB *-ku* "you" (2 f. sg. acc. suff.) (→ GAG §42g-k)

-ki → also *-kim*

kī "like; how?; as" **1.** prep.: "like"; "according to"; "for" (a price); "on account of"; before infin., *kī lā mekê* "without negligence", *kī šakān bilte* "by imposing tribute"; MB *kī qāt*, jB *kī ša* "instead of" **2.** interrog. adv.: "how?", NA PNs before prec. "How should I ...?"; → *kiyā*; *maṣû* I G 6 **3.** conj. usu. + subjunct. [NB GIM] temporal: "when" before pret., perf., pres., stat. **4.** condit.: NB "if" before perf., pres.; *kī* introducing oath = neg., e.g. *kī undeššer* "if I abandon" = "I will not abandon", *kī lā* = pos. (*kī adi* before pres.); *kī ... kī* "whether ... or"; *ša'ālu kī* "to ask" etc. "whether" **5.** MB "because" **6.** "that" after vb. of knowing, saying, swearing **7.** "just as", usu. *kī ša*; > *kīam* etc.; *kīkī*; *kīma*, *kīmê*; *kē*; *kišūma*; → *akanna* I; *akī*; *kīnanna*

kīa → *kīam*; *kiyā*

kiā'im in *k. u k.* "here and there" Mari; also Am. *ki-ia-am ... ki-ia-am*; → *kīam*

kiakī "thus"? OB(poet.)

kīam, *kīa*, Mari also *kêm*, M/NB also *kâ(m)* "so, thus" [UR5.GIM] **1.** of way of speaking, writing, calculating etc.; "etc., and so on"; *šī lū k.* "so be it (for ever)"; OB *šumma lā kīamma* "if it is not the case", MA *ū lā kīa* **2.** O/MA *k.-ma* "just so, in the same way" **3.** OB as pred. ~ "it is", *warḫum kīam* "it has been a month"; + pron. suff. *kīašša* "she is like that" **4.** after prep., *ina/ana k.*, OA *akkīam*, OB(N.Mes.) also *ikkêm* "hence, in consequence"; *aššum k.* "for that reason, purpose" **5.** *k. ... k.* "once ... another time, now ... then", of person *k. k.* "so-and-so" **6.** O/jB interrog. "how (much)?"; < *kī* + *-am*; > *kâmma*; → *akia*; *kiā'im*; *kīaššu*

kīa(š)šu Bab. lex. = *kīam* + *-šu* "in that way"

kiāšum, jB *kâšu* "to help" O/jB, esp. infin. "assistance, support"; > *kišamma* ?

kibaltu (a kind of semiprecious stone) jB lex.

kibalû, *kipalû* "rebel land" jB lex.; < Sum.

kibarru "boat of inflated skins"? NA/jB

kibasu → *kibsu* II

kibbātu → *kibbu* II

ki(b)bu(m) I; pl. *ki(b)bāni* (an object) Bab., NA; of gold; < Sum.?

kibbu(m) II; lex. pl. f. "burn mark, brand"? Bab.; Mari (an extispicy procedure)?; < *kabābu* II

kibegûm "initial state" OB math.; < Sum.

kibiltu uncl. jB lex.; → *kabālu*

kibinû (syn. for) "father" jB lex.

kibirru(m); pl. m. & f. **1.** Bab. ~ (a weapon) **2.** Bab. lex. "taper, fire-brand"; < Sum.

kibittum → *kabittu* 1

kiblu → *kiplu*

kibnu → *kipnu*

kibrātu → *kibru*

kibrītu, *kubrītu* "sulphur" M/jB [PIŠ$_{10}$(=KI.A).(^{d})ÍD; PIŠ$_{10}$.^{d}ÍD.LÚ.RU.GÚ; also *kibri*-^{d}ÍD (folk etym.)] as drug, of various colours; rit., om.; *išāt k.* "fire of s."

kibru(m), *kipru(m)*; pl. m. & f. "bank, shore, rim" [PIŠ$_{10}$(=KI.A)] of river, canal, sea, as safe place; "rim" of oil cup; "border, edge" of furniture, boat; of part of body, *k. īnim* "rim (=white) of eye"; in *kibrāt erbetti(m)/arba'i(m)* [UB.DA.LÍMMU(.BA)] "the four edges" of the world, jB also *kibrātum* alone [UB.MEŠ] "the world"

kibrû, *kubarû* ~ "old man" jB lex.

kibrûm → also *kiprum*

kibsu(m) I; pl. m. & f. "track, footprint" [KI.UŠ] **1.** "tread, imprint" of foot, *k. redû* "to follow a track", *ša kibsi* "tracker" (NA → *rādiu* 2); "droppings" of animal, as drug; MA "rung" of ladder, jB "step"; *k. šēpē* "soles of feet" **2.** "track, route" of person, animal, *k. šakānu* "to make o.'s way"; transf. "mode of life, behaviour, course of life" **3.** math. "way of calculation"; OA *kibsātum* "deducted amounts"; < *kabāsu*

kibsu II, NB also *kibasu* (a garment) M/NB usu. of deity

kibšum I (or *kipšu*) "donkey foal"? OA

kibšu II (or *kipšu*) (a fungal mould) jB as skin-complaint; *zēr k.* as drug

kibšû (or *kipšû*) (a bird) jB lex.

kibtu(m); pl. *kibātu*, Mari *kabātum* "wheat" Bab., NA [(ŠE.)GIG(.BA); NB also GIG.BI]

kīdam "to the outside" OB; < *kīdu*

kidadabru (a plant) jB lex.

kīdānu(m), *kīdiānu* adv. "outside" Bab., MA of buildings *ša/ana k.* "exterior"; of persons "away" from home, family, land; as prep. "outside" gate etc.; < *kīdu* + *-ānum*

kīdānû "external" MB of wall; < *kīdānu* + *-ī*

kidapasse → *kindabašše*

kiddum → *kīdu*

kiddudû → *kidudû*

kidennu → *kidinnu*

kīdiānu → *kīdānu*

kidil- → *kidinnu*

kidimuri → *kadmuru*

kidinētu "forest" jB lex.

kidinnu(m), *kidennu(m)*, *kidīnu* ~ "protection, aegis" OB(Susa), M/NA, M/NB [UBARA; in PNs also BAR] at Susa ~ "divine protection" for person; later also privileged status (incl. tax exemption) of cities and their citizens, *amēl/āl k.* "exempted man/city"; in PN *Kidin-DN* (NB also *Kidil-* before *Ellil*, *Iltar*); jB "protective watch"; < Elam.; > *kuddunu*; *kidinnû* I, *kidinnūtu*

kidinnû I; f. *kidinnītu* "protégé(e)" M/NB, esp. as (f)PN; < *kidinnu*

kidinnû II (or *kitinnû*) **1.** NB (a fabric, textile)? (→ *kidintu*) **2.** j/NB (a metal object) **3.** NB (a payment or delivery)

kidinnūtu "exempt status, protection" j/NB, NA esp. in *k. kaṣāru*, *k. šakānu* "to establish (s.o.'s) exemption"; < *kidinnu*

kidintu f. var. of *kidinnû* II 1 ?

kidīnu → *kidinnu*

kīdītu "exterior part" O/jB [SA] om. (a part of the liver); pl. *kīdêtum*, *kīdiātu* ~ "outlying establishments"; < *kīdû*

kidkidru → *kukkudru*

kidmuri → *kadmuru*

kidrûm → *kadrû*

kīdû(m) "exterior" O/jB of part of geometrical figure; "external" of plaster on wall; astr. of moon's halo; MB as fPN "(Woman) from outside"; < *kīdu* + *-ī*; > *kīdītu*

kīdu(m), OB also *kiddum*; pl. m. & f. "outside, countryside", esp. as opp. to in the city; as habitat of plants, animals; "outside" of building, of human body; > *kīdam*; *kīdānu*, *kīdānû*; *kīdû*, *kīdītu*

kidudû, *kiddudû* pl. tant. "rites" jB, NA [KI.DU.DU] of ritual in temple, freq. with *parṣū*; < Sum.

kigallu(m) "socle, pedestal" OAkk, Bab., NA [KI.GAL] of building, statue; "(foundation of earth =) underworld", also in DN *Ereš-kigal*; < Sum.

kigallu → also *igigallu*; *kagallu*

kiga(l)lû → *kikallû*

kigamlum, OA also *kugamlum*, M/NA *gugamlu* "animal pen" Ass., OB; OA for donkeys, MA lambs

kigullatu (desig. of a woman) jB, among paupers etc.

kigullû ~ "place of destruction" jB lex.; < Sum.

kigurrum (a mathematical body) OB; < Sum.?

kiḫullû "mourning rites" jB [KI.ḪUL]; also "mourning place"; < Sum.; → *giḫlû*

kikā "thus, like"? Am.; < W.Sem.

kika(l)lû, *kiga(l)lû* "hard ground" Bab. [KI.GÁL(.LA)]; < Sum.; → *kagallu*

kikamunu "third in line" Nuzi [3-*mu-nu*] of person for duty; < Hurr.; → *kukumnu*

kikarpu "three-year-old" Nuzi, of animals; < Hurr.

kīkī, *kēkē*, *kīkīya* "how?" M/jB in exclamation; < *kī*

kikittu mng. unkn. jB lex.

kikiṭṭû "ritual procedure" M/jB [KÌD.KÌD(.DA/BI)]; < Sum.

kīkīya → *kīkī*

ki(k)killu → *kilkillum*

kikkimû, *kikkišû* (desig. of a reed artefact) jB lex.; < Sum.

kikkirânu(m), *kikkiriānu*, *kirkirânu*, *kilkil/rânu*, *kiškirânu*, *kiškalânu*, MB(Bogh.), Ug. *kirkiriyannu* "pine or juniper seeds" O/jB, MA [ŠIM.ŠE.LI/LÁ(.BABBAR)]

kikkišu(m), NA *kikkisu* "reed fence, wall" O/jB, NA [GI.SIG]; as enclosure for field, orchard; as hut for ritual

kikkišû → *kikkimû*

kiksu ~ "splinter of wood" jB lex.

kikunannum, *kipunannum* (an item of dress) OA

kikunnûm → *gegunnû*

kikurrû ~ "temple foundation" jB; < Sum.

kilallān, *kilallū(n)*; f. *kilattān*, OA also *kilaltān*, OB gen. *kilettīn* "both" [MAŠ.TAB.BA] of persons, things, as subst. or adj.; with pron. suff., e.g. OA *kilallākunu* "both of you"; OB st. abs. *kilalal kilalal* "in pairs"; → *kalû* II

kilāmu → *gilāmu*

kilattān → *kilallān*

kilâtu pl. tant. "barrage" M/NB in watercourse; < *kalû* V

kildu → *kišdu*

kilī- → *kalû* II

kilibbu "total" jB lex.?; < Sum.

kilibbum → also *kilimbu*

kilidar (desig. of horse) MB, also as name of horse

kililānu → *karānu* 4

kilīliš "as with a wreath" jB with vb. of surrounding; < *kilīlu*

kilīlu(m) "wreath" OAkk, Bab., NA [GILIM] **1.** head ornament for humans, gods, of silver, gold; OAkk, OB transf. desig. of DN in PNs **2.** jB, NA, NB also *killilu* "parapet" of wall, building **3.** Bab. lex. (a kind of rush)? **4.** *(iṣṣūr) k.* (an owl); ^{d}*K.* (a female demon); > *kilīliš*; *kullulu* II, *kulīlum* II; → *kulūlu*

kilimbu, *kilibbum*, *kilimmu* "reed bundle" O/jB [GI.GILIM]; < Sum.

kilimmu → *kilimbu*

kilippû → *kuluppû*

kilītum "restraint" Mari, as function of door; < *kalû* V

kilkilânu → *kikkirânu*

kilkillum, jB *ki(k)killu* (a reed structure) O/jB, for rituals

kilkirânu → *kikkirânu*

killatu → *kullatu* I

killilu → *kilīlu* 2

killilû → *kulīlītu*

killu(m) mng. uncl. **1.** OB ext. (part of liver)? **2.** jB lex. in *aban killi* (a stone)

killu → also *ikkillu*; *kīlu* I

kilpum I "profit"? OA

kilpu II mng. unkn. NB

kilsukku (or *kirsukku*, *ḫabsukku*?) (part of plough) jB lex.

kilṣu ~ "(physical) contraction" jB comm.; < *kalāṣu*

kiltappu → *gištappu*

kīlu I, NB *killu* "enclosure, confinement" M/NB [KI.ŠÚ] of prisoner; *bīt k.* "prison"; *ša k.* "prisoner"; *iṣṣūr k.* "cage-bird"; < *kalû* V; → *k.* II

kīlum II "finale" of song Mari; = *k.* I ?

kilūbu "(bird) cage, trap" Am.; < W.Sem.

kilullû ~ "massacre" jB lex.; < Sum.?

kilupinnum → *kulupinnum*

kilzappu → *gištappu*

-kim, *-ki* "to you" (2 f. sg. dat. suff.) (→ GAG §42g-h)

kīm → *kīma* 3

kimâ adv. "outside" jB; < *kawûm* I

kīma "like; when, as, that" [GIM] **1.** "like", in similes; "according to" measure, word, decree etc.; math. "equal to", "equal in rank to"; "as" of person's rôle, number's function **2.** "in place of, instead of", *ša kīma PN* "PN's representative(s)"; *kīma kunukki* "instead of a seal" **3.** OB *kīm(a) inanna* "right now", *kīma* *šalāšīšu* "just three times", *kīma pānīšu* "at once"; Am. + adv. "... as possible", e.g. *kīma mādiš* "as much as possible" **4.** before infin. "in order to", *kīma libbika lā marāṣim* "so that you should not feel insulted"; OA *kīma itappulim ittanapulūniāti* "they will pay us as far as possible"; OB *kīma lā nabšî* "as though it had not occurred"; "instead of" doing s.th.; "in spite of" doing s.th.; "as soon as", *kīma aṣê šamši* "as soon as the sun rises/rose" **5.** adv., OB after *ša* "from time to time, on occasion"; *ašar kīma šapārim* "wherever he may send" **6.** conj. "when" (NA + indic.) **7.** conj. "because", "in such a way that" **8.** conj. "that" after vb. of saying, knowing **9.** conj. "as" in comparative clauses, *kīma tīdû* "as you know", also *ana kīma*, *akkīma*; *kīma ša* "just as though"; < *kī* + *-ma*; → *kīmê*; *kīmū*; *kūm*

kima' "how much?" NB; < Aram.

kima(ḫ)ḫu(m), *gimāḫu* "grave, tomb" Bab., NA [KI.MAḪ]; *bīt k.* "mausoleum"; < Sum.

kīmānû → *kīmū*

kimarru → *gamarru*

kīmatu → *kimtu*

kimdu(m) (a kind of cloth) OB, Ug., jB$^{?}$; < *kamādu*

kīmê "like; as, that" Alal., Am., Nuzi, Bogh., Ug. **1.** prep. "like", "according to" **2.** conj. (freq. + indic.) "when", "if"; "because"; "that" after vb. of saying etc.; "in order that"; "as, in the way that"; < *kī* + *-mê* II

kimek (part of a vehicle) jB lex.

kimiltu "wrath, anger" M/NB of deities [DIB; DINGIR.ŠÀ.DIB.BA]; < *kamālu*

kimirtu(m) "sum, total" Bab. esp. math.; < *kamāru* IV

kimītu "bondage" jB; < *kamû* II

kimkimmu, *kinkimmu* **1.** jB "wrist (joint)" **2.** lex. (syn. of taboo)

kimmagātu pl. tant. (a kind of textile) MB

kimru(m) "layer(ing), heap(ing)" O/jB, NA of dates; NA $^{(udu)}$*k.* (a sacrificial sheep); Am. (a festival); < *kamāru* IV

kimrum → also *gimru*

kimṣu(m), *kinṣu*, *kiṣṣum* "shin, lower leg" Bab., NA [DU$_{10}$.GAM] **1.** "shin, calf" of human, left, right, also du.; of animal, constellation; of boot **2.** Nuzi (a measure of length, = *eṣemtu*, 3/4 cubit) **3.** "support", OB of DN in PN; math. of three-dimensional body; Nuzi (part of a lock); → *kamāsu* II

kimtu(m), *kintum*, *kīmatu* f. "family" [IM.RI.A] *bīt k.* "family house"; → *kīmu*

kīmu "family" jB; → *kimtu*

kīmū, NB also *kīmānû* "instead of" Bab., M/NA; as prep. OB *kīmūšu/ša* "instead of him/her"; "in return for"; Nuzi "as" share, gift etc.; → *kīma*; *kimuḫlu*; *kūm*

kimuḫlu "substitute"? Nuzi; < *kīmū* + Hurr. *-uḫlu* ?

kimûtu "bondage" jB; < *kamû* II

kimzūru mng. unkn. jB in *k. ša amēlūti* "human *k.*" as drug

-kin(a) "your" (2 f. pl. gen. suff.) (→ GAG §42g-k)

kīna, *kēna* "yes!" OA; < *kīnu*

kinaḫḫu; Hurr. pl. *kinaḫḫena* "purple" Nuzi in minas; garments *ša k.*; < PlN Kinaḫ(n)i ?

kinakata adv.? mng. unkn. MA

kinaltu → *kiništu*

kīnanna "so, thus" Am., Nuzi, Bogh.; → *kī*; *inanna*

kinartu → *kiništu*

***kināši(m)** "to you" (2 f. pl. dat. pron.) (→ GAG §41f)

-kināši(m) "to you" (2 f. pl. dat. suff.) (→ GAG §42g-k); jB also acc.

kinaštu → *kiništu*

kināti "you" (2 f. pl. acc. pron.) Bab. unattested (→ GAG §41f); OA dat.

-kināti "you" (2 f. pl. acc. suff.) Bab. (→ GAG §42g-k); OA dat.

kinattu(m), *kinātu*; pl. m., later also f. *kinātātu* **1.** "employee, menial"; as coll. "staff"; OB(Chagar Bazar) *sūt k.* (a *sūtu*-measure); **2.** j/NB, NA business or prof. "colleague"

kinattūtu "colleagueship" jB; Am. "personnel"; < *kinattu* abstr.

kinātu → *kinattu*

kīnātu → *kīnu*; *kittu* I

kinayyātu pl. tant. (a present, payment or offering) j/NB, NA

kinburru (a nest)? jB of a bird; < Sum.

kindabašše, *kindabasse*, *kidapasse* etc. ~ "loincloth" M/NA

kingallu "leader of assembly" jB epith. of Nabû; < Sum.

kingu → *kinkum* I

kīniš "reliably, genuinely" OAkk, Bab. "faithfully, truly"; "duly, legitimately"; "righteously"; < *kīnu*

kiništu, *kinaštu*, *kinaltu*, *kinartu* "priesthood, religious staff" NB [LÚ.UKKIN]; < *kanāšu* II

kinītum I (a kind of emmer) Mari

kinītu II (or *qinītu*) "concubine"? jB lex.

kinkimmu → *kimkimmu*

kinkum I, j/NB *kingu* "sealing" Bab., of bag, door; OB "sealed tag"; < *kanāku*
kinkum II (a festival) OB; (name of 6th month at Ešn.)
kinnanû (syn. of) "father" jB lex.
kinnārum; pl. f. ~ "lyre" Mari, Ug.; < W.Sem.
kinnāruḫuli "lyre player" Alal.; < *kinnārum* + Hurr. *-uḫ(u)li*
kinnaškarakkum → *kannaškarakkum*
kinnikêm "over there" Mari
kinnû, *ginnû*, *gennu* "mountain" M/NB *nēreb(i) k.* "mountain pass"; < Sum.
kinsigu → *kinsikkum*
kinsigubbû (one present at afternoon meal) jB lex.; < Sum.
kinsikkum, *kissikkum*, *kinsigu*, *kinzigu* "late afternoon" Bab. [KIN.SIG]; < Sum.
kinṣu → *kimṣu*
kinšu "slope" j/NB, constructed round house, field; < *kanāšu* I
kintillû "completed job" jB; < Sum.
kintum → *kimtu*
kinturru → *kitturru* I
kīnu(m), Ass. *kēnu(m)* "permanent, true" [GI(.NA); GIN, esp. in PNs; ZI.DA] **1.** "permanent" of health, life etc.; of part of liver, station of planet, temple **2.** "reliable, true" of word, command; of person, servant, partner "honest"; "loyal", "righteous" of king **3.** "legitimate" of son, ruler; math. "correct", also of standard measures; < *kânu*; > *kīna*, *kittu* I; *kīniš*; *kīnūtu*
kinūnatu (a tree) jB lex.
kinūnu(m), M/NA *kanūnu*; pl. f. "brazier" [KI.NE; NB also KI.NE.NE] of copper, silver etc.; MA "oven" of brick; (a festival) esp. as name of 10th month, Mari, Nuzi, NA [ITI.AB (→ *Ṭebētu*)]; also in PNs; > *Kinūnû*
Kinūnû; f. *Kinūnītu*; *Ki/anūnāya* "born on the *Kinūnu* festival" M/NB, NA [KI.NE(.NE)- ; NA ITI.AB-]; < *kinūnu*
kinupḫušši mng. unkn. Nuzi; < Hurr.
-kinūšu → *-kunūši*
kinûtu ~ "nickname" jB comm. of word for illness; < *kanû*
kīnūtu, NA *kēnūtu* "loyalty, steadfastness" NA, NB; < *kīnu*
kinzigu → *kinsikkum*
kipalallu (a piece of furniture) Am.
kipalû → *kibalû*
kiparu (an official at Susa) Bab.(Elam); < Elam.
kipattu "vulva"? jB in *šapat k.*
kipdu, *kipidu* "plan(s), efforts" jB, esp. with *šuddû* "to make s.o. abandon plan"; < *kapādu*
kipilu → *kiplu*
kipkippu (a bird of prey)? jB
kiplu, *kiblu*, NA *kipilu*? "twisting, twine" M/jB of rope; decorative "twine" on whip, on door; of withies, as packaging material; also (part of body)?; < *kapālu*
kipnu (or *kibnu*) (a plant) jB lex.
kippatu(m) "circle, hoop, ring" Bab., M/NA [GAM; math. also KA.KEŠDA] **1.** math. "circumference; circle" **2.** "perimeter" of heaven and/or earth; of baldachin **3.** "ring" of metal; held by ruler; of door; "handle, grip" of vessel, musical instrument; (feature on liver) **4.** *kakkab k.* (a star) **5.** "tendril, twining stem" of vine **6.** *k. lemutti* "ring of evil"; < *kapāpu*
kippu(m) "loop, trap" O/jB, NA as trap for birds, animals; pl. "loops" of intestines of sacrificial sheep, "(resultant) omens"; < *kapāpu*
kipputtātu pl. mng. unkn. Susa, a device for casting lots or sim.
kiprum (or *kib/prûm*) (an object or substance) OB
kipru → also *kibru*
kipsu → *kipṣu*; *kispu*
kipṣu, *kipsu* "constriction, contraction" jB ext.; < *kapāṣu* II
kipšanti mng. unkn. Nuzi in *ša k.*, desig. of chariot
kipšu → *kibšu* I.II
kipšû → *kibšû*
kīpu; pl. *kīpāni* (a linen cloth) NB
kipuālu, *kupuālu* (a kind of tamarisk) jB lex.
kipunannum → *kikunannum*
kiqillutu "rubbish dump" NA; < Aram.
kirādu(m) (leather container) O/jB for oil
kirānu → *karānu*
kirāru mng. unkn. OB(Alal.), as MN
kirassu → *kirissu*
kirbānu(m), *karbānum*, *ki/urbannu* "lump (of earth)" Bab., NA [LAG] **1.** "clay lump" in symbolic acts, *k. nasākum/nadûm/ḫepû* "to throw/cast/break a lump"; *k. laqātum* "pick up lumps"; mag., math. **2.** of other materials, "lump" of lapis lazuli, salt **3.** *k. eqli* [LAG GÁN/A.ŠÀ] (a plant, phps.) "camomile"; also ~ (a grasshopper)
kirenzi "proclamation" Nuzi; < Hurr.
kirgunnu (a container) jB lex.
kiri(b)bu (or *kiri(p)pu*) (a garment) jB lex.; → *kiribinnu*
kiribinnu (a garment) NA lex.; → *kiribbu*

kiribtu "blessing" M/NB, NA from deity; *k. DN* "one blessed by DN" freq. in PNs; < *karābu* II

kiribu → *kiribbu*

kirību "blessed one" NB in PN; < *karābu* II

kirikarum (a bird) OB

kiriktu "collection, accumulation" M/NB of water at regulator; < *karāku*

kirimaḫḫu "park" jB/NA, NB [GIŠ.KIRI6.MAḪ] of botanical garden at Nineveh; city sector at Uruk; < Sum.

kirimmu "(crook of) arm" M/jB; as protection to child, supplicant etc.; also du.

kirinnu/û ~ "clay lump" M/jB lex., of potter; < Sum.?

kirinnu → also *girimmu* 2

kirinnû → *kirinnu*

kirippum (an oil jar) Mari

kirippu → also *kiribbu*

kirissu(m), MA *kirassu* ~ "hairpin, clasp"? O/MA, O/jB [GIŠ.KIRID(=ŠÌR)]; < Sum.

kirîš, kirīšum → *kirû*

kirītum I (a container) OB, for foods

kirītu II **1.** (a rope) jB lex., for boat **2.** NB pl. *kirâta* (an ornament in gold) (or → *kirratu*)

kirītu → also *qirītu*

kirium → *kirû*

kirkirânu, kirkiriyannu → *kikkirânu*

kirlammu (a container) jB lex.; < Sum.

kirmaḫḫu (or *ge/irmaḫḫu*) "large oven, kiln" jB lex.; < Sum.; → *kīru* I

kirnāya (desig. of a coat) NA lex.

kirratu(m) (or *girratu(m)*) (an ornament) OAkk, Mari, in gold; MB, attached to chair; → *kirītu* II 2

kirrētu (a kind of meat) jB lex.

kirru(m), *kīru* (a big jar) [(DUG.)KÍR; OAkk DUG.GIR; Bogh. DUG.GÍR.GÁN/KIŠ] for liquids; of stone, metal; < Sum.; → *kerru*; *kirratu*

kirsukku → *kilsukku*

kīrtu "daze, coma"? jB lex.; < *kâru* II ?

kirû(m), OA *kirium*, term.-adv. *kirîš, kirīšum*; pl. m. & f. "(fruit) plantation, orchard" [GIŠ.KIRI6; Mari also GIŠ.KI.SAR] esp. of date palms; < Sum.

kīru(m) I, *kēru* f. "oven, kiln" Bab. [GIR4] OB esp. for bitumen; < Sum.

kīru II (an official) NB

kīru → also *kirru*

kisal (a weight) NA/jB [KISAL] prob. 1/20 shekel

kisalbarakku "outer court" OB(N.Mes.), Mari; < Sum.; → *kisallu*

kisallu(m), MB also *kisellu*; pl. f. "forecourt" Bab., M/NA [KISAL] of temple, palace, house; *k. nāri* "river foreshore"; < Sum.; → *kisalbarakku*; *kisalluḫḫu*;*kisalmāḫu*

kisallu → also *kiṣallu*

kisalluḫḫatu(m) "female courtyard sweeper" O/jB [MUNUS.KISAL.LUḪ]; < *kisalluḫḫu*

kisalluḫḫu(m) "courtyard sweeper" O/jB [KISAL.LUḪ]; < Sum.; > *kisalluḫḫatu*; → *kisallu*

kisalluḫḫūtu "rôle of courtyard sweeper" Nuzi, Bogh. [KISAL.LUḪ-]; < *kisalluḫḫ(at)u* abstr.

kisalmāḫu(m) "main court" Bab. [KISAL.MAḪ] of temple; < Sum.; → *kisallu*

kisbu → *kupsu*

kisellu → *kisallu*

kisibirrītu(m), *ki(s)sibirru(m)*, *kusibirrītu*, M/NB *ku(s)sibirru*, Ass. *kisibarru(m)* "coriander" [(Ú.)ŠE.LÚ(.SAR)]; M/NB also a metal object ?

kisiggû, *kisikkû* pl. tant. "funerary offerings" jB; < Sum.; → *kisikkum*

kisikkum (a vase) Mari; = *kisiggû* ?

kisikkû → *kisiggû*

Kis(i)līmu (9th Bab. month) M/NB [ITI.GAN (.GAN.NA); OB rdg. uncert.]; > *kissilīmû*

kisilīmû → *kissilīmû*

kisillu → *kiṣallu*

kisimmu ~ "sour milk"? Bogh., jB [(Ú.)GA/ḪAB]; < Sum.

kisimtum (a vegetable) OB; < *kasāmu*

kisinnu (a bronze object) MB(Alal.)

kisintu → *kisittu*

kisirru (a tool) NB

kisirtu "wall facing" Mari, M/jB(Ass.) of stone, brick; on quay-wall, city-wall, tower, building; < *kasāru*

kisittu(m), *kisintu*, *kišittu* "branches, boughs (of tree)" Bab., M/NA of cedar; for fuel; "stem" of reed, of stag's horn; transf. "descent" of person, city, *k. ṣâti* "primeval ancestry"; "descendant, offspring"; < *kismu*

kisītu (or *gis/ṣītu*) (a weapon) Nuzi; < *kasû* III ?

kiskibirru, *kiškibirru* (a trap)? or "kindling wood" jB lex.; < Sum.

kiskilātu (or *kiškilātu*) pl. tant. (a musical instrument)? jB/NA; → *kiski'u*

kiskilili (a demoness); → *lilium*

kiskirru(m), *kiškirru(m)* (a wooden board) Bab.; NB (a type of temple contribution (recorded on a wooden ledger))

Kiskī(s)sum (3rd? month) Mari, OB(Ešn.)

kiskisum (a wooden siege implement) Mari

kiski'u (a musical instrument)? jB lex.; → *kiskilātu*

kislaḫû "threshing floor" jB lex.; < Sum.

kislaqqu → *kizalāqu*

Kislīmu → *Kisilīmu*

kislum, *kaslu* (part of body) O/jB, NA of human; animal; to right and left of backbone; OB *kisil ritti* "side? of hand" (or → *kiṣallu*)

kismu(m) "cutting" O/jB; Mari "stubble"?; jB lex. (a growth of leeks)?; < *kasāmu*

kispu(m), Nuzi, NA, NB *kipsu*; Nuzi pl. f. "funerary offering" (to ancestors) Bab., NA [KI.SÌ.GA] food, drink *ana k.*; *k. kasāpu* "to make a funerary offering"; *ūm k.* "day of funerary offering"; > *kasāpu* II

kispu → also *kupsu*

kissatu(m) I, NB also *kiššatu* "fodder" Bab., NA for domestic animals, birds; NA, NB *rab k.* "fodder-official"; jB *k. ṣerri* 'snake-fodder' (a plant); < *kasāsu* ?

kissatu II "(action of) gnawing" jB; of fire; *k. (libbi)* (an illness); < *kasāsu*

kissikkum → *kinsikkum*

ki(s)silīmû "born in *Kislīmu*" MB in fPN *Kissilīmītum*; < *Kisilīmu*

kissu (part of a plough and a chariot) MB

kissu → also *kīsu* I.II; *kiššu*

kissû → *kisû*

kissugu (a fish) jB mag.

kissuku → *kišukku* II

kissurratu → *kisurratu*

kistum (topog. term)? OB

kisum → *kizum*

kisû(m), *kissû(m)* "footing, plinth" Bab. [KI.SÁ] around base of building, gate, wall; < Sum.

kisû → also *kizû*

kīsu(m) I, *kissu* (a kind of reed) O/jB lex. [GI.ZI] (a reed; an object made of reed); < Sum.?

kīsu(m) II, *kēsu*, *kissu*, *kīšu* f. "money-bag; money" [(KUŠ.)NÍG.NA4] of leather, for gold, silver; *k. ša tamkāri* "merchant's money-bag"; transf. (sum of money as capital investment); *aban k.* (stone weight); *nāš k.* (merchant); jB "(gardener's) bag"

kīsu III, occas. *kīšu* "binding, bonds" M/NB; *kīs libbi* "heart constriction" (a medical complaint); < *kasû* III

kisukku → *kišukku* II

kisurratu, *kissurratu*, OB also *kiturratum* (a reed pipe)? Bab. as musical instrument

kisurrû(m), *kisurru*, *kasurru*; pl. m. & f. "border, territory" Bab. [KI.SUR] "boundary" of field; "ground plan" of building; "territory"; < Sum.

kiṣallu(m), *kis/ṣillu*, *kisallu* f. "ankle" O/jB [ZI.IN.GI] of human; left, right; of animal; "astragalus, knucklebone" as "jacks, fivestones"

kiṣaru → *kiṣru*

kiṣillu → *kiṣallu*

kiṣiptu "calculation" jB, NA; < *kaṣāpu*

kiṣirtu(m) **1.** jB med. ~ "thickening, constriction", also NA *kaṣirtu* **2.** O/jB ext. (a feature on liver) **3.** OB "rental payment" **4.** jB (a kind of construction) **5.** M/NA (a kind of document, phps.) "envelope, case-tablet"; < *kiṣru*

kiṣru(m), occas. *kiṣaru*; pl. usu. m. "knot; concentration, group; rental" [KA.KEŠDA; KÉŠ(.DA); Ì.KEŠDA] **1.** "knot, bonding" of reed-stem, string; "joint" of arm, finger; "clasp" etc. of shoe, container; of mountains *k. šadî*, pl. f. *kiṣrāt š.* "natural rock, bedrock" **2.** "concentration, conglomeration" of tangled reed; "lump" of material; "accumulated wealth"; "group, band" of men, esp. military, OB *k. (šarrim)*, NA *k. (šarrūti)* "(royal) contingent", pl. also f.; *rab k.* "centurion"; astr. "group" of stars; "crossing" of path with ecliptic ? **3.** transf. *k. libbi* "anger" of deity, person; *k. zikrūti* "concentrated manliness"; *k. DN* "strengthened by DN", esp. in PNs **4.** OAkk, Bab. "rental (payment)"; NB (a collection of dues); < *kaṣāru*

kiṣṣatu, *giṣṣatu* "hair loss, shedding of skin" M/jB med.; < *kasāsu*

kiṣṣu(m) "shrine" [ITIMA] as residence of deity; M/NA also desig. of (holy) city

kiṣṣum → also *kimṣu*

kiṣṣuru "interlocked, entwined" jB of iconographic elements; < *kaṣāru* Gt

kīṣu I "flayed" jB; < *kâṣu*

kīṣu(m) II "coolness" OAkk, Bab. *k. (ūmi)* "cool (of day), evening"; < *kaṣû* III

kīša → *kīšamma*

kišab(k)u → *kušabku*

kišādānuššu "on his neck" jB; < *kišādu* du.

kišādu(m); pl. f. "neck; bank" [(UZU.)GÚ] **1.** of human, deity, statue; du. "(both sides of) neck", "back of neck" (as recipient of load, yoke); as place of necklace, seal etc.; of animal **2.** OB f. (a neckcloth) **3.** "necklace", "(stone worn at) neck, neckstone" **4.** "bank, shore" of sea, water-course, also du. "both banks" **5.** (part of a wheel)

kišaḫû (an offering) jB lex.; < Sum.

kīšam in *k. ... k. ...* "either ... or ..." OA

kīša(m)ma, MB *kīša*, jB also *kašāme* "forgive me" O/jB as interj., implying polite contradiction; < *kiāšum* imper.?

kišarānum, *kiše/irānum* (an edible item) OA

kišdu, MA *kildu* "acquisition" O/MB, MA; jB in *k. eperi* (an illness); lex. "limit, boundary"; < *kašādu*

kišerānum → *kišarānum*

kišertum, *kišeršum* "bondage, captivity" Early Mari, OA; OAkk *bīt k.* "prison"; < *kašāru* ?

kišḫi "chair" jB lex.; < Hurr.

kišibbu, *kišippu* "seal(ing)" jB; < Sum.

kišibgallu "seal-owner" OB, jB lex. [KIŠIB.GÁL]; < Sum.

kišinnu → *kiššanu*

kišippu → *kišibbu*

kiširanum → *kišarānum*

kiširru(m) "success"? OA *lā ša k.* "unsuccessful, failure"; jB of DN *ālik k.* "helper"?; < *kašāru* ?

kiširtu (a food)? NB; < *kašāru* ?

kišīrum (or *qišīrum*) mng. uncl. OB math.

kišittu(m) "achievement, acquisition; conquest" [KUR(-)] **1.** pl. OA, OB "acquisitions" (other than by purchase) **2.** "conquest" of land, town; "items acquired by conquest, spoil", also freq. *k. qāti*, of town, property, population **3.** *k. ilim* (a serious illness); < *kašādu*

kišittu → also *kisittu*

kišītu ~ "rebellion" jB lex.

kiškalânu → *kikkirânu*

kiškanû, MA *kiškanā'u* (a tree) M/NA, M/NB [GIŠ.KÍN]; growing at Eridu; used as wood, drug; < Sum.

kiškattû(m), *kiškittû(m)*, NA/jB *kitkittû*, pl. f. *kitkitāte* [GIŠ.KIN.TI] **1.** "(industrial) kiln" **2.** "craftsman" Bab., NA esp. military craftsman; OB *bīt k.* "workshop"; < Sum.

kiškibirru → *kiskibirru*

kiškilātu → *kiskilātu*

kiškirânu → *kikkirânu*

kiškirru → *kiskirru*

kiškittu jB lex. **1.** (part of a ship's keel) **2.** (a leather item)

kiškittû → *kiškattû*

kišpu(m) "sorcery, evil spell" Bab., M/NA usu. pl. [UŠ$_{11}$; UŠ$_{11}$.ZU] *k. paš/ṭāru* "to dispel sorceries"; *qāt k.* causing illness; < *kašāpu*

kišṣappum → *gištappu*

kiššanu, *ki(š)ši/ennu* (a leguminous vegetable) Ass., O/jB [GÚ.NÍG.ḪAR.RA]

kiššatu(m) I "totality, world" Bab., M/NA [KIŠ; ŠÚ; ŠÁR; KI.ŠÁR.RA] **1.** before subst. "totality, all of", *k. nišī* "all people" etc. **2.** alone "the world, universe"; *šar k.* "king of the world" **3.** of river "full flood", esp. *mīl k.*; → *kašāšu* I

kiššatu(m) II "emmer" O/jB [ÁŠ(.A.AN) (→ *kunāšu*)]

kiššatum III (a garment) OB

kiššatu → also *kissatu* I

kiššātum, *ḫiššātum* pl. tant. "debt-slavery; distraint" OB of persons, property; "indemnity" for lost property; < *kašāšu* I

kišše/innu → *kiššanu*

Kiššītu(m) "of Kiš" O/jB epith. of Ištar; < PlN Kiš

kiššu(m), *kissu* "(reed-)bundle" O/jB [GI.SA]; also math. "truncated cone"; < Sum.

kiššū pl. tant. ~ "exercise of power"? O/jB; < *kašāšu* I

kiššû "empowered, authorized" jB; < *kiššū(tu)* + *-ī*

kiššūtu "exercise of power, authority" M/NB, NA [ŠÚ; KIŠ] *k. ṣabātu/epēšu/bêlu* "to seize/exercise/take control of power"; *āl k.* "capital city"; of king "personal authority"; < *kašāšu* I

kīšu → *kīsu* II.III

kīšū pl. tant. ~ "pain(s)" jB

kišubb(ān)îš "into a waste" jB; < *kišubbû*

kišubbû(m), NA also *qišubbû*, NB *gi/ušubbû* "waste ground" [KI.ŠUB.BA] *k. petû* "to bring w.g. into cultivation"; NB *eqel k.* "waste field", "waste (building) plot"; < Sum.; > *kišubbānîš*

kišubû "ending of hymn" jB [KI.ŠÚ.BI(.IM)]; < Sum.

kišukkiš "in captivity" jB; < *kišukku* I

kišukku I "captivity" j/NB(lit.); < Sum.; → *k.* II

kišukku II, NA *ki(s)suku* ~ "grating"? j/NB, NA; = *k.* I ?

kišūma (or *kīšuma*) "so, thus" Am., Ug.; < *kī*

kitbarattu ~ (bed-frame) jB lex.

kitekarû "prostitute" Bogh. lex.; < Sum.

kiterru → *kitru* II

kitimtu "secret, mystery" Ug., of scribal craft; < *katāmu*

kitinnû → *kidinnû* II

kitintu → *kitītu* I

kitirru → *kitru* II

kitītu(m) I, *kitin/ttu*, NA *qitītu* "linen robe" Bab., NA; < *kitû*

kitītu II (a metal tool) MB

kitkittû → *kiškattû*

kitmu(m) O/jB **1.** "cover(ing)" of bed, vehicle **2.** (a musical interval sounded by strings 6 + 3); also (a lyre-string); < *katāmu*

kitmulu "very displeased" jB; < *kamālu* Gt

kitmuru "piled up" jB of treasure; of disease?; < *kamāru* IV Gt

kitmusu "kneeling, squatting" jB; < *kamāsu* II Gt

kitpudu "cunning" jB, of spells; < *kapādu* Gt

kitpulu "entwined" jB, of snakes; of wrestler?; < *kapālu* Gt

kitpulūtu in *kitpulūssunu* "in an entwined state" jB; < *kitpulu*

kitru I "help, reinforcements" j/NB, NA *ana k. šapāru/alāku* "to send/go for reinforcements"; "ally"; also of DN in PNs; > *katāru* I ?

kitru II, *kite/irru* ~ "legacy, bequest" Nuzi; < Hurr.?

kittabru (or *kittapru*) (syn. for arm) M/jB [ŠE]; also (a growth)? on lung, face; < *abru* II ?

kittu(m) I, later also *kē/ītu*, Ass. *kettu(m)*; pl. *kinātum* etc. "steadiness, reliability, truth" [NÍG.GI.NA; jB also NÍG.ZI; GI.NA]; pl. ~ sg. **1.** "stability, solidarity" OB of work, transf. "stable conditions" **2.** "reality", *ina k.* "really, truly", acc. "honestly!, indeed!", "reliability, truth" of omens; *zēr k.* "true, legitimate heir", esp. in PNs **3.** "loyalty" of subject, slave **4.** "righteousness, justice", *šar/dayyān/dīn k.* "just king/judge/verdict"; (d)*K.* as DN; *lā k.* "iniquity", *ana lā k.* "unjustly" **5.** "truth", NB *ina kittišu* "sincerely"; *lā k.* "untruth, lies"; < *kīnu*

kittu II (or *qittu* ?); pl. *kitāta* (a stand, support)? NB

kitturru I, *kinturru*, *katurû* "toad, frog" O/jB lex.; also "(stone figure of) frog"

ki(t)tu(r)ru II (a kind of chair or stool) jB/NA; *ša k.-šu* "chair person"; Nuzi → *kutturu* 2; < Sum.

kitû(m) "flax; linen" [(TÚG.)GADA; occas. GIŠ.GADA] **1.** as plant; *zēr k.* "linseed" **2.** "linen fibre", *qê k.* "linen thread" **3.** as textile "linen"; *išpār k.* "linen weaver" **4.** "linen garment"; jB *k. isinni* "festival of linen clothing", *labiš k.* "one entitled to wear linen"; Nuzi, NB "linen" for bed clothes; < Sum.; > *kitītu* I

kītu(m), *kētu* (a reed mat) OA, M/jB [GI.KID]; < Sum.

kītu → also *kittu* I

kitullu (a troop formation)? jB(Ass.)

kiturratum → *kisurratu*

kitu(r)ru → *kitturru* II

kiūrum I (desig. of shrine at Nippur) OB lex.; < Sum.

kiūru II (a metal basin) jB, NA [KI.ÙR]; < Urar.

kiūru III "ground, earth" jB lex.; also (chthonic deity of Lullubu)?; < Urar.

kiūšu "step, tread" M/jB lex.; < Sum.

ki'utukku syll. wr. not attested (an incantation) jB lex. [KI.^{d}UTU(.KAM)]; < Sum.

kiyā "how much?" OB; → *kī* 2

kiyaḫum adv.? mng. uncl. OB lex.

kizalāqu, *kiz/sla(q)qu*, NB *kasilaqqu* ~ "treasure, treasury" NA, NB; of goddess

kizapuzzu (an object) Qatna, of gold; < Hurr.?

kizeḫḫuru (a functionary) Nuzi; < Hurr.

kizibiannu → *zibibiānum*

kizinû → *gizinakku*

kizirtu "lock of hair, pigtail" NA; < *kezēru*

kizītu (or *kizzutu*) mng. uncl. MA in *sūti ša ki-zi-ti* (a kind of *sūtu* measure); also (an emblem)?

kizla(q)qu → *kizalāqu*

kizum (or *kisum*) ~ (a pastry)? Mari

kizû(m), NB also *kisû*, Nuzi, Ug. also *kazû* ~ "animal-trainer" Bab. [(LÚ.)KUŠ$_7$] later esp. associated with horses, "groom"; > *kizûtum*

kizûtum "job of a *kizûm*" Mari; < *kizû*

kizzāniš mng. uncl. jB

kizzānû, *gizzānû*; f. *k/gizzānītu* (desig. of star, phps.) "goat"(-star)? jB; < *kizzu* I

kizzatu(m), *gizzatu*(m) ~ "deduction, curtailment"? Bab., NA **1.** OB transf. "curtailment, retrenchment"? due to famine **2.** "deduction"? from yield of field, "diminution"? of field **3.** pl. NA, NB (reserved land)?; < *gazāzu*

kizzatu → also *kizītu*

kizziḫu mng. unkn. Qatna, desig. of golden pin; < Hurr.?

kizzu I, *kazzu*, *gizzu* "(young male) goat" jB [MÁŠ.ZU]; > *kizzānû*; → *gazāzu*

kizzu II (a cloak for offering ceremony) MB

-knu → *-kunu*

-ku → *-ki*; *-kum*

kū → *kūm*

kû(m), O/MA *ku(w)ā'u(m)*, jB also *kumma/u*; f. *kattum*, OA *ku(w)ātum*; pl. m. *kuttun*, *kuttīn*, OA *ku(w)ā'ūtum*; f. *kâttun*, *kuttum* "your; yours" O/MA, O/jB **1.** with subst., OA esp. before, *kuwātum têrtaka* "your instruction", OB after, *ṣuḫārē kuttīn* "your lads" **2.** alone "yours" **3.** as pred., OA *kaspum lā kuā'um* "the silver is not yours"; OB *kûmma* "is yours", "is in your control/gift"; NA → *ikkû*

kuānu → *kânu*

kuāšim, Ug., M/NA *kuāša/u* "to you" (2 m. sg. dat. pron.) OAkk, O/MB, M/NA; after *a(na)*; also Bogh. for gen.; NA for acc.; → *kâšim*

kuāti, jB *kuāta* "(of, to) you" (2 m. sg. pron.) OA, jB lex., as acc., gen., dat.; → *kâti*

kuātum, kuā'u → *kû*

ku'ātu → *kuyātu*

kuba'ātum pl. (a topog. term) OA (or → *kupātum* ?)

kubādu → *kubātu*

kubarinnu, *kubarindu* (a vessel) jB lex.; → *kapparinnu* ?

kubartu(m) (heavy garment)? O/jB; < *kubārum*

kubarû → *kibrû*

kubārum "thick, heavy" OAkk as PN; < *kabāru*

kubārum → also *gubārum*

kubāsu (a foodstuff) MB; < *kabāsu*

kubātu, *kubādu* "veneration" j/NB, NA; "honorific ceremony"; < *kabātu*

kubbu → *quppu* II

kubbû(m) I, Nuzi also *ḫubbû* "sewn" O/jB; < *kubbû* II

kubbû II, NB *ḫubbû* "to sew" M/NB, NA; *birma k.* "sew" s.th. with (= acc.) coloured thread; NB "sew" s.th. "on"; > *kubbû* I; *kabbā'um*; *mukabbû*

kubbudu → *kubbutu*

kubbulu(m), *kumbulu(m)* "crippled" O/jB [AD4] of humans, sheep; < *kabālu*

kubburu(m) "very thick" O/jB lex., and in PNs; < *kabāru*; → *kabbaru*

kubbusum "downtrodden" OB; < *kabāsu*

kubbušu (or *kuppušu*) (a cake) NB

kubbuttu; pl. *kubudāti* "honorific gift" Am., Ug.; < *kabātu*

kubbutu(m), *kubbudu*, Ass. *kabbutu(m)* **1.** "very heavy, solid" **2.** "very honoured"; < *kabātu*

kubbu'u D mng. unkn. jB lex.

kubdum → *kubtu*

kubrītu → *kibrītu*; *kuprītu*

kubru(m) "thickness" O/jB, M/NA; as dimension, also "diameter"; "thickest part" of tail, horn, arm; "fattest" of sheep-flock, "mass" of army; < *kabāru*

kubsu (or *k/qub/psu*) mng. unkn. Ug. in *eqlēt kubsāti*

kubšānu (a crested bird) jB; < *kubšu*

kubšu(m) occas. f. "headcloth, turban" [(TÚG.)SAGŠU] **1.** "turban" worn by man, by king, god; NA *ša kubšēšu* "turban-purveyor" **2.** "crest" of bird in *kubši barmat* [SIPA.TIR.RA.MUŠEN] **3.** Qatna "cap" of seal **4.** "top" of part of body, of heart (*libbim*), lung (*ḫašîm*), *k. kimṣi* "kneecap"?; > *kabāšu*; *kubšānu*, *kubšuḫuli*

kubšuḫuli "turban-maker" MB(Alal.); < *kubšu* + Hurr. *-uḫ(u)li*

kubtu(m), Mari *kubdum* **1.** "lump, clod" O/jB, NA [IM.DUGUD] of clay; "ingot" of lead, copper; Mari "(net) weight" **2.** jB "heavy yield, tribute"; < *kabātu*

kūbu(m) I, *qūpu* "foetus" [NÌGIN] esp. $^{(d)}$*K.* as DN

kūbu(m) II (or *kūpu(m)*) (a building) jB

kūbu III (a drinking vessel) Am.; < Eg.

kubuddā'u(m) ~ "honorific gift"? Mari, Emar; < *kabātu*

kubukku(m) f.; du. *kubukkān* "strength" OB(Susa)?, jB; of god, man

kuburrû(m) "thickness, reinforcement" Bab., as dimension; j/NB "projection", of gate tower; < *kabāru*

kubussû(m) (a kind of legal decree) OB(Susa) esp. *k. kabāsum*, *k. šakānum* "to promulgate a decree"; *warki k.* "after the decree"; < *kabāsu*

kubūsu(m) (or *kupūsu(m)*) ~ (a handle)? O/jB on door, box

kubuttû "abundant wealth" j/NB; < *kabātu*

kudādu(m), *gudādu(m)* "very small, tiny" j/NB lex.; as PN (also OAkk, OA ?)

kūdanu(m), *kūdannu*, Ass. *kūdunu*, gen. *kūdini* "mule" Bab., M/NA [ANŠE.GÌR.NUN(.NA); NA abbr. GÌR; OB ANŠE.LA.GU ?]

kudāru, *kuddāru* (kind of terrain)? NA; *rab k.* (an official)

kudāru → also *kudurru* I

kuddāru → *kudāru*

kuddilu, lex. also *kuddulu* ? (a garment) MA

kuddu (a container) jB lex., of wood, of reed; < Sum.

kuddubbû mng. unkn. jB lex.; < Sum.

kuddulu → *kuddilu*

kuddunu D "to seek sanctuary" jB; < *kidinnu* denom.

kudimeru, *kudime/arānu* (a plant) jB lex., med.

kudimmu(m), *kuttimmu(m)* (a herb) Ass., jB yielding "salt"; seeds sown across destroyed city

kūdin(i) → *kūdanu*

kudkuddu (a plant) jB lex.

kuduḫtaš (a prof.) OB(Susa)

kuduktu I; pl. *kudkētu* (a unit of measure) Nuzi, for textiles and wool

kuduktu II mng. unkn. j/NB

kūdunu → *kūdanu*

kuduppānu "(a kind of) pomegranate" M/jB [GIŠ.NU.ÚR.MA.LÀL?/KU$_7$.KU$_7$]

kudurrānu (a crested bird) M/NB; [NÍG.DU-*nu*] also as PN; → *kudurru* II ?

kudurru I, NA *kadurru*, NB also *kudāru*; pl. m. & f. "carrying frame, (builder's) hod" NA, j/NB [NÍG.DU] for hay, bricks, mud; NA "(earth-carrying) labour (obligation)"; Nuzi (a wooden container); NB *k. tikki* "neck-*k*." mng. uncl.; < Hurr.?; > *kadāru* IV ?

kudurru II; pl. m. & f. "boundary; boundary stone" M/NB [NÍG.DU] *k. kunnu, naṣāru, nukkuru* "to fix, observe, change boundary"; *k. nasāḫu* "to remove boundary stone"; M/NB(Ass.) "territorial limits"; > *kadāru* III; → *kudurrānu*

kudurru III "eldest son" M/NA, M/NB [NÍG.DU; BÚLUG]; usu. in PNs; < Elam.

kugamlum → *kigamlum*

kug(u)rûm "granary-supervisor" OB [KA. GUR$_7$]; < Sum.

kuḫātu → *kuyātu*

kuiḫku (container for oil) Am.; < Eg.

kukittu; pl. NA *quqinētu* ~ "inappropriate location"? jB/NA lex., ext.

kukkadru → *kukkudru*

kukkallānu, *gukkallānu* ~ "of fat-tailed type" jB lex.

kukkallu(m), *gukkallu(m)* "fat-tailed sheep" Bab., MA [GUKKAL]; < Sum.

kukkānītu (a garden plant) j/NB; → *kukku* I

kukku(m) I, *gukku* f. "(a kind of) cake" Ass., jB [GÚG; jB NINDA.KA.DÙ]; < Sum.

kukku II, *kūku* (part of a balance) jB lex.

kukkûm "darkness" O/jB lex.; as desig. of nether world; < Sum.

ku(k)ku(b)bu, NA also *kukkupu, quqqubu*; pl. m. & f. **1.** M/NA, M/NB (an offering vessel, phps.) "rhyton" for liquids, of metal, stone **2.** jB lex. "pig's stomach"

ku(k)kudru(m), *kukkadru, kidkidru* "sheep's stomach" O/jB lex., ext.

kukkupu → *kukkubbu*

kukkurratum → *kurkurratu*

kukkušu(m), *kakkušu, kukkuštu(m)* (a low quality flour) O/jB, also *qēm k.*; *k. (ša) buqli* "malt-flour"; < Sum.

Kukkuzannum → *kurkuzannu*

kukru → *kukuru*

kuksu (a garden tool) jB lex.; < Sum.

kūku → *kukku* II

kukubu → *kukkubbu*

kukudru → *kukkudru*

kukudum → *gugutum*

kukullu → *kakkullu*

kukumnu "three-year-old" Nuzi, of ox; < Hurr.; → *kikamunu*

kukunnû → *gegunnû*

kukuru(m), *kukru* (an aromatic tree) [ŠIM/GIŠ. GÚR.GÚR; ŠIM.KU$_7$.KU$_7$] (an aromatic product from the tree), also med., mag.

kukūsum (part of body) OB lex.

kukutu (or *kukūtu*) (a reed artefact) Am.

kukutum → also *gugutum*

kula'e (a garment) Nuzi

kula'ūtu "delay, procrastination"? Bogh. in *k. epēšu*; < *kalû* V (or = *kulûtu* ?)

kulbāb(ān)iš "like ants" j/NB; < *kulbābu*

kulbabtu "female ant" Bogh. lex.; < *kulbābu*

kulbābu, Bogh. also *kulbību* "ant" jB, NA [KIŠI$_{8/9}$]; eggs, earth of ants as drug; > *kulbabtu*; *kulbābāniš*

kulbannu → *kalbānu*

kulbattu → *kulmittu*

kulbību → *kulbābu*

kuldu (or *k/qultu*) (a copper object) Am.

kulīlānu (a plant) jB lex.; < *kulīlu* I

kulīl(ī)tu, *killilû* "dragonfly" jB; < *kulīlu* I

kulilû (a kind of curtain)? jB lex.; < *kulīlu* III ?

kulīlu I, *kulilû* "dragonfly" jB; *mīl k.* "flood bearing dragonfly (corpses)"; > *kulīlītu*; *kulīlānu*

kulīlum II "small crown, headband" Mari, of silver; < *kilīlu* dimin.

kulīlu III, *kulullu/û* "fish-man" jB [KU$_6$.LÚ. U$_{18/19}$.LU]; in myth; "(figure of) fish-man" in copper, clay; < Sum.; > *kulilû*?

kulinaš mng. unkn. Nuzi, desig. of textile; < Hurr.

kullānum (or *qullānum*) (a metal item) Mari

kullānu → also *kullu* I

kullaru I "Kullar-juniper" jB lex.; < PlN Kullar

kullarum II (a disease) OB mag.

kullatān "universally" NB(lit.); < *kullatu* I; → *mītūtān*

kullatu(m) I, Bogh. also *killatu* "totality, all of ..." OAkk, Bab.(lit.); absol. "whole (world)"; before subst., pron. suff. "all of ..."; < *kalû* II; > *kullatān*

kullatu(m) II "clay pit" O/jB [KI.GAR], for figurine clay etc.

kullizu(m) "ox-driver; plough-ox" OAkk, Bab. **1.** "ox-driver" [(LÚ/ÉRIN.)ŠÀ.GU$_4$], *lišān k.* "ox-driver's slang"; occas. of woman **2.** "plough-ox" [GU$_4$.ŠÀ.GU$_4$]

kullizūtum "rôle of ox-driver" OB [GU4.ŠÀ. GU4- ; NAM.ŠÀ.GU4-]
kullu I; pl. *kullāni* "nut(-kernel)" NA
kullu II "hoe" jB lex.
kullu(m) III, Ass. *ka''ulu(m)* **D** "to hold" [DIB] (stat. NB only) **1.** "hold, be holding" s.th., in the hand; "hold up" roof; "hold on to, hold back"; "be in possession of" country, property, field; "hold ready" offering etc., "have available"; NA *(ina qāti) k.* "consider, take" value (as given); "maintain, keep to" cult, righteousness; "bear in mind" words, dream; "have tenure of" office, prebend; "wear" garment; of things "contain"; of person, body "have, suffer from" illness; of month "bring, be characterized by" rain, eclipse **2.** *rēša(m) k.* of people, things "be at s.o.'s disposal", "be ready, be at the service of, serve"; "look after, care for, pay attention to" **Dtn** iter. **Dt** pass. of D OA of silver "be retained" *išti kaspim*; "be held back, restrained" **Dtt** NA "be restrained"; > *mukillu*; *takiltum* II; → *tākaltu*
kullultu "coronation, crenellation"? jB ext.; < *kullulu* I
kullulu I "veiled, covered" M/jB of bride; < *kullulu* II
kullulu(m) II **D** "to veil, crown" O/jB, M/NA face, lips, in distress; MA "crown" king; jB stat. of gate "is crowned" with crenellations **Dt** pass. of D; < *kilīlu*/*kulūlu* denom.; > *kullulu* I, *kullultu*; → *kutamlalu*
kullumu(m), Ass. *kallumu(m)* **D** "to show, display" [IGI] **1.** "show s.th. to s.o." (= 2 acc.), "make s.th. apparent, reveal", "expose" to light **2.** abstr. obj. "show s.o." anger, love, power **3.** "make s.o. experience" trouble, hunger, profit **4.** + infin., subord. clause "show how to ..., where ..." **5.** "instruct, teach" person, horse **Dtn** iter. **Dt** pass., of thing "be revealed"; of person "be informed of" **DR** OB **Š** "reveal" a sign, a fact **Štn** iter. **ŠD** → *muškallimu*; > *kallimum*; *kullumūtu*; *mukallimtu*; *muškal=limu*; *taklīmu*, *taklimtu*
kullumūtu "exhibition, display"? jB in *bāb k.* "gate of *k.*"; < *kullumu*
kulmandu → *zermandu*
kulmašītu(m) (a cultic prostitute) Bab. [NU. BAR]
kulmāšum → *kulpāšum*
kulmittu (or *kulbattu*) (a vessel) NB
kulpāšum, also *kulmāšum* ? (a divine weapon) OB
kultāru → *kuštāru*
kultību → *kuštībum*
kultu → *kuldu*; *kuštu*
kulû → *kalû* II; *kulu'u*
kulullu/*û* → *kulīlu* III
kulūlu "crown" M/NA, j/NB as mark of royalty; "veil"?; "crenellation" of gateway towers; > *kullulu* II; → *kilīlu*
kulūmum → *kalūmu*
kulupinnum, *kilupinnum* mng. uncl. OA, phps. "sickle", or unit of measurement, for straw
kuluppu (a worm) jB
kuluppû, *kilippû* (a bird) jB
kulûtu "rôle of a *kulu'u*"? MB(Susa); → *kula'ūtu*
kulu'u(m), *kulû(m)* (male cultic prostitute) OAkk?, Bab., NA, esp. of Ištar, also in PNs; > *kulûtu*
-kum, *-ku* "to you" (2 m. sg. dat. suff.)
kūm, *ku(m)mu(-)*, *kū*, *kūmī-*, *ikkūm*, NB also *akkū* "instead of" NA, NB, occas. jB **1.** prep. "in place of", "in exchange for", also *ina*/*ana k.* **2.** conj. + subjunct. "instead of" doing s.th. (= pres.); "since, in view of the fact that" (+ pret., stat.) **3.** adv. "instead", "in return", also *ina k.*; → *kīma*; *kīmū*
kumaḫu (a plant) jB lex.
kumānu (a surface measure) MA, MB(Alal.), Nuzi (= 1/6 *ikû*; Nuzi 1/2 *awiḫaru*); Ass. also linear measure (= 10 *purīdu* ?); < Hurr.?
kumāru; pl. f. **1.** (a kind of terrain) M/NA, j/NB **2.** (desig. of precious stones) NB; < *kamāru* IV ?; → *qumāru*
kumāṣu ~ "bush offering refuge"? jB lex.
kumbulu → *kubbulu*
kumdilḫi (a functionary) OB(Susa); < Elam.
kūmī- → *kūm*
kumirtu (a priestess) jB; < Aram.; → *kumru*
kumiru mng. uncl. Am.; < W.Sem.
kumma → *kû*
kummaru (a white garment) jB lex.
kummu(m) I "cella, shrine" [AGRUN] "innermost room" of shrine, also of house, palace; in gener. "shrine, temple"; also term.-adv. *kummiš*
kummu II "(the cuneiform sign) KUM" jB
kummu → also *kû*; *kūm*
kummu- → *kūm*
kummulu "very angry" jB; < *kamālu*
kummusu "fearsome"? jB lex.; < *kamāsu* II
kumru(m) "priest" O/MA, Mari [OA GUDU4]; → *kumirtu*
kumšillu → *kunšillu*

kumteniwa mng. unkn. Nuzi, in topog. desig.; < Hurr.
kumû (a water bird, phps.) "pelican" jB
kūmu(-) → *kūm*
kumurrû(m) "heaping up" O/jB **1.** math. [UL.GAR; GAR.GAR] "addition" **2.** jB "piling up, accumulation" **3.** jB lex. "laying out" of dates to ripen; < *kamāru* IV
kumūru → *gumūru*
kumušā'u mng. unkn. Nuzi
-kun → *-kunu*
kunaggu → *kunangum*
kunaḫi (a building) Ug.
kunangum, *kunaggu* (a metal drinking vessel) OB [wr. KU/GU.NA.(AN.)GI4]
kunaštu mng. uncl. jB; < *kunāšu* ?
kunāšu(m), jB also *kunšu*, Nuzi, Bogh. *kunīšu* f.; pl. freq. m. "emmer" [OAkk ÁŠ.AN; Bab. ÁŠ.AN.NA; j/NB, NA (ŠE.)ÁŠ.A.AN (→ *kiššatu* II)]; > *kunaštu*?
kunāšunu, NA *kanāšunu* "to you" (2 m. pl. dat. pron.) M/NA
***kunātunu** "you" (2 m. pl. acc. pron.) MA
kunā'u → *kunûm*
kundirāšu, *kundarāšu*, *kandiršu* (a piece of apparel) NA
kundulum (a bronze vessel) OB; → *kandalu*
kungu I (a kind of house) jB lex.
kungu II, *gungu* (a kind of rush) jB lex., med.
kungušakkum (desig. of a servant) Mari
-kuni "your" (2 m. du. gen. suff.) OAkk
kunibḫu, *kunibu* (a garden plant)? j/NB, NA
kuni(n)nu(m) (a basin for liquids) O/jB, of stone, metal, bitumened basketry; *qanû k.* "drinking-straw"; < Sum.
kunīšu → *kunāšu*
kunkunnu mng. unkn. jB lex.
kunnir (a window) jB lex.
kunnu "fixed" M/NB, NA; "firmly established" of table, heir; "fixed in place" of bolt; "confirmed" of statement, "loyal"; astr. "correct"; < *kânu* D
kunnu → also *kânu* D; *kūnu*
kunnû "cared for, cherished" j/NB of person; jB lex., of textile "well-finished"; < *kanû* D
kunnupu (or *kunnubu*) **D** mng. unkn. jB lex.
kunnūtu "care, cherishing" j/NB; < *kunnû*
kunsaggû "turning-point, apogee"? jB of planet's course; < Sum.
kunšillu, *kumšillu* "carder" M/jB **1.** "carding-comb" or "teasel" for fabric **2.** MB as prof. desig. "carder", also abbr. *kun*8 **3.** lex. (part of the body)
kunšu(m) "ball" of wool jB
kunšu → also *kunāšu*
-kunu, *-kun*, OA also *-knu*, NA *-kanū* before *-ni*, NB after *n* or *m* also *-gunu* **1.** "your" (2 m. pl. gen. suff.) **2.** Ass. also "(to) you" (2 m. pl. acc., dat. suff.)
kunûm, *kunu'um*, MA *kunā'u* "your(s)" (2 m. pl. pron. adj.) O/MA; f. as subst. "your (affair)" etc.; → *ikkanû*
kūnu, *kunnu* "firmness" M/NB, NA [GIN] in *k. qāti* "fixed procedure"; *k. libbi* "loyalty"; *k. kussî* "permanence of throne"; < *kânu*
kunukku(m); pl. m. & f. "seal" [(NA4/IM.)KIŠIB; Nuzi also NA4] **1.** "(cylinder) seal" **2.** "seal impression, sealing, bulla" **3.** "sealed (tablet)", NB *ina kanāk k. šuāti* "at the sealing of that document" **4.** ext. "vertebra" of sheep (and associated muscle) [also UZU.KIŠIB]; med., of human *k. kišādi/eṣemṣērim* "neck/backbone vertebra"; > *kanāku*
kunūši(m) "to you" (2 m. pl. dat. pron.) O/jB
-kunūši(m), NB also *-kunūšu*, *-ka/inūšu*, after *m* also *-gunūšu* "to you" (2 m. pl. dat. suff.) Bab.; M/NB also acc.
kunūti "you" (2 m. pl. acc., gen. pron.) OA, OB; OA also dat.; → *kâtunu*
-kunūti, arch. OB also *-kunūt* "you" (2 m. pl. acc. suff.) O/jB; OA dat.
kunu'um → *kunûm*
kunzu (a leather bag) jB, for aromatics
kunzubu → *kuzzubu*
kupanna mng. unkn. Nuzi
kupartu "expiation" NB; < Aram.
kupatinnu, *kuptatinnum*, *ka/uppatinnu*, *kuppitannu* "globule, pill" O/jB [NU.KÁR.KÁR] as golden ornament; med., mag., of clay; < *kapātu* ?; → *kuppittu*
kupātu(m) ~ "corn(field)"? OA, j/NB, NA; more than one word ? (→ *kuba'ātum*)
kupīrātu pl. tant. ~ "swabbings" jB rit.; < *kapāru* II
kupīru "bitumen"? NA for building; → *kupru*
kupītu I (a marsh-bird) jB, NA; < *kupû*
kupītu II (animal dropping)? jB lex.
kupkudum (a reed artefact) OB
kuppatinnu, kuppitannu → *kupatinnu*
kuppātu (a kind of building) Nuzi; < *quppu* II pl.?
kuppittu; pl. *kuppinēti* jB var. of *kupatinnu* ?

kuppu; pl. m. & f. "cistern, water-source" M/jB, *mê kuppāni ša šadê* "water from mountain springs"

kuppû(m) I "eel"? O/jB [GÚ.BÍ.KU6]; *marti k.* "eel's gall" as drug; also (a bird), (a snake); < Sum.

kuppû II "snow, ice" NA

kuppupu(m) "very bent" Bab.; as PN; < *kapāpu*

kuppurtum → *kupurtum*

kuppušu → *kubbušu*

kupputtu (a measuring vessel) j/NB; < *kupputu*

kupputu "conglomerated" j/NB of parts of liver; (desig. of carnelian); < *kapātu*

kuprītu(m) (or *kubrītu(m)*) mng. uncl. O/MB; < *kupru* ?

kupru(m), *kupuru* "bitumen, pitch" Bab., M/NA [ESIR/ÉSIR.UD.(DU.)A] usu. in dry form; for building, ship, figurine; > *kapāru* III; *kuprītum*?; → *kupīru*

kupsu, *kuspu*, *kisb/pu* "husks, bran" M/NA, M/jB [DUḪ.ŠE.GIŠ.Ì] usu. of sesame; *k. dišpi* "honey remnants", i.e. "wax"; Ug. *k. paššūri* "table crumbs"

kupsu → also *kubsu*

kuptatinnum → *kupatinnu*

kupû ~ "reed thicket" jB; > *kupītu* I

kūpu → *kūbu* II

kupuālu → *kipuālu*

kupulḫu (a linen cloth)? NB

kupuršinnum, *kurup/bšinnu(m)* (desig. of gold) OA, Bogh.; < Hitt.?

kupurtum (or *kuppurtum*) "anointment" OB (Susa); < *kapāru* II

kupūsu → *kubūsu*

kurabdu (a plant) jB lex.

kurādu (an implement) jB lex.

kurangu, *kuraggu* "rice" jB, NA

kūrapānu "neck-protector" NB; < OPers.

kurartu, *g/kura/ir/štu* (a skin complaint, phps.) "boil"? jB med.; < *kurāru*

kurāru(m), *gurāru* O/jB **1.** "glowing ashes" **2.** (a boil, carbuncle)? [GIR.GIG; occas. GIG.GIR]; > *kurartu*

kurassû → *kuruštû*

kuraštu → *kurartu*

kurbannu → *kirbānu*

kurbasi (a kind of thistle)? jB lex.

kurbu f. "blessing" jB; < *karābu* II

kurdillu (a kind of cucumber; a fruit) jB lex.

kurdinnu (or *kurtinnu*) (an evil-smelling plant) jB lex., NA

kurdiššu (a storage facility for straw) M/NA

kurduppum → *gurduppum*

kurgarrânu (a kind of stone) jB; < *kurgarrû*

kurgarrû (a cultic performer) M/NA, M/NB [(LÚ.)KUR.GAR.RA] freq. with *assinnu*; bearing sword and mace; *rab k.* "chief *k.*"; NA f. [MUNUS.KUR.GAR.RA] = *kurgarrātu* ?; < Sum.; > *kurgarrânu*, *kurgarrûtu*

kurgarrûtu "function of the *kurgarrû*" NB; as prebend; < *kurgarrû*

kuriallum (a functionary)? OA; → *kurniyallu* ?

kuribinnu (a kind of land)? Nuzi; < Hurr.

kurību (an ethereal spirit) NA/jB freq. ^{d}*K.*; "(figure of) a *k.*" of silver etc.; → *karābu* II

kur(i)giqu (part of a building) jB, rdg. unkn. phps. *mat(i)giqu*

kuriguru → *kanagurru*

kurillu → *kurullu* I

kuriltû → *kuruštû*

kurinnu → *kurrinnu*

kuripinnu (a kind of terrain)? Nuzi

kurissu; pl. f. ~ "leek" NA; → *karašu*

kurištu → *guristu*; *kurartu*

kurītu(m) "shin, tibia" Bab. [GÌR.PAD.DU/DA.LÚGUD.DA] of sheep, ox etc.; OB *k. kappim* "wing-bone" (desig. of part of liver ?); < *kurû* ?

kurkanû (a medicinal plant) M/NB, NA [Ú/ŠIM.KUR/KUR4.GI.RÍN/RIN.NA] as drug; root of *k.*

kurkatta(m) "like a goose" jB; < *kurkû*

kurkizannu → *kurkuzannu*

kurkû(m) "goose" Bab., NA [KUR.GI.MUŠEN; NB also MUŠEN.KUR.GI]; as tribute, offering; med. *šaman k.* "goose-fat"; < Sum.; > *kurkatta*

kurkudum mng. unkn. OB, as PN

kurkurrānu (desig. of a sheep) jB lex.

kurkurratu(m), *kukkurratum* (a vessel) OAkk, O/jB; for honey, wine; < *kurkurru*

kurkurru jB, NA **1.** lex. (a bird) **2.** (a vessel), of copper **3.** astr. (a phenomenon associated with stars); > *kurkurratu*

kurkuzannu(m), *kurkizannu* "piglet" O/jB, M/NA [ŠAḪ/ŠÁḪ.TUR]; as PN, also *Kukku=zannum*

kurmatu → *kurummatu*

kurmittu "butterfly"? jB

kurmu → *kurummu*

kurniya(l)lu (a functionary) Ug.; → *kuriallum* ?

Kurnugi "The Underworld" Bab. lex.; < Sum.

kurpīsu → *qurpissu*

ku(r)rinnu; pl. f. (a neck ornament) M/jB, NA

kurru(m) I occas. f. "(measure of dry capacity:) gur, kor" OAkk, Bab., OA [GUR] OB *kur kittim* "normal gur", loc.-adv. *kurrum* "per gur"; *k. šaqālu* "to weigh the gur"; Bab. as measure of ship's capacity; < Sum.; → *kursisakkatum*

kurru II (part of body, phps.) "pelvis" jB; med. left, right

kurru(m) III "tanning fluid" Bab., NA

kurru → also *kūru* III

kurrû(m); st. abs. du. *kurriā/kurrâ* "short" OB, Bogh., jB as pl. of *kurû*; < *kurû*

kursallum, *kuršullum* (a basket) Bab. of reed; also, as an ornament; < Sum.

kursānum → *gusānu*

kursimtu, *kurṣimtu*, *kursittum*, jB *kurs/ṣindu*, *kurṣiddu*, NA *kussimtu* ? "scale, plate" O/jB **1.** of snakeskin **2.** (a tool) **3.** for scale-armour **4.** NA on door ?

kursimtu → also *kuṣīmu*

kursindu → *kursimtu*

kursinnu(m), Bogh. *kuršinnu*; pl. m. & f. "ankle"; of human, sheep; as cut of meat; MB "astragalus", as game; lex. (an object)

kursinnum → also *gusānu*

kursisakk(at)um; pl. f. "grain-container" OB, of 1 gur; < Sum.; → *kurru* I

kursissu → *kurusissu*

kursittum → *kursimtu*

kursû → *kuruštû*

kurṣibtu → *kurṣiptu*

kurṣiddu → *kursimtu*

kurṣimatu → *akuṣīmu*

kurṣimtu → *kursimtu*; *kuṣīmu*

kurṣindu → *kursimtu*

kurṣiptānu (a plant) jB lex.; < *kurṣiptu*

kurṣiptu (or *kurṣibtu*) "butterfly" jB, NA; *k. alpi* (a flower); *k. eqli* "nettle"? [GI.ZÚ.LUM.MA] lex., med.

kurṣû(m) "fetter" Bab., OA [Nuzi GIŠ.GÌR] of copper, for feet; *k. purrurum/ḫepû* "to loosen/ break bonds"; NB (an ornament) "chain" of gold; jB desig. of a star

kuršinnu → *kursinnu*

kuršullum → *kursallum*

kurtinnu → *kurdinnu*

kurû(m); f. *kurītu(m)* "short" OAkk, Bab. [LÚGUD(.DA)] of things, part of body, time; as subst. "short (person), dwarf", also as (f)PN; transf. medical complaint *libbī kuri* "my heart is short"; < *karû* II; > *kurītu*?, *kurrû*

kūru I "depression, torpor" jB, NA [Ù.SÁ] of physical and mental apathy; NA *k. ēnē* "weak-sightedness"; < *kâru* II

kūru(m) II f. "kiln, furnace" Ass., OB for metal, glass; *uqnê/abnē k.* "kiln-made lapis lazuli/ stone" i.e. (blue) glass

kūru(m) III, *kurru* (part of a reed) jB

kūrum IV (a short reed mat) Bab. lex.; < Sum.

kurubšinnu → *kupuršinnum*

kurūbu (a bird) jB lex.

kurukku, *karakku* (a bird) M/jB

kuru(l)lu(m) I, *kurillu* "sheaf, stook" O/jB, M/NA; "(single) sheaf", coll. "sheaves, the harvest"; MA, Nuzi (a harvest festival); Mari pl. f. "bundles" of vine-prunings; → *k.* II

kurullum II ~ "catastrophe, death-toll" Mari; = *k.* I ?

kurullum III (a spice)? OAkk, OB

kurultû → *kuruštû*

kuru(m)mānu (a vessel, or kind of fruit)? Am., of ivory

kurummatu(m), *kurmatu* "food allocation, ration" [ŠUK(.ḪI.A)] for human, deity, animal; OB *eqel k.* "field for subsistence"; "bread (ration)", OA silver, tin as "ration"; → *kurummu*

kurummu (or *kurmu* ?) jB, by-form of *kurummatu* ?

kurumtu (a stone) Ug.

kuru(n)nu(m) (a kind of beer) Bab.(lit.) [KURUN.NAM/NA] offered to deity; drunk by men, in ritual; < Sum.

kuruppu(m) "(vegetable) basket, hamper" Bab.; also a reed structure; NB in *māšiḫu ša k.* as measuring unit for grain, dates, legumes and onions

kurupšinnu → *kupuršinnum*

kurusi(s)su(m), *kursissu* (a rodent) O/jB, esp. fond of sesame

kurussu "strap" M/jB; of leather; also "band" of copper; < *karāsu*

kurussû → *kuruštû*

kuruš (a spice) jB lex.; < Kass.

kuruštā'u "fatted animal" MB, Nuzi, of sheep; < *kuruštû*

kuruštû(m), *gurušsû*, MA *kuru/iltû*, *kuru/assû*, *kursû* (fodder for fattening) O/jB, MA; usu. in *ša k.* "animal-fattener" [LÚ.KU7]; < Sum.; > *kuruštā'u*, *kuruštumma*

kuruštumma in *k. epēšu* "to fatten" Nuzi; < *kuruštû*

kurzaḫḫu; Hurr. pl. *kurzaḫḫena* mng. unkn. Nuzi, in topog. desig.; < Hurr.

kurzidakkum "flour-basket" OB; < Sum.

kusa, *kusi* in *kusa/i yāmi* "algae"? jB, liter. "sea-covering"; < W.Sem.

kusannu → *gusānu*

kusāpu **1.** jB "crumb, scrap" of bread [PAD] **2.** NA "bread" [NINDA.MEŠ (→ also *akalu* 1)]; < *kasāpu* I

kusarikku(m), *kusarakku*, *ḫusarikku*, Bogh. *kušariḫḫu* "bison" OAkk, Bab.(lit.) [GU$_4$.A. LIM; GU$_4$.ALIM] jB also ^{d}*K.*; *ṣalmē k.* "images of bison"; astr. (a star)

kusāsū pl. tant. "gums" or "chewed bits"? jB; < *kasāsu*

kusi → *kusa*

kusibirr(īt)u → *kisibirrītu*

kusigau → *kusīqu*

kusīgu → *ḫusīgu*

kusīpānû → *kusīpu* II

kusīpu I; pl. m. & f. "bread (crumbs)" j/NB; < *kasāpu* I

kusīpu II, *ka(s)sīp/bu* (a plant) jB lex., med.; pl. (or derivative ?) *kusīpānû*, *kassibānû/u*; jB lex. desig. of a snake

kusīqu, *kusigau* (a garment) jB lex.

kusītu(m), Bogh. *kušītu* "robe" [TÚG.BAR. DUL/DUL$_{5/8}$]; OA fine (*raqqātum*), of Akkad; Am. of linen; NB for divine statue; < *kasû* III

kusīu (a headband) jB lex.; < *kasû* III

kuspu in *kusup libbi* "heartbreak"? NA; < *kasāpu* I

kuspu → also *kupsu*

kussalili (a functionary) Nuzi

kussimtu → *kursimtu*

kussīum → *kussû*

kussu (an ornament) Qatna, of gold, attached to disc

kussû(m), OAkk, OA *kussīum* f. occas. m. "chair, stool, throne" [(GIŠ.)GU.ZA; (GIŠ.)AŠ. TE; (GIŠ.)AŠ.TI] as piece of household furniture; "seat" in boat, chariot etc.; OA "saddle" on donkey; *k. serdê*, *k. ša ḫarrāni* "travelling seat, sedan-chair"; Nuzi *k. ša ebēri* "sedan-chair"?; *k. šapiltum* "low chair, stool"; judge's "seat"; king's "throne", transf. *kussûm kussīam išannan* "one throne (= dynasty) will rival another"; deity's "throne"; NB *bīt k.* "throne land, royal estate"?; *nīd k.* (part of liver); < Sum.; → *kuzā'u*

kussusu "gnawed (reed)" jB lex.; < *kasāsu*

kusû mng. unkn. jB lex.

kusullum (a wooden object) OB

kusummû (a garment) jB lex.

kūṣānû → *kūṣāyu*

kuṣā'u "spillage"? MA; < *kuṣṣû*

kūṣāyu(m) "of winter"? Bab., of harvest, pig; NB of date palm, also *kūṣānû*; < *kūṣu*

kūṣi (a plant) jB lex.

kuṣibi (a garden herb) NB

kuṣillātu (an illness)? jB lex.

kuṣimānu → *akuṣīmu*

kuṣīmu(m), *kurṣ/simtu* (a bent stick) O/jB; as part of door

kuṣippum (or *g/kuzippum*); pl. f. mng. unkn. OAkk

kuṣīrum (or *kuzīrum*) (a binding)? OB; < *kaṣāru* ?

kuṣṣu → *kūṣu*

kuṣṣû D "to tilt" NA a bowl for libation; > *kuṣā'u*

kuṣṣû → also *kūṣû*

kuṣṣudu ~ "cripple(d)" jB; < *kaṣādu* ?

kuṣṣulu (or *kuzzulu*) D mng. unkn. jB lex.

kuṣṣuru(m) "thoroughly knotted" O/jB; < *kaṣāru* D

kuṣṣuṣu(m) "(one) crippled by lack of hand"? O/jB lex.; < *kaṣāsu* I

kūṣu(m), *kuṣṣu(m)* "coldness, winter" [EN.TE. (EN.)NA; ŠED$_7$] "cold temperature", "cold weather"; med. "chill, shivering"; "winter (-time)", OB *ina k. k. ibašši* "there will be cold weather in the winter"; < *kaṣû* III; > *kūṣāyu*; *kūṣû*

kūṣû, *kuṣṣû* adj. "winter('s)" j/NB, of sheep, vegetable; NB "winter stores"; < *kūṣu*

kuṣu'u (an animal)? jB lex., equated with *muš'u*

kušabku(m), *kišab(k)u*, *kušābu* (a thorny tree, shrub) O/jB [GIŠ.AB.BA] OB for fuel; < Sum.

kušaḫḫum → *ḫušaḫḫu*

kušānu → *gusānu*

kušāpu; pl. m. & f. "sorcerous materials" jB; < *kašāpu*

kušariḫḫu → *kusarikku*

kušartu "repair, patch" M/NB; < *kašāru*

kušāru ~ "reed stalk" Bab. mag.; also lex. (a shelter); < *kašāru* ?; → *kušru* I

kušēr(āt)u → *kušīru*

kušgugalû (a drum, liter.) 'skin of great ox' jB [KUŠ.GU$_4$.GAL-]; < Sum.

kušḫāru (a wall) jB lex.

kušīru(m), *kušēru*; lex. pl. f.? "success, profit" O/jB, NA; st. abs. *lā kušīr* "profitless"; < *kašāru*

kušītu → *kusītu*

kušpa'e (an edible item)? Nuzi; < Hurr.; → *kušupḫa*

kušraḫḫum ~ (leather strap) OB, for chariot; < Sum.

kušru I, *kuzuru* (a plant) j/NB, NA [Ú.KU.GAG (or *tuš-rú* ?)] as drug; → *kušāru*; *tušru*

kušru II ~ "ingot" NB of silver, copper

kušrum III (component of a boat) OB

kuššatu(m) (a garment) OA, Bogh.

kuššikku (a clay) jB lex.

kuššû/u mng. unkn. jB lex.; < *kašû* II ?
kuššudu "chased (off)" jB of bird, person; < *kašādu* D
kuššuku (prof. desig.) OB(Susa); < Elam.
kuštappu → *guštappu*
kuštāru(m), jB freq. *kultāru*; pl. m. & f. "tent" Bab.; *bīt ṣēri k. šarrūtišu* "desert house, his royal tent"; *(Aḫlamû) šūt k.* "tent people"; OB PlN *Kuštārātum*
kuštībum, *kultību* "(kind of) shovel" O/jB
kuštu, *kultu* (a kind of grass) M/jB
kušû ~ "crab" j/NB(lit.) [KÚŠU]; < Sum.; → *alluttu*
kūšu "skin" jB lex.; < Sum.
kūšum → also *qūšum*
kušuḫannu (a wooden object) Nuzi; < Hurr.?
kušupḫa, **kušuppara** (kinds of bread or pastry) Nuzi; < Hurr.; → *kušpa'e*
kušurrā'um "restitution" OAkk, in *šībūt k.* "witnesses to r."; < *kašāru*
kušurru mng. unkn. jB
kutāḫu; pl. m. & f. ~ "spear, lance" NA
kutallānu(m) "backward" jB adv. in *kutallānikka* "behind you"; OA as PN; < *kutallu*
kutallu(m) "back" [GÚ.TÁL; GÚ.TAR] **1.** "back of head" of human, animal; jB *mukīl k.* "supporter, helper" **2.** "back" of lung, ear etc.; "rear" of chair, building, army etc.; *ina/ana k.* "behind" as prep., as adv., st. abs. *ina kutal* **3.** of time, *k. šatti* "end of year", *ina k.* "later" **4.** NA, NB *(ša) k.*, NB pl. f., also Mari? "reserve" soldier, NB also "spare (ox)"; < Sum.; > *kutallūtu*, *kutallānu*
kutallūtu "position as reserve" NB; < *kutallu* 4
kutamlalu, *katamlalu* mng. uncl. jB lex.; → *kullulu* II
kutānum, occas. *kutīnum* (a textile) OAkk, OA, Mari; or *qutānum* ?
kutāṣu (a log)? jB lex.
kūtātu → *kūtu*
kutatupḫuḫlu (a functionary) Nuzi; < Hurr.
kutimmūtu "position as goldsmith" NB [LÚ.KÙ.DIM-], as prebend; < *kutīmu*
kutīmu(m), *ku(t)timmu(m)* "goldsmith, silversmith" Bab. [(LÚ.)KÙ.DÍM; NB usu. KÙ.DIM]; < Sum.; > *kutimmūtu*
kutkim mng. unkn. MB in skins of *k.*; < Kass.?
kutlālu mng. unkn. jB lex.
kutlānum (a bird) OB
kutlu(m); pl. f. ~ "rail, fence, side-wall"? Bab., MA of oven
kutmā'išu (a container) Ug., of bronze
kutmānu ~ (a tamarisk)? jB lex.
kutmu(m) "cover, covering" O/jB [DUL] in *k. libbi* "stomach tissue" of animal; < *katāmu*
kutpû "black frit" M/jB [(NA4.)AN.ZAḪ.GE6]
kutrannu (or *qutrannu*) (an object) Nuzi
kuttenašwe (desig. of cattle) Nuzi; < Hurr.
kuttim (prof. desig.) Nuzi
kuttimmatu "female charcoal-burner" jB mag.
kuttimmu "charcoal-burner" jB lex.
kuttimmu → also *kudimmu*; *kutīmu*
kuttu → *kūtu*
kuttumu "covered over" j/NB; of bride "veiled"; of ship "with deck"; of land "inaccessible"; < *katāmu*
kutturu **1.** OB(Alal.) (a class of person)? **2.** Nuzi (a wooden object) = *kitturru* II ?
kuttutu mng. unkn. jB lex.; phps. = *ḫuttutu*
kūtu(m), *kuttu(m)*, *kutû*; pl. m. & f. "jug, can" for liquids O/jB, M/NA [(GIŠ/DUG.)UD+MUNUS+KAB] of wood, clay, copper; transf., elephant's "trunk"
kutullu → *kuzullu*
kutultu mng. unkn. jB lex.
kutumdu → *kutumtu*
kutummu(m) "cover(ing)" Bab., OA; for axe; of reed, leather for interior of boat; "protection, covering garment" for person; "outer sheath" of reed stem; < *katāmu*
kutumtu, *kutumdu* ~ "covered basket"? jB; < *katāmu*
kutuniwe mng. unkn. Nuzi; desig. of yoke-team; < Hurr.
kutūtum; pl. *kutu'ātum* "security" OA; < *katā'um*
kuwāti → *kuāti*
kuwā'um → *kû*
kuyātu, *ku'ātu*, *kuḫātu* (a plant) M/jB, as drug; Qatna, as ornament in gold, lapis lazuli
kuzābum "alluring" OB in fPN *Kuzābatum*; < *kazābu* I
kuzallu(m), OB also *guzālum*; pl. f. "shepherd" O/MA, O/jB; *(waraḫ) K.* (3rd month) Ass.
kuzā'u "throne" jB lex.; < Sum.; → *kussû*
kuzāzu jB **1.** "wood-wasp" **2.** (a goat); < *gazāzu* ?
kuzbānītu "alluring" M/jB, of goddess; as fPN; < *kuzbu*
kuzbānu (a bird) jB lex.; < *kuzbu*
kuzbu(m) ~ "attractiveness, (sex) appeal" Bab. [ḪI.LI] "charms" of woman, goddess, *za'nat kuzbam* "is laden with allure"; female genitalia; "sexual potency" of male; transf. of field, water, temple; < *kazābu* I
kuzippu, *guzippu* "cloak" M/NA

kuzippum → also *kuṣippum*

kuzīrum (cultic person) jB; < *kezēru*

kuzīrum → also *kuṣīrum*

kuzubtum "flattery, seduction"? OA, of words; < *kazābu* I

kuzullu(m), *kutullu(m)*, *guzullu* "bundle of reeds" Bab.

kuzuru → *kušru* I

kuzzalûm → *guzalû*

kuzzisallum (a basket) OB; < Sum.

kuzzubu(m), *kunzubu* "very charming, attractive" OA, O/jB, of goddess; as fPN; OA of speech; jB also desig. of illness; < *kazābu* I

kuzzulu → *kuṣṣulu*

L

la prep. jB(Ass.), NA, NB **1.** spatially "from" a place **2.** in *la qātī/ē* "from" a person **3.** Emar "to"; < W.Sem.; > *lapāni*

lā "not, no; without, un-" [NU] **A.** negation of individual words: adj. *lā damqu* "not good", *lā šû* "not his own", ptcp. *lā mupparkû* "unceasing", subst. *lā kittu* "injustice", adv. *lā pīqam* "not once"; + infin. gen. or st. abs. e.g. *lā maḫār* "irresistible"; + gen. "without", OB *kasap lā kanīkim* "silver without a tablet", OA *lā šībē* "without witnesses", OAkk *lā šurrātim* "no lies"; NA *dibbī lā dibbī* "unspeakable things", NB *amāt lā amāt* "every single word"; Ass. *lā* ... *lā* "neither ... nor" **B.** negation of clause, placed immediately before pred.: **1.** subord. clauses before subjunct. (OA also inverted *lā ša* + vb.) **2.** condit. clauses (→ *šumma* 1) **3.** oaths before subjunct. (j/NB pos. statements → *kī* 4; *šumma* 2; GAG §185j) **4.** in interrog. clauses **5.** in proh. before pres., stat. **6.** Ass. as negation of main clause, OA also → *ula*; *lā* ... *lā* ... "neither ... nor ..."; before subst. for emphasis, e.g. NA *lā kusāpē takkal* "she eats no bread at all" **7.** OAkk, Bab. rarely as strong negation of main clause (→ *ul*), OAkk *manāma lā illik* "no one at all went", NB *lā āmur* "I definitely did not see", OB *lā tutta* "you surely will not find" **C.** in comb.: **1.** *ša lā* "without", esp. "without agreement of" s.o.; "except for" **2.** → *adi* 3; *ana* I 13, *alla*; *ezib*; *ina* 7, *illā*; *lāman*; *šumma* 4

la'ābu(m), *le'ēbu* ~ "to harass" O/jB **G** (*i/i*) of demons etc. "afflict" person, lung; jB of *la'bu/li'bu* "infect" s.o. **D** "infect" s.o. with *l.* illness **N** pass. "be infected"; > *li'bu*, *la'bum*, *la'ībum*; *tal'abum*?

la'āmum → *lêmu*

la'āšu(m) ~ "to dirty, defile"? jB lex. **G**; **D**; > *li'šu*, *la'šu* II, *lā'išu*; *lu'aštu*

la'ātu "to swallow (up)" Bab. **G** (*u/u*) of persons, animals **D** ~ G; → *alātu*; *ma'lātu*

la'ā'u → *le'û*

labābu(m) "to rage" O/jB **G** (*a/u*) of person, demon **Š** caus., of fever "make s.o. rage" **Št** OB "exert o.s."? **N** "become furious" of flood, "be feverish"? of lips; > *libbātu*; *labbibu*; *šalbābu*; *šalbubu*; *nalbubu*, *nalbābu*

labāku(m) "to be(come) soft" OAkk, O/jB, MA **G** (*i/i*) of part of body; of bow "be supple"; of drugs, in liquid **D** "make soft, soften up" part of body etc.; drugs in liquid **Dtn** iter. of D **Š** ~ D "soften, soak"; > *labku*; *labbuku*; *lubku*; *lubkānu*

labanātu "incense" jB

labānu(m), NB also *le/abēnu* "to spread, stroke" **G** (*i/i*; NA perf. *issibin*) **1.** "stroke" part of body, esp. nose (*appa*), gesture of submission, respect [KIR4.ŠU.GÁL] **2.** "spread out" (mud to make) bricks, *libittam l.* "make bricks", *agurra l.* "make baked bricks", also absol.; jB/NA "brick over" **D** MA, jB lex. ~ G 2 "cover, reinforce with brickwork" **Š** caus. of G 1 jB *appa l.*; caus. of G 2 "have bricks made", also NA "cause to brick over"; > *labnu* I; *libnu*; *lābinu*, *labbinu*?; *libittu*; *lubbundu*, *labbūnu*; *nalbanu*, *nalbattu*, *nalbanatta*

labânu → *labiānum*

labāriš j/NB **1.** in *l. alāku* of buildings "to become old, dilapidated" **2.** in *l. ūmē* "in days to come" (in future), "with the passage of time" (in past); < *labāru*

labarmanna ~ "for the future, henceforth" Bogh.

labāru(m) "to be(come) old, long-lasting" **G** (*i/i*) [TIL] of persons "live long, live to a great age"; of city, food, work "become old"; of time "last long"; *labār (dūr) ūmī* "long duration; longevity; distant future"; *labār palê* "long reign"; in PNs *-lilbir*, *-lilbur* (→ *bâru* III) **Gtn** iter. jB *litabbur dadmī* "long survival of (separate) settlements" **D** "make long-lived, long-lasting" [TIL; also LIBIR.RA], of god "give" s.o. "long life", "make" s.o.'s life, reign "last long"; of man "hold" e.g. sceptre "for a long time", OB *kussâm ulabbar* "will hold the throne for long"; ellipt. "live long" **Dt** "be allowed to live long, reach old age" of person, building **Š 1.** caus. "bring to old age, allow to last long" reign, priesthood **2.** of person, building "become old, dilapidated"; > *labīru, labīriš, labirtu, labīrūtu*; *labāriš*; → *lubāru*; *labarmanna*

Labāṣu, *Lapāṣu* (a disease demon) jB [dDÌM.ME.A] as demon, as disease

labāšu(m) "to clothe o.s." **G** (*a/a*, jB *i/i*) "put on" garment (= acc.); stat. "wears, is wearing", *ṣubātam lā labšāku* "I wear no clothing"; transf. "is clad in" fear, soreness, radiance etc.; Nuzi for D "clothe" s.o. **Gt 1.** stat. transf. "is clad in" sickness, fear etc.; of object "is overlaid with" gold etc. **2.** OA, OB "provide with clothing" **3.** liter. "get dressed (in)" [MU4.MU4] **D** "clothe" [MU4.MU4], "provide with clothing" esp. as gift; transf. OA "enclose" tablet in envelope; MB/MA "face" wall with bricks; NB "overlay" object with metal; "wrap" s.o. with leprosy **Dt** "clothe o.s. with, put on" garment etc. **Š** "clothe, array" transf. with greenery, fear etc.; "overlay, bedeck" with precious metal **Št** "clothe o.s. with"; stat. "is clothed with" **N** ~ G "put on" garment (= acc.), also transf. light, justice; stat. "is clad in"; > *labšu, labšūtum, libšu, lubšu, lubāšu, lubūšu, lubuštu*; *labbašu*?, *lubbušu*; *litbušu*; *nalbašu*; *talbīšum, talbuštu*

labātu (a kind of wool) jB lex.

labātu → also *labtu*; *lapātu*

lābatu(m), jB *labbatu* "lioness" OAkk, O/jB as epith. of goddess; in fPN *Ši-lābat*; < *lābu*

labaṭu, *lapiṭu* (a plant) jB lex., comm.

labā'u → *lawûm* II

labbānātu → *kalbānātu*

labbānu → *alappānu*

labbašu (prof. desig.) NB; < *labāšu* ?

labbašūte → *lubbušu*

labbatu → *lābatu*

labbibu "very furious" jB of weapon; < *labābu*

labbinu (a fly) jB lex.; < *labānu* ?

labbiš → *lābiš*

labbu 1. ~ "weak"? OB of oxen **2.** (desig. of low quality dates) j/NB [GIŠ.GIŠIMMAR.BUR ?]

labbu → also *lābu*

labbuku "softened, steeped" MA of aromatics; < *labāku* D

labbūnu; pl. f. (a stand or pedestal)? M/NA for statues; in *bīt* (d)*l.* (a religious building); also in PN; < *labānu*

labbušu → *lubbušu*

labēnu → *labānu*

labertu → *labirtu*

labēru → *labīru*

labērūtu → *labīrūtu*

labiānum, *labânu*, NA *lib/pânu* "neck(tendons)" O/jB, M/NA [SA.GÚ] of human, animal

lābinu(m), NB *lēbinu* "brick-maker" Bab. esp. *lābin libitti(m)*; < *labānu*

labīriš "of old" OB in *ištu l.*, *ina l.* "for a long time"; < *labīru*

labirtum, *labertum* OB **1.** "long-standing property" esp. of fields **2.** "long-standing, old debt" [LIBIR] **3.** "earlier time"; < *labīru*

labīru(m), *labēru(m)*, jB also *labru*; NB f. also *labištu* "old" [LIBIR(.RA); TIL] of objects, food, drink etc.; of building; "former, previous, long-standing" of field, person, king etc.; "old-established" of customs, measures; of tablet, in col. as subst. *kīma labīrišu* "according to its original" [LIBIR.RA.BI.GIM]; as subst. "former time", *kīma l.*, *ina l.* "(as) in the past"; < *labāru*; > *labīriš, labirtu, labīrūtu*

labīrūtu, *la/ebērūtu* "old age" M/jB(Ass.), Bogh., NA of person, building *l. alāku* "to grow old, become dilapidated"; Bogh. *kī l.* "as of old"; < *labīru*

lābiš, *labbiš* "like a lion" M/jB; < *lābu*

labištu → *labīru*

lābišu (a plant) jB lex.

labittu → *labnu* I; *libittu*

labītu in *l. ilabbi* fig. etym. of guard, "makes the round" NA; < *lawûm* II

lābiu → *lāmû*

labku; NA f. *labaktu* "soft" M/NB, NA **1.** Nuzi "supple" of bow **2.** MB "moist" of plaster; NB in subst. use "moistening" of soil **3.** NB (a type of beer) **4.** NA "tender" of meat; < *labāku*

labniš "as (if using) throwsticks"? jB(Ass.); < *labnu* II

labnu I; f. *labittu* "(spread) flat" MA, jB of face, nose; "moulded" of bricks MA; (a type of basket) jB lex.; < *labānu*

labnu II, *libnu* "throwstick" jB lex.; > *labniš*

labru → *labīru*

labṣum "foreigner"? OB lex.

labšu "clothed" jB esp. in *labiš kitê* "linen-wearer" (a temple official); Nuzi "worn" of clothes; < *labāšu*

labšūtum "clothed state" OB in *labšūssa* "clothed" of woman; < *labšu*

labtu(m), also pl. *labātu* "(oven-)parched grain" O/jB, NA [NA. ŠE.SA.A]

labû, *lebû* "to howl, whine, squeal, cry out" jB **G** (*u/u*, also *i/i*) of dog, pig etc.; of sick person "cry out", of baby; of wind in stomach; of house "creak"; *zubbi labê* (a type of fly) jB lex. **Gtn** iter. of invalid; > *lābû*

labû → also *lawûm* II

lābu(m), OAkk, OA *lab'um*, jB also *labbu* "lion"; also transf. as desig. of god, king, demon; > *lābatu*; *lābiš*

lābu → also *li'bu*

lābû adj. "howling, bleating" jB lex.; < *labû*

lab'um → *lābu*

la'bum adj. "suffering from *li'bu* disease" OB lex.; < *la'ābu*

la'bu → also *li'bu*

labubi(t)tu (a plant) j/NB

labūnu → *labbūnu*

labussu → *lubuštu*

ladinnu, *ladnu*, *ladunu* (an aromatic, phps.) "ladanum resin" j/NB, NA

ladiru → *aladiru*

lâdiru "fearless" MB/MA for *lā ādiru*

ladnu → *ladinnu*

lâdu(m), NA *luādu* "to bend down" O/jB, NA **G** (*ū*) of wrestler; tree; path; of part of exta; NA "bow" in shame ?

ladunu → *ladinnu*

la'ēbum → *la'ībum*

lagabbiš "like a lump" jB; < *lagabbu*

lagabbu(m) "lump, clod" OA, O/jB lex.; < Sum.

lagāgu "to cry out" jB lex. only **G**; **D**

lagallum, *laga(r)ru(m)* → *lagaru*

lagarturru "apprentice *lagaru* priest" NB; < Sum.

lagaru(m), *lagarru*, *lagallum* (a priest) Bab., Susa; < Sum.

laga(š)takkaš (desig. of horses) M/NB; < Kass.

lagā'u, *lagû* "scale, dirt, scum" jB on lips, ears, scalp; in bitumen oven

lāginu (an agricultural occupation) jB lex., also *lāgin išitti* "rich, important"

lagu mng. unkn. jB lex. in *abšu lagu* (a kind of legume)

lagû → *lagā'u*

laḫābu, *leḫēbu* ~ "to rumble, growl" MA, jB **G** (*i/i*) of patient's belly, horse, wolf **Štn** "cause to growl continuously"

laḫādu → *laḫātu*

laḫagu (a plant) jB lex., med.

laḫamu → *laḫmu*

laḫāmu(m) I, *leḫēmu* "to be hairy" O/jB **G** stat. only *šārta la/eḫim* "is covered in hair" **D**, **Š** lex. only; > *laḫmu*, *laḫīmu*; *luḫḫumu*

laḫāmu II **G** unattested **D** j/NB "to brew" beer from malt or dates

laḫanatu, *laḫandu* → *laḫantu*

laḫangiddû (a slender flask) jB lex.; < Sum.

laḫannu(m); pl. m. & f. (a flask) Bab., M/NA [DUG.LA.ḪA.AN] of pottery, stone, metal; < Sum.; → *laḫiānum*

laḫantu, *laḫanatu*, *laḫandu* (a bird) jB lex.; of girl in song

laḫarûm, **laḫarītum** (desig. of a garment) OB

laḫaruḫšum, *laḫaruššu*, *laḫaruška/u* "quiver (on chariot)" O/jB

laḫāšu(m) "to whisper" O/jB **G** not attested **Gt** jB "pray in a whisper" **D** "whisper" **Dtn** Mari iter. **Dt** jB "whisper to o.s."; > *liḫšu*; *Mulaḫḫišu*

laḫātu (or *laḫād/ṭu*) mng. unkn. jB lex. **D**; **Š**

laḫḫinu → *alaḫḫinu*

laḫḫinutu (a female official) M/NA; < *laḫḫinu*

Laḫḫum (a month) Mari, OB(Susa)

laḫiānum (a vessel) OB = *laḫannu* ?; > *laḫiyānātu*

laḫīmu "hairy" jB lex.; < *laḫāmu* I

laḫi(y)ānātu(m) pl. tant. (a kind of shell) O/jB; < *laḫiānum*

laḫmu(m), *laḫamu* **1.** 'hairy' jB lex.; OB as PN **2.** (a mythical being) OAkk, Bab. guardians of sea, sky, earth, *apsû*; "(statue, image of) *l.*"; < *laḫāmu* I

laḫru(m) m. & f. "sheep", mostly f. "ewe" OAkk, Bab., NA [(UDU.)U8]; lit. "flocks", also deified *Laḫar*

laḫšātu f. pl. (implements)? NB of iron

laḫšu → *lašḫu*

laḫtangiddû (a narrow beer vessel) jB lex.; < Sum.

laḫtanu(m); pl. f. (a beer vat) OA, O/jB [LAḪTAN]; < Sum.

laḫtu "pit" jB lex.

laḫû I "jaw(s)" M/jB
laḫû II "dry wood" jB lex.; < Sum.
lāḫu "young shoot" jB lex.; < W.Sem.
la'ībum, *la'ēbum* "suffering from *li'bu* disease" OAkk as PN; < *la'ābu*
lā'ir(i)ānu, *lāwirānu(m)* "standing water" O/jB; → *awirānum*
la'īš "like a small child" jB; < *la'û*
lā'išu(m) "oppressive, merciless" O/jB of goddess, death; < *la'āšu*
lā'ium → *lē'û*
lakādu(m) "to run" O/jB **G** (*i/i*) of person, animal; > *lākittu*
lakānum (or *laqānum*) (a type of sheep)? OA, also as PN
lakbum (or *lakpum*, *laqb/pum*) (a vessel) OB lex.
lākittu "(a type of) boat" jB lex. (liter. 'runner'?); < *lakādu*
lakku (or *laqqu*) (a vessel) Qatna of silver
lakpum → *lakbum*
lakû(m) I "weak" of person, "suckling" of animal, child; also as fPN *Lakītu(m)*; of date palm; < *lakû* II; → *la'û*
lakû(m) II "to be(come) weak" OA, O/jB **G** (*i/i*) of person, foundation **D** "weaken" s.o.; > *lakû* I
lakû III "crooked" jB lex.; < Sum.
lâku → *lêku*
lalagu → *lallangu*
lalā'iš "like kids" jB; < *laliu*
lalānû "indigent, powerless" jB lex.; > *lulânû*?
lalânû "flourishing" jB of person; "luxuriant" of garden; < *lalû* I
lala'u mng. unkn. jB
lalā'u → *laliu*
lālēnu, *lālenna* in *ina l.* "above (in document), *supra*" NB; < Aram.
lalgar "cosmic (underground) water, *apsû*" jB
lalikkû → *liligû* I
laliu(m), *lali'u*, *lalû(m)*, *lalā'u(m)* "kid, young goat" O/jB, MA [MÁŠ.TUR]; also OA, OB *Laliya* as PN; > *lalā'iš*
la(l)langu, *lalagu* (a leguminous vegetable) jB lex.
lallarātu pl. tant. "lamentation" jB; < *lallaru*
lallariš "like a mourner" jB; < *lallaru*
lallāriš "like honey" jB; < *lallāru*
lallartu(m), *lallarītu* "female mourner" O/jB; also as desig. of bird, insect; of squeaky shoe ?; < *lallaru*
lallaru(m) "(professional) mourner" O/jB; also (a bird); desig. of owl, cricket etc.; > *lallarātu*; *lallartu*; *lallariš*
lallāru "white honey" jB; also transf., of lips; > *lallāriš*
lallašu mng. unkn. OB lex.
Lallubû(m), *Lanlubû*, jB also *Lullubû* (a month) O/jB; 6th month, OB(Susa); 7th month, jB astr.; OB fPN at Susa *Lallubītu*
lalšagakku "midwife" jB lex.; < Sum.
lalû(m) I "plenty, exuberance" OAkk, Bab., NA [LA] **1.** "plenty, wealth; abundance" of luxury, vegetation **2.** "exuberance, (sexual) charms, attractions" of woman, goddess, rarely also man; of god, man "prime of life" etc.; OB also pl. f. as PN; *l. malû* "to be full of charms", *l. šebû* "to be satisfied, sated with attractions" of woman, life, palace etc. **3.** "desire" for s.th., to do s.th.; "longing" for god; > *lalânû*; *lalûtu*; *lulû* I; *lullû* II
lalû II "to bind"? jB lex.
lalû → also *laliu*
lalûtu(m) "vigour, prime of life" OB as PN, jB of man's middle age; < *lalû* I
lāma, M/jB also *lām*; before pron. suff. *lāmi/u-* "before (in time); in front of" OAkk, Bab., OA **1.** prep. "before" person; "before" an event, *lāma eṣēdim* "before reaping", *lām libbiya* "before I wish"; > *ellāmu-* **2.** adv. OAkk, OB before pret. "not yet"? **3.** conj. "before" + subjunct.
lamādu(m) "to learn" **G** (*a/a*; imper. *limad*) [ZU] "learn, come to know" a fact, a matter (esp. with obj. *ṭēmum*, *awātum*); "learn" how to do s.th.; "comprehend, understand"; OA "recognize, acknowledge" a claim, obligation; OA, O/jB "know (sexually)" **Gtn** iter. "(repeatedly) ascertain" s.th.; OA "repeatedly study" tablet, MB(Shechem) "study" (as apprentice) **Gt** **1.** "learn thoroughly, completely", esp. stat. **2.** recipr. OB "get to know one another" **D** **1.** "inform" s.o. of s.th. (= 2 acc.) **2.** "teach" s.o. a fact, a craft etc. **3.** OA "charge" s.o. with an expense **Š** M/jB, NA "have" s.o. "learn" s.th. **N** of command, plan, demon "be comprehended, fathomed"; > *lamdu*; *limittum*; *lummudu*; *mulammidu*; *talmīdu*
lam(a)ḫuššû f. (a ceremonial garment) Bab., Am., Bogh. [TÚG.NÍG.LÁM]; < Sum.
lamamaḫḫu "human-headed bull colossus" jB(Ass.) [dLAMMA.MAḪ]; < Sum.
lamāmu I "to chew" jB **G** (*a/u*) of animal, person **D** ~ G ? "masticate" alum
lamāmu II, *lemēmu* "to test"? MB, NA in glass manufacture
lāman "not yet" jB lex.; < *lā* + *-man*

lamānu → *lemēnu*

lamaqartu, *lamaqurtu* (a container of standard capacity) NA for fish

lamassannu ~ "fortunate, blessed" MB of correspondent's superior; < *lamassu*

lamassatu(m) "tutelary goddess" O/jB [^{d}LAMMA]; also "(image of) tutelary goddess", e.g. *l. Ištar* "figurine of Ištar"; *l. īni* "pupil" of the eye; OAkk, OA, OB also fPN; < *lamassu*

lamassu(m) f. "(female) tutelary deity" [^{d}LAMMA]; freq. in PNs; as source of good fortune, *l. rašû* "to have personal god, i.e. good fortune"; OB lex. *awīl l.* "lucky man"; OB *Mardukma lamassaka* "Marduk is your personal deity"; *l. māti* "tutelary deity of land"; "(image of, figurine of) *l.* deity"; in NA palaces (a type of sphinx) also [MUNUS.^{d}LAMMA]; *aban l.* (a precious stone); > *lamassannu*, *lamassatu*

lamaštu(m), NA also *lamassu* (a demoness) [^{d}DÌM.ME] attacking esp. new-born and sucklings; also in *aban l.*, *šam(mi) l.* (kinds of stone, plant)

lamattu "ant" jB lex.

lâmātu in *ša la-mat-su* "one with no true claim" jB; also lex. (an interj.); < *lā* + *awātu*

lamdu "experienced" jB; of virgin *lā lamittu*; < *lamādu*

lamḫuššû → *lamaḫuššû*

lāmi- → *lāma*

la'miš "like ashes" jB; < *lāmu*

lammu I, *lummu* (a tree) M/jB, NA; < Sum.

lammu II jB **1.** (desig. of the underworld) **2.** ^{mul}*l.* (a star); < Sum.

lammudu → *lummudu*

lammunum → *lummunu*

lamniš → *lemniš*

lamnu → *lemnu*

lamsīsu, *lamsisû* (a brewing vat) jB; < Sum.

lamṣatānu "fly-bitten"? MB as horse's name; < *lamṣu*

lamṣu, *lamṣatu(m)*, *namṣ(at)u* (a big fly) O/jB [NIM.SAḪAR.RA]; also med., "fly(-bite)", esp. *lamṣat ḫilāti*; > *lamṣatānu*

lamû (a branch) jB lex.

lamû → also *lawûm* I.II

lāmu, *la'mu* "glowing ashes" Bab. esp. with *belû*/*bullû* "to (be) extinguish(ed)"; > *la'miš*

lāmu- → *lāma*

lāmû, *lēmû*, NA *lābiu* M/NB, Nuzi, NA adj. **1.** Nuzi of witness "walking round" land **2.** "surrounding" (with obj.); < *lawûm* II ptcp.

la'mu → *lāmu*

lamutānu, *lamutu*, *lautānu* m. & f.; f. *latānu*, mostly pl. "slave(s), retainer(s)" NB

lamuttu → *lemuttu*

lamutu → *lamutānu*

lâniḫu → *aniḫu*

Lanlubû → *Lallubû*

lānu(m) "form, stature" Bab., NA [ALAN] "outward form" of human; "height, size" of person, deity, image, tree, ark; mag. "(image of) human form"

lānu → also *karānu* 4

lanuqānu (part of a statue)? MB

lapān(i) "in front of" j/NB spatially; with vb.s of fleeing, fearing etc. "from before"; taking, stealing "from" s.o.; attitude "towards, with regard to" s.o.; occas. commanded, engendered "by" s.o.; < *la* + *pānu* I

lapānu(m) "to be(come) poor" **G** (*i/i*, occas. *u/u*) [ÚKU] of persons **D** "make poor, impoverish"; > *lapnu*; *lupnu*; *lappanu*; *luppunum*

lapāpu(m) "to wrap around" Bab. **G** (pres. *ilappap*) med., mag. with wrappings (*lippī*) etc. **D** ~ G ?; > *lippu*

Lapāṣu → *Labāṣu*

lapātu(m), *labātu* "to touch, take hold of" **G** (*a/u*) [TAG] **1.** "touch" person, part of body; also with sexual connotation; transf. OA "touch" s.o.'s ear, in court; "involve, call in" palace (officials); "undertake" job (*liptu*) **2.** "(wrongly) lay hands on" property etc. **3.** "attack (with violence), grasp violently" o.'s throat (in oath-taking); with knife, sword, whip etc. **4.** OB "levy, call up" troops **5.** OA, OB math. "inscribe, enter (on tablet)" **6.** "affect with, harm with" fire, damp, pest, disease etc. **7.** "apply" s.th. to s.th. (= 2 acc.), "smear, anoint" s.th. with (= *ina*) e.g. bitumen, oil, blood etc. **8.** stat., of omen etc. "is unfavourable" **9.** of omen "affect" s.o., "be applicable to" s.o. **10.** MB of sun "touch" the sky, "rise" **Gtn** [TAG.MEŠ] iter. of G 6, 7 **Gt** [TAG.TAG] **1.** ~ G 5 OA "write down, enter (on tablet)" **2.** ~ G 7 "smear" s.th. with s.th. (= 2 acc.), ellipt. "infect" weapon (with poison) **D** [TAG.TAG; TAG.MEŠ] **1.** ~ G "grasp" throat (~ G 3), "touch" part of body "roughly", "play" stringed instrument, "make contact with" dirt, pollution, genitals **2.** "have bad effect on" s.th., "upset" situation, omen **3.** OA, OB "delay", stat. "is delayed"; ellipt. "tarry, make a stop" **4.** OA "write" message, answer, tablet etc. to s.o. **5.** "sprinkle, fumigate" with liquid, incense etc. **6.** NA ~ G 6 of eclipse "affect" land **Dtn** iter. of D 4 "repeatedly write" tablets **Dt** pass. of D 3 OB "be delayed" **Š** [ḪUL.MEŠ; TAG.TAG] "ruin, destroy, plunder" land, city, building; gods, people, images; cult; "pound up" in mortar **Št**^{1} [ḪUL(.MEŠ)] pass. of Š **Št**^{2} caus. of pass. OB "allow to be touched" **N** pass. of G [TAG.TAG] of work "be undertaken"; of possession "have hands laid on, be appropriated"; OA "be entered, recorded" as (= acc.) surety; "be affected" by weevils, by fire, by injury; of salt "be applied" to fish; > *laptu* I; *laptānu*; *liptānu*; *liptu*, *lipittu*; *lupputu*; *mulappitu*, *talpittu*; *nalpatu*, *nalpattu*; *šalputtu*, *šulputu*

lapiṭu → *labaṭu*

laplaptu(m) "thirst"? OB lex., jB, NA

lapnu(m); f. *lapuntu*, *laputtu* "poor; pauper" [ÚKU; NÍG.NU.TUKU] as adj. (opp. = *šarû* I) and subst.; NB as fPN; < *lapānu*; > *lappanu*

lappanu "very poor" jB; < *lapnu*

lappānu → *alappānu*

laptānu "tainted" jB with blood etc.; < *laptu* I

laptānû "turnip-coloured" jB lex. of stone; < *laptu* II

laptu(m) I; f. *lapittu* "touched, affected" Bab., NA [TAG] of limb "injured"; animal, wood "affected" by disease, insects; of omen "unfavourable"; of lyre "struck, played"; < *lapātu*

laptu(m) II, *liptu* "turnip" Bab., NA [LU.ÚB.SAR] also lex., med. *lapat armanni* (a plant); > *laptānû*; → *labtu*

lâpu → *liāpum*

laputtû(m), *luputtû* ~ "lieutenant; overseer" OAkk, Bab., OA [NU.BÀNDA/BÀN.DA] a military officer; also as epith. of deities, rulers; < Sum.

laqāḫu "to take" Am.; < W.Sem.; = *leqû* II

laqalaqa → *laqlaqqu*

laqānum → *lakānum*

laqātu(m) "to gather up, glean" **G** (*a/u*, NA pres. *ilaqqut*) of humans, animals "pick up, collect" clods, seeds, flour, animals; human tears; of bees "gather" honey; "take away by force, subdue" enemies, descendants etc. **D** ~ G "gather together hastily" commodities, troops etc.; "plunder, strip" house **Dtn** iter. (or pl. obj.?) **Š** caus. of G "cause to collect, gather up" **N** pass. of G "be taken away by force, destroyed"; > *laqtu*; *liqtu*; *lāqitu*, *lāqittu*; *laqqātum*; *luquttûm*; *malqatu*

laqā'u "to suffer" NA; < Aram.

laqā'u → also *leqû* II

laqbum → *lakbum*

Lā-qēpu → *qīpu* 1

lāqiānu "buyer" MA; < *leqû* II

lāqittu(m) "female collector" OB of grain; of clods; < *laqātu*

lāqitu(m) in *l. ki/urbānī(m)* "clod-collector" O/jB [LÚ.LAG.RI.RI.GA]; < *laqātu*

laqlaqqatu → *laqlaqtu*

laqlaqqu, *laqalaqa*, *raqraqqu* "stork" jB [RAG.RAG.MUŠEN; A.RAG.MUŠEN]; also desig. of vulva

laqlaqtu, *laqlaqqatu* (a skin complaint) jB med., on head

laqpum → *lakbum*

laqqātum "gatherer" OAkk as PN; < *laqātu*

laqqiqu (a stone) jB lex.

laqqum mng. unkn. OB lex., desig. of person

laqqu → also *lakku*

laqtu "gathered, gleaned" jB of seed; transf. "destroyed"; < *laqātu*

lāqtum ? mng. unkn. OB

laqû → *leqû* II

lāqu → *līqu* I

laradu → *lardu*

larandu (a big cat) jB

lardu, *laradu* (a grass, *Nardus*) j/NB, NA [Ú.KI.KAL.ḪI.RI/RÍ(.IN)] in field, as drug, as soap; → *ḫerīnum*

larindu → *lurmûm*

laripu (a linen garment) NB

larsīnum, *larsinnu* f. "hoof" O/jB of animal; of pig, as drug; OB lex. *ša larsīnātim* "club-footed"?

larû(m) "branch, twig" O/jB, MA [PA] of plant; as ornamental design; ext., in sheep "branch" of rib, of vein

lārum → *lēru*

laruššu mng. unkn. jB in *laruš tâmti* "sea *l.*"

lasāmu(m) "to run" Bab., M/NA **G** (*u/u*) [KAŠ$_4$] of god, human; of animal, bird; "gallop"; "serve as a runner" NA, of army service **Gtn** [KAŠ$_4$.KAŠ$_4$] iter., of demons, animals **Š** caus. OB lex.; > *lasmu*; *lismu*; *lassamu*, *lussumu*; *lāsimu*

lāsimu(m) **1.** "swift" of horses, knees (*birkā*) jB **2.** "runner, courier" Bab., NA [OB LÚ.KAŠ$_4$.E; later (LÚ.)KAŠ$_4$] as official; also as PN; ^{d}*L.* (a deity); < *lasāmu*

lasmu(m) "speedy" M/NA, jB [KAŠ$_4$] of animal; of feet; < *lasāmu*

lasqum, *lašqu* (a kind of pastureland)? Mari, MB, MB(Ass.)

lassamu "speedy, nimble" NA of feet; < *lasāmu*

lašḫu, *laḫšu* "gum(s)" jB; *l. šaplû* "lower g."

lāši → *laššu* I

lašlašu "valueless" NA of words; < *laššu* II

lašqu → *lasqum*

laššu I, NA also *lāšu/i* "(there) is not, are not" Ass., occas. Bab.; OA *kīma emārū laššûni* "as there are no donkeys", 2 f. stat. *laššuāti*; NA *niqittaka lū laššu* "may you have no anxiety", *šumma ibašši šumma laššu* "whether there is or not", absol. *laššu* "no!"; < *lā* + *išû*

laššu(m) II "absent; alien"? OA, O/jB; > *laššūtu*; *lašlašu*

laššūtu (response that there is not) MA; < *laššu* II

lašû (part of body) jB lex.

lāšu → *laššu* I; *la'šu* I

lâšu I "to knead" Bab. **G** (*ū*) [SILA$_{11}$(=ŠID)] dough, clay etc.; > *līšu*

lâšu II "to lick"? jB lex.; > *melēštu*

la'šu I, *lāšu* (a copper ore) jB lex.

la'šu II "polluted" jB; < *la'āšu*

latāku(m) "to try out, test" **G** (*a/u*) food, drink; animal, person; opinion, mathematical exercise; "question" s.o.; "be circumspect"; jB mag. *šaman l.* (a type of oil) **D** ~ G "test" s.th.; > *latku*; *litku*, *litiktu*; *maltakum*, *maltaktu*

latānu → *lamutānu*

latā'u → *letû* II

latku(m) "tested, checked" jB, NA of textile, metal, drug; < *latāku*

lattu (a container of standard capacity) NA for fish

latû → *letû*

lâtu → *lītu* II

lâṭu(m) "to confine, keep in check" Bab., NA **G** (*ū*) with bridle, stock; of animal "wrap itself round"; of god "encircle" world; of ring "enclose" enemy; "bind up" weapons **D** ~ G "encircle, enclose" world, enemy; > *līṭu* I, *līṭūtu*; *malūṭu*

la'u → *karānu* 4

la'û(m) "small child; baby(ish)" OA, O/jB [LÚ.TUR] as adj. and subst.; OB as PN, and fPN *La'ītum*; of reed; > *la'îš*; → *lakû* I

la''upum I "wrapped in cloth" OA of textiles; < *la''upum* II

la''upum II **D** "to wrap in cloth" OA; > *la''upum* I

lautānu → *lamutānu*

lawā'um → *lawûm* II

lāwirānu → *lā'iriānu*

lawītum "encirclement, siege" OB in *āl lawītika* "city you are besieging"; < *lawûm* II

lawûm I, *lamû* "besieged" OB of land; Nuzi "fenced" of threshing floor; < *lawûm* II

lawûm II, *lamû*, OAkk, OA *lawā'um*, M/NA *labā'u*, *labû* "to surround; besiege" **G** (*i/i*; NA perf. *assibi*) [NIGIN; NÍGIN] **1.** "surround, encircle" s.th. with (= acc., also *ina*) s.th., with wall, ornament, mag. with lime, flour, astr. with halo (*tarbāṣa*) **2.** "encircle, besiege" city, enemy etc. **3.** "wrap up" in cloth, string etc. **4.** "go round" in survey; in cult; of animals **5.** Nuzi of witness "walk round (the land of)" s.o. **6.** NB "keep company" with (= *itti*) **7.** of part of liver, weather, incense "turn round, veer round" **Gtn** iter. of demon "continually encircle" s.o.; of part of liver "repeatedly be wound round" **Gt** jB "be wound round (each other)", stat. (*tilmi*) "is surrounded" **D** "surround"; OA "wrap" **Š** [Nuzi NIGIN (.MEŠ)] "encircle" building with brickwork, wall, ornament; "cause to besiege"; "make" s.o. "walk round", Nuzi "survey" (field); NB "bring by circuitous route" **N** **1.** "be besieged" **2.** OA "embrace one another"; > *lawûm* I, *labītu*, *lawītum*; *lāmû*; *liwītum*, *līmu* II, *limûtu*; *mušelwû*; *nalbētu*; *nalbân*; *talmītu*

lazānu → *lezēnu*

lazāzu "to endure, persist" jB **G** (pres. *ilazzaz*) [ZAL(.ZAL)] of rains; illness **Gtn** ~ G; > *lazzu*, *lazziš*; *luzzuzum*; *lezû* II

lazziš "persistently" jB [ZAL-*iš*]; < *lazzu*

lazzu "enduring, persistent" M/NB, NA [ZAL.ZAL] of rain, injury, illness; < *lazāzu*; > *lazziš*

lê → *karānu* 4

le'āmu → *lêmu*

le'ā'um → *le'û*

lebēnu → *labānu*

lebērūtu → *labīrūtu*

lēbinu → *lābinu*

lebû → *labû*

lēbu → *lību*; *li'bu*

le'ēbu → *la'ābu*

leḫēbu → *laḫābu*

leḫēmu "to consume" Am., j/NB **G** (*i/i*) food or drink

leḫēmu → also *laḫāmu* I

lē'îš jB in *lā lē'îš* "like an incompetent"; < *lē'û*

lekû, *lequ* "to go" **G** jB lex.

lêku(m), *lâku* "to lick (up)" O/jB **G** (pres. *ilêlâk*) of person, animal **D** of cow "lick" hide; > *malāku* I?

lemēmu → *lamāmu* II

lemēnu(m), Ass. *lamānu(m)* "to be(come) bad" **G** (*i/i*; stat. *lemun*; NA pret. also *ilmun*) [ḪUL] "become" (stat. "is") "unsatisfactory", "unfavourable", "unlucky"; of heart, person "be malevolent", "become angry" towards (= dat.) **Gtn** of heart "repeatedly become angry" **Gt** stat. "is very angry, malevolent" **D** **1.** "make" s.th. "unfavourable" e.g. word, fate **2.** "do evil, treat" s.o. "badly" **3.** "trouble, burden" s.o.'s heart, o.s. **Dtn** OB "repeatedly trouble" s.o.'s heart **Dt** "become angry with one another" **Št** "become hostile to one another" **ŠD** jB "make difficult"; > *lemnu*, *lemniš*, *lemuttu*, *lemuttānu*; *lemmenu*; *lumnu*, *lumnānû*, *lumnatta*; *lummunu*, *lummuttum*; *nelmenu*

lemmenu "very bad" jB; < *lemēnu*

lemmu → *lēmu*

lemniš, OA, OB *lamniš* "badly" Bab., OA; esp. *l. epēlāšu(m)* "to treat badly"; < *lemnu*

lemnu(m), OAkk, O/MA also *lamnu(m)*; f. *lelamuttu(m)* "bad" [ḪUL] person, demon, animal; illness, curse etc.; day, wind, word, action; of taste or smell; as subst. (pl. also *lemnū*) "evil person, enemy"; *mimma lemnu* "all that is evil", also as demon [NÍG.ḪUL]; < *lemēnu*; > *lemuttu*, *lemniš*

lemû(m) I "to consume" O/jB, Mari **G** (*e/e*) food and drink

lemû(m) II "to be unwilling" OB, Bogh. **G** stat. only *lemi/u* "is unwilling"; > *lēmu*; → *muā'um*

lēmu, *lemmu* "disobedient (one)" M/jB; < *lemû* II

lēmû → *lāmû*; *lē'û*

lêmu(m), OAkk *la'āmum*, NA *le'āmu*? "to consume, eat and drink" **G** (*ē*; OAkk pres. *tala''am*) of human, of lamb; jB *akla u šikara lā ilêm* "should not consume bread or beer"

lemuntu → *lemuttu*

lemuttānu "scoundrel" NB; < *lemuttu*

lemuttu(m), *lemuntu(m)*, Ass. usu. *lamuttu(m)* "evil, wickedness" [ḪUL- ; MUNUS.ḪUL] often pl. *lelamnēlātu* (OB also *lennēti*), of bad intentions, words, actions; OA *l. alākum* "to intend, plot harm"; "misfortune" of weather, flood etc.; Bab. *bēl l.* "adversary"; OB lex. *ša l.* "evildoer"; *iṣṣūr l.* (a bird, owl); < *lemnu*; > *lemuttānu*

lennētu → *lemuttu*

lēpu → *lību*; *lipium*; *līpu*

leqû I "adopted" jB lex.; < *leqû* II

leqû(m) II, *laqû(m)*, OAkk, Ass. *laqā'u(m)* "to take, take over" **G** (*e/e*) [TI; ŠU.TI; ŠU.BA.AN.TI(.MEŠ)] **1.** "take hold of" weapon, earth etc., "take delivery of" animal **2.** "be in receipt of, take over" goods, money, ground, slave, bribe, document **3.** "receive" share, ration, bequest **4.** "take away with o.s., take off" gift, person; vent. "bring, fetch" **5.** "take away, carry off" booty, captives etc. **6.** idioms: "adopt" child, brother; "take" as wife, for slave; *qāt/qātāti PN l.* "stand surety for PN"; of planet *kakkaba leqât* "contains, absorbs star"; *parṣa/ī l.* "perform ritual(s)"; of part(s) of body *šāra leqe/â* "suffers from draught; from wind" **7.** "accept" abstr. obj., prayer, wish; judgement; name; office, function; math. "take" number etc.; → *šēṭūtu* **8.** OB "get to know" s.th. **9.** Am. also G pass. forms **10.** Ug. in *ša laqē išāti* "fire tongs" **Gtn** iter. of G **D** Ass. ~ G pl. obj. **Š** caus.; esp. of G 7 "cause to take office, appoint" s.o. **N** pass. of G 1-5 **Ntn** iter. OA; > *leqû* I; *lēqû*; *lāqiānu*; *liqûtu*; *lūqu*; *luqūtum*; *melqētu*; → *laqāḫu*

leqû → also *lekû*

lēqû "foster father" O/jB; < *leqû* II

lēru, *līru* , OA *lār(um)* (a gold paste) j/NB, OA, NA measured by weight

lēšu → *līšu*

letû I "split, divided" jB lex. of wood, reed; < *letû* II

letû(m) II, *latû*, MA(Ug.) *latā'u* ? "to split" Bab., MA? **G** (*e/e*) part of body; stat. of parts of liver "are split"; "divide" into portions **D** "shatter" skull, legs, mountain, stone **N** OB "be divided" *ana šina* "in two"; > *letû* I; *lutû*

lētu(m), *lītu* f. "cheek; side" Bab., MA [TE] **1.** "cheek" *l. maḫāṣu(m)* "to slap"; *šārat l.* 'cheek-hair', i.e. "beard"; *l. nadû(m)* 'to drop o.'s cheek' i.e. "give o.'s attention" to, also "be careless" **2.** transf. "side" of parts of entrails; of building, wall, gate **3.** M/jB as prep. *ina l.* "beside", *ana l.* "to" s.o.'s "presence", *adi l.* "up to" s.o., *ištu l.* "from" s.o.; > *ellēt*?; → *lītu* I 1

lētu → also *lītu* I

leṭû → *luṭû* 2

lēṭu → *līṭu* II

le'û(m), OAkk, OA *le'ā'um*, MA *la'ā'u* "to be able, powerful" **G** (*i/i*, *e/e*) (→ GAG §106t) [ZU; in PNs also DA, Á.GÁL] **1.** after (occas. before) infin. "be able" to do s.th., *ebēram ul il'û* "they were unable to cross"; before subst.

"be competent to do, master"; absol. "be able", also with second vb.; NA, NB(Ass.) of king, god *kī ša ila''ûni* "as he chooses" **2.** "be (more) powerful" than s.o. (= acc.), *ina dīnim ile''išunūti* "he defeated them in the lawsuit"; "gain power over" s.o. (= acc.) **R** Mari **Gtn** iter. of G 1 OB **Gt** OA "be competent, capable" with respect to s.th. **Š** OB of gods "give power to, empower"; > *lē'û, lē'îš, lē'ûtu; lītu* I, *lītānû; tele'û, telītu* I, *telūtu*?

lē'u(m), *lēyu, lû* "board" [GIŠ.ZU; GIŠ.DA; GIŠ.LE.U5(.UM)] **1.** "(writing-)board" of wood infilled with wax; DN *nāš l.* "holding a writing-board", *l. ša balāṭi* "b. of life" **2.** "(wooden) board" of door, chariot, plough; "sheet, plaque" of metal

lē'û(m), OAkk *lā'ium*, OB also *lēyûm*, NB also *lēmû*; MA f. *lā'ittu* "powerful, competent" [Á.GÁL; in PNs also DA, ZU] of deity, king; of worker, doctor "competent"; + gen. "skilled in" s.th., soldiers *lē'ût qabli* "skilled in battle"; in PNs, of deity, father, brother; *lā l.* "weak, powerless"; < *le'û*; > *lē'îš, lē'ûtu*

lē'ûtu(m), OB also *lēyûtum* "competence, skill, power" Bab., NA [Á.GÁL- ; ZU-] "power" of god, king; "victory" in lawsuit; "skill" of craftsman, scribe; *lā l.* "incompetence"; < *lē'û*

lēyu → *lē'u*

lēyûm → *lē'û*

lēyûtum → *lē'ûtu*

lezēnu, Ass. *lazānu* "to ridicule, jeer (at)" Bab., NA **G** (*i/i*) person; "speak" word "slanderously" **D** ~ G; < *aluzinnu* denom.?

lezû I "persistent" MB of injury; < *lezû* II

lezû II "to continue, be persistent" jB **G** (*u/u*); > *lezû* I; → *lazāzu*

liāpum, *lâpu* mng. unkn. **G**; **D**

liāru → *tiālu*

liātu → *lītu* II

li'atu "saliva"? Bogh. lex.

libânu → *labiānum*

libāru(m), *lipāru, lupāru, lipir* (a fruit (tree)) OA, O/jB, Elam, Bogh. [GIŠ.MI.PÀR/PAR4]

libāru-šūši 'let them catch sixty' (a plant) jB lex.; → *bâru* I

libbānu "inside" Mari, M/jB [ŠÀ-*nu*] adv. "within", of region, halo, lung, also *ana l.*; + pron. suff. *libbānuššu* "within it"; < *libbu* + *-ānu*

libbātu(m) pl. tant. "rage, fury", esp. *l. malû* "to be filled with anger, angry" against s.o. (= gen.), *libbātini lā imalla* "let him not be angry with us"; < *labābu*

libbâtu → *narbâtu* 2

libbilibbi → *libbu* B 3; *līpu* 2

libbu(m) "inner body; heart" [ŠÀ] **A. 1.** "inner body, internal organs" of human, animal "womb", *ša l.-ša* "foetus"; *ṣīt libbi* "offspring" of father **2.** "heart" of human; of animal, in extispicy, as meat portion; (parts → *dūru* I 3, *papānu* 2, *rēšu*) **3.** *l. īni* "iris"? **4.** as seat of emotions, thought, memory "mind, mood, spirit"; joyful, angry, sorrowful; of loyalty → *gamāru* II Gt, D; peaceful, fearful; *ina l. bašû* "to be in" s.o.'s "thoughts", *ina l. šakānu* "to take to heart" **5.** as seat of will, *šumma l.* "if it is wish of" s.o., *kī l.* "according to wish" of s.o., *ašar l.* "where" s.o. "wishes"; *mutu libbiša* "a husband of her choosing"; *lā l. ili(mma)* "against god's will; alas", OB *ul libbī* "I don't want to"; NB *ina ḫūd libbišu* "of his own free will" **6.** OA pl. "attitude" towards s.o. **7.** "courage", *l. nadānum, l. šakānu* "to encourage", *l. nasāḫu(m)* "discourage" **B.** transf. **1.** "content" of letter, statement **2.** "interior" of city, palace, sea etc., "pith" of reed **3.** "heart" (= various parts) of date palm, NB also *lib(bi) libbi* **4.** (an ornament) of metal, stone **5.** NA *akal l.* (a pastry)? **6.** OB "weft" **C.** in prep. expressions **1.** *ina l.* (after *ša* without *ina*) [ŠÀ.BA for *ina libbi(ša/šu)*]; *ša libbi(ša/šu)* "in(side), within" of space, time; "from among"; "from out of"; OA "incumbent on"; NA, NB "by means of", "in exchange for"; NB oath "by" DN; NA "at the time of" s.o. **2.** loc.-adv. (usu. *libbū*) "from out of, belonging to" group, larger quantity; NB "in the same way as, just like" **3.** *ana l.* "into, towards"; "as addition to"; "against, in opposition to"; "on account of, because of"; NB "(in exchange) for" **4.** *ultu/ištu/issu l.* "from (out of)"; of time "since" **5.** *adi l.* "until"; "as far as" **D.** adv. etc. **1.** *ina l.* "in there, therein" **2.** "from out of it/them" **3.** NB *ina libbi kī* "because of the fact that" **4.** *ana l.(-ma)* "to the interior"; > *libbānu*

libbū → *libbu* C 2

libbuḫu → *ellabbuḫḫu*

libburšu (part of a house) Nuzi

libittu(m), Am. also *labittu*; j/NB st. constr. also *libnat* "mudbrick" [SIG4]; coll. "mudbrick(s)"; also of metal, dung, "block" of pressed figs; "brickwork" (often *libnatu*), "mudbrick building"; < *labānu*

libītu → *liwītum*

liblibbi → *libbu* B 3; *līpu* 2

libnat(u) → *libittu*

libnu, *lipnu* in *libin appi* "stroking of the nose" M/jB, gesture of submission; < *labānu*

libnu → also *labnu* II

libšu(m) "raiment" OB(poet.); < *labāšu*

lību, *lī/ēb/pu* adj. mng. unkn. Bogh., jB of hide

li'bu(m), *lī/ēbu*, *la'bu(m)*, *lābu* (a serious disease with associated fever) O/jB [DIḪ]; also *l. (ṣibit) šadî*; as demon; ext. (a spot affected by *l.* disease); < *la'ābu*

līdānu "chick, young bird" M/NB of ducks etc.; MA, jB "child (of a slave girl)"; < *līdu*

lidātu → *littu* I

liddanānu (a plant) jB lex.

liddatu → *littu* I

liddu → *līdu*

līdiš "day after tomorrow" NA in *ina l.*, *illīdiš*; → *allītiš*; *ullītiš*

līdu(m), *liddu* "child, offspring" O/jB of humans; < *walādum*; > *līdānu*

ligimû(m), *nigimmû*, *nagimu* "kernel, sprout" O/jB of palm tree, barley; transf. of humans, animals; jB *illigimīya* "in my youth"; < Sum.

liginnu(m) f. "(type of) tablet" Bab., NA [(IM.)GÍD.DA] Mari in administrative context; j/NB, NA "school exercise tablet", *l. qabû* "to recite text"; < Sum.

ligittu "crooked furrow" jB lex.; < Sum.

lignu (or *liknu*) (a wooden container)? NA

liḫburu (a garden herb) NB

liḫmu "muddy water" Bogh. lex.; → *luḫāmum*

liḫšu "whisper(ing)" jB, NA as prayer, malicious rumour; < *laḫāšu*

Likkaše (a month) OB(Alal.)

liknu → *lignu*

liktirik (a garment) OB(Susa)

līlâ "in the evening" M/jB; < *līlum*

līlâtu → *līliātum*

lildu → *lišdum*

līlēn in *in līlēn* "in the evening" Mari; < *līlum*

līliātum, *līlâtu(m)* pl. tant. "evening" OAkk, Bab. [KIN.SIG]; also "evening (meal)"; *līliattam*, *līlâtan* "in the evening"; *waraḫ Līlâtim/Lilliātim* (1st month) Mari; < *līlum*

lilibu (part of horse-trappings) jB lex., of leather

liligû 1. also *lalikkû* "colocynth" jB [ÚKUŠ.LI.LI.GI] 2. (a bird) jB [LI.LI.GI.MUŠEN]; < Sum.

lilissu(m); pl. m. & f. "kettledrum" Bab., NA [LILIZ; also LI.LI.ÌZ] of bronze, esp. rit.; < Sum.

lilium, *lilû*; f. **lilītu(m)**, and **ardat lilî** (storm demons) O/jB [*lilû* = LÍL.LA.EN.NA/NU; LÚ.LÍL.LÁ; *lilītu* = MUNUS.LÍL.LÁ; KI.SIKIL.LÍL.LÁ; *ardat lilî* = KI.SIKIL.LÍL.LÁ; KI.SIKIL.UD.DA.KAR.RA]; singly, pl. (*lilû*), in pair (*lilû lilītu*), and as triad; OB *ina ṣīt lilîm* "at the rising of the *l.*"; < Sum.; → *kiskilili*; *wardatum*

lillânītu (a plant) jB lex.; < *lilliannum*

lillânu → *lilliannum*

lillatu → *lillu* I

lilliannum, *lillânu*; pl. f. "stalk with ripe ears" O/jB [ŠE.LILLAN]; > *lillânītu*

Lilliātum → *līliātum*

lillidu(m); f. *lillittu(m)* "offspring" 1. of humans, coll. "children, offspring"; of animals 2. as age category, of sheep "(recently sexually) mature" [SILA4.GUB; f. KIR11.GUB], of pigs; < *walādum*

lillu(m) I; f. *lillatu* "idiot" OAkk, OA, O/jB [(LÚ/MUNUS.)LIL] also as PN; Nuzi, of horse; > *lillūtu*

Lillu(m) II Bab. 1. (a demon) 2. (a god)

lillūtu "idiocy" M/jB in *l. šūluku* "to reduce to idiocy, incapacitate"; < *lillu* I

lilum (desig. of a sheep)? Mari

lilû → *lilium*

līlum "evening, night" OB; > *līlâ*, *līlēn*, *līliātum*

līm; nom. *līmu*, NA also *li'mu*; also Pre-Sarg.; pl. *līmī* "thousand" [LIM] OA *10 līmē*; OB, Alal. occas. abbr. to *li*; NA *adu (1) li'mišu* "1,000 times", also jB *ana līmā*; NA *rab 1 līm* "captain of 1,000"

limā → *lumā*

limittum; pl. *limdātum* ~ "thing(s) notified, promised item(s)" OB in pl. of gifts; < *lamādu*

limītu → *liwītum*

līmu(m) I, *limmu* "eponym (of year)" Ass.; also "eponymate", *ina šanê limmišu* "in his second eponymate"; OA *bīt l.* "office of the eponym official"

līmu II "environs"? NB of town; < *lawûm* II

līmu III, *li'mu* "family, tribe" jB lex.

līmu → also *līm*

li'mu → *līm*; *līmu* III

limûtu ~ "encirclement"? jB lex.; < *lawûm* II

lipânu → *labiānum*

lipāru → *libāru*

līpi līpi → *līpu* 2

lipiltu → *lipištu*

lipir → *libāru*

lipiškigû (an internal disease) Ug.; < Sum.

lipiššatu "female genitalia" jB

lipištu(m), *lipiltu* O/jB, NA [(UZU.)NU] 1. om. "male genitalia" 2. "sperm" of human; jB lex. transf. "offspring" 3. (a sperm-like secretion) in body of human, sheep 4. (a part of the exta) 5. (a plant)

lipittu(m) **1.** ~ "work-levy" OA **2.** (a disease)? M/jB; < *lapātu* G 4.6

lipium, *lipû(m)*, *līpum*, *lēpu* "(animal) fat; tallow" Bab., NA [(UZU.)Ì.UDU] in sacrificial animal; as ingredient, commodity; material of figurine; *l. magarri* "axle-grease"; *l. amēlūti* "human fat"; of plants; → *lupû*

līp līpi → *līpu* 2

lipnu → *libnu*

lippu "wrapping" M/NA, jB, of cloth; med. "tampon; wad" of wool; < *lapāpu*

liptānu "warty" MB, name of horse; < *liptu*

liptu(m); pl. f. [(NÍG.)TAG] **1.** "undertaking, job", "offering", in PNs "creation" of DN **2.** in *l. qāti/ī* "handiwork", (ritual) "undertaking" **3.** "attack" of illness; *l. ilim*, *l. Erra* "plague" **4.** *lipit napištim* "throat-grasping", i.e. treaty (→ *lapātu* G 3) **5.** "mole, wart" on human, animal, entrails; < *lapātu*; > *liptānu*

liptu → also *laptu* II

lipû → *lipium*

līpu(m), *lēpu* "descendant, scion" [NUNUZ] **1.** MB *l. rebû* "great-great-grandson"; jB *lā līp šarri* "not of royal descent"; pl. "descendants" **2.** *līp(i) līpi*, *lib(bi)libbi* [ŠÀ.BAL.BAL] "great-grandson", "descendant" of king, scribal family; of Šamaš, as son of Sîn; < *elēpu*

līpu → also *lību*; *lipium*

liqtu(m) "gathered material; selection" Bab., M/NA desig. of quality of gold, textiles, OB oil; "gleanings" of grain, usu. pl. f.; *liqit ṣupri* "nail parings"; "(textual) excerpts", pl. m. & f.; MA *rab liqtāni* (an official); OB as PN "Foundling"; Nuzi for → *liqûtu*; < *laqātu*

līqu(m) I, *lāqu* in *l. pî*, also *alīq pî*, *elāq pî* "palate" O/jB

līqu II "steering paddle"? NB; < Aram.

liqûtu(m) "adopted child" O/jB; < *leqû* II

liriša (a prof.) OB(Elam)

līru → *lēru*

lisakkû → *lišakkû*

lismu(m) "running, race" O/jB, NA esp. in cult; *ša l.* "runner"; < *lasāmu*; → *lisnu*

lisnu mng. uncert. NA = *lismu* ?

lissūsu (a plant) MA; seed of *l.*

lišakkû (or *lisakkû*) mng. unkn. jB in *māmīt l.* "oath by *l.*"

lišānu(m) f. "tongue, language" [(UZU.)EME] **1.** "tongue" of human, animal (pl. m.); as instrument of prayer, malice; *l. šakānu* "to engage in discussion" **2.** "language"; jB, NA *bēl l.* "one who knows a (foreign) language" **3.** "speech, statement"; *ša l.* "informer, informant"; Nuzi "judicial deposition"; jB "synonym list" **4.** transf. "tongue (of flame)"; "blade" of implement **5.** M/jB, NA *l. kalbi* "hound's-tongue, *Cynoglossum*" [Ú.EME.UR.GI$_7$], NB ^{mul}*l. k.* (a star)

lišdum, *lildu* "cream" O/jB

lištāḫu → *šiltāḫu*

līšu, NA *lēšu* "dough" M/NB, NA [NÍG.SILA$_{11}$(=ŠID).GÁ] of emmer; *ina l. kuppuru* "to cleanse with dough"; figurines of d.; Am., Bogh. "(fruit) paste"; < *lâšu* I

li'šu "desecration" NA; < *la'āšu*

lītānû "victorious" MB in PN; < *lītu* I

litbušu "clothed; clothing"? jB lex.; < *labāšu* Gt

liti, *litum* (desig. of kind of silver) OA

litiktu(m) "test" OA, O/jB; esp. (a measuring vessel); < *latāku*

lītiš mng. unkn. NA

litku "test, means of testing" jB; < *latāku*

littu(m) I, *liddatu*; pl. *lidātu* "descendant, progeny" OAkk, M/jB, NA of god; king etc.; < *walādum*

littu(m) II; pl. *littētu(m)* "stool" Bab., M/NA [GIŠ.ŠÚ.A]

littu(m) III ~ "old age" Bab.; > *littūtu*

littu → also *lītu* I.II

littû (a net) jB lex.; < Sum.

littūtu "(extreme) old age" j/NB, NA *l. alāku*, *kašādu*, *šebû* "to live to, reach, be satisfied with extreme old age"; < *littu* III

litum → *liti*

lītu(m) I, *littu*, Bogh. also *lētu*; M/jB pl. *lītātu* "power, victory" [NÍG.È] **1.** "sphere of authority", OA commercial, OB administrative "province"; Mari "(army) corps" (or *lētu* ?) **2.** "power, strength" from deity, esp. in PNs **3.** "victory", *l. šakānu* "to establish victory" over (= *eli*); *lītāt šarrūtīya* "my royal victories"; *ina l.* "victoriously, in triumph"; < *le'û*; > *lītānû*

lītu(m) II, *littu*; pl. *liātu*, *lâtu* "cow" [ÁB; GU$_4$.ÁB; NB also ÁB.GAL; pl. (GU$_4$.)ÁB.ḪI.A, ÁB.GU$_4$.ḪI.A etc.]; pl. also "cattle" (coll.); < *lī'um* I

lītu → also *lētu*

liṭṭu mng. uncl. jB

liṭṭu → also *līṭu* I-III

līṭu(m) I, *liṭṭu* "hostage" O/jB, NA; liter. 'confined', Bogh. pl. *līṭūtu*; as subst., pl. *līṭū*; < *lâṭu*; > *līṭūtu*

līṭu II, *liṭṭu*, *lēṭu*; pl. *liṭṭētu* (a garment or cloth) M/NA, M/NB as bed covering; white

līṭu III, *liṭṭu* "sketch, drawing" NA

līṭūtu "rôle as hostage" M/jB(Ass.) *ana l. ṣabātu* "to take as hostage"; < *līṭu* I

lī'um I, *lû(m)* "bull" O/jB offered, slain, eaten; also as wooden figure; heavenly "bull"; lex. also = lion; > *lītu* II

lī'um II (a word for food) OB

liwā → *lumā*

liwītum, M/NB *limītu*, M/NA *libītu* **1.** OA "packaging, wrapping" **2.** "circumference, rim" of eye, armour, chariot **3.** "limits, extent, area" of field, building **4.** jB *ina l. ūmimma* "within the compass of one day" **5.** "enclosure" round field, garden; *igār l.* "enclosure wall" **6.** "environs" of town, palace, canal; M/jB kings, lands in "surrounding area" **7.** NA "entourage" of king; < *lawûm* II

lū, in prec. *lu-*, *li-*, Ass. also *la-* "let it be; or" [ḪÉ] **A.** ptcl. expressing wish **1.** + pret. = prec. (only OA before 1 pers. pl., → *i*) "let me, you, him" etc. do s.th.; with interrog. force "should I, he ...?" etc., concessive "even if ...", potential "should he ..., then ..." **2.** occas. + perf. **3.** + 2 pers. pres., *lū taḫassas* "you should think" **4.** + stat. and forms of *izuzzum*, *edû* II etc. **5.** in nominal clauses, *atta lū mutīma* "may you be my husband", NA *ḫannūte lū ina pānīka* "may these be before you" **6.** M/NA *lū lā* in proh., + pres., + stat. **7.** in unfulfilled condit. clauses, + pret. or stat., *lū īde* "had I known" **8.** in concessive clauses, + pret., perf., stat., *lū tattadnā* "even though you have given" **B.** ptcl. expressing affirmation **1.** *lū* + pret. "verily", usu. in roy. inscr. **2.** in oaths, asseverations (→ GAG §185), + subjunct. (OAkk, OA); + indic.; + subst. **C.** "or", freq. *ū lū*; *(ū) lū ... (ū) lū* "either ... or" [ḪÉ ... ḪÉ]; between substs. and clauses **D.** Am. "if"; > *lūman*; *lūmē*

lû → *karānu* 4; *lē'u*; *lī'um* I

luādu → *lâdu*

luāmum "to harangue" s.o. OA **G** (*ū*) **Dtn** "repeatedly harangue"?

lu'aštu(m) "dirty straw" Bab. lex.; < *la'āšu*

lu''ātu → *lu''û* I

lubādu (or *lubāṭu*) (a disease) jB

lubalakkum ~ "man on duty" OB lex.; < Sum.

lubānu → *lupānu*

lubartum "garment" OB; < *lubāru*

lubāru(m), O/MA *lubēru(m)* "garment" [TÚG.ḪI.A] freq. of linen; for god, for *kalû* priest; med., mag. "piece of cloth, rag"; *bīt l.* "clothes chest" jB lex.; > *lubartum*; → *labāru*

lubāšu(m) "clothing" OA, O/jB; < *labāšu*

lubāṭu → *lubādu*

lubbatum mng. unkn. OB

lubbâtu → *narbâtu* 2

lubbundu "brickwork" NB of lintel; < *labānu*

lubbunû "incense"? NB

lubbušu; NA *labbušu*, pl. *labbašūte* "clothed" j/NB, NA of unshorn sheep; "uniformed" of soldiers; < *labāšu* D

lubēru → *lubāru*

lubkānu (oil used for lubrication)? jB lex.; < *lubku*

lubku(m) "salve, lubricant" O/jB; *napšalti l.* "softening ointment"; NB pl. f. *lubkēti*; < *labāku*

lubru I (a kind of date palm) jB

lubru II (prof. desig.) Nuzi

lubšu "clothing" jB; also "covering" of young reed; < *labāšu*

lubultu → *lubuštu*

luburu mng. unkn. jB lex. in *bīt l.* (a woolsack)?

lubuštu(m), later *lubultu*, NA *la/ubussu* "clothing, garment" [SÍK.BA; later TÚG.ḪI.A] **1.** gener. "dress, outfit", "clothing allocation, ration" **2.** specific "garment"; coll. "clothes", *l. birmi/e* "multicoloured clothing" **3.** j/NB "(ceremony of) clothing (the images)", pl. *lubūšā/ētu* **4.** transf. sheep's "coat", door's "covering", footstool's "cover"; < *labāšu*; → *lubūšu*

lubūšu(m) "garment", also "dress, outfit" (~ *lubuštu* 1); NB = *lubuštu* 3; < *labāšu*

luddu mng. unkn. jB; → *duqdu*

ludû(m) (desig. of a field) O/MB

ludû → also *luṭû*

luduttu → *lu'tu*

lugalara(us)sû (a royal retainer) jB lex.; < Sum.

lugšu → *lukšu*

lugû (a door) jB lex.

luḫāmu(m) "mud" OB incant.

luḫḫu (part of entrails)? jB

luḫḫum → also *lu'u*

luḫḫumu "with long-haired coat" jB lex., of ox; < *laḫāmu* I

luḫmû → *luḫummû*

luḫšû(m) (a temple functionary) Mari, jB [LÚ.SÍK.BAR.RA]; < Sum.

luḫummû(m), lex. also *luḫmû* "silt, mud" O/jB

luḫumû → *lummû*

luḫusīnum (an object) OA

lu''ītu → *lu''û* I

lukānu in *ina lukānumma* mng. unkn. NB

lukkuku D mng. unkn. jB lex.

lukkusu (or *lukkuṣu*) **D** mng. unkn. jB lex.

lukšu (or *lugšu*) ~ "conifer needles"? jB [GIŠ.EREN.SÍG ?]

lukšû (a garment) jB lex.?
lūku (a tree) Bogh. lex.; < Sum.
lukurgallu "chief lukur-priestess" jB lex.; < Sum.
lulânû "weakling" jB lex.; < *lulû* II or *lalānû* ?
lulidānītu → *luludānītu*
lulīmītu (a siege-instrument)? jB
lulimmu → *lulīmu*
lulimtu (a jewel)? jB of *elmēšu* stone, of gold
lulīmu(m), *lulimmu* "red deer, stag" Bab., NA [LU.LIM]; also a constellation [MUL.LU.LIM]; transf. of ruler, e.g. *l. eršu* = "wise prince"
lulītum, *lullītum* mng. unkn. OB
lūlītu "arrowhead" NB of iron, bronze; < Aram.
luliu → *lulû* II
lullakku (a beer vat) jB lex.; < Sum.
lullītum → *lulītum*
lullû(m) I "primeval man" O/jB [LÚ.U$_{18/19}$.LU] created by gods; desig. of Ut-napišti; < Sum.
lullû II **D** "to enrich, endow with plenty" M/NB, NA, land with luxuries, trees with fruit; < *lalû* I denom.; > *lullû* III
lullû III "luxurious, beautiful" M/jB; < *lullû* II
lullû IV "false"? jB
Lullubû → *Lallubû*
lullubūtu (a plant) jB lex.
lullumtum, *lulluntu* (a travel and battle garment) OAkk, Mari, jB
lulmû "earring" jB; < Sum.
lulû(m) I "plenty, luxury, splendour"? j/NB *l. malû*/*mullû*, *šumallû* "to be laden/load, fill with abundance, splendour" divine image, temple, ship; < *lalû* I
lulû(m) II, Ass. *luliu(m)* f. "slag"? Ass., O/jB [KÙ.GAN; KÙ.ÁM] of metals; NA of glass; < Sum.?; > *lulânû*?
lūlu f. mng. unkn. OB
luludānītu, *lulidānītu* (a stone) M/jB
luludānû (a prof. desig.) jB lex.
lulumtu, *luluntu*, *luluttu* (a plant) jB
lulūtu (an animal)? Am. in descr. of vessel
lulūtu → also *alulūtum*
lumā, *limā*, *liwā* ptcl. mng. unkn. Bogh., jB lex.
lumaḫḫu **1.** (a purification priest) jB [LÚ.MAḪ] **2.** also *lummāḫu* ~ "chief, ruler" jB lex.; < Sum.
lumakku → *lummakku*
lūman O/jB modal adv. **1.** in *l. lā* "were it not for", *l. lā kâti* ... "but for you ..." **2.** + vb. "if only ...!" **3.** Bogh. *l.* ... *l.* ... "were it that ... or that ..." in unreal clause; < *lū* + *-man*
lumāšu, *lumaššu* "constellation" j/NB [LÚ.MAŠ(-)]; also $^{mul/múl}$*l.*; forming zodiac

lūmē mng. uncl. Ug.; phps. "would that ..." or "if perhaps ..."; → *lū*
lummāḫu → *lumaḫḫu* 2
lu(m)makku (a minor priest) O/jB lex.
lummu(m) I (a small drinking-vessel) O/jB, NA [ÚTUL.TUR]; < Sum.
lummu II **D** "to dissolve"? jB alum, wax, honey
lummu → also *lammu* I
lummû, *luḫumû* (a spider or snail) jB [MUL.DA.MUL]
lummudu; Ass. *lammudu*, pl. *lammadūti* **1.** NA "taught" of words **2.** jB lex. in *lā l.* "uninitiated" of calf (sexually), "untried" of plough; < *lamādu*
lummunu(m), OA *lammunum* "very bad" OA, O/jB of man "very unfortunate, oppressed"; of road, fate; OA of copper; < *lemēnu*
lummuṣu **D** mng. unkn. jB comm. stat. of eyes
lummuttum "misfortune" OB; < *lemēnu*
lumnānû "evilly inclined" jB; < *lumnu* + *-ān* + *-ī*
lumnatta "evilly" jB [ḪUL-*at-ta*]; < *lumnu*
lumnu(m) "evil, misery" [ḪUL] of evil action, thought towards s.o.; *bēl l.* "adversary"; s.o.'s "evil plight"; *l. amāru* "to experience ill fortune"; *l. libbi(m)* [ŠÀ.ḪUL] "sorrow, misery", astr. "eclipsed state"; (a name of the planet Mars) [MUL.ḪUL]; < *lemēnu*; > *lumnatta*; *lumnānû*
lupānu, *lubānu(m)* (a terebinth) OAkk, jB
lupāru → *libāru*
lupnu(m) "poverty" O/jB; < *lapānu*
luppu(m); pl. m. & f. **1.** O/jB (a leather bag) [KUŠ.LU.ÚB] **2.** jB lex. (a part of the scales); < Sum.
luppunum "very poor" OB lex.; < *lapānu*
lupputu; also f. *lupputtu* in subst. use "tainted, soiled" jB [ŠU.LÁL], esp. of dirty bandages; < *lapātu*
lupû mng. unkn. j/NB; (a fish), or = *lipium* ?
luputtû → *laputtû*
lūqu ~ "(state of) hostage"? Am.; < *leqû* II
luqumā mng. unkn. NB
luquttûm "activity of gleaning"? OB; < *laqātu*
luqūtum; pl. *luquātum* "goods" OA, usu. in transit; < *leqû* II
lurimā'u etc. → *lurmûm*
lurmu(m) "ostrich" Bab., NA [GA/GÁ.NU$_{11}$.MUŠEN; GÁ.NA.MUŠEN] *pel l.* "ostrich egg"; *ša pel l.* "ostrich-egg vessel"
lurmûm, MA *lurimā'u*, *lurinnu*, *lurīnu*; f. *lurimtu(m)*, NB *lu/arindu* "pomegranate", as fruit; as tree, NB *gapnu ša l.* "branch of p."; as wood for tool; as decorative element, of

carnelian, silver; NB f. as fPN; var. of → *nurmû*

lurpiānum, *lurpânu*, *lurpâdu* (a mineral)? O/jB

lurrakkûm; f. *lurrakkītum* (a culinary profession) Mari, OB lex.

luršu (prof. desig.) OB(Susa)

lurû(m) "man with feminine voice"? O/jB

lusan, OB *lušanu* (a musical instrument, or part of it) O/jB

lussumu "very fleet" NB as PN; < *lasāmu*

lušanu → *lusan*

lušmu mng. unkn. MA in *bīt l.*

lušû "grease" jB lex.

luttu → *luṭṭu*

lutû "twig" j/NB of apple, poplar etc., in ceremonies; < *letû* II

lūtu(m), *lu'tu* "debility; (a disease)" O/jB

lu'tu, *luduttu* (a wooden implement) jB lex.

lu'tu → also *lūtu*

luṭṭu(m), *luttu(m)* (a cup or bowl) O/jB, NA; < Sum.

luṭû(m) **1.** Bab. [GÍR.ZU] (a dagger) **2.** jB lex., also *ludû, leṭû* (a sharp part of a reed)

lu'u(m), *luḫḫum* "throat, oesophagus" O/jB of human, bird; blocked

lu''û I; f. *lu''ūtu*, *lu''ītu* "sullied, dirty" j/NB of person, hands, in ritual context; of street; f. pl. *lu''âtu* in subst. use; < *lu''û* II

lu''û(m) II **D** "to sully, make dirty" Bab., esp. in cult **Dt** pass. of D; > *lu''û* I; *malû* II; *tal'ītu*

lu''umu adj. mng. unkn. jB

luzzuzum mng. unkn. OB lex., desig. of man; < *lazāzu*

M

-ma, also *-me*, *-mu* ptcl. and conj. (*-me* Am.; NA, NB rarely after *e* or *im*; NA before *-ni* (→ *ayyakamēni*, *matimeni*); *-mu* NB, occas. jB, esp. after *u*) **1.** to stress single words esp. pred. of nominal clause **2.** "and" between main clauses or infin.s, NA rare (→ GAG §§123a, 126, 158-60)

mā "what!" ptcl. introducing and continuing dir. speech; "indeed", esp. expressing indignation; M/NA "this means:"; → *magana*; *muk* I

-mā interrog. ptcl. O/jB (→ GAG §123b)

ma'ādu → *mâdu*

ma''altu → *mayyaltu*

ma''ālu → *mayyālu*

ma'āru → *wârum*

ma'assu → *mādu*

ma''assu → *mayyaltu*

ma'attu → *mādu*

ma'da → *mādu*

madādu(m) I "to measure (out)" **G** (*a*/*u*) [ÁGA] "measure out, pay" grain, other dry and liquid commodities; "survey" field, border **Gtn** iter. of G **Gt** stat. "is balanced, equal" **D** = G; "measure" building, person; NA *birti ēnē maddudu* (NB *ina birīt īnī muddudu*) 'measure between the eyes', i.e. "give s.o. strict orders" **Š** caus. of G "have measure out, pay" **N** of produce "be measured out"; fields "be measured, surveyed"; > *middatu*; *mādidu*, *mādidūtu*; *mindu* II; *namaddu* I, *namdattum*, *muddû*?

madādu II NB **G** (*i*/*i*) ~ "to escape" (from = acc.); "avoid" (s.th. = acc.); < Aram.

madagallûm (a type of boat) OB; < Sum.

madakku, *madāku* "(wooden) mortar" jB lex. *kak m.* "pestle"; (part of a loom); < *dakāku* I

madaktu "(military) camp; expeditionary force" j/NB, NA *m. šakānu*, *nadû* "to make, pitch camp"; NB *ana m. alāku* "to take the field", *(*LÚ*) ālik m.* "conscript"; PlN *Madaktu* (in Elam); < *dâku*

madāku → *madakku*

madallu(m) (or *matallu(m)*) **1.** O/jB (a precious stone) **2.** OAkk(Sum.) (a copper object)

madālu "to preserve in salt" NA **G** (*i*/*i*), meat; > *madlu*; *midlu*; *muddulu*

madananu → *madnanu*

Madānu(m), *Mandānu* DN "the Divine Judge" Bab. [^{d}DI.KUD] jB; also = Marduk, Enlil; < *diānum*

madārum I ~ "chief, noble" Mari; > *madārūtum*

madāru(m) II mng. unkn. O/jB om., med. **G** (*i*/*i* ?) stat. (a condition of eyes) **D** stat. (a condition of exta); > *midru* II?

madārūtum (status of a *madārum*) Mari; < *madārum* I

madattu → *maddattu*

madbareš "into the steppe" jB; < *madbaru*

madbaru(m), *mud(a)buru* "steppe, desert" Mari, M/NB, NA; NA in PN; < W.Sem.?

maddānum, *mandānu* (a bread basket) OB, jB lex.; < *nadānu* II

ma(d)dattu(m), *mandattu* "payment, obligation" Ass., M/NB; OA (an allotment, a quota); Ass., Bogh., Ug. "tribute"; MB "delivery quota" of textiles; NB (compensatory payment to make up for lost work-time); NB(Nippur) "supplementary payment, commission"; < *nadānu* II

maddatu → *middatu*

maddu → *mādu*

maddû in *m. kussî(m)* (part of the liver) OB; = *mandû* II

madgaltu "observation tower; border post" MA, Bogh.; *bēl m.* "commander of the border post"; < *dagālu*

madgalu "observation"? NA; < *dagālu*

mādidu, *mandidu* "measuring official (for grain etc.)" M/NB, NA [LÚ.(Ì.)ÁG]; NB as family name; < *madādu* I

***mādidūtu**, *mandidūtu* "office of the measuring official" NB [LÚ.MAN.DI.DI-]; < *madādu* I

mādiš, M/NB also *ma'diš* "greatly, very" Bab., OA; OB *m. ūmī* "for many days"; < *mādu*

mādiyā "pregnant"? NB; < Aram.

madlā'um, *madlû(m)* "bucket" OAkk, Bab.; < *dalû* II

madlu "salted" NA; < *madālu*

madlû → *madlā'um*

madnanu, MB also *madananu* **1.** jB lex. "strength" **2.** MB (type or part of chariot); < *danānu* II

madû → *medû*

mādu(m), later also *ma'du*, *mandu*, NA *maddu*; f. *mattu(m)*, *ma'attu*, NA also *ma'assu* "many, numerous, significant" [ḪI.A(.MEŠ); MEŠ]; f. pl. abstr. "much, many things"; m. pl. in lex. "plural" (sign, forms); acc. as adv. "very"; < *mâdu*; > *mādiš*, *ma'dû*, *mādūtu*

mādû → *ma'dû*; *mandû* I

mâdu(m), *ma'ādu*, OAkk, Bab. also *miādu(m)* "to be(come) many, numerous" **G** (*ī*; *i/i*) [ḪI.A] OAkk, OB in PNs; jB *eli ... m.* "become more than"; NA *ina muḫḫi ... m.* "become too many for" **Gtn** iter. of G **Š** "make numerous, increase"; "make more numerous"; "do too much" **N** "become very much, become increased"; > *mādu*, *mādiš*, *ma'dû*, *mādūtu*; *mu'uddû*; *nam'adum*, *namattu*; *šum'uttu*; *mušmīdu*

ma'du → *mādu*

ma'dû, *mādû* "(large) quantity, wealth, abundance" j/NB; NB *(a)kī mādê* "very much"; < *mādu* + *-ī*

ma'dû → also *mandû* I

madušsu (a plank)? jB lex.; < Sum.

mādūtu "numerousness" Am. in *kī(ma) mādūti* "very much"; < *mādu*

magāgu, *maqāqu* "to spread, stick out, protrude" M/NA, M/jB **G** (*a/u*) of beggar "hold out" the hand; "have cramps, spasms"; stat. "is tense"; of animals "cover, mate" **Gtn** iter. of G "have repeated cramps" **D** = G of limbs "stiffen, project", of penis "be erect"; NA "impale"? **N** lex. (*nam(a)gugu*) "suffer cramp"; > *mangu* II; *mungu*; *mangāgu*; *namungatu*; → *makāku*

magal "very (much), greatly" Bab., M/NA(lit.) [UL4.GAL]

magallatu "parchment scroll" NB; < Aram.

magallatu-karra "maker of parchment scrolls" NB; < Aram. + OPers.

magallum (a big boat) Mari; < Sum.

magana ~ "now; please" OB; < *mā* + *gana* ?; = *gana*

magannu I (or *makannu*), *magānu* "gift" Nuzi etc. also in PN; as Aram. lw. NA *ina m.*, *im-magāni* "gratuitously, in vain", NB *ana m.* "gratis"; < Indo-Iran.; > *magannūtu* I

magannu II (a location)? MB(Alal.); > *magan=nūtu* II

magannūtu I (or *makannūtu*) "gift" MB(Alal.), Nuzi; < *magannu* I

magannūtu II mng. unkn. MB(Alal.); < *magannu* II

magānu → *magannu* I

magarāniš → *maqrāniš*

magarrānu (a type of horse) MB

magarru(m), Nuzi also *mugarru* "wheel" Bab., NA [GIŠ.UMBIN]; also "waggon, chariot"; < *qarāru* ?; → *mugerru*

maga(r)rûm "travel provisions on a ship" OB [MÁ.GAR.RA]; < Sum.

magāru(m) "to consent, agree" **G** (OA, OB, occas. jB *a/u*, later *u/u*, NA pret. *immagur*) [ŠE(.GA); AŠ] **1.** stat. "is in agreement"; "allows, permits"; "is agreeable (to), convenient (for), suits (s.o.)"; hemerology, of day, time "is favourable" **2.** "agree with" (s.o. = acc.) **3.** after neg. "not consent" (to = acc. or *ana*), "disagree with"; NA and NB in hendiad. "refuse, be unwilling to" **4.** OB of woman "be submissive, compliant, yield to (s.o.)" **5.** of deity "hear, answer" a prayer, "grant" a request, also in PNs, PlNs and names of buildings **Gtn** iter. of G **Gt** recipr. "agree with one another, settle on"; stat. "are in (mutual) agreement" [ŠE.ŠE.GA] **D** OA "bring to agreement, make agree"; jB "reconcile" **Dt** ? prob. Gtn **Š** **1.** OB "cause to agree" **2.** "make (s.th.) agreeable" **Št** OB "bring into harmony, reconcile" people, feelings **N** **1.** OB "consent (to s.th.)" **2.** "agree" (with s.o. = *ište*, *itti PN*) **3.** "reach, make an agreement" **4.** "have (o.'s request) granted" **5.** Bogh. "receive, accept gladly" a present **Ntn** iter. of N OA, jB "be repeatedly acceptable"; > *magru*, *māgiru*; *migru*; *mitgāru*, *mitguru*, *mitgurtu*; *mundagru*; *tamgertum*, *tamgurtu*

magattu; pl. *magaṭāta* "scraper (for bricks)" NB; < Aram.

maggalum → *mangālu*

maggārum → *maqqārum*

maggu "tight, taut" MA, reins; < *magāgu*

magikû "provider" jB lex.

magillu(m), *magīlu(m)* OAkk, jB **1.** (type of boat), barge **2.** lex. (name of a mythical being)

maginnu; pl. f. *maginnāta* "(wide-brimmed Greek hat)" NB

magīrtum, *migīrtu* "challenge, insult"; < *giāru*

māgiru(m) "submissive, compliant" Bab., OB also in PN [ŠE.GA]; *lā m.* "unobliging, uncooperative, unwilling"; < *magāru*

magīṣu (a type of boat) jB lex.

Magmaru (a month) Ug.; < Ug.

magrāniš → *maqrāniš*

magrītu(m) "spite(ful act), malice, abuse" Bab.; < *gerû*

magru **1.** MA "willing" **2.** M/NB "friendly, favourable", in PN [ŠE.GA]; of water; month; < *magāru*

magrû "insulting" O/jB lex.; < *gerû*

magšaru(m) Bab. **1.** "superior strength" **2.** (a battleaxe); also (part of the liver)?; < *gašāru*

magû(m) mng. unkn., (a metal)? lex., OAkk?

magullāyā (desig. of a group of villagers) NB; < *magulû* ?

magulû (a big raft) jB [GIŠ.MÁ.GU.LA] to transport bull colossi ; < Sum.

magurgurru "ark" M/jB; < Sum.

magušu "magus, Magian" NB; < OPers.

magzazu "shearing blade"? jB lex.; < *gazāzu*

maḫabbum (or *maḫappum*) (s.th. by a canal)? OB

maḫadum → *maḫḫatum*

maḫāḫu(m) "to soak, steep (in liquid); dissolve in liquid" O/jB, M/NA **G** (*a/u*) [DIR] of earth, clay, excrement; clay figurines in urine; of plants; stat. of fog; "cause" eyes "to swell" (through rubbing) **Gtn** iter. of G **D** = G ? **N** pass. of G; > *miḫḫu* I, *miḫḫatu*

maḫālu mng. unkn. jB lex.

maḫan (a type of wooden chest) Am.; < Eg.

maḫappum → *maḫabbum*

maḫari "tomorrow" Am.; < W.Sem.

maḫariš → *maḫriš*

maḫāriš **1.** OAkk "in order to receive" **2.** jB "in order to confront"; < *maḫāru* + *-iš*

maḫarû → *maḫrû* I

maḫāru(m) "to face, confront; oppose; receive" **G** (*a/u*, pret. NB also *inḫur*, Ass. also *iḫḫur*) [IGI] **1.** "oppose"; "face" (an enemy = acc.); "set o.s. against" wind; "dam up, impound" a river; of obstacle "obstruct, stand in s.o.'s way" **2.** "appeal to" (s.o. = acc.) judge, king, deity, also in PN **3.** "receive, accept" goods, money, interest, ransom, tribute, present, also in PN; *ana šīmi, ana kaspi m.* "buy", esp. *nadānu u m.* "do business"; "receive" defamation, slander, calumny; "answer"? a prayer, "receive" s.o.; "meet with" misfortune **4.** "take upon o.s." bad omen, trouble etc. **5.** "correspond, equal" in size, rank; also in PN; "please"; OB stat. *īnam m.* "pleases the eye", NA *ina pān PN maḫir*; "become attractive, pleasing" (for = acc.) **6.** jB "compare with, equal"? **Gtn** iter. of G **Gt** recipr. of G → N, "attack each other"; astr., celestial bodies "enter conjunction" or "enter opposition"; O/jB of length, breadth etc. "become equal to each other", OB math. [ÍB.SÁ]; of horns of the moon "become proportionate, symmetric"; om., of signs "harmonize, agree"; "become square" **D** **1.** as G 2 "appeal to" **2.** "send, travel upstream" **3.** M/jB "drive against the wind" **4.** "place, lay down opposite" **5.** OA, jB "present, offer" **6.** OB(Susa) "make demands on, require"? **7.** "mix" ingredient into liquid glass **Dtn** iter. of D 5 "present again and again"; astr. "rise again and again"? **Š** caus. of G [GABA.RI] **1.** "cause s.o. to meet (with)" trouble **2.** "face" wind **3.** "receive" goods, money etc., "present" offerings [GABA.RI] **4.** jB "recite, recount" **5.** jB, NA "make equal" **6.** NA "make proportionate (to)" good deed **Štn** OA "let receive again and again" **Št** **1.** jB "oppose, confront" (s.th. or s.o. = acc.) **2.** "compare o.s. to, put o.s. on the same level with" **3.** jB "equate with, put in the same category with" **4.** "make, be equal (with one another)" height, depth **5.** math. "square" a number or length [NIGIN; ÍB.SÁ; MB UR.KA.E] **N** **1.** pass. of G "be opposed"; of goods etc. "be accepted, received"; of prayers "be answered"; "be confronted" (with = acc.) **2.** recipr. "meet one another, collide"; of interest "become equal to each other"; > *maḫru* I; *meḫru* I, *meḫrû*, *meḫrūtu*, *meḫertu*, *meḫratum*, *meḫretu*; *muḫru*; *maḫāriš*; *maḫīru*, *maḫīriš*, *maḫīrtu*; *māḫiru*, *māḫirtu*, *māḫirānu*; *maḫḫiru*; *muḫḫuru*, *muḫḫuriš*, *muḫḫurtu*; *muḫurrā'um*; *miḫḫūru*; *mitḫāru*, *mitḫāriš*, *mitḫartu*; *mitḫurtu*; *namḫaru*, *namḫartu*, *namḫāru*; *šumḫurtu*; *tamḫāru*, *tamḫāriš*, *tamḫartu*, *tamḫīru*

māḫāru "tomorrow" MB(Ta'annak); < W.Sem.

maḫāṣu(m) "to beat; weave" **G** (*a/a*; NA perf. → GAG §96h) [SÌG; RA] **1.** "beat" human being, animal, limb; idiomatic expressions OA *qātam m.* "refuse to accept", Nuzi *pūt PN m.* "vouch for, guarantee"; "put in (fetters); wound, smite"; *pan, panāt PN m.* "defeat utterly"; of deity, demon "strike, inflict" with a disease **2.** "drive in" object; "play, beat" musical instrument, toy; OA "smash, divide" silver, "cut" prices; "ram" a boat; "beat down" crops; "cut" reeds **3.** "weave" textile **4.** with 2 acc. *mayyārī m., šer'a(m) m.* "plough" a field; "apply" colour, stamp to s.th. **5.** *qaqqad, rēš eqli m.* "plough a (fallow) field"; "sprinkle" with liquid; *qaqqada(m) m.* "undertake work, process"; Nuzi of land "border on, abut"; OA "bring down" price **Gtn** iter. of G **Gt** (pret. *imtaḫaṣ*, MB onwards *imt/daḫḫeṣ*) "beat each other, fight" **D** [SÌG.SÌG] "beat, belabour; wound"; of animal tail "twitch"; Am. "cover" with gold; NA "slaughter"; "mark out" border with posts; of pain "hurt, stab" **Š** "cause to beat"; NA "sow discord" **Št 1.** lex. of part of the liver "become detached"? **2.** pass. of Š "let o.s. be beaten" **N** [RA] "be beaten (up); wounded; smashed; slaughtered"; of vegetation "be beaten down"; of peg "be driven in"; NB = Gt "fight"; > *maḫṣu; meḫṣu, miḫiṣtu; maḫiṣātu; māḫiṣu, māḫiṣānu, māḫiṣtu, māḫiṣ-pūtūtu; muḫḫuṣu; mitḫuṣu, mitḫuṣūtu; mundaḫṣu, mundaḫṣūtu; mušamḫiṣu, mušamḫiṣūtu; namḫaṣu, namḫaṣtu; tamḫuṣu, tamḫīṣu*

māḫāt → *māḫī*

maḫatum → *maḫḫatum*

maḫātum (a relative, phps.) "aunt" OA; < *maḫā'um*

maḫā'um (a relative, phps.) "uncle" OA; > *maḫātum*

māḫāziš "into the city" jB; < *māḫāzu*

māḫāzu(m) (or *māḫazu*), occas. *maḫzu* 'place of taking' [KI.ŠU.PEŠ5] **1.** "shrine, cultic centre"; "(market) town"; OAkk also a PlN; Nuzi "quay" **2.** jB ~ "spring, basin"; < *aḫāzu*; > *māḫāziš*

maḫdalu mng. unkn. jB lex.; < *ḫadālu* I

maḫdu/û mng. unkn. jB lex.

maḫḫadum → *maḫḫatum*

maḫḫaltu(m) "sieve" O/jB [GI.MA.AN.SIM. NÍG.ÀR.RA]; < *naḫālu* I

maḫḫalu (a basket or box)? O/jB, MA; < *naḫālu* I ?

maḫḫatum (or *ma(ḫ)ḫad/tum*) (an object of reed) OAkk

maḫḫiru "willingly receiving"? jB; < *maḫāru*

maḫḫītu → *maḫḫūtu*

maḫḫu "exalted" jB; < Sum.

maḫḫû(m), *muḫḫû(m)* "ecstatic, prophet" OAkk, Bab., NA [LÚ.GUB.BA]; also OB (a bird); < *maḫû*

maḫḫuriš → *muḫḫuriš*

ma(ḫ)ḫurtum → *muḫḫurtu*

maḫḫuru(m) OA for → *muḫḫuru*; *Maḫḫur-ilī* (4th month); < *maḫāru*

maḫḫūtiš "like a female ecstatic" jB; < *maḫḫūtu*

maḫḫûtiš in *m. alāku* "to become frenzied, ecstatic" jB; < *maḫḫû*

maḫḫūtu(m), *muḫḫūtum, maḫḫītu* "female ecstatic, prophetess" OAkk, O/jB [MUNUS. GUB.BA]; < *maḫḫû*

māḫī, *māḫāt, mārā* "one-twelfth of a shekel" NB; < Aram.

maḫilumma mng. unkn. Nuzi in *m. epēšu*

māḫirānu, NB also *māḫirnu* "the one who received, recipient" MA, NB; < *māḫiru* + *-ān*

maḫīriš "at the market" jB; < *maḫīru*

māḫirnu → *māḫirānu*

maḫirtu (a bone of the leg) Bogh., jB

maḫīrtu(m) "market price, current value, exchange rate" Mari; < *maḫīru*

māḫirtu(m), OB also *mēḫirtum* **1.** OAkk "recipient (f.)" **2.** O/jB, NA "(boat) moving upstream"; *ana m.* "upstream; wrong way"; "passer-by coming in o.'s direction (f.)" **3.** jB lex. (a kind of door); < *māḫiru*

maḫīru(m), *makīrum*; pl. m. & f. [KI.LAM; GÁN.BA] **1.** Bab., NA "exchange rate, market price", OB *bīt m.* ~ "shop"; NB *m. nabû* "to announce the exchange rate (valid for a sale)", *m. epēšu* "to complete a transaction", *ṭuppi ša m., kunuk m.* "exchange-rate document" **2.** jB, NA "trade" **3.** OA, O/MB "market", *rabi m.* "market-overseer", Bab., OA, NA *bāb m.* "market gate", also desig. of city quarter; < *maḫāru*

māḫiru(m) "opponent, antagonist, enemy; one who faces; recipient" [GABA.RI]; < *maḫāru*; > *māḫirtu, māḫirānu*

māḫiṣānu "the one who struck" MA; < *māḫiṣu*

māḫiṣātu pl. tant. (a wooden calculator, phps.) "abacus" j/NB; < *maḫāṣu*

māḫiṣ-pūtūtu "guaranty" NB; < *maḫāṣu*; → *pūtu* 1

māḫiṣu(m); f. *māḫiṣtu, māḫištu* **1.** Bab., NA "beater, striker" [LÚ.GIŠ.PAN.TAG.GA] (a person who brands and castrates? animals for slaughtering); Nuzi, NB *māḫiṣ pūti* "guarantor, bondsman", *māḫiṣ-pūtūtu* "warranty"; Mari *māḫiṣ qaqqadim* "accuser" **2.** Bab. "weaver" **3.** jB "hunter", NA/NB "archer"; < *maḫāṣu*

māḫītu "whip" OB, M/NA

maḫlašu(m), *maḫlišu* (a bronze scraper)? Mari, MA; < *ḫalāšu*

maḫnaqu (a sling, noose)? lex.; < *ḫanāqu*

maḫra, *maḫri* "in front"; "before"; "earlier" Bab.; < *maḫru* II

maḫraṣu(m) ~ "(battering) ram" O/jB; (a wooden piece of equipment) NA; < *ḫarāṣu*

maḫrašu, lex. once *marḫašu* (a post for fastening things to) jB; < *ḫarāšu* II

maḫrātu(m) pl. tant. "front part, forepart; first instalment; bow (of boat)" O/jB; < *maḫru* II

maḫri → *maḫra*

maḫriš, jB *maḫariš* "in front of" OAkk, jB; < *maḫru* II

maḫrītu, maḫrīum → *maḫrû* I

maḫru(m) I **1.** jB "(s.th.) that can be faced, withstood" **2.** "received"; < *maḫāru*

maḫru(m) II "front" [IGI] **1.** subst., of place: "front, presence"; of time: "past (time)" **2.** in prep. expressions (→ GAG §115j): *(ina) maḫar* "before (s.o.), in the presence of (s.o.)"; *ana maḫar* "before (s.o.), into the presence of (s.o.)"; *adi m.* "up to, in the direction of" jB, NA(roy. inscr.); *ištu m.* "from (s.o.)"; > *maḫra, maḫrātu, maḫriš, maḫrû* I

maḫrû(m) I, *maḫrīum*; f. *maḫrītu(m)*; MB also *maḫarû*, j/NB also *muḫrû* [IGI] **1.** "first; former, earlier; previous, older" **2.** "next, future" **3.** Mari in adv. use *maḫrû/êmma* "promptly"; < *maḫru* II + *-ī*

maḫrûm II (a type of spade) OB; < *ḫerû* II

maḫsû → *meḫsû*

maḫsûtu (a wooden object) NA lex.; < *ḫesû* ?

maḫṣu(m) "beaten, smitten" O/MA, O/jB of people "beaten"; of nails, posts "driven in"; of metal "hammered"?; "woven"; of a boat "rammed"; < *maḫāṣu*

maḫšalum, *maḫšulu* (a pestle)? OA, MB; < *ḫašālu*

maḫtûtum mng. unkn. OB; < *ḫatû* III ?

maḫû(m) "to rave" O/jB **G** (*i/i*, orig. *u/u* ?) **Gtn** iter. of G **N** "become frenzied"; > *maḫḫû, maḫḫûtiš, maḫḫūtu, maḫḫūtiš*

mâḫum "to set out, depart"? OB **G** (pret. *imūḫ*)

maḫzirāmu pl. "requirements" Am.; < W.Sem.

ma'irītu → *mārītu*

ma'išu (a kind of sheep)? MA

ma'ītu; pl. *ma'ītātu* "garden"? MB(Alal.), NB

maka → *ammaka*

makaddu, *makkadu, maqaddu, manqudu* **1.** jB lex. (a wooden stick or spatula)? **2.** MB(Alal.) (a copper object); < *kadādu*

makaḫu (or *maqaḫu*) "enclosure"? Nuzi

makāku "to extend, spread (out)" j/NB **G** (*a/u*) *irtu m.* "expand (the chest)", *qātu m.* "stretch out o.'s hand; raise o.'s hand against (= *ana*)"? **D** = G ?; → *magāgu*

makallu, *mangallu* (topog. term) Nuzi

makallû "anchorage, berth" j/NB; also ~ "irrigation dyke"?; < *kalû* V

mākaltu(m), NA *mākassu*; pl. *mākalātu(m)*, OB also *mākaltātum* "wooden dish" O/jB, M/NA [(GIŠ/DUG.)DÍLIM.GAL]; < *akālu*

makalu → *mangālu*

mākalum (a knife) Mari; < *akālu*

mākālu(m), *mākālû* "meal, food" Bab., NA; < *akālu*

makanaktu → *maknaktu*

makannu → *magannu* I

makannūtu → *magannūtu* I

makānu(m) ~ "emplacement"? O/jB; < *kânu* ?

makarrû (a type of boat) NB; < Sum.

makāru(m) I, *mekēru, megēru* "to irrigate, water" Bab., NA, with 2 acc. **G** (OB *a/u*, later *i/i*) fields; heart with wine **D** = G **Dt** pass. "become flooded" **Š** "let (water) irrigate (the fields), provide irrigation" **N** pass. of G "be irrigated"; > *makrum* I; *mikru* I; *mēkiru*; *namkaru*; *tamkīru*

makāru(m) II "to do business, use for commerce"? OA, Ug., j/NB **G** jB; OA "plan ahead, make dispositions freely, have s.th. entirely at o.'s disposal" **D** NB "buy (with silver)"? **Št** = G ?; > *makkārum, mākiru; makkūru, namkūru; muštamkiru; tamkāru, tamkārūtu, tamkārānû, tamkārašše*

mākassu → *mākaltu*

makāsu(m) "to levy customs or rental dues" O/jB, M/NA, Ug. **G** (*i/i*, OB mostly *u/u*) **N** pass. of G; > *maksum; miksu, mikiltu*?; *mākisu*

makāṣu, *makaṣṣu* "slaughtering block" jB; < *kâṣu*

makāšu mng. unkn. jB lex. **Gt**

makâtu → *makūtu*

makdādu (a scraper)? jB lex.; < *kadādu*

makdaru mng. unkn. MA; < *kadāru* II ?

makdû (a wooden bucket)? jB lex.

makiltu → *makištu*

makilu(m) (or *maqilu(m)*) (a type of weapon) OAkk, jB

makīrum → *maḫīru*

mākiru → *makkārum*

mākisu(m) "tax-collector" O/jB, M/NA **1.** OB "collector (of tenancy dues)" [EN$_7$.KU$_6$/GIR] **2.** "collector of taxes, customs dues" [LÚ.NÍG.KUD.DA]; < *makāsu*

makištu, *makiltu* (a type of conifer) jB lex.

makittu → *makkītu*

mākiu → *mēkûm*

makka → *ammaka*

makkadu → *makaddu*

makkaltu → *makkastu*

makkannu (a container) jB lex.

makkannû, *manga(n)nûm* (a cripple) O/jB lex.

makkanû "(originating) from Makkan, in Makkan style" jB lex.

makkarāniš "as with a donkey-goad" jB; < *makkaru* + *-ān* + *-iš*

makkaru "donkey-goad" jB lex.; > *makkarāniš*

makkārum, *mākiru(m)* "merchant, dealer" OA, jB; < *makāru* II

**makkastu*, *makkaltu* "wood-cutting" MB; < *nakāsu*

makkasu 1. M/jB (a knife) **2.** MA, M/NB, Am. (a bowl) **3.** NB "cut (dates of good quality)"; < *nakāsu*

makkāsu (a prof. or occupation) jB lex.

makkītu(m), *makittu* "(processional) boat" Bab. [GIŠ.MÁ.GÍD.DA]; OB *ša m.*, pl. *šūt m.* "bargee"; < Sum.

makkû, *meqiu* (a pole)? jB lex.; → *makūtu* II ?

makkūru(m), *ma(k)kurru* jB also f. "property, possession(s)" [NÍG.GA]; < *makāru* II

makkūru → also *makūru*

makkūtu (a type of boat) jB lex.; < Sum.

makkūtu → also *makūtu* II

maklalu, *muklalu*, (or *ma*/*uqlalu*) (a type of garment) M/NA, Bogh.

maklûtu "anchorage, berth" jB; < *kalû* V

maknaktu, *makanaktu* "seal" NB; < *kanāku*

maknakum, *maknākum* "sealed container, room" OA; < *kanāku*

makraku "bandage" lex.; < *karāku*

makrasû, *(ša) makratti* (a type of table) Nuzi

makriš (a part of a chariot) OA

makrum I "irrigated" OB; < *makāru* I

makru II "advice"? jB lex.

makru III "red spot" jB lex.

makrû(m) "red" OA, Mari, jB; name for planet Mars; Mari of copper

maksum "taxed" OB, of donkey; < *makāsu*

maksû(m) "(medical) bandage; fetter, shackles" O/jB; < *kasû* III

maksūtu 1. j/NB "binding; bandage" **2.** NB (a religious ceremony) **3.** NA (a wooden stand)?; < *kasû* III

makṣāru(m); pl. m. & f. **1.** OB (a mathematical procedure) **2.** jB "snaffle" for horse **3.** NB "bundle" of straw etc.; < *kaṣāru*

makû I, *māku(m)*; NA pl. *makiūte* ~ "destitute, poor"? Bab., NA; NA also "missing"; > *makûtu*; → *akû* I; *makû* II.III

makû(m) II, *mākum* "want, lack, need" O/jB; < *makû* III infin.; → *ammaki*

makû(m) III "to be absent, missing" OB, jB, NA **G**; **Š** "cause to go missing"; > *makû* I?, II

makûm IV (or *maqûm*) "to spy" Mari **G**; > *mākûm*

makû → also *mekû* V

māku → *makû* I.II

-māku suff. indicating unreality or potentiality Am., Bogh., occas. jB; < Hurr.?

mākûm (or *māqûm*) ~ "reconnoitrer, scout" Mari; < *makûm* IV

makūḫu(m) (a type of textile) OA, Nuzi, Ug.

makurru → *makkūru*; *makūru*

makūru(m), *makurru*, *makkūru*, *maqurru* f. "(processional) boat" O/jB [GIŠ.MÁ.GUR$_8$] "boat"; mag. "(model of a) boat"; "gibbous moon"; (a constellation); OB math. (biconvex figure); < Sum.

makūtu I (a type of bread)? OB

makūtu(m) II, *makkūtu*; pl. *makâtu* "staff, pole, post" Bab. (pole for a well, shaduf?); NB [DÌM.ME ?] "pillar; punt pole"; (a bread or cake); jB (a bone); → *makkû*

makûtu "destitution"? NA/jB; < *makû* I

mala I, *mali*, *mal*, *malla*/*u*, NB *malu-* "as much as" **1.** prep. before pron. suff. and subst. "as much as, equivalent to"; before infin. "as much as necessary to"; *ana mala*, *ammala* "in accordance with" **2.** *mala*/*i ša* OB "everything that"; NB "just as much as", "such as (s.th.) is" **3.** rel. pron. "as much as; everything that" and sim. (→ GAG §§48j, 168f-h), *mimma mala* "everything that"; NB *mamma mala* "everyone who"; < *malû* III st. constr.; → *ammal*; *ammar*

mala II, *mali*, MA *malla* "once; one" **1.** Ass. "once" **2.** OB, MA, Nuzi, jB before units of measure "one"; > *malama*; *malani*; *malmala*, *malmališ*

malâ → *malû* I 4

malādu → *walādum*

malāḫu(m) I, *malaḫḫu* "sailor; shipwright" [(LÚ.)MÁ.LAḪ$_{4/5}$] jB *lišān m.* "sailors' jargon"; NB as family name; *zê m.* "excrement *m.*" (a plant); < Sum.; > *malāḫūtu*

malāḫum II (a container)? OA

malāḫu III "god" jB lex.; < W.Sem.

malāḫu IV "to tear out" M/jB, NA **G** (*a/u*) **D** "reduce (s.th.) to fibres, shred"; astr. "flicker" **N** "be torn out"; > *malḫu*?; *milḫu*, *miliḫtu*; *muluḫḫû*; → *malā'u*

malāḫūtu "sailor's trade" NB [LÚ.MÁ.LAḪ4-]; < *malāḫu* I

malā'iš "in abundance, fully" OB; < *malû* III

malākiš "in order to advise" jB; < *malāku* II

malāku(m) I **1.** O/jB (a cut of meat) **2.** jB lex. (a bush)?; < *lêku* ?

malāku(m) II "to discuss; advise" **G** (*i/i*) [GALGA] "advise (s.o., s.th.)" with 2 acc.; Am. "look after, mind" with *ana* **Gtn** iter. of G **Gt** "discuss (with others), confer (about s.th.); consider, ponder" **D** Mari "advise, exhort" **N** "be advised; consider; discuss (with others)"; > *milku*, *miliktum*, *malkum* II; *malākiš*; *mallākum*; *māliku*, *māliktu*; *mitluku*, *mitluktu*; *mumtalkum*, *mundalkūtu*; *tamlāku*; *tamtalku*

malāku III "to rule (over s.o.)" Ug.; < W.Sem.; > *namlaktum*; → *malku* I

mālaku(m) I "walk, way; course" OAkk, Bab., NA "access road, walkway; march, route; stage (of march); river-bed"; NB *mālak Sîn* "lunar orbit"; < *alāku*

mālakum II "messenger" OB; < W.Sem.

malallu → *ma'lalum*

malallû(m), *mallû* (a type of freight boat) O/jB [(GIŠ.)MÁ.LAL]; < Sum.

malallû → also *manalalû*

mālaltu(m), OB also *ma'laltum* (a post or beam) O/jB [DÌM.TUR.TUR]; < *alālu* II

malalû → *ma'lalum*

malālu(m) I "to eat o.'s fill; pillage, loot; consume" O/jB **G** (*a/u*) **Št** NB "carry off from everywhere"?; > *millatum*

malālu II (a part of the body) jB

ma'lalum, *mālalu(m)*, *malallu*, *ma(l)lalû* ~ "wooden mortar"? O/jB; < *alālu* II ?

malâm ~ "on an equal basis" OB(lit.); < *malû* III

malama "once again" MA; < *mala* II

malamališ → *malmališ*

malani "once" NA; < *mala* II

mal'ānum "entirely, totally" OA; < *malû* III

malāsu, *malāšu* "to pluck (out), tear out" jB **G** (*a/u*, *i/i*) **D**; > *mullušum*

malāšu → *malāsu*

malātu mng. unkn. O/MB, jB lex. **G**; **Gt** of entrails; > *miltu*

malâtu "the entire offerings (for a period)"? NB; → *malītu*

ma'lātu, *mallātu*, *mal'ātu* "root of the tongue" jB; < *alātu* (*ma'lātu*, *mallātu*), *la'ātu* (*mal'ātu*)

malāṭu → *malūṭu*; *mulluṭu*

malā'u "to tear out"? jB **G**; = *malāḫu* IV ?

malā'um → also *malû* IV

malbašu → *nalbašu*

maldadu ~ "curtain"? jB, in boat; NA; < *šadādu*

maldaḫu → *mašdaḫu*

maldara, *maldariš* → *masdara*

maldaru → *masdaru*

maldu → *mašdu* I; *waldum*

malemmū → *melemmu*

mal'etum "possibility, option"? OA; < *le'û*

malgû, *malgâtum* "from Malgûm" O/jB, of vessel, song, musical instrument; < PlN

malgūtu (topog. term) NA

malḫu (desig. of a stringed instrument) jB lex.; < *malāḫu* IV ?

mali → *mala* I.II

malia → *malû* I

maliḫum → *malku* I

māliktu(m) "adviser, counsellor (f.)" O/jB; < *māliku*

maliku → *malku* I

māliku(m) "adviser, counsellor" [(LÚ.)GALGA; LÚ.AD.GI4.GI4]; Mari also of worshipped ancestors; < *malāku* II; > *māliktu*

malikūtu(m), *malkūtu* "rulership, rule" Bab.; < *malku* I

malīliš "like a pipe?" jB; < *malīlu*

malīlu (a wind instrument, phps.) "pipe" jB [GI.GÍD (→ also *ebbūbu*)]; > *malīliš*

mālittu → *wālittum*

malītu; pl. *malâtu*. **1.** jB (a lament) **2.** j/NB (a ritual vessel); < *malû* I f.; → *malâtu*

malium → *malû* I

Malkānum (2nd? month) Mari; < *malku* I

malkatu(m) "ruler (f.), queen" OAkk, M/jB; < *malku* I

malkittu → *maškittu*

malku(m) I, *maliku(m)* "prince, king" not OA ?; also a demon, spirit ?, OB also *maliḫum*; > *malkatu*, *Malkānum*, *malikūtu*; → *malāku* III

malkum II "advice" OA *m. ṣabātum* "to take a decision"; < *malāku* II

malkūtu → *malikūtu*

malla → *mala* I.II

mallaḫtu, *mullaḫtu* (a type of saline grass) jB lex.

mallākum "adviser" early OB in PN; < *malāku* II

mallalû → *ma'lalum*
mallatu "bowl, dish" jB
mallātu → *ma'lātu*
mallittu mng. unkn. jB lex.
mallu → *mala* I
mallû → *malallû*
mallūtu "balancing payment, final instalment"? MA; < *malû* IV D
malmala "singly, once"? jB lex.; < *mala* II
malmališ, *mammališ*, *malamališ* "correspondingly, equally" Bab.; *m. zâzu* "to share equally"?; < *malmala*
malmallu → *mulmullu*
malmalu (a type of beer) jB lex.
malqatu(m) (tool for gathering dates) O/jB; < *laqātu*
malqētu → *melqētu*
malsûtu → *massûtu*
maltakal → *maštakal*
maltaktu(m) "test, check" O/jB; *bilat maltakti* "(officially) assayed talent"; OB "sand-clock"; < *maltakum*
maltakum, *maštaku* "test, check" OB; < *latāku*; > *maltaktu*
maltītu → *maštītu*
maltu(m) (a type of bowl) OAkk, O/jB and in Sum. texts
maltû → *martû*; *maštû*
mâltum → *mayyaltu*
maltūtu → *maštūtu*
malṭaru → *mašṭaru*
malṭītu → *mešṭītu*
malṭû → *mešṭû*
malu- → *mala* I
malû(m) I, **malium*, OA *mal'um*; f. *malītu* "full, complete, sated" [SA5] **1.** of objects and measurements **2.** of gramm. forms **3.** of time **4.** *malia*, *malâ mê* "dropsical" [A.GAL.LA.TI.LA] **5.** OB *maliam* "totally, entirely"; < *malû* IV
malû II, often pl. "matted, dirty (body) hair" M/NB; < *lu''û* II
malû(m) III "abundance, fullness" Bab. [SA5] *malê irti* "success"; NB *m. ṣabātu* "to reach (healthy) fullness"; < *malû* IV infin.
malû(m) IV, OAkk, O/MA *malā'um* "to be(come) full; fill up (with = acc.)" **G** (*a/a*) [SA5] of canal, land "fill up with" water, earth etc., also people; also of containers, human and animal organs, the human body; stat. "is full of" radiance, fertility etc. **Gtn** iter. of G **D** [SA5] "fill (up)" (with = acc.); "inlay"; *qātum-*, *ana qāt PN m.* "hand over, entrust"; "put s.o. (or s.th.) under s.o."; of time "fulfil, reach fullness"; of measurement "do in full"; "pay in full"; *mullû nadānu* "pay the full amount"; "nock" a bow; OB(Susa) "enlarge, add" **Dtn** iter. of D **Dt** pass. of D **Š** "cause to become full" (of = acc.) and = D **Št** "deliver in full; complement; provide (with = acc.)" **ŠD** poet. for D **N** NB pass. for Dt; > *malû* I.III, *mala* I, *malâm*, *malā'iš*, *mal'ānum*; *malītu*, *malâtu*; *mīlu*, *mīlūtum*; *milītu*; *mūlu*; *mulā'u*; *mullû* I, *mallūtu*; *nemlû*?; *tamlīu*, *tamlītu*
mal'u → *malû* I
maluktu → *amaluktu*
malūṭu(m), *maluṭṭu*, *malāṭu* "ring, clasp, fastening (device); stocks, pillory" O/jB lex.; < *lâṭu*
māmilūtum mng. unkn. OB(Susa)
māmīnu(m) "why?; what?!" Am., Bogh; < W.Sem. *mā* + *mīnu* I ?
māmiš "like water" NB; < *māmū*
māmītu(m); pl. *māmâtu* "oath; curse" [NAM.ÉRIM/RIM; SAG.BA] leg. "(asseverative) oath" of vassals and subjects; "(promissory) oath"; om., mag., med. "(broken) oath"; "curse" following the breaking of an oath; as a demon; *qāt m.* (a disease); < *wamā'um*; → *tamītu*
mamlu, lex. once *meamlu* adj. ~ "impetuous, fierce"? j/NB; < *wamālum* ?
mamlūtu ~ "impetuosity" MB; < *mamlu*
mamma → *mamman*
mamma- → *mammannu-*
mammališ → *malmališ*
mamman, *mamma(m)*, OB occas. *manman*, NB also *mammu*, *mammāma*, Nuzi *mammamma* "somebody, who(so)ever", with neg. "nobody"; OAkk → *mammāna*, NA → *memēni*; < *man-man/ma*; → *mammannu-*; *manāma*
mammāna, occas. *mammānan* "who(so)ever" OAkk and occas. later for *mamman*; OAkk with neg. "nobody"
mamma(n)nu-, *mamma-*, NA *mummu(n)nu-* with poss. suff. "whosoever, anyone of" s.o. NA, NB; → *mamman*
Mammītu(m) (name of a goddess); OAkk, Bab. *waraḫ M.* (a winter month); < *mammû*; → *mumītu*
mammu(m), *mammû*, *mâmu*, *meammu* "tiara" O/jB; → *meānum*
mammu → also *mamman*
mammû(m), *mummu* "frost, ice" O/jB; also (a copper mineral); < Sum.; > *Mammītu*
mammû → also *mammu*
mamṣāru → *namṣāru*
māmū, *māwū* pl. "water" OB, M/jB(poet.); > *māmiš*; → *mû* I

mâmu → *mammu*

man → *mannu* I

-man suff. indicating unreality after stressed word O/jB, esp. in condit. clauses (→ GAG §§152d, 170h); OA → *-min*; → *lāman*; *lūman*; *šummaman*; *ulāman*; *ullāman*

Mana (a month) OB(N.Mes.)

ma'na "hey!" OB(lit.)

manāḫtu "resting-place" NA; < *nâḫu*

mānaḫtu(m); MA pl. also *māneḫātu* "weariness, fatigue; toil, work" Ass., O/jB **1.** gener., *m. amāru* "to suffer hardship" **2.** "(expenditure of) labour and materials; equipment for work"; *m. šakānu* "to invest labour"; *m. apālu*, also *nadānu*, *mullû* "to pay expenses, compensate for expended labour"; *m. leqû* "to recover costs of labour" **3.** pl. "proceeds (of labour); earnings" **4.** "cultivated field, orchard" **5.** MB(Alal.) "vassal service"; < *anāḫu* I

mānaḫu ~ *mānaḫtu* Susa, j/NB; Susa "earnings"; j/NB "hard labour"; < *anāḫu* I

manakuttu mng. unkn. jB lex.

manal(al)û, *malallû* "official in charge of weighing" jB lex.; < Sum.

manāma, Ass. *mannāma*, *manamma* "somebody; who(so)ever"; *m. lā* "no-one"; *m. (ša)* "whoever"; → *mamman*

manan mng. unkn. OB in *ana m.*, phps "why?" or "although"

manantu (a type of storage building) jB lex.

manānu pl. tant. "nerves"? jB

manât(um) **1.** OB(Susa) (a mathematical variable) **2.** NB "accounting"; < *manû* IV

manā'um → *manû* II.IV; *menû*

manda → *minde*; *Ummān-manda*

mandānu → *Madānu*; *maddānum*

mandattu → *maddattu*

mandētu "(result of) reconnoitring, report, information" NB; *m. šapāru* "to report"; < Aram.

mandidu → *mādidu*

mandidūtu → *mādidūtu*

mandittu (a wooden object) jB; < *nadānu* II ?

mandītu **1.** j/NB "surprise (attack)"? **2.** NB "(metal) attachment" for furniture etc.; < *nadû* III

mandu → *mādu*

mandû I, *ma'dû*, *mādû* (a pole)? jB lex.; → *muttû*

mandû II "emplacement" OB, Bogh.; in *mandī kussî* (a part of the liver); < *nadû* III; → *maddû*; *nīdu*

māneḫātu → *mānaḫtu*

mangāgu "fibres of the date palm" j/NB; < *magāgu*

mangallu → *makallu*

mangālu, *makalu*, OB *maggalum* mng. unkn. Bab., assoc. with door; < *nagālu* ?

manga(n)nûm → *makkannû*

mangāru(m) I (a large basket) OB [GI.GUR.IN.NU.DA]

mangāru II, also *mangāṣu* (< **nagāṣu* ?) ~ "advice"? jB lex.; < *nagāru* II ?

mangu I, *mannagu* (a type of bean)? j/NB [TÈ]

mangu II (a skin disease) jB; < *magāgu*

manḫalu "entrance, entering" NB; < Aram.

māni "how much, many?" Am.; < W.Sem.

maniātum → *minītu*

maninnu (a type of necklace) Qatna, Alal., Am.; < Sanskr.?

mānitu m. & f. "(gentle) wind, breeze" jB

manman → *mamman*

mannagu → *mangu* I

mannāma → *manāma*

mannašam adv. mng. unkn. OA

manniki "(so) be it" Mari; < Hurr.

mannu(m) I, OAkk, NA also *man*, NA also *ma''u* "who?"; in PN; with pron. suff.; indir. questions; *m. ša* "who(so)ever; everyone who", "each, every (single) person"; *m. šanâmma* "anyone else"; → *attamannu*; *attimannu*; *mamman*

mannu II "what?" Am.; < W.Sem.

mannummê, *mannumma* "who(so)ever" MB (Alal.), Am., Nuzi, Bogh., Ug.; with neg. "nobody"; Ug. "everybody"; → *mīnummê*

manqudu → *makaddu*

mansû → *massû*; *maššû* I 3

manṣartu → *maṣṣartu*

manṭaru "fibre, bast" NB; < Aram.

manû(m) I "counted" Bab.; *lā m.* "countless"; < *manû* IV

manû(m) II, OAkk, OA *manā'um* "mina (c. 480 grams)" [MA.NA; MB, NA also abbr. MA] of metal; wool; dates etc.; NA *m. ša PlN/šarri* "(standard) mina of PlN/the king"; "a mina-weight"; jB *man ṣelaḫru* "small mina (= 1/3 shekel)"; NB astr. *m.* = four hours; < *manû* IV

manû III, *mānu* (a kind of wood) jB lex., syn. of *ēru* II; < Sum.?

manû(m) IV, OAkk, OA *manā'um* "to count, calculate; recite" **G** (*u/u*, later often *i/i*) [ŠID] **1.** "count, enumerate, list"; "calculate; wait (a number of days); charge; debit" **2.** "count as (= *ana* or *-iš*), count among (= *itti*)"; "change into" **3.** *ina/ana qātē m.*, or loc.-adv. *qātu-* + pron. suff. *m.* "deliver, surrender s.o. (to)"

4. "recite" hymn, incantation **Gtn** iter. of G **D** = G **Dt** pass. of D **Š** "cause to count; cause to deliver" **N** pass. "be counted, calculated; delivered"; > *manû* I.II, *mānu*, *manâtum*, *manûtu*; *mīnu* II, *minānu*?, *minītu*, *minûtu* I; *munūtu*

manû → also *menû*; *munû* I

mānu in *ana lā māni* "countless" NA/jB of booty; prisoners; < *manû* IV

mānu → also *manû* III

mânu "to supply (with food)" j/NB, NA **G**; > *mu''untu*, *ma''uttu*

manunûm mng. unkn. OB; < Sum.?

manûtu "count(ing), standard" NB [ŠID] in *(ina) m. ša PlN*; < *manû* IV; → *minûtu* I

manzaltu → *mazzaztu*

manzassu, *manzaštum* → *mazzaztu*

Manzât → *Manziat*

manzattuḫlu, *mazzattuḫlu* "policeman" Nuzi; < Hurr.; > *manzattuḫlūtu*

manzattuḫlūtu "the office of policeman" Nuzi; < *manzattuḫlu*

manza'tum (a wooden implement) Early Mari

manzazānu → *mazzazānum*

manzazānūtum → *mazzazānūtum*

manzaz pānū(t)tu → *mazziz pānuttu*

manzaztum → *mazzaztu*

manzazu → *mazzizu*; *nanzāzu*

manzāzu → *mazzāzu*

manzeš, *manziaše* jB(NA) **1.** (a stone) **2.** (a metal container)?; < Urar.?

Manziat, *Manzât*, also *Manzīt* "rainbow" OAkk, Bab., NA [^{d}TIR.AN.NA] also DN; occas. in PN; astr. (a stellar nebula)?

manzû, *ma(z)zû* (a type of drum) jB [MEZE(ÁB×ME.EN); ME.ZÉ]; < Sum.

maprû (a (silver) vessel) Am.

maqaddu → *makaddu*

maqaḫu → *makaḫu*

maqaltānu (a priest)? NA; < W.Sem.?

maqalūtu → *maqlūtu*

maqāqu → *magāgu*

maqarratu "bale (of straw)" NA, NB; < *qarāru* ?

maqartu (desig. of vessel) NA, NB; phps. "cooling" vessel; < Aram.

maqartu → also *waqrum*

maqāru → *waqārum*

maqātu(m) "to fall" [ŠUB] **G** (*u/u*; perf. NA *ittuqut*) **1.** liter. "fall, drop"; of soldier in battle "die"; "fall down (before s.o.); plunge; collapse"; "pounce on, rush at"; "fall into s.o.'s hands" **2.** transf. "fall into (the heart); catch (the eye)"; j/NB, NA *ina pî m.* "fall from the mouth = be declared solemnly" **3.** of event "befall", with *ana* or dat. "happen to s.o."; of illness, misfortune "attack, strike s.o."; of inheritance "fall to s.o."; "invade, raid" a country **4.** of person, information "come, appear, arrive"; of thought "occur to, come to mind" **5.** "run away, desert, defect" (to = *ana pān*) **6.** of tax, etc. "be abandoned", of glow "fade; of flesh, charms "waste away" **Gtn** iter. of G **D** "declare as falling due"; ~ "cause to waste away" **Š** "cause to fall, cause s.o.'s downfall, ruin s.th. or s.o., wreck"; "cause to fall to s.o."; "cause to be dropped"; OA "assign, forward"; > *maqtu*, *maqittu*, *maqtam*, *maqtiš*, *maqtūtum*; *māqittu*; *miqtu*, *miqittu*; *muquttû*; *muqqutum*; *mušamqittu*, *šumqutttu*

maqāṭu, *maqāṭutu*; pl. *maqāṭāti* (a garment) NA

maqilu → *makilu*

maqittu "dilapidation, disrepair" jB(roy. inscr.); < *maqtu*

māqittu "missile" jB lex.; < *maqātu*

maqlalu → *maklalu*

maqlālu 'small thing', syn. for "vulva" jB lex.; < *qalālu* I

maqlû **1.** jB, NA "burn(ing), combustion", esp. in ritual **2.** jB lex. "roasting oven"; < *qalû* II

maqlūtu(m), NA also *maqalūtu* "burn(ing), conflagration" O/jB, NA [GÍBIL]; "burnt offering"; < *qalû* II

maqqabu, *maqqibu* "hammer" Am., Ug.; < W.Sem.

maqqadu, *muqqadu*, *mūqadu* "(right of) pasture" Ug.; < Ug.; → *nāqidu*

maqqaḫā du. "tongs" Ug.; < Ug.

maqqārum, *maggārum* "chisel" OB; < *naqāru* ?

maqqātum pl. (a plant) OB

maqqibu → *maqqabu*

maqqītu(m) "libation; vessel for libation" Bab. [BAL-]; < *naqû*

maqqû(m), Bogh. *meqqû*; NB pl. *maqqānû* "libation (vessel)" Bab., M/NA; < *naqû*

maqrāniš, *mag(a)rāniš* "on threshing floors" jB; < *maqrānu*

maqrānu(m) "threshing floor" OB; (a month) Mari, OB(Ešn., Chagar Bazar); < *qarānu*; > *maqrāniš*

maqrattu(m) "threshing floor" OB(Susa), Nuzi; < *qarānu*

maqtam "suddenly" Mari; < *maqtu*

maqtarum "censer" OB; < *qatāru* II

maqtiš "suddenly"? jB; < *maqtu*

maqtu(m) "fallen" Bab., NA [ŠUB]; of person, animal "fallen, defected, deserted"; of fruit, architecture "dropped, collapsed"; "sudden"; < *maqātu*; > *maqtam*, *maqtiš*, *maqittu*, *maqtūtum*

maqtūtum "collapsed state" Mari; < *maqtu*

maqûm → *makûm* IV

māqûm → *mākûm*

mâqu mng. unkn. NA **G** (*ū*)

maqurru → *makūru*

mar → *ammar*

mārā → *māḫī*

marāḫu(m) "to allow to become spoiled"? OB, jB lex. **G** grain **D** lex. **N** of grain "be spoiled"; > *marḫum*; *merḫu* II; *murḫu*?

marā'iš → *marû* II G

māraku(m) "length; full extent" O/jB; < *arāku*

maraqqum → *marrāqum*

marāqu(m) "to rub s.th. smooth; grind s.th. (down)" Bab., NA **G** (*a/u*) **1.** "rub s.th. smooth; scrape off"; "polish" beam; "whet, sharpen" tooth; transf. "wipe out" city **2.** "grind"; "pulverize" drug; cuneiform tablet **D** = G "grind"; NB "clear o.s." of claims **Dtt** NA "be pulverized, ground down" **N** pass. of G "be scraped, rubbed away"; > *marqu*; *mirqu*, *miriqtu* I; *murqu* I?, II; *murruqu*, *murruqūnu*, *mumarriqānu*; *tamrīqātu*

marāru(m) I "to be(come) bitter" **G** (*i/i*) [SES] of substances, food etc.; transf. of person "be bitter"; of punishment, weapon "be heavy, bitter; prevail" **Gtn** iter. of G [SES.MEŠ] **D** "make bitter"; stat. "is embittered" NB; "scrutinize closely" **Dt** pass. of D **Š** "make bitter" weapons in battle; > *marru* I, *martu*, *marratu*; *murru*, *murrānu*?; *murāru*, *murārītu*; *marraru*; *marruru*; *murrurtu*; *tamrīrum*, *tamrirtu*

marāru(m) II "to break up (by digging)" O/jB **G** (*a/u*) also transf. "overturn" **N** pass. of G

marāru III ~ "to go away, depart" Am., Ug. **G** (*u/u*) **Š** "chase away"; < Ug.

marāsu "to mix; mash" jB, NA **G** **1.** (*a/u*) "mix" **2.** (*i/i* < Aram.) "crush" **D** in comm.; > *marsu* I; *mersu*

marāṣu(m) "to be(come) ill; be(come) arduous, difficult" **G** (*a/a*, NB *u/u*; stat. *maruṣ*, Ass. *mariṣ*) [GIG] **1.** stat. of person, animal "is/was ill", "suffers" (from = acc.), (in = acc.); "become ill" **2.** "worry; care for", stat. "is distressed, grieved, worried" often with *libbu* as subj.; "worry" (about = *ana* or dat.) **3.** "displease" (s.o. = *eli*) **4.** "be(come) difficult, oppressive, unpleasant", stat. of work etc. "is oppressive"; "become annoying" **Gtn** iter. of G "fall ill repeatedly"; with *libbu* "worry incessantly" **D** "offend, hurt; worry s.o."; OB as Š "do in an offensive manner, make (s.th.) hurtful" **Š** caus. of G "cause to suffer; make ill"; "infect" a place; "expose to an eclipse (of the moon)"; "hurt, offend"; "do in an offensive manner"; "torment; affect s.o. badly, give s.o. a hard time"; stat. jB of terrain "is very difficult"; "cause to displease" (s.o. = *eli*) **Št¹** "be hurt, troubled" **Št²** "exert o.s., take trouble" **ŠD** Am. with *libbum* "distress o.s."; > *marṣu*, *marṣiš*, *maruštu*, *marṣūtu*; *marrāṣu*; *murṣu*; *namraṣu*, *namraṣiš*; *šumruṣu*

marašu → *maršu* 2

marāšu → *warāšum*

mārat banûtu → *māru* 3

maratû "in Marad style"? Mari; < PlN

mar'atum → *mārtu*

marāṭu "to scratch; scrape off" M/NA, M/jB **G** (*a/u*); also ~ "overuse, make excessive use (of)" **D** = G **N** "be scratched"; > *merṭu*

marā'um → *marû* II

mār banî, mār banûtu → *māru* 3

marbiqatum (a piece of jewellery)? Mari; < W.Sem.

marda(n)nu (a porridge or pudding)? jB lex.

mardatu(m), M/NA *mardutu* "rug, tapestry" Ass., O/MB; > *mardatuḫulu*

mardatuḫ(u)lu ~ "rug weaver"? MB(Alal.), Nuzi; < *mardatu* + Hurr. *-uḫ(u)lu*

mardītu M/NA, M/NB(Ass.) **1.** "bed" of river **2.** "stage" of march, *bīt m.* "road-house"; < *redû* I; → *merdītu*

mardû "successor" jB; < *redû* I

mardutu → *mardatu*

margānum, *marga/unnu*, also *margūlu* (a resinous bush; also its resin) O/jB; → *argānum*

margirānu → *merginānu*

margû(m) **1.** OB (an animal, phps.) "bear"; > *margūtu*? **2.** OB (a topog. desig.); → *sagû* III

margūlu, margunnu → *margānum*

margūṣu(m) (a resinous bush) O/jB also as a drug

margūtu (an animal)? jB lex.; < *margû* 1 ?

marḫa(l)lu(m) (a variety of carnelian)? O/jB, Qatna, Am.

marḫanû (a tree)? jB lex.

marḫaṣu, NB also *warḫaṣu* **1.** M/NB, NA "rinse, lavage" [RA]; med., mag. **2.** j/NB "drain(pipe)" of chariots, terraces; < *raḫāṣu* I

marḫaṣu → also *maḫrašu*; *marḫušu*

marḫītu(m) "mate, wife" O/jB; < *reḫû*

marḫum mng. unkn. OB describing a feature of the liver; < *marāḫu*

marḫušu(m), *marḫašu(m)* 'of Marḫaši' **1.** OAkk(Sum.), O/jB (a stone) "marcasite" **2.** Mari (a wood) **3.** Ug. "marcasite (bowl)" for oil; < PlN

mariakītum mng. unkn. OB

marīnum, *marinnu* (a leather article) O/jB; < Sum.?

marišmara, *marišmalû* (a plant) jB

mārītu(m), jB also *ma'irītu* "(s.th.) from Mari" Mari; jB lex.; → *mērītu*

mari(y)annu, *maryannu* (a caste of warriors) MB(Alal.), Bogh., Ug.; < Sanskr.

markabtu "chariot" Ug.; < W.Sem.; → *narkabtu*

markastu "compress, poultice"? jB med.; < *rakāsu*

markasu "bond, tie; rope" Bab. [DUR] **1.** "(ship's) painter", NB pl. *maškasātu* **2.** "closure" of door **3.** "bond" of brickwork **4.** transf. of goddess, palace; jB *PlN markas šamê u erṣeti* "PlN, the bond of heaven and earth"; < *rakāsu*

markutum (a wooden object) Mari

marmaḫḫu(m), *arma(ḫ)ḫu* (a fruit tree) O/jB

marmaḫḫūtu "office of the *pašīšu* priest" jB

marma(r)ru "strong" jB lex.

marmēnu (a drink) NA

marnu'ātum (a farinaceous food) OA

marqantu (a weapon) jB

marqītu(m) I "refuge" O/jB; < *raqû*

marqītu II "vegetation" jB lex.; < *warāqum*

marqu "ground, pulverized" Nuzi, jB/NA, salt, glass; < *marāqu*

marrāqum, *maraqqum* (a prof.) OB lex.

marraru "very bitter" jB; < *marāru* I

marrāṣu "sickly" jB; < *marāṣu*

marratu(m) "bitter thing" **1.** lex. and in Sum. texts (desig. of a date palm) **2.** j/NB, NA "the sea" (incl. southern marshes), NB (the Mediterranean) **3.** "rainbow" [IM.SES-*tum*] **4.** lex. (a chain)? **5.** (a bird); < *marru* I

marru(m) I "bitter" [SES] of food and drink; of the mouth; transf. of wind, weapons; pl. *marrūtu* (a type of onion); < *marāru* I

marru(m) II "shovel, spade" Bab. [(GIŠ/URUDU.)MAR] also as symbol of Marduk and Nabû; < Sum.

marruru(m) **1.** OA "bitter flour" **2.** MA "closely scrutinized"; < *marāru* I D

marrūtu → *marru* I

marsattu(m); MA pl. *marsanātu* "a (soaking) vat" OAkk, MA, NB?; < *rasānu*

marsu I "mixed" jB lex.; < *marāsu*

marsum II (part of the equipment of a chariot)? OA; → *maršu* 1

marṣadu (a copper object or mineral) jB lex.; < *raṣādu*

marṣā'u "awl"? Am.?, jB lex.

marṣiš "bitterly, sadly; laboriously" j/NB [GIG-*iš*]; < *marṣu*

marṣu(m); f. → *maruštu*, Bab. later also *marultu*, OA *marištum* "sick; troublesome" [GIG; TU.RA] of lament "bitter"; "difficult, severe"; of terrain "difficult"; < *marāṣu*; > *marṣiš*, *marṣūtu*

marṣūtu(m) in *marṣūssu* **1.** OB "in his trouble" **2.** jB "in his illness"; < *marṣu*

mār-šarrūtu → *māru* 1

marše'urrû → *še'urrû*

maršidātum pl. (a stone) Mari; < *rašādu*

mār šipri, *mār šiprūtu* → *māru* 4

maršītu(m) "property, possessions, livestock" O/jB, Nuzi, Ug.; < *rašû* I

maršu(m) **1.** "leather strap" Ass., Mari, M/jB, of bag, sandal, harness (→ *marsum* II); Mari pl. f., attached to net **2.** lex. (a bed), also *marašu* (→ *muruš*) **3.** Bogh. (a garment)

maršu → also *waršum*

martakal → *maštakal*

martātum "Martu woman"? OAkk

martianni "men, warriors" Nuzi; < Sanskr.?

martu(m), Bogh. *mertu* "gall bladder; bile" [ZÍ; also EŠ ?] also transf., e.g. NB to drink *m.* before s.o. = to despise s.o.; *aban m.* "gall stone"; < *marru* I

martû, *mertû*, *maltû*, NB *maštû* (a tree) Bab. [GIŠ.MA.NU.TUR.TUR]; a pole, part of a cart; < *retû* II ?

mārtu(m), OAkk, OA(lit.) *mar'atum*, pl. *maruātum*; OA *mer'a/etum*, pl. *meru(w)ātum*, *merâtum*; jB also *mērtu*, NB also *māštu* "daughter; girl" [DUMU.MUNUS]; NA *m. rabītu* "eldest daughter"; *m. šarri* "princess"; transf. to express a relationship, e.g. in PN "daughter" (of a deity); jB *m. ilāni* (a priestess); *m. banûtu* → *māru* 3; lex. *m. Ištar* (an animal); *m. šamê* (sulphur); jB *m. rē'î* "locust"; *m. eqli* (a plant); *mārat palḫi* (plant name); *m./mārti uppi* (part of a palm tree); NA *m. lipê*, *nāre* (figurine)?; NB *m. n šanāti* "n years old"; *m. šanat* "one year old"; < *māru*; > *mārtūtu*

marturrû "small vehicle" jB; < Sum.

mārtūtu "(adoptive) daughterhood" Nuzi [DUMU.MUNUS-]; < *mārtu*

marû(m) I, Ass. *mar'u(m)* "fattened, fat" [NIGA(=ŠE)]; "slow", jB gramm. of Sum. verbal forms (opp. → *ḫamṭu*); < *marû* II

marû(m) II, OAkk, Ass. *marā'um* "to fatten; do slowly" **G** (*i*/*i*) animals, organs; OAkk *marā'iš* "in order to fatten" **Gtn** iter. of G "delay repeatedly" **Š** "supply with fodder, fatten" **Št** "give in abundance" **N** NA uncl.; > *marû* I; *mīru* II; *mārû*, *mārûtum*; *mušamrû*; *imrû* I; *namrā'um*, *namriātum*, *namrītu*?; *šamrû*

marûm III "to examine"? Mari **G**

māru(m), OAkk, Ass. *mar'u(m)*, OA mostly *mer'um*, jB also *mēru*, Nuzi also *nāru* "son, descendant; boy" [DUMU; later often A, in col. PEŠ.GAL] **1.** *m.* *ṣeḫru*/*rabû* "younger/elder son"; Nuzi "adopted son"; *mār māri(m)* "grandson"; *mār aḫi(m)*, *aḫāti(m)* "nephew"; *mār šarri(m)* "prince", NA "crown prince", *mār-šarrūtu* "status of crown prince" **2.** of social or geographical origin: "member of, belonging to", in *mār āli(m)* "citizen", *mār PlN*; *mār bīti(m)* "member of the house(hold), house slave", NB "household administrator"; OB *mār bīt ṭuppim* "government scribe"; *mār ēkallim*; *mār māti(m)* "native (of a region)" **3.** of membership of class or prof.: *mār awīlim* "free man", OB *mār muškēnim*; *mār bārîm* "diviner" etc.; M/NA [A/DUMU.SIG/SIG5] phps. *mār damqi* "nobleman", usu. as charioteer ; NB *mār banî* "free man", *mār banûtu* "status of a free man", with MUNUS = *mārat banûtu* ? **4.** "who has to do with" (s.th.) and sim. in OB *m.* *abullim* 'porter' (i.e. court official)?; NB *m.* *amēl sīsî* "(horse) groom", *m.* *zēri* "field labourer"; *mār šipri(m)* [LÚ.A.KIN; LÚ.KIN.GI4.A] "delegate, envoy", *mār šiprūtu* "rôle as envoy; exchange of envoys" **5.** "boy, young friend, darling", Ug. addressing subordinates **6.** as desig. of age or size, e.g. *m.* *šatti* "yearling, one-year-old"; of animals "kid, lamb, chick" etc. **7.** *m.* *libitti* (plant name); > *mārtu*, *mārtūtu*; *mārūtu*

māru → also *āru* I

mārû(m) "animal fattener" O/jB, Nuzi [(LÚ.)NIGA(=ŠE)]; *bīt mārî* "fattening shed"; < *marû* II; > *mārûtum*

mâru "to buy"? NB **G** (*i*/*i*); < Aram.?

mâru → also *wârum*

mar'u → *marû* I; *māru*

maruktu → *amaluktu*

maruṣtu, *maruštu(m)*, j/NB also *marultu* "evil, distress" [NÍG.GIG] *m.* *amāru* "to experience trouble"; *ina maruštim* "reluctantly"; < *marṣu*

maruštu → *maruṣtu*; *waršum*

mārūtu(m), OA *mer'uttum*, MA *mar'uttu*, *māruttu* "status of son" [DUMU-] *ina m.* *nasāḫu* "to disinherit"; "status of adopted son (or daughter)", *ana m.* *leqû*/*šakānu* "to adopt", *ana m.* *nadānu* "to put up for adoption"; < *māru*

mārûtum "fattening (technique)" OB; < *mārû*

maryannu → *mariyannu*

marza'u, *marziḫu*, *marzû* (a priest)? Am., Ug.; → *marṣa'u*

masabbu(m), *masappu(m)* (a basket) Bab., Ug., NA [(GI.)MA.SÁ.AB]; also (a cultic object)

masablu'urrâku "street-sweeper's basket" jB lex.; < Sum.

masāḫum OA **D** "to treat with contempt"; stat. of metal "is of inferior quality"; > *massuḫum*

masāku(m), *mašāku* "to be(come) bad, worsen" Ass., O/jB **G**; **D** "make s.th. bad" **Š** "consider as bad" **N** "be made bad", "turn out bad"; "be blamed"; > *masku*; *masiktu*; *muskum*?; *mussuku*; *musukkû*

masappu → *masabbu*

māsartu → *māšartu*

masārum (or *maṣ*/*zārum*) ~ "to obstruct, impede"? OA **G** (*a*/*u*); stat. "is not available"? **N** ? pass. of G; > *maṣirum*?; *muṣārum*?

masāru → also *maṣāru*

masâtu "washbasin" jB lex.; < *mesû* II

masā'u → *mesû* II

masdara, *maldara*, *mas*/*ldariš*, *mešdariš* "continuously, always" Am., jB; < *masdaru*

masdaru, *maldaru* **1.** MA "duration; permanence" **2.** jB lex. (a knife)?; < *sadāru*

masennu → *mašennu*

masḫartum (a vessel for oil) OA, OB; < *saḫāru*; → *masḫātum*

masḫaru(m) (a vessel)? OAkk(Sum.), jB lex., NB; < *saḫāru*

masḫarūtum mng. uncl. Mari; < *saḫāru*

masḫastum uncl. OB; < *saḫāšu* ?

masḫātum (a beaker) OB, scribal error for → *masḫartum* ?

masiktu(m), Bogh. etc. *mašiktu* "badness, bad feelings, reputation" O/jB, MA; MB(Alal.) *bēl mašikti* "criminal"; < *masku*

masirum → *maṣirum*

masīru ~ "clay, mud" (as wall plaster)? jB, NA; < *sêru* ?

masiu → *mesû* I

maskannu → *musukkannu*

maskartum → *maškartum*

maskiltu → *baskiltu*

masku(m), *mašku* "bad, evil" O/jB; OB as PN "Ugly"; < *masāku*; > *masiktu*
maslaḫtu(m), *masraḫtu* (a libation vessel) Bab. [DUG.A.SÙ]; < *salāḫu* I
maslaḫu(m), *masraḫu* (a libation tube) O/jB; med. "urethra"; < *salāḫu* I
maslaqtu (a cooking pot) jB lex.; < *salāqu* I
masla'tu "infection, epidemic" M/jB; < *salā'u* I
masla'u "pitcher, jug" jB lex.; < *salā'u* I
masmakannu → *musukkannu*
masmas (a plant) jB
masnaqtu "inspection" j/NB; < *sanāqu* I
masradum (a pack-saddle) OA; < *sarādu*
masraḫtu → *maslaḫtu*
masraḫu → *maslaḫu*
massaku(m) 1. OB ~ "tow-rope" for boat **2.** NA mng. unkn., textile item in pairs; < *nasāku*
massaku → also *maštaku*
massāru "saw" jB; *bēl m.* (epith. of Ninsar); < *nasāru*
massātum "princess, queen" OA; < *massû*
massiš (horse trappings)? MB; < Kass.
massītu → *maštītu*
massu (a conscript labourer) Alal., Am.
massum → also *maṣṣum*
massû(m), OA *massu'um*, jB also *maššû*, *ma/ensû*; f. *massūtum* "leader, expert" Bab. (lit.), O/MA [MAS.SÙ]; < Sum.; > *massātum*; *maššûtu* II
massû → also *maššû* I 3
massuḫum ~ "inferior quality" OA of metal; < *masāḫu* D
massusu mng. unkn. NB
massūtu "washing" MA; < *mesû* II D
massūtum → also *massû*
massûtu, *malsûtu* **1.** MB "call"? **2.** j/NB "reading out, lecture"; < *šasû*
massu'um → *massû*
masû → *mesû* I
māsū → *mēsū*
mas'um → *mesû* I
ma'su mng. unkn. jB
masūktu "mortar" jB; < *sâku*
masuššû (topog. term)? MB
maswātu (a type of tree) Ug.; < Ug.?
maṣādu (a melting pot) Ug., jB; < *ṣâdu* II
maṣallu; pl. f. "sleeping place, shelter" for shepherds etc. M/jB; NA, of tomb; < *ṣalālu*; → *muṣallu*
maṣarrītum (a vessel) Mari; < *maṣarru*
maṣarru(m) (a vessel) O/jB, NA; < *ṣarāru* I
maṣāru(m), also phps. *maz/sāru* Bab. **G** (*a/u*) ~ "to stride about"? **D** (< *miṣru* denom.?) "enclose, mark boundaries (of)"; "limit" time **N** (phps. different word?) ~ "become compact"?; > *maṣirum*?; *muṣārum*?; *namṣāru*

maṣārum → also *masārum*

maṣā'um → *maṣû*

maṣēn → *maṣi*

maṣḫatu(m) (a kind of flour) Bab., M/NA [ZÌ.MAD/MA.AD.GÁ]; < *ṣaḫātu* I

maṣi, also (+ subjunct. *-n(i)*?) *maṣīn*, *maṣēn* "(but) since, in view of" NA in *issu m.* "since", "as if"?; *kī m.* "correspondingly, accordingly" (→ also *maṣû* G 6.7); < *maṣû*

maṣiḫu "middle"? NB; < Aram.?

māṣilu (a musician, phps.) "cymbalist" Ug.; < W.Sem.

maṣirum (or *mas/zirum*) in *annakam m.* (a variety of tin) OA; < *masārum* or *maṣāru* ?

maṣīru (a shipping due) NB; < Aram.?

maṣītu "(that which is) sufficient" jB; < *maṣû*

maṣlālum (or *maṣlalum*) mng. unkn. OB in PN; < *ṣalālu*

maṣraḫtu (an emblem) jB lex.; < *maṣrāḫu*

maṣrāḫu(m) O/jB, NA **1.** "socle for (divine) symbols" **2.** "socle" of the gall bladder, phps. "bile-duct"? [SUR]; < *ṣarāḫu* II

maṣṣartu(m), Am. also *manṣartu* "observation, guard" [EN.NUN/NU.UN] OA *rabi maṣṣar(ā)tim* "captain of the guards"; *ša m.*, *bēl m.* "guard, watchman", NB *bīt m.* "guardroom"; *m. naṣāru(m)* "to stand guard", also astr. "observe"; "watch" of the night, st. abs. *maṣṣarat* "at first watch"; "cultic watch"; *m. ḫašîm* 'guard of the lungs' (= "bronchia"?); "depot, warehouse"; "safe custody; proper care"; < *naṣāru*; > *maṣṣarūtu*

maṣṣaru(m), NA *maṣṣuru* "guard, watchman" [(LÚ.)EN.NUN; (LÚ.)EN.NU(.UN)] in comb., e.g. Am. *m. šarri* "king's guard"; *m. abullim* "gatekeeper"; *m. qišātim/qišti* "forest guard"; *m. eqlim* "field guard"; of deities and divine images *m. šulmi(m) u balāṭi(m)* "guardian of health and life"; *m. ṭīdi* 'guardian of clay' (= a worm); < *naṣāru*

maṣṣarūtu(m) "safekeeping" O/jB; < *maṣṣartu*

maṣṣum, *mass/zzum*? OB **1.** (a garment) **2.** (rash, eczema)?

maṣṣuru → *maṣṣāru*

maṣû(m), OAkk, Ass. *maṣā'um* "to correspond, comply with (s.th.); be sufficient, suffice" **G** (*i/i*) **1.** after *mala*, NA *(am)mar* (of field etc.) "be as much as it amounts to, is worth"; "be worth as much as s.o. else"; *mala*, *ammar libbi- m.* "achieve wishes"; after infin. "be able to" **2.** with *ana* or dat. "reach" o.'s goal; stat. "is sufficient" **3.** with acc. "reach" a number or a time **4.** OA "take responsibility for" **5.** with *kīma* "become equal to" **6.** *kī maṣi* "how much (does it correspond to)?", math. also after prep. (→ *maṣi*) **7.** absol. *maṣi* "it is enough!", also in PN; OA before *laqā'um* and *ṣabātum* "be ready, in a position to take" **D** "make available, provide" (→ *wuṣṣûm*), OB *qātam m.* "make o.s. available, get involved" **Dt** OA "be made available" **Š** caus. of G "cause to/let correspond"; "cause to suffice"; jB "prepare (properly)"? drug mixture; NA "be able to" **Štn** uncl. **Št 1.** "set about doing s.th." **2.** stat. "is within reach, available"; > *maṣi*, *maṣītu*; *miṣītum*; *muštamṣû*

mâṣu(m) "to churn, make butter"? O/jB **G**; > *namāṣu*; *namūṣu* ?

mâṣu → also *wiāṣum*

maṣullultu → *ṣulultu* I

mašaddu, *mešeddu*, Nuzi *mašandu*; NA pl. f. "(yoke-)shaft" M/NB; jB astr. "shaft (of the waggon-star = Ursa Major)"; < *šadādu*

mašādu(m) "to beat; full (cloth, wool)"? Bab., OA [SA] **G** (*i/i*, OA *a/u*) OA "full"? textiles; jB "massage"; of demons etc. "strike" with disease; "crush, press in"? foetus, organs **D** "massage"? **N** pass. of G "be stricken, have a stroke"; > *mašdu* II; *mišdu*, *mišittu*

mašāḫu(m) I "to measure" land, buildings M/NB **G** (*a/u*) "measure, mete out" commodities; also Mari "count" people ? **Gtn** "measure out to each" **D** = G **N** "be measured"; > *mašḫu* I.II; *mašīḫu*; *mišḫu* I, *mišiḫtu*; *māšiḫum*, *māšiḫānu*; *mumaššiḫu*; *namšāḫu*; *tamšīḫu*; → *mašā'u*

mašāḫu II ~ "to flash, shine, glow" [SUR] jB **G** (*u/u*) of star, meteor; > *mišḫu* II

mašāku → *masāku*

mašallu(m) (a groove, channel, conduit)? OB, jB lex.; < *šalālu* II ?; → *mušlālu*

mašallû (a boat) jB lex.; < Sum.

maš'altu "questioning, interrogation" j/NB; also (a type of commentary); < *šâlu* I

mašālu(m), MB also *mešēlu* "to equal" **G** (O/jB *u/u*, jB also *a/a*, MB *i/i*) stat. "is equal" (to = *ana*); "become equal" (to = *ana*, *-iš* or dat.); MB "become equal", i.e. "smooth", of the sea; "be(come) halved, bisected" of time, grain; the moon **D** "make equal, proportionate"; with *ana* "equalize in value", "equal s.o."; "make s.th. similar, match"; "reproduce, copy" **Dt** "find o.'s match" **Š** "make s.th. equal" **Št** "place on a level" (with = acc.) **N** "attain the equivalent condition"?; > *mašlu*; *mišlu*, *mišlānū*, *mišla*; *mušālu*; *muššulu*, *muššultu*; *tamšīlu*, *tamšiltu*; *miššulu*?

maš'alu (an oracle)? Ug.; < *šâlu* I

mašandu → *mašaddu*

mašānum (an object of precious metal) OAkk and in Sum. texts; → *maššânu*, *mušānum* ?

maš'anum → *mešēnu*

mašarrû "dream" jB lex.

māšartu, NB *māsartu* "inspection, (military) review" M/NA, NB; NA *ēkal m.* "Review Palace, arsenal"; < *ašāru*

mašāru(m) "to drag (across the ground)" OA, O/jB **G** (*a/u*) garments; Nuzi leg. "drag (the hem of a garment)" to confirm the validity of an agreement; "teasel" fabric; "drive" a vehicle **Gtn** of animal "drag" tail "to and fro"; "drag s.o. to death" with animals; OA "delay, draw out" action, treatment **D**, **Dtn**, **Dt** → *wašārum* **Š** caus. of G; > *mašru*; *mišertu*; *māširum*; *mašīru*; *tamšāru*; *namšartu*

ma'šaru "tithe" Ug.; < Ug.

mašāšu(m) "to wipe off; clean" O/jB **G** (*a/u*) **D** "clean"? **Dt** pass. of D **N** pass. of G; > *maššu*; *māšištu*; *mašištu*?

mašātu "to itch" jB **G** stat.; > *maštu*

maš'atu (a plant with thorns) jB

mašā'u(m) "to take away by force, rob" **G** (*a/u*, jB once *i/i*) [KAR] from s.o. = acc.; "abduct s.o."; "loot, pillage, ransack" country, building; stat. "is robbed" **Gtn** iter. of G **D** → *muššu'u* **Š** "let s.o. be robbed, cause to be robbed" **N** "be taken away by force"; "be looted, ransacked"; "be stolen"; > *maš'u*; *miše'tu*; *maššī'u*; *maššûtu* I?

mašā'u → also *mašû* II

mašdaḫu, *maldaḫu* "procession (street)" j/NB; < *šadāḫu*

mašdu I, *maldu* ~ "edge"? of bed, river j/NB

maš'enum → *mešēnu*

mašdu I, *maldu* ~ "edge"? of bed, river j/NB

mašdu II "dressed"? f. pl., of hair jB lex.; < *mašādu*

mašdû (a stone) jB

mašēltu → *mešēltu*

mašennu, *mašēnu*, Nuzi, NA *masennu* (an administrator, a manager) Nuzi, NA, NB [(LÚ.)AGRIG ? (→ *abarakku*)]

maš'enum → *mešēnu*

maš'ertum mng. uncl. OA

māšerum → *māširum*

mašgabarû, **mašgabû** (types of sacrificial goat) jB lex.; < Sum.

mašgallu "billy goat" jB lex., NB; → *daššu*
mašgallû "pertaining to a billy goat" Nuzi
mašgašu(m), *maškašu(m)* (a battle mace)? O/jB; < *šagāšu*
mašgibillû → *mašgizillû*
mašgikīdu → *aškikītu*
mašgizillû, *mašgibillû* (a sacrificial goat) jB [MÁŠ.GI.IZI.LÁ/LÁL]; < Sum.
mašgubbu "sexually mature goat" jB lex.; < Sum.
mašḫaltappû (a priest performing sacrifices)? jB; < Sum.?
mašḫaltu "(type of) sieve" jB; < *šaḫālu*
mašḫalu(m) "(type of) sieve" O/jB, M/NA; < *šaḫālu*
mašḫantu, *mašḫandu* (a waistband, sash)? jB; < *šaḫānu*
mašḫaṭu "stairs, ladder" M/jB; MB PlN *Mašḫaṭ-šarri*; < *šaḫāṭu* I
mašḫu I "measured, surveyed" NB; < *mašāḫu* I
mašḫu(m) II **1.** OAkk(Sum.) (a beer mug) **2.** Qatna, Am. (a bead)?; < *mašāḫu* I
mašḫu III "god" M/jB; < Kass.
mašḫudû (a class of people)? jB lex.
mašḫulduppû "scapegoat, kid as expiatory sacrifice" jB [MÁŠ.ḪUL.DÚB(.BA)]; < Sum.; → *ḫultuppû*
mašḫurannu (a garment) Ug.
mašḫuru, gen. *mašḫiri* (a textile) MA; < *saḫāru* ?
mašiānu → *maššânu*
māšiḫānu "the one who surveyed" MB; < *mašāḫu* I
mašīḫu; pl. also f. (a measure of capacity, varies from 30 to 54 *qû*, ~ 1 *pān*) NB; < *mašāḫu* I
māšiḫum "surveyor" OB lex.; < *mašāḫu* I
mašiktu → *masiktu*
maširru (a wooden vessel) jB lex.
mašīru (a wheeled vehicle) MA, M/jB; < *mašāru*
māširum, *māšerum* "a teaseller of cloth" OB lex.; < *mašāru*
mašiš "in oblivion, forgotten" OB; < *mašû* I
māšiš "on both sides" jB; < *māšu*
mašištu modal ptcl. jB; < *mašāšu* ?
māšištu f. "polisher" jB lex.; < *mašāšu*
mašītu, *maššītu* "twin sister" jB; < *māšu*
mašītu → also *mašû* I 1
maškabum; pl. f. "camp" Mari; < W.Sem.
maškadu (an illness of the joints, arthritis?) jB
maškadu → also *aškadu*
maškakātu(m) pl. tant. "harrow" O/jB [GIŠ.GÁN.ÙR]; < *šakāku*

maškantu "ingredients, materials" jB; < *šakānu*
maškantu → also *maškattu*
maškanu(m) 'place of putting' **1.** "threshing floor" [KISLAḪ; MAŠ.GÁN] OB; pl. also f. **2.** "place, site, settlement"; OB PlN *Maškan-RN* etc.; om. of parts of the liver; of the moon **3.** "fetter, shackles, chain"; OB as mark of a slave **4.** NB "security, pledge", also *bīt m.*; *m. šakānu* "to pawn, pledge"; *m. ṣabātu* "to take as pledge" **5.** Ass., Urar. (túg)*m.* "tent"; < *šakānu*; → *maškantu*; *maškattu*
maškānum "deposit" OA; < *šakānu*
maškanūtu "state of pledge" NB *ana m. šakānu* "to pledge"; *ana m. ṣabātu* "to take as pledge"; < *maškanu* 4
maškartum, *maskartum* (a piece of jewellery) OAkk, OB
maškartum → also *mašqartum*
maškasu → *markasu*
maškašu → *mašgašu*
maškattu(m), NA *maškantu* "depot; account" except OB; OAkk "depot"; O/MA "account", *m. šakānu(m)* "to open an account"; M/NB "depot; stores", PlN *Maškanāti*; NA *maškanti uqnî* "substitute lapis lazuli"?; < *maškanu*
maškēnu → *muškēnu*
maškirtum (a drinking vessel) Mari; < *šakāru*
maškiru → *maškaru*
maškittu, *malkittu* "sacrificial table, altar" jB, NA; < *šakānu*
mašku(m) "skin" [KUŠ] of human; "hide" of animal; "leather"; "peel, skin" of fruit, plant; jB *m. ḫurāṣi* "gold overlay"; > *muššuku*
mašku → also *masku*
maškūnum mng. unkn. OA
maškuru Ass., NB *maškiru* "(inflatable) animal skin" NA, NB? [KUŠ.BAR.RA] for swimmer or raft; < *šakāru* ?
mašlatu "knife (of a basket weaver)"; < *salātu* II
mašliu → *mašlû*
mašlu(m) "half" O/jB; jB *ūm mašil* "midday" [UD.SA9.ÀM]; O/jB *mūši mašil* "midnight"; OB of length, width; < *mašālu*
mašlû(m), *mešlûm*?, OAkk, MA *mašliu(m)* **1.** OAkk, MA "(leather) bucket"; OAkk pl. f. **2.** OB "leather wrapper" for textiles **3.** jB (a wall socle)?; < *šalû* I
mašmašgallum "chief exorcist" OB lex.; < Sum.
mašma(š)šu "incantation priest" M/NA, M/NB [(LÚ.)MAŠ.MAŠ]; also as epith. of deity; → *wāšipum*
mašma(š)šūtu "conjuration; function, work of an incantation priest" jB, NA [MAŠ.MAŠ-] *m.*

epēšu "to perform an incantation"; of deity *DN bēl m.-ti*; < *mašmaššu*

mašna "for the second time" Ug.; < *šanû* III

mašqalillu, *mašqaliltu* "suspension"? jB; < *šuqallulu* ?

mašqaltum OA, OB **1.** "weighing out; payment" **2.** "balance, scales" **3.** "weight, pendant"; < *šaqālu*

mašqalu "weight" Am.; < W.Sem.; → *šaqālu*

mašqartum (or *maškartum*) (an agricultural implement) Mari, OB(Ešn.)

mašqītu(m) O/jB, NA **1.** "watering place", "irrigation outlet"; "drink, (medicinal) potion" **2.** (leather enema bag); < *mašqû*

mašqium → *mašqû*

mašqū → *warqum* 2

mašqû(m), OAkk *mašqium* "watering place" OAkk, O/jB; "sprinkling vessel, watering can"; < *šaqû* III

mašqûtu j/NB **1.** (a watering vessel) **2.** "potion"; < *mašqû*

mašraḫū pl. tant. ~ "good health"? OB; < *šarāḫu* I

mašraktu "votive offering" NA(Urar.); < *šarāku*

mašrītu, *mešrītu* "riches, wealth" Bogh., jB; < *mašrû*

mašru "teased" of textile, "roughened" of skin, door MA, M/jB; < *mašāru*

mašrû(m), *mešrû* "riches, wealth" [NÍG.TUKU]; also pl.; Bab. in PN; med. transf. "excrement"?; jB *bēl m.* "rich man"; *iṣ m.* "date palm"; astr. *kakkab m.* "Sirius"; < *šarû* II

maššakku → *muššakku*

maššaktu (a kind of income payment) NB

maššânu, NA *mašiānu* "tongs" M/NA; NB wooden; < *našû* II ?; → *mašānum*

maššartu(m) "deduction, withdrawal; foodstuffs set aside" Bab.; NB (a remuneration for temple officials); astr. "diminution" of lunar visibility; < *našāru* I

maššaru (a container)? jB lex.; < *našāru* I

maššatum (a metal weapon)? OAkk

maššītu(m) 'carrying (to)', "delivery" OA, M/jB [ḪI] MB "delivery" of commodities; "ingredient(s)" of drugs, in glass recipe; < *našû* II; → *maššû* I

maššītu → also *mašītu*

mašši'u(m) "rapacious, predatory" O/jB; < *mašā'u*

maššiyannu (a sash)? Ug.; < Hitt.; → *aššiyannu* ?

maššu "polished, shining" M/jB, Am.; < *mašāšu*

maššû(m) I **1.** OB (a carrying basket or board) [GI.GUR.DA (→ *gigurdû*)] **2.** jB (a suction tube) **3.** also *massû*, *mansû* (a symbol or signal) [MAS.SÙ]; < *našû* II

maššû II "forgetful" jB; < *mašû* II

maššû → also *massû*; *māšu*

maššûtu I mng. uncl. MA, MB; < *mašā'u* ?

ma(š)šûtu(m) II **1.** OB(Susa) (a royal donation document) **2.** jB "sovereign dignity"?; < *massû*

maštakal, OB *ammaštakal*, jB also *mal/rtakal* (an alkaline plant) O/jB, NA [(Ú.)IN.NU.UŠ; Ú.IN$_6$.ÚŠ/UŠ]

maštaktu (or *maštaqtu*) (a wooden object) OB lex.; → *maltaktu*

maštaku(m), *massaku*, *meštaku* "chamber; cell" Bab.(lit.) [AMA], of humans, deities

maštaku → also *maltakum*

maštaqtu ~ "constriction" jB med.; < *šatāqu*

maštaqtu → also *maštaktu*

maštītu(m), MA, M/jB also *maltītu*, NA *massītu* **1.** O/jB, MA "(allowance of) drink" **2.** NA "drinking vessel"; < *šatû* II

maštu(m) (an itching skin condition) O/jB; < *mašātu*

maštû(m), jB also *maltû* "drinking vessel; drink" O/jB; < *šatû* II

maštû → also *martû*

māštu → *mārtu*; *māšu*

maštûtu(m), M/jB *maltūtu* **1.** OB "weaving", in *bīt m.* "weaving shed" **2.** O/jB "textile"; < *šatû* III

mašṭaru, *malṭaru* **1.** M/NB, NA "inscription" **2.** MB pl. f., jB "medical prescription"; < *šaṭāru* II

mašṭû → *mešṭû*

mašû(m) I; f. *mašītu(m)* **1.** Bab. "forgotten", f. also subst. "forgotten thing(s)"; (a part of the gall bladder) **2.** jB ^{u}*mašû* (a plant name); < *mašû* II

mašû(m) II, Ass. *mašā'u(m)*, NB occas. *wašû* "to forget" **G** (*i/i*) "forget" s.th., also in PN; "forget, leave (s.th.) behind"; "forget about"; OA, OB in hendiad. "forget o.s., (do s.th.) unintentionally" **Gtn** iter. of G **D** OA, OB "allow to sink into oblivion"; jB → *wussûm* **Š** "cause, allow to forget" **N** "be forgotten, neglected"; > *mašû* I, *mašîš*; *maššû* II; *mīšu* I; *mišûtu*?; *tamšītum*; → *mīšītum*

mašû → also *māšu; mesû* II G

māšu(m), *ma(š)šû*; f. *māštu* "twin (brother/sister)" [MAŠ.TAB.BA] OAkk, Bab. of human, OAkk as PN; of deity; image; astr. (the constellation Gemini) [MUL.MAŠ.TAB.BA],

$^{\text{d/mul}}$*m.* (name of a star in the constellation Hercules ?); of objects; ^{ú}*māštu* (a plant name) [prob. Ú.MAŠ.TAB.BA]; < Sum.; > *māšiš*, *mašītu*

mâšu → *muāšu*

maš'u → "destitute, robbed" jB; < *mašā'u*

mašûtu → *maššûtu* II

mat → *mati*

mât → *me'atu*

matāḫu "to lift" M/NA **G** (*a/u*) "pick up, lift" objects for transport; "collect" person, thing; "lift, raise" eyes; *rēša m.* "lift s.o.'s head" for an office; "lift, help s.o. up"; of the new moon "ascend" **D** = G ? **N** "be lifted"; of moon, stars "ascend higher"

matallu → *madallu*

matāqu(m) "to be(come) sweet" O/jB, NA **G** (*i/i*) **D** "make sweet, sweeten"; > *matqu*, *mutqu* I, *mutqû*, *mutqītu*, *mutāqu*, *mutāqūtu*

matār → *watār*

mataru → *watrum*

matāru(m) **G** stat. only "is spotted, speckled" O/jB

matāru → also *watārum*

mate → *mati*

matēma → *matīma*

mati, *mate*, also *mat*, *immati/e* (= *ina m.*), *ammati* "when?"; *ad(i) m.*, OA, MA(Ug.) *qadu mate*, NA *adi immat(e)* "until when?", also in PN; as conj. "when" (→ GAG §174e); > *matīma*, *matimê; matmatma, matimeni*

mat(i)giqu → *kurigiqu*

matīma, *matēma*, *matime*, *immatī/ēma* "ever; always" [UD.KÚR.ŠÈ] **1.** in questions "at any time, ever"; in pos. sentences "sometime"; with neg. "never" **2.** "always" in the past **3.** "for ever" in the future; *ana m.* "for ever"; < *mati*; → *mutima*

matimatima → *matmatma*

matime → *matīma*

matimê, *immatimê* "whenever" MB(Alal.), Am., Nuzi, Bogh.; < *mati* + *-mê* II

matimeni "ever" NA, with neg. "never"; < *matīma*

mātitān "all countries" j/NB(lit.) **1.** jB loc.-adv. "in all lands" **2.** gen. subst. "of all lands"; < *mātu* I (→ GAG §61q)

matliḫšum, *matlišḫum* (a strap, belt) OA

matmatma, *matimatima*, *matummatumma* "ever and ever" OB, Mari

matnu(m) "sinew, tendon; string (of a bow)" O/jB, NA; also used as a drug ?

matqanu "stand, tripod" Nuzi, j/NB; < *taqānu*

matqu(m); f. *matuqtu* "sweet" [KU$_7$.KU$_7$] of food etc.; of skin diseases; NB in fPN *Matuqtu*; < *matāqu*

matqû (an iron object) NB

matraktu(m) (a stone hammer)? Bab. lex.; < *tarāku*

matru → *watrum*

mattu → *mādu*

mattûm → *muttû*

mātu(m) I f. "land, country" [mostly KUR (pl. KUR.KUR); OAkk, OB KALAM; OAkk, NB(roy. inscr.) also MA.DA] **1.** sg. "(own) home country, territory"; in names of countries, DNs, PNs; "flat country" in contrast to mountain; "land" in contrast to sea; "(foreign) country, territory"; "inhabitants of a country"; "area of" surface of entrails, e.g. *māt ubāni(m)* "area of 'finger'", *māt (ubān) ḫašî* "a. of lung", *māt tākaltim* "a. of stomach" **2.** pl. f. "the countries" of a region; "all countries"; > *mātitān*

mātu(m) II m. ~ "sacred precinct"? O/jB

mâtu(m), OAkk, Ass. *muātu(m)* "to die" **G** [mostly ÚŠ (NB often wr. GAM)] stat. of humans and animals "are/were dead"; "fall" in battle; "be put to death, killed, executed"; of body tissue "become gangrenous"; of tree "die"; NA stat. "is exhausted, spent"?; OA of document "become invalid" **Gtn** pl. subj. "die one after another, consecutively" **Š** "put (s.o.) to death, kill; kill (involuntarily)"; "destroy" plants, harvest; > *mītu*, *mītānû*, *mītūtu*, *mītūtiš*, *mītūtān*; *mayyitānu*; *mušmītu*; *mūtu*, *mūtānu*; *muttatu* II; *muātiš*; *ittīl-imūt*

mâtu → *me'atu*

matummatumma → *matmatma*

matuqtu → *matqu*

maturru(m) "(little) boat" O/jB [GIŠ.MÁ.TUR]; < Sum.

matušû (desig. of Marduk's boat) j/NB [GIŠ.MÁ.(U$_5$.)TUŠ.A]; < Sum.

maṭā'u → *maṭû* II

maṭiš adv. "little" jB lex.; < *maṭû* I

maṭium → *maṭû* I

maṭrû **1.** Am., jB (a handle)? **2.** NB "welt, weal"?; < *ṭerû*

maṭṭaltu "mirror image, reflection; counterpart" jB; < *naṭālu*

maṭṭalu "reeds used for kindling" jB lex.; < *naṭālu* ?

maṭṭi → *maṭû* II

maṭû(m) I, OA *maṭium* "small, little; insignificant, low-value" [LAL]; *pīam m. šakānum* "to speak humbly" (to s.o. = *ana*); < *maṭû* II

maṭû(m) II, OAkk, Ass. *maṭā'u(m)* "to be(come) little" **G** (*i/i*) [LAL] of water level "become low"; of yield, possessions etc. "become less, lessen, diminish"; "grow scarce, be in short supply"; esp. as opp. to *(w)atāru(m)*; stat. "is lacking, wanting"; *pī X maṭi* "X is humiliated"; math. "become less" (than = *ana*), *maṭi* "minus" in *X* LAL *Y* (rdg.?); "need, be in need" (of = acc.); "be defective"; of sight "fail, deteriorate"; of humans "waste away, be emaciated" **D** "reduce, curtail" [LAL], stat. "is restricted in o.'s ability" (to do s.th.); *pī X muṭṭû* "humiliate X" **Dt** "be reduced; impeded" **Š** "lessen; neglect, disregard (s.o. or s.th.)", "treat badly, insult" **Št** "suffer reduction, meet with loss"; stat. OB "is despised"; > *maṭû* I, *maṭîš*; *mīṭu*, *miṭītu*; *muṭû*, *muddû*?; *muṭṭû*; *imṭû*, *inṭatta*; *šamṭû*; *tamṭītu*

ma'u(m) **1.** OB (a bird) **2.** jB lex. (a part of the tongue)

ma''u → *mannu* I

ma'û(m) ~ "to push (s.th.) away"? **G** ? OB bolt; NA uncl. **D** **1.** ~ "throw, hurl down"? **2.** "praise"?

mā'u I ~ "ruler"? jB

mā'u II "excrement" jB lex.

mā'ū → *mû* I

mâ'u(m) "to vomit (bile)" O/jB **G** (*a/a*) **Gtn** iter. of G

mâ'u → also *muā'um*

mā'unnu "dwelling, habitation" Am.; < W.Sem.

ma''uttu; pl. *ma''utāti* "subsistence? (field)" NA; *rab m.* (official in charge of *m.*); < *mânu*; = NB *mu''untu* ?

māwū → *māmū*

mayyākum "place of copulation"? OB(Gilg.); < *niāku* ?

mayyaltu(m), *mâltum*, *ma''altu*, NA *ma''assu* "bed; stable" O/jB, NA **1.** "bed" [(GIŠ.)KI.NÁ] **2.** "litter, sedan (chair)"? [GIŠ.MAR.ŠUM] **3.** NA *ma''assu* "stable"; < *nâlu*

mayyālu(m), *ma''ālu* "bed, resting place" Bab., M/NA [(GIŠ.)KI.NÁ] euph. for "grave"; *m. muš(īt)i* "bed for the night"; *bīt m.* "bedroom"; OB om. (part of the gall bladder); *m. Ištar* (a type of grass); < *nâlu*

ma(y)yāru(m) "breaking up (of the soil)"? Bab. [APIN.ŠU.KIN] *m. maḫāṣu* "to plough (a field)"; "field ploughed with a *m.*"; j/NB "plough" (employed for this); < *nêru* ?

mayyitānu "moribund"? jB; < *mâtu*

māzaḫu → *mēzeḫu*

mazāqu "to suck" jB, NA **G** (*a/u*) **D** "suck out" **Dtt** pass. of D **Š** "let suck"; > *mizqu*; *muzīqātu*; → *namzāqu*

mazaru (a garment) Ug.; < *mazāru* ?

mazāru (to treat wool in a certain way) O/jB **G**; > *mazru*, *mizru*, *mazaru*?

mazāru → also *masārum*; *maṣāru*

mazā'u I (a leather bag)? NA

mazā'u(m) II, *mazû* "to press, squeeze" Ass., jB **G** (OA *i/i*, jB *a/u*) "press out" beer; "crush" drugs in oil **D** MA "rape" a woman **N** pass. of G "be pressed out"; > *mazû* I; *miz'u*, *mēzû*; *munzu'um*; *namzītu*

maziānu (a racecourse for horses)? MA

mazirum → *maṣirum*

mazītum → *mazû* I

maziu (a metal vessel) NA; → *manzû*

mazium → also *mazû* I

mazkûtu "clearance of an obligation" NB; < *zakû* II

mazlagum "trident, fork" OA

mazpān → *mazzizu*

mazru ~ "felted"? jB lex.; < *mazāru*

mazrūtu, *ma(z)zarūtu*, *mazruttu* **1.** Bab. "basket" (of a gardener etc.) **2.** NA "(area or state of) cultivation", esp. *ina m.* ; < *zarû* II

mazû(m) I, OA *mazium* "pressed" OAkk, OA, jB [KAŠ.ŠUR.RA] as subst. OAkk, jB; OA f. *mazītum* "excessively pressed, cheap beer"; (desig. of bread); < *mazā'u* II

mazûm II mng. unkn. OB(lit.) **G** (*u/u*) **Dt** jB ?

mazû → also *manzû*; *mazā'u* II

mâzu(m) **G** unattested **Dt** Bab. "to refuse" to do s.th.

mazūru "fuller's stick" jB lex.; < *zâru*

mazzaltu "clearing (out)" NB; < *nazālu*

mazzaltu → also *mazzaztu*

mazzālu(m) (a pouring vessel) for water, oil O/jB; < *nazālu*

mazzarūtu → *mazrūtu*

mazzassu, *mazzaštu* → *mazzaztu*

mazzattuḫlu → *manzattuḫlu*

mazzazānum, *manzazānu(m)*, *mazzuzānum*, OB(Alal.) also *mazzazzānum*, Susa *munza= zānum* "security, pledge" O/jB; < *mazzāzu*; > *mazzazānūtum*

mazzazānūtum, *manzazānūtum* "(state of being a) pledge" OB of slave; < *mazzazānum*

mazzaz pānū(t)tu → *mazziz pānuttu*

mazzaztu(m), *mazzaštu(m)*, *manzaz/štum*; M/NB *manzaltu*, pl. freq. *manzalātu*; MA *mazzaltu*, NA *man/zzassu* "position; post"; OAkk(Sum.) "office"; NB "term of office, shift" [KI.DAG ?]; *bēl m.* "office-holder"; jB astr. "position" of divine constellations; "position" at court, in the cult etc.; of cultic object; MB pl. *mazzalāt taqrubti* "battle stations"; < *mazzāzu*

mazzazu → *mazzizu*; *nanzāzu*

mazzāzu(m), *manzāzu(m)* "position" [mostly KI.GUB; also NA] "abode, location" of living being; "position; post"; med. "faeces" or "flatulence"?; astr. "position" of star, planet, constellation, "phase" of the moon; om. (an ominous constellation); ext. (mark on the lobus sinister); "socle, stand" of stele, statue etc.; jB "running board" of chariot; math. [KI.GUB(.UŠ)] uncl.; "pledge, security" mostly *mazzazānum*; < *izuzzum*

mazzazzānum → *mazzazānum*

mazziz pānū(t)tu, *man/zzaz pānū(t)tu* (→ GAG §59a) "position as a courtier" M/NA, M/NB

mazzizu, *mazzazu*, *manzazu* "standing" (earlier → *muzzazu*), in comb. M/NA, M/NB *m. pāni*, NB realized as *mazpān* (a courtier) [LÚ.GUB.BA.IGI]; NA *manzaz ēkalle* (a courtier); < *izuzzum* G ptcp.; → *mazziz pānuttu*; *nanzāzu*

mazzum → *maṣṣum*

mazzû → *manzû*

mazzuzānum → *mazzazānum*

-me → *-ma*; *-mi*

mē → *me'atu*

-mê I after voc. and pron. "hey!" jB

-mê II forms indir. interrog. pron.s, ptcl.s etc. in Am., Nuzi, Bogh., Ug. etc.; → *anummamê*; *ayyišammê*; *ayyummê*; *kīmê*; *mannummê*; *matimê*; *mīnummê*

-mê → also *-mî*

meamlu → *mamlu*

meammu → *mammu*

meānum, *mênu*, *minnu* "tiara" O/jB; < Sum.; →*mammu*

me'atu(m), *mât*, also *mē*, O/MA *mētu(m)*; pl. *me'ātu(m)*, *mâtu(m)*, Mari *mêtum* "(one) hundred" [ME] as numeral; followed by object counted or unit of measure; NB *rab mē* "centurion"; OA loc.-adv. *(ana) mētum n* "n per cent"; → *mētā*

meburku(m) "halfa grass" OAkk, jB; folk etym. < *mû* I + *burku*

mēdedu "thorn" jB lex.; < *edēdu*

mēdeḫtum ~ "spotted condition"? of gall bladder OB; < *edēḫu*

mēdelu "bolt, bar" M/NB [GIŠ.ŠU.DEŠ]; < *edēlu*

mediru → *midru* III

medû, NA *madû* ~ "to become visible" M/NB, NA **G** stat. "is known" (→ *edû* II G) **D** "look after; observe"; "take friendly notice" (of s.o.); "look up to"; NB "watch" **N** NB "become clear"

medutu (desig. of animal hides) Nuzi

megēru → *makāru* I

mēgiru → *mēkiru*

mēgûtu(m) "negligence" O/jB; < *egû* III

meḫānātu → *meḫû* I

meḫertu, *miḫirtu* **1.** M/jB "produce, income, production" **2.** M/jB "complaint against" **3.** jB *ina meḫerti-* "upstream of" **4.** MA "(woman) of equal rank"; < *maḫāru*

meḫḫu → *miḫḫu* I.II

mēḫirtu → *māḫirtu*

meḫratum OA **1.** "copy" of tablet, oath **2.** "equivalent" usu. in silver; < *maḫāru*

meḫretu(m), NA, occas. NB *meḫratu* "opposite side; front" Bab., NA [IGI- ; GAB] **1.** after prep. *ina m.* "opposite"; *ana m.* "towards the opposite side, against"; also *adi m.*, *ištu m.* **2.** without prep. "opposite" **3.** as prep. "toward(s)"; "in the presence of" **4.** "façade, frontage (of a building)"?; < *maḫāru*

meḫrītu → *meḫrû*

meḫru(m) I, *miḫru(m)*; pl. m. & f. [GABA.RI] **1.** "copy, duplicate" of tablet **2.** "answer" **3.** musical "refrain, response" [GIŠ.GI4.GÁL] **4.** "equivalent", math. "equal number"; "(person) of equal status"; of omen "counterbalance" **5.** NA "colleague", esp. *qanni m.* "among colleagues" **6.** for → *meḫretu* **7.** "weir, barrage" **8.** "presentation" (type of offering) **9.** "adversity, unfavourable incident"; < *maḫāru*; > *meḫrû*, *meḫrūtu*

meḫru II (a conifer) jB, NA

meḫrû(m) "(of) equal (rank)" OB, f. *meḫrītu* as fPN; < *meḫru* I + *-ī*

meḫrūtu, *meḫruttu* "equal rank" Am., Bogh.; < *meḫru* I

meḫsû(m), *maḫsû* (a metal cup with a lid)? O/jB; < *ḫesû*

meḫṣu(m), *miḫṣu(m)* "blow; textile" [SÌG] **1.** "blow, strike"; "attack" of demon **2.** Nuzi "welt, weal" **3.** "thrust, impact" of tool, weapon **4.** "prick, sting, bite" of animal, plant **5.** "doorpost"? **6.** (type of engraved gem)? **7.** "(woven) fabric, textile" [TÚG.SÌG]; < *maḫāṣu*

meḫû(m) I; occas. Aram. pl. *meḫānātu* "storm" Bab. *ša m.* said of Adad; *tīb(ût) m.* "onset of a storm"; transf. of battle etc.

meḫûm II "evening (offering)" OAkk, OB(Elam); → *tamḫû*

mēkeku (a wooden scraper) jB lex.; < *ekēku*

mekēlu mng. unkn. jB, NA?, NB? **G**; **D**
mekēru → *makāru* I
mēkiru, *mēgiru* "irrigator" jB lex.; < *makāru* I
mekku, *mikku* (type of glass) Ug., NA
mekkû(m), *mikkû(m)* O/jB **1.** (a reed sieve) **2.** "drumstick" or "stick (for a hoop)" **3.** (part of animal's harness) lex. **4.** (type of tool) lex.
mekû(m) I (or *mēkû(m)*?) ~ "instruction"? OAkk, jB
mekû II, *mikû* (a bitter plant) jB
mekû III (a type of song) jB lex.
mekû IV (a siege instrument) Bab. lex.
mekû(m) V, *makû* "to neglect" O/jB, Mari, Am. **G** (*i/i*) "neglect" s.th.; "be negligent" (towards = *ana*) **Dt** = G ? **Št 1.** ~ "pacify"? a country **2.** of part of the lung, mng. unkn.; > *mēkûm*; *mikītu* I; *temkûm*
mēkûm, *mākiu* "inactive, idle man" OB, NA; < *mekû* V
mēkû → also *mekû* I
mēkûtu(m) "want, lack, shortage" jB; < *ekû* II
melammu → *melemmu*
melammû (a shining garment) jB; < *melemmu*
mēlelu "play" jB; < *mēlulu*
melemmu(m), also *malemmū*, M/NB *melammu*, mostly pl. "fearsome radiance, aura" Bab.(lit.) [ME.LÁM] of deity, demon; *m. našû(m)* "to wear *m.*"; of king *m. šarrūtim* "royal radiance"; of temple; of planet Saturn; of person "glow of health, healthy glow"; < Sum.; > *melammû*
mēleṣu(m) ~ "excitement, exhilaration"? O/jB; < *elēṣu*
melēštu, *melīštu*, *mēseltu* (part of the tongue)? jB lex.; < *lâšu* II
mēlītu, *mēlittu* "step, stairway" Mari, jB; < *elû* III
melqētu(m), Ass. *malqētu* (a tax or perquisite)? O/jB, MA [ŠU.TI.A]; < *leqû* II
melṭītu → *mešṭītu*
melṭû → *mešṭû*
mēlû(m) "height, altitude" Bab. [SUKUD] **1.** "(measured) height" of door etc. **2.** "ascent, way up"; "step" of staircase, ladder **3.** "high place, hill"; < *elû* III
mêlu "poultice (hung round neck)" jB, NA; < *e'ēlu* ?
meluḫḫû "of Meluḫḫa (type)" jB lex.; < PlN
mēlulāyu "playful" jB lex.; < *mēlulu* + *-āy* (→ GAG §56p)
mēlultu(m) "game, play" O/jB, Nuzi; of cultic games, sport; transf. of battle; < *mēlulu*
mēlulu(m) "to play" (with = acc.) O/jB, NA (pret. *immelil*, Ass. *immalil*, pl. *immel(i)lū*; imper. *melil*; ptcp. *mummellum*) irreg. vb.; > *mēlelu*, *mēlultu*, *mēlulû*, *mēlulāyu*, *mummellu*

mēlulû "player, actor" jB; < *mēlulu*
memēni, also *mimīlēnu*, *menimeni* "somebody, who(so)ever" NA for → *mamman*; with neg. "nobody"; more rarely for *mimma* "something, any(thing)"; with neg. "nothing"
memītu, *memētu* jB lex. **1.** (term for a girl) **2.** (a plant)
mendiu (a musical instrument) jB lex.; < Sum.?
mēneštu "weakness, famine" jB; < *mēnešu*
mēnešu ~ "weakness" NA; < *enēšu*; > *mēneštu*, *mēnešūtu*
mēnešūtu "(condition of) weakness" M/jB; < *mēnešu*
menimeni → *memēni*
mensû → *massû*
menû(m), *manû(m)*, OAkk *manā'um* "to love" OAkk, O/jB **G** (*i/i*) OAkk in PN **D** lex. "flatter"?; > *mēnum*?; *minûtum* II; *mumannûm*
mēnum "love"? OAkk subst. in PN; < *menû* ?
mênu → *meānum*
menuniānum (a type of textile) OA
mēqiqānu → *miqqānu*
mēqītu "eye paint" Am., Bogh.; < *eqû*
meqiu → *makkû*
meqqû → *maqqû*
mēqûm "cosmetics" OB; < *eqû*
mērānu → *mīrānu* I
mērânu → *mērênu*
mērânû → *mērênû*
mēraštum → *mēreštu* I
mērašu → *mērešu* I
mer'atum → *mārtu*
merdītu, *merdētu*, *mardītu* j/NB **1.** lex. *m. ḫurri* mng. unkn. **2.** NB (a cultic ceremony or procession) **3.** lex. (a stepladder) [GIŠ.MAḪ]; < *redû* I
mēreḫtu "aggressiveness, insolence" j/NB; NB in PN; < *erēḫu*
mēreltu → *mēreštu* II
mērênu(m), *mērânu* "nakedness" O/jB; of country "barrenness"; esp. loc.-adv. with pron. suff. *mērênuššu* "in naked, wasted state" O/jB; < *erû* III
mērênû, *mērânû* "naked" jB; < *mērênu* + *-ī*
mereššû "naked" jB; < *eriššī-* and *mērênu* (mixed form)
mēreštu(m) I, OA *mēraštum* "planting, cultivation" OA, O/jB [APIN-] OA "sowing time"; OB *eqlum m.* "arable land, farmland"; < *mērešu* I
mēreštu II, *mēreltu* "wish, need" M/NB "daily needs, requisites, necessaries"; "consignment" of silver or commodities; NB in col. *ina mērešti* "with intent, deliberately"; < *erēšu* II

mērešu(m) I, Ass. *mērašu* "cultivated land" Bab., M/NA "(year of) cultivation" opp. to fallow; *bīt m.* "cultivated land"; < *erēšu* I

mērešu II "wisdom" jB; < *eršu* I

mērešu III "desire" MB; < *erēšu* II

mer'etum → *mārtu*

merginānu, *me/irgirānu*, jB(Ass.) *margirānu* (a medicinal plant) M/jB; → *merzīnu*

merḫum I (an official, phps.) "judge" OAkk, OB; OAkk in PN; > *merḫūtum*

merḫu(m) II, *mirḫum* "ergot, stye (in the eye)" O/jB; < *marāḫu*

merḫu III mng. unkn. MB

merḫūtum "office of the *merḫum*" Mari; < *merḫum* I

merītu(m), *mirītu(m)*, *mer'ītu* "pasture" O/jB; < *re'û*

mērītu(m), *mīrītu(m)* "musical instrument from Mari" OAkk, O/jB; OAkk, OB in Sum. texts; < PlN; → *mārītu*

mer'ītu → *merītu*

mermeri mng. unkn. Ug.

merqu → *mirqu*

merrītum mng. unkn. OB

merrū jB **1.** lex. "wind" **2.** (a type of song); < Sum.

merrû (a plant) jB lex.; var. of → *errû* ?

mersu(m), *mirsu(m)* (a cake) ingredients: dates, sesame, oil etc. [NINDA.Ì.DÉ.A/ÀM]; OB fPN *Mersīya* "Little cake, 'Sweetie pie'"; < *marāsu*

mertu → *martu*

mertû → *martû*

mērtu → *mārtu*

merṭu "scrapings"? jB; < *marāṭu*

meru "hundred" OB(Susa)

mēru → *māru*; *mīru* I

mērû "pregnancy" jB; < *arû* IV

mer'um → *māru*

mer'uttum → *mārūtu*

meruwātum → *mārtu*

merzīnu (a medicinal plant) jB; → *merginānu*

mēsallu(m), jB usu. *emesallu* (desig. of salt) O/jB; < Sum.; → *ummisallu*

mēseḫtu "allocation (document)" jB lex.; < *esēḫu*

mēseltu → *melēštu*

meserru → *misarrum*

mēsertu "confinement, siege" jB; < *esēru* II

mēseru(m) "confinement; enclosure" O/jB; OB "imprisonment"; *bīt m.* (ritual enclosure); "(feeling of) isolation"; < *esēru* II

mesītu(m) **1.** OB(Susa) 'purification', "clearing" of claims **2.** jB "water for washing"; < *mesû* II

meskannu → *musukkannu*

meskertum "barrage, dam"? OB; < *sekēru* I

messam → *misissam*

messētu "distance" O/jB lex.; < *nesû* II

messû (a trap)? jB lex.

messûtu "identification" MB; → *wussûm*

mesû(m) I, Ass. *mas'um*, *masiu(m)*, *masû* "washed, clean, pure" [LUḪ] of object, substance; OB fPN *Mesītum*?; of metal, mineral "refined, purified"; OB(Susa) leg. "cleared"; < *mesû* II

mesû(m) II, Alal., Ug. also *ma/ešû*, Ass. *masā'u(m)* "to wash, clean(se), purify" **G** (*i/i*) [LUḪ] "wash"; "wipe away" tears, blood; "refine" metal, mineral; OB(Susa) "clear" of claim **Gtn** iter. of G [LUḪ.MEŠ] **D** "purify, cleanse" → *wussûm* **Dt** pass. of D "wash o.s." **ŠD** "wipe away" **N** of crime "be washed away"; > *mesû* I; *mesītu*; *mīsu* I; *musâtu*; *masâtu*, *massūtu*, *massu'um*; *nemsû*, *nemsētu*; *tamsûtu*?

mēsu(m), *mēšu* (a type of tree) O/jB [GIŠ.MES (→ *musukkannu*)]; → *mēšu*; *mišena*

mēsu → also *mīsu* I

mēsū, *māsū* pl. tant. "cult, rites" M/NB; → *mīsu* I

mêsu, *mêšu* MA, j/NB **G** of god "to hurl down" human; "crush" stone, plant; "destroy" **N** pass. of G

mêsu → also *mêšu*

mesukkannu → *musukkannu*

mesukku **1.** jB, NA (a bird, phps.) "falcon" **2.** MB (pl. f. *mesukkēti*), Am. (bird-shaped jewellery)

meṣḫarūtu → *meṣḫerūtu*

meṣḫēriš "during childhood" O/jB; < *ṣeḫēru*

meṣḫerūtu, *meṣḫarūtu* "childhood, youth" j/NB; < *ṣeḫēru*

meṣirānu (desig. of horse) NA

meṣirtum in *ša m.* (an occupation) OB lex.

mēṣiru "drawing"? NA; < *eṣēru*

meṣiuri (a plant) jB lex.

mēṣu → *wīṣum*

mêš "where?" jB; → *êš*; *īš*

mēšariš → *mīšariš*

mēšaru → *mīšaru*

mēšarūtu → *mīšarūtu*

mešdariš → *masdara*

mešdugudû → *meštegudû*

mešeddu → *mašaddu*; *mešētu*

mešedi → *mešētu*

mešēltu(m), *mu/ašēltu*, OA *mašāltum*; pl. *mešēlētu* "whetstone" O/jB [NA4.BAR.DÙ.E ?]; < *šêlu*

mešēlu → *mašālu*; *mušālu*

mešēnu(m), OAkk *maš'anum*, OA *maš'enum* "sandal, shoe" OAkk, Bab., OA; < *šênu*; → *mišena*

mešēqu(m) "strickle" O/jB for levelling grain in measuring-vessel; OB *šīq m. kabrim/raqqim/bīrūyim* "heavy/light/medium level measure"; < *šêqu*

mēšeriš → *mīšariš*

mēšeru → *mīšaru*

mēšeštu → *mīšertu*

mešētu(m), *mēšītu(m)* ~ "opening, passageway in a wall"? OA, OB, Bogh., Ug. **1.** OB, Susa math. mng. unkn. in surface calculations **2.** OA (a narrow storeroom) **3.** Hitt., Ug. in LÚ *mešēdi, mešetti* (an official, phps. orig. in charge of a storeroom ?); *rab m.* (overseer of the *m.*)

mešgûm "rabies" Mari; < *šegû* II

mešḫa(t)tu → *mišiḫtu*

mēšītu → *mešētu*

meškalallû (a table) lex.; < Sum.

meškalû (a type of door) jB lex.

meški (a type of door) jB lex.

mešlu → *mišlu*

mešlûm → *mašlû*

mešrêtu pl. tant. "limbs" M/NB [Á.ÚR]; < *šarû* II

mešrītu → *mašrītu*

mešrû → *mašrû*

meštaku → *maštaku*

meštegudû, *meštegurrû*, *mešt/dugudû* (a heavy table) jB lex.; < Sum.

mešṭītu, *me/alṭītu* ~ "assignment, ration" j/NB; < *šeṭû* II; → *mešṭû* 3

mešṭû(m), *melṭû*, *mišṭû*, *maš/lṭû* Bab. **1.** "drying (process); dried state", *šīr m.* "dried meat"; *nūn(ē) m.* "dried fish" **2.** jB "bedstead"? **3.** NB = *mešṭītu*; < *šeṭû* II

mešû → *mesû* II

mēšu (a club of *mēsu* wood)? jB

mēšu → also *mēsu; mīšu*

mêšu(m), *mêsu* "to disregard, scorn" Bab. **G** (pret. *imēš*, *imīš*, *im'eš*) "neglect" deity, human; "fail" in o.'s duty **Gtn** iter. of G **D** = G **N** "be neglected"; > *temēšu*

mêšu → also *mêsu*

mešurru (a topog. term) NA

mētā "a hundred times" OA; → *me'atu*

mētaqtu → *mēteqtu*

mētaqu → *mētequ*

mētellu "lordship, power" jB; < *etellu*; → *mēzezu*

mētellūtu(m) "rulership, power of a ruler" O/jB; < *etellu*

mēteqtu, NA *mētaqtu* "march-past, advance" MB, NA; < *etēqu*

mētequ(m), NA *mētaqu* "route, passage" O/jB, NA of troops, vehicles; < *etēqu*

mētu → *me'atu*; *mītu*

mêtum → *me'atu*

meṭēnu(m) ~ "flour bin" OAkk(Sum.), O/jB; < *ṭênu*

meṭlūtu "manhood" M/jB; < *eṭlu*

mēṭu (a divine garment in the cult) NB

mēṭu → also *miṭṭu*

me'um (a bird) OB

mēzeḫu, *mē/āzaḫu* "sash" j/NB, for divine statues, priests; < *ezēḫu*

mēzezu ~ "wrath, fury" M/jB; < *ezēzu*; → *mētellu*

mēzû "beer brewer" Bab. lex.; < *mazā'u* II

mezura, *misuru* (material of armour) Nuzi; → *mizru*

-mi, *-me* suff. in citation of dir. speech (→ GAG §123c)

-mî, *-mê* ptcl. in interrog. clauses

miādu → *mâdu*

miammu → *mimmû*

middatu(m), *mindatu(m)*, *maddatu* "measure" of volume, length, area, time Bab., NA *qan m.* "measuring reed"; *m. ša ammati ša erî* (a bronze measure of 1 cubit); "dimension, measure" of body, limb; < *madādu* I

midde → *minde*

midduḫ/'ru → *minduḫru*

midinu → *mindinu*

midirtu; pl. *midrāti* "garden plot" jB; < *midru* I

midlu "process of salting; salt meat" Bab. lex., NA; < *madālu*

midru(m) I (a type of land) OA, Ug., jB; > *midirtu*

midru II (a disease)? jB; < *madāru* II ?

midru III, *mediru* (a type of bread) M/NA

migīrtu → *magīrtum*

migru(m) "consent, approval, agreement" OB *ina m.*, jB *ana m.* "voluntarily"; MA *lā migir* "against o.'s will"; j/NB *ina migir libbi* "gladly"; OA pl. f. *ina migrāti* "on (s.o.'s own) accord, initiative"; OB in PN; "who is favoured by, favourite of" a deity etc. OAkk, OB in PN; of king; < *magāru*

miḫḫu(m) I, *meḫḫu(m)*, *miḫḫatu* (a type of beer) used for libations O/jB, NA; < *maḫāḫu*

miḫḫu II, *meḫḫu* mng. unkn. jB

miḫḫūru(m) "offering" OAkk(Sum.), OB, NB; < *maḫāru* D (→ GAG §55o) *miḫiltu* → *miḫiṣtu*

miḫirtu → *meḫertu*

miḫiṣtu, *miḫiš/ltu*; pl. *miḫṣātu*, NB also *miḫilētu* "strike" M/NB **1.** "blow; wound"; jB river name ^{íd}*Miḫṣat-Era*; (an abrasion on the gall bladder) **2.** "(cuneiform) wedge; sign" [GÙ/GU.SUM]; < *maḫāṣu*

miḫru → *meḫru* I

miḫṣu → *meḫṣu*

mikdu mng. unkn. jB lex.

mikiltu "percentage due on produce"? MB; < *makāsu* ?

mikītu I "neglect, absence"? j/NB; < *mekû* V

mikītu(m) II (or *miqītu(m)*) mng. unkn. OB, Am.

mikku → *mekku*

mikkû → *mekkû*

miklu mng. unkn. NA

mikru(m) I "irrigation; irrigated land" O/jB; < *makāru* I

mikru II (or *miqru*) "(horse's) girth-strap"? Nuzi, jB

miksu(m); pl. f. & m. "tax (on produce)" Bab., M/NA [NÍG.KUD.DA] **1.** OB "due" payable by tenant **2.** "duty, tax"; MB *bīt m.* "tax depot"; M/NA "customs duty"; *m. kāre nēbere* "quay and ferry dues"; NB (shipping dues), $^{(lú)}$*rab m.* "tax collector, inspector"; < *makāsu*

mikûm ~ "seductive (feminine) charm(s)" OB of Ištar

mila, *mili* "times" Am. in *7 u 7 m.*; < W.Sem.

mildu → *wildum*

milḫu "extraction, tearing out" NA; < *malāḫu* IV

milḫu → also *mil'u*

mili → *mila*

miliḫtu "(cattle) theft"? jB; < *milḫu*

miliktum "advice" OB(lit.); < *malāku* II

milītu "corpulence" OB; < *malû* IV

milku(m); pl. f. "advice, counsel; resolution, intelligence" [GALGA] "advice" given by deity, in PN; NB *ina zêri lā m.* "with unconsidered hate"; of person, king "reason"; "council", jB *bīt m.* "council hall"; "plan, decision"; < *malāku* II

millatum "looting, pillage" OB om.; < *malālu* I

millu mng. unkn. jB

miltu mng. unkn. jB lex.; < *malātu*

mīlu(m), NA *mil'u*; pl. *mīlū*, NA *mil'āni* Bab., NA **1.** "high water, flood(ing)" [ILLU; A.ZI.GA; A.MAḪ] *mīl kiššati* "maximum level of high water"; transf. *m. bēri* "mile-high flood" of speech **2.** "fullness" *m. irti(m)* 'fullness of the chest' = "success"; OB *ina mīl libbi* "lightheartedly"?; < *malû* IV; > *mīlūtum*

mil'u, *milḫu* f. "saltpetre" M/jB, NA [(NA_4.)AN.NE]

mil'u → also *mīlu*

mīlūtum in *mê mīlūti* "flood waters" OB math.; < *mīlu*

mimē/īnu → *memēni*

mimma, Am., Nuzi, NB also *mimmu/i* and sim. "anything, something; everything, all" [NÍG.NAM] **1.** "something"; *m.* + subst. "any"; *m. lā*, *m. ul* "nothing; not at all"; adv. *m. lā m.* "somehow" **2.** "every(thing), total(ly), all" rarely of persons; *m. annîm* "all this"; *m. ša* "all that" **3.** as rel. pron. "all that"; *m. šumšu* "anything", *m. š. ul(a)*, *lā* "nothing at all" **4.** Nuzi, Am., Ug. *mimmu/i/a šum/nšu* often with second pron. suff. "all that belongs to"; < *mīn(u)* I + *-ma*; > *mimmû*; NA → *memēni*

mimmāmu/a/i "everything, all" O/jB(lit.); < *mimma*

mimmi → *mimma*

mimmu → *mimma*; *mimmû*

mimmû, Am. also *miammu*, partly declined **1.** before gen. or pron. suff. "all, anything (of)" possessions; "all things", OAkk in PN; OA "anything of/from" **2.** rarely absol. "all, everything"; *m. mala* "all that" **3.** as rel. pron. "all that"; "whatever"; < *mimma* (→ GAG §48f)

-min ptcl. indicating unreality OA, esp. in condit. and final clauses; *šumma-min* "if it were that ..." (→ GAG §§152d, 162a); O/jB → *-man*

mīnam → *mīnu* I

minānu ~ "reckoned"? jB; < *manû* IV ?

minâtu → *minītu*

mindatu → *middatu*

minde, *midde*, also *manda* "perhaps" Bab., Am., Bogh.; OB etc. in PN; < *mīn īde* "what do I know?"; Mari etc. → *wuddi*

mindinu(m), *midinu(m)* and sim. (a wild cat, phps.) "tiger" or "cheetah" O/jB [UR.$ŠUB_5$(=NÚMUN)]

mindu I (a plant) jB lex.

mindu II "measured amount, ration" NB; *bēl m.* "quartermaster"?; < *madādu* I

mindu → also *mundu*

minduḫru, *midduḫ/'ru* "residue, sediment"? MA, jB ?

miniḫû mng. unkn. jB lex.

minītu(m); pl. OB *mi/aniātum*, Mari *minêtum*, later *minâtu* "measure, dimension" Bab., NA [ŠID] **1.** sg. jB "reckoning"; NB astr. "measurable part" **2.** pl. "(normal) dimensions"; *eli m.* "beyond measure"; *ana m.* "in relation to, according to"; NB *ṭupšar minâti* "architect"?; "(period of) time, moment" **3.** pl. "limbs, physique" [UB.NIGIN/NÍGIN.NA]; < *manû* IV

minnu → *meānum*; *mīnu* II

minsu, *minsi* "why?" M/NB(lit.); NB in PN; < *mīn(u)* I + *-šu(m)*; → *miššum*

mīnšu → *mīnu* I; *miššum*

minu "who?" Am.; < W.Sem.

minû (a pustule)? jB lex.

mīnu(m) I, Bab. mostly *mīnû(m)* "what?" [math. EN.NAM; M/NB also EN(.NA)] OAkk, OB, MA, Nuzi, NB in PN; with *ina*, OB *immīnim*, MB *ina m.* "with what?", jB *immīnê* "how, by what means?"; *ana m.* (MA *ana'īni*), *aššum m.* and sim., OB also *mīnam* "why?"; with pron. suff.; *mīnum ša* "what is it that?"; NA, NB before rel. clause *m. ša*, NB also *m. kī* "whatever; all that"; > *minsu*, *miššum*; *mīnummê*; *mimma*, *mimmû*, *mimmāmu*; *minde*; *mūnu* I; → *ammīni*; *māmīnu*; *miššam*

mīnu(m) II, NA also *minnu* "number" Bab., NA; *(ana/ina/ša) lā m.* "without number, countless"; NB "payment (by instalments)"?; < *manû* IV; → *almīn*

mīnû → *mīnu* I

mīnummê "all (of), each (of)" MB(Alal.), Am., Nuzi, Bogh., Ug. occas. for → *mimma*; *m. ša* "all that"; Bogh. "whatever; everything that"; < *mīnu* I + *-mê* II; → *mannummê*

minûtu(m) I Bab., M/NA [ŠITI(.MA)] **1.** "count(ing); number" **2.** math. "calculation" **3.** astr. "calculated time", esp. *lā m.* of unexpected appearance **4.** jB *m. nikkassi* "settlement (of accounts)" **5.** "recitation" of incantation **6.** "form, physique"; < *manû* IV; → *manûtu*

minûtum II "desire, love" OB lex.; < *menû*

minzer, *minzaḫar* (a term for a horse) MB; < Kass.

minzû mng. unkn. MB

mipāru → *gipāru*

miqittu(m) "(down)fall" [RI.RI.GA; ŠUB] "collapse" of building; "strike (of lightning)"; "attack (of disease)"; "fallen (soldier), corpse"; "deaths of livestock, epidemic (among animals)"; "dead animal; carcass"; < *miqtu*

miqītu → *mikītu* II

miqqānu, *mēqiqānu* (an insect, phps.) "moth" jB

miqqu "hole, cavity" jB lex.

miqru → *mikru* II

miqtu(m); pl. *miqtū* "fall" [ŠUB]; "collapse" of wall; OB, NA (pl. *miqtāni*) "driftwood", "(plant) detritus" on river; "fall" of meteor, star, OB *miqit parzillim* "fallen piece of (meteoric) iron"; "incidence" of fire, Gira, rit. *miqit mê u išāti* "onset of water and fire"; OA *miqit niggallim* 'falling of the sickles' i.e. "(start of) harvest"; jB "dry rot" on wall; OA "what fell to (s.o.)", i.e. money, profit; *miqit pî(m)* 'what fell from the mouth' = "impudence, effrontery", *m. pî rašû* "to become impudent"; *m. ṭēmi* "despair; loss of reason"; in desig. of diseases "failure"? of part of the liver; *m. errī*, *m. libbi* (intestinal diseases), *m.* or *miqit šamê* 'fallen from the sky', phps. "falling sickness, epilepsy"? [AN.TA.ŠUB.BA; → *antašubbû*]; name of demon *Miqit*; < *maqātu*

mīrānu(m) I, *mērānu(m)*, later also *mūrānu* "young dog, puppy" OAkk, Bab. [UR.TUR(.RA)]; "cub" of lion or hyaena; Nuzi transf. in PN; < *mūru*

mīrānu II (a plant) jB lex.

mirgirānu → *merginānu*

mirgu (an alliaceous plant, phps.) "leek" j/NB

mirḫum → *merḫu* II

miriqtu(m) I; pl. *mirqētu* "damaged part" of building O/jB; < *marāqu*

miriqtum II (a container) OB

mirītu → *mērītu*

mirqu, *merqu* **1.** MB (a type of flour) **2.** jB/NA (a fine glass); < *marāqu*

mirsu → *mersu*

mirtum (an agricultural tool) OB

mīrtum "breeding cow" OB; < *mīru* I

mīru(m) I, *mēru* "breeding bull" O/jB; OB in Sum. texts only; of deity; OB(Susa) "breeding ram?"; > *mīrtum*

mīru II "fattening (process)" j/NB; < *marû* II

mīru III, *mūru(m)* (part of the intestines) O/jB

mīru IV mng. unkn. jB lex.

mirûtu in *ana mirûti* "for viewing, to see" (the king) Am.; < W.Sem.?

misarrum, *mi/eserru(m)*, also *musarrum*; pl. m. & f. "belt" [KUŠ.E.ÍB]; also "(metal) band" decorating doors

misissam, *messam* "sheep's stomach" Bogh., jB lex.

misissānu (a plant) jB lex.; < *misissu*

misissu, *mišissu*, MB *missam* in *m. tâmti* "meerschaum, sepiolite" M/jB

missam → *misissu*

missātu mng. unkn. jB lex.

mīsu(m) I, *mēsu* "washing; purification; (a type of refined metal)" O/jB [LUḪ] *kasap m.*

"refined silver"; *mīs qātē* "(ritual) hand-washing"; *mīs pî* "mouth-washing" [KA.LUḪ.ḪU/Ù.DA] of sacrificial animal; of human; of divine statue; < *mesû* II; → *mēsū*

mīsum II (a kind of fish) OB

misuru → *mezura*

miṣaru, miṣirru → *miṣru*

miṣītum "equivalent" OB; < *maṣû*

miṣratu → *iṣratu*

miṣru(m), *miṣirru, miṣaru*; pl. m. & f. Bab., M/NA **1.** "border, boundary"; NB *bēl m.* "(adjoining) neighbour"; "boundary mark"; "band, dividing line" on figurine etc.; jB pl. f. "limit" of time (→ *maṣāru* D) **2.** "territory, region"; *ana m. māti turru* "to reconquer" **3.** M/NA (an ornament); > *maṣāru* ?

miṣrû → *muṣrû*

mīṣu → *wīṣum*

mīṣūtamma ~ "as a small company"? Am.; < *wīṣum*

mišaḫu → *mišḫu* I.II

mišariš → *išariš*

mīšariš, *mī/ēša/eriš* "in justice, justly" M/jB; < *mīšaru*

mīšarru → *mīšaru*

mīšartu(m) "justice" OAkk, jB; OAkk as PN; < *mīšaru* ?

mišaru NB for → *išaru* I

mīšaru(m), also *mēša/eru(m), mīšarru(m)* "justice" [NÍG.SI.SÁ] **1.** of deity, esp. Šamaš; as DN **2.** *m. šakānu(m)* "to establish just order, bring about justice"; OB (royal decree promulgating justice) **3.** OB(Alal.) *araḫ m.* (a month) **4.** OB (a part of the body)?; < *ešēru*; → *mīšartu*

mīšarūtu in *m. alāku* "to obtain justice" jB [NÍG.SI.SÁ-]; < *mīšaru*

mišdu(m) **1.** OB (part of a doorpost) **2.** jB rit. "massage"; < *mašādu*

mišertu(m), *miširtum*, NB *me/išeštu* (a small net) Bab. lex.; < *mašāru* ?

mišertu → also *miširtu*

mīšertu(m), *mīširtu(m)* **1.** O/jB lex. "standard *qû*-measure, vessel (holding 1 sila)" **2.** OB (regular festival contribution of flour); < *ešēru*

miševtu → *mišertu*

miše'tu(m) "forcible removal; pillage" Ass., M/jB; < *mašā'u*

mišḫa(t)tu → *mišiḫtu*

mišḫu I, *mišaḫu* "measured area" for building assignment NB; < *mašāḫu* I

mišḫu II, *mišaḫu* "flash, illumination" jB; ~ "train" of meteor, star; "glitter" of fabric; "glow" of person; < *mašāḫu* II

mišḫu III mng. unkn. jB rit.

mišiḫtu, *mi/ešḫa(t)tu*; pl. *mišḫātu* "measurement; dimension" j/NB "size, length" of building; "distance"; NB "measured (plot)" of land; < *mašāḫu* I

miširtu(m), *mišertu(m)* "produce (of the sea and rivers)" O/jB

miširtum → also *mišertu*

mīširtu → *mīšertu*

mišissu → *misissu*

mišittu "(medical) stroke" j/NB "apoplectic stroke; coronary"; of parts of the body "paralysis (caused by a stroke)"; *m. rābiṣi* (stroke caused by the *r.* demon); < *mašādu*

mišītu "oblivion" jB; < *mašû* II

mišītum "confusion" OB; < *ešû* IV

mišla adv. "in half" OA; < *mišlu*

mišlānū pl. tant. **1.** "half (shares)" of profit O/jB [ŠU.RI.A; also IGI.2.GÁL.LA.A?] **2.** (a drainage tile) lex.; < *mišlu*

mišlu(m), *mešlu*; pl. m. & f. "half; middle, centre" [BAR]; OB loc.-adv. *mišlum* "half"; NA pl. f. *ina mešlāti ša MN* "in mid-MN"; < *mašālu*; > *mišla, mišlānū*

mišmunnu "sealed bulla" Nuzi; < Hurr.

mišqu (a drinking vessel)? Ug.; < Ug.

miššam "where to?"? jB lex.; → *ayyiša*; *mīnu* I

miššum, *mīnšum* "why?" OAkk, OA; OB lex.; OAkk in PN; < *mīnu* I; → *ammīni*; *minsu* (→ GAG §67g)

miššu → also *mīnu* I

miššulatam mng. unkn. Mari

miššulu mng. unkn. jB lex.; < *mašālu* Gt ?

mištannu "head money, reward (for capture)" MB(Alal.); < Indo-Iran.?

mištû → *meštû*

mišu "army, troops" Am.; < Eg.

mīšu I, *mēšu* **1.** MB "oblivion" **2.** NB (joint of meat)?; < *mašû* II

mīšu II "night" Am.; → *mūšu*

mišuḫḫu (a dye)? Nuzi, for textiles; < Hurr.

mišurum I (an object in a temple)? OA

mišurum II (an official)? Nuzi

mišûtu mng. unkn. jB lex.; < *mašû* II ?

mitaḫṣūtu → *mitḫuṣūtu*

mītānû "deceased" NB; < *mītu* + *-ān* + *-ī*

miteku (a weapon)? jB lex.

mitgāru "favourable, propitious" j/NB [ŠE.GA]; < *magāru* Gt

mitgurtu(m) "agreement, mutual understanding" Bab. [ŠE.ŠE.GA; MUNUS.ŠE] *lā m.* "discord; disobedience"; < *magāru* Gt

mitguru(m) **1.** OB "(previously) agreed"? **2.** Bogh., jB "harmonious"; < *magāru* Gt

mitḫāriš "in the same manner" O/jB [TÉŠ.BI] to take, distribute, pay "in equal shares"; "simultaneously"; "similarly"; "altogether, totally"; < *mitḫāru*

mitḫartu(m) **1.** OB math. "(side of a) square" [ÍB.SÁ; LAGAB?] **2.** O/jB "totality", "mankind"; *mitḫarta* "altogether"; < *mitḫāru*

mitḫāru(m) "corresponding (to one another); like (one another)" [LAGAB]; "symmetric(al), proportionate, of the same size" [TÉŠ.BI.MEŠ]; of fever "equally high"; "uniform, homogeneous, even"; "of equal rank, equivocal"; "square"; of features "regular", OAkk also in PN; "proportionate to"; M/NA *ana mitḫār* st. abs. "equally, one-to-one"; of periods of time "(of) equal (length)"; *lā m.* "diverse, of uneven quality" [NU.TÉŠ.A]; < *maḫāru*

mitḫa(ṣ)ṣūtu → *mitḫuṣūtu*

mitḫummu → *mutḫummu*

mitḫurtu "convergence, coincidence; harmony" j/NB astr. "conjunction, opposition" of celestial bodies; "joining of waters"; *lišān m.* "harmony of languages", DN *sāniq(u) m.* "who controls the *m.*" of languages, of Nabû, Ninurta, Nergal; "(harmonious) mankind"?; < *maḫāru*

mitḫuṣu "fight, combat" M/jB, NA; also ref. to hunting; < *maḫāṣu* Gt

mitḫuṣūtu, NA also *mitḫa(ṣ)ṣūtu*, *mitaḫṣūtu* "battle" jB/NA; with *sedēru* "to line up (troops) for combat"; with *epēšu* "to fight, wage war"; < *mitḫuṣu*

mitinnu → *mītu*

Mitirunnu (a month) Nuzi; < Hurr.

mitluktu "advice, deliberation" j/NB; < *malāku* II

mitluku "circumspect, prudent" j/NB; < *malāku* II

mitru I "strong, powerful" jB, of opponent

mitru II **1.** jB lex. (a reed)? **2.** Nuzi (a tree)?

mitrû (a garment)? MB; < *mudrû* or Ug.?

mītu(m), Ass. *mētu(m)*, Nuzi once *mitinnu* "dead" [ÚŠ, NB often wr. GAM; BA.ÚŠ] transf. of the (politically) powerless, of city or country; "dead person; dead animal"; "apparition of dead person"; OA "insolvent"; Emar pl. (as if subst.) *mītū*, of ancestors; < *mâtu*; > *mītānû*, *mītūtu*, *mītūtiš*, *mītūtān*

mītūtān "the dead (gener.)" NB; < *mītu*; → *kullatān*

mītūtiš "like death" jB in *ikšuddū* (= *kašādu* G) *mītūtiš* "they became (still) as death"; < *mītūtu*

mītūtu(m) "(state of) death" Bab., NA; "(form of) death" in *m. qātēšu/ramannišu* "suicide"; < *mītu*; > *mītūtiš*

miṭētu → *miṭītu*

miṭirtu, also *miṭru*, jB also *miṭratu* "watercourse, canal; a type of irrigation" M/jB

miṭītu(m), *miṭētu(m)*, Nuzi also *miṭūtu* "decrease, reduction" Bab., M/NA; "reduced yield, shortfall"; "shortage; loss" of troops, animals, materials; "under-performance" of work; OB "flaking, peeling off" of colour, coating; NB *miṭītī* "my humble self"; < *maṭû* II

miṭratu → *miṭirtu*

miṭru → *miṭirtu*

miṭṭu(m), *mīl/ēṭu* (a divine weapon) OAkk, O/jB, NA [GIŠ.TUKUL.DINGIR] OAkk, OB in Sum. texts; also as cultic object

mīṭu(m) **1.** O/jB "low level" of water **2.** OB "loss" during transport; < *maṭû* II

mīṭu → also *miṭṭu*

miṭūtu → *miṭītu*

mīya, *mīyati*, *ema'e* "who?" Am.; < W.Sem.

mizqu (a bowl)? Ug., jB; < *mazāqu*

mizru "felt"? jB lex.; < *mazāru*; → *mezura*

miz'u, *mīzu*, OB(Alal.) *mizzu*? (a sweet alcoholic drink) jB, NA; < *mazā'u* II

-mu → *-ma*

mū → *muk* I

mû I, OAkk, OA *mā'ū* pl. tant. "water" [A(.MEŠ); also A.ḪI.A] *mê kabrūtim* "mass of water"; *m. nāri* "river water", *m. mūši* "dew"; in names of canals; "watering place"; rit. *mê qāti* "water for (washing) the hands"; OA *ša mā'īšu* (desig. of gold, textiles); of other liquids: "(body) fluid(s), secretion", "amniotic fluid", *mê marti* "gall"; "sap" of plant; *mê šēri* "meat broth"; in representations as a decorative element; → *māmū*

mû II pl. tant.? "(cultic, cosmic) order, rules" Bab.; OB in PN; < Sum.; → *ella-mê*

mû III '*mu*-word' jB lex.; desig. of ptcp.s; < *mu-*

mû IV sg. (an object) OB

mu'arrirum "auxiliary force" Mari; < *na'arruru*

mu'āru "man" jB

muāšu "to check"? NA; < Aram.

muātiš "towards death" OA; < *mâtu*

muātu → *mâtu*

muā'um in *lā m.* "not to want (to)" OA **G** after infin.; after subst. in acc. rare **Gtn** iter. of G; → *lemû* II

mubabbilum; pl. *mubabbilūtu* "juggler" or "acrobat"? OB; < *babālu* D; > *mubabbilūtum*

mubabbilūtum "rôle of juggler" Mari; < *mubabbilum*

muballiṭānu "that keeps alive; maintainer" MA; < *balāṭu* II D

muballi(ṭ)ṭum mostly f. **1.** OB "cage" for a lion **2.** Mari (part of a canal, phps.) "weir" **3.** lex.

"life?-boat" **4.** Am. "smelling bottle" **5.** OB as fPN; < *balāṭu* II D

mubannītum "benefactress" OB; < *banû* II D

mubannû, *mubennû*; pl. *mubannî*, Aram. *mubanniya* 'who beautifies', "preparer of offering tables"? j/NB [LÚ.DÍM] i.e. temple cook; < *banû* II D

mubannûtu "office of the *mubannû*" NB; < *banû* II D

mubarrimu "worker of coloured textiles" NA lex.; < *barāmu* I D

mubarrītum "observation corps"? Mari; < *barû* I D

mubarrû **1.** "commentary"? **2.** (a temple? official) NB; Bogh. *rab m.* "overseer of the *m.*"; < *barû* I D; → *mubirru*

mubassiru(m), NA also *mupassiru*; pl. *mubassirū* "messenger" Mari, NA; < *bussuru*

mubattiru (a worm or grub)? jB; < *butturu* II

mubbibum; pl. *mubbibū* "census official" Mari; < *ebēbu* D

mubbirtu "(female) accuser" NA; < *abāru* III

mube'išu → *mubêšu*

mubennû → *mubannû*

mubêšu, *mubeššu*?, *mube'išu*? "implement for stirring" MA; < *bêšu* D

mube'u (or *mupe'u*) (an official, phps.) "investigator" Nuzi in LÚ *m.*; < *bu''û* II ?

mubirru/û (a prof.) MB; = *mubarrû* ?

mūbû "thickness" NA; < *ebû* II

mudaburu, *mudabiri* → *madbaru*

mūdādum "beloved" OB as PN only; < W. Sem.?; → *madādu* II

mudakkiu (a (metal) object) NA; < *dekû* II D ?

mudakkû → *mudekkû*

mudalliḫu (an official)? NB; < *dalāḫu*

mudammiq(a)tu(m) (a wooden implement) O/jB, NA; < *damāqu* D

mudammiqu (a craftsman)? Mari; < *damāqu* D

mūdânūtu in *lā m.* "ignorance" NA; < *mūdû*

mudarriktu "woman thresher" NA; < *darāku* III D

mudasû(m) "list of names, register" O/jB [MU.DA.SÁ]; < Sum.

mudatu (payment due from a *mudu*) Ug.; < *mudu*

mūda'um → *mūdû*

mudāyû, *mudû* (a wooden object) jB lex.; → *amūdāya*

mudbaru → *madbaru*

muddu → *mudu*; *mundu*

muddû "deficit, arrears"? Nuzi; → *muṭû*

muddû → also *mūdû*

muddultu → *mundultu*

muddulu(m), *mundulu* "salted? (meat)" OAkk (Sum.), jB; < *madālu* D

mudekkû, *mudakkû* ~ "inciter, agitator"? MB; < *dekû* II D

mudeššû "life-giver" OB lex.; < *dešû* D

mudidlû, *mudidlu*, *mudillu/û* "individual line" jB lex. of text

mudiṣṣum "deceptive, oppressive"? OB lex.; < *dâṣu* D

mudrû (a mourning garment)? jB lex.; < Sum.; = MB *mitrû* ?

mudu (or *muddu*), esp. *m. šarri* (a courtier), "acquaintance" of the king Ug.; > *mudatu*; → *mūdû*

mudûm (a garment) OAkk(Sum.); < Sum.?

mudû → also *mudāyû*

mūdû(m), OAkk *mūda'um*, OA *mūdi'um*, occas. *muddû*; pl. *mūdû*, NB *mūdânê*; f. st. constr. *mūdeat*, *mūdât* "knowing, wise" [(GAL.)ZU] with dependent gen. "knowing, aware of (s.th.)"; "experienced"; *mūdût qabli*, *tāḫāzi* "battle-tested, experienced in combat" soldiers; *m. kalâma* etc. "omniscient" in divine and royal epith.s; absol. "intelligent, knowing"; "competent, well-versed"; "expert"; "acquaintance"?; *lā m.* "stupid, ignorant"; stat. "is learned" OAkk in PN; "is versed" (in = acc.); < *edû* II G ptcp.; > *mūdûtu*, *mūdânūtu*; → *mudu*

mu'dû → *mu'uddû*

mudulu (a pole)? jB lex.; < Sum.

mūdûtu(m) "knowledge, awareness (of s.th.)" Bab.; < *mūdû*

mu'erru(m), *muwerrum* ~ "leader (of an assembly)" O/jB [GAL.UKKIN.NA; (LÚ.)Á.GÁL] (an official); of deities, esp. Papsukal; OB as PN; < *wârum* D

mu'errūtu "leadership (of an assembly); command" M/NB; of kings; of Marduk; < *mu'erru*

mu'ertum; OB pl. *mu'erētum* "order, commission" for goods ? OA, OB; < *wârum*

mugabbû → *mukabbû*

mugallitu(m) "troublemaker; intimidator" Bab.; < *galātu* D

mugammertu 'that gathers'?, i.e. "the sea" jB lex.; < *gamāru* II D

mugammerum "collector" of soldiers, i.e. "conscription officer"? OB; < *gamāru* II D

muganniṣum ~ "haughty, sneering person" OB lex.; < *ganāṣu* D

mugarru → *magarru*

mugdašru, *mugdešru* "powerful" j/NB; < *gašāru* Gt
mugerru "two-wheeled vehicle, chariot; wheel" M/NA [GIŠ.GIGIR ?]; *nangar m.* "cartwright"; < *qarāru* ?; → *magarru*
muggu → *mungu*
mugguru **D** "to tear down" NA, building; < Aram.
muggušu(m) **D** mng. unkn. O/jB
mugi(l)lu (a container)? MA in *m. ša urqe* "*m.* of greens"
mugu, Bab. mostly *mungu* in *rab m.* (a high official) NA, NB
mugu → also *mungu*
mugubbû → *immugubbû*
muḫabbiltu 'that damages', i.e. (a bad omen)? jB; < *ḫabālu* II D
muḫaddûm "who gives delight, joy" OB as PN only; < *ḫadû* III D
muḫa''idu "watcher" jB lex.; < *ḫiāṭu* D
muḫālum (a foodstuff)? OA
muḫarrišu mng. unkn. jB lex.; < *ḫarāšu* I or II D
muḫaṭṭipum mng. unkn. OB; < *ḫaṭāpu* D
muḫeššû mng. unkn. jB lex.; < *ḫašû* IV D
muḫḫelṣītum "slippery ground" OB; < *neḫelṣû*
muḫḫu(m) "skull; top" from OAkk on [UGU] **1.** as subst. "skull", med. also "brain"; "surface" of organs; "upper part" of object; OB math. (upper width or surface-area of a body) **2.** after prep. (→ GAG §115h): *ina muḫḫi*, *muḫ* "on, in, on top of"; "over, above"; of debt, duty "incumbent on", OB *ina m. PN šasûm* "to call s.o. to account"; talk, laugh, write "about"; live "at s.o.'s expense" **3.** "with regard to, concerning; on account of"; NB "in accordance with"; Am. often *muḫḫi* on its own **4.** *ana m.* "in addition to", math. "plus", "with respect to", "toward(s)"; "until"; "onto" (s.th. or s.o.); "per"; "against"; "referring to" **5.** M/NA *ša muḫḫi X* "official in charge of X" **6.** as adv. M/NB, NA: *ina m.* "(up)on it"; "over, above it"; "in addition"; "about it, on that subject"; *ana m.* "upon it"; "in addition"
muḫḫû → *maḫḫû*
muḫḫuriš, NA *maḫḫuriš* "as an offering" jB, NA(roy. inscr.); < *maḫāru* D
muḫḫurtu, OA *ma(ḫ)ḫurtum* "opposite, facing (side)" OA, M/jB; < *maḫāru* D
muḫḫuru "offering" MA, jB; MA *Muḫḫur-ilī* (8th? Ass. month); < *maḫāru* D; OA → *maḫḫuru*
muḫḫuṣu; f. *muḫḫuṣ/štu* "provided with fittings"? jB lex.; < *maḫāṣu* D

muḫḫūtum → *maḫḫūtu*
muḫru **1.** jB (an offering) **2.** NA "appeal"; (a prayer) **3.** jB (a cultic building) [KUN.SAG (.GÁ)]; < *maḫāru*
muḫrû → *maḫrû* I
muḫtanbu "growing" jB; < *ḫanābu* Gt
muḫterkun "female (animal)" jB lex.; < Elam.
muḫtillû (a garment) M/NB
muḫurrā'um "receipt" of commodities OAkk; < *maḫāru*
mu'irtu ~ "subject, dependant"? Bogh.(Hitt.)
mu'irtuttu ~ "government, administration" Bogh.(Hitt.)
muk I, *muku*, also *mū* NA after 1 sg. to introduce dir. speech; → *mā*; *nuk* I
muk II (a plant) jB lex.
mukabbirum, *muktabbirum* "boaster, exaggerator" OB lex.; < *kabāru* D, Dtn
mukabbû, *mugabbû* "stitcher, tailor" j/NB [LÚ.TÚG.KAL(.KAL)]; < *kubbû* II
mukallimtu "scholarly commentary" j/NB, NA [NÍG.PÀ.DA]; NB (an extract from the land register)?; < *kullumu*
mukallu → *mukkallu*
mukannišum "subjugator, subduer" OB, MA in PN; < *kanāšu* I D
mukānu(m) (part of a loom)? O/jB
mukanzibtu (a water clock) jB lex.; < *kazābu* I D
mukarrisu, NB *mukarrišu* (a metal vessel for liquids) NA, NB; < *karāsu* D?
mukarṣītu (a metal item, phps.) "cooler" NB; < *kaṣû* III D ?
mukaššidu "pursuer, persecutor"; < *kašādu* D
mukattimtu **1.** jB rit. (a net)? **2.** jB lex. (desig. of a door); < *katāmu* D; → *kātimtu*
mukiddum mng. unkn. OB lex.; < *kâdu* I or II D
mukillu(m), st. constr. *mukīl* "holder, support, grip" Bab. **1.** of objects (a vessel stand); *m. dalti* 'holder of a door'; *m. šipri* (a sleeve)?; *m. rēši(m)* (part of the liver) **2.** of person, deity, demon: *m. abbūti* "intercessor, advocate"; *m. appāti*, *ašâti* "chariot driver, rein-holder"; *m. bābi(m)* "gatekeeper"; *m. rēši(m)* "constant attendant", *m. rēš damiqtim* "good spirit", *m. rēš lemutti(m)* "evil spirit" [SAG.ḪUL.ḪA.ZA]; < *kullu* III
mukinnu(m) "witness" Bab.; NB *m. šarri* mng. unkn.; < *kânu* D
mukinnūtu "testimony, evidence" j/NB, NA; < *kanû* D
mu(k)kallu, *gukallu* (a priest or scholar) jB
mukkidu jB lex., syn. of *ukkudu*

mukku, *muqqu* "poor quality, waste wool" O/jB lex.; < Sum.

muklalu → *maklalu*

mukru (or *muqru*) (a loincloth) lex.

muktabbirum → *mukabbirum*

muktaššaššu "overpowering" jB; < *kašāšu* I Rtn

muku → *muk* I

mulabbiṭu mng. unkn. jB

Mulaḫḫišu "Whisperer" as name of god jB/NA; < *laḫāšu* D

mulammidu "master (of an apprentice)" jB lex.; < *lamādu* D

mulappitu (an implement) NA; < *lapātu* D

mulā'u(m) ~ "complementary payment" to fill a quota O/MA; < *malû* IV

muldamû (or *muldamulû*) (an invertebrate) Bab. lex., syn. of *lummû*

mulīgu → *mulūgu*

mulku "kingship"? Am.; < W.Sem.

mullaḫtu → *mallaḫtu*

mullilu(m) "purifier" O/jB, NA **1.** (a priest) **2.** (a cultic? cleaning implement) [SANGA$_4$]; < *elēlu* II D

mullītum "she who raises" OB of Ištar in fPN; < *elû* III D

mullû(m) I "filling (up), replenishment" Bab., Nuzi, Bogh. "compensation"; NB *m. mullû* "to make compensation (for)"; Ug. "compensation (blood money)"; < *malû* IV D

mullû(m) II (an object) OB; < Sum.

mulluqtum mng. unkn. OB in fPN

mullušum "with the hair plucked/torn out" OAkk in PN; < *malāsu*

mulluṭu (a desig. of a person) jB lex.

mulmullu, *malmallu* "arrow" M/NA, M/jB

mult... → *mušt...*

multarriḫu → *muštarḫu*; *muštarriḫu*

mulṭu → *mušṭu*

mūlu "fullness" O/MB in PN; < *malû* IV

mūlû(m) O/jB, Bogh., NA [DU$_6$] **1.** "height" **2.** "rise, hill(ock)"; Mari, of acropolis **3.** "climb, ascent"; < *elû* III

mulūgu, *mulīgu* (a type of dowry) M/NB, Nuzi

mulūgūtu ~ *mulūgu* Nuzi

muluḫḫû 'tearing out' jB om. uncert.; < *malāḫu* IV

mulūḫum, *mulū'um* ? (a type of wood)? OA

mulûtu? "rule(rship)" NB; < Sum. mulu + *-ūtu*

mulū'um → *mulūḫum*

mum (an emblem of Ea) MB

muma''eru; f. *muma''ertu* "commander, ruler; satrap" j/NB, NA [LÚ.GAL.UKKIN]; < *wârum*

muma''erūtu "office of satrap" [LÚ.GAL.UKKIN-] NB; < *muma''eru*

mumannûm "flatterer"? OB lex.; < *menû* D

mumarriqānu, *mumarraqānu* "guarantor" NB; < *marāqu* D; → *murruqūnu*

mumarrītu → *muwarrītum*

mumassû → *muwassûm*

mumaššiḫu (a measuring instrument)? jB lex.; < *mašāḫu* I D

mumaššû → *muwassûm*

mumbium "boaster, braggart"? OB lex.; < *ebû* II D

mumerrītu → *muwarrītum*

Mumītu jB DN; = *Mammītu* ?

mummallittu → *walādum* D

mummātu → *mummu* II

mummellu "actor?, player" jB lex.; < *mēlulu*

mummenu (a trader)? jB lex.

mummertu, *mummirtu* "(female) matchmaker; procuress" MA; < *amāru* I D

mummidu(m) mng. unkn. OB lex. and as PN; < *emēdu* D?

mummilu "stirring, exciting; whirling; obscuring"? jB of deities; lex. of storm; < *wamālum* D

mummirtu → *mummertu*

mummu I ~ "life-giving force"? M/NB, NA of deities, e.g. Ea, Ištar, Papsukal, Marduk; DN ^{d}*Mummu*, the vizier of Apsû; MB (a symbol of Ea); jB "destination, use, purpose"?; (a school), *(bīt) m.* ~ "(sculpture) workshop of a temple"; jB *mār m.* "pupil, apprentice scribe"; < Sum.

mummu(m) II; pl. *mummātu*? (a scraper)? O/jB

mummu III "someone, something" Bab.

mummu IV "noise"? jB

mummu → also *mammû*

mummu(n)nu- → *mammannu-*

mumt... → also *mund...*, *munt...*

mumtalkum, *mundalku*, NA *muttalku*; f. *muttaliktu* Bab., NA **1.** "deliberate, circumspect" **2.** "counsellor, sage"; < *malāku* II Gt

munabbûm, *munambû(m)* (a lamentation priest) O/jB lex.; < *nabû* II D

munaggiru(m), *munan/mgiru(m)* "denouncer, informer" O/jB; < *nagāru* II D

munaggirūtu "activity of a denouncer" jB; < *munaggiru*

muna''išu "veterinary surgeon" jB; < *nêšu* D

munāmātu → *munattu*

munambû → *munabbûm*

munamgiru → *munaggiru*

munammiru → *munawwirum*

muna(m)mū ~ "abundance"? jB

munangiru → *munaggiru*

munappiḫtum "bellows"? OB; < *munappiḫu*

munappiḫu(m) "lighter of fires; rumour-monger" O/jB lex.; < *napāḫu* D

munappilum "digger" OB lex.; < *napālu* I D

munaqqītu "libation vessel" NA; < *naqû* D

munaššiku; f. *munaššiktu* "biting (dog)" jB; < *našāku* D

munattu; pl. *munāmātu* "morning slumber" jB; adv. *munattiš* "awake"

munawwirum, *munammiru* "brightening, cheering (person)" OB in PN only, jB lex.; < *nawāru* D

mundabru (or *mundapru*) ~ "powerful" jB lex.; < *dabāru* Gt ?

mundagru "compliant" jB; < *magāru* Gt

mundaḫṣu, *mundaḫḫiṣu*, NA *muttaḫṣu* "fighting; fighter" jB, NA; < *maḫāṣu* Gt

mundaḫṣūtu "soldiering" M/NB; < *mundaḫṣu*

mundalku → *mumtalkum*

mundalkūtu "deliberation, circumspection" M/NB; < *mumtalkum*

mundapru → *mundabru*

mundu(m), *muddu(m)*, *mindu* (a type of flour) OAkk, Bab. [NÍG.ÀR.RA]

mundultum, *muddultum* (a type of bed) Bab. lex.

mundulu → *muddulu*

munedû → *immunedû*

muneḫḫu "who repulses, subduer" Ass., M/jB; < *nê'u* D; → *munē'u*

munērtum "murderess" OB lex.; < *nêru* D

munē'u in *siparri munē'e* mng. unkn. NB; → *muneḫḫu* ?

mungapru "superior"? jB lex.; < *gapāru* N

mungu, NA *mu(g)gu* (a disease causing) "cramp, stiffness" jB; < *magāgu*

mungu → also *mugu*

munḫiatum mng. unkn. OB, as field name

munīqu "lamb" or "kid" NB; < *enēqu*; → *unīqu*

munnabtu(m); f. *munnabittu(m)*; pl. *munnabtū*, MB(Alal.) also *munnabātu*, Ug. *munnabtūtu* "fugitive, refugee"; Ass., M/NB also as PN; < *abātu* II N (→ GAG §97l); > *munnabtuttu*

munnabtuttu "refugee status" Bogh.; < *munnabtu*

munnagru "hired man" NA; < *agāru* N

munnarbu, *munnerbu* "fugitive, runaway" jB; "fleet(-footed), swift" of deity, demon, king; < *nērubu*

munnišu "weakening, debilitating" jB; < *enēšu* D

munt... → also *mund...*

muntāqu → *mutāqu*

-munu "(n-)placed; (n-)year-old" Nuzi; < Hurr. suff.

munû I, *manû* (a type of bed) jB lex.; < Sum.(Emesal)

munû II (a foot disease) jB

mūnu I "what?" NA occas. for → *mīnu* I; in PN

mūnu II "larva, caterpillar" jB, NA [ZA.NA]

munūtu(m); pl. *munuātu* "(ac)count(ing)" Ass., OB; OB "check, count(ing)"; OA "quota, dividend"; < *manû* IV

munutukû "childless, without issue" M/jB [MU.NU.TUKU]; < Sum.

munutukûtu "childlessness" M/jB [MU.NU.TUKU-]; < *munutukû*

munzazānum → *mazzazānum*

munzêtu → *musâtu*

munziqu → *muzīqu*

munzirrū → *muzzirrū*

munzizu → *muzzazu*

munzu'um "squeezed dry, exhausted"? OB lex.; < *mazā'u* II D

mupaddû "(sheep) offering for the naming (of s.o.)" jB lex.; < Sum.

mupaḫḫirum "who gathers, collector" OB; in PN; < *paḫāru* II D

mupallisum "who diverts, interferes" OB; < *palāsu* D

mupallišum "breacher" OB lex. in *mupalliš bītātim* "burglar"; < *palāšu* D

mupaqqirānu "claimant" NB; < *baqāru* D

muparriṭu (a butcher)? Bogh.; < *parāṭu* D

mupassiru → *mubassiru*

mupaṣṣû, *mupeṣṣû* "washerman, cleaner" NB; < *peṣû* II D

mupašširu(m) OB lex. **1.** (profession concerned with textiles) **2.** in *m. šunātim* "dream-interpreter"; < *pašāru* D

mupattilum "(yarn-)twister" OB; < *patālu* D

mupattītu 'opener' (an implement for cultivation) jB lex.; < *petû* II D; → *mupettûm*

mupazzirum "smuggler" OA; < *pazāru* D

mupeggû "slanderer"; < *pagû* II D

mupeṣṣû → *mupaṣṣû*

mupettûm "person regulating a sluice-gate"? OB lex.; "open-mouthed"? OB in PN; < *petû* II D; → *mupattītu*

mupe'u → *mube'u*

muppalsiḫum (an occupation) OB; < *napalsuḫu*

muppalsu "looking (benevolently) on (s.o.)" jB; < *palāsu* N

mupparkû → *naparkû* II

mupparšu "flying, winged" OB, jB; of bird, Anzû; *Mupparšu* (name of Marduk's horse); < *naprušu* II

muppišānu "who committed" (sorcery) MA; < *epēšu* II D

muppišu; f. *muppištu* "who does s.th. to (s.o.), harms (s.o.)" jB, NA "bewitcher, sorcerer, sorceress"; "slanderer"; NA "dealer, agent"?; < *epēšu* II D

muppiš(ū)tu "witchcraft, spell" jB; < *muppišu*

muqabbû "who laments; wailer" jB lex.; < *qabû* II D

mūqadu → *maqqadu*

muqallilum "who belittles, humiliates" OB, jB; < *qalālu* I D

muqallipum "dehusker (of grain)"? OB lex.; < *qalāpu* D

muqallûm "roaster (of grain)" OB lex.; < *qalû* II D

muqappil zê 'roller-up of dung' = "dung beetle" jB lex.; < *kapālu* ? + *zû* I

muqarribum → *muqerribum*

muqāru(m) mng. unkn. O/jB; also as PN

muqattertu "censer, thurible" j/NB; < *qatāru* II D

muqerribum, OA *muqarribum* "transporter, delivery agent" OA, OB; < *qerēbu* D

muqi(p)pu(m) "guarantor" OAkk, jB lex.; < *qiāpu* D

muqlalu → *maklalu*

muqqadu → *maqqadu*

muqqelpītu(m), *muqqalpītu(m)* (vessel) "going downstream" O/jB; OB *ša m.* (captain of a boat moving downstream); *ana m.* "downstream"; "from top to bottom, from top to toe"; < *neqelpû*

muqqu(m) I ~ "weakened, wearied" O/jB; < *muqqu* II

muqqu(m) II "to weary, tire; wane" O/jB; OB "obliterate, disregard" fault, crime; "be slack", "delay" journey, action; of person "age"; MB in PN; stat. jB of troops, limbs "are slack"; > *muqqu* I

muqqu → also *mukku*

muqqutum **1.** OB lex. "wasted (through a disease)" **2.** Mari mng. uncert.; < *maqātu* D

muqru → *mukru*

muqtablu "fighter" Bab.; < *qitbulu*

mūqu → *emūqu*; *muqqu* I

muquttû(m) ~ "claim falling due" Bab.; < *maqātu*

murabbiānu, *murabbânu* **1.** MA "foster-father" **2.** NA "educator, tutor"?; < *rabû* II D; → *muribbānu* ?

murabbītu(m) "foster-mother" O/jB; < *rabû* II D

mūra(d)du, occas. *murradu* "descent, way down" j/NB; < *warādum*

murakkisu "binder of sheaves" jB lex.; < *rakāsu* D

mūraku, Nuzi also *mūruku* "length" M/jB, Am., NA [GÍD(.DA)]; < *arāku*

murammiktum "washbasin" OB; < *ramāku* D

murammiku → *muremmiku*

murammû (a tool) NB used for brick-making; < *ramû* III D ?

mūrānu → *mīrānu* I

murappidum "one who makes difficulties" OA; < *rapādu* II D

muraqqītu "(woman) maker of perfumes, spicer" M/NA, NB; *rab muraqqiātu* "chief of the female perfume makers"; < *muraqqiu*

muraqqiu, *muraqqû* ~ "maker of perfumes, spicer" M/NA [(LÚ.)Ì.RÁ.RÁ]; < *ruqqû*

murārītu "vegetable plot"? MA; < *murāru*

murāru(m), **murartu** (a bitter vegetable, phps.) "endive, chicory" O/jB; < *marāru* I; > *murārītu*

muraššû I 'who does wrong' j/NB **1.** "quarreller, cantankerous person" **2.** "wild cat" [SA.A.RI] f. *muraššītu*; NB as PN; < *rašû* III D

muraššû II (a worker) NB

murattib(t)u "soaking vessel" = "mash tun"? MB, jB lex.; < *ratābu* D

murdinnu → *amurdinnu*

murdû → *murudû*

murdudû (a plant) Bogh., jB [Ú.MUR.DÙ.DÙ; Bogh. MUL.DÙ.DÙ]; < Sum.

murēdu → *murīdu*

muremmiku, NB also *murammiku* ? "bath attendant"? MB(Hana); < *ramāku* D

murḫu, *murru*, *murikua* (a garment) lex.; < *marāḫu* ?

muribbānu (a function or prof.) NA/NB; → *murabbiānu* ?

murīdu, *murēdu* (a function or prof.) Bogh. Hitt.

mūridum "person descending"? OB; < *warādum*

murikua → *murḫu*

murinnākum mng. unkn. OB; < Sum.

murkigû (pulmonary disease) Ug.; < Sum.

murkunaš (a garment)? Nuzi

mūrnisqu "select young animal; war horse" jB/NA; < *mūru* + *nisqu* (→ GAG §59a)

murqannu → *murruqūnu*

murqu I ~ "intellect, reason" jB; *lā m.* "lack of reason; foolishness"; < *marāqu* ?

murqu II NB occas. for *murruqu*

murqu → also *wurqum*

murradu → *mūraddu*

murrānu(m), NB lex. *u(r)rānu*, jB lex. also *ḫurrānu* **1.** jB, NA (a tree or shrub) [GIŠ.MA.NU.SIG$_7$.SIG$_7$], jB also *amurrānu* **2.** OAkk(Sum.) (source of an oil); = 1 ? **3.** lex. (a stone (object))?; < *murru* ?

murraqūtu "release, clearing from claims" NB; < *murruqu* 2

murratum (or *ḫu/arratum*) (a weapon)? OAkk

murriḫu "urgent" jB in *ūm murriḫti* "hasty, urgent storm"; < *arāḫu* I D

murru Ass., M/NB, Am., Bogh. **1.** "bitterness" **2.** "myrrh" [(GIŠ.)ŠIM.SES]; < *marāru* I; > *murrānu*?

murru → also *murḫu*

murrû I **D** "to be silent" jB lex.

murrûm II 'one who uncovers' OA in *murri qablītim* "uncoverer of the jar" (to do accounts); < *erû* III D

murrû → also *arû* VI D

murruqu NB **1.** of silver "refined" **2.** "released from claims" **3.** "clear, intelligible"; < *marāqu* D; → *murqu* II

mu(r)ruqūnu, *murqannu* etc. NB for → *mumarriqānu*

murrurtu "slander"? Ug.; < *marāru* I D

murrutu (or *ḫurrutu* ?) (a plant) NB used to make flour during famine

murṣu(m); pl. *murṣānu* "illness, disease" [GIG] of various parts of the body, e.g. *muruṣ qaqqadi* "head disease, headache", *m. šinni* "dental infection"; *m. libbi(m)* "heartache, sorrow, distress"; < *marāṣu*

murta''imu "thunderer" (name of Adad) jB lex. (< NA for **murtammimu* ?); < *ramāmu* Gtn ?

murtâmu, jB lex. also *muštamû*; mostly in pl. *murtâmū* "loving each other, lovers, friends" M/jB; < *râmu* II Gt

murtappidu(m) "wandering, roving" O/jB; of animals, of ghost of a dead person [KIP-*du* ?]; of weapon; < *rapādu* II Gtn

murtaṣnu ~ "thunderous, roaring" of Adad jB; ^{d}*Murtaṣnu* (name of Adad); < *raṣānu* Gt

murtaššû "who wrongs continuously"? jB lex.; < *rašû* III Dtn

murte'âtu → *re'û* Gt

mūrtu, *mūštu* "young female animal" MA, MB; < *mūru*

mûrtu → *wu''urtum*

murû "rainstorm" Ug. lex.; < Sum.

mūru(m) "young animal; young bull; foal (of donkey or horse)" [DÙR]; also transf. of king; lex. *mūr mê* (an insect); > *mūrnisqu*, *mūrtu*

mūru → also *erium*; *mīru* III

mur'u (an official)? Nuzi, Ug.; < Ug.; > *murūtu*

mur(u)dû(m) "lattice, grating" O/jB in river; "(golden) filigree"; < Sum.

mūruku → *mūraku*

murūma pl. (a textile) Ug.

muruqūnu etc. → *murruqūnu*

muruš "bed" jB lex.; → *maršu* 2

murušû "man" jB lex.; < Sum.?

murūtu "function of *mur'u* official" Nuzi; < *mur'u*

murzānum, *muruzānum*, *murzīnum* (a wooden object) OAkk(Ur III), OB

murzumurza (or *ḫa/urzuḫa/urza*$^?$) (a garden plant) NB

musabbiktu "woman basket-weaver" jB lex.; < *sabāku* D

musaḫḫiptu (a hunting net) jB lex.; < *saḫāpu* D

musaḫḫirtum mng. unkn. OB fPN ?; < *saḫāru* D ?

musaḫḫiru "buyer, buying agent" NB; *rab m.* "head of the buying agents"; < Aram.

musaḫḫûm "troublemaker"? OB in PN; < *seḫû* D

musakkiltu (or *musaqqiltu*); pl. *musakk/qqilātu* (topog. term) NA, rdg. uncert.; < *sak/qālu* D or *akālu* Št ?

musalliḫtu; pl. *musalliḫātu* (a libation vessel) M/NB, NA; < *salāḫu* I D

musallimu "conciliable, placatable" jB; < *salāmu* II D

musammeḫtu "woman mixer" (of dough$^?$)? NB; in *bāb m.* (name of a gate$^?$); < *samāḫu* D

musaqqiltu → *musakkiltu*

musarriru → *sarāru* D; *sarrirum*

musarrum → *misarrum*

musarrû → *mūšaru*

musarû (a disease)? jB lex.

musarû → also *mušarû*; *mūšaru*

musārum → *muṣārum*

musassiānu "who has proclamation made" MA; < *šasû* D

musâtu, *munzêtu* "(used) washing water" j/NB "toilet, lavatory"; *bīt m.* "lavatory"; *rābiṣ m.* "demon of the lavatory"; < *mesû* II

musazkirum → *mušazkirum*

musellûm "supplicant" OB lex.; < *sullû* I

museppûm "supplicant" OB lex.; < *suppû* II; → also *suppû* I D

musiktu (or *mušiktu*) (a stone object) Ug. lex.

musiqqum "who makes narrow, confines" OB lex.; < *siāqum* D

muskum "s.th. bad, s.th. evil"? OB; < *masāku* ?

musku → also *mušku*

mussaḫ(ḫi)ru **1.** OB(Susa) (a household utensil) **2.** jB "(benignly) turned to(wards s.o.)", of goddess; < *saḫāru* Gtn, N

mussa''ītu → *mušta''ûtu*

mussâtu → *esû* D

mussipu ~ "scoop" MA; < *esēpu* D

mussiru(m) **1.** MA (part of a stove) **2.** lex. (part of a plough, phps.) "seed funnel" **3.** Mari, jB lex. (a cultic functionary); < *esēru* II D ?

mussû → *mesû* II D; *wussûm*

mussuku "wretched, pitiful"? jB; MA also PN; < *masāku* D

musukkannu, *mes(uk)kannu*, occas. *mas(ma)kannu*, *(u)sukkannu* "Magan-tree", phps. "*Dalbergia sissoo*" Bab., NA [GIŠ.MES. MÁ.KAN.NA (→ *mēsu*)]; < Sum.?; → *usukannu*

musukkā'ū → *musukkû*

musukku(m), *usukku*; f. *(m)usukkatu* "ritually unclean; impure person" O/jB [Ú.ZÚG; f. MUNUS.Ú.ZÚG]; < Sum.

musukkû, OA *musukkā'ū* pl. tant. **1.** OA, OB "poor quality (silver)"? **2.** OB mng. unkn.; < *masāku*

muṣabbi(t)tu **1.** jB lex. (part of a loom) **2.** NB (a bronze implement); < *ṣabātu* D

muṣa''irānu, *muṣârānu* "frog" Qatna, jB [BIL.ZA.ZA]; med. also used as drug; "(figurine of a) frog"

muṣallu NA for → *maṣallu* or *muṣlālu* ?

muṣallu → also *muṣṣālu*

muṣallû "liar, evildoer" jB lex.; < *ṣelû* I D

mūṣâne → *mūṣû*

muṣappertu 'she who shapes', i.e. "woman hairdresser"? jB lex.; < *ṣapāru* D

muṣappiu "dyer" NA; < *ṣapû* II D

muṣârānu → *muṣa''irānu*

muṣarriḫtum "wailing woman"? OB; < *ṣarāḫu* I D; → *ṣarriḫtum*

muṣarrirtu(m), *muṣarrištu*; pl. *muṣarrirātu* (a libation vessel) O/jB, NA, usu. metal; < *ṣarāru* I D

muṣārum (or *musārum*) (a metal object) OA; < *masārum* or *maṣāru* ?

mūṣā'u → *mūṣû*

muṣeḫḫu → *muṣiḫḫu*

muṣiḫḫu(m), *muṣeḫḫu(m)* "clown, jester" O/jB lex.; < *ṣiāḫu* D

muṣiptu; pl. *muṣipēti* (a garment) NB; < *ṣuppu* II ?

mūṣium I (a departure tax) OA; < *waṣûm*; → *mūṣû*

mūṣium II (an official) OA

mūṣiu → also *mūṣû*

muṣlālu(m) "siesta(-time); midday" Bab. [AN.BIR9(=NE)]; acc. as adv. "at noon"; < *ṣalālu*; → *muṣallu*; *šumṣulu*

muṣrû, *miṣrû* "Egyptian" jB lex.

muṣṣabru → *muzzapru*

muṣṣāltu, *muṣṣēltu* jB lex. **1.** (a term for the gall bladder, phps.) "gallstone" **2.** (a mineral); < *muṣṣālu*

muṣṣālu, *muṣallu* "quarrelsome; troublesome" jB; of a stone; < *ṣâlu* Gt ?; > *muṣṣāltu*

muṣṣēltu → *muṣṣāltu*

muṣṣû → *maṣû* D; *mūṣû*; *wuṣṣûm*

muṣṣuṣu → *muzzuzu*

muṣû(m) (a garment) OA?, M/NB; *pān m.* (part of the garment); < *wuṣṣûm* ?

mūṣu "exudation" jB **1.** lex. (a stone) **2.** med. "discharge" at the foreskin

mūṣû(m), M/NA *mūṣā'u*, NB also *muṣṣû*, Ug. *mūṣiu*?; NB pl. *mūṣâne* "exit" Bab., M/NA [KI.È; ZAG.È; KI.TA.È.A]; "way out"; "going out, departure"; "escape route", *ša lā mūṣê* "inescapable"; "outflow, outlet"; NB "exit tax", a canal charge; astr. "rising" of star; "yield" (< W.Sem.); OB *m. šattim* "end of the year"; < *waṣûm*; OA → *mūṣium* I

mūša → *mūšu*

mušabbištu mng. unkn. jB lex.

mušabšû "that calls into existence; creator" jB lex.; f. also DN; < *bašû* Š

mūšabtu (a room in a house, phps.) "toilet" jB; < *wašābum*

mūšabu(m) "dwelling, domicile, abode; seat (of honour), throne"; < *wašābum*

mušadbibu, *mušedbibu* **1.** MB "that causes s.o. to litigate" **2.** j/NB, NA "that causes s.o. to speak (sedition)"; < *dabābu* II Š

mušadbibūtu "instigation" NA; < *mušadbibu*

mušaddinum "tax collector" OB; < *nadānu* II Š

mušaddû "that causes negligence"? jB; < *nadû* III Š

mušadgil(ann)u "who transfers ownership (of s.th. to s.o.)" NB; < *dagālu* Š

mušādiru "frightening" jB; < *adāru* II Š

mušaggišum "murderer" OB lex.; < *šagāšu* D

mušaḫḫinu, *mušeḫḫinu*; NB pl. *mušaḫḫinānu* "brazier, stove" j/NB [ZABAR.ŠEN.DIL. KÚM.MA]; < *šaḫānu* D; → *mušeḫḫittu*

mušaḫḫitum mng. unkn. Mari

mušāḫizu(m) "who gives instructions; trainer" Bab.; < *aḫāzu* Š

mušaḫlilu "that causes to shout with joy" jB; of bull; < *alālu* III Š

mušaḫripu "early ripening (date palm)" jB lex.; < *ḫarāpu* I Š

mušākilu(m) 'that lets eat, feeds' Bab., M/NA **1.** "supplier of food" to people **2.** "feeder, fattener" of animals, birds **3.** Mari, Bogh.(Hitt.) (a kind of knife); < *akālu* Š
mušākilūtum "feeding (of animals)" OB; < *mušākilu*
mušālittu "midwife" jB lex.; < *walādum* Š
mušallilu "plunderer" jB lex.; < *šalālu* I D
mušallimānu "delivery man"? M/NA, NB; NA "healer"?; NB as a prof.; < *mušallimu*
mušallimu(m) O/jB **1.** Mari "that delivers safely; safe-conduct, escort" **2.** jB stat. of deity "safeguarding, preserving (s.o.'s) health"; < *šalāmu* II D
mušallû → *muššallû*
mušalmû → *mušelwû*
mušālu(m), Am. *mešēlu*; jB pl. f. "metal mirror" [NÍG.ŠU.ZABAR]; also (a wooden object); < *mašālu*
mušalwû → *mušelwû*
mušamḫiṣu, *mušanḫiṣu*; pl. *mušam/nḫiṣū*, *mušamḫiṣūtu* "inciter to fight, troublemaker" NA, NB; < *maḫāṣu* Š
mušamḫiṣūtu "sedition" NA; < *mušamḫiṣu*
mušamqi(t)tu; pl. *mušamqitātu* OB "(agricultural) sieve"; jB lex. *ša m.* (an agricultural worker); < *maqātu* Š
mušamrû "that fattens" animals jB lex. of Adad; < *marû* II Š
mušamšû "wandering by night, wakeful" jB; < *šumšû*
mušanḫiṣu → *mušamḫiṣu*
mušanmirtu "lamp" NA; < *nawāru* Š
mušannītu, *mušennītu*; pl. *mušennētu* "dam" diverting water flow NB; < *šanû* IV D
mušannû(m) mng. unkn. OB lex., NB; < *šanû* IV D ?
mušānum (a wooden object) OB; → *mašānum*
mušappiktu (vessel for pouring) oil? jB lex.; < *šapāku* D
mušappilu(m) "that lowers" OB lex., jB; < *šapālu* D
mušapšiḫu (part of a door) NB; < *pašāḫu* Š
mušapšiqtu "having difficulty" in childbirth Bogh., jB; < *pašāqu* Š
mušapzertu 'that hides' jB lex. (term for a door) lex.; < *pazāru* Š
mušaqqiltu "scales" NB comm.; < *šaqālu* D
mušaqqû I "that raises" jB; < *šaqû* II D
mušaqqûm II "(man) that waters" animals Mari; < *šaqû* III D
mušarbidu 'that makes roam'? jB lex., desig. of official ?; < *rapādu* II Š ?
mušardû "leaking" jB, of basket; < *redû* I Š
mušāridum → *mušarriṭum* I
mūšarišam "per *mūšar*-measure" OB; < *mūšaru* (→ GAG §67g)
mušarkisu "(military) procurement officer"? NA/NB; < *rakāsu* Š
mušarkisūtu "office of *mušarkisu*" NA; < *mušarkisu*
mušarqidu "dizzying"? jB; < *raqādu* Š
mušarriṭum I (or *mušāridum*) (prof. connected with trade) OA; < *šarāṭu* D ?
mušarriṭu II "that tears" (garments) OB lex.; < *šarāṭu* D
mušarrû → *mūšaru*
mušartu mng. unkn. Bogh. in *ašar m.*
mušaru → *išaru* II
mušarû, *musarû*, NA also *muššarû*; pl. *muššarê*, NA also *muššarāni* "(royal) inscription" M/NB, NA [MU.SAR]; < Sum.
mūšaru(m), *muš/sa(r)rû* "(flower, vegetable) bed" Bab. **1.** "garden(-plot)" OB *ana m. šakānim* and sim. "to divide up in beds" **2.** (surface measure = 12×12 cubits) [SAR] **3.** (cubic measure = 12×12×1 cubits) [SAR] **4.** jB (term for) "buttocks"; < *ešēru* or Sum.?; > *mūšarišam*
mušašnû "regulated, diverted" NA of canal; < *šanû* IV Š
mušaṭpilu "calumniator" jB; < *ṭapālu* Š
mušāṭu(m) "combed-out hair; carded wool" O/jB [SÍK.ŠAB]; also "(cloth of) carded wool"?; < *mušṭu*
mušazkirum, *musazkirum* "official swearing in (a witness), taking an oath (from s.o.)"? Mari; < *zakāru* Š
mušazziqu "troublemaker" jB; < *nazāqu* Š
mušazzizum "(person) that makes (s.o.) attend" (an accounting procedure)? OA; < *izuzzum* Š
mušēbirtu mng. unkn., phps. "ferry" NA; < *mušēbiru*
mušēbiru(m) **1.** OB "that brings (s.o.) across" the water **2.** MB (an aqueduct)?; < *ebēru* I Š
mušedbibu → *mušadbibu*
mušēdû ~ "that informs"? jB lex.; of deity; < *edû* II Š
mušeḫḫinētu pl. "stoves" NB (pl. of *mušeḫḫinu* or *mušeḫḫittu*); < *šaḫānu* D
mušeḫḫinu → *mušaḫḫinu*; *mušeḫḫinētu*
muselbû, *muselimu* → *mušelwû*
mušēlītu → *mušēlû* 6
muselmû → *mušelwû*
mušēltu → *mešēltu*
mušēlû 'that raises' M/NB **1.** (a doorkeeper) **2.** "winnower" **3.** (priest performing incantation for the dead), "necromancer" **4.** (an (agri-

cultural) implement) **5.** (part of door closure) **6.** (a cloud formation), also f. *mušēlītu*; < *elû* III Š

mušelwû, *mušelmû*, *mušalw/mû*, occas. *mušelbû*, *mušelimu* "(field) surveyor" Nuzi; < *lawûm* II Š

mušēniqtu(m); pl. *mušēniqātu*, Alal. *mušēniqtāti* "wet nurse" [UM.ME.GA.LÁ] of woman, goddess, also "mother animal suckling"; < *enēqu* Š

mušennītu → *mušannītu*

mušēpišu(m) "overseer, foreman" Bab. "organizer of a ritual"; NB "workshop"?; < *epēšu* II Š

mušēpišūtu(m) **1.** OB "supervision, direction of work" **2.** jB "organization? of a ritual"; < *mušēpišu*

mušeqqilum "(deity) in charge of weighing" (in the nether world)? OB(Susa); < *šaqālu* D

mušēribtum 'that brings in' (desig. of a feeder canal) OB; < *erēbu* I Š

mušēridum 'that conveys down' OB; *mušērittu* "oesophagus" jB; < *warādum* Š

mušērišu ~ "cultivation inspector" MB; < *erēšu* I Š

mušērittu → *mušēridum*

mušērtu(m) **1.** Mari "overlooking window"; also "overlooking" in jB *apti m.* **2.** jB 'she who leans in' (name of a demon); < *šurru*

mušēṣītum 'that brings out' (desig. of a drainage channel) OB; < *mušēṣû*

mušēṣû, *mušēṣi'u* **1.** NB "drain"; pl. *mušēṣānû* **2.** NA (an ornament)? **3.** OB "one who leases, tenant" **4.** OB, Mari, NB (an official); < *waṣûm* Š

mušēšertu "palm broom" jB lex.; < *ešēru* Š

mušēšeru jB **1.** "that puts in order" **2.** "draining freely" of water ? **3.** mng. unkn. lex.; < *ešēru* Š

mušētiqtu 'that lets pass' mng. unkn. NB; < *etēqu* Š

mušēzibtu **1.** in *ša mušēzibti* "shield-bearer" NA **2.** "life-belt"? NB; < *mušēzibu*

mušēzibu(m) "saving, rescuing; saviour"; of deity in PN [MA, NB (*mu*-)KAR]; of human; < *ezēbu* Š

mušgallu, *muššugallu* 'great serpent', (mythical beast) jB [MUŠ.GAL]; also used as a drug ?; < Sum.

mušḫalṣītu, *mušḫelṣītu* "slippery place"?; < *neḫelṣû* Š

mušḫīštum 'that makes hasten'? OB of goddess; < *ḫiāšum*

mušḫuššu(m) ~ "serpent-dragon" Bab. [MUŠ.ḪUŠ] (a mythical monster) jB; (a constellation); < Sum.

mušiḫḫu (a water-clock) jB lex.; < *šiāḫum* I D

mušīḫtum (a vessel) Mari; < *šiāḫum* I D

mušiktu → *musiktu*

mušimmu → *šiāmu* D

mūšiš "at night" jB; < *mūšu*

mušītiš (or *mušītaš*), *mušītan* "during the night-time" jB; < *mušītu*

mušītu(m); pl. *mušiātu*, *mušâtu* "night(-time)" [GE$_6$]; acc. "at night"; rit., invoked as person; < *mūšu*

muškallimu "teaching, explaining" jB stat.; < *kullumu* ŠD

muškallu (a large fish net) jB lex.; error for *šuškallu* ?; < Sum.?

mūškaṣât "at night towards morning" OB lex.; < *mūšu* + *kaṣâtu*

muškēnu(m), *maškēnu*; Mari f. *muškettum* ? "dependant, bondsman of the palace; poor man" OAkk, Bab., NA [MAŠ.EN.GAG; MAŠ.GAG.EN] OB leg. (a social class) contrasted with *awīlum* and *wardum*; jB, NA "pauper"; < W.Sem.?; > *muškēnūtu*; → *šukênu*

muškēnūtu(m) O/jB, Bogh., NA **1.** "dependence on the palace, status of a *muškēnum*" **2.** "impoverishment, poverty", *m. alāku* "to sink into poverty, become poor"; < *muškēnu*

muškinnu (a belt)? jB lex.

mušku, *musku* (a tree and its wood) jB, NA

muškû 'snake-eater' jB lex., desig. of a bird of prey; < Sum.

mušlaḫḫūtu "art of the snake charmer" jB lex.

muš(la)laḫḫatu jB **1.** "female snake charmer" [MUŠ.LAḪ$_4$(.LAḪ$_4$)] **2.** lex. (a worm)?; < *mušlalaḫḫu*

muš(la)laḫḫu "snake charmer" M/jB [(LÚ.) MUŠ.LAḪ$_{4/5}$; once MUŠ.LAḪ$_6$]; < Sum.

mušlālu(m) (archit. construction, phps.) "staircase(-gate)" Ass., OB; < *šalālu* II ?; → *mašallu*

mušmaḫḫu (a mythical serpent) jB [MUŠ.MAḪ]; < Sum.

mušmīdu "making numerous" jB lex.; < *mâdu* Š

mušmītu "murderous, death-bearing" jB as epith. of deity; < *mâtu* Š

mušnigum (or *mušniqum*) mng. unkn. OB om., substance filling spleen

mušpalu(m) "depth" of an excavation; "depression (in the ground)", "lowland" O/jB [TÙN/TÚL.LAL]; < *šapālu*

mušpīšu "conjurer"? jB lex.

mušqalpītu mng. unkn. jB; < *neqelpû* Š

muššakku(m), *maššakku* "incense" O/jB used by dream-interpreter, as opiate ?
mu(š)šallû (a clay tube, pipe)? NB
muššarrūtu "craft of wood inscriber, engraver?" Bogh. lex.; < Sum.
muššarû → *mušarû*
muššāru(m) (a semiprecious stone, phps.) "serpentine" Bab., M/NA [(NA4.)MUŠ.GÍR; MB NA4.NÍR.MUŠ.GÍR ?]; *m. zaqāni* (a variety of *m.*); *īn m.* "'eye'(-stone) of *m.*"; < Sum.?
muššipu (an incantation priest) jB; < *wašāpum* D
muššu "(female) breast" Qatna, jB, *akal m.* (breast-shaped roll, loaf of bread)?
muššû → *mašû* II D; *wussûm*
muššugallu → *mušgallu*
muššuku "leathery" jB; < *mašku*
muššultu "likeness, replica"; < *mašālu* D
muššulu(m) 'made to resemble' OAkk, M/NB, NA **1.** OAkk as PN **2.** "image, likeness" of (sick) person, object **3.** "mirror"; < *mašālu* D
muššuru mng. unkn. Am.
muššuru → also *wašārum* D; *wuššurum*
muššu'tu; pl. *muššuātu* "ointment" jB; < *muššu'u*
muššu'u D "to rub" part of body jB, with s.th. = acc. **Dtn** iter. of D; > *muššu'tu*
muštabbabbu(m) "blazing"? OA, O/jB of Lamaštu and other demons; jB lex. ᵈ*Muštabbabbu*; < *šabābu* I Rt
muštābiltu(m), *multābiltu* jB **1.** (desig. of the tongue)? **2.** *šumma m.* (name of commentary series on liver omens) **3.** OB (type of due or tax); < *wabālu* Št
muštablakkitum "sheaf-turner" OB lex.; < *nabalkutu* II Štn
muštabrītu, *muttabrītu* 'enduring', i.e. "seaworthy ship" jB lex.; < *bitrû* II Št
muštaddinu 'that ponders' jB lex. of deliberate person ; < *nadānu* II Št
muštaggišu → *muttaggišu*
muštaḫalqu ~ "deserter" NB; < *ḫalāqu*
muštaḫḫizum "infectious" Mari; < *aḫāzu* Štn
muštaḫlilu → *muttaḫallilu*
muštaḫmiṭu → *ḫamāṭu* III Štn
muštaḫṭu, *multaḫṭu* "escapee, survivor" j/NB(Ass.); < *šaḫāṭu* I Gt
mušta''ītu → *mušta''û*
muštakkitum (a trader)? OA; < *šakātu* Dtn
muštālu(m), *muštēlum*, *multālu* "who considers; deliberate" Bab.; of deity, in PN; of king; Mari f. pl. as subst. "discussions"; jB m. as subst. "adviser, councillor"; < *šâlu* I Gt

muštālūtum, *multālūtu* "consideration, deliberation" O/MB; of deity, king; OB "conference, council"; < *muštālu*
muštamkiru "trader" jB lex.; < *makāru* II Št
muštamṣû "that makes an effort" jB; < *maṣû* Št
muštāmû "who considers well, gives careful thought" jB; < *awûm* Št
muštâmu → *murtâmu*
muštannintu → *muštašnintu*
muštannû "hostile" jB; < *šanû* IV Gtn
muštappitu "treacherous" jB; < *šapātu* Gtn
muštaprišu → *muttaprišu*
muštapṣu(m) "wrestler" O/jB; < *šapāṣu* Gt
muštapšiqtu "(woman) having difficulty (in childbirth)" MA, jB; < *pašāqu*
muštaptinnu, *multaptinnu* (a potter's tool) jB lex.; < Sum.?
muštaptu "treacherous" jB lex.; < *šapātu* Gt
muštaptūtu "treachery" jB; < *muštaptu*
muštarḫu, *multarḫu*, Bogh. *multarriḫu* **1.** M/NB(Ass. roy. inscr.) "presumptuous, arrogant" **2.** Bogh., NB of deity "proud, noble"; < *šarāḫu* I Gt
muštarḫūtu, *multarḫūtu*, Bogh. *multa/erriḫūtu* "arrogance" MB, Bogh.; < *muštarḫu*
muštarīlu (name of planet Mercury) j/NB [prob. MUL.UDU.IDIM.GU4.UD]
muštarriḫu(m), *multarriḫu* "praising o.s.; self-important, conceited" O/jB; MB in PN of deity "proud"; < *šarāḫu* I Gtn/Dt
**muštarriḫūtu* → *muštarḫūtu* Bogh.
muštarriqu 'that steals in', i.e. "(secret) lover" jB; < *šarāqu* I Gtn
mušta(r)rištu (a bird) Bogh. lex.
muštasḫip(t)u, *multasḫip(t)u* (a stone) jB; NA [NA4.MUNUS.LA] also as a drug; < *saḫāpu* Št
muštašīmu → *šummu* II Št
muštaškinu, *multaškinu* jB lex. (desig. of god, of potter's tool); < *šakānu* Štn
muštašnintu, Susa *muštannintu* (part of the liver) jB; < *šanānu* Št
mušta''û; f. *mušta''ītu* "idle, at leisure" MB fPN; < *šuta''ûm*
***mušta''ûtu**, *multa''ûtu*, *multa''ītu*, NA *mussa''ītu* "leisure, relaxation" M/jB(Ass.), NA; < *mušta''û*
muštēbilum mng. unkn. OA; < *wabālu* Št
muštēlum → *muštālu*
muštēmiqu(m), *multēmiqu* "devout supplicant" Bab.(lit.); < *emēqu* I Št
mušte(n)nium **1.** OB lex. (a vessel) **2.** jB *muštēnû*, *muštennû* "having reached puberty; nubile" jB; < *enû* III Št ?

muštēpišu; f. *muš/ltēpiš/ltu* jB **1.** "sorcerer, bewitcher; sorceress" **2.** adj. "crafty" of fox ; < *epēšu* II Št

muštēpišūtu, *multēpišūtu* "magical ritual" jB; < *muštēpišu*

muštērtum "waking time, morning" Mari; acc. "in the morning"; < *êru* Št

muštēšertu, MA *multēšertu* **1.** jB "(woman) having normal childbirth"; < *ešēru* Št^1 **2.** MA "repair, maintenance", of chariot; < *ešēru* Št^2

mušte''û "repeatedly searching, deliberate" jB; < *še'û* Gtn

muštezzibu → *ezēbu* Štn

mušti(n)nu(m) "urethra" O/jB; *aban m.* "bladder stone"; OAkk mng. unkn.; < *šiānum* Gt

mūštu → *mūrtu*

muštinnu (a plant) jB lex.

mušṭu(m), *mulṭu* f.; pl. *mušṭātu* "comb" [(GIŠ.)GA.RÍG] *m. šīpātim* "wool comb"; OB *šinni m.* "tooth of a comb"; > *mušāṭu*

mūšu(m) "night" [GE$_6$]; acc. *mūša(m)* "at night"; *mūšamma* "yesterday night"; Mari *mūšam mūšānima* "at dead of night"; *urru/a/i u mūšu/a/i* and vice versa *mūšurrī* "day and night, continuously"; *šāt m.* "night-time", also (the second watch of the night); *maṣṣarti, maṣṣarāti ša m.* "watch(es) of the night"; *ina mūši mašil, mašli* "at midnight"; > *mūšiš*; *mušītu, mušītiš*; *šumšû*; → *mīšu* II; *muškaṣât*

muš'u (an animal) jB lex., equated with *kuṣu'u*

mušumma mng. unkn. OB

mūšurrī → *mūšu*

muta''imu → *mute''imu*

mūtamû → *mūtawûm*

mūtānu(m) "epidemic, plague" Bab., NA [NAM.ÚŠ.MEŠ; ÚŠ.MEŠ]; < *mūtu*

mūtaplu(m), *mutappilu(m)* "that intercedes for; intercessor" in PN, of deity; < *apālu* I Gt(n)

mutaqqinu (a gardening tool)? NB; < *taqānu* D

mutāqu(m), *muttāqu*, *muntāqu* "confectionery, sweetmeat" Bab., NA; *ša m.(-šu)* "confectioner" [(LÚ.)NINDA.KU$_7$.KU$_7$]; < *matāqu*; > *mutāqūtu*

mūtaqu; pl. *mūtaqātu* "passage(way), street" j/NB; < *etēqu*

mutāqūtu "service as a confectioner" NB; < *mutāqu*

mūtawûm, jB *mūtamû* ~ "eloquent"? O/jB lex.; < *awûm* Gt

mute''imu, *muta''imu* "master, ruler, prince" NB(Achaem.); < *tu''umu* II

mutellum → *muttellum*

muterru jB, NA '(re)turner' **1.** lex. (a bolt) **2.** lex. (wooden part of a fowler's net) **3.** NA "poker" **4.** *m. gimilli* "avenger" **5.** *m. ṭēmi* "adviser; agent"; < *târu* D; *mutērtu*

mutērtu(m); pl. *muterrētu* Bab. **1.** "leaf of a door"; pl. "double door"; NB *bīt m.* "portico" **2.** (a fowler's net); < *muterru*

muthummu, *mithummu* "fruit(s), product(s) of a garden" M/jB [NÍG.SA.SA(.ḪI.A)]

muti(ma) "ever" OA, Bogh.; → *matīma*

mutinnu → *muttinnu*

Mutir (a month) OAkk

mutkû mng. unkn. jB lex.

mutlellû "that rises; lofty, exalted" j/NB, of deity; < *utlellû*

mutnennû "who prays much, pious" M/NB; < *utnēnu* II

mutqītu (a sweet bread)? NA; < *mutqû*

mutqu I "sweet thing, sweetness" jB in akal m. "sweet bread"; < *matāqu*; → *mutqû*

mutqu II "head louse" jB

mutqû(m) "sweet bread" Bab. [NINDA. KU$_7$.KU$_7$?]; < *matāqu*; > *mutqītu*; → *mutqu* I

muttabbiltu jB **1.** "female servant" **2.** ~ "furniture" **3.** lex. pl. (a slide for battering ram) **4.** lex. (a hunting net); < *muttabbilu*

muttabbilu(m) "servant" O/jB; < *wabālu* Gtn

muttablakkatum "rebellious" OB; < *nabalkutu* II Ntn

Muttabriqu → *barāqu* Ntn

muttabrītum mng. uncl. Mari

muttabrītu → also *muštabrītu*

muttaddinu "salesman, seller" jB lex.; < *nadānu* II Gtn

mutta'du, *muttādu* ~ "attentive, submissive" jB; < *na'ādu* Gt

muttaggišu(m), once *muštaggišu* "bustling, restlessly busy" O/jB of human, demon; < *nagāšu* Gtn

muttaḫ(al)lilu(m) and sim. "roaming around; prowler, vagabond" Bab.; < *ḫalālu* III Ntn

muttaḫṣu → *mundaḫṣu*

mutta'ilu mng. uncl. jB; < *itūlu* Gtn

muttakkipu "goring" jB of demon; < *nakāpu* Gtn

muttaklu "trusted person" jB; < *takālu* N

muttakpu "goring" jB of animal, storm; < *nakāpu* Gt

muttalku → *mumtalkum*

muttalliktu(m); pl. *muttallikātu(m)* 'regularly moving' **1.** OA, O/jB (a mobile group); "expeditionary force"; (a group of harvest-collectors)?; (a group of herdsmen); OA uncert. **2.** MB/MA, NA "course, way"; OB math. (a coefficient); jB (slide, rails for battering ram) **3.** Bogh., jB (a sliding door); < *muttalliku*

muttalliku "mobile, movable, agile" jB; of person "roaming, restless"; "travelling"; lex. of oven "portable"; "movable furniture"; < *alāku* Gtn

muttallītum → *muttellû*

muttallu/û → *muttellum*

muttallūtu "superiority" Bab. lex.; < *muttellu*

muttan(an)biṭu "bright, shining" jB; < *nabāṭu* Gtn

muttaparšidu → *muttaprašš̌idu*

muttaplisu ~ "inspector" OB lex.; < *palāsu* Ntn

muttaprašš̌idu, *muttaparšidu* "fugitive, homeless" jB; < *naparšudu* Ntn

muttaprirru "roaming around" jB; < *parāru*

muttaprišu, *muštaprišu* "winged, flying" M/jB [DAL.DAL] of bird, insect; transf. of fire; < *naprušu* II Ntn

muttāqu → *mutāqu*

muttarrittum; pl. *muttarridātu(m)* "perpendicular (line)" OB math.; abbr. *mu-ut*; < *warādum* Gtn

mu(t)tarrītu (a woman hairdresser)? jB lex.

muttarrûm, *muttarrium* "guide; leader (of a caravan)" OA, OB; < *warûm* II Gtn

muttāru (a canal) jB lex.; < *wârum* Gt

muttašrabbiṭu "drifting about" jB; < *našarbuṭu* Ntn

muttaššiṭu "arrogant"? jB; < *wašāṭum*

muttatiku "habitual fornicator" jB lex.; < *niāku* Gtn

muttatu(m) I "half" of parts of the body etc.; field; number of objects, people; OB occas. "one-third"; OA (a half-container on one side of a donkey; half of a standard donkey's load ?)

muttatu II "dead (animal)" NB; < *mâtu*

mutteklemmû "ever-frowning" jB; < *nekelmû* Ntn

mu(t)tellum, *muttallu/û* ~ "princely, noble" Bab.(lit.) of deity; of human, in PN; of falcon; of divine or human speech, order etc.; > *muttallūtu*

muttellû, *muttillû* ~ 'that roams around' jB, NB?; OB f. *muttallītum* (a servant)?; < *ne'ellû* Ntn

mutte(r)rītu (a tool) jB lex.

muttetendu "conspiring, conspirator" jB; < *emēdu*

muttikku, *muttīku* (person suffering from a venereal disease)? jB lex.; < *niāku* Gtn; → *muttatiku*

muttillû → *muttellû*

muttil(t)u (a demon) jB [KIN.GAL.UD.DA]; < *itūlu* ?

mu(t)tinnu "choice wine" jB; < Sum.(Emesal)

muttiš "in front, before (s.o.)" O/jB; < *muttu*

muttu(m) "front (part)" OA, O/jB; Bogh. "front side" of the body; with poss. suff. "before (s.o.)";> *muttiš*

muttû(m), *mattûm* (a pole) O/jB lex.; → *mandû* I

mutturu → *watārum* D

mutu(m) [DAM] m. **1.** "husband", *m. aḫāti* "brother-in-law"; in PNs **2.** "man, warrior"; > *mutūtu* I

mūtu(m) "death" [(NAM.)ÚŠ]; jB ^{d}*Mūtu* (demon Death); *m. šīmti(m)*, *m. ilišu* "natural death"; OB *aran mūtim* "capital punishment"; *bīt m.* "grave"; < *mâtu*; > *mūtānu*

mutuššu (a warrior) jB lex.

mutūtu(m) I O/jB **1.** "status of a husband" in *ana aššūtim u m. aḫāzum*, *nadānum* "to take, give as wife and husband" **2.** "manliness, bravery"; < *mutu*

mutūtu II mng. unkn. NA

muṭa''imu, *muṭe''emu*, *muṭe"e'u.* "lawgiver" NB(roy. inscr.); → *ṭēmu* denom.?

muṭappilu(m) "slanderer"; < *ṭapālu* D

muṭā'ū → *muṭû*

muṭe''emu → *muṭa''imu*

muṭībtu 'that beautifies', (desig. of a door) jB lex.; < *ṭiābu* D

muṭṭarridum? (a transporter) OA; < *ṭarādu* Gtn

muṭṭû "very little, too little" Bab.; < *maṭû* II

muṭû(m), Ass. pl. tant. *muṭā'ū* "deficit, missing sum; deficiency, shortage" Ass., O/jB [NA LAL- ?]; < *maṭû* II; → *muddû*

mu'(ud)dû "(large) quantity; multitude" jB/NA; < *mâdu*

mu''untu "rations, sustenance" NB; < *mânu*; NA → *ma''uttu*

mu'uru in *m. ṣēri* "hunting" MB(Ass.); → *bu''uru* I

mu''uru → *wârum* D

muwarrītum, M/jB *muma/errītu*, *namrītu* (a weapon or tool) O/jB, Am., Nuzi; < *arû* VI D

muwassûm, *mumass/ššû* ~ "inspector of slaves"? O/jB lex.; jB of DN [MAŠ.ŠU.GÁL]; < *wussûm*

muwerrum → *mu'erru*

muza''iztu "distributer" MB as fPN; < *zâzu* D

muzakkûm 'cleaner' Mari, desig. of an implement; < *zakû* II

muzannibu (or *musannipu*) mng. unkn. OB lex.

muzaqqipu (an agricultural occupation) OB lex.; < *zaqāpu* D

muzibbu 'letting flow' j/NB, desig. of a water-clock; < *zâbu* D

muzībtu "drainage" NB; < *zâbu*
muzīqātu (a disease)? jB lex.; < *mazāqu*
muzīqu, *munziqu* "raisin" M/NB [(GIŠ.) GEŠTIN.UD.A]
muzzapru (or *muṣṣabru*) "very bad" (or "malicious") jB of lips, words, person; < *zapāru* (or *ṣabāru* I) Gt
muzzazu(m), *muzzizu(m)*, *munzizu* "standing" (later → *mazzizu*) **1.** OAkk, pl. *muzzāzū* "witness" **2.** OA ~ "guarantor of appearance"? **3.** "standing (on duty), serving", OB *muzzaz bīti* "servant"; *muzzaz ēkallim* "courtier"; *m. bābi* (a tax collector) **4.** OB f.pl. *muzzaztum* (part of a necklace); < *izuzzum*

muzzerrū, *munzerrū* "enemies" O/jB; < *zêru* Gt

muzzizu → *muzzazu*

muzzuzu (or *muṣṣuṣu*) **D** mng. unkn. jB lex.

N

na- as nominal prefix → GAG §56b, c, h

-na **1.** OAkk, OB subjunct. suff. GAG §83c **2.** OB in prohibition after *lā*

na'ādu(m) "to be attentive, concerned" **G** (*i/i*) "pay attention" (to = *ana*); "be concerned, worry" (about = *ana*); stat. "is worrying(ly bad)" of physical condition, disease, assets **Gtn** iter. "be constantly worried" **Gt** "watch carefully"; "observe strictly" (divine) order **D** OA, OB "alert, notify" s.o. (about = acc.), "inform, advise" (of = acc.); Bogh. "start a war"? **Dtn** "alert in each case", Am. "start wars repeatedly" **Š** OA "indicate to s.o. the inadmissibility, impropriety of an action"; OB, j/NB "inform"; NA (of deity) mng. unkn.; MB → *âdu* Š **Štn** OA iter. of Š; M/NA mng. unkn.; > *na'du*; *na'diš*; *nayyādu*; *ni'ittum*; *mutta'du*; *ta''ittu*

na'ādu → also *nâdu*

na'ālu(m) ~ "to moisten" O/jB **G** (*i/i*) eye, tree; > *na'īlu*; *nīlu* II; *nayyālu* II?

na'āmu(m) ~ "to advance boldly"? jB **G** (*i/i*) of soldiers; > *nā'imum*

na'āpu(m) "to be(come) dry, wither" O/jB **G** (*u/u*) of land, wood **Gtn** iter. of G of roots "wither repeatedly" **Dt** "be made to wither"; > *na'pu*; *nīpu*

na'arruru(m) **N** "to go to assist, bring reinforcements" OB, Am. (→ GAG §101g-i); > *ne'rāru*, *ne'rārānum*, *nērārūtu*; *mu'arrirum*; → *arāru* III Ntn

na'āru(m) "to roar, snarl" O/jB **G** of lion, demon **D**, **Dt** = G; > *nā'eru*; → *naḫāru* II

na'āsu(m) "to chew up, gnaw" O/jB **G** (*i/i*) drugs **D** = G

na'āṣu → *nâṣu*

na'āšu "to have difficulty breathing, wheeze"? M/jB **G** (*i/i*) **D** = G ?; > *ni'šu*

na'āšum → also *nêšu*

na'ā'um → *nê'u*

nababtu mng. unkn. jB lex.

nabābu "to play the flute"? jB **G** (*u/u*)

nabādiš → *napādiš*

nabāḫu "to bark" j/NB **G** (*u/u*) of dog, demon **Gtn** iter. of G **D** ~ G

nabākum (or *nab/pāk/qum*) "to bring (in, along)" OB(lit.) **G** (*i/i*, *a/u*) a person

nābališ, *nāpališ* "on dry land" jB; convert "into dry land"; < *nābalu*

nabalkattānu jB "insurgent, rebel"; NB "contravener (of contract)"; < *nabalkattu*

nabalkattu(m) "crossing" Bab., NA [KI.BAL; NB BAL] "crossing" of terrain; (illegal) "crossing" of wall, "burglary"; "(ladder) for crossing, climbing"; "uprising, insurrection, desertion"; "reversal, retreat"; NB "fallow part" of field; NB astr. "excess"; "revolution" of planet; < *nabalkutu* II

nabalkutu(m) I "having crossed over" O/jB; "having exceeded" a certain age; "inverted, awry" of part of body; < *nabalkutu* II

nabalkutu(m) II, *nubalkutu* "to cross over" **N** [BAL; Nuzi KI.BAL] (Mari stat. also *nabalkat)* **1.** "cross, traverse" terrain, mountain, frontier, "ford" a canal, also transf.; "go across", vent. "come across" **2.** jB of witchcraft etc. "befall" (s.o. = acc.); *ina libbi- n.* "come into o.'s mind" **3.** Mari "change o.'s mind", "go over" to s.o.'s side; "revolt, defect" (from = acc.; *eli*, *ṣēru-* ; *ana muḫḫi*; *itti*) **4.** "resist" an order; "oppose" (s.o. = acc.); "be in breach of contract" **5.** of parts of the body "turn over, be inverted"; of earthquake; "roll" eyes; "turn" to flee **6.** jB *nabalkut dīni* "perversion of justice" **7.** of interest rate "change" **8.** "overflow", NB "go beyond, exceed", also math., astr.; OB of delivery "pass time limit"? **Ntn** iter. of N [BAL.BAL; BAL.MEŠ] **Š** caus. "send" or "bring across, transport" cattle?, ships; "forward" letters; "transfer (s.th.) into (another container)"; "copy" text; "cause, allow to defect"; "foment rebellion"; *pī ... š.* "incite (s.o. to do s.th.)"; OA "cause to commit breach of contract"; "displace, upset, remove" object, frontier; "overthrow" throne, government; "reverse, overturn" judgement; "make ineffective" spell; NA "extend past time limit" **Štn** iter. of Š OA "repeatedly transport" letter; "try repeatedly to move" **Št** Mari pass. of Š "be transported"; Nuzi mng. unkn.; > *nabalkattu, nabalkattānu, nabalkutu* I; *šutabalkuttu; muttablakkatum; muštablakkitum* (→ GAG §110c-d)

nabālum (part of a chariot) Early Mari; → *nubālum* ?

nābalu "dry land, mainland" MA, M/NB [PA.RI.IM]; < *abālu*; > *nābališ*

nabāqum → *nabākum*

nabāru, *nabārtu(m)* "(fish-)trap" O/jB, "cage" for lions etc.; < *bâru* I

nabāsiš "like red wool" jB; < *nabāsu*

nabāsu(m), *nabassu, nabāšu, napāsu* "red(-dyed) wool" Bab., NA [SÍK.ḪÉ.MED/ME.DA]; > *nabāsiš*

nabaššuḫum → *namaššu'um*

nabāšu → *nabāsu*

nabāṭu(m) "to be(come) bright, shine" Bab. **G** (*u/u*) of celestial body, divine weapon **D** "make bright" **Dt** pass. of D **Š** "make shine" face, statue; temple façade, building, object **Št** jB "be illuminated, lit" **N, Ntn** (mostly *i/i*) iter. of G "(repeatedly) come alight"; > *muttananbiṭu; nibṭu; nambaṭu*

naba'um (type of reed mat)? OAkk(Sum.)

nabā'u(m) ~ "to rise, well up"? O/jB **G** (*u/u*) of Tigris flood; > *nābi'u* I; *namba'u; nib'u*

nabā'um → also *nabû* II; *nābi'u* II

nabāzu "to bleat" jB **G** (*u/u*) of goat

nabbillu → *nappillu*

nabbu → *nābu* II

nabḫatum → *napḫatum*

nabḫātum → *naḫbātu*

nabiḫum (a gold ornament)? OAkk(Sum.), OB

nābiḫum → *nābi'u* I

nabirium → *nabrium*

nabīum → *nabû* I

nābi'u(m) I, *nābiḫum* "who rises, revolts" O/jB; < *nabā'u*

nābi'u II, *nāpi'/ḫu* "plunderer" jB, of city, land

nablaltum "mixing vat" Mari; < *balālu*

nablālu (a reed stirring-stick)? NB; < *balālu*

nablāṭu(m) **1.** O/jB "subsistence" **2.** jB "healing, cure", *meḫiṣ lā n.* "incurable wound"; < *balāṭu* II

nabliš "like a flame" O/jB; < *nablu* I

nablu(m) I "flash of fire, flame; fire-arrow" O/jB, also as DN; transf. and in simile of rainbow, king, dog; jB (a flame-symbol)?; > *nabliš*

nablu II (desig. of wool) NB; < Aram.?

nablu III (a vessel)? jB

nabnītu "creation" M/NB, NA(lit.), by god(s); "(all) creation, creatures"; "progeny" of king; "product(ion)" of gold, image; "shape, figure, physique" of king, statue; < *banû* IV

nabramu (a piece of furniture) lex.; < *barāmu* II ?

nabraqqu → *namruqqu*

nabrartu, *naprartu* (a reed mat) jB lex.; < *barāru* or *parāru* ?

nabrarû, *naprarû* "plain, open country" jB; < *barāru* or *parāru* ?

nabrītu(m) I **1.** OA (an object) **2.** jB lex. (part of plough); < *nabrû*

Nabrītum II "Born on the day of the *nabrû* offering" OB fPN; < *nabrium*

nabrītum III ~ "inspection" OA; < *barû* I; → also *nebrītu*

nabrium, *nabrû(m), nabirium* OAkk, Bab. **1.** OAkk(Sum.) (an offering, a festival) **2.** OAkk, OB(Ešn., N.Mes.) (a month) **3.** jB lex., NB (a copper vessel)?; > *Nabrītum* II

nabrû, *naprû* (part of plough) jB lex.; > *nabrītu* I

nabrû → also *nabrium*

nabruqqu → *namruqqu*

nabšium "deposit" OAkk, OA; *ana n. ezābum, nadānum* "to leave, hand over on deposit"; < *bašû*

nabṭû, *nebṭû* ~ "horizon" jB; < *bedûm* ?

nabû(m) I, *nabīum* "called, authorized person" of king; in PN "called" by a deity; Bab., M/NA as DN [dAG; dMUATI]; also a star; < *nabû* II

nabû(m) II, OAkk, OA *nabā'um* "to name; nominate; decree" **G** (*i/i*) [SA4] "name" persons, things, places (+ 2 acc.); "invoke" deity; with *mala* "(as much as) is named", i.e. "exists"; "call s.o. (to s.th.)" of deity, esp. in PN; of deity "nominate" king/deity to his/her office; "decree, ordain" rulership, fate, judgement; NB "declare" conversion rate **D** "lament, wail" **Š** "cause to name" **N** "be named"; "be called (upon)"; > *nabû* I; *nību* I, *nibītu*, *nibûtu*; *nubû*; *munabbû*; *tabbītum*

nabû → also *nebû* I.II

nābu(m) I, *nēbu* "insect eggs" **1.** O/jB "nit", jB also as drug **2.** lex. "butterfly eggs"

nābu(m) II, *nabbu* "deity, god" Bab.; < Elam.

nābudu → *abātu* II N

naburriš "like battlements" jB; < *naburru*

naburru (or *napurru*) "battlement(s)" jB(Ass.); > *naburriš*

nābutum "escaped; fugitive" OB; also PN ?; < *abātu* II N

nābutu → also *abātu* II N

na'butu → *abātu* II N; *naḫbutu* I.II

nadabaktu → *natbaktu*

nadabāku → *natbāku*

nadādu(m) **G** (*i/i*) NB "to cede, give way"? < Aram.? **D** OA "search for"?; MA "drive together, round up"? horses; > *nidittum*?

nadāku → *nadāqu*

nadal (or *naṭal*) (a garden plant) NB

nadāniš "for giving" OAkk; < *nadānu* II

nadānu I "gift" M/NB, Bogh., Ug. "gift, payment, tribute"; < *nadānu* II infin.

nadānu(m) II "to give" **G** (pres. OAkk and occas. later *inaddan*, Bab. *inaddin*, *inan/mdin*, Ass. *iddan*; perf. *ittadin*, Ass. *ittidin*, pl. *ittadnū*, NB, M/jB rarely *ittannū*, vent. MB onwards *ittanna*, NB also *ittannu*; pret. *iddin*, vent. wr. OB in PN, MA rarely *idinna(m)*; NB before pron. suff. also *inaddaššu*, *taddaššu*; imper. OAkk, Bab. *idin*, pl. *idnā*, NB *innā*, Ass. *din*; Am. also W.Sem. pass. *iú-da-an/na*; Bogh. also Ass. forms (→ GAG §102j-l)) [mostly SUM; in PNs MU, AŠ] **1.** of person "give, hand over, offer"; "pay" silver, interest; "leave, cede" s.th. to s.o.; "put at s.o.'s disposal" soldier, porter; "deliver"; "give s.o. (in marriage)"; of deity "grant" offspring, (long) life, prosperity; "confer, bestow" rulership on king; "commit, entrust (to s.o.)" sceptre, land; "deliver" enemy; "give" order, advice, reason **2.** "sell", also *ana kaspim*, *ana/aš-šīmim* *n.* **3.** *awātam*, *qabâm* *n.* "promise" **4.** math. "give" a result **5.** with *ana* + infin. or acc. infin. "allow, permit" to do s.th. **6.** with parts of the body: with *idu* O/jB "endeavour", NA "give o.s. up"?; with *libbu* "encourage"; *pānī* *n.* "turn the face toward", "give attention to", NB "reveal o.s."; Mari, Am. "get ready to travel (to)"; *pâ(m)* *n.* "give o.'s consent"; OA *šēpē* *n.* "set out" for **Gtn** iter. of G "give, grant repeatedly"; "sell repeatedly" **Š** "cause to give", esp. "collect, make to pay" tax, debt etc.; "recover" silver, payment **Štn** iter. of Š OB "collect repeatedly" **Št**^{1} OB "be collected" **Št**^{2} (pres. mostly *uštaddan*, rarely *uštanaddan*) [SUM.SUM.MEŠ] jB "intermingle" liquids; "exchange (advice) with one another, confer"; "ponder" **N** "be given, granted"; "be delivered"; "be sold"; > *nadnu*, *nadīnu*, *nadintu*; *nidnu*, *nidintu*; *nādinum*, *nādinānu*, *naddinu*, *nādittu*, *nādinatu*; *nadānu* I, *nadāniš*; *nudunnû*; *maddānum*, *maddattu*, *mandittu*?; *mušaddinum*, *muštaddinu*; *muttaddinu*; *šadduttu*; *tadduntu*; → *tadānu*

nadāqu (or *nadāku*) mng. unkn. jB lex.

nadarruru → *darāru* I N

nadāru(m) I "to be wild, furious" O/jB **G** stat. of demons **N** [ŠU.ZI] inchoative "become wild, go on the rampage" of animal, god, demon **Ntn** iter. of N [om. also IDIM(.MEŠ)]; > *nadru*; *nanduru* I

nadārum II "to vow" OB; < W.Sem.

nadāšum mng. unkn. OB lex.

nadā'um → *nadû* III

nadbāku → *natbāku*

naddinu "generously giving"? jB lex.; < *nadānu* II

nādiānu "the one who laid out" a garden MA; < *nadû* III

nadimmu (a stone-cutting tool) jB lex.; < Sum.

nādinānu(m) "the one who gave" Bab.; "seller"; Nuzi "deliverer, supplier"; < *nādinum*; → *tādinānu*

nādinatu "(woman) who has sold" NB; < *nadānu* II

nadintu(m), *nadittu(m)* "gift" O/MB; < *nadnu*

nadīnu "extra, additional gift"? NB; < *nadnu*

nādinum "giver, donor; seller" OAkk, OB, Nuzi; < *nadānu* II

nadiru → *nadru*

na'diš "attentively, piously" jB; < *na'du*

nadittu → *nadintu*

nādittu "(female) seller" NB; < *nadānu* II

nadītu(m) **1.** OAkk, Bab. "'fallow' (i.e. childless) woman" [LUKUR]; OB "celibate (priestess)" (→ *gagû*) **2.** O/jB lex. (a warehouse) **3.** OA "deposited document"; < *nadû* I

nadium → *nadû* I

nadnu "given" NB in PN; < *nadānu* II; > *nadintu*; *nadīnu*

nadru(m), *nadiru* "wild, aggressive" O/jB; < *nadāru* I

nadû(m) I, OAkk, OA *nadium* "placed, laid (down)" [ŠUB] **1.** of document "deposited"; jB of foundation "laid"; of saliva "spat out" **2.** OB of bag "dropped"? **3.** of field "fallow"; of building, city, region "deserted, abandoned" **4.** lex. (desig. of headdress)? **5.** lex., of person "fallen"?; < *nadû* III

nadû II, *nādu* (a stele)? lex.; < Sum.; → *narû*

nadû(m) III, OAkk, OA *nadā'um* "to throw (down); lay down" **G** (*i/i*) [ŠUB] **1.** "throw s.o., s.th." esp. into (= *ana* or acc.) fire, water, prison; "cast" lot, net; of hot oil "bubble" **2.** "emit, throw up, expectorate" bile, mucus, "spit"; "sweat, discharge" moisture etc.; "utter" noises, "recite" incantation **3.** "drop" prey; "throw off, shed" skin, clothes; "let drop" parts of the body; of bird "let hang" wings; *aḫa(m) n.* "be idle" **4.** "knock over, upset"; "knock out" teeth; "repel" army **5.** "reproach s.o. (= *eli*) for s.th., accuse s.o. (= *eli*) of" **6.** "reject, desert"; "disobey, ignore" orders; "neglect" field; "abandon" house, nest; "stop, give up (doing s.th.)" **7.** "lay down"; "pour, fill (in)" liquids, flour, earth; OA "lay down, deposit" goods; M/NB "lay" foundations; "lay out" building, garden, sleeping place, abode; "pitch" camp; "lay" eggs **8.** "impose"; "(put) load" (on) animal; with 2 acc. "put s.o." in chains; "put on" jewellery; "fasten" a lock, bolt; "set" fire (to); "bring about" need, trouble; with *qātu* "lay hands on s.o., s.th.", "desecrate" temple; "write, set down" in writing; OB math. "put in, enter" number; MB "launch" boat; "apply" irrigation water **9.** various: OA with *īnu* "keep (o.'s eyes) on, be attentive"; OB *ina napištim n.* "put in mortal danger"; NB with *libbu* "take s.th. to heart"; "recommend s.th. warmly"?; M/jB "apply, put on" colour; Nuzi "sentence s.o. to" **10.** stat. of person "is lying down, laid up, ill"; *ana dīnim nadi* "is in dispute, at issue"; Qatna of gem "is set, mounted"; Am. of metal "is incorporated" **Gtn** iter. of G [ŠUB.ŠUB] OA *qātam itaddûm* "deposit the respective share(s)"; stat. "is covered with" spots etc. (= acc.) **Š** caus. of G "cause (s.o.) to give up, force s.o."; "hinder s.o." in doing s.th.; "bring to a standstill" **Štn** iter. of Š, NB "leave fallow repeatedly" **Št** pass. of Š **N** pass. of G "be thrown (away), laid down" [ŠUB]; > *nadû* I, *nadītu*; *nādiānu*; *nīdu*, *nidītu*, *nidûtu*; *mandû* II, *mandītu*; *mušaddû*; *nuduā'um*; *nuddiātu*; *šaddu'atum*; *taddītum*

nadû IV **D** "to cast s.o. out, expel" Am.; < W.Sem.

nadû → also *naṭû* IV

nādu(m), *nayyādu* f. **1.** OAkk, Bab., NA "(water-)skin" [KUŠ.ÙMMU(=A.EDIN.LAL)] **2.** Mari "leather pouch" [KUŠ.EDIN.NA]

nādu → also *nadû* II; *na'du*

nâdu(m), *na'ādu* "to praise, celebrate" **G** (pres. *inâd*, pl. *inaddū*, pret. *inād*, M/NB also *ina''ad*, *i''ud*; prec. *lu-'a₄-ad* OB in PN) [I; NÍ.TUKU] "extol" deity, king in PN **Gtn** iter. of G NB **D** = G **Dtn** iter. of D "praise repeatedly" **Dt** "be praised" **Št** "sing praises antiphonally" **N** "be praised"; > *šanūdu*; *šutanīdû; tanīdu*, *tanattu*, *tanittu*;

na'du(m), *nādu* "attentive, reverent" Bab.; of king, deity; OB of dog "watchful"; jB horse, king *na'id qabli* "devoted to battle"; < *na'ādu*; > *na'diš*

naduḫḫu → *natuḫḫu*

nadunnû → *nudunnû*

na'duru, *nanduru* "darkened, obscured, eclipsed" jB; < *adāru* I N

nadušu ~ "scion, offspring" jB

na'eltu mng. unkn. jB lex.

nā'eru(m), *nā'/ḫiru*, *nē'iru* "roaring" O/jB of lion (figure), deity; "screeching" of bird; < *na'āru*

nagabbiš "into the depths of the water" jB; < *nagbu* I

nagabbu → *nagbu* I

nagabtum → *naqabtum*

nagābum ~ "to store up"? Mari; < W.Sem.?; > *nagbu* II

nagāgu(m) "to bray, bellow, bawl" O/jB **G** (*a/u*, *u/u*) of donkey etc., demon, human sufferer; > *nuggatu*; *naggigu*; *tangagtu*?

naga(ḫ)ḫu jB **1.** lex. (a plant name) **2.** *n. šatti* (a disease) **3.** ~ "barbarian"

nagallum (or *naqallum*) (a title or function of a person) OB

nagalmušu ~ "lofty, exalted"? jB lex.; → *šagalmušu*

nagaltû, *negeltû* "to awake, wake (up)" intrans. M/jB (pret. *iggeltu*, later also *iggelti*, Ass. *iggalti*; jB perf. (vent.) *ittegeltâ*) (→ GAG §110i)

nagālu ~ "to glisten, (be a)glow" M/jB **G** of star, animal **D** "make glow" **N** of star; of person "glow"; transf. of heart, liver "burn"; > *nangulu*; *naggālu*; *mangālu*?

nagamarūte → *nagmuru*

naga(p)pu(m) **1.** O/jB "sheaf, bundle" **2.** Mari mng. unkn.

nagargallu "master joiner" jB of deity; < Sum.; → *nagāru* I

nagarruru → *qarāru* N

***nagaršû N** (or *garāšu* N ?) ~ "to run about in confusion" jB **Š** "confuse, upset" offerings ?

nagāru(m) I, *nan/mgāru*, *naggāru* "joiner, carpenter" [(LÚ.)NAGAR] maker of furniture, doors, boats; M/NA *n. pāši* "adze-worker"; NA *n. mugirri* "wheelwright, cartwright"; NB as family name; < Sum.; > *nagārūtu*; → *nagargallu*

nagāru(m) II **G** NA mng. unkn. **D** "to denounce" O/jB; > *nāgiru*, *nāgirtu*, *nāgirūtu*; *mangāru* II?; *munaggiru*, *munaggirūtu*; *taggertum*

nagārūtu (prof., craft of the carpenter) jB, NA; < *nagāru* I

nagāšu(m) "to go to(wards)" O/jB **G** (*u/u*) of men, animals **Gtn** (*i/i*) "wander, travel about" [DAG.DAG] **D** jB of woman mng. unkn. **Dtn** jB "roam around" **N** ~ G jB; > *nugušša*; *muttaggišu*

nagbu(m) I, *nagabbu* **1.** OAkk, Bab., NA "underground water" [IDIM], "source, head-waters" of a river; deified [^{d}IDIM] (= Ea) **2.** Bab. "(the) whole, entirety" of wisdom, cult; of people; > *nagabbiš*

nagbu(m) II ~ "stored" Mari, jB lex., of grain; < *nagābum*

naggalapu → *naglabu*

naggālu "glowing" MB in PN; < *nagālu*

naggāru → *nagāru* I

naggigu, *nangigu*, *nāgigu* "that brays, braying" jB lex., of donkey, man; < *nagāgu*

nagimu → *ligimû*

nāgirtu "(female) herald" jB, of goddess; < *nāgiru*

nāgiru(m) "(town) crier, herald" [LÚ.NIMGIR, NA often LÚ.NÍMGIR, 600(=DIŠ+U)]; also of deities, transf. of animals; jB, NA (a high official), *n. rabû* "chief herald", *n. ēkalli* "palace herald"; < *nagāru* II

nāgirūtu, *nammigirūtu* (office of the herald) jB; < *nāgiru*

nagiṣṣu → *namgiṣṣu*

nagītu "district" j/NB; also in PlNs; NB *bāb n.* (a city gate or quarter in Uruk); < *nagû* I

nagiu → *nagû* I

naglabu(m), NA also *nag(ga)lapu* Bab., M/NA **1.** "razor, shaving blade" [GÍR] **2.** "hip", du. "flanks" of animal [(UZU.)MAŠ.SÌLA; OB also ŠU.I]; astr. (part of moon); < *gullubu* II

nagmaru(m) **1.** OB "final payment" **2.** M/jB "end" (of a month) **3.** MB "completion" of work; < *gamāru* II

***nagmuru**; pl. *nagamarūte* "completed, finished"? NA; < *gamāru* II N

nagum (a bird) OB

nagû(m) I, NA *nagiu*; pl. *nagû*, NA *nagiāni* "region, district; coastal area" Bab., M/NA; jB "island"?; > *nagītu*

nagû(m) II, *negû* "to sing joyfully, carol" O/jB **G** (*u/u*, jB also *i/i*) **Gtn**; > *nūgu*; *nigûtu*; *tamgītu*

nagubinakku (a stone vessel) jB lex.; < Sum.

nāgurtu "hire"? NA, of persons; < *agāru*

naḫabû → *naḫbû*

naḫalaptu → *naḫlaptu*

naḫa(l)littu (a garment)? MA; rdg. uncert.

naḫallu(m), *naḫlu(m)* "stream, wadi, gorge" Bab., M/NA; OB also in PlN

naḫallulu → *ḫalālu* III N

naḫalṣû → *neḫelṣû*

naḫālu(m) I "to (pass through a) sieve, sift" O/jB **G** (*a/u*) **D** ~ G lex.?; > *naḫlu*; *neḫlu*; *nuḫḫulu*; *maḫḫalu*?, *maḫḫaltu*

naḫālum II "to share out, transfer property" (to s.o. = acc.) **G** (*i/i*) Mari **D** ? OB ext. mng. unkn. **N** pass. of G ? Mari; < W.Sem.; > *niḫlatum*

naḫanṣû in *karān n.* (a type of wine) NA

naḫaptu → *naḫḫaptu*

naḫarbušu "to freeze" intrans.? jB **Ntn** iter.; < *ḫurbāšu* denom.

naḫarmumu "to break down, collapse" M/NB **N**; **Š** "cause to collapse"

naḫarmuṭu(m) **N** "to dissolve, melt, disintegrate" intrans. O/jB, of ice, tablet, person, dream **Š** trans. "melt, dissolve"; also transf., enemy

naḫaršušu N ~ "to collapse" jB **Š** caus.

naḫāru(m) I ~ "to be shrivelled, withered"? O/jB, MA **G** MA stat. of document "is invalid"? **D** "make shrivel, cause to wither"?; transf. "invalidate"; → *na'āru* D **Dt** "be made to shrivel"?; > *naḫru*; *nuḫḫuru*?

naḫāru(m) II "to snort" jB **G** (*u/u*); > *naḫīru*; *nāḫiru*, *nāḫirānu*, *neḫru*; *nuḫḫuru*?; → *na'āru*

naḫāsu(m), j/NB *neḫēsu* "to (re)cede; return" Bab. **G** (*i/i*) [LAL] of troops "withdraw, yield"; of entrails "recede, be sunken"?; in chariot malfunction → *narkabtu*; of flood "subside, abate"; MB of wall "cave in"; NB "deduct"; NB "flow back", of payments into treasury; of field "revert (to s.o.)"; "withdraw, shrink from" (an oath); j/NB of celestial bodies "retrograde"; Am. "halt, stop s.o." **Gtn** jB iter. "subside repeatedly" of flood **Gt** jB "pale, blanch"? **D** ~ "retch"? (**Dt** → *duḫḫusu* Dt) **Š** NB **1.** "send back, return" (s.o. or s.th.) **2.** "let recede"; > *naḫsu*; *niḫistu*

naḫāšu(m) "to be(come) luxuriant" Bab., MA **G** (*i/i*) "prosper, thrive, be healthy", also in PN; infin. "health, prosperity"; Nuzi "be pleasing" to s.o. **D** "grant prosperity, health", NB also in PN **N** OB lex. "become prosperous, happy"?; > *naḫšu*; *nuḫšu*, *nuḫšānu*; *nuḫāšu*

naḫātu(m) "to be(come) small, diminished" O/jB **G** (stat. *naḫut*) "be of inferior quality", of field; with *libbu* "be(come) despondent, fainthearted" **D** "diminish, reduce"?; "castrate"? bulls; "clip" wings; > *naḫtu*; *neḫtu*?; *nuḫḫutu*; *niḫittu*?; *taḫḫittu*?

naḫbaltu "pit(fall)"? jB; < *naḫbalu*

naḫbalu(m) "trap" O/jB "pitfall" for lions etc., "box-trap"; *n. tâmti* "trap of the sea"?; < *ḫabālu* IV; > *naḫbaltu*

naḫbaṣu (an oil flask) jB, NA; < *ḫabāṣu* II ?

naḫbaštum (a reed object) OAkk(Sum.); < *ḫabāšu* II

naḫbašu (a chaff-cutter)? jB lex., NB; < *ḫabāšu* II

naḫbātu(m), *nabḫātum*, *naḫpātum* (a leather or reed carrying-case) OAkk(Ur III), O/jB; < *ḫabû* IV

naḫbû, *naḫabû* (a drinking vessel) M/NB, NA; NB *ša naḫbêšu* (a drinks vendor) as family name; < *ḫabû* III

naḫbutum I "migrated"? OB in *kakkum n.* (feature on part of the liver); < *ḫabātu* III N ?

naḫbutu II "robbery"? NA; < *ḫabātu* I

naḫellu (part of a cup) Qatna; < Hurr.?

naḫḫaptu (or *naḫaptu*) (a garment) NA

naḫḫasu → *naḫsu*

naḫḫu ~ "rent" NB for garden, house

naḫḫuḫu (a container) MB

nāḫirānu "snorter, puffer" MB as PN; < *nāḫiru*

naḫīru(m) "nostril" Bab., M/NA [KA.BÚN]; MB/MA "spout" for water; < *naḫāru* II

nāḫiru 'snorter' MA, M/jB **1.** MB/MA ~ "dolphin" **2.** jB lex. (a bird); < *naḫāru* II

nāḫiru → also *nā'eru*

naḫīṣum (or *na'/ḫīṣ/sum*) (a prof.) OB lex.

naḫlaptu(m), *naḫlapu*, later *naḫalaptu*, Nuzi occas. *naḫnaptu* **1.** "garment, cloak, coat" [(TÚG.)GÚ.È(.A); NA TÚG.DUL/DÙL] Bogh. *ēpiš n.* (a tailor); lex. *n. ūri* "loincloth" **2.** NB brick "facing, cladding" (of ziggurrat) **3.** NA *n. pēmi* (a cut of meat); < *ḫalāpu* I; → *taḫlaptu*

naḫlu(m); f. *naḫiltu* "sieved; strained" **1.** Bab., MA of corn etc. **2.** lex. of textile "open-work"? **3.** MB lex. (desig. of diseased skin); < *naḫālu* I

naḫlu → also *naḫallu*

naḫmaṣu (a stand for a cauldron)? NB; < *ḫamāṣu*

naḫmum (an ominous sign) Mari

naḫnaḫatu "(nasal) septum"? NA

naḫnaptu → *naḫlaptu*

naḫparum (a wrap)? OAkk; < *ḫapāru* I ?

naḫpātum → *naḫbātu*

naḫpum adj. mng. unkn. Mari, of finger; < *nakāpu* ?

naḫpû (a tool, phps.) "(clod-)breaker" jB lex.; < *ḫepû* II

naḫramum, in pl. *naḫramū* "blanket" or "cloak"? OB; < *ḫarāmum* I; → *nāramu*

naḫru ~ "withered, shrivelled"? jB lex. of wood; med., of patient "wasted, emaciated"?; *muruṣ n.* (desig. of a disease); < *naḫāru* I

naḫsu(m), *naḫḫasu* "(very) thin, narrow" O/MB; of fabric "delicate, fine"; of arrow "pointed, sharp"; < *naḫāsu*

naḫṣabum (an object made of silver)? Mari; < *ḫaṣābu* I ?

naḫšu(m) "thriving, healthy; lusty" OAkk, O/jB; OAkk, OB as PN; f. pl. *naḫšātu* "haemorrhage"; < *naḫāšu*

naḫtu "small, slight" j/NB **1.** "young (bird)" **2.** lex. (a part of the entrails)? **3.** lex. (a type of garment); < *naḫātu*; → *neḫtu*

naḫû mng. unkn. Am.

nāḫu(m), *nuḫḫu* "pig's fat, lard" OAkk, OA, O/jB [Ì.ŠAḪ]

nâḫu(m), OAkk, Ass. *nuāḫu(m)* "to rest" **G** [ḪUN.GÁ] **1.** "be at rest, become restful"; of celestial bodies "be still"; of fire "burn steadily"; of a maniac "quieten, calm down"; of ritual "stop"; of country, battle "be pacified", MA, MB also in fPN; "calm o.s., relent" of deity, also of human anger, excitement **2.** jB mng. unkn. **D** "calm (s.o.), appease, placate" deities; "pacify" a country; "soothe, sedate" pain, anger; "extinguish" fire; "settle" (i.e. draw back ?) a curtain **Š** ~ D "soothe" the heart **N** of a patient "come to rest"; > *nēḫu*, *nēḫtu*, *nēḫiš*; *nūḫtu*; *nuḫḫu*; *tanēḫu*, *tanēḫtu*; *tanūḫtum*?; *manāḫtu*

naḫurutu → *nuḫurtu*

naḫūtum, *na'ûtum* ? (a type of onion)? OB

nā'ikānu "the one who had intercourse" MA; < *niāku*

na'īlu "flooded valley" Bab., MA; < *na'ālu*

nā'imum "bold" OB PN; < *na'āmu*

nā'iru → *nā'eru*

na'īs/ṣum → *naḫīṣum*

na'ištum → *napištu*

nak(a) → *annaka*

nakabtum → *naqabtum*

nakādu(m) "to beat, throb" Bab., MA **G** (*u/u*) "be frightened, anxious"; of the heart "pound, beat" **Gt**, **Gtn**; (**D** → *naqādu* D) **Š** OA, NB "make" the heart "throb", "worry (s.o.)" **N** OB (pres. *u*) "be anxious"; > *nakkadu*

nakalmû → *nekelmû*

nakālu(m) "to be(come) skilful, artful, clever" Bab., NA **G** (*i/i*) "be clever, skilful"; NB mng. uncert.; *niklu n.* jB "outwit, dupe" s.o., NA, NB "be insidious, deceive" **D** "make skilfully"; NB *nikiltu n.* "trick" s.o. **Š** jB "cause to make (s.th.) skilfully"; > *naklu, naklūtu, nakliš; nakīlum; niklu, nikiltu; takkīlū; takkalātu*

nakamaru → *nakmaru*

nakāmu(m) "to heap, pile (up)" Bab., OA **G** (*a/u*, OA, M/jB also *i/i*) "amass, accumulate" goods, tribute **D** ~ G **N** pass.; > *nakmu* I, *nākimum*?; *nikmu, nikimtu; nakkamtu*

nakāpu(m) "to push, thrust" Bab., NA **G** (*i/i*) [DU7] of horned animals "gore, butt"; transf. "touch, abut"; "mutilate, stub" finger; (as var. of *naqābu*) "pierce, stab" with a weapon; "penetrate (sexually), deflower" **Gtn** iter. of G "push forward, advance repeatedly" in battle; "push aside, away"; of mountains "abut" **Gt** [DU7.DU7] of animals "butt each other"; transf. of rulers "fight each other, battle"; of storm "shake s.th. thoroughly, knock about"; of water "surge, break over s.th. or s.o." **D** "knock down, push away"; "butt"; > *nakpu; nākipu; nikpu, nikiptu* I; *nakkapu, nakkaptu, nakkāpû; takkiptu; muttakkipu, muttakpu; naḫpum*?

nakaru(m); f. *nakartu(m)*, NB *nakaštu* "strange, unknown; enemy" OAkk, Bab., NA [(LÚ.)KÚR] OB also PN; of planet Mars; < *nakāru*; → *nakru*

nakāru(m) "to be(come) different, strange, hostile" **G** (*i/i*; stat. *naki/ar*) [KÚR] "change (in appearance)"; of plan, order "change"; "be(come) estranged", "grow angry"; "rebel, revolt" (against = *itti*, NA *issi*); NB *bēl nakāri* "enemy"; "be at feud with"; "deny" a statement, with neg. "confirm"; "contest, dispute"; "deny s.o. s.th., refuse" **Gtn** iter. of G [KÚR.KÚR] "keep changing o.'s mind"; of flame "flicker, waver"; of constellation "change position repeatedly"; "move house repeatedly" **Gt** recipr. "become (each other's) enemies" **D** [KÚR] "change, alter" words, names, prices, plans; "improve"; "give up" a vice; "eliminate, remove" (seat of) a disease; "remove, abolish" king(ship); "hand s.th. on"; "transfer, move s.o. elsewhere"; "remove" from office; "shift, (re)move" objects; clothes; "clear" a building site, ruins; "clear out" brazier, vessel; "move" domicile etc.; OB stat. "is strange, outlandish"; NA "make enemies of"; W.Sem. *nukkir* "made hostile" **Dtn** iter. of D [KÚR.KÚR] **Dt** pass. of D "be changed, removed"; Bogh. "be horrified, panic-stricken"? **Š** "make enemies of, cause enmity between"; > *nakru, nakaru, nakkarum, nakriš, nakrūtu; nikaru; nukru, nukurtu; nukurrû; takkīrum*

nakāsu(m) "to cut, fell" [KUD] **G** (*i/i*) **1.** "fell, cut down" trees etc.; "cut, trim" beams; "knock, cut off"; Nuzi, NB "partition off" field; "cut off" dates from tree; "cut through" s.th., esp. garment, hem (in legal context) **2.** "sever" parts of the body; with *qaqqadu* "decapitate", *napištu* ("throat; life"); OB transf. "keep away, hold off"; "kill, slaughter" people, animals **Gtn** iter. of G **D** ~ G esp. with pl. or du. objects; also "chop, hack to pieces"; MA "mutilate"; "slaughter" **Dt** of sacrificial animal "be slaughtered" **N** pass. of G; > *naksu, nakistu*?, *niksu; nikkas*?; *nakūsu*?; *nukāsu; nākisu; nukkusu* I; *makkasu, makkastu*

nakaštu → *nakaru*

nakāšu(m) "to set aside" OA, O/jB **G** (*i/i*) Mari "turn away" envoys; "leave unused" field, female breasts; "set" fire to s.th. (= 2 acc.) **D** = G **Ntn** ?; > *nakištu*?; *nikištum*?

nakbartu (a thick garment) MB; < *kabāru*

nakbasu(m), *nakbassu* **1.** O/jB "step" of a staircase **2.** M/NA, Nuzi (a mat) **3.** Mari "sole" of foot; < *kabāsu*

nakbatu(m) "weight, combat power" of troops O/jB [DUGUD; IDIM], esp. om.; also "main body" of army; < *kabātu*

nakdu → *nakkadu*

nakiltu → *naklu; naksu*

nakīlum mng. unkn. OB; < *nakālu* ?

nakimtu → *nakmu* II

nākimum OB as PN; < W.Sem. or *nakāmu* ?

nākipu "goring" jB; < *nakāpu*

nakiru → *nakru*

nakistu (or *nakištu*) mng. unkn. jB lex.; < *nakāsu* (or *nakāšu*)

nākisu, NB also *nēkisu* **1.** NA, NB "butcher" **2.** NA "woodcutter"; < *nakāsu*

nakištu → *nakistu*

nak(ka)du ~ "(still) twitching, pulsating" of liver jB; < *nakādu*

nakkamtu(m), j/NB also *nakkant/du* "treasure, stores; treasury, storehouse" Bab., M/NA; also *bīt n.* "storehouse"; NA of horses "reserves"; < *nakāmu*

nakkaptu(m) "brow, temple" Bab. [SAG.KI]; often du.; also of sheep; < *nakāpu*

nakkapu(m) **1.** jB (projecting part), "tip" of foot, lung **2.** NA (or *nakuppu*, wr. *na-ku-pu*) after measurement "in circumference" **3.** OA (a caulking tool)?; < *nakāpu*

nakkāpû(m) "goring, liable to butt" OB [DU_7×DU_7]; < *nakāpu*

nakkarum "hostile" OB; < *nakāru*

nakkatu (or *naqqatu*) (a type of land) Nuzi

nakku(r)ru mng. unkn. OA; → *namkūru*; *naqquru*

nakkūru → *namkūru*

nakkuššu "substitute (worker)"? OB(Alal.), Nuzi; < Hurr.

naklamû → *nekelmû*

nakliš "artistically, skilfully" M/NB; < *naklu*

naklu; f. *nakiltu* "skilful, elaborate, clever" Bab., NA; < *nakālu*; > *nakliš*; *naklūtu*

naklūtu "ingenuity" jB; < *naklu*

nakmartu(m) **1.** OB math. "sum, total" **2.** jB (an ailment)?; < *kamāru* IV

nakmaru(m), NB also *nakamaru*, NA *nakuaru* (a basket, pannier) Bab., NA for textiles, liquids etc.; < *kamāru* IV

nakmasu mng. unkn. jB; < *kamāsu* I ?

nakmu I "heaped (up)" jB; med. "accumulated" matter in a body; < *nakāmu*

nakmu II (or *naqmu*); f. *nak/qimtu* mng. unkn. O/jB (desig. of people)

nakmû, Mari *nakwûm* "roasting implement" O/jB; < *kawûm* II

nakpu "mutilated, crushed"? jB of finger; < *nakāpu*

nakramu, NB *nakrimu* (leather container for liquids) MA, NB; < *karāmu*

nakriš "like an enemy" jB; < *nakru*

nakru(m), *nakiru(m)*, NB *nekru* "strange, foreign" [KÚR] of language, city, people; "hostile (person); enemy"; OB lex. *ša nakirti* "enemy"; < *nakāru*; > *nakriš*, *nakrūtu*; → *nakaru*

nakrūtu "hostilities" jB; < *nakru*

nakruṭu "mercy"; < *karāṭu* N

naksu(m); jB f. *nakiltu* "cut (off)" Bab., NA [KUD]; of tree "felled"; of limb "severed"; of animal "slaughtered"; < *nakāsu*

naktamtu(m) **1.** OA, jB lex. (vessel with) "lid" **2.** OAkk, jB lex. (a door); < *katāmu*

naktamu(m) **1.** O/jB "cover, lid" **2.** lex. in *n. pî* "horse's bit"; < *katāmu*

naktu (a textile) Ug.

nakû (stopper, plug)? Am.

nâku "to browse on"? jB **G** of elephants

nâku → also *niāku*

nakuaru → *nakmaru*

nakuppu → *nakkapu* 2

nakūsu mng. uncert. jB in *n. nakis*; < *nakāsu* ?

nakwûm → *nakmû*

nalabanu → *nalbanu*

nalabâna → *nalbân*

nalāšu(m) "to (fall as) dew" O/jB **G** (*u/u*) of demon in simile **D** "bedew"; < *nalšu* denom.

nalbābu "rage, fury" jB; < *labābu*

nalbân, *nalabâna* "all around" M/NA; < *lawûm* II

nalbanatta "like a brick mould" jB; < *nalbattu*

nalbantu → *nalbattu*

nalbanu(m), later also *nal(a)ba/inu* "brick mould" Bab. [GIŠ.Ù.ŠUB]; OB math. (a coefficient); < *labānu*; → *nalbattu*

nalbašu(m), Am. also *malbašu* "cloak, coat" O/jB [TÚG.MAḪ]; *n. ṣēni* "sheep's fleece"; *n. šamê* [AN.MA] 'cloak of the skies', i.e. "cloud cover"; < *labāšu*

nalbattu(m), *nalbantu*; pl. *nalbanātu* "brick mould" OAkk, Bab., NA [GIŠ.Ù.ŠUB]; Mari also "frame" for gems; < *labānu*; > *nalbanatta*; → *nalbanu*

nalbētu ~ "wrap(ping), overlay" M/NA of textile, gold; < *lawûm* II

nalbinu → *nalbanu*

nalbubu "furious, raging" jB; < *labābu*

naldar → *naltar*

nāliš "like a deer" jB; < *nālu*

nalmu, *nermu* ~ "foundation" jB lex.

nalpattu(m) **1.** OB math. "given value" of a number **2.** Bab. (shallow bowl, jar) [GIŠ.DÍLIM.TUR]; < *lapātu*

nalpatu, *nalpitu* (a metal tool) Mari; < *lapātu*

nalšu, *naššu(m)*, *namšu* "(nocturnal) dew" Bab., NA [ŠÈG]; > *nalāšu*

naltar, *naldar*, *nātar* (a type or quality of gold) NB

naltiptu → *naštiptum*

nālu(m), *nayyalu* "roe deer"? O/jB, M/NA [DÀRA.MAŠ.DÀ]; > *nāliš*

nâlu(m), *niālu(m)* "to lie down (to sleep)" **G** (pret. *inăl*, pres. *inâl*, *inêl*; stat. OA, Nuzi *nāl*) [NÚ] "lie down" to die; stat. "is lying down" sick etc. **D** (pret. *unīl*, MA *una''il*) "lay, strike down" soldiers **Š** **1.** "lay s.o. down" [NÚ]; "lay out" for burial; "spread out" substances for mag. purposes; lex. "lay, spread out" corn for cleaning? **2.** "flatten" a city **3.** "preserve" s.th. in salt or sand; > *nīlu* I; *nayyālu* I; *mayyālu*, *mayyaltu*; → *itūlu* (→ GAG §107i-m)

na'lu(m), *ne'lu(m)* (a disease) Bab.

namaddu(m) I, *namandu(m)*, Bogh. *namm=an/ddu* **1.** Bab., OA "measuring vessel" [NB DUG.NÍNDA ?] **2.** M/NA "measurement, dimension", pl. f.; < *madādu* I

namaddu II "darling, loved one" Ass., M/jB; < *madādu* II

nam'adum "(large) quantity, amount, number" OA; < *mâdu*

namallu, *namullu* "plank-bed" jB lex.; < Hurr.

namālu(m), *namlu* "ant" O/jB, Am.; OB also (f)PN

namandu → *namaddu* I

namanšu'um → *namaššu'um*

namānu (a medicinal plant) jB

namārītu, *namirātu*; pl. *namārātu* "daybreak, third watch of the night" jB [EN.NUN. ZALAG.GA]; < *nawāru*

namarkû, *nemerkû* "to be late, be delayed" M/NB, NA **N** (pret. *immerki*, Ass. *immarki*, pres. *immerekki*, Ass. *immarakki*) esp. on journey; also of stars; "fall behind, default" (with payments or obligations) (concerning = acc.) **Š** caus. of N "delay s.o."; < *warkûm* denom.?

nāmartu "appearance" jB; OA of first sighting of moon; < *amāru* I

namaru (a quiver)? jB lex.

namāru "clearing, path" jB; < *nawāru*

namāru → also *nawāru*

nāmaru(m), *nāmeru* **1.** OAkk, O/MB, Qatna, Am., NA "mirror" **2.** OAkk, MB (a garment) **3.** Ass., jB "watch-tower"; jB *bīt n.*; < *amāru* I

namāṣu, *nemēṣu* "(butter) churn" jB lex.; < *mâṣu*; → *namūṣu*

namašiatum mng. unkn. OB

namaššu'um, *namaššuḫum*, OAkk(Ur III) *nab/waššu'/ḫum*, OB *namanšu'um* (a garment) OAkk, OA, OB

namāšu(m) "to set (o.s.) in motion, start out" **G** (*u/u*) on journey, campaign; Ug. *dīna n.* "bring a lawsuit" (*itti* = against s.o.) **Gt** "move towards each other"? **D** "make s.o. move, set s.th. in motion"; NA "depart" (ellipt.); Ug. "initiate" lawsuit (→ G) **R** OB lex. (→ *nammušīšu*); > *nammaštû*

namattanni (a herdsman)? MB(Alal.); < Hurr.

namattu "increase, enlargement"? MA; < *mâdu*

namā'um → *namû* II

nambas/ṣum → *nambazum*

nambattu rdg. uncl. (wr. *nam*-BAD-*tú*) (a ghost)? jB lex.

nambaṭu (a bright mark)? jB; < *nabāṭu*; → *nambazum*

namba'u "source, spring" M/jB; < *nabā'u*

nambazum (or *nambas/ṣum*) mng. unkn. OB; = *nambaṭu* ?

nambūbtu, *nambūmtu* "wasp" jB; → *nūbtu*

namburbû "apotropaic ritual" j/NB, NA [NAM. BÚR.BI]; < Sum.

namdālu, *nandālu* "millipede" jB lex.

namdattum "(amount) measured, paid" OB; < *madādu* I

namerimburrudû (ritual to remove a curse) jB [NAM.ÉRIM.BÚR.RU.DA]; < Sum.

nāmeru → *nāmaru*

namgaru → *namkaru*

namgāru → *nagāru* I

namgiṣṣu, *nagiṣṣu* mng. unkn. JB

namgugu → *magāgu* N

namḫartu(m), *namḫaru* "receipt(s), takings" O/jB [ŠU.TI.A ?]; *n. ēkallim* goods "received by palace"; measure, weight *ša n.* "for receipts"; < *maḫāru*

namḫarû **1.** jB lex. (container on cart)? → *ḫarû* I **2.** jB (a poisonous plant); < Sum.

namḫāru(m) (a vessel) OAkk, Bab.; often of metal, for flour, beer etc.; < *maḫāru*

namḫaṣ(t)u(m), NA *nanḫaṣ(t)u* (a wooden pole) O/jB, NA; < *maḫāṣu*

namiratu → *nawiratum*

namirātu → *namārītu*

namirtu → *nawiratum*

namiru → *nawru*

namkaru(m), M/NB mostly *namgaru*, also *namqaru* "irrigation canal, reservoir"? Bab.; MB, NB also in PlN *Na(m)k/gar-DN*; < *makāru* I

namkattum mng. unkn. Mari

namkūru(m), *namkurru*, Bogh. also *nan/kkūru*, often pl. "property, possession(s), capital" O/jB, M/NA [NÍG.GA]; O/MB *rēš n.* "liquid capital, available funds"; jB lex. *n. īnī* (an expression for mirror); < *makāru* II

namlaktum, usu. pl. "(governed) territory, realm" Mari; < *malāku* III

namlu → *namālu*

namman/ddu → *namaddu* I

nammar → *nimru* I

nammaštû(m), *nammaššû(m)*, *nammaštu* **1.** Bab.(lit.) "moving things, animals" [NÍG.KI ?; A.ZA.LU.LU; NÍG.ZI.GÁL] *namaššê (ša) ṣēri* "wild animals" **2.** Mari, jB [Á.DAM] (a human settlement) ; < *namāšu* ?

nammigirūtu → *nāgirūtu*

nammû (a headband, headdress) jB lex.

na(m)mušīšu(m), *nam(mu)šūšum*, *namšīšu* ~ "mobile, agile" O/jB; jB *alāku n.* "to pass away, die"; < *namāšu* R or Sum.?

nampašu → *nappašu*

namqaru → *namkaru*

namrāṣiš "with hardship" jB; < *namrāṣu*

Namra-ṣīt → *nawru*

namrāṣu(m) "hardship, difficulty" Bab.(M/NA) of terrain, experience; < *marāṣu*

namrâtum → *namriātum*

namrā'um, usu. pl. "fattening" OB; < *marû* II

namriātum, *nawriātum*, *namrâtum* f. pl. OB, Ug. **1.** "fat(tened) animals, fatstock"; *ša namriātim* "official in charge of fattening animals" **2.** (a festival)? (→ *namrītu*); < *marû* II

namrīrum, *namrirru* "awe-inspiring radiance" OAkk, Bab.(lit.); usu. pl.; of deities, demons, kings, temples; < *nawāru*

namriš "splendidly, brilliantly" j/NB; < *nawru*

namrītu (a festival) OB; < *marû* II or *nawāru* ?; → *namriātum* 2

namrītu → also *muwarrītum*

namru → *nawru*; *nimru* I

namrû → *namrā'um*

namruqqu, *nabru/aqqu* (a medicinal plant) M/jB

namruratu → *namurratu*

namrūtu "mother-of-pearl"? jB/NA; of the sea (*ša tâmti*); < *nawru*

namsītu → *nemsētu*

namsû → *nemsû*

namsuḫu, *nemšaḫu* "crocodile" MA, MB; Qatna as figurine; < Eg.

namṣabu → *naṣṣabu*

namṣartu, *naṣṣartu* (a storage vessel) j/NB; < *naṣāru* ?

namṣāru(m), Ug. *mamṣāru* **1.** OAkk, Bab. "sword" [GÍR.GAL]; also transf. for deities **2.** lex., Ug. (a squared stick, mace)? **3.** lex. (desig. of a canal); < *maṣāru*

namṣ(at)u → *lamṣu*

namša (an alabastron) Am.; < Eg.

namšāḫu(m) (leather container for cosmetics)? O/jB; < *mašāḫu* I

namšarratu mng. unkn. Am.

namšartu; pl. *namšarāte* "threshing-sledge"? MA, Am.?; < *mašāru*

namšāru, *namšāšu* "stomach" jB lex.

namšiḫu → *naššiḫu*

namšīšu → *nammušīšu*

namšu → *nalšu*

namšūšum → *nammušīšu*

namtaggû "sin" jB lex.; < Sum.

namtallûm, *nantallû(m)* "(solar, lunar) eclipse" OB; < Sum. nam-dalla ?; → *antallû*

namtaru(m), *namtarru* "fate" OB lex., M/jB [NAM.TAR]; as desig. of demon or underworld god; < Sum.

namtullu → *nattullu*

namû I; pl. *namûti* "living in the steppe, steppe-dweller" Ug.; MB(Alal.) (desig. of a social group); < *nawûm* I + *-ī*

namû II, OAkk *namā'um* (a copper object) OAkk ?, Nuzi, jB

namû → also *nawûm* I.II

nāmu (a bird call or noise) jB

namuggatu → *namungatu*

namū'iš (to turn) "into a wasteland" jB; < *nawûm* I

namulḫu (a plant) jB lex.

namullu → *namallu*

namundu mng. unkn. jB lex.

namungatu, *namuggatu* "(state of) paralysis" MB; < *magāgu*

namurratu(m), jB also *namruratu* "awe-inspiring radiance" OAkk, Bab.; of deities, kings, weapons; < *namurru*

namurru(m) "awe-inspiringly radiant" OAkk, O/jB; of deities also in PN; of kings, weapons; < *nawāru*; > *namurratu*

nāmurtu, NB *nāmuštu* "audience gift, present" M/NA, M/NB; < *amāru* I; → *tāmartu*

nāmurtu → also *nanmurtu*

namūṣu (a tool) jB lex.; → *namāṣu*

namušīšu → *nammušīšu*

nāmuštu → *nāmurtu*

namūtu(m), jB(NA) *numuttu*, *na/u'ūtu* ~ "derision, mockery" O/jB, MA; *n. epēšu(m)* "to deride, mock", *ēpiš n.* "scorner, mocker"

namûtu "desolation, wasteland" jB; *n. alāku* "to turn into, become wasteland", *n. šūluku* "to turn s.th. into wasteland, make desolate"; < *nawûm* I

namzāqu(m), *nanzāqu* "key" O/jB [GIŠ.E11; NÍG.GAG.TI]; *ša n.* (a doorkeeper, person in charge of keys)

namzītu(m), *nanzītu*, NA *nazzītu* "mash tub" OAkk, Bab., NA [DUG.NÍG.DÚR.BÙR]; < *mazā'u* II

nanaḫu → *ananiḫu*

nanaptum (or *nānaptum*) (a type of rope) Mari

nanbû (a garment) jB lex.

nandālu → *namdālu*

nanduru I "very wild, furious" jB; < *nadāru* I

nanduru II "intertwined" jB of features on liver; < *edēru* N

nanduru → also *na'duru*

nangāru → *nagāru* I

nangigu → *naggigu*

nangu (a vessel)? NB

nangugu → *agāgu* N

nangulu, *nankulu*, *nengulu* "glowing" jB of star; ^{d}*Nengultu*, *Neggultu* (name for planet Venus); < *nagālu* N

nanḫas(t)u → *namḫaṣtu*

nanḫuzu ~ "inflamed, burning" jB of demons; < *aḫāzu* N

naniḫu → *ananiḫu*

naniqu (a plant)? jB lex.

nankulu → *nangulu*

nankūru → *namkūru*

nanmurtu(m), *nāmurtu* ? O/jB **1.** "meeting, confrontation" of armies etc. **2.** "heliacal rising" of star, planet; < *amāru* I N

nannābu "offspring, seed" Bab., NA; < *enēbu*

nannāriš "like the moon" jB; < *nannāru*

nannartu "light of the sky, luminary" M/jB; epith. of Ištar; < *nawāru*

nannāru(m) "light of the sky; moon" **1.** Bab. epith. of Sîn, folk etym. of Nanna [$^{(d)}$NANNA/NÁN.NA(*-ru/ri*); U4.SAKAR] **2.** jB (a bird); < *nawāru*

nannû(m) "command, behest" O/jB(poet.) with loc.-adv. + pers. suff. "at" s.o.'s "command"

nansītu → *nemsētu*

nansû → *nemsû*

nanṣabu → *naṣṣabu*

nanšaḫû, *nanšuḫû* (an iron tool) NB

nanšû → *naššû*

nanšuḫû → *nanšaḫû*

nantallû → *namtallûm*

nanzāqu → *namzāqu*

nanzāzu, *manzazu* M/NB **1.** "that stands (in attendance)" before (= *maḫri-*) s.o. **2.** pl. *nanzāzū* "attendant, courtier" **3.** "position (of honour); prominent position" of deities; < *izuzzum* G, N; → *mazzizu*

nanziqu → *nazziqu*

nanzirum → *nazziru*

nanzītu → *namzītu*

nanzû → *naššû*

napādiš, *nabādiš* "for the purpose of separating" (from the empire)? jB; < *napādu* II ?

napādu(m) I (a wooden clamp)? OAkk, O/MB; < *pâdu*

napādu II "to separate, cut off" O/jB lex. **G**; **D**; > *nipdu*; *napādiš*?

napāgu ~ "to go into hiding, disappear"? OB lex., M/jB **G**

napāḫu(m) "to blow; light up; rise" Bab., NA **G** (*a/u*) [MÚ] **1.** med. "blow" a drug into eye etc. **2.** "kindle, light" fire, oven; of parts of the body "become inflamed" or "swollen" [BAR7] **3.** of celestial bodies, esp. the sun "light up, appear" [KUR]; also in PN; *napāḫ šamši* "sunrise, east"; Nuzi of month "begin" **Gt** jB "catch fire, be ablaze" **D** [MÚ] "wheeze, gasp"; jB of snake "hiss" (at) [BÚN]; of wind "blow gustily ?"; trans. "ignite" beacon, also stat. "is ignited"; of parts of the body "become inflamed, swollen" **Dt** pass. of D "be ignited" **Št** MB "blow at each other"? in a game **N** pass. "be blown at, fanned" [MÚ], jB "be incited" of rebellion; of fire, torch "be ignited"; astr. "light up" **Ntn** iter. of N [MÚ.MÚ] "be ignited repeatedly"; "shine repeatedly"; "be(come) inflamed, swollen repeatedly"; > *napḫu*; *nipḫu*; *nappaḫtu*; *nappāḫu*, *nappāḫtu*, *nappāḫūtu*; *nuppuḫu*; *munappiḫu*, *munappiḫtum*; *tappuḫtum*; *tanpaḫu*?

napākum → *nabākum*

nāpališ → *nābališ*

napalkû "(having become) wide"? jB; < *nepelkû*

napalkû → also *nepelkû*

napalsaḫtum, *napalse/uḫtu(m)* ~ "low stool" O/jB; < *napalsuḫu*

napalsuḫu(m), *naparsuḫu* "to fall to the ground, squat, grovel" Bab. **N** of humans, statue, chariot **Š** "make prostrate"; > *napalsaḫtum*; *muppal=siḫum*

napaltu → *napaštum*

nāpaltu(m) "answer" OA, O/jB; OB in PN; < *apālu* I

napalṭû "to pass, go past" M/jB **N** of weapons "miss" target **Š** caus. of N

napālu(m) I "to dig out, hack down, demolish" **G** (*a/u*) "dig out, up", OAkk "quarry" stones; jB of dog "dig s.th. out"; "gouge out" eyes;

"hack down, demolish" cities, buildings **D** ~ G "search, rummage through"; of animals "forage, rootle"; "turn up (the soil of)" a garden; "gouge out" eyes, "blind" **N** astr., of star, mng. unkn. (→ *n.* II ?); > *niplu* II?; *nipiltu* I; *nāpilu*; *nuppulu*; *nappaltu* I; *munappilum*

napālu(m) II "to pay balance" OA, O/jB **G** (*a/u*); astr. "give way", of day to night, and vice versa **Gtn** iter. of G **D** = G **Š** "cause s.o. to pay balance" **N** pass.? (→ *n.* I ?); > *nipiltu* II; *nappaltu* II; *tappīlātu*

napālu III "to fall" Am. G (imper. *nupul*); < W.Sem.

nāpalû "interpreter, translator" jB; *nāpalê ṭūb kabatti* "that imparts joy to o.'s heart"; < *apālu* I

napāpum → *apāpu* N

napāqu(m) **G** lex. **Gtn** MA of husks "to harden"? **D** med. "be constipated", of nose, bronchial tube "become blocked"; → *nuppuqu* **Dtn** iter. of D

napāqum → also *nabākum*

naparaḫtu → *napraḫtu*

napardû I, *neperdû* "shining brightly" M/jB, esp. of day; < *napardû* II

napardû II, *neperdû* "to shine brightly" M/NB, NA **N** of day, deity; of mind, mood "be cheerful" **Š** "lighten, illuminate" darkness; "make cheerful, cheer up" person, mood, heart; > *napardû* I

naparkû I, *neperkû* "ceasing, inactive" M/NB; *lā n.* "ceaselessly, unremittingly"; < *naparkû* II

naparkû II, *na/eperkû(m)* "to cease, stop doing" s.th. Bab. **N** (pret. *ipparku*, NB also *ipparki*) "leave off work"; "become inactive"; *idā ... n.* "leave s.o.'s side, desert s.o."; of hymns, offerings "cease, be discontinued"; *lā n.* "be incessant, constant", *lā mupparkû* "ceaseless(ly)"; OB(Bogh.) trans. "neglect" **Ntn** of eyes, speech "fail repeatedly" **Š** O/MB "allow to cease", MB tribute, offering; > *naparkû* I

naparqudu(m) "to lie on o.'s back, lie flat (against)" O/jB **N** esp. om. of parts of body, features of liver **Ntn** iter. of N; > *purqidam*

naparrurtu, Susa *napurratu* "divergence, dispersal" jB om., Susa; < *parāru* N

naparruru → *parāru* N

naparsuḫu → *napalsuḫu*

naparšudiš "(in order) to escape" jB; < *naparšudu*

naparšudu(m) "to flee, escape" Bab., M/NA **N** "escape (from = *ina*)"; Ass. *(Ip)paršidu*, as PN; transf. *ina qātī n.* "fall into desuetude" **Ntn** iter. of N "run away repeatedly"; "(attempt to) flee from time to time"; > *naparšudiš*; *muttaprašidu*

napāru mng. unkn. Elam **G**; **Š**; < Elam. denom.?

napāsu → *nabāsu*

napāṣu(m) "to push away, down; smash, abolish" **G** (*a/u*) "push s.o. down, away"; *qātam n.* "push (s.o.'s) hand away" = "refuse o.'s consent"; "convulse, jerk" of limbs; "crush" objects, grain; "beat s.o. up"; OB "defer (payment) of" accounts **Gtn** of jaws, lips "snap repeatedly", "flop about repeatedly" **Gt** "beat each other"? **D** ~ G "crush" grain, "smash" door; "beat" wings; transf. pl. obj. "kill, smite" enemies, offspring; OA "defer payment of" accounts **Dt** "thrash about"; > *napṣu*; *nipṣu*; *nappāṣu*; *nuppuṣu*; *tappīṣu*

napaštum, MA *napaltu*; pl. *napšātu* "life; throat" OAkk, O/MA (Bab. → *napištu*; → also *napuštu*); OAkk in PN; OA *ša n.* "provider"; MA *bēl napšāte* (avenger of a life); < *napāšu* I

napāšu(m) I "to breathe; be(come) wide" **G** (*u/u*) [PEŠ5; PA.AN] "draw breath, calm down"; OAkk, OB also in PN; "snort"; MA of horse "pause for breath"; OB of disease "ease off"; jB of organ "distend, expand", of fever "spread"?; OA "stand up for o.'s claim(s), make a claim"; jB of harvest, food "become plentiful, abundant" **Gtn** iter. of G; OA "make claims repeatedly" **D** "make wide" canal; "make productive, fertile" garden; "let breathe freely, relax" heart; "air" garments **Dtn** of deity "expand" domination "overall" **Dt** of land, place "be widened, enlarged" **N** Mari "ease up, become easier", of assignment; > *napšu* I.III; *nipšu* I; *napīšu*, *napaštum*, *napištu*, *napuštu*; *nupūšu*; *nappašu*; *tappištum* I

napāšu(m) II "to pluck, pick (wool)" Ass., jB **G** (*a/u*) NA "pluck" rose **D** ~ G **N** "be plucked apart", also in simile; transf. of oil; > *napšu* II; *nipšu* II; *nāpištu*; *tappištu* II; *tappaštu*

napātu "to look at"? jB(Gilg.) **G** (*a/u* ?)

nāpatu (a vessel, bucket) jB lex.

napdû **1.** MA/MB "fastening" (rope, band?) **2.** jB lex. (a mat) **3.** jB lex. ('elephant hide'?, a plant); < *padû* ?

naperkû → *naparkû* II

napḫartum "sum total"? OB; < *napḫaru*

napḫaru(m) "total, sum; (the) whole, entirety" [(ŠU.)NIGIN/NÍGIN; PAP] construed absol., as st. constr. before nouns, or with pron. suff. **1.** in additions "sum total"; "sub-total" [PAP]; Mari pl. f. *napḫarātu* "totals" of troops **2.** "entirety"

of people, countries, objects, rites etc.;
< *paḫāru* II; > *naphartum*

naphatum (or *nabhatum*) (a wooden object)
OAkk

naphu(m) "blown on" Bab. **1.** O/jB of fire,
"kindled", also transf. of quarrel; "shining,
bright" **2.** NB *naphāti* "kindling"? **3.** lex. (a
plant); < *napāhu*

nāpilu(m), *nappilu* **1.** NA (a siege implement for
demolishing walls) **2.** OB (an excavator)?;
< *napālu* I

napištu(m), *napšatu(m)*, OB also *na'ištum*
"throat, life" OAkk ?, Bab. (Ass. → *napaštum*;
→ also *napuštu*) [ZI] **1.** "throat" of humans,
animals; O/jB *napištam lapātum* "to grasp
(o.'s) throat" in oath-taking; *napšāt martim*
(part of the gall bladder), *n. ubānim* (part of
liver); OB, Qatna *ša (pāni) n.* "pendant"
2. "(essence of) life", often pl.; O/jB in PN
Uta-napištim (also -*na'ištim*); *balāṭ napšāti*
"preservation of life"; *n. šakānu* "to give up the
ghost"; *(awāt, dīn) n.* "matter of life (and
death), lawsuit (deciding over) life (and
death)"; OB *bēl n.* "protector" **3.** "living,
livelihood, subsistence" **4.** "living being",
"self"; Bogh. pl. "personnel, staff" **5.** jB lex.
"neckerchief"?; < *napāšu* I; → *šiknat napišti*

nāpištu "female wool-plucker" jB lex.;
< *napāšu* II

napīšu(m) "breath(ing)" Bab. [PA.AN]; OB also
"breathing (space)" granted by deity; "scent,
aroma"; *ša n.* "censer"; < *napāšu* I

napkapu mng. unkn. NB

naplaqtum, *naplāqu* "slaughtering knife" OAkk,
jB; < *palāqu*

naplastu(m), *naplaštum* **1.** O/jB "blinker,
blinder (for animals, slaves)"; O/MB also
feature of liver [IGI.BAR] **2.** Mari (a kind of
payment); < *palāsu*; → *naplāsu*

naplāsu(m) "look, glance" O/jB; Mari =
naplastu "blinker (for animals)"; om. (feature
on liver) [IGI.TAB] = *naplastu*; < *palāsu*

naplaštum → *naplastu*

napluḫātum in *rēš n.* mng. unkn. OB(poet.);
< *palāḫu* ?

nappaḫānu mng. unkn. jB

nappaḫ(t)u M/jB [BUN/BÚN] **1.** "bellows"
2. "bladder" or "prostate gland"?; *ḫiniq(ti) n.*
"urinary retention" **3.** "rebellion"; < *napāḫu*

nappāḫtu "female smith, metalworker" NA;
< *nappāḫu*

nappāḫu(m) "smith, metalworker" [(LÚ.)
SIMUG] "(gold-, copper-, bronze-)smith", NB

as family name; *n. ḫurāṣi* "goldsmith"; *n. erê*
"coppersmith"; M/NA, NB *n. siparri*
"bronzesmith"; jB Ea *ša n.* (Ea as patron deity
of smiths); DN *dN.* (desig. of Ea); *bīt n.*
"smithy"; MB PlN *āl nappāḫi*; < *napāḫu*;
> *nappāḫtu, nappāḫūtu*

nappāḫūtu "trade of smith" Nuzi; < *nappāḫu*

nappaltu I "(building) rubble, excavated debris"
j/NB [IM.BAL]; < *napālu* I

nappaltu II ~ "balance, balancing amount"? MA
"share (of harvest)"?; j/NB astr. (difference in
arithmetical sequence)?; < *napālu* II

nappalu → *nappillu*

nappāṣu, *nappāṣtu* "wooden beater, club"? jB
lex.; MA PN *Nappaṣāni*; < *napāṣu*

nappašu, *nampašu* "air hole" Ug., j/NB **1.** lex.
"venthole" of an oven; "opening" in a wall,
canal **2.** (a type of) "window" **3.** "nasal opening"; < *napāšu* I

nappatum ? (a type of land)? OB lex.

nappaṭu (a small oven, brazier) jB; OB lex.?

nappillu, *nabbillu*, *nappalu* "caterpillar(s)" jB

nappilu → *nāpilu*

nappītu(m) **1.** O/jB, NA "sieve" [GI.MA.AN.SIM]
2. jB lex. (desig. of a snake); < *napû* II

nappû(m) "sieve" Bab. [GI.ŠÀ.SUR]; < *napû* II

nappu'um ? mng. unkn. OA

napraḫtu(m), *naparaḫtu* (a fermenting vessel)
Bab.; < *parāḫu*

napraku "bolt, (cross)bar" jB [GIŠ.ŠU.GI₄]
"bolt", part of door lock; transf. of blocked
mouth; "barrier, obstacle"; < *parāku*

naprartu → *nabrartu*

naprarû → *nabrarû*

napraṣu(m) (a tool, phps.) "chisel" OA, O/jB;
also transf. of DN *n. parakkim* "chisel? of the
dais"; < *parāṣu* I or II ?

naprû → *nabrû*

naprušu I "flying" jB; of insect, bird;
< *naprušu* II

naprušu(m) II "to fly" Bab., NA **N** [DAL] Am.
in simile of messenger "speed, rush"; of
humans "flee" (like birds) **Ntn** "fly about"
[DAL.DAL] of birds; of demon; of grain "fly
everywhere"; transf. of humans **Nt** jB of
disease "fly away" **Š** "let fly" bird, arrow; in
simile "cause (humans) to fly" like birds **ŠD** as
Š in simile "let fly" **Štn** iter. of Š "repeatedly
shoot" javelin; > *naprušu* I; *mupparšu*;
muttaprišu

napsamu(m) "nose bag" Mari, MA, jB;
< *pasāmu*

napsaqu, *napšaqu* (reinforcing beam of chariot)? jB; < *pasāqu*

napṣu(m) "crushed" O/jB; of date palm (shoot); of sinew "bruised, damaged"; OB of payment "deferred, remitted"?; < *napāṣu*

napšaltu → *napšaštu*

napšaqu → *napsaqu*

napšartum (treated grain) OB [BÚR]; < *napšāru*

napšaru → *napšuru*

napšāru(m) O/jB **1.** (agricultural tool for treatment of grain, phps.) "winnowing basket" **2.** (type of harrow) **3.** (desig. of the) "uvula"?; *(šīri) n.* "thymus (gland)"?; < *pašāru*; > *napšartum*

napšaštu, *napšaltu*; pl. *napšal/šātu*; NA also *napšiltu* "(bowl for) ointment(s), salve" jB, NA [GIŠ.DÍLIM.Ì.ŠÉŠ]; < *pašāšu*

napšatu → *napištu*

napšiltu → *napšaštu*

napšu(m) I "wide, plentiful, ample" Bab.; of garment; of food, prosperity "abundant"; fDN *Napušti*; < *napāšu* I

napšu(m) II "plucked" jB; of wool; < *napāšu* II

napšu III "life, breath" jB; < *napāšu* I

napšû → *bašû* N

napšurtu "dissolution, release" of anger jB; < *pašāru* N

napšuru, *napšaru* "appeasement, forgiveness" jB, NA; < *pašāru* N

naptanu(m) "meal(-time)" [NÍG.DU; KIN.SIG; BUR] often cultic, also royal "banquet"; *n. šēri, lilâti* "morning, evening meal"; *bīt n.* "banqueting house, room"; < *patānu* I

naptaqu "(metal) mould"? jB lex.; < *patāqu* I

naptētu "key; small saw" jB lex.; < *petû* II

naptû, *neptû* "key, opening device" jB lex.; < *petû* II

napṭartu(m), NB *napṭaštu*, Bogh. also *napṭertu* **1.** Mari "desertion" (of soldiers) **2.** jB (type of key), NB in PlN ? **3.** OB, Bogh. (desig. of class of woman); < *paṭāru*

napṭaru(m) "(type of) acquaintance, guest-friend" O/jB, NA; *bīt n.* ~ "lodgings, guest-house"; < *paṭāru*

napṭarūtu(m) "position of a *napṭar(t)u*"? O/MB; < *napṭartu* or *napṭaru*

napṭaštu, napṭertu → *napṭartu*

napṭiru jB/NA error for *ipṭiru* ?

napṭu(m) "naphtha" Bab., NA [Ì.KUR.RA; Ì.ḪUL]

napû I "sieved" jB [SIM]; < *napû* II

napû(m) II "to sieve, sift" Bab. **G** (*i/i*) [SIM] grain, drugs; > *napû* I; *nāpû*; *nappû*, *nappītu*

napûm → also *nepûm*

nāpû 'sifter' (desig. of a caterpillar) jB lex.; < *napû* II

nâpu I "to sway, shake"? jB **Dt** of sky "be shaken"

nâpu II "to make additional payment" NB; < *nūptu* denom.?

na'pu "dry, dried" jB; < *na'āpu*

napultu → *napuštu*

napurratu → *naparrurtu*

napurru → *naburru*

napuštu, *napultu*; pl. NA *na/upšāte* "life; throat" M/NA, M/NB [ZI] often pl., MB in PN *Ut-napušti*, also "(threat to) life"; Nuzi, jB lex. "(it is) vital, urgent"; MA *n. lapātu* "to grasp (s.o.'s) throat"; < *napāšu* I; → *napaštum*; *napištu*

napzaram "clandestinely" Mari; < *pazāru*

naqabâtu, naqabiātu → *naqbītu*

naqabtum (or *naq/g/kab/ptum*) (a stable, fold, pen)? OAkk(Sum.)

naqābu(m) "to penetrate sexually, deflower" O/jB **G** (*a/u*) **D** ~ G ?; → *nakāpu* G

naqādu(m) "to be in danger(ous condition)" Bab. **G** stat. (*naqud*, *naqid*) "causes concern, is critical" **D** stat. "is alert, anxious"; > *naqdu*, *naqdiš*, *naquttu*; *niqittu* I; → *nakādu*

naqallum → *nagallum*

naqalpû → *neqelpû*

naqarruru → *qarāru* N

naqāru(m) "to demolish; scratch" **G** (*a/u*) "demolish, pull down" cities, buildings etc., esp. with *epēšu(m)* "tear down and rebuild"; "break up, dismantle" ship; "destroy" inscription; "hew out" a path; "break, smash" ribs, objects; NB "fell"? palm trees; "scratch, scarify" face; "carve, engrave" words, image; "scrape up" dirt; of wool mng. unkn. → *nuqāru* ? **Gtn** iter. of G, OB prec. [ḪÉ.GUL.GUL] **Gt** lex. "scratch each other"? **D** "demolish" shrines; of bird "scratch (up)" earth; "cause tearing pain to" s.o. **Š** "cause (s.o.) to wreck, destroy (s.th.)" **N** "be demolished, pulled down" of buildings, divine images; > *nāqiru*; *niqru*, *niqirtum*; *nuqāru*; *naqquru*; *maqqārum*?

naqā'u → *naqû*

naqbaru "burial place, grave" jB, NA; < *qebēru*

naqbītu(m); NA pl. *naqabiātu*, *naqabâtu* "utterance" O/jB, NA; esp. "wording (of a prayer)"; < *qabû* II

naqdiš "in a critical condition" jB; < *naqādu*

naqdu "one in critical state, critical(ly ill); solicitous" jB; < *naqādu*; > *naqdiš*, *naquttu*

nāqidu(m); pl. m. & f. "stock-breeder, herdsman" [(LÚ.)NA.GAD] of sheep, goats, cows; also as PN and in PlN; as epith. of kings and gods; MA *rab n.* "overseer of the shepherds"; > Sum.; > *nāqidūtu*; → *maqqadu*

nāqidūtu "position, task of a herdsman" M/NB; transf. of king "pastorate"; < *nāqidu*

naqimtu → *nakmu* II

nāqiru "(wall) hook"? jB; < *naqāru*

naqītu "libation" jB; < *naqû*

naqmītu, *naqmūtu* "burning, conflagration" jB; < *qamû* II

naqmu → *nakmu* II

naqmūtu → *naqmītu*

na(q)qabu (a hammer) Emar

naqqatu → *nakkatu*

naqquru(m) "scratched" OA "incised" of wooden tablet; MB(Alal.), Nuzi horses "with (ownership) marks"?; < *naqāru* D

naqrabu(m) **1.** OA "closeness" of time, or place? **2.** M/jB(Ass.) "fight(ing zone), battle (field)"; < *qerēbu*

naqû(m), Ass. *naqā'u(m)* "to pour (a libation), sacrifice" **G** (*i/i*) [BAL] beer, water, wine, flour; *nāq mê* [A.BAL] "pourer of water" for the dead; "shed" tears, blood; "sacrifice" animals; Ug. *ša naqî* (an official)? **Gtn** iter. of G **D** ~ G **N** pass. "be poured out, sacrificed"; "be showered" (with = acc.); > *naqītu*; *nīqu* I; *maqqû*, *maqqītu*; *munaqqītu*; *taqqītum*

nâqu(m) I "to cry (out), wail" O/jB **G**; > *tanūqātu*

nâqu(m) II, *nuāqu* "to run, go" O/jB **G** of men; of light "go forth" **D** MA(roy. inscr.) "set in motion" reversal of fortune

naquttu "critical situation, (state of) distress" j/NB(post-Sargon II); *kī n.*, NB *(a)kī n.* "out of need"; *n. rašû* "to fall on hard times"; NB also in PN; < *naqdu*

nārabtum → *nērebtu*

narābu(m) "to soften, dissolve" (intrans.) OA, O/jB **G** (*a/u*) [DIG] stat. (*narub*) of wool, parts of the body "are (too) soft" **D** "soften" parts of the liver; > *narbu*; *nurbu*; *nurrubu*

nar'amātu(m) pl. tant. **1.** OB(Susa) *ina n.-šu/ša* "of his/her free will, voluntarily" **2.** MB *(āl) n.* "favourite (city)"; < *râmu* II

narāmtu(m) "beloved, favourite (woman)" OAkk, Bab., OA [ÁG-] (st. constr. *narāmat*, *naramti*, NB also *narmat*); OAkk, OB in PN; also of goddesses; of places; < *narāmu*

nar'amtu, *nar'antu*; pl. *narāmātu* (a weapon, phps.) "javelin" M/NA; < *ru''umu*

naramû → *narmû*

narāmu(m) "loved one; love" OAkk, Bab., OA [KI.ÁG] **1.** of humans "beloved (of a deity)", also in PN; of deities, of cities, temples **2.** NB of deity "who loves" **3.** "love (of, for)" **4.** OB(Alal.) *ina narām libbīšu* "voluntarily, of his own free will"; < *râmu* II; > *narāmtu*, *nar'amātu*

nāramu(m) "blanket" or "cloak"? O/jB; < *arāmu*; → *naḫramum*

nar'antu → *nar'amtu*

nārāru, *na'rārum* → *ne'rāru*

nārārūtu → *nērārūtu*

na'ratu → *nārtu* II

narāṭu(m) "to sway, tremble" Bab., NA **G** (*u/u*) OB of sacrificial animal; MB of patient; jB/NA of feet, hands "tremble"; of earth, mountains "shake" **D** "shake (s.o.), make (s.o.) tremble"; of deity "cause (earth etc.) to shake"; NA/jB "upset s.o." **ŠD** ~ D; > *nāriṭu*; *nirriṭu*; *nurruṭu*

narbaqu (a hoe) jB lex.; < *rapāqu*

narbāṣu "lair (of an animal)" O/jB; < *rabāṣu*

narbâtu pl. tant. "end(ing), cessation" jB **1.** *lā n.* of offerings "never-ending" **2.** lex. (name of 7th month), possibly to be read *li/ubbâtu*?; < *rabû* III

narbu(m); f. *narubtu(m)*, OA *naribtum* "soft" OA, O/jB; of textiles, parts of the liver, women; OB as (f)PN; < *narābu*

narbû(m) "greatness" O/jB; also in PN; pl. "great achievements, deeds, feats" of the gods; < *rabû* II

narbûtu "greatness" jB/NA; < *narbû*

nardamtu "track, footpath" jB lex.; < *nardamu*

nardamu jB **1.** "mooring pole" **2.** lex. "track, footpath"; < *radāmu*

nardappu jB **1.** lex. (a seeding apparatus) **2.** "mantrap, clamp"

nargallatu "female chief musician" NA; < *nargallu*

nargallu(m) "chief musician" OAkk, O/jB, NA [(LÚ.)NAR.GAL]; < Sum.; → *nāru* II

nargītu, *nargātu* (a headband) M/jB

nargu(m); jB pl. *nargātu* "(cedar) cone" OA, jB

nariku (or *nariqu*) (a vessel) MB(Alal.) of bronze

narinnu (a plant) jB lex.

nariqu → *nariku*

nāriš "like a river" jB; < *nāru* I

naritum (part of a cow)? OB

nāriṭu(m), *nāriṭṭu* "marsh, swamp" O/jB; also transf. (to lie in) "the mire", (be in) "difficulty"; < *narāṭu*

nariu (a measure used for wool) Nuzi

nariyarpu "five-year-old" Nuzi; < Hurr.

narkabtu(m) "chariot" [GIŠ.GIGIR] for war, hunt, ceremony; Nuzi *rākib n.* "chariot driver"; jB/NA *n. tāḫāzī* "war chariot", *bēl n.* "chariot owner" (→ *berkabtu*); cultic, divine "chariot" of gods; *n. ūmi* "storm-chariot" of Marduk; *bīt n.* lex. (part of a chariot)?, NB "chariot estate" (military fief); *neḫēs n.* "(backwards) rolling of the chariot"? (desig. of a physical malfunction); (the constellation Auriga) [MUL.GIŠ.GIGIR]; < *rakābu*; Ug. → *markabtu*

narkabu(m), NB also *naškabu* "(upper) grindstone" Bab., MA; < *rakābu*

narkamu (or *narkumu*) (a decorative object on furniture) MA

narmaktu **1.** M/NA, M/jB "washbasin"; of bronze; for oath **2.** rit. or med. "bath"; Bogh. *bīt n.* "bathhouse"; < *ramāku*

narmaku(m) **1.** OA "(cultic) washing" in MN *Narmak(a)-Aššur* **2.** Bab. "washbowl, bathtub" [DU_{10}.ÚS.SA] of bronze; < *ramāku*

narmat → *narāmtu*

narmû(m), *naramû* "dwelling" of deities Bab.; < *ramû* II

narpastum "threshing shovel" OB lex. in *ša n.* "thresher"; < *rapāsu*

narpasu "threshing shovel"? jB [GIŠ.MAR. ŠE.RA.AḪ]; < *rapāsu*

narpašû, *narpašu* ~ "broadening" jB om.; "extension (of battle)"?, or "expansion (of intestines)"; < *rapāšu*

narqītu I "place of refuge" jB; < *raqû*

narqītu II "perfume" jB; < *ruqqû*

narru (a criminal) jB lex.

narrubu → *nērubu*

naršiddu → *naršindû*

naršindatu, *naršimdatu*, *naršinnatu* (a sorceress) jB; < *naršindû*

naršindû, *naršiddu* (a sorcerer) jB; > *naršindatu*

naršinnatu → *naršindatu*

naršītu (a canal) jB lex.

nārtu(m) I "ditch, canal" OB, M/NA [ÍD-]; < *nāru* I

nārtu(m) II, Ass. *nuartu(m)*, MB *na'ratu* ? "female musician" Bab., M/NA [MUNUS.NAR]; < *nāru* II

narṭabtum (an irrigation apparatus)? OAkk; < *raṭābu*

narṭabu(m) **1.** OB [SÚN] "soaking vessel", container for beer mash **2.** jB "beer mash"; < *raṭābu*; → *nardappu*

narû(m), OA *naruā'um* "stele" [(NA4.)NA.RÚ.A; NA.RU; NA4.RÚ.A; MB also NÍG.NA]; OA, OB (publicizing inscriptions, decrees); M/NB (boundary stone); < Sum.; → *nadû* II; *nariu*

narû → also *nariu*

nāru(m) I f., NA m. "river, watercourse, canal" [ÍD in PlN and names of canals; pl. OB ÍD.ÍD; ÍD.DA.ḪI.A]; (= the Euphrates) in *Eber nāri* "Transpotamia"; OB in ordeal as DN (river deity) [dÍD], also in river ordeal; jB (the river of creation); NA *mārat n.* [DUMU.MUNUS.ÍD] 'daughter of *n.*' (a demon); transf., as desig. of aureole? round moon, of features of exta; > *nārtu* I, *nāriš*; *šiddi-nārāya*

nāru(m) II, Ass., Nuzi *nu'āru(m)*, MB *na'ru* "musician" [(LÚ.)NAR]; jB Ea *ša n.*; < Sum.?; > *nārtu* II; *nārūtu*; → *nargallu*

nāru(m) III mng. unkn. OA?, OB in PN

nāru → also *māru*

nâru → *nêru*

na'ru → *nāru* II

naruā'um → *narû*

narūqum, *naruqqu* f. "leather bag" OAkk, OA, O/jB [KUŠ.A.GÁ.LÁ]; OA as measure for grain etc., "investment capital" esp. of gold

narûtu(m) (a variety of malt) OA, jB

nārūtu(m) "profession of musician; musicianship" Bab. [NAR-]; < *nāru* II, *nārtu* II

nasāḫu(m) "to tear out" **G** (*a/u*) [ZI] **1.** "pull out" plants, nails; "pull out (of a cover)", "draw" sword; "uproot" foundations, buildings; "dig up, excavate" earth; "tear out" eyes, organs, inner being; stat. with *libbu* also transf. "is torn out"; "abolish" kingship, seed **2.** "take away, remove"; "exterminate, wipe out" humans; "pull off" clothes, headgear; "clear out" oven (pipe), canal; "eradicate, remove (the seat of)" a disease, "remove" a spell, a demon; **3.** "raise" taxes; "withdraw" money **4.** "take away" animals; "disinherit"; "evacuate" city; "deport" s.o.; "send s.o. away; dismiss, transfer" from a service; "remove" s.o. from an office; "dethrone, unseat" a government; "move" residence **5.** "dismiss, quash" a charge; "remove" obstacles; "take from s.o., relieve s.o. of" a burden; "dispose of, deal with" a matter (*awātu*) **6.** "copy" text **7.** NA "carry out" a sacrifice **8.** OB math. "subtract" [also BA.ZI], *nāsiḫ šiddim, pūtim* "subtrahend" **9.** with *qātu* "take away (o.'s hand)" = "deprive s.o. (of help), deny s.o. (help)"; "refuse, deny s.o. (partnership)" in a business venture; "reject (surety)" **10.** ellipt. "strike (a tent ?)" = "set out, depart" **11.** ellipt. (of time) "pass, elapse"

[BA.ZAL(.LA)] **Gtn** iter. of G "repeatedly draw" weapon **D** ~ G [ZI.ZI; ZI.MEŠ] "uproot, tear out, draw, copy" etc.; NA 'extract (from o.'s heart)' = "invent, fabricate" **Dt** pass. of D **Š** caus. of G Bab. "cause to reject" a charge; "remove" sins; OA "let withdraw" money; "have s.o. removed" **Štn** or Št "dig, clear out repeatedly" a canal **Št¹** pass. of Š "be made to withdraw" s.th. **Št²** "seek out, select" **N** pass. "be extracted, torn out" [ZI]; "be removed" from register; NA astr. mng. unkn.; > *nasḫu*; *nisḫu* I, *nisḫatu*, *nisiḫtu*; *nusḫu* II; *nasīḫu*, *nasīḫūtum*; *nāsiḫu*; *nusāḫu*; *nassiḫu*; *nussuḫum*; *tassuḫtu*

nasāḫu → also *našāḫu*

nasāku(m), *našāku* "to throw (down)" **G** (*u/u*, j/NB also *i/i*) [ŠUB] **1.** "throw" grain onto threshing floor; "throw s.th., s.o." into fire, river; NB *ina kīli n.* "throw into prison" **2.** "throw down, drop" a burden; "deposit" goods **3.** of wind, disease "flatten s.o., prostrate" **4.** "throw off, put behind o.s." slander, evil; mag. "throw (behind o.s.)"; "reject" agreement; NB "give up" paternity; **5.** "shoot" an arrow; "eject, throw out, belch forth" slaver **6.** *a/ina muḫḫi* ... *n.* "impose, enjoin (a task) on s.o." **Gtn** iter. of G **Š** "cause (s.o.) to throw; remove, eliminate"; "allow to be thrown away" documents, name, inscription; "repeal, abolish" order, contract, MB tribute; "render ineffective, inoperative" calumnies, a star's brightness; "allow to shed, remove" yoke, burden; "abandon, give up" land, grave **Št** pass. of Š (→ also *nasāqu* Št) **N** pass. "be thrown down"; > *nasku*; *nasīku* I; *nisku*; *massaku*

nasāqu(m) "to choose, select" **G** (*a/u*, NA *i/i*) animals, objects; of words esp. stat. "are well chosen" **D** ~ G **Š** "let choose" **Št** "put, keep in order" (or = *nasāku* ?) **ŠD** ~ D; > *nasqu*; *nisqu*, *nisiqtu*; *nasīqum*, *nasīqūtum*; *nassiqu*; *nussuqu*

nasarruru → *sarāru* N

nasaru → *nasru*

nasāru "to saw" **G** (*u/u* ?) NB uncert. **D** ~ G ? lex.; < Aram.?; > *nasru*?; *massāru*

nasāsu(m) "to lament, wail, moan" Bab. **G** (*u/u*, OB also *a/a*) of humans, deities; of cattle "low" **D** ~ G; transf. of thunder "growl"?; > *nassu*, *nassiš*, *nasištu*?; *nissatu*, *nissatiš*; *tassistu*; → *nazāzu*

nasāsu → also *našāšu* I

nasā'um → *nesû* II

nasbu (or *nas/ṣb/pu*) "sleeve" jB lex.

nasbû (a vessel) jB for beer; < *sabû*

nasḫapu(m) (a basket) Bab.; < *saḫāpu*

nasḫiptu, *našḫiptu*; pl. *našḫipē/ātu* (a shovel) j/NB; < *saḫāpu*

nasḫu(m) "torn, pulled out, uprooted" O/jB, MA [ZI] of plants; "copied out" on tablet; OB "discharged" from an office; MA, jB "deported"; < *nasāḫu*

nasḫuru "favourable attention" of a deity Bab.; < *saḫāru* N

nasiḫtu → *nasḫu*; *nisiḫtu*; *nasištu*

nasīḫu(m) **1.** OB, lex. "displaced person, labourer" **2.** NB "deportee"; as family name; < *nasāḫu*; *nasīḫūtum*

nāsiḫu 'one who removes' jB lex.; < *nasāḫu*

nasīḫūtum "deportation" Mari; < *nasīḫu*

nasīkātu → *nasīku* I.II

nasikku → *nasīku* II

nasiktu → *nasku*

nasīku I **1.** jB "that was cast down; fallen (person)" **2.** M/jB pl. f. *nasīkātu* "faraway lands"; < *nasku*

nasīku II, *nasikku*; pl. m. & f. "sheikh, tribal leader" M/NA, j/NB; < Aram.?

nasīkūtu "position of a sheikh" NA; < *nasīku* II

nasīqum (or *nāsik/qum*) (an agricultural worker) OB; < *nasāqu* ?

nasīqūtum (service of a conscript labourer) OB; < *nasīqum*

nasistum → *nasištu*

nasīsum (or *nazīzum*) (a garment) Early Mari; → *nasištum*

nasištu(m), OA *nasistum*, lex. also *nasiḫtu* (an under-garment) OA, jB lex.; < *nassu* ?; → *nasḫu*

nasku, *našku* "thrown down" jB "abandoned, deserted; far-flung" land(s); "fallen, exhausted"; f. as subst. *nasiktu* NB math. "horizontal, level"; *na/isiktu* lex. (desig. of a cart); < *nasāku*

naslamum "state of peace" with s.o. OB; < *salāmu* II

nasmītu → *naṣmītu*

naspantu, *nas/špant/du*, *naspa/ittu* "devastation" M/NB, NA [KUŠ₇-] **1.** M/jB *abūb n.* "devastating flood"; *šar n.* "king of destruction"; Ninurta *ša n.* **2.** jB lex. (desig. of gruel); < *sapānu*

naspanu (a levelling tool, harrow)? OB, jB lex.; < *sapānu*

naspattu → *naspantu*

naspittum "mourning (ritual)"? OA; < *sapādu*

naspittu → also *naspantu*

naspu → *nasbu*

naspuḫtu "dispersal, disintegration" Bogh., jB om., of house, land; < *sapāḫu* N

nasqu(m) "chosen, choice, precious" Bab., NA; troops; precious stones; words; OB [IGI. SAG.GÁ] "select quality" wool; MA fPN *Nasiqtu*; Nuzi *ina pī n.* "voluntarily"?; < *nasāqu*

nasrāmu (a wooden tool) NA; < *sarāmu*

nasru(m), *nasaru(m)* **1.** (hook or peg for suspension) OB of reed; jB/NA of wood or metal, for meat; *bīt n.* (meat store) [É.UZU] **2.** (desig. of a garment) [TÚG.NÍG.GAB.DAB] MB lex.; < *nasāru* ?

nassapu(m) OAkk, jB **1.** (a measuring vessel)? **2.** (a net)?

nassiḫu (desig. of a buyer, trader) jB lex.; < *nasāḫu*

nassiqu "choosy, fastidious" jB; < *nasāqu*

nassiš "plaintively" jB; of raven's croak; < *nassu*

nassu "groaning, wretched" O/jB; < *nasāsu*

nasû → *nesû* I.II

naṣabātu → *naṣbatu*

naṣābu(m) I "to suck" O/jB **G** (*a/u*, *u/u*) liquids; "lick" finger **D** ~ G **N** pass.; > *naṣṣabu*

naṣābu II "to place, put" Am. **Gt** (*ittaṣab*); < W.Sem.

naṣarruru → *ṣarāru* I N

naṣartu → *naṣru*

naṣāru(m) "to guard, protect" **G** (*a/u*) [ÙRU; in PN PAB] **1.** "watch over" houses, estates, possessions, gardens; animals; "guard s.o."; *maṣṣarta(m) n.* "stand guard, keep watch (for s.o.)" **2.** "be on o.'s guard (against s.th.)"; "take care, mind"; "watch" o.'s words; "observe" the sky **3.** "look after, protect" humans, cities, countries **4.** "preserve" a woman's virginity; "keep" secrets **5.** "be mindful of, observe, obey" orders, decrees, oaths **6.** "keep (in mind), retain" words, prayers **Gtn** iter. of G **Gt** "be careful, on o.'s guard" **D** ~ G Am. **Š** caus. of G "guard", "appoint a guard over", OA, OB "put in safekeeping"; "commit s.th. to memory"; "obey, observe (well)" orders etc. **Št** Mari "be on the alert" **N** "be protected" OAkk in PN; "be observed"; > *naṣru*, *naṣriš*, *naṣarūtu*; *niṣrum*, *niṣirtu*; *nuṣrum*; *nāṣiru*; *nāṣirtu*; *namṣartu*?; *maṣṣaru*, *maṣṣartu*, *maṣṣarūtu*

naṣarūtu "treasure" NB; < *naṣāru*

naṣaṣu (a stone) jB lex.

naṣbaru; pl. *naṣbarānu* (a door mounting) NB of metal; < *ṣabāru* II

naṣbatu(m), NA *naṣabātu* **1.** Bab., NA (a coat) **2.** NB (a metal coating) for divine statues? **3.** MA (a festival)? **4.** OA "handle" of a cup; < *ṣabātu*

naṣbu → *nasbu*

naṣbû(m) (a qualification of real estate)? OB/MA(Hana)

naṣirtu → *naṣru*

nāṣirtu (desig. of a door) Bab.; < *naṣāru*

naṣīru(m) "clamour, wailing" Bab.

nāṣiru(m) "guard, guardian" O/jB; also as epith. of deities; M/NB, NA as PN; < *naṣāru*

naṣmadu **1.** jB "harness, yoked team" **2.** Mari (a headband); < *ṣamādu* II

naṣmattu(m); pl. *naṣmadātu* "bandage, poultice" O/jB [(NÍG.)LAL; LÁL (→ *niglallu*)]; < *ṣamādu* II

naṣmītu (or *nasmītu*) (part of the liver)? jB; < *ṣamû* II (or *samû* II ?)

naṣmû(m) "thirst" Mari; < *ṣamû* II

naṣnaṣu (a bird) jB

naṣpadu "floating rib" of a sheep jB

naṣpu → *nasbu*

naṣraptu(m) "crucible; dyeing vat" Bab. [NÍG. TAB]; ext. (a depression in the liver); < *ṣarāpu* I

naṣrapu, *našrapu* j/NB **1.** jB astr. (a group of stars in Perseus) **2.** NB (a joint of meat) **3.** jB lex. "seed, descendant"?; < *ṣarāpu* I ?

naṣriš "safely" MB(Alal.), Am.; < *naṣru*

naṣru(m); f. *naṣirtu*, Bogh. once *naṣartu* "guarded, under surveillance"; "kept, preserved"; "protected"; "kept secret"; f. as subst. "treasure" (→ *niṣirtu*); OAkk PN *Naṣrum*; < *naṣāru*; > *naṣriš*

**na(ṣ)ṣ* → *našû* II (Ass. forms)

naṣṣabu(m), *nan/mṣabu*, *nuṣṣabum*, *nunṣabu*; pl. f. Bab., NA **1.** "drain pipe" **2.** (a type of cucumber); < *naṣābu* I

naṣṣartu → *namṣartu*

naṣû(m), *neṣû* "to tear down; scrape" O/jB; plaster off house walls; med. "slit open" sore

nāṣu "plumage, feathers" jB

nâṣu(m), *na'āṣu* "to look down on, despise" O/jB, Am. **G** (*a/a*); also stat., of house "is mean" **D** ~ G

-nâš → *-niāšim*

našāḫu(m), *nasāḫu* "to have diarrhoea" O/jB **G**; > *nišḫu* I; *naššiḫu*

našāku(m) "to bite" O/jB **G** (*a/u*, also *i/i* ?) [ZÚ.KUD]; "bite, gnaw" o.'s tongue, lips (in anger); "bite off" nose etc. **D** "bite up, crunch"; of shoes "pinch"; > *nišku*; *munaššiku*

našāku → also *nasāku*
našallulu → *šalālu* II
našappu(m) 1. OB (a basket) 2. NB (a metal bowl)
našāpu(m) "to blow (s.th.) away" O/jB, NA **G** (*u/u*) "winnow" corn; transf. "scatter"; of beer → *našpu* **D** OB "winnow" sesame; "strip, clear off" field, wall plaster **N** "be blown away"; > *našpu*; *nušaptum*
našāqu(m) "to kiss" **G** (*i/i*); stat., of parts of body "are entwined" **Gt** "kiss each other" **D** ~ G **Š** caus. of G **N** "kiss each other"; > *naššūqītu*
našarbuṭu(m), *našarbuṣu* **N** "to flit, chase about" O/jB lex. **Ntn** iter.; > *muttašrabbiṭu*
našāru(m) I "to deduct, take s.th. from s.th., reduce" **G** (*a/u*) "cut off" part of a field from s.o. (= acc.); "remove, withdraw" silver, goods (from = acc.), "draw off" liquid, flood waters; "reduce, diminish"; astr. ellipt. of moon "wane" **D** ~ G "separate off, put aside", "diminish" **Dt** pass. of D "be weakened" **Š** OA "have (silver) deducted"; Mari "draw off" river **N** OB of barley "be removed, withdrawn"; NB of earth "be excavated"; "be badly affected, reduced"; > *nišru*, *nišertu*; *nušertu*; *nušurrû*; *nušurtum*; *maššaru*, *maššartu*
našāru II "to pour out" M/jB **G** (pres. *inaššar*) oil; transf., plenty
našāšu I, *nasāsu*, *nazāzu* "to shake" O/jB **G** (*i/i*); of lizard "wriggle" **D** of sheep "shake" its tail; "toss" hair; "flap" wings; of fish "wriggle"?; "rock" baby ?
našāšu II "to sniff" jB lex. **G** (*i/i*) of lizard; > *naššišu*
našā'u → *našû* II
našbaṭu "trimmed palm-frond" jB; < *šabāṭu* II
nâši → *nâšin*; *niāši*
-nâši → *-nâšin*; *-niāšim*
nāšiānu "that carried off" MA; < *nāšû*
nâšin, *nâšni* "to us" (1 pl. dat. pron.) Nuzi, Bogh.; after *an(a)*; < *niāši* + *-ni(m)*
-nâšin "us" (1 pl. acc. suff.) MA, MB, Bogh.; → *-niāti*
našītu → *našû* I
nāšītu, *nāšiu* → *nāšû*
naškabu → *narkabu*
našku → *nasku*; *nišku*
naškupû (a garment)? Nuzi
našlamtu "complete payment, final instalment" MA; MB PN *Našlandu* ?; < *šalāmu* II
našlaptu "illicit removal"? OB of goods; < *šalāpu*

našmaḫtum ~ "breach of trust"? OA, pl.; < *šamāḫu* II
našmaḫum ~ "exuberance, pleasantness" OB, pl.; < *šamāḫu* I
našmaṭu "plucked item"? jB lex.; < *šamāṭu* I
našmum (a pastry) Mari
našmû → *nešmû*
nâšni → *nâšin*
našpaktu (a jug)? jB; < *šapāku*
našpaku(m); pl. m. & f. "storage vessel; storeroom" 1. OA, O/jB (storage jar for oil etc.) [Ì.DUB] 2. O/MB "granary, silo"; "storeroom" [É.UŠ.GÍD.DA; (É.)Ì.DUB; also É.DUB ?] 3. O/jB "capacity" [also É.ÙR.RA ?] 4. jB med. (a swelling)? of the joints; < *šapāku*
našpakūtu "storage (place)" OB [(É.)Ì.DUB-]; < *našpaku*
našpand/tu → *naspantu*
našpartum I (a garment) OAkk; → *našparum* I
našpartu(m) II, O/MA also *na/ešpertu(m)*, NB also *našpaštu* "message, commission" O/MA, Mari "written message, letter"; M/jB "mission, embassy"; OB DN *ᵈNašpartum*; NB "instruction, assignment", *n. šullumu* "to carry out an errand, fulfil a mission", *n. alāku* "to conduct business" for s.o., *ālik n.* "business manager, agent", *ina n.* "on behalf of"; *ša n.* "person under commission"; < *šapāru*
našpartu III (a bird) jB comm.
našparum I (a garment) OAkk; also *našpariš* "for a *n.*"; → *našpartum* I
našparu(m) II "messenger, envoy" Bab. [OB freq. NA.AŠ.PAR/BAR]; < *šapāru*
našpaštu, *našpertu* → *našpartu* II
našpiku (a garment)? Nuzi
našpiltu "residue" jB lex., of malt; < *šapālu*
našpu 'blown away' (desig. of type of thin beer) jB [SIG/SIG5]; also *šikar n.*, *billatu našiptu*; < *našāpu*
našpuḫu → *sapāḫu* N
našramu (a chisel or knife)? jB lex.; < *šarāmu*
našraptu "burning; crucible"? jB lex.; < *šarāpu*
našrapu "fire box" jB as part of kiln; < *šarāpu*
našrapu → also *naṣrapu*
našrapūtum mng. unkn. OB lex.
našru "eagle" jB lex.
našša (a vessel) Am.; < Eg.
naššiḫu, *namšiḫu* "suffering from diarrhoea" jB lex.; < *našāḫu*
naššīkum → *niššīku*
naššišu "sniffing"? OB lex.; < *našāšu* II
naššu → *nalšu*

naššû, jB *nanšû*, NB *nanzû*? "carrier" Bab.; OB lex. "porter"; NB (a lever)?; < *našû* II

naššūqītu f. "(malevolent) kisser" jB of demon; < *našāqu*

naštiptum, j/NB *naltiptu* "bandage" Bab.; < *šatāpu*

naštuq "(leather) bag, purse" NB; < Gk.?

naštaptum (a configuration on the liver) Early Mari ext.; < *šaṭāpu*

našû(m) I "lifted, raised" O/jB of eye; *našiam*/*našâ rēši(m)* "(with) the head held high"; < *našû* II

našû(m) II, OAkk, Ass. *našā'u(m)* "to lift, carry" **G** (*i*/*i*) (M/NA stat. 1 sg. *naṣṣāku*, 3 f. sg. *naṣṣat*, 3 pl. vent. *naṣṣūni* etc.; perf. 3 pl. *ittaṣṣū*, 1 sg. vent. *attaṣṣa*, 3 sg. *ittaṣṣa*; imper. *iṣṣā(ni)* etc.) [ÍL; j/NB also GUR17] **1.** "lift up, raise" object, part of body (→ also 5); transf. "raise s.o. up", "install" in an office, "induct" priest(ess); "raise" s.o. from poverty; math. *ana X n.* "multiply by X"; ellipt. "lift" baggage = "set out, depart", of water "rise", of body "be bloated" **2.** "carry, bear" basket, child etc.; stat. "is carrying, holding" weapon, symbol, musical instrument etc.; of tree "bear" fruit; "be imbued with" radiance, poison; transf. "bear" grief, punishment, responsibility; "support, maintain" s.o. with food **3.** "carry, transport", vent. "bring" s.o., s.th., offering, tribute, rent; transf. NB *ṣibûta n.* "make request"; Bab. of heart "bring" s.o. to do (= *ana*) **4.** "take away" s.o., s.th.; vent. "bring away"; NA "take" loan, purchase; Ug. *n. ū nadānu* "transfer ownership" to s.o. **5.** in idioms: Nuzi *ilāni n.* "swear by the gods"; + *qātu(m)* "lift" the hands in supplication (→ *nīšu* I); "hold" s.th. in hand = "control"; + *īnu(m)* "lift" o.'s eyes to s.th. = "covet"; *pāna*/*ī n.* "long for (= *ana*)"; + *rēšu(m)* "lift" the head = "honour" s.o., "take care of" s.o./s.th., "examine, inspect", NA "need, require; be ready"; M/NB *rēš eqli*/*zēri n.* "take over field"; + *pūtu(m)* NB "stand in for", leg. "be guarantor for" s.o. **Gtn** iter.; ellipt. of spleen "rise repeatedly"; "support" s.o, "maintain" wife, family; OB math. "multiply" **Gt** OA pres. "pick up, collect" **Š** caus. of G (NA pres. 3 pl. *ušaṣṣū*) "cause to lift" hands in prayer; "cause to carry" **N 1.** pass. of G "be lifted, raised" **2.** ellipt., of demon, tide "rise" **3.** ingress. "pick up, collect" OA freq.; > *našû* I; *nīšu* I, *nišītu*; *nišûtu*; *naššû*; *nāšû*, *nāšiānu*; *maššânu*?; *maššû* I, *maššītu*; *taššiātum*, *taššītu*?

našû → also *nešû*

nāšu (a type of beer) NB; *ša n.-šu* "beer brewer, seller", also as family name

nāšû, Ass. *nāšiu* "bearing; bearer"; jB lex. "fruit-bearing" tree; f. OB "consecrator" of priestess; M/NA, Nuzi "porter"; OB *nāš(i) biltim* "tenant of a field owned by the state"; jB *nāš patri* 'sword-bearer' (= "servant"); < *našû* II

nâšu(m), Ass. *nuāšu* "to rock, shift" Bab., NA **G** (*ū*) [TUKU4] (intrans.) of earth, mountains; of building, wall, teeth "be(come) loose, shaky"; "quake" with fear; transf. of person "shift, give way", of field ownership "be transferred" **D** [TUKU4] (trans.) "shake" head, part of body, the earth etc.; "shift" object, disease, person from place; Mari also intrans. "shift o.s." **Dt** pass. of D

nâšu → also *niāši*

našuma mng. unkn. Qatna

našwe (a class of people) Nuzi; also PN; < Hurr.

natāku(m) "to drip" O/jB, NA **G** (*u*/*u*) [BI.IZ] of rain "(fall in) drop(s)"; of poison "trickle, ooze" from mouth **Gtn** iter. "trickle repeatedly, trickle away" **D** "(let) drip" [BI.IZ] **Dtn** iter. of D **Š** ~ D **Štn** iter. of Š; > *nitku* I; *nātiktu*; *tattiktu*; *tīku*

natakušri, metath. *tanakušri* mng. unkn. Nuzi; < Hurr.

natallu (part of the body) jB lex.

natanu (a tool) jB lex.

natāpu → *naṭāpu*

nātar → *naltar*

natāru ~ "to split open" j/NB **G** lex. **D** "cleave, demolish" mountains; stat. of jaw, intestine "is split" **Š** ~ D (more freq.); > *nutturum*

natbaktu, NA *nadabaktu* ~ "sluice" **1.** MB (part of an irrigation system) **2.** jB "waterfall, ravine" **3.** NA cultic = *natbāku* 4; < *tabāku*

natbāku(m), NA, NB also *nad(a)bāku* 'pouring' **1.** OB (depot for grain) **2.** M/NA ~ "allocation" of commodities ? **3.** MB, NA, NB "layer, course" of bricks **4.** M/jB, NA "(mountain) gully" (→ *natbaktu* 3) **5.** M/NA "decanting, libation"; < *tabāku*

natḫi in *bīt n.* (a chapel)?; PN *Natḫaya*, PlN *Bēlat-natḫa* NA; < Hurr.?

natḫuḫlû (a class of women) Nuzi; < Hurr.

nâti → *niāti*

-nâti → *-niāti*

nātiktu 'dripper' (a libation vessel) jB lex.; < *natāku*

nattullu, Bogh. *namtullu* ? **1.** M/NB (part of harness) **2.** NB astr. (part of the Yoke star) [MUL.ŠUDUN.ANŠE] *natû* → *naṭû* IV

nātu(m) "handle" OAkk, jB lex.; of wood, for sickle, knife

natuḫḫu (or *naduḫḫu*) mng. unkn. jB lex.

naturru ~ "chisel"? jB lex.

naṭal → *nadal*

naṭālu(m) "to look" **G** (*a/u*) [IGI; IGI.GÁL; IGI.DU8] "(be able to) see"; "look, gaze"; OB transf. "have view, opinion"; OA of deities "witness", OB in PN; "look at" (= dat., *ana*), "set o.'s mind to" s.th.; "inspect" offerings, fields, "observe" the sky, "experience" dreams, visions, sorrow; "regard, consider" s.o. as s.th.; "see fit"; stat. "is visible"; of parts of the liver "face" **Gtn** iter. **Gt 1.** "look at each other", of parts of the liver "face each other"; transf. OB of goods etc. "be of equal value", OA *ana itaṭlim nadānum* "sell for cash" **2.** OB om. "look away" **D** Mari "examine thoroughly" **Š** caus. "show, let s.o. experience" **Št** pass. of Š Bab. "be shown", "be made to experience" **N** "be seen, visible"; > *niṭlu*; *nāṭilu*; *naṭṭalu*; *maṭṭalu*?; *maṭṭaltu*

naṭāpu(m), *natāpu(m)* "to tear out" O/jB **G** (*i/i*) "tear out" plants, tongue **Gtn** iter. **D** ~ G "uproot" people; plants **N** Mari of wool "be plucked"?; > *naṭpu*; *niṭpu* I; *nuṭṭupum*

naṭā'u → *naṭû* III.IV

naṭbaḫu(m) 1. OA "butcher's knife" **2.** jB lex. "chopping block"; < *ṭabāḫu*

naṭīlu (a small ladle) NB; < Aram.

nāṭilu "seeing" Bab. of eyes; *lā n.* [IGI.NU.TUKU; IGI.NU.GÁL] "blind", also transf.; < *naṭālu*; → *iginutukû*

naṭpu "torn out" j/NB lex. of plant; NB mng. unkn., of words, jB of a priest ?; < *naṭāpu*

naṭṭalu "seeing, with (good) sight"? Bogh. lex.; jB ext. mng. unkn.; < *naṭālu*

naṭû(m) I "suitable, suited" OAkk, O/jB, NA of rites "fitting, right, proper"; of sailor "qualified"; *ina naṭê* "in an appropriate manner"; *lā n.* "unsuited, inappropriate"; f. sg. & pl. *lā naṭū/âtu/i* "improprieties"; < *naṭû* III

naṭû II "beaten" MA of human; < *naṭû* IV

naṭû(m) III, *naṭā'u(m)* "to be suitable, proper" **G** stat. only; of words "are suitable"; of deed "is appropriate"; of terrain "is suited"; MA of tablet *ana ḫīpe n.* "is fit for breaking"; > *naṭû* I

naṭû(m) IV, *natû(m)*, *nadû(m)*, Ass. *naṭā'u* "to hit, beat" Bab., M/NA **G** (*u/u*, *i/i*) "beat, whip" humans, horses **D** ~ G of tongue, mng. unkn. **Š** "cause to beat" **N** "be beaten"; > *naṭû* II; *niṭâtu*, *niṭûtu*

nāṭu (a religious ritual)? NA

nâṭu (to have a bowel disorder) jB **G** (*a/a*); > *nīṭu*

na'û(m) Bab. **G** mng. unkn. **D** "to set in motion, animate" s.th.

na'ûm → also *niā'um*

nā'u(m) (a stone) O/jB lex.; < Sum.

nâ'u ~ "to belch"? jB lex. **G**

na'ūtu → *namūtu*

na'ūtum → *naḫūtum*

nawāru(m), *namāru*, OAkk stat. *nabir* "to be(come) bright, shine" **G** (*i/i*; Am. stat. also *namur*) [ZÁLAG; astr. also BU] of celestial bodies; without subj., e.g. *ina namāri* "at dawn"; of parts of the liver "be light"; of eyes "shine (with joy)", of face, heart, mind "be(come) cheerful, glad"; of deity, human "be cheerful"; OB "celebrate (festival)"; stat. "is favourable"; of confused sign "become clear"; of employee "be excellent" **D** "make bright" [ZÁLAG] liter., of deities "illuminate" lands, city; "lighten" darkness; ellipt. of eclipse "become light"; "make shine, resplendent"; Mari "clear" reeds; NB "uncover, expose" foundations; jB "ignite" brazier; transf. "make s.o. glad, cheerful"; "clarify" confusion; Mari "enlighten" s.o. **Dt** pass. of D "be made bright" **Š** "cause to shine, become bright", "shine, polish"; "ignite" torch; transf. "gladden" eyes, heart **ŠD** ~ D "lighten, gladden" **N** Am. of eyes "brighten" (OB → *amāru* I N); > *nawru*, *nawiratum*, *namriš*, *namrūtu*; *namāru*; *namrītu*?; *nīru* II; *nimru* II, *nimurtu*; *namārītu*; *numūru*; *nūru* I, *numru*; *nummuru*; *namurratu*, *namurru*; *namrīrum*; *nannartu*, *nannāru*, *nannāriš*; *nuwwurum*, *munawwirum*; *mušanmirtu*; *tawwertum*?

nawaššu'/ḫum → *namaššu'um*

nawatum → *nawītum*

nawen(a) (part of a chariot)? Nuzi; < Hurr.

nawir(a)tum, *namir(a)tu* "brightness, light" O/jB [ZÁLAG] *n. šakānu* "to bring about brightness"; < *nawru*

nawirum → *nawru*

nawītum (or *nawa/utum* ?) (a pedestal used in cult)? OB

nawriātum → *namriātum*

nawru(m), (*nawirum* ?), *namru*, *namiru* "bright, shining" [ZÁLAG] of celestial bodies, as divine epith.; jB PlN *Namra-ṣīt* [dAŠ.IM5/ÍM.BABBAR]; of eyes, face "shining, radiant"; of metal, precious stones, textiles "bright(ly coloured)"; transf. of employee, goods "excellent, good quality"; (a stone) [NA4.ZÁLAG]; (a plant name); lex. (a bird); < *nawāru*; > *nawiratum*, *namriš*, *namrūtu*

nawûm I, *namû(m)* m. & f. "pasturage; steppe" O/jB [A.RI.A; A/Á.DAM] OB "(area, members of) nomadic encampment"; M/jB "steppe, desert, deserted regions"; > *namû* I; *namû'iš*, *namûtu*; *nawûm* II; *numû*

nawûm II, *namû* "to turn into desert" **G** stat. "is desolate" **D** "lay waste" field, city **Dt** pass. of D **N** "become desert"; of temple "become a ruin"; < *nawûm* I denom.

nawutum → *nawītum*

nayāru → *niāru*

nayyabtu "floating rib" or "cartilage at the tip of the rib" jB ext.

nayyādu "careful"? jB; < *na'ādu*

nayyādu → also *nādu*

nayyaktu "(woman) given to sexual intercourse" jB; < *niāku*

nayyalu → *nālu*

nayyālu I "reclining" jB; < *nâlu*

nayyālu II (person dispossessed of land)? M/NA, Ug., j/NB; Ug. (a fief holder whose land is taken away); NB *bīt n.*; < *na'ālu* ?

nayyāš → *niāši*

nazaginnakku (a lapis lazuli vessel) jB lex.; < Sum.

nazālu(m) "to pour out, drain away" Bab., NA **G** (*a/u*) water, molten glass etc.; > *mazzālu*, *mazzaltu*; *nizlu*

nazāmu(m) "to moan, complain" Ass., O/jB **G** (*u/u*) OA "complain, grumble" **Gtn** iter. **D** ~ G; "make s.o. complain" **Dt** "groan, growl"; "raise complaints against" s.o. or s.th. **Dtt** NA for Dt **Š** Nuzi "cause to groan"?; > *nazmātu*; *nizmatu*; *izzimtu*; *tazzimtu*

nazāpum mng. unkn. OB **G** (*i/i*)

nazāqātu pl. "troubles, vexations" NB; < *nazāqu*

nazāqiš "to s.o.'s sorrow"; < *nazāqu*

nazāqu(m) "to creak; be vexed" **G** (*i/i*) of humans "be vexed, annoyed"; "worry"; Mari of field "be troublesome"; jB of door etc. "creak, squeak"; of snake "hiss"? **R** Mari **Gtn** iter. **Š** "annoy, upset" s.o. **Štn** iter. of Š; > *nazqūtum*; *nizqu*, *niziqtu*; *nazāqiš*, *nazāqātu*; *nāziqu*; *nazziqu*; *mušazziqu*; *tazzīqum*

nazarbubu(m) ~ "to (tremble with) rage" O/jB **N** of monsters

nazāru(m) "to revile, curse s.o." Bab., NA **G** (*a/u*, jB occas., NA *i/i*) "curse" deity, s.o., s.th.; "abuse, insult" **Gtn** iter. **Š** NA "render detestable" **N** jB pass. "be abused, cursed"; > *nazru*; *nizirtu*; *nazziru*; *izzirtu*, *izziru*; → *ezēru*

nazāzu(m) "to make a swishing sound" Bab. **G** (*u/u*) of tree; of pig "grunt, snort"; OB of snake "hiss"? **D** "hush" a child ?; > *nazzizu*; → *nasāsu*

nazāzu → also *našāšu* I

nazbaltum "load" OB; < *zabālu*

nazbalum "(standardized) load, daily rate of transporting" OB math. [ÍL] in *n. libittim* "*n.* of bricks", of earth etc.; < *zabālu*

nāzinum (a metal projectile) Mari

nāziqu "creaking" jB; lex. of door; of wind "howling"; < *nazāqu*

nazīzum → *nasīsum*

nazmātu pl. "troubles, vexations" jB; < *nazāmu*

nazqūtum "worry, sorrow" OB; < *nazāqu*

nazru(m) "cursed" O/MB; < *nazāru*

nazuz → *izuzzum*

nazūzu "canebrake" jB lex.

***nazziqu**, *nanziqu* "plaintive, querulous"? O/jB; < *nazāqu*

nazziru, *nanzirum* "given to cursing" O/jB; < *nazāru*

nazzītu → *namzītu*

nazzizu "hissing" OB, of snake; < *nazāzu*

-ne → *-nim*

ne'āru → *nēru* I; *nêru*

ne'āšum → *nêšu*

neā'um → *nê'u*

nēbaḫum, *nēbeḫum*; pl. f. (a kind of payment) OB

nēbaḫu → also *nēbeḫu*

nēbartu → *nēbertu*

nēbaru → *nēberu*

nēbeḫu(m), *nebḫu*, Susa, M/NA *nēbaḫu(m)* "band" Bab., M/NA [TÚG.ÍB.LÁ; NA also ÍB.LÁ] "belt, sash" for person, horse, divine image; "frieze" on buildings; < *ebēḫu*

nēbeḫum → also *nēbaḫum*

nēbertu, Ass. *nēbartu(m)* "crossing(-place)"; "process of crossing" sea, river, OA "ferry(-due)"; "far side, opposite bank"; < *ebēru* I

nēberu(m), *nēperu*, Ass. *nēburu(m)*; pl. f. **1.** "crossing, ford"; in PlN; Mari pl. "ferrying right(s)"? **2.** "ferry(boat)" [GIŠ.MÁ.DIRI.GA]; *ša n.* "ferryman" **3.** astr. (planet Jupiter) [mul/dSAG.ME.GAR ?]; also as name of North star ?; < *ebēru* I

nēbettu ~ "sash, girdle" j/NB [(TÚG.)DÁRA]; < *ebēṭu* II

nebḫu → *nēbeḫu*

nebrītu(m), OA *nabrītum* "hunger(-ration)" OA, O/jB [ŠÀ.SUD] **1.** OA "(minimum) ration, fodder" for donkey; OB for prisoner **2.** M/jB "hunger, famine"; < *berû* II

nebṭû → *nabṭû*

nebû I, *nabû*; f. *nabītu*, *nebūtu* "shining, brilliant" M/NB [SA4] of stars, deities; transf. of dogs; MB as fPN; < *nebû* II

nebû(m) II, *nabû* "to shine, sparkle" Bab. **G** (*i/i*) of stars, deities, in PN; > *nebû* I

nēbu → *nābu* I

ne'ellû **N** "to roam around" jB **Ntn** (*ite'(el)lû*) iter.; > *muttellû*

negeltû → *nagaltû*

neggultu → *nangulu*

negû → *nagû* II

neḫelṣû(m), *ne/aḫalṣû* **N** "to slip, slide" O/jB, NA of person, foot; on ice; "slide down" a tree; transf. "slip (up), make error"; of foundation, parts of liver "slide out of place" **Š** "cause to slip"; > *muḫḫelṣītum*, *mušḫalṣītu*; *itaḫliṣū*, *itaḫlaṣānu*

neḫēsu → *naḫāsu*

nēḫiš "calmly, quietly" jB; < *nēḫu*

neḫlatum → *niḫlatum*

neḫlu "(process of) sifting, sieving"? jB; < *naḫālu* I

neḫrārānum → *ne'rārānum*

neḫrārum → *ne'rāru*

neḫru "wheezing, snorting" M/NB; also Ug. (a disease); < *naḫāru* II

neḫsu I, occas. *nikkassu* ~ "inlay" NA in precious metal

neḫsu II (a garment) OB(N.Mes.)

neḫtu "young"? jB of a bird; < *naḫātu* ?; → *naḫtu*

nēḫtu(m) "calm, peace" O/jB [NE.ḪA; NE.ḪU] *šubat n. šūšubum* "to let dwell in security"; < *nēḫu*

neḫûm I adj. mng. unkn. OB; < *neḫû* II

neḫû(m) II mng. unkn. Bab. **G**; > *neḫû* I

nēḫu(m) "calm, peaceful" Bab., NA; of wind and water; *šubtu(m) n.* "peaceful dwelling"; < *nâḫu*

nē'iru → *nā'eru*

nekelmû(m), *neklemû*, *nakalmû*, *naklamû* **N** "to frown at, regard malevolently" Bab., NA of divine, royal displeasure; of demon etc. **Ntn** iter. **Š** caus.; > *mutteklemmû*

nēkemtu(m) "removal" **1.** "forcible removal, plundering" **2.** om. "displaced part"? of feature on the liver **3.** OB oil om., mng. uncl. **4.** (a planetary phenomenon); < *ekēmu*

nēkepum (a tool or container) OAkk(Sum.), OB lex.; < *ekēpu*

nēkisu → *nākisu*

neklemû → *nekelmû*

nekru → *nakru*

nelbītu mng. unkn. Bogh. lex.

nēlepu(m), *nēlebum*, *nēleptu* (a brewing vessel) O/jB; < *elēpu* or *alāpu* ?

nelmenu(m), OB(Susa) metath. *nenmelu* "misfortune"? O/jB; < *lemēnu*

nēltu → *nēštu*

ne'lu → *na'lu*

nemašu, *nemazu* "tree"? jB lex.

nēmedu(m), Ass. *nēmudu(m)* "that on which one leans" **1.** of deity in PN "support" **2.** "base, socle" for cultic symbol **3.** "base" of DN, desig. of sanctuary, of city **4.** "(back)rest" of furniture; *(kussê) n.* "chair with back" **5.** (an astronomical term) **6.** (a medical term); < *emēdu*; → *nēmettu*

nēmel "because" NA with subjunct.; < *nēmelu*

nēmelu(m), Ass. *nēmulu(m)*; pl. f. "profit, benefit" [Á.TUKU]; OB *ul nēmel* "there is no profit"

nēmequ(m), Ass. *nēmuqu* "wisdom, sagacity" Bab., M/NA [NAM.KÙ.ZU] "civilising knowledge"; "skill(ed craftsmanship)"; NA "cunning"; < *emēqu* I

nemerkû → *namarkû*

nemēṣu → *namāṣu*

nēmettu(m), Ass. *nēmattu(m)* **1.** OB "levy, imposition" **2.** OB "(cause for) complaint", *n. rašûm* "to complain" **3.** "crutch"; "support" of wall; transf. of DN in PN, PlN **4.** NB astr. mng. unkn. **5.** Ass. "back(rest)" of a chair; NA "couch" [GIŠ.NÁ]; < *emēdu*; → *nēmedu*

nemlû(m) "throat"? O/jB lex.; < *malû* IV ?

nemra'u (a textile or garment)? jB/NA lex.

nemsētu(m), Am., Nuzi, Bogh., Ug. also *namsītu*, *nansītu*, *nensītu* "wash-basin" O/jB; < *mesû* II

nemsû(m), *namsû*, *nansû* "wash-basin" Bab. [NÍG.ŠU.LUḪ.ḪA] of metal; "washing tank" of wood, of reeds; Mari "cistern"?; < *mesû* II

nemšaḫu → *namsuḫu*

nemûm ~ "to be strange, disturbing"? OB(lit.) **G** of dream

nēmu → *nīmu*

nendabbum → *nigdabbum*

nenegallu (an insect) jB lex., med.; < Sum.

nengulu → *nangulu*

nēniu → *nīnû*

nenmelu → *nelmenu*

nensītu → *nemsētu*

nenšûm "confused" OB of bird; < *ešû* IV N

nentû N "to overlap" or "go parallel with each other"? jB, astr. of stars **Ntn** (pret. *ittentu*) iter. of stars; of animals

nenu (a dirty bandage, rag) jB lex.

nēnu → *nīnu*

-nēnu → *-nīni*

nenzu mng. unkn. NA desig. of copper

nepārum → *nupāru* I

nēpašu → *nēpešu*

nepātu "meadow, outskirts"? jB lex.

nepelkû(m), *napalkû* **N** "to be(come) wide (open)" Bab. (stat. *nepelku*); jB of eyes; OB of part of the liver "expand"; jB of horns of the moon "be wide apart"; of branches; of people "spread out" **Š** (infin. *šupalkû*) "open wide" mouth, door; "widen" road, waterway; jB astr. of constellation; > *palkû, napalkû*

nēpeltu → *nēpeštu*

neperdû → *napardû* I.II

nēperētum pl. tant. "food provision" OB for human, animal; < *epēru*

neperkû → *naparkû* I.II

nēperu → *nēberu*

nēpeštu(m), jB also *nēpeltu* "work(manship), performance" O/jB [DÙ-] **1.** "activity, procedure" of ritual, medical treatment, mathematical calculations; OB "(agricultural) production" **2.** "(method of) construction, workmanship" **3.** "account, financial statement"; math. "enumeration"? **4.** lex. (bag for carrying metals); *ša n.* (man with *n.* bag) **5.** jB lex. (a disease)?; < *epēšu* II

nēpešu(m), NA *nēpušu* Bab., M/NA **1.** "activity; procedure"; math., mag. "procedure, instructions" **2.** "tool, implement"; M/NA "(siege) machine" **3.** OB(Ass.) "(method of) construction"; < *epēšu* II

nēpišum (package of precious metal) OA; < *epēšu* II

nepītum f. "woman distrained (for debt)" OB, freq. wr. ^{munus}*n.*; < *nepûm*; → *nipûtum*

nēpītu(m) "baking trough" OB, Elam, Nuzi?; < *epû* II

nepṣûm (or *nepsûm*) (an intestinal illness)? OB lex.; < *peṣû* II ?

neptû "opening, breach" M/jB; in wall, in liver; < *petû* II

neptû → also *naptû*

nepûm, *napûm* "to distrain, take as pledge" OB **G** person, animal; often with *nipûtum* **Gtn** iter.; > *nepītum, nipûtum*

neqelpû(m), *ne/aqalpû(m)* **N** "to float, glide (along/down)" O/jB, MA [DIRI] of watercraft "sail, float downstream"; of objects on water; of clouds, wind "drift" **Ntn** iter. [DIRI.MEŠ] of boat, water; of invalid "become dizzy repeatedly"?; of eye "roll around"? **Š** "sail" boat, cargo "downstream"; > *muqqelpītu; mušqalpītu*

nēr, *nēru, nīru* "600" Bab. [GÉŠ+U] OB *nēr ṣābī* "600 troops"; "host, army"? jB lex.; *ana n.-šu/ša* "all; totally"

nērabu → *nērebu*

ne'rārānum "reinforcing" Mari, of troops; < *ne'rāru*

ne'rāru(m), *na'rārum, nē/ārāru* "aid, help" O/jB; M/NA in PN [ÉRIN.TÁḪ/TAḪ] esp. military support, "reinforcements"; from deities, in PN; jB also "ally"; Am. *bēl n.* "helper"; < *na'arruru*; > *nērārūtu, ne'rārānum*

nērārūtu, *nārārūtu* "aid, help" M/jB, Bogh. [ÉRIN.TAḪ-] esp. of military support; < *ne'rāru*

nerdû → *nerṭû*

nērebtu(m), OAkk *nārabtum* "entrance, entry" OAkk, Bab., Elam, Ug. **1.** "entrance" of building **2.** "pass" (giving access to mountain), also of feature of liver; OB as PlN (= Ishchali) **3.** as name of festival ?; < *nērebu*

nērebu(m), Ass. *nērubu* "entrance" of house, land; "(mountain) pass"; (feature of liver); as name of land; < *erēbu* I

nērebūtum "entrance" OB ext., as feature of liver; < *nērebu*

nermu → *nalmu*

nerpû (a pole, part of a well)? jB lex.; < Sum.

nerrubu → *nērubu*

nērtānītu f. "murderous" jB mag. of sorceress; < *nērtu*

nērtu(m) "murder, killing" Bab., OA; *ēpiš n.*, *ša n.* "murderer"; < *nêru*

nerṭû (or *nerdû*) "sin, misdemeanour" jB [NIR.DA]; < Sum.; → *šertu* I

nēru I, Ug. *ne'āru* ? (dimension of a field) Ug.?, jB; OAkk in DN ?

nēru II (a tree) jB lex.

nēru III (a bird)? jB lex.

nēru → also *nēr*

nêru(m), *nâru(m)*, OAkk *ne'ārum* "to strike; kill" OAkk, Bab. **G** [SAG.GIŠ.RA] "hit; kill" enemies, NA, NB in PN; "fell" a tree; OAkk,

OB "smite, defeat" enemy, city **D** ~ G; > *nērtu, nērtānītu*; *munērtum*; *mayyāru*?

nērubtu(m) "flight, rout" Bab., esp. om.; < *nērubu*

nērubu(m), *ne/arrubu* **N** "to flee, escape" O/jB (*u/u*) of person, animal; > *arbu* 2; *arbūtu* 2.3; *munnarbu*; *nērubtu*

nērubu → also *nērebu*

nesâtu → *nesû* I

nêsekku → *nêšakku*

nēseptu(m) **1.** Bab., NA (a container) **2.** OB (a type of rental agreement); < *esēpu*

nēsepu, Ass. *nēsupu* **1.** NA "shovel, fire-rake" **2.** NB (a container of standard size) for liquids; < *esēpu*

nesîš "at a distance, from afar" j/NB; < *nesû* I

nesû(m) I, *nessû(m)*, *nasû* "far, distant" Bab. of land(s); of king "remote"; transf. of object, ship "from afar, exotic"; f. pl. *nesâtu* "far-away place, distance"; of time "remote"; < *nesû* II

nesû(m) II, *nasû*, OA *nasā'um* "to be distant; withdraw" (from = acc., *ina*, *eli*) Bab., OA **G** (*e/e*) [BAD] **1.** stat. "is far from" s.o.; transf. of deity's heart **2.** "distance o.s. from, depart from"; esp. of demon, god "abandon" person, body (*zumru*); of fear, disease; absol. of person, demon etc.; of horse "shy"; also = D "remove" **Gtn** iter. of G **D** "take away; remove" earth, emotions; "deport" people **Š** "make s.o. or s.th. recede; drive away" evil etc. **ŠD** ~ Š "remove" guilt **N** "depart, leave" [BAD] of god, disease etc.; > *nesû* I, *nesîš*, *nesûtu*; *nusâtu*; *messētu*

nēsu → *nēṣu*

nēsupu → *nēsepu*

nesûtu "distance" jB; < *nesû* II

neṣbettu "finger" jB lex.; < *ṣabātu* ?

neṣû → *naṣû*

nēṣu, *nēsu* "strong"? jB, NA

nêšakku(m), NB also *nêsekku* (a priest; a dignitary) Bab. [(LÚ.)NU.ÈŠ]; < Sum.

nêšakkūtum (office of *nêšakkum*) OB [NAM.NU.ÈŠ]; < *nêšakku*

nešalpû, *nešelpû* **N** "to glide, slither" jB; of snake

nešbû I "satiety, satisfaction" jB; < *šebû* I

nešbû II "putrid"? Ug., jB mag., of blood

nešelpû → *nešalpû*

*(-)****nêšim*** → *(-)niāšim*

nešmû(m), *našmû* "hearing" O/jB; med. "sense of hearing"; < *šemû*

nešpertu → *našpartu* II

nēštu, *nēltu* jB **1.** "lioness" [MUNUS.UR.MAḪ]; lex. *zumbi n.* (a fly) **2.** (desig. of a star or constellation); < *nēšu*

nešû(m), *našû* "to vomit"? O/jB lex. **G**; **D** ~ G; > *nušû*

nēšu(m) "lion" [UR.MAḪ; UR.A]; epith. of deities; *n. (ša) qaqqari* "chamaeleon"?; astr. (desig. of constellation) "Leo" [MUL/MÚL.UR.MAḪ/A]; > *nēštu*

nēšu → also *nišu*; *nīšu* II

nêšu(m), *ne'āšum*, OAkk *na'āšum* "to live, revive" OAkk, O/jB **G** [Bogh. TI.LA] OAkk also in PN; O/jB of invalid "recover" **Š** "keep alive, sustain"; > *nīšu* II; *muna''išu*; *tenēštu*; → *na'āšu* D; *nâšu* D

netbītum "mobilization place" Mari; < *tebû*

nētentu (a mixing tool)? M/jB lex.; < *etēmu* ?

nêti → *niāti*

-nêti → *-niāti*

netmertu (a box with a lid)? jB lex.; < *temēru*

nētu (a wooden object)? jB lex.

nêtu I "to enclose, surround"? jB **G** stat., of feature in entrails; > *nītu*, *nītiš*

nêtu II "to chop"? jB lex.

nê'u(m), *ne'û*, OAkk *na'ā'um*, OA *neā'um* "to turn back" (trans. and intrans.) OAkk, O/MA, O/jB **G** *irtam n.* "turn s.o.'s breast = put to flight", also refl. "flee"; "counteract, deflect" oath; "staunch" bleeding; "satisfy, allay" hunger **D** ~ G **N** "be turned back"; MA of ship "capsize, overturn"; > *muneḫḫu*, *munē'u*?; *nu''u*

nezû "to void" urine, excrement jB **G** of human, animal **Ntn** iter.

-ni I Ass. subjunct. suff.

-ni II "me" (1 sg. acc. pron. suff.)

-ni III "our" (1 pl. gen. suff.); → *-nīni*

-ni → also *-nim*

niā'attum → *niā'um*

niāku(m), *nâku* "to have sexual intercourse with" **G** med. *muruṣ nâki* "venereal disease" **Gtn** iter. of G **Š** "permit intercourse" **N** pass.; > *nīku* I.II, *nīktu*; *nā'ikānu*; *nayyaktu*; *muttikku*; *muttatiku*; *mayyakum*?

niālu → *nâlu*

niāru, *ni/ayāru* "papyrus" M/NB, NA; NA *kerkē n.* "rolls of p."; also in PlN; NB also "parchment"

-niāš → *-niāšim*

niāši(m), OB also *nayyāš*, j/NB *nâši/u* "to, for us" (1 pl. dat. pron.); Bab. after *an(a)*; jB also for gen., acc.; → *nâšin*; *nīnu*; *yâšinu*

-niāšim, Mari *-nêšim*, OAkk *-niāš*, NB also *-nâš(i)*, *-nši* "to, for us" (1 pl. dat. suff.)

niāti, Mari etc. *nêti*, O/jB also *nâti* "us" (1 pl. acc. pron.); "of us" (gen.); OA also dat.; → *nīnu*; *yâtinu*

-niāti, *-nêti*, M/jB *-nâti* "us" (1 pl. acc. suff.); OA also dat.

niā'um; f. *niattum*; OA pl. *niā'uttum*, *niā'attum*; OB *nûm*, f. *nuttun/m*, pl. once *nuātum*; lex. *ni/a'ûm* "our" as adj. for emphasis instead of poss. suff.; in pred. use "ours"; → *innû*; *nīnu*

niazu in *iṣṣūr n.* (a bird) Bogh. lex.

nib → *tāwi*

nibatu mng. unkn. jB lex.

nibītu(m) Bab. **1.** "naming, nomenclature"; *n. šumi* "giving of name"; *n. zakāru/nabû* "to call to a vocation" as king; "invocation" of god **2.** "(one) nominated" by a deity etc.; < *nabû* II

nibiu → *nībû*

nibrārum (or *niprārum*) (a textile) OA

nibṣu ~ "young bird, fledgling" j/NB

nibṭu(m) "brightness, radiance" jB, NA?; < *nabāṭu*

nibu → *yānibu*

nibûm → *nib'u*; *nipûm*

nību(m) I, *nimbu*, NA also *nīpu* "naming" OAkk, Bab., NA **1.** "name, designation", *n. šattim* "year name" **2.** "amount" of silver etc., Mari "nominal value" **3.** "number", jB *lā nība*, *ša lā nībi* "without number, countless" **4.** OA, jB "declaration" ?; < *nabû* II

nību II "small piece"? M/jB of precious metals

nību → also *nib'u*

nībû, *nibiu* (a feature on the spleen, lungs) O/jB

nib'u(m), *nip'u(m)*, *nibûm*, NA *nību* "(s)welling up" O/jB, NA of water, spring; of vegetation, *n. erṣeti/eqli* ~ "wild growth" on fields; *n. balti* (a plant); < *nabā'u*

nibûtu "naming" jB of DN; < *nabû* II

nibzu "(a kind of) document" NA, NB described as Assyrian, Aramaic

nidabû → *nindabû*

nidaḫulušḫu (or *nitaḫulušḫu*) (a copper object) Nuzi; < Hurr.

nidbû → *nindabû*

nidintu(m), *nidittu(m)*; OB st. constr. also *nidnat* "gift, dowry" Bab. [NÍG.SUM.MU; NB SUM-, NÍG.SUM] also in PNs; NB *nidinti šarri* "income, property of the king"; < *nadānu* II

nidittum, *nitittum* "recoil, fear"? Bogh. lex.; < *nadādu* ?

nidittu → also *nidintu*

nidītu(m) Bab. **1.** OB, NB "unbuilt, waste plot" **2.** j/NB (an astronomical term) **3.** OB *n. appim* "crestfallenness, despondency"?; < *nadû* III

nidnakku → *nignakku*

nidnu(m) "gift" O/jB [Ug. SUM(.MEŠ)]; OB in PN "(divine) gift"; OB *n. pîm* "promise, pledge"; < *nadānu* II

nidûm mng. unkn. OB ext.

nīdu(m) "l(a)ying, throwing (down)" Bab. [ŠUB]; jB "(cumulus) cloud"?; NB (a claim); *nīd(i) aḫi(m)* "negligence", *n. a. išû/rašû(m)* "to be(come) negligent, lazy"; *n. erši* "bedridden state"; *n. giḫlê* "mourning"; ext. *n. kussî(m)* 'emplacement of throne' (part of the liver); *n. libbi* 'cast-off of womb', i.e. "foetus"?; *n. qabli* (descending tune)?; jB lex. *n. rapši* "winnowed grain"; *n. ru'ti* "flow of saliva"; *n. ṭēmi* "faint-heartedness"; < *nadû* III

nidûtu(m) "abandonment" Bab. [KISLAḪ ?] "uncultivated state, waste land"; lex. in *n. Ea* (a fish); < *nadû* III

nigarruru mng. unkn. jB lex.

nigdabbum, *nendabbum* (a food ration) OB in cult; < Sum.; → *nindabû*

nigdabbūtum "office of presenting *nigdabbum* offerings" OB [NAM.LÚ.NÍG.DAB.BA]; < *nig=dabbum*

ni(g)dimdimmû ~ "physical form, shape; manufactured object" jB lex. of human; < Sum.

niggallu(m), *ningallu*, NA *ingallu* "sickle" [URUDU.(ŠU.)KIN; Nuzi, NB NÍG/NI.GÁL.LA] of copper, iron etc.; OA used for payments, also as desig. of harvest time; OB *waraḫ n.* (a month); < Sum.

niggallû (a type of property) jB lex.; < Sum.

niggaru in *bīt n.* "storehouse" jB, of shrine; < Sum.

niggirgiddû (a watering can)? jB lex.; < Sum.

niggulû (something big)? O/jB lex.; < Sum.

nigimmû → *ligimû*

nigiṣṣu, Bogh. *ningiṣṣu*; pl. f. "crack, crevice" M/jB [KI.(IN.)DAR]; lex. *ṣēr n.* (a type of snake); lex. *šāt n.* (a plant)

nigītum (or *nikītum*, *nig/kittum*) (a resinous plant) OAkk(Sum.)

nigkalagû, nikkalagû ? (a drum) jB [URUDU.NÍG.KALA.GA]; < Sum.

niglallu, *niglaltu* (a bandage) jB lex.; < Sum.; → *naṣmattu*

niglum (a garment) OB; < Sum.?

niglussû (a vessel) jB lex.; < Sum.

nignakku(m), *nignaqqu(m)*, *nidnakku* "censer, incense burner" Bab., M/NA [NÍG.NA]; < Sum.

nignerûm "false claim" OB; < Sum.

nigsagilû "substitute, replacement" jB [NÍG.SAG.ÍL/GIL-]; of substitute king; mag., of figurine; < Sum.

nigsiliqqu (a table or tray) jB lex.; < Sum.

nigûtu(m), *ningûtu*; pl. *nigâtu* "joyful song, musical celebration" O/jB; *n. epēšu, šakānu* "to hold a festival, make music"; < *nagû* II

nigzalladû (a copper object) jB lex.; < Sum.

niḫistu "retreat" NB **1.** "backflow" of goods, payments **2.** "change of mind, relenting"? of deity in PN **3.** astr. "stationary point"?; < *naḫāsu*

niḫittu (desig. of precious metal) MB; < *naḫātu* ?; → *ni'ittum*

niḫītum mng. unkn. OB of lion

niḫlatum (or *neḫlatum*) ~ "transferred property" Mari; < *naḫālum* II

ni'ittum ~ "dangerous situation, predicament"? Mari; < *na'ādu*

nikaru ~ "outsider" Emar; →*nakāru*

nikaruru ? (a plant) jB lex.

nikasu → *niksu*

nikiltu "skill" j/NB, NA "cleverness, ingenuity", often pl.; "artful design, skilful execution" of work; "scheming, cunning"; < *nakālu*

nikimtu "heaping up" M/jB "accumulation" of property; med. also pl. (a swelling)?; < *nakāmu*

nikiptu I "blow, affliction" jB in *n. Sîn* (a disease); < *nakāpu*

nikiptu(m) II (or *niqiptu(m)*) "spurge, *Euphorbia*"? (a shrub with male and female flowers, milky juice) OAkk, O/jB, NA [ŠIM.^{d}NIN.URTA; ŠIM.^{d}MAŠ]; used in med. and mag.; *šaman n.* "oil of spurge?"

nikištum "contribution"? OA; < *nakāšu* ?

nikittu → *nigītum*

nikītum → *nigītum*

nikkalagû → *nigkalagû*

nikkas st. abs. "half-reed" Bab. **1.** as measure of length, OB = 3 cubits; NB *n. qanê* "3.5 cubits" **2.** NB as area measure = 3.5 cubits of surface ~ 6.125 sq. metres; < *nakāsu* ?

nikkassamumma, *nissakkamumma* in *n. epēšu* "to do the accounts" Nuzi; < *nikkassu*

nikkassu(m), often pl. "account(s); property" [NÍG.KA9/KA] **1.** "(statement of) account"; in idioms OA *n. šasā'um* "to claim settlement of account(s)"; Bab., NA *n. epē/āšu*, MA *n. ṣabātu* "to balance accounts"; *ina n. šakānu* "to submit, make s.th. available for accounting"; *ina n.* "at (the time of) the accounting"; *rab n.* "comptroller"; Elam *bīt n.* "counting house"; NB math. "(result of a) calculation" **2.** NB "possessions, wealth"; *rab n.* "administrator of property" **3.** Bab. (an emblem of Šamaš) [GIŠ.NÍG.KA9]; < Sum.; > *nukkusum* II; *nikkas=samumma*

nikkassu → also *neḫsu* I

niklu "skill" M/jB in *n. libbi* "ingenuity"; j/NB, NA "craftiness, deception"; < *nakālu*

nikmu "accumulation" of property Ug.; < *nakāmu*

nikpu(m) "thrust" OAkk ?, O/jB **1.** *n. alpim* "goring of ox" **2.** om. *n. ubāni* mng. uncl. **3.** OAkk liver model "abutting surface"?; < *nakāpu*

niksu, NB also *nikasu* "cutting (off)" M/NA, M/NB [KUD] **1.** "slaughter" of animal, jB *n. immeri* "sheep carcase"; jB *nikis patri* "dagger-cut"; NB "incision" **2.** "cut, piece" of meat, wood, cloth; *n. qaqqadi* "severed head"; Nuzi of land "plot, sector", also "reduction"; MB *n. karî* (fee for) "cutting open a grain pile"; "breach, gap" in a wall; < *nakāsu*

nīktu in *muruṣ n.* "venereal disease" jB; < *niāku*

nīku I "(sexually) known, lain with" MA, jB; < *niāku*

nīku II "fornication, sexual intercourse" jB; < *niāku*

nikurtum → *nukurtu*

nīlu(m) I "lying down" O/jB lex. of man, tree; < *nâlu*

nīlu(m) II, *ni'lu* "wetness, moisture" O/jB **1.** "flooding" of field **2.** human, animal, god's "semen" **3.** astr. mng. unkn.; < *na'ālu*

-nim, M/NB *-ni*, M/NA *-ne* after pl. forms **1.** "to me" (1 pl. dat. suff.) **2.** vent. affix; *-*nim-ni* > Bab. *-ninni*, Ass. *-nenni*; → *-am*

nimar → *nimru* II

nimbu → *nību* I

nimgallu "big fly" jB (desig. of a siege engine); < Sum.

nimmullu (a kind of fly)? jB; < Sum.?; → *nuḫḫullu*

nimra'u (a garment) NA lex.

nimru(m) I, *namru, nammar* ~ "leopard" O/jB [PIRIG.TUR; → *Ukaduḫḫa*]; also as desig. of demon; (a constellation)?

nimru(m) II, OAkk *niw(a)rum* "light" OAkk, Ass., OB(N.Mes.); (st. constr. *niw/mar, nimu/er*) of a deity, esp. in PN; < *nawāru*

nimšū pl. tant. "sinews" O/jB of sheep

nimšulu, *niššulu*; pl. f. "fish spawn"? jB lex.

nīmu(m), *nēmu(m)* (a fodder grass) O/jB

nimurtu in *epšēt(i) nimurti* "friendly doing(s), festive activities"? MB/MA of a temple; < *nawāru*

nindabû(m), *nid(a)bû* "(food) offering" [NIDBA(=PAD.^{d}INNIN)]; < Sum.; → *nigdabbum*

nindanu(m) **1.** "rod, pole" as a measure of length, Ass., O/jB = 12 cubits; NB = 14 cubits (~ 7 metres) **2.** jB ~ "(cultic) prescription, instruction"?

ningallu → *niggallu*

ningibit mng. unkn. OB lex.

ningiṣṣu → *nigiṣṣu*

ningûtu → *nigûtu*

nīni → *nīnu*

-nīni, *-nēnu* "our" (1 pl. gen. suff.) NB for *-ni* III

nīniu → *nīnû*

ninkummu (a type of deity; a temple official) jB; also as DN; < Sum.

ninnigum mng. unkn. OB lex.

ninnum → *nīnû*

nīnu, later also *nīni*, NA *nēnu* "we" (1 pl. nom. pron.); as emphatic subject, in pred. use; Nuzi, Bogh. for acc. etc.; → *anīnu*; *niāti*, *niāši*; *niā'um*

nīnû(m), *ninnum*, Ass. *nīlēniu* (a medicinal plant, phps.) "*Ammi*" Bab., NA [(Ú.)KUR.RA(.SAR)]

Nipas (desig. of a festival) OA

nipdu "cutting (off)"? jB; < *napādu* II

nipḫu(m) "(the act of) lighting, flaring (up)" Bab., M/NA **1.** "rising, shining" [KUR; MÚ] of fire "burning, blazing"; of celestial bodies "rising", *nipiḫ Šamaš* "sunrise, east"; MA fDN *Šarrat-nipḫe*; in PNs **2.** om. "(blazing, flaring up of) anger, quarrel" [IZI.GAR]; "row, fight"; pl. f. "dispute" among seers **3.** "controversial omen", i.e. sign which will produce unclear results **4.** "(sun) disc, ornamental boss"; < *napāḫu*

nipiltu I "s.th. dug up" jB; < *napālu* I

nipiltu(m) II "payment in settlement" OA, O/jB; < *napālu* II

niplu(m) I "shoot, sapling" O/jB

niplu(m) II ~ "visible part of the moon" O/jB; < *napālu* I ?

nipqū pl. "excrement, defecation" jB; < Aram.

niprārum → *nibrārum*

nipru "scion, offspring" M/jB

nipṣu(m) "smashing, shattering" O/jB **1.** med. *n. šer'āni* (condition of sinews)? **2.** *n. erî* (copper fragments) **3.** (a meteor. phenomenon) **4.** Mari in *nipiṣ nikkassī* "clearance of accounts"; < *napāṣu*

nipšu(m) I "breathing, scent" Bab., NA "snorting" of the bull of heaven; "odour, stink, scent"; *n. šattim* mng. unkn. OB(lit.); < *napāšu* I

nipšu II "tuft" M/jB, NA of wool; < *napāšu* II

nipûm (or *nibûm*) mng. uncert. OB

nīpu(m), *ni'pu* "dried wood" M/jB, NA; < *na'āpu*

nīpu → also *nību*

ni'pu → *nīpu*

nipûtum "debt slave, distrainee" OB often wr. ^{munus}*n.*; as "pledge"; *n. wuššurum* "to set free a d."; < *nepûm*; → *nepītum*

niqdu(m) (a plant) OAkk, NB

nīqētum → *nīqu* I

niqiptu → *nikiptu* II

niqīqu "copulation" jB lex.; → *nīqu* II

niqirtum "demolition" (a coefficient) OB math.; < *naqāru*

niqittu I "anxiety" M/NB, NA, *n. rašû* of illness "to become critical", of person "to get worried", of statue etc. "to get damaged"; MB *kī n.* "in concern, anxiously"; < *naqādu*

niqittu II "retaliation, satisfaction" NA; < Aram.

niqium → *nīqu* I

Niqmum I (a month) OB(N.Mes.), Mari; < W.Sem.

niqmum II "revenge" Mari; < W.Sem.

niqqu "fig seed"?; (a type of flour)? jB lex.

niqru(m) "(wood salvaged from) demolition" O/jB; < *naqāru*

nīqu(m) I, *niqû(m)*, OA also *niq'um*, *niqium*; pl. m. & f. "offering, sacrifice" [(UDU.)SISKUR/SÍSKUR; Mari, Elam AMAR.AMAR.RE] of sheep, ox, commodities, jB also "libation" of water, beer; *ša n.* "sacrificer"; < *naqû*

nīqu II "copulation" jB lex.; → *niqīqu*

niq'um → *nīqu* I

niqūdatum, *niqūdu*, *niquddu* (a marsh bird) Bab.; also as PN

nirāḫu (a kind of snake) jB [MUŠ.TUR]; < Sum.

niraniṯḫu (a chair cushion)? Nuzi; < Hurr.

nirašše, *nirišše/i* (desig. of a canal) Nuzi; < Hurr.

nirātu mng. unkn. MB

niringum mng. unkn. OB lex.

nirišše/i → *nirašše*

nirit(e), *ina n.* ~ "because" NA

nirriṭu "fear" NA; < *narāṭu*

nirru(m), *nīru* **1.** j/NB (a rope or braided string)? **2.** MB, Nuzi (an identifying mark on ear, back of animals)

nīru(m) I "yoke, crossbeam" [GIŠ.ŠUDUN/ ŠUDUN4; GIŠ.GIŠ; ext. AL.TI/TE] **1.** "yoke" for animal teams; *ša muḫḫi n.* (ornament for a yoke) NA; transf. "(political) yoke, domination, rule" **2.** "(door) lintel" **3.** O/jB (part of the liver, lung) **4.** "yoke-star" = Arcturus (and parts of Boötes) [MUL.MU. BU(.KÉŠ.DA)]

nīru II "light" MA in PNs, jB; < *nawāru*

nīru III "prayer" jB lex.

nīru → also *nēr*; *nirrum*

nirwe (a commodity measured by vol.) Nuzi; < Hurr.

Nisaba, *nissaba/u* "grain (goddess)" [^{d}ŠE.NAGA; ^{d}NAGA] **1.** (grain goddess) **2.** jB "grain"; < Sum.

nisaggu → *nisannu*

nisaḫu → *nisḫu* I

nisakku, nisangu → *nisannu*

nisannītum f. "born in the month *Nisannu*" MB as fPN

nisa(n)nu(m), *nissa(n)nu(m)*, *nisakku*, *nisan/ggu* Bab., NA **1.** O/jB "offering (of first fruits)", also *n. šattim* **2.** (1st Bab. month) [ITI.BÁR.ZAG.GAR; later ITI.BÁR; jB occas. ITI.BAR(.SAG.SAG)]; < Sum.

nisapti mng. unkn. Nuzi

nisbat (or *nis/zb/pat*) mng. unkn. OAkk(Susa)

nisḫatu(m) (a tax levied on imported goods) OA; < *nasāḫu*

nisḫu(m) I, *nisa/iḫu*; pl. f., NA *nisḫāni* "extract(ion)" Bab., NA **1.** 'act of extraction': OB pl. "evacuations"; *ṣāb nisḫātim* "people torn away (from work), runaways"; NB ~ "(advance) payment" for workers; *n. ša PlN* (local tariff or due date$^{?}$); astr. "orbital velocity"? [ZI] **2.** 'result of extraction': OB "(what is) torn out, stubble" of plant; "excavated earth, material taken (from s.th.)"; "(concentrated) extract"? of oil; "(choice) cut" of meat; j/NB, NA "section of a tablet series"; < *nasāḫu*

nisḫu II, *nišḫu* mng. unkn. MB(Alal.), Nuzi

nisḫu → also *nišḫu* I

nisiḫtu **1.** OB "desertion" of troops **2.** (lex. also *nasiḫtu*) j/NB (a temple tax, temple dues); < *nasāḫu*

nisiḫu → *nisḫu* I

nisiktu → *nasku*

nisiqtu "selection, choice" j/NB, NA; of stones, *aban n.* "precious stone"; < *nasāqu*

nisku "shot" MB; in *n. qanê* "arrow shots"; < *nasāku*

nispat → *nisbat*

nisqu(m) "choice, selection" **1.** OAkk, OB lex. (a class of people) **2.** "best quality" of animals, textiles, stones, trees; "high level" of scribal art; < *nasāqu*; → *mūrnisqu*

nissaba/u → *Nisaba*

nissakkamumma → *nikkassamumma*

nissa(n)nu → *nisannu*

nissatiš "in lamentation" jB; < *nissatu*

nissatu(m), occas. *niššatu* "wailing, lamentation" O/jB, NA [SAG.PA.LAGAB]; *ša n.* "mourner" jB; < *nasāsu*

nisūtu → *nišūtu*

niṣirtu(m) "treasure; secret" Bab., NA [MUNUS.ÙRU(-); ÙRU-*ti*] **1.** "treasure, wealth"; *bīt n.* "treasury"; *n. ēkalli* "palace treasure" (→ *naṣru*) **2.** NB(lit.) of city etc. "protection, (place of) shelter" **3.** jB *(ašar) n.* "hidden, secluded place" **4.** "secret (knowledge)", esp. scribal **5.** astr. "hypsoma" of a planet or star, also *bīt n.*? **6.** ext. *n. ḫašê* (part of the lung); < *naṣāru*

niṣrum "protection" OAkk as PN; < *naṣāru*

nīṣu mng. unkn. jB med.

nišertu(m), *niširtu(m)*, NB also *nušertu* "deduction, removal" Bab.; OB "plot" of land "taken away"; < *našāru* I

nišḫu(m) I, *nisḫu* "diarrhoea" O/jB; < *našāḫu*

nišḫu II (a reed pipe)? jB lex.

nišḫu → also *nisḫu* II

niširtu → *nišertu*

nišiš "like a human" jB; < *nišu*

nišītu(m) "lifting, raising, elevation" O/jB "elevation to, installation in" priestly office; *n. (īni/īnī) DN* "raising (of the eyes) of DN" = "(object of) glance, chosen person of a deity"; (a condition causing palms to die)?; < *nīšu* I

nišku(m), Ug. *našku*; pl. f. "bite" O/jB [KA (.TAR)] "bite" of dog, mouse, snake; transf. of shoe (mng. uncl.), death, "pain"? inflicted by objects; MB *n. pî* "mouthful, morsel"; < *našāku*

nišru(m) **1.** OA "instalment" **2.** Bab. "deduction" **3.** NA "stone block"?; < *našāru* I

niššatu → *nissatu*

niššīku(m), *naššīkum* (a title of Ea) O/jB; also wr. [^{d}NIN.ŠI.KÙ]

niššikūtu "rank of the god Ea" jB [^{d}NIN.ŠI.KÙ-]

niššulu → *nimšulu*

nišu(m), *nīšu*, *nēšu*; mostly pl. *nišū*; f., Mari, j/NB, NA also m. "people" [UN.MEŠ] "humanity"; "population, populace" of a deity, land, "subjects" of a king; "relatives, kin, family"; *nīš(ī) bīti(m)* "domestic servants"; > *nišiš*; *nišūtu*

nīšu(m) I "lifting, raising" [ÍL; ZI.GA; MU] *nīš rēši(m)* 'lifting of the head' i.e. "honour, recognition"; ext. (desig. of part of the exta); *nīš qāti(m)* 'hand-lifting' (a type of prayer) [ŠU.ÍL.LÁ(.KÁM/KAM)? (→ *šu'illakku*)], *n. q. našû/rašû* "to pray"; *nīš īnī* "glance (of favour)", "favourite", "discretion", OAkk in PN; *nīš libbi(m)* "desire", esp. "(sexual) libido" [ŠÀ.ZI.GA]; *nīš gabarî* (desig. of a musical interval; a mode); < *našû* II

nīšu(m) II, *nēšu* "(oath on the) life" [MU; mag. ZI] *nīš ili(m), ilāni, DN, šarri(m) zakāru(m)/tamû* "to swear by the life of ..."; mag. "(oath on, invocation of a deity's) life", *n. X lū tamâta/tummû* "be conjured!/to conjure by oath on X"; mag. "(broken) oath" as source of malign influence; < *nêšu*

nīšu III (a technical term of reed- or basket-work) jB lex.

nīšu → also *nišu*

ni'šu "difficulty in breathing, wheezing" jB; < *na'āšu*

nišūtu(m), *nisūtu*, OA *nišuttum* "relative(s) (by consanguinity or marriage)" Bab., OA [IM.RI.A; UZU.SU]; M/jB "personnel" of palace, temple; < *nišu*

nišûtu "installation" jB of king, priest in office; < *našû* II

nitaḫulušḫu → *nidaḫulušḫu*

nit(i)ru "nitre, sodium" jB, NA

nītiš "like a siege" jB; < *nītu*

nitittum → *nidittu*

nitku(m) I "dripping, drop" jB; of blood, wine etc.; < *natāku*

nitku II, *nutku* (a mineral or frit) MB, Ug.

nitru → *nitiru*

nittu "burglar, thief" jB; also as compound *nittâmēlu*

nitû mng. unkn. jB lex.

nītu(m) **1.** Bab. "encirclement, enclosure"; usu. in *n. law/mû(m)* "to enfold s.o. in grasp", "surround" troops etc.; "encircle, besiege" city **2.** (a part of the intestines) **3.** jB lex. ~ "silence"?; < *nêtu* I

ni'tu (a weapon)? Ug.; < Ug.

niṭâtu f. pl. "beatings" jB; < *naṭû* IV

niṭlu(m) "look; view" Bab., NA **1.** "look, gaze"; *niṭil īnī* "the (act of) looking at", "blink of the eyes" = "moment"; MB *ana niṭli ēnī* "under s.o.'s eyes" **2.** "(eye)sight, vision"; *n. našû* "to take away s.o.'s sight" **3.** "appearance" of wall **4.** OB transf. "(point of) view, judgement"; *šumma niṭilka/ki, kīma niṭlika* "if/as you see fit"; < *naṭālu*

niṭpu I "place of tearing up" jB of reed; < *naṭāpu*

niṭpu II (an ornament) NB

nīṭu(m) "bloody faeces" O/jB [RI.RI]; < *nâṭu*

niṭûtu(m) "thrashing, beating" O/jB; < *naṭû* IV

ni'u **1.** jB "lord, master" **2.** jB lex. (a musical instrument)?

ni'ûm → *niā'um*

niwaru (or *niweru*) "(legal) portion, share"? OB(Alal.), Nuzi; < Hurr.?

niwarum → also *nimru* II

niweru → *niwaru*

niyāru → *niāru*

nizil → *nizlu*

niziqtu(m) "worry, grief" O/jB, Elam; in omens, laments etc.; < *nazāqu*

nizirtu jB **1.** "(the act of) cursing, curse" **2.** "(the object of) curse", of person, animal "accursed" by (= gen.) god; < *nazāru*

nizlu, *nizil* in *bīt n.* "drained land" NB; < *nazālu*

nizmatu(m) "desire, objective" Bab.(lit.); *n. kašādu(m)* "to attain o.'s goal"; < *nazāmu*

nizqu both "creaking" of a waggon and "sorrow", in word-play jB; < *nazāqu*

-nši → *-niāšim*

nu → *nuk* I

nûm → *niā'um*

nuāḫu → *nâḫu*

nuāqu → *nâqu* II

nuartu → *nārtu* II

nu'āru → *nāru* II

nuāšu → *nâšu*

nuātum → *niā'um*

nuā'um → *nuwā'um*

nuazu, *nubazu*, *nūzu* (a variety of dates) j/NB

nubalkutu → *nabalkutu* II

nuballu M/jB **1.** "(eagle's) wing"; also as form of snare ? **2.** military "vanguard"?

nubālum "carriage, vehicle" OB, Mari, Alal. [GIŠ.GIGIR]; → *nabālum* ?

nūbalum "dry land" OB; < *abālu*

nubāru → *nupāru* I.II

nubattu(m) "evening (rest)" Bab., M/NA **1.** as time of day, *nubattam* "in the evening"; "eve of a festival; vigil ceremonies" **2.** "evening meal", MA "evening offering" **3.** "(over)night stop (-ping place)", *n. šakānu*, NB *bâtu* "to halt for the night"; MB, NB in PN; NB also pl. *nubattātu* mng. uncert.; < *biātum*

nubātum mng. unkn. OB

nubāzu → *nuāzu*

nubi "10,000" Nuzi; < Hurr.

nūbtu(m) "honey-bee" Bab. [NIM.LÀL]; also as fPN; → *nambūbtu*
nubû "lament, wailing" O/jB, NA; *ša n.* "mourner"; < *nabû* II
nūbu (a cucurbitaceous plant) jB lex.
nuddiātu pl. tant. (a foodstuff)? jB; < *nadû* III
nudinnû, nudnû → *nudunnû*
nuduā'um; pl. f. "deposition, notification"? OA; < *nadû* III
nudunnû(m), MA *nudunnā'u*, NA *nadunnû*, *nundunû, nudnû*, NB also *nudinnû* "marriage gift" to bride from bridegroom, or her father, "dowry"; jB also transf.; < *nadānu* II
nug → *nuk* II
nugatipu (a festival)? MA; in *n. ša Ištar*
nuggatu, occas. *nukkatu* "rage, anger" jB; < *nagāgu*
nūgu "jubilation" M/jB; < *nagû* II
nuguššû ~ "stir, bustle" jB; < *nagāšu*
nuḫar "high temple, ziggurrat" j/NB
nuḫāru (a flower)? jB lex.
nuḫāšu "luxuriant, prosperous" NB as PN; < *naḫšu*
nuḫatimmatum, *naḫatimmatum* "female cook" OB; < *nuḫatimmu*
nuḫ(a)timmu(m) "cook" [LÚ.MUḪALDIM (=MU)]; *bīt n.* "kitchen"; NB *rab n.*; as family name; < Sum.
nuḫatimmūtu(m) "job, position as a cook; cook's prebend" Bab. [LÚ.MUḪALDIM-]; < *nuḫatimmu*
nuḫḫu "calm(ed)" jB; of water(s); < *nâḫu*
nuḫḫu → also *nāḫu*; *nu''u*
nuḫḫubu (or *nuḫḫupu*) "arrogant"? jB of fox
nuḫḫullu 'evil fly' O/MB; < Sum.; → *nimmullu*
nuḫḫulu ~ "covered in scars, scarred"? NB as PN; < *naḫālu* I
nuḫḫupu → *nuḫḫubu*
nuḫḫuru ~ "emaciated, skinny"? M/NB; MB as a horse's name, NB as PN; < *naḫāru* I or II ?
nuḫḫuṣu D "to shake"? jB lex.
nuḫḫutu NB **1.** "cut off, struck off" of silver **2.** mng. unkn. of linen; < *naḫātu* D
nuḫḫuṭu D ~ "to hiccup"? jB
nuḫpuru (a garment) Nuzi; < Hurr.
nuḫsu → *nusḫu* I
nuḫšānu "luxuriant, prosperous" NB as PN; < *nuḫšu*
nuḫšu(m) "abundance, plenty; fertility" [ḪÉ.NUN] "fruitfulness" of fields; "plentiful harvest"; in PNs; < *naḫāšu*
nuḫtimmu → *nuḫatimmu*
nūḫtu(m) "calm, peace" Mari; < *nâḫu*
nūḫu(m) **1.** OA, O/jB (a leather pouch for oil) **2.** Nuzi, Hurr. pl. *nūḫena* (a fabric impregnated with grease) **3.** OB (a prof.)
nuḫurtu(m), NA also *naḫurutu* (a variety of asafoetida) Bab., NA [(Ú.)NU.LUḪ(.ḪA)(.SAR); NA4.NU.LUḪ.ḪA; also Ú.NU.LAḪ.ḪA] med., seed, husk, root, resin used; also (desig. of a disease)?
nuk I, *nuku*, *nu* "saying:" NA ptcl. introducing dir. speech after 1 pers. vb.; → *muk* I
nuk II (or *nug*) (a plant, bulrush ?) jB
nukaribbatum "female gardener" O/jB [MUNUS.NU.GIŠ.KIRI6]; < *nukaribbu*
nukaribbu(m) (or *nukarippu(m)*), OA *nuk(i)ribb/ppum*, NB *nukuribb/ppu* "gardener, date-grower" [(LÚ.)NU.GIŠ.KIRI6]; *rabi n.* "head gardener"; < Sum.
nukaribbūtu(m), NB also *nukuribbūtu* "gardening work; date cultivation" Bab. [(LÚ.)NU.GIŠ.KIRI6-]; < *nukaribbu*
nukarippu → *nukaribbu*
nukāsu; pl. f. "cut of meat" NB; < *nakāsu*
nukatu → *nukkatu*
nukdu → *nuqdu*
nuk(i)ribb/ppum → *nukaribbu*
nu(k)katu, *nuktu* (an aromatic plant)? jB lex.
nukkatu → also *nuggatu*
nukkusu(m) I "cut (in pieces)" O/jB; of garments, flesh; < *nakāsu* D
nukkusum II "to balance accounts"? OAkk; < *nikkassu* denom.
nukru(m) "curio(sity)" Mari; < *nakāru*
nuktu → *nukkatu*
nuku → *nuk* I
nukuribb/ppu → *nukaribbu*
nukurrû, OA *nukurrā'ū* pl. tant. "denial" OA, O/jB; OA *ana n. šakānum* "to deny, disavow" s.th.; "contested, denied amount" of silver; < *nakāru*
nukurtu(m), OAkk, OB also *nikurtum* "enmity, hostility" [MUNUS.KÚR; NAM.KÚR ?; Am., Bogh. also (LÚ.)KÚR] "act of aggression"; pl. "hostilities, war"; *māt n.* "enemy country"; *bēl n.* "enemy"; Am., Bogh., Ug. *n. epēšu, ṣabātu* "to fight, be hostile"; < *nakāru*
nuku(š)šû (a door fitting) j/NB [(GIŠ.)NU.KÚŠ.Ù] of wood, metal; upper, lower; < Sum.
nuldānum (a local ruler) OB(N.Mes.); < *walādum*
nuldānūtum (rôle of *nuldānum*) OB(Shemshara); < *nuldānum*
nullānu → *nullâtānu*

nullānū pl. tant. "fraud, deception" OB; < *nulliātum*

nullānūtum "treachery" OB in *n. epēšu* "to act treacherously"; < *nulliātum*

null(ât)ānu "vile, treacherous" jB; < *nulliātum*

nulliātum, *nullâtu* pl. (sg. rare) "maliciousness; foolish talk, foolishness" O/jB [KA.NU.GAR.RA] with vb.s for speech "calumny, slander"; > *nullānū, nullānūtum, nullâtānu*

numātum, *nuwātum* sg. "movable goods, possessions" OB

numītu ~ "pasturage"? NB

nummuru "very bright, brilliant" NB as PN; < *nawāru*

numru "brightness" M/jB; MB *n. libbi* "cheerfulness, gaiety"; om. (a light mark on the spleen)?; < *nawāru*

nūmtu → *nūptu*

numû "wasteland"? jB lex.; < *nawûm* I

numunnu "seed(ing), sowing" jB; < Sum.

numūru "torch" jB, NA; < *nawāru*

numuttu → *namūtu*

nundunû → *nudunnû*

nungulû (a copper object) jB lex.; < Sum.; → *nunnu*

nungurtu (a property, property value) NB

nunnatu (a copper object) M/jB; < *nunnu*

nunnu(m), *nūnu*, *nunûm* (a copper object) O/jB; < Sum.; > *nunnatu*; → *nungulû*

nunṣabu → *naṣṣabu*

nunûm → *nunnu*

nūnu(m) "fish" [KU6]; sg. also coll., *n. tiāmtim* "sea fish"; *n. (ḫ)isê* "pressed fish" → *ḫesû*; *n. ḫupê* "mashed fish"; *n. ṭabti* "salted, cured fish"; *šaman n.* "fish oil"; jB DN *Nūnu* (fish deity); astr. [MUL/MÚL.KU6] the constellation Piscis Austrinus, also another star or constellation

nūnu → also *nunnu*

nun'u (a table) jB lex.

nunūtu → *anunūtu*

nunzûm "ignorance" OB; < Sum.

nupāru(m) I, *nepārum*, *nubāru*, OB occas. *nurpārum*; pl. f. "prison, workhouse" Bab.; also *bīt n.* MA, MB(Alal.), Nuzi

nupāru(m) II, *nubāru* "heart, (frame of) mind" Bab.; of deity, also in PN; of humans

nuppuḫu(m) "swollen, inflamed" O/jB; of parts of the body; < *napāḫu* D

nuppulu "blinded; one-eyed" jB ?; < *napālu* I D

nuppuqu(m) **D** "to pay attention" OAkk in PN, jB lex.

nuppuṣu "crushed" jB lex.; of beer-wort; < *napāṣu* D

nuppu'um D mng. unkn. OA

nupšatu → *napištu*

nūptu, occas. *nūmtu* "(supplementary) gift, payment" j/NB, esp. NB leg.; also in PNs; < Aram.?; > *nâpu* II ?

nupūšu "airing" MA; < *napāšu* I

nuqāru; pl. f. "low-quality wool" O/jB; < *naqāru*

nuqdum "spot (on the skin)" OB

nurbu "soft place, tender part" MA, jB; of food, plants, earth; transf. of moan ?; < *narābu*

nurētu mng. unkn. NB astr.

nurimdu "pomegranate" Am.; → *nurmû*

nurmagallu "big pomegranate" jB lex.; < Sum.; → *nurmû*

nurmânu "bead (in the shape of a pomegranate)" Qatna; < *nurmû*

nurmû, Nuzi *nurumu* "pomegranate" M/NB, NA [(GIŠ.)NU.ÚR.MA]; as tree, as fruit; as ornament, in stone, metal; *aban n.* "pomegranate pip"; → *lurmûm*; *nurimdu*; *nurmagallu*; *nurmânu*

nurpārum → *nupāru* I

nurpiannuḫlu (a prof., rank)? Nuzi; < Hurr.

nurrubu(m) "very soft" O/jB [Susa DI.GI] of skin (defects), parts of organs "yielding"; OB as PN; < *narābu*

nurruṭu "quivering" jB of spear; < *narāṭu* D

nuršu (a copper object) MB

nūru(m) I "light" [ZÁLAG; IZI.GAR] of sun etc.; of deity, king; *n. amāru* "to see the light, be freed"; *n. kullumu* "to free"; "daylight, daybreak", *ina n.* "at dawn"; "lamp", also *šā(t) n.* (Mari pl. *šāt nūrātum*), *šannūri(m)*, Nuzi *šannūru*, NB *bīt n.*; NA "shine, gleam" of stones; om. (a light spot on an organ); (a type of song); < *nawāru*

nūrum II (a garment) OAkk

nurumu → *nurmû*

nurwe (a type of wood)? Nuzi; < Hurr.?

nurzānu (desig. of physical trait) NA as PN; < *nurzu*

nurzu ~ "throat" j/NB of sick person; as cut of meat "narrow part"?; of canal bank; > *nurzānu*

nusāḫu "extract(ion)" NA pl. m. (a grain tax); pl. f. "torn-out (pieces)"?; < *nasāḫu*

nusâtu pl. ~ "waste pieces" jB, of stone chippings; < *nesû* II

nusḫu(m) I, NB also *nuḫsu* (a container) OAkk, Bab. of reed, leather, clay; also in Sum. texts

nusḫu(m) II (a category of field) MB; < *nasāḫu*

nussu (a clay container) M/jB

nussuḫum (a wooden object)? OAkk(Sum.); < *nasāḫu* D

nussuqu(m) "select(ed), chosen" jB; of objects "choice"; of speech, advice "well-chosen"; < *nasāqu* D

nuṣābu (a medicinal plant)? M/jB med. etc.

nuṣrum "protection" OB in PNs; < *naṣāru*

nuṣṣabum → *naṣṣabu*

nušābātum pl. mng. unkn. OB; < *nuššubum*

nušābu (or *nušāpu*) "cushion" Nuzi

nušaptum "blown away" OB brewing term; < *našāpu*

nušāpu → *nušābu*

nušertu → *nišertu*

nušḫu; pl. f. (a nut) MA, jB

nuššubum D mng. unkn. OB; > *nušābātum*

nušû(m) jB **1.** lex. (a plant) **2.** pl. ~ "vomit, sputum"?; < *nešû*

nušurrû(m) "reduction, diminution" Bab. [BA-] *n. šakānum* "to reduce s.th."; < *našāru* I

nušurtum "portion"? OB; < *našāru* I

nutāpu ~ (old wood) jB lex.

nutia[...] ~ "first, principal" jB lex.

nutku → *nitku* II

nuttum → *niā'um*

nuttûm I (a seed funnel)? OB lex.

nuttûm II **D** "to tear apart"? Mari; < W.Sem.?

nuttulu mng. unkn. jB lex.

nuttun → *niā'um*

nutturum mng. uncert. OB lex.; < *natāru* D

nuṭṭupum "uprooted"? OB f. *Nuṭṭuptum* as fPN; < *naṭāpu* D

nūṭu (a leather bag) NB

nu''u "turned back" MB/MA in *lā n.* "irresistible"; < *nê'u* D

nu'û, nû'u → *nuā'um*

nu'ūtu → *namūtu*

nuwašši(we) mng. unkn. Nuzi; MB(Alal.) in PN; < Hurr.

nuwātum → *numātum*

nuwā'um *nuā'um*, *nu'û* (or *nû'u*?) "unintelligent; barbarian" OA as desig. of native Anatolians; M/NB "stupid (person)"; > *nuwā'uttum*

nuwā'uttum in *n. epāšum* "to carry out affairs of natives" OA; < *nuā'um*

nuwwurum "brilliance" OB of DN; < *nawāru*

nūzu → *nuazu*

P

pa'āṣiš "in order to crush" OB; < *pa'āṣu*

pa'āṣu(m), *pêṣu(m)*, *pâṣu* "to break up, crush" O/jB, NA **G** (pres. *ipa''aṣ*, *ipêṣ*, *ipâṣ*) plants, minerals; transf. "smite" land, person **D** ~ G drugs; NA ~ "abduct, make disappear" animals, slaves **Dtt** NA pass. of D **N** pass. of G NA, of gypsum? **Ntn** "be repeatedly crushed", transf., of heart; > *pa'ṣu*; *pa'āṣiš*; → *pâšu*

padakku; pl. f. (a grain storage facility) NA

padānu(m), *paddānu* f. & m. "way, path" OAkk, Bab.; also transf. "way (of life)"; ext. (a part of the liver) [GÍR; OB also KA.GÌR]

padattu(m) ~ "form, frame" Bab. of human physique

paddānu → *padānu*

paddi'u(m) "unfortunate person"? O/jB

padduga(n)nu(m), NA *pandugānu* (a cultic ceremony, meal) Ass.

padû(m), *pedû* "to spare, set free" O/jB(lit.) **G** (*i/i*) of deity "absolve, be merciful"; > *pīdu* I, *pidītum*; *pādû*; *napdû*?

pādû "forgiving" M/jB(lit.) in *lā p.* "relentless, merciless" of deity, king, demon, illness, weapon; < *padû*

pâdu(m) "to confine, imprison" O/jB **G** (*ā*; jB occas. *ī*) person, with fetters (= acc.), in house, inside city; "take captive"; transf., of illness, evil, darkness **D** "keep in confinement", person, ox **Š** Mari, caus. of G "have s.o. bound" **N** pass. MB "be imprisoned"; > *pādūtum*; *pīdu* II; *napādu* I

padûtu mng. uncl. NB

pādūtum "imprisonment, arrest" OB; < *pâdu*

pagalu (a libation vessel) NA (nom. *pagulu*, pl. *pagelē*) of gold; for wine

pagālu, *pakālu* "to be strong" j/NB **G** lex. only **D** "make strong" esp. stat. of deity, person; of date palm; > *paglu*; *puggulu*

pagdarû mng. unkn. jB lex.; < Sum.

paggar → *pagru*

pagītu → *pagû* I

paglu "strong, huge" j/NB, of animal, log, dyke; < *pagālu*

pagrā'um, *pagrûm* (a kind of sacrifice) Mari in *nīq p.* "*p.* offering"; Dagan *bēl p.*; < *pagru*

pagru(m), NB also *paggar*; pl. *pagrū*, jB also f., NB also *pagrānu* "body; corpse" Bab., NA [AD6 (also = *šalamtu*)] **1.** "body" of human; also "self, person" **2.** "corpse" of human, "carcase" of animal; jB *p. asakki* (name of a star); > *pagrā'um*

pagrûm → *pagrā'um*

pagû(m) I; f. *pagītu*, *pagūtu* "ape" O/jB, M/NA [UGU.DUL/DUL6.BI] as tribute, in art; med., hair, bone etc. of ape; (desig. of human); O/jB (a musical instrument) [SA.LI]; → *bazītu*

pagû(m) II, *pegû* ~ "to slander, lie"? O/jB **G** lex.; > *mupeggû*; *pīgu*

pagūgu mng. unkn. jB lex.

pagūmu(m); pl. m. & f. (a harness strap)? O/jB, MA of leather; for horses

pagūtu → *pagû* I

paḫādu "to be in terror" Ug. **G** (*u/u*); < W.Sem.

paḫāḫu "to be weakened, abate"? j/NB, NA **G** of fever; of kingship; > *paḫḫu*?

paḫallu(m) "thigh" O/jB; *ina birīt paḫalliya* "on my lap"; OB as PN, MB PN *Paḫallānu*

paḫantarru, *paḫattarru* (a blanket) Alal., Nuzi, Bogh., Ug.; < Hurr.

paḫanu "prince" jB lex.; < Elam.

paḫarḫulû (a wooden object) Nuzi; < Hurr.

paḫāru(m) I "potter" [LÚ.BÁḪAR] also OAkk as PN, M/NB as family name; *utūn p.* "potter's kiln"; ᵈ*P.* (patron god of potters); < Sum.

paḫāru(m) II "to gather" **G** (*u/u*) [NIGIN] "gather, assemble" (intrans.), of people, city, land; of goods, silver "accumulate"; of smoke, sweat "collect", Mari *paḫārumma p.* of wall "be completely assembled" **Gtn** iter. **D** "bring together, assemble" (trans.) [NIGIN], people, (population of) land; goods, commodities, waters **Dtn** iter. of D **Dt**, **Dtt** NA, **DRt** Mari pass. of D "be gathered"; "come together, assemble" **Š** OB "gather" ears of corn; > *puḫru, puḫriš; puḫḫuru; mupaḫḫirum; napḫaru, napḫartum; tapḫarum, tapḫīrum, tapḫūrum, tapḫurtu*

paḫasēmunu (a plant)? NB

***paḫāsu(m)** (or *paḫāṣ/zu(m)*) mng. unkn. O/jB **G** unattested **D** lex. only **Ntn** (*u/u*) ~ "to be constantly disappointed"?

paḫaš → *pīḫātu* I 2

paḫattarru → *paḫantarru*

pāḫatu, pāḫātu → *pīḫātu* I

pāḫatūtu → *pīḫātūtu*

paḫā'um → *peḫû* II

paḫāzu mng. uncl. NA, NB **G** (*i/i*) **Š** caus. NA; > *paḫḫizu; paḫḫuzû*

paḫāzu → also *paḫāsu*

paḫḫizu, *pāḫizu* ~ "presumptuous person"? NA; < *paḫāzu*

paḫḫu (or *paḫu*) mng. uncl. MA, desig. of wood; < *paḫāḫu* ?

paḫḫulu mng. uncl. NB

paḫḫuru → *puḫḫuru*

paḫḫuzû ~ "insolent"? NB; < *paḫāzu*

paḫīdu, *peḫīdu* (a kind of flour) MB

pāḫizu → *paḫḫizu*

paḫnu ~ "substitute"? MA

paḫu → *paḫḫu*

paḫû → *peḫû* II

pāḫu "sleeve"? jB lex.

pāḫu → also *pūḫu*

paḫuru mng. unkn. Nuzi

paḫussu (a women's garment) Alal., Nuzi

paiḫu ~ "clear" Nuzi, of plot of ground

pa'īṣu → *pa'ṣu*

pā'iš → *pû* I 8

pakālu → *pagālu*

pakartu (desig. of a woman)? jB med.

pakāru ~ "to present" jB **G** (*i/i*) lamb; → *pukkuru*

pakku(m) I ~ "consideration, sagacity" Bab. (lit.); *bēl p.* "wise person", *ṣūḫ lā p.* "foolish laughter"

pakku II (a metal object) NA

pakru → *bakru* II

pakuttu ~ "wooden stave" O/jB; < Sum.

palādu I (a garment) jB lex.

palādu II mng. unkn. jB

Palae, *Palai* (a month) Alal., in *waraḫ P.*

palaggu → *balangu*

palāḫu(m) "to fear, revere" **G** (*a/a*; imper. *pilaḫ*; stat. OAkk, OB occas. *paluḫ*) [MUD] absol. "be afraid", infin. *p. rašû* "become afraid", also "act reverently"; *ana napištiya aptalaḫ* "I feared for my life"; "fear" s.o., s.th., "revere, worship" deity; "behave respectfully towards" s.o., "serve" s.o. **Gtn** iter. of G **Gt** stat. "is terrifying"; "be constantly reverential" **D** "terrify" of ghost etc.; NA *bēl palluḫi* "person to be intimidated" **Dtn** iter. jB "repeatedly terrify" **Dt** pass. OB "be terrified, become afraid" **Š** jB "make" people "afraid, reverent"; stat. *ramānšu šupluḫ* "has made himself reverent" **N** ~ G NA "be(come) fearful, reverent"; > *palḫu, palḫiš; pulḫu, puluḫtu, pulḫītu; pulīḫātum; puluḫḫûm; palluḫu*?; *pallaḫum; tapliḫtu; napluḫātum*?

Palai → *Palae*

palakku → *balangu*

palāku(m) "to divide off, demarcate" Bab. **G** (*a/u*) field etc.; *pilka(m) p.* "demarcate a sector" **D** ~ G **ŠD** NB "have" meat allocation "divided up" **N** NB of 'meat-portion' of constellation "be divided up"; > *palku; pilku* I; *pālikum; pallākum*

palāku → also *palāqu*

palālum "to guard, watch over" OA, O/jB **G** (*i/i*) person; absol. "be watchful, on guard" **Ntn** OA "constantly watch over" s.o.; > *pālilu; pallallûm; pillatu*

palâmu, *paliyāmu* (a royal robe) jB lex.

palaqqu → *balangu*

palāqu(m), *palāku(m)* "to slaughter, strike down" M/NB **G** (*i/i*, later also *a/u*) animal, person (OAkk in PN ?); stat. of part of body "is smitten" **Gtn** NB "repeatedly slaughter" people **D** pl. obj. "slaughter, smite down" animals, people **Dt** pass. of D, of oxen "be slaughtered" **N** pass. of G, of ox "be slaughtered"; > *palqu; pulluqu; naplaqtum*

palāsu(m) "to look (at)" **G** (*a/u*) occas.; "look" at, towards (= dat., OA acc.) s.o.; OAkk in PNs (wr. *ip-lu*$_5$?) **D** "direct vision, divert attention" of animal, person; esp. stat. of person "is deflected, inattentive" **Dt** "divert o.'s attention" **Š** caus. "cause s.o. to see" s.th., "experience" a loss **N** freq. [IGI.BAR] "see" s.th.; "look, gaze" at (= dat.) s.o., esp. with benevolent intent; also of demon etc., malevolently; "consider, take into consideration" **Ntn** iter. O/jB esp. "examine, check over" fields, animal; "constantly gaze at" (to determine will of) deity; > *itaplustu*; *mupallisum*, *muppalsu*; *naplāsu*, *naplastu*

palāšu(m) "to perforate" **G** (*a*/*u*) [BÙR; GAM] "make breach in" wall, house; "bore, drill through" stone; "pierce" nose etc.; ext., of part of liver, stat. also absol. "is pierced" **D** ~ G "breach" house etc.; OB "break into" enemy land; "pierce", MA esp. pl. obj.s; "bore" holes in door, for well; Mari transf. "forge ahead with, get on with" work ? **Š** caus. OB **N** pass. of G of building etc. "be breached"; of stone, nose "be pierced"; > *palšu*; *pilšu*; *pallišu*, *pālišu*, *pallissu*; *mupallišum*

pālātu → *pāštu*

palatuššu (a title of Enlil) OB

palā'u (desig. of Elam. troops) jB lex.

palā'um → also *palû*

palgiš "like a ditch" jB; < *palgu*

palgu(m) "ditch, canal" [PA5] usu. for irrigation; *p. kirî* "plantation ditch"; *ṭīd p.* "mud from ditch"; > *palgiš*

palḫiš "fearfully, reverently" Bab.(lit.); < *palḫu*

palḫu(m) "fearful" Bab., NA **1.** "frightful, causing fear", of snake, cry; *palḫam zīmī* "of fearsome appearance" **2.** "frightened; reverent"; < *palāḫu*

pālikum "divider"? OB lex., desig. of textile worker; < *palāku*

palīlu(m) (a textile) OA, Nuzi

pālilu(m) "guardian, watchman" OAkk, OA, O/jB; except OA, only in PNs and as DN *Pālil*; < *palālu*

pālišu 1. MA "borer", a tool **2.** jB f. *pālištu(m)* (a spear) **3.** jB [NÍG.BÙR.BÙR] (a plant); < *palāšu*

pālītum "garment from Pala" OA

paliyāmu → *palâmu*

palku "divided, demarcated" jB, of dyke; of textile; < *palāku*

palkû "wide, broad" M/NB of desert, courtyard; "wide-open" of eyes; transf. of wisdom, understanding, knowledge; goddess *palkât uzni* "of great wisdom"; "wise, accomplished" of person ; < *nepelkû*

pallaḫum, *pallaḫûm* "very reverent" OB lex.; < *palāḫu*

pallākum "(field-)demarcator"? OB, as PN; < *palāku*

pallallûm mng. uncl. OB lex., a prof. connected with birds; < *palālu*

pallissu "female stone borer" NA [MUNUS.NÍG. BÙR.BÙR]; < *pallišu*

pallišu(m) 1. OB "housebreaker, burglar" **2.** NA [LÚ.NÍG.BÙR.BÙR] "(stone) borer"; < *palāšu*; > *pallissu*

palluḫu "fearsome"? jB of an image; < *palāḫu* ?

palluḫur → *pallūru*

pallukku, *pa(l)lu(k)ku* "double pin, rod" jB, Ug. lex.; also part of loom ?; < Sum.

palluk/*gu* → *ballukku*

pallurtu → *išpallurtu*

pallūru, *palluḫur*? (a cut of meat) NB

pallūṣītu → *ballūṣītu*

palqu "slaughtered, killed"? j/NB; of fish; < *palāqu*

palsû (or *balsû*) (a feature on the liver) jB; < Sum.

palṣu → *balṣu*

palšu(m) "pierced" O/jB [BÙR] of seal; Alal. "breach(ed place)"; < *palāšu*

palti(n)gu (a travelling-chair) jB lex.

paltu (a class of woman)? jB lex.

pāltu → *pāštu*

palû(m), OAkk *palā'um* "period of office" [BALA] **1.** "reign" of king, of dynasty; "dynasty", *šubat*/*āl p.* "dynastic seat/city"; M/NA "regnal year"; OB lex. *bēl p.* "office holder" **2.** OB (a staff); also as symbol of rule, in PNs; < Sum.

palû → also *pelû* II

palugu, *palukku* → *pallukku*; *ballukku*

pampallu (a woollen cloth) Nuzi; < Hurr.?

pāmu mng. unkn. jB lex., syn. of noise ?

pān → *pāna*; *pānu* I.II

pāna, NA also *pān* adv. **1.** "previously, earlier"; *kī ša p.* "as before", *eli ša p.* "more than before"; *ina*, *ištu*/*ultu p.* "in, since earlier times"; *ūmī p.* "earlier days" **2.** "in front", *pāna u arka* "before and behind"; *ālik p.* "leader"; < *pānu* I

pānâ adv. "first" jB, in time; < *pānû*

panagû (a kind of bronze)? jB lex.

panāgu → *panāku*

panakkum "triangle inscribed in one-third of a circle" OB math. [PAN ?]; < Sum.

panāku, NA *panāgu* **G** (*i*/*i*) jB "to decorate with a boss or knob"? **D** M/jB "overlay" or "rivet"? with gold ornament; < *pinku* denom.?

panānikum, *panānigum* (a pastry)? OB lex.; → *pannigu* ?

panantu ~ (a wooden peg)? NA lex.

pānānu(m) "previously, before" OA, OB, Am., Ug. etc.; *ištu*, *kīma p.(-ma)* "since, as (it was) before"; < *pānu* I; opp. → *aḫarrum*

pānānûm adj. "previous" OB; < *pānānum* + *-ī*

pānātu f. pl. "front" Susa, Nuzi, j/NB, NA [IGI-] **1.** spatially: "front side, frontage" of building, field, orchard etc.; "van" of army; "forepart" of neck; acc., loc.-adv. as prep. "in front of, before", jB *pānāssu* "before him" **2.** temporally: loc.-adv., *ina p.* "before" s.o.('s time); *(ina) pānāt* "before" (beginning) an action, j/NB *pānātūa* "before me, my (arrival)"; < *pānu* I

pānâtu → *pānītu* I

panā'um → *panû*

panbillu → *banbillu*

Pandānu 'Chesty' MB, as PN; < *bāmtu* II

pāndu → *bāmtu* I.II

pandugānu → *paddugannu*

pandunum (a pastry or bread) OB lex.

pāni adv. "previously, before" MA; < *pānu* I

pāniš **1.** jB "in front" **2.** OA "in advance"; < *pānu* I

pānišam adv. "first, as first action" OA; < *pānu* I

pānītu(m) **1.** Ass., OB, Am., Nuzi "earlier (time)"; *i(na) pānītim*, OA *pānītam* "previously"; *kī p.* "as before", pl. Susa *ša pānâti u warkâti* "of earlier and later (times)", Nuzi *ippānâtimma* "previously"; Am. *eli ša pānâti* "more than before" **2.** OB *pānīt kunukkiya* "my previous document"; < *pānû*

pānīu → *pānû*

pannarum, OB *pannerum* "brush"? OA, OB, for animals

pannigu, *pi(n)nigu*, MA *pu(n)ni/ugu* (a pastry or bread) M/NA, j/NB [NINDA.DÌM; NINDA.DÌM/DIM$_{10}$.ME; NINDA.DIM$_{11}$.MA]; → *panānikum* ?

panpānu (a shrine or cultic installation) jB lex., mag.

pāntu → *bāmtu* II

panû(m), OA *panā'um*, NB *penû* "to face; be ahead" **G** (*u/u*) OA "turn o.s." to(wards) (= *ana*, dat.) s.o.; Bab. (also *a/a*, *i/i*) "go in front, go ahead", "forestall, anticipate" s.o.; stat. "is in front of" s.th.; NB "receive" payment "in advance" **D** OA "forward" s.th. to s.o. "urgently", "give" s.th. "priority"; < *pānu* I denom.

pānu(m) I "front", pl. "face" [IGI] **1.** liter.: "face" of deity, human, animal, figurine; med. white, black, red etc. **2.** conveying emotions: joyful, benevolent; bright; malevolent, darkened; downcast **3.** ~ "(person's) presence", *p. X amāru* "to visit" s.o., s.th.; *p. naṭālu*, *še'û*; *p. dagālu* "to attend to, serve, obey" s.o. **4.** of intentions, attention: *p. suḫḫuru* "to turn o.'s face, favour" away from, towards; OA *ana ālim pānūšu* "he intends (to go) to the City"; OB *kīma (ṭēm) pānīka* "in accordance with your intentions"; MA *ašar pānūšani* "wherever she will"; NA, NB *pān šarri maḫir* "it is in accordance with the king's will"; *pānī/pānam šakānu(m)* "to set o.'s face" to(wards), "determine, intend" to do s.th.; "direct" s.o. (else) towards **5.** *p. w/babālu(m)* "to forgive, indulge" s.o. **6.** transf. of place: "front" of ship, furniture, textile; army; of part of body; NB *bīt pāni* "front room" of building; *p. u (w)arki/u* "before and behind"; "surface" of steppe, sky, water; "front side, frontage" of field, watercourse, land; *ālik pāni* "leader"; *p. X ṣabātu(m)* "to take the lead of X" **7.** transf. of time: *pān šatti(m)* "early part of year, spring"; *ūmē p.* "earlier days", *šar p.* "previous king", *ālik p.* "predecessor"; *ša/ina/ultu p.* "of/in/since earlier times", *eli ša p.* "more than before" **8.** after prep.s (also *pān*, *pāniš*, *pānuššu* etc.): *ina p.* "in presence of, in front of, in vicinity of"; "from before, in consequence of"; NA, NB of loans, personnel "at the disposal of"; *ana p.* OA, OB "for" s.o., "at s.o.'s disposal"; "on s.o.'s account, on behalf of"; "opposite", "in return for"; later "before, into the presence of" s.o.; MA "on behalf of" s.o.; *ištu/issu/ultu p.* "from" somewhere, s.o. **9.** misc.: jB *bēl pāni* "nouveau riche"; OB *ina pānīkunu* "from what is available to you"; *pān X* "up to", "to the full amount of"?;*p. išû/rašûm* "to be(come) clear", also *p. u bāba(m) ul īšû* "cannot be exactly identified"; math. *p. X puṭur* "form the reciprocal of X"; > *pāna*, *pānâ*, *pānānu*, *pānānûm*, *pānātu*, *pāni*, *pāniš*, *pānišam*; *pānītu*, *pānû*; *panû*; → *buppānī-*; *lapāni*

pānu(m) II (a basket; a measure of capacity) [GI.GUR] **1.** (a (large) basket) OA for tablets, copper etc., OB for grain, MB for tablets [GI.GUR.IM.MA ?] **2.** Bab. "bushel" (a dry capacity measure) [PI] OB = 60 *qû*, NB = 36 *qû* = $^{1}/_{5}$ *kurru* **3.** NB (an area measure) = 10,800 sq. cubits (Babylon), 10,000 (Uruk)

pānû(m), Ass. *pānīu(m)* adj. "first, earlier; front" [IGI] **1.** "first" arrival, ship, messenger; OA *išti pānîmma* "with the first (messenger)" **2.** "earlier, previous" king, creditor; period of duty; consignment, tablet, words, property; NB "(born) first, older"; OB pl. *pānûtuni* "our ancestors" **3.** "front", of part of body, locks of hair; < *pānu* I + *-ī*; > *pānâ, pānītu*

panušḫu → *penušḫu*

papaḫḫu "mountains, the east" Nuzi; < Hurr.

papāḫu(m); pl. m. & f. "cella, shrine" [PA.PAḪ] in temple, in house; also *bīt p.*

papallibbi → *papānu* 2

papallu "shoot, sprout" j/NB; liter. of tamarisk etc.; transf. "offspring, scion"; < Sum.

papānu **1.** lex., med. (a kind of rush or sedge) **2.** MA, jB in *papān libbi, papallibbi* (part of body, swelling of stomach) of human, of animal

papaššarri (desig. of a silver vessel) Alal.

papatu (a wooden object) Alal.

papḫaldaru mng. unkn. jB lex.; < Sum.

pappaltu ~ "porridge" MA; jB lex., med. (desig. of discharged semen); < *pappāsu*

pappardaliu(m), *pappardilû(m)* "agate"? [(NA4.)BABBAR.DILI; NA4.BAR6.BAR6.DILI]; < Sum.; → *papparmīnu*

papparḫītum, papparḫû, papparḫuātu → *parparḫû*

papparmīnu (a semiprecious stone) j/NB, NA [(NA4.)BABBAR.MIN5]; < Sum.; → *pappar=daliu*

papparum "white area" OB, on agate (*pappardalium*); < Sum.

pappāsītu (a white lime) M/NB [BA.BA.ZA.dÍD]; < *pappāsu* + *-īt*

pappāsu(m) f. ~ "porridge" OAkk, Bab., NA [BA.BA.ZA] esp. *p. buqli* "malt gruel"; NB (an allowance for officials); < Sum.; > *pappaltu; pappāsītu*

pappirum → *bappiru*

pappu(m) I; pl. m. & f. "lock?/strand? of hair" O/jB of human; *pappāt īni* "eyelashes"; also (a stone)

pappum II "(the sign) PAB" OB

pappû (desig. of a person) jB lex.

paprum (an object) OA

paqadu → *paqdu*

paqādu(m) "to entrust; care for; appoint" **G** (*i/i*) [Am. only NU] **1.** "entrust, hand over" s.o., s.th. to (= *ana*, dat.) s.o.; "confide, assign" task, person, animal to s.o. to be taken care of **2.** "take care of" person, animal, house(hold), country etc.; OB "allocate" ration etc. "to" s.o. (= acc.) **3.** "check" extispicy, "review" troops, booty, horses **4.** j/NB, NA "appoint" person to office; "charge, commission" s.o. with task **Gt** "behave cautiously"; M/NB stat. "is concerned" about (= *ana*) s.th., s.o. **D** ~ G **1.** "entrust, hand over" pl. obj. **2.** "check, oversee" **3.** "look after, care for" shrine **4.** "assign" persons "to tasks" **5.** "appoint" official **Dt** NB(Achaem.) "exert o.s." **Š** caus. **1.** "cause to entrust" **2.** MB "give" temple "into care" **N** pass. **1.** "be entrusted" **2.** "be cared for" **3.** j/NB "be appointed" **4.** jB om., of event "be checked, confirmed"?; > *paqdu; piqdu, piqittu, piqittūtu, piqanānu; pāqidu; puquddû; pitqudu*

paqarānu → *bāqirānum*

paqāru → *baqāru*

pāqat → *pīqat*

pāqātu → *pāqu* 2

paqdu(m), NB freq. *pa(q)qa(d)du, paqūdu* **1.** "entrusted"; *paqid/paqdat* ([SUM-*at*]) *qāti* "handed over"; NA *paqid dullu* "charged with work" **2.** NB as subst. "entrusted, appointed (official)", pl. *paqdūtu, paqūdānu, paqūdē* **3.** NB *ana p. manû* "to reckon as pledge"; < *paqādu*

pāqidu(m) "carer" (for s.o.) O/jB; of child, ghost *p. ul/lā išû* "has none to care (for him)"; < *paqādu*

pāqirānu → *bāqirānum*

pāqiru "claimant" M/jB; < *baqāru*

paqqaddu → *paqdu*

pa(q)qāyu "mat-weaver" M/NB

paqru → *baqru*

pāqu **1.** f. *pāqtu* NA mng. uncl., epith. of Ištar **2.** pl. tant. *pāqātu* jB lex. (a fine-meshed hunting net); (a reed sieve); < *piāqum*

pâqu → *piāqum*

paqūdu → *paqdu*

paquttu → *puquttu*

parab → *parasrab*

parādu(m) I "to be scared, terrified" **G** (*i/i*, M/NB also *u/u*) [MUD] of person, OA, OB esp. *libbum* as subj.; stat., of dream "is frightening" **Gtn** iter. [MUD.MUD]; of ritual recitation "be nervous, diffident" **Gt** stat., NA of words "are frightening" **D** "terrify"; stat. jB med., of innards **Dtn** iter. **Dt** pass. "be scared"; NB of ritual recitation "be nervous, diffident" **Š** caus. MB "make" opponent "terrified" **ŠD** "terrify"; > *pardu, pardiš; pirittu; purrudum; pitrudu*

parādu II **N** "to separate o.s., cut o.s. off" NB, of gods; < W.Sem.

paragum mng. unkn. OB

paraḫšītum (a musical instrument) Mari; < *paraḫšûm*

parahṣûm, *parašû(m)* "of Marḫaši" Mari, OB lex.; < PIN; > *parahṣītum*

parahu (a wild equid) jB lex.; < W.Sem.

parāhu ~ "to ferment" jB **G** lex. only **D** lex. "ferment" (trans.), beer; > *naprahtu*

parāhu → also *parāku*; *parā'u* I

parakānum → *pirikānum*

parakkatannu (an object) Am., of gold

parakku(m), Mari also *perekkum* "cult dais; sanctuary" Bab., M/NA [BARAG] **1.** "chapel, shrine"; transf. "cult" **2.** post-OB "dais" for statue, altar, throne; *āšib p.*, *bēl p.* "occupant of dais" **3.** *p. šīmāti* "dais of destinies", also desig. of platform in courtyard **4.** jB(roy. inscr.) "(royal) dais, palace" **5.** Nuzi, Am. (a stool upholstered in fleece or gold); < Sum.

paraktum "sail"? OB; → *paruktu*

parāku(m), NA also *parāhu* "to lie across, obstruct" **G** (*i/i*, occas. *a/u*) [GIB] **1.** of star, part of body, animal etc. "lie, be placed across"; "block" gate etc.; stat. + acc., *padānam parik* "lies across the path"; math. "lie transversely" **2.** transf. "obstruct", "make difficulties", absol. and for s.o. (= dat., *ana pān(ī)* etc.) **3.** "hinder, thwart" s.o. **4.** "hold" foot, head "in between"; "place" obstruction "across"; "put cross-wise"; med. "rub in transversely" **Gtn** iter. [GIB.MEŠ] **D** ~ **G 1.** OB "close off, bring to an end" matter, accounts **2.** "lay s.th. across, transversely"; stat. "lies transversely"; astr. of moon "go into opposition" **3.** "block" door, street, "thwart, oppose" s.o. **4.** stat. of face "has transverse markings" **Š** caus. of G M/jB(Ass.) "put s.th. in opposition" to s.o. **Štn** OB "repeatedly set up in opposition" to s.o. **N** [GIB] **1.** "stand in the way" of (= *ana pānī-*, dat.), "oppose" **2.** "be blocked in" **Ntn** "constantly oppose, stand in s.o.'s way"; > *parku*, *pariktu*, *parkiš*; *perku*, *piriktu*; *parriku*, *parriktu*; *purukkû*; *napraku*; *šapraku*

parallum → *burullum*

para(m)māhu 'pre-eminent dais' jB [BARAG. MAH] for deity's throne etc.; desig. of temple; < Sum.

parāmu "to shred" NA **N** of shoes; < Aram.?

parapše (a kind of field) Alal.

paraqītu → *barraqītu*

parāqu "to divide off, separate" jB **G** stat. of gods "are staying away"

parāru(m) "to be dissolved, broken up" OA, O/jB **G** (*u/u*, Bogh. also *i/i*) liter. of food; transf. med. of part of body "become powerless", of senses (*ṭēmu*) "be confused"

Gt ~ N ? **D** "disperse, scatter" army, band, assembly, family etc.; library; ashes, liquid; "distribute, share out" rations, land; OA "break" fetters; "smash" potsherd, shrine, rock; stat. of part of body "is quite powerless", of sense, evil "is dispersed"; stat. of moon "appears ragged"? **Dt** pass. "be smashed"; "be distributed" **N** (infin. *naparruru(m)*) [DIR] of group "be scattered, disperse"; OB of individual "become homeless"?; of potsherd "be smashed" **Ntn** of people, demons, animal "roam around, in all directions"; of eyes "rove"; > *parru* II; *purruru*; *muttaprirru*; *naparrurtu*, *napurratu*, *nabrarû*?, *nabrartu*?

parāru → also *šuparruru* II

paras ~ "fraction" OB; < *parāsu*

parasiggû → *barasiggû*

parasrab, *parab* ('big fraction', i.e.) "five-sixths" jB lex.; < *paras* + *rabû* I

para(s) ṣehru "one third (of a shekel)" Nuzi; < *paras* + *ṣehru*

parasu → *parsu*

parāsu(m) I "to cut (off); decide" **G** (*a/u*) [KUD] **1.** "cut off, withhold" offerings, sustenance; "keep away" evil; *šēp X p.* "exclude" enemy etc. from land, temple etc. **2.** "wean" child **3.** "pick out, select" person, animal, grain; "set aside" timespan **4.** "stop" tears, diarrhoea **5.** "block" way, esp. *alakta p.*; "break off" journey, activity; stat. "is discontinued"; "cut off, abolish" parturition, noise of humanity **6.** "divide up, section" part of body, space, container; "set s.o. at variance" with god; stat. "is divided, split", ellipt. of oil "be divided, split up"; "divert" watercourse **7.** *(w)arkata(m) p.* "establish facts" of a case, "investigate" **8.** "decide", *purussâm/dīnam p.* "reach decision; pass judgement"; absol. "arbitrate" between persons; NB *eli/ina muḫḫi X p.* "decide against" s.o., "condemn s.o. to" s.th. (= acc.) **Gtn** OB "continually block" s.o.'s way **Gt** stat. **1.** jB "are separate" from each other **2.** of result "is indecisive, inconsistent" **3.** NB of offering "is discontinued entirely" **D** ~ **G** [KUD.MEŠ] **1.** "cut off, separate" s.o. **2.** "cut off, cease" delivery **3.** "divide up, section" part of body, corpse etc. **4.** = **G 7** *(w)arkata(m) p.* "establish facts" **5.** "decide" absol. **Š** caus. **1.** of G stat. "causes" path, feet etc. "to be cut off; excluded" **2.** of G 7 + *warkatum* "cause to establish facts" **3.** "get rid of" blemish **N** pass. of G [KUD] **1.** "be cut off, withheld; cease" of offering, rain etc., person's presence, greetings; with *šēp* "be excluded" **2.** of way etc. "be cut off" **3.** OA of persons "separate from one another; be divorced" **4.** of facts (*warkatum*) "be established" (→ G 7) **5.** "be decided"; NB of price "be fixed"; > *parsu*; *persu*, *pirištu*; *pirsu*; *parīsu* I?, II, *parrisānu*?; *purussû*; *pārisu*; *parrisu*; *purrusum*; *pitrusum*, *pitrustu*; → *paras*; *parasrab*; *paras ṣeḫru*

parāsu II **Dt** "to spread out" NB of troops; < Aram.

parāṣu(m) I "to breach; lie" **G** (*a/u*) **1.** "breach" wall **2.** transf. "breach, contravene" oath **3.** NB "deceive, tell lies to" s.o. **D** NB "tell lies" **Š**, **Štn** mng. uncl. **N** pass. of G **1.** OB of breach "be breached" **2.** jB of oath "be contravened"; > *perṣu*, *piriṣtu*; *parriṣu*; *parrāṣu*; *napraṣu*?

parāṣu II "to carry out ritual" Alal., jB, NA **G** NA *nēpešē p.* "perform rites" **D** ~ G Alal., jB **Dt** pass. of D of rites "be performed" **N** ~ Dt; < *parṣu* denom.; > *napraṣu*?

paraššannu "pertaining to a trained horse" Nuzi; < Hurr.

paraštinnu mng. unkn. jB lex.

parašû → *paraḫšûm*

parāšu(m) "to flatter" O/jB **G** (*a/u*) of person, mouth **D** jB lex. "make flattering"; > *purrušiš*

parāšu → also *naprušu* II

parattitinnu (part of whip-handle) Am.

parattu ~ "dry land" jB lex.

parāṭu "to tear, clear away"? jB, NA **G** (*a/u*) stat., of part of liver "is torn away"?; astr. of heavenly body ~ "flicker"?; NA "clear away" meal; > *muparriṭu*

parā'u(m) I, *parāḫu* "to cut off, slice through" O/jB, NA **G** (*a/u*) stone, root, thread, harvest; head, hand, lips; transf. life **D** ~ G jB; belt, vein, vegetation; life **N** pass. of G, of thread, root "be cut through"; > *par'u*

parā'u II "to sprout" NA **G** (*u/u*) of plant; < *per'u* denom.; > *piri'tu*

parā'um → also *parû* III

para'urum (desig. of a homosexual) Alal.

pardannu (an illness) jB

pardēsu "enclosed garden" NB, work on; for wine; < OPers.

pardiš "fearsomely" jB; < *pardu*

pardu(m) O/jB **1.** "afraid, fearful", of person, dove **2.** "frightening, terrifying", of dream, omen; < *parādu* I; > *pardiš*

pargāliš → *pargāniš*

pargallu (desig. of sacrificial animal) NB

pargāniš, MB(Susa) *pargāliš* "on the meadow" M/NB, as place for contented cattle; < *pargānu*

pargānīu, *pargānû*, MB(Susa) *pirqānû* "meadow-grazed" M/NA, desig. of sheep; < *pargānu*

pargānu "meadow" jB lex.; > *pargāniš*; *pargānīu*

pargānû → *pargānīu*

parḫu mng. unkn. MB, desig. of roofing ?

parḫudû (a class of person) Bab. lex., also *ša p.*

pariangu "harpoon"? MB(Ass.)

parīdu mng. unkn. NB, a commodity

pariktu(m) **1.** Bab. "cross-wall"? **2.** lex. pl. "cross-furrows" **3.** Mari pl. "obstructions, hindrances" **4.** MB *ina p.* "in opposition" **5.** j/NB "violent act, violence" **6.** NA "blockage, barrier"; < *parku*

pāriqānu → *bāqirānum*

parīsu(m) I, *parissu*, *parīšu*; pl. m. & f. **1.** Bab. "rudder, boat-pole", also transf. as desig. of helping deity; Nuzi "pole" for mat support **2.** jB lex. (part of the structure of a boat); < *parāsu* I ?; > *parrisānu*

parīsu(m) II "half *kurru*" OAkk(Ebla), OB, Alal., Bogh.; freq. abbr. *pa*; < *parāsu* I

pārisu **1.** jB lex. "divider", desig. of door **2.** NB/NA "decisive" of word **3.** NB (a prof.); < *parāsu* I

parišḫu, *parušḫu* mng. unkn. Ug.

parišû (a garment) NB

parīšu → *parīsu* I

parittannu → *barittannu*

paritu → *baritu*

parītu → *parûtu*

parkiš "cross-wise" O/jB [GIB-]; < *parku*

parku(m) "transverse" **1.** OB "cross-ploughed" of field **2.** "lying across" of part of liver, astr. of figure (*uṣurtu*) **3.** "blocked" of way **4.** NA as subst. "injustice, crime"; < *parāku*; > *pariktu*; *parkiš*

parkullu(m), *purkullu* "seal-cutter, lapidary" Bab., M/NA [(LÚ.)BUR.GUL]; < Sum.; > *pur=kullūtu*; → *parkulluḫuli*

parkulluḫuli, *purkulluḫuli* = *parkullu* Alal.; < Hurr. form

parkuttum → *parputtum*

parmusānu ~ "bridegroom"? jB

parparḫû, *papparḫû*, *papparḫītum*; MA pl. *papparḫuātu* (a herb, phps.) "purslane, *Portulaca* species" Bab., MA [BABBAR. ḪI(.SAR)]; < Sum.; → *puḫpuḫu*

parputtum, *parkuttum* (a stick)? OB(Susa)

parraqītu → *barraqītu*

parrāṣu "liar" jB lex.; < *parāṣu* I

parratu "she lamb" MA, j/NB [UDU.BAR.MUNUS]; < *parru* I

parriḫtu → *perriḫtu*

parriktu "strut, cross-bar" jB lex., of bed; < *parāku*

parriku(m) **1.** M/jB epith. of gods, of kings, mng. uncl. **2.** lex., desig. of weapon, of person, mng. uncl.; < *parāku*

parrisānu pl. "boatmen" jB; < *parīsu* I

parrisu 'much separating'? jB lex., desig. of wolf; < *parāsu* I

parriṣu "lying" jB; NA "criminal" [LUL]; < *parāṣu* I

parru I "(male) lamb" j/NB [UDU.BAR.GAL]; > *parratu*; → *p.* II

parrum II "weaned" Mari, of sheep; < *parāru*; = *p.* I ?

parru → also *barrum* II; *pāru* II

parrû(m) I **1.** OA "base, common" **2.** jB "(homosexual) lover"; < *parû* III

parrû II (kind of emmer broth) jB lex.; < Sum.

parsigu → *barasiggû*

parsīgu, *parsikkum* → *paršīgu*

parsiktu(m), *paršiktum* "bushel measure" O/jB [GIŠ.BA.RÍ.GA] (~ *pānu* II) of DN; *p. kittum* "official *p.*"; (part of a barge); < Sum.

parsīmum, *parṣīmum* mng. unkn. OB in *p. šatti* "*p.* of the year"

parsu(m), NB also *parasu* "cut off" [KUD] of building, place "separate"; NB of fields "lying apart"; of baby, animal "weaned"; OA "confidential, private"; jB "rare, exquisite"?; < *parāsu* I; → *paras*; *parasrab*; *paras ṣeḫru*

parsûm → *barsûm*

parṣīmum → *parsīmum*

parṣu(m) "office; (cultic) ordinance" [GARZA; OB also MAR.ZA] **1.** "office, post"; *bēl p.* "office-holder"; *p. šarrūti* "rôle of king"; OB purchased; old, new; "(symbol of) office" **2.** usu. pl. "cultic ordinance(s), rites"; *p. epēšu*, *šuklulu*, *šūšuru*, *mašû* "to perform, carry out perfectly, set in order, forget rites"; *p. lā simātišunu* "rites inappropriate to them"; OA (a tax)?; also "cultic (object)" **3.** usu. pl. (~ Sum. me) "cosmic ordinances, divine functions", i.e. attributes and functions of deity, underworld, ruler etc. **4.** Alal., Am., Bogh. "custom, tradition"; > *parāṣu* II

paršamūtu → *puršumu*

parša'u → *perša'um*

paršīgu(m), *parsīgu(m)*, *parsikkum* "headdress, turban" OAkk, Bab., OA [(TÚG.)BAR.SI; jB TÚG.BAR.SIG] in red (wool); *p. ūmakkal* "everyday headdress"; OB also (part of boat); < Sum.

paršiktum → *parsiktu*

paršu(m) "excrement" O/jB of animals

paršumu NA **D** (pret. *uparšim*) "to outlive" s.o. **Dtt** (pres. *uptataršam*) "reach a great age"; < *puršumu* denom.

paršumu → also *puršumu*

paršu'u → *perša'um*

parû(m) I, Mari st. abs. *pār* "mule" Bab., NA [ANŠE.KUNGA; jB also GÌR ?]

parû II "base, common" jB lex.; < *parû* III; > *parûtu*

parû III, OA *parā'um* ~ "to speak basely"? **G** jB lex. mng. uncl. **D** OA "contaminate, alloy" metal; "abuse" deity, "blaspheme"; > *parû* II; *parûtu*, *parītu*; *parrû* I; *purûm*

parû IV "to vomit" jB **G** (*u/u*) med., om., also "excrete"; of animal **Gtn** iter. of G **Š** med. "cause to vomit"; > *parūtu* III; *purâtu*

pāru(m) I "hymn" O/jB, to deity

pāru(m) II, *parru*, *bāru* "skin, hide" O/jB, of animal; lex. (a sleeve)?; < Sum.

pāru III ~ "product" jB lex.; *p. nūbtu* "product of bee, honey"; → *per'u*

pārum IV (a container of 1 bur capacity) OB math.

pāru V (an official) MB(Alal.)

pâru(m) I "to seek" OA, O/jB **G** (*ā*) "look for" s.o. **Gtn** iter. MB "search for" tools **Gt** OB "seek out" s.o.'s stature; road

pâru II **D** jB stat. mng. uncl.

par'u "sliced through" jB, of belt; < *parā'u* I

par'um → also *per'u*

parūgu (unit of stored seed-corn) jB, NA

paruktu "sail" NB for boat; of wool; < Aram.; → *paraktum*

parūru (a drug) jB

parušḫu → *parišḫu*

paruššu (a sharp stick) jB; < Sum.

parūtu I, *paruttu* (a kind of alabaster) M/NB for palace construction; in mag.

parūtu(m) II "(a kind of) quiver"? O/jB

parūtu(m) III "vomit(ed matter)" jB; < *parû* IV

parûtu, *parītu* "baseness, slander" jB lex.; < *parû* II

parzillu(m) "iron" [AN.BAR] for tools, weapons, ornament; as tribute, in rit.; NB transf. cattle *ša p.* "of iron (i.e. permanent stock)"

parziqqu (a tool) jB lex.

parzīziš → *tamzīziš*

pasa'(a)du (a money-chest)? NB

pasāḫu(m) O/jB **G** not attested **D** "to drive away" evil, "reject"? words **N** Mari "march on, advance"?; > *paseḫtu*

pasālu(m) "to turn (away)" (intrans.) O/jB, MA **G** (*i/i*) stat. of foot "is turned out"; of omen "change"; OB *pisilti kaspim paslāku* "I am in financial difficulties"; MA "renege" on a contract; jB "divert" route **D** stat. of limbs "are distorted"; > *pisiltu*; *passalum*; *pussulu*

pasāmu(m) "to veil" O/jB **G** (*i/i*) woman; "cover" mouth **D** ~ G stat. "is veiled" **Dt** pass. "veil o.s."; > *pussumu*; *pusummu*; *napsamu*; *pasuttu*; *tapsimtum*; → *paṣānu*; *pesēnu*

pasāqu(m) mng. unkn. O/jB; > *pussuqu*?; *napsaqu*

pasāsu(m), NA occas. *pašāšu* "to erase" Bab., NA **G** (*a/u*) "cancel" instruction, judgement, oath; ominous sign; sin, penalty; "destroy, flatten" town **D** ~ G of storm "destroy, flatten"; "erase, rub out" document; "annul, cancel" judgement, sin, omen **Dt** pass., of wall "be flattened, collapse"; of document "be erased"; of oracle, sin "be annulled"; > *passu* II; *pissatu*; *pussusu*; *pasūsātu*

paseḫtu "(part of) the intestines" jB lex.; < *pasāḫu*

pasillu; f. *pasillatu* (a kind of sheep) Bogh., j/NB [UDU.AS4.LUM] for sacrifice

pasiqqû "(narrow?) canal" jB lex.; < Sum.

paskāru (a headdress) Am., Nuzi

pasku mng. uncl. MB, desig. of leather

pasnannu → *paznannu*

pasnaqu → *pisnuqu*

paspasu "duck" M/NB [UZ.TUR.MUŠEN] Nuzi *rē'i p.* "duck-keeper"; OA, Nuzi as PN; j/NB(lit.) in omen, as sacrifice; NB f. [UZ.TUR.MUNUS.MUŠEN] = *paspastu* ?

pasqu, *pašqu* ~ "(interior) ledge, cornice" jB(Ass.)

pasqû, *pašqû* (a tool) jB lex.

pasru(m) ~ "pole" O/jB, NA; wooden, for chariot etc. (or var. of *paššuru*)

passalum "distorted"? OB, as PN; < *pasālu*

passu(m) I "doll; pawn, gaming piece" O/jB [ZA.NA] male; of bronze, clay; *mēlulti p.* "game with pawns", of battle

passu II (a kind of reed) jB lex.; < *pasāsu*

passûm → *pessû*

passuku **D** "to clear (away), clear out" NA, debris, earth from river; people

passurtu → *bussurtu*

passuru → *bussuru*

pasû mng. uncl. jB **G** (*a/a*) of demon "to press" on chest ?; "press" drugs ? **D** lex.; "crush"? colours; > *tapsû*?

pāsū pl. tant. "(interior) part(s)"? Nuzi of bow, chariot; jB of intestines

pasuntu → *pasuttu*

pasūsātu "obliteration"? jB, effect of Lamaštu; < *pasāsu*

pasuttu(m), jB also *pasuntu*; pl. *pasumātu* "(kind of fowling) net"? O/jB; also on ship; < *pasāmu*

paṣādu(m) "to cut into, slice" O/jB, NA **G** (*i/i*) stone **D** ~ G "cut through" mountain; transf. people **Dt(t)** pass. of D, NA of temple "be ruptured"?; > *puṣādū*

paṣāmu mng. unkn. jB **G** (*a/u*)

paṣānu(m) "to cover up, veil" O/MA **G** (*i/i*) OA "conceal" s.th. **D** MA "veil" a woman **Dt** pass. of D; > *paṣṣunu*, *puṣūnu*; → *pasāmu*; *pesēnu*

paṣāṣu mng. uncert. **G** jB lex.; NA of person "to disappear"? ; > *paṣṣu*, *puṣāṣû*?

paṣiu → *peṣû* I

paṣṣu "absent, missing" NA; < *paṣāṣu*

paṣṣunu "veiled" MA, of woman; < *paṣānu*

paṣû → *peṣû* I

pāṣu → *pa'ṣu*

pâṣu → *pa'āṣu*

paṣ'um → *peṣû* I

pa'ṣu(m), *pāṣu*; NB *pa'īṣu*, *payīṣu* "crushed, broken up" Bab. **1.** O/jB of sesame, ingredients; as subst., pl. *pa'ṣānu* brewer's "crushings" **2.** NB "disbanded, off-duty" of troops; < *pa'āṣu*

paṣuddu → *puṣuddu*

pašāḫiš "in restfulness" jB; < *pašāḫu*

pašāḫu(m) "to cool down, rest" **G** (*a/a*, also *i/i*; OAkk, OA imper. also *pišaḫ*) [SED] **1.** "calm down" of horse after exercise; "abate" of illness, anger, esp. divine wrath **2.** "be at rest, take rest" of people, troops; "stand" of concoction **Gtn** OB "repeatedly gain relief", sexually **D** "pacify, appease"; "give relief" to invalid; "allow" concoction "to stand", "cool off"?; NB "rest" field **Dt** pass. of illness "be assuaged" **Š** "cause, allow to rest"; "calm, pacify" heart (*libbu*), mood (*kabattu*) etc., also ellipt. "rest" (intrans.); "unstring" bow **Štn** iter. "constantly assuage" **Št** pass. of mood "be assuaged" **ŠD** "calm, pacify" **N** "come to rest, achieve peace" **Ntn** of mood "constantly become assuaged"; > *pašḫu* I, *pašāḫiš*;

mušapšiḫu; *šupšuḫiš*; *tapšaḫu*; *tapšīḫu*; *tapšuḫtu*

pašālatti adv. "crawling"; < *pašālu* + *-atti*

pašallu(m) "(a kind of) gold" OAkk, Bab., OA

pašālu(m), *pešēlu* "to crawl" O/jB **G** (*i/i*) of captives etc. **Gtn** iter., on all fours **Š** OB "make wriggle" like fish in basket; > *pašālatti*; *pišiltu*?

pašālu → also *bašālu*

pašanum (a bird) OB

pašānu "to yank, pull violently"? jB **G** (*i/i*) ears

pašāqu(m) "to be narrow; be difficult" O/jB, NA **G** (*u/u*) of part of body "become narrow"; stat. of crossing, demon "is difficult, troublesome" **D** stat. of water "is confined, hemmed in"; NA mng. uncl. **Š** **1.** caus. (rare) jB "make difficult", jB lex. "defeat" **2.** intrans. (denom. < *šupšuqu*) "be in difficulties, have a hard time"; stat. of road, ascent "is difficult", of crime "is grievous", of plan etc. "is hard to grasp"; of worker, woman in childbirth "suffer severe exertion" **Štn** intrans., of heaven and earth "be repeatedly constricted"; transf. "be repeatedly reduced to hard straits" by battle **Št** intrans., of woman in childbirth "suffer severe exertion" [PAP.ḪAL.ME(Š)], of invalid "go through a hard time"; > *pašqu*, *pašqiš*; *pušqu*; *šapšāqu*; *šupšuqu*, *šupšuqiš*, *šupšuqtu*; *mušapšiqtu*, *muštapšiqtu*; *tapšiqtu*

pašarānu mng. uncl. jB om.

pašartu "threshing" or "sale (of grain)" jB; < *pašāru*

pašāru(m) "to release, free" **G** (*a/u*) [BÚR] **1.** "loosen" (soil of) field, (husks? from) grain; knot **2.** OB "sell?, dispose of" grain, commodities, land, person; MA "issue"? or "withdraw"? grain; NA "convert" into currency **3.** Ug., Am., Alal. "free" captive **4.** "solve, resolve" dispute; "undo, release" spell, curse, oath; "dissipate" anger; "interpret" dream **5.** Mari, absol. ~ "disengage o.s.", NA "free" o.'s feet, i.e. "move off" **6.** NB stat. of heart "is free (of anxiety), at ease" **7.** Urar. "dedicate" animal to deity **Gt** jB "mutually disclose" desires **D** ~ G "dispel, disperse" cloud, evil, spell; "unravel" thread; "interpret" dream; "disseminate" lies **Dt** pass. "be loosened", "be dispelled" **Š** "cause to dispel" illness, evil forces; "cause" heart (= sexual restraint ?), knot "to be loosened" **N** [BÚR] pass. of G; "be sold"; of weather "clear up"; of deity, person, heart "become reconciled to, forgive"; "be released, freed" from demon **Ntn** iter.; > *pašru*; *pišru*, *pišertu*, *pašīru*, *pašīratti*, *pišīriš*; *pašartu*; *pašurtu*; *pāširu*, *pāšertu*; *puššurtum*; *mupašširum*; *napšāru*, *napšartum*, *napšuru*, *napšurtu*; *tapšūru*, *tapšertu*

pašāšu(m) "to anoint" **G** (*a/u*) [ŠÉŠ; med. also EŠ] person, part of body, divine image, stele etc., horse, with (= acc. or *ina*) oil; "smear" door with oil, wall with mud **Gtn** iter. [usu. ŠÉŠ.MEŠ; EŠ.MEŠ] **Gt** "anoint o.s." OA, O/MB **D** ~ G "anoint" s.o.; "oil" straw; "smear with" mud **N** (occas. *i/i*) "anoint o.s." with (= acc.), "be anointed"; > *paššum*; *piššatu*; *pašīšu*, *pašīšūtu*; *pušištum*; *napšaštu*

pašāšu → also *pasāsu*

pašāṭu(m) "to erase" **G** (*i/i*) [LAL] inscription; stat. of part of liver "is obliterated, invisible"?; NB "lay out" brick (< Aram.) **D** ~ G "erase" text, drawing, document; stat. of part of liver "is obliterated"; "cancel, revoke" words **Š** OB "cause s.o. to erase" **ŠD** ~ Š ? jB; > *pāšittu*

pāšertu 'loosener' NA **1.** as fDN **2.** ~ "dehusker", a tool; < *pāširu*

pašḫu I "resting, restful" jB; < *pašāḫu*

pašḫu II, *puašḫu*; pl. f. (a kind of javelin) NA for hunting

pašidu mng. unkn. jB lex.

pašīratti "secretly" NB; < *pašīru* + *-atti*

pašīru, *pišīru* "a secret" M/NB; of knowledge; "secrecy", *ana p. šakānu* "to place in hiding"; < *pašāru*; > *pašīratti*; *pišīriš*

pāširu(m) **1.** OA "retail merchant" **2.** NB "dream interpreter" **3.** jB "dissolver" of spells etc.; epith. of water in mag. **4.** (a plant); < *pašāru*; > *pāšertu*

pašīšu(m) 'anointed' (a priest) OAkk, O/jB, MA? [GUDU4]; < *pašāšu*

pašīšūtu(m) "rôle of *pašīšu* priest" O/jB

pāšittu(m) "obliterator" O/jB, epith. of Lamaštu; < *pašāṭu*

pašku I (a bird) jB lex.

pašku II **1.** j/NB "wooden block, stump" **2.** NB "clod (of earth)"

pašqiš "with difficulty" jB; < *pašqu*

pašqu "narrow" M/NB(lit.) **1.** of space "narrow, confined" **2.** of way, terrain "steep, difficult" **3.** transf., of condition "severe, hard"; f. as subst. *pašuqtu* "dire straits"; < *pašāqu*

pašqu → also *pasqu*

pašqû → *pasqû*

pašru j/NB, NA [BÚR] **1.** of ground "loosened"?; of mud "dissolved"; of grain "dehusked"?; of heart "appeased" **2.** Urar. of votive offering "dedicated"; < *pašāru*

pašru → also *pasru*

paššiššu "apprentice"? Nuzi, of gardener

paššum "anointed" OB, of priest ?; < *pašāšu*

paššurmāḫu "high table" jB [GIŠ.BANŠUR.MAḪ], used in cult; < Sum.

paššuru(m), OB?, M/NA also *pasru(m)*; Nuzi pl. f. "table" [(GIŠ.)BANŠUR] as domestic furniture, of wood, precious materials; in temple "(offering) t."; *p. gerri* "travelling t."; *p. dīnim* "judgement t."; *p. rakāsu/paṭāru* "to lay/clear t." for meals; *p. ḫidâti* etc. "celebratory t."; OB *p. qaqqadim* "headrest" or "headboard"?; M/jB transf., desig. of king, goddess = "table (servant)"; < Sum.

paštatum mng. uncl. OAkk

pāštu(m), *pāltu*; jB pl. also *pālātu* "axe, adze" O/jB [URUDU.DUR10.TAB.BA] of copper; carried by deity; < *pāšu*

pašû(m) "to exhale" OA, O/jB **G** (*u/u*) transf. OA "rebuke" s.o.; OB of god *pīam lā kīnam p.* ~ "breathe, convey bad statement"; med. "break wind" **Gtn** jB ~ "repeatedly pant"; > *pašūtu*

pāšu(m) "axe, adze" [GÍN]; for battle, hunting; of butcher, barber; as symbol, in gold, copper; > *pāštu*

pâšu "to break up, crush" M/jB **G** (*a/a*) ingredients **D** ~ G; → *pa'āṣu*; *puāšu*

pašultu (a kind of knife)? jB

pašūmu → *pusummu*

pašunu (a legal expert) Nuzi; < Hurr.

pašuqtu → *pašqu* 3

pašurtu "sale" jB in *p. maḫīri* "sale of goods"; < *pašāru*

pašūtu "expectoration"? NA; < *pašû*

patāḫu(m) "to puncture, bore through" Bab., NA **G** (*a/u*) wall, oven, part of body etc. **D** ~ G; NB "stab (and kill)" cattle **Dt** jB "stab one another"; > *patḫu*; *pitḫu*; *puttuḫum*; *patīḫu*?

patakkātu → *pattakkātu*

patālu(m), *petēlu* "to twine" O/jB **G** (*i/i*) "twist" rope etc.; stat. of part of liver "is entwined, twisted"; "wrap round, entwine" with wool, fat **D** "wrap round, wind; twist (yarn)" **N** pass. of G "be twined" **Ntn** OB of intestines "be repeatedly entwined"; > *pitiltu*; *puttulu*; *mupattilum*

patānu(m) I "to dine" O/jB **G** (*a/u*); *naptanam p.* "eat a meal"; med. *balu(m)/lā patān* "without dining, on an empty stomach" **Gtn** iter. Mari **Š** caus. of G; > *patnu* I; *putānātum*; *iptennu*; *naptanu*

patānu(m) II, *petēnu* "to become strong; strengthen" Bab., NA **G** (*i/i*) of person, ground "sustain, resist" pressure; NA, NB of deity "encourage, support" **D** "strengthen"; > *patnum* II, *patniš*; *pitnu*; *pattānu*; *taptānu*?

patāqu(m) I, NB also *petēqu* "to shape, create" Bab. **G** (*i/i*) "form" brick, brickwork, wall, building; statue etc.; "cast" metal; "create" heaven, earth, mankind etc. **D** ~ G OB "cast" silverwork **Š** NB "cause to mould" bricks **N** of bricks "be moulded"; of statue, metal "be cast"; of humanity "be created"; > *patqum*; *petqu*; *pitqu*, *pitēqu*, *pitiqtu*; *naptaqu*

patāqu II "to drink" jB **G** (*i/i*), beer

patarītum (a tool) Alal., of bronze

patarru(m), *pattaru* "(battle) mace"? OAkk, O/jB of copper, bronze

patā'um → *petû* II

patḫu "holed" jB, of discarded shoe; < *patāḫu*

patīḫu(m), *patīḫatu(m)* "bag, sack" O/jB, of leather; < *patāḫu* ?

patinnu(m) ~ "sash, band" Bab., for headdress; as part of blanket

patiprāsu, *patparāsu* (a judicial official) NB; < OPers.

patīru(m) "sack" O/jB of leather

patium → *petû* I

patniš "strongly" jB; < *patnum* II

patnu I "eaten" jB, of meal; < *patānu* I

patnum II, *pet(e)nu* "tough, resistant" Bab., of person, animal; of wall, beam; < *patānu* II; > *patniš*

patnu III (a piece of furniture)? Nuzi

patparāsu → *patiprāsu*

patqum "formed, built" OB of mud wall; < *patāqu* I

patrānu 'sword-plant' (name of a plant) M/jB [GÍR-] lex., med.; < *patru*

patru(m) "sword, dagger" [GÍR] as weapon; *p. šibbi* "dagger (worn in) belt"; as divine symbol, esp. OA *p. ša Aššur*; "knife" of butcher, leather-worker etc.; > *patrānu*

pa(t)takkātu (desig. of humanity) jB

pattānu "supporter, strengthener" NB epith. of DNs in PNs; < *patānu* II

pattarānu (an ornament)? Nuzi, of bronze

pattaru → *patarru*

pattiš "like canals" jB; < *pattu* I

pattu(m) I, *pātu*; pl. *patātu(m)* "canal" Bab., M/NA; as name *Patti-ṭuḫdi*, *-mēšari* etc.; > *pattiš*

pattu(m) II "border (district)" Mari, NA(roy. inscr.) [ZAG]; *ša patti PlN* "on the borders of PlN"; < *pāṭu* f.

pattu → also *pātu*

pattû I "(a kind of) chest" j/NB, of reed; < Sum.

pattû II "open(ed)" M/NA [DUḪ.MEŠ], f. *pattūtu* desig. of chariot; < *petû* II D Ass.; jB → *puttû*

patû → *petû* I.II

pātu(m), *pattu* "edge, rim" Am., NA, NB [ZAG] of textile, helmet; *ša p. lā išû* "limitless"; NB *ina p. dabābu* "to speak aside"; < *pû* I f.; → *piātum*; *pattu* II, *pāṭu*

pātu → also *pattu* I

pâtum → *pūtu*

pat'um → *petû* I

paṭāmum "to enclose in fat" OB stat., of part of entrails

paṭāru(m) "to loosen, release" **G** (*a/u*) [DUḪ] **1.** "loosen, untie" package, sealing; dress, fetters, bonds, belt; "unhitch" animal **2.** "clear away" offering, table; "vacate" forts **3.** "uncover" head, loins; "slacken, relax" hand('s grasp), jaw etc.; stat. of part of liver "is loose" **4.** "clear, dispel" evil, sin, punishment, illness, debt etc.; "disperse" army formation, "break" contract **5.** "release, free" person from bondage, soldier from service; "ransom, free" captive, slave; field etc. from pledge **6.** "discontinue" activity, "cancel" document **7.** math. "find" reciprocal **8.** ellipt. OB of troops etc. "break (camp), move on"; Am., jB etc. "go away, move off"; O/MB "desert, shirk" work, "secede" from king; of animal "break loose"; of oil, smoke "dissolve, disperse" **Gtn** iter. OB of oil "disperse in all directions" **D** ~ G [DUḪ.MEŠ] **1.** "unhitch" oxen **2.** "separate, cut off" hem, hair **3.** "clear away" building, rocks; person from road **4.** "dismantle, loosen" joints of door, bridge etc.; "release" springs of water **5.** stat. of part of body "is split, broken up"; sinews "are slackened" **6.** math. "solve, resolve" task **7.** "dispel, break" norms, regulations; mag. knot, power; sin, curse **8.** "release" boat; "set free, ransom" person; of god "forgive" s.o. **Dtn** jB "repeatedly slacken" joint **Dt** pass. of D; NB of wall "be loosened, collapse"; of limbs "be slackened"; of pain, omen "be dispelled"; "be ransomed" **Š** caus. (of G 1, 3, 4, 5, 8) **ŠD** jB "disperse" battle **N** pass. of G [DUḪ] "be loosened, untied", of ship "slip anchor"; of table "be cleared away", of camp "be struck"; of loins "be ungirt"; of ground "be loosened"; of sin, punishment etc. "be dispelled", "abate, disappear"; of troops "move away"; of pledge etc. "be freed"; math. "be (re)solved"; > *paṭru*; *piṭru*; *paṭīru*; *puṭāru*; *pāṭeru*, *pāṭerānu*; *puṭṭuru*; *puṭūru* II; *ipṭiru*; *napṭaru*, *napṭartu*, *napṭarūtu*; *taptartum*, *tapṭertu*, *tapṭīru*

pāṭerānu "the one who released/s" MA; < *paṭāru*

pāṭeru(m) **1.** Mari "deserter" or "demobilized (soldier)" **2.** jB lex. f. *pāṭertu* 'that which undoes' (a word for door); < *paṭāru*

paṭīru; pl. m. & f. "portable altar" j/NB, NA [GI.DU8] esp. rit.; < *paṭāru*

paṭru "released" j/NB; of plough "unhitched"; of shoe etc., loins "loosed"; of breast (*irtum*) "enfeebled"; < *paṭāru*

paṭṭu → *pāṭu*

paṭû (or *ḫaṭṭû*) mng. unkn. jB in col., desig. of a tablet ?

pāṭu(m), Ug. also *paṭṭu* "border; district" Bab. [ZAG] of city, land; OB *pāṭ erbettim* "the four borders" of the world; cosmic *p. šamê u erṣetim* "border(s) of heaven and earth"; "edge" of part of liver; > *pattu* II

pa'û, *paya* (a bird) jB, of Tiāmat

pā'um → *pû* I.II

pa''ugu "taken away" MA, of tablets; < *puāgu* D Ass.

pawera/e "lord, great one" Am.; < Eg.

paya → *pa'û*

payīṣu → *pa'ṣu*

pazāru(m) "to hide o.s., be hidden" Ass., O/jB **G** jB in comm.; Mari "conceal o.s." **D** "hide, conceal" s.o., s.th.; OA "smuggle" silver etc., Mari ellipt. "go, act secretly"; jB *alāku puzzuru* "go secretly" **Dt** pass. of D OB "be concealed" **Št** OB "hide s.o. away", "shelter, protect" **ŠD** OB "shelter" **N** OA "conceal o.s."; > *pazru*, *pazriš*; *puzru*; *pazzurtu*, *puzzuru*; *mupazzirum*; *mušapzertu*; *tapzertu*; *napzaram*

paziru → *pazru*

pazitu "vizier" Am.; < Eg.

paznannu (or *pasnannu*) mng. unkn. Am., desig. of gold

pazriš "in secret" jB; < *pazru*

pazru, Alal. *paziru* "concealed" Alal., jB; < *pazāru*

Pazūzu (a demon) jB, NA; *qaqqad Pazūzāni* "*P.* heads"

pazzurtu(m) **1.** OA "concealment", *ašar p.* "place of concealment" for goods etc. **2.** NA *ana p.* "secretly"; < *pazāru* D

pe'ālu → *bêlu*

pedû → *padû*

pe'ettu → *pēmtu*

pegû → *pagû* II

pēgu "taken away" NA, of city, field; < *puāgu*

peḫīdu → *paḫīdu*

peḫītum "sealed store"? Mari; < *peḫû* I

peḫlum mng. unkn. Mari

peḫû(m) I "sealed, closed; stupid" O/jB [SAG. GI4] **1.** "closed off" path, gate, house **2.** of person "stupid"; < *peḫû* II

peḫû(m) II, OA *paḫā'um*, NB also *paḫû* "to close up, seal" **G** (*i/i*) [ÚŠ] part of body; house, wall, chest, with clay, bitumen; "caulk, seal" boat, oven; "block" canal, with wall; "shut in" s.o., s.th., "shut up, seal up" s.th., in wall, dough; jB transf. stat. of ordinances "are contained" in house; NB of guilt, crime "is forgiven" **Gtn** iter. of G **D** ~ G "seal up" nostrils, gate; "shut in, seal away" person, s.th. **Š** OB caus.? **N** pass. of G [ÚŠ] "be sealed up"; of road "be blocked", of ship "be caulked"; > *peḫû* I, *peḫītum*; *pīḫu*, *pīḫātu* II?; *pēḫû*

pēḫû(m) "caulker" Bab., of ship; < *peḫû* II

peḫūnu "incompetent builder, jerry-builder"? jB lex.

pekušḫu (a wooden object) Nuzi; < Hurr.

pelludû(m), *billudû* "cult(ic rites)" Bab., of deity, city; lex. *ša p.* "cultic officiant"; < Sum.

pelû(m) I, lex. also *pēlu(m)* "(light) red" O/jB (lit.) of blood, ant, stone; < *pelû* III

pelû(m) II, *palû* "egg" Bab. [NUNUZ] of bird, as food; of Anzû, ostrich; of tortoise, fish, snake, ant

pelû III "to be red" Bogh., jB **G** (*i/i*) of face, hair; moon, rainbow **N** "become red" of ripening dates ?; > *pelû* I

pēlu → *pelû* I; *pīlu*

pêlu → *bêlu*

pēmtum, *pēnt/du*, *pettu*, M/NA *pe'ettu*; pl. *pe'enāti* "charcoal" [NE]; for cooking, offering etc.; > *pendû*?

pēmu(m), *pēnu* "(upper) thigh" Bab. [ḪÁŠ.GAL; (UZU.)ÚR] of deity, person; sheep, horse; as meat; OB *bāmat p.* "half, one side of thigh"

pendû, *pindû(m)* **1.** Bab [GUG] (mark on skin, phps.) "mole" or "birthmark"; on face; on baby; OB as PN **2.** Bab., NA [(NA4.)^{d}ŠE.TIR] (a red? speckled stone) in mag.; for jewellery, as building stone; transf., MB of king *p. namāri* "stone of illumination" **3.** lex. (a tree); < *pēmtum* + *-ī* ?

pēndu → *pēmtum*

peniḫuru "field surveyor" Nuzi; < Hurr.

penišḫu → *penušḫu*

pennigu → *pannigu*

pēntu → *pēmtum*

penû → *panû*

pēnu → *pēmu*

pênu "to grind" Nuzi, jB **G** flour

penušḫu, *penišḫu*, *panušḫu* (a metal vessel) Nuzi; MA of silver, bronze; < Hurr.

penzer → *pizzer*

penzu(r)ru(m) mng. unkn. O/jB lex.

peqqû "colocynth" j/NB lex.; NB nom. unit. *peqqūtu* in garden

pequm mng. unkn. Mari **G** (perf. *ipteqe*)

per'āsu → *per'āzu*

per'ašum → *perša'um*

per'āzu (or *per'āsu*) (a material) Am., for tool, pin

perdum (a kind of equid) OA

perekkum → *parakkum*

pēretu → *pērtu*

perḫu → *per'u*

periprušḫu (a metal object) Nuzi, of bronze; < Hurr.

perku(m), *pirku(m)*, NB also *pišku* **1.** Bab., M/NA "transverse line", math. in geometrical figure; OB "frontier" of urban district; Nuzi "short side" of field (= *pūtu*); Ass. *ina p.* "across", *ana p.* mng. uncl.; NB *p. ša nāri* "canal barrage"? **2.** NA, NB "crime, injustice"; < *parāku*

perniqqu(m) (a mythical weapon)? O/jB; as feature of liver

perriḫtu (or *parriḫtu*) mng. uncl. NB as desig. of woman

perru(m), *pirru(m)*, *pīru* **1.** O/jB mng. uncl. **2.** MA of troops ~ "enrolment", also *bēl p.* **3.** NA ~ "payment collection, tax delivery"; "corps" of troops ?

persannu → *peršannu*

persa'u → *perša'um*

persu(m), *pirsu(m)* "division" Bab. **1.** Mari [KUD] "section" of troops, *rabi p.* "section commander" **2.** jB lex. "sector" of orchard **3.** jB lex. (a part of the entrails) **4.** "cutting" of thread, "cessation" of flood **5.** "section" of text, "partial tablet"; < *parāsu* I

perṣaduḫḫu, *perṣeduḫḫu* (a balsam) MA; < Hurr.?

perṣu(m), *pirṣu(m)* "breach" O/jB in wall, canal bank; < *parāṣu* I

peršannu, *persannu* (a building or plot of ground) Nuzi ?

peršantu → *pursandu*

perša'um, OAkk *per'ašum*, jB *parša'u*, *pa/uršu'u*, *persa'u*, *puru'zu* etc. "flea"; also as PN; > *puršatta*?

pertā(we) mng. unkn. Nuzi; < Hurr.

pērtu(m), *pēretu*, NB also *pēštu* "hair (of head)" of humans; *p. gu/allubu* "to shave the head"; jB *p. ḫarrāni* 'hair of the wayside' (a plant)

pēru → *pīru*

per'u(m), *perḫu*, OAkk, OA *par'um*, NB also *perwu* "bud, shoot" [NUNUZ] **1.** "bud, shoot" of tree, plant; MA as stone ornament; *p. kalbi* 'dog's shoot' (a plant) **2.** transf. "scion, descendant(s)" of human; freq. in PNs; > *parā'u* II; → *pāru* III

perullum → *burullum*

pērūrūtu(m) "mouse" O/jB [PÉŠ.TUR]; also (a bird)?; OB, as fPN

peruzzu (or *perușșu*) (a textile) Alal., Nuzi; < Hurr.

perwu → *per'u*

pesēnu "to cover up, veil" NB **G** (*i/i*) facts, words; "conceal" person, animal **D** ~ G NB **N** pass. of G "be kept secret"; > *pesnu*; → *pasāmu*; *pașānu*

pesnu "concealed" NB; *ina pesindu* "secretly"; < *pesēnu*

pessû(m), *passûm* "lame, limping" Bab. [BA.AN.ZA] of human, Am. of stone figure; of sheep, damaged by neglect; transf. "crippled" of tree, jB lex.

pesû ~ "to rejoice" jB lex. **G**

peș**û(m)** I, *paș'um*, *pașû(m)*, Ass. *pașiu(m)* "white" [BABBAR] **1.** as colour: of wool, textile; animal('s hide), parts of liver; of men, women as PN; of plant, tree; of food, drink; stones, metals; star, heavenly phenomena, clouds **2.** of land: OB "clear" (for cultivation)?; O/MA *qaqqerē p.* "clear ground plot" (NA → *pușû*); < *peșû* II

peș**û(m)** II "to be white" Bab. **G** (*i/i* or *e/e*) [BABBAR] **1.** of animal('s coat), person, part of liver, spittle, planet etc. **2.** of field "be clear"; of fire "be white(-hot)"; of person "turn pale"; of vegetation "be blanched, wasted" **D** "make white" **1.** j/NB "blanch" vegetation **2.** jB "bring" fire "to white heat" **3.** OB "clear (ground for)" garden; > *peșû* I; *pūșu*; *pușû*; *pūșāya*, *pūșammūtu*; *mupașșû*; *nepșûm*?

pêșu → *pa'āșu*

pešēlu → *pašālu*

pēštu → *pērtu*

pētân birki "swift runner" jB (liter. 'knee opener') of man; horse, lion; < *pētû* + *-ān* +*birku*

petēlu → *patālu*

petenu → *patnum* II

petēnu → *patānu* II

petēqu → *patāqu* I

pētḫallu; pl. m. & f. "riding horse" M/NA, M/NB (liter. 'crotch opener'); also coll. and pl. "cavalry"; *ša pētḫalli*, *pētḫallāti* "rider, cavalryman"; < *pētû* + *ḫallu* I

petîš adv. "openly"? jB astr. comm.; < *petû* I

petītu → *petû* I 3

petnu → *patnum* II

petqu "cast"? NB in *lā p.* "not struck"?, desig. of silver; < *patāqu* I

pettu → *pēmtum*

petû(m) I, *patû(m)*, OA *patium*, *pat'um* "open" [BAD] **1.** of road, entrance etc.; part of body, eye, ear, transf. *p. uzni* "wise" **2.** of package, letter, shoe; "open (in shape)" of cuneiform sign **3.** *(lā) petītu(m)* "(un)mated" of female animal [GÌŠ.NU.ZU] **4.** "arable" of field **5.** "ready for action" of weapon **6.** "flowing" of water **7.** jB lex. "wise" **8.** OA "far distant" of time; < *petû* II

petû(m) II, *patû*, OAkk, OA *patā'um* "to open" **G** (*e/e*) [BAD; astr. also TAG4] **1.** door, gate; grave, house, room; container; "undo" lock, package **2.** "expose, open up" foundation; "unsheathe" weapon; "dehusk" barley; "unroll" rope; "broach, start on" wine, grain etc. **3.** "lay open" road, watercourse, mountains; "start" water flowing, "open up" well, spring; "bring" field "into cultivation" **4.** parts of body as obj.: lips, mouth (= speak); ear(s) (= hear, (give to) understand); eyes (= see, (give to) understand); *pānī p.* "make s.o. cheerful, satisfied"; *qātam p.* "be generous"; *upnī p.* "open fists" i.e. "pray"; *ida/ī p.* "get ready for battle"; *ḫalla p.* "open crotch" i.e. "ride" (→ *pētḫallu*); *purīdu p.* "run"; with *birkā*, *sūnu*, *ūru* "open 'knees', lap, groin" sexually **5.** transf. "reveal" words, secret; o.'s sins, heart **6.** NA ellipt. of star "move into distance" **Gtn** iter. [BAD.BAD; BAD.MEŠ] **D** ~ G "open"; "undo" lock; "bring" field "into cultivation"; NA "inaugurate, found" city; with *uznu* "inform, instruct", OA also ellipt. without *u.* "inform"; "expose, reveal" part of body, words etc.; NA "move s.o. away", "dismiss" from post; OB stat., of ornament "is finished? with" gold **Dt** pass. of D "be opened"; "be brought into cultivation" **Š** caus. of G **Št**¹ pass. of Š OB "be made to open up" **Št**² OB "express o.s. openly" to s.o., "specify explicitly" amounts **ŠD** jB(poet.) ~ D **N** pass. of G [BAD] "be opened"; "be unsheathed", "unrolled"; of secret "be revealed"; NB of land "be opened up, freed (from hostilities)"; Mari of rains "commence" **Ntn** iter.; > *petû* I, *petîš*; *pītu* I; *pūtu* II; *pētû*, *pētûtu*; *puttû*, *pattû* II; *mupettûm*, *mupattītu*; *šaptûm*; *naptû*, *naptētu*, *neptû*; *taptû*, *teptītum*; *pētân birki*; *pētḫallu*

pētû(m) 'opener' O/jB lex.; **1.** "door-opener, porter" **2.** (a wrestler) **3.** "thresher"; < *petû* II

pētûtu "rôle of revealer"? jB, of scribal craft; < *pētû*

piāqum, *pâqu* "to make narrow, tight" O/jB **G** OB ellipt. "screw up" (eyes, to see); stat. of eyes; of mesh "be close, fine" **D** "compress" substance ?; > *pīqu*, *pīqa*, *pīqat*; *pāqu*; *pūqu*; → *puqqu*

pi'āsu → *pi'āzu*

piātum "side" Mari, in topog. descr. of city, district; < W.Sem.?; → *pātu*

pi'āzu, *pi'āsu*, occas. *pur'āsu* (a small rodent) jB lives in a hole, gathers food; also (a small fish)

pidānu "assay" (of gold) NB

pidarānu (or *piṭarānu*) mng. unkn. jB

piddu → *pīdu* II

pidītum "pardon, indulgence" OB; < *padû*

pīdu I "pardon, indulgence" jB, NA; < *padû*

pīdu II, *piddu* ~ "imprisonment" jB lex.; < *pâdu*

pigû **1.** jB lex. (a plant) **2.** NA (a drum)?

pīgu "lying, deception"? MA, M/jB; < *pagû* II

pīḫātu(m) I, *pāḫātu(m)*, M/NA *pāḫutu* "responsibility; province" Bab., M/NA [NAM] **1.** *p. našû(m)*, OB *ana p. izuzzum* "to bear a r., be responsible", *p. apālu(m)* "meet a r.", *ana p. šakānum* "make (s.o.) responsible"; *bēl(ū)*, *šūt pīḫātim* "responsible official(s)" **2.** M/NA, M/NB "province", *bēl p.* "provincial governor" (NA, NB also without *bēl*, NB also *b. paḫaš*); < *puḫḫu*; > *pīḫātūtu*

pīḫātu II (a dark-coloured garment) j/NB; < *pīḫu* ?

pīḫātūtu, NA *pāḫatūtu* "provincial governorship" jB(Ass.), NA [(LÚ.)NAM-]; < *pīḫātu* I

pīḫu(m), *pī'u* "beer-jar" Bab. [PIḪU; jB DUG.KA.GAG], OB also as liquid measure; NB *p. ša šadî* (a type of beer); < *peḫû* II

pikallullu "aperture in oven" jB lex.

pikarsinnu mng. unkn. Nuzi, in desig. of gold vessel

pikru → *bikru*; *piqru*

pilaggu → *balangu*

pilaḫā'u mng. unkn. Nuzi

pilakku → *pilaqqu*

pilāniš "like limestone" jB; < *pīlu*

pilaqqu(m), *pilakku(m)* "spindle" O/jB, NA [(GIŠ.)BAL] for spinning wool; as ornament in gold, lapis lazuli; *qaqqad p.* "head of spindle"; (a kind of stone, phps.) "belemnite" [NA4.BAL]; *p. Ištar* ~ "wood-wasp"; NA as PN ?; < Sum.?

pilaqquḫuli "(female) spinner" Alal.; < *pilaqqu* + Hurr. *-uḫ(u)li*

pilāyānu pl. mng. unkn. OB

pilku(m) I; pl. m. & f. "demarcated zone, sector" O/jB, NA of field-holdings; NA "work-sector" of construction; < *palāku*

pilku II "feudal service" Ug.; < Ug. *pa* + *ilku* I ?

pillatu(m) "stolen goods" O/jB; < *palālu*

pillu I mng. unkn. jB lex.

pillu II, *pilû* (a kind of wine)? jB lex.; < Sum.?

pillû (a plant, phps.) "mandragora" M/jB [GIŠ/Ú.NAM.TAR; Ú.NAM.TAL] *inib/zēr p.* "m. fruit/seed"; *p. zikaru* "male m."

pilludû → *pelludû*

pillurtu → *išpallurtu*

pilpilânu (a homosexual)? jB; < *pilpilû*

pilpilû "homosexual lover" jB lex.; < Sum.; > *pilpilânu*; → *pippilû*

pilšu(m) "breach" [BÙR; jB also GAM] in wall of house, city; in body, liver "perforation", *p. appi*, *uzni* "nostril, ear-hole"; in seed funnel, stone; < *palāšu*

piltu (a container)? OB(Susa)

piltu → also *pištu*

pilû → *pillu* II

pīlu, *pēlu*, *pūlu* "limestone" M/NB, NA; for buildings, stone vessel; "(single) limestone block"; *ša p.-šu* "limestone dealer"; > *pīlāniš*

pīlu → also *pīru*

pindû → *pendû*

pingu → *pinku*

pinkarannu (desig. of horse) Nuzi

pinku(m), *pingu* **1.** Bab. "knob, boss", on seal, ornament **2.** Bogh. lex. (a bird); > *panāku*?

pinnanāru mng. unkn. jB lex.

pinnartu, *punnartu* "rennet cheese"? jB lex.

pinnāru(m) "rennet cheese"? O/jB; as PN

pi(n)nigu → *pannigu*

pinnu, NA *pīnu* ~ "button, stud" Qatna, Nuzi, NA; bronze, in horse-trappings; gold, in jewellery

pinze/ur → *pizzer*

pīpī → *pû* I 3

pi(p)pilû "sin" jB lex.; → *pilpilû*

pīqa(m), *pīqi* ~ "on (one) occasion" jB; esp. of hypothetical cases; *pīqa ... pīqa* "now ... then"; *(ina) p. lā p.* "on repeated occasions"; < *pīqu*; → *pīqat*

piqanānu ~ "agent, executor"? NB; < *piqnētu* (NB *piqittu* pl.)

piqannu → *piqqannu*

pīqat, *pāqat* "perhaps" O/jB, esp. OB; Ug. also *p. ... p.*; < *pīqu*; → *pīqa*

pīqātu → *pīqu*

piqdu "allocation, consignment" M/NB, of goods, payment; < *paqādu*

pīqi → *pīqa*

piqittu(m); pl. *piqdātu(m)*, NB *piq(i)nētu*, NA *piq(it)tātu* "allocation, check" Bab., NA [SI.LÁ; SI.IL.LA/LÁ] **1.** esp. OB "allocation" of commodities for s.o.'s maintenance **2.** "check, stock-take", "review" of troops; "verification" of extispicy **3.** "appointment, mandate" **4.** "administrative responsibility"; < *paqādu*

piqittūtu "post of responsibility" NB; also *bēl-p.*; < *piqittu*

piqnētu → *piqittu*

pi(q)qannu "droppings (of sheep, gazelle)" jB [A.GAR.GAR]; med. as drug; in om.

piqru (or *pikru*) (a game) MB

pīqu(m) "narrow, tight" M/jB of pass, well, mouth; as subst. "strangulation"?; f. pl. *pīqātu* "narrow places"? OB lex.; < *piāqum*; > *pīqa*, *pīqat*

pirakānum → *pirikānum*

pirākum (a structure) OA

pirankumma in *p. epēšu* "to flee" Nuzi; < Hurr.

pirassum (a water vessel) OB

pirḫa (a plant) jB lex.

pirīdu → *purīdu*

piriduḫ → *pirizaḫ*

piriduluš (a plant) jB lex.; < Kass.?

piriggunû(m) (a coloured stone) Mari, jB [NA4.PÌRIG.GÙN.NU] lex., mag.; < Sum.

pirikānum, *pi/arakānum* (a textile) OA

pirikkum (a symbol or cultic installation) OA of Aššur, OB; → *parakku* ?

pirikkum → also *pirikum*

piriktu(m) ~ "opposition, violent act"? O/jB; also a technical term in brewing; < *parāku*

pirikum, *pirikkum* "chatterer" OB lex.

piriltu → *pirištu*

pirimaḫ (a plant) jB lex.; < Kass.

pirindu ~ "slice" j/NB of pomegranate; as food

pirinzaḫu, *purunzaḫu* (a word for) "frog" jB comm.

piriṣtu(m) "falsity, falsehood" Bab.; "lie(s)"; "false claims, expectations"; < *parāṣu* I

pirištu(m), *piriltu* "secret" (subst.) Bab., M/NA [AD.ḪAL]; *p. naṣāru*, *petû*, *šūṣû* "to keep, release, let out a secret"; *ina p.* "in conclave"; *šammi p.* (a plant); < *parāsu* I; → *bītu* 5; *ērib-bīt-pirištūtu*

pirīt pirīt → *birīt birīt*

pirittu(m) "terror" Bab., OA [ŠÀ.MUD]; OA "imputation(s), threat(s)"?; jB *idāt p.* "terrifying omens"; < *parādu* I

piri'tu "shoot, sapling" NA, of palm tree; < *parā'u* II

pirizaḫ, *piriduḫ* (a plant) jB lex.; < Kass.

Pirizzarru (a month) OB(Hana)

pirku → *perku*

pirmaḫ, *purma/uḫ*, *pir(zu)muḫ* (desig. of horses) MB; < Kass.

pirqānû → *pargānīu*

pirqu I "claim" Nuzi; of property *p. rašû* "be subject of a claim"; < *baqāru* (with metath.)

pirqu II, *pišqu* "redemption" NB, of person from pledge; < Aram.

pirru → *perru*

pirsānu mng. unkn. O/jB lex.

pirsu; f. *pirsatu* "weaned" M/NA, MB of children; MA also of animals; also MB as (f)PN; < *parāsu* I

pirsu → also *persu*

pirṣatu "deceit" NA; < *parāṣu* I

pirṣu → *perṣu*

pīru(m), *pīlu*, *pēru*; pl. m. & f. "elephant" Bab., M/NA [AM.SI]; *mašak p.* "elephant hide"; *šinni p.*, *š. ša p.* "ivory"

pīru → also *perru*

pirzumuḫ → *pirmaḫ*

pisannu → *pišannu* I

pisi(l)lūtum (or *piṣ/zi(l)lūtum*) mng. unkn. OA

pisiltu(m) ~ "misadventure"? O/jB of financial straits (→ *pasālu* G); om. in apodoses *ana ḫarrāni(m) p.* "an adversity for the trip"; < *pasālu*

pismu mng. uncl. jB lex. **1.** (a disease of sheep)? **2.** (part of lyre)?

pisnāqu → *pisnuqu*

pisnuqiš "wretchedly" jB; < *pisnuqu*

pisnuqu, *pisnāqu*, *pasnaqu* ~ "feeble, wretched" j/NB; also as subst.; > *pisnuqiš*

pispisu "bug"? NA

pissatu "erasure" jB; < *pasāsu*

pīsu(m); pl. m. & f. "shovel"? Bab., for winnowing [GIŠ.LAGAB.MAR; GIŠ.MAR.ŠE.BAD ?]

pisurru(m) (part of a goose) O/jB; med. *qilpu ša p.-šu* "skin of its *p.*"

piṣallur(t)u → *pizallurtu*

piṣi(l)lūtum → *pisillūtum*

piṣīru(m) mng. unkn. OB lex., jB om.

piṣṣer → *pizzer*

piša'iš(ḫu) mng. unkn. Am., Nuzi, in desig. of whip; < Hurr.

pišanna mng. uncl. Nuzi, *ša p.* desig. of men

pišannu(m) I, *pisannu(m)*; pl. m. & f. "box, chest" Bab., NA [(GIŠ/GI.)PISAN; GIŠ.PÍSAN] usu. of reed (gi*p.*), also wood (giš*p.*); for food, clothing, cups, tablets; (parts of a door), upper, lower; NA "gutter" on roof; < Sum.; → *p.* II

pišannu II (a bag) NB, of wool, linen, for temple property; = *p.* I ?

pišaru mng. unkn. OB lex.

pišertu(m), *piširtu(m)* "release" O/jB [BÚR-] **1.** "loosening" of soil; lex., of grain husks ? **2.** "sale, disposal" of harvest produce etc. **3.** "dispelling, release" of sorcery etc.; "(materials used in) dispelling ritual"; < *pašāru*

pišiltu (a clay lump)? jB; in, from tablet ?; < *pašālu* ?

pišīriš "clandestinely" MB(Ass.); < *pašīru*

piširtu → *pišertu*

pišīru → *pašīru*

pišittu mng. unkn. jB lex.

pišku → *perku*

pišmatum (or *wišmatum*) mng. unkn. OB

pišqu → *pirqu* II

pišru(m); pl. f. "release; interpretation" Bab., NA [BÚR] **1.** "ritual to dispel" sorcery, evil etc.; *iṣ p.* "magic staff" **2.** "interpretation" of omen, dream etc.; < *pašāru*

piššatu(m) "ointment" Bab., NA [Ì.BA; OB also Ì.ŠÉŠ] **1.** "ointment, salve", *p. šurmēnim* "cypress-oil" **2.** "ointment allocation, ration" **3.** Am. "(box for) ointment"?; < *pašāšu*

pištu(m), *piltu* "abuse, scandal" O/jB; *p. uppušu* "to treat s.o. abusively"; jB *pišātu* "abusive songs"; < *wapāšum*

pita(ḫ)ḫa mng. unkn. Nuzi, flour for *p.*

pitakku (a building)? Nuzi

pitēqu, *pitqu* "offspring" jB lex.; < *patāqu* I

pitḫu "perforation" M/NA, j/NB in wall; "stab wound" in flesh; < *patāḫu*

pitiltu(m) "string, cord" O/jB, NA [ŠU.SAR], of palm-fibre; < *patālu*

pitinkak ~ "glove"? Am., as pair

pit(i)pabaga "mess-mate" NB, of king; < OPers.

pitiqtu(m) "mud wall, mud masonry" O/jB [IM.DÙ.A], usu. round field etc.; in mathematical texts; *p. patāqu* "to form a mud wall"; < *patāqu* I

pitnu(m) "box; (a musical instrument)" **1.** [(GIŠ.)NA5] "(strong-)box, casket" of wood, stone, ivory; on chariot, in bathroom **2.** "string" of a musical instrument; (an instrument); < *patānu* II

pitqu(m) "casting" **1.** of metal, *p. erî, kaspi* "cast copper, silver" etc. **2.** "mould(ing)" of baked brick (*agurru*) **3.** ~ *pitiqtu* "mud wall" [NB IM.DÙ.A] **4.** "(sheep)fold, pen" **5.** poet. of human, "formation, creation" of DN; < *patāqu* I

pitqu → also *pitēqu*

pitqudu, NB *putqudu* "cautious, prudent" M/NB of ruler, official etc.; < *paqādu* Gt

pitru(m) **1.** Bab. (unbuilt plot, waste space) **2.** jB med. ~ "stomach lining"? [DUḪ]

pitrudu "frightened" jB of speech; < *parādu* I Gt

pitrustu(m), *pitruštu(m)* "inconsistent result" O/jB om.; jB ext. [freq. DUḪ- ; DUḪ.UŠ(.A)], of self-contradictory omina; < *pitrusum*

pitrusum "separate, placed apart" Mari, of spots on liver; < *parāsu* I Gt

pitruštu → *pitrustu*

pittallenni (a class of person) Alal.; < Hurr.

pitti "just as, in the way that" NA + subjunct.; < *pittu* I

pittu I ~ "area, vicinity" M/NA, M/jB, *ina pit* "near to"; of woman *pittiša* "of her rank"; M/NA "sphere of responsibility"; jB, NA *(ina) pitti(mma)* "on account of", "instead (of)", "accordingly", NA also *ip-pitti(mma)*; NA *ap-pitti* "according to" (NB → *appitti*); > *pitti*

pittu II mng. unkn. jB comm.

pittu → also *pītu* II

pītu(m) I, *pitûm* "opening, aperture" Bab., NA [BAD] of door, gate; in wall, quay; of part of body; "clasp" for necklace; *p. pāni* "clear solution" to problem; *p. purīdi(m)* "(first) stride"; *p. pî* "opening of the mouth" [KA.DUḪ. Ù/ḪU.DA] (dedicatory ritual); (a tuning of the harp); OB *kīma pītim* "instantly, by return"; OB in MN *Pīti-erṣetim*; < *petû* II

pītu(m) II, *pittu* "bundle" Bab., NA as measure of sesame, garlic etc.

pitūtu; pl. *pituāte* (a headdress) NA, *p. rakāsu* "to tie a *p.*"

piṭarānu → *pidarānu*

piṭātu → *piṭṭātu*

piṭru(m) "release" O/jB [DUḪ] **1.** as feature of liver (→ *paṭāru* G 3) **2.** "untying" of knot **3.** "clearance" of table **4.** *lā p.* "without respite" **5.** OB (a stone); < *paṭāru*

pi(ṭ)ṭātu pl. tant. "archers" Am., Ug.; < Eg.

pīum → *pû* I.II

pī'u → *pīḫu*

piyāmu, *piyānu* ~ "strong" jB lex.

piyapiya (a plant) jB lex.

pizallur(t)u (or *piṣallur(t)u*) "gecko" M/jB [MUŠ.DÍM.GURUN.NA; MUŠ.DA.GUR4.RA; Bogh. MUŠ.DÍM.KUR.RA] red, white etc.; also (a plant) [Ú.AM.SI.ḪAR.RA.NA]

pizi(l)lūtum → *pisillūtum*

pizzer, *penzer*, *pinze/ur*, *piṣṣer* (a plant) OAkk, jB; → *upinzer*

pizzerium (an object) OAkk, of gold

pû(m) I, OAkk, OA freq. *pā'um*, *pīum* (also OB); pl. f. "mouth" [KA; Ug. also KA×U; jB also MÚRUB] **1.** of deity, human; as speech organ, *ina p. qabû(m)* "to speak", *ina p. šakānu(m)* "to put" words "into s.o.'s mouth"; of words *ina p. (w)aṣû(m)* "to be uttered", → *ṣītu* 2; OA *ša pā'ē* ~ "informant"; *ša pî* "word, statement", also *šūt pî* "oral tradition" of interpretation **2.** "muzzle, beak" of animal, bird **3.** "statement, command"; *pâ ištēn šakānu* "to make unanimous, achieve consensus", *p. itti X šakānu* "to reach agreement with" s.o.; → *maṭû* I.II; *p. nadānu* "to promise"; *ana p. X (w)ašābu(m)* "to dwell obedient to" s.o.; "talk, rumour", *ina p. nišī* "in popular report", NB *ana pīpī ša X* "according to X" **4.** om. *pû(m) (lā) kīnu(m)* "(un)reliable statement" **5.** "wording" of tablet; *ana/kī p.* "in accordance with text" of document; OB *ezub pī ṭuppišu* "not counting what is recorded on his tablet" **6.** *ana/kī pī* "with respect to", "in view of", "in proportion to"; Bab. *(ana) pī šulpi(m)* = "cultivated (for grain)" **7.** "opening, aperture" of part of body, O/jB lex. of womb; "mouth" of watercourse, NA also pl. *piāte*; "entry, access" to road, mountain pass, building; of pot, bag, box, furrow; Qatna "setting"? of jewel **8.** transf. "maw, teeth" (of battle, death); *(ina) p. patri(m)* "(at) the mouth of the sword"; jB *pā'iš karāši* ~ "from the thick of battle" **9.** of time, "start"; MA *pī namāre* "at break of dawn"; > *pātu*

pû(m) II, *pā'um*, *pīum* "chaff" [IN.BUBBU]; esp. as symbol of worthlessness *ištu p. adi ḫurāṣim* "from chaff to gold"

pûm → also *bûm*

puādum (or *puāt/ṭum*) mng. unkn. OA **G** obj. word (*awatam*)

puāgu(m) "to take away forcibly from" s.o. (= acc.) Ass. **G** goods, person, land; NA *eqlu pēgāku* "I am deprived of the field" **D** → *pa''ugu*; > *pēgu*

puašḫu → *pašḫu* II

puāšu(m) mng. uncl. Ass. **G** phps. "to reach agreement" or "disagree"

puati (or *puwati*, *bu(w)ati*) (a ring)? Am., Ug.

puāt/ṭum → *puādum*

pudru → *putru*

pūdu(m), *būdu(m)*; pl. f. mng. unkn. O/jB, desig. of sheep

pūdu → also *būdu* I-IV

puggum → *buggum*

puggulu, *pungulu*, *pukkulu(m)* "very strong, massive" O/jB; of power, deity, temple, part of loom; < *pagālu*

puglānu (a plant) jB lex., med.; < *puglu*

puglu(m) "radish" Bab. [Ú.GA.TIN]; in garden; desig. of part of liver; > *puglānu*; → *buqlu*

pūgu(m) "net" O/jB; OB also as curtain ?

pugudātu "bridle, rein(s)" NB; < Aram.

pugurru → *bugurru*

puḫādu(m) "lamb" [SILA4; Mari also SILA4.NÍTA; jB freq. UDU.SILA4] *p. miḫir ummišu* "lamb equal of its mother"; Bab. also (a fish) [KU6.SILA4]; > *puḫattu*

puḫālu, Am. *puḫīlu* "male animal, stud" M/NB, NA; of ram, bull [UTUA], stallion, elephant, duck; also of zoomorphic vessel

puḫarrinnu ~ (a mark)? Nuzi, on horse; < Hurr.?

puḫattu(m) "female lamb" O/jB [MUNUS.SILA4]; < *puḫādu*

pūḫātu → *pūḫtu*; *pūḫu*

puḫdinu mng. unkn. Mari, of gold

puḫḫan (an official)? Alal.

puḫḫu(m) **D** "to exchange" O/jB, NA; *iddin upīḫ* "he gave in exchange" **Š** Bogh. "substitute" word in formula; > *pūḫu*, *pūḫtu*; *pīḫātu* I, *pīḫātūtu*; → *pūḫizzaru*; *pūtuḫḫu* ?

puḫḫuru, NA *paḫḫuru* "assembled" M/NB, NA; < *paḫāru* II D

puḫīlu → *puḫālu*

pūḫizzaru, *pūḫukaru* "exchange equivalent" Nuzi, for field etc.; < *pūḫu* + Hurr. *-izzar/-ukar*

puḫlalû → *buḫlalû*

puḫmaḫu "blind-worm"? jB lex.

puḫpuḫḫû/u "squabble, brawl" M/jB, *p. ina bīt amēli iššakkan* "*p.* will take place in a man's house"

puḫpuḫu, *purupuḫu*, NA *purpuḫinnu* "purslane" jB, NA lex., med.; → *parparḫû*

puḫriš "in assembly, together" OB, Am.; < *puḫru*

puḫru(m); pl. f. "assembly" [UKKIN] **1.** "(formal) assembly" of gods, people, for decision-taking, judicial proceedings; MB *bīt p.* "council house"?; *awāt p.* "decision of the Assembly" **2.** "gathering" of clan, family, people, land; OB st. abs. *puḫur(ma)*, MA *ina puḫrišunu* "all together" **3.** "totality" of gods, kings etc.; *p. erṣeti* "the whole earth", *puḫur šer'āni* "all the sinews"; *puḫuršu* "his whole being"; < *paḫāru* II; > *puḫriš*

puḫtu(m) (a copper object) OB, jB lex., NA?

pūḫtu(m) "item of exchange" O/jB; leg. in transaction; (a type of document)?; rit. "substitute"; < *pūḫu*

pūḫu(m), occas. *pāḫu*; pl. m. & f. "exchange; substitute" [KI.BÉ.GAR; OB also KI.BA.GAR.RA]; *ana p.* "in exchange, as a substitute", *ana pūḫ eqlim, kirîm* "in exchange for a field, orchard"; *p. ša amtim* "exchange for a maid"; freq. pl. *ana pūḫāt(im)* etc.; Ug., M/NA of loans *ana/ina p.*; mag., rit. "substitute", *šar pūḫi* "substitute king"; < *puḫḫu*

pūḫukaru → *pūḫizzaru*

puḫur → *puḫru*

puḫutepi "scribal apprentice" OB(Susa); < Elam.

pukdu → *puqdu*

pukku(m) (a wooden ring or ball)? O/jB, used in game with *mekkû*

pukkulu → *puggulu*

pukkuru D "to fetter, tie up" j/NB hands, person; < Aram.

pūku → *būku*

pukuli; Hurr. pl. *pukulinena* (a tree)? Alal., Nuzi; < Hurr.

pulaḫli (a prof. desig.) Alal.; < Hurr.

pulḫānu (a plant) jB lex.

pulḫātu → *puluḫtu* 2

pulḫītu(m); also pl. *pulḫâ/êtu* ~ "distress, consternation"? Bab.(lit.), visible on lips; < *pulḫu* ?

pulḫu "fearsomeness; fear" M/NB **1.** jB(Ass.) freq. pl., esp. *p. melammī* "terror of radiance" of god, king **2.** NB "fear of, respect for" lord; < *palāḫu*; > *pulḫītu*?

pulīḫātum pl. tant. "anxiety" OB, in *bīt p.*; < *palāḫu*

pulilu (a building)? Alal.

pulluqu (or *pulluku*) "slaughtered" MB, of calves; < *palāqu*

pulqu → *pušqu*

pultu (desig. of a lamb) Bogh. lex.

pūlu → *pīlu*

puluggu → *pulungu*

puluḫḫûm "frightful appearance" OB m.pl.; Bogh. f.pl. *puluḫḫêtu*; < *palāḫu*

puluḫtu(m) "fear(someness)" Bab., NA [NÍ] **1.** "fear", *p. rašû* "to be terrified"; *p. ēkalli* "respect for the palace", *p. ilāni* "veneration of the gods" **2.** "fearsomeness", often pl. *pulḫātu*; *lābiš p.* "clad in fearsomeness"; of deity, king, lion, weather, underworld; < *palāḫu*

pulukkiš "like a mountain peak" NA/jB; < *pulukku*

pulukku(m) "needle; stake; boundary" Bab. [BULUG] **1.** "(metal) needle, pin"; st. abs. (not) "even a pin"; jB(Ass.) "mountain pinnacle" **2.** "boundary stake", "boundary"; *p. šamê u erṣeti* "limits of heaven and earth"; < Sum.; > *pulukkiš*; → *pulungu*

pulungu, *pulumgu*, *puluggu* "boundary" M/NA(lit.); var. of *pulukku*

pumidi (desig. of person) Alal.

punānu (or *bunānu*) (a plant) jB med.

pungulu → *puggulu*

punnartu → *pinnartu*

punnigu, *punnugu* → *pannigu*

punnunu → *bunnunu*

punzurtu → *puzzuru*

pūpatu (a plant) NA, as drug

pupuri (a container)? Alal., of copper

pupuwalli "ruin"? Bogh.; < Hitt.

puqdatu → *puquttu*

puqdu (or *pukdu*) (part of a plough) jB lex.

puqdû, *puqiddû* → *puquddû*

puqqu(m) D "to pay attention to" OAkk, Bab., NA "be attentive, obedient" to s.o. (= acc.; *ana*, term.-adv., dat.), esp. in PNs to deity; to king, to brilliance (of god), to judgement; OB "respect" deadline; "observe" instruction **Dt** stat. "regularly attends to"; NB *ana epēši ... pituqqāk* "I am assiduous to build ..."; → *piāqum* D

pūqu(m) "defile, cleft" O/jB **1.** of river valley **2.** of sheep, human "cleavage" at rear, jB also du.; < *piāqum*

puquddû(m), NB also *puq(id)dû* "(formal) delivery; legal consignment" Bab. [SI.LÁ]; < *paqādu*

puqurrā'u → *buqurrû*

puqurru → *buqurru*

puqurrû → *buqurrû*

puquttu, *puqdatu*, NA *paquttu* "thorn" M/NA, M/NB [GIŠ.LAGAB] **1.** (a thorny weed), in waste places; as drug **2.** metal "spike", in jewellery, as tool; ext. entrails *kīma p.* "like a thorn"?

purādu(m) **1.** (a large type of carp) Bab. [SUḪUR.KU$_6$]; mag. as part of composite beings **2.** pl. f. *purādātu* mng. uncl. jB comm.

purāku (a fabric) Nuzi; for furniture etc.

purallum → *burullum*

pur'āsu → *pi'āzu*

purâtu "vomit(ed matter)" jB; < *parû* IV

purdātu (or *purṣātu*, *burd/ṣātu*) f. pl. (gemstones)? jB lex.

purdû (or *burdû*) (a copper object) NA

purgû → *burgû*

purīdu(m), *puriddu*, *pirīdu*; MA pl. f. "leg" Bab., M/NA [PAP.ḪAL] **1.** of human; du. "lap", *birīt p.* "lap"; as adv. *p. alāku* "to run", *p. šuzuzzu* "to set up" figurine "in running posture"; *p. petû* "to open legs", i.e. "run" **2.** "leg" of animal **3.** Nuzi, Ug. ~ "pace" as linear measure, NB = 3 cubits **4.** MA, MB(Alal.) (a surface measure) **5.** jB lex. (a bird)

purissû → *purussû*

purišatum? (desig. of a textile) Mari

purkītu → *burkūtu*

purku → *burku*

purkullu → *parkullu*

purkulluḫuli → *parkulluḫuli*

purkullūtu "lapidary's craft" j/NB [(LÚ.)BUR.GUL-]; < *parkullu*

purkūtu → *burkūtu*

purmaḫ, *purmuḫ* → *pirmaḫ*

purpuḫinnu → *puḫpuḫu*

purqidam adv. "on(to) the back, supine" jB, of human posture; < *naparqudu*

purru; Hurr. pl. *purrena* mng. uncl. Alal., desig. of land-holding; = *pūru* II ?

purru → also *pūru* I

purrû I adj. mng. unkn. Bogh., jB lex.

purrûm II **D** mng. unkn. OAkk

purrudum "terrified" OB; < *parādu* I

purruru; f. also *purruštu* "dispersed, scattered" M/jB; of family, pot; "dismantled"? of equipment; < *parāru*

purrusum mng. uncl. OB; f. pl. *purrusētum*, desig. of cows; < *parāsu* I

purrušiš "flatteringly" OB; < *parāšu*

purrušu mng. uncl. jB lex., desig. of meat

pursaggu/û → *bursaggu*

pursandu, *peršantu* (a material) MB, in desig. of gold ring, stone vessel

pursāsu(m) ~ "(rear) lock of hair" O/jB, on figure

pursiktu → *buršiktu*

pursilû "1 *qa* vessel" jB [BUR.SÌLA]; < Sum.

pursindu, *pursittu*; pl. *pursimētu* (or *bur...*) ~ "vein"? jB, Ug. in *p. dāmi* "*p.* of blood"

pursītu(m), lex. *pursû* "(offering) bowl" [DUG.BUR.ZI]; of clay, wood, metal, stone; < Sum.; → *pūru* I

pursû → *pursītu*; *purussû*

purṣātu → *purdātu*

purṣimd/tu → *burṣimtu*

puršas/šillu → *buršašillu*

puršatta "like a flea" OB(Susa); < *perša'um* ?

puršiktu → *buršiktu*

puršumtu, *puršuntu* "old woman" jB; < *puršumu*

puršumu(m), NA *paršumu*, pl. *paršalumūte* "old (man)" O/jB, NA [NA (LÚ.)AB.BA]; NA f.pl. *paršumāte* "greyness" of beard; > *paršumu*, *puršumtu*

puršuntu → *puršumtu*

puršušallû → *buršašillu*

puršu'u → *perša'um*

purûm "abuse" OA, esp. *p. šakānum* "to abuse" s.o.; < *parû* III

pūru I, *purru* "(stone) bowl" MA, M/jB [BUR]; esp. *šaman p.* "oil from bowl"; for food, butter; of 3 gur; < Sum.; → *burgû; burmāḫu*; *bur=saggu*; *burzigallu* etc.; *pursītu*

pūru(m) II "lot" Ass., Nuzi, Emar, NB; MA *p. salā'u* "to cast a lot"; M/NA "(plot of land chosen by) lot"; NA "lot" for selection of (eponym's) name, "eponymate"; → *purru*

puruḫlibnu (an aromatic essence) NB; < Aram.

purukkû ~ "backlog in payment"? MB, NB; < *parāku*

purullum → *burullum*

purunzaḫu → *pirinzaḫu*

purupuḫu → *puḫpuḫu*

purussā'um → *purussû*

purussu → *burussu*

purussû(m), OA *purussā'um*, j/NB also *pur(is)sû* "decision" [EŠ.BAR] on course of action; leg. *p. parāsum* "to pass a verdict", NB *p. dīni* "legal verdict"; of divine dispositions, *p. šamê u erṣeti* "d.s of heaven and earth", *bīt p.* "house of destinies"; of omens *p. kīnu* "reliable, firm d."; < *parāsu* I

purusutattesu (an official) NB; < Gk.

puru(t)tum (or *buru(t)tum*) (a garment) OAkk

puru'zu → *perša'um*

pusikku → *pušikku*

pusmu, *pussu* "sleeve" jB lex.

pussulu(m) "crippled" OAkk, O/jB; of foot, person, also as PN; (a kind of lapis lazuli); OAkk, desig. of copper vessel; < *pasālu*

pussumu, *pussunu(m)* "covered up, veiled" OAkk, jB; of goddess; f. (also *pussuttu*) lex. as subst., desig. of bride; OAkk as PN; < *pasāmu*

pussuqu mng. uncl. jB lex., epith. of place; < *pasāqu* ?

pussusu "erased, cancelled" jB lex.; < *pasāsu*

pussuttu → *pussumu*

pus'um "heavy perspirer"? OB lex.

pusukku → *busukku*

pusummu, *pusumtu*, OA *pusūnum*, MA *puṣūnu*, jB also *pašūmu* "veil" O/MA, jB; < *pasāmu*; *paṣānu*

pūṣā'a → *pūṣāya*

puṣādū pl. ~ "cuts (of meat)" NB; < *paṣādu*

pūṣā'ītu → *pūṣāya*

puṣammūtu "laundry work" NB; < *pūṣāya*

puṣāṣû pl. mng. uncl. j/NB, phps. "crumb(s), chopping(s)"; < *paṣāṣu* ?

puṣā'u → *pūṣāya*; *puṣû*

pūṣāya, *pūṣā'a*; f. *pūṣā'ītu* "launderer; laundress" NA, NB; < *pūṣu*; > *pūṣammūtu*

puṣû(m), MA *puṣā'u* "whiteness" OA, Mari desig. of a kind of gold; M/NA in *qaqqarē p.* "clear(ed) ground" for building (OA → *peṣû* I 2); < *peṣû* II

pūṣu(m) "whiteness; white spot" Bab. [BABBAR] on body, stone, planet; of mature grain *še' pūṣi* [NB ŠE.UD.E.DÈ]; < *peṣû* II; > *pūṣāya*, *pūṣammūtu*

puṣuddu, *paṣuddu* "mongoose"? jB lex.

puṣūnu → *pusummu*

pušḫatti "like a rat?" jB

pušḫu ~ "rat"? jB, NA; > *pušḫatti*

pušikku(m), Nuzi *pusikku(m)* "carded wool" Bab., OA [SÍK.GA.RÍG.AK.A]

puširtum, *pušiltu* "malt residue" O/jB lex.; < *pašāšu*

pušku "span" NA, NB as linear measure, 1/6 cubit; < Aram.

pušqu(m), MB also *pulqu* "narrowness; straits" [PAP.ḪAL] **1.** "narrow place", *p. ḫuršāni* "mountain defile"; "constriction" in liver **2.** transf. "hardship, (dire) straits", also pl.; PN *Uṣi-ina-pušqī* "He escaped from trouble"; < *pašāqu*

puššānītu → *buššānītu*

puššurtum "solution"? Mari, for illness; < *pašāru*

putānātum f. pl. (a bread or pastry) OB; < *patānu* I

pūtānu/û "with (high) brow"? MA as PN; < *pūtu*

putinnu → *butinnu*

pūtiš "opposite"? OB in *pūtiš nāri* "opposite the river"; < *pūtu*

putqudu → *pitqudu*

putru(m) (or *pudru(m)*) "animal droppings, dung" Bab., NA; crushed, in baskets; jB med.; NA *p. sūqi* "street dung" desig. of pigeon

puttu ~ "prince" jB lex.; *šikar p.* (a kind of beer) jB med.

puttû "opened" jB; mng. uncl. as desig. of a kind of cooked meat; desig. of leek; "flowing" water; < *petû* II; M/NA → *pattû* II

puttuḫum "pierced" OB of sieve, box; < *patāḫu* D

puttulu "twisted, twined" jB, of parts of liver; < *patālu* D

pūtu(m) I f.; pl. OB *pâtum*, MA, MB *pūtātu* "forehead, brow" [SAG.KI; SAG; ZAG] **1.** of person: in legal procedures, with *ebēbu*, *elēlu* etc. "to be clear, clear s.o." of claims, O/MB *p. emēdu(m)* "to guarantee", *p. maḫāṣu* "to act as guarantor", *p. (eṭēri) našû* "to bear responsibility for (payment)"; *pūssu ikabbit* "he will be honoured" **2.** of animal, bird: j/NB rit. *p. immeri lapātu* "to touch the sheep's brow"; math. *p. alpim* 'ox's forehead' = "trapezoid" **3.** "front (side)" of plot of land (opp. of long side (*šiddu*)), of river, sea; "frontage" of building; "front" of furniture **4.** NB *pūt zitti* "preferential share" **5.** *ina/ša pūt* "opposite", spatially, topog.; NA "in the presence of"; MB "because of, on account of"; NA "in respect of, in requital for"; > *pūtānu*, *pūtiš*; → *māḫiṣ-pūtūtu*

pūtu II "opening" NA in *pūt upni* "prayer bowl"; < *petû* II; *upnu*

pūtuḫḫu "responsibility" NA in *p. našû* "to be responsible" for duty, for payment; → *puḫḫu* ?

puṭāru(m) "grazing bull"? O/jB; < *paṭāru*

puṭṭuru "released" j/NB; NB of slave, house; lex. *p. īni* (a bird); < *paṭāru*

puṭūru I (a mushroom)? NA

puṭūru II "release, ransom" jB lex., NB; < *paṭāru*

puwati → *puati*

puzriš → *puzru* 1

puzru(m), *puzuru*; pl. f. "concealment" [PUZUR4; PÙZUR; Ass. MAN] **1.** OAkk, OA, OB "shelter" of deity, in PNs and PlNs, e.g. *Puzriš-Dagan* "Under the protection of D."; *Puzur-DN* **2.** "concealment, hiding-place", *p. ṣabātum, aḫāzu(m), emēdu(m)* etc. "to take refuge"; *ina p. šakānu* "to stow s.th. away"; *ina p.* "secretly" **3.** *puzur bīti* "secret part of house", "recesses" of words, mountains; ext. (part of liver); jB *puzur nūni* uncl. (OB → *budūru*); < *pazāru*; → *bussurtu*

puzzuru(m); MB f. *punzurtu* "concealed" O/MB of divine dwelling; as (f)PN; < *pazāru D*

Q

qa → *qû* II

qa'ālum ~ "to gather"? Mari, troops

qabaltīu, NA *qabassīu* "central" M/NA [MÚRU-]; < *qabaltu*

qabaltu(m), NA *qabassu*, *qabsu* "middle" Bab., NA [MÚRU-] spatially, *qablat*/*qabalti*/*qabsi āli* "city centre"; NA, NB as prep. "among"; lex. in *q. qaqqadi* mng. uncl.; < *qablu* I

qabāru → *qebēru*

qabassīu → *qabaltīu*

qabassu → *qabaltu*

qabātu → *ḫabātu* IV

qabā'u → *qabû* II

qabbaṣu → *gabbaṣu*

qabbā'u(m) "reporter?, informer?" OB, as official; < *qabû* II

qabbiru ~ "burial priest" jB lex.; < *qebēru*

qabbum → *gabbu* I

qabḫu (or *qapḫu*) (a vessel) NA, of copper

qābiānu(m) "the speaker (of particular words)" NA; OA in PN ?; < *qabû* II

qābiš "like a dyke" jB; < *qābu*

qabītu "spoken, expressible" jB, in *lā q.* "unspeakable (things)"; < *qabû* II

qābītu f. "speaker" NA, of Ištar; < *qabû* II

qabla "(in) the middle" OB in *alpum ša q.* [GU4.ÁB.MÚRU] "central ox" (of team); Mari as prep. *ina q.* "in the middle of"; OA *i(q)-qabla* "in the middle"; < *qablu* I

qablāni "central part" OAkk in *in q.* "in the middle of"; < *qablu* I

qabli "in the middle of" OAkk; < *qablu* I

qablītu(m) "centre, central part" [MÚRU-] **1.** "central part" of chariot, door; OB interval of 2nd and 5th lyre-strings; also a lyre-tuning; "middle" of body, hand, organs **2.** "interior, inside" of land, heaven; astr. "node"; OB *ina q.* "within" liquid, herd **3.** jB lex. of Sum. vb. infix **4.** "middle (watch)" of the night; also *maṣṣartu q.* [EN.NUN.MÚRU(.BA)] **5.** OA, Mari (a container) of wood, metal; OA *q. errûm* "to uncover the *q.*" (→ *murrûm* II) **6.** NB (a garment) **7.** OB "balance, scales" **8.** transf. in *qablīt šanîm mullû* "make up the other's portion"; < *qablû*

qablīu → *qablû*

qablu(m) I "hips; middle" [MÚRU] **1.** "hips, waist" of human, god, animal, also du.; *(ṣubātu/e) ša q.* "loincloth"; *q. rakāsu* "to gird loins" i.e. "to fit out, equip"; *q. paṭāru* "to ungird loins" OB of freeing slave, jB of ceasing work, also for battle; transf. du. (part of gall) **2.** "belt, girdle"? **3.** "middle"; of parts of body, objects, building, city, sea etc.; of time, *q. ūmi*/*mūši* "middle of day/night", also loc.-adv. e.g. *qablu ūmi*; *ina q. tidūki* etc. "in the midst of battle"; *nīd q.* → *nīdu*; > *qabla*, *qablāni*, *qabli*; *qabaltu*; *qablû*, *qablītu*

qablu(m) II f. & m. "battle" [MÚRU; OB also ŠEN.ŠEN] *q. epēšu* "to do battle"; *q. lā maḫār* "irresistible onslaught"; (f)DN *bēl(et) q.* "lord/lady of battle" as title; > *qitbulu*, *muqtablu*

qablu III "plantation" of trees NA [MÚRU]

qablû(m), OAkk, O/MA *qablīu(m)* "central" [MÚRU-] of field, gate, beam etc.; jB lex. of plough-ox; of parts of exta; NB of action "intermediate" in time; gramm. "infixed"; of textiles etc. "middling", "of medium quality"; < *qablu* I

qabru(m) "grave, tomb" OA, O/jB [URUGAL (=AB×GAL)]; > *qebēru*

qabsu → *qabaltu*

qabû I "animal pen" j/NB; for sheep, geese etc.; OB(Susa) mng. uncl.; > *qabuttu*

qabû(m) II, OAkk, Ass. *qabā'u(m)* "to say, speak, command" **G** (*i/i*) [DU11; DU11.GA; E] **1.** "speak" (absol.) to s.o. (= dat.); esp. before dir. speech, or *kī'am* ("thus"); "promise, agree"; comm. of word etc. "mean, imply" **2.** "say, pronounce" word, decision, judgement; good, evil; prayer, cry; "instruct, command", of deity "decree" life, death **3.** "recount" deeds etc. **4.** "name, call (by name)" field, river etc.; "designate, nominate" s.o. **5.** with acc. infin., e.g. OA *šaqālam qab'āti* "you (f.) are directed to pay" **6.** infin. as subst. "promise; prayer; agreement; speech; instruction"; *qabâm šakānu(m)* "make promise", "give undertaking", om. "make a prognostication"? **Gtn** iter. **D** O/jB "wail, lament" **Š** caus. of G; of exorcist "make" patient "recite"; NA "have order given" **N** pass. OA *ša naqbu'im iqqibi* "what was to be said was said"; > *qabītu*; *qābītu*, *qābiānu*; *qību*, *qibītu*; *qubû*; *muqabbû*; *naqbītu*; *taqbû*?; *qabbā'u*

qābu "dyke" jB lex.; > *qābiš*

qâbu → *qâpu*

qabūru → *qubūru*

qabuttu "(animal) stall" NA for donkeys, NB for sheep, birds etc.; < *qabû* I

qabūtu; NA pl. *qabuāti* "bowl" NA, NB for liquids

qadādu(m) "to bow down" OAkk, Bab. **G** (*u/u*, Bogh. also *a/u*) *appīl/a-*, *kišād- q.* "bow face, neck" (in dejection); of temple *rēšāšu q.* "bow its head"; jB absol. "bow o.s."; Mari transf. "be inclined to, compliant with" **Gtn** [GAM.GAM] *kišādsu q.* "repeatedly bow his neck"; of date palm **D** trans. *appa-*, *lētā- q.* "bow face, cheeks", transf. "subject" enemy at o.'s feet **Š** caus. *appa- š.* "make s.o. bow face"; > *qaddu*, *qaddiš*, *qaddadāniš*; *qiddatu*; *qiddu*?

qadāpu mng. unkn NB **G** (*i/i*)

qadaruttu? mng. uncl. NA

qadāšu(m) "to be(come) pure" OAkk, OA, Bab. **G** lex.; Am. of deity; Ug. stat., of house "is cleared" (of claims?) **D** "purify", OAkk oil; cultically, person, animal, implement, OA in judicial ritual; Mari "dedicate as *qadištum*" **Dt** pass. of D "cleanse o.s."; > *qaššu*, *qadištu*; *qadšūtu*, *quddušu*; → *qašādu*

qadā'um (or *qatā'um*) ~ "to consent"? OA **G** (or = *katûm* II "to become poor")?

qaddadāniš, *qadd(ān)iš*, *qiddadāniš* adv. "bowed down, bent over" O/jB of person's gait; < *qaddu*

qaddu(m) "bowed down, bent over" O/jB lex., of date palm, part of body; < *qadādu*

qadi → *qadum*

qadiltu → *qadištu*

qadilû, *kadilû* ~ (a cloak) jB lex.

qadištu(m), MA, MB *qadiltu*, NA *qadissu*, Mari also *qaššatum* (a type of priestess) [(MUNUS.)NU.GIG]; MB also as fPN; < *qaššu*; → *qašdatu*

qadma ~ "in presence of" OAkk; < *qadmu*

qadmiš "previously" jB; < *qadmu*

qadmu(m) **1.** OB "former time" **2.** O/jB as desig. of god, usu. pl.; lit. phps. "pre-eminent"; > *qadmiš*; *qudmu* etc.; → *aqdamum*; *qadūmum*

qadru → *kadru*

qadšūtu "status of a *qdš*-cultic servant" Ug.; < *qaššu*; → *qašdūtu*

qadu → *qadum*

qadû(m) I "owl" O/jB [URU.ḪUL.A.MUŠEN]; *q. iṣṣūr Ea* "owl, bird of Ea" calls *tukkutukku*; blood of *q.* as drug; > *qadû* II

qadû II "to screech like an owl" O/jB **G** (*i/i*, Mari *u/u*) **D** in comm., mng. uncl. (**N** → *qâdu* N); < *qadû* I denom.

qadû III (a kind of bread) MB; → *qadūtu*

qadû → also *qadūtu*

qâdu "to ignite" M/jB **G** (*ū*; lex. also *qiādu*) fire, torch etc.; "set fire to" building, tree; MB stat. transf., of mood "is fired, ardent" **N** pass. (pret. *iqqadi*) jB of fire "be ignited"; > *qīdātu*

qadum, *qadu*, OA freq., jB occas. *qadi* "together with, including" O/MA, O/jB, M/NB(lit.) **1.** as prep. with subst.; OA *qadi-ma tertika* "following your instructions" **2.** with pron. suff. OA *qadi-a/ni/šu-ma* "with me/us/him"; O/MB *qaduššu*, *qadukku* "with him", "with you" **3.** of place, time "as far as, up to" **4.** as conj. Mari "until", "because", *q. lā* "before"; MA *q. balṭutūni* "as long as she is alive"; NA etc. → *adi* 1

qadūmum (desig. of an adze) Mari, in *pāš q.*; → *qadmu*

qadurtu mng. unkn. NA

qadūtu(m), *qaduttu*, *qadû*? "silt; dregs, lees" O/jB, NA [IM.GÚ] as material for wall-plaster; of deposit in eyes; as drug; *q. šikāni* "river-silt"?; *q. adatti* (dirt from bird's nest) as drug; *q. šikari* "beer-dregs"; NA *akal q.* (a kind of bread), pl. *qaduāti*

qaḫālum "to assemble" (trans.) Mari **G** (*i/i*); < W.Sem.?

qakdâ/û → *kaqdâ*

qalālu(m) I "to be(come) light, weak, slight" **G** (*i/i*) [LAL] in quantity "be(come) (too) few, (too) small"; of limbs "be light", i.e. feel right; of wine "be poor quality"; of word, of person "be lightly regarded, despised", also *qaqqad X iqallil* "X will be belittled" **D** "reduce" amount, payment; "produce poorly, spoil" garment, beer; "despise, humiliate, dishonour" person, also *qaqqad X q.*; of pig "defile" **Dtn** iter. of D, also of Dt **Dt** pass. of D, of slave "be humiliated"; > *qallu* I, *qallatu*, *qalliš*, *qalluttu*; *qallalu*; *qulālu*, *qalullā'um*; *qullulum*; *maqlālu*; *muqallilum*; → *qallissu*

qalālu II NA **Nt** *attaqallalla* "I hang down"; → *šuqallulu*

qalāpu(m) "to peel" Bab., NA **G** (*a/u*) reed, onion; "hatch" bird from egg, "strip off" covering; "skin" lizard etc. **D** ~ G "strip of, free from" husk, covering, skin **N** pass. of G, of onion "be peeled"; > *qalpu*; *qilpu*; *qulpu*; *qalīpu*; *quliptu*; *qallupu*

qaldu → *qašādu*; *qašdu*

qāli mng. unkn. MA

qalīpu (a plant) jB lex.; < *qalāpu*

qâliš "silently" jB; < *qâlu*

qalītu usu. pl. "parched grain" M/NA [ŠE.SA.A] as food, also for horses; < *qalû* I

qālītum f. "roaster" **1.** OB "(female) grain-parcher" **2.** NA (vessel for parching); < *qalû* II

qallalu; NA f. phps. *qal(las)su* "very small" NA, NB; of child, object; silver "of low value"; NB pl. *qallalūtu* "slave boys"; < *qallu* I

qallatu(m) "female slave" Bab., esp. NB; < *qallu* I

qallissu "slave girl" NA; also "urgent" or "slight"?; < Aram. *qallīlā* ?

qalliš "lightly" jB; of oath-taking etc.; "slightly"; < *qallu* I

qallu(m) I, NA also *qālu* "light, little, slight" Bab., NA [NA QÀL] **1.** "light" of vehicle, implement, vessel, troops; NA of "light" mina, talent etc. (opp. *dannu*); transf., of oath, illness **2.** "small" of person, animal, building etc. **3.** "few" of animals, "little" of water **4.** "slight, unimportant" of word; of person, esp. NB "slave" [LÚ.QÀL] **5.** lex. "impure"; < *qalālu* I; > *qallatu*, *qalliš*; *qalluttu*; *qallalu*

qallu II "forest" Am., jB

qallû (or *gallû*) "(human) genitals" jB; < Sum.

qallupu "peeled" NA, of figs; < *qalāpu* D

qalluttu "slavery, service"? Ug.; < *qallu* I 4

qalmu "small" jB lex.

qalpu "stripped, peeled" M/NB [BAR] of tree, reed; of fish "scaled"; of textile "worn"; < *qalāpu*

qalqallu (a grill, brazier) jB lex., of clay or metal

qalqālu (desig. of spices) M/jB med.

qaltu → *qaštu*

qalû I "roasted, parched" M/NB, NA [BIL; BÍL] of plant, meat; NB of metal "refined"; jB of person "burnt"; < *qalû* II

qalû(m) II "to roast; burn" **G** (*u/u*, later also *i/i*) [GÍBIL; jB also BIL] persons, sacrifice, figurine; city, clothing; medical ingredients; NA "refine" silver; *išātam/ina i. q.* "burn with fire"; also intrans., of fire **D** ~ G "roast" grain; "burn" harvest, door, city **N** pass. of G; > *qalû* I, *qalītu*; *qīlu*; *qilûtu*; *qālû*, *qālītum*; *qullû*; *maqlû*, *maqlūtu*

qālu ~ "thick"? jB lex.

qālu → also *qallu* I

qālû "roasting (oven)" jB lex.; < *qalû* II

qâlu(m) "to pay attention; be silent" Bab., M/NA **G** (*ū*) [ME.ME (pl.)] "attend" to s.o., s.th., to order, to words; "respect, look after" s.o.; Am. "be silent", M/jB, NA "keep silent" (about s.th.) **Gtn** iter.; esp. infin. *qitayyulu* "anxious silence" **Š** OB, esp. Mari "make s.o. aware of, attend to" s.th.; > *qâliš*; *qūltu*, *qūlu*; *qayyalu*

qâlu → also *qiālu*

qalullā'um "disrespect" OA, pl.; < *qalālu* I

qamāmu, *kamāmu* "to stand up" jB lex. **G** of hair, or trans. "dress" hair?; > *qammatum*, *qimmatu*

qamḫurû "palm pith" or "bud" jB lex.

qammatum (a priestess) Mari; < *qamāmu*

qamû I "burnt, parched" jB; < *qamû* II

qamû(m) II "to burn (up)" **G** (*i/i* or *u/u*) building, city; enemies (occas. figuratively); transf. "burn" heart, NB of saltpetre "consume" brickwork **D** ~ G liter. and transf. **Dt** pass. jB of flesh "be burned up" **Š** NB "cause" fire (*Gira*) "to burn" s.th.; > *qamû* I; *qimītu*; *naqmītu*

qamû → also *qemûm*

qanānu(m) "to nest" O/jB, NA **G** (*a/u*, also *u/u*, jB also *i/i*) of bird "make a nest" obj. *qinnu*, also transf. of persons; absol. of bird "nest"; < *qinnu* denom.; > *qannu* I, *qanīnu*

qanānu → also *kanānu*

qanā'u → *qanû* II

qandalu (a metal object) Mari, of silver; = *qandalû* ?

qandalû (an irrigation pipe) NB; < *qanû* I + *dalû* II; → *qandalu*

qanduppu (an insect, phps.) "leech" lex. in *q. margutu*

qanīnu "(built) nest"? jB lex.; < *qanānu*

qānītu mng. unkn. NA, an object; < *qanû* II ?

qannā'u "jealous" Bogh.; < W.Sem.; → *qenû*

qannu I "built" jB lex. of a nest; < *qanānu*

qannu(m) II f. "fringe; border" [SI] **1.** "fringe, hem" of garment **2.** "horn" (usu. → *qarnu*) **3.** j/NB "animal pen, stall" **4.** M/NA, Nuzi "boundary, borders", "environs" **5.** NA as prep. etc. *q. aḫā/ē'iš* "together; mutually"; *issi q.* "instead of"; *ina q. meḫrīya* "in association with my colleagues"; *(ina) q.* as conj. "as soon as" + subjunct.; = *qarnu*

qannun(t)u → *qunnunu*

qan šalālu(m), *qan šalāli* (a type of reed) Bab., Bogh. [GI.ŠUL.ḪI(.A)] med., rit., mag.; < *qanû* I + *šalālu*

qan ṭuppi(m), *qanṭuppu*, *qarṭuppu*; pl. m. & f. "writing reed, stylus" Bab., NA [GI.DUB.BA]; *bēl q.* as divine epith.; also *q.*, as divine symbol of Nabû etc., as brand on animal, slave; < *qanû* I + *ṭuppu*

qanû(m) I; pl. m. & f. "reed, cane" [GI; OB pl. m. GI.ḪI.A] **1.** as plant, in reed-beds; → *qan šalālu*; *q. ṭābu* "sweet reed" [GI.DÙG.GA], an aromatic **2.** as building, or craft material, e.g. *q. šipri* 'work-reed'; NA *ša muḫḫi qanâte* "reed officer" **3.** as shaft of weapon; "arrow" **4.** as musical "pipe"; "tube" of stone, metal **5.** as part of weighing-scales **6.** as measuring instrument, *q. mindati*; as metrological unit = 6 (NB 7) cubits, half nindan (c. 3 metres); NB "(square) reed" = 49 sq. cubits, also desig. of "house plot"; > *qandalû*, *qan ṭuppi*

qanû(m) II, *qanā'u* **G** **1.** OB (*i/i*) "to keep possession of" slave etc. **2.** NA (*u/u*) "to acquire" **D** MB mng. uncl. **N** OA of house "be acquired"?; > *qinītu*; *qānītu*?

qanūnum → *ganūnum* II

qapālu → *kapālu*

qapḫu → *qabḫu*

qapīru (a container) NA for fish, dates; < Aram.

qappatu(m) "(palm-leaf) basket" Bab. [GI.GAM.MA]; *ēpiš q.* "basket-maker"; → *quppu* II

qapsīdum (or *gap/bsīdum*) "edge (of garment)"? OB

qapû "to turn upward" NB **G** stat., of part of nose; < Aram.

qāpu (a stone item) Bogh.

qâpu(m), NA also *qâbu* "to fall down, collapse" Bab., NA **G** (*ū*) [DIRI]; also "sag" of wall, beam **D** stat. "is completely collapsed" **Š** caus. stat. "was allowed to collapse"; > *qayyapu*; *quppu* I

qâpu → also *qiāpu*

qaqānu (a sea-bird) jB lex.

qaqdâ/û → *kaqdâ*

qaqqadānu loc.-adv. "on its head, headlong" jB; < *qaqqadu*

qaqqadānû(m); f. *qaqqadānītu* "with large head" [SAG.DU-]; of human, esp. as (f)PN; OB also transf. "prominent"; lex. as desig. of bird, locust, plant, vegetable; < *qaqqadu*

qaqqadu(m), *kaqqadu(m)*; pl. f. "head; capital" [SAG.DU; SAG] **1.** liter. "head" of human, deity, animal, figurine etc. **2.** "person", "self"; OA pl. "(serving) man" **3.** "leading person", freq. pl., as community leaders **4.** "upper part, top" of object, part of body, building etc.; "crown" of date palm **5.** "beginning" of time-period; "starting point" in field; "original, initial amount"; "capital" in silver, grain etc.; *q. rēdîm* "the original (holder of office of) soldier" **6.** jB $^{(na_4)}$*q.* (a stone) **7.** Mari *q. rašûm* "to get the upper hand, get ahead" **8.** OA "poll-tax"; > *qaqqadānu*, *qaqqadānû*, *qaqqadû*; *kaqdâ*?

qaqqadû (or *sagdû*) "headband" jB lex.; < *qaqqadu* (or Sum.)

qaqqariš "(down) to the ground" jB(roy. inscr.), of destroyed building; of supplicant; < *qaqqaru*

qaqqaršu(m), *kaqqaršu* "onto the ground" OA, O/jB, usu. with *maqātu(m)* ("to fall"); *q. manû* "to raze to ground"; < *qaqqaru* (→ GAG §67g)

qaqqaru(m), *kaqqaru(m)*; pl. m. & f. "ground, earth" [KI] **1.** "the earth" as opp. to sky, sea; jB as desig. of underworld ? **2.** "(the) ground" as a surface **3.** "terrain, territory", *q. nakri* "enemy territory", *q. dannum* "difficult terrain" **4.** "(plot of) ground", esp. for building(s) **5.** "stretch, extent of land", esp. in measurements, e.g. *X bēr qaqqaru* "X miles distance" **6.** astr. "district" of constellation **7.** "base, floor" of boat, brazier etc. **8.** ext. (part of liver) **9.** "(blank) space" on cuneiform tablet **10.** Nuzi, Ug. (desig. of wool, textile) mng. uncl.; > *qaqqariš*, *qaqqaršu*

qaqqullu → *kakkullu*

qaqû(m) (a bird) Bab.; → *qaquttu*

qāqullu (a plant, phps.) "*Elettaria cardamomum*" M/NB, providing wood for divine symbol; *išid q.* "root of *q.*", *qēm q.* "flour from *q.*"; also (a bird)

qāqultu (a divine symbol) NA

qaquttu (a bird) jB lex., sim. to *qaqû*

qarābu "battle" NA(jB), esp. *q. uppušu* "to do battle"; < Aram.

qarābu → also *qerēbu*

qarādu(m) "to be warlike" **G** stat. → *qardu* **D** "strengthen, encourage" weak person; > *qardu, qardūtu; qurdu; qarrādu, qarrādūtu; qurādu, qurādūtum; qitrudu; taqrīdu*

qarādu → also *garādu*

qarāḫu "to freeze" NA **G** (*u/u*) in *qarḫu q.* "frost freezes"; > *qarḫu*

qarāmu "to cover, overlay with (= acc.)" M/NA **G** stat. *ṣarpa qarim* "is overlaid with silver" **D** jB lex., mng. unkn.; > *qermu*

qarānu(m), *garānu(m)* "to stack up, pile on" Bab. **G** (*a/u*) straw, tribute etc. **D** ~ G "store up" grain, oil; wealth; "pile up" corpses **Dt** pass. of D **Št** "store up", "heap up" goods etc.; > *qurunnu, qurunniš; qitrunu; taqrintu; maqrānu, maqrāniš*

qarāru(m), *garāru(m)* "to writhe, grovel" Bab., NA **G** (*u/u*) stat., of water, part of liver etc., house roof "be wavy, ribbed"; of animal "roll, wallow", of soldiers "grovel" **Gtn** iter. of G **D** "drip, trickle" liquid down, esp. med. **Š** caus. "make s.o grovel" (→ *šugarruru*) **N** (*naq/garruru*) ~ G "grovel", "roll (on ground)"; of water "roll, meander?"; Mari of word "stir" in heart **Ntn** iter., of man, snake, bird, part of exta; > *qarru; qarūru; qirīru; qāriru; qarrāru?; qarrurtu; qurruru; taqrirtu; maqarratu?; magarru?, mugerru?;* → *išqarrurtu*

qarāšu(m), *garāšu* "to chop up" Bab., NA **G** (*a/u*) [KÍD] wood, meat **D** ~ G "knock down"? dates; "chew up" tongue; > *qeršu* I; *qurraštu; qarrišu; qaršum?*

qarā'u → *qerû*

qarbāte pl. mng. uncl. NA, with pron. suff.

qarbatu → *qerbetu*

qarbītu (a cultic garment) NB; < *qerbû* ?

qarbu → *qerbu* II; *qurbu*

qarbûm → *qerbû*

qarbuḫu (a plant) jB lex.

qarda(m)mu, occas. *qurdāmu* "enemy, adversary" jB

qardanānu → *karatnannu*

qardu(m); f. *qarittu* "valiant, heroic", of deity, king, heart etc.; jB f. pl. as subst. "heroism"; < *qarādu*

qardu → also *gardu* I

qardumum → *gardumum*

qardūtu "heroism, warriorhood" M/NA, M/NB; < *qardu*

qarḫu; pl. f. "ice, frost" jB, NA; < *qarāḫu*

qāribu (an edible bird) NA

qāriru(m) mng. uncl. OB?, Nuzi; < *qarāru*

qarittu → *qardu*

qarītu(m), *qirītu* "grain-store" Bab., M/NA [ÉSAG]; MA, Nuzi *bīt q.* "granary"; NB also for dates

qarītu → also *qerītu*

qariu → *qarû*

qarnānû; f. *qarnānītu* "horned" Bogh., jB; lex., desig. of wild bull; of sprouting malt; of alkali; < *qarnu*

qarnu(m); du. & pl. f. "horn" [SI] **1.** of animal, esp. as drinking vessel; of figurine etc.; on temple; of deity **2.** transf. "power" of human; "horn(-shaped feature)" of heavenly body; "shoot" of plant, tree; in oil-stain; on part of liver, of body; on ship, cart **3.** "fringe" of garment (usu. → *qannu* II), also transf. *q. šībâti* "threshold of old age"; > *qarnānû, qarnû, qurnātum*; = *qannu* II

qarnû, *qarrānû* "horned" jB; desig. of sheep, fetters; of salicornia (*uḫūlu*); < *qarnu*

qarrādu(m); pl. also *qarrādūtu* "warlike; hero, warrior" [UR.SAG] of god, king; "warriors" in army; jB of heart, mind "heroic"; < *qarādu*

qarrādūtu(m) "heroism" Bab., NA; < *qarrādu*

qarrānû → *qarnû*

qarrāru; pl. f. (a garment) NA; < *qarāru* ?

qarratḫu (a plant) jB lex.

qarrātu(m) pl. (a festival in Aššur) Ass. in MN *waraḫ/uraḫ Qarrātim*; OA also sg. "invitation"?; < *qerû*

qarrišu, *qarsu* (a caterpillar) jB; < *qarāšu*

qarru "crooked"? jB, epith. of track (*kibsu*); < *qarāru*

qarruḫu "bald"? NA, of old animal; < Aram.

qarrurtu (a leather object) M/NA; < *qarāru*

qarrutu mng. unkn. jB lex.; OA → *qarrātu*

qarsu → *qarrišu*

qaršum mng. uncl. Mari, epith. of textiles; < *qarāšu* ?

qartappu → *kartappu*

qarṭuppu → *qan ṭuppi*

qarû, *qariu* "invited" NA of guests; < *qerû*

qarû → also *karû* I; *qerû*

qāru (an ornament) M/NA in gold

qarūru subst. "rolling back, recession"? jB, of waters; < *qarāru*

qaspu (or *qazpu*) (an iron implement) NA

qaṣirtu (or *kaṣirtu*) mng. unkn. MB lex.

qaṣṣabitti → *qātu* 9

qaṣûm → *kaṣûm* II

qašādu(m) "to be(come) pure" O/jB, MA **G** stat. **D** "purify", "consecrate" person; > *qašdu*, *qašdatu*, *qašdūtu*; *quššudu*; → *qadāšu*

qašbu "dried dates" NB; < Aram.

qašdatu(m) Mari, jB var. of *qadištu*; < *qašdu*

qašdu(m) "pure, holy" O/jB, of deity, temple, offerings; < *qašādu*; > *qašdatu*, *qašdūtu*

qašdūtu "status of a *qdš*-cultic servant" jB lex. var. of *qadšūtu*; < *qašdu*

qašittum (a net) O/jB lex.

qaššatum → *qadištu*

qaššu(m); f. *qadištu* "holy; dedicated" OA, O/jB; OA of building, as desig. of cultic personnel; jB as epith. of river; < *qadāšu*; *qadištu*; *qadšūtu*

qaštu(m), *qaltu* "bow" [GIŠ.PAN] **1.** for hunting, battle; Akkadian, Cimmerian **2.** *awīl/ṣāb(ē) q.* etc. "archers, archery units" **3.** *eqēl/bīt q.* "bow-field/estate" (of military colonists) **4.** MB, NA *bīt q.* "bowcase" **5.** "bow-star" [MUL/MÚL.PAN] (= Canis maior without Sirius ?) **6.** math. (a geometrical figure)

qaštu → also *qištu*

qâšu → *qiāšu*

qāta(qāta) → *qātu*

qatālum "to kill" OB, esp. Mari **G** (*a/u*) in *ḫâram/ḫârī q.* "kill ass(es)" to solemnize treaty **Š** caus. of G; < W.Sem. *qtl*

qātam "at once, immediately" Mari, in *qātam ana qātassumma*; < *qātu*

qātamma "just so, just as" Mari, MB(Alal.), Am., Bogh.; "in the same way as"; Mari also *qātam q/kātamma*; < *qātu*

qatānu(m) "to be(come) thin, narrow" **G** (*i/i*; stat. *qatan*) [SIG] of door, wall foundation, part of body; transf., of illness, voice **D** "make thin" file of soldiers; > *qatnu*; *qatunu*?; *qutnum*; *qutānu*, *qutandu*; *qattanu*; *qattinu*?, *qattinnūtu*?; *quttunum*

qatāpu(m), Mari *q/kaṭāpum* "to pluck" **G** (*a/u*) fruit from tree, also transf. "enjoy" sexual charms; "pluck" threads, from textile; "crop, pick off" head from oath-breaker, warriors out of battle **D** ~ G "pluck, pick off" fruit, warts **Dt** pass. of D **N** "be plucked"; > *qatpu*; *qitpu*; *qātipum*

qātaqāti → *qātu* 11

qatāru I "incense" NA, NB (pl. f.); < *qatāru* II infin.

qatāru II "to smoke" (intrans.) Bab., NA **G** (*u/u*) of fire, incense, cloud; transf. of person "be gloomy, depressed" **D** "smoke" (trans.) [SAR]; "burn" incense, "fumigate" s.o., s.th. with incense (= 2 acc.); "blacken with smoke", also transf. with illness, with depression **Dtn** iter. of D "repeatedly fumigate" **Dt** pass. "be blackened, darkened"; "be fumigated" **Š** caus. of G "make" flame, cloud, incense "smoke"; > *qatru*; *qutru*, *quturtu*; *qatāru* I, *qutāru*; *qutturu*; *qatrānu*?; *qutrēnum*; *maqtarum*; *muqattertu*; *taqtīru*

qatattu → *qatnu*

qatā'um → *qadā'um*; *qatû* II

qātīma "although"? OB; < *qātu*

qatinnu → *qattinu*

qātipum "(cloth-)plucker" OB lex.; < *qatāpu*

qātišam "hand by hand"? OB; < *qātu*

qatnu(m); f. *qatantu(m)*, *qatattu* "thin" [SIG] of thread, textile etc.; "slender" of person, part of body; "narrow" of street, gate; "weak" of beer; "fine, delicate" of craftsmanship; NA "junior" (< Aram.); < *qatānu*; > *qattanu*; → *qattinu*

qatpu(m) "plucked" OA, of textile; jB of fruit; < *qatāpu*

qatrānu "cedar resin"? jB lex.; < *qatāru* II ?

qatru "smoky" jB of oven; < *qatāru* II

qattanu(m) "very thin" O/jB of fibres, parts of body; < *qatnu*

qa(t)tinnūtu "status of a *qatinnu*" NA; < *qattinu*

qattinu, NA *qatinnu* (a rural class) M/NA, M/NB, also as PN; < *qatnu* ?; > *qattinnūtu*

qattītu mng. unkn. Bab. lex.

qattunu → *quttunum*

qatû I "ended, completed" j/NB of work, object; of education, training; "final" of result, report; < *qatû* II; > *qatûtu*

qatû(m) II, OAkk *qatā'um* "to come to an end, finish" OAkk, Bab. **G** (*i/i*) [TIL] of time, life, journey etc.; of drink etc. "be exhausted"; of person "(almost) die, be finished"; of building, work, accounts "be completed"; of tablet "is finished" in col. [also AL.TIL]; NA stat. of heart "is total(ly devoted)" to king; *lā qatê* "endlessly" **D** "bring to an end" [TIL], "destroy" person, land; "use up fully" food, water; "complete" period of time, sleep, meal; astr. ellipt. of eclipse, heavenly body "complete (its course)"; "pay", "carry out" work etc. "in full", NB in hendiad. "(do s.th.) in full" **Dt** pass. of

D "be completed, come to an end"; NB of claim, house "be achieved"; OB of grain *ina eṣēdi uqtatattû* "has been fully harvested" **Š** "complete" regnal years, (harvest on) field; "bring" life "to an end" **Št** pass. of Š; also "bring to completion"?; > *qatû* I, *qatûtu*; *qītu*; *quttû*, *quttûtum*; *taqtītu*

qātu(m) f.; du. *qātān* "hand" [ŠU; later ŠU.2 freq. for sg.] **1.** "hand" of human, deity; "paw" of lion; *ša q.* Am., Ug. f. "bracelet", NA "(bowl) for hand(-washing)"; O/jB *šāt q.* "(wooden) handcuffs"; *mīs qāti/ē* "(ritual) hand-washing"; *q.* + *emēdu* D "to lay hands" on s.th.; OA *q. maḫāṣum* "reject a request"; *q. nadû* "lay hands on" s.th., s.o.; *q. nasāḫu* "withdraw o.'s hand, cease an action", "reject a pledge"; *q. našû* "raise o.'s hand(s)" in prayer, *nīš qāti(m)* "hand-raising" (a prayer); *q. ṣabātu* "take hand(s)" to guide or help s.o., OB transf. *q. iṣabbat* "takes leave"; *q. šakānu* "lay hands on", also OA, NB *q. šakānu (ina muḫḫi)* "confiscate"; *q. turru* "guide s.o.'s hand away", MB "make s.o. renounce" a claim, jB "restrain s.o. from doing" s.th.; *q. (w)abālu(m) ana* "raise o.'s hand against", "start to do" s.th. **2.** OB "span" as measure of length **3.** "handle" of tool etc. **4.** transf. as source of action, power etc.: "hand(writing)", esp. in col.; Qatna "handiwork"; "achievement", "sphere of power, responsibility" etc.; *ina q.* "in/from s.o.'s possession, control"; ~ "influence" of god, demon as cause of illness, misfortune **5.** OA *qātum*, *ša q.* "of current quality, normal" of metal, textiles, *annak qātim* "disposable tin"; *ina qātim* "at hand, available" **6.** "list" on tablet; *q. aklim*, *šê* "list of bread, grain", workers etc. **7.** "share, portion" **8.** (unit of measurement), OB for palm fibres, NB for linen **9.** NA, NB *qāt ṣibitti*, NA also *qaṣṣabitti* "stolen goods; red-handed" **10.** usu. pl. *qātātu(m)* "surety, pledge" [ŠU.DU$_8$/DÙ.A], OA "guarantor"; OB *q. leqû* "to stand surety" for (= *ana*) s.o.; NA *bēl q.* "guarantor" **11.** in prep. & adv. use: OA *qāta qāta* "proportinately"; MA *ana qāt*, *aqqāt* "more than, over and above"; *ina qāt* "by agency of, through"; Mari *qātam ana qātim*, *qātaqāti* etc. "at once, immediately"; NA *qātāya* "(myself) in person", *šapal*, *šapla/i qāti* "underhand, secretly"; > *qātam*, *qātamma*; *qātišam*; *qātīma*; → *izqātu*; *šinqātu*

qatunu (a mountain plant) jB(MA$^?$) med.; < *qatānu* ?

qatûtu "state of completion" MB; < *qatû* I

qaṭāpum → *qatāpu*

qaṭû ~ "to come up" to (= *ana*) NB; < Aram.

qāṭû "wood-cutter" NB; < Aram.

qa'u → *qû* II

qâ'u → *gâ'u*

qawali (or *kawali*); pl. *q/kawalena* (an object in gold) MB(Alal.); < Hurr.; → *kawalzuru*

qāyipānu(m) "the lender, creditor" O/MB, MA; < *qāyipu*

qāyipānūtu(m) "function of the lender" O/jB in *q. epēšu(m)* "to act as the lender"; < *qāyipānu*

qāyipu "lender, creditor" jB lex.; < *qiāpu*

qayyalu(m) "attentive" O/jB, of worshipper etc.; also as desig. of a demon; < *qâlu*

qayyapu "tottering, liable to collapse" NB of wall, earth; < *qâpu*

qayyašu "generous, liberal" jB; < *qiāšu*

qayyātu(m), *gayyātu*, *ka'ātu*, *kâtu* (a parched grain product) Bab.

qazan (or *kazan*); pl. *q/kazanena* (a kind of wood)? MB(Alal.), as material of furniture; < Hurr.

qazpu → *qaspu*

qebēru(m), Ass. *qabāru* "to bury" Bab., M/NA **G** (*i/i*) human, animal, figurine, object **D** ~ G "bury"; transf. "wrap up (as though for burial)"; ext. stat. of liver etc. "is convoluted"? **Dt** pass. of liver "be rolled up"? **N** pass. of corpse "be buried"; < *qabru* denom.; > *qebru*; *qēbiru*; *qubūru*, *qubirtu*; *qabbiru*; *naqbaru*

qēbiru "burier" jB; < *qebēru*

qebru(m) "buried" O/jB, of human; *eṭemmu lā qebru* "unburied ghost"; < *qebēru*

qēltu → *qīštu*

qēmītu "female grinder" NB, in *bīt q.*; < *qemûm*

qemûm, *qamû* "to grind" Bab. **G** (*i/i*) grain; transf. of demons "pulverize, destroy" land; < *qēmu* denom.?; > *qēmītu*

qēmu(m) "flour" [ZÌ(.DA); MB(Susa) also ZI.DA] from grain; for marking ground; NB (a rental payment on crown land); "powder, flour" of plants, nuts, date-stones etc.; > *qemûm* ?

qenû "to be jealous" jB **G**; > *qinû*; → *qannā'u*

qēpu → *qīpu*

qēpūtu → *qīpūtu*

qerbatu → *qerbetu*

qerbēnum, *qerbēnu/a* adv. "inside" Bab. "in the interior" of human body; of building; NB astr. as prep. "inside"; < *qerbu* II

qerbetu(m), *qa/erbatu(m)* "environs (of a settlement), meadowland"; < *qerbu* II

qerbiš I O/jB **1.** "nearby, close at hand" **2.** "instantly, forthwith"; < *qerbu* I

qerbiš II "inside" O/jB, as adv., as prep.; < qerbu II

qerbītu(m) "centre, interior" Bab.; of body, esp. "womb"; of liver; of ark; jB *q. ūmi* "midday", NB *ina q.* "from among"; < *qerbû*

qerbu(m) I; f. *qerubtu(m)* "near" Bab., of land, people; NB "on hand, available" of commodities; as subst. "relative"; of time: NB *ana qerbi*, MB in PNs *ina q.* "quickly, soon"; < *qerēbu*; > *qerbūtum*; Ass. → *qurbu*

qerbu(m) II, OA freq. *qarbum* "centre, interior" [ŠÀ] **1.** "centre" of town; "interior" of building, OA esp. *qe/ara(b)-bītim*, as storeroom; of heaven (*šamê*), mountains (*šadî*), land (*māti*); jB of boat **2.** "interior, inside(s)"; OA "contents" of wrappings; "intestines" of human, animal body (usu. pl.) [med., ext. ŠÀ.MEŠ]; *q. qattanūtu/kabbarūtu* "small/large intestine"; MB "womb" in fPN **3.** transf. "inner being, mind", "contents, meaning" of words **4.** jB *q. suluppi* "date flesh" as drug **5.** *q. mušīti* "midnight" **6.** in prep. use *ina qere/ab* "within, inside, among"; Bab. loc.-adv. *qerbu(m)*, with suff. *qerbuš(šu/ša)* "therein, thither"; also *ša, adi, ištu/ultu, ana q.* etc.; > *qerbēnum, qerbiš* II, *qerbītu, qerbû, qarbītu*?; *qerbetu*

qerbû(m), OB also *qarbûm* "internal" O/jB of house-wall, tablet, geometrical figure; < *qerbu* II

qerbūtum "nearness" Mari, in *ūm qerbūti* "recently"; < *qerbu* I

qerdu → *gerdu*

qerēbu(m), Ass. *qarābu(m)* "to be/come close" G (*i/i*, arch. OB *a/a*, OA, NB, occas. jB *u/u*; stat. *qerub*, Ass. *qurub*) [KU.NU] **1.** stat. "is close, at hand" of people, transf. of social relationship; of field, land, building; of commodities "are available"; of person "is present"; transf. "is involved, concerned" in s.th.; of time "is imminent" **2.** of person, deity, star "approach, come close to" s.th., s.o.; of demon etc., with hostile intent; to woman, with sexual connotation; leg. "make an appearance" before official, lawcourt **3.** of army, traveller "arrive"; of day; of word "come to mind"; of animal "be presented" for sacrifice; of part of body "be able to reach" **4.** M/jB *ana aḫāmiš q.* "come together (in alliance)" **5.** MB, NA "get started on (= *ana*)" work, activity **6.** leg. "make claim on" s.o.; "lay claim to" s.th.; Ug., Am. "take action against" s.o. **Gtn** iter. **Gt** **1.** "come close to one another", stat. "are close to each other" in battle **2.** "come close up", stat. "is imminent" **D** "bring, present" gift, tribute, offering, meal; "bring s.o. before" king, official, "produce" witness, "introduce" s.o.; abstr. "be in close relationship" to s.o.; ellipt., of person, animal, star "approach" (intrans.); "escort, lead" person towards (= *ana, adi*); "bring up" troops; "allow" evil etc. "near"; OA "address" a word to s.o.; OA "pay preferentially" to s.o.; stat. "is imminent"; NA "combine" ominous signs **Dtn** iter. **Dt** pass., mng. uncl. **Š** "present (a request)" to s.o.; "attach" s.th. to s.o. **Štn** iter. of Š "constantly present (request), pray" **Št** "come close to", "follow closely" **N** MA(Bogh.), NA ~ G 6 "lay claim" to s.th., s.o.; > *qerbu* I, *qerbiš* I, *qerubtum, qerbūtum*; *qurbu, qurbiš, qurbūtu*; *qurrubu*; *qitrubiš*; *muqerribum*; *naqrabu*; *taqribtu, taqrubtu, taqrību*; *teqrūbatum*

qeremu → *qermu*

qerītu(m); pl. also *qerrētu*?; Ass. *qarītu* "banquet, feast" O/jB, M/NA [KAŠ.DÉ.A]; *q. šakānu*, NA *epāšu* "to hold a feast"; *ina q. ašābu* "to sit down to a feast"; < *qerû*

qermu, *qeremu* (a garment) NA, NB; also adj., of wool; < *qarāmu*

qerqīsum (a container) OB; or PlN ?

qerqišu (a tree)? NA/jB; = *gergiššu* ?

qersu(m) (a wooden compartment or vehicle)? OB?, NA

qeršu(m) I ~ "strip, band" OAkk, Bab., NA of silver, bronze; MB (túg)*q.* "shawl"?; lex., "(leather) strap"?; "strip" of meat; (a kind of bread or pastry); < *qarāšu*

qeršum II (a kind of payment) OB(Susa), Mari

qerû(m), Ass. *qarā'u(m)* "to call, invite" G (*i/i*, O/MA *a/a* ?) person to meal, deity to offering, enemy to battle; OB of deity "call s.o. (to fate)" euph. of death **D** j/NB "call up, invite"; > *qarû*; *qarrātu*; *qerītu*; *qirītu*; *qurrû*

qerubtum "vicinity" OB; < *qerbu* I

qēṣu "summer" Am.; < W.Sem.

qēšu → *qīšu* II

qettā'u "reed-cutter" NB; < Aram.

qiādu → *qâdu*

qiālu(m), *qâlu* "to fall" OA, O/jB **G** (*ī*) of reed **D** "fell" enemy

qiāpu(m), *qâpu* "to (en)trust; believe" **G** **1.** "trust" a person **2.** "believe, credit" person, word; also absol. **3.** "verify" fact **4.** "entrust" task, object to s.o.; "make loan, extend credit to" s.o. **Gtn** OA iter. of G 4 **D** **1.** OAkk "act as guarantor for" s.o. **2.** Bogh. "give credence"? **Št2** Mari "borrow, take out a loan" **N** OB **1.** of person "be given credit" **2.** OA of goods "be entrusted" **3.** of heart, i.e. intentions "be trusted"; > *qīpu*, *qīpūtu*, *qīptu*; *qāyipu*, *qāyipānu*, *qāyipānūtu*; *muqippu*

qiāšu(m), *qâšu*, OB once *qiātum* "to give, present" **G** (*ī*) [BA; NÍG.BA] objects, field, slave; of deity "grant" life, characteristics; freq. *qištam q.* "give as a gift" **Gtn** OB lex. only **D** jB/NA pl. obj. *qīšāti q.* "bestow gifts on" s.o. **Dt** pass. of D "be presented"; > *qīšu* I, *qīštu*; *qayyašu*

qiātum → *qiāšu*

qibītu(m) "speech; command" Bab., NA [DU_{11}(.GA); NB PNs also E] "utterance, statement"; "command"; "prayer, request"; freq. *q. pî* with same mng.s; < *qabû* II

qību "command; statement" M/NB, NA [ME.A (or ME-*a*); DU_{11}(.GA)] "command, instruction"; "pronouncement" of diviner, exorcist, NA pl. *qibâni*; *q. šakānu* "to make, issue a statement"; < *qabû* II

qīdātu pl. (of *qittu*?) "kindling" jB/NA of beacon; < *qâdu*

qiddadāniš → *qaddadāniš*

qiddatu(m) "bending down, declination" O/jB **1.** of person, esp. pl. "being crouched down" (in anxiety) **2.** *ina*/*ana q.* (*nārim*) "downstream (on river)"; med. *ana q.* "downwards" of applying salve **3.** *q. ūmi* "evening, afternoon" [UD.GURUM.MA] **4.** *q. ša nurmî* (pomegranate product); < *qadādu*

qiddu, *qindu* "vault (of sky)"? jB lex.; < *qadādu* ?

qidḫu rdg. uncl. (an illness) jB; = *qudḫu* or read *saḫḫu* II ?

qilā'ūtum → *qilûtu*

qilītu, *qullītu* (a plant) jB lex.

qilpu "rind, skin" M/NB [BAR] of grain, date, onion etc.; metal "overlay"; "worn cloth"; < *qalāpu*

qiltu (an alkaline plant) jB, NA; "lye, alkali" in bowl

qiltu → also *qištu*

qīltu → *qīštu*

qīlu "burning; burn-mark"? NA; < *qalû* II

qilûtu, Mari *qilā'ūtum* ? "burning" Bab. [GÍBIL] "incineration"; (incant. against) "burn(ing)"; "firewood"; MB "roasting"; < *qalû* II

qimītu "burning, incineration" M/jB(Ass.) in *q.* ^{d}*Gira*; < *qamû* II

qimmatu(m) "tuft, plume" Bab., MA [SUḪUR] "tuft, lock (of hair)"; "crest, crown" of tree, reed, moon; (decorative element on capital of column); < *qamāmu*

qimmu (a kind of furniture)? NA

qindu → *qiddu*

qinītu "acquisition, property" NA; < *qanû* II; pl. → *kinayyātu* ?

qinītu → also *kinītu* II

qi(n)nanzu → *qinnāzu*

qinnatu(m) "buttocks, rump" [GU.DU/DI; GÚ.DU] of human, animal; NB *qinnat andi*^{sar} 'maid's rump' (a herb); Bogh., Nuzi topog. "rear", *ina q.* "behind", "back" of quiver; → *qinniš*

qinnāzu(m), *qi(n)nanzu* f. "whip" O/jB, NA [KUŠ.ÙSAN)]; OB transf. (an agricultural work team)

qinniš "backwards" NA; → *qinnatu*

qinnu(m) "nest" [GÙD] of bird, snake; transf. of human home; f., human "family, clan"; > *qanānu*

qinû(m), NA *qin'u*, *qi'u* "envy" Bab. lex., NA; *bēl q.* "envious person"; < *qenû*

qīptu(m) "trust; loan" [ŠU.LAL] **1.** "belief, credence" in person, in fact **2.** "position of trust", "appointment" **3.** OA, OB, NA "loan, credit", *ana q. nadānum* "to give on credit"; *bēl q.* "creditor" **4.** NB *bīt q.* mng. unkn. **5.** Bogh. for *qīpu* 2 "representative"; < *qiāpu*

qīpu(m), NA *qēpu* **1.** adj. "believable" in PN *Lā-qēpu(m)* "Incredible" **2.** "entrusted", esp. M/NA, NB as subst. "representative", freq. of king; [LÚ.TIL.(LA.)GÍD.DA; also TI.LA.GÍD, TIL.LA.AN.GÍD.DA]; < *qiāpu*

qīpūtu(m), *qēpūtu* **1.** OB "position of trusted agent" **2.** M/jB "function of representative"; < *qīpu*

qirīru "wick"? NA, for lamp; < *qarāru*

qirītu "announcement" MA; < *qerû*

qirītu → also *qarītu*; *qerītu*

qīrtum "bitumen" Mari; < *qīru*

qīru; pl. f. "(liquid) bitumen, pitch" M/NA; > *qīrtum*

qišīrum → *kišīrum*

qiššû(m); pl. m. & f. "cucumber" O/jB, NA [ÚKUŠ(.SAR)]; Am. *aban q.* "cucumber-shaped oil flask"; lex. *patar q.* (a sword)

qištiš "like a forest" jB; < *qištu*

qištu(m), M/NB also *qiltu*, occas. *qaštu*; pl. *qišātu(m)* "forest, wood" [GIŠ.TIR] *q. erēnim* "cedar forest"; *maṣṣar q.* "forest guardian"; lex. *q. (ša) qaqqadi* (desig. of hair on head); < *qīšu* II

qīštu(m), later also *qī*/*ēltu* "gift, present" [NÍG.BA], also as dedication to deity; < *qiāšu*

qīšu(m) I "given" in PNs; NA(roy. inscr.) *ki qīšūte* "as dedicated gifts"; < *qiāšu*

qīšu(m) II, *qēšu* "forest, wood" O/jB [GIŠ.TIR]; > *qištu*, *qištiš*

qišubbû → *kišubbû*

qītāyû "concluding" jB of section of text; < *qītu*

qitbulu Gt "to engage in combat" Ug.; < *qablu* II denom.

qitītu → *kitītu* I

qitmu(m) "black paste" O/jB [IM.SAḪAR. GE6.KUR.RA]

qitpu(m) "gathering, plucking" OA in *qitip karānim* "grape-harvest"; Bab. "gathered (dates)"; < *qatāpu*

qitrubiš "in close combat" O/jB; < *qerēbu* Gt

qitrudu(m) "very warlike" Bab.(lit.); < *qarādu*

qitrunu (or *gitrunu*) "accumulating (wealth), miserly" jB; < *qarānu*

qittu → *kittu* II; *qīdātu*

qītu(m) "end" Bab., M/NA(lit.) [TIL] of day, year, reign etc.; "termination" of life; of line of text; < *qatû* II

qi'u → *qinû*

qû(m) I "flax; thread, string" Bab., NA(lit.) [GU] **1.** as plant; DN *bānû še'i u qê* "creator of grain and flax" as staple crops **2.** "thread", spun; woven; spider's "web"; of feature on liver etc. ~ "filament"; "(builder's) line", *kīma qê* "straight"; astr. (meteor. phenomenon); < Sum.; > *qû'iš*

qû(m) II, OB also *qa'u*; OA pl. f. *quātum*; st. abs. *qa* (a capacity measure) "*qa*" (~ 1 litre) [SÌLA] **1.** as measuring-vessel, OB *qâm ša Šamaš*, oil *ina qê kittim* "in a standard *q.*"; lex. [DUG/GIŠ.SÌLA] **2.** as capacity unit, usu. one-tenth of *sūtum* **3.** NB as unit of area **4.** OB, NA (measure of thickness of trees)

qubātu → *qubbatu*

qu(b)batu mng. unkn. MB, NA

qubbû → *qubû*; *qu''û*

qubbuḫu → *gubbuḫu*

qubbulu D 1. NB "to accept"; < Aram. **2.** OB, Am. ~ "to fight"?

qubbutu D mng. unkn. jB lex.

qubirtu, *quburtu* "(snake's) lair"? jB; < *qebēru*

qubsu → *kubsu*

qubû(m), *qubbû* "lamentation" O/jB; < *qabû* II

quburtu → *qubirtu; kupurtum*

qubūru(m), NA *qabūru* "grave, burial place" Bab., NA; OB also "funeral, funerary gift"; < *qebēru*

qudāšu(m), *qudaštu*, NA *qudassu* "(ear?)ring" NA, NB; OAkk as PN

quddadu → *quddu* II

quddu I; pl. f. "(kind of) axe" j/NB, NA; of copper, iron

quddu II, *quddadu* (a tamarisk product) jB lex.; < Sum.

quddušu "purified, consecrated" M/jB; of sheep, cultic paraphernalia, building; < *qadāšu*; → *quššudu*

qudḫu rdg. uncl. (an illness) jB; → *qidḫu*

qudīni → *udīni*

qudmēnītu mng. uncl. jB; < *qudmu* ?

qudmiš, *qudmī-* "in front of" O/jB(poet.) *q. DN* "before DN", *qudmišunu* "before them"; < *qudmu*

qudmu(m), *qudumu* **1.** of place: O/jB(lit.) "front (side)", *ana q.-* "before, in presence of" s.o.; M/jB "leader, precursor" **2.** of time: jB "primeval" of city; < *qadmu*; > *qudmiš*, *qudmû*; *qudmēnītu*?

qudmû(m) "primordial" M/NB(lit.) of temple, ritual; "first, front" O/jB of lyre-string; < *qudmu*

qudru (or *qutru*), *qud/tratu* (a plant) jB/NA [Ú.KI.AN.IM] *zēr q.* "*q.* seed" in medical texts; < *qutru* ?

qudumu → *qudmu*

qû'iš "like threads" jB; < *qû* I

qulālu(m) "belittlement, disgrace" Ass., j/NB usu. pl.; OA *q. epāšum*, jB/NA *q. šakānu* "to disgrace, bring dishonour on" s.o.; < *qalālu* I

quliptu(m), Ass. *qulāptu* "skin of scales" O/jB, MA [BAR] of fish, snake, of constellation Piscis = shooting star?; of human skin complaint, *q. ēnē* "cornea"?; "bark" of tree, "cortex" of reed, "husk" of grain, *ša q.* "(barley) dehusker"; < *qalāpu*

qullānum → *kullānum*

qullītu → *qilītu*; *qulliu*; *qullû*

qu(l)liu(m), NB *qullû*; pl. m. & f. (a vessel) OB, M/NA, NB, of bronze; of clay

qullu(m), *qūlu* (a large ring) OB of door; M/NA, NB of copper, silver

qullû "roasted, burnt" NA, NB; NA *qullītu* "parched grain"; NB of butter; < *qalû* II D

qullû → also *qulliu*

qullulum "despised, little valued" OB, of house(hold); NB of person, NA f. *qallussu* as fPN ?; < *qalālu* I D

qullutu D mng. unkn. jB lex.

qulmû(m); pl. m. & f. "(kind of) axe" OAkk, Bab. [OAkk, OB GUL.ME] of copper, iron; "(model) axe" held by figurine

qulpu "rind, bark"? jB, NA

qulqulliānu, *qulqullânu* (a plant, phps.) "cassia" M/jB, NA, seed and root used in med.; < *qulqullu* ?

qulqullu(m) **1.** OA (a form of packaging) **2.** OB mng. uncl. **3.** MB (a textile); > *qulqulliānu*?

qultu → *kuldu*

qūltu(m) "silence" O/jB; OB *bīt q.-šu* "his house of silence, i.e. tomb"; < *qūlu*

qūlu(m); pl. f. "silence" O/jB [NÍG.ME.GAR] of disaster, despair; *q. libbi* "peace of mind"?; < *qâlu*; > *qūltu*

qūlu → also *qullu*

qumaḫḫu "cattle"? jB; < Sum.

qumāru ~ "shoulder and upper arm"? M/jB, of human; (part of constellation Cygnus)?; → *kumāru*

qumāšu (or *qumāštu*); only pl. *qumāšātu* attested "capital (of a column)"? M/NA

qummālu(m), *qummānu*, *qummāru* ~ (a skin complaint) O/jB; jB (a condition affecting sesame); > *qummānû*, *qummārûtu*

qummānu (a sheep) jB lex.

qummānu → also *qummālu*

qummānû, *qummārû* "leprous" jB, lex. of person; desig. of sheep; < *qummālu*

qummāru → *qummālu*

qummārû → *qummānû*

qummārûtu "case of leprosy" jB lex.; < *qummāru*

qummû → *qu''û*

qummušu D mng. unkn. jB lex.

qumqummatu (desig. of a sorceress) jB

qunātā "woad (*Isatis tinctoria*)" NB; < Aram.; → *qunû*

qundu (a plant; a wooden item) jB/NA?

qunduḫu (desig. of a settlement) jB lex.

qunnabru "fetters" jB

qunnabtu(m) "hemp plant" OAkk ?; NB as fPN

qunnabu "hemp" NA, NB; ^{šim}*q.* as aromatic; also as fPN

qunnunu(m), MA *qannunu* "rolled up" OAkk, MA, M/jB; of hair "curly, rolled"?; of person, also (f)PN *Qannun(t)u* "With curly hair"?; → *kanānu*

qunnupu D mng. unkn. jB lex.

qunû "of lapis lazuli colour" NB var. of *uqnû*, of wool etc.; → *qunātā*

qununnītu (a kind of wool) NB (or f. pl. *qununnētu* ?); < *uqnû*

qupātu pl. tant.? (a kind of flour) MA

quppatum "box" OB; for grain; < *quppu* II nom. unit.

quppu I "collapsed" j/NB of wall; < *qâpu* D

quppu(m) II; pl. m. & f. "box, chest" Bab., M/NA; of reed, of wood; for food, silver, tablets; "(bird) cage"; NB *ša muḫḫi q.* "cashier"; Nuzi, as attachment for chair (or *kubbu* ?); > *kuppātu*?; *quppatum*; → *qappatu*

quppû "sharp knife, scalpel" M/jB; of doctor, for self-mutilation; Emar, of table

qupputtu → *kupputtu*

qupsu → *kubsu*

qūpu → *kūbu* I

qūqānu(m), *gūqānu* (a worm) O/jB **1.** lex. (a worm) **2.** lex., med. (an eye-disease) [IGI.GU.LÁ]

quqinētu → *kukittu*

quqqubu → *kukkubbu*

quqû(m) (desig. of a snake) OB; M/NA as PN ?

ququbinnu (a medicinal plant) jB lex.

qurādu(m) "hero, warrior" [UR.SAG] of god, king, soldiers; < *qarādu*

qurādūtum "heroism" OB; < *qurādu*

qurāštu (a cut of meat) jB lex.; < *qarāšu*

qurbiš "recently" Mari; < *qurbu*

qurbu(m), NA also *qarbu*; f. *qurubtu* "near" Ass. **1.** of time: OA *ana ūmē qurbūtim* "within a short while" **2.** of place: MA "close" **3.** transf. MB(Alal.), NA of person "follower, retainer" (→ *qurbūtu*), "relative"; NA of commodity "available"; < *qerēbu*; Bab. → *qerbu* I

qurbūtu "closeness" NA in *ša q.* (later without *ša*) "close follower, bodyguard"; NB also *(ša) qurrubūti/u*; < *qurbu*

qurdāmu → *qardammu*

qurdu(m) "warriorhood, heroism"; pl. "heroic acts"; of god, king etc., freq. in PNs; jB "(song of) beau geste"; < *qardu*

qurnātum pl. "horned goddesses"? Mari; < *qarnu*

qurnû (a herb, phps.) "marjoram" jB; → *urnû*

qurpi(s)su(m), *qursi(p)pu(m)* (or *q/kurpīsu* ?) "helmet" Bab., NA; usu. of bronze, also iron, silver

qurqurratu(m) "female metal-worker" O/jB, of goddess, witch; < *qurqurru*

qurqurru(m) "metal-worker, esp. coppersmith" Bab. [TIBIRA]; > *qurqurratu*, *qurqurrūtum*

qurqurrūtum "copper-working" Mari; < *qurqurru*

qurqurû (a soup)? jB lex.

qurrû "called together, summoned" jB of deities; < *qerû* D

qurrubu NB **1.** "brought close, presented" of sacrifice; f. pl. as subst. "presents" **2.** → *qurbūtu*; < *qerēbu* D

qurrudu → *gurrudu*

qurruru(m), *gurruru* **1.** OB as PN, mng. unkn. **2.** NB of vessel "leaky"?; < *qarāru*

qursi(p)pu → *qurpissu*

quršu → *guršu* I.II

qurû (a length of wood) jB

qurunnatu mng. unkn. jB, epith. of cross (*išpallurtu*)

qurunniš, *gurunniš* "into a heap" jB; < *qurunnu*

qurunnu(m), *gurunnu(m)*; pl. f. "heap" Bab., NA(lit.), usu. "pile" of corpses, NB of bricks; MB of sesame; < *qarānu*

qusāyu (desig. of sheep) NA

qušartu mng. unkn. MA

quššudu "very holy, sanctified" MB(Ass.), jB of temple, offering; < *qašādu*; → *quddušu*

qušû (a deity's robe) jB lex.

qūšum (or *kūšum*) (a stone) Mari

qutandu (a cut of meat) NB, from sacrificial animal; < *qutānu*

qutānu(m) 's.th. thin' **1.** OAkk as PN? **2.** OAkk, Mari, OA → *kutānum* (a textile) **3.** OB (a piece of wood) **4.** NA, NB pl. f. "(a narrow) strip" of field; < *qatānu*

qutāru "incense; fumigation" j/NB, NA; < *qatāru* II

qutīnum → *kutānum*

qutītu → *qutû*

qutnum 'thinness, s.th. thin' OAkk, O/jB [SIG] **1.** OAkk, OB as desig. of textile? **2.** O/jB ext., desig. of constriction in liver, gall; < *qatānu*

qutrannu → *kutrannu*

qutratu → *qudru*

qutrēnum, *qutrinnu*; pl. f. "incense (offering)" Bab. [NA.NE; OB NA]; Ug., Nuzi *ša q.* "incense-vessel, censer"; < *qatāru* II

qutru(m) "smoke" [NE] from incense, oven, conflagration; "fog"; < *qatāru* II; > *quturtu*; *qudru*?

qutru → also *qudru*

quttû "completed" Ug., jB, of workmanship; < *qatû* II D; > *quttûtum*

quttunum, NA *qattunu* "very thin" OB lex. of person, also PN; NA of textiles; < *qatānu*

qutturu "smoked, smoky" jB lex.; < *qatāru* II D

quttûtum "completion, finished state" OB; < *quttû*

qutû, *gutû*; f. *qutītu* jB **1.** "Gutian" of stone; fig; of person, pejoratively **2.** lex. "Cuthaean" of chariot-type

quturtu(m) **1.** Mari "smouldering (spot)" **2.** NB "smoke"; < *qutru* nom. unit.

qu''û(m), *quwwû*, *qummû*, *qubbû* **D** "to await; wait for (= *ana*, dat.)"; "wait on" s.o. in service, "trust in" s.o.; *rēša q.* "look after, take care of" s.o., s.th., also ironically "take care of, i.e. deal with, call to account"; → *waqûm*

R

ra'ābu(m), NB also *raḫābu* "to shake, tremble" **G** (*u/u*); of parts of body, door-jambs; esp. with wrath, "be angry" of deity, person **Gtn** iter. "tremble continually" **Š** caus. "make s.o. shake", "make angry" **Št** pass. "be made to tremble", of flatulence "rumble"; "be(come) irritated"; > *ra'bu*, *ra'batu*; *rūbu* I; *ra'ību* I, *ra'ibtu*, *ra'ībāniš*; *ru'ubtu*; *ra''ābum*; → *râbu*

ra''ābum "very trembly" OB as PN; < *ra'ābu*

ra'āmu → *râmu* I.II; *ru''umu*

ra'āmuttu, *râmuttu*, *ri'āmuttu*? "friendship" Am.(Mit.); < *râmu* II

ra'āsu → *râsu*

ra'āṣu → *râṣu*

ra'ātum → *rittu*

ra'āzu, *rêzu* ~ "to inlay"? jB lex. **G** with carnelian; > *rā'izu*?

rab, *rabi* "chief, overseer of" Bogh., j/NB, NA; < *rabû* I; → *rabû* I 6 and under second words; note abstr. forms *rab-banûtu*, *rab-bītūtu*, *rab-kiṣirūtu*, *rab-puḫrūtu*, *rab-sikkatūtu*, *rab-šerkūtu*, etc.

rabābu(m) "to be weak, submissive" Bab., NA **G** (*u/u*, *i/i*) of person, foundation; of hand "be slack"; Mari "be poor?" of flour **D** "make submissive"; "uproot" tree ? **Š** ~ D "make submit"; stat. "is obedient"; ellipt. "relax" (o.s.) **ŠD** poet. ~ D; > *rabbu*, *rabbiš*, *rabbumma*; *šarbābu*, *šarbābiš*

rabā'iu "fourth" MA, of lot; < *rebû*

rabāku(m) "to boil down, decoct" O/jB **G** (*a/u*) med., drugs, in wine, beer etc. **D** ~ G; > *ribku*; *rabīku*

ra'bāniš → *ra'ībāniš*

rabannu, *rabânu* → *rabiānum*

rabāqum mng. unkn. OB **G** (*i/i*) of cattle **Dt** ~ G, of cattle

rabarabaru; pl. *rabarabrānu* (a functionary)? NB; < Iran.

rabāṣu(m) "to sit, be recumbent" of animals **G** (*i/i*) [NÚ], also of reptiles, birds; of person "camp, lie in wait", of demon "lurk"; transf. of house, of unused weapons, of flour; of eyes "stare" **Gtn** iter.; OA of person "regularly sit on, i.e. retain" copper; of incense "hang low persistently, settle" **Š** "allow to sit" (in pasture); "make" troops "camp"; > *rabṣu*; *rubṣu*; *rābiṣu*, *rābiṣūtu*; *narbāṣu*; *tarbaṣu*

rabāšum "to raise objections, protest"? OA **G** (*a*?/*u*); > *ribšum*

rabât → *rabiat*

ra'batu "fit of rage"? jB, *r. irši* "he suffered a fit of rage"; < *ra'ābu*

rabā'u → *rabû* II.III

rabbannu → *rabiānum*

rabbat "10,000" Mari, *5 rabbātim* "50,000" (homers of grain); < W.Sem.; → *ribbatu* II

rabbi → *erbe*

rabbiš "gently, softly" O/jB, of rainfall, speech; < *rabbu*

rabbu(m) "soft, gentle" OAkk, O/jB, of person, hand; wool, garment; transf. of forgiveness, sleep; < *rabābu*; > *rabbiš*; *rabbumma*

rabbû(m) "very big" Bab. [GAL.GAL] of things, people; Mari *awīlī rabbûtimma* "a great many men"; NB (a big kind of cake); also as pl. form of *rabû* I ?; < *rabû* I; > *rabbûtu*

rabbumma adv. "gently" OA, Mari; OA "by easy instalments"; < *rabbu*

rabbûtu(m) "greatness, grandeur" O/jB, of deity; also pl. *rabbâti*; < *rabbû*

rabi → *rab*

rabiāna "for the fourth time" Nuzi; < *rebû*

rabiānum, *rabânu(m)*, NA *ra(b)bannu* "mayor" O/jB of town, village; NA (high foreign official), pl. f. *rabbannāti*; < *rabû* I

rabiat, *rebiat*, *ra/ebât* "a quarter" O/jB [IGI.4.GÁL; Susa 4-] *r. šamnim* "a quarter of the oil"; OB *ana rabiātim* [NAM.IGI.4.GÁL.LA] rental "at 25%"; < *rebû*

rabīku, *rapīqu* "(a kind of) decoction" M/jB [KAM.KU.DA] esp. med.; < *rabāku*

rābiṣu(m) (an official, liter. "lurker") [MAŠKIM; MÁŠKIM] OA "bailiff", of palace, of individual; OB judicial officer; Ug., Am. a royal official; transf. of god, spirit "invigilator" of s.o., of throne, gate; of demon *r. murtappidu* "roaming *r.*", *r. nāri/ūri* "*r.* of river, roof"; s.o. has hand, foot of *rābiṣi*; < *rabāṣu*

rābiṣūtu(m) OA *rābiṣuttum* "rôle of *rābiṣum*" OA, O/jB; < *rābiṣu*

rabîš "greatly" Bab., NA [GAL-*iš*] of divine orders, commissions; speak, trust, consider "greatly"; M/jB(Ass.) *r. ašābu* of king on throne "to sit in majesty"?; < *rabû* I

râbiš "quakingly" jB; < *râbu*

rabītu(m) **1.** OB "capital city" **2.** Ug. "queen" **3.** esp. pl. "great thing(s)"; < *rabû* I

rabiu → *rabû* I

rab-sikkatūtu (or *rab-šikkatūtu*) mng. uncl. jB

rabṣu(m) "recumbent" O/jB of cattle; of (ill?) human; < *rabāṣu*

rab-šikkatūtu → *rab-sikkatūtu*

rabû(m) I, *rabiu(m)* "big" [GAL] **1.** in size, vol.; of units of measure, e.g. *ammatu r.* "the big cubit" **2.** of festival, meal, accounting, share "major"; MA *taḫūmu r.* "major boundary" **3.** abstr. of punishment, wisdom, name, fame etc. **4.** "great" of deity, king etc., *ilū rabûtum* "the great gods", fDN *rabīt Igigi* "the great(est) of the Igigi **5.** "old, adult", *aḫu(m) r.* "elder/eldest brother"; st. abs. *ṣeḫer rabi* "young and old" **6.** of person, official "noble, grandee"; st. constr. "chief ..., overseer of ..." e.g. *rab aškāpē* "chief leather-worker", *rab ešerti* "decurion", *rab puḫri* "chairman of assembly", *rab birti/ēkalli* "fort/palace commander", *rab būli/miksi* "supervisor of cattle/taxes" (→ also *rab*); NB *rab bānê* [LÚ.GAL.DÙ] "building inspector"?, also as family name; < *rabû* II; > *rab*, *rabîš*, *rabītu*, *rabûtu*; *rabbû*, *rabbûtu*; *rabiānum*; *parasrab*

rabû(m) II, *rabā'u(m)* "to be big, to grow" **G** (*i/i*) [GAL; stat. also GAL.ÀM] **1.** "be big", "be too big"; "be bigger", stat. "is big" **2.** "grow", of tree, ear; Ass., NB of money, debt "accumulate interest" **3.** "grow up, become adult" of person; OB *adi rabiāku* "until I am of age", Nuzi *rabi* "he is senior", Mari girls *irtabê* "have grown up" **4.** transf., abstr. "be(come) great" of deity, king, demon; of word, sin, name etc. **Gtn** "constantly grow, become great" of deity, of divine command **D** **1.** "bring up" child, *ana murabbītišu* "to the woman who brought him up"; also animal, plant, date-plantation **2.** "promote" s.o. in office, "advance" ahead of (= *eli*) s.o. **3.** "increase" space, payment, friendship **4.** abstr. "make great, magnify" word, throne etc. **Dt** "be made superior to" s.o., of goddess **Š** "make great"; liter. "extend" building site; "raise, bring up" child, to kingship; usu. transf., abstr. "augment, aggrandize" kingship, domination, cult, weapons; "elevate, promote" s.o.; "magnify, praise" s.o.('s deeds, qualities) **Štn** iter., of name "be constantly magnified" **ŠD** ~ **Š** **N** "swell, become enlarged"? jB lex. **Ntn** OB of interest "constantly accumulate" **Rt** OB math. "increase occasionally" *mala urtababû* "as many as have severally increased"; > *rabû* I, *rab*, *rabîš*, *rabītu*, *rabûtu*; *rabbû*, *rabbûtu*; *rubû*, *rubûtu*, *rubātu*, *rubūtu*; *rubbû* I.II; *rūbu* III; *rabiānum*; *murabbiānu*, *murabbītu*; *narbû*, *narbûtu*; *šurbû*, *šurbûtu*; *tarbû*, *tarbûtu*, *tarbītu*; *parasrab*

rabû(m) III, *rabā'u* "to set" of heavenly body Bab., M/NA **G** (*i/i*) [ŠÚ; astr. also GAL, GIR5]; *ina pān šamši rabê* "before sunset"; *r. šamši* "the West"; *šamšu irta/ebi* "the sun has set"; of moon (Sîn), stars **Gtn** astr. [ŠÚ.ŠÚ] iter. of G **D** **1.** "submerge" field, cloth, plant under water **2.** "douse, extinguish" fire; > *rību* II; *rūbu* II; *narbâtu*

rabû → also *rebû*

rābum (a vessel)? OAkk; → *rību* IV

râbu(m) Ass. *ruābu(m)* "to quake" **G** (*ū*) [ŠÚ] of heaven, earth; of things; of person, from fear **D** "make" heaven, earth "quake"; "shake" foundations, building etc.; "make s.o. tremble" from fear; of witch "activate" sorceries **Š** MB/MA "make tremble"; > *rību* I; *râbiš*; → *ra'ābu*

râbu → also *riābu*

ra'bu(m) ~ "raging" Bab.; < *ra'ābu*

rabūšene "(in) 4th year" NA, i.e. 3 years ago; < *rebû* + *šattu*

rabūtu → *rebû*

rabûtu(m) "greatness" O/jB [GAL-] of deity, men; chariot *simat r.* "symbol of greatness"; *kīma rabûtika* "in accordance with your generosity, nobility"; < *rabû* I

radādu(m) "to chase, pursue" Bab., M/NA **G** (*a*/*u*) individual, army **D** lex. only; > *raddu*; *raddādu*

radāmu mng. unkn. M/jB **G** stat., of foetus **D** OB, uncert. **Š** MB(Ass.) "cause" flood, blood "to flow"; > *nardamu*

rādāniš "like a rainstorm" jB; < *rādu*

radāpu "to pursue" NA, NB **G** (*i*/*i*) animals, people; NA before second verb "do quickly"; < Aram.; > *radpi*; *ridpu*

radā'u → *redû* I

raddādu "pursuer, persecutor" jB; < *radādu*

ra(d)didu (a garment) NA

raddu "pursued" jB; of donkey; < *radādu*

raddu → also *rādu*

rādiu(m) **1.** OA ~ "(caravan) guide" **2.** NA [LÚ.UŠ] *rādi kibsi* "tracker"; "driver, herder" of animals; (a work foreman)?; < *redû* I; Bab. → *rēdû*

radpi, *radpu* "quickly" NB; < *radāpu*

rādu(m), occas. *raddu* "rainstorm, cloudburst" Bab. [AGAR$_5$] *r. illak*, *izannun* "a rainstorm occurs"; jB *ina rādi tik šamê* "in a rainstorm poured from heaven"; > *rādāniš*

râdu(m) "to quake, shake" O/jB **G** (*ū*) of wall, part of body; jB, from fear **Gtn** iter. of man ?

ragābu "to be afraid" Am. **G**; < W.Sem.

ragāgu I ~ "to be(come) mischievous" jB **G** (*i*/*i*) of mankind; > *raggu*, *raggiš*; *riggatu*; *ruggugu*; *targīgu*

ragāgum II (or *raqāqum*) mng. unkn. OB **G** (*a*/*a* or *a*/*u*)

ragāmu(m) "to shout; prosecute, raise claim" **G** (*a*/*u*, *u*/*u*; j/NB perf. also *irtagu'*/*w*) [KA.GÁ.GÁ] **1.** "exclaim, shout to" s.o.; NA "declaim"; of Adad "peal" **2.** Mari "call for" s.th., "call up" troops **3.** "make claim" against s.o. (= *ana*, dat.) *aḫum ana aḫim ul iraggam*; "claim s.th." from s.o. (= *ana*); NB "sue" s.o. (= acc.) **Gtn** iter. OA, Mari **Gt** OA "raise claims against each other" **Š** MB "cause to raise claims"; > *rigmu*, *rigimtum*; *rugummû*, *rugummānû*; *rāgimu*, *rāgimānu*; *raggimu*, *raggimtu*; *arugimānum*; → *targumannu*

ragāšum **G** not attested **N** OB (*i*/*i*) "to be excited, disturbed"?, of Adad

raggimtu, *raggintu* (an oracle priestess) NA, of Ištar; < *raggimu*

raggimu 'shouter' j/NB, NA desig. of an oracle priest; < *ragāmu*; > *raggimtu*

raggintu → *raggimtu*

raggiš "like a villain" jB; < *raggu*

raggu(m), jB also *rangu* "wicked, villainous" of evildoers, criminals; demons; < *ragāgu* I; > *raggiš*

rāgimānu, *rāgimannu* "claimant" OB(Susa); < *ragāmu*

rāgimu jB as DN ^{d}*R.* "shouter", of Adad; < *ragāmu*

raḫābu → *ra'ābu*

raḫāḫu(m) "to mix"? O/jB lex. **G** (*a*/*u* ?)

raḫāṣu(m) I "to flood; wash" **G** [RA] **1.** (*i*/*i*) of Adad "flood" field etc.; stat. of part of liver "is submerged"; transf. of god, demon, king "overwhelm" land etc.; of person "rush", of horse "race" **2.** (*a*/*u*) "wash", rit. "cleanse"; "bathe", stat. "is drenched" in blood **Gtn** [RA.RA] iter. of G 1 and 2 **Gt** OB "race towards one another" **D** ~ G, Ug. of rain god **Š** caus. of G 1 "make hasten", of G 2 "make wash" **N** pass. of G 1 (*i*/*i*) of field "be flooded", of G 2 (*a*/*i*) of plough, chariot "be washed", "be drenched" **Ntn** ~ Gtn "constantly flood" (trans.); > *raḫṣu*; *riḫṣu* I, *riḫiṣtu*; *raḫīṣu*, *rāḫiṣu*, *raḫḫiṣu*; *marḫaṣu*

raḫāṣu(m) II "to trust" OAkk, NA, NB **G** (*i*/*i*, Bab. *u*/*u*) OAkk "entrust" matter to s.o.; "trust, trust in" s.o., s.th.; *ana muḫḫi šarri raḫṣāku* "I trust in the king" **Š** caus. "make s.o. trust" in s.o.

raḫāṣum III ~ "to hold a debate" Mari **G** (*a*/*a*; *i*/*i*) esp. *riḫṣam r.*; > *riḫṣum* II

raḫāšu(m) "to move, be in motion"? Bab. **G** of people **Gtn** (*u*/*u*) OB ? (**Š** W.Sem. Hif'il: Am. *iarḫiša* "set in motion")

raḫātu (or *raḫāṭu*) mng. unkn. jB/NA **G** (*u*/*u*), of stone

raḫḫātu f. (an illness) jB, liter. "pourer"?, as sorceress; < *reḫû*

raḫḫiṣu "racer" jB, of onager, draught animal, demon; < *raḫāṣu* I

raḫīṣu "threshing-floor" jB lex., for straw; < *raḫāṣu* I

rāḫiṣu(m) **1.** M/jB, of Adad "flooder" **2.** OB "(clothes) cleaner"; < *raḫāṣu* I

rāḫītu, *rāḫium* → *rāḫû*

raḫṣu **1.** jB ext. "submerged" **2.** jB "washed down"?; < *raḫāṣu* I

raḫta (a vessel) Am., of gold; < Eg.

raḫû → *reḫû*

rāḫû(m), OAkk *rāḫium* "pourer, discharger" OAkk, O/jB **1.** OAkk as river name **2.** lex. "inseminating" **3.** mag. "creator", *rāḫītu* "creatress", of demon; < *reḫû*

râḫu → *riāḫu*

ra'i, *ra'u* ~ "definitely, without question"? O/jB lex.

rā'i'annu → *rā'imānu*

ra'(ī)bāniš adv. mng. uncl. jB with *šasû* ("to call"); < *ra'ību* I or *ra'bu* ?

rā'ibānum, *rā'ibannu* (a substitute)? O/jB; < *riābu*

ra'ibtu, *ri'ibtu* "shivering" jB, as illness; < *ra'ābu*

ra'ību(m) I, OA *ri'ībum* "shivering, cramp"? OA, O/jB grips (*ṣabātu*) s.o.; *bēl r.* (an enemy), lex.; also *qāt* ^{d}*R*. "hand of *Ra'ību*" (a medical diagnosis) (or = *r.* II ?); < *ra'ābu*

ra'ību II, *rību* (desig. of the Igigu) jB; < *riābu* ?; → *r.* I

rā'imānu, NB occas. *rā'i'annu* "one who loves" j/NB, NA "lover of" s.o., s.th.; < *râmu* II

rā'imānû "amorous" jB, stat. *rā'imānī* "is amorous"; < *rā'imānu* + *-ī*

ra'īmu(m) "loved, beloved" OAkk, Bab. esp. in PNs; < *râmu* II

rā'imu → *râmu* II G

rā'imūtum "friendship" OB; < *râmu* II

rā'izu, *râzum*? (a pronged implement) O/jB, 1 to 4 prongs; < *ra'āzu* ?

rakābu(m), NA occas. *rakāpu* "to ride" **G** (*a/a*; imper. *rikab*) [U5] **1.** "mount, ride on" chariot, boat, animal; of gods "ride" wind, storm etc. **2.** "mount (sexually)" of animal, man **3.** transf., of parts of body etc. "be superimposed", of moon "cover, eclipse" star **4.** OB of ploughshare (*šinnum*) "cut furrow" **Gtn** iter. "repeatedly mount (sexually)" **Gt** [U5.U5] **1.** "mount each other (sexually)" **2.** of parts of liver, stars "be superimposed on each other" **D** **1.** "fertilize" palm-grove **2.** mng. uncl., "install?" seed-funnel **Š** [U5] **1.** "load" goods, men on ship, animal for transport, "transport" **2.** "make s.o. ride" horse etc. **3.** "cause to mount (sexually)" **4.** *šinnam š.* caus. of G 4 **Št** caus. of Gt; > *rakbu*, *rakbû*?; *rikbu*, *rikibtu*; *rukūbu*; *rākibu*; *rakībum*; *rakkābu*, *rakkābūtum*; *rukkubum*; *ritkubu*; *narkabu*, *narkabtu*; *šurkubu*; *šutarkubu*; *tarkībum*, *tarkibtum*, *tarkubtu*

rakāku mng. unkn. jB **G** stat., of temple

rakānu(m) mng. unkn. O/jB lex. **G**; > *rakīnum*

rakāpu → *rakābu*

rakasu → *raksu*

rakāsu(m), Bogh., Alal. occas. *rakāšu* "to bind" **G** (*a/u*) [KEŠDA] **1.** "tie" s.th. on to s.th., "moor" boat, "attach" animal to yoke, plough, "bind" amulet, wool, medical dressing to person, baby to wet-nurse, silver into hem; "bind on, round" weapons, clothing, "bandage" invalid; transf., illness, evil; stat. of part of body, liver "is attached" **2.** "tie up, together" package, sack, commodities, reeds **3.** "bind" with fetters **4.** "install, insert" s.th.; "enrol" person, horse in army; "join together, construct" foundation, fort; NB *riksa r.* (operation in wall-repairs) **5.** "prepare, set ready" bread, cups; "lay, set" table; *riksa r.* "set out (components of) offering(-ceremony)" **6.** *riksa*/*rikista r.* "conclude treaty", Ass. "issue an ordinance"; *awāta r.* "impose" (s.o.'s) word, orders **7.** of obligation, esp. OA *kaspum i(na)/išti qaqqad X rakis* "X is liable for the silver"; "deliver s.th. under a contract"; "obligate, commit (s.o.) for" a length of time; "commit, contract" s.o. to employment, task **Gt** stat. **1.** "are tied together, attached to each other" **2.** of illness "is permanently bound" to (= *itti*) s.o. **D** ~ G [KEŠDA. MEŠ] "tie on to"; "bind round, accoutre with" weapons, rings; "bind up, bandage"; "pack up"; "assemble, fit together, construct" building, doors, forts etc.; "make s.o. liable" for payment; *riksāti(m) r.* "conclude agreement"; "oblige s.o. by contract" to do s.th.; of god "hold s.o. liable" for sins **Š** caus. of G **N** pass. "be girt" of loins, "be attached" to (= *itti*) s.o.; "be joined, fitted together"; OB "be banded together, conspire" **Ntn** iter.; > *raksu*; *riksu*, *rikistu*; *rukkusu*; *rikkusatum*; *markasu*, *markastu*; *murakkisu*; *mušarkisu*, *mušarkisūtu*; *tarkistum*, *tarkīsu*

rakbu(m) "mounted messenger"? O/jB [RÁ. GABA]; also *r. imēri(m)* [jB U5] "donkey rider" as messenger; < *rakābu*

rakbû "mounted messenger" NA [(LÚ.)RA. GABA]; < Sum. or *rakābu* ?

rakībum (a canal)? Mari; < *rakābu*

rākibu(m) "rider" Bab.; OB also as PN; *r. narkab(ā)ti* "charioteer", at Nuzi also social rank; lex. (also *rakūbu* ?) of sexually mature animal "mounting"; < *rakābu*

rakīnum (an agricultural worker)? OB lex.; < *rakānu*

rakissu, *rakisu* → *raksu*

rakkābu(m) O/jB **1.** "sailor, crew" **2.** of animal "ready to mount (sexually)" **3.** (part of harrow); < *rakābu*

rakkābūtum "(provision of) crew" OB, boat rental; < *rakkābu*

rakkasūte → *rukkusu*

raksu, NA also *raka/isu*, Am., Bogh. occas. *rakšu*; f. *rakissu* "bound, tied" M/NB, NA [LAL] of basket "plaited"; "tied on"; "tied up, packaged"; "harnessed"; "built in, join(t)ed together"; of worker "hired, contracted"; NA (type of conscript); < *rakāsu*

râku "to pour out, away" M/jB **G** (pres. *tarâk*); liquids **D** ~ G

rakūbu (term for young)? jB lex.

rakūbu → also *rākibu*

rakūpu → *rukūbu*

rākūsā pl. "construction workers" NB of bridge; < Aram.

ramāku(m) "to bathe, wash o.s." **G** (*u/u*) [TU5] of person "wash in (= acc.)", *mê ina ramākika* "when you wash in water"; *dāma r.* "be bathed in blood"; "dilute, soak" drugs in water, beer **Gtn** iter. **Gt** stat. "is drenched in", of chariot wheel in blood etc. **D** "bathe, wash in (= acc.)" (trans.) [TU5], person, animal; Mari "prune"? vine **Dtn** iter. of D **Dt** "be washed, drenched" **Š** "cause" lock "to be drenched" in oil; > *ramku*, *ramkūtu*; *rimku*; *rumīkātu*; *rummukum*; *murammiku*, *murammiktum*; *tarmīku*, *tarmiktum*; *narmaku*, *narmaktu*

ramāmu(m) "to roar, growl" O/jB **G** (*u/u*) of person, animal; of Adad, i.e. thunder; of battle, illness, drum, earth, building(s) **Gtn** iter. [MU7.MU7] of Adad; > *rimmu*; *ramīmu*; *rāmimu*; *murta''imu*?

ramāmu → also *râmu* II

ramannu → *armannu*; *ramānu*

ramānu(m), Ass. usu. *ramunu(m)*, M/NB also *ramannu*, *remānu*, *ramnu*; O/MA pl. f. "self" [NÍ] *ramānšu* "himself, itself", *ramānī*, Ass. *raminī* "myself"; *ana r.*-, loc.-adv. *ramānuš* etc. "for himself etc.", also "for himself alone, by himself"; *ana r.*, loc.-adv. *turru* "to convert to o.'s own, appropriate", also *ana īdi r. turru*; *ina r.*- "alone, independently, at o.'s own expense"; after st. constr. or *ša*, e.g. NA *šaknu ša rami/āniya* "my own appointee", OB *ina qāt r.-ya* "with my own hand", *ina*, *kīma ṭēm r.-šunu* "according to their own assessment; initiative"; MA animals *ramanātušunu* "their own bodies" of gold; Mari *ana ramānimma* "independently, all by (him)self"

ramāṣu "to enclose, mount"? Bogh., jB **G** lex. only; > *tarmāṣu*?

ramā'u → *ramû* III

ramīmu(m) "roar, rumbling" O/jB, of Adad, chariot etc.; < *ramāmu*

rāmimu "roarer" jB in DN ᵈ*R.*, of Adad; < *ramāmu*

rāmimu → also *râmu* II G

ramīṭu (a spot or mark)? jB med. [UD.A]

ramku(m); pl. *ramkū* and *ramkūtu* 'bathed' (a priest) Bab.(lit.); of Ea, Eridu; < *ramāku*

ramkūtu "post of *ramku* priest" jB

ramnu → *ramānu*

ramû(m) I "slack, released" Bab.; of man, sheep; of unstrung bow, of thread; < *ramû* III

ramû(m) II "to throw" Bab. **G** (*i/i*) [RI] **1.** "cast down, lay down" silver, bitumen **2.** "cast over s.o., invest s.o. with (= acc.)" fear, radiance etc. **3.** "pitch (and occupy)" dwelling, *šubta r.* "establish a residence", of god, king "occupy, take up occupation of" temple, palace etc. **Š** caus. of G **ŠD** ~ Š jB "cause to occupy" cult-centre **N** pass. "be invested with" fear; > *rimītu*; *narmû*

ramû(m) III, occas. *remû*, Ass. *ramā'u(m)* "to slacken, become loose" **G** (*u/u*) of parts of body, sinews; foundations, bandage **Gtn** iter., med. of parts of body **D** **1.** "release, let go" binding; "slacken" parts of body, "loosen" clothing; Mari ellipt. "loosen ropes, i.e. move on"; "release" lock **2.** "clear away" offerings; "absolve" guilt, sin, "pardon" **3.** OA "give s.th. up, relinquish"; NA "leave, abandon" s.o., "leave s.th. behind", "quit" a place **4.** NA "set free, release", with second verb "allow" to do s.th. **Dtn** jB of bird "repeatedly lets droop" wing **Dt** "become slack"; Mari *qātum urtammaššunūšim* "control over them has been slackened"; > *ramû* I; *rimûtu*; *rummû*; *murammû*?; *tarmītu*

rāmu, *ra'mu*? "(be)loved" jB, NA, of/by Ištar, the people; < *râmu* II

râmu(m) I, NA *ra'āmu* "love" Bab., NA of deity, person for king, brother, woman; *muruṣ r.* "venereal disease"; "love-making" of animal, in potency incantations; < *râmu* II infin.

râmu(m) II, Ass. and occas. later Bab. *ra'āmu(m)*, occas. *ramāmu* "to love" **G** (*ā*; *a/a*) [ÁG; jB also KI.ÁG(.GÁ)] of deity, person "love" s.o., s.th., "make love to"; freq. in PNs, e.g. *DN-rā'im-kitti/zēri/šarri* "DN loves justice/seed/king", NB also *-rāmim-*; of sheep, its lamb; of dog, its master; *ašar i/tarammu* "wherever he/you desire" **Gtn** iter. OA, Am.; NB *ašar ir/štâmu* "wherever he desired" **Gt** **1.** OB "love permanently"? **2.** jB "love one another" **D** of dog, "fawn, fondle" **Dt** recipr. "fondle one another" **Š** caus. of G **N** pass. of G "be loved, caressed"; > *rāmu*; *ra'īmu*, *rîmu*, *rîmtu*; *ra'ūmtu*, *rûmtu*; *râmu* I, *ra'āmuttu*; *rīmātum*; *ru'āmu*; *rā'imānu*, *rā'imānû*; *rā'imūtum*; *rayyāmum*; *ritūmum*; *ir'emum*; *murtâmu*; *nar'amātu*, *narāmu*, *narāmtu*; *tarāmu*, *tartāmū*

râmu III, Ass. *riāmu* "to present to, endow" M/NB, NA **G** (*ī*) M/NB "make gift of" land etc. to s.o. (= acc.); *rīmūta r.* "present as a gift"; NA "excuse, remit"; > *rīmu* II; *rīmūtu*; *tarīmtu*

ra'mu → *rāmu*

râmuttu → *ra'āmuttu*

rangu → *raggu*

rantarra (an object) Nuzi; < Hurr.?

rapādu(m) I, *rupādu* (a disease of the joints?) O/jB [SA.AD.GAL]; of humans, *šam(mu/i) r.* "drugs for *r.*"; also lex., of sheep

rapādu(m) II "to roam, wander" **G** (*u/u*) absol., of person, gazelle; + acc. *ṣēra r.* "roam the desert" etc. **Gtn** (jB occas. *i/i*) iter. of demon etc. "constantly roam" desert etc., also *ina kamâti/sūqi r.* "wander in the outback/street"; transf. med., of tongue **D** **1.** OA "keep s.o. moving" **2.** jB ellipt. of spasm "make (body) move" **3.** Mari "do s.th. actively, persist" **Š** caus. of G **Št** or **Štn** ~ Gtn, of restless weapon; > *ripittu*; *murappidum*; *murtappidu*; *mušarbidu*?; → *rapdum*

rapaltu → *rapaštu*; *rapšu* I

rapāqu(m) **G** (*i/i*) **1.** O/jB "to hoe" field, garden **2.** M/NA "fix" with nails, "rivet"?; transf. "fasten" enemy's neck with fetter **D** ~ G **1.** jB "hoe" field **2.** NA "fasten" in fetters; OA transf. "exert pressure on" debtor; > *rapqu*; *ripqu*; *rupuqtum*; *rapīqum*; *rāpiqu*; *ruppuqum*?; *narbaqu*

rapāsu(m) "to beat, thresh" O/jB, MA **G** (*i/i*) "hit" s.o., animal, with s.th., "clap" o.'s hands; "beat, belabour" s.o.; "thresh" grain; OB transf. of expenditure "ruin" s.o. **N** pass., lex. only; > *ripsu* I; *rāpisum*; *narpasu*, *narpastum*; *tarpīsu*?

rapaštu(m), *rapaltu* ~ "loin, lower back" [GIŠ.KUN; ÚR.KUN] of human ~ "pelvic region, small of back"; of animal "haunch, rump?", also (^{uzu})*r.* as cut of meat, "chine"; astr. (^{mul})*r.* (part of constellation); < *rapšu* I

rapāšu(m) "to be(come) broad, expand" **G** (*i/i*, occas. *u/u*; stat. *rapaš*) [DAGAL; jB also PEŠ] **1.** of object, door, space, part of exta "be wide" **2.** of river "widen, become wide"; transf. of property, herds etc. "be(come) extensive", of land, population "expand" **3.** of understanding etc. (*ḫasīsu*, *libbu*, *pānū* etc.) "be great, deep, generous" **Gt** jB stat., infin. "be very wide, broad" etc. **Gtn** OB "widen repeatedly" of part of liver **D** [DAGAL; PEŠ; TÁL] **1.** "give s.th. (a specific) width" **2.** "widen" path, "extend" city, land, property, family etc. **3.** "scatter afar" seeds **4.** "give copiously" gold, advice, wisdom **5.** NA of king *uzna/u urappaš* "use wisdom abundantly" **6.** jB ellipt. "take wide steps"? **Dt** pass. of D jB "be extended" **ŠD** poet. ~ D jB "widen" ditch; > *rapšu* I, *rapšiš*, *rapaštu*; *rupšu*; *rappašu*; *ritpāšu*; *narpašû*; *tarpašû*

rapātu (or *rapāṭu*) mng. unkn. jB **G** (*a/u*), obj. drugs

rapā'um, OB *rapûm* **G** **1.** OA mng. unkn., obj. silver **2.** OB "to heal" in fPN *Tarpi-Annunītum*; → *ripûtu*

rapdum (or *rapṭum*) (a cripple)? OB lex.; → *rapādu* II

rapīqum mng. uncl. OB; (a food)?; pl. f. (a plot of ground)?; < *rapāqu*

rapīqu → also *rabīku*

rāpiqu(m) "hoer" O/jB; < *rapāqu*

rāpisum "thresher" OB; < *rapāsu*

rappašu "very wide" M/jB; < *rapāšu*

rappu(m) "hoop, clamp" O/jB used as shackle; transf. of deity, king "band" shackling enemy, people; astr. ^{mul}*r.* (a constellation); < Sum.

rapqu "hoed" jB lex.; < *rapāqu*

rapšiš "widely" j/NB, "over wide area"; < *rapšu* I

rapšu(m) I; f. *rapaš/ltu(m)* "wide, extended" [DAGAL] of building, object, road; sea, sky, earth; "extensive" property, army, population; "great, deep" heart, understanding etc.; < *rapāšu*; > *rapaštu*, *rapšiš*

rapšu(m) II; pl. f. "winnowing shovel" Bab, OA?; of wood

rapṭum → *rapdum*

rapûm → *rapā'um*

raqābu ~ "to decay" NA **G** not attested **Š** caus., mng. uncl.; > *ruqbu*?, *ruqbūtu*

raqādu(m) "to dance, skip" Bab., NA **G** (*u/u*) of human, animal; of part of body, "jerk" **Gtn** iter. **D** "make s.th. dance"? **Š** "make skip" etc., of illness, "cause spasms"?; "make" s.o.'s heart "jump"; jB/NA rit., obj. cakes, mng. uncl. **ŠDt** ~ D, infin. *šutraqqudu*, mng. uncl.; > *riqdu*; *riqittu*; *raqqidu*; *mušarqidu*

raqāqu(m) "to be(come) thin, fine" **G** (*i/i*) [SAL.LA] of parts of liver, of body; of hair "be sparse"; of oil "get thinner" **Gtn** of part of liver "become ever thinner" **D** "roll out thin", drugs, gold leaf; > *raqqu* I, *raqqatu* I; *ruqqu* II; *raqqaqu*; *ruqququ*

raqāqum → also *ragāgum* II

raqā'u → *raqû*

rāqidum → *raqqidu*

raqqaqu "very thin" jB, NA; < *raqāqu*

raqqatu(m) I **1.** OA, O/jB (a fine garment) [TÚG.SAL.LA] **2.** NB (a thin decorative plate) **3.** OB as fPN *Raqqatum* "slim"; < *raqqu* I

raqqatu II "river-flats" j/NB of land beside river

raqqidu(m), also *rāqidum* ? "(cultic) dancer" O/jB; also (desig. of a donkey); < *raqādu*

raqqu(m) I "thin, fine" OA, O/jB [SAL.LA] of part of body, object, textile; palm tree; offering-vessel; hand-writing; "slim" of grain-measure; < *raqāqu*; > *raqqatu* I

raqqu(m) II "tortoise, turtle" O/jB [BAL.GI (.KU6); BA.AL.GI.KU6] *qulepti r.* "tortoise-shell" as drug; PlN *Nagīte-raqqi* "Tortoise-district"; as figurine

raqqû "oil-perfumer" O/jB, NA [ŠIM.SAR; (LÚ.)Ì.RÁ.RÁ]; < *ruqqû*

raqqû → also *ruqqû*

raqqûtu; pl. *raqquāte* "spice(s)" NA; < *ruqqû*

raqraqqu → *laqlaqqu*

raqtu → *saltu* II

raqû(m), NA *raqā'u* "to hide, give refuge to" O/jB, NA **G** (*i/i*) fugitive slave; Nuzi "dismiss, send away" **Gtn** iter. **D** ~ G **N** "hide (o.s.), take refuge" **Ntn** iter. of N; > *riqītu* I; *marqītu* I, *narqītu* I

rāqu → *rīqu* I

râqu → *riāqu*; *rêqu*; *ruāqu*

raquddu, *raqundu* (an implement) NB; of iron

rāqūtu → *rīqūtu*

rasābu(m), *rasāpu(m)*, NB occas. *rašābu* "to smite" Bab., NA **G** (*i/i*) city, enemy, with weapon **D** ~ G "beat down, fell" criminal, enemy; "thrash" limbs; > *risbu*, *risbatu*, *risibtu*

rasānu(m), *raṣānu*, NB *resēnu* "to soak, steep" Bab., NA **G** (*a/u*, NB *i/i*) in (usu. = *ina*, also acc.) water, milk, oil etc.; > *risnu*, *risittu*; *rasīnū*; *rāsinu*, *rāsinūtu*; *marsattu*

rāsānu → *rāšānu*

rasāpu → *rasābu*

rasīnū pl. tant ~ "dough lumps" j/NB, MA?; < *rasānu*

rāsinu, *rēsinu* "tanner"? NB; < *rasānu*

rāsinūtu, *rēsinūtu* "activity of tanner" NB, *r. epēšu*; < *rāsinu*

rāsum "detachment" Mari, of troops; < W.Sem.

râsu(m), *rêsu*, *ra'āsu*, *râšu(m)*, *rêšu* "to strike, smite" OAkk, O/jB(lit.) **G** (*a/a*) of meteor "hit" ground, "strike" s.o. **D** ~ G "smite" lands, enemies; > *rīsu*

ra'su, occas. *re'su*, NB *rāšu* "sheikh" NA, NB, of Chaldaeans; < Aram.

raṣādu(m) "to watch from hiding, spy"? O/MB **G** (*i/i*) of enemy; > *marṣadu*

raṣānu(m) ~ "to be powerful (of voice)" O/jB **G** (*u/u*) lex. **Gtn** of cries "sound out repeatedly" **D** stat. "is given powerful voice"? of deity **Dt** of Adad, drum, "rumble loudly"; > *raṣmu*!; *ruṣṣunu*; *murtaṣnu*

raṣānu → also *rasānu*

raṣāpu "to build" Ass., Am., Bogh., Ug. **G** (*i/i*) house, wall, ziggurrat; tower of skulls; NA *paṭṭer riṣip* "clear (site) and rebuild" **D** ~ G Ug., houses?; > *raṣpu*; *riṣpu*, *riṣiptu*

raṣāṣu ~ "to cry" jB **G** (*u/u*)

raṣi(t)tu (or *raṣṣutu*) (a reed object) MA

raṣmu ~ "loud-voiced" jB, NA, of deity, demon, king; < *raṣānu* (!)

raṣpu "built" NA, of houses; < *raṣāpu*

raṣṣatu → *raṣittu*

raṣṣiṣu "chicken" NB; < Aram.

raṣûm Š OB ~ "to give" house "in payment"?; → *tarṣiātum*

râṣu(m), *ra'āṣu* "to rush (to help)" O/jB **G** (*ū*; jB perf. *išta'uṣ*) "go to aid" s.o. (= *ana*, dat.); OB *qablum irūṣa ana bābika* "battle rushed to your gate" **D** jB "shed"? tears; > *rūṣu*; *rīṣu*; → *rêṣu*

rašābu(m) ~ "to be terrifying" O/jB **G** (stat. *rašub*) of deity etc. **D** lex. only; > *rašbu*; *rašubbu*, *rašubbatu*; *rišibtu*

rašābu → also *rasābu*

rašādu "to found, lay foundations of" Bab., NA (**G** MB stat. "is founded" **D** jB stat., both uncert.) **Š** "lay" foundation (*išdu*, *temennu*, *uššu*); "found" wall, building, residence; "establish" throne, reign, priesthood, name etc.; < *išdu* denom.; > *rašdu*; *maršidātum*; *šuršudu*

rašāku(m) "to dry out" O/jB **G** lex. (intrans.) **D** "dry out" (trans.), building; stat. of tongue, part of exta "is dried out"; > *rišiktu*; → *ruššukum*

rāšānu, *ra'šānu*, occas. *rāsānu* (a skin complaint)? jB, of humans, cattle, sheep

rašašim OB om. for *rāš(i) ašîm* "headache sufferer"?; < *rašû* I + *ašû* I ?

rašāšu ~ "to glow (with heat)"? jB **G** (*u/u*) of substance in kiln **D** "heat up"?

rašā'u → *rašû* I.III

rašbu(m) ~ "terrifying" Bab.(lit.), of deity, temple, city, flood, battle; < *rašābu*

rašdu "firmly founded" jB, of shrines; < *rašādu*

rāšilūtu "luck, divine favour" Am., NA; < *rāši ili* + *-ūtu*

rašû(m) I, OAkk, Ass. *rašā'u(m)* "to acquire, get" **G** (*i/i*) [TUKU] **1.** "become owner of, come into possession of" property etc. **2.** "acquire" brother, friend; "get" strength, help, (divine) protection, repute (*šuma*); wisdom, advice **3.** "come to have" claim, grounds for complaint, credit against s.o., "be owed" s.th. by s.o., *ša elīya taršû* "which I owe you" **4.** "experience, be affected by" need, wish, fear, anger, compassion, *nīd aḫi r.* "become negligent", OA also absol. "get worried" **5.** → *idu* 4; *pānu* I 9; *qaqqadu* 7; *ṣītu* 4 **Gtn** iter. [TUKU.TUKU; Nuzi TUKU.MEŠ] **Š** caus.; "cause, arrange for s.o. to get" son, friend etc.; "supply s.o. with" field, commodity; of deity "endow" s.o. with strength etc.; "secure" justice, verdict, mercy, forgiveness; "cause to suffer" punishment, pain, interest **Štn** iter., OB *pānam šutarši* "make clear repeatedly"; > *rāšû*, *rāšilūtu*; *maršītu*; *rašašim*?; → *rašûtu*

rašû II "to be(come) red" j/NB **G** (*i/i*) of feet, of mucus **Dt** "become red" of face; > *rišûtu*; *rūšum* III; *ruššû*

rašû(m) III, *rašā'um* ~ "to slacken" **G** (*u/u*) OA, OB, sinews; Mari ellipt., transf. "weaken (stance), acquiesce"? **D** OB, jB ~ "harass" **Dtn** iter. "constantly maltreat" **Dt** pass. of D; > *rešûm*?; *muraššû* I; *murtaššû*; *taršītum*

rāšu → *ra'su*; *rēšu*

rāšû(m), occas. *rešû*; f. *rāšītu* **1.** OB lex. "rich, well-off" **2.** NB [LÚ.TUKU-] "creditor" (→ *rašûtānu*); < *rašû* I

râšu → *râsu*; *riāšu*

rašubbatu(m) "terrifying appearance" Bab.(lit.), of deity, demon, king, weapon; < *rašubbu*

rašubbu ~ "terrifying" M/NB(lit.) of deity, temple, king etc.; < *rašābu*; > *rašubbatu*

rašûtānu, *rešûtānu* "creditor" NB; < *rašûtu*; → *rāšû* 2

rašūtu (a garment) NB

rašûtu, *rešûtu* "credit" NB [TUKU-] *ša r.* *ša abīya ina muḫḫišunu ibaššû* "of whom my father is a creditor"; *r. eṭēru* "to pay (amount of) credit"; < Aram. or *rašû* I ?; > *rašûtānu*

rašûtu → also *rišûtu*

ratāmu "to whisper"? jB **G** lex. only

ratātu "to tremble" jB **G** (*u/u*) of person, part of body; > *ratītu*; *rattitu*; *ruttutum*

ratītu (a shivering sickness) jB; < *ratātu*

rattitu "shivery" jB; < *ratātu*

ratuttu (a kind of anenome)? jB [Ú.GI.RIM. BABBAR ?]

raṭābu(m) "to be damp" Bab. **G** (only stat. and infin.) of food, part of liver; of dates "are fresh" **D** "moisten" malt, ground, dates; OB *ṭuppam r.* "moisten, i.e. erase tablet"; > *raṭbu*; *ruṭbu*, *ruṭubtu*; *riṭbu*, *riṭibtu*, *ruṭibtu*; *ruṭṭubu*; *muraṭṭibtu*; *narṭabu*, *narṭabtu*

raṭāpu(m) "to continue" or "to begin" O/jB **G** (*u/u*) work; jB sexual intercourse (with = dat.); Mari, Bogh. with second verb in infin. "continue/begin" doing s.th., *arṭup bakâm* "I continued/began to cry", *baqāmam irṭup* "he continued/began to pluck"

raṭbu(m); f. *raṭubtu*, Mari also *raṭa/ibtum* "damp, fresh" Bab., bread, fruit, meat, wood; "wet, irrigated" fields; < *raṭābu*

raṭû → *retû* II

rāṭu(m); pl. f. "water-channel, pipe" O/jB, M/NA [ŠÌTA] "irrigation channel"; "pipe" for irrigation, drainage; "tube" of metal; "oesophagus", "channel" of eye, womb, liver

râṭu(m) mng. unkn. O/jB **G** (*ā* ?)

ra'u → *ra'i*

ra'û → *re'û*

rā'um → *rū'u*

rā'û → *rē'û*

râ'u "to befriend" jB, MA? **G**; **Gt** "become partners to each other" **D** lex. only ?; < *rū'u* denom.

ra'ūmtu(m), *ru'ūmtu* "beloved" OAkk as fPN; jB epith. of goddess; < *râmu* II; → *rûmtu*

rayyāmum ~ "friend" OB; < *râmu* II

raziqātu ~ "garden plants"? jB lex.

razû **N** (*u*) "to make off, scram" Ug.; < W.Sem.

râzum → *rā'izu*

re'ābum → *riābu*

re'āmu → *rêmu*

rē'âtu → *rē'ītu*

rebâ/ênē → *rebû* 2

rebât, *rebiat* → *rabiat*

rebētu → *rebītu*

rebībītum (part of body) Mari; → *rebītu* 2

rebîš **1.** jB "fourthly" **2.** NB "four times"; < *rebû*

rebītu(m), Ass. *rebētu(m)* **1.** "square, piazza; open space" in city [SILA.DAGAL(.LA)]; desig. of Akkad, Uruk; *r. āli(m)* "city square", *r. abul PlN* "PlN Gate Square"; Ass.(roy. inscr.) "district, precincts", e.g. *r. Dēr*, *Ninua* **2.** as part of body ~ "abdomen" (→ *rebībītum*), also *r. šinnēšu* "palate"?; < *rebû*; → *rību* V

rebû(m), *rabû*, Nuzi etc. *rubû*; f. *re/abūtu(m)* "fourth; a quarter" **1.** usu. before subst. "fourth", *ina rebūtim šattim* "in the fourth year"; MA *ina rabūtešu* "for the fourth time"; jB *ina rebî* "fourthly" **2.** fraction, f. & m. [IGI.4.GÁL(.LA)] "one-quarter", OA *rebūt erîm* "a quarter of the copper"; M/NB "quarter (-shekel)" [4-*ut/tú*], *3 rebât* "three-quarters"; NA *ana rabûttišu irabbi* "will bear interest at 25%"; NB *rebû* "(field subject to) 25% tax", pl. *rebâ/ênē*; < *erbe*; > *rabā'iu*; *rabiat*; *rabiāna*; *rabūšene*; *rebîš*, *rebītu*, *rību* V; *rubu'ā*, *rubu'û*; *rubbu'um*

redîš "in succession" jB ext.; < *redû* I

rēdītum (a payment)? OB; < *rēdû*

redû(m) I, Ass. *radā'u(m)* "to accompany, lead, drive, proceed" **G** (*e/e*, *i/i*, OAkk *a/a*) [UŠ] **1.** "accompany, escort" s.o. **2.** "lead, take", vent. "bring" s.o. somewhere **3.** "drive" horses, asses, cart, boat, "herd" cattle, sheep etc. **4.** "convey" goods, booty, divine symbol **5.** Bab. ~ "appropriate, claim possession of", *warkat PN r.* "succeed to PN's estate" **6.** "pursue, chase" enemy etc.; "follow" tracks, customs **7.** "lead, direct" troops **8.** ellipt. "proceed, be on the way", *arki r.* "follow after", Ass.(roy. inscr.) "march"; astr. of planet "advance" **Gtn** [UŠ.UŠ; UŠ.MEŠ] iter. of G **Gt** jB **1.** recipr. of G of parts of liver "follow each other"? **2.** "lead away" **D** "add", "make additional payment of" commodities, animals, land etc.; *eli nišēša nišē lure/addi* "I added people to its people"; *šuma ul uraddi* "I did not add a line (of text)"; NB *uraddēma aballuṭ* "I am getting healthier" **Dtn** MB(Ass.) "make repeated additions" **Dt** pass. of D "be added" **Š** caus. **1.** "have s.o. convey s.th." **2.** "make s.o. follow" path etc. **3.** "cause" water, canal, blood "to flow (out)"; absol. of invalid "defecate", of demon "spray" (poison?) **4.** "make" constellations "follow on" **Št¹** pass. of Š OB of water "be released, channelled" **Št²** OB "follow along" a road, also ellipt. "proceed"; OB ~ "help" s.o. "along", "do a favour"; jB "persist" in illness **ŠD** ~ D "add" jB(poet.) **N** pass. of G "be led away", of animals "be driven"; "be pursued"; of house "be appropriated"; > *rīdu* I, *ridûtu*; *redîš*; *rēdû*, *rēdûtum*, *rēdītum*, *rādiu*; *ruddû*; *mardû*; *mardītu*, *merdītu*; *mušardû*; *šurdû*, *šurdûtu*; *terdû*, *terdītu*

redûm II "to be suitable" OB **G** (*u/u*, occas. *i/i*); with infin., *ana ṣabātim ireddû* "they are suitable for taking"; boat *ula ... eredduniāšim* "is not suitable for us"; sheep ... *ana ṣibûtim ireddû* "meet the requirement" **Gtn** iter. "serve repeatedly" **N** ~ G "be found suitable"; > *riddu*

rēdû(m) **1.** Bab. [UKU.UŠ] "soldier, private", freq. acting as police; *qaqqad rēdîm* [UKU.UŠ SAG] "original (i.e. not substitute) private" **2.** M/NB [LÚ.UŠ] ~ "administrator" **3.** M/jB "pursuer, persecutor" **4.** jB "accompanying (ox)"?; < *redû* I; Ass. → *rādiu*

rēdûtum in *rēdûssuma lillik* "let him perform his military service" OB; < *rēdû*

rēḫāniš "as the remnant" jB; < *rēḫu*

rēḫtu(m), *rīḫtu(m)* "remainder" [ÍB.TAG4] *rēḫat būlim* "the rest of the cattle", pl. *rēḫāti* "left-overs (of temple offerings)"; NA, NB in PNs, *DN-r.-uṣur* "DN protect the rest"; < *rēḫu*

reḫû(m), *raḫû* "to pour out; have sexual intercourse with" Bab.(lit.) **G** (*i/i*, *e/e*) **1.** of liquid, river, sleep "flow over" s.o.; trans. "pour" sleep, liquid "over" **2.** of man, "copulate with, inseminate", girl *ša lā reḫâtu* "has not been inseminated"; transf. of god, seed plough "inseminate" earth **3.** of father, demon etc. "engender, procreate" **Gtn** iter., of diseases "repeatedly affect" s.o. **Gt** lex., recipr. **D** jB "sprinkle" with oil, "pour" magical liquid "over" s.o. **N** pass. mng. uncl.; > *riḫītu*; *riḫûtu*; *ruḫû*; *rāḫû*; *raḫḫātu*; *marḫītu*

rēḫu(m), *rīḫu(m)* "remaining, left over" Bab., NA; *rēḫūtešunu* "the remainder of them"; as subst. "the rest", pl. freq. *rēḫānu* "those remaining"; < *riāḫu*

rē'i-alpūtu "post of oxherd" NB [LÚ.SIPA. GU4-], as prebend; < *rē'û* + *alpu* I

re'indu "beloved" NB as fPN; < *re'mu*

rē'ītu(m) "shepherdess" OAkk, O/jB, epith. of goddesses; also fPN; < *rē'û*

rē'ium → *rē'û*

rekmu mng. unkn. jB, epith. of weapon

rēltu → *rīštu*

remānu → *ramānu*

rēmānû → *rēmēnû*

rēmēnānû "compassionate" jB; < *rēmēnû* + *-ān*

rēmēnû(m), Ass. *rēmānû* "merciful" Bab., NA, of deities; occas. of human; < *rēmu* + *-ān* + *-ī*

rēmtu "womb" jB [ARḪUŠ], of foetus *rēmassu* "its womb"; < *rēmu*

remû → *ramû* III

rēmu(m), *rīmu* "womb; compassion" [ARḪUŠ] **1.** "womb" of woman; goddess, *rīmu ālid* *napḫari* "the womb which bore all"; "(representation of) womb"; *aban r.* "womb stone", lex. **2.** "compassion, mercy" of deity, king; *r. rašû(m)/šakānu(m)* "to be merciful/act mercifully"; jB *nīq rēmi u šulmi* "offering for mercy and well-being"; < *rêmu*; > *rēmēnānû, rēmēnû; rēmtu; rēmūtu*

rēmu → also *rīmu* I

rêmu(m), Ass. *re'āmu(m)* "to be merciful, have compassion on" **G** [ARḪUŠ] of deity, freq. in PNs; *ul irēmanni ištarī* "my goddess has not had mercy on me"; of king, authority "forgive" **Gt** OA "be mutually accommodating" **Š** NB "make s.o. merciful" to (= dat.) s.o.; > *rēmu, rēmēnānû, rēmēnû; rēmtu; rēmūtu*

re'mu "friend, loved one" NB; < Aram.; > *re'indu*

rēmūtu "pardon" NA(roy. inscr.) *r. šakānu* "to decree s.o.'s pardon"; < *rēmu*

rēmūtu → also *rīmūtu*

rēqēnum "from a distance" OB in *ina r.-ma*; < *rēqu*

rēqu(m), *rēqû(m)* "far, distant" Bab.(lit.) in space; in time, NB *ištu ūmī rēqūti* "from distant days"; < *rêqu*

rêqu(m) "to be distant, go far off" OAkk, Bab. **G** (*ē*; stat. usu. *rūq*, OB also *rēq*) **1.** stat. "is distant", of place, person; of journey "is long" **2.** "go far away from (= acc. or prep.)" place, person; transf. NB, of decision "be remote"; NB of water "be too far (down)" to draw (*ana sâbu*) **Gt** jB "go off away" **D** "keep s.o. at a distance", OAkk name of wall *Murīq-* "Fender-off of ..."; OB "banish" from palace **Š** **1.** "send s.o. away from" **2.** "allow to move away from"; > *rūqu, rēqu, rūqiš, rēqēnum*; Ass. → *ruāqu*

resēnu → *rasānu*

rēsinu → *rāsinu*

rēsinūtu → *rāsinūtu*

rêsu → *râsu*

re'su → *ra'su*

rēṣu(m) "helper" [Á.TAḪ] (OB poet. and later, nom. freq. *rēṣū-* before pron. suff.) of god, freq. in PNs; of persons, OB *rēṣka* "your helper"; "(military) support", jB *adi rēṣēšu* "with his allies"; < *rêṣu*; > *rēṣūtu*

rêṣu(m) "to help" O/jB **G** e.g. PN *Sîn-rēṣam* "Help me, Sîn" **D** ~ G MB *ī nura'iṣ* "let us help" one another; > *rēṣu, rēṣūtu*; → *râṣu*

rēṣūtu(m) "help, assistance" [Á.TAḪ]; jB *ana rēṣūt aḫāmeš* "to their mutual support"; *rēṣūt awīlim* (etc.) *alāku(m)* "to go to s.o.'s assistance"; < *rēṣu*

rēšātu → *rīštu*

rēšētu → *rēštu*

rēšiš "like a slave" jB; < *rēšu* 6

rēštu(m); pl. *rēšētu*, NA *rīšāti* "beginning; point; prime" [SAG] **1.** OB "beginning" of month; "first instalment" of rent **2.** "top", "peak" of mountain, "head" of bed **3.** "prime quality" of oil, OA as subst., also pl. **4.** NA, NB pl. [SAG.MEŠ] "first-fruits?" as offering **5.** of deity *ana rēšēti šakānu/šūṣû* ~ "to exalt"? king etc. **6.** *atmû rēšēti* "human race" (mng. uncl.); < *rēšu*; > *rēštû*

rēštu → also *rīštu*

rēštû(m) "first, pre-eminent, prime" Bab., NA [SAG; jB occas. SAG.KAM] **1.** "first" in time; in series, of tablet; "first(-born)" of god, king, calf **2.** "pre-eminent" of deity, person **3.** "prime, first-class" of animal, food, drink; of fruit, phps. also "earliest (in season)"; clothing **4.** "primeval" city; "original" wall, foundation, cult; < *rēštu* + *-ī*

rešûm "reckless, inconsiderate" OB lex.; < *rašû* III ?

rešû → also *rāšû*

rēšu(m), *rāšu(m)* "head; beginning; slave" [SAG] **1.** "head" of person; of animal, esp. in representations, OB *kās r. alpim, ṣabītim* etc. "ox, gazelle's-head cup"; transf. in idioms (occas. du.) *r. šapālu/šaqû* (s.o.'s) "head is low/is high", *rēssu našû* "to care about him; require, need, call on him", *r. šuqqû* "to honour"; → *kullu* III 2; *ina r. izuzzu(m)* "to stand by, assist" s.o.; OB DN *ili rēšiya* "my personal god" **2.** O/jB *šūt r.* ~ "courtiers", M/NB *ša r.* (a court official); MA du. *ša rēšēn*, NA *ša r.* [LÚ.SAG] "eunuch" **3.** "top, upper part" of building; "peak" of mountain; "upper border" of country, "top" of door, furniture, "head" of bed; "upper side, tip" of part of body; transf. *ana r. šakānu* "to promote"; horizontally "head" of canal, bridge; *r. eqli(m) kašādu(m)* "to reach head of field", i.e. destination **4.** "beginning"; in time *r. šatti(m)/(w)arḫi(m)* "b. of year/month", *r. šarrūti* "accession year"; of activity *r. nikkassē* "b. of accounting", *r. kisrišu* "his first payment", *r. tāmarti* "first visibility", *r. šipti* "start of incantation"; OB math. *r. še'im* etc. "initial, original amount of grain" etc.; OB *rēšam, ina rēši(m)* (OB occas. du. *rēšīn*), *ištu/ultu/issu r.* "earlier, from the start" **5.** "top quality, the best"; OA ~ "available amount, level" of goods, payment **6.** O/jB "slave" [also SAG.ÌR]; > *rēšiš, rēštu, rēštû, rēšūtu; rūštu*

rēšu → *râsu*

rešûtānu → *rašûtānu*

rēšuttu → *rēšūtu*

rešûtu → *rašûtu*

rēšūtu(m), Ass. *rēšuttu* "slavery" Bab., MA, Ug. [NAM.SAG] NB *r. epēšu* "to serve" (gods); *r. alāku(m)* "become a slave; perform service"; < *rēšu* 6

retû(m) I "fixed, installed" O/MB of door, wheel; < *retû* II

retû(m) II, occas. *raṭû* "to drive in, fix" Bab., NA **G** (*i/i*) "drive in" nail etc.; "fix in place", foundations with bitumen and baked brick, doors **Gtn** iter. **D** ~ G "drive in" nail, stake; "install" stele, doors; "fix" eyes; "impale" s.o. on stake **N** "be fastened" of sword; > *retû* I; *martû*?; *tertītu*

rētu ~ "strength" jB lex.

re'û(m), M/NA *ra'û*, M/NB also *rey/wû* "to pasture, tend" **G** (pres. *ire''i*, *irê*, pret. *irē*) [SIPA] sheep, cows; "(allow animals to) graze" field, plants (= acc.); transf. of god, king "tend" human(s) **Gtn** iter. **Gt** "constantly pasture, tend", sceptre *murte'ât nišē* "which constantly tends the people" **N** NB of cattle "be herded, grazed"; > *rītu*; *rē'û*, *rē'ītu*, *rē'ûtu*; *merītu*

rē'u "angry" Bogh. lex.; < W.Sem.

rē'û(m), *rēyû(m)*, OAkk *rē'ium*, *rā'û(m)* "shepherd, herdsman" [(LÚ.)SIPA] of sheep, cattle, donkeys, horses, pigs, NA camels, M/NB birds etc.; *rab(i) r.* "chief shepherd"; transf. god, king as "shepherd" of humanity, the land; Mari, Bogh. ext. (a part of the liver); also lex. (a bird) [SIPA.MUŠEN], *mār(at) r.* (a grasshopper); < *re'û*; > *rē'ītu*, *rē'ûtu*; *rē'i-alpūtu*

rē'ūtu → *rīmūtu*

rē'ûtu(m) "shepherdship" Bab., NA [SIPA-] sheep *ana r.* "for pasturage", NB *mār-r.* "position as member of shepherds" as prebend; of king, *r. epēšu(m)* "to exercise rôle of shepherd", *r. tenēšēti* "shepherdship of humanity" etc.; jB "animals being pastured, herd"; < *rē'û*

rewû, *reyû* → *re'û*

rēyû → *rē'û*

rēzu → *ra'āzu*

riābu(m), *râbu*, OAkk *re'ābum*? "to replace, requite" **G** (*ī*) [SU] **1.** "replace, restore" s.th. to s.o. (= dat., *ana*); MB *ul rībāk* "I am not repaid", *rība r.* "pay compensation"; of deity esp. in PN "restore" brother(s) (in compensation) **2.** O/jB "pay back, requite", *gimilla(m) r.* "return a favour", god *irâbšu lumnu* "will pay him back with evil" **D** OA "replace" losses **Dt** OA "be recompensed"; MB of favour "be requited" to s.o. **Š** caus. of G OB; > *rību* III; *ru'ubbā'um*; *rā'ibānum*; *ra'ību* II?; *muribbu*; *tarībtu*; → *Rībatu*

riāḫu(m), *râḫu* "to remain, be left over" **G** (*i*) of commodities, animals, people, also math., astr. **D** "leave over, allow to remain" **Š** ~ D, esp. imper. "spare!" in PNs *Šurīḫ(a)-DN*; > *rēḫu*, *rēḫtu*, *rēḫāniš*; *rūḫu*; *ruḫḫu*

riāmu → *râmu* III

ri'āmūtu → *ra'āmuttu*

riānum (a tree) OAkk, OB?, used for masts ?; → *iliānum*

riāqu(m), *râqu* "to be empty; be unemployed" **G** (*ī*; stat. Bab. *rīq*, Ass. *rāq*) [SUD] **1.** "be empty", of house, granary, boat etc.; field *mê rīqat* "is without water"; transf. of word "be meaningless" **2.** of persons, animals, plough "be without work", "be free" for (= *ana*) s.o.; *adi tariqqū* "until you are free"; of days "be empty, unoccupied" **D 1.** "make empty, empty out" jar etc. **2.** OB "leave" cattle "unemployed" **Š** ~ D "empty, unload" vessel, ship; NA "release" s.o., from employment; OB "allow" cattle "to be unemployed"; > *rīqu* I, *rīqūtu*; *terīqtu*

riāšu(m), *râšu* "to rejoice" **G** (*ī*; jB pres. pl. occas. *iruššū*) [SÙ] of deity, temple, land, freq. in PNs; of person, s.o.'s face (*panūšu irtīšū*), tree **Gtn** iter. MB **Gt** jB "rejoice constantly" **D** "give cause for rejoicing, celebration" to **Š** "cause to rejoice"; > *rīšu*, *rīštu*, *rīšiš*

riātu "ventive" jB lex., of Sum. infixes; < *warûm* II

rībatu(m) "compensation" as PN abbr. from names composed with *riābu*

ribbatu(m) I, occas. *ribbetum* "arrears, backlog of payments" O/jB [LÁL+GAG; LÁL+U; LAL+U; LÁL.ḪI.A] in silver, animals etc.; *bēl ribbēt awīlim* "man's creditor"; *ribbāti ša DN* "arrears owed to DN"

ribbatu II "10,000" Alal., *1 ribbat* (shekels) of silver, gold; < W.Sem.; → *rabbat*

ribbetum → *ribbatum* I

ribku(m) "concoction, infusion" O/jB rit., med.; < *rabāku*

ribšum "protest"? OA in *ribšē epāšum* "to make objections"?; < *rabāšum*

rību I "earthquake" M/NA, M/NB; < *râbu*

rību II "setting" of heavenly body j/NB, *ina niphi u r.* "at rising and setting"; stone *kīma r. šamši* "like sunset"; < *rabû* III; → *rūbu* II

rību III; pl. m. & f. "replacement, requital" OAkk, Bab. "(gift in) substitution"; "compensation"; < *riābu*

rību(m) IV (a vessel) OA, M/jB [DUG.DAL.GAL] of pottery, bronze; → *rābum*

rību V "square" Bogh. lex., for *rebītu*

rību → also *ra'ību* II

riddu, *rīdu* "(good) conduct" O/jB; *āḫiz r.* "well-behaved"; < *redûm* II

ridpu "pursuit" NA; < *radāpu*

rīdu(m) I Bab. [UŠ] **1.** NB "driving, droving" of animal **2.** "succession" of prince **3.** "pursuit, persecution", *bēl(et) r.-ya* "my persecutor"; < *redû* I

rīdu II (desig. of meat, flour) M/jB

rīdu → also *riddu*

ridûtu(m) Bab., NA [UŠ-] **1.** O/jB "appropriation, (right of) succession", *r. redû(m)* ~ "to administer s.o.'s domain" **2.** j/NB, NA "succession" (to throne), *mār ridûtišu* "his heir-apparent", *bīt ridûti* (crown prince's palace) **3.** jB "pursuit, persecution" **4.** jB *ūm ridût(i) Ištar* "day of procession? for Ištar"; < *redû* I

rigāmu mng. unkn. NA, unit of measure for vegetables

riggatu "villainy" NA/jB; < *ragāgu* I

rigibillum (a wooden instrument)? OAkk(Sum.)

rigimtum ~ "claim, request" OB, for payment, ration; < *ragāmu*

riglum (or *rik/qlum*) (an object) OA

rigmu(m); pl. f. "voice, cry, noise" [GÙ] "voice" of deity, human; "cry" of animal, bird etc.; *r. Adad* "thunder"; "noise" of natural phenomena, weapons, feet, fire, musical instruments; "pronunciation" of cuneiform wedge; *r. šakānu(m)* "to raise o.'s voice" against (= *elī*, *ina muḫḫi*), "make remonstration"; < *ragāmu*

riḫiṣtu, *riḫiltu* "flooding" M/jB [RA-], usu. *r. Adad* "flooding of Adad", "storm-flood"; < *raḫāṣu* I

riḫītu(m) "pouring out, insemination" Bab., esp. in PNs; < *reḫû*

riḫṣu(m) I "flood(ing)" O/jB, NA [RA; GÌR.BAL] from storm, cloud-burst; Mari transf., of military assault ?; *Adad ša r.*, $^{d}R.$ "god of storm-flood", *urpat r.* "cloud causing storm-flood"; (feature on liver); < *raḫāṣu* I

riḫṣum II "public debate" Mari, esp. in *r. raḫāṣum*; < *raḫāṣum* III

rīḫtu → *rēḫtu*

rīḫu → *rēḫu*

riḫûtu(m) "progeny; sperm" O/jB [A.RI.A] "insemination, sperm", *r. amēlūti* "human semen" as drug, of ox (*alpi*), pig (*šaḫî*); *riḫût PN* "progeny of PN"; *r. Šakan* "*r.* of Šakan, i.e. wild beasts", *r. Šulpaea* "*r.* of Šulpaea, i.e. epilepsy, epileptic" etc.; < *reḫû*

ri'ibtu → *ra'ibtu*

ri'ībum → *ra'ību* I

ri'ītu → *rîtu*

rikasu → *riksu*

rikbu(m) Bab. [U5] **1.** "crew" of ship **2.** ~ "attachment" on seed-plough, lyre; "superstructure" on ziggurrat; ~ "growth" on liver etc. **3.** on palm tree "male inflorescence"?, "stage of growth"?; < *rakābu*

rikibtu M/jB **1.** "copulation"? **2.** ~ "spur" of animal, bird in *r. ayyāli* "stag's spur" (an aphrodisiac), *r. arg/kabi* "spur of *a.* bird", as drug; < *rakābu*

rikistu, *rikiš/ltu* "treaty, pact" M/NB, usu. between states; jB also "conspiracy"; < *rakāsu*

rikkusatum? "bundle"? OB, of plants; < *rakāsu*

riklum → *riglum*

riksu(m), Alal., Bogh. also *rikšu*, NB also *rikasu*; pl. m. & f. "binding, knot, bond" [DUR; (KA.)KEŠDA] **1.** "band, belt, tie" as (part of) clothing; NB *rikis qabli* 'loin-girding' (payment for military service); "poultice, bandage"; "tie, binding" of sheaf, furniture, door etc.; "muscle, sinew" etc. in body; cosmic "band, bond", holding together heaven, earth, seas etc.; "package, bundle" of goods, reeds, vegetables **2.** "joining, fitting together"; "joint(s), construction" of wall, building; "assemblage, composition" of offerings; "band, integration" of people, "group" of texts, instructions **3.** "agreement, treaty, decree"; in private transactions "contract", freq. pl. f.; OB "contract(ually agreed sum)"; MB, NB "treaty", Nuzi, j/NB private "contract"; M/NA "decree, (palace) ordinance"; < *rakāsu*

rīmāniš "like a wild bull" O/jB; < *rīmu* I

rīmānu/û "bull-like"? NA, NB, epith. of king; < *rīmu* I ?

rīmātum pl. "love" OAkk, from Ištar; < *râmu* II

rimītu "residence, dwelling" M/NB(Ass.) for god, king; < *ramû* II

rimku(m), NA *rinku* "bath, bathing ceremony" Bab., NA [TU5], med., rit. "bathing procedure"; *bīt r.* "bath-house" (a ritual series); *mê r.* "bathing water", *r. tabka* "spilled bath-water"; < *ramāku*

rimmatum ~ "maggot"? OB; → *erimmatu*

rimmu(m); pl. f. "roaring, murmur" O/jB of person, dog, thunder, forest; < *ramāmu*

rīmtu(m) "wild cow" O/jB [SÚN] hunted; as epith. of goddess; < *rīmu* I

rîmtu(m), OAkk *rîntum*, NB *rîndu* "beloved" (f.) OAkk, Bab., of goddess, women, esp in fPNs; < *râmu* II

rimṭu (an illness) NA

rīmu(m) I, *rēmu* "wild bull" [(GU4.)AM] hunted; *qaran r.* "bull's horn"; desig. of god, king, temple; NA ᵈ*Rīmē* "divine bulls"; representations of *r. kadru/nadru/ekdu* "rearing/ wild/furious bull"; > *rīmtu, rīmāniš, rīmānu*?; → *ri'mu*

rīmu(m) II "gift" of god, in PNs, e.g. *Rīmuš* "His gift", *Rīm-Anum*; < *râmu* III

rīmu → also *rēmu*

rîmu(m) "beloved" OB, MA, in PNs [ÁG]; < *râmu* II

ri'mu jB lex., W.Sem. for *rīmu* I

rimûtu (kind of paralysis) M/jB med., mag., *r. rašû* "to get, suffer paralysis"; < *ramû* III

rīmūtu, NB also *rēm/'ūtu* "gift, present" M/NA, M/NB "grant, donation", freq. by king, MA pl. *rīmuāte*; NA *kī r.* "as a gift"; NB "(free-will) gift", freq. *ana r. ana nudunnû* "for gift (or) dowry"; PNs *Rīmūt-DN* "Gift of DN"; < *râmu* III

rîndu → *rîmtu*

rinku → *rimku*

rîntum → *rîmtu*

rinzu (a kind of bewitchment)? jB

ripḫu(m) "swelling" O/jB, as complaint of sheep, patient; → *ruppuḫum*

ripittu ~ "straying, errancy" O/jB; *ḫarrān r. alākum* "to go on a straying journey"; < *rapādu* II

ripqu(m) **1.** OB pl. f. "hoed land"? **2.** jB (a hoeing song)? **3.** MA (an ornamental fixture)?; < *rapāqu*

ripsu I 'threshing(s)' (a kind of groats) jB lex.; < *rapāsu*

ripsu II "vapour, haze" NA

ripûtu "healing" Am.; < W.Sem.; → *rapā'um* 2

riqdu mng. uncl. j/NB; desig. of a stool, of a silver oven; < *raqādu*

riqittu (a dance) jB lex.; < *raqādu*

riqītu(m) I, *riqittu* "(ruminant's third) stomach" Bab.; also med., of human; < *raqû*

riqītu(m) II (scented oil) OB, MA; < *ruqqû*

riqlum → *riglum*

riqqu "votary" NB, person dedicated to temple; *rab r.* "overseer of the votaries"; < Sum.; > *riqqūtu*

riqqu → also *rīqu* II; *ruqqu* I

riqqūtu "position of votary" NB; < *riqqu*

rīqu(m) I, Ass. *rāqu(m)* "empty; unemployed" [SUD] **1.** "empty" container, house, hand(s), "unloaded" donkey, boat; transf. "empty" word(s), letter **2.** jB gramm. "omitted, lost" consonant etc. in Sum. **3.** of days "free of work, unoccupied"; astr. *ūmu r.* "moon-less day"? **4.** of person, animal "unemployed, free"; NB "work-shy"; < *riāqu*; > *rīqūtu*

rīqu(m) II, *riqqu* "aromatic substance" [ŠIM (.MEŠ/ḪI.A)] freq. pl.; as commodity, in foundation deposit, also rit., med.; *gimir r.* "all aromatic trees" in park, *r. ṭābūte* "sweet aromatics"; > *ruqqû*

rīqūtu(m), M/NA *rāqūtu* "emptiness" O/jB, M/NA [SUD] freq. in acc. of condition *rīqūssu/sīna* etc. **1.** "in an empty state", "empty" of ship, container etc. **2.** "empty-handed", *rīqūssu ul ittallak* "he shall not leave empty-handed" **3.** OB "freedom from work", *ina lā rīqūtim(ma)* "having no free time" **4.** OB om. (desig. of alternative apodosis); < *rīqu* I

risbatu(m) "brawl" O/jB; < *rasābu*

risbu(m) ~ "blow, beating" O/jB; < *rasābu*

risibtu "beating, battering" jB; < *rasābu*

risittu, *riṣittu*; pl. Mari *risnātu*, NB *ris(in)nēti* "soaking" Bab., (beer mash); lex., NB "tanning process", "tanned leather"; < *rasānu*

risnu(m) "soaking" O/jB; *r. ša aškāpi* "tanner's fluid"; "soaked ground"?; < *rasānu*

rīsu, *rissu* "beating, battering" jB; < *râsu*

riṣiptu "construction, masonry" NA, of ziggurrat; < *raṣāpu*

riṣittu → *risittu*

riṣpu "building" jB lex.; < *raṣāpu*

rīṣu(m) "help, assistance" Bab. [Á.TAḪ] *r. ilim* "divine aid"; ext. *kak r.* (part of liver); *ālik(at) r.* "helper"; < *râṣu*

rīšāti → *rēštu*

rišâtu → *rišûtu*

rīšātu → *rīštu*

rišibtu "terror, awe" MB(Ass.), *rišibtu bēlūtiya* "in the awesomeness of my domination"; < *rašābu*

rišiktu "desiccation" jB med., of flesh, head; < *rašāku*

rīšiš "joyfully" O/jB; < *riāšu*

rišītum → *rišûtu*

rīštu(m), *rēštu*, occas. *rēltu*; usu. pl. *rī/ēšātu* "rejoicing, celebration" [ÁR.I.I ?] *r. šakānu* "to hold a celebration", *r. malû* "be given over to rejoicing"; < *riāšu*

rīšu(m) "celebrated" O/MB, of god; < *riāšu*

rišummāni ~ "naked"? jB lex.; < *erû* III ?

rišûtu(m), *rišītum*, occas. *rašûtu*; pl. *rišâtu* "redness, reddening" OAkk, O/jB; as illness, skin complaint; < *rašû* II

ritkubu M/jB **1.** [U5] "copulating with each other", of animals **2.** of ox with two "superimposed, entwined" bodies; < *rakābu* Gt

ritpāḫum, *ritpuḫum* "two-handed" OB lex; → *ruppuḫum*

ritpāšu "very wide" j/NB; heaven; understanding etc.; < *rapāšu*

ritpuḫum → *ritpāḫum*

rittu(m); pl. see 7, "hand" [KIŠIB; KIŠIB.LÁ] **1.** of human *r.* (loc.-adv.) *tamāḫu* "to hold in the hand", also transf., *tamḫat rittušša* "she holds in her hand"; for carrying out actions; cut off, as punishment; bearing slave-brand, "wrist" for ring; NB transf. "possession" **2.** "paw" of animal, Anzû **3.** "handle"; $^{\text{na}_4}$*r.* "stamp-seal"; j/NB astr. $^{(\text{mul})}$*r. gamli* (a constellation) **4.** OB ~ "opportunity, feasibility", *kīma rittimma* "as occasion arises"; *ul rittum* "there is/was no opportunity" (→ *redûm* II ?) **5.** NB *ina (muḫḫi) iltēt r.* "in one go, all in one" **6.** "plough"?, esp. M/NB in *alap r.*; *bīt r.* (land-concession from temple or crown) **7.** Early Mari pl. *ra'āt(um)* as linear measure ?

rîtu(m), *ri'ītu* "pasture" Bab., M/NA [SIPA-] for sheep; for horses (*sīsî*), cattle (*alpī*); *r. u mašqītu* "pasture and watering-place"; Nuzi *riwītenā* (Hurr. pl.) for horses ?; < *re'û*

ritūmum "love-making" OB; < *râmu* II Gt infin.

riṭbu (a marsh plant)? jB lex.; < *raṭābu*

riṭibtu(m) "wetness, wetting" O/jB; house *r. immar* "will suffer from damp"; "watered land, irrigable fields"; < *raṭābu*

rīṭu mng. unkn. jB lex.

ri'ūtu → *rīmūtu*

riwītu → *rîtu*

rû → *erû* I; *rū'u*

rū'a → *rū'u*

ru'āmu(m) "love" O/jB(lit.) "(sexual) charm" of woman; jB "love-making", gift *kī r.* "out of love, for love"; < *râmu* II

ruāqu(m) "to be distant, go far off" Ass. **G** of person, OA of silver **D** OA "allow (silver) to be at a distance"; Bab. → *rêqu*

ru'ātu → *ru'tum*

rū'atum → *rūtum*

rubatu → *urbatu* II

rubātu(m) ~ "princess"; as fPN; as title of goddess; OA of indigenous (Anatolian) ruler; < *rubû*; → *rubūtu*

rubā'u → *rubû* I

rubā'ūtum → *rubûtu*

rubbu → *rūbu* I

rubbû I "brought to full growth" NB, of vine; < *rabû* II D

rubbû II ~ "increase" MB; NA "interest" on silver etc.; < *rabû* II D

rubbu'um "to quadruple" OB **D** stat. *lū rubbu'ūkum* "let them be increased fourfold for you"; < *rebû* denom.

rubṣu(m) O/jB **1.** animal's "litter, bedding" **2.** "dung (from floor of stall)" **3.** lex. (syn. for womb)?; < *rabāṣu*

rûbtu → *ru'ubtu*

rubû(m), O/MA *rubā'u(m)* ~ "prince" [(LÚ.) NUN] **1.** Ass. "king, ruler", OA of king of Aššur, M/NA esp. of earlier, later rulers **2.** Bab. "king", "noble"; as title of DN; < *rabû* II; > *rubātu*, *rubūtu*, *rubûtu*

rubû → also *rebû* I; *rubu'û*

rūbu I, *rubbu* "anger, turmoil" M/jB of deity; pl. "raging, turmoil" of sea; < *ra'ābu*

rūbu II "setting" NA, of planet; < *rabû* III; → *rību* II

rūbu III "adulthood" NA; < *rabû* I

rubu'ā "four each" O/MB; < *rebû*

rubu'īu → *rubu'û*

rubūtu "(divine) queen" jB; < *rubû*; → *rubātu*

rubûtu(m), OA *rubā'ūtum* "rulership" Bab., OA [NUN-]; of humans, gods; OA *r. ṣabātum* "to seize the kingship"; *ūmī rubûti* "days of rule", *šamnē r.* "oil of kingship"; < *rubû*

rubu'û, *rubu'īu*, *rubû* M/NB **1.** "four-year-old" [MU.4], of animals **2.** "of team of four", of plough, chariot; < *rebû*

ruddû "added to, increased" NB, of offering; < *redû* I D

rūdu (part of the head)? Susa

rugbu(m), NB also *rugubu*; pl. f. "loft, room on roof" Bab. [É.ÙR.RA] OB, rented; NB *bīt r.* "upper storey"; > *ruggubu* II

ruggû(m) ~ "to make false claim" O/jB **D** against s.o. (= acc.) for (= *ana*) s.th.

ruggubu(m) I "with roof-room" Bab.; *bītu (lā) r.* "house with(out) second storey"; transf. lex. of wind mng. uncl.; < *ruggubu* II

ruggubu II "to put on an upper storey" jB **D** on ark; < *rugbu* denom.; > *ruggubu* I

ruggugu "very wicked" jB; < *ragāgu* I

rugubu → *rugbu*

rugummānû "legal claim" MA; < *rugummû* + *-ān*

rugummû(m), OAkk, OA *rugummā'um*; pl. freq. *rugummâni* "claim"; *r. (ul) īšu* "is (not) liable to claim"; *r. nasāḫu* "to reject a claim"; "(sum) claimed", *r. apālum* "to pay a claim"; < *ragāmu*; > *rugummānû*

ruḫḫu "left over; special?" j/NB, of animals, fruit; < *riāḫu*

ruḫḫupu **D** mng. unkn. jB process applied to malt

ruḫû(m) "sorcery, philtre" O/jB [UŠ11] freq. with *kišpu* and *rusû*; *r. zīrūti* "spells of hatred"; *bēl r.-ya* "my bewitcher"; < *reḫû*

rūḫu "(special) remnant"? NB; < *riāḫu*

rū'iš "for (his) friend" OB; < *rū'u*

rukkubum "fertilized" OB of date palm, orchard; < *rakābu* D

rukkusu; NA pl. *rakkasūte* "well fitted together" M/jB of house, door; NA of horses "harnessed"?; < *rakāsu* D

rukūbu(m), NA also *ru/akūpu* "vehicle" Bab., NA; i.e. **1.** "chariot", e.g. *r. šarrūtišu* "his royal vehicle" **2.** "boat" [GIŠ.MÁ.U5] pl. f., for procession, king, god, MB *ša r.* "boatman" **3.** of animal, "mount"; camels *rukūpišunu* "their mounts"; < *rakābu*

rûmatu → *rûmtu*

rumīkātu "waste bath-water" jB; < *ramāku*

rummû "released, slackened"? NB; < *ramû* III

rummukum "bathed" OB lex.; < *ramāku* D

rûmtu, *rûntu*, occas. *rûmatu* "beloved" (f.) M/NB of woman, goddess; < *râmu* II; → *ra'ūmtu*

rûntu → *rûmtu*

rupādu → *rapādu* I

ruppuḫum adj. mng. unkn. OB lex., of hand; → *ripḫu*; *ritpāḫum*

ruppuqum mng. unkn. OB as PN; < *rapāqu* ?

rupšu(m) "width, breadth" [DAGAL] as dimension; NB pl. f.; jB lex. in plant names mng. uncl.; < *rapāšu*

rupultu → *rupuštu*

rupuqtum ~ "a rivet" OA, in silver; < *rapāqu*

rupuštu(m), *rupultu* "phlegm, spittle" O/jB, MA [ÚḪ] of person, animal, Tiāmat; MA ~ "scum" on decoction

ruqbu (or *ruqpu*) (a kind of wool)? jB lex. in *šipat r.* "*r.* wool"; NA, desig. of silver, mng. unkn.; < *raqābu* ?

ruqbūtu in *ruqbūta ušallakki* "I shall make you decay" jB; < *raqābu*

rūqiš "(from) afar" M/jB; < *rūqu*

ruqpu → *ruqbu*

ruqqu(m) I, Am. *riqqu*; pl. m. & f. "cauldron" [(URUDU.)ŠEN (→ *šannu*)] of metal, usu. copper/bronze; Nuzi, of 30 minas bronze, of ox (*ša alpi*) weighing 101 minas; jB *bīt r.* (room housing cauldron)

ruqqu(m) II "thinness; thin place, part" O/jB [SAL.LA] med. *r. uznē* "thin part of ears"; ext. of (parts of) liver, lung etc.; < *raqāqu*

ruqqû, Ass. *raqqû* "to process oil" MA, M/jB **D** by adding aromatics etc.; "add aromatics to, perfume"; < *rīqu* II denom.; > *raqqû*, *raqqûtu*; *riqītu* II; *muraqqiu*, *muraqqītu*; *narqītu* II; *tarqītu*

ruqququ "very thin" jB lex.; < *raqāqu*

rūqu(m) "distant" [SUD] **1.** of place: land, mountain; heaven; gods, people, Ut-napištim, Medes; of road "long"; as subst. "the distance", freq. f. pl., *ana rūqēti* "into the distance"; transf. of heart "deep, unfathomable" **2.** of time: "distant" days, years, also = long life; *līpu r.* "remote descendant"; < *rêqu*, *ruāqu*

rusâtu → *rusû*

rusrussu → *rušruššu*

russû(m) ~ "to dissolve"? O/jB **D** earth; person, by sorcery **Dt** pass. of enemy land, witch (mng. uncl.); > *rusû*

rusû(m), occas. *rušû*; pl. m. & f. "dissolution?; sorcery" O/jB [UŠ11] of field; usu. (a kind of sorcery); < *russû*

ruṣṣunu ~ "loud-voiced" jB, epith. of goddess, person; < *raṣānu*

rūṣu(m) "help" OAkk, NB in PNs; < *râṣu*

rušbātum (or *rušpātum*) mng. unkn. OA

rūšiš mng. uncl. jB comm.

rušpātum → *rušbātum*

rušruššu, occas. *rusrussu* (a plant) jB lex., med.

ruššu → *rūšu* I

ruššû(m) "red" Bab. [ḪUŠ(.A)] of gold, sun, bronze; grain, fruit; of bloody urine; of divine countenance; < *rašû* II; → *ḫuššû*

ruššukum (or *ruššuqum*) **D** ~ "to fix" or "overlay" Mari, metal-working term

rūštu(m) "top quality; best oil" Bab., NA **1.** "first class" [SAG] in *šaman r.* "first class oil" **2.** "first class oil" [Ì.SAG]; < *rēšu*

rušû → *rusû*

rūšu(m) I, *ruššu* "dirt" O/jB, under fingernail, under threshold; < *warāšum*

rūšum II "door-lintel" Mari; < W.Sem.

rūšum III "redness" OB lex.; < *rašû* II

rušumtu, *rušunt/du* "wet mud, silt" jB; *ina r. nadû* "to be stuck in the mud"

ru'tītu, *ruttītu* "sulphur" M/jB [ÚḪ.^{d}ÍD; UŠ$_{11}$ (.^{d}ÍD)] "river-spittle" as drug etc.; → *ru'tum*

ruttu → *rūtu*

ruttuḫu D mng. unkn. jB lex.

ruttutum "shivery"? OB lex.; < *ratātu*

rutûm mng. uncl. Mari, in pl.

rūtum, *ruttu(m)*, *ru'tu*, OA *rū'atum*? "companion, associate" (f.); also as fPN; Ištar *r. ilāni*; < *rū'u* f.

rūtu → also *ru'tum*

rûtum → *rū'ūtu*

ru'tum, *rūtu(m)*; pl. *ru'ātu* "spittle" OAkk, O/jB [ÚḪ]; *r. nadû(m)* "to spit", *ina pîšu r. illak* "saliva flows in his mouth"; freq. in mag.; "sap" of plant; → *ru'tītu*

ru'tu → also *rūtum*

ruṭbu(m) "dampness" O/jB lex.; < *raṭābu*

ruṭibtu "dampness" jB [KI.DURU$_5$] **1.** "damp ground", "irrigated field" **2.** (an illness, phps.) "dropsy", *r. marāṣu/našû* "to suffer from *r.*"; < *raṭābu*; → *ruṭubtu*

ruṭṭubu "wetted through" jB lex.; < *raṭābu*

rūṭu "half-cubit, span" NA [LAL] esp. to measure children's height; < *(amma)r* + *ūṭu*

ruṭubtu "dampness" jB lex. (= *ruṭibtu*); < *raṭābu*

rū'u(m), *rûm*, *rū'a*, occas. *rā'um* "colleague, friend"; *ina bīt rū'išu ašrum* "place (for him) in his colleague's house"; *rū'a kaššāpat* "my associate is a witch"; > *rūtum*; *rū'ūtu*, *rū'iš*; *râ'u*

ru'ubbā'um "replacement" OAkk, of cow etc.; < *riābu*

ru'ubtu, *rûbtu* "rage" j/NB; < *ra'ābu*

ru'ūmtu → *ra'ūmtu*

ru''umu D ~ "to strike off" jB Anzû's 'hands'; > *nar'amtu*

rū'ūtu(m), *rûtum*, *ru'uttu* "friendship, association" O/jB, *r. epēšu(m)*, *banûm* "to form a friendship"; < *rū'u*

S

sa'ābu (or *sa'āpu*) mng. unkn. jB med. **G** (*i*/*i*)

sa'ālu, *sâlu* "to cough" jB lex., med. **G** (*u*/*u*) **D** "cough protractedly"; "cough" matter "up" **Št** "be made to cough"; > *suālu*

sa'āpu → *sa'ābu*

sa'atum (a tax or payment) OA

sabā'iu "seventh" MA [7-*ú*]; < *sebe*

sabāku(m) "to interweave" OB **G** (*i*/*i*) transf. "bring into company of" s.o. **D** "plait"; > *sābikum*; *musabbiktu*

sabālu → *zabālu*

sabarru → *saparru*

sabāsu → *subbusu* II; *šabāsu*

sabāṣu → *šapāṣu*

sabât → *sebītum*

sabā'u(m) "to rock, quake; lurch" O/jB, NA **G** (*u*/*u*) intrans., of sea, water, earth; chariot, dog; dragonfly; of man, in fear **D** "make to rock, rock" trans., sea; med., person **Š** "cause to quake"; > *sābi'u*; *sabbi'u*; *sibi'tum*

sa(b)babu → *sabūbu*

sabbasû → *šabbasû*

sabbi'u mng. unkn. jB lex.; also f. *sabbi'tu*; < *sabā'u*

sabbu → *sā'u*

sabībum mng. unkn. OB as PN

sabību → also *sabūbu*

sābikum "plaiter"? OB as PN; < *sabāku*

sabillûm (a kind of net)? OB lex.; < Sum.

sabirru → *šawirum*

sabītu(m), *šebītu(m)* "(kind of) lyre" OAkk, O/jB

sābītu(m) "female brewer, alehouse keeper" O/jB [MUNUS.(LÚ.)KURUN/KÚRUN.NA]; *bīt s.* "alehouse"; also as fPN; < *sābû*

sābi'u "billowing" jB; < *sabā'u*

sābi'u → also *sābû*

sablum "work team" Mari; < W.Sem.

sabsinnu "sack-maker" NB; < *sabsû*

sabsinnūtu "craft of sack-making" NB; < *sabsinnu*

sabsu → *šabsu*

sabsû, *sabsu'u*, *šabšû* "sack-maker" OB PN, jB lex.; > *sabsinnu*, *sabsinnūtu*

sabsuttu → *šabsūtu*

sabsu'u → *sabsû*

sabu (or *sapu*) mng. uncl. Nuzi in *sabumma epēšu*; < Hurr.

sabû(m) ~ "to brew beer" OA, M/NB **G** also sesame? **D** ~ G; Nuzi "assign" corn "for brewing"?; > *sību*; *sibûtu*; *sābû*, *sābītu*, *sābûtu*; *nasbû*

sābu (a red stone) M/jB lex., mag.

sābû(m), *sēbû*, *šību*, *sā*/*ēbi'u*, OAkk, OA *sābium* "brewer, innkeeper" [LÚ.KURUN/KÚRUN.NA, j/NB also .NAM] OB also as PN; *bīt s.* "alehouse"; *šikar s.* "brewer's beer"; < *sabû*; > *sābītu*, *sābûtu*; → *ṣēbûm*

sâbu(m), *sâpu* "to draw" water Bab. **G** (*a*/*a*) **Gtn**? iter.

sabubânu → *zibibiānum*

sabūbu, *sabību* (or *sa(b)babu*?) "(grain of) cumin" NA as gold ornament; → *zibibiānum*

sabûtu → *sibûtu*

sābûtu(m) "brewing (business)" O/MB; < *sabû*

sadādu I **G** jB stat. "is provided with"? of part of liver, with features **D** j/NB "to provide for, support" person, date palm, sheep; > *suddu*

sadādum II "to make a raid" Mari **G** (pret. *isdud*); > *sādidu*; *saddum*?

sadāḫum (or *saṭāḫum*) mng. unkn. OB lex. **G**

sadāru(m), j/NB also *sedēru* "to place in order; do regularly" Bab., M/NA **G** (O/MB *a/u*, otherwise *i/i*) **1.** in place: stat. "are in a row"; "put" entries on tablet "in order"; "arrange in order" offering-stands, troops, horses etc. **2.** in time: "use regularly", "carry out (action) regularly", treatments, rituals, + *alākum* "come/go regularly"; stat. "is constantly attentive" to (= *ana*), "follow s.o. (= acc.) constantly"; of event "take place regularly"; OB *ina sadāri* "regularly" **D** ~ G OB in hendiad. "(do s.th.) regularly"; M/jB(lit.) "do/bring/send etc. regularly"; NA, NB "put s.th. in order, arrange s.th. properly"; > *sadru*, *sadirtu*, *sadriš*; *sidru*, *sidirtu*; *sadīru*; *sudduru*; *masdaru*, *masdariš*, *masdara*; *tasdīru*

sādātu → *sādu* I

sa(d)dalum rdg. uncert. (a metal object) OA

saddanakku(m), *s/šandanakku(m)*, *šaddan=akku*; pl. f. "administrator of date orchards" O/jB [SANTANA]; < Sum.

saddinu, *šaddi(n)nu* (a tunic)? Am., Nuzi, NA, NB; multicoloured; of linen; Nuzi in pairs

saddum "razzia" Mari; also "(plunder of) a raid"; < W.Sem.?; → *sadādum* II

saddu → also *ṣaddu*

sadēya (an animal from Egypt) NA

sādidu(m) "raiding party" O/jB; < *sadādum* II

sadirtu "battle line" NA; < *sadru*

sadīru "(ordered) group, section" M/jB of animals; "section" of text on tablet; "band" of colour in stone; < *sadāru*

sādīu "(animal) at pasture" Nuzi; < *sādu* I

sadriš "regularly" jB; < *sadru*

sadru(m), NB also *sedru* "in order, regular" Bab., NA of trees "in rows", of song "in sections", of battle-line "drawn up"; of flood, deliveries etc. "regularly happening"; < *sadāru*; > *sadriš*; *sadirtu*

sādu I, NA *sa'du*; pl. f.? "meadow, pasture" j/NB, NA; > *sādīu*

sādu II (a gold alloy)? NA, NB; → *sādūtu* ?

sâdu(m) "to smite" O/jB(poet.) **G** (*a/ā*) enemy

sa'du "help" jB; < Aram.; → *sêdu*

sa'du → also *sādu* I

sādūtu (a colour)? MB desig. of garment; → *sādu* II ?

sa'eru → *sa'aru*

sagallu(m) (a muscle, tendon) O/jB [SA.GAL (.LA)] OB lex. (neck muscle); jB med., hemerology "hamstring"; also an illness thereof; < Sum.

sagalluḫu (a plant) jB lex.

sagānu "governor" NB; < Aram.

sagarrûm (a stringed instrument) OB lex.; < Sum.

sāgātu → *sāgu* I

sagbānu → *šagbānu*

sagbu(m), *sagbû(m)* (or *sakbu/û(m)*) (a class of soldier) O/jB

sagbû "first, foremost" jB lex.; < Sum.

sagbû → also *sagbu*

sagdilûm "single, bachelor" OB; < Sum.

sagdû → *qaqqadû*

sagdullu (a headdress) jB lex.; < Sum.

sagēru → *sakru*

sa(g)gilatu "sedge tuber" jB, NA? [GIŠ/Ú.TU9.NIM] as drug; ornament?; of gold

saggilûm → *sangilûm*

saggu → *šaggu*

sagiddûm (a stringed instrument)? OB lex.; < Sum.

sagiqqu → *sakikkû*

sāgittu "priestess" NB; < Aram.

sagrikkum (or *sakrikkum*); pl. f. "straw bale" OB; < Sum.

sagû I "to cause distress to, trouble" MB(Ass.), jB, NA **G** of oath; stat. "is troubled"

sagû II "menstrual towel"? jB

sagû III (desig. of a bear?) in jB *sagummargû*

sagû → also *sāgu* II

sāgu I; pl. f. (a skirt, kilt) M/NA, MB?; of workman, soldier; NA *ša sāgātešu* "kilt-dealer"

sāgu(m) II, *sagû* "sanctuary, cella" Bab.; *s. nēmedi*, *s. parakki* "altar, dais-chamber"

sagulûm (a snare) OB lex.; < Sum.

sagummargû, *sagû margû* (a musical instrument)? jB lex.

saḫāḫu(m) "to be terrified" OA, Bab.(lit.) **G** (*u/u*) of person, country **D** OA "frighten"

saḫallētu → *šaḫallû*

saḫālu(m), *seḫēlu* "to prick, pierce" **G** (*a/u*, occas. *i/i*) of weapon, thorn etc.; transf. of pain, sorceries, toothache, also *saḫāl/šaḫāl šīri* "annoyance" **D** ~ G **Dtn** iter., of spears **N** pass., liter. and transf.; > *saḫlu*; *seḫlu*; *siḫiltu*

saḫamḫu → *zaḫamḫu*

saḫāmu(m) "to trouble, oppress" OB **G** not attested? **D** "oppress, give trouble to" s.o. **N** "be troubled" Mari (unless G ?); > *saḫmu, saḫimtu*

saḫānu jB **G** mng. unkn. **D** "to draw" dagger

saḫānum → also *zaḫānum*

saḫaptu "devastation" jB, of land; < *saḫāpu*

saḫāpu(m) "to envelop, overwhelm" Bab., M/NA **G** (*a/u*) [ŠÚ] of flood, smoke, net; transf. of radiance, fear, demon, suffering; "spread" net etc. "over" s.o.; "overturn" chariot, ship, bowl etc. **D** ~ G of radiance etc., demon "overwhelm"; "overcome"? mountain; "overwhelm" s.o., OB transf. with words (*ina awâtim*), jB with (= acc.) epilepsy, fear **Š** jB "cause" radiance, fear "to overwhelm"; "cover" s.th. "with" s.th. (= 2 acc.) **Št** jB stat. of livers "are made to overlie each other" **N** [ŠÚ] pass. of G **Ntn** iter. mng. uncl.; > *saḫpu, saḫiptu; sāḫipu; seḫpu, siḫiptu, saḫaptu; musaḫḫiptu; muštasḫiptu; nasḫapu, nasḫiptu*

Saḫarātum (or *Zaḫarātum*) (a month) OB(Ešn.)

saḫargû, *šaḫargû* "mudguard" M/jB on chariot; < Sum.

saḫār(i), *saḫār ūmi* "in the evening" O/jB; < *saḫāru*

saḫarmuddû ~ "body"? jB lex.; < Sum.

saḫarru → *šaḫarru* II

saḫaršubbûm, *saḫaršuppû*, occas. *suḫaršuppû*, NA also *šaḫaršuppû* "leprosy" Bab., NA [SAḪAR.ŠUB.BA] *s. lubbušu, mullû, katāmu* etc. "to wrap, infect, cover etc. with leprosy"; < Sum.

saḫartum → *saḫertum; siḫirtu*

saḫaru "tower" NA; < Aram.

saḫāru(m) "to go around, turn; search; tarry" **G** (*u/u*) [NIGIN] **A.** of living beings **1.** "turn round, turn back", of army; of city etc. "change" political allegiance; of deity "turn to, favour" s.o.; "care for"; with *idu* "turn to s.o.'s side", "align o.s. with" **2.** "go (a)round", esp. in search of s.th./s.o., "search for"; mag. ~ "seek out, i.e. bewitch" s.o. **3.** OA "tarry, delay", esp. stat. "is held up"; "await" s.o. **4.** NA in hendiad. "again" **B.** of things, processes etc. **1.** "turn" (intrans.), "move round", stat. "is turned", of parts of liver, hair, star, wind etc. **2.** "stay around, persist" **3.** stat. "is surrounded by" s.th. (= acc.); also trans. "lie round" of ominous features **Gtn** [NIGIN.MEŠ] iter. of G, esp. A 2 "constantly seek out", "seek to help" s.o. **D** [NIGIN] **1.** "send" s.o., head "round" town, villages for public display; stat. "is round, encompasses" of hair, part of liver **2.** "make" s.o. "return, retreat", "turn back" embassy, attack etc.; Mari "turn" s.o. "out, evict"; NA "bring back, return (trans.)", in hendiad. + *nadānu* "give back", "restore" s.th. to o.'s possession; Mari "(re)convert" building to other purpose **3.** with parts of body, "turn" o.'s back, in flight; *kišādam s.* 'turn the neck' i.e. "attend", OB "apply o.s." to work, jB "give attention to s.o." malevolently of demon, benevolently of protector; "divert o.'s eyes, head" to other matter; *pānī s.* "turn o.'s face" to attend, "turn face away" in displeasure, rejection, "towards" s.o. in reconciliation **Dtn** jB error for Gtn?; MA infin. of garment (*ša tusaḫḫuri*), mng. uncl. **Š** caus.; OA of G A 3 "make s.o. tarry"; OB "convert (mood of)" troops; "make" wall, canal "surround" city, orchard etc. **Št** **1.** "surround s.th. on all sides" with (= acc.) **2.** stat., of troops "stand in a circle"; of bodies "lie round one another" **N** [NIGIN] **1.** "turn back, come back" of person, animal, word, illness etc. **2.** of deity, king "turn towards, favour" s.o.; freq. in PNs **3.** OA in hendiad. "do" s.th. "again" **Ntn** iter., esp. "search out constantly", "be constantly in attendance on"; > *saḫru; saḫertum; seḫru, siḫirtu; saḫāri; sāḫiru, sāḫertu; saḫḫaru, saḫḫiru, saḫḫertu; suḫḫuru, suḫḫurtu; suḫurrā'um; masḫaru, masḫartum, masḫar=ūtum; mašḫaru?; mussaḫru; musaḫḫirtum?, mussaḫḫiru; nasḫuru; šusḫuru, šusḫurtu; tasḫīru, tasḫirtu*

saḫār ūmi → *saḫāri*

saḫāšu(m) "to catch in a net" jB lex. **G**; > *seḫšu; sāḫišum, masḫastum*?

saḫatennū → *šuḫatinnū*

saḫātu I (a bush)? jB lex.

saḫātum II "pitfall, trap" Mari; for lion; < W.Sem.

saḫā'um → *seḫû*

saḫertum, OA also *saḫartum* (goods on the market) OA, OB; < *saḫāru*

sāḫertu(m) Bab., NA **1.** 'favourer', desig. of goddess (< *sāḫiru* f.) **2.** M/NB, NA (desig. of heifer) [(GU₄.)ÁB.NIGIN] **3.** MB (desig. of canal) **4.** "enclosure wall" of house, garden **5.** "reflex? bow" Mari, lex.; < *saḫāru*

saḫḫa(r)ru, NA also *si(ḫ)ḫāru*; NB pl. *saḫḫarrānu* (an offering bowl) M/NB, NA [(DUG.)BUR.ZI.TUR] of stone, metal

saḫḫaru "convoluted" jB of intestines; < *saḫāru*

saḫḫertu "(female) peddler" Mari, jB, NA [MUNUS.ZILULU]; < *saḫḫiru*

saḫḫiru(m) "peripatetic" Bab., NA of demon, ghost; as subst. "peddler", *(ilu) saḫḫiru* (an ecstatic)?, also NB PN; < *saḫāru*

saḫḫiš "like a meadow" jB; < *saḫḫu* I

saḫḫu I "(water-)meadow" M/jB; > *saḫḫiš*

saḫḫum II (a physiological feature, phps.) "swelling" or "scar" OB ext.; also jB, unless to be read *qidḫu*

saḫḫu → also *salḫu* II; *sanḫu*

saḫḫû (a stone) M/NB mag., med.

saḫimtu "valley"? jB; < *saḫmu*

saḫindu "yeast"? jB; < Sum.

saḫiptu (a female cultic personage) MA, jB; < *saḫpu*

sāḫipu "swooping" O/jB of birds; < *saḫāpu*

saḫirru → *šaḫarru* II

sāḫiru(m) "turning" Bab., M/NA **1.** "returning", of boomerang **2.** "searcher", desig. of demon (or 'favourer' → *sāḫertu*) **3.** "petty merchant, peddler" **4.** "convoluted", of entrails **5.** (lower element of door pivot) **6.** (a shoe strap) **7.** NB (a canal) **8.** NA (part of a bed) **9.** "one who cares" (→ *zākirum*); < *saḫāru*; > *sāḫertu*

sāḫirum → also *zākirum*

sāḫišum "ensnaring" OB of net; < *saḫāšu*

saḫītu → *siḫītu* I

saḫlânu (a plant) jB lex., med.; < *saḫlû*

saḫlium, usu. *saḫlû* f. pl. (a cultivated plant, phps.) "cress" [ZÀ.ḪI.LI(.SAR); ZÀ.ḪI.LI.A(.SAR); O/MB also ZÀ.AḪ.LI(.A)(.SAR)] pounded; cultivated; as drug; NB also wr. *saḫ*-DA (= *lê*); > *saḫlânu*, *saḫlûtu*

saḫlu(m) "pierced" Bab. of part of body; of person (mng. uncl.); < *saḫālu*

saḫlûtu "(single) cress? seed" jB, in descr. of spot; < *saḫlû*

saḫmaštu(m), occas. *šaḫmaštum* "rebellion, uprising" Bab.(lit.); also lex. (a thorny plant)?

saḫmu "pressed in" Nuzi, jB; of fruit (mng. uncl.); Nuzi as subst., (a topog. depression)?; < *saḫāmu*; > *saḫimtu*

saḫnātu "ear (of corn)"? jB lex.

saḫpu **1.** jB of emblems "overthrown"? **2.** MA of bow "wrapped, encased"; < *saḫāpu*; > *saḫiptu*

saḫru "turned" jB; of part of liver; < *saḫāru*

saḫsaḫḫātum, *saḫsaḫḫūtum* mng. unkn. OB lex.

saḫṭu "(a kind of) grasshopper" jB lex.

saḫû → *seḫû*; *siḫītu* I

sāḫum → *šāḫu*

saḫ'um "rebellious" OA; < *seḫû*

saḫūnu **1.** NA (a spice or vegetable) **2.** jB (a kind of beer)

sā'idum "helper" O/jB in PNs; < → *sêdu*

sakādum → *zaqādum*

sakakkum ? mng. uncl. Mari, in *ṭupšar s.* (a confidential scribe)

sakāku(m) "to block" Bab. **G** infin. (pass.) *sakāk uzni* "ear blockage"; stat. "is blocked", transf. of meaning "is impenetrable" **D** stat. of person "is hard of hearing", of ear "is blocked" **Dt** of ears "be blocked" **Ntn** OB "act deaf"?; > *sakku* I, *sakkiš*; *sakīku*; *sukkuku*, *sukkukūtu*; *sikkatu* II?

sakālu(m) I "to acquire, hoard" Bab. **G** (*i*/*i*) esp. *sikiltam s.* "acquire possessions" **D** ~ G jB lex.; > *sikiltu*; *sukkulu*; → *musakkiltu*

sakālu II ~ "to balk, get stuck" or "to rear, shy" jB **G** (*i*/*i*) of horse in yoke; of statue in procession; of part of door bolt **Gtn** iter., of bolt; → *musakkiltu*

sakānu **1.** Am. **G** (pret. *i*) "to see to, care for" **2.** Mari **D** "to settle, keep settled" people; < W.Sem.

sakānum → also *šakānu*

sakāpu(m) I, *zakāpu*?, NB *sekēpu* "to push down, off, away" Bab. **G** (*i*/*i*) "push off" ship from land; "launch" logs on water; "push back, fend off" person, evil; "push down, overthrow" enemy, city, land etc.; of gods "overthrow" kingship; "overturn" throne **D** ~ G OB "reject" s.o. **Dt** pass. of water "be driven back" **N** pass. OB of bitumen "be launched"; > *sakpu* I, *sakiptu*?; *sikiptu*, *sukiptu*?; *sukuptu*; *sakkāpu*

sakāpu(m) II "to rest, lie down" Bab. **G** (*u*/*u*; *i*/*i* ?) **D** MB stat. "are put to rest" **Dt** NB of flocks "be lain down"; > *sakpu* II; *sākipu*

sakāru → *sekēru* I

sakātu(m) "to be silent" Bab. **G** (*u*/*u*) of persons **D** NB "silence" s.o.

sakbu → *sagbu*

sakbû → *sagbu*

sakēru → *sakru*

sakikkû, *sagiqqu(m)*; usu. pl. (a muscular ailment) O/jB, NA [SA.GIG] as title of omen series; also ~ "symptom(s)"; Mari "(amulets for) *s.* ailment"?; < Sum.

sakīku(m) "(mud, silt) deposits" Bab. in river, canal; < *sakāku*

sākinu, *sakinnu*, *sakkinu* "prefect, governor" OB(Alal.), Ug. [LÚ.GAR]; < W.Sem.; → *sūkinu*

sakiptu "rejection"? jB; < *sakāpu* I ?

sākipu "resting" jB in *lā s.* "unrelenting"; < *sakāpu* II

sakirru → *šakirru*

sakīru → *sakru*

sākiru → *sēkiru*

sakkāpu "pusher" jB lex., term for part of door lock; < *sakāpu* I

sakkarû → *sikarû*

sakkinu → *sākinu*

sakkiru (or *šakkiru*) mng. unkn. jB lex.; < *sekēru* I ?

sakkiš "dully"? jB of thunder; < *sakku* I

sakkiu → *šakkû*

sakku(m) I "blocked; deaf" Bab. of canal; of person, also as DN; < *sakāku*

sakku II (component of quivers, doors, columns) Nuzi, NA, of gold, silver; of clay ?

sa(k)kum → also *zakû* I 2

sakkû(m) I, *sakku* ? (cultic rites) Bab. of person; of gods; *paššūr s.* "offering table" in family shrine; < Sum.

sakkû II (or *šakkû*) mng. unkn. jB; astr. in *bīt s.*

sakkû → also *šakkû*

sakkuku → *sukkuku*

sakkušakûm (or *sakkušaqûm*) (kind of offering) OB(N.Mes.)

sakkuttu → *sankuttum*; *takkussu*

saklalu mng. uncl. O/jB; < Sum.?

saklu(m) "simple, imbecile"; *lišānu sakiltu* "speech-handicapped"; "incompetent" of charioteer; as PN; of Gutians

sakpu(m) I "pushed away" Bab., of person "rejected" by god, family; NB, of troops "pushed back, scared off ?"; < *sakāpu* I

sakpu II "resting" jB; < *sakāpu* II

sakrikkum → *sagrikkum*

sakru, *sag/kē/īru*, NB *šagīru* ~ "refined" M/NA, jB; desig. of gold; < *sekēru* II; → *šagīru*

sakrû(m) (or *saqrû(m)*) (a kind of terrain)? OB

sakrumaš; jB pl. f. (a chariot officer)? M/jB, early NB [LÚ.KIR$_4$.DAB (→ also *kartappu*)]; < Kass.

sâku(m), *zâku(m)*, NA *suāku*, jB also *šāku* "to pound, pulverize" O/jB, M/NA **G** (*ū*) [SÚD] plants etc. in med., rit. **D** ~ G **N** pass. of G OB of oil-bubble; > *sīku*, *sīktu*; *masūktu*

sakullu → *sugullu*

sakuttum → *sankuttum*

salādu → *salātu* II

salaḫum → *salḫu* I 2

salāḫu(m) I, *šalāḫu* "to sprinkle (with)" liquid O/jB **G** (*a/u*) [SUD] water, oil etc.; *dīmātišu qaqqara isallaḫ* "he sprinkles the ground with his tears"; stat., of parts of liver, of body, star etc. "is covered with drops" **D** ~ G; also absol. "sprinkle" eyeball, "lustrate" kid, purification rite (*šuluḫḫu*) **N** pass. "be sprinkled" with (= acc.); > *salḫu* I; *sāliḫu*, *sāliḫtu*; *sulluḫum*; *maslaḫu*, *maslaḫtu*; *musalliḫtu*

salāḫu(m) II, *salā'u*, *šalāḫu*, *šelēḫu* ~ "to jerk, twitch" O/jB **G** (*i/i*) of hair, part of liver **D** Mari stat. "is paralyzed"?

salālu(m) ~ "to clear out, clear away"? O/jB **G** (Bogh. pres. *isallal*, jB pret. *islil*) of demon "clear out" body; of bird "pluck? out" feather **D** ~ G corn-store; feather; stat. of lawsuit "is wound up"? **Dt** pass. of D; > *sullulu*?

salamaḫum (a garment) OB

salāmum I "amity, friendly relations" OB; < *salāmu* II infin.

salāmu(m) II, NB *selēmu* "to be(come) at peace (with s.o.), amicable" Bab., M/NA **G** (*i/i*, occas. *a/a*) [SILIM] of god with (= *itti*) human(s); "make peace", stat. "is at, keeps peace", *bēl s.* "one at peace with" s.o. **D** "conciliate, propitiate" angry deity, enemy; "soothe" anger; "bring peace to" s.o.; absol. "create peace" **Š** NB "make s.o. be at peace"; > *salmu*, *salmāniš*; *silmu*; *salāmum* I; *salīmu*, *salīmiš*; *Sulāmum*; *sulummû*; *sullumu*; *musallimu*; *naslamum*; *taslimtu*

salāqu I "to boil" O/jB **G** (*a/u*) lex., med. **D** ~ G ? **Dtn** iter. **N** pass. of G; > *salqu*; *silqātu*; *silqu* I; *sulāqu*; *maslaqtu*

salāqu II, *selēqu* "to climb up" NB; < Aram.

salātu(m) I, *sallātu* "family, clan" Bab. [IM.RI.A; ŠU.SA.A] esp. *kimtu u s.* "family and clan"; "head-count" of cattle; > *salûtum*

salātu(m) II, *salādu*, *šalāṭu* "to slit, slice through, split" Bab., NA **G** (*a/a*, *i/i*) wood, branch, horse's ear, crenellations; "cut off, separate" troops, person; of god, guardian spirit "desert" s.o. **D** ~ G "trim away" or "split" threads, meat, fingernails; transf., complex problems; of water "erode" bank; stat., of part of liver **N** pass., transf. of man "be cut off" (mng. uncl.); > *saltu* I; *siltu* I, *silittu*; *mašlatu*

salā'u(m) I "to sprinkle; slander" **G** (*a/u*) water, on s.o. (= acc.); *bīt salā' mê* (ritual of purification), MA vessel *ša salā'i* "sprinkler"; transf. OB "infect", OA "sully" s.o. with accusation, "slander" **Gtn** iter. **D** ~ G mag. "besprinkle" **N** pass. **1.** OA "be slandered" **2.** Bab. med. "be infected, sicken (intrans.)" [LÍL]; transf. "be tainted" by scandal etc. **Ntn** iter. [LÍL.LÍL] jB med.; OB of expectant mother "keep feeling sick"; > *sil'u*, *sili'tu*; *masla'u*, *masla'tu*; → *šalā'um*

salā'u(m) II "to leave uninformed" Ass. **G** (*i/i*) deceitfully; NA "deceive, tell lie (to)" **Gtn** iter. NA **Š** NA "disdain, neglect" (< Aram.?); > *sal'ū*; *silītu* II; *sullû* II; *taslītu*

salā'um III mng. unkn. OAkk **G** (*i/i*)

salā'u → also *salāḫu* II

salbagīnu → *sapalgīnu*

salḫu(m) I "sprinkled, damp" **1.** OB of lamb still wet behind the ears [SILA4.SÙ.A; SILA4.BU.A ?] **2.** Mari (also *salaḫum*), MA of irrigated area; < *salāḫu* I

salḫu(m) II, *saḫḫu* (a garment) O/MB; of red wool

salḫūtum mng. uncert. OB

sāliḫtu (an object, phps.) "sprinkler" MB; < *salāḫu* I

sāliḫu(m) "sprinkler" O/jB of paths, prof. desig.; < *salāḫu* I

salīmiš "in peace" j/NB; < *salīmu*

salīmu(m), *silīmu*; pl. f. "peace, amity" Bab., M/NA [SILIM] *s. šakānu(m)*, *epēšu(m)* "to make peace"; "peace (mission, overture)"; *ina s.* "in peace"; *ana s.* "for (making) peace"; NA *s. kiššati* "world peace"; OB *salīmātum* "(words of) peace"; *bēl s.* "one at peace with" s.o., "ally"; "peace" with god, esp. *s. rašû* "to acquire divine pardon"; < *salāmu* II; → *šalmu* II; *šulmu* 4

sālimu → *salmu*

saliqu → *salqu*

salittu → *salmu*

salītu "net" j/NB, NA for animal, fish; < Aram.

salku → *šalgu*

sallaḫurû (or *šallaḫurû*) (container for seed-corn)? jB lex.; < Sum.

sallatu → *šillatu* I

sallātu → *salātu* I

sallewe → *zallewe*

sallu ~ "tray" O/MB(Alal.), NA; for fruit etc.; MB(Alal.) of bronze; usu. ^{giš}*s.*, also of silver, gold

sallûm → *sullû* I

salmāniš "in friendly mood"? jB; < *salmu*

salmu, *sālimu* "peaceful, friendly" M/NB, NA of goddess (*salittu*), of night-time; as subst. "one at peace, ally", pl. *salmūti* and *salmē*; < *salāmu* II; > *salmāniš*; → *šallāmu*; *šalmu* I

salqu, *saliqu* "boiled" j/NB, NA of meat, also subst. "boiled (meat)", pl. *salqāni*; (a brew) pl. f. *saliqāte*; < *salāqu* I

saltu I "trimmed" jB lex. of reed; < *salātu* II

saltu II (or *raqtu*) (a legume) jB, Ug. lex.

salṭiš mng. unkn. jB astr.

salṭu → *šalṭu* III

salû → *salā'u* I.II.III; *šalû* I.II.III

sâlu mng. unkn. jB **N** of eyes

sâlu → also *sa'ālu*

sal'ū pl. "ignorance"? OA *i(na) s.* "unchecked"?; OB adj. *sal'ūti* ?; < *salā'u* II

salule → *zalule*

saluppu → *suluppu*

salûtum "family relationship" OB(N.Mes.); < *salātu* I

samādiru "flower" NA, *šaman* ^{šim}*s.* "oil of blossom"; < Aram.

samādu(m), NB *semēdu* "to grind (finely)" Bab., OA **G** (*u/u*) barley, sesame; *šipir samādim* "grinding work"; jB stat., transf. of part of entrails **Gtn** iter., OB; > *samdu*; *simdu*; *samīdu* I; *sumīdātu*; *sāmidu*

samaḫḫu (a net)? jB lex.; < Sum.

samāḫu(m), Nuzi *semēḫu*, D occas. *šummuḫu* "to mix" (intrans.) Bab., M/NA **G** (*a/u*, Nuzi *i/i*) of metals, troops; "be joined" of parts of liver; Nuzi "share" in property; jB "have intercourse", man with ox; (trans.) "mix" s.th. with water (*ana mê*) **D** "mix" (trans.) drugs, ingredients, horses, lands; Am., Bogh. stat. of ornament "is encrusted with"; MA "confuse" field borders; Nuzi, Ug. "give share" of property **Dt** NA usu. **Dtt** Nuzi "receive share", Bogh., NA "perjure o.s."; > *samḫu*; *sāmiḫum*; *summuḫu*; *musammeḫtu*

samāku(m) "to cover up, bury" O/jB, M/NA **G** (*a/u*) with earth; boundary; canal, with weeds; MA of rapist "constrain"? **D** ~ "smother, incapacitate"? person, fort; NA "support" (< Aram.) **N** OB of canal "become smothered, overgrown" by weeds; > *samku*, *sankātu*?, *samkūtu*; *simku*?; *sumuktu*

samallu → *samullu*

samālu(m); OA pl. f. (a cup) OA, jB

***samānâ** "eighty" not attested in syll. wr.

***samānēšeret** "eighteen" not attested in syll. wr.

samāna-ešrû, *samaššurû* "eighteenth" NB; < **samānēšeret*

samāne, Ass. *šamāne*; f. *šamānat*, *saman(ū)tu* "eight", *samanti ūmē* "eight days"; *samāne šanātim* "eight years"; OB(Tell Haddad) *samāninammatim* "eight cubits" (→ *ammatu* I); jB *šārī samānūti* "eight winds"; > *samnu* I, *samānû*; *samānūtu*; *sumuntu*, *sumuttu*?; *summunu*; *sumunû*; *samāna-ešrû*

sama(n)num → *samullu*

samānû "eighth, one-eighth"; < *samāne*; → *samnu* I

samānūtu "octet" jB; < *samāne*

samaru (an ornament)? jB

samārum (or *zamārum*) ~ "to set aside, separate off" OA **G** (*i/i*) silver, goods etc.

samāsu(m) (a bush)? O/jB lex.; → *samḫasu*

samaššurû → *samāna-ešrû*

samāšu(m) ~ "to hide" O/jB **G** (*a/u* or *u/u*) lex., jB(lit.) **D** Mari "conceal" person, animal **N** Mari "be hidden" or "hide o.s.", from census; > *simištum*; *sumšu*?

samā'u → *samû* II

samdakkum → *santakku*

samdu(m), *sandu* "ground, milled" O/jB; < *samādu*

sameqa (a plant) jB lex.

samḫasu(m) (or *samḫaṣu*) (a bush) O/jB lex.; → *samāsu*

samḫu "mixed" jB, of censers "assorted"?; < *samāḫu*

samīdu(m) I; pl. *sa/emmīdātu(m)* (a fine flour) O/jB freq. ^zíd^*s*.; < *samādu*

samīdu(m) II, *simīdum*, *s/šamīṭu* (a soapwort)? O/jB, M/NA [Ú.KUR.ZI(.SAR)]; in sacks; *zēr s.* "seed of *s*." as drug; occas. wr. ^ú^*s*. or *s*.^sar^

sāmidu(m) "grinder; miller" O/jB, M/NA; also as PN; < *samādu*

sāmiḫum "(wine-)mixer"? Mari, prof. desig.; < *samāḫu*

samīnu(m), *sammānum* (a garden herb or spice) O/jB

samîš "like one undecided"? jB; < *samû* I

samītu; NA pl. *sayyāte*? ~ "wall-plinth, revetment" j/NB, NA?

samīṭu → *samīdu* II

sāmiṭu → *šāmiṭu* I

samku "buried" jB lex. syn. of "dead"; < *samāku*

samkuttum → *sankuttum*

samkūtu "infilling"? Mari; < *samāku*

sammaḫūte → *summuḫu*

sammānum → *samīnu*

sammatu mng. unkn. jB, an animal ?

sammīdātu → *samīdu* I

samminnu (a quality of barley) Nuzi

sammītum (a lyre) Mari; < *sammû* f.

sammu → *sāmu*

sammû(m) "lyre, harp" Bab. [(GIŠ.)ZÀ.MÍ]; *šer'ān s.* "lyre-string"; *nāš/nārē/šūt s.* "lyre-player(s)"; transf. to describe large hands, jB; < Sum.; > *sammītum*

sammuḫu → *summuḫu*

sammūtu "fragrance"? jB, of cedars

samnu(m) I; f. *samuntu(m)* "eighth" [8- ; 8.KAM; OB also KI.8] as ordinal; < *samāne*; > *Araḫ= samna*; → *samānû*

samnu II "oath" jB

samrūtum; pl. *samrātum*, OA *samruātum* "nail" OA, OB of copper; also ^giš^*s*.

samsammu O/jB lex. **1.** (a drum) **2.** (a bird); < Sum.?

sāmtu(m), *sānd/tu*, NA *sa'tu* "redness" **1.** *s. maḫāṣu* "to colour red" **2.** M/NA "dawn" **3.** "carnelian" (also other red stones ?) [(NA4.)GUG]; *s. kūri*, *qalītu* (artificial red stone) **4.** OA "red wool" **5.** NB (a tree)?; < *sāmu*

samṭu → *šamṭu* II

samû I ~ "undecided, vacillating" M/jB; < *samû* II

samû II ~ "to vacillate, be undecided" j/NB, NA **G** (*u/u*) of person; politically "be undependable"; NB "be inept"; jB of ship "drift" **Gtn** NA of feet "deviate, stray" **D** ~ "cause to stray, lose direction"; > *samû* I, *samîš*; *sūmum* II; → *naṣmītu*

samû → also *šamû* I

sāmu(m), occas. *sa'mu*, Mari also *sīmum*, Ug. *šāmu*; f. j/NB also *sāndu* "red, brown" [SA5] of wool, cloth, hide; skin, coat of animals; of human as PN; fruit, beer; stone, metal, (*ḫurāṣu*) *s.* "red gold"; cloud, star etc.; < *siāmum*; > *sāmtu*; *sūmu* I

sâmu → *siāmu*

sa'mu → *sāmu*

samukānu (a siege implement) OB, Mari

samullu(m), *samallu(m)*, Sum. *sama(n)num* (a tree) Bab., OA

samuntu → *samnu* I

samūnu (a prayer) jB lex.

sanābu → *sanāpu*

sanamuḫlu (a functionary) Nuzi; < Hurr.

sanannu → *šanannu*

sanānu mng. unkn. **G** jB lex. **D** "make flow" in channel ?; > *sanninu*

sanapu (a plant) jB lex.

sanāpu(m) (or *sanābu(m)*) "to tie on" O/jB **G** (*i/i*) weapon to body; pin to head **D** stat. mng. uncl.; > *sinbu*, *sinibtu*; *sunāpu*?; *sānipum*; *sannāpum*

sanāqu(m) I, NB also *senēqu*, Ug. occas. *šanāqu* "to check; approach" **G** (*i/i*) [DIM4 (.MÀ)] **1.** "check" that s.th. is correct, weight, amount, statement, persons; text; "test, keep control of" s.o.; stat. "is in order", "is obedient, under control" **2.** "come near, approach, be upon" s.o.; of season, event, harvest; stat. "is at hand, available"; "approach" judge, court, for judgement; "advance claim" on s.th.; "approach, advance on" s.o. with hostile intent; of parts of liver etc. "stretch up to" **Gt** stat. "is near" **D** ~ G 1 "check, control" goods, quantities, work, (activities in) palace etc.; "cross-examine, interrogate", "exhort, counsel" s.o.; stat., ext., astr., mng. uncl. **Dt** pass. of D "be checked, controlled" **Š** caus. of G 2 "make s.th. reach" s.o., "arrive" **N** pass. NB "be checked"; MB "be interrogated"; > *sanqu, saniqtu; sanqūtu; siniqtu; sāniqu, sunnuqu; masnaqtu; tasniqtu*

sanāqu II "to lack, be in need of" NB stat.; < Aram.; > *sunqu*

sanāšu, *šanāšu, sanāsu*? "to stick in, drive in" jB, NA **G** (*i/i*) sword into heart **Gtn** NA ellipt. "stake out" camp? **D** ~ G "drive" reed etc. "into" heart etc.; > *sunnušu*

sanbuku ~ "bunch, spray" NA, of fruit

sandanakku → *saddanakku*

sandâniš "like a bird-catcher" NA/jB; < *(u)sandû*

sandu → *samdu*

sandû → *usandû*

sāndu → *sāmtu; sāmu*

sangil(i)mud, *sangirmud* (a bluish stone) j/NB, NA [NA$_4$.SAG.GIL.MUD]

sangilûm, *saggilûm* "difference, discrepancy" OB in metrology; < Sum.

sangirmud → *sangilimud*

sangu; pl. *sangāni* (mountain track)? NA/jB

sangûm (a metal object)? OB

sangûm → also *šangû*

sangûtu → *šangûtu*

sanḫu, *saḫḫu* (part of an ornament) NB, pendant, of gold, silver

sanḫulḫazakku, *sanḫulḫazû* (the demon *mukīl rēš lemutti*) jB; < Sum.

Sāninu MB PN; < *zanānu* II ?

sānipum "binder" OB as PN; < *sanāpu*

saniqtu "verified fact" Mari, jB; < *sanāqu* I

sāniqu "controller" jB, "one who controls" s.o.; lex., f., syn. for door; < *sanāqu* I

sankallu(m) "foremost" O/jB **1.** OB of gods **2.** [(NA$_4$.)SAG.KAL] (a precious stone); < Sum.

sankātu ~ "intrigues"? NA; < *samku* ?

sankidabbû (a head illness) jB [SAG.KI.DAB.BA]; < Sum.

sankuddû (a kind of fish) jB lex.; < Sum.

sankullu(m) **1.** (a mace) OAkk, jB [SAG.GUL; SAG.KUL.LA] **2.** jB astr. [SAG.KUL.LA/LI] "globe-lightning"; < Sum.

sankuttum, *sakkuttum*; pl. *sankunātum* ~ "remainder, residue" OB [SAG.KUD] of grain, animals, gold; < Sum.

sannāpum "binder" OB as PN; < *sanāpu*

sannigû "list of stock" O/jB [SAG.NÍG.GA] rdg. uncert.; < Sum.; → *namkūru*

sanninu ~ "slanderous" M/jB; < *sanānu*

sannu (a fishing net) jB lex.

sanqu(m) "checked" [DIM$_4$(.MÀ)] of commodities; OB math. "recalculated to normal unit"; "verified" of statement; of official, also as PN; j/NB "obedient; disciplined", *lā s.* "disobedient"; < *sanāqu* I

sanqû (a grade of dates) Ug.(lit.); < Sum.

sanqūtu "prudence, obedience" jB *s. alāku* "to behave in an obedient manner"; < *sanāqu* I

sansannum → *sassannu*

santak(ka/u), *sattak(ka/u)* "continuously, regularly" M/NB(poet.)

santakku(m), *sattakku(m)*, occas. *samdakkum* "triangle, wedge" Bab. **1.** "triangle" [SAG.DÙ] math. **2.** "triangular shape, wedge" lex., of troop formation **3.** "cuneiform wedge" [SANTAK$_4$], esp. *s. takāpu* "to imprint a wedge"; < Sum.

santakku → also *santakka*

santappu "protective cover"? jB lex.; < Sum.

santašurrû (a stone) jB lex.; < Sum.

sāntu → *sāmtu*

santukullu (top part of weapon) OB lex.; < Sum.

sapādu(m) "to mourn" O/jB **G** (*i/i*) for s.o. (= dat.); *irta s.* "beat breast"? **Gtn** iter., transf. of date palms **Š** "cause to mourn"; > *sipdu, sipittu; naspittu*

sapāḫu(m), occas. *šapāḫu* "to scatter, disperse" **G** (*a/u*) [BIR] oil; earth, grain, animals; people, family, land, troops; transf. "frustrate" plan, acts; stat. "are spread" of parts of body **Gtn** iter. OA "continually frustrate" s.o.'s intentions **D** "squander" goods, estate; "spend freely"; "scatter" salt, dust, (beads of) necklace; "splash" water etc. "over" s.th. (= acc.); "disperse, break up" sheepfold, army, population; "frustrate" plans; *arna s.* "disperse guilt/sin"; "debilitate" limbs; NA stat. of water "is dissipated" (wr. *ṣappaḫūni*) **Dtn** iter. **Dt** pass., of property (*bīt awīlim*) "be squandered" **N** [BIR] **1.** pass. of G "be scattered, dispersed"; "be squandered" **2.** "disperse" (intrans.), of demon "evaporate";

> *saphu, saphūtu; siphu, sipihtu; sapīhūtu; sappāhu, sappihu; suppuhu; naspuhtu*

sapāku G not attested **N** NA ~ "to be ensnared" **Ntn** iter. jB "writhe" of invalid

sapalgīnu, *saplagīnu, salbagīnu* (a plant) jB lex.

sapalu → *saplu; supālu*

sapannu(m) "flatland, plain" Bab., NA between mountains; reed-swamp; *s. tâmti* "coastal plain"; < *sapānu*

sapānu(m) "to flatten, lay flat" Bab., NA **G** (*a/u*) field (for sesame cultivation), also obj. sesame, and absol.; tents; grindstone; "overturn, cast down" stele, image; of flood, enemy, gods, weapons etc. "flatten" land, transf. "overwhelm, swamp" enemies **D** MA stat. "is worn, damaged"? **Š** caus. of G "cause to overthrow" **N** pass., of road, place "be flattened, levelled"; > *sāpinu, sipnu; naspanu, naspantu; sapannu*

sapāqu 1. NA "to be sufficient" of garrison **2.** NB lex. "to be able, strong"; < Aram.; > *sapqu*

sapāriš "as with, like a net" jB; < *sapāru*

saparru(m), *sabarru, šaparrum* f. "cart" Bab., M/NA [GIŠ.GAG.LIŠ/SÌLA; jB GIŠ.GAG.LIŠ.LAL; NB GIŠ.GAG.SI.LAL, GIŠ.SA.PAR]; < Sum.?

saparru → also *sapāru*

sapāru(m), *saparru, šaparru* "(deity's) net" O/jB [SA.PÀR] in hunting, for enemies; *s. manzât* "*s.* of rainbow"; < Sum.; > *sapāriš*

sapdinnum (or *saptinnum*) (a fine textile) OA

saphu(m) "scattered, dispersed" Bab., NA [BIR] of population, family, animals; palm trees; f. "scattered material" of malt, wheat ?; "expanded" of lex. list [BIR.MEŠ]; < *sapāhu*

saphūtu(m) "dispersal, diaspora" O/jB *s. awīlim* "dispersed humanity"; < *saphu*

sapīhūtu mng. uncl. jB lex.; < *sapāhu*

sapīnatu, NA *šappīnatu* "boat" NA, NB; < Aram.

sāpinu "flattener" MB desig. of a stone; of a demon; < *sapānu*; → *šāpinum*

sāpiu → *sēpû*

saplagīnu → *sapalgīnu*

saplišhu (a desig. of meat offerings) NA

saplu, *sapalu* "bowl, dish" M/NA, M/jB of copper, bronze; for oil

saplu → also *šaplu* II

sapnu "paw" jB, of lion

sappāhu 1. MB "scatterer" as PN **2.** MA *ša s.*, desig. of bowls; < *sapāhu*

sappandu (a resinous tree)? jB lex.

sappartu, *šappartu* "point, tip (of horn)"? Bogh., jB of ox, goat etc.

sappāru(m), *šappāru(m)* (a wild animal, phps.) "wild ram" Bab.; < Sum.

sappatu → *šappatu*

sappihu "wasteful, spendthrift" jB; < *sapāhu*

sappu(m) I (a bowl) OA, O/jB; of metal; MB on chariot, of wood; → *šappu*

sappum II (a lance) OB [ŠA.U$_4$.ŠA; ŠA.U$_{18}$.ŠA]

sappu III (or *šappu*) "scraper"? jB lex.

sappu → also *zappu*

sapqu "able, competent" NB lex.; < *sapāqu*

sapsapānu "moustachioed" M/jB, as PN; (a fish); (a plant); < *sapsapu*

sapsapu; pl. f. "moustache" MA, jB [TÙN.BAR] of human; MA "fringe" of garment; > *sapsapānu*; → *sassaptu*

saptinnum → *sapdinnum*

sapu → *sabu*

sapû → *sepû* II

sāpû → *sēpû*

sâpu → *sâbu*

sapulhu (a container) NA; < Hurr.?

saqādum → *zaqādum*

saqālu ~ "to take away"? jB **G** (*a/u*) persons from s.o.; → *musakkiltu*

saqāpu → *zaqāpu*

saqāru → *zakāru; zaqāru*

saqātu (a bird) j/NB [GÌR.GÍD.DA.MUŠEN] eats dates

sāqirum → *zākirum*

saqqāya, *šaqqāya* "sack maker" NB; < *saqqu*

saqqu(m) "sack(cloth)" Bab., OA; > *saqqāya*

saqrû → *sakrû*

saqtu → *zaqtu*

sāqu(m) "thigh" OAkk$^?$, jB; → *sīqu* II

sâqu → *siāqum*

sarabu → *šarbu* II

sarādu(m) "to tie up" OA, O/jB **G** (*i/i*) lex., OA "pack" a donkey; > *sardum; sāridu; surrudu; masradum*; → *serēdu*

sarāhiš "in ruins" jB of temple; < *sarāhu*

sarāhu(m) "to destroy, ruin" Bab., NA **G** (OB *i/i* ?, NA pres. *isarra/uh*) mng. uncl. **D** ~ G "demolish" structure; life, limbs **Dt** pass. of D **N** NB "be ruined"; > *serhu; sarāhiš; tasrihtu*

sarāmu(m) ~ "to cut open" O/jB **G** (*i/i*) roof, skull; stat., of part of liver "is parted"?; > *sirimtu; sarramtu; nasrāmu*

sarāmû (an archit. fitting)? NA

saranātu pl. (a wooden item) NA

sarāpu ~ "to sup" M/jB **G** of person consuming porridge **D** mng. unkn. lex.

sarāqu(m) "to strew, sprinkle, pour" **G** (*a/u*) [DUB] grain, incense, flour, esp. in rit.; transf. OB "cast s.o. down" before DN ? **N** pass.; > *serqu*; *surqēnum* ; → *zarāqu*

sarartu ~ "treachery" M/jB; < *sarāru*

sarāru(m), MB occas. *ṣarāru* "to be false" **G** only stat. and infin., of person "be a liar, dishonest", of statement, dream, document "be false" **D 1.** "deceive" s.o. **2.** "lie, tell lie" **3.** "act dishonestly" **4.** "contest, declare s.th. false" **N** (*nasarruru*) "be proved false"; > *sarru* I, *sarriš*, *sarrūtu*, *sartu*, *sarta*, *sartatti*; *surri*, *surriš*, *sursurtu*, *surru*, *surrātu*, *surrātānum*; *sarartu*; *sarrarum* I, *sarrirum*; *surrurtum*; *tasrīru*

sarbu "tallow, fat" jB lex.

sarbu → also *šarbu* I

sardium, *sardû* (a song of blessing) O/jB; < Sum.

sardum "packed, loaded" OA, of donkey; of baggage; < *sarādu*

sardû → *sardium*

sarḫullu (or *šarḫullu*) (a musical percussion instrument) jB, of copper

sariam, *sariānu* → *sariyam*

sāridu(m) "packer, donkey-driver" OA, jB lex., of donkeys; *ša s.* "packer's expenses"; < *sarādu*

sarirû (a portable object)? jB

sari(y)am, *siri(y)am*, *siri*, *še/iryam*, Ebla *sari(y)ānum*, MA *sariānu*, NB *šir'am*, *šir'annu*, Bogh. *siriyanni*; pl. f. "(coat of) armour" M/NA, M/NB for men, horses; of leather and copper, NB ^{túg}*s.* "(woollen) tunic"; < Hurr.

sarkatu → *sarqatu*

sarkidum → *zarqidum*

sarku (a class of soldier) Am., Bogh., Ug.; < Hitt.

sarku(p)pu(m), *serkuppu* ~ "reed marsh" OAkk, jB lex.

sarmānu pl. or du.? ~ "hands, handles" j/NB lex.; → *sarmā'u*

sarmāšum, *sermāšu* "grain heap, sheaf"? O/MB; OB *ša s.* (an agricultural worker); < Sum.?

sarmā'u ~ "(fore)arm"? jB, M/NB; Emar as linear measure; → *sarmānu*

sarme "forest" jB lex.; < Hurr.?

sarnum (or *zarnum*) mng. unkn. OA

sarqatu(m), *sarkatu(m)* "abomasum with duodenum"? O/jB lex., ext.

sarqidum → *zarqidum*

sarrāmānu → *serrēmānu*

sarramtu "splitter, (wooden) wedge"? Nuzi; < *sarāmu*

sarrāriš → *sarrārum* I

sarrartu (or *zarrartu*) (open country)? MB

sarrārum I "criminal" OAkk, OB; esp. seditious; OAkk PN *Ḫusus-sarrāriš* "Think on the rebel(s)"; < *sarāru*

sarrāru II (pin on a waggon) jB lex.

sarrarû (or *šarrarû*) (a malformed reed)? jB lex.

sarrātu → *sarru* I; *sartu*

sarriqu → *zarriqu*

sarrirum (or *[mu]sarrirum* ?) "deceitful" Mari; < *sarāru*

sarriš "maliciously" O/jB; < *sarru* I

sarru(m) I, *sāru*, *ṣarru* "false; criminal" [LUL] of person "dishonest"; "criminal"; of city, person "false, rebellious"; desig. of planet Mars [MUL.LUL.LA]; "false" of tablet; of barren date palm; math., "provisional" of figure before final calculation; as PN; < *sarāru*

sarru(m) II, *zarru(m)*, *sāru*, *zāru* "grain heap, stack" O/jB; *ša s.* (agricultural worker); < Sum.; > *zarriš*

sarru(m) III, *zarru* (crescent-shaped piece) O/jB **1.** (a box, chest) **2.** (a depression in lung)? **3.** (a component of cartwheel); < Sum.?

sarrû → *surrû* II

sarruru D "to pray to, worship" NA **Dtn** iter.; > *surāru*

sarrūtu(m), *sarruttu* OA, OB, Am., Nuzi "dishonesty, treachery"; < *sarru* I

sarsannu → *sassannu*

sarta adv. "dishonestly" MB; < *sartu*

sartatti/u "fraudulently" NA, NB; < *sartu*

sartennu, *sartinnu* , Nuzi also *širtennu*? "chief judge" Nuzi, j/NB, NA; < Hurr.

sartu(m), *ṣartu*, NB *saštu*; pl. *sarrātu(m)* "falsehood, dishonesty, crime" [LUL-], *kī s.*, *ina s.* "dishonestly"; NA "penalty (for crime)"; *šībūt/kunuk/ṭuppi sar(rā)tim* "false testimony/ document"; < *sarru* I f.; > *sartatti*

sarûm ~ "early, in advance"? OA

sarûm → also *zarû* II

sāru "fan, fly-whisk" NA, *s. šētuqu*, *ka''û* "to wave fan"

sāru → also *sarru* I.II; *šāru*

sâru(m) "to rotate, dance" O/jB **G** (*ū*) of person; animal; wind, water "whirl" **D** *sûrta surru* "set up in a circle" reed bundles; > *sûrtu*

sar'u mng. unkn. jB med.

sasallu → *šašallu*

sasā'u → *šasû*

sasinnu(m), *sisinnu*, O/MB(Alal.) *šašš/ssinnu* "bowyer, bow-maker" Mari, OB(Alal.), M/NA, Susa, M/NB [(LÚ.)ZADIM]

sasiu "invited" NA subst., of guests; < *šasû*; > *sasûtu*

saskû(m), *sasqû(m)*, *t/šas/šk/qû* (a fine flour) O/jB [(ZÌ.)EŠA; OB also ZÌ.TIR.A] esp. in rit.; < Sum.?

saslum mng. unkn. OB lex.; also as PN

sasqû → *saskû*

sassannu(m), *sansannum*, Nuzi *sarsannu* (plaited reed artefact) O/jB desig. of a hunting basket, *ša s.* (a trapper); a whip-handle; a musical instrument ?

sassaptu "eyelashes, eyebrow"? jB lex.; → *sapsapu*

sassatu "grass, turf" M/NA, M/jB [Ú.KI.KAL]; < *sassu*

sassu(m) "base, floor" Bab., NA **1.** OB math. "base" of figure **2.** "floor(-boards)" of chariot [KI.KAL] **3.** "sole" of shoe, "bottom" of container; part of an axe **4.** jB ${}^{\text{ú}}$*s.* for *sassatu* "grass"; > *sassatu*; → *sassumma*

sassû → *šasû* D

sa(s)sukku 1. Nuzi (a functionary) **2.** jB (a bird)

sassullu → *sasullu*

sassumma in *s. epēšu* ~ "to lay bricks out" Nuzi; < *sassu* + *-umma* ?

sa(s)surtu "model womb"? MA, of tin/lead; < *šassūru* ?

sassūru → *šassūru*

sasû → *sasiu*; *sasûtu*; *šasû*

sāsu(m) 1. "moth" [UR.ME], OA textiles *sāsam laptu* "affected by moth"; also as PN and fPN *Sāsatum* **2.** Ug., jB (a stone) [NA4.NÍR.ZIZ]

sasullu (or *sassullu*) (a textile) Nuzi

sasuppu → *šušippum*

sasûtu mng. unkn. NA in *ša s.*, desig. of deity; < *sasiu*

saṣḫar(t)u "youth" jB lex.; < W.Sem.

saštu → *sartu*

sāt → *šāt*

satālu "to plant" jB(Ass.) **G** (*i/i*) reed-bed; > *šitlu*

sataru(m), *zataru*, *s/zateru* (a herb, phps.) "thyme" or "savory" Mari, M/jB

satarušššu, *satruššu*, *sazaruššu* (a kind of terrain) Nuzi; < Hurr.

sateru → *sataru*

satruššu → *sataruššu*

sattak(ka) → *santakka*

sattakku → *santakka*; *santakku*; *sattukku*

sattum → *zātum*

sattukku, *šattukku(m)*, *šantukku*, *sattakku* "regular delivery, regular offering" Bab., NA [SÁ.DUG4; Mari, MB also SÁ.SAG]; Mari "(non-cultic) deliveries"; elsewhere mostly ref. to temple offerings; *s. DN* "regular offerings for DN"; *s. MN* "*s.* of MN"; *s. X* "*s.* comprising X", e.g. dates, oil, grain; *immer s.* "*s.* sheep"; NB family name *Rē'i-s.* "Shepherd of *s.* (sheep)"; *ša s.* "person in charge of *s.*"; < Sum.

sātum → *zātum*

sâtu → *sūtu* I

sa'tu → *sāmtu*

saṭāḫum → *sadāḫum*

saṭāru → *šaṭāru* II

sâṭu mng. unkn. jB lex. **G**

sā'u(m), *sabbu* **1.** Mari, jB lex. (a tree) **2.** Bogh., jB "mud"

sâ'u(m) "to cry out (in pain); wince"? O/jB **G** (*isā'*)

sa'ūdum (a tree) Mari

saumbulu "seal" NB; < Gk.

sa'uru (or *sa'eru*); pl. f. (an ornament) NA, of gold; → *šu''uru* I.II

sa''uru → *šu''uru* II

sawûm ~ "desert" OB

sāwum (or *sāyum*) ~ "cup" Mari, of gold

sayyītu → *samītu*

sazaruššu → *sataruššu*

Sê' → *Sîn*

se'āru → *sêru*

seba → *sebe*

***sebâ** "seventy" not attested in syll. wr.

sebât → *sebītum*

sebe, *seba*, OA **šabe*, MB(Alal.) *šeb'i*; f. *sebet(tu)* "seven", *sebet ūmim sebe mušiātim* "seven days (and) seven nights"; > *sebîšu*, *sebītum*, *sebû*, *sebūtum*, *sabā'iu*, *sebêšer*, *sebettu*, *subu'īu*

sebêšer "seventeen" OB; < *sebe* + *-šer*

sebettu "group of seven, heptad"; DN [${}^{\text{d}}$IMIN(=7).BI] *(Ilū-)Sebettu/i*; < *sebe*

sebiat → *sebītum*

sebîšu, OA *šabîšu*, jB also *šibîšu*, Am. *šib'ettān(a)* etc. "seven times"; freq. *adi s.-šu*; < *sebe*

sebītum; st. abs. *sebiat*, *se/abât* "one-seventh" OB; < *sebe*

sēbi'u → *sābû*

sebû(m), *šibû*, *šabû*; f. *sebūtu(m)* "seventh" Bab., NA?; NB also "one-seventh"; < *sebe*; *sabā'iu*

sēbû → *sābû*

sebūtum "seventh day (of month)" OB; < *sebû*

sedēru → *sadāru*

sediš → *šediš*

sedru → *sadru*; *sidru*

sēdum ~ "red"? OB lex.

sêdu "to support, assist" NB; < Aram.; → *sa'du*; *sā'idum*

se'du → *si'du*

segû "to roam, wander" NB **G** gener. "go, go along" with; NB "proceed" according to law **Š** caus. "make s.o. go along" with s.o.; "enforce" law; < Aram.; > *sēgû*

sēgu (a game) MB

sēgû "restless" of ghost jB; < *segû*

seḫēlu → *saḫālu*

seḫḫu (an object) NA, of precious stone

seḫlu, *siḫlu* "thorn, spine" jB, NA of plant, fish; transf. "stab" of pain, illness; < *saḫālu*

seḫpu, *siḫpu*; MB pl. f. "covering; surface" M/NA, M/NB **1.** "covering, overlay" Am. of chariot in gold; "bark, bast" as covering for bow [(GIŠ.)BAR.KÍN]; of leather **2.** "surface, extent" of heaven, earth, lands **3.** "flattening", *s. mūti* "f. by death", *ana s. pānišu* "flat on his face"; < *saḫāpu*

seḫru(m), *siḫru(m)* **1.** "bend, turn" of river, horse **2.** "mercy, favour" of deity, in PN **3.** "frame, setting, rim" for gems, wheel etc. **4.** Ass. "region, district" **5.** (a stone) [NA4.Á.ŠUBA]; < *saḫāru*

seḫseḫī "at dusk" OB lex.; < Sum.?

seḫšu(m), *seḫtum* "gathered-up" O/jB of tablet "invalid(ated), void"; < *saḫāšu*

seḫû(m), *saḫû(m)*, OA *saḫā'um* "to rise up, revolt" Bab., OA **G** (*i/i*) of individuals, lands **D** "wreck, ruin" table, foundations, boundary (-stone); "destroy, desecrate" building, carving; transf. cult, person **Dt** pass. "be ruined, desecrated" **N** "fall into confusion"; jB(Ass.) "foment rebellion" **Ntn** lex. "be constantly confused"; > *saḫ'um*; *sīḫu* I, *siḫītu* I; *sēḫû*; *suḫḫû*; *musaḫḫûm*

sēḫû "dissenter, challenger" NB leg., against contract; < *seḫû*

sekēpu → *sakāpu* I

sekertu → *sekretu*

sekēru(m) I, *sakāru(m)* "to shut off, block up" **G** (*i/i*) [ÚŠ] water(course), street; nose, lips, man (of urinary blockage) **D** ~ **G** "dam" canal; "block" mouth, part of liver **Dt** "be blocked" of ears **N** "be blocked up" of watercourse, part of body; OA "shut o.s. away" **Ntn** [ÚŠ.ÚŠ] med. "be persistently blocked" of part of body, urine;

> *sekru* I, *sekretu*; *sikru*; *sukurtum*; *sēkiru*, *sēkirūtu*; *sikkūru*; *sakkiru?*; *meskertum*

sekēru II "to heat" in an oven O/jB, NA **G** (*i/i*) [ÚŠ], med. "stew" ingredients; NA "fire" bricks; Mari, NA (a treatment in goldworking); > *sakru*; *sekru* II

sēkiru(m), *sekkiru*, OAkk *sākirum* (a canal-worker) OAkk, O/jB [OB LÚ.A.IGI.DU₈] in charge of maintenance of dykes, dams etc.; < *sekēru* I

sēkirūtu "damming work" jB; < *sekēru* I

sekkiru → *sēkiru*

sekretu(m), *sekratu*, *sekertu(m)*, *sekru(m)* "enclosed (woman)" Bab., NA? of class of women [OB (MUNUS.)SÉ.(E.)EK.RUM/RU.UM; also MUNUS.UŠ ?]; name, desig. of goddess; MB, jB(Ass.) of royal concubine, pl. "harem"; < *sekru* I; → *sikru* 2

sekru I "closed off, up" jB of canal; < *sekēru* I

sekru II "warmed" jB of liquid; < *sekēru* II

sekru → also *sekretu*

sekû "deaf" jB lex.

selēmu → *salāmu* II

selēqu → *salāqu* II

sellu, *sillu* "basket" M/NB [GI.GUR.SAL.LA] esp. for bread, dates; *qan s.* (a kind of arrow)?; jB(Ass.) (an archit. feature, phps.) "archivolt"

selû → *šelû* III

semēdu → *samādu*

semēḫu → *samāḫu*

semeru "ring" M/NB [ḪAR] in chain, fetter; as ornament; → *simirtu*; *šawirum*

semmīdātu → *samīdu* I

senēqu → *sanāqu* I

senkurru → *simkurru*

sennu → *šannu*

sepēru "to write (in Aramaic script)" NB; < Aram.; > *sipru* II

sepīru, *sepirru* "interpreter-scribe (of Aram.)" NB [LÚ.A.BAL; LÚ.KUŠ.SAR ?]

sepiu → *sēpû*

sepû I (a type of beer) NA; < *sepû* II

sepû II, *sapû* "to pluck, pull"? jB **G** wool, hair **Gtn** med., "persistently pluck"? hair of head; > *sepû* I; *sēpû?*

sepû(m) III mng. unkn. O/jB **G** of dragonfly on flooded land (**D** → *suppû* I)

sēpu (a cereal) NA; esp. *akal s.* "s. loaf"

sēpû, *sēpiu*, MA *sāpiu* "felt-worker" M/NA, jB; < *sepû* II ?

seqru → *zikru*

serapu → *serpu*

sērāšu → *sīrāšu*

sērāšû → *sīrāšû*

serbittum (or *serpittum*) (a fish) OB

serdīum "of olive wood"? OB, of a bow; < *serdu*

serdu(m) "olive tree" [OB SÉ.ER.DU(.UM); Ug. GIŠ.GI.DÌM(.MA)] *šaman s.* "olive oil"; NA "olive(s)"; > *serdīum*

serdû(m) **1.** OA, OB (kind of contract) **2.** j/NB "carrying-pole" for litter; < Sum.

serēdu "to make a bandage" jB [LÁ]; → *sarādu*

serḫu "debris" NB in *s. epērī* "eroded soil"; < *sarāḫu*

serkuppu → *sarkuppu*

sermāšu → *sarmāšum*

sermu → *zermu*

sernaḫ (a garment) MB; < Kass.

serpittum → *serbittum*

serpu, *serapu* "shearing knife" NB of iron

serqu(m), *šerqu*, once *surqu*, NB *sišqu* "strewn offering" of flour etc.; *s. mūši* "night-time offering"; deities *māḫirū s.-ya* "receiving my offering"; < *sarāqu*

serramannu (or *zerramannu*) (desig. of horses) Nuzi

serrāmu → *serrēmu*

serrēmānu, Ug. *sarrāmānu* 'onager-coloured' Ug., jB [NA4.ZA.GÌN.ANŠE.EDIN.NA] (kind of lapis lazuli); < *serrēmu*

serremtu "female onager" jB [MUNUS.ANŠE.EDIN.NA]; < *serrēmu*

serrēmu, NA *serrāmu* "onager" M/NB, NA [ANŠE.EDIN.NA] hunted; in omens; in similes, running, rolling; > *serremtu*; *serrēmānu*

serru → *zerru* III

serserrum (a weapon)? OB

seršu (a topog. term)? jB lex.

sēru → *se'ru*

sêru(m), Ass. *se'āru(m)* "to plaster, smear" **G** (*ē*) wall, roof, barrage; (part of) body with liquid (= acc.); MA "rub down" horse **D** "smear, anoint" s.o. with substance; > *se'ru*; *sīru* I; *masīru*?

se'ru, *sēru* "plastered" MA, jB of pottery ~ "covered with a clay slip"; < *sêru*

sesseru(m) "young child" O/jB

sētu → *sītu*

sêtu → *šētu* II

se'û ~ "to press down" M/jB **G** (*i/i*) part of liver; stat. of body; transf. "suppress, oppress" land, enemy etc.; > *si'ûtu*

Sî' → *Sîn*

siāmu(m), *sâmu* "to be red, brown" **G** (stat. *sām*) [SA5] of textile, hide; part of body, heavenly bodies; fire **D** "redden, dye red" hides; > *sāmu*, *sāmtu*; *sūmu* I, *sūmtu*; *sīmūtu*

siānātu, *siyānātu*, *ziānātu* (a covering) Nuzi; of leather, wool

siānu, *siyānu* "temple" O/MB(Elam); < Elam.

siāqu(m), *sâqu* "to be(come) narrow" Bab., NA **G** (stat. *sīq*, NA *sāq*) of part of body; river; transf. of life, land "be straitened" **Gtn** NB of structure "stay closely aligned with" **D** "make (too) narrow, reduce"; "straiten, reduce" life, enemy; > *sīqu* I, *sīqiš*?; *sūqu*, *Sūqāya*, *sūqāqû*; *musiqqum*

siāṣu → *šiāṣum*

sibarātum → *ṣibarātum*

sibbatu → *zibbatu*

sibberru → *sippirû*

sibbirru, *simbirru*, *sinb/pirru* (a tree) jB; also aromatic product thereof; → *šibburratu*

sibbu → *sippu*

sibburratu → *šibburratu*

sibibiānu → *zibibiānum*

sibirru → *šibirru*

sibittu → *sebettu*

sibi'tum "irresoluteness"? OB; < *sabā'u*

sibkarû (or *sipkarû*) (an object) NA, NB of metal

sibru → *sipru*

sibsātu → *šibsātu*

sibsīrum (or *sipsīrum*) mng. unkn. OB in *s. sīsîm* "*s.* of a horse"

sibtum → *ṣibtum* IV

sību(m) "brew (of beer)" O/jB [KURUN.NA]; *bīt s.* "brewery"; < *sabû*; > *sibûtu*

sību → also *šību*

sibûtu(m), *sabûtu*, *šebûtu* "(process of) brewing" O/jB, Nuzi; *bīt s.* "brewery"; in MN *(w)araḫ s.*; < *sību*

sidāte (copper implements) NA

sidirtu "row" M/jB, NA *s. šakānu* "to draw up line of battle"; *s. sadāru* "to form a row"; < *sadāru*

sidru "row" jB, NA "line of battle"; "row" of gods; "register" of carving; NB transf. "regular offering"; < *sadāru*

sidû (a topog. term)? jB lex.

si'du (or *se'du*) (kind of mistletoe)? jB lex.

sidūrum (a stone)? OB

sigaggurītu → *siggaggurītu*

sigaru → *šigaru*

sigba(r)rû "(priest) with long hair" jB [LÚ.SÍK.BAR(.RA)]; < Sum.

si(g)gaggurītu(m), *singanga/urītu(m)* (part of foot) O/jB

siggūrum → *singurru*

siggu → *sinkum*

sīgu → *sīku*; *sinku*

si(ḫ)ḫāru → *saḫḫarru*

siḫiltu(m) "thorn, sting" O/jB; transf. "pain"; < *saḫālu*

siḫiptu jB **1.** in *s. DN* (an illness) **2.** *s. litti pagarti* "*s.* of a *p.* cow" mng. uncl.; < *saḫāpu*

siḫirtu(m), OAkk *saḫartum* [NIGIN-] **1.** OB math. "circumference"; NB "surroundings", *igār s.* "enclosure wall" of temple **2.** Bab. "area, district" **3.** "entirety" of people, land etc., *a(na) s.-šu* etc., *s. ēkalli* "all the palace", *s. ummānī* "all the workforce" etc.; *s. amūti* "the entire liver"; < *saḫāru*

siḫītu(m) I, jB also *saḫītu* "rebellion" OA, jB; < *seḫû*

siḫītum II (a process for treating barley)? OB for beer

siḫlu → *seḫlu*

siḫpu → *seḫpu*

siḫru → *seḫru*

siḫtum → *seḫšum*

sīḫu(m) I "rebellion" Bab., NA; *bēl s.* "rebel", *s. epēšu* "to rebel"; < *seḫû*

sīḫu(m) II, *šīḫu* "wormwood (*Artemisia*)"? Bab.; as drug

sīḫu III (or *zīḫu*) "captivity, detention"? Nuzi

sīḫu → also *šāḫu*

siḫūnu (a kind of wool) NB

siḫūru (an aromatic plant) jB

sikallītu (a tool) NB

sikanšarrum → *sikaššarrum*

sikānu → *sikkānu* I

sikarû(m), *sakkarû* ~ (palm-bark spikes)? O/jB

sikaššarrum, *sikanšarrum*, *sikišarrum*? (a stone) OA, in pl.

sikdu (a kind of mantis) M/jB

sikidû (a kind of sheep) jB lex.; < Sum.

sikillu, *usikillu*, Ug. *(e)šigillu* M/jB **1.** (a plant) [Ú.SIKIL] as drug, called *šam tēlilte* "purification plant" **2.** (a semiprecious stone)? [NA4.SIKIL]; < Sum.

sikiltu(m) "acquistion(s), (hoarded) property" O/jB, MA; also in PNs; < *sakālu* I

sikinūnu → *sukannīnu*

sikiptu(m) Bab. **1.** "repulse" of enemy etc.; *s. šakānu* "to repel" **2.** "rejection" by deity, esp. in PNs; < *sakāpu* I

sikišarrum → *sikaššarrum*

sikkannu → *sikkānu* I.II

si(k)kānu(m) I, *sikkannu*; pl. f. "(boat's) steering paddle, rudder" O/jB [GIŠ.ZI.GAN]

sikkānu(m) II, *sikkannu*; pl. f. (sacred boulder or stele) OB(N.Mes.), Mari, Bogh., Emar

sikkānum III (an attendant) Mari; < *sikkum*

sikkatu(m) I, Ass. also *s/ziqqutu* "peg, nail" [(GIŠ/URUDU.)GAG] of wood, copper; part of chariot, door, lock; NB "blade" of plough; "stake" in ground, as boundary-marker, Mari *ša s.* "surveyor"?; math. "cone, pyramid"; "foundation cone, peg" in wall, esp. Ass. archit. ornament, of stone, terracotta etc. (→ *karru* II); *rab(i)/tupšar/ša sikki/āti* (official titles); *s. ṣēli(m)*, Mari also *si(q)qa(ṣ)ṣēli* "breastbone" [GAG.TI] of human, animal; → *s.* II

sikkatu(m) II, *šiggatu* (a serious illness) O/jB; = *s.* I or < *sakāku* ?

sikkatu(m) III "yeast"? O/jB for beer; OB *s. rubbûm* "to cultivate yeast"

sikkatūtu → *rab-sikkatūtu*

sikkum (or *si(q)qu(m)*?) "hem, fringe" OA, OB of garment, *s. ka''ulum/ṣabātum* "to hold/seize hem" in supplication; OB *ša s.* (a messenger); > *sissiktu*; *sikkānum* III

sikkû → *šikkû*

sikkūru(m), Ug. *s/šukū/īru*; pl. m. & f. "bar, bolt" [GIŠ.SAG.KUL] of wood, copper, for lock; on door, waggon; transf. of heaven, *Ebeḫ s. māti* "Mt. Ebeḫ, bolt of the land"; part of womb; *s. šaqīli* [GIŠ.SAG.KUL.LAL/LÁL] (a kind of bolt); < *sekēru* I

sikmu(m) (a payment)? O/MB; pl., for apprehending a fugitive

sikru(m) **1.** Bab. "dam, barrage" **2.** OB "seclusion (in cloister)" **3.** NA med. "scab" behind ears; < *sekēru* I; → *sekretu* log.

sikšu I, *šik(i)šu*, *zikšu* (side-pole of chariot cab)? O/jB [Á.KÁR.GIŠ.GIGIR]

sikšu II (a topog. term) jB lex.

sīktu → *sīku*

sīku(m) "pounded" O/jB, MA ? of plant seed; m. & f. as subst. "pounded substances, powder"; of person ~ "disabled"?, also as PN; < *sâku*

siladagurrû mng. uncl. jB lex.; < Sum.

sil(a)gazû (an offering vessel of 1/2 *qû* capacity) M/jB [DUG.SÌLA.GAZ] to be broken after use; < Sum.

silakku, *silaqqu* (a village)? M/jB

sila(m)māḫu(m) (a ceremonial garment) OAkk(Ur III), jB; < Sum.

sīla(m)mu (a kind of grass) jB lex.

silaqqu → *silakku*

silaru(m) (a spice)? OAkk, jB lex.

silgazû → *silagazû*

Sililītu(m) (a month) O/jB, (10th month) OB(Susa); → *ṣililītu*

sililllu, *sulillu* (a tree) jB lex.

silīmu → *salīmu*

sili(q)qu mng. unkn. jB lex.

silittu "offtake" jB, of canal; < *salātu* II

silītu(m) I, occas. *šelītu* "afterbirth; womb" O/jB [ÙŠ] of woman, animal

silītu II; pl. *siliāti* "lie, false accusation" NA; < *salā'u* II

sili'tu(m), *silītu(m)* "sickness, disease" O/jB, NA [LÍL]; < *salā'u* I

sillaru → *zillaru*

sillatu → *išqillatu*

sillātu → *šillatu* I

sillikuḫli "witness" Nuzi; < Hurr.

sillitum → *šillatu* I

sillu → *sellu*

sillû → *ṣillû* II

sillūnum, *sillunnu* "old" O/MB, MA of person; of cattle; < Hurr.

sillurmû, *Sîn-lurmâ* "night/day blindness" jB; → *sinnūru*

sillušiḫuru mng. unkn. Nuzi; < Hurr.

silmu "peace"? jB; < *salāmu* II

silqātu (a boiled liquid) j/NB; < *salāqu* I

silqu(m) I **1.** OA "animal for slaughter" **2.** Bab., NA boiled food, esp. "boiled meat"; < *salāqu* I

silqu II; pl. f. (a vegetable, phps.) "mangold" jB

siltu I ~ "sliver (of wood), chip" jB; < *salātu* II; → *silittu*

siltu II (a kind of groats) j/NB, NA

sīlu I, *sūlu* (a tree) jB lex.

sīlu II, *šīlu* mng. unkn. jB lex.

sil'u "sprinkling, lustration" MA, jB; med. also "micturation"; < *salā'u* I

silukannu → *zilukannu*

silullû → *zilullû*

simakku(m), *simāku* (a shrine) Bab.

simannu → *isimmānu*; *simānu* I-III

simānu(m) I, *simannu*, Ass. *simunu* "(right) occasion, season" Bab., M/NA *s. zēri (arāši)* "time for sowing"; NB *s. ša maṣṣartišu* "time for his watch"; jB, NA *ina lā s.-šu* "at the wrong moment" for s.th.; NB astr. "time" in gener.; NA *(i(na))simin* + subjunct. "when"; < *wasāmum*; Ug. → *šimānu* II

Simānu(m) II, *Simannu* (3rd Bab. month) Bab., M/NA [OB ITI.SIG4.A; later ITI.SIG4, occas. ITI.SIG4.GA]

simānu III, *simannu* (a craftsman) NB mending lyres

simānû "born in the month *S.*" MB, NA PN; → *isimmānu*

simātu (or *simattu*) mng. unkn. NA lex. (part of intestines)

simbatu → *zibbatu*

simberru → *sippirû*

simdu(m), *sindu* (a flour) OAkk, j/NB, NA; < *samādu*

simētu → *sītu*

simḫu mng. unkn. jB

simīdum → *samīdu* II

simirtu (a ring on the plough) jB lex.; → *semeru*

simištum "a secret" Mari; < *samāšu*

simkadrû → *sinkadrû*

simkātu f. pl. mng. unkn. MA; < *samāku* ?

simkurru, *senkurru* (a hunted animal) M/NA

simmagir, OB in PlN *Dūr-Su/immukri* (a minister of the Bab. king) j/NB [LÚ.U4. SAKAR.ŠE.GA (as though = *Sîn-magir*)]; *bīt s.* (his house); *šanû ša s.* (his deputy); < Elam.?

simmānû → *isimmānu*

simmatānû mng. unkn. NA of horses

simmatu → *summatu*; *zimmatu*

simmiltu(m) "stair(case)" [(GIŠ.)KUN4/5; once GIŠ.I.BAL]; OA leading up citadel, esp. *rabi s.* (a high Anatolian official); *bīt s.* "stair-room, stair-well"; NB *s. dūri* "siege-ladder"; M/jB (Ass.) of mountain ascent; *s. šamāmī* "ladders to heaven"; > *summulu*

simmu(m) "wound, lesion" Bab., NA [GIG] of surgeon's incision; *s. lazzu, ṣarrišu, matqu* "persistent, spreading, sweet (i.e. discharging ?) wound"

simru → *šimru*

simtu(m) "appropriate symbol, characteristic" [ME.TE] before abstr. nouns "symbol, proper sign" of s.th., *s. ilūti/šarrūti* "symbol of divinity/royalty"; bread *s. balāṭi* "material substance embodying life"; inscriptions *s. tanādātim* "tangible sign and assurance of fame"; horse manoeuvres *s. taḫāzi* "appropriate to battle"; "symbol" or material item "characteristic of, appropriate to" a person, grave *s. mītūti* "proper attribute of the dead"; king *s. DN* "proper (person) for DN"; OB animals, women *s. ēkallim* "palace property"; *simāti(m) šitakkunu(m)* "to adorn (temples) in appropriate manner"; pl. "proper customs"; *lā s.*, pig *lā s. ēkurri* "not proper to a temple"; *ašar lā simātešu* "place inappropriate, unbefitting to him"; < *wasāmum*

simtu → also *šimtu*

sīmu → *sāmu*; *sūmu* I

simurrûm, *šimurrû(m)* "from Simurrum" OB, Ug. lex. of grindstone; jB of kind of pig; < PlN

Simut "(planet) Mars" jB; < Elam.

sīmūtu ~ "redness" jB med.; < *siāmu*

Sîn, NA also *Sē/ī'* "the moon(-god)" Bab., M/NA [^{d}EN.ZU; $^{(d)}$30]; "moon", esp. jB astr.; > *sînu*; → *Su'ēn*

sinbu(m), NA *sinpu* "sanitary towel" O/jB, NA for women; also desig. of a foundling; < *sanāpu*

sindakku mng. unkn. jB

sindu → *simdu*

sindû "Indian" jB(Ass.) as desig. of timber tree; < Sanskr.

singanga/urītu → *siggaggurītu*

singu → *sinkum*

singurgurtu (or *ešgurgurtu*) (a bird) jB

singurru(m), *zingurrum*, *siggūrum* (a fish) OAkk, O/jB [NÍNDA×?.KU$_6$; ZI.GUR.KU$_6$]

sinibtu (or *siniptu*, *zinibtu*) (a membrane on lung) jB; < *sanāpu*

siniqtu(m) "check, control" OB, jB lex. [DIM$_4$-?]; < *sanāqu* I

sinkadrû, *simkadrû* (a yellowish mineral) jB; < Sum.

sinkum?, *singu*, NA phps. *siggu* "discarded wool" Bab., NA?

Sîn-lurmâ → *sillurmû*

Sîn-magir → *simmagir*

sinnatum ~ "spear, lance"? O/jB, Mari; ^{gis}*s*.; *ēpiš s*. "spear-maker"; < *sinnu* I

sinniltu → *sinništu*

sinnisāniš → *sinnišāniš*

sinnissu, *sinniš* → *sinništu*

sinnišāniš, *sinnisāniš* "into a woman" M/jB; < *sinništu*

sinnišānu (an effeminate cult performer) jB; < *sinništu*

sinništu(m), MA, M/jB also *sinniltu*, NA *sinnissu* (or → *issu*?), Bogh. *šinništu* "woman" [MUNUS]; st. abs. in *zikar u sinniš* "male and female"; also of animals; qualifying date palm, stones, etc.; > *sinnišu*, *sinnišānu*, *sinnišāniš*; *sinnišūtu*

sinnišu "female" jB; < *sinništu*

sinnišūtu (NA → *issūtu*) (rôle of female) jB; *epēš s*. [NAM.MUNUS.A] "to have sexual intercourse"; < *sinništu*

sinnu I (a metal object) M/NB; > *sinnatum*; → *sinnutu*

sinnu II ~ "withdrawal"? jB, NA

sinnurbûm, *sinnubbû*? ~ "weak-sighted person"? O/jB lex.

sinnūru "weak sight"? Bogh.; → *sillurmû*

sinnutu (or *sinnūtu*) ~ "brand"? NA; → *sinnu* I

sinpirru → *šibburratu*

sinpu → *sinbu*

sinqu → *sunqu*

sinsû mng. unkn. jB lex.

sinûm → *zinû*

sînu "moon"? jB lex.; < *Sîn*

sinundu → *sinuntu*

sinūnītu (term for mucus)? jB comm.

sinuntu, *s/ṣinundu* "swallow" M/jB, NA [SIM.(MU.)MUŠEN]; MB *pī s*. "swallow's beak" in descr. (of leg)? of bed; desig. of a constellation, a fish (→ *sinūnu*); → *šinūnūtu*

sinūnu(m) "'swallow-fish'" O/jB [SIM.KU$_6$]; → *sinuntu*

sipālu → *supālu*

siparātum → *ṣibarātum*

siparru(m), Nuzi *siperru*? "bronze" [ZABAR; OB(Susa) also ZA.BAR]; OA pl. "bronzes, bronze items"; NA, NB "fetters", also *s. parzilli* "iron fetters"!

sipdu; pl. f. "wailing, mourning" jB; < *sapādu*

siperru → *siparru*

sipḫu(m) **1.** Mari (a metal vessel) **2.** Emar (desig. of field) **3.** jB "scatterings" of barley **4.** jB "dusk"? **5.** f. pl. OA mng. uncl.; < *sapāḫu*

sipiānu → *zibiānu*

sipipiānu → *zibibiānu*

sipiḫtu mng. uncl. jB; < *sapāḫu*

sipittu(m) "mourning (rites)"; *s. šakānu(m)* "to institute mourning ceremony"; *s. šuṣruḫu* "to have" people "wail lamentation"; < *sapādu*

sipkarû → *sibkarû*

sipnu "flattening" NB, of sesame cultivation; < *sapānu*

sippīḫu (an agricultural operation)? NB; < Aram.?

sippirû (a fruit (tree)) jB; → *sibbirru*

sippu(m), *sibbu* "(door-)jamb" Bab., M/NA [ZAG.DU$_8$] *s. bābāni*, to left and right of doorway; of city gate; Ass. "buttress" in city-wall; (vertical member) of table, bed etc.; "(reed-)stem"; ext. (edges of 'palace-gate' in liver)

siprītu (a textile) NA; → *ṣipirtu* III ?

sipru I ~ "debris"? j/NB

sipru II "document" NB; < Aram.; → *sepēru*

sipsatu → *šipšatu*

sipsīrum → *sibsīrum*

sipšatu → *šipšatu*

sipšu (a topog. term) jB lex.

siptum → *ṣibtum* IV

sipû (a mourning garment) jB lex.

sīpu I "(act of) prayer" jB(Ass.); → *suppû* II

sīpu II mng. unkn., phps. (an insect) NA

siqar → *zikru*

siqdīum → *šiqdīum*

siqdu → *šiqdu*

sīqiš "narrowly"? jB; < *sīqu* I ?

siqqatu → *sikkatu* I

siqqu → *sikkum*

siqqurratu → *ziqqurratu*

siqru → *zikru*

siqsiqqu → *ziqziqqu*

sīqu I "narrow, tight" M/NB of ship; garment; MB *ina sīqti* "in a short while"?; *napišti s.* "straitened life"; < *siāqu*

sīqu II "thigh"; du. & pl. "lap" M/NA; → *sāqu*

sīqu → also *zīqu* I

sīrāšītum, Nuzi *sīrāsūtu* "female brewer" OB(Susa), Nuzi; < *sīrāšû*

sīrāšu, *sērāšu*, *sīrīšu*, *šīrīsu*, Bogh. *šīrāš* "(a kind of) beer" Bab.; st. abs. as DN ^{d}*Sīra/iš*; < Sum.?; > *sīrāšû*, *sīrāšītum*, *sīrāšûtu*

sīrāšû(m), *sērāšû(m)*, OAkk *šīrāšûm*?, *sīrēšû*, *surrāšû* "brewer" [LÚ.LUNGA/LÚNGA/LÙNGA; NB LÚ.KUL.LUM/LA]; NA, NB *rab s.* "chief brewer"; < *sīrāšu*

sīrāšûtu(m) "(activity of) brewing" Bab. [LÚ.LUNGA/LÙNGA-]; also "brewer's prebend"; < *sīrāšû*

sīrātu → *sīru* II

sirendu → *sirimtu*

sīrēšû → *sīrāšû*

siri(am) → *sariyam*

siriānum → *ziriānum*

***sirimtu**, *sirendu* (a utensil or tool) MB; < *sarāmu*

sir(i)pi, *sirpiš*; pl. *sirpame* "brown (horse)" MB; < Kass.

sīrīšu → *sīrāšu*

siriyam, siriyanni → *sariyam*

sirku (or *sirqu*) (a fortification) jB

sirpi, sirpiš → *siripi*

sīru(m) I, *šēru* "(wall-)plaster" Bab., NA [IM.BAD]; also of oven; < *sêru*

sīru(m) II, NB *zīru*; pl. f. "awning, (reed-) shelter"

sīru III (an official) NA

sīrum IV (a tax revenue)? Mari

siruribu mng. unkn. MA, desig. of garments

sisalḫu, *siserḫu* (desig. of sheep, cattle) NA; < Hurr.?

sisānu → *zizānu*

sisātu (a plant) jB lex.

siserḫu → *sisalḫu*

sisinnu → *sasinnu*; *sissinnu*

sisītu → *šisītu* I.II

sisium → *sisû*

sisrinnu → *sissirinnu*

sissiktu(m), NA also *š/zišš/zziktu* "hem, fringe" [TÚG.SÍG] of cloak; esp. as symbolic portion, *šārtum u s.* "hair and fringe" as tokens, *s. batāqum* "to cut off hem" in divorce, also in mag.; as substitute for seal; for securing dowry; *s. ṣabātu* "to supplicate"; < *sikkum*

sissimtum? mng. unkn. OB lex.

sissimu → *sissiru* I

sissinnu(m), NB also *šissinnu*, *sissintu*, *šissintu* ?; pl. m. & f. "date-palm spadix" [GIŠ.AN.NA.GIŠIMMAR] with fruit, *fDN ša kīma s. suluppū armū* "fDN whom dates clothe like a spadix"; used as broom; NB usu. transf., (remuneration for gardener); astr. (desig. of a constellation); *s. libbi* (a plant); Nuzi (a silver object, in pairs)

sissirinnu, *sisrinnu* (a building)? jB lex.

sissiru I, *sissimu* (a storeroom) jB lex.

sissiru II "child" jB lex.

sissu ~ "ulcer, abscess" jB lex.

sisû(m), OAkk *sīsum*, OA *sisium* "horse" [ANŠE.KUR.RA; ANŠE.PA+GÍN; NA also KUR] OA *rabi s.* "horse-master"; Alal., NB *rē'û (ša) s.* "horse-herder"; *bīt s.* "stable", NB "horse fief"; NB *mār s.* "charioteer"; OA, Bogh. *rabi s.* (a court official); *kakkab s.* (a star); *s. ša tâmti* 'sea-horse', desig. of *nāḫiru* fish; → *eliya ša sīsê*

sišabu ~ "cultic meal(-time)" jB lex.

siškūru ~ "cultic meal(-time)" jB lex.; < Sum.

sišqu → *serqu*

si'šu "canal in spate"? jB

sitmātu mng. unkn. jB lex.

sittu → *sītu*; *šittu* II.III

sittūtu pl. "those remaining" jB(Ass.), NB; < *šētu* II

sītu(m), *sētu(m)*, *sittu*, *simētu* "projection, salient" O/jB [BÀD.SI] of city-wall, on house; OB transf., of feature on spleen; lex. (an insect)

si'ûtu "pressure, oppression" NB, political; < *se'û*

siyānātu → *siānātu*

siyānu → *siānu*

siyû (a plant) jB lex.

sû(m) I (a hard stone) Ass., O/jB; used for grinding

sû(m) II (a kind of reed mat) O/jB

sû → also *zû* II

suādu(m), *suwādu* (an aromatic plant, phps.) "sedge(-tubers)" Bab. [(ŠIM/GIŠ/Ú.ŠIM.)MAN. DU; Ú/ŠIM.IM.MAN.DU; (GIŠ/ŠIM.)IM.DI/DU; (GIŠ/ŠIM.)EN.DI] med.; oil of *s*.

suāku → *sâku*

suālu "cough; phlegm" M/jB med., om.; < *sa'ālu*

subālu → *supālu*

subandu (or *supandu*) mng. unkn. NB, desig. of a sum of silver

subbum → *zubbu*

subbû (or *suppû*) adj. mng. uncl. MB, descr. of building

subbusu I "gathered together" NB, of troops; < *subbusu* II

subbusu II **D** "to call together, assemble" NB, troops; < Aram.; > *subbusu* I

subu'īu "seven-year-old" Nuzi [7-]; < *sebe*

subu(r)rītu f. "Subarean" jB, desig. of cart; of fruit; < PlN Subartu

suddu "care, maintenance" NB, of person; < *sadādu* I

suddû "one-sixth of a shekel" NB [6-]; → *šediš*

sudduru **1.** jB lex. of bowl "set about" with stones **2.** f., transf., as fPN; < *sadāru* D

sudurru "backside, rump" jB of human; < Sum.

sudūru(m), Ug. *šudururu* ~ "ornament" O/jB, *s. ilūti* "o. of divinity"; OB as PN ?

suduštu "(plough with team of) six" jB lex.; < *šediš*

Su'ēn, *Su'īn* "moon(-god)" OAkk, O/MA; in MN *walurah̯ S.*; OA du. "moon(-symbol)", of bronze; → *Sîn*

su'eššu ~ "tiny"? jB lex.

sugagātu pl. mng. unkn. jB om. in apodoses

sugāgum "sheikh, tribal representative" Mari; also OB as PN; < W.Sem.

sugāgūtum "post as sheikh" Mari; sheep, silver payments re *s*. of PN, of PlN; < *sugāgum*

sugallītu → *šugallītu*

sugāru (a type of clay) jB lex.

suginnu → *sumkīnu*

sugû "famine" M/NB, NA [SU.GU$_7$]; < Sum.

sugullu(m), *sukullu(m)*, NA *sakullu*; pl. m. & f. "herd, cattle" Bab., M/NA [ÁB.GU$_4$.ḪI.A ?] of cattle, horses, gazelle; NA *rab sakullāte* "overseer of herds"

sugulluh̯lu ~ "cattle officer" Nuzi; < *sugullu* + Hurr. *-uh̯lu*

sugullurtannu (a payment for cattle)? Nuzi; < *sugullu* + Hurr. *urtannu*

sugūnum (an ornament) Mari, on drinking-vessel

suh̯aršuppû → *sah̯aršuppû*

suh̯attānu (a job title)? NB

suh̯ātu "armpit" M/NB, of human; Mari transf., "protective embrace"; NB also as archit. term for recessed doorway; → *šah̯ātu* I

suh̯erra → *suh̯īru*

suh̯h̯u ~ (a mat) j/NB; as part of door; < Sum.

suh̯h̯û "confused" jB; < *seh̯û* D

suh̯h̯urtu "retreat, repulse" M/jB [NIGIN-] of army; *s. šakānu* "to effect a retreat"; < *sah̯āru*

suh̯h̯uru "curved" jB; < *sah̯āru*

suh̯irrah̯h̯u mng. unkn. jB lex.

suh̯īru, *suh̯erra* "foal" M/NA, MB(Alal.), Nuzi of donkey, horse; < Hurr.

suh̯ru (part of a well) j/NB

suh̯ru → also *šah̯ūrum* II

suh̯sīlu → *suh̯su*

suh̯su, *šuh̯su*, *su'su*? "bed" jB; also (a kind of grasshopper), esp. *s/šuh̯sīlu(m)* "god's *s*."; *s. Ištar* (a plant)

suh̯um → *ṣuh̯um*

suh̯ullatu (a garden plant) NB

suh̯umbi mng. unkn. jB in *nah̯laptu s.*

suh̯ummu mng. unkn. M/jB

suh̯uppatum, *šuh̯uppatu(m)*, *šuh̯uptu*, lex. once *šah̯uppatu* "boot(s)" O/jB, O/MA [OB KUŠ.ŠÚḪUB; M/jB (KUŠ.)ŠUḪUB]; Mari esp. *mešēn s.*; for men and women; < Sum.

suh̯uppum I, *šuh̯uppu* ~ "rim, tyre" Bab. of waggon(-wheel); (a ring of reed-plants); < Sum.

suh̯u(p)pum II ~ "storage, store"? OA, esp. *ina s. laqā'um* "to take from stock"

suh̯urh̯ena mng. unkn. MB(Alal.), desig. of wood; < Hurr.

suh̯urmāšu "(mythical) goat-fish" M/NB, NA [SUḪUR.MÁŠ(.KU$_6$)] also "(constellation) Capricorn" [MUL.SUḪUR.MÁŠ.KU$_6$]

suh̯urrā'um, *suh̯urrû* "(political) reversal" OAkk, jB; < *sah̯āru*

suh̯uššu(m) "young date palm, palm-shoot" O/jB [GIŠ.GIŠIMMAR.TUR(.TUR)]; < Sum.

Su'īn → *Su'ēn*

su'ītum "from land of Su"? OB epith. of Ištar

sukannīnu(m), *šukannunnu*, NB *sikinūnu* "dove, pigeon" Bab., NA [TU.KUR$_4$.MUŠEN; MB also TU.KUR.MUŠEN] for meal, as offering

sukannu → *sukinnu*; *usukannu*

sukinnu(m) (or *suqinnu(m)*), *sukannum* "lane, narrow path" O/MA; OA through mountains for smuggling; MA in town

sūkinu "commissar" Am.; < W.Sem.; → *sākinu*

sukiptu mng. unkn. jB lex.; also OB fPN ?; < *sakāpu* I ?

sukīru → *sikkūru*

sukkal-atû "superintendent doorman" jB lex.; < Sum.; > *sukkal-atûtu*; → *atû* II; *šukkallu*

sukkal-atûtu "gatekeeper superintendency" NB [LÚ.SUKKAL-NI.GAB-] as prebend; < *sukkal-atû*; → *atûtu*

sukkallatu "female minister" jB [MUNUS.SUKKAL]; < *šukkallu*

sukkallu → *šukkallu*

sukkalmaḫḫu(m) "chief minister" O/jB [LÚ.SUKKAL.MAḪ] title of men, of god; also as ruler of Elam; < Sum.; > *sukkalmaḫḫūtu*; → *maḫḫu*; *šukkallu*

sukkalmaḫḫūtu "office of chief minister" OB; < *sukkalmaḫḫu*

sukkīnum → *sumkīnu*

sukkir "king" OB(Susa); < Elam.

sukkisukki (a functionary)? OB(Susa); < Elam.

sukku(m) "shrine, chapel"; NA, NB also in PN *Sukkāya*; < Sum.

sukku → also *usukku*

sukkuku(m), Ass. *sakkuku* "deaf; mentally handicapped" [GÉŠTU.LAL; Ú.ḪUB]; also as PN; < *sakāku* D

sukkukūtu, NA *sakkukūtu* "deafness, idiocy" jB, NA; < *sukkuku*

sukkulu "grabbing" jB, in ^{d}*S*. (name of Marduk's dog); < *sakālu* I D

suku → *zuku*

sukullu → *sugullu*

sukuptu(m) "repulse" Bab., of army; < *sakāpu* I

sukurtum "(trade) embargo, suspension" OA; < *sekēru* I

sukūru → *sikkūru*

sukusi → *zuguzi*

sulāqu (a garment) jB lex.; < *salāqu* I

sulā'um mng. unkn. OB(lit.)

sulḫum (part of the hand) OB lex.

sulḫû → *šalḫû* I

sulillu → *silillu*

sulilû → *zilullû*

sulladû (a kind of meat)? jB lex.; < Sum.

sullû(m) I, OA *sallûm* **D** "to appeal" to s.o., "pray to" s.o. **1.** OA, OB "appeal" to (= *ana*) s.o. for (= acc.) s.th. **2.** OAkk, Bab. "supplicate, pray to" deity **Dtn** iter. of G 2; > *sulû* I; *musellûm*; → *ṣullû*; *teslītu*

sullû II ~ "impudence, deception" jB, NA; < *salā'u* II

sullû → also *sulû* I.II; *šulû*

sulluḫum "lustrated"? OB, as PN; < *salāḫu* I D

sullulu(m) mng. uncl. O/jB of house; → *salālu*; *ṣullulum* I

sullumu "reconciled"? MB f. as fPN ?; < *salāmu* II D

sullunu I "very plentiful" NB; < *sullunu* II

sullunu II **D** "to make plentiful" jB lex.; > *sullunu* I

sulsullu → *sussullu*

sulû I, *s/šullû* "prayer" jB, usu. after *suppû*; < *sullû* I

sulû(m) II, *sullû* "bait" O/jB, lamb for wolf etc.; < Sum.

sulû → also *šulû*

sūlu, *sul'u* (a payment) Nuzi, MB

sūlu → also *sīlu* I

sul'u → *sūlu*

su'lu (a glass-making tool) NA

suluḫḫû → *sulumḫû*

sulukannu (a food-container) NA

sulumḫû(m), *zulumḫû*, *s/zuluḫḫû*, Mari *sulūḫum* (a kind of long-fleeced sheep) Bab., NB as offering; O/jB also (a sheepskin garment); < Sum.

sulummû, *sulummā'u(m)* "peace-making, peace (treaty)" Bab., MA *bēl s.* "ally"; *ina s.* "in peace-time"; < *salāmu* II

suluppu(m), NA *saluppu*; Nuzi pl. f. "date" [ZÚ.LUM; OB occas. ZU.LUM; later ZÚ.LUM.MA, abbr. ZÚ]; *aban s.* "date-stone"; *mê s.* "date-juice"; *qilip s.* "date-skin"; < Sum.

sumaktar, *sumuktar*, *sumakti* "half-bred" M/NB **1.** desig. of horse, donkey, bird **2.** (a resident alien)?; < Kass.

sumāšum, *sumāsu* (a sea-fish) O/jB lex.

sumginnu → *sumkīnu*

sumīdātu, *summiddītu* (a kind of flour) j/NB; < *samādu*

sumītum (or *zumītum*) (desig. of a building) OB(Susa)

sumkīnu(m), *sukkīnum*, *sum/nginnu*, *su(k)kinnu*, *su(g)ginnu* ~ "rot, decayed matter" Bab. of grain, wood, copper decay; < Sum.

sumkurānu → *sunkuršānu*

summāniš "like a dove" jB; < *summu* I

summatu(m), MA also *simmutu*, Ug., Bogh. *šummatu* "(female) dove, pigeon" [TU.MUŠEN (→ *summu* I)]; *kī(ma) s. damāmu* etc. "to coo (mournfully) like a dove"; as fPN; *zê s.* "dove excrement" as drug; *kišād s.* "dove's neck" as desig. of gem; (desig. of a fish); < *summu* I

summiddītu → *sumīdātu*

summiš "like a (male) dove" jB; < *summu* I

summu(m) I, NA *su''u* "(male) dove, pigeon" Bab., NA [TU.MUŠEN (→ *summatu*)]; cooing *kīma s.*; NA "dove(-figurine)" of gold; > *summatu*, *summāniš*, *summiš*

summu II "moment, time"? jB lex.

summuḫu, Ass. *sammuḫu*, pl. *sammaḫūte* "mixed, miscellaneous" M/NA, Bogh.; < *samāḫu* D

summulu "stepped" jB lex.; < *simmiltu*

summunu "one-eighth" NB; "eighth share"; "one-eighth *qû* measure"; < *samāne*

sumqu → *sunqu*

sumšu mng. unkn. jB lex.; < *samāšu* ?

***sūmtu**, *sūntu* "red wool" NA lex.; < *sūmu* I

sūmu(m) I, NA *su'mu*, Nuzi *sīmu* "redness; red spot" O/jB [SA5; Susa TIR] *s. nadi* "r. is present"; *s. itaddûm* (*nadû* Gtn) "to cover with red spots"; < *sāmu*

sūmum II "indecision" OB; < *samû* II

su'mu → *sūmu* I

sumukku mng. unkn. jB lex.

sumuktar → *sumaktar*

sumuktu(m) "covering"? OAkk, jB; < *samāku*

sumun[dû?] (a field plant) MB; = *šumuttu* ?

sumuntu "plough with team of eight" jB lex.; < *samāne*

sumunû **1.** MB "eight-spoked" of wheel **2.** NB "eight-year-old" of donkey; < *samāne*

sumuttu "(payment of) one-eighth"? NB in dates; < *samāne*

sunāpu (or *sunābu*) (a sanitary towel) NA lex.; < *sanāpu* ?

sunduru → *ṣuddurum*

sunginnu → *sumkīnu*

sungirtu, *sungiru* (a meadow plant) j/NB; as drug, as famine food

sunguru mng. unkn. jB

sunkuršānu, *sumkurānu* (a marsh bird) jB lex.

sunnu → *sūnu* II

sunnuqu "checked" O/jB "reduced" of rations, "narrow" of street; < *sanāqu* I D

sunnušu, *šunnušu* "pierced, perforated" M/jB, of garment; < *sanāšu* D

sunqu(m), Ass. also *sumqu*, *suqqu*, *sinqu* "famine" Bab., NA [Ú.GUG]; < *sanāqu* II

sūntu → *sūmtu*

sunû (a door-fitting) NB, of copper

sūnu(m) I; pl. f. "loin, lap" [ÚR] in sexual relations; as place for receiving, keeping, dispensing s.th.; as place of protection; OB *ṣubāt s.* "loincloth"; of animal, esp. as cut of meat

sūnu II, NB also *sunnu*; pl. m. & f. (a cloth trimming or sim.) Bab., MA [(TÚG.)ÚR; TÚG.TÙN]

sunukru → *zunukru*

supālu(m), OAkk *sapalum*, *sipālu*, *subālu* "(a) juniper" OAkk, O/jB [Ú.ZA.BA.LAM/LÁ/LU/AL; OB ZA.BA.LUM]; oil of; as drug

supandu → *subandu*

supannum → *suppannum*

supāqu (a garment) NA lex.

supargillu → *supurgillu*

suparinnu (a bronze object) jB lex.

supīrātu ~ "trimmings"? NA of linen; < Aram.?

supīrātu ~ "trimmings"? NA of linen; < Aram.?

supku → *zupku*

su(p)pannum (a container)? OA of bronze, silver

suppīnum, *suppinnu(m)*; pl. m. & f. (a builder's tool) Bab.

suppûm I **D** OB "to abduct" slave(-girl) **Dt** "be abducted"

suppû II, Bogh. lex. also *šuppû* **D** "to pray, supplicate" Bab. to deity (= acc. or *ana*, *-iš*); jB(Ass.) "beseech" king **Dtn** iter.; > *supû*; *museppûm*; *tespītu*; → *sīpu* I

suppû → also *subbû*; *supû*

suppuḫu "scattered" j/NB, of palm trees; of seed-plough (mng.?); < *sapāḫu* D

supqu → *zupku*

supû, *suppû* "prayer, supplication" M/NB [SÍSKUR] to deity, esp. *s. teslīti*, *s. sulû* etc.; occas. to king; < *suppû* II

supuḫru → *šupuḫru*

supuqtu (an object) NA

supurgi(l)lu, *šapargillu*, NA *supargillu* "quince" M/NA, jB [GIŠ.ḪAŠḪUR.KUR.RA]

supūrītu "(lamb) of the fold" jB lex., i.e. young ?; < *supūru*

supurtum (or *ṣupurtum*) (a topog. feature) OB; < *supūru* ?

supūru(m) "sheepfold" Bab.(lit.) [AMAŠ] for sheep and goats; also cattle; *s. Šakan*, *Dumuzi*; *immer s.* "sheep from fold"; "(animals in the) fold", *s. ruppušu* "to extend the fold (i.e. flock)"; desig. of city of Uruk; "halo" round moon; > *supurītu*; *supurtum*?

sūqāqû, NA *s/šūqāqu*; pl. f. "street, lane" M/jB, NA; < *siāqum*; → *sūqu*

suqāru (desig. of a path)? jB lex.

Sūqāya "from the street" i.e. "foundling"? NA, NB as PN, fPN *Sūqā'ītu*; < *sūqu*

suqinnu → *sukinnu*

suqqu → *sunqu*

suqtu(m), *zuqtu* f. "chin" O/jB of person, Mari *s. lapātum* "touch s.o.'s chin" (a gesture of solidarity); astr. ~ "projection" from halo ?

sūqu(m), NB also *šūqu*; pl. m. & f. "street" Bab., NA [SILA; E.SÍR]; *ina s.* also "publicly"; *s. rapšu*, *qatnu* "wide, narrow s."; in Uruk *s. ilāni* "s. of the gods"; *sūq erbetti* "fourways, square", mag. *eper/ḫaṣab s. e.* "earth/sherd from crossroads"; < *siāqum*; > *Sūqāya*; → *sūqāqû*

surāru "prayer" NA; < *sarruru*

surā'um, *surāyum* → *zurāyum*

surdû "hawk, falcon" M/jB, NA [SÚR.DÙ.MUŠEN] in omens; "(figure of) hawk" of gold etc.; < Sum.

surinakku, *še'urinnakku* (a kind of bat) jB lex.

surinnu (a plant) jB, NA

surmaḫḫu "chief lamentation-priest" jB; < Sum.; → *surrû* II

surqēnum, *surqinnu* "strewn offering" Bab; < *sarāqu*

surqu → *serqu*

surramma OA (ptcl. reinforcing prohibition); → *surri*

surrašû → *sirāšû*

surrātānum "liar"? OB lex.; < *sarāru*

surrātu(m) pl. tant. "lies, crimes" OAkk, Bab., NA; also "unjust legal proceedings"; < *sarāru*

surri, lex. *surru* **1.** OA *surri* + prec. "as soon as" (... then ...) **2.** Bab. *ana s.*, jB also *adi s.*, ~ "forthwith, soon"; > *surriš*; *sursurtu*; → *surramma*, *assurri*; *issurri*

surriḫumunû (a table) jB lex.; < Sum.

surriš, *ṣurriš* "quickly, soon" M/jB; < *surri*

surru(m) "deceit, falsehood" OA, OB; < *sarāru*

surru → also *surri*; *sūru*; *ṣurru* II

surrûm I D "to check, confirm" OA, OB

surrû II (a lamentation-priest) jB lex.; < Sum.; → *surmaḫḫu*

surrudu "packed up" M/jB, of donkey; < *sarādu*

surrurtum mng. unkn. OB; < *sarāru* D

sursumbum → *ṣurṣuppu*

sursurtu, *sursu(r)ru* ~ "suddenly" jB; < *surri*

sûrtu, *su''urtu* "circle" jB; *s. sâru* "to make a circle"; < *sâru*

surû(m), *sūru* (a foreigner)? OB, O/MB(Alal.), Am.

sūru, *surru* "canal, ditch" j/NB [SÙR]; < Sum.

sūru → also *surû*

surūdu (part of sheep) jB

suru(m)mu(m) "bowels"? O/jB

susānu (a vessel) NA, of silver

susānu → also *šušānu*

susapinnu, *šusapinnu* "best man" M/jB, accompanying bridegroom

susapinnūtu "rôle of best man" Ug., silver payment for *s.*

susbû (a priest) jB lex.; < Sum.

susbûtum "rôle of *s.* priest" OB

sussānum mng. unkn. OB lex.

sussu(k)ku (a functionary) Nuzi; < Hurr.?

sussulaḫḫu (or *zuzzulaḫḫu*) (an object) Nuzi, of bronze; < Hurr.

sussullu(m), NB also *šussullu*, *sulsullu*, Nuzi usu. *sussulku*; Nuzi pl. *sussulkannu* ~ "chest, box" OAkk, Bab., NA [GIŠ.BUGIN/BÚGIN.TUR] of fisherman; Nuzi, for bread, meat; NB for beer; NA, NB of silver

sūsu "antelope" NA; < Eg.

sūsu → also *šūšu*

su'su → *suḫsu*

susupallu mng. unkn. jB lex.; < Sum.

suššu mng. unkn. NB

suššuru, *šūšuru* (a bird) jB

sūtān → *šūtānu*

sūtānānu → *šūtānānu*

sūtannu, *sūtānu* → *šūtānu*

su(t)tinnu → *šuttinnu*

sutû → *šutû* I

sūtu(m) I, Bogh., Nuzi also *šūtu*; pl. *sâtu*, NA *sūtāte* (a capacity measure) "seah"; (a container); (a payment) [(GIŠ.)BÁN] **1.** (a measuring container) usu. = 10 *qa*; of wood, clay, copper; small, big; *s. kittim* "right *s.*", *s. maṭītim* "(too) small *s.*"; of DN, of city-gate, of palace; for offerings, rations, taxes **2.** NB also (a surface area) = 6 *qa* **3.** (a capacity measure) [BÁN; 2 *s.* = BÁNMIN; 3 *s.* = BANEŠ; 4 *s.* = BANLIMMU; 5 *s.* = BANIA]; OB *(ana) sūtum* [BÁN.TA.ÀM] "per *s.*" **4.** Bab. (a form of payment), OB commodities paid by merchants; NB (rental payment) in dates etc.; NB *bīt s.* "rented property"; NA?, NB *rab s.* "overseer of *s.* payments"

sūtu II (part of plough)? OB

sūtu III (a briar) jB lex.

sūtu → also *šūtu* II

su''u → *summu* I

su''urtu → *sûrtu*

su''usu D mng. unkn. jB; stat. of condition of person; → *suḫsu*

suwādu → *suādu*

suwar (or *ṣ/zuwar*) ~ "in the matter of ..."? OB

Ṣ

ṣabābu, *ṣapāpu* "to flutter (about)" jB **G** (*u/u*) of bird "flutter"; "flap" wings; transf. "fuss over, care for" **D** "spread" wings **Š** "teach" fledglings "to spread" wings **N** of horse "be agitated"? **Ntn** "flutter about"; > *taṣbubtum*

ṣabālu → *zabālu*

ṣabāriš "for speaking" jB; < *ṣabāru* I

ṣabāru I "to twinkle; blink; mutter" M/jB, NA **G** (*u/u*) of star; of eye "blink, wink (maliciously)"; of demon, bird "twitter, chirp"; of snake "rustle" or "hiss"? **Gtn** iter. of G **Gt** (infin., stat., imper. *tiṣb...*) "speak" **D** MB "be startled"?; jB lex. of intestines "suffer contractions"? **Š** "cause to spread" news, instructions **Nt** ~ Gt ?; > *ṣabru*, *ṣabāriš*; *ṣabburītu*; → *muzzapru*; *ṣapāru*

ṣabāru(m) II "to bend, twist"? O/jB, NA **G** (*a/u*) "spin" of spindle; limbs; stat. "has plaited hair" **D** ~ G ? mng. unkn. of field-bank **Š** NA "make" body "spin" like a spindle **Štn** "shape" shield "by repeated bending" **Ntn** of man "twist o.s. up continually"; > *naṣbaru*

ṣabat "starting from" Nuzi; in time, place; < *ṣabātu* imper.

ṣabātu(m), Ug. *ṣabāṭu* "to seize, take; hold" **G** (*a/a*) [DAB] **1.** obj. living things: "seize" person, by force, legally; "hold captive"; "hold s.o. responsible"; "catch s.o. at"; of sleep, desire, illness, bad luck etc. "overtake, overcome" s.o.; "capture, catch" animal; NA "adopt" foundling **2.** obj. part of body: "grasp"; foot, in supplication; hand, in support; mouth, to silence s.o.; *ina libbi ṣ.* "plan" s.th.; ext. of part of entrails "enfold" **3.** obj. inanimate: "grasp, hold" tool, weapon, reins; goods; "seize" hem (*sissiktu*) as symbolic act; "confiscate" goods; "enclose", "set, fix" gems; *batqu ṣ.* "make a repair"; "hold fast" door, ship; of vessel "contain" amount; of wind, crop disease "affect"; "usurp, take" throne; "take possession of" house, land, city; "occupy, adopt" position; "undertake" journey, "take" route; M/NA, MB "draw up" (sealed) document (*kunukku*, *ṭuppu* etc.) **4.** obj. abstr.: "take away" potency; "keep hold of" life, decrees; Ass. "fix (in writing), record"; NA, NB *malâ ṣ.* "become healthy", jB *mērê ṣ.* "become pregnant"; "take on, over" parenthood, office, responsibility; "make" statement (*awātam*); "reach" decision; of mercy "affect" s.o.; "take on" work, expedition; "settle" accounts; "carry out" offering, violence; "undertake, begin", *dīna ṣ.* "go to court" **Gtn** iter. of G [DAB.DAB; DAB.MEŠ] "continually engage in" prayers **Gt** (infin. etc. *tiṣb...*) [DAB(.DAB)] "hold one another", "wrestle", "be locked in combat", "engage in litigation"; of parts of body, liver etc. "be interlocked, grown together"; "hold fast" hand, emblem; stat. of ox **D** ~ G [DAB; DAB.DAB; DAB.MEŠ] also "enclose, bind, set" with metal (bands); "fasten" roof-beams, thread; "occupy" city; "block" road; "claim" protection (*kidinnu*) **Dtn** iter. "repeatedly take possession of" **Dt** pass. of D Am. "be captured" **Š** caus. of G [DAB] "direct" s.o.'s attention (*pānū*) towards (*ana*); "equip, provide with" income, pasturage, water; often ellipt. "put in place, install" door; "launch" ship; "post" guard; "install" gate-sculptures; "settle" inhabitants; "cause to catch" fire, "ignite"; "make s.o. (start to) do s.th." **Štn** "make grasp repeatedly" **Št^1** pass. of Š NB of work "be started on" **Št^2** "make o.s. take", OA "gather up" silver; OB "get" troops, animals, tools "ready"; "execute" plan, decision **N** pass. of G [DAB]; ~ Gt OA, OB "seize one another", "litigate" **Ntn** iter. of N OA "be repeatedly in litigation" **Nt** ~ Gt "be interlocked, grown together"; of teeth "lock each other"; > *ṣabtu; ṣabat; ṣibtu* I, *ṣibittu, ṣibtātu*?; *ṣābitu, ṣābitānu; ṣabbutītu; ṣubbutu; muṣabbittu; naṣbatu; šuṣbuttu; tiṣbutu, tiṣbuttum;* → *neṣbettu; ṣubātu, ṣubātiš; taṣbâtu*

ṣabā'um, *ṣabûm* "to take the field" OB **G** (*a/u* ?) of troops **D** OAkk "put army into the field"; → *ṣābu*

ṣabā'u → also *ṣapû* II

ṣabbu → *ṣābu*

ṣabbû → *ṣubbû*

ṣabburītu ~ "female mutterer" jB; < *ṣabāru* I

ṣabbutītu "(evil) female seizer" jB of goddess; < *ṣabātu*

ṣabbutu → *ṣubbutu*

ṣabiātum, *ṣibiātum* pl. tant. "wishes, designs" OB; < *ṣabû* II

ṣabību (or *zabību*) (a wooden object) jB

ṣābitānu(m) "captor, one who seized" O/MB, MA; < *ṣabātu*

ṣabītu(m) "gazelle" Bab., M/NA [MAŠ.DÀ]; med. gazelle's excrement, part of body as ingredient; *rēš ṣ.* "head of gazelle" on vessels; *šinni ṣ.* "gazelle's tooth" (a stone); lex. (a desig. of snakes, fish)

ṣābitu **1.** "recipient" **2.** NB (a tool for gripping) **3.** 'holding', i.e. magnetic, as epith. of *šadânu* stone; < *ṣabātu*

ṣābītu → *ṣāpītu*

ṣabru(m) ~ "blinker, winker, one who blinks, winks" O/jB, MA lex. also as PN; < *ṣabāru* I

ṣāb-šarrūtu "royal service" NA; < *ṣāb-šarri* (→ *ṣābu*)

ṣabtu(m) "captured; taken" [DAB]; of captive person, bird; MB "put to work"; of silver, oil "received"; MA of tablet "drawn up"; < *ṣabātu*

ṣabûm I "wished for, expected" OB; < *ṣabû* II

ṣabû(m) II, *ṣebû* "to wish (for)" Bab. **G** (*i/i*) corn, silver; "want"; NB "request, desire" **Gtn** iter. of G med. of intestines "have chronic urge" to pass water; > *ṣabû* I; *ṣabiātum, ṣibûtu; taṣbâtu*?

ṣabû → also *ṣabā'um; ṣābu*

ṣābu(m), Mari also *ṣabûm*, with pl. *ṣābuyū*, NB also *ṣabbu* "people; troops" [(LÚ.)ÉRIN(.MEŠ)] construed as sg. and pl.; *ṣ. qašti* "archers", *ṣ. narkabti* "chariot-troops" etc.; *ṣ. šēpē* "foot-soldiers"; *ṣ. ēkalli* "palace personnel"; *ṣ. eleppi* "ship's crew"; *ṣ. ṣēri* "desert folk"; *ṣ. šarri* "royal troops"; > *ṣāb-šarrūtu;* → *ṣabā'um*

ṣābû "dyer" NB; < Aram.?

ṣabûtu → *ṣibûtu*

ṣadānu (a bush, shrub) jB, NA lex., med.; in garden; *ṣadā'ūri* "roof *ṣ.*"? (→ *ṣadūru*)

ṣādānu → *ṣīdānu*

ṣadāru ~ "to be (placed) askew, slant"? jB **G** of part of body **D** "make" eyes "squint"?; stat. of nose, mouth, dentition "is crooked"; > *ṣuddurum*

ṣaddu(m), *ṣādu, saddu* "(wooden) signal, sign" Bab.; lex. *ša ṣ.* "man with sign(board)"?; as divine symbol, astrological sign, portent

ṣadīdu "antimony" jB, NA

ṣadû(m) "to receive as sustenance" O/jB **G** not attested **Gtn** "be regularly nourished with" **D** "equip s.o. with provisions, supply with food"; *ṣudê ṣ.* "make provision for"; > *ṣidītu; ṣudû*

ṣādu → *ṣaddu*

ṣâdu(m) I "to prowl, roam; turn" O/jB, NA **G** (pret. *iṣūd*) of person "roam around"; of storm, cloud, divine word; of door, person "turn about, around"; of part of body "twitch" **Gtn** "roam about" [NIGIN, or also for G ?] of storm, animal, person; of part of body "continually turn, twitch" **D** "turn" part of body **Dtn** iter. of D [NIGIN]; of demon "twist" face; > *ṣūdu* I; *ṣīdānu; ṣā'idu, ṣayyādu, ṣayyudû; ṣu''udum*

ṣâdu II, *ṣuādu(m)* "to melt (down)" Ass., M/jB **G** (pret. *iṣūd*) of metal, glass "melt, become molten"; transf. of Sirius "turn red" like molten copper **D** "melt, refine" metal; transf. "destroy" land; > *ṣīdu; ṣūdu* II; *maṣādu;* → *ṣā'idu*

ṣaduq "right, true" Am.; < W.Sem.

ṣadūru? (a tree) jB final syll. uncl.; → *ṣādānu*

ṣaḫarru → *ṣaḫḫaru*

ṣaḫartu → *ṣeḫertu; ṣeḫru* I

ṣaḫāru → *ṣeḫēru*

ṣaḫātu(m) I "to press, squeeze" Bab., NA [ŠUR] **G** (*a/u*) "press out" oil, wine, juice etc. **D** ~ G also transf. "put pressure on, oppress, blackmail, pressgang" s.o. **N** pass. of G also Ug. of person "be hard pressed"; > *ṣaḫtu; ṣāḫitu; ṣāḫitūtu; ṣāḫittu; ṣuḫḫutu; maṣḫatu;* → *ṣāḫit-ginûtu*

ṣaḫātu II "to wish, desire" NA **G** "want" field; > *ṣaḫittu* I.II

ṣaḫḫartu → *ṣeḫḫertu*

ṣaḫḫaru(m), NB also *ṣaḫarru* **1.** Bab. (a kind of grain) **2.** j/NB "minor crop"; < *ṣeḫēru*

ṣaḫḫaru → also *ṣeḫḫeru*

ṣaḫḫirum (a desig. of copper) OA; < *ṣeḫēru* ?

ṣaḫḫurum "very small" OA; < *ṣeḫēru*

ṣāḫit-ginûtu "office of offerings-oil-presser" NB [(LÚ.)Ì.ŠUR.GI.NA-]; < *ṣāḫitu* + *ginû* I

ṣaḫittu I, *ṣiḫittu* "wish, desire" NA, NB; < *ṣaḫātu* II

ṣaḫittu II "she who is desired" NA in fPN; also *Lā-ṣ.* "Undesired one" fPN; < *ṣaḫātu* II

ṣāḫittu(m) "female oil-presser" OAkk, NA?; < *ṣāḫitu*

ṣāḫitu(m) "oil, wine-presser" **1.** "oil-presser" [(LÚ.)Ì.ŠUR; OB also ŠUR.RA] *ṣ. ginê* "oil-presser for regular offerings" **2.** "wine-presser" lex. [NB ŠUR.GEŠTIN]?; < *ṣaḫātu* I; > *ṣāḫitūtu*, *ṣāḫittu*, *ṣāḫit-ginûtu*

ṣāḫitūtu "office of oil-presser" NB [LÚ.Ì.ŠUR-] in temple; < *ṣāḫitu*

ṣaḫru → *ṣeḫru* I

ṣaḫtu "pressed, squeezed" M/jB [ŠUR(.RA)] of wine (*karānu*); < *ṣaḫātu* I

ṣāḫu (or *zāḫu*), *ṣ/zā'u* "oven (for oil processing)" jB lex.

ṣâḫu → *ṣiāḫu*

ṣaḫurānūtu "(time of) youth" NA; < *ṣeḫēru*

ṣaḫurtu → *ṣuḫurtu*

ṣā'idu(m), *ṣayyidu* "roaming, restless" O/jB of demon, dog; "roving" fugitive; also as PN; (a kind of bird); (a desig. of kind of gold) (< *ṣâdu* II ?); < *ṣâdu* I

ṣala(b)ittu (a plant) jB, Bogh. lex., med.

ṣalālu(m) "to lie (down), sleep" Bab., NA **G** (*a/a*; imper. *ṣilal*) [NÚ] of humans, gods; "lie" with, sexually; "be still, peaceful"; of animals; "lie still" in death; of ruin, in desertion; of quay, in inactivity; *lā ṣ.* "sleeplessness, insomnia" **D** Mari "see in o.'s sleep"? **Š** "allow to sleep, rest; put to sleep"; > *ṣallu* I, *ṣallūtu*; *ṣālilu*; *ṣallallu*; *maṣallu*, *maṣlālum*; *muṣlālu*; *šumṣulu*

ṣalāmu(m) "to be(come) black; be(come) dark" **G** (*i/i*) [GE$_6$] of part of body; transf. of face, lips "become dark" with anger; of incense, oil, metal; of star, moon **Gtn** iter. of G **D** [GE$_6$.MEŠ] "turn s.th. black"; transf. of face "turn dark" with anger; "blacken" with calumnies **Dt** of star "be darkened, obscured" **Š** "cause to become dark" **Ntn** ~ Gtn ?; > *ṣalmu* I, *ṣalmāt qaqqadi*; *ṣulmu*; *ṣulāmu*; *ṣallamu*, *ṣallamtu*, *ṣallāmum*

ṣalāpu(m), *ṣelēpu* "to cut (at an angle)" O/jB **G** (*i/i*) "cut open, dissect" animal; "cross out" text ?; "distort" justice ?; stat. of heart "is crooked, wicked" **D** ~ "cut up (into portions)"; stat. "is wrong"?; > *ṣalpu*, *ṣaliptu*; *ṣilpum*, *ṣiliptu*; *ṣulpu*; *ṣulāpu*; *ṣullupu*; *šuteṣlipu*

ṣalā'u, *ṣalû* "to throw, lay (down)" M/NA, Nuzi **G** (*i/i*) "cast" a lot; "lay (down)" threshold, clothes, invalid; "set up" throne; "miscarry, abort" foetus; "cast off" yoke; stat. "lies, is situated" **Š** "cause to miscarry, abort" foetus

ṣalbatānu "planet Mars" M/NB, NA

ṣalbu → *ṣalpu*

Ṣaliltum, Gasur *Ṣalul* (a month) OAkk

ṣālilu(m) "sleeping, resting" O/jB of person; "one who sleeps with" s.o.; *lā ṣ.* "unsleeping"; < *ṣalālu*

ṣaliptu, *ṣiliptu* "lying, dishonesty" M/NB of speech, actions; < *ṣalāpu*

ṣalla(l)lu (a night bird) jB [Ù.KU.KU.MUŠEN]; < *ṣalālu*

ṣallamtu, *ṣallamdu* 'black thing' jB **1.** (a stone, basalt or sim.) **2.** lex., med. (a bush, castor-oil ?) **3.** lex. (a night bird) **4.** (a black snake) [MUŠ.GE$_6$]; < *ṣallamu*

ṣallamu "black, very dark" j/NB; "black (people)" [GE$_6$.MEŠ]?; of sheep, donkeys; < *ṣalāmu*

ṣallāmum "black (one)" OA of pack-asses; of a kind of copper; < *ṣalāmu*

ṣallu(m) I "sleeping" Bab. "sleeping person"; of animal; < *ṣalālu*

ṣallu II; pl. also *ṣallānu* "(animal-)skin, leather" NA, NB often with KUŠ as det.; NA *ša ṣallišunu* "leather-sellers"

ṣallû → *ṣullû*

ṣallulu → *ṣullulu* II

ṣallummû ~ "comet" jB lex., astr.

ṣallūtu "(state of) sleep" jB; < *ṣallu* I

ṣalmānu → *ṣalmu* II

ṣalmāt qaqqadi(m) "the black-headed ones", i.e. "mankind" Bab. [OB SAG.GE$_6$; M/jB SAG. GE$_6$.GA/A]; < *ṣalmu* I

ṣalmu(m) I "black, dark" [GE$_6$] of textiles, animals, skins, hair; of person "black(-haired)", also as PN; of plant, wood, stove; astronomical phenomena; < *ṣalāmu*

ṣalmu(m) II; pl. NA, NB *ṣalmānu/i* "effigy, image" [ALAN; NU; OAkk DÙL] "figure" (in round or relief, large or small statu(ett)e, figurine, inscribed image); of god, king, person, demon; in metal, stone, clay, wax etc.; transf.

"constellation"; "representation" of death; "likeness" of brother, god

ṣalpu, *ṣalbu* "sliced, crooked" M/jB of fish "sliced up"; "crooked, wicked"; < *ṣalāpu*

ṣāltu(m), *ṣē/iltum*, NA *ṣassu* "combat, strife, discord, quarrel" [DU$_{14}$] domestic, military, legal "strife"; ^{d}*Ṣ*. goddess of battle; *ṣ. epēšu* "to (engage in a) fight"; *bēl ṣ.* "legal opponent"; < *ṣâlu*

ṣalû → *ṣalā'u*

ṣâlu(m), *ṣêlu(m)* "to fight, quarrel" OAkk, Bab., OA **G** "(pick a) fight, start conflict, legal contest"; stat. "be at strife" with **Gtn** iter. of G **Gt** (stat. *teṣul*) "fight one another" in war, law; "be quarrelsome, pugnacious" **Št** "put into conflict with one another"; > *ṣāltu*; *ṣālūtu*; *ṣūlātu*; *muṣṣālu*, *muṣṣāltu*

Ṣalul → *Ṣaliltum*

ṣalūlu → *ṣulūlu*

ṣālūtu, *ṣēlūtu* "contest, conflict" jB in *ṣ. epēšu* "to start a fight"; < *ṣâlu*

ṣamādu I; jB pl. *ṣamādāni* "team" of mules j/NB; < *ṣ.* II infin.

ṣamādu(m) II, NB also *ṣemēdu* "to tie up; yoke, hitch up; bind up" **G** (*i/i*) [LAL; LÁL] "harness, yoke up" animal, plough, chariot; "equip, get ready" person, troops, supplies; "gird, tie on" clothing, weapon; "attach, apply (bandage)" **Gtn** iter. of G [LAL.LAL; LÁL.MEŠ] **D** ~ G "connect" watercourses; "apply" bandage "to" s.o. **Š** "cause to hitch up" horse to chariot; "have equipped" **Štn** iter. of Š **Št**^{2} OB "link" watercourses "together"; > *ṣamādu* I, *ṣamdu*; *ṣimdu* I, II$^{?}$, *ṣimdatum*, *ṣimittu*; *ṣindītu*; *ṣummudu*; *naṣmadu*, *naṣmattu*

ṣamar → *zamar*

ṣamāru(m) "to wish, strive (for)" **G** jB **Gt** (infin. etc. *tiṣm*...) j/NB "strive for doggedly, persistently" **D** ~ G "strive" for (= *ana*; dat.); "plot" against s.o. (= *ana*; dat.); "aim for, plan"; absol. "strive, make effort"; > *ṣummirātu*; *ṣumru*, *ṣimru* I$^{?}$; *ṣumurtum*$^{?}$; *taṣmertu*

ṣamāru → also *ṣemēru*

ṣamātu "to transfer (property), sell" Ug. **G** stat. "is transferred, sold" [ŠÁM.TIL.LA(.ŠÈ)] **D** ~ G; < Ug.

ṣamā'u → *ṣamû* II

ṣamdu(m), *ṣa/endu* "bound up; equipped" Bab. of silver "readied"; of chariot, plough "hitched up"; of animal "harnessed"; of army "equipped"; (a condition of part of liver); < *ṣamādu* II

ṣamiu → *ṣamû* I

ṣammudu → *ṣummudu*

ṣamû(m) I, *ṣamiu* "thirsty" O/jB; < *ṣamû* II

ṣamû(m) II, Ass. *ṣamā'u* "to be(come) thirsty, thirst for" (= acc.) Bab., NA **G** (*u/u*) **Gtn** iter. of G **D** "make thirst(y)" man; horses **Š** "keep thirsty, deprive of drink"; > *ṣamû* I; *ṣūmu*, *ṣummû*, *ṣumāmu*, *ṣumāmītu*; *naṣmû*, *naṣmītu*?

ṣamuṣīru (a plant) jB lex.

ṣanāḫu "to excrete (fluid), have diarrhoea" jB **G** (*a/u*) **Gtn** iter. of G; > *ṣinḫu*

ṣandu → *ṣamdu*

ṣanduru → *ṣuddurum*

ṣanṣar → *zanzar*

ṣānum → *ṣēnu* III

ṣânu, *ṣênu(m)* "to fill up, bloat" with (= acc.) liquid etc. Bab.(lit.) **G** (*a/a*, *e/e*) with poison, disease; with fear **Gtn** iter. of G **D** NA mng. uncl. **N** NB of canal "be filled up" with silt

ṣânum → also *ṣênu*

ṣa'nu "flock" Bab. lex.; < W.Sem.; → *ṣēnu* III ?

ṣapāḫu → *sapāḫu* D

ṣapānu "to shelter, recover, rescue" Am. **G**; < W.Sem.

ṣapāpu → *ṣabābu*

ṣaparatu, *ṣaparu* → *ṣapru* II

ṣapāru(m), *ṣepēru* "to press down; wink" O/jB, NA **G** (*a/u*, later also *i/i*) **1.** "wink" eye **2.** stat. of facial feature "is flat, depressed"; "make hollow, dent in" cloth; "press down" thumb onto script; "inlay, inset" gems; "press in"? medicament; of demon "push in" intestines **Gtn** iter. of G 1 **D** ~ "make impression on"; NB "brand" cattle; > *ṣapru* I; *ṣipirtu* I; *ṣapparrû*$^{?}$; *ṣuppuru*; *muṣappertu*; → *ṣabāru* I

ṣapītu (or *zapītu*) (a kind of rush) NB

ṣāpītu, *ṣābītu*; pl. *ṣāpâti* "watch-tower" NA, NB for siege; < Aram.

ṣapiu → *ṣapû* I

ṣapparrû "malicious gossiper" jB; < *ṣabāru* I or *ṣapāru* ?

ṣappuḫu **D** "to squeeze out" NA; < Aram.

ṣapru(m) I "pressed in, down" O/jB; of heart ~ "troubled"; < *ṣapāru*

ṣapru II, *ṣaparu*, *ṣap(a)ratu* (a spice) jB lex.

ṣapšiš (or *zabšiš*) "like a *ṣ.* garment" jB; < *ṣapšu*

ṣapšu (or *zabšu*) (a garment) j/NB (OAkk [TÚG.A.SU] here ?); > *ṣapšiš*

ṣapû(m) I, *ṣepû*, MA *ṣapiu* "soaked, dyed" Bab., MA of irrigated field; plants, malt; textiles (lex. *ṣepûtu*, or subst. *ṣipûtu* ?); < *ṣapû* II

ṣapû(m) II, *ṣabā'u* "to soak, drench" Bab. **G** (*u/u*) fields with water; malt, groats etc.;

textile; basket with bitumen **D** ~ G **N** pass. of G of body in water; > *ṣapû* I; *ṣīpu* I; *ṣupû*, *ṣubītu*; *ṣuppû*; *muṣappiu*

ṣapūnu "north" NB; < W.Sem.

ṣar in *ṣar maḫāṣu* "to strike hard" NB; < Aram.

ṣarâ → *zarâ*

ṣarābu → *ṣarāpu* I

ṣarādu → *ṣarātu*

ṣarāḫu(m) I "to cry out, wail, complain" Bab. **G** (*a/u*) "keen, lament, sing lamentation" **Gtn** iter. of G **Š** "make weep, lament"; > *ṣarḫu* II, *ṣarḫiš*; *ṣerḫu* I, *ṣerḫiš*, *ṣiriḫtu* II; *ṣāriḫu*; *muṣarriḫtum*?

ṣarāḫu II "to light up, flare up" (intrans.) jB **G** (*u/u*, once *i/i*) [SUR] of star, demon **Š** "make" lightning, firebrand "flash"; > *ṣarḫu* III; *ṣerḫu* II; *ṣarriḫum*; *maṣrāḫu*, *maṣraḫtu*; *muṣarriḫtum*?; → *ṣ*. IV Š

ṣarāḫu III "to heat up" (trans.) M/NA, M/jB **G** (*a/u*) water; stat. of sick person "is feverish, hot with fever", transf. "is incensed, hot with anger, boiling with rage" **D** "keep warm" horse **N** of spices, innards; invalid; angry person's liver (*kabattu*) "become hot"; transf. "start to boil with rage" **Ntn** "continually get fever, have a chronic fever"; > *ṣarḫu* I; *ṣerḫu* III, *ṣiriḫtu* I; *ṣurḫu*; *taṣraḫu*; → *ṣ*. IV Š

ṣarāḫu IV ~ "to send" Bogh., jB **G** (*a/u*) person, ship **D** ~ G **Š** jB "have" battle "prepared"? (or *ṣ*. II or III ?)

ṣarākum ~ "to gut, disembowel" OB **G** stat. of sheep

ṣarāmu(m) "to make an effort, strive" Bab., NA **G** (*i/i*) in hendiad. "try to" **D** ~ G *ṣ*. *kašādu* "achieve, reach" s.th.; > *ṣermum*, *ṣirimtu*; *ṣarramum*

ṣarāpu(m) I, NB also *ṣarābu* "to burn, fire; dye (red)" **G** (*a/u*) "smelt and refine" metal; "fire, bake" clay tablet, brick; "dye" textiles, ivory, leather, mountain with (= acc.) red (colour), blood etc. **D** ~ G "burn (up)" drug, person in fire; of stomach "give burning pain"; of cheeks "burn" with tears; transf. "torture" o.s.; "dye (red)"; "make" stone "glow" **Dtn** iter. of D **N** pass. of G "be fired; reddened"; > *ṣarpu*; *ṣerpu* I.II, *ṣerpētu*, *ṣiriptu*; *ṣurpu*; *ṣarīpu*; *ṣāripu* I?, II; *ṣurrupu*, *ṣarruputtum*; *naṣrapu*?, *naṣraptu*; *šuṣrupu*

ṣarāpu(m) II ~ "to be loud, resound" O/jB **G** (*u/u* ?) of desire "cry out" **D** "cry out loudly" **Š** "make" lamentation "resound"; > *ṣarpiš*

ṣarāru(m) I, *ṣerēru* "to flash; drip" Bab., NA **G** (*u/u*, NB also *a/u*) [ŠUR] of star, sun etc. "twinkle, flash"; of demons; of body fluids "drip, ooze, trickle" **D** NA "drip (liquid), make libation" **N** (infin. *naṣarruru*) lex. mng. uncl. **Ntn** of Mars "flash repeatedly"; > *ṣarru*; *ṣurāru* I; *ṣāriru* I; *maṣarru*, *maṣarrītum*; *muṣarrirtu*

ṣarārum II "to pack up" OB **Š** "have packed" clothes

ṣarāru → also *sarāru*

ṣarāšu(m) **G** jB mng. unkn. **D** OB ~ "to spread out, give out rays"? like a star; jB of tree "sprout out, put out (shoots)"; transf. of descendants; "continue" treatment; > *ṣaršum*; *ṣeršu*; *ṣuršu* 1; *ṣarraštu*, *ṣarrišu*; *ṣurrušum*

ṣarātu(m), *ṣarādu* "to fart" O/jB **G** (*i/i*, *u/u*) of human, animal **D** "fart continually"; > *ṣāritu*

ṣarbatu(m), *ṣerbe/atu(m)* "poplar" [GIŠ.ÁSAL (A.TU.GAB.LIŠ)] the tree; also "poplar wood"

ṣarbu(m) "poplar" Bab. in DN *Bēl-ṣarbi* jB lex. [GIŠ.ÁSAL]; M/NA in DN *Bēlat-ṣ*.

ṣarḫiš "plaintively" jB; < *ṣarḫu* II

ṣarḫu(m) I "hot" O/jB, M/NA of water, ground; food; fever; "hot-tempered" mule; < *ṣarāḫu* III

ṣarḫu II "wailing" jB epith. of cry (*rigmu*); < *ṣarāḫu* I

ṣarḫu III "flashing" jB of star; < *ṣarāḫu* II

ṣāriḫu(m) "wailer" (a lamentation priest) O/jB lex.; < *ṣarāḫu* I

ṣarīnu → *zarīnu*

ṣarīpu "dyed (red) sheep" Nuzi; < *ṣarāpu* I

ṣāripu I, *ṣēripu* (or *ṣa/erīpu*); pl. *-ūtu* (a kind of court personnel) Bogh., Ug.; < *ṣarāpu* I ?

ṣāripu II "dyer" NA, NB in *ṣārip dušê* "leather-dyer"; < *ṣarāpu* I

ṣāriru I "flashing red" **1.** M/NB (a gold alloy) **2.** jB (a star, constellation) [MUL.AN.TA. ŠUR.RA]; < *ṣarāru* I

ṣāriru(m) II (a lamentation priest) O/jB

ṣāritu, *ṣarritu* "farter" jB; < *ṣarātu*

Ṣarpānītu → *Zarpānītu*

ṣarpiš "loud and bitterly" Bab. of wailing; < *ṣarāpu* II

ṣarpu(m); NB f. also *ṣarriptu* "burnt, reddened, refined" Bab., M/NA "fired, baked" of pottery, brick, tablet [AL.ŠEG$_6$.GÁ (or = *bašlu* ?)]; "dyed (red)" of water, skin; "refined" of metal; MA also as subst. "silver" (→ *ṣurpu* 3); < *ṣarāpu* I; → *Zarpānītu*

ṣarramum "very keen, eager, striving hard" OB as PN ?; < *ṣarāmu*

ṣarraštu(m) (a bush, shrub) O/jB lex.; < *ṣarāšu*

ṣarratu → *ṣerretu* I

ṣarriḫum "shining" OB epith. of Ištar; < *ṣarāḫu* II; → *muṣarriḫtum*

ṣarriptu → *ṣarpu*

ṣarrišu "spreading" MB of wound; < *ṣarāšu*

ṣarritu → *ṣāritu*

ṣarru "flashing" jB of stars; "dripping"? of water; (a kind of reed basket); < *ṣarāru* I

ṣarru → also *sarru* I; *ṣerru* II

ṣarrupum → *ṣurrupu*

ṣarruputtum "(silver) refining" OA; < *ṣurrupu*

ṣarṣar → *zanzar*

ṣarṣartu, *ṣarṣaru* "forest, wood" jB lex.

ṣarṣaru(m) I (a large snake) O/jB; OB also as DN ?; < *ṣerru* I

ṣarṣaru II (a holy water vessel)? jB, NA

ṣarṣaru → also *ṣarṣartu*; *ṣāṣiru*

ṣarṣa'tu mng. unkn. jB lex.

ṣarṣuppu → *ṣurṣuppu*

ṣaršum (desig. of ill person)? OB lex.; < *ṣarāšu*

ṣartu → *sartu*

ṣarû (a part of date palm)? jB lex.

ṣâru → *ṣīru* I; *ṣurrum* IV

ṣar'u "snake" jB lex.; < W.Sem.?

ṣassu → *ṣāltu*

ṣāṣiru(m), *ṣarṣaru*, *ṣa(ṣ)ṣarum* ? "cricket, grasshopper" Bab., NA; also as PN

ṣaṣumtu, *ṣaṣund/tu*, *ṣaṣu'tu* (a medicinal plant) M/jB (= *aṣuṣimtu*)

ṣâtiš → *ṣiātiš*

ṣâtu → *ṣiātu*

ṣā'u I (a kind of field) Ug.; < Ug.

ṣā'u II (a stone vessel) jB lex.

ṣā'u → also *ṣāḫu*

ṣa''upu → *ṣuppu* I.II

ṣawārum "neck" OAkk

ṣawwûm D "to speak"? OA

ṣayyādu "vagrant; hunter" jB; < *ṣâdu* I

ṣayyaḫu(m) "enjoyable, sumptuous" O/jB of meal, place, sight etc.; < *ṣiāḫu*

ṣayyāḫu 'laugher' (a bird); < *ṣiāḫu*

ṣayyattu mng. unkn. NB

ṣayyidu → *ṣā'idu*

ṣayyudû "roving, roaming" jB of demon; < *ṣâdu* I

ṣayyuḫû "grinning fiendishly" jB of demon, goddess; < *ṣiāḫu*

ṣe'ānu → *ṣēnu* III; *ṣênu*

ṣebû → *ṣabû* II

ṣēbûm (a prof. desig.)? Susa (= *sābû* ?)

ṣeḫertu(m), *ṣaḫartu(m)* **1.** Bab., NA "(little) girl" [MUNUS.TUR ? (→ *ṣuḫartu*)] **2.** OAkk "small goods" [TUR.TUR]; < *ṣeḫru* I; → *ṣeḫḫertu*

ṣeḫēru(m), OAkk, Ass. *ṣaḫāru(m)* "to be(come) small, young, little" **G** (*i/i*) [TUR; jB also AL.TUR]; j/NB infin. *ṣeḫēru* "(time of) youth"; of population, prosperity etc. "be reduced"; of organs, people "be small, shrink"; of person "be under age, a minor"; OA "be deducted" **Gtn** iter. of G [TUR.TUR; TUR.MEŠ] "get ever smaller, less" **D** fact. of G [TUR] "deduct" silver etc.; "reduce, squander, deplete" property, flocks; "reduce" land, population; "work, fashion, whittle away, use (up)" stone; stat. "is too small"; NB "break up (into lumps)"?; > *ṣaḫurānūtu*; *ṣeḫru* I, *ṣeḫertu*, *ṣeḫrūtu*; *ṣeḫru* II; *ṣuḫru*, *ṣuḫurtu*; *ṣuḫāru*, *ṣuḫartu*; *ṣuḫurrû*; *ṣaḫḫaru*, *ṣaḫḫirum*?, *ṣaḫḫurum*; *ṣeḫḫeru*, *ṣeḫḫertu*; *ṣuḫḫuru*, *ṣuḫḫuriš*; *meṣḫēriš*, *meṣḫerūtu*; → *paras ṣeḫru*

ṣeḫḫertu(m), MA *ṣaḫḫartu* **1.** O/MB, MA "young girl" [OB MUNUS.TUR ?] **2.** Bab. "minor crops" [Mari TUR.TUR ?] **3.** Bab. "small pieces"? of wood, stone; < *ṣeḫru* I; → *ṣeḫertu*

ṣeḫḫeru(m), Ass. also *ṣaḫḫaru* "tiny, diminutive, very small" OAkk, O/jB, M/NA [TUR.TUR] of things; of animals, people "very small, young"; pl. "little children", O/MB "child(-workers)"; < *ṣeḫru* I

ṣeḫḫu ~ "battle fury"? jB

ṣeḫḫutu → *ṣuḫḫutu*

ṣēḫiš, *ṣīḫiš* "laughing, with laughter" jB; < *ṣīḫu*

ṣeḫru(m) I, *ṣaḫru(m)* "small; young" [TUR(.RA); BÀN(.DA)] of things, animals, persons "small"; of animals, persons "young"; of persons "minor, under age"; of brother, sister "younger"; of king "the Second"; of persons "lowly"; of scribe, merchant etc. "junior"; as subst. "child; servant"; *ṣa/eḫer rabi* "young and old, small and great"; Bab. *(ak)kī(ma) ṣeḫri* "in short order, quickly"; < *ṣeḫēru*

ṣeḫru II "(time of) youth" jB; < *ṣeḫēru*

ṣeḫrūtu "(time of) youth" jB; < *ṣeḫru* I

ṣēḫtu → *ṣīḫtu*

ṣēlāniš, *ṣēlēniš* "sideways" jB; < *ṣēlu*

ṣēlānû "with prominent ribs" jB lex. epith. of ox; < *ṣēlu*

ṣēlēniš → *ṣēlāniš*

ṣelēpu → *ṣalāpu*

ṣellu → *ṣēlu*

ṣēltum → *ṣāltu*

ṣelû(m) I "to insult" O/jB **G** woman **Gt** recipr. "insult each other" **D** ~ G MB(lit.); > *muṣallû*

ṣelû II "to ignite" jB **G** obj. incense (*qutrinnu*) **Š** "make s.o. burn" incense; > *ṣilûtu*?

ṣēlu(m), *ṣīlu(m)*, *ṣe/illu(m)* f. "rib" [TI] of human, animal; as cut of meat; "side, flank" of part of liver; "edge" of sherd, sword etc.; *šār ṣ.* "side wind"; "side" of ship, chariot, house; OB lex. *ša bīti ṣ.* "neighbour"?; > *ṣēlāniš*, *ṣēlānû*, *ṣēlû*

ṣēlû; f. *ṣēlītu* "on its side, sideways" jB of script; < *ṣēlu*

ṣêlu → *ṣâlu*

ṣēlūtu → *ṣālūtu*

ṣemēdu → *ṣamādu* II

ṣemēru(m), *ṣamāru* "to swell up, be swollen, bloated" O/jB **G** stat. only attested, of part of body **D** stat. ~ G stat.; > *ṣimru* II, *ṣimertu*

ṣendu → *ṣamdu*

ṣennetān → *ṣinnatān*

ṣennettu → *ṣernettum*

ṣennu → *ṣēnu* I

ṣēnu(m) I, *ṣīnum*, *ṣe/innu* "evil, malevolent" Bab.(lit.) of person; disease; locusts; > *ṣīnu* I; → *ṣinnarabu*

ṣēnu II "loaded, filled" jB lex. of basket etc.; < *ṣênu*

ṣēnu(m) III, OAkk *ṣānum*, NA *ṣe'ānu* f. "flock, sheep (and goats)" [USDUḪA; OB also US5.UDU(.NÍTA)] construed as sg. and pl.; → *ṣa'nu* ?

ṣênu(m), OAkk *ṣânum*, NA *ṣe'ānu* "to load (up)" OAkk, O/jB, NA **G** "load" ship, waggon etc. with (= acc.), "heap up" meal, offering; "pile on" incense, aromatics; > *ṣēnu* II, *ṣiyānu*

ṣênu → also *ṣânu*

ṣepēru → *ṣapāru*

ṣepû → *ṣapû* I

ṣe'pum, *ṣēpum*; pl. f. "sealed letter" OB

ṣēr → *ṣēru*

ṣerba/etu → *ṣarbatu*

ṣerdu (a musical interval sounded by strings 4 and 6) Ug., jB

ṣerēru → *ṣarāru* I

ṣerḫiš "with shouting" jB; < *ṣerḫu* I

ṣerḫu(m) I "shout, lamentation" O/jB [BALAG. DI] "lament"; *ēpiš/ša ṣ.* "singer of lamentations"; < *ṣarāḫu* I

ṣerḫu II "flash, sudden illumination, flare" jB [SUR] astr. of heavenly bodies; *ṣ. šakānu* "to flare up suddenly"; < *ṣarāḫu* II

ṣerḫu III "fever(ish) heat" jB lex., med.; < *ṣarāḫu* III

ṣerīpu, *ṣēripu* → *ṣāripu* I

ṣēriš Bab.(lit.) **1.** prep. "towards, against" s.o., "above, over" s.o. **2.** "in the steppe" **3.** "upon him"; < *ṣēru* + *-iš*

ṣērītu f. "open country" OB(Susa), Nuzi, jB [Nuzi EDIN.NA/MEŠ]; < *ṣērû*

ṣermum "effort, goal, desire" Mari; < *ṣarāmu*

ṣernettum, *ṣennettu(m)*, *ṣennītu*, *ṣinnatu* (a skin disease) O/jB

ṣerpētu (a barley soup) O/jB with milk or oil; < *ṣarāpu* I

ṣerpu(m) I **1.** Bab., M/NA "red wool", also *ša ṣ.*, *šīpāt ṣ.* **2.** jB "red spot" **3.** Mari "(red) dye"; < *ṣarāpu* I

ṣerpu II **1.** j/NB "fired (clay)" of tablet, figurine **2.** Qatna *ḫurāṣu ṣ.* "refined gold"; < *ṣarāpu* I

ṣerrāniš I "like a snake" jB; < *ṣerru* I

ṣerrāniš II "through the doorpost socket" M/jB; < *ṣerru* II

ṣerratān, *ṣerretān* du. (a pair of wooden objects) jB lex.; < *ṣerretu* I

ṣerretu(m) I, *ṣerratum*, NA *ṣarratu* "nose-rope, leading rope" OAkk, Bab., NA liter. of animal; captives; transf. *ṣ. nīšī* "control of people"; *ṣ. šamê (erṣeti)* "cosmic retaining rope"; *ṣ. šamê* also "Milky Way"?; > *ṣerratān*

ṣerretu II, once *ṣurrītu* "mane"? jB of lion; astr. "corona, halo"? round star

ṣerretu(m) III "concubine, subsidiary wife" O/jB [DAM.TAB.BA]; < *ṣerru* III ?

ṣerretu → also *ṣertu*

ṣerriš mng. unkn. jB lex.

ṣerru(m) I, *ṣē/īru(m)* "snake" [MUŠ] in similes; in representations; *ṣ. karāni*, *šadî*, *qinni*, *gušūri* "wine, mountain, nest, beam snake" etc.; *aban ṣ.* "snake stone"; *šam ṣ.* "snake plant"; as constellation, "Hydra"? [dMUŠ]; > *ṣerrāniš* I, *ṣerriš*?; *ṣarṣaru* I

ṣerru(m) II, *ṣarru* "socket for doorpost" O/jB upper, lower; > *ṣerrāniš* II

ṣerru III M/jB **1.** "enmity" in *bēl(et) ṣ.* "enemy" **2.** "enemy"; > *ṣerretu* III?

ṣerru → also *ṣīru* II

ṣeršu "offshoot, growth" jB of fungus; astr. of moon's horns; < *ṣarāšu*

ṣertu(m), *ṣerretu* "nipple, teat, udder" O/jB of woman, goddess; demon, animal; *ṣ. parīsi* "nipple of punting-pole"; *ṣ. šamê* "udders of heaven" transf., source of rain

ṣēru(m) "back, upperside; steppe, open country" [EDIN(.NA); Bogh. also LÍL] **1.** "back" of man, horse, fish; of parts of exta; of mountain **2.** in prep., adv. phrases: *ina ṣēr*, *iṣṣēr* OA, O/jB "on(to), over, towards, in(to) the presence of";

eli ṣēr jB(lit.) "over"; *ana ṣēr, aṣṣēr* OA, O/MB "to(wards), in addition to", Am. "against" s.o.; loc.-adv. *ṣēruššu(n)* roy. inscr. Sargon II-NB "(up)on, against"; *ṣēr* roy. inscr. after 700 BC "(up)on, above, over and above, in addition to, against, to(wards)"; *ana ṣēr(um)ma, aṣṣērma* OB "in addition, furthermore"; *aṣṣēr* + subjunct. OA, OB "in addition to the fact that" **3.** "steppe, open country" opp. to city (*ālu*); as abode of demons, wild beasts; battlefield; place for ritual; location of fields; *ša ṣ.* "steppe-dweller"; *bīt ṣ.* "tent"; DN *Bēl(et)-ṣ.* **4.** Nuzi, jB *ālik ṣ.* (a type of soldier); > *ṣēriš, ṣērītu, ṣērû, ṣêru*?; → *eṣemṣēru*

ṣēru → also *ṣerru* I

ṣērû "desert policeman"? j/NB [LÚ.EDIN-*u*]; < *ṣēru*

ṣêru(m) "to spread out, widen, broaden (out)" (intrans.) O/jB of part of liver, palm tree; < *ṣēru* denom.?

ṣētu(m), *ṣītum* "bright light, heat" Bab., NA [UD.DA] of sun, moon, stars; "light" and "heat" of day; Am. *ina ṣ.* "in the open air"; NB *ina ṣ. šamši* (a specification of time); "heat" as illness, esp. *ḫamāṭ/ḫimiṭ ṣ.* "sunstroke"?; < *ṣuā'u* ?

ṣētu → also *ṣītu*

ṣê'u, *ṣêyum* ~ "to repulse" O/jB, NA **G** horses, chariots; > *teṣētu*

ṣī → *ṣī šamši*

ṣiāḫu(m), *ṣâḫu* "to laugh; cry" **G** (*ī*; pres. once *aṣayyaḫ*) of person, god; of the heart (*libbu*); also in PNs **Gtn** iter. of G also of bird **D** "amuse, make laugh"; stat. "is amusing"; > *ṣīḫtu, ṣīḫu; ṣēḫiš; ṣūḫu, ṣūḫānû; ṣuḫḫum; ṣayyaḫu, ṣayyāḫu, ṣayyuḫû; muṣiḫḫu*

ṣiāru → *ṣīru* I; *ṣurrum* IV

ṣiātiš, *ṣâtiš* "for ever, for the future" M/jB; < *ṣiātu*

ṣiātu(m), *ṣâtu* **1.** "distant time" [UL] of past time, esp. *ūm ṣ.* "primeval days", *āl ṣ.* "primordial city"; of future, *ana ṣ./aṣṣ., ana/adi ūm ṣ., ana/adi ṣât ūmē* etc. "for ever after", *mê ṣ.* "ever-running water" **2.** jB, NA "commentary (on words excerpted from text)" [UD.UL.DÙ.A; once UL]; < *ṣītu* pl.

ṣibarātum (or *s/ṣib/parātum*) (a domestic utensil) OA

ṣibaru, *ṣiburu* (a bitter plant, phps.) "aloe" jB, NA lex., med.

ṣibāru I (a wooden peg) jB lex.; om. (a peg-like growth, feature)

ṣibāru(m) II ~ "sparrow" O/jB lex.

ṣibatannūtu ~ "fief, land-holding"? MB

ṣiba(t)tu (a harp)? j/NB

ṣibbiru → *ṣippiru*

ṣibbu (a mark) jB lex.; < Sum.

ṣibiātum → *ṣabiātum*

ṣibittu(m) "seizure" **1.** "captivity, imprisonment" [once EN.NU.UN] *bīt ṣ.* "prison"; *ša (bīt) ṣ.* "prisoner" **2.** "capture" by demon etc.; NA, NB *qāt ṣ./qaṣṣ.* "stolen property" or "caught red-handed"? **3.** NB "enclosure, basin" for irrigation water **4.** jB "work procedures, training"? **5.** Mari ~ "disagreement"?; < *ṣabātu*

ṣibtātu, *ṣibtētu* "fetters"? NA, NB of iron; < *ṣabātu* or Aram.?

ṣibtu(m) I; pl. f. "seizure" [DAB; MÁŠ (→ *ṣ.* II); Ì.DAB$_5$] **1.** "seizure" of (i.e. by) god, demon etc., i.e. illness; absol. "seizure" (= epilepsy ?) **2.** OB "seizure, confiscation" of ship **3.** NB "captivity" (= *ṣibittu*) **4.** OB "holding" of land **5.** NA, NB ? "occupation" of land, town **6.** MA, M/NB "withdrawal, taking" **7.** "(act of) grasping", OA *ṣ. niggalli(m)* "harvest-time"; jB, NA *ṣ. tulê* "grasping breast" in oath ceremony; *ṣ. appi* "moment"; *ṣ. qātē* "(thing) held in hand", NB *ina ṣ. qātē* "fettered" **8.** jB "capacity" of container **9.** Bab. *ṣ. ṭēmi(m)* "decision, decisive action", esp. with *išû(m), rašû(m)* "to come to a decision, start work, get to work" **10.** "setting" for precious stone (or *ṣ.* II ?); < *ṣabātu*; → *ṣ.* II 3; *ṣ.* III

ṣibtu(m) II "(addition =) interest" [MÁŠ (→ *ṣ.* I)] **1.** "interest" on silver, grain etc.; also "its interest" [MÁŠ.BI]; *ṣ. Šamaš* "interest of Š." **2.** Bab. ext. "processus papillaris" on liver **3.** M/NB, NA (a tax on cattle); *rab ṣ.* (a collector of cattle taxes) (or *ṣ.* I ?) **4.** OA "appendix" to tablet; < *waṣābum*; → *ṣ.* I 10; *ṣ.* III

ṣibtu(m) III (= *ṣ.* I or II ?) NB **1.** (a garment, esp. for cult statues) [MÁŠ] **2.** (a kind of loaf)

ṣibtum IV (or *s/ṣ/zib/ptum*) mng. unkn. OA

ṣiburu → *ṣibaru*

ṣibûtu(m), *ṣabûtu(m), ṣubûtu*; jB pl. *ṣibûtātu* "wish, desire, need, plan" Bab. [(Á.)ÁŠ] *mala ṣ.* "as much as wanted, needed"; *awīl, bēl ṣ.* "person required"; *ana ṣ. šakānu* "to need" s.th.; *ṣ. epēšu(m), kašādu(m)* "to accomplish desire, execute plan"; *ṣ. nadû(m)* "to abandon plan"; NB "request, demand" of king and others; < *ṣabû* II

ṣīdānu, *ṣ/šādānu* "(attack of) vertigo" M/jB [NÍG.NIGIN; TU.RA.NIGIN/NÍGIN.NA ?] also as name of demon; < *ṣâdu* I

ṣiddu(m), *ṣindu* in *ṣ. (u) birtu(m)* "proletariat, common people" O/jB

ṣidītu(m) "(travel) provisions" Bab. [NINDA. KASKAL; NB ZÍD.DA.KASKAL ?]; < *ṣadû*; NA → *eṣidītu* ?

ṣīdu "molten" j/NB of silver; as subst. in pl. *ṣīdānu* "silver ingots"; < *ṣâdu* II

ṣīḫiš → *ṣēḫiš*

ṣiḫittu → *ṣaḫittu*

ṣīḫtu(m), *ṣēḫtu(m)* "laughter" O/jB in pl. "flirtations, amusements, delights"; jB also "weeping, distress"; < *ṣiāḫu*

ṣīḫu "laughter" jB lex.; < *ṣiāḫu*; > *ṣēḫiš*

ṣilatalānu (a plant) jB lex.

ṣilbu → *ṣillibu*

ṣiliānum (a container, esp. for tablets) OA

ṣililītu (a bird) jB lex.

ṣiliptu(m) "(diagonal) dissection" Bab. [BAR.TA; BAR.NUN] math. "diagonal" of trapezium, rectangle, "hypotenuse" of triangle; NB astr. "(equalizing) correction"; < *ṣalāpu*

ṣiliptu → also *ṣaliptu*

ṣillaḫta → *zillaḫta*

ṣillānû jB **1.** "shade-loving" of plant **2.** "shady" of house, roof **3.** "throwing shadows" of torch; < *ṣillu*

ṣillāte pl. ~ "shelters" NA; < *ṣillu* ?

ṣil(li)bu (a cultic item)? NA med., rit.

ṣillîmaḫḫu mng. unkn. Bogh.; < *ṣillû* II ?

ṣillu(m) "shade, shadow; protection" [GISSU (=GIŠ.MI); MI] "shade" of tree, building, forest; "shadow" of smoke, transf. of king, god; (a dark spot on eye); "canopy" on boat; (a feature of liver); NA *ša ṣ.* "sun-shade"; transf. "protection" of god, king etc., of rivers, temples etc., esp. in PNs; > *ṣillānû*, *ṣillûm* I; *ṣillūlu*; *ṣullum*; *ṣillāte*?; → *ṣulūlu; ṣullulu* I.II

ṣillu → also *ṣēlu*

ṣillûm I "surrounded by shadow, hooded"? OB lex. of eye; < *ṣillu*

ṣillû(m) II, *ṣullûm*, *ṣullium*, *sillû* f. "thorn" [DÁLA(=IGI.GAG)] also "spike of palm leaflet"; "needle, pin", esp. "(chastity) pin"; NB "(iron) spike"; > *ṣillîmaḫḫu*?

ṣillūlu(m) "shelter, protection" OAkk, OA, O/jB also in PNs; < *ṣillu*

ṣillurtu (a kind of tree, phps.) "chaste tree, *Vitex agnus-castus*" jB(Ass.) lex.

ṣi(l)lūru (a kind of wool) jB lex.

ṣilpum (a kind of (dried ?) fish) OB; < *ṣalāpu*

ṣīltum → *ṣāltu*

ṣīlu → *ṣēlu*

ṣilûtu "burning (of incense)"? jB; < *ṣelû* II ?

ṣimdatum, *ṣindatu* "regulation, ordinance" Bab.; also (a kind of treaty); *ṣ. šarrim* "royal decree"; *warki ṣ.* "after the edict"; *ṭuppi ṣ.* "edict tablet"; < *ṣamādu* II; → *ṣimdu* I; *ṣimittu*

ṣimdu(m) I, *ṣindu*; pl. m. & f. "binding; (yoke-)team" OAkk, Bab. [NÍG.LAL; LAL ?] "belt" for wrestler; med. "bandage"; plough, chariot "team"; (an archit. fastening); "fixed plan, programme"; < *ṣamādu* II; → *ṣ.* II

ṣimdu(m) II, *ṣindu*, NB *ṣindû* "3 *sūtu* (vessel)" Bab., OA as measure [BANEŠ], st. abs. *ṣimid* (OB = c. 25 litres); "3 *sūtu* vessel" [(GIŠ/ DUG.)BANEŠ]; = *ṣ.* I ?

ṣimertu(m) "swollen state, bloatedness" O/jB; < *ṣemēru*; → *ṣimru* II

ṣimid → *ṣimdu* II

ṣimittu(m), NA once *ṣimmittu* "binding; (yoke-)team" Bab., M/NA [NÍG.LAL; LAL] "cross-beam" of yoke; "team" of horses, oxen, M/jB(Ass.) *ṣimdat*, *ṣimitti nīri* "yoked team"; "pair" of clothing, armour; < *ṣamādu* II

ṣimru I ~ "wealth" jB comm.; < *ṣamāru* ?

ṣimru II jB = *ṣimertu*; < *ṣemēru*

ṣimtu (a kind of beer) NA lex.

ṣindatu → *ṣimdatum*

ṣindītu (a wooden ring on plough)? jB lex.; < *ṣamādu* II

ṣindu → *ṣiddu*; *ṣimdu* I.II

ṣindû → *ṣimdu* II

ṣingabrû (a red stone) NB, from Sogdia; < Elam.

ṣinḫu "loose excretion" Bogh. lex.; < *ṣanāḫu*

ṣinnaḫtiru(m), *ṣinnaḫte/uru(m)* (a stomach complaint) O/jB lex., med.; < *ṣanāḫu* ?

ṣinnar(a)bu (a large grasshopper) jB lex.; < *ṣēnu* I + *erbû*

ṣinnarbubtu "reed node" Bogh., jB

ṣinnatān, *ṣe/inna/etān* du. (a pair of wooden objects) O/jB lex.; < *ṣinnatu*

ṣinnatu, *ṣinnetu* (a wind instrument) j/NB of wood, reed; > *ṣinnatān*

ṣinnatu → also *ṣennettu*

ṣinnetu → *ṣinnatu*

ṣinnu → *ṣēnu* I

ṣīnu(m) I "wickedness" O/jB lex.; < *ṣēnu* I

ṣīnu(m) II "help, assistance" O/jB, MA? lex.; also in PNs

ṣīnum → also *ṣēnu* I

ṣinundu → *sinuntu*

ṣiparātum → *ṣibarātum*

ṣipirtu I "(topog.) depression, trough" MB; < *ṣapāru*

ṣipirtu II, NB *ṣipištu* (a gem stone) j/NB; < *ṣipru* ?

ṣipirtu III (an item of clothing) NA, NB; NA *išpar ṣiprāte* "weaver of *ṣ*."; < Aram.?; → *siprītu*

ṣipištu → *ṣipirtu* II

ṣippa(r)rātu I "morning" NA; < Aram.

ṣippa(r)rātu II (an ointment)? Am.(Eg.) in *bīt ṣ*. "box for *ṣ*."

ṣipparu (a bronze/copper object) NB

ṣippatu(m) I "fruit orchard" Bab.(lit.); → *ṣippūtu*

ṣippatu(m) II O/jB **1.** (a kind of reed) **2.** (a vegetable); < *ṣippu* ?

ṣippatu(m) III; OB pl. also *ṣippētum* ? "(pine-)cone" O/jB "cone" of pine (*ašūḫu*); of silver, gold; "fish-bone"

ṣippiru (or *ṣibbiru*) (a kind of field) Ug. in *eqlēt ṣ*. "*ṣ*. fields"; < Ug.

ṣippu (a vegetable) jB lex.; > *ṣippatu* II?

Ṣippu → also *Ṣip'u*

ṣippūtu (or *zibbūtu*) (a tree) NA; → *ṣippatu* I

ṣipru(m); pl. f. "point, spike" Bab. "beak" of bird; "point" of triangle, horn; "coma" of comet; (a pointed ornament in stone, metal); > *ṣipirtu* II?

ṣiptum → *ṣibtum* IV

ṣīpu I "submersion, soaking, drenching" M/NB, NA; of irrigated field, cooked meat; "dyeing" of brick, textile; < *ṣapû* II

ṣīpu II (a salt)? MB(Ass.)

Ṣip'u(m), *Ṣippu* (a month) O/MA, NA lex.

ṣipûtu → *ṣapû* I

ṣīrānu/û → *ṣīru* I

ṣiriānum → *ziriānum*

ṣiriḫtu I "inflammation" j/NB med. of fever, eyes; transf. of anger; < *ṣarāḫu* III

ṣiriḫtu(m) II "lamentation, wailing" O/jB; < *ṣarāḫu* I

ṣirimtu(m) "effort, intention" O/jB; < *ṣarāmu*

ṣirīnu (a metal object)? MB

ṣiriptu ~ "reddening, discoloration (of skin)"? M/jB lex., med.; < *ṣarāpu* I

ṣīriš "supremely, eminently" O/jB; < *ṣīru* I

ṣirûm I (a domestic item) OB

ṣirû II "brim, edge" j/NB with *malû*; of vessel, canal in *ana ṣ. malû/mullû* "to be/make full to the brim"; transf. of person "to be at end of tether"

ṣīru(m) I "exalted, supreme, splendid, outstanding" [MAḪ] often in stat.; "high(-quality), tall" of door, ship, column; transf. "exalted" of deity, king, wild cow; holy items etc.; river, building, dais, shrine; rites, wisdom etc.; command, name; "high-ranking", NA as subst. "envoy" [LÚ.MAḪ], pl. *ṣīrānu/û*; > *ṣīriš*, *ṣīrūtu*, *ṣurrum* IV

ṣīru II, *ṣerru* (a carpenter's tool) O/jB lex.; < Sum.

ṣīru III, *ṣūru* mng. unkn. jB lex. in *ṣīr/ṣūr muṣlāli* "*ṣ*. of siesta-time"

ṣīru → also *ṣerru* I

ṣīrūtu(m) "supremacy, exaltedness" O/jB of king, deity; < *ṣīru* I

ṣiṣītu (a part of loom, phps.) "shuttle" Ug., jB

ṣiṣnu (or *ṣiṣṣal* ?) "fish larva(e)"? jB lex.

ṣiṣṣatu (a floral ornament) Qatna; < W.Sem.

ṣiṣṣippu "water-clock" jB lex.; < Sum.

ṣiṣṣu(m) (a wooden bar)? O/jB for neck and hand fetters

ṣiṣṣu → also *zizzum*

ṣiṣû → *ṣuṣû*

ṣī šamši(m) "sunrise" O/jB rare for *ṣīt šamši* (→ *ṣītu* 3)

ṣītān, *ṣītaš* "at sunrise, in the east" j/NB [GIŠ.NIM] *ina ṣ. u šīlān* "in the east and the west", *ultu ṣ. adi šīlān* "from the east to the west"; *Ṣītaš* (a month = *Simānu*); < *ṣītu*

ṣītiš "in the east" jB; < *ṣītu*

ṣītu(m), *ṣētu(m)*; pl. → *ṣiātu* "exit; (sun-)rise; issue" [È] **1.** "exit, issuance" of abscess, spring-water; "place of origin" **2.** "(new) growth" of plant; 'that originating from': trees from mountain, person from womb (*ūru*); *ṣīt libbi* "offspring"; word from mouth *ṣīt pî* "utterance" **3.** "(sun-)rise" [^{d}UTU.È(.A); È] (→ *ṣī šamši*), also as time of day; "the east" **4.** "issue" of commodities, "debit, loss" [ZI.GA]; "departure" of person; *ṣ. rašû(m)* "to make off, decamp" **5.** OB "exit tax"? [BA.ZI]; jB lex. *ṣīt kišādi* "neck opening"; < *waṣûm*; > *ṣītān*, *ṣītiš*; *ṣiātu*, *ṣiātiš*

ṣītum → also *ṣētu*

ṣi'ûtu mng. unkn. jB lex.

ṣiyānu "incense" jB lex.; < *ṣênu*

ṣû (or *zû* ?) mng. unkn. jB lex.; → *ṣī šamši*

ṣuādu → *ṣâdu* II

ṣuā'u "to dry" MA **G** stat. of textiles "are dry"; > *ṣētu*?

ṣubabû(m), *ṣumbabû* "conifer bud" O/jB

ṣubārum, *ṣupārum* "slave"? OA, or a PN ?; < *ṣubrum* ?

ṣubātiš "with, into a garment" jB; < *ṣubātu*

ṣubātu(m) "textile, garment" [TÚG]; OA mostly "textile, cloth"; Bab. mostly "garment, clothing"; "cortex"? of palm tree; < *ṣabātu* ?

ṣubâtu → *ṣubītu*

ṣubbîš "in order to observe" OB; < *ṣubbû*

ṣubbītu → *ṣubītu*

ṣubbu → *ṣumbu*

ṣubbû(m), Ass. *ṣabbû(m)* **D** "to observe (from a distance), inspect, check, look at" Bab., O/MA people, building work, divine image; damage; text; also in PN **Dt** pass. of D "be recognizable" **Št** **1.** "carry out according to plan, execute thoroughly" **2.** "stare fixedly"; > *ṣubbîš*

ṣubbulu → *zabālu* D

ṣubbutu(m), Ass. *ṣabbutu* **1.** OB lex. "lame, paralysed" **2.** NB "arrested"? **3.** MA "drawn up" of tablets **4.** jB/NA "successive" of favourable days; < *ṣabātu* D

ṣubītu, *ṣupītu*, once *ṣubbītu* NB **1.** "dyed wool" **2.** "irrigation, soaking"; < *ṣapû* II

ṣubrum f. ~ "(domestic) servants, labourers, slaves" OA; > *ṣubārum*?

ṣu'bu → *ṣuppu* III

ṣubûtu → *ṣibûtu*

ṣudannu, ṣudānu → *ṣudiānum*

ṣudātu (or *ṣudâtu*) (a part of cart) jB lex.

ṣūdātu, ṣuddu → *ṣūdu* II

ṣuddurum, *ṣunduru*, once *sunduru*, NA *ṣanduru* "squinting, cross-eyed"? O/jB, NA also as PN; < *ṣadāru* D

ṣudiānum, *ṣudinnu*, *ṣuda(n)nu* **1.** O/jB lex. (a tree) **2.** jB mag. (a stone)

ṣudû pl. tant. "rations, provisions" Bab. *ṣ. gerrim* "journey provisions"; rit., for figurines; NB for ducks; < *ṣadû*

ṣūdu I "whirling" M/jB in *ṣūd pāni* "giddiness, vertigo" [IGI.NIGIN.NA]; < *ṣâdu* I

ṣūdu II, *ṣuddu* "molten metal" NA, NB; pl. *ṣūdāte* "castings"; < *ṣâdu* II

ṣudūru (a ceremonial garment) jB lex.

ṣūḫānû "smiling" jB; < *ṣūḫu*

ṣuḫartu(m) "girl; young woman; female servant" OAkk ?, O/MA, O/jB [MUNUS.TUR (also = *ṣeḫertum* ?); OB also MUNUS.LÚ.TUR.RA ?]; < *ṣuḫāru*

ṣuḫāru(m), *ṣuḫārû* "boy, male child; servant" OAkk ?, OA, O/jB [(LÚ.)TUR; MB also (LÚ.)KAL.TUR ?; Nuzi TUR ?]; < *ṣeḫēru*; > *ṣuḫartu*; → *ṣuḫru* 1

ṣūḫētu → *ṣūḫu*

ṣuḫḫum "laughable, trivial" Mari of meal; < *ṣiāḫu* D

ṣuḫḫu → also *ṣūḫu*

ṣuḫḫuriš adv. to *ṣeḫēru* D or *ṣuḫḫuru* ? OB

ṣuḫḫuru "very small, tiny, minuscule" jB; < *ṣeḫēru* D

ṣuḫḫutu(m), once *ṣeḫḫutu* "squeezed, pressed" OAkk, O/jB of eye condition; esp. as PN; < *ṣaḫātu* I D

ṣuḫilu, *ṣuḫitu*, *ṣuḫlu* (a messenger)? MB; < Elam.?

ṣuḫru(m) "youth(s)" **1.** OA "(the) children" as coll. to *ṣuḫāru* **2.** Bab. "(time of) youth"; pl. f. *ṣuḫrētu* "young days"; < *ṣeḫēru*

ṣuḫum (or *s/zuḫum*) (a desig. of person) OB

ṣūḫu(m), *ṣuḫḫu*; pl. f. "laugh, laughter" Bab. also "(object of) amusement"; "love play", stone, drug, incantation of *ṣ.*, i.e. aphrodisiac; < *ṣiāḫu*

ṣuḫurrû "reduction" OB in accounting, pl. f.; jB of population; < *ṣeḫēru*

ṣuḫurtu, NA often *ṣaḫurtu* "the young, youth(s)" M/NB coll. "youth(s)", also "young man"; NA (abbr. *ṣa*) "young man"; < *ṣeḫēru*

ṣulāmātu (or *zulāmātu*) mng. unkn. jB comm.

ṣulāmu 'Blackie' (a bird; a tree) jB lex.; < *ṣalāmu*

ṣulāpu mng. unkn. jB in *šinni* ("tooth") *ṣ.*; < *ṣalāpu*

ṣūlātu pl. tant. "battle, combat" j/NB(poet.); < *ṣâlu*; → *ṣulultu* II

ṣullium → *ṣillû* II

ṣullum "protection" OB(Susa); < *ṣillu*

ṣullû, *ṣallû* **D** "to beseech, pray to" j/NB, NA deity; "supplicate" king; leg. "appeal to" king **Dtn** iter. of D jB, NA; > *ṣulû*; → *sullû* I; *teslītu*

ṣullû → also *ṣillû* II; *ṣulû*

ṣullultu → *ṣulultu* I

ṣullulum I "roofed"? OB of house; < *ṣullulu* II ?; → *sullulu*

ṣullulu(m) II, NA *ṣallulu* **D** "to roof over, cover " Bab., NA "roof" house, room with (= acc.) beams, mats etc.; "make" sky "into roof"; "place" beams "as roof"; "cover over; obscure" sky, parts of liver; stat. of language "is obscure"; transf. "give protection" of deity to man, official to king; < *ṣulūlu* denom.; > *ṣullulum* I?; *taṣliltu*

ṣullupu "divided" into half lines ? jB of tablet; < *ṣalāpu* D

ṣulmu(m) "blackness, black spot; black wood" [GE_6] "black spot" on stone, body, eye, heavenly body; *ṣ. īni* "iris", *ṣ. pāni* "anger, rage"; "dark cloud, rain cloud"; "black wood, ebony"; < *ṣalāmu*

ṣulpu ~ "misdeed" Bogh.; < *ṣalāpu*

ṣulû, *ṣullû* "supplication, prayer" j/NB, NA to deity, king; also in PNs; < *ṣullû*

ṣulultu I, once *ṣullultu* "roofing, covering" j/NB for temple; (mostly a part of exta, phps.) "diaphragm" [AN.DÙL-]; < *ṣulūlu*

ṣulultu II (a syn. for battle) jB lex.; error for *ṣūlātu* ?

ṣulūlu(m), NA *ṣalūlu* "roof, canopy" [AN.DÙL; OA also DÙL] "shelter, canopy"; transf. of forest; "roof" of temple etc.; "aegis, protection" of deity, king; as epith. of deity; lex. (a clay sealing)?; > *ṣullulu* II; *ṣulultu* I; → *andullu*; *ṣillu*

ṣumāmītu(m), *ṣu(m)māmī/ētu(m)*, NB *ṣumāma'ītu* "(severe) thirst" Bab., NA causing death; *eqel/qaqqar ṣ.* "land of thirst"; < *ṣūmu*

ṣumāmu "thirst" j/NB; < *ṣūmu*

ṣumbabû → *ṣubabû*

ṣumbiru (an object) Am.

ṣumbu(m), NA also *ṣubbu*; pl. m. & f. "wheel; waggon" Bab., NA [(GIŠ.)MAR.GÍD.DA] esp. j/NB(Ass.) "(Elamite) waggon" in army

ṣumlalû(m), Aṣs. *ṣumlaliu(m)* (a spice plant) [ŠIM.GAM.MA; also ŠIM.GAM.ME; (GIŠ.)GAM. MA]

ṣummāmītu → *ṣumāmītu*

ṣummirātu(m), *ṣummu/erātu(m)*, NA *ṣumrātu* "desires, aims" O/jB, NA [ŠÀ.SÌ.SÌ(.KE)] usu. with *kašādu(m)* "to achieve (o.'s goal)"; < *ṣamāru*

ṣummu → *ṣūmu*

ṣummû "thirst" j/NB, NA; NB also transf. *ṣ. ša šipirtu* "longing for a letter"; < *ṣamû* II

ṣummudu, NA *ṣammudu* "equipped, harnessed" jB, NA of plough, vehicle; < *ṣamādu* II D

ṣummunu → *zummunu*

ṣummur → *ṣumru*

ṣummurātu, *ṣumrātu* → *ṣummirātu*

ṣumru(m) "desire, purpose" O/jB; Mari *ina ṣumur mīnim* "to what purpose?" (or *ṣummur* < *ṣamāru* D infin.); < *ṣamāru*

ṣūmu(m), *ṣummu* "thirst" Bab., NA [Ug. IMMIN.MEŠ]? *ṣūm mê* "thirst for, lack of water"; *ašar*, *qaqqar ṣ.* "land of thirst"; < *ṣamû* II

ṣumurtum mng. unkn. OB lex.; < *ṣamāru* ?

ṣunduru → *ṣuddurum*

ṣunnu mng. unkn. jB lex.

ṣupārum → *ṣubārum*

ṣupītu → *ṣubītu*; *ṣupû*

ṣuppā(n) du.? "60 cubits" (= c. 30 metres) Bab. [1/2.ÉŠ; 5.NINDA(.DU)]

ṣuppatu I (a pool, pond)? MB

ṣuppatu II ~ "layer of combed wool" NB garment material; < Aram.; → *aṣuppātu*

ṣuppu I, MA *ṣa''upu* ~ "decorated, overlaid, clad, covered" M/NA, M/jB of gold, silver items; of furniture; textiles; < *ṣuppu* II

ṣuppu II, MA *ṣa''upu* ~ "to decorate, inlay ?, overlay ?" O/jB, M/NA; MA also "rub down"? horse with oil; > *ṣuppu* I; *muṣiptu*

ṣuppu(m) III, NA *ṣu'bu* "white sheep"

ṣuppû "soaked"? NB of dates; < *ṣapû* II D

ṣuppuru(m) O/MB **1.** of sheep's fleece "straggly, in strands" **2.** Nuzi of armour "grooved, serrated"; < *ṣapāru* D

ṣupru(m), *ṣupuru*; pl. f. *ṣuprātu(m)*, once *ṣuprānu* "(finger/toe-)nail; claw; hoof" [UMBIN] of humans, deities; *ša ṣ.* "nail-cutter"; mag. *liqit ṣ.* "nail clipping"; "nail(-impression)" on tablet; "claw" of bird, animal, demon; "foot" of furniture; "hoof" of sheep, cow, horse; "claw" of saffron plant; → *ṭupru*

ṣupû "soaked (material)" M/jB; med. from river; MB f. *ṣupītum*, desig. of chariot; < *ṣapû* II

ṣupurtum → *supurtum*

ṣupuru → *ṣupru*

ṣurārītum → *ṣurārû*

ṣurāru I "libation" NA of wine; < *ṣarāru* I

ṣurāru II "bundle, money pouch" NB; < Aram.

ṣurārû, *ṣurāru(m)*, once *ṣurīrû*; nom. unit. *ṣurīrītum*, *ṣuririttu*, OAkk *ṣurārītum* "lizard(s)" OAkk, O/jB [EME.ŠID; EME.DIR] construed as m. sg., f. sg. and m. pl.; med. *qaqqad*, *zê ṣ.* "head, excrement of lizard" as ingredient; of steppe, wall; with two tails; also as PN

ṣurbu (a garden herb, a kind of fennel ?) NB; < Aram.

ṣurḫu "heat, fever" jB, NA; < *ṣarāḫu* III

ṣuririttu, *ṣurīrītum*, *ṣurīrû* → *ṣurārû*

ṣurpu(m) **1.** O/jB in *ṣurup libbi(m)* "burning of heart" as illness **2.** MB in *ṣ. zišagalli* "flash? of inspiration"? **3.** Qatna, MB(Alal.), Ug. "refined (silver)" (= *ṣarpu*); < *ṣarāpu* I

ṣurrānītu "*ṣurru*-like stone" jB [NA4.GUG.ZÚ]; < *ṣurru* I

ṣurriš → *surriš*

ṣurrītu → *ṣerretu* II

ṣurru(m) I "obsidian, flint" Bab., MA [NA4.ZÚ] for ornament; black, white, yellow/green varieties; as blade; *ṣ. kūre* "kiln (i.e. artificial) *ṣ.*"; (a kind of glaze); > *ṣurrānītu*; *ṣurtu*

ṣurru(m) II, once *surru* "interior, heart" Bab., NA as part of human body; "heart, mind, mood"; transf. of Ištar *ṣ. tāḫāzi* "essence? of battle"; in loc.-adv. "interior, middle"

ṣurru(m) III (a drinking vessel) Mari, Alal.

ṣurrum IV **D** "to exalt" OB; < *ṣīru* I
ṣurrû "split" NB of palm fronds; < Aram.
ṣurruḫu I ~ "built high" jB lex.; < *ṣurruḫu* II
ṣurruḫu II **D** ~ "to build high" jB; > *ṣurruḫu* I
ṣurrupu, OA *ṣarrupum* "refined" OA, jB of silver; < *ṣarāpu* I D
ṣurrušum "notched, jagged"? OB ext. of part of liver; < *ṣarāšu* D
ṣurṣuppu(m), OB *sursumbum*, MB *ṣarṣuppu* (a container with knobs) OA, O/jB
ṣuršu(m) **1.** NB "sprout, shoot"?; < *ṣarāšu* **2.** OA, OB (a metal vessel)
ṣurtu "flint (blade)" jB; < *ṣurru* I
ṣurtu → also *uṣurtu*
ṣurûm (a plant, phps.) "opopanax" Mari
ṣurû → also *zurû*
ṣūrum "cliff, rock" OB
ṣūru → also *ṣīru* III; *ṣu'ru*
ṣu'ru, *ṣūru* "back" Am.; < W.Sem.
ṣuṣimtu → *aṣuṣimtu*
ṣuṣû(m), once *ṣiṣû* "reed-thicket" O/jB
ṣuṣūlu (a plant) jB med. (= *ṣuṣūnu* ?)
ṣuṣūnu (a tree or shrub) NA with fruit
ṣu''udum ~ "whirling" OB of storm; < *ṣâdu* I D
ṣu''upu → *zu''upu*
ṣuwar → *suwar*

Š

-š → *-ša*; *-šu*

ša, OB occas. *še* "who(m), which; (s)he who, that which; of" etc. (det. pron.) **1.** (→ GAG §§137-8) before gen. "of" (after subst.; after pron. suff.; also before subst.), jB lex. "with reference to, (with the meaning) of; (when said) of"; (before infin.) "fit to (be), due to (be)"; (before *lā* + infin.) "not to be, which cannot/should not be"; (in PN) "(the deeds) of" DN; (in prof. desig.) "he of", i.e. the man in charge of; *ša X-šu* = "the X-man"; (before prep.) e.g. *ša libbi*, *ša muḫḫi*; *ša lā* "without; in the absence of" **2.** (→ GAG §§164-8) rel. pron. before subjunct. or nominal clause "who, whom, which" (also with no antecedent); OAkk as acc. only; followed by subst. + pron. suff. "whose"; by vb. + dat. pron. suff. "to whom"; in comb. with other conj.s esp. j/NB, NA, e.g. *adi ša*, *akī ša*, *kīma ša*, *ištu ša* etc.; "that, according to which"; "with respect to the fact that …", "because"; → *iššā*; *šalânû*; *šāt*; *šu*; *šūt* I

-ša, *-š* "her" (3 f. sg. pron. suff. after subst.)

šā "the two of" OAkk, du. of *šu*

ša'ālu → *šâlu* I

ša'āmum → *šâmu*

ša'āru(m) "to win, conquer" OAkk, OB, Mari **G** (*a*/*a*)

šabā- → *šaptu*

šabābu(m) I "to glow; be parched" O/jB **G** (*u*/*u*) of lips **Gtn** of eyes; > *šibūbu*; *muštabbabbu*

šabābum II ~ "to proclaim"? OB **G** (*a*/*u* or *u*/*u*)

šabāḫu "to settle, be deposited" jB **G** (*u*/*u*) of dust **Š** of eyes ~ "be covered"; > *šibḫu*; *šabīḫu*

šabāḫu → also *šapāḫu*

šabalbalû "(psychological) confusion" (as illness) jB [ŠÀ.BAL.BAL-]; < Sum.

šabartu "block, bar" of copper MA; < *šebēru*

šabāru → *šebēru*

šabāsu(m), *sabāsu(m)*, *šabāšu(m)* "to be angry" **G** (*u*/*u*, jB also *a*/*u*; stat. Bab. *š*/*sabus*, OA *sabis*) with = *eli*, also *itti*, *išti*; jB *kišāda š.* "turn (neck) away in anger" **Gtn** iter. of G **Š** "make angry"; > *šabsu*, *šabsiš*; *šibsātu*; *šabbasû*

šabāsu → also *šabāšu*

šabāṣu → *šapāṣu*

šabāšu(m), *šabāsu*, *šapāšu* "to gather" Bab., NA **G** (*a*/*u*, M/jB occas. *u*/*u*) "collect" grain taxes; NB "round up" cattle; mag. "scoop up" soil **D** "gather together", "collect" taxes **N** pass. of G; > *šabšātum*, *šibšu*

šabāšu → also *šabāsu*

šabattu(m), NB *šabbatu* (a garment) Mari, MA, Am., Nuzi, Ug., NB

šabattu → also *šapattu*

šabātu → *šapāṭu* I; *šaptu*

Šabāṭu I (11th Bab. month) OAkk, Bab., NA [OB ITI.ZÍZ.A; later ITI.ZÍZ(.A.AN)]

šabāṭu(m) II "to beat, sweep (away)" OA, O/jB **G** (*i*/*i*) of wind, demon, illness "strike"; "sweep" roof, house [SAR] **Gtn** mng. uncert. **N** "be blasted" by wind; > *šibṭu*; *našbaṭu*; *šabbiṭu* I.II

šabā'u → *šebû* I

šabbaliltu → *šambaliltu*

šabbasû, *sabbasû* "very angry" M/jB; < *šabāsu*

šabbatu → *šabattu*; *šappatu*

šabbilu, *šambilu* (a plant) M/jB

šabbiṭu I "staff, sceptre" jB; < *šabāṭu* II

šabbiṭu II (desig. of soldiers) jB lex.; < *šabāṭu* II

šabbu (desig. of beer) NB

šabburtu "broken up, ploughed land" NA; < *šebēru* D

šabburum "broken" OA desig. of good quality copper; < *šebēru* D

ša(b)bušatta adv. mng. unkn. MA

šabdu → *šaptu*

šabe → *sebe*

šabīḫu ~ "layer" of dust or mist? jB astr.; < *šabāḫu*

šabikû (a type of headgear) jB lex.

šabirru → *šawirum*

šabîšu → *sebîšu*

šabītum (or *šapītum*) (a commodity) OA

šabium, *šabû* adj. mng. uncert. O/jB of cedar in rit.

šabī'um "(one who is) satisfied" Mari; < *šebû* I

šabrātu "female interpreter of dreams" jB; < *šabrû* II

šabru → *šebru*

šabrû(m) I (a temple official) OAkk, O/jB [ŠAPRA]; < Sum.; > *šabrûtu*

šabrû II "interpreter of dreams" jB; > *šabrātu*

šabrûtu "function of a *šabrû*" jB; < *šabrû* I

šabsiš "angrily" jB; < *šabsu*

šabsu(m), *sabsu(m)* "angry, turned away in anger" Bab. esp. of gods; also with *kišādu* ("neck"); < *šabāsu*

šabsû "man midwife, accoucheur" jB, NA lex.; OB as PN ?; < Sum.; → *sabsû*

šabsūtu(m), *tabsūtu(m)*, jB also *šabšūtu*, M/NA *sabsuttu* "midwife" Ass., O/jB [MUNUS.ŠÀ.ZU]; < Sum.; > *tabsûtum*

šabšātum f. pl. "taxes collected" OB; < *šabāšu*

šabšû → *sabsû*

šabšūtu → *šabsūtu*

šabtu → *šaptu* pl.

šabû → *sebû*; *šabium*; *šapû* II.IV; *šebû* I; *šubû* I

šâbu(m) "to tremble, quake" Bab.(lit.) **G** (*ū*) of gods in fear, like reeds; of the heavens **D** caus. of G "make vacillate"

šâbu → also *šiābu*

šābultum → *šēbultu*

šābulu(m) "dried (out), dry" Bab., OA [phps. ḪÁD.A; ḪÁD.DU] of grain, fruit, meat, blood; vessel; tablet; "withered, shrivelled", also OB as PN; < *abālu* Š

šaburru (or *šapurru*) "beam" of a boat NB

šabušatta → *šabbušatta*

šadādu(m) "to drag" [GÍD(.DA)] **G** (*a/u*, M/jB; pret. occas. *irdud*) **1.** "tow" chariot, cart, ship, yoke; *ša ša(d)dādi* "rickshaw" **2.** "stretch" a rope, ellipt. "survey" house, field etc. **3.** "draw" line, boundary; "draw" curtain etc.; "pull" ear, nose; "stick out" tongue, lips, also "tear out" tongue **4.** "draw down", "draw up"; "draw in, bring in, fetch" troops, animal, "produce" witnesses **5.** "draw away; drag off", also intrans. "move away" **6.** astr. ellipt. "extend (time)" i.e. "be late"; "have patience"; "endure" anger, "bear" guilt, punishment; *ana libbi- š.* "consider earnestly" **7.** intrans. "extend, stretch" of property, parts of body, exta **Gtn** iter. of G **Gt** "tug, pull in both directions" OB **D** "tug, drag" **Š** caus. of G **N** pass. of G **Ntn** pass. of Gtn; > *šaddu* I; *šaddidu*, *šādidu*; *šaddādu*; *šadittu*; *mašaddu*; *šiddu*, *šiddatu* I; *maldadu*

šadāḫu(m) "to walk, stride, move forward" Bab.(lit.) **G** (*i/i*) esp. in processions; "pass along" street (= acc.) etc.; of arrow "fly, speed"; of stars, clouds **Gtn** iter. of G of troops "march" **Gt** "march" of troops **D** "pass along" road, through reed thicket **Š** caus. of G "lead in procession" **Ntn** ~ Gtn; > *šaddiḫu*; *išdiḫu* I; *mašdaḫu*

šadālu(m) "to be(come) wide" Bab.(lit.) **G** (*i/i*) stat., of door; of understanding "is broad"; of people "multiply" **D** "widen, increase" building, cultivation, boundaries; descendants; years of life **Dt** pass. of D; > *šadlu*; *šuddulum*

šadâniš "like a mountain" NA, NB(lit.) [KUR.MEŠ-*niš*]; < *šadû* I

šadânu(m) I, OA *šaduānum*, NB *šaddânu* "haematite" Bab., OA, NA [(NA4.)KA.GI.NA; NA4.KUR-*nu*]; *š. ṣābitu* [DAB(.BA)] "magnetite, lodestone"; < *šadû* I ?

šadânu II (a disease) jB

šādānu → *ṣīdānu*

šadaru → *šaddaru* II

šadāšium "sixth" OA; < *šediš*

šaddabakku → *šandabakku*

šaddādu "boat-tower" NB; < *šadādu*

šaddādu → also *šadādu* G

šadda(g)gad → *šaddaqda*

šaddalu → *šandalum*

šaddanakku → *saddanakku*

šaddânu "east" Nuzi; < *šadû* II

šaddânu → also *šadânu* I

šaddaqda(m), *šaddaqdi(m)*, NB *šadda(g)gad*, NA *šaddaqdiš* "last year" [MU.IM.MA]; < *šattu* + *qdm* (→ GAG §72c)

šaddaru I, *šitarru* (a grass) jB lex.

ša(d)daru II mng. uncert. jB comm.

šaddattunu mng. uncert. NA

šaddā'u → *šaddû'a*

šaddidu(m) "hauler, tower" Bab. of men "boat-tower" [LÚ.GÍD.DA] (→ *šādidu*); of cattle "draught(-animal)", also f. *šaddittu(m)*; < *šadādu*

šaddiḫu "far-reaching" jB(lit.) of s.o.'s arms; < *šadāḫu*

šaddi(n)nu → *saddinu*

šaddu(m) I; f. *šaddatu(m)* Bab., OA **1.** "taut, elongated" **2.** uncert. mng.; < *šadādu*

šaddu II; pl. *šaddānu* (a chest or container) M/NB, NA of wood, for gold, precious objects

šaddû → *šadû* I.II

šaddû'a, *šaddā'u* O/jB **1.** "mountain-dweller"; f. *Šaddā'ittu* MA as fPN **2.** "mountain detritus"; < *šadû* I

ša(d)dū(ā)'iš "like a mountain" j/NB; < *šadû* I

šadduntum → *šadduttu*

šadduppû → *šanduppû*

šadduttu(m), *šadduntum*, *šanduttum*, *šanduntum* "exaction (of payment)" OB; < *nadānu* II Š

šaddū'utum (a commercial tax) OA; < *nadû* III Š

šādidu(m) Bab. **1.** "boat-tower" [(ÉŠ.)GÍD], OB also *š. ašlim* (→ *šaddidu*) **2.** "tow rope" **3.** *š. ašli, eqli* "surveyor" **4.** NB *š. ša sisê* (a type of transport personnel); < *šadādu*

šadipu (or *šaṭipu*) (a small wooden object) NB

šadittu "sedan chair" jB lex.; < *šadādu*

šadīum → *šadû* II

šadlu; f. *šadiltu*; f. pl. NB(roy. inscr.) once *sadliātim* "broad, spacious" j/NB of earth, sea, gate; understanding, heart; "extensive" troops, possessions, gifts; < *šadālu*

šadû(m) I, *šaddû*, OAkk, OA, OB *šadu'u(m)*, gen. OAkk *šadwim*; st. constr. *šad(i)*; pl. m. & f., also *šadân(u)* **1.** "mountain(s)" [KUR; ḪUR.SAG (→ *ḫuršānu*); SA.TU] also transf. as epith. of gods, cities, temples; esp. in PN as refuge; *š.-šu emēdu* "to disappear" **2.** lit. "open country, desert" **3.** (a myth. locality corresponding to Sum. kur); > *šadâniš*, *šaddūā'iš*; *šaddû'a*; *šadû* II; *šadûssu*

šadû II, *šaddû*, OAkk *šadīum* "east; easterner; east wind" [IM.KUR.RA; KUR-*ú*; IM.3]; NB *bīt š.* "east wing" of a house; < *šadû* I + *-ī*; > *šaddânu*

šadû III (a mineral component of glaze) jB

šadû IV **N** "to be rejected" NB; < Aram.

šaduānum → *šadânu* I

šaduppu(m) (a tablet basket) jB lex.; < Sum.

šadurnû → *šurdunû*

šadûssu "into the mountain" jB; < *šadû* I

šadu'u → *šadû* I

ša'erru → *ša'irru*

šagā mng. unkn. NB

šagabigalzu, *šakabigalzu* (a plant) jB lex., med.; < Kass.

šagāgu "to stiffen, be tense" jB **G** stat. of joints, sinews **Ntn** "stiffen continually"; > *šaggu*; *šiggatu*

šagalmušu, *šakalmušu* "fear"? O/jB; → *nagalmušu*

šagaltu → *šaggaštu*

šagālu(m) ~ "to misappropriate" O/jB **G** (*i/i*); > *šigiltu*

šagalûtu "deportation" NA; < *šuglû*

šagammu(m), Mari *šigammu* "upper door hinge"? O/jB

šagāmu I "clamour, roaring" jB; < *šagāmu* II infin.

šagāmu(m) II, OB once *šagānum* "to roar, shout" O/jB, NA **G** (*u/u*) [GÙ.DÉ] of gods, demons; king; thunder; animals; waterfall; of house, wall "make a noise"; med. of ear, head "buzz, suffer tinnitus" **Š** caus. of G **Štn** iter. of Š; > *šigmu*, *šigmiš*; *šagāmu* I, *šagantu*; *šagīmu*, *šagimmatu*, *šaggumūtu*; *šāgimu*; *šugummû*

šaganakku → *šakkanakku*

šagantu "roaring" MB; < *šagāmu* I

šagānum → *šagāmu* II

šagapīru → *šagapūru*

šagapūriš "majestically" OB; < *šagapūru*

šagapūru(m), *šaggapūru*, *šagapīru* "mighty, majestic" Bab.(lit.), Ug., Bogh. epith. of deities; > *šagapūriš*

šagarû "hunger" jB; < Sum.

šagarû → also *šakarû*

šagassum "robber" OB lex.; < Sum.

šagaṣṣu (or *šagāṣu*) (a bat-like bird or animal) jB lex.

šagaštu → *šaggaštu*

šagāšu(m), OA, OB also *šakāšum* "to kill, slaughter" [OB GAZ?] **G** (*i/i*) of god, king, demon; "slaughter" animal; OB also "maltreat"; OA transf. *raman-*(acc.) *š.* "make every possible effort" **D** as G **N** "be killed"; OA ~ "be ruined"; > *šagšu*; *šaggišu*, *šāgišu*; *šaggāšu*, *šaggāšû*, *šaggaštu*; *šigištum*; *mašgašu*; *mušaggišu*

šagbānu(m) (a disease) O/jB lex., med.; < Sum.?

šagga(m)maḫḫu → *šangammāḫu*

šagganakku → *šakkanakku*

šaggapūru → *šagapūru*

ša(g)gaštu(m), *ša(g)galtu* "slaughter, murder" Bab., M/NA; OB lex. *ša š.* "murderer"; < *šagāšu*

šaggāšu(m); f. *šaggaštu* "murderer" O/jB of demons, fate, men; < *šagāšu*

šaggāšû "murderous" jB; < *šagāšu*

šaggišu "murderous; murderer" j/NB of men; also mythical draught animal; < *šagāšu*

šaggu, *saggu* "stiff, tense" M/jB of muscles, tendons; < *šagāgu*

šaggûm → *šangû*

šaggumūtu "yelling, wailing"? jB; < *šagāmu* II

šaggûtum → *šangûtu*

šagigannakku (a vessel) jB lex.; < Sum.

šagiggu → *šagikku*

šagigu(r)rû(m) "free-will offering" Bab. [ŠÀ.GI(4)/IGI.GURU6(-)] sheep, grain etc.; < Sum.

šagikku, *šagiggu* j/NB **1.** "spleen" [UZU.ŠÀ.GIG] **2.** (a vessel); < Sum.

šagiltum → *šigiltu*

šagimmatu "roar, cry" jB; < *šagāmu* II

šagimmu → *šagīmu*

šagimtu → *šakintu*

šagīmu, *šagimmu* "roaring, clamour" jB of gods; men; < *šagāmu* II

šāgimu MA, jB of lion "roaring", of donkey "braying", of storm "thundering"; < *šagāmu* II

šagīru (an impurity in gold) NB (or → *sakru* ?)

šāgišu "murderer" jB; < *šagāšu*

šaglû → *šuglû*

šagšu(m) "slain; afflicted, oppressed" O/jB; < *šagāšu*

šagûm → *šegû* I

šagubbu (a vessel) jB lex., used in brewing; < Sum.

šagunnu (a vessel) jB lex.

šagurrû "compassion" jB lex.; < Sum.

šagușșu (a vessel) jB lex.

šaḫâ "at an angle" (to each other) jB; < *šaḫātu* I

šaḫādum "to give, present" OB **G**; < W.Sem.

šaḫāḫu(m) "to become loose, fall out; disintegrate; disappear" **G** (*u*/*u*) of hair, wool; teeth; gemstones; med. gall-, kidney stones; flesh; of people "become powerless"? **Gtn** iter. of G **D** "waste" flesh, body; "make (hair) fall out"; OA "corrode" metal **Dt** pass. of D **Ntn** "suffer continual loss" (of hair or teeth ?); > *šiḫḫatu*; *šaḫḫīḫu*; *išḫiḫatum*?

šaḫallûm; pl. Ug. *saḫallētu*? (a vessel)? OB, Ug.; < Sum.?

šaḫālu(m) "to sieve, filter" **G** (pres. *išaḫḫal*) **D** lex.?; > *šaḫlu*; *šiḫlu* I; *šiḫiltu*; *šāḫilu*; *mašḫalu*, *mašḫaltu*; → *saḫālu* G

šaḫa[mēlu?] "pig-man" jB lex.; < *šaḫû* I + *awīlu*

šaḫānu(m) "to be(come) hot" Bab. **G** (*u*/*u*; stat. *šaḫun*) of weather; heart **Gt** (also *a*/*a*) "warm o.s. in" (= acc.) sun's heat (*ṣētu*) **D** "heat up" person, water, medicine **Dt** pass. of D **N** "become hot"; > *šaḫnu*; *šuḫnu*; *šuḫīnu*; *mušeḫḫittu*; *mašḫantu*; *mušaḫḫinu*

šaḫ api → *šaḫapu*

šaḫapiš "like a wild boar" jB [ŠAḪ.GIŠ.GI-*iš*]; < *šaḫapu*

šaḫappu (a fish) jB lex.; < Sum.

šaḫapu, *šaḫḫapu*, *šaḫ api* "wild boar" O/jB, MA [ŠAḪ.(MEŠ.)GIŠ.GI(.MEŠ/ḪI.A)]; < *šaḫû* I + *apu* I; > *šaḫapiš*

šaḫargû → *saḫargû*

šaḫarru I, *šuḫarru*, *šuḫarrû* ~ "porous"? Ug., jB **1.** of vein in eye **2.** of pottery vessels [SÁḪAR]; also f. as subst. *šaḫarratu*, *šuḫarratu* jB lex.; < Sum.; → *šuḫurru*

šaḫarru(m) II, *šaḫirru(m)*, *saḫa*/*irru*; pl. m. & f. **1.** (a net for carrying straw, barley etc.) OA, O/jB [SA.ḪIR] **2.** (worker using a *š.*), OB lex. also *ša š.*; < Sum.

šaḫaršuppû → *saḫaršuppû*

šaḫartu(m); pl. *šaḫarrātum* ~ "legging(s)" Ass., Ug.

šaḫāru mng. unkn. jB lex. **G**

šaḫātu(m) I; jB pl. also *šaḫātātu* "armpit; side; corner" OA, O/jB of person; bird; house, town; land; OA transf. "assistance, support"; > *šaḫâ*

šaḫātu II (a fetid plant) jB lex.

šaḫātu(m) III, jB also *šaḫāṭu* "to be afraid; fear, hold in awe" **G** (*u*/*u*) **Gt** stat. "is much in awe" **D** "scare, intimidate" **Dt** pass. of D; > *šaḫtu*, *šaḫtiš*; *šiḫittu* III

šaḫātu(m) IV, *šaḫāṭu* "to wash (off, away), rinse, wipe down" **G** (*a*/*u*) also jB mag. "smear" a paste, dust on s.th.; OA transf. "clear" debts ? **D** "wash s.o. down" with beer, water; OA "clear" of obligations **Dt** "wash o.s. down with" **Š** OA "have cleared" of obligations **N** "be washed off, washed away"; transf. in battle "be wiped out"; > *šiḫittum* I

šaḫāṭu(m) I "to jump (on); attack; escape" OAkk, Bab. [GU4.UD] **G** (*i*/*i*; jB pres. once *itaḫḫiṭ*, perf. once *iltikiṭ*) of humans, animals "jump"; "jump out, escape"; "jump on to, attack"; of animal "mount, cover" sexually; of parts of body "pulse, twitch, jerk"; "run away"; of headdress "fall off"; of heavenly bodies "rise"; "skip, omit" lines of verse **Gtn** [GU$_4$.UD.MEŠ] "jump about", "jump in succession", "continually attack", "spring up continually", of fire, lightning; med. "constantly pulse, throb" **D** "attack" **Š** caus. of G "make arise, cause s.o. to jump across" river **N** "be attacked"; > *šeḫṭu*; *išḫiṭum*; *šāḫiṭum*; *mašḫaṭu*; *muštaḫṭu*; *šaḫḫuṭītu*

šaḫāṭu(m) II "to tear away, off, down" **G** (*a/u*) "take off" garment, headdress; "flay" skin; "cast off, remove" guilt, evil; darkness (of eclipse); "form" bricks (by drawing off mould) **D** as G "tear down" roofbeams; of parts of body mng. uncl.; "draw" sword **Š** caus. of G **N** "be removed, stripped off" **Ntn** iter. of N; > *šaḫṭu*; *šiḫṭu* II

šaḫāṭu III (or *šeḫēṭu*) "to be angry, rage" NB **G** (*i/i*) *libbu š.*; > *šuḫṭu*

šaḫāṭu → also *šaḫātu* III.IV

šaḫḫaḫu → *šaḫšaḫḫu*

šaḫḫapu → *šaḫapu*

šaḫḫīḫu; f. *šaḫḫiḫtu* jB **1.** ~ "dissolving, passing" of kidney stone **2.** (an illness); < *šaḫāḫu*

šaḫḫītu, *šaḫḫūtu* "sailing boat" jB [GIŠ.MÁ.ŠÀ.ḪA] (also mag.) model "boat"; < *šaḫḫû*

šaḫḫu (a wooden object)? MA; → *šāḫu*

šaḫḫû(m), *šaḫû* (a linen canvas cloth) Bab., Mari, Bogh. [TÚG.ŠÀ.ḪA]; < Sum.; > *šaḫḫītu*

šaḫḫūtu → *šaḫḫītu*

šaḫḫuṭītu f. "who keeps attacking" jB of sorceress; < *šaḫāṭu* I

šaḫi(l)lu "bucket" NB; < Aram.

šaḫilu; pl. f. (a garment)? NA, NB

šāḫilu "strainer" Mari; "irrigation filter"? NB; < *šaḫālu*

šaḫirēn du.; pl. *šaḫirātum* (an article of footwear or part of one) OA

šaḫirru → *šaḫarru* II

šaḫittu → *šiḫittu* II

šāḫittu (a type of priestess) jB lex.

šāḫittum → also *šiḫittum* I

šaḫītu(m) "sow, female pig" Bab. [MUNUS.ŠAḪ]; < *šaḫû* I

šāḫiṭum "attacker"? OB mng. uncl.; Mari *mār š.* "raider"; < *šaḫāṭu* I

šaḫlātum → *šeḫlātum*

šaḫlu(m) "sieved" OA, jB; < *šaḫālu*

šaḫluqtu(m), Bogh. also *taḫluqtu* "destruction, annihilation; disaster" OAkk, O/jB(lit.) [NÍG.ḪA.LAM.MA; NAM/NÍG.GILIM.MA; ŠA$_4$.ZÁḪ]; < *ḫalāqu* Š

šaḫmu mng. unkn. MA/jB

šaḫmaštum → *saḫmaštu*

šaḫnu; f. *šaḫuntu* "warm" MA?, NB in fPN; < *šaḫānu*

šaḫpu (a metal alloy)? Am.

šaḫrabbūtu "devastation" NB; < *ḫarābu*

šaḫrartu I "deathly hush" jB; < *šuḫarruru* II

šaḫrartu II "devastation" jB; < *šuḫruru*

šaḫratu → *šārtu*

šaḫrûm (an insect)? OB lex.

šaḫsasuttu "recollection, reminder" NA; < *ḫasāsu* Š

šaḫšaḫḫu(m), *šaḫḫaḫu* "slanderer, scandal-monger" O/jB

šaḫšūru → *ḫašḫūru*

šaḫtiṣu → *šaḫtuṣu*

šaḫtiš "reverently, humbly" MB; < *šaḫtu*

šaḫtu, *šaḫṭu* "reverent, humble" M/NB as royal epith.; < *šaḫātu* III

šaḫturrû "piglet" jB; < Sum.

šaḫtuṣu (or *šaḫtiṣu*) mng. unkn. MA

šaḫṭu(m); f. *šaḫittu* "stripped"? of fruit, wood OA, jB; < *šaḫāṭu* II

šaḫṭu → also *šaḫtu*

šaḫû(m) I, Ug. *šeḫû* "pig" **1.** [ŠAḪ; ŠÁḪ] "pig, boar"; jB lex. *š. qaqqari* (an insect) **2.** OB, lex. [GIR.KU$_6$] (a fish) **3.** astr. (a constellation or star, phps.) "Delphinus" [MUL.ŠÁḪ]; < Sum.; > *šaḫītu*; → *šaḫamēlu*; *šaḫapu*

šaḫû II mng. unkn. jB lex.

šaḫû III mng. uncert. jB **G** (*i/i*) of raven (**D** → *šuḫḫû* II-IV)

šaḫû → also *šaḫḫû*

šāḫu(m), OAkk *sāḫum*, *šīḫu(m)*, *sīḫu*, MA *šaḫḫu*?; pl. f. "basin" OAkk, O/jB, MB(Alal.), M/NA [ZA.ḪUM] for drinking or cooking; usu. of metal

šāḫû "upright"? of chest Am.; < Eg.?

šâḫu "to blow" **G** (*ī*) of wind; > *šēḫu*, *šēḫānu*; → *šêḫu*

šâḫu → also *šiāḫu* I

šaḫumaš (a copper object) MB

šaḫunnu "appeasement" jB; < Sum.

šaḫuntu → *šaḫnu*

šaḫuppatu → *suḫuppatum*

šaḫurratu(m) "deathly hush" O/jB also pl.; < *šuḫarruru* II

šaḫurru mng. unkn. jB lex.

šaḫurrurum → *šuḫarruru* II

šaḫurtu mng. unkn. OB(Susa)

šaḫūru(m) I, MA also *šuḫūru* cultic 'summit building'; in Babylonia, shrine on summit; in Assyria, subsidiary building; also *bīt š.* as part of temple; < Sum.

šaḫūrum II, jB *šuḫāru, š/s/z/tuḫru*, also *šiḫru* (a part of the foot) O/jB in *š. šēpi(m)*

šā'iltu(m) **1.** "female diviner" OAkk, OA, O/jB [MUNUS.ENSI] **2.** "praying mantis" jB lex.; < *šā'ilu*

šā'ilu(m) **1.** "asker, one who asks" jB **2.** "dream interpreter" O/jB, NA [LÚ.ENSI]; Am. also "augur" (bird-omen diviner) **3.** "praying mantis" jB lex.; < *šâlu* I

šā'imum "buyer" OA; < *šâmu*

ša'irru, *ša'erru* (a wooden object) jB

šā'iru mng. unkn. Am., jB

ša'ītu (a small liquid measure) Ug.

šā'iṭu(m) "water-drawer"? OB lex., jB; < *šâṭu* I

šâka "you" (2 m. sg. obl.) jB(poet.) (→ GAG §41i-j); → *kâšim*; *kâti*

šakabigalzu → *šagabigalzu*

šakadu "heroic" jB lex.

šakāku(m) "to harrow; thread (on string)" O/jB, MA [UD.DU] **G** (*a/u*) **1.** "harrow" field **2.** "string" beads, gems on string or wire; MA "thread" ears together as punishment **Gtn** OA iter. of G **Gt** OB transf. of fruitless action, uncl. **D** as G 1 and 2 **N** "be strung together"; > *šakku*; *šikkatu* II; *šakīkātu*; *šākikum*; *maškakātu*; *šikkūtu* II

šakalmušu → *šagalmušu*

šakāmu(m) I mng. unkn. OB, NB in PNs, jB lex.

šakāmum II vb. (an activity involving textiles) OB; > *šikimtum*

šakānu(m), Mari also *sakānum*; occas. *šakāmu* ? "to put, place, lay down" [GAR; occas. MAR] **G** (*a/u*) **1.** "set in place" image, stele; ritual equipment, furniture; "deposit" document; "plant" tree, plant; "put on" jewellery, clothing; Am., Ug. "put" to the flames, burn; M/NB *ana utūni š.* "melt down" **2.** stat. *šakin* "is placed, is located, is present" om. of parts, marks, signs; places, water, boundaries; of people "are settled" **3.** "provide, supply with" (= 2 acc.), stat. "is supplied with" of people with jewellery, weapons, hairdo; field, subsistence; "is provided" with part of body, e.g. demon, monstrous birth with head, tail etc.; "apply" plaster to building; "equip" with life, understanding, "mark" with brand **4.** "place" foot, hand etc.; transf. OB(Susa) "place" hand and tongue = "to pledge"; ear, eye, face = "attend" **5.** "put" person(s) on stake, in lap etc.; "appoint, assign, install" to office; "place" as pledge **6.** math. "put down" a number etc. **7.** "impose" tax; victory **8.** "fix, arrange, contrive" time, festival, boundary; assembly, consultation **9.** "confer, issue" decision, pardon **10.** "pronounce, issue" word(s), statement, oath, OB ellipt. "declare, inform" **11.** "make, conclude, establish" agreement, treaty, friendship **12.** "create, cause, bring about" good, evil, light, dark; peace, plenty; flood, trouble, need; freedom, protection; murder, rebellion; defeat; ominous result; cessation of work **13.** "carry out, organize" actions, activities; OB ellipt. "treat, process" dates; NB *ina ṭābti š.* "preserve, salt" **14.** "make, install, set up, establish" road, nest, dwelling, garden plot, account, name i.e. succession **15.** *ana X š.* "convert to, change into", "use as" **Gtn** iter. of G (jB imper. *tišakkan*) [NB GAR.MEŠ ?] **Gt** "place permanently, enduringly", esp. jB var. of G **D** jB/NA "appoint as *šaknu*"? **Š** **1.** caus. of "to place" etc. **2.** caus. of "is present" (*šakin*) "make to be present"; "cause to settle, camp"; "make reside" fear of god in s.o.; "cause to be provided with" **Štn** iter. of Š 2 **N** pass. of G "be put"; of goods "be deposited"; *zīm, pān X naškunu* "have the appearance of, look like"; MB, Am. "come together with s.o."; "become" **Ntn** iter. of N [GAR.GAR]; > *šaknu, šakintu, šaknūtu, šakin ṭēmi, šakin ṭēmūtu*; *šiknat napišti*; *šiknu, šikittu*; *šukuttu* I; *šukānu*; *šākinu, šākinūtum*; *šukunnû*; *šakkinu*; *maškanu, maškānum, maškanūtu, maškattu, maškittu*; *muštaškinu*; *iškinū*; *maškantu*; *šakinnu*; *šikinnu* II; *šikintu*; *taškuttu*?

šakartu "drunkenness" NA; < *šakāru*

šakarûm, *šagarû* (a metal object) Mari, MB(Alal.), Bogh.

šakāru "to be(come) drunk" M/jB, NA **G** (*i/i*) **Gtn** iter. of G **D** "make drunk"; > *šakru* I; *šākiru*; *šakartu*; *šakkarû* I, *šakkurû*; *šakrānû*, *šakkarānû*; *šikaru, šikriš*; *maškuru*?; *maškirtum*

šakāsum "to dry out" (trans.) OB **G** (*u/u* ?) **D** "dry, dry off" **Dt** "be dried off"

šakāṣu(m) ~ "to be wild(-eyed)"? OA; Bogh., jB lex. **G** infin. only **Gt**; > *šakṣu*

šakāšum → *šagāšu*

šakattû(m) (a garment) OAkk, OB, western MB [GADA/TÚG.ŠÀ.GA.DÙ; Bogh. TÚG.ŠÀ.GA.(AN.)DÙ/DUM; GADA/TÚG.ŠÀ.GADA(.DÙ), also GADA.DÙ]; < Sum.

šakātu(m) I ~ "to fetch"? OA, NA **G** OA stat. only **Š** caus. "have fetched"; also OA *pūrī š.* "cast lots"; > *muštakkitum*

šakātu II mng. unkn. jB **G** (*i/i*) **D** only lex.

šakīkātu f. pl. "strung row" MB of aromatics; < *šakāku*

šākikum "one who strings beads" OB lex.; < *šakāku*

šakillu (a wooden structure) NB; also pl. f. as PlN, canal name

šakimtu mng. unkn. jB lex.

šakinnu "date palm sapling" jB lex.; < *šakānu*

šakintu, *šakittu*, NA also *šagimtu* **1.** MB *šakittu* "accumulation" of water **2.** NA (a female official) [MUNUS.GAR] esp. in harems **3.** jB → *šaknu* 1; < *šaknu*

šākintu → *šākinu* 2

šakin ṭēmi, M/NA also *šikin ṭēme*, OB(lit.) *šakinṭēmûm* (a minor administrator); later "provincial governor" Bab., NA [LÚ.GAR.UŠ$_4$] mostly in Babylonia; < *šaknu* + *ṭēmu*

šakin ṭēmūtu "governorship" NB [LÚ.GAR.-UŠ$_4$-]

šākinu(m) 'that places' O/jB **1.** "date palm cultivator" **2.** jB f. *šākintu* "she who performs" ritual; < *šakānu*

šākinūtum "date palm cultivation" OB; < *šākinu*

šakirru; pl. Ug. *sakirrātu* "churn" O/jB for milk; < Sum.

šakirû(m), *šakirūtu(m)* "henbane"? OAkk, O/jB, NA [Ú.ŠAKIRA; Ú.ŠÀKIRA] med., om.; < Sum.

šākiru; pl. *šākirūtu* "drunkard" NA; < *šakāru*

šakirūtu (a type of ritual equipment) jB

šakirūtu → also *šakirû*

šakišānu (a bronze object) MB(Alal.)

šakittu → *šakintu*; *šaknu* 1

šakkabakku(m) (part of a box)? OB, Mari; < Sum.

šakkadirru I, *šikkidirru*, also *šikkê terri* ~ "marten" jB [^{d}NIN.KILIM.TIR.RA]; → *šikkû*

šakkadirru II, *šikkaterru* (a kind of lizard) jB [KUN.DAR]

šakkanakku(m), M/NB also *šakkanku*, Aššur also *ša(n)ganakku*; pl. also f. *šakkanakkātu(m)* **1.** "(military) governor" [(LÚ.)GÌR.NÍTA; NISAG; MB pl. GÌR.NÍTA.GÌR.NÍTA] also as royal title; of underworld deity *š. erṣeti* **2.** OB (a feature of the exta); > *šakkanakkūtu*

šakkanakkūtu "governorship" NA(roy. inscr.); < *šakkanakku*

šakkanku → *šakkanakku*

šakka(n)nu (a type of reed) jB lex.

šakkarānû "drunken, bibulous" jB; < *šakāru*

šakkarû(m) I "drunken, bibulous" O/jB lex.; < *šakāru*

šakkarû II (a stone tool of the reed worker) OB lex., jB

šakkinu(m) **1.** OB (a contractor for date production) **2.** jB lex. (a musician); < *šakānu*

šakkinūtum (date production contract) OB

šakkiru → *sakkiru*

šakkiu → *šakkû*

šakku(m) I "harrowed" O/jB of fields; < *šakāku*

šakku II (a type of wood) MB

šakku III (a garment) Susa

šakku(m) IV (a vessel) Mari; jB lex.

šakkû (or *sakkû*), *š/sakkiu* (a headdress) jB lex.

šakkû → also *sakkû* II

šakkukum (a belt) OA

šakkullu (a wood used for furniture)? M/NA, M/NB, Nuzi [GIŠ.ŠÀ.KAL; NA ŠAG$_4$.UL$_4$] used for chairs, wheels etc.; < Sum.?

šakkurû "drunkard" jB lex.; < *šakāru*

šaklulu → *šuklulu* I.II

šaknatu → *šaknu* 1

šaknu(m) "placed, deposited etc.; governor" **1.** adj., f. *šakintum*, *šakittu(m)*: "deposited", "laid out" garden, building plan; *šaknat*, *šakin napištim/napšātu* "living being(s)"; "equipped (with)" seal **2.** subst.: "appointee", pl. *šaknūti* [LÚ.GAR-*nu-ti/e*; GAR.KUR], esp. Bab., M/NA "governor", *š. māti* "provincial governor"; NA "(military) official"; "representative"; < *šakānu*; > *šaknūtu*; *šakin ṭēmi*

šaknūtu "governorate" M/NB [LÚ.GAR- ; (LÚ.) GAR.KUR-]; < *šaknu*

šakrānû; pl. *šakrānûtu* "drunkard" NA; < *šakāru*

šakru I "drunk; drunkard" jB, NA; < *šakāru*

šakru II "handle" MA, Am.(Mit.) e.g. of bucket

šakṣu(m), Bogh. also *šekṣu* ~ "scowling, glowering" OA in PN, M/jB, also in pred. use; < *šakāṣu*

šakšum → *takšium*

šaktum → *šaqtum*

šaktumu "left covered" NA, of vessel; < *katāmu* Š

šâku → *sâku*; *šâqum* II

šakudu → *šukudu*

šākultu → *šūkultu*; *tākultu*

šākulu → *šūkulu*

šakummû ~ "anxiety"? jB lex.; < Sum.

šakurrum → *šukurru*

šakurû mng. unkn. jB comm.

šākussu → *šūkultu*

šakuttu → *šukuttu* I

šakūzu, Nuzi *šakuzzu* (a bronze object) Nuzi, jB lex.

šalābbīti → *šalāmu* I 2

šalabila (a plant) jB; corrupt form ?

šalādi (a plant) Ug. lex.; corrupt form ?

šalāgu(m) "to snow" Mari, MB **G** (pres. *išallag*); < *šalgu* denom.

šalāḫu(m) "to pull out, uproot" Ass., Am., jB **G** (*a/u*) joint; OA "withdraw" from a partnership, *qaqqad- š.* "withdraw o.s., back out"; OA "dispatch" wares **D** OA as G

šalāḫu → also *salaḫu* I.II

šalakdānum "(a type of) mouse" OB(Susa) lex.; < Sum.

šalāliš "surreptitiously" MB; < *šalālu* II

šalālu(m) I "to carry off, plunder" [IR; LAḪ$_4$] **G** (*a/u*) "carry off" animals, captives, booty; "sack, plunder" city, land **Gtn** "repeatedly carry off" **D** as G ? lex. **N** pass. of G; > *šallu*; *šallūtu*; *šallatu* I, *šillatu* II, *šallatiš*; *šālilu*; *mušallilu*

šalālu(m) II "to creep, slither" O/jB **G** lex. only **N**, **Ntn** (*našallulu(m)*, *itašlulu(m)*;→ GAG §101g) [NIM.NIM] "crawl (continually)" of snake, worm; med., uncert. mng. of parts of body; > *šalāliš*; *mašallu*?, *mušlālu*?

šalālu(m) III "to commit an act of impudence" OA; jB lex. **G** (pres. *išallal*) **Gt** as G **D** lex. only; > *šillatu* I; *šillannû*

šalālu → also *qan šalālu*

šalamdu → *šalamtu*

šalamtiš, NB *šalamtaš* "like a corpse" j/NB

šalamtu(m), M/NB also *šalamdu*; pl. *šalmātu* "corpse" (lit.) [AD$_6$ (also = *pagru*)] of human being, god

šalāmu I (as subst.) **1.** MB, Am. [SILIM-] "peace, well-being" **2.** *šalām(u) bīti*, *šalābbīti*, also *šullum bīti*; pl. *šalām bītānu* "well-being of the temple" (a cultic ceremony) NA, NB [SILIM-*mu* É-] **3.** NB *lā šalām(u)* "incorrect, unseemly behaviour" **4.** *š. šamši* "sunset; west" M/jB(Ass.), Am., jB; < *šalāmu* II infin.

šalāmu(m) II "to be(come) healthy, intact" [SILIM(=DI); NB GI] **G** (*i/i*, OAkk, Mari also *a/a*) **1.** of people, lands etc. "be(come) healthy, well"; freq. in PNs; "have success etc." in commerce, in law; OB of woman "be safely delivered (of)" child (= acc.); of people, caravans, ships, tablets "get to destination safely" **2.** of sum of money, tablet, part of body, liver "be complete, perfect"; of life, temple "remain intact" **3.** of spell, sheep-shearing, work, house, rites "be completed, finished"; of event "come to pass" **4.** MA, NB "be satisfied with, be paid off in full with" **5.** of omen "be favourable" **6.** Ug. stat. "is at peace" (for *salāmu* II) **D** "keep well, intact; pay off in full", of god sustaining persons, esp. in PNs; "give well-being" of house, city, land; "look after well"; "keep in order, administer"; "heal, improve"; "deliver safely, in good order"; "hand over, pay in full"; "meet (claim) in full, make restitution"; "complete, carry out in full" responsibilities, commands; "make ready, finish"; "complete, reach end of" a period of time **Dtn** astr. uncl. **Dt** Mari "be entrusted, commissioned"? **Dtt** NA pass. of D ?; > *šalmu* I.II; *šalimtu*, *šalmiš*, *šalmūtu*, *šalimuttu*; *šulmu*, *šulmāniš*, *šulmānu*, *šulmānūtu*; *šalāmu* I; *šallāmu*; *šullumu*, *šullumtu*; *šulummû*; *našlamtu*; *tašlimtu*; *mušallimu*; *mušallimānu*; → *šalamtu*; *šalummu*; *tašlamtu*

šalânū- "without" NB, with pron. suff. *šalânūa*, *-ukka*, *-uššu*, *-unnu* "without my/your/his/our permission"; < *ša* + *lā* + *-ān*

šalāpu(m) "to pull out, draw, unsheathe"; Ass. "wipe" O/jB, M/NA **G** (*a/u*, once *i/i*) "tear out" tongue; "draw" sword etc.; "extract" person, brick **D** as G "tear out, away; take out" **N** of tongue "be pulled out"; of dagger "be drawn"; > *šilpu*, *šiliptum*; *šālipu*, *šāliptu*; *našlaptu*

šalāqu(m) "to cut open" OAkk, O/jB, NA **G** (*a/u*) sheep, leather bottle, shoe, mouth, of god ref. to childbirth **D** as G "cut open" camels; "lacerate" garment; > *šilqum*; *šulluqu*; *tašliqtu*

šalāš st. abs.; f. *šalāšat*; nom. f. *šalaštu(m)*, MA, M/NB *ša/elaltu*, NA **šalassu* "three" [3(=EŠ$_5$, more rarely EŠ$_{16}$)] (→ GAG §69); > *šalāš...*, *šalš...*; *šālišu*; *šulultu*, *šuluštu*; *šulšu*; *šullušu* I, *šullušiš*, *šullul*; *šullušû*; *šulūšā*, *šulūšā'um*; *šulušīu*; *šušlušu*; *šušalšum*; *tašlīšu*

šalāšā, *šelāšā*, OB also *šalāšu* "thirty" [30]; < *šalāš*; > *šalāšā'û*, *šalāšû*

šalāšā'û, *šalāšāmû* "one-thirtieth" NB [30-*'u-ú*]; < *šalāšā*

šalāšī-, NB *šelāšī-* "thrice, three times" OA (*ana*) *š.-šu*; OB *adi*, *ana*, *kīma š.-šu*; M/jB *š.-šu*; NB *adi š.-šu*; < *šalāš*

šalāšiu "third" M/NA; also "of third size"; < *šalāš*

***šalaššer**; f. *šalaššeret* "thirteen" OB; < *šalāš* + *ešer*

šalaššerītum "one-thirteenth" OB (st. constr. *šalašeriat*); < *šalaššer*

šalaššerû "thirteenth" MB; < *šalaššer*

šalaššumma in *š. epēšu* "to adopt as daughter" Nuzi; < Hurr.

šalaštu → *šalāš*

šalāšu(m) "to do for a third time, three times" **G** (OA, OB *i/i*, j/NB *a/u*) **D** as G work on field, march, divination; "make threefold" thickness; math. "multiply by three" **Š** "make triple" yarn; < *šalāš*

šalāšu → also *šalāšā*

šalāšû, *šelāšû* "thirtieth day of month" jB; < *šalāšā*

šalatti(n)num (an illness) OB, jB lex.

šalāṭu(m) I "to rule, be in authority" **G** (*a/u*, NA, also jB *i/i*) "rule, control" person(s); "have (political/commercial) control over"; OA stat. "is available" **Gt** "be more powerful"; "have precedence" **D** OA **Dt** "be authorized, impose o.'s authority" **Š** "give authority over"; > *šalṭu* I.II; *šalṭiš*; *šalṭāniš*; *šulluṭu*; *šitluṭu*, *šitluṭiš*

šalāṭu(m) II "to cut (into)"? Bab. **G** (*a/u*) foot; earth; > *šilittu*

šalāṭu → also *salātu* II

šalā'um ~ "to wrong, do wrong" OA **G** (*a/a*); → *salā'u* I

šalā'u → also *šalû* II

šalbābu **1.** "wise"? (a title of Marduk) jB also as epith. of other gods **2.** of sword = *šalbubu*; < *labābu*

šalbubu(m) "furious" O/jB; as epith. of Enlil; < *labābu*; → *šalbābu* 2

šalgu(m), Mari once *salku* "snow; sleet"; > *šalāgu*

šalḫiu → *šalḫû* I

šalḫu (a linen garment for divine statues) j/NB

šalḫû(m) I, *šalḫiu*, O/jB *šulḫû(m)*, *sulḫû* "outer wall, enceinte" Bab., M/NA [BÀD.ŠUL.ḪI]; < Sum.?

šalḫû II, *šulḫû* (a wooden grille)? jB lex.

šālibu → *šālipu*

šaliḫatu (an aromatic) NB

šaliḫtu mng. uncert. jB

šālilu "plunderer" jB lex.; < *šalālu* I

šalimtu(m), NA also *šalintu*, NB *šalindu* **1.** Bab., NA "well-being", *š. šaknat* "good fortune is decreed" to s.o. **2.** j/NB, NA "righteousness" **3.** "favourable area, side" of the exta; < *šalmu* I

šalimuttu (a temple payment)? MA; < *šalāmu* II

šalindu → *šalimtu*

šālinnu(m) **1.** OA (a type of sheep) **2.** MB (a metal object)

šalintu → *šalimtu*; *šalmu* I

šalippūtum → *šeleppūtu*

šāliptu (a utensil) NA; < *šalāpu*

šālipu, *šālibu* (a profession) NA; < *šalāpu*

šališium "three-year-old" OA of animals; < *šalāš*

šalištum "group of threee" OA; < *šalāš*

šalištum → also *šalšu*

šālišu(m) "third" OA, OB(Susa); < *šalāš*

šalittu → *šalṭu* I.II

šallabā/īnu → *šallapānu*

šallaḫurû → *sallaḫurû*

šallāmu "friend" Ug. for *salmu*; < *šalāmu* II

šallapānu, *šallabā/īnu*, *šellebēnu* (a grass)? M/jB lex., med.

šal(la)pittu jB lex. **1.** (a clay plaster) **2.** (shoes so treated)

šallariš "as (with) wall plaster" NB

šallaru, Ass. *ši/ellaru(m)* **1.** "wall plaster" **2.** jB lex. (a type of groats)

šallatālu mng. unkn. jB lex.

šallatiš "as booty" jB in *š. manû* "to reckon as booty"; < *šalālu* I

šallatu(m) I "plundered thing(s), booty" [NAM.RA; OAkk NAM.RA.AK; jB NAM.RI]; of people; "despoliation" of divine statues; OB lex. *ša š.* "captor" or "captive"; < *šalālu* I

šallatum II (a heavy cloth) OAkk for chariots

šallatu → also *šillatu* I

šallaṭu → *šalṭu* III

šallu "plundered; (taken) captive" M/NA, M/jB people, gods; also possessions; < *šalālu* I

šallum/ntu → *šullumtu*

šallurānu "noise of wailing"? jB lex.

šallurtum "plum"? OB as fPN; < *šallūru*

šallūru(m), Nuzi also *šannūru* (a fruit, phps.) "plum" Bab., NA [GIŠ.ŠENNUR] tree, fruit; in med.; OB also as PN; < Sum.

šallussu → *šullušu* I 2

šallūtu "state of captivity" MB(Ass.) in *šallūssu(nu)* "in captivity"; < *šallu*

šalmātu → *šalamtu*; *šalimtu*; *šalmu* I

šalmiš "well, in safety" M/NB; < *šalmu* I

šalmu(m) I; f. *šalim/ntu* "intact, healthy, sound" [SILIM(=DI)] animal, person; "solvent, prosperous"; "undamaged, complete" tablet, ship etc.; "sincere, correct" speech; "favourable" omen, dream, month, day; jB *lā šalimtu/šalmātu* "lies; insincere words"; < *šalāmu* II; > *šalmūtu*, *šalmiš*, *šalimtu*; → *salmu*

šalmu II "peace" Am. for *salīmu*; < *šalāmu* II

šalmūtu(m) "well-being, health, good condition" Bab., esp. with pron. suff. in adv. use, e.g. *šalmūssa/u* "in good condition"; < *šalmu* I

šalpittu → *šallapittu*

šalputtu, jB lex. *šulputtu* "ruination" M/NB [ḪUL]; of home, city, land; < *lapātu* Š

šalšā'a → *šalšāya*

šalšāmi → *šalšūmi*

šalšatu → *šalšu*

šalšāya, *šalšā'a* "third brother, son" j/NB; < *šalšu*

šalšene → *šaluššani*

šalšerīšu "thirteen times" OB; < *šalāš*

šalšiānu/i, Nuzi *šaššiāna* "for the third time" M/NA, Nuzi; < *šalšu*

šalšiš "thirdly" Bab.; < *šalšu*

šalšu(m), *šaššu(m)*; f. *šalištum*, *šaluštu(m)*, *šalultu*, NA *šalussu*, MB also *šalšatu* **1.** "third" [3.KAM(.MA)]; *š. qatnu*, *uḫrim* (desig. of lyre strings); *šalšatu* (a musical interval) **2.** "one-third" [IGI.3.GÁL; ŠUŠANA ? (→ *šuššu* I du.)] OB st. abs. *ana šaluš* "at one-third"; OA *ana šalšīšu* "into three parts", f. pl. OA, OB "portion of one-third", of beer, proportion of 1:3, jB "tax of one-third"; < *šalāš*; → *šulšu*; *šulultu*; *šuluštu*; *šaluštu*

šalšūma (a bronze object) Ug.

šalšūmi, NA *(iš)šaššūme*, Am. *šalšāmi*, Nuzi also *šalušmu* "the day before yesterday" O/MB, NA; NA in *(it)timāli (iš)šaššūme* "in the recent past"; < *šalšu* + *ūmu* I

šalšūtī-, *šaššūtī-* "for the third time" M/NB e.g. *šalšūtīya/šu*; < *šalšu*

šalti → *šatti*

šāltum "interrogation" OB; < *šâlu* I

šalṭāniš "in triumph" j/NB with *alāku* Gtn; < *šalṭu* I

šalṭiš "imperiously, triumphantly, with authority" Bab.(lit.); < *šalṭu* I

šalṭu(m) I "authoritative; having authority" Bab., MA also as PN; OA *ana š. šakānum* "to treat harshly"?; < *šalāṭu* I; > *šalṭāniš*, *šalṭiš*

šalṭum II "freely available" OA of goods; as subst. f. pl. *šalṭātum* "available (goods)"; also of merchants mng. uncl.; < *šalāṭu* I

šalṭu III, *šallaṭu*, NA *salṭu* "bow-case" NA, NB of leather; < Aram.

šalû(m) I, *salû* "to submerge, immerse o.s. in" Bab. **G** (mostly *i/i*) in river ordeal; transf. of lines on palm "are sunken"? **Gtn** iter. of G **Š** "subject s.o. to the river ordeal"; > *šalû* IV; *mašlû*; → *šīlu* I

šalû(m) II, *salû*, NA *šalā'u*, NB *šelû* "to fling, cast away" Bab., NA **G** (mostly *u/u;* pres. also *išalla*) "throw" spittle; weapon; earth, soil; "cast off" child by sale; of heart "devoted"? to king; "pelt" s.o. with s.th. (= 2 acc.) **D** "pelt" with rain **N** pass. of G; > *šilūtu* I

šalû III, lex. *salû* "to tear to pieces"? jB **G** (*i/i*) **D**

šalû IV "submerged" jB crops; < *šalû* I

šâlu(m) I, *ša'ālu(m)* "to ask" **G** (pres. OB and occas. jB *išâl*, pl. *išallū*; otherwise *iša''al*; pret. *išāl*, *iš'al*) "ask, question (s.o.)"; "ask about, inform o.s. about" esp. *šulum X š.* "ask after s.o.'s health"; Mari, Am. "call to reckoning, punish" **Gtn** iter. of G "ask around, repeatedly"; "interrogate, cross-examine" **Gt** "ask o.s., consider, reflect" about s.th. (= acc.); "consult, take advice"; "cross-question" s.o. about s.th. (= 2 acc.) **D** "(cross-)question" **N** "be questioned"; > *šāltum*; *šā'ilu*, *šā'iltu*; *šitūlu*; *šitūltu*; *maš'alu*, *maš'altu*, *muštālu*, *muštālūtum*

šâlu II "to rejoice" jB **Dt** only (3 f. *tultīal*); > *tašīltu*

šâlu → also *šiālu*

šalultu → *šaluštu*

šalummatu(m) ~ "radiance" Bab., Bogh., Ug. [SU.LIM; SU.ZI] of deities, king, temple, cult furnishings; weapons; heavenly body; Qatna (a type of metal jewellery); < *šalummu*

šalummu "radiant" jB, NA of deity; king; > *šalummatu*

šaluppû (part of intestines)? jB lex.; < Sum.

šalussu → *šalšu*

šalussû (part of intestines) jB lex.; < Sum.

šaluš → *šalšu* 2

šalušene → *šaluššani*

šalušmu → *šalšūmi*

šaluššani, Ass. *šal(u)še/ine* "the year before last" OB, Nuzi, NA; < *šalšu* + *šattu*

šaluštu, *šalultu* "group of three" jB lex.; < *šalšu*; → *šalištum*

šamādu mng. unkn. M/NA, jB **G** (*i/i*) **D** stat. MA "are attached"?

šamagu(m) (an illness) OB

šamāḫu(m) I, once *šamāku* "to grow, flourish; be magnificent" **G** (*u/u*; stat. *šamuḫ*) of deity esp. in PNs, kingship; of vegetation; of people "flourish, attain extraordinary beauty or stature" **D** "make flourish" people; also in PNs; "make huge" **Dtn** iter. of D **Ntn** for Gtn ?; > *šamḫu*, *šamḫatum*, *šamḫiš*; *šumḫu*; *šammaḫu*; *šummuḫu*; *našmaḫum*

šamāḫum II ~ "to break an agreement" OA **G** (*u/u*); > *našmaḫtum*

šamakātā "onions" NB; < Aram.

šamāku → *šamāḫu* I

šamallû(m), OAkk, OA *šamallā'um*; jB also *šamlû* 'purse-bearer' **1.** Bab., OA "merchant's assistant" [LÚ.ŠÁMAN.LÁ]; also as PN **2.** j/NB, NA "(scribal, priestly) apprentice, novice" [LÚ.ŠÁMAN.MÁL.LÁ; (LÚ.)ŠAB.TUR]; < Sum.

šamallûtu(m) **1.** OB, Nuzi "position of merchant's assistant" **2.** NB "apprenticeship" [LÚ.ŠÁMAN.LÁ-]; < *šamallû*

šamāmiš "to heaven" Bab.(lit.) also "like heaven"; < *šamāmū*

šamāmu ~ "to injure" jB **G** (*a/u*) of demon; of part of body "cause (s.o.) pain" **D** as G **Ntn** "become injured"? jB lex.; > *šimmatu*

šamāmū "heavens" Bab.(poet.) for *šamû* I; NB *ina šamāmū libbi* "in the inmost part of the heart"?; < *šamû* I; > *šamāmiš*

šamānat, šamāne → *samāne*

šamanu → *šamnu*

šāmarītu mng. unkn. jB

šamāru(m) I "to rage, be furious" Bab., NA **G** (*u/u*; stat. *šamur*) of deity, demon; sorcerer, warrior; horse; snake; river **Gtn** ? iter. of G **Gt** OB ~ "be troublesome"; M/jB "be furious, attack furiously" **D** as G NA in PN of Adad **Š** jB "make rage" weapon; heart; "put (horses) to gallop"; > *šamru* I, *šamriš*; *šumru*; *šammaru*; *šitmuru*, *šitmuriš*, *šitmāru*

šamāru(m) II O/jB **G** "to gloat"? over (= *eli*; *ina muḫḫi*) s.o. **Gtn** iter.? for Gt "praise" **Gt** (imper. also *tišmar*; prec. also *lištammar*) "praise (god)" esp. in PNs, prayers **D** = Gt ? lex.

šamašīšu (a bronze object) Ug.

šamaškillānu (a type of onion) jB lex.

šamaški(l)lu(m), *šusikillu*, Mari also *šumatkilu* (a type of onion) Bab., NA [SUM.SIKIL.(LUM.) SAR; in Mari also SUM.KI.SIKIL, SUM.SIKIL.LA, SUM.SAR.SIKIL; NA also Ú.SUM.SIKIL(.SAR); NB also ŠE.SUM.SIKIL]; < Sum.

šamaššammū, *šamšamū* "sesame" [ŠE.GIŠ.Ì; Mari, OB(Rimah), MA, Nuzi ŠE.Ì.GIŠ(.MEŠ); OAkk GIŠ.Ì]; mostly pl.; < *šaman* + *šammī* 'plant-oil'?

šamātu, *šemētu* "to mark (with sign of ownership), brand" Mari, M/NB; Mari "paint" **G** (*i/i*; stat. 3 f. *šendet*) sheep, cattle; slaves, deserters; house **D** jB lex.; < *šimtu*, > *šāmitu*, *šendu*

šamātu → also *šamāṭu* I.II

šamâtu → *šamiātum*

šamāṭu(m) I, *šamātu(m)* "to tear away, tear down" **G** (*a/u*) flowers, twigs, dates; objects; excess of share; "snatch (s.o.)" from need **D** as G of storm "pluck" quills from wings **Št** mng. unkn. **N** pass. of G; > *šimṭum*; *šāmiṭu* I.II; *šummuṭu* I; *našmaṭu*

šamāṭu(m) II, *šamātu* ~ "to be sunken, flattened"? O/jB **G** (stat. only) of part of body, exta **D** "flatten"?; > *šamṭu* I; *šummuṭu* II

šamā'u → *šemû*

šamā'ū → *šamāmū*; *šamû* I

šamāyû(m) "heavenly, from heaven"? **1.** O/MB, MA$^?$ as PN, also OB fPN *Šamāyâtum* **2.** jB *šamāyâtu*, *šimmāyâtu* (a mineral); < *šamû* I

šambaliltu(m), *šabbaliltu*, *šammu baliltu* "fenugreek" [Ú/ŠE.SULLIM(.SAR)]; → *šammu*

šambilu → *šabbilu*

šāme'ānu "hearsay witness" MA; < *šemû*

šameru → *šawirum*

šamêša → *šamû* I

šamḫatum, *šamkatum*, *šamuḫ/ktu(m)* O/jB **1.** "prostitute"; as fPN in Gilg. **2.** "voluptuous" as fPN; < *šamḫu*

šamḫiš "proudly"? jB; < *šamḫu*

šamḫu(m), once *šanḫu*; f. *šamuḫtu(m)* "luxuriant, lush" O/jB; of vegetation; "prosperous" of persons; as PN; "luxuriant" pasture; < *šamāḫu* I; > *šamḫatum*, *šamḫiš*

šamḫūtu mng. unkn. jB lex.

šamiātum, *šamâtu(m)* f. pl. "rain" OB; < *šamû* II

šaminānu → *šamnānu*

šāmitu "brander, marker" NB of slaves etc.; < *šamātu*

šamīṭu → *samīdu* II

šāmiṭu I, *šamiṭṭu*, *sāmiṭu*, *šumittu* (an alkaline plant) jB; < *šamāṭu* I

šāmiṭu(m) II (an occupation involving processing barley) OB lex., jB; < *šamāṭu* I

šamkānum I "servant" OAkk (as PN), OA, OB

šamkānum II mng. unkn. OB topog. desig.

šamkatum → *šamḫatum*

šamlû → *šamallû*

šammaḫu "very prosperous" O/jB; < *šamḫu*

šammāḫu "large intestine; paunch" jB; < Sum.

šammaktum mng. unkn. OAkk fPN ?, OB PlN

šammānum (a snake) OB

šammaru "very furious" jB of god, demon; < *šamāru* I

šammaṣu → *šamūṣu*

Šamme(na) (a month) MB(Alal.); < Hurr.?

šammirānû mng. uncert. jB

šammu(m) **1.** "plant(s); grass, herb" [Ú] as pasture, fodder; *š. kirî* "garden plant"; med., mag. *š. ša alādi* "birth plant" as medicinal herb; *š. Šamaš* "sunflower" jB [Ú.^{d}UTU]; "herbal infusion" to be drunk **2.** "emery" O/jB [NA$_4$.Ú]; > *šamaššammū*; *šambaliltu*

šammû mng. unkn. jB

šammūtum mng. unkn. OB math.

***šamnānu**, *šaminānu* 'fatty' NB of dates; < *šamnu*

šamnu(m), NA also *šamanu* "oil; fat; cream" [Ì(.MEŠ); Ì.GIŠ (→ also *ellu* II)] culinary and for anointing (mostly sesame, in Ass. occas. olive); for divination; *š. ṭābu(m)* "fine oil"; aromatic "oil" of trees, e.g. myrtle, cedar; "grease" from bitumen; "mineral oil"; animal "fat"; *š. libbim* "stomach fat"; from fish, bird, snake; mag. "cream" of cow; Am. *bīt š.* "oil container"; > *šamnānu*; *šummunu*; → *šamaššammū*

šamriš "furiously, impetuously" O/jB deity, king, demon; < *šamru* I

šamru(m) I "furious, impetuous" O/jB, NA deity, king, demon; tempest, flood, light; onslaught, weapons; < *šamāru* I; > *šamriš*

šamru II (a plant) jB lex.

šamrû "fattened" MA; < *marû* II

šamšāli → *amšāli*

šamšamū → *šamaššammū*

šamšatu(m) "(sun-)disc" [AŠ.ME; ᵈUTU.MEŠ] as cult ornament, usu. of metal; astr. "parhelion; paraselene"; < *šamšu*

šamšiš, *šaššiš* "like the sun" jB [ᵈUTU-]; < *šamšu*

šamšu(m), later also *šanšu*, *šaššu* OB occas. f. "sun; sun-god; (sun-)disc; gold" [ᵈUTU; astr. 20; AŠ.ME] **1.** "sun" (→ *erēbu* I G; *šalāmu* I;*waṣûm* G 3); epith. or desig. of god, king; other person as protector, patron **2.** "Šamaš" **3.** "day(time)"; OA *ina šamši* ... "on the day that ..., as soon as ..." **4.** "sun(-disc)" as symbol, jB pl. *šam/nšānu*, also *šanšānāti* **5.** *šaššu* poet. "gold" **6.** lex. *aban š.* (a stone weight); > *šamšatu*; *šamšiš*; *šaššāniš*; *šaššantu*

šamtaknaya → *šumatakānu*

šāmtum; pl. *šāmātum* "purchase"? OA, OB ?; < *šâmu*

šamṭu I, *šanṭu* "torn loose" j/NB **1.** lex. of grain **2.** (a fabric of *šimṭu* wool)?; < *šamāṭu* II

šamṭu II, *samṭu* (a foreign name for the acacia) jB in plant list

šamṭû "weakened" MA, of eyes; < *maṭû* II

šamû I, *šamā'ū*, Am., Ug. etc. *samû*, NB also *šawû* mostly pl. tant. "sky, heaven" [AN] **1.** as natural phenomenon and as seat of gods; OB *šamêša*? "heavenwards"; jB upper, middle, lower heaven; *kīma š.* "as high as the sky" **2.** NB golden "baldachin"; *š. pî* "roof of mouth"?; *š. libbi* mng. uncl.; > *šamāmū*, *šamāmiš*; *šamû* II; *šamāyû*

šamû(m) II f.; pl. *šamâtu(m)* "rain" O/jB [AN]; < *šamû* I; > *šamūtu*, *šamiātum*

šamû → also *šawû* II; *šemû*

šāmu(m) "purchased" Ass. [(LÚ.)ŠÁM]; NA *mār š.* (a social class); < *šâmu*

šāmu → also *sāmu*

šâmu(m), *ša'āmum* "to buy, purchase" (from = *itti*, *išti/u*) [ŠÁM; MB IN.ŠI/ŠE.(IN.)SA₁₀] **G** (pres. *išâm*, *išammū*, OAkk, OA *iša''am*; pret. *išām*, OAkk, OA, MB *iš'am*; stat. *šām*, *ša'im*) **Gtn** iter. of G (imper. pl. *tišāmā*) "make separate purchases of" **N** (OA pres. *iššaʼʼam*, pret. *iššiʼim*) pass. of G; > *šā'imum*; *šāmu*, *šāmtum*, *šāmūtum*; *šīmu* I.II, *šīmūtu*; *šiāmātu*; *šāyimānu*, *šāyimānūtu*

šâmu → also *šiāmu*

ša-muḫḫi-ālūtu "town supervisorship" NB; < *ālu* I

šamuḫtu → *šamḫatum*; *šamḫu*

šamuktu → *šamḫatum*

šamunakku (a type of flour) jB lex.; < Sum.

šamūṣu, *šammaṣu* (a plant) jB lex.

šamūšu(m) "second string (of lyre)" O/jB [MB wr. *šá*-GI₆(=*mūšu*)]; < Sum.

šamuttu → *šumuttu*

šamūtu(m) f. sg. "rain" O/jB; Gilg. "rain" of wheat, fish etc.; *š. ṭuḫdi* "rain of plenty"; < *šamû* II

šāmūtum "purchase" OA *kasap š.* "purchase money"; < *šâmu*

šanā "two each, two by two" OA; < *šina* II

šanadu → *šannadu*

šanādu/û → *šanūdu*

šanāḫu → *šanā'u*

šanā'iyu "second; of second rank, size" MA [2-]; < *šanû* I

šanakkum (or *šanaqqum*) (a container for grain)? OA

šanannu, *sanannu*, *ašannu* "chariot-archer" MB(Alal.), Ug.; Ug. pl. *-ma*; Hurr. suff. *-ḫe*; < Ug.

šanānu(m) "to equal, rival" [SÁ(=DI)] **G** (*a/u*) "be(come) equal to s.o.", "put (o.s.) on a par with"; of temple "reach up to" the sky; astr. "be level with"; *lā šanān* "incomparable, without rival" [NU.SÁ.A] **Gtn** iter. of G "compete with severally"; of Gt "continually contest" **Gt** (jB pret. also *ištanun*) "equal one another, compete, contest" [SÁ.SÁ; OAkk UR.UR] with (= *itti*) god, death etc.; absol. pl. "compete"; om. "be alike"; as G "reach up to" **D** OA "replicate, bring in equivalent numbers of" witnesses; Am. erron. for G "be equal"? **Dt** Am. "struggle" of soldiers **N** "be compared, comparable" with (= *itti*); esp. neg. "be incomparable, unrivalled" of lordship, onslaught, command etc.; > *muštašnintu*; *šinnatu*, *šinintu*; *šāninu*; *šitnunu*, *šitnuntu*; *šannunātum*; *tašnīnu*, *tašnintu*

šanaqqum → *šanakkum*

šanāqu → *sanāqu* I

šanassu(m) "every year, annually" OB; < *šattu*

šanāṣu ~ "to sneer, scoff at" Bab. **G** (*i/i*) also of animal "bare the teeth at" **Gtn** Am. *iltannaṣ* ? iter. of G; > *šinṣu*

šanāšu → *sanāšu*

šanat → *šattu*

šanātu (or *šanâtu*) (oil-bearing aromatic plant) MA

šanātu → also *šattu*

šanâtu → *šanātu*

šanā'u, *šanāḫu*, *šanû* ~ "to block, block off" jB, NA **G** (*a/u*) "stifle"; "block" with dry matter **Gtn** iter.? **D** stat. of eyes "are suffused" with blood **Dt** ~ D stat.; > *šini'tu*

šanā'u → also *šanû* III.IV

šana''udu → *šanūdu*

šanā'um "for a second time" OA; "at two" (minas ?); → *šanā*

šandabakku(m), *šaddabakku* Bab. **1.** OB, Mari "chief accountant" [GÁ.DUB.BA] **2.** M/NB (the governor of Nippur) [LÚ.GÚ.EN.NA] **3.** Ug., jB "calculation table(t)"; < Sum.; > *šandabakkūtu*

šandabakkūtu(m) "post of chief accountant" Mari; "governorship of Nippur" MB [GÚ.EN.NA-]; < *šandabakku*

šandalippu → *šindilippu*

šandalum, *šaddalu*; pl. f. (a copper vessel) OB, Mari; jB lex. [ŠEN.DIL; ŠEN.DA.LÁ]; < Sum.

šandanakku → *saddanakku*

šandilippu → *šindilippu*

šanduntum → *šadduttu*

šanduppu(m), OA *šadduppum* "ring"; "(detention) ring, shackle" for prisoner; "(ornamental) ring" in stone

šanduppû, *šadduppû* "son" jB lex., also in col.; < Sum.

šanduttum → *šadduttu*

šanênu → *šaniānu*

šangagallu "high priest" jB lex.; < Sum.

šanga(m)māḫu, *šagga(m)maḫḫu* (an exorcist) jB [(LÚ.)SÁNGA.MAḪ with graphic var.s] esp. of god Kusu; as title of prominent exorcists; < Sum.

šanganakku → *šakkanakku*

šangû(m), *šaggûm*, OA *sangûm* "priest, temple manager" [(LÚ.)SANGA; É.BAR] *š. rabû*, *šaniu* "chief, deputy *š.*"; Ass. as royal title; < Sum.

šangûtu(m), *šaggûtum*, NA also *sangûtu* "priesthood, post of *šangû*" O/jB, M/NA [SANGA-]; in Assyria of royal function

šanḫu → *šamḫu*

šaniānu, *šaniyānu*, Nuzi *šani(y)āna*, jB also *šanênu* "secondly, for the second time"; < *šanû* I

šāninu(m); f. *šānintu* "rival; of equal birth" [jB ZAG.DU/DI] in PNs; *š. ul īšu* "is unrivalled" of DN, kingship, palace etc.; < *šanānu*

šanîš I "secondly" O/jB "for the second time"; "again"; "as also"; < *šanû* I

šanîš II "otherwise; or else" O/jB, NA [MAN-] om., comm., astr. of alternative interpretations or versions; < *šanû* II

šanīta(m) → *šanītu* I.II

šanittum → *tanittu*

šanītu I "a second time" jB; also OB, MA *šanītam*; < *šanû* I

šanītu(m) II "something other" OA, O/jB **1.** adv. acc. *šanīta(m)* to introduce new subject **2.** "s.th. strange, hostile" (also pl.); < *šanû* II

šaniu → *šanû* I.II

šaniyānu/a → *šaniānu*

ša(n)nadu(m), once *šanudû* (an illness) O/jB

šannasru mng. unkn. jB lex.

šannā'um "hater" OB

šannu(m), *šunnu*, *šennu*, *šēnu*, Am. also *sennu*; pl. f. *šannātu(m)* (a metal kettle or cauldron) Bab., OA [phps. ŠEN (→ *ruqqu* I)]

šannunātum f. pl. "presentation (of witnesses)" OA; < *šanānu* D

šannūri → *nūru* I

šannūru → *šallūru*; *nūru* I

šannu'u → *šunnû*

šansuku → *šumsuku*

šanšāla → *amšāli*

šanšantu → *šaššantu*

šanšānu, *šanšu* → *šamšu*

šantu → *šattu*

šantukku → *sattukku*

šanṭu → *šamṭu* I

šanu- → *šunu*

-šanu- → *-šunu*

šanû(m) I, OAkk, Ass. *šaniu(m)*; f. *šanītu(m)* "second, next" [2.KAM(.MA)] of officials "deputy" [LÚ.2-]; "next, the following" day, month etc.; "second (in quality)", "second (in size)"; < *šina* II; = *š.* II ?; > *šaniānu*; *šanîš* I, *šanītu* I; *šanûti*; *šanûtī-* ; *šanā'iyu*; → *šanû* III

šanû(m) II, Ass. *šaniu(m)* "(an)other" [MAN] also "different, strange; inimical, evil", in pl. "outsiders"; *mannum š.* "who else?"; *šanûmma* "any other", also term for planet Mars; *ašar šani(u)mma* "anywhere else"; < *šanû* IV; = *š.* I ?; > *ašaršani*; *šanîš* II, *šanītu* II

šanû(m) III, *šanā'u(m)* "to do twice, do for a second time" **G** (*i/i*) often in hendiad. before second vb. (Am. after or without other vb.); OAkk PN *Išni-ilum* "God repeated" **D** "repeat, report" speech, fact, dream to (= *ana*; dat.) s.o.; "repeat" an action, "do again" also in hendiad.; "remeasure" s.th. (and make payment) OA cloth, Bab. grain **Dtn 1.** Mari "repeat (request) yet again" in hendiad. **2.** OB "measure out again, severally" **Dt** pass. OB of grain "be remeasured" (and paid out); jB "maintain o.s."? **Št** O/jB "duplicate" action **1.** "double" in hendiad. (pay back etc.); of parts of body "be duplicate" **2.** "repeat, do again"; also in PN *Uštašni-ilum* (1 or 2 ?); < *šina* II, *šanû* I denom.; > *šunnû*; *tašna*, *tašnītu*, *tašnû*; *šutašnû*; *mašna*

šanû(m) IV, *šanā'u(m)* "to be changed, become different" [MAN] **G** (*i/i*) of road, border; position; work; price, amount; physical appearance; illness; rule(r); regulation, words; plan; *ṭēm X išanni* "the mood of X changes", *šanê ṭēmi* "change of mind, vacillation"; *libbum š.* of heart "change"; NB "diverge from" s.o. **Gtn** iter. "change continually" of invalid's face; esp. with *ṭēmum* **Gt** stat. "is contradictory" **D** "change" (trans.) [NB GI.GI] "change position of" boundary stone, dwelling; "change" fate; clothing; words, name; judgement; heart (*libbu(m)*), mind (*ṭēmu(m)*); stat. "is very strange, different" of tongue, person **Dtn** iter. with *ṭēmu(m)* **Dt** pass. of D of face, mind "be changed"; Mari "be postponed" **Š** as D "alter" statement, agreement; *ṭēmu(m) š.*; "relocate" building site, watercourse; > *šanû* II, *šanîš* II, *šanītu* II; *šinītu* I; *šunnâtu*; *mušannû*?, *mušannītu*; *mušašnû*; *muštannû*

šanû(m) V ~ "to run, trot" O/jB **G** of man; donkey; ox **Gtn** iter. of G of horse; > *šānû*

šanû VI "to sluice, apply water to" Mari, M/NB **G** (*u/u*, also *i/i*) door; NB "seal, plaster over" mud roof afresh **D** as G "wash over, flood"; > *šinītu* II

šanû → also *šanā'u*

šānû(m) "runner, trotter" O/jB lex. [(LÚ.) KAŠ4(.E)] of man; of foal; < *šanû* V

šânu → *šiānum*

šanudû → *šannadu*

šanūdu, *šanādu*/*û*, *šana*/*u''udu*, *ša*/*unundu* "illustrious, heroic" jB; < *nâdu* Š

šanu(n)katu "princess, queen" jB lex.; also of goddess

šanûti adv. "a second time" Susa, Am.; < *šanû* I

šanûtī-, *šanuttē-* + pron. suff. "for the second time" M/NA, M/jB e.g. *šanûtēka taḫaššal* "you crush a second time"; also *ina š.-*; frozen form *(ša) šanûtīšu*; < *šanû* I

šanu''udu → *šanūdu*

šanzātu, *šazzātu* mng. unkn. Am. of jewellery

šapāḫu(m), *šabāḫu* ~ "to sprinkle" O/jB **G** (pres. *išappaḫ*) flour, ashes, drugs **D** as G flour

šapāḫu → also *sapāḫu*; *šuppuḫum*

šapaḫūtu mng. unkn. jB in *ina šapaḫūtika*

šapāku(m) "to heap up; pour on" [DUB; once LAL] **G** (*a/u*) earth, (of gods) the mountains; stat. of clouds "are piled up"; grain etc.; seed, transf. of gods, also in PNs; "pour" liquids, molten metal; OA "invest" capital **Gtn** iter. of G "pour repeatedly, in various places" e.g. precious substances in rit. **Gt** OA "put on deposit, in store" metal, textiles etc. **D** as G "pile up" corpses, mountains, grain; "pour" oil, "cast" bronze **Š** caus. of G **N** pass. of G; of subjects "be prostrated"; of invalid's limbs "be limp" **Ntn** [DUB.MEŠ; DUB.DUB ?] iter. of N; > *šapku*; *šipku* I, *šipiktum*, *šipkātu*, *šipkūtum*; *šupku*; *šapīku*; *išpiku*; *mušappiktu*; *našpaku*, *našpaktu*, *našpakūtu*; *šupukkû*

šapal → *šaplu* II

šapālu(m) "to be(come) deep, low" [KI.TA; SIG; astr. also BÙR] **G** (*i/i*) "be deep" of well, river, ditch etc.; "be sunken" of eyes; ears; part of liver; "reach lowest point" of moon, stars; building; flame; mountain; "be lowly, humble"; "humble o.s."; "be depressed" of heart, mood; "be low" of price (opp. = *šaqû* II), "suffer a loss" in business **Gtn** "become progressively lower" of doors, foundations **D** "dig deep"; "lower" water table; stat. "are low" of heavenly bodies, parts of body; ellipt. "be placed deep" of features on liver, eyes etc.; "bring down" amniotic fluid; "bend down, incline" face; "humble, humiliate" s.o.; "suppress" opinion (*libbu*); "reduce, lower" price **Dtn** iter. astr. "stay constantly low" **Dtt** NA "move downstream" **Š** caus. of G "bring low, abase" **N** of person, speech "be humbled"; > *šaplu* I.II, *šapiltu*, *šapliš*, *šaplānu*, *šaplāniš*, *šaplû*, *šaplītu*; *šuplu*; *šupālu*, *šupālû*, *šupālītu*, *šupālānu*; *šappalu*; *šuppulu*, *šuppultu*; *šušpulu*; *mušpalu*; *mušappilu*; *našpiltu*; *tašpiltu*

šapāpu(m) ~ "to move along" jB(lit.), O/jB lex. **G** (f. imper. *šuppī*) **D** lex. mng. uncl.

šapargallu (a large fishing net) jB lex.; < Sum.

šapargillu → *supurgillu*

šaparru → *saparru*; *sapāru*

šapartu(m), NA once *šipartu*; pl. *šaprātu(m)* "pledge" Ass., Nuzi; OA *ana š. nadā'um* "to pledge" house etc., *š. ka''ulum* "to hold as pledge"; M/NA *kī š.* "as a pledge" (*šakānu* "to deposit", *ka''ulu* "to hold", *ušābu* "to live" with creditor); *š. paṭāru* "to release from a pledge"; NA *ana š.* "as a pledge" (*kammus(at)* "is living"; *akālu* "to enjoy" a field); < *šapāru*; → *šapru* I 2

šapāru(m) "to send; send (a message), write (to)" [KIN] **G** (*a/u*) with dat. or acc. of recipient: goods; person; tablet; word, decision, message (*šipirtu*); true, false, friendly, hostile messages; help; OA, OB with acc. infin. "send (instruction)" to do s.th.; "send (word)" written or spoken; OB *šapāram šapārum* "send message"; "govern, administer" weavers, land, people **R** Mari **Gtn** iter. of G [KIN.KIN; KIN.MEŠ] "repeatedly send"; also "repeatedly instruct, brief (s.o.)"; "continually govern" (**Gt** → *šitpuru*) **Š** OB "cause to write" **Št** M/jB(Ass.) "govern" **N** pass. of G "be sent, be sent as a message"; > *šapru* I; *šipru*, *šipirtu*, *šiprūtu*; *šāpiru*, *šāpirūtu*, *šāpirtum*; *našparu* II, *našpartu* II; *tašpartu*; *šapartu*; → *šipāru*

šaparziqqu (a wind) jB; → *zīqu* I

šapāṣu(m), *šabāṣu*, *šapāsu*, *sabāṣu* ~ "to clasp, enfold; grip, twist"? O/jB **G** (*i/i*) with arms, legs **Gt** "grapple, wrestle" **D** "keep enfolded"; stat. "is enfolded" by (= acc.); > *šipṣu*; *šitpuṣu*; *muštapṣu*; *šapṣu*

šapāšum mng. unkn. OB lex.

šapāšu → also *šabāšu*

šapattu(m), *šabattu* "15th day of month" OAkk, Bab., OA [UD.15.KAM]; also "period of 15 days, fortnight"

šapātu "to be malicious, treacherous" jB lex. **G**; **D**; > *muštappitu*, *muštaptu*, *muštaptūtu*; *šappitu*

šapātu → also *šapāṭu* I; *šaptu*

šapāṭu(m) I, *šapātu(m)*, once *šabātu* "to give judgement, exercise authority" O/jB **G** (*i/i*) absol. and with obj. (*dīnam*, *šipṭam*); > *šipṭu* I; *šāpiṭu*, *šāpiṭūtum*

šapāṭum II ~ "to inform strictly, reprimand" OB **G** (*a/u*); > *šipṭu* II

šapā'um → *šapû* III

šapīku; pl. f. 'piling up' M/NB "deposit" of grain; of river silt; < *šapāku*

šapiltu(m) **1.** "lower (part); inner (part)" OA, O/jB [KI.TA] of parts of the body; of garments, objects **2.** "the remainder, rest" O/jB [ÍB.TAG4] of persons; of commodities, assets; math. "remainder" after subtraction **3.** "second in rank, assistant" lex. **4.** "anvil-stone"; < *šapālu*; → *šaplu* I

šāpinum mng. unkn. OAkk; → *sāpinu*

šāpirtum "mistress, lady" OB; < *šāpiru*

šāpiru(m) "giver of instructions" [(LÚ.)UGULA] **1.** "ruler" said of kings **2.** "governor, controller" said of officials; gener. "administrator, boss"; *š. mātim/PlN/nārim* "(provincial) governor; controller of land, city, canal"; "controller" of people, troops; esp. NB "overseer" of craftsmen etc.; < *šapāru*

šāpirūtu(m) **1.** "post of *šāpiru*" OB, Mari **2.** "sovereignty" M/jB(Ass.); < *šāpiru*

šapītu (a bird) jB lex.

šapītu(m) → also *šabītum*; *šapû* I.V

šāpiṭu(m) **1.** "district governor" OB, jB lex. **2.** "judge" as epith. of Šamaš jB; < *šapāṭu* I

šāpiṭūtum "governorship, jurisdiction" Mari; < *šāpiṭu*

šapium → *šapû* I

šapku(m) "heaped up, poured out" O/jB "banked up" of earth; of cloud; Am., jB "cast" of metal objects; < *šapāku*

šapla → *šaplu* II

šaplān → *šaplānu* 2

šaplāniš "underneath, below" jB; < *šaplu* II

šaplānu(m) "underneath; beneath, under" [KI.TA(-)] **1.** adv.: "(down) below; downstream"; also *ana*, *ina*, *ištu š.*; also "inwardly, in secret" **2.** prep., also *šaplān*: "beneath, under; downstream from"; Nuzi "west of"; also *ana*, *ina*, *ištu š.*, with pron. suff.; *š. šēpi* "sole of the foot"; < *šaplu* II

šaplâtu → *šaplītu*; *šaplû*

šapliš "below; down(wards)" [KI.TA] esp. in *eliš u šapliš* "above and below"; = "in the netherworld", "on earth"; "downwards; downstream"; OA "lower in value"; < *šaplu* II

šaplītu(m) "lower part; inside" Bab. [KI.TA(-)] esp. of parts of the exta; OB(lit.) "the netherworld"; pl. *šapliātu*, *šaplâti* [KI.TA(-); KI.TA.MEŠ] "below" as opp. to *elâtu*; "netherworld"; "inmost, hidden thoughts"; < *šaplû*

šaplīu → *šaplû*

šaplu(m) I; f. *šapiltu* "low(er); lowly" OAkk, O/jB, NA of sea, land; "low" stool; "lowly" person; < *šapālu*; → *šapiltu*; *šappalu*

šaplu(m) II, NA also *saplu* "underside, bottom" [KI.TA] OB "arrears"; in prep. use *(ina, ištu, ana) šapal*, NA often *šapla*; jB, NA also loc.-adv. with pron. suff. *šaplū'a, šapluššu* etc.; transf. "under" control, charge of, "at" the feet of, "under" the oath of; NA *šapal, šapla/i qāti* "secretly"; < *šapālu*; > *šaplānu, šaplāniš, šapliš, šaplītu, šaplû*

šaplû(m), Ass. *šaplīu(m)*, once *šiplû* "lower" [KI(.TA)] "lower(-lying)" (opp. to *elû* "upper") of buildings, objects, parts of body; land, sky, world; "of lower quality"; of plots of land "lower" side (mostly south and east), also math. of figures; "suffixed" of Sum. gramm. elements; < *šaplu* II

šappalu(m) "low" O/jB; used as pl. of *šaplu* I; < *šapālu*

šappartum (a part of the chariot) Mari

šappartu → also *sappartu*

šappāru → *sappāru*

šappatu, *šabbatu*, NB also *sappatu* (a pottery vessel) OB(Alal.), M/NA, j/NB for wine, vinegar; NB also of bronze ?; < *šappu*

šappīnatu → *sapīnatu*

šappitu "treacherous" jB; < *šapātu*

šappu(m) (a vessel, prob.) "bowl" [(DUG.)ŠAB] for oil, wine, beer, flour, honey; of clay, metal, stone; > *šappatu*; → *sappu* I

šappu → also *sappu* III

šappultu mng. unkn. jB comm.

šapraku (a household object) NB; < *parāku*

šapru(m) I; pl. *šaprūtu/e*, NA also *šaprāte* **1.** OB, Am., jB, NA "envoy, messenger" **2.** NA var. of *šapartu* "pledge"; < *šapāru*

šapru(m) II "thigh" O/jB, Elam, Bogh. [ḪÁŠ] of persons, esp. *š. maḫāṣu* "to strike the thigh" as gesture; of animals; transf. of part of cart

šapṣu, *šepṣu*, *šipṣu* "recalcitrant, obstinate" M/NB of judge; animal; "difficult" of mountain, "intransigent" of enemy, land; words; in subst. use, f. pl. *šapṣētu* "resistance"?; < *šapāṣu*

šapšāqu(m) "constraint, hardship" Bab.(lit.) of human condition(s); M/jB(Ass.) of mountain tracks; < *pašāqu*

šapšu f. "sun" Ug. [dUTU]; < Ug.

šaptu(m), occas. *šabdu* f.; du. *šaptā(n), šaptī(n)*, *once šabā-*; pl. *šapātu*, once *šabātu* "lip; rim" [NUNDUN; occas. SUN4] **1.** of humans, animals; *š. elītu, šaplītu* "upper, lower lip"; (as speech organ) *ina š. šakānu* "to utter" **2.** transf. "words, opinion"; *š. šemû* "to listen to" s.o.; *zikir, siqir š.* "pronouncement"; god *š.-ka* "your spokesman" **3.** "rim" of vessel, jewel; cistern; "crest" of wall; "bank" of canal; Nuzi "edge" of path, field etc.

šaptum → also *šīpātu*

šaptûm ~ "open(ed up)" OA, of shoes; < *petû* II Š

šapṭu, *šepṭu* (desig. of high quality) j/NB wool, sheep; timber

šapû(m) I, f. *šapītu*; OA *šapium, šap'um*; du. Mari *šapu(w)ān* **1.** "padded, thick" OA, Mari, jB lex. of hides, textiles, belts, shoes **2.** of vessels, uncert. mng. jB lex.; < *šapû* II ?; → *šupû* II

šapû(m) II, *šepû(m), šabû* "to be dense; thick; loud" O/jB **G** (mostly *u/u*) **1.** of clouds "be dense", stat. "is obscured (by clouds)"; of darkness; transf. of words; of face, eyes "cloud over"?; of fire "smoke" **2.** of noise "be(come) loud", of land "make loud noise" **Gtn** "repeatedly smoke"; "repeatedly flare up"; also astr. **D** O/jB *rigma(m) š.* "make loud noise" **N** of noise (*rigmu*) "become loud"; > *šapû* I?; *šitpû*; *šapû* V

šapû(m) III, *šepû(m)*, OAkk, OA *šapā'um* "to be silent" OAkk, OA, O/jB **G** (*u/u*) **Gt** as G (more freq.) **D** "silence" enemies, "suppress" revolt; > *šāpû, tašpītum*

šapû IV, *šabû*, once *šepû* "to wrap up, seal up" M/jB [GAG.GAG-] **G** (*i/i*) rit., med. with leather; door, with string; transf. "envelop" in darkness; > *šupû* I; *šibītu*

šapû V; f. *šapūtu, šapītu* "dense" jB of clouds; "swelling" of sound; < *šapû* II

šapûm → also *šepûm*

šāpû "enemy, obdurate foe" j/NB; < *šapû* III

šāpû → also *šūpû*

šap'um → *šapû* I

šapuḫru → *šupuḫru*

šapūlu(m), Bogh. *šapullu* "groin, inner thigh" O/jB [jB ḪÁŠ.GAL] of humans; left, right (also du.); *šārat š.* "pubic hair";→ *šapālu*

šapurru → *šaburru*

šapûssu → *šupēltu*

šaqālu(m) "to weigh, pay; balance, suspend" [LAL; Ì.LÁ.E (= *išaqqal*)] **G** (*a/u*) **1.** "weigh" substances, objects **2.** "weigh out, pay" silver, tax, interest; transf. of Šamaš "assess" lands; "dispense, allocate" demons, suffering, mourning **3.** "mete out (sparingly)" rain **Gt** [LÁL] "be in balance, equal" of day and night; astr. "be in opposition, conjunction"; "be equal" of man to god **D** **1.** "weigh" **2.** OA "pay out" silver, payment, tribute **3.** O/jB (denom. from *šaqlu*) "make scarce" rain **Š** "cause to pay" OA, OB, MB(Alal.) **N** "be weighed, paid out"; "be meted out (sparingly)" of rain, flood; > *šaqlu*; *šiqlu*; *šuqlum* I, *šuqultu*; *šāqilu*; *šitqulu*, *šitqultu*; *mašqaltum*; *mušaqqiltu*; *mušeqqilum*; → *mašqalu*; *šuqallulu*

šaqāqu (a bronze object) jB lex.

šaqāru "to pierce" jB **G** (*i/i*) of demon **D** as G of arrow; also of person, with (= *ina*) arrow

šāqâtu → *šāqûtu*

šaqā'u → *šaqû* III

šāqilu(m) (wooden lock or bolt) Bab.; < *šaqālu*

šaqîš "high up" j/NB in heaven; of statues and buildings "on high"; "loudly" of laugh; bird; < *šaqû* I

šaqītum "irrigated land" Mari; < *šaqû* III

šāqītu(m) "female cup-bearer" [OAkk MUNUS. SAGI; Am. MUNUS.DÉ; NA MUNUS.KAŠ.LUL]; < *šāqû*

šāqiu → *šāqû*

šaqlu(m) "weighed out; scarce" O/jB of grain, metal; rain; barley *šaqlūssu* "even if scarce"; < *šaqālu*

šaqqāya → *saqqāya*

šaqtum (or *šaktum*) mng. uncl. OB in boundary descr.

šaqû(m) I "high, elevated" [LAL; jB also AN.TA. GÁL] of god, place, mountain, building; "in high place" of city; ground; "of high rank" of tribe; "prominent, sublime"; < *šaqû* II

šaqû(m) II "to be(come) high, elevated" [LAL; jB also NIM; astr. also E_{11}, AN(.TA)] **G** (*u/u* and *i/i*; stat. *šaqu* and *šaqi*) of gods, men; places; crops; parts of body, esp. *rēšu(m)* "head"; buildings; "go upstream", "rise" of sun etc.; of price, rank, position; stat. "is sublime" of lordship, strength, words etc. **Gtn** [NIM.MEŠ] of heavenly body "repeatedly rise"; of heel "walk with a springy gait" **D** "raise up" person, torch; "exalt, extol" god, person; kingship, throne, name; "take upstream" boat; absol. "travel upstream"; "raise high" building; terrace; of moon "raise" star above itself; *rēša/ī š.* "raise head" i.e. "exert o.s."; "look after" s.o.; "raise" eyes, hands, tail; price **Dtn** iter. of D **Š** "exalt, elevate" god, human; terrace; command; "praise" **Št(n)**? jB lex. **N** ~ G "rise" of price **Ntn** mng. uncl.; > *šaqû* I, *šaqîš*; *šūqu* I; *šušqûtu*, *šušqûm*; *tašqītum*; *mušaqqû* I

šaqû(m) III, OAkk, Ass. *šaqā'u(m)* "to give to drink, irrigate" [NAG] **G** (*i/i*) "give (drink) to" to man, animal (= 2 acc.); "soak" textile; *dimta š.* "weep tears"; "irrigate" field, also of rain, "fill" cistern "with" water **Gtn** [NAG.MEŠ] iter. of G **Š** caus. of G **N** Mari pass. of G; > *šaqûm* IV, *šaqītum*; *šāqû*, *šāqītu*, *šāqûtu*; *šīqu* I, *šiqītu*; *mašqû*, *mašqītu*, *mašqûtu*; *mušaqqûm* II

šaqûm IV "irrigated" OB, field; < *šaqû* III

šaqû V (a spade) jB lex.

šāqû(m), Ass. *šāqiu(m)* 'giver to drink' **1.** "butler, cup-bearer" [(LÚ.)ŠU.SÌLA.DU$_8$; (LÚ.)KAŠ. LUL; also MB TIN.LUL; OB(Rimah) ŠU.DU$_8$. SÌLA.A; OB(Alal.) LÚ.SÌLA.(ŠU.)DU$_8$ (.A)]; *rab šāqê* "chief cup-bearer" (high official) [LÚ.GAL. ŠU.SÌLA.DU$_8$; (LÚ.)GAL.KAŠ. LUL; LÚ.GAL.ŠU. DU$_8$.A] **2.** Nuzi "irrigator" **3.** (a piece of brewer's equipment); < *šaqû* III

šâqu(m) I (an operation performed on textiles) **G** jB lex. **D** OB

šâqum II (or *šâkum*) vb. mng. unkn. OB **G** (pret. *išāq*)

šâqu III mng. unkn. Bogh., jB lex. **G**

šâqu IV "to tremble"? jB lex. **G**

šaqummatu, *šuqummatu* "(deathly) hush" jB to pour, cast "silence" over etc.; < *šaqummu*

šaqummiš "quite silently" O/jB *š. wašābum* "to sit in silence"; of demon, roam "in silence"; *š. īmi* "became silent"; < *šaqummu*

šaqummu(m) "quite silent" O/jB esp. of places; also "secluded, quiet"; < *šuqammumu* II; > *šaqummatu*, *šaqummiš*

šāqûtu(m) esp. *š. mê* "irrigation work" Bab.; NB also *šāqâtu*; < *šāqû* 2

šar → *ašru* III 5

šār, *šāru* "3,600" Bab., Ass.(roy. inscr.) [ŠÁR] as indefinitely large number of years, miles etc.; *adi š.* "for all time; everywhere"; < Sum.; → *šuššār*

šarābu "to wander about" jB **G** (pres. *išarrab*)

šarāḫu(m) I "to take pride in, make splendid" Bab. **G** (pret. *išruḫ*; stat. *šaruḫ*) kingship; stat. "is proud, splendid" of god, man; form, appearance, gait; palace, torch **Gt** ~ "show pride" **D** "make proud, splendid; glorify" gods, king; divinity, kingship; praise, splendour, command, battle; rites, offerings; buildings; stat. "is overweening" of behaviour **Dtn** "repeatedly praise" **Dt 1.** pass. of D "be glorified" **2.** "praise o.s." esp. in PNs; "be overweening, boast" **Š** "glorify"; "make splendid" **Ntn** Mari "become overweening"; > *šarḫu*, *šarḫiš*, *šarraḫu*, *šarraḫūtu*, *šarraḫû*; *šurruḫu* I; *šitrāḫu*, *šitruḫu*, *šitarḫu*; *šutarruḫūtu*; *mašraḫū*; *muštarḫu*; *muštarriḫu*; *šušruḫu*; *tašriḫtu*, *tašrīḫū*; *muštarḫūtu*; *muštarriḫūtu*

šarāḫu(m) II "to pull up" jB **G** (pret. *išruḫ*) a plant

šarāḫu III "to mark, brand" Nuzi, NB **G** (pret. *išruḫ*) animals, hides; > *šarḫītu*

šarāku(m) I "to present, give" OAkk, Bab., NA [OAkk A.MU.(NA.)RU; SAG.RIG$_7$; GÁ] **G** (*a/u*; pret. once *išrik*) of gods "bestow, entrust" men, districts; weapons, insignia; prosperity etc.; fame, might; long life, wisdom; righteousness; also "bestow" evil, loss; of men "present, dedicate" statue, offering; person; grain, dowry etc.; "put at the disposal of, in the power of" s.o. **Gtn** iter. of G **Š** caus. of G **N** pass. of G "be presented", "be put in the power of" s.o.; > *šerku, šerkatu, šerki-ilūtu, šerkūtu, šeriktu; šarrāku, šarrāktum; mašraktu*

šarāku II "to suppurate, discharge pus" jB **G** (*i/i*) **Gt** (*ištarik*); < *šarku* denom.

šarāku III mng. unkn. jB lex.

šaramaiddu → *šarmadu*

šarammu → *tarammu* I

šarāmu(m), NB *šerēmu* "to trim, peel off" **G** (*a/u*; j/NB *i/i*) grindstone, seal(ing); tablet from envelope; "hack" weeds from field; "prune" palm, reeds **D** "trim" beams; animal's horn; > *šarmu; širmu, šerimtum; našramu*

šarānu(m) **1.** OAkk (a wood) **2.** jB (a medicinal plant)

šārānu "wind-bag, flatulent" jB [IM-]; < *šāru* I

šarāpu(m) "to burn, burn away" [GÍBIL] **G** (*a/u*) wood; oil; incense; tablet, figurine, city; corpse; OB stat. "is feverish" **D** as G **N** "be consumed by fire", of fire "be ignited"; > *šarpu* I.II; *šurpītu, šurpu; šuruptu; našraptu, našrapu*

šarāqu(m) I "to steal" **G** (*i/i*; occas. *a/u*) goods, people, animals; field; *šurqam š.* "steal (stolen) goods", *ina šurqi š.* "steal by theft"; OA of official "confiscate"; Ug., Bogh. absol. "be a thief" **Gtn** iter. of G "steal constantly from" palace; "constantly arrogate to o.s."; "do s.th. by stealth", also in hendiad. **N** of persons "be abducted"; OA "be confiscated" (from = dat.); > *šarqu, šarqiš, šāriqānum, šarqūtu; šerqum; šurqu, šurqiš; šarriqu; šarrāqu, šarrāqānu, šarrāqiš, šarrāqāniš, šarrāqītu, šarrāqūtu; šitarqum; muštarriqu; muštarqu*

šarāqu(m) II "to be ready"? O/MB **G** stat. only

šarāqu(m) III ~ "to cook" **G** meat Akk. lw. in Sum. **D** MB "fuse, cast" glass

šarāru(m) I ~ "to go ahead" Bab. **G** (*u/u*) in battle; in prayer; of food supplies "go off, deteriorate"? **Gtn** iter. of G of sign on liver **D** "encourage"?; > *šarriru*

šarāru(m) II (a human activity) Mari **G** not attested **Gtn** *ana ramānišu/ka ištanarrar*

šarāru III mng. uncert. jB **G** (*u/u*, also *a/u*) ext., om. **D** ext. **Ntn**

šarāṣu "to clutch, claw onto"? jB lex. **G; Gt**

šaraš(a)rānum → *šaršarānu* I

šarāṭu(m) "to tear, shred" Bab., NA **G** (*a/u*) garments (in grief); skin **D** as G "rend" garments; "tear" skin **Dt** pass. of D **N** "be rent, torn apart"; > *šurruṭu; šerṭu; šurāṭum; mušarriṭu* I$^?$, II

šarā'u → *šarû* II

šarbābiš "impotently" jB with *naḫarmumu*; < *šarbābu*

šarbābu "impotence" jB with *naḫarmumu*; < *rabābu*

šarbašši "cushion"? OB(Emar); < Hitt.

šarbillu "storm" jB

šarbiš "like a chill rain" jB; < *šarbu* II

šarbu I (or *sarbu*) mng. unkn. NA

šarbu II, NA *sarabu*; NA pl. f. "rainy season, cold" jB, NA; *š. u ṣētu* "wet and dry weather"; > *šarbiš*; → *šurīpu*

šarbu III (a metal) MA

šarbû (or *šarpû*) "rabid" OB lex., jB

šardappu (a part of a harness) Bogh., j/NB, NA; of leather; of metal

šardunû → *šurdunû*

šaressu → *ašarēdu*

šargadarānu, *šargada* (a plant) jB lex.

šargānu "mighty" jB lex.

šargītu (a child's game) MB

šarḫiš "proudly, splendidly" O/jB; < *šarḫu*

šarḫītu f. "branded" NB of cow; < *šarāḫu* III

šarḫu(m); f. *šaruḫtu(m)* "proud, splendid" Bab, NA of gods; kings; sheep; commands; rites; < *šarāḫu* I

šarḫullu(m) (a metal implement) Mari; jB lex., NB

šarḫullu → also *sarḫullu*

šāriqānum "the thief" Mari; < *šarāqu* I

šāriš, *šārišam* "in the wind" jB; < *šāru* I

šarium → *šarû* I

šarku(m) ~ "pus, suppuration" Bab., NA [LUGUD]; > *šarāku* II

šarmadu, *ašarmadu*, Ug. *šaramaiddu* (a medicinal plant) M/jB [(GIŠ.)Ú.GUR$_5$.UŠ]

šarmu "lopped, trimmed" jB lex.; of palm; term for a $^1/_2$ *qû* measure; Am. of ornaments; < *šarāmu*

šarnagu (a plant) jB

šarnuppu (persons receiving rations) jB; < Elam.

šarpu I Nuzi, NA for *šurpu* "burning"; "incineration of corpses"; < *šarāpu*

šarpu II adj. "with burn wounds" Nuzi of horse; < *šarāpu*

šarpû → *šarbû*

šarqiš "secretly, by stealth" jB; < *šarqu*

šarqu(m); f. *šariqtu(m)* "stolen" OB, Nuzi of slave; cattle; < *šarāqu* I; > *šarqūtu*, *šarqiš*

šarqūtu "theft" NA; < *šarqu*

šarra (an object) Am.

šarrabtu (a female demon)? jB

šarrabtû, *šarrabṭû* (an official) OAkk, Bab., Am.; also name of underworld demon; < Sum.

šarrabu (a demon) M/jB

šarraḫu "very proud" M/jB of gods; men; < *šarāḫu* I

šarraḫû ~ "very proud" jB; < *šarāḫu* I

šarraḫūtu "bragging" MB, a child's game; < *šarāḫu* I

šarraktum → *šarrāku*

šarraku (or *šarrāku*) (a class of persons) O/MB(Alal.); > *šarrakūtu*

šarrāku(m); f. *šarraktum* (a class of persons) OAkk, OB, Mari; jB lex. esp. in city name *āl-šarrākī* [URU.SAG.RIG7]; < *šarāku* I

šarrakūtu "function of a *šarraku*" MB(Alal.), Ug.; also *kasap š.* payment; < *šarraku*

šarrāpūtu (a game) MB

šarrāqāniš "like a thief" jB; < *šarrāqu*

šarrāqānu(m) "the thief in a particular case" OB, Nuzi; < *šarrāqu*

šarrāqiš "like a thief, in secret" j/NB; < *šarrāqu*

šarrāqītu "female thief" jB as epith. of Ištar; < *šarrāqu*

šarrāqu(m), OA *šarruqum* "thief" [(LÚ.)NÍ.ZU] *kīma š.* "stealthily"?; < *šarāqu* I; > *šarrāqiš*, *šarrāqāniš*, *šarrāqānu*, *šarrāqūtu*, *šarrāqītu*

šarrāqūtu(m) "theft" OB, also Ug. "stolen goods"; < *šarrāqu*

šarrarû → *sarrarû*

šarratu(m) "queen" [GAŠAN; MUNUS.LUGAL; UN.GAL; NA also 20-]; of deities, humans; *š. kibri* "queen of the river-bank", a bird; < *šarru*; > *šarratūtum*

šarratūtum, *šarratuttu* "queenship" Mari, Bogh., Ug. [MUNUS.LUGAL-]; < *šarratu*

šarrena (a cultic image) Nuzi; < Hurr.

šarriqu "thieving" OB; NA f. *šarriqtu*; < *šarāqu* I

šarriru(m) "deferential"? OB lex., jB; < *šarāru* I

šarriš in *Šarriš-takal* "Trust-in-the-king" OAkk PN; < *šarru*

šarrišarru → *šaršerru*

šarru(m); pl. *šarrū*, *šarrānu* "king" [LUGAL(.E); 20; BÁRA; 180+20; Elam 150; once GÚ.GAL, GIŠ.GIŠIMMAR] **1.** of deities and humans; *š. rabû* "Great King"; "king" of a country, city; OA *šarrānē šaniūtim* "other king(let)s"; *š. ḫammā'u* "usurper"; OB *ša š.* "king's representative"; NA *ḫarrān š.* "royal road" **2.** "first quality" of textiles etc. **3.** lit. male "beloved"; > *šarratu*, *šarratūtum*, *šarriš*, *šarrūtu*

šarrum → also *šerru*

šarrû → *šurrû* II

šarrubānu (a cucumber) Ug. lex.

šarrumma → *šurrumma*

šarruqum → *šarrāqu*

šarrūtu, Ass. *šarruttu(m)* "kingship, reign" [LUGAL- ; 20- ; NAM.LUGAL(.LA); NAM.20] of deities, humans *š. epēšu* "to exercise kingship"; appoint, choose *ana š.* "to/for kingship"; insignia, attributes of k.; *kunuk/unqi š.* "royal seal"; *āl/šubat š.* "royal city, residence"; *š. rabītu* "'Great King'-ship"; OA *lubūš š.* "first quality garment"; < *šarru*; → *arad-šarrūtu*

šaršabiṭṭu (a tree) jB lex.; OB [NE.DU.KU]

šaršarānum I, *šaraš(a)rānum*, *šerešrānum* (a capacity measure) OA, smaller than a *karpatum*

šaršarānu II "rebel" NA, NB

šaršarratu → *šeršerratu*

šaršarru → *šaršerru*

šaršāru → *šaššāru*

šaršerru, *šaršarru*, *šarrišarru*, *šeršerru*, *ša/eššeru* "red paste" jB, NA [IM.SA5]

šaršubbû (or *imsaršubbû*) (a kind of tablet) Ug.?, jB lex.; < Sum.

šārtu(m), Bogh. also *šaḫratu*, Am. *šērtu* "hair; (animal's) pelt" [SÍK; SÍK.ÙZ; also MUNSUB, MÚNSUB] head, beard, body "hair" of humans (sg. & pl.); "an (individual) hair"; of deities, figures, mythical beings; "coat, hair; pelt" of animals esp. goats (*š. enzi*); of lion, pig, donkey; on spleen; "plumage" of bird; "hair" as material (weighed); "awn" on grain; → *šu''uru* I

šarû(m) I, OA, arch. OB *šarium* "rich" [NÍG.TUKU] "wealthy" (opp. = *lapnu*); jB(lit.) "copious" of foliage, shade; < *šarû* II; > *šarûtu*

šarû(m) II, Ass. *šarā'u(m)* "to be(come) rich" [NÍG.TUKU] **G** (*u/u* and *i/i*) of persons "be, become wealthy" **Gtn** iter. of G **D** "make rich"; "give generous measure" of fodder **Š** "make rich"; > *šarû* I, *šarûtu*; *mašrû*, *mešrêtu*; *mašrītu*

šāru(m) I, jB once *sāru*; pl. also f. "wind; breath" [IM] good, bad; goes (*alāku*), blows (*ziāqum*) etc.; specific winds as compass points

→ *amurru* 4, *elû* II, *ištānu*, *šadû* II, *šūtu* II; *ana šār erbetti* "to the four winds"; transf. "(wind =) nothing, lies"; *ana š. turru* "to annihilate"; "breath; air; flatulence"; > *šāriš*; *šārānu*

šāru II; pl. *šārūtu/a* "hostile, enemy" Am.

šāru III (or *šâru*) mng. unkn. jB lex.

šāru → also *šār*

šâru "to slander" Am. **G**; **D**

šâru → also *šāru* III

šaruptu → *šuruptu*

šarūriš "with brilliance" jB

šarūru(m) **1.** "brilliance, ray" [ŠE.ER(.ZI)] of sun, moon etc.; deity; temple; ext. (a fraying, radiating feature of liver)? **2.** "tendril" of cucumber [ŠAR.ZI.MEŠ]; (a type of melon)

šarûtu(m) "richness, wealth" Mari, jB; < *šarû* I

šārūtu "post of singer" Am.; < W.Sem.

šarzuā'īum (a garment) OA

šarzuḫu (a plant) jB lex.

šasā'um → *šasû*

šasbūtu (or *šas/ṣb/pūtu*) (a plant)? jB lex., NA

šaskû → *saskû*

šasnibi, *šišanibe* (a vegetable) NA, NB

šaspūtu → *šasbūtu*

šasqû → *saskû*

šassā'u(m); f. *šassā'ītu(m)* "shouter, wailer" O/jB of wailing goddess; cow; "wailing" of a lament; < *šasû*

šassinnu → *sasinnu*

šassukkatu "female accountant" (of the underworld) jB epith. of goddess

šassukku(m) "accountant" OAkk, O/jB [SAG.DU$_5$]; < Sum.

šassūru(m), *šasurru*, *sassūru*, *šaturru*; pl. f. [ŠÀ.TÙR] **1.** "womb" of humans, deities, animals; personified mother goddess, Qatna also of stone **2.** (an insect); < Sum.; > *sassurtu*?

šasû(m), OAkk, OA *šasā'um*, M/NA *sasā'u* "to shout, call (out); read (out)" [GÙ- ; DÉ; GÙ.DÉ] **G** (*i/i*, pret. *išsi*, *issi*, later often *ilsi*, Mari once pres. *itassi*; OB imper. often *tisi*) **1.** of men "shout"; also of animals, storm, heaven "cry, roar, sound"; (shooting) star "make a sound"; "cry out" in anger, sorrow etc.; of baby, invalid **2.** "call out" song, lamentation; of herald "announce" **3.** "call" to s.o. (= dat.); "address, appeal to" god, king; "call on, call in" god, representative; leg. "summon, subpoena"; "invite" **4.** "demand, call for" s.th. **5.** "lay a claim" against (= *eli*, *ina muḫḫi*; Susa, Nuzi *ina (w)arki*) **6.** "call" by name, by (foreign) word; "name" **7.** "read (out)"; *nikkassī š.* "settle accounts" **Gtn** [GÙ.GÙ(.MEŠ)(-); GÙ.DÉ.MEŠ(-); GÙ.DÉ.DÉ(.ME/MEŠ)(-); GÙ.DÉ.GÙ.DÉ(-)] iter. of G, esp. "read, study" tablet, stele **D** only MA "have a proclamation made", MA also infin. *sassû* "pronouncement" **Dtn** erron. for Gtn Mari "lay claims against" **Š** caus. "make cry out, call to" s.o., "make (s.o.) declare" **N** pass. of G; > *sasiu*, *sasûtu*; *šīsu*; *šisītu* I; *šassā'u*; *massûtu*; *musassiānu*; *tassītum*; → *šāṣû*

šasurru → *šassūru*

šaṣb/pūtu → *šasbūtu*

šāṣû "croaker" jB lex. (desig. of crow); → *šasû*

šâṣu → *šiāṣum*

šâš I "to her" OB(poet.) for *šâšim*

šâš II "which" NB(Achaem.)

šâša "to her" (dat.); "that, the same" (acc.) late jB, NA for *šâši*

šašallu(m), NA *sasallu* **1.** "tendon of the hoof or heel" **2.** "back"? [(UZU.)SA.SAL] of humans (med. often du.); of animals "(fleece from) back"; "(meat of) back"; ext. (a part of liver); < Sum.

šašappum (royal title in Elam) OB(Elam)

šašappūtum "post of *šašappum*" OB(Elam)

šašarû (an official) Nuzi

šâši(m) "to her" (dat.); "her" (acc.); "that, the same" (f.) Bab.; OB(Susa) "him"; → *šâš* I; *šâša*; *šī*; *šū*

šâšina "those; the same" (f. pl. acc., gen.); → *šâtina*; *šina* I; *šināšim*

šāšitānu, *šāšitūnu* (an illness) M/jB

šāšītu "lantern" NB; < Aram.

šāšitūnu → *šāšitānu*

šaškallum → *šuškallu*

šaškillulu (desig. of a person) OB lex.; < Sum.?

šašmiš, OB *šašniš* "(in)to combat" O/jB

šašmu, OB *šašmûm* ? "(single) combat" Bab. (lit.) *š. epēšu* "to do battle"; > *šašmiš*

šašniš → *šašmiš*

šašrītu mng. unkn. jB lex.

šaššāniš "like the sun" jB; < *šamšu*

šaššantu, *šanšantu* "small sun disc" jB; < *šamšu*

ša(š)šānum (a metal object) OAkk

šaššāru(m), OB also *šuššārum*, OA *šeššērum*, Bogh. *šaršāru* "a saw" [URUDU.ŠUM.GAM.ME] of bronze, iron, silver etc.; as symbol of Šamaš; *šinni š.* "tooth of saw"

šaššaṭu(m) (a disease of the joints) O/jB med., mag.; also of sheep; *(šam) š.* "plant, drug for *š.*"?

šaššeru → *šaršerru*

šaššiāna → *šalšiānu*

šaššinnu (a type of gem) Qatna

šaššinnu → also *sasinnu*

šaššiš → *šamšiš*

šaššu → *šalšu*; *šamšu*

šaššūgu, *šuššūg/qu* (a tree) Bab., NA [GIŠ.MES. GÀM; GIŠ.SÙḪ.NA] as source of timber; twig of *š.* as drug; in plantation

šaššūme → *šalšūmi*

šaššumma in *š. epēšu* "to forfeit" Nuzi (with *uštu*, *ina* "from"); house, share of inheritance; also of judges "order to forfeit"

šaššūtē- "for the sixth time" M/NA *š.-šu*; < *šediš*

šaššūtī- → *šalšūtī-*

šāšu (a metal tool) Nuzi

šâšu(m) "(to/of) him" Bab., NA; OB dat. after *ana*; M/jB acc., dat., gen.; j/NB also nom.; Nuzi also for pl. "them"; → *šū*

šâšunu, once *šâšun* "(to/of) them; those" M/NB acc., dat., gen.; "those, i.e. those same"; → *šuātunu*; *šunāšunu*; *šunūši*

šašurum (a headdress)? OB lex.

šāt, occas. *šāti/u*, *sāt*, f. sg. "who(m), which; of" OAkk, OA, O/jB **1.** occas. as rel. pron. "which" **2.** before gen. "of", PN *Šāt-DN* "She of DN"; → *šāt urri*, *šāt mūši* "(the watches) of dawn, night", "daytime, night-time"; *šāt qāti* "handcuff"; *šāt tibni*, *šāt kapri* (names of birds); → *ša*; *šât*

šât f. pl. "who(m); of" OAkk as rel. pron. and before gen.; < *šāt* pl.

šâta "that, this same" OAkk(peripheral) occas. for *šâtu*

šatāḫu "to stretch out" (intrans.) jB **G** (*a/u*) **D** "make grow long"; > *šitḫu*

šatakku "a (kind of) hole"? jB [ŠÀ.TAG]; < Sum.?

Šatalši (a month) MB(Alal.); < Hurr.?

šatammu(m), *šattammu(m)* "administrator; government auditor" Bab., NA [(LÚ.)ŠÀ.TAM; OB pl. often ŠÀ.TAM.E.NE] of palace, city, temple, house; NA, NB esp. "chief administrator" of temple, also of city of Dēr; < Sum.?

šatammūtu(m) "post of *šatammu*" Bab., NA [LÚ.ŠÀ.TAM-]

šatānu "to urinate" jB **G** (*i/i*) of men, animals; "urinate on" (= *ana*); < *šiānum* Gt

šatāpu ~ "to cut out, hollow out" jB **G** (*i/i*); > *šatpu*; *šitpu*; *šitiptu*; *naštiptum*

šatāqu(m) "to split, crack (off)" O/jB, Mari, MA [DAR] **G** (*a/u*) esp. om. of parts of liver and lung; OB "separate" hem **D** jB stat. of watercourses "are gouged into" mountain, of parts of body "are cracked, fissured"? **N** Mari "be split"?; > *šatiqtu*; *šitqu* I; *šuttuqum*; *maštaqtu*

šataru (a fine garment) jB lex.

šatā'u → *šatû* II

šāti → *šāt*

šâti "(of) him; that, this" Bab. (acc., gen.); "that, this same" (m. & f. acc., gen.); → *šêtu* I; *šī*; *šū*

šâtina "those, these same" M/jB(Ass.) (f. acc., gen.); < *šuātina*; → *šināti*

šatiqtu (a vessel) j/NB; < *šatāqu*

šatpu(m) "excavation, pit, hollow" O/jB [PÚ.SAG] esp. math. in calculation of vol.; < *šatāpu*

šatta(m) "this year" Ass., O/jB [Ass. MU(.1.KAM); NB MU.AN.NA.ÀM ?]; < *šattu*; → *šatti*

šattammu → *šatammu*

šattetaumma in *š. epēšu* mng. uncert. Nuzi; < Hurr.

šatti, occas. *šatta/u* in *ana š.* "thereupon, therefore" M/NB(lit.), also *aššatti/a*, *ina šatti*; < *šuāti*

šattišam(ma), *šattiša* "year by year; yearly" [MB (Ass.) MU-*šàm-ma*, MU.AN.NA-*šam*]; < *šattu*

šattu(m), *šantu(m)* f., occas. m.; pl. *šanātu* "year" [MU; MU.AN.NA; OA MU.X.ŠÈ; Bogh. etc. MU.KAM; jB MU.1.KAM] *šattum* (loc.-adv.), *ina/ana/ša šatti* "yearly", *šanat* (st. abs.) "one year", also after prep. (*ana*, *ištu*), also with poss. suff.; "(time of) year, the season"; *pān(i) š.* "spring"; *warkiāt/arkât š.* "later part of year"; *rēš š.* "new year"; NB *mār š.* "one-year-old" of animals; *qīt š.* "end of year"; *šatta(m) (ana) šatti(m)* etc. "year by year"; pl. "years = span of time", e.g. "years" of plenty; > *šatta*, *šatti= šamma*; *šattussu*; *šanassu*; → *rabūšene*; *šaddaqda*; *šaluššani*

šattu → also *šû* I; *šatti*

šattû → *šattūtu*; *šātû*

šattukku → *sattukku*

šatturru → *šāt urri*

šattussu "yearly" j/NB [MU.AN.NA-*us/ú-su*]; < *šattu*

šattušḫum (a drinking vessel)? Mari

šattūtu, *šattû* (a leather object) jB lex.

šatû(m) I "knotted, woven" O/jB; < *šatû* III

šatû(m) II, Ass. *šatā'u(m)* "to drink" [NAG] **G** (*i/i*, pret. later *ilti*, NA *issi*) of human, god, animal; of plant, of field "be watered"; of cultivators "have access to water rights" **Gtn** iter. of G [med. NAG.NAG; NAG.MEŠ] **Š** caus. of

G OA (usu. → *šaqû* III); > *šātû*; *šitû* II; *šutû* IV; *maštû*, *maštītu*

šatû(m) III "to knot together, weave" Bab. **G** (*u/u*) "weave" spider's web; "entangle" weapons in threads (*qê*); stat. of lines on hand "intersect"; "join" battle **D** as G Mari "weave" garment **Š** caus. of G **N** pass. of G of thread (*qû*) "be woven"; > *šatû* I, *šatûtu*; *šetâtu*; *šītu* II, *šitû* III?; *šutû* I; *šuttūtu*; *maštūtu*

šātu → *šāt*

šātû(m) (or *šattû(m)*) "drinking much" OB lex., jB; < *šatû* II

šâtu "him; that, this same" O/jB; O/MB (acc.) "him", "that, this same"; jB(Ass.) (acc., gen., occas. nom.) "that, this same"; → *šâta*; *šū*

šâtu → also *šêtu* II; *šu'ātu*

ša'tu, *za'tu* (a type of thorny plant) jB

šatubbû "ardent desire" jB lex.; < Sum.

šatummum → *šutummu*

šatumû "rain" jB lex.; < Sum.

šâtunu, *šâtun* "those, these same" OB(Ešn.), M/jB(Ass.) (m. acc., gen.); < *šuātunu*; → *šunūti*

šāt urri(m), *šaturru(m)*, *šatturru* 'that of the dawn' = "third watch of the night" Bab., NA [EN.NUN.UD.ZAL(.LA/LE)]; < *šāt* + *urru*

šaturru → *šassūru*; *šāt urri*

šatûtu "weaving" MA; < *šatû* III

šaṭāpu(m) "to preserve (life), rescue" OAkk, Bab. **G** (pret. *ištup*) esp. in PNs "save" people, life; > *šaṭpum*; *naštaptum*

šaṭāru I, NA *šaṭṭāru*; NB pl. *šaṭārānu* "(piece of) writing; copy, exemplar; written document" j/NB, NA; < *šaṭāru* II infin.

šaṭāru(m) II, Nuzi also *saṭāru* "to write (down)" [SAR; IN.SAR; in col. AB.SAR(.ÀM), GIŠ, GUB] **G** (*a/u*, NB pret. also *ilṭar*; NA imper. also *šuṭar*) "inscribe" tablet, stele; "copy"; "formulate" a document; "write down; put in writing" name, fact, oath; "list" troops; of Šamaš 'write' omen, on liver **Gtn** NB iter. of G **D** "put down in writing, list" facts, information **Š** caus. of G **N** pass. of G of year-name "be written"; of tablet, seal "be inscribed"; > *šaṭāru* I; *šaṭru*; *šiṭru*, *šiṭirtu*; *šaṭṭiru*; *mašṭaru*

šaṭāṭu "to rip open" jB **G** (*a/u*) of snake "tear open" body **D** as G ?

šaṭipu → *šadipu*

šaṭpum "rescued" OAkk as PN; < *šaṭāpu*

šaṭru(m) "written, inscribed" Bab. [SAR] esp. *šumu(m) š.* "written name"; of stele "inscribed"; Mari *ṣābum šaṭrūtum* "listed troops"; < *šaṭāru* II

šaṭṭāru → *šaṭāru* I

šaṭṭiru "eager to write" jB lex.; < *šaṭāru* II

šaṭû → *šeṭû* II

šâṭu I "to pull, tow" j/NB(lit.) **G** (pret. *išūṭ*) yoke; "haul" beams; "exert" o.s. **D** as G "draw" yoke; > *šā'iṭu*

šâṭu II "to despise, ignore" M/NB **G** (pret. *išūṭ*) "ignore" people, words; "neglect" duty; Am. also pass. forms (*tu-*, *u-* etc.) "be disloyal"?; → *šêṭu*; *šiāṭu*

ša'u (a wooden part of a waggon) MB

šâ'u(m) "to fly" O/jB **G** (pret. *išū'*) of birds; of men "like a bird" (*iṣṣūriš*) **Gtn** "fly around, back and forth" **D** of wind uncl.; → *šê'u* II

ša''uru → *šu''uru* II

šawarum → *šawirum*

šawinum (an illness) OB

šawirānu ~ "ring-shaped"? jB; < *šawirum*

šawirum, *šawarum*, OB often *šeliwerum*, *šelilameru*, NA *š/sabirru* f. "ring" OA, NA, O/jB [ḪAR] "torc" for hand, foot; of silver, gold, copper; also as PN; > *šawirānu*; *šuwwurum*; → *semeru*

šawû I "roasted" OB(Susa), jB of kid; < *šawû* II

šawûm II, *šamû*, occas. *šemû* "to roast" Bab. **G** (*i/i*) (intrans.) Mari of lion *išātam išwi* "roasted in the fire"; of malt; locusts **D** trans.; > *šawû* I; *šumû* I; *šumamtu*

šawû → also *šamû* I

šāyimānu(m) "purchaser, he who made the purchase" O/jB; < *šâmu*

šāyimānūtu "status of purchaser" jB; < *šâmu*

šazamû; pl. f. "Zamuan (wine-jar)" NA; < *ša* + PlN

šazbussu "consignment, delivery" NA of food, clothing; < *zabālu* Š

šazzātu → *šanzātu*

šazzuztum "representation; (business) representative" OA; < *izuzzum* Š

še → *ša*

-še → *-šim*; *-šu*

šeāru → *ši'āru*

še'āru → *šêru*

še'ā'u → *še'û*

šeberu → *šebru*

šebēru(m), OAkk, Ass. *šabāru(m)* "to break" **G** (*i/i*) bolt, bow etc.; "break up" clods, field, grain; bone, limb, neck; wing; persons ("break up" troops ?; "break" resistance ?); "break, contravene" words **D** as G "break up" statues; "break" bones, Nuzi "injure" ox **Dt** pass. of D of army "be broken up" **N** pass. of G [ḪAŠ;

also GAM] **Ntn** iter. of N; > *šebru*; *šibirtu*; *šabburum*, *šabburtu*, *šubburu*; *šabartu*

šēbētu → *šībtu* I

šeb'i → *sebe*

šebirbirredû (an offering of barley) jB [ŠE.BIR. BIR.(RE.)DA-*a*/DÈ-*e*]; < Sum.

šebirru (a building material) NB

šebirtu → *šebru*; *šibirtu*

šebītu → *sabītu*

šebru(m), *šeberu*, *šibru*, *šabru*; f. *šebirtu* "broken" O/jB [ḪAŠ] of wood, beam, chair, reed; bones, parts of body; "broken up" clods, turds; < *šebēru*

šebû(m) I, *šabû(m)*, Ass. *šabā'u(m)* "to be full (of = acc.); be replete, satisfied (with)" **G** (*i/i*) of human, animal with food, drink; "be fully paid, satisfied with" money; with sleep, (long) life (*balāṭa*), old age (*šībūta*), roaming (*atalluka*), plenty (*lalû* etc.) **Gtn** iter. of G **D** "fill with, satisfy with (= acc.)"; "give" animals "their fill" to eat, drink; "satisfy, pay in full" with money, goods etc.; long life, plenty **Dt** pass. of D OA "be fully satisfied with (= acc.)" payment **N** ingress. "become satiated"; > *šib'um*; *šabī'um*; *šebû* II; *šibbû* I; *šubû* III; *nešbû* I; *tašbītum*

šebû(m) II; f. *šebītu* "satisfied, sated" O/jB also *lā š.* "insatiable"; < *šebû* I

šēbu → *šību*

šēbultu(m), OAkk *šābultum*, OB *šībultum* "despatch, consignment" esp. OA of goods; *š. PN* "gift from PN"; < *wabālu* Š; → *šūbultu*

šeburtu (a colour)? NA(Tell Halaf) of wool

šēbuttu → *šībūtu*

šebûtu → *sibûtu*

šēbūtu → *šībūtu*

šeda'um, *šuda'um* (a prof. or title) Oakk

šeddu → *šēdu* I

*__šediš__, OB *sediš* st. abs.; f. *še/iššet*, *šiššat* "six"; *šeššet ūmū* "six days"; > *šedištum*; *šeššīšu*; *šeššu*; *šeššiš*; *šeššātu*; *šadāšium*; *šaššūtē-*; *šuššu* I; *šudušīu*; *šudūšum*; *šiššat*; *suduštu*; *suddû*

šedištum "group of six" OA; < *šediš*

šedû, *šēdu* "sprout" jB, NA lex.; < Sum.

šēdu(m) I, *šīdum*, occas. *šeddu* "protective deity; luck" Bab., NA [^{d}ALAD; A.RÁ] often with *lamassu*; *š. rašû* "to acquire *š.*"; good, protective *š.*; *š. bīti(m)* "household god"; "personal god" of individual, e.g. *š. šarrim* "*š.* of the king"; *šēduššu* "under his protective deity"; figur(in)e, representation of *š.*; also evil *š.*, e.g. *š. lumnim*, *lemnu*; *š. sanî* "deputy *š.*"

šēdu II (a plant) jB lex.

šēdu → also *šedû*

šeduštum → *šeššu*

še'ēru mng. uncert. jB **G** unattested ? **Gtn** iter. of G of demons, obj. thresholds

šegû I, Mari *šagûm* "wild, aggressive" O/jB; < *šegû* II

šegû(m) II "to be wild, rave" O/jB **G** stat. of dog "is rabid" **N** (pret. *iššegu*, *iššegi*) "become wild, start raving" [IDIM] of animals, woman **Ntn** iter. of N of animals; goddess; > *šegû* I; *mešgûm*

šegû → also *šigû*

šegu(n)nû(m) "grain crop" O/jB(lit.) [ŠE.GU.NU; ŠE.GÙN.NU]; < Sum.

šegušsu, *šegūšu* → *šigūšu*

Šeḫali (a month) Nuzi; < Hurr.

šēḫānu, *šīḫānu* (an ecstatic) jB [Á.KAM]; < *šēḫu*

šeḫēqu "to sneeze"? jB **G** (*i/i*)

šeḫeru, *šiḫiru* "morning" jB lex.; < W.Sem.

šeḫetnu/i, *šeḫtenu*, *šeḫtuni* (a fraction) Nuzi; < Hurr.

šeḫēṭu → *šaḫāṭu* III

šeḫlātum, *šaḫlātum* (a vegetable) Mari

Šeḫli (a month) Nuzi; < Hurr.

šeḫlum, *šiḫlu*, *šillu* "high water"? Bab. lex.

šeḫtenu → *šeḫetnu*

šēḫtu; pl. *šēḫātu* "incense burner" M/NA of metal; used in cult; *š. šarrû* "to start a *š.*"; *š.* for purification (*tēlisse*); for wine

šeḫtuni → *šeḫetnu*

šeḫṭu(m), *šiḫṭu(m)* "jump, attack; (astronomical) rising" Bab., NA [GU$_4$.UD] "attack" of lion, snake; "raid, razzia", *ḫarrān š.* "raiding expedition"; *š. šamši(m)* "sunrise"; astr. as term for Mercury; < *šaḫāṭu* I

šeḫû → *šaḫû* I; *šēḫu*; *šêḫu*

šēḫu, *šīḫu*, occas. *šeḫû* "wind, breath" M/jB, Am. *š. ṭābu* "favourable wind" of king; med. "air, breath" in body, head; "inspiration", *ša šēḫi* "ecstatic"; < *šâḫu*; > *šēḫānu*

šēḫu → also *šīḫu* I.III

šêḫu (or *šeḫû* ?) **N** "to be agitated"? jB of people (*nišū*); → *šâḫu*

šē'iqum (an official controlling measurement of grain) OB; < *šêqu*

še'ittu, *še'ītu* → *še'tu*; *ši'ītum*

šekaruḫḫu, *šekarû* (a copper object) Nuzi in pairs

šeklinnu (desig. of goats) Nuzi; < Hurr.

šekṣu → *šakṣu*

šēlabiš "like a fox" jB(Ass.); < *šēlebu*

šēlabu → *šēlebu*

šelaltu → *šalāš*
šelappāyu → *šeleppāyu*
šelappû → *šeleppû*
šelāšā → *šalāšā*
šelāšī- → *šalāšī-*
šelāšû → *šalāšû*
šēlebu(m), *šellebu*, Ass. *šēlubu* "fox" [KA5.A] in fables, proverbs, similes; → *karānu* 4; a star (*g* in Ursa Major) [MUL.KA5.A]; as PN; OB, jB lex. (a kind of fish); OB, jB lex. (a bird or locust); > *šēlabiš*, *šēlebūtu*
šēlebūtu, *šīlibūtu* "vixen" O/jB [MUNUS.KA5.A]; < *šēlebu*
šelēḫu → *salāḫu* II
šelenāyu (type of worker or soldier) MA; < Hurr. or gentilic from PlN
šeleppāyu, *šelappāyu* (a type of craftsman)? M/NA, Nuzi; *rab š.* "overseer of *š.*"; < gentilic ?
šeleppû(m), *šilippû*, NA *šelappû* **1.** "turtle" [NÍG.BÚN.NA(.KU6)]; also as model in gold **2.** (a type of snake)
šeleppūtu, *šalippūtum*; pl. *šeleppūtātu(m)* "she-turtle" OAkk, O/jB; also *š. ša tābali* 'turtle of dry land' = "tortoise"
šelippūtu, *šeliptu* → *šelliptu*
šelītu → *silītu* I
šellaḫurû → *sallaḫurû*
šellaru → *šallaru*
šellebēnu → *šallapānu*
šellebu → *šēlebu*
šelli(n)tannu (an official or functionary, phps.) "authorized agent" Nuzi, stat. *šelli(n)tannāku* "I am ..."; < Hurr.?
še(l)liptu, also NB *šelippūtu* (a metal implement) jB lex., NB
šelluḫlūtu "status of a *šiluḫlu*" Nuzi; < *šiluḫlu*
šēltu, NA *šēssu*; pl. *šēlātu* "sharp blade, point" jB, NA of scraper, sword; mountain peaks *kīma š. patri* "like the point of a dagger"; < *šêlu*
šelû I mng. uncert. jB lex.; < *šelû* II
šelû II mng. uncert. O/jB **G** of tooth, features of exta **Gt** lex. **D** lex.; > *šelû* I
šelû III, *selû* "to be neglectful; neglect" NB **G** (*u*/*u* and *i*/*i*) "be neglectful" of (= *ana*/*ina* (*muḫḫi*)) oath, guard-duty etc.; "neglect" (+ acc.) sin, ration-payment; > *šilûtu*
šelû → also *šalû* II
šēlu, *še'lu* "sharpened" M/jB of weapons; < *šêlu*
šēlu → also *šīlu* I
šêlu(m) "to sharpen, whet" O/jB **G** weapons; teeth **D** as G of troops before battle; > *šēlu*, *šēltu*, *šēlūtu*; *mešēltu*
šêlu → also *šiālu*
še'lu → *šēlu*
šeluḫansirru (a stage in the growth of barley) jB lex.; < Sum.
šēlūtu "pointed blade" jB(Ass.) of weapons, in similes; < *šêlu*
šēlūtu → also *šēlū'atum*
šēlū'utum, *šēlūtu* Ass. (Bab. → *šūlūtu* II) **1.** OA, pl. *šēlū'ētum* "upward consignment" (to Anatolia) **2.** MA "material brought up, scum" **3.** NA "votive gift" of objects; esp. of female votaries; *mārē š.* "sons of votaries"; < *elû* III Š
šemāḫu → *šimāḫu*
šemeru → *šawirum*
šemētu → *šamātu*
šēmētu → *šēmu*
šemmium, *šemmû*, also *šemmueum*, *šemmeau*, *šenmeû* "that constantly hears, listens" OB lex., MB of men; gods, also in PNs; < *šemû*; → *šēmû*
šēmtu → *šīmtu*
šemu → *šumu*
šemû(m), *šamû*, OAkk, Ass. *šamā'u(m)* "to hear" [GIŠ.TUK; also ŠE.GA; NA in PNs ḪAL] **G** (*e*/*e*; imper. *šime* and *šeme*; NB prec. also *lušmu*, perf. *altemu*; NA imper. *še'i*, perf. pl. *issa''ū*) **1.** of men, gods; of judge "hear" a case; of ears (*uznāya*) **2.** "hear" a tablet, have it read to one **3.** "be informed of", "learn of" s.th. **4.** "listen to" s.o.; "obey" person, command **5.** "understand" speech; of gods "hear, accede to" prayer, freq. in PNs **R** Mari **Gtn** (also *ištanammi*, imper. *tišamme*) iter. of G "hear, listen to constantly"; "read" tablet, letter "carefully"; "hear on separate occasions" **Gt** NB "make a mutual agreement" **D** NA stat. "is made to hear, is informed" **Š** caus. of G; "read" tablet to s.o.; "report" to s.o. **Štn** iter. of Š **Št** "cause to hear successively" ref. to more than one hearer **N** "be heard, obeyed, listened to"; "become known"; > *šēmû*, *šāme'ānu*; *šemmium*; *nešmû*; *tešmû*, *Tašmētu*
šemû → also *šawû* II
šēmu, also f. pl. *šēmētu* "fat, grease" jB lex.
šēmû(m) "hearer; that hears" Bab. [ŠE(.GA)] *lā š.* "disobedient"; of god "not attentive" to prayers; < *šemû*; → *šemmium*
šena → *šina* II
šenamašan → *šinašan*
šendu, *šindu*; f. *šemittu*; f. pl. *šendētu* "branded, marked" NB of sheep; < *šamātu*
šengallu, *šengannu* (a cooking vessel) jB lex.; < Sum.

šenmeû → *šemmium*

šennu → *šannu*

šenû(m) mng. unkn. O/jB **G**, an action or movement

šēnu(m) I f.; freq. du. "sandal(s), shoe(s)" [(KUŠ.)E.SÍR/SIR; NA phps. KUŠ.DA/DÀ. E.SIR/SÍR]; jB lex. (a type of fish); > *šênu*

šēnu II, *šīnu* (a wooden part of a waggon) Nuzi

šēnu → also *šannu*

šênu "to put on (shoes)" jB **G** (*e*/*e*) with acc. *šēnu*; < *šēnu* I denom.; > *mešēnu*

šēpānu- → *šēpu*

šēpītu(m), *šīpītu* "foot", transf. "lower end" Bab., NA [GÌR-] of furniture; of dam, terrace; of statue; topog. "lower side" of field etc.; < *šēpu*

šepṣu → *šapṣu*; *šipṣu*

šepṭu → *šapṭu*

šepûm, *šapûm* "to ask, question (s.o.)" OB **G** (*i*/*i*) **D** "cross-question" **Š** caus. of G

šepû → also *šapû* II-IV

šēpu(m), OB often *šīpum* f., often du.; pl. *šēpēlātu(m)* "foot" [GÌR; OAkk phps. DU; ext. also AŠ ?] (loc.-adv. with pron. suff. *šēpilaššu*, *šēpū'a* etc.; du. *šēpānuššu*) of human, animal, bird; *ina š.* "on foot"; seize (*ṣabātu*) in supplication; kiss f.; cut off f. of enemy, foreigner, from territory = repel invasion; dust of f.; NA *šēpēya* "my own" chariot, troops etc., *ša šēpē* "personal"; transf. *šēp PN* "(at) the foot of PN" = OA under his control, in his caravan; OB = under his responsibility; "(furniture) foot"; *kīma šēpīšunu* "according to their rank" Nuzi, NB; "foot" of mountain; of constellation, cloud; ext. (a feature on liver); > *šēpītu*, *šêpu*

šêpu "to stride"? jB lex. **G**; < *šēpu* denom.

šepua mng. unkn. Nuzi

šeqqatu → *šiqītu*

šeqtu (a date tax)? NB; < *šêqu* ?

šeqû mng. unkn. Ug. lex.

šēqu I (a vessel) MB

šēqu II adj. mng. uncert. jB pl. of arrow

šêqu(m) "to level off" O/jB **G** grain in measuring-vessel; > *šīqu* II; *šē'iqum*, *mešēqu*

šer → *šerru*

-šer → *–šeret*

šēra → *šēru* II

šerammuḫḫu "north" Nuzi; < Hurr.

šer'ānu(m), also *šir'ānu(m)* "vein, artery; ligament, tendon; nerve" [SA(.A)] in human and animal body; "sinew" for bow, armour, musical instrument; OB "allocation of work" (same word ?)

šer'azum, *tu*/*ar'azu* (a nut tree)? O/jB

šerbillu (a tree) jB lex.; < Sum.

šerdannu, *širdannu* (type of person) Am., Ug.

šerdingirgallakku (a divine hymn) jB; < Sum.

šerēmu → *šarāmu*

šerešrānum → *šaršarānum*

-šeret, *-šer* "ten" in compound numerals, e.g. *ištēnšeret*, *šinšeret*, *ḫamiššeret*; < *ešer*; → *-šerīšu*; *-šerû*

šergiddû (a Sum. song) jB [ŠÈR.GÍD.DA]; < Sum.

šergûm "adorned"? OAkk

šerḫānu → *šer'ānu*; *širḫānu*

šerḫu → *šer'u*

šerḫullum → *šurḫullu*

šeriktu(m), *širiktu(m)* "present, grant, offering; dowry" Bab., NA [NB PNs RU-] *ana š. šarāku(m)*; NB husband's "(wedding) gift"; < *šarāku* I

šerimtum, *širimtu*, NB *širindu* **1.** OB as PN mng. unkn. **2.** NB "cutting; weeding" on field; < *šarāmu*

šeriš "violently" jB; < *šēru* I

-šerīšu "ten times" in compound numerals, e.g. *ištēnšerīšu*, *erbēšerīšu*; < *ešer*; → *-šeret*

šeri'tu, *šer'ītu* (a divine garment) j/NB, NA; presented to temple

šerkatu, *šiškatu* "female temple oblate" NB [MUNUS.RIG$_7$]; < *šerku* I

šerk(i)-ilūtu, *šiški-ilūtu* "position, status of temple oblate" NB; < *šerku* I + *ilu*

šerku(m) I, *širku(m)*, NB also *širaku*, *šišku* **1.** OAkk, OB in PNs ?; MA "gift, (part of) dowry"; Ug. (a tax) **2.** j/NB "temple oblate" [LÚ.RIG$_7$]; *rab š.* "overseer of the oblates"; also in PNs; MA also (a palace functionary); < *šarāku* I; > *šerkatu*, *šerki-ilūtu*, *šerkūtu*

šerku(m) II, *šerkû* "string" (of dried fruit) OAkk, OB, Ug. lex., jB of figs, apples etc.

šerku III mng. unkn. jB lex. of reeds

šerku IV (a capacity measure)? jB lex.

šerkû → *šerku* II

šerkugû (a Sum. song) jB [ŠÈR.KÙ.GA-]; < Sum.

šerkūtu, *širikūtu* "position of temple oblate" NB [LÚ.RIG$_7$-]; < *šerku* I

šermum → *širmu*

šernamennakku, **šernamgalakku**, **šernamginakku**, **šernamurunakku** (types of Sum. songs) jB; < Sum.

šernu(m), *širnu(m)* **1.** (a wooden chariot part) OB, M/NA **2.** (a container) Mari (= 1 ?)

šerqum "stolen goods" OA ; < *šarāqu* I

šerqu → also *serqu*

šerru(m), OA also *šarrum*; Nuzi pl. also f. "(young) child" [LÚ.TUR; TUR.DIŠ] "baby"; "child" (of s.o.); OB, Elam "descendant", also *šer(ri) šerri(m)* "descendant(s)"

šeršānum (a cult song) OB in *ša š.* (a cultic singer); < Sum.

šeršerratu(m), *šeršerretu*, Ass. *šaršarratu(m)* "chain, set of rings" Ass., O/jB [(URUDU.) ŠÈR.ŠÈR; M/jB also URUDU.MÚRU. ŠÈR.ŠÈR]; OA du.; esp. used as fetters; < *šeršerru*; > *šuršurrātu*

šerše(r)ru(m), *širširum* "link (in chain)" OAkk(Sum.), O/jB; ext. (a feature on spleen, kidney etc.); > *šeršerratu*

šeršerru → also *šaršerru*; *šerru*

šērtu(m) I, *šīrtu(m)* "guilt, crime; punishment" OAkk, Bab. [NIR.DA] often "guilt and penalty"; "vice"; "offence" against (= gen.) king, god; heavy, great; impose (*emēdu*, *šakānu*), bear (*w/zabālu*), release (*paṭāru*, *tabālu*) etc.; → *nerṭû*

šērtu(m) II, *šīrtu(m)* "morning" Bab., M/NA [Á.GÚ.ZI.GA (→ *šēru* II)]; *šērtam*, *ina šērti(m)*, Mari *in šērtēn* "in the morning"; *ina šērti*, *iššērta* also = "tomorrow morning"; pl. *ina/ša šērēti* (NA *šērāti*) "in the morning hours"; *Ištar ilat šērēti* "goddess of dawn", Venus; < *šēru* II

šērtu(m) III, *šīrtum* "bar" O/jB; as part of locking mechanism; of gold

šērtu → also *šārtu*

šerṭu(m), *širṭu(m)*, NB *šišṭu* ~ "cloth strip, rag, tatter" OAkk, Bab., NA; < *šarāṭu*

šerû I ~ "to take refuge" O/jB **G** (*i/i*) of bat in crevice **D**, **Dtn** lex. only

šerû II ~ "to lay down" O/jB, NA **G** (*i/i*) beam; stat. of vegetation on mountain-side; feature on liver **D** as G lex.; > *šēru* V

šerû III "to redeem"? NB **G** (*i/i*) o.'s share

šerû IV mng. uncert. Ug. **G** (*a/a*)

-šerû(m) "...teenth" in compound numerals, e.g. *ištēnšerû*, *erbēšerû*; < *ešer*; → *-šeret*

šēru(m) I ~ "fierce" O/jB god; demon; weapon; > *šēriš*

šēru(m) II, *šīru* "morning" Bab. [Á.GÚ.ZI.GA (→ *šērtu* II); NB KIN.NIM]; "morning star, dawn"; *šēra*, *ina šēr(i(m))* "in the morning"; *maṣṣarti š.* "morning watch"; *naptan š.* "morning meal"; OB, O/MB(Alal.), Bogh., Ug. *urra(m) šēra(m)* "later on, in the future"; > *šêru*, *šērtu* II; Ass. → *ši'āru*

šēru(m) III "song, chant" O/jB [KI.RU.GÚ]; also (a musical interval); < Sum.

šēru IV (a kind of mat) jB lex.; also OAkk *šīrum* ?

šēru V adj. mng. uncert. jB lex.; < *šerû* II

šēru VI subst. mng. unkn. jB lex.

šēru VII subst. mng. unkn. jB lex.

šēru → also *sīru* I; *šīru*

šêru(m), NA *še'āru* "to rise early" **G** (*e/e*) esp. in hendiad. "do s.th. in the morning"; with *šumšû* "spend all day" **Gtn** iter. OA; < *šēru* II denom.; → *šurru*

šer'u(m), *šir'u(m)*, *še/irḫu(m)* f. "furrow" OAkk, Bab. [AB.SÍN]; *š. šakānum*, *maḫāṣu*, *petû* "to put in furrows"; *eqel š.* "field with furrows"; as source of produce; OAkk(Nuzi) = $^1/_3$ ell; OB(Susa), MB in MNs; part of the constellation Virgo

še'ru "(pock-)marked" jB; → *šu''uru* II

šerwanaše, *širwanaše* mng. unkn. Qatna of gold cup; < Hurr.

šeryam → *sariyam*

šesanû (a container) OB

šēssu → *šēltu*

šešanu → *šišnu*

šešgallu, *šešgulû* "big brother, elder brother" j/NB [(LÚ.)ŠEŠ.GAL] term for a high priest; freq. in col.; < Sum.

šešgallūtu "post of *šešgallu*" jB [LÚ.ŠEŠ.GAL-]

šešgulû → *šešgallu*

šešimtu; Hurr. pl. *šešimtena* (a leather object) Nuzi; < Hurr.

šešmittu (a stone) Qatna

šeššanna/u → *eššēšu*

šeššātu, *šiššātu* "with six (spokes or yoked animals)" MB, MB(Alal.), Nuzi, jB lex.; also with Hurr. suff. *šeššātupḫe*; < *šediš*

šeššektu → *šiššiktu*

šeššeku (a bird) jB lex.; < Sum.

šeššeru → *šaršerru*

šeššērum → *šaššāru*

šeššet → *šediš*

šeššiktu → *šiššiktu*

šeššiš "sixfold" OB; < *šediš*

šeššīšu, *šiššīšu* "six times" OA, OB [A.RÁ.6-*šu*; 6-*šu*]; < *šediš*

šeššu(m), *šiššu(m)*; f. OA *šedištum*, OB *še/iduštum* **1.** "sixth" [6-] **2.** "one-sixth"; < *šediš*

šeštum mng. unkn. OB lex.

šeštuḫlu (an official) Nuzi; < Hurr.

šēšû(m), occas. *tēšû* (a small net) O/jB; *ša š./t.* "hunter or fowler using nets" OB lex.

šetâtu f. pl. (a garment) Ug.; < *šatû* III

šetertu mng. unkn. NB agricultural term

šêti → *šêtu* I

šetiptu → *šitiptu*

šētiš "as with a net" jB; < *šētu* I

šetru mng. unkn. MB(Susa)

šettu "sin, act of negligence" j/NB; < *šêṭu*; > *šettūtu*; → *šeṭṭu*

šettu → also *ši'ītum*

šettūtu "sin" jB; < *šettu*

šetû → *šitû* II; *šêtu* II

šētu(m) I f.; pl. *šētētu* "(hunting) net" Bab. [(GIŠ.)SA] knotted, for gazelle, deer; bird; in battle, for men; also transf.; *ša š.* "hunter or fowler using nets" OB lex.; > *šētiš*

šētum II (a textile) OB

šêtu I, *šêti* "that, this same" Mari m. & f., acc., gen.; → *šâti*

šêtu(m) II, *sêtu(m)*, OB also *šiātum*, Bogh. lex. *šâtu* "to be/leave remaining" (trans. & intrans.) OAkk, OA, O/jB **G** (pret. *išē/īt*, pres. *išêt*, jB also *išettu/i*) in account-keeping; in PNs, curses, prayers "leave s.o. alive"; "leave (to stand)" of vessel; "be remaining, escape, be left" **D** OA mng. unkn.; > *šittu* II, *sittūtu*

še'tu(m), *ši'tu(m)*, *še'ittu(m)*, *še'ītu* "mattress, bolster" O/jB, M/NA of bed, chair; < *šê'u* I

šeṭṭu "crime, evil deed" jB; < *šêṭu*; → *šettu*; *šēṭum*

šeṭû I "wide open" jB of pit; < *šeṭû* II

šeṭû(m) II, *šaṭû* "to spread out" j/NB **G** (*i/i*) corpses, trees, like malt (*buqlu*) **Gtn** distrib. of G jB **Š** (jB *ušelṭi*) caus. of G; > *šeṭû* I; *mešṭītu*, *mešṭû*

šēṭum "crime, evil deed" OB; < *šêṭu*; > *šēṭūtu*; → *šeṭṭu*

šēṭu → also *šīṭu* I

šêṭu(m) "to miss (accidentally); neglect, despise, commit crime" Bab. **G** "spurn, disregard" person; oath, enemy; "sin, do evil"; > *šettu*, *šettūtu*, *šeṭṭu*, *šēṭum*; *šēṭūtu*; → *šâṭu* II; *šiāṭu*

šēṭūtu(m), OA *šēṭuttum*, O/jB also *šīṭūtu(m)* "scorn, neglect" OA, O/jB in *š.* (of s.o.) *leqû(m)/laqā'um* "to scorn, spurn (s.o.)"; < *šēṭum*

še'u(m) f. (phps. to be read *û(m)*) "barley; grain" [ŠE(-*um/am/im*)(.MEŠ); NA phps. ŠE.PAD.MEŠ] gener. "barley", OA phps. "wheat"; pine "kernel"; "grain" as a unit of measure

še'û(m), Ass. *še'ā'u(m)*; also *šê'u* "to seek (out)" **G** (forms → GAG §106t) "seek" s.th., advice, life; from s.o. (= acc.); OA leg. "call on" s.o. for help; a person (in friendship), fraternally (*ana aḫḫūtim*); god (for help); "seek (to do)" harm; poet. "probe, scrutinize" plans etc. **Gtn** [KIN.KIN] iter. and distrib. "seek constantly for, seek for in various places", esp. "visit" places (*ašrī*, *ašrāti*) "assiduously"; "strive constantly for" throne; of demons "search out (s.o.) continually"; "follow, strive after" behaviour, command; life, good, evil; "seek out" favourable day, wind; "be assiduous (in reverence) towards; be solicitous (for the welfare of)" **Gt** uncert. **D** as G "seek" s.o., "seek help from" s.o. **Dtn** jB lex. = Gtn ?; > *mušte''û*

šē'u, *šī'u* "neighbour" jB esp. *š. bābi* "one who frequents the door", "regular visitor"; < *še'û*; > *šī'ūtum*; f. → *ši'ītum*

šê'u(m) I ~ "to pad, upholster" O/jB, MA **G** only stat. *šē'* of pillow etc. "is stuffed with (= acc.)"; > *še'tu*

šê'u II "to fly" jB(Ass.) **G** of king, troops on campaign (var. of → *šâ'u*)

šê'u → also *še'û*

še'urinnakku → *surinakku*

še'urrû (or *marše'urrû*) "winnowing shovel" jB lex.; < Sum.

šewerum → *šawirum*

šezibbu → *šizbu*

šēzubtum "relief, holiday" OB; < *ezēbu* Š

šēzuzu "very fierce" j/NB of god, dragon; < *ezēzu*; → *šūzuzu*

ši "of" OAkk gen. of *šu* "he of"

-ši "her" (3 f. sg. acc. suff.) (→ GAG §42g-k)

-ši → also *-šim*

šī "she; that, this same" Ass. rare [BI] "she" before vb.s, giving emphasis, *šīma* "it is she who ..."; Mari *šī lā šī* "this or that"; "that, this same" (of f. nouns); OB *lā šī* "(s.th.) unseemly"; > *šīt*, *šīti*; → *iššī*; for acc. etc. → *šâti*, *šiāti*, *šuāti*; *šâši*, *šiāšim*, *šuāšim*

šiābum, *šâbu* "to be(come) old" OA, O/jB **G** of person, animal **Gtn** "become ever older"; > *šību*, *šībūtu*; *šībtu*

šiāḫum I, *šâḫu* "to grow (tall)" O/jB **G** (pret. once *išūḫ*; O/jB also *iš(t)ēḫ*) of gods, men, animals, birds; trees, plants, mountains; of men "grow, be great" in wisdom (*ina tašīmti*) **D** mng. uncert.; > *šīḫu* I, *šīḫtu*; *šuḫḫu* I; *mušiḫḫu*, *mušīḫtum*; *tašīḫu*?

šiāḫu II mng. uncl. NA

šiālu(m), *šâlu*, also *šêlu* "to coat, smear" Ass., O/jB **G** wall with components of plaster **D** ~ G OA **Dt** pass.? OB

šiāmātu(m) pl. tant. "purchased goods, commercial stock" O/MA; OA silver etc. *ana š.*

"for (buying) purchased goods"; MA "(real estate acquired by) purchase"; < *šâmu*

šiāmu(m), *šâmu* "to fix, decree" [NAM] **G** (ptcp. → D) *šīmta(m)*, *šīmāti(m) š.* "make o.'s will, testament", "bequeath"; "decree (s.o.'s) fate"; *šīmat balāṭi, marušti* (etc.) *š.* "decree a fate of life, trouble etc." for s.o. (= dat.); *ana šīmti(m) š.* "decree as (s.o.'s) fate"; "decree" strength, wisdom; festival; purchase price **Gt** "decree for ever"? **D** usu. ptcp. st. constr. *mušīm*, pl. *mušimmū* for G ptcp. (→ GAG §104k) **N** pass. of G "be decreed"; "be specified" for ritual purpose; > *šīmtu*

šianātu (a textile) Nuzi; wool for *š.*

***šiānum**, *šânu* "to urinate" M/jB **G**; **Gt** as G **Gtn**; > *šīnātu*; *muštinnu*; *šatānu*

šiāqum mng. unkn. OB **G** (*išīq*, *ištīq* only)

šiāriš "in the morning" OB(poet.)

ši(')āru(m), *šiyāru*, *šeāru* "morning" Ass. (Bab. → *šēru* II); OA *ina šiārim*, MA pl. f. *ina šiārāte*, NA *ana/ina/iš-šiāre* "in the morning(s)"

šiaru[...] (a metal object) Ug.

šiāṣu(m), *šâṣu*, NA also *siāṣu* "to decline, wane" O/jB, NA **G** of prosperity, water level, daylight **N** ingress.

šiāš(im) "to her" OB; → *šī*

šiāti, lex. also *šeāti* "(of) her; that, this same" OAkk, Ass., OB "her" (acc.); "of her" (gen.); OA also dat.; "that, this same" message, slave girl, tablet etc., M/NA *ina šattimma šiāti* "in that same year"; OA *aššiāti* "therefore" (< *ana* I + *š.*); → *šī*

šiātum → *šētu* II

šiāṭu "to be(come) neglectful" NA **G** (stat. *šēṭu*) towards the rituals (*ana nēpešē*); > *šīṭu* I; → *šâṭu* II; *šēṭu*

šibartu → *šibirtu*

šibā'u, *šipā'u* (a ration) Nuzi of barley, tin

šibbu(m) I, *šippu(m)* "belt" Bab. "(sword-)belt"; "girdle" of birth-stones

šibbu(m) II (a fierce mythical snake) MB(roy. inscr.), jB; also in comparisons

šibbu III, *šību* (a disease) O/jB

šibbu IV mng. uncert. NB

šibbu V mng. unkn. jB lex.

šibbû I (provisions) jB lex.; < *šebû* I

šibbû II in *ša š.* (desig. of a person) OB lex.

šibburratu, *sibburratu*, Bogh. also *šinburratu* (a plant, phps.) "rue (*Ruta*)" M/jB [Ú.LUḪ. MAR.TU/TÚ]; as drug → *sibbirru*

šib'ettān(a) → *sebîšu*

šibḫu "deposit, layer" jB (with *šabāḫu* Št); *š. mūti* "pall of death"; < *šabāḫu*

šibibânu, *šibibiānu* → *zibibiānum*

šibirru(m), *šipirru*, occas. *sibirru* "shepherd's staff; sceptre" Bab., M/NA [GIŠ.ŠIBIR] "staff" carried by shepherds (as weapon); of gods, kings "(ceremonial) staff, sceptre", with crown or mace (*ḫaṭṭu*); of ivory, among booty; < Sum.

šibirtu(m), *šebirtum*, NA *šipirtu*, Ug. *šibartu* "piece, block" OAkk, Bab., NA [KÙ.PAD. DU/DA?; LAGAB] "block, lump" of silver, copper, gold; of lapis lazuli; "lump" of malt, as drug; < *šebēru*

šibīšu → *sebîšu*

šibittu "dill (*Anethum*)" NB

šibītu (or *šipītu*) "suture, seam" jB in garment, building, skull; < *šapû* IV

šibqātu, *šibqētu* f. pl. tant. "plan" M/NB also in PN; → *šibqū*

šibqu (or *šipqu*) (part of a doorpost) jB lex.

šibqū pl. tant. "scheme, plan; trick, plot" Bab. esp. with *še'û* G(tn) "to initiate hostile schemes"; → *šibqātu*; *šiqpu*

šibru (a plant) jB

šibru → also *šebru*

šibsātu, *sibsātu* f. pl. tant. "anger, angry rejection" M/jB esp. *š. ili* "divine rejection"; < *šabāsu*

šibšatu → *šipšatu*

šibšu(m) (an agricultural tax) from OAkk on; on various cereals, sesame, NA esp. on straw; *š. eqli(m)* "tax on a field"; < *šabāšu*

šibtu (or *šiptu*) (a cup) jB lex.

šībtu(m) **1.** O/jB also pl. *šībātu*, *šēbētu* "greyness, grey hair" **2.** "old woman" [MUNUS.ŠU.GI] **3.** OB "female witness"; < *šību*

šibṭu "blow; epidemic" M/NB, NA **1.** ~ "epidemic, plague" (→ also *šipṭu* I.II); of plague god (*bēl š.*); f. pl. *šibṭātu(m)* **2.** "gale, blast" of wind; med. *š. šāri* (a disease); < *šabāṭu* II

šibû → *sebû*

šību(m), *šēbu*, *sību*, *šīpu*; f. *šībtu* "old (person); elder; witness" [(LÚ/MUNUS.)ŠU.GI/GI4(.A); (ERÍN.)AB(.BA)] **1.** "old" of men, animals; as subst. "old man"; astr. constellation Perseus **2.** "elder" of community (*š. ālim*), PlN, land etc.; pl. usu. *šībūtu(m)* **3.** "witness" [OAkk AB×ÁŠ (reduplicated = pl.); OB LÚ.(KI.) INIM.MA(.BI); Nuzi, Ug., NA (LÚ.)IGI]; OB pl. usu. *šībū*; jB ext. "textual witness"; < *šiābu*; > *šībtu*; *šībūtu*

šību → also *šibbu* III; *šib'um*; *šīpu* II.III

šību → *sābû*

šib'um, *šību* "satisfaction" O/jB; < *šebû* I

šibūbu "spark, scintillation" jB lex.; < *šabābu* I

šībultum → *šēbultu*

šībūtu(m), *šēbūtu*, Ass. *šī/ēbuttu(m)* [(NAM.) AB.BA; ŠU.GI- ; NB LÚ.AB.BA.MEŠ] **1.** "old age" of men, i.e. long life; "condition of old age", i.e. senility, also of buildings **2.** "function as witness" **3.** "testimony", e.g. *š. nadānum* "to give testimony", *ṭuppum ša š.* "tablet acting as t."; < *šību*

šidaḫu(m) ~ "healthy appearance"? O/jB of face, figure

šidallu → *šitaddaru*

šidapu (a type of leather) NB for shoes

šiddatu I (a stand for a large vessel) j/NB of wood, silver; on a ship; < *šadādu*

šiddatu(m) II mng. unkn. O/jB

šiddātu → *šiddu* 2

šiddi-nārāya "riverbank dweller" NA; < *šiddu* + *nāru* I

šiddu(m) "side, edge; curtain" **1.** "(longer) side" [UŠ] of fields, buildings etc. (opp. = *pūtu*); upper/lower (*elû/šaplû*); math. of rectangle; "side" of right-angled triangle; of parts of body; of implement, furniture; piece of cloth; M/NA, M/jB "side, bank" of river, canal, sea; of mountain **2.** "stretch; stage" of road; ~ "district"; esp. *š. māti* "length and breadth of land"; Mari pl. f. *šiddāt ēkallim* "palace area"; MB(Alal.), Emar as surface & linear measure **3.** "curtain, cover", *š. šadādu* "to draw c."; MA on chair; *bīrīt šiddī* "cubicle surrounded by curtains" jB rit., mag. **4.** *šiddāt ṭupšarrim* "measurement of scribe" OB(Elam.); < *šadādu*; → *šiddi-nārāya*

šīdum → *šēdu* I

šid'u → *šit'u*

šiduri "girl" jB lex. also as fPN in Gilg.; < Hurr.

šiduštum → *šeššu*

šigammu → *šagammu*

šigarriûm → *šugarriā'um*

šigaru(m), *sigaru* "(wooden) clamp" [(GIŠ.) SI.GAR] "(neck-)stock" for captives; "door lock, bolt", also transf. e.g. *š. šamê* "bolt of heaven"; jB *ša š.* "guardian of the lock"; < Sum.

šiggatu mng. unkn. jB; < *šagāgu*

šiggatu → also *sikkatu* II

šiggi(a)nnu (a tree or its wood) Nuzi

šiggû mng. unkn. jB

šigguštu, *šimguštu* (a garden plant) M/jB lex., med.

šigilikûm (or *šigiliqûm*) (an official)? OB

šigillu → *sikillu*

šigiltu(m), OB also *šagiltum* ~ "misappropriation" Bab. esp. to take (*ekēmu*, *našû* etc.) *ana/ina š.*; < *šagālu*

šigištum "slaughter, killing" OB; < *šagāšu*

šigmiš "loudly" jB(poet.); < *šigmu*

šigmu "noise" jB; < *šagāmu* II; > *šigmiš*

šigû, *šegû*, once *šimgû* (a cry of lamentation) Bab. *š. šasû*; *ana š. erēbu* "to enter (a temple) to (recite) *š.*"; as desig. of prayer; also in PNs

šigugāru (a type of stone) jB lex., med.

šigūšu, *šegūšu*, *šeguššu* **1.** O/jB (a type of barley) [ŠE.MUŠ$_5$] bread, flour of *š.* **2.** jB lex. (a kind of apple tree)?; < Sum.?

šiḫānu (an official) NA lex. [LÚ.KA.TAR]

šīḫānu → *šēḫānu*

šiḫaṭu → *šiḫṭu* II 1

šiḫḫatu "disintegration, flaking off" M/NB of decaying wall plaster; of pottery vessel; *š. šīri* "wasting of the flesh"; < *šaḫāḫu*

šiḫiltu "filtered liquid" jB; < *šaḫālu*

šiḫilu → *šiḫlu* II

šiḫiru → *šeḫeru*

šiḫittum I, occas. *šāḫittum* "clearance of debts" OA; < *šaḫātu* IV

šiḫittu II, *šaḫittu* f. adj. mng. unkn. of plants Ug. lex., jB lex.

šiḫittu III; pl. *šiḫṭātu* "fear" jB; < *šaḫātu* III

šiḫittu IV (a household item) NB

šiḫlu I "sifting(s)" jB, of precious stones; < *šaḫālu*

šiḫlu II, *šiḫilu* ~ "second" M/NA; of person "substitute"?; of goods "second-rate"?; < Hurr.?

šiḫlu → also *šeḫlum*

šiḫrum "strap" Mari, jB

šiḫru → also *šaḫūrum* II

šīḫtu "sprout, shoot" jB lex.; < *šiāḫum* I

šiḫṭu(m) I (a kind of fodder) OB, M/jB lex.

šiḫṭu II **1.** NB, also *šiḫaṭu* "hide" of sheep etc. **2.** jB "discard" of clothing; < *šaḫāṭu* II

šiḫṭu → also *šeḫṭu*

šīḫu(m) I, *šēḫu* "grown (tall)" Bab., NA of gods, men, physique; "full-grown, tall" of lettuce, trees, beams; "lofty" of mountains; < *šiāḫum* I

šīḫu(m) II (part of a garment; of a chariot) O/MB

šīḫu III, *šēḫu* (an insect) jB lex.

šīḫu IV ~ "farmstead, estate" NB

šīḫu → also *sīḫu* II; *šāḫu*; *šēḫu*

ši'ītum, *še'ītu*, *še'ittu(m)*, *ši/ittu(m)*, *šettu* "neighbour (f.)" O/jB; also "secondary wife"; < *šē'u*

šikanu → *šiknu* 3

šikaru(m), *šikru(m)* "beer; alcoholic drink" [KAŠ(.ḪI.A/MEŠ)]; j/NB also *š. suluppī* "date wine"; in Syria usu. "(grape) wine"; *š. šadî* (a wine); *bīt š.* "tavern"; NB *rab š.* (official in charge of brewery); < *šakāru*

šikimtum mng. unkn. OB (desig. of garment); < *šakāmum* II

šikin napišti → *šiknat napišti*

šikinnu(m) I; pl. f. (container for oils etc.) O/jB; also a stone flask; also jB lex. mng. unkn. of birds; < Sum.

šikinnu(m) II (a net) O/jB lex.; *ša š.* "fisherman who uses a *š.*" OB lex.; < *šakānu*

šikintu ~ "allocation" NA; < *šakānu*

šikin ṭēmi → *šakin ṭēmi*

šikišu → *sikšu* I

šikittu(m); st. constr. *šikitti*, *šiknat* "form; layout" **1.** "form, shape" of gods, men, animals etc.; "layout, construction(-plan)" of walls, houses, buildings **2.** OAkk, jB "creation" of mankind, "appointing" by gods **3.** OA, pl. *šiknātum* "agreement" **4.** M/NB "garden plot"; < *šakānu*; → *šikintu*; *šiknat napišti*

šikkaterru → *šakkadirru* II

šikkatu(m) I, *šiqqatu(m)* "flask" OA, O/jB [DUG.ŠAGAN] often for oil; (miniature) of stone as ornament

šikkatu(m) II **1.** OB pl. "harrowed (land)" **2.** OB, Mari; jB lex. "tassel; trimmings" on clothing **3.** jB lex. ~ "date palm fibre" **4.** Mari, jB lex. "string of beads"; < *šakāku*

šikkatūtu → *rab-sikkatūtu*

šikkê terri, *šikkidirru* → *šakkadirru* I

šikku → *šīkum*

šikkû(m), NA *sikkû* "mongoose" Bab., NA [^{d}NIN.KILIM] also as PN; a star [MUL.NIN.KILIM]; *š. terri* → *šakkadirru* I; > *šikkūtu* I; *šikkukūtum*

šikkukūtum 'little mongoose' (part of the arm) OB; also (a cut of meat); < *šikkû*

šikkurratu (a reed or rush) jB

šikkūtu(m) I f. "female mongoose" OB, NB; also as fPN; < *šikkû*

šikkūtu II "string of beads" jB; < *šakāku*

šiklu mng. unkn. Nuzi

šiknat napišti(m), *šikin napišti(m)* "(things endowed with life =) living things" Bab., NA(lit.) [NÍG.ZI.GÁL]; < *šiknu* + *napištu*

šiknu(m) **1.** "act of putting, setting", "imposition" of building on site; ship on water; ring on person; "application" of fire, of feet i.e. "access"; "(first) laying out" of plot, field; of plants; "appointment" to office; "imposition, issue" of commandment; "operation, effectuation" of designs, signs **2.** "form, appearance, nature" of buildings, living beings, tree, plant, clothes; *abnu*/*šammu š.-šu* "the appearance of the stone/plant is:" (scientific series); "nature" of illness **3.** also *šikanu*; pl. *šiknātu* "deposit, sediment", *š. nāri* "river silt", "layer" of cloud, of blood ? **4.** NA in *rab šiknāni* mng. unkn.; < *šakānu*

šikriš "for beer" OB in to thirst "for beer"; < *šikaru*

šikru(m) "haft, hilt" O/jB of weapon; transf. of feature on liver

šikru → also *šikaru*

šikṣu(m) "ulcer, abscess" O/jB lex., ext.

šikšu → *sikšu* I

šiktu (or *šiqtu*) m. ~ "slag" MA, M/jB

šīkum (or *šikkum*) (a desig. of copper) OA

šīlān, *šillān* usu. *ina š.* "in the sunset, in the west" j/NB [GIŠ.ŠÚ] freq. after *ṣītān*/*š*; < *šīlu* I

šilangītu (a freshwater fish) jB lex.

šilannu (desig. of textiles; of arrows) Nuzi; < Hurr.?

šilašu (an animal) jB lex.

šilḫak "strong" jB lex.; < Elam.

šilḫu (woollen part of a chariot harness) MB

šīlibūtu → *šēlebūtu*

šiliḫtu **1.** jB lex. (a plant) **2.** NB (part of a canal) at Nippur; also in PlN

šilina (a gem) Qatna; of gold, agate; < Hurr.?

šilingu, *šillumgu* (a bird) jB lex.

šilipkā'um, *šilipkī'um*, *šulupkā'um*, *šulupkī'um* (a type of textile) OA, OB

šilippû → *šeleppû*

šiliptum "withdrawal" OB of merchants from association; "removal" of a child from the womb; < *šalāpu*

šilipu → *šilpu*

šiliqqu (a bird) jB

šilittu "split piece" of reed jB lex.; ~ "offshoot, scion"? of paternal line, of king MB(Ass.); < *šalāṭu* II

šillān → *šīlān*

šillannû "unashamed" jB; < *šillatu* I

šillaru → *šallaru*

šillatu(m) I, NB *šallatu*, OB lex. *sillitum*, jB also *sallatu*; pl. *sillātu* "impudence, shamelessness" [KA.É.GAL] OA "villainy" also pl.; speak "iniquity", *š. pî* "slander"; < *šalālu* III

šillatu II "booty" j/NB [NAM.RA]; < *šalālu* I

šillu (a basket or quiver)? jB lex.

šillu → also *šeḫlum*

šillumgu → *šilingu*

šilpu(m) "withdrawal; thing withdrawn" O/jB *šilip rēmim* "withdrawal from womb" = new-born baby; *šilip šarpi* of stone mng. unkn.; also adv. *šil(i)pu* mng. unkn. of marching, sending troops; < *šalāpu*

šilqum "split piece" OB lex. of reed; < *šalāqu*

šiltāḫānu "'arrow-man'" NA, as DN; < *šiltāḫu*

šiltaḫḫu → *šiltāḫu*

šiltāḫiš "like an arrow" jB of man, fox; < *šiltāḫu*

šiltāḫu(m), *šiltaḫḫu*, MA phps. *lištāḫu* "arrow" Bab., M/NA [(GIŠ.)GAG.(U4/Ú.)TAG.GA; Ug. GI.GAG.KUM.TAG.GA]; as weapon; *qaqqad š.* "arrowhead"; as epith. of DN; astr. "Sirius" [MUL.GAG.SI.SÁ]; > *šiltāḫānu*, *šiltāḫiš*

šīlu(m) I, *šēlu* "depression, concavity" O/jB [BÙR] ext. "hollow, perforation" in liver etc.; on new-born baby; < *šalû* I ?; > *šīlān*

šīlu II "brother" jB lex.

šīlum III (a water craft)? jB

šīlu → also *sīlu* II

šiluḫlu (class of person, phps.) "conscript" MA, Nuzi; < Hurr.; > *šelluḫlūtu*

šilūtum I "thrown-up material" OB math.; < *elû* III Š

šilūtu(m) II; pl. *šilâti* "shot" MA of bow; < *šalû* II (or → *šēltu* ?)

šilūtu III mng. unkn. jB lex. as DN

šilûtu "neglect, carelessness" NB; < *šelû* III

-šim, *-ši*, MA *-še* "to her" (→ GAG §42g-h)

šimāḫu(m), *šemāḫu(m)*, *šimaḫḫu* "boxthorn" OB lex.; jB, NA, med.

šimānu I (a temple estate, benefice ?) jB lex., NB; NA in *rab šimāni*

šimānu II = *simānu* I ? Ug. *ina š.* "at the (right) time"

šimarātu f. pl. (part of a building) MB(Ass.)

šīmātu → *šīmtu*; *šīmu* I

šimbizidû "antimony paste" jB lex., med. [ŠIM.BI.ZI.DA (→ *guḫlu*)]; < Sum.

šimertu (an illness) jB, NA

šimeru → *šawirum*; *šimru*

šimešlu, *šimeššalû* → **šimiššalû**

šimēta, *šimētān* → *šimītān*

šimgu → *šingu* II

šimgû → *šigû*

šimguštu → *šigguštu*

šimikapšu (a mark on sheep) Nuzi; < Hurr.

šimiru → *šawirum*; *šimru*

šimiššalû, *šimeššalû(m)*, *šimšalû*, *šimšallu*, *šimešlu* "(type of) box-tree"? Bab., NA [(GIŠ.) ŠIM.ŠAL] as tree; more freq. as aromatic

šimītān, *šimētān*, *šimēta* "(in the) evening" M/jB [AN.USAN/ÚSAN]; also *ultu*, *ina*, *adi š.*; < *šiwītum*

šimītān → also *šimtān*

šimittu (a precious object) M/NB; gold for *š.*

šimittu → also *šumuttu*

šimītu → *šiwītum*

šimmatu "paralysis" Bogh., jB, NA from scorpion; of flesh, sinews; stones (*abnū*) for *š.*; < *šamāmu*

šimmāyâtu → *šamāyû* 2

šimmugallu "chief incantation-priest" jB; < Sum.

šimrānu (a plant) jB

šimriš mng. uncert. MB of nocturnal ceremony; as name of horses; < Kass.

šimru, *simru*, Nuzi *šime/iru* "fennel" M/NB as food, drug; *qēm š.* "flour of? f."

šimšallu, *šimšalû* → *šimiššalû*

šimtān, *šimītān* jB lex. var. of *šimtu*

šimtu(m), *simtu(m)*, Nuzi *šind/tu* "mark, token; colour, paint" OAkk, Bab. [(KUŠ.)ŠE.GÍN; KUŠ.ŠE.GIM Mari, lex.; MA also ŠE.ŠEN] **1.** "ownership mark", *š. šakānum* "to put a mark" on animal, field, brick; *š. išātim* "brand"; *š. uzni* "ear-mark"; also "birthmark" **2.** "branding iron" **3.** "colour, paint", weighed; for wooden objects, skins; as drug; du. OB *šimtāša* (= healthy cheeks)?; > *šamātu*; → *šimtān*; *šendu*

šīmtu(m), also *šēmtu*; st. constr. *šīmti*, occas. *šimit* "what is fixed; will, testament; fate, destiny" [NAM; NAM.TAR] OA "fixed (amount)"; "last will, testament", Nuzi *ṭuppi š.* "bequest tablet"; "fate, destiny" of (= decreed by) s.o.; god (fixer) of "fate(s)", lord of "fate(s)"; "destiny, lot" of (= decreed for) s.o.; *ūm š.* "predetermined day", *ūm lā š.* "premature death"; "(fate =) death, day of death"; *ana š. alāku(m)* = "to die a natural death"; < *šiāmu*; → *ṭupšīmātu*; *šimumaku*

šimṭum, jB *šinṭu*, Nuzi *šintu* "plucked wool" OB, Nuzi, jB lex.; also *šimṭā/ētu* f. pl. mng. unkn. OB, jB; < *šamāṭu* I

šīmu(m) I; pl. m. & f. "purchase (price); goods for commerce" [ŠÁM; ŠÀM; NÍG.ŠÁM] **1.** "purchase"; *š. šâmum* "to make a purchase"; *ana š. n/tadānum* "to sell", *š. leqûm*, *šâmum* "to buy"; OA *bēl š.* "person who has received the price"; M/NA *mār/ša š.* "man bought (as slave)" [LÚ/DUMU.ŠÁM] **2.** "(purchase) price" of animal, food etc.; *šīmšu* "his price"; *akal š.* "bought bread", *ana š. gamri* [MB ŠÁM.TIL.LA.BI/NI.ŠÈ], *ana šīm gamer* (st. abs.) "for the full price" **3.** OA, OB "wares, commercial goods", also "commerce, trading"; OAkk, OB, MA, Ug., Am., "(property acquired by) purchase" [ŠÀM.MEŠ]; *ṭuppi/kanīk šīmātim* "purchase document"; MB *šīmāte epēšu* "to engage in commerce"; < *šâmu*; > *šīmūtu*

šīmu II "purchased" jB lex.; < *šâmu*

šimumaku "last testament, will" Nuzi *ṭuppu ša š.*; < *šīmtu* + Hurr. suff.

šimurrû → *simurrûm*

šīmūtu "purchasing venture" j/NB; < *šīmu* I

šin → *šina* I.II

-šin → *-šina*

šina I, NB also *šin(i)* **1.** "they" (f. pl. nom.); before vb. to give emphasis, *šinama* "it is they who ..."; as pred. ... *šina* "they (are) ..." **2.** "those, these same" (nom.; of f. nouns); → *iššini*; for acc. etc. → *šâšina*; *šināšim*; *šināti*

šina II, *šena* "two" [MIN; MIN5] (st. constr. *šin*; f. *šitta*); *ana šina* (divided) "in(to) two"; *adi šina* "twice"; *šin šīmišu* "double his price"; > *šanā*, *šanā'um*; *šinīšu*, *šittān*; *šanû* I, *šanîš* I, *šanītu* I, *šanûti*, *šanûtī-*, *šanā'iyu*, *šaniānu*; *šanû* III etc.; *šinašan*; *šiniānu*; *šinnû*; *šunā'a*; *šinšeret*, *šinšarium*; *šunu'tu*; *šunu'û*

-šina, OB(poet.) *-šin*, OA also *-šna* "their (f.)" (→ GAG §42g-k); Ass. also acc. "them (f.)"

šinaḫilu(m) "second (rank, class)" OA, Nuzi of persons "deputy, second-in-command"; of textiles, furniture, wheat "of second quality"; < Hurr.

šinaḫiluḫli "person attached to the deputy"? Nuzi of persons; < *šinaḫilu*

šinaḫilūtum "office of *š.*" OA; < *šinaḫilu*

šinamātu mng. unkn. Nuzi, woman *ša š.*; < Hurr.

šinamû (a functionary) NB *š. ša* PN, *ša* PlN

šinamumma ~ "double, twice" Nuzi [2-] in *š. epēšu* "to pay twofold"; < Hurr.

šinamuna "twice, twofold" Nuzi, also *ana š.*; < Hurr.

šinamunu, *šinamušu* "deputy, representative" Nuzi; < Hurr.

Šinanūtum → *šinūnūtu*

šinapšumma in *š. epēšu* ~ "to be false"? Nuzi, of testimony; < Hurr.

šinarpu "two-year-old" Nuzi of animal; < Hurr.

šinašan "both of the two, each of the two" jB; also OB *šenamašan*; < *šina* II

***šināšim** "to them (f.)", unattested; → *šina* I

-šināši(m) "to them (f.)" Bab. (→ GAG §42g, j)

-šināt "(to) them (f.)" (acc., dat.) OAkk, arch. OB

šinâtena → *šinītu* II 1

šināti, NB also *šinēti* **1.** "them" (f. pl. acc.) not attested **2.** "those, these same" (acc., gen.; of f. nouns); OB *lā š.* "not belonging, inappropriate, improper (actions, words)"; → *šina* I; *šinātina*

-šināti, NB also *-šinēti* "them (f.)" Bab.; dat. "to them (f.)" OA

šinātina "those, these same" (acc., gen.) MA; = *šināti*

šinātu f. pl. mng. uncert. MA for horses; → *šinītu* IV

šīnātu(m) pl. tant. "urine" OAkk, Bab. [KÀŠ(.MEŠ)] of human, animal; < *šiānum*

šinatumma in *dīna š. epēšu* "to appeal against a verdict" Nuzi; < Hurr.

šinbiltu (a plant, phps.) "spikenard, *Nardus stricta*" jB lex.

šinburratu → *šibburratu*

šindilippu, *šindissu*, *šanda/ilippu* (topog. term)? jB

šindu → *šendu*; *šimtu*; *šimṭum*

šine(p)pât, *šine(p)piat*, *šinepêt(um)* → *šinipu*

šinēti → *šināti*

šinētu → *šini'tu*

-šinēti → *-šināti*

šingu I ~ "village, farmstead" j/NB

šingu II, *šimgu*; pl. *šingātu* mng. uncert. M/NA

šini → *šina* I

šiniānu; f. *šiniāntum* (desig. of sheep) OB ?; < *šina* II ?

šinintu ~ "equality"? jB in *lā šininti ēkalli* (person) "not up to, worthy of the palace"; < *šanānu*

šinipu; f. OB *šine(p)piat*, *šine(p)pât*, *šinepêt(um)*, jB *šinipât(u)*, *ši(n)nipât*, NB *šinnipētu*; OA, OB, jB also du. *šinipā/ī/ē* "two-thirds" (→ GAG §70i) [ŠANABI; OB also ŠA.NA.BI] math. *šinip šinipīya* "2/3 of my 2/3" i.e. 4/9; jB *šinipassu* "two-thirds of him" (Gilg.); NB *šinnipētu* "two-third (length)" reed-stems

šinišḫu (topog. term) Nuzi; < Hurr.

šinīšu "twice"; math. *ana/adi š. šakānum*; *ana š.*, OA *aššinīšu* "in two"; Ass. *ana š.* before pl. tant. nouns = "two"; < *šina* II

šinītu(m) I "alteration" O/jB in *š. ṭēmi(m)* ~ 'change of plan'? (a medical condition) [DIMA.KÚR.RA]; < *šanû* IV

šinītu(m) II **1.** OA (pl. *šiniātum*), MB(Alal.) (Hurr. pl. *šinâtena*) "dyed textile"; OB lex. *ša š.* "dyer" **2.** NB "(clay) roof-sealing"; < *šanû* VI

šinītu III (a type of leek) jB lex.

šinītu IV (a type of flour) MB; → *šinātu*

šini'tu, *šinētu* "blockage" of throat ? jB med.; < *šanā'u*

šinnānu "toothed" jB lex. of reeds; of pomegranates; < *šinnu* I

šinnatu "similarity, equality (with = gen.)" jB; *DN š. Anim* "DN the equal of An"; of king, *š. apkalli*; of palace; < *šanānu*

šinni → *šinnû*

šinnipât, *šinnipētu* → *šinipu*

šinništu → *sinništu*

šinnu(m) I; pl. f.; freq. du. "tooth" [ZÚ; Bogh., Am. KA×UD] of humans, gods; animals, demons etc.; *š. (pīri)* "elephant tooth, ivory"; transf. of feature on carapace, intestine; "tooth" on saw, comb; "point, blade" of hoe, harrow, plough; stool, battering-ram; jB lex. ZÚ *kalbi* 'dog's tooth' (a plant); > *šinnānu*; → *šinqātu*

šinnu II mng. unkn. NB

šinnû, *šinni* "two each" Bab. [2.TA.ÀM]; < *šina* II

šinnūtu mng. unkn. NB

šinqātu 'hand-tooth' i.e. "finger" jB lex.; < *šinnu* I + *qātu*

šinṣu "taunting, scoffing" MB as children's game; < *šanāṣu*

šinšarium, *šinšerû(m)*, NB *šinzerû*, *šiššurû* Bab. [12-] **1.** "twelfth" **2.** "one-twelfth" of sheep; of day (as prebend); < *šinšeret*

šinšeret "twelve" OB (otherwise wr. 12); < *šina* II + *-šeret*

šinšerû → *šinšarium*

šinšinnu → *šunšunnu*

šinšu mng. unkn. jB

šintarpu "seven-year-old" Nuzi of donkey; < Hurr.

šintu → *šimtu*; *šimṭum*

šintunnu "seventh" Nuzi; < Hurr.

šinṭu → *šimṭum*

šīnu → *šēnu* II

šinuntum, *šinunītum*; pl. OA *šinunuātum* (a type of leather or a leather object) OA, Mari

šinūnūtu(m), *šunūnūtu* "(type of) swallow" Bab. [MUL.ŠÍM.MAḪ] also as fPN, OB once *Šinanūtum*; astr. star(s) in Pisces and Pegasus; → *sinuntu*

-šinūtu → *-šunūti*

šinuzza ~ "horse trappings" OB(Alal.) of silver

šinzerû → *šinšarium*

šīpānu (an archit. feature) MB

šiparru → *šipāru*

šipartu → *šapartu*

šipāru(m), *šiparru* Bab. **1.** "regulations, instructions" of god(dess), of battle **2.** "assembly"; < *šapāru* ?

šipassu(m), *šipatsu* "clay sealing, sealed bulla" O/jB, M/NA; OB *š. nadûm* "to attach", MA *maḫāṣu* "to strike off a sealing"

šipāṣu (part of chariot or horse trappings) NB

šipatsu → *šipassu*

šīpātu(m), occas. *šūpātu* pl. tant., occas. construed as sg.; OA *šaptum* "wool, fleece" [SÍK(.MEŠ/ḪI.A); M/NBalso SIK ?]; from sheep; jB also of cotton, trees *nāš š.*

šipā'u → *šibā'u*

šipḫu (a part of the kiln) jB

šipiktum mng. uncert. OB lex.; < *šapāku*

šipipiānu → *zibibiānum*

šipirru → *šibirru*

šipirtu(m), NB often *šipištu*; pl. *šip(i)rātu(m)*, *šip(i)rētu* "message, letter, instruction" Bab., M/NA **1.** "message" conveying "instruction" or "report"; "letter", *š. šarri* "royal letter", NB with det. IM/KUŠ "document (on) clay (tablet)/leather (scroll)" **2.** j/NB pl. *šip(i)rētu* "chancery, official archive" **3.** pl. *šiprātum* = *šipru* "(agricultural) work", Mari *ša š.* "chargé d'affaires" **4.** Nuzi also "pledge, security"; ; < *šapāru*

šipirtu → also *šibirtu*

šipiṣu → *šipṣu*

šipištu → *šipirtu*

šipītu → *šibītu*

šīpītu → *šēpītu*

šipkātu(m) f. pl. "heaping up, storage, stores" **1.** OA "investments, deposits" with/on behalf of another **2.** OB *š. ebūrim* "storage of harvest" as a season or time limit **3.** math. "number of bricks" in a length of wall **4.** OB (brewing term) **5.** jB lex. "cast form"?; < *šapāku*

šipku(m) I "heaping up, pile; storage; casting, formation" Bab., NA [DUB] **1.** *š. eperī* "heap of earth", also of tells; *š. baṣṣī* "heap of sand", i.e. sand dune; "bulk, solidity" of mountains; *š. uššī* "foundations"; *š. šamê* "base of sky, horizon" **2.** "casting" of metal, transf. of persons, i.e. birth **3.** in *mašak š.* (a type of leather); < *šapāku*

šipku(m) II (a term for cereals) OB, Mari

šipkūtum mng. unkn. OB ref. to grain; < *šapāku*

šiplû → *šaplû*

šippu, *šīpu* **1.** "red spot" jB astr. **2.** (red) "decoration on garments" M/NB

šippu → also *šibbu* I; *šīpu* II

šipqu → *šibqu*

šipru(m); pl. *šiprū*, Mari also *šiprānu*; f. pl. → *šipirtu* "sending, mission; work" [KIN] **1.** "mission", esp. in *mār š.* "messenger"; OAkk, OA also *šiprum* "messenger" **2.** "work", *š. epēšum* "to do work"; MA *šipar šarri* "royal corvée"; "work" on s.th. e.g. MA *šipar narkabtim*; "skilled work, skill" e.g. of Enki, *š. aḫāzu* "to acquire skill" **3.** "action"; "characteristic activity" of woman etc.; *š. lemnu* "unfavourable action" of gods towards man; "effect, affliction" of illness; "plan, scheme"; *š. kašādu* "to achieve intention" **4.** "(piece of) work, artefact, manufacture"; *š. qāti(m)* "handiwork"; of temple "fabric"; < *šapāru*

šiprūtu(m) **1.** OA as coll. "messengers" **2.** O/jB *ana š. ezēbu(m)* "to leave as a pledge"; < *šapāru*

šipsatu → *šipšatu*

šipṣu(m), *šepṣu*, *šipiṣu*; pl. f. "obstinacy, non-compliance; force" Ass., jB *š. šakānu* "to engage in violence"; < *šapāṣu*

šipṣu → also *šapṣu*

šipšatu, *šipsatu*, *sipš/satu*, occas. *šupšatu* "(length of) wood, beam"? M/NA, jB [GIŠ.ŠÚ.A?] of door, window; "railings, posts" for race-track

šiptu(m) f. "incantation, spell" Bab., NA [ÉN; TU$_6$] *rēš š.* "beginning of the spell"; *š. balāṭim* "spell for life"; of DN; of (i.e. against) disease; to cast (*nadû*), recite (*manû*) a spell etc.; OB lex. *ša š.* "magician"; < *wašāpum*

šiptu → also *šibtu*

šipṭu(m) I "judgement; verdict, sentence" Bab., NA *š. u purussûm*; *š. šakānu* "to impose a verdict"; Šamaš, *bēl š.*; < *šapāṭu* I

šipṭu(m) II f. "threat, strict order, reprimand" Mari, j/NB; *š. nadānum, dunnunum* "to make, emphasize a threat"; < *šapāṭum* II

šīpu I (a yellow paste) jB [ŠIM.BI.KÙ.GI]

šīpu(m) II, *šippum*, *šību* (a part of the roof) Bab. overlaid with gold, silver; at base of door

šīpu III, *šību* in *š. nadû* "to produce a discoloration" in bread, garment, wound jB

šīpu → also *šēpu*; *šību*; *šippu*

šiqātu f. pl. (a song) jB

šiqdīum "of almond wood"? OAkk lex., of spear; < *šiqdum*

šiqdu(m), *šuqdu*, *siqdu* "almond (tree)" [GIŠ. EŠ$_{22}$(=LAM×KUR)] as timber; *š. matqu* "sweet almond"; *šaman š.* "almond oil"; > *šiqittu*; → *duqdu*

šiqittu "almond tree" M/jB; < *šiqdu* nom. unit.

šiqītu(m); Ug. *šiqqatu*, *šeqqatu* "irrigation" O/jB also "irrigation channel"; OB(Susa) "irrigated land"; < *šaqû* III

šiqlānum (a desig. of silver)? OA

šiqlu(m) "shekel" [GÍN] **1.** weight: 1/60 mina (= 8 grams) (st. abs.) *šiqil*; MB(Alal.), Ug. 1/50 mina; jB *ina š. šeḫri/rabî* **2.** capacity measure: 1/6 *qû* **3.** surface measure: 1/60 *mūšaru*; < *šaqālu*

šiqpu; pl. *šiqpētu* "trick, stratagem" jB lex.; < *šibqū* metath.?

šiqqatu → *šikkatu* I; *šiqītu*

šiqqu(m), *šīqu* (a fish condiment) O/jB [AL.ÚS.SA]

šiqšiqqum (a bird) OB

šiqtu → *šiktu*

šīqu I, Nuzi also *šiqû*; pl. f. "watering, irrigation" M/NA, M/jB of fields; *mê šīqi/šīqāti* "irrigation water"; Nuzi *eqlu (lā) šiqû* "(non-)irrigated field"; < *šaqû* III

šīqu(m) II "levelling off" (of grain in measuring vessel) O/jB in *šīq mešēqim/qātim* "levelled by scraper/by hand"; jB f. pl. "(vessels) levelled full"; < *šêqu*

šīqu III (an illness); *šam š.* "plant of (= against) *š.*" jB

šīqu → also *šiqqu*

šir (a metal object) Mari

širaku → *šerku* I

šir'am, *šir'annu* → *sariyam*

šir'ānu(m) "son" jB lex.; OAkk as PN

šir'ānu → also *šer'ānu*

šīrāš → *sīrāšu*

šīrāšûm → *sīrāšû*

širdannu → *šerdannu*

širḫānu, *šerḫānu* "current, flood" jB lex.; → *šer'ānu*

širḫu → *šer'u*

širiānu (a cake)? Nuzi

širiat (a type of bread) NA

širiktu → *šeriktu*

širikūtu → *šerkūtu*

širimtu, *širindu* → *šerimtum*

širinnatu, Nuzi *širinnitu* "snaffle, horse's bit" MB, Am., Nuzi

šīrīsu → *sīrāšu*

širkētu pl. adj. (desig. of wool) jB lex.

širku → *šerku* I

širmu(m), Mari also *šermum* **1.** jB lex. "vessel with the capacity of 1 *sūtu*" **2.** Mari, usu. *š. qarni(m)* lit. 'horn trimming', desig. of a cup; < *šarāmu*

širnu → *šernu*

širraḫu "man" jB lex.
širrum → *šīru*
širširum → *šeršerru*
šīrtu → *šērtu* I-III
širṭu → *šerṭu*
šīru(m), *šēru*, OB also *širrum*, MA, MB also *tīru*, often pl. "flesh; body; entrails (omen)" [UZU(.MEŠ)] "meat" of animals; organ *š. lawi* "is surrounded in flesh"; *mê š.* "meat broth"; "ominous part" examined in extispicy; "omen"; *š. lemnum* "unfavourable omen in entrails" etc.; human "flesh"; as famine food; in med., om.; *š. ṭābu*, *ṭūb š.* "good physical health"; OB "a person, individual"; "genetic stock", *lā šīr* "not of (our) flesh", *š. ramāni* "of own flesh"; *š. u dāmu* "flesh and blood"; OB deeds are sweet *ana š. DN* "to the person of DN, DN himself"?; "corporeal identity", stone becomes *ana š. ili*, *mēsu*-tree is *š. ili*
šīru → also *šēru* II.IV
šir'u → *šer'u*
širumaku mng. uncert. Nuzi in exchange contract; < Hurr.
širumma in *š. epēšu* "to give corroborative testimony" Nuzi; < Hurr.
širwanaše → *šerwanaše*
širyam → *sariyam*
šisirum → *šiziru*
šisītu(m) I, *tisītum*, *sisītum* "cry, clamour" O/jB, NA "proclamation" of herald, city; of work-song; "shout" of battle, of mourning; "cry" of DN; "roar" of waterfalls; < *šasû*
šisītu(m) II, *šišītu*, *tisīsu*, *tis/ṣītu*, Ass. *sisītu* "(hand/foot) joint" O/jB, M/NA *š. ritti* "wrist"; "ankle, hock" of sheep, cow
šissinnu, *šissintu* → *sissinnu*
šīsu(m), *šisû(m)*, OB also *tīsûm* "cry" O/jB; "summons" by palace; on field; also *ūm š.*; < *šasû*
šīṣūtu (an inferior quality of dates) jB; → *šuṣu*
šišaḫu (a mineral) jB lex.
šišanibe → *šasnibi*
šišanu → *šišnu*
šišītu(m), once *šišittu* "skin, layer, film" Bab., NA med., ext. "film, membrane" on lungs, liver etc.; *š. arāmu* "to be covered in a membrane"; transf. "film" of oil; astr. (a meteor. phenomenon); lex. (a plant)
šišītu → also *šisītu* II; *šišûm*
ši'ši'u mng. unkn. NA
šiškatu → *šerkatu*
šiški-ilūtu → *šerki-ilūtu*
šišku → *šerku* I
šiškur → *tiskur*
šišnu, *ši/ešanu* (a grass) jB lex.
šiššat st. constr. "one-sixth" OB; *š. rabât* "one-twenty-fourth"; < *šediš*
šiššātu → *šeššātu*
šiššektu → *šiššiktu*
šiššet → *šediš*
šiššiktu, *še/išši/ektu* jB lex. **1.** (a stone) **2.** (a wind); < Sum.?
šiššiktu → also *sissiktu*
šiššu(m) "silence, stillness" O/jB
šiššu → also *šeššu*
šiššûm mng. unkn. OB
šiššurû → *šinšarium*
šišṭu → *šerṭu*
šišûm; f. *šišītum* (person with eye disease) OB lex.; < Sum.
šīt O/MA, Am., Nuzi, Bogh. **1.** "she" (nom. pron.) for emphasis *šītma* "it is she who ..."; as pred. ... *šīt* "... is she" **2.** "that, this same" (nom.; of f. nouns); < *šī*; → *šīti*
šitaddaru(m), *šitaddalu*, lex. also *šidallu*, Emar lex. *tišattalu* "Orion" O/jB [(MUL.)SIPA.ZI.AN.NA]
šitarḫu "very proud, splendid" of gods, king jB; < *šarāḫu* I Gt
šitarqum "disappearance"? in OAkk curse formula *adi šitarqišu*; < *šarāqu* I
šitarru → *šaddaru* I
šit'āru(m), *tit'āru*, once *tityāru* "variegated, iridescent" of eyes O/jB
šitektumma mng. unkn. Nuzi in *š. epēšu* phps. "to manumit" slave; < Hurr.
šitḫu(m) **1.** (an atmospheric phenomenon) jB astr. **2.** (a feature of the liver) Mari, jB; < *šatāḫu*
šīti NA, also NB **1.** NA "she, it" (nom. pron.) **2.** NB "that, this same"; < *šī*; = *šīt*
šitimgallu "master builder" j/NB; < Sum.
šitimmāḫu "master builder" jB lex.; < Sum.
šitiptu(m), *šetiptu* "excision"? O/jB lex.; < *šatāpu*
šitlu(m) "sprout, seedling" O/jB lex.; < *satālu*
šitlû mng. unkn. Bogh. lex.
šitluṭiš "triumphantly" jB; < *šitluṭu*
šitluṭu "triumphant" j/NB of Nabû, Ninurta; < *šalāṭu* I Gt
šitmāru, occas. *šitmarru* "very wild" jB god; horse; < *šamāru* I Gt
šitmu "log of wood" Nuzi
šitmuriš "wildly, passionately" jB; < *šitmuru*
šitmuru "very wild" jB, NA of battle, cavalry, river, god; < *šamāru* I Gt
šitnuntu "combat" jB battle; debate; < *šanānu* Gt
šitnunu "combative" jB of deities; "hard-fought" victory; < *šanānu* Gt
šitpu(m) "pit, excavation" OB; jB lex.; < *šatāpu*

šitpû "surging, flaring" jB of fire, torch flame; < *šapû* II Gt

šitpuru "to outfit o.s., attire o.s. with" jB **Gt** only infin., stat., imper., also transf., e.g. mountain *šitpurat puluḫtu* "is shrouded in terror"

šitpuṣu ~ "quarrelsome" jB lex.; < *šapāṣu* Gt

šitqu I "split, crack" jB "crack" in liver; *š. irti* (part of breastbone); of stones *š. šadî* "quarried from mountain"; (a leather pouch)?; < *šatāqu*

šitqu II (a sanctuary) jB

šitqultu jB astr. **1.** "opposition, conjunction" **2.** "equinox" [LÁL-]; < *šaqālu* Gt

šitqulu "sufficient"? jB of bread; < *šaqālu* Gt

šitrāḫu "very proud, splendid" M/NB epith. of gods, kings; < *šarāḫu* I Gt

šitrum ~ (a textile) OA

šitrudu mng. unkn. M/jB **Gt**

šitruḫu "very proud, splendid" jB; < *šarāḫu* I Gt

šittān "two-thirds" O/jB, Bogh.; < *šina* II

šittu(m) I, occas. *šiṭṭu* "sleep" Bab. good, bad; → *šuttu*

šittu(m) II, *sittu(m)*; pl. *š/sittātum, š/sītātum*; jB st. constr. *sītalet* "remnant, remainder" [ÍB.TAK4] "rest" of silver, field, grain; math. "remainder"; as PN "(sole) remnant"; < *šêtu* II

šittu III (or *sittu*) (a kind of meat) jB lex.

šittu(m) IV "excrement" O/jB; < Sum.

šittu → also *ši'ītum*

šitû(m) I (a garden plant) Bab. also *šitê kasî*

šitû II, *šetû* "drinking" Bogh., Am.; < *šatû* II

šitû III (an eye ailment) jB; < *šatû* III ?

šītu I "reins" jB lex., for horse

šītu II ~ "textile" NA; < *šatû* III

šit'u (or *šid'u*) (a bird) jB

ši'tu → *še'tu*

šitūltu(m) "discussion, consultation; deliberation" Bab.; < *šâlu* I Gt

šitūlu(m) "deliberation; consultation" Bab.; < *šâlu* I Gt

šiṭirtu(m), *šiṭertu(m)* "writing; document" Bab. *š. ṭuppi* "writing on tablet"; Bogh. "document, written record"; transf. *š. šamê/šamāmī* "(writing in heaven =) stars" (→ *šiṭru*); < *šaṭāru* II

šiṭru(m) "(piece of) writing" Bab., NA [SAR] "inscription", *š. šumi(m)* "written name"; transf. *š. šamê, burūmê* "stars" (→ *šiṭirtu*); (a song), "performance of *š.* song"; < *šaṭāru* II

šiṭṭu → *sittu* I

šīṭu I, NA also *šēṭu* "careless" jB lex., NA; < *šiāṭu*

šīṭu II mng. unkn. jB lex.

šīṭūtu mng. uncert. j/NB

šīṭūtu → also *šēṭūtu*

šiu "little"? jB

ši'um (a bird) OB

šī'u → *šē'u*

šiuḫiwe mng. unkn. Nuzi; < Hurr.

šī'ūtum "rôle of neighbour" jB; < *šē'u*

šiwerum → *šawirum*

šiwiātum f. pl. mng. unkn. OB in incantation

šiwītum, *šimītu* "evening" O/MB; > *šimītān*

šiyāru → *ši'āru*

šiyataltapše (a feast day)? OB(Alal.), also Nuzi *šiyataltašše*; in *ūm š.*; < Hurr.?

šiyû ~ "strength" jB lex.

šizbānu, Ug. lex. *zizbannum* ? **1.** "milk-fed" lamb jB lex. **2.** (a plant) M/jB lex., med. with milky sap ?; < *šizbu*

šizbu(m), *ši/ezibbu*, NA *zizibu* "milk" Bab., M/NA [GA(.MEŠ)] in med., rit., om.; also "milky fluid" in gall bladder etc.; *ša š.* "suckling, unweaned" of humans, animals; NA *ša zizibišu* "milkman"; > *šizbānu*

šizirum (or *šisirum*) (an object) OA

šizû "one-third cubit" OB, jB

-šna → *-šina*

-šnu → *-šunu*

šu OAkk, OB(poet.) **1.** before gen. "(he/it) of", also O/MA, O/MB in PNs **2.** before rel. clause "who, whom, which" (later becomes *ša*); → *šā*; *ši*; *šūt* I

-šu, occas. *-š(e)* **1.** "his" (3 m. sg. gen. suff.); in multiplicatives "times" → e.g. *šinīšu*; NA *ša X-šu* "the X-man" → e.g. *šizbu* **2.** "him" (3 m. sg. acc. suff.) (→ GAG §42g-k)

-šu → also *-šum*

šū "he; that, this same" OAkk, Bab., NA [BI; NB in PNs also MU] **1.** "he" before vb.s, giving emphasis, *šūma* "it is he who ..."; *šū* ... "he is ..."; as pred. ... *šū* "... is he" **2.** "that, this same", *awīlum šū* "that man" (→ GAG §41); → *agāšū*; *iššū*; *šūt* II; *šūtu* I; for acc. etc. → *šâti, šâtu, šuāti*; *šâši, šâšu, šuāšim*

šû(m) I, O/MA *šu(w)ā'u(m)*; f. *šuattum/šuātu, šattu(m), šuttum*; m. pl. *šuttun*, OA *šuā'ūtum*; f. *šuāttum* "his, hers; belonging to him/her" O/MA, O/jB [UR5], OB *še'am šuâm* "grain of his own"; *wardim lā šêm* "a slave not his own" etc.; OA *ḫurāṣum šuā'um* "the gold is his"; Bab. also *lā š(u)attu(m)* "inappropriate" behaviour, "untoward" events

šû II (a stone) M/jB [(NA4.)ŠU.U] mag., med., often *š. zikar u sinniš* "male and female *š.* stone"

šûm III, *šu'u* "sheep" OB, jB [phps. UDU (.NÍTA)] for sacrifice; > *šu'ātu*

šû → also *šuḫûm* I; *šu'u*

šūa "that, this same" (acc., gen.) OAkk for later *šuāti*

šuadumma mng. unkn. Nuzi in *š. epēšu* for field; < Hurr.

šuanatḫu (a prof. or occupation) Nuzi; < Hurr.

šuanuḫna mng. unkn. Nuzi (desig. of blankets); < Hurr.

šuāru(m) ~ "dance" O/jB(poet.)

šuāš "on him/her" (m. or f.?) OAkk in PN *Šuāš-takal*

šuāša MA **1.** "her" (3 f. sg. acc.) **2.** "that, this same" (f. sg. acc.)

šuāšim "to him, to her" (3 m. & f. sg. dat.) OB; → *šī*; *šū*

šuāšu(m) **1.** "to him, him" M/NA (3 m. sg. dat.); jB (3 m. sg. acc.) **2.** "that, this same" MA, NB (gen.); jB (acc.)

šuāti, *šuātu*, OA, NB often *šuwāti*, NB also *šu(w)āta* m. & f. [BI; UR5(.MEŠ); NB MU. ME(Š), MU- (< *šumu*)] **1.** "him; her; it", OA *ša kīma šu(w)āti* "his representative" **2.** "that, the same" j/NB (acc., gen.); NA (also nom.); *ana šuāti* "therefore"; NB also pl.; > *šatti*; → *šī*; *šū*; *šūa*

šuātina "those, the same" (f. pl. acc., gen.) jB(Ass.); > *šâtina*

šuattum → *šû* I

šuātum, *šu'ē/ītu* "lady, mistress" OAkk, j/NB epith. of goddesses; < *šuwā'um*

šuātu → also *šû* I; *šuāti*

šu'ātu, *šâtu* "ewe" O/jB; < *šûm* III

šuātunu "those, the same" (m. acc., gen.) M/jB(Ass.); > *šâtunu*

šuā'u → *šû* I; *šuwā'um*

šubabītu, *šupapītu*, *ušpapītu* (an insect) jB lex.

šubāḫu mng. unkn. jB

šubakilu (person with a physical or moral defect) jB

šubalkutu → *nabalkutu* II

šubarīum, *šubarû*; f. *šub(a)rītu(m)*, *šubur(r)ītu* "from Subartu, in the style of Subartu" OA, O/jB, Mari

šubarrû, occas. *šuparrû* ~ "(tax) exemption" j/NB of king *š. šakānu* "to institute an amnesty"; of gods, to confirm, increase "freedom" (from burdens); "released, exempted person"; < Sum.

šubarrûtu(m), Bogh. *šuparruttu* "release" O/jB of slave

šubaru(m) (a wood) OAkk, Mari [GIŠ.ŠUBUR]

šubarû → *šubarīum*

šubā'u → *šumû* I

šubbatu → *šuppatu*

šubbû → *šapû* II D; *šebû* I D

šubbuḫu D mng. uncert. NB; → *šuppuḫum*

šubburu(m) "broken" Bab. of cart, tool; NB of horses; < *šebēru* D

šubbutu D "to accommodate" (person) NB; < *šubtu* I denom.

***šube''û(m)** (or **šubê'u(m)*) ~ "to rush upon"? O/jB, MA (*ušbī'*, *uštebī'*, *ušba''i*) of flood, snake (→ GAG §109i, j, l)

šubiltu → *šubultu*

šūbiltu → *šūbultu*

šubrītum → *šubarīum*

šubšulum "boiled" OB *kuprum š.* "boiled asphalt"; < *bašālu* Š

šubtu(m) I, *šuptu(m)* "seat, dwelling" [KI.TUŠ; TUŠ; DAG] **1.** "dwelling place", *š. nēḫtu* "peaceful dwelling" (for subjects); *š. ramû*, *nadû* etc. "to set up, take up dwelling"; "(human) settlement"; "quarters, military position" for troops; "residence" of king; god's "residence" in temple, in heaven, in *apsû*; "lair, nest" of animal, bird **2.** "seat; site; foundation"; "base (for divine symbol); altar-base"; "support" for vessel; "position, placement" of ear, of feature on liver etc. **3.** jB "(animal) trap, pitfall"; < *wašābum*; > *šubbutu*

šubtu II (or *šuptu*) (a garment) MB, Am.

šubtum III; pl. *šubātum* (a surface measure) OA

šubû(m) I, NA also *šabû* (a semiprecious stone) Bab., NA [NA4.ŠUBA] seal of *š.*, esp. in mag.; *š. arqu* "yellow *š.*"

šubû II (or *šupû*) ~ "slander" jB lex.

šubû III "satiety" jB lex.; < *šebû* I

šubû → also *šumû* I; *yašibum*

šūbu "rush" M/NA(roy. inscr.) to flatten (*ṇiālu* Š) enemy *kīma š.* "like rushes"

šububu (a weapon or tool) Am.

šubultinbi "young" jB(Ass.) in col. *šam(al)lû š.* "young assistant"; < *šubultu* + *inbu*

šubultu(m), *šubiltu*; pl. *šubullātu* "ear, spike (of corn)" O/jB, MA as smallest thing: (not even) "an ear of corn"; as star name "Spica"; → *šubultinbi*

šūbultu(m), *šūbiltu* "consignment; gift" Bab. (OAkk, OA in PNs) *ṣimdat š.* "regulation on conveyance"; "s.th. sent by/from"; "gift" sent to recipient; < *wabālu* Š; → *šēbultu*

šubulu (a piece of jewellery) Mari

šuburru(m) "rump, bottom" O/jB [DÚR] of humans; *š. marṣu* "illness of posterior", *bāb š.*

"anus"; NB "bottom" of a field; OB math. "base" of figure

šūdadu, *šudātu* "lover" jB

šudarāru mng. unkn. jB lex.; < *darāru* I ?

šudātu → *šudādu*

šuda'um → *šeda'um*

šuddû → *tuddû*

šuddudu (part of a waggon)? MB

šuddulum, *šum/ndulu* "very wide, spacious" Bab.(lit.); earth, terrain; temple; heart; of offerings "plentiful"; < *šadālu* D

šuddurum → *šunduru*

šudgultu → *šudugultu*

šudingirrakku 'god's hand' (a serious illness) jB [ŠU.DINGIR.RA]; < Sum.

šudlupu "sleepless; troubled" jB of sufferers; of groans; < *dalāpu* Š

šudugultu "transferred property" NB for *šudgultu*; < *dagālu* Š

šudururu → *sudūru*

šudušīu, *šudušû* "six-year-old" Nuzi, NB of horse, ass; < *šediš*

šudūšum "six" OB; < *šediš*

šudutinnu (archit. term)? MA

šūdûtu, Nuzi also *šūšûtu* "announcement, edict" jB, Nuzi; Nuzi *arki š.* "after the official announcement"; of palace (*ēkalli*), new (*eššu*); < *edû* II Š

šu'ētu → *šuātum*

šugallā'um (an official) OAkk [ŠU.GAL4.LÁ(-); ŠU.LÁ+GAL4(-)]; < Sum.

šugallītu(m), *sugallītu(m)* (desig. of goddess) O/jB

šugānû → *tugānû*

šugarriā'um, occas. *šugarruwā'um*, *šigarriûm* (a metal tool) OA; as symbol in judicial proceedings

šugarrû, *šugurrû* (a processed form of dates) NB as payment in kind

šugarrû → also *šugrû*

šugarruru(m) "to roll" O/jB, MA seal on tablet; stick across body; "allow" animals "to roll (on ground)"; < *qarāru* Š; > *šugurruru*

šugarruwā'um → *šugarriā'um*

šuggudum mng. unkn. OB lex.

šugguru(m) "to cheat, lie" O/jB **D**, **Dt**; > *tašgertu*

šugidimmakku 'hand of the ghost' (an illness) jB [ŠU.GIDIM(.MA)]; < Sum.

šugillu mng. unkn. Nuzi

šuginakku → *šuginû*; *šu'iginakku*

šuginû(m), *šugunûm*, occas. *šuginakku* (a type of offering) OB, Mari; jB lex. [ŠU.GI.NA] of animal; oil, bread, beer etc.; *ša š.* "person in charge of *š.*"; < Sum.

šugipunu (a textile) Nuzi

šugītu(m) (a class of women) O/jB [(MUNUS.) ŠU.GI] able to marry; < Sum.; → *šugû*

šuglû, NA *šaglû* "deported" NA, NB; < *galû* II; > *šagalûtu*

šuglutu, *šugludu* "very frightening" jB of flood, palace; < *galātu*

šugru → *šukru*

šugrû(m), *šugurû(m)*, *šugarrû(m)* "basket" Bab.; < Sum.; → *šugarrû*; *šukurû*

šugû(m) "old man" O/jB lex.; < Sum.; → *šugītu*

šugû → also *šukû*

šugummû ~ "buzzing"? NA; < *šagāmu* II

šugunûm → *šuginû*

šuguppum mng. unkn. OB lex.; < Sum.

šugurru(m) **1.** (a mat)? OB **2.** "roll" jB of salt meat; < Sum.

šugurrû → *šugarrû*

šugurruru adj. mng. uncert. NB of donkey; < *šugarruru*

šugurû → *šugrû*

šuḫ "on the subject of, à propos" NA

šuḫalulu mng. unkn. MB(Susa) in descr. of road

šuḫarratu "deathly hush" jB *š. tabkat* "silence is poured out"; < *šuḫarruru* II

šuḫarriš "in silence" jB; → *šuḫarruru* II

šuḫarru/û → *šaḫarru* I

šuḫarruru I "silent" jB; < *šuḫarruru* II

šuḫarruru(m) II, *šuḫruru*, *ša/uḫurruru(m)* "to be deathly still" OAkk, O/jB, NA **Š** (pret. *ušḫarrir*, pres. *ušḫarrar*, early OB 2 sg. *tašḫarrar*; stat. *šaḫur*, *šuḫarrur*) of gods, humans; s.o.'s face; desert (*ṣēru*), palace; storm **Št** as Š "be quite silent"; > *šaḫurratu*, *šuḫarratu*, *šuḫarriš*, *šuḫarruru* I, *šaḫrartu* I

šuḫāru → *šaḫūrum* II

šuḫatinnū, *šuḫutinnū*, Ug. *saḫatennū* pl. tant. "(a type of) onion" OA, O/jB [ZA.ḪA.TIN.SAR]

šuḫattu(m); pl. *šuḫattātu* (a cloth, rag) Bab., M/NA used for wiping; (as plant name) *š. tinūri* "*š.* of the oven"

šuḫātu mng. uncert. jB(Susa) of piglet

šuḫēḫunu → *šukênu*

šuḫḫānu (a type of plough) NB *(epinnu) š.*

šuḫḫarampašḫa "wet nurse's compensation" Nuzi; < Hurr.

šuḫḫelu mng. unkn. Nuzi, phps. "offcuts" of textile; < Hurr.

šuḫḫiṭṭātu mng. unkn. jB comm.

šuḫḫu I "very long" jB of wooden rafters; < *šiāḫum* I D

šuḫḫu(m) II "buttock; stand, trestle" Bab. of men (also du.); animals; "stand" for a drum; a part of the intestines

šuḫḫu III (a festival) OB(Alal.) in *ūm š.*

šuḫḫû I "destroyed" jB of temples; < *šuḫḫû* II

šuḫḫû(m) II **D** "to remove" O/jB freedom, document; cloth in rit.; > *šuḫḫû* I

šuḫḫû III, occas. *šu''û* **D** "to have (illicit) sexual intercourse" O/jB with (= *itti*); stat. of priestess **Dt** pass. of D esp. of priestess; > *tašḫītu*

šuḫḫû IV **D** of mud "to spoil, ruin" a garment jB

šuḫḫurum → *šu''uru* I.II

šuḫīnu "brazier"? O/jB; < *šaḫānu*

šuḫītu → *šuḫû* II

šuḫnu "heat" jB lex.; < *šaḫānu*

šuḫru mng. unkn. jB lex.

šuḫru → also *šaḫūrum* II; *šūru* I; *šu'ru*

šuḫrûm ~ "gleanings"? Mari

šuḫrubtu "waste land" jB of uncultivated ground; pl. *šuḫrubātu*, of temple; < *ḫarābu* Š

šuḫruru **Š** "to lay waste, reduce to silence" jB marshes, dwellings **Št** pass. of city; > *šaḫrartu* II

šuḫruru → also *šuḫarruru* II

šuḫsīlu, šuḫsu → *suḫsu*

šuḫtu(m) "verdigris, patina, rust" O/jB, NA [SAḪAR.URUDU] on copper sword; used in mag. and ointments; *šuḫat ḫurāṣi* "*š.* on gold"?; also a plant

šuḫṭu "anger" OA, jB; *š. libbi(m)*; < *šaḫāṭu* III

šuḫûm I, jB *šu'û*, also *šû* (a disease) OB, jB

šuḫû II; f. *šuḫītu* adj. mng. unkn. Am. of bed, chariot

šūḫu(m) "(small) cucumber" jB lex.

šuḫulḫu (a type of wool)? Nuzi; < Hurr.

šuḫummumu ~ "deathly hush" jB lex.

šuḫunni (a piece of furniture)? Nuzi; < Hurr.

šuḫuppatu → *suḫuppatum*

šuḫuppu → *suḫuppum* I

šuḫuptu → *suḫuppatum*

šuḫuraptu mng. unkn. Nuzi; < Hurr.

šuḫurru(m) "porous vessel" O/jB of pottery; → *šaḫarru* I

šuḫurruru → *šuḫarruru* II

šuḫurum mng. unkn. OB lex.

šuḫūru → *šaḫūru* I

šuḫutinnū → *šuḫatinnū*

šu('i)ginakku "barber" O/jB [(LÚ.)ŠU.I.GI.NA]; < Sum.

šu'illakku '(prayer of) raised hands' j/NB, NA [ŠU.ÍL.LÁ(.KAM/KÁM) (→ *nīšu* I)] *š. našû*, *epēšu* "to perform", *manû* "to recite a *š.*"; < Sum.

šu'ītu → *šuātum*

šukāmu(m) "scribal art" or "stylus"? Bab.(lit.) DN *āḫizu š.* "who has learnt/holds *š.*"; given to king by DN

šukannunnu → *sukannīnu*

šukānu "ornament, jewellery" OAkk, M/NB, NA *š.* of kingship; of troops; for decoration of DN; as grave goods; < *šakānu*

šukarumma in *š. epēšu* ~ "to give in exchange"? Nuzi; < Hurr.

šuka''unu → *šukênu*

šukbusu ~ "ramp" jB stand on *š.*; < *kabāsu* Š

šukdu (or *šuqdu*) mng. unkn. jB; → *šiqdu*

šukênu(m), jB also *šukennu*; OAkk, Ass. *šuka''unu(m)* (pres. also *uškân*); Am., Nuzi, Bogh., Ug., Emar **šuḫēḫunu* (→ GAG §109i-j) "to prostrate o.s." [KI.ZA.ZA] before god, king; before freq. = dat. suff.; MA in introduction to letters *(n)ultaka''in* "I/we bow" (before my/our lord); OA "submit to" document, functionary; → *muškēnu*

šukīru → *sikkūru*

šukītu (part or type of vehicle) Nuzi; < Hurr.

šukītuḫlu (a kind of soldier) Nuzi; < *šukītu* + Hurr. *-uḫlu*

šukkallu(m), *sukkallu(m)* "(a court official); minister" [(LÚ.)SUKKAL] king's minister; (in Elam) a ruler of a district; MA *š. rabiu*, NA *š. dannu* "chief minister"; M/NA *š. šaniu* "deputy minister"; of gods e.g. *Bunene š. Šamaš*; < Sum.; > *šukkallūtum*; *sukkallatu*; → *sukkalatû*; *sukkalmaḫḫu*

šukkallūtum "post of *š.*" Mari; < *šukkallu*

šukkammu mng. uncert. NB

šukkû **D** Bogh. lex. **1.** "to cleanse" **2.** "to pray"?

šukkultu "dregs, scrapings" jB from pots; < *šukkulu*

šukkulu(m) **D** "to wipe down, wipe out" O/jB, M/NA with cloth; sandals with beard **Dtn** iter. **Dt** pass.; > *šukkultu*

šukkuptu mng. unkn. jB lex.

šukkuṣu "wild"? jB lex.

šukkuštu (a plant name) jB rdg. uncert.

šuklû → *šuglû*

šuklultu "completion; completeness" jB of decor; "form" of human body; < *šuklulu* II

šuklulu(m) I, Ass. *šaklulu(m)*; NA pl. *šaklalūte* "complete, perfect" [ŠU.DU$_7$] of things; temples, cult; "entire, uncastrated" of sacrificial animals;

OA in *qātam š. nadā'um/itaddûm* "to deposit a full share"; < *šuklulu* II

šuklulu(m) II, Ass. *šaklulu(m)* **Š** "to complete, make/do completely"; "create perfectly" humans, form, statue; house, city etc.; of woman "carry" a child "to full term"; "perform perfectly" cult etc.; OA "provide" s.th. "completely" **Štn** "always perform perfectly" cult **Št** pass. of Š of house "be completed"; "have complete success"; > *šuklulu* I; *šuklultu*

šuknušu "humble" jB of king towards gods; < *kanāšu* I Š

šukru (or *šug/qru*) mng. unkn. MA in *šukri ēnēšunu* (stone objects); → *šu'ru* ?

šukrû → *šukurû*

šukû(m), *šugû* "doorpost" Bab.; < Sum.

šukubbe; pl. *šukubbena* mng. uncert. MB(Alal.) of chair, footstool; < Hurr.

šukubtu(m) (or *šukuptu(m)*) **1.** (a class or category of persons) MB(Alal.) **2.** uncert. mng. Mari, MB(Alal.)

šukuddāku "(temple) fisherman" j/NB; < Sum.

šukuddākūtu "profession of temple fisherman" jB; < *šukuddāku*

šukudu(m), also *šakudu*, *šukuddu* **1.** O/jB, Nuzi "arrow" [GAG.SI.SÁ] **2.** Bab. "Sirius" [MUL. GAG.SI.SÁ] **3.** jB lex. "sharp end of a spindle"

šuku(k)ku (a land measure) MB(Alal.)

šūkultu, M/NA *šākultu*, NA *šākussu* "feeding; meal, banquet" M/NA, M/NB, MB(Alal.), Ug., Emar as ceremonial feast; "fodder" for animals; f. pl. "left-overs"?; NB "fattening shed" for sheep; < *akālu* Š

šūkulu(m), MA *šākulu* "fed, fattened" Bab., MA of domestic animals; "steeped, tanned" of hides; < *akālu* Š

šukunātu f. pl. mng. unkn. Bogh. lex.

šukunnā'um → *šukunnû*

šuku(n)niš adv. mng. unkn. jB(Ass.) of speaking

šukunnû(m), *šukunnum*, OAkk *šukunnā'um* **1.** OAkk, OB "estimated yield; cultivation agreement" [GAR.RA; NÍG.GAR(.RA)] of dates; + *šakānu(m)*; of grain **2.** M/jB "blasphemy, false accusation" [NÍG.GAR] against god, man; < *šakānu*

šukunu (an allocation) Nuzi, Ug. of grain etc., also of animals for palace

šukuptu → *šukubtu*

šukurgallu(m) "big lance" OB(N.Mes.); jB lex. [GIŠ.ŠUKUR.GAL]; < Sum.

šukurru(m), Mari also *šakurrum* OAkk, O/jB, NA [GIŠ.ŠUKUR] **1.** "lance, spear" **2.** (a household utensil) **3.** (a metal peg or rivet); < Sum.

šuk(u)rû(m) mng. unkn. O/jB lex.; < Sum.

šukūsu(m) I, *šukussu* "subsistence (field)" O/jB [A.ŠÀ.ŠUKU] assigned to temple or palace employee; < Sum.

šukūsu(m) II (a divine headdress) O/jB

šukuttu(m) I, NA also *šakuttu* "adornment, jewellery" of women, deities; gold, silver; st. constr. usu. *šukutti*, but also jB *šuknat mūši* "the jewellery of the night" ref. to moon; < *šakānu*

šukuttu II (or *šuquttu*) mng. uncert. NB of sacrifices

šulāpu (an ornament, phps.) "knife blade" NB; < Aram.

šulbû (part of a door-lock) jB lex.

šulgum (a container) Mari

šulḫum I (a textile) OA

šulḫu II (a cake)? Nuzi

šulḫû(m) I (an ailment) O/jB

šulḫû II (a scribe) jB lex.

šulḫû → also *šalḫû* I.II

šulḫullum → *šurḫullu*

šulilanni ~ "mankind" jB lex.

šulīpum (an object) OAkk

šulītu → *šūlūtu* I

šullaḫu; pl. *šullaḫena* (a vessel) MB(Alal.)

šullāmu (desig. of horses and mules) NA; < Aram.

šullānu(m) ~ "pockmarked, wart-covered"? O/jB also OAkk, Bab. as PN ?; < *šullu*

šullu(m), *šūlu* "(big) wart, pockmark"? O/jB on human body; of a feature on the exta; > *šullānu*

šullû → *sulû* I

šullum bīti → *šalāmu* I 2

šullul "one-third (of a shekel)" NB; < *šullušu* I

šullultu → *šullušu*

šullumāniš → *šulmāniš*

šullumānu → *šulmānu*

***šullumtu**, NB *šullundu*, NA *šallum/ntu* "completion, final payment" NA, NB; < *šalāmu* II D

šullumu mng. uncert. j/NB as PN; < *šalāmu* II D

šullundu → *šullumtu*

šulluqu "(with) lacerated (ear)" MB of horse; < *šalāqu* D

šullušiš ~ "in thirds" jB of hair; < *šullušu* I

šullušu(m) I **1.** (= vb. adj. *šalāšu* D) "trebled, tripled, threefold" j/NB; Ug., jB land "worked for a third time"; Mari in *kaspam/ḫurāṣam šulluš* ~ "decorated? with silver/gold" **2.** (as subst., f.) j/NB *šullultu* "one-third"; *šullultašu* "one-third of him"; NB *šullulti 1 šiqil kaspi* "one-third shekel of silver"; NA *šallussu* [ŠUŠANA-], *š. ša 1 qa* "one-third *qû*" **3.** NB f. pl. *šullultātu* "one-third shares"; < *šalāš*; > *šullul*; *šullušiš*, *šullušû*

šullušum II (a type of log) OB

šullušû "made of or with (something) tripled" jB lex.; < *šullušu* I

šullušû → also *šulušīu*

šulluṭu "triumphant" jB of DN; < *šalāṭu* I D

šulmāniš, jB also *šullumāniš* "in peace" Bab.(lit.); < *šulmu*

šulmānu, NA also *šulmannu*, NB also *šullumānu*; pl. f. "greeting-gift" M/NA, M/NB; M/NA, NB often as bribe or inducement; NB to gods; Am., Ug., also jB "well-being, health"; < *šulmu*

šulmānūtu "gift, present" jB; < *šulmānu*

šulmu(m) "completeness; well-being" [SILIM (=DI)] **1.** "completeness, intact state" **2.** "well-being, health, safety" esp. in letter-headings **3.** "greeting, good wishes (for well-being)"; MB, NA "greeting ceremony" for king; "message of greeting" **4.** Ug., NB "peace" (→ *salīmu*) **5.** "setting" of sun; "fall" of dynasty etc. (< *šalāmu* I 4) **6.** om. ~ "bubble" **7.** ext. (a crease on the sheep's liver); < *šalāmu* II; > *šulmānu*, *šulmāniš*, *šulmānūtu*

šulpu(m) I "stalk, straw" Bab. "stem" of cereal plant; "stubble" esp. *pī šulpi(m)* of fallow fields; "drinking straw"; (a wind instrument), *ša š.* "player of *š.* instrument" OB lex.

šulpu II (a vessel) j/NB, NA of gold, silver

šulpu III mng. uncert. jB om.

šulputtu → *šalputtu*; *šulputu*

šulputu(m); f. *šulputtu* "defiled, ruined" O/jB of divine statues; city; land; < *lapātu* Š

šulsudu → *šuršudu*

šulšān → *šuššu* I du.

šulšu "one-third" j/NB; < *šalāš*; → *šalšu; šuššu* I du.

šulû(m), later *sulû*, *sullû* "street, lane" Bab. esp. jB in *sūqu u sulû*; < Sum.

šūlu(m) I (a demon) O/jB *š. lemnu* "evil spirit"

šūlu II ~ "reed stem" Nuzi, for arrows

šūlu III "cough" jB

šūlu → also *šullu*

šūlû(m) I "raised, high" Bab. **1.** of cow "served, covered" (sexually) **2.** NB of heaven; < *elû* III Š

šūlû II "ordeal"? jB lex.

šul'u "small"? jB lex.

šuluḫḫatu ~ "drizzle"? jB om.; < *šuluḫḫu* ?

šuluḫḫu(m) usu. pl. "purification rite" (lit.) [ŠU.LUḪ(.ḪA)] pure *š.*; to carry out properly (*ešēru*), purify (*ebēbu* D), establish *š.* rites; also with → *salāḫu* I G, D; < Sum.; > *šuluḫḫû*; *šuluḫḫatu*?

šuluḫḫû(m) (a bowl for hand-washing) M/jB [ŠU.LUḪ]; < *šuluḫḫu*

šuluḫtu "despatch, consignment" Am.; < W.Sem.

šūluku "brought to readiness" jB lex. of malt; < *alāku* Š

šulultu f. adj. "third" Nuzi for *šalultu* (→ *šalšu* f.); < *šalāš*

šulultu → also *šuluštu*

šulummatu (part of lung) jB right, left

šulummu (a leather part of the harness) Mari

šulummû "good condition" j/NB in *š. māti*; < *šalāmu* II

šulupkā'um, *šulupkī'um* → *šilipkā'um*

šuluš → *šulluš*

šulušā "three each" OA, O/jB [3.TA.ÀM]; < *šalāš*

šulūšā'um "threefold"? OA; < *šalāš*

šulušīu(m), *šulušû(m)*, *šullušû*; f. *šulušītu* "three-year-old" Bab., MA, Nuzi [MU.3; 3-] of animals; < *šalāš*

šuluštu, *šulultu* "one-third" jB; < *šalāš*; → *šalšu*

šulušû → *šulušīu*

šulutu (a plant) jB lex. equated with *aššultu*, *uššultu*

šūlūtu I, NB also *šūlītu* M/NB; MB mng. uncl.; j/NB "garrison", also *ṣābē š.*

šūlūtu(m) II **1.** "votive gift" j/NB; Mari of persons **2.** "summons"? MB; < *elû* III Š; Ass. → *šēlū'atum*

šuluṭṭu (a preparation of aromatics) jB

-šum, *-šu* "to him" (3 m. sg. dat. suff.), usu. after vent. (→ GAG §§42g-k, 84b)

šumakkû → *šumekkû*

šumamtu "parched grain" jB lex.; < *šawû* II

šumat(a)kānu, *šumutkānu*, *šumutkunaya*, *šamtaknaya* (a title, phps. a tribal name)? NB

šumatkilu → *šamaškillu*

šumdu mng. unkn. JB

šumdulu → *šuddulum*

šumekkû (a tool) jB lex., also *ša šumakkî* (a prof.); < Sum.

šumēla(m), *šuwēlam*, *šumēli/u* "on the left" Bab., NA [(Á.)GÙB; 150]; < *šumēlu*

šumēlu(m), *šumīlu(m)* "the left" [GÙB; Á.GÙB.BU; 150; Susa 16; Qatna also GÙB.BA] "the left side" of body, object, place; (opp. =

imittu I); *šumēlukki* "to your left"; "left hand"; "left wing" of army etc.; > *šumēla*, *šumēlû*

šumēlu → also *šumēla*

šumēlû(m) "left-hand" O/jB [Á.GÙB(.BA/BU)(-)] "(standing) on left"; as PN "left-handed"?; jB of table, part of body; lex. (a kind of *šubû*-stone); < *šumēlu*

šumēnu(m), *šu(n)minnu* (a stone) Bab., Emar, Ug. lex.; med. as drug; < Sum.

Šumeru(m), OB lex. also *Šuwerum* **1.** "Sumer" [EME.GI7] **2.** jB, NA "Sumerian (language)"; *š. aḫāzu* "to learn Sumerian"; *lišān š.* "Sumerian language"; as lex. gloss; "Sumerian (text)"

šumerû 1. jB lex. "a Sumerian" **2.** jB "(scribe in) Sumerian"; < *Šumeru*

šumešam → *šumišam*

šumgallu → *ušumgallu*

šumḫu(m) "luxuriance, plenty" Bab.(lit.) of vegetation; transf. of population, descendants; < *šamāḫu* I

šumḫurtu 1. jB mng. uncert. **2.** jB, Susa ext., adv. acc. *šumḫurta(m)* ~ "oppositely"; < *maḫāru* Š

šumīlu → *šumēlu*

šuminnu → *šumēnu*

šumišam, *šumešam* "name by name" OB, Mari; < *šumu* + *-išam* (→ GAG §67g)

šumittu → *šāmiṭu* I

šumkalatḫu ? (a bronze object) Nuzi; < Hurr.

šumkū, *šunkū* pl. tant. "onions" Ass.

šumma, NA also *šummu* "if" (NB only lit.; → *kī* 4) [BAD; om., med. DIŠ; UD (also OB 360+40; MAŠ; AŠ); NA also MU (< *šumu*)] **1.** introducing condit. clauses in indic.: "if" (→ GAG §161) **2.** introducing oaths, with subjunct. M/NA, M/jB (OB with indic.): *šumma lā* = pos., *šumma* = neg. oath **3.** *šumma* ... *šumma* "whether ... or" (→ GAG §§161b-c, 180b); ext. "either ... or"; MB also *(u) šumma* "or rather ..." **4.** OA *š. libbika* "if you wish"; *š. lā* "without, in the absence of" **5.** NA introducing indir. questions, with subjunct. "whether, if" (→ GAG §180b) **6.** Am., Nuzi, Bogh. conj. "when" **7.** Bab., Am., NA adv. "now see, truly"; > *šummaman*; *šummu* I

šummaman, *šummamin*, *šumman* "if" (introducing unreal conditions) OA, O/jB e.g. in PN *Šumman-lā-DN* "If there had not been DN", *šumman lā kâti* "if it had not been for you"; < *šumma* + *-man*/*-min*

šummannu(m) I "halter, tether" O/jB [ÉŠ.LÁ] for humans; animals; NB (as part of a water-hoisting device)

šummannum II, *šumunnum* mng. unkn. OB mag.

šummannu III "gift, present" jB lex.

šummānum "defect"? Mari

šummatu → *summatu*

šummu I "a *šumma*-clause; law, edict" jB; < *šumma*

šummu(m) II **D** "to ponder, reflect" O/jB; OB "think, consider" **Št** mng. uncert. O/jB only in PNs e.g. *Luštašīm-ilī*; *Muštašīm*; > *tašīmtu*

šummu → also *šumma*; *ušummu*

šummuḫu(m), jB lex. also *šummuku* "very luxuriant" Bab.(lit.), Mari; O/MB in PNs; NB of forest "lush, verdant"; of gifts "very plentiful"; < *šamāḫu* I D

šummuḫu → also *samāḫu* D

šummuku → *šummuḫu*

šummunu D not attested **Dt** (only *ussatmin*) pass. "to be oiled, rubbed with oil" NA; < *šamnu* denom.

šummuṭu I "trimmed off" jB lex. of date branch; < *šamāṭu* I D

šummuṭu II "laid flat" jB, of butterfly at rest; < *šamāṭu* II D

šumna (a servant)? Nuzi; < Hurr.

šumnašušḫu; pl. *šumnašušḫena* (a container) Nuzi; < Hurr.

***šumquttu**, *šunqu(t)tu* "adjustment, deduction" NB; < *maqātu* Š

šumru "fury, furiousness" MB(Ass.) in *š. tāḫāziya* etc.; < *šamāru* I

šumruṣu(m); f. OB also *šumruštum* "very painful, suffering" O/jB of situation; road; words; heart; < *marāṣu* Š

šumsuku, MA *šansuku* "deprived" MA, jB; < *nasāku* Š

šumṣulu(m), MB also *šunṣulu* **Š** "to spend the day in rest" O/jB freq. with *šumšû*; → *muṣlālu*; *ṣalālu*

šumšû(m), MB also *šunšû* **Š** "to spend the night; do s.th. at night" O/jB [GE6.ZAL] astr. "last through the night"; < *mūšu* denom.; > *mušamšû*

šumu(m), jB occas. *šemu*, NB also *šu'u*; pl. m., also *-ānu*; NA pl. also f. "name; son; line of text" [MU] **1.** "name" of person; *š. šaṭru* "written name" in inscription; of statue, building, mountain; "word for" stone, plant etc.; *kunuk*, *aban š.-ya* "seal, stone with my name" **2.** "(good) name, repute, fame"; *š. šakānu(m)* "to establish reputation"; *š. ṭābu*, *damqu* etc. "good repute" **3.** idiomatic usages: *ana šum(i)* → *aššum* "on account of"; *mimma šumšu* "anything whatever"; (after subst.) *šumšu/a* "any" OA, OB **4.** "son, succession" esp. in PNs **5.** "line (of text)" [MU.NI; MU.(ŠID.) BI(.IM) in col.] OB *šanû(m) šumšu* "a variant thereto is ..."; *ḫīp 1 š.* "break of one line"; (in col.) *n š.* "(total) n lines"; > *šumišam, šumû* III

šumû I, MA *šubā'u*, NA *šuwû, šubû* "roast meat" M/NA, M/NB [UZU.KA.NE] esp. in rit. and offerings; MA *ša šubā'e* (a roasting pan or spit); < *šawû* II

šumû(m) II "handle (of tool)" O/jB

šumû III "name tag" jB lex. of clay; < *šumu*

šūmū pl. tant. "garlic" [(Ú/ŠE.)SUM.SAR]; seeds of *š.*

Šumuḫalše (a month) MB(Alal.); < Hurr.?

šumunnum → *šummannum* II

šumutkānu, šumutkunaya → *šumatakānu*

šumuttu(m), MA, Bogh., Ug. *šamuttu*, occas. *šimittu* (a red vegetable, phps.) "beetroot" O/jB, MA [(Ú.)SUMUN.DAR(.SAR); jB also Ú.SU.AN. DAR(.RA)]; also *zīr š.* "seed(s) of *š.*"; < Sum.?; → *sumundû*

šum'uttu "(textual) addition"? jB; < *mâdu* Š

-šun → *-šunu*

šunā'a, *šu(n)nāya* "two each" NA [2-*a-a*]; < *šina* II

šunamerimmakku 'hand of the curse' (an illness) jB [ŠU.NAM.ÉRIM/MA-]; < Sum.

šunannu (a piece of furniture) Alal., NA of wood

šunāšunu "to them" (m. pl. dat.) NA

šunatu, šunātu → *šuttu* I

šunātunu "those, the same" (acc.) M/NA

šunāya → *šunā'a*

šunāzi (a medicinal plant) jB

šundu I conj. "when, while" Nuzi, jB usu. with subjunct.

šundu II (a type of wool) NB

šundulu → *šuddulum*

šunduru(m), *šuddurum* mng. unkn. Mari

šungallu → *ušumgallu*

šunḫu, *šun'u, šūnu, šunuḫu* (a medicinal plant) jB

-šuni → *-šunu*

šunī "they two" (m. du. pron.) Am.

-šunī "of them two" (m. du. gen.) OAkk, Am.; "them two" (m. du. acc.) OAkk, Am.

šunīš "on them two" OAkk in PN *Šunīš-takal*; < *šunī* + *-iš*

-šunīšim "to them two" (m. du. dat.) OAkk

šunīti **1.** "them two" (m. du. acc. pron.) OAkk **2.** "those two" (m. du. pron. adj.) OA

-šunīti "them two" (m. du. acc.) OAkk

šunium → *šunûm* I

šunkū → *šumkū*

šunminnu → *šumēnu*

šunnâtu f. pl. "alteration, change" jB *ina lā šunnâte* "without change"; < *šanû* IV D

šunnāya → *šunā'a*

šunniru → *šurīnum* I

šunnu(m) mng. uncert. O/jB **D** and **Dt**

šunnu → also *šannu*

šunnû, NA *šannu'u* "doubled" jB, NA; < *šanû* III D

šunnuqu mng. unkn. jB lex.; var. of *šūnuqu* ?

šunnušu → *sunnušu*

šunnūtu → *šunu'tu*

šunqu(t)tu → *šumquttu*

šunṣulu → *šumṣulu*

šunšû → *šumšû*

šunšudu → *šuršudu*

šunšunnu (or *šinšinnu*) mng. unkn. jB lex.

šunu, NA also *šanu-* before subjunct. *-(u)ni* **1.** "they" (3 m. pl. nom.) before vb.s, giving emphasis, *šunuma* "it is they who ..."; in pred. use ... *šunu* "they are ..." **2.** "those, these same", *awīlū šunu* "those men"; → *aššunu*; *iššunu*; for acc. etc. → *šunūši*; *šunūti*

-šunu OAkk, Bab.(poet.) also *-šun*, OA, O/jB also *-šnu*, *-šuni* **1.** "their" (3 m. pl. gen.) **2.** "them" (3 m. pl. acc.) Ass., also occas. OAkk, O/jB for Bab. *-šunūti*; MA, jB occas. "to them" (dat.); NA also *-šanu-* before subjunct. *-(u)ni*

šunûm I, *šunium* "theirs, belonging to them" OA, OB *lā šunium* "(s.th.) not theirs"; → *iššunû*

šunû II (a tree, phps.) "chaste tree, *Vitex agnus castus*" M/jB [GIŠ/Ú.ŠE.NÚ.A; GIŠ.ŠE.NA.A; GIŠ.ŠE.NU] seed, root etc.; < Sum.

šunû III mng. unkn. Bogh.

šūnu, šun'u → *šunḫu*

šūnuḫiš "with much trouble" jB; < *šūnuḫu*

šunuḫu → *šunḫu*

šūnuḫu "much troubled, wearied" jB of petitioner, worshipper; speech, prayer; < *anāḫu* I Š; > *šūnuḫiš*

šunundu → *šanūdu*

šunūnūtu → *šinūnūtu*

šūnuqu "milk-giving" MA of ewe; also jB mng. uncert. of plant; < *enēqu* Š

šunūši(m) "to them" (3 m. pl. dat.) OB; → *šunu*

-šunūši(m), once OB(poet.) *-šunūt* "to them" (3 m. pl. dat. suff.)

šunūti, NB also *šunūtu* **1.** "them" (3 m. pl. acc.) **2.** "of them" (3 m. pl. gen.) OA, OB after st.

constr., *ša*, *kīma* **3.** "those, these same" (acc., gen.); → *šunu*

-šunūti, NB *-šu/inūtu* **1.** "them" (3 m. pl. acc. suff.) **2.** "to them" (3 m. pl. dat. suff.)

šunūtu → *šunūti*

-šunūtu → *-šunūti*

šunu'tu, *šunnūtu* "two(-animal) plough" jB lex.; < *šina* II

šunu'û(m) "two-year-old" Bab. [MU.2; 2-] of animals; < *šina* II

šupālānu "lower or western border or district" Nuzi, also loc.-adv. *ina šupālāniššu*; < *šupālu*

šupālītu **1.** "undergarment" Am., NA, NB [TÚG.KI.TA] **2.** jB "foundation"?; < *šupālû*

šupalkû → *nepelkû* Š

šupālu(m) 1. OB "depression, low-lying area" **2.** in adv. use OB, Mari *šupālu*; Nuzi, j/NB *šupāl(a)*, Nuzi also *šupalli* "below" (Nuzi = "westwards"), also *ina š.*, *ana š.* "downwards" **3.** in prep. use *šupāl(u/a)*, also *ina/ištu š.*, *šupāluššu* "beneath" (Nuzi = "west of"); Am., Bogh., Ug. *ana šupāl(i) šēpī* "beneath the feet of" (= submission) [KI.TA]; Am., NB *šupāl(u/i) šēpī* "footstool"; < *šapālu*; > *šupālānu*, *šupālû*

šupālû(m); f. *šupālītu*, NB *šuppallītu* "lower" Bab., M/NA of buildings; topog. of sea, watercourse; town; field; < *šupālu*; > *šupālītu*

šupapītu → *šubabītu*

šuparrû → *šubarrû*

šuparruru I; f. *šuparrur/štu* "spread out" jB of net; heaven; foliage; sheep (mng.?); < *šuparruru* II

šuparruru(m) II **Š** "to spread out" O/jB [BÀRA(.GA)] net; wings; cloth; stars **Štn** iter. of Š; > *šuparruru* I

šuparruštu → *šuparruru* I

šuparruttu → *šubarrûtu*

šuparzuḫu **Š** "to make abundant" j/NB "make abundant" offerings; "provide abundantly for" shrine etc.

šupātu → *šubtu* I

šūpātu → *šīpātu*

šupa''ultu → *šupêltu*

šupa''ulu → *šupêlu*

šupa''ussu → *šupêltu*

šupe''ilu "exchanged" Nuzi of fields; < *šupêlu*

šupellu → *šupêlu*

šupêltu(m), *šupe''ultu(m)*, MA *šupa''ultu*, NA *šupa''ussu*, *šapûssu*, NB also *šupûltu* "exchange" [ŠE.BAL] *ina/ana/akī š.* "as an exchange"; *ana š. X* "in exchange for X"; of grain, field etc. "item exchanged"; Nuzi *ṭuppi š.* "exchange document"; "substitute"; < *šupêlu*

šupêlu(m), *šupellu(m)*, OA *šupa''ulu(m)* **Š** "to exchange, overturn" Bab., OA [ŠU.BAL] **1.** "exchange" s.th. for s.th. else (legally); "switch" items; populations; OA "convert into" (= acc.), barley into malt **2.** "turn over, overthrow" nest; person, on bed; established order; offerings; commands; *lā mušpēlu* "irreversible"; "bring round" (to o.'s side) **Št** **1.** pass. of Š **2.** act. "exchange with one another"; "overturn" commandment (as Š 2); "bring round" to o.'s side; > *šupe''ilu*; *šupêltu*

šupe''ultu → *šupêltu*

šupḫatu (a gold object) Qatna

šūpîš **1.** OB "in order to make apparent" **2.** jB "openly, publicly"; < *šūpû*

šupiu (an ornament) Qatna, of lapis lazuli

šupku "foundation, substructure" M/jB [UL.ḪÉ] of terrace; *š. šadî* "mountain base"; *š. šamê* "foundation of heaven"; < *šapāku*

šuplu(m) "depth" Bab. [BÙR; math. GAM; astr. SIG] "deepness", *š. erṣeti*, *mê* "depth of the earth, water" etc.; (as measured dimension, esp. math.) "depth"; astr., of moon, planet "(greatest) negative distance (below the ecliptic)" (→ *šūqu* I); < *šapālu*

šuppatu(m), *šubbatu* "rush, sedge"? Bab. in canals; with seven nodes

šuppu (a topog. term) NB

šuppû → *suppû* II; *šapû* III D; *wapûm* Š

šuppuḫum D "to incite" OB

šuppultu mng. uncert. jB lex., med.; < *šapālu*

šuppulu "very deep" M/jB of ditch; also OAkk "very short" of stature as PN; < *šapālu* D

šupšatu → *šipšatu*

šupšikkum → *tupšikku*

šupšuḫiš "in order to be peaceful"? jB; < *pašāḫu* Š

šupšuqiš "very laboriously; under difficult circumstances" jB; < *šupšuqu*

šupšuqtu "woman labouring (in childbirth)" M/jB [MUNUS.LA.RA.AḪ]; < *šupšuqu*

šupšuqu "very laborious" M/jB of terrain; of person "in difficulties"; < *pašāqu* Š

šuptae mng. unkn. Nuzi; < Hurr.

šuptu → *šubtu* I.II

šuptumma mng. unkn. Nuzi in *š. epēšu* an activity related to garments; < Hurr.

šupû I (a wrapper)? jB; < *šapû* IV

šupû II; f. pl. *šupêtu* "thick, padded"? NB of cloths; → *šapû* I

šupû III mng. unkn. jB lex.

šupû → also *šubû* II; *yašibum*

šūpû(m), NA *šāpû* "made apparent, resplendent, famous" Bab., NA [È] of deities, heavenly bodies; king; cities; < *wapûm* Š; > *šūpîš*

šupuḫru, *supuḫru*, once *šapuḫru* (a variety or part of the cedar) MA, M/jB [GIŠ.EREN.BAD] med. as material

šupukkû (a type of ration) jB lex.; < *šapāku*

šupûltu → *šupêltu*

šuqallulu(m) Š "to hang (down)" (intrans.) [LAL] (pret. *ušqallil*, pres. *i/ušqallal*; stat. *šuqallul*) of bag; copper on scales; part of body; bat; snake; clouds from sky; (trans.) "allow, cause s.th. to hang, be suspended"; > *šuqullālu*; *mašqalillu*?; *ašqulālu*; → *qalālu* II; *šaqālu*

šuqammumu I "silent" jB; < *šuqammumu* II

šuqammumu(m) II Š "to be(come) silent, still" O/jB, Bogh., MA (pret. *ušqammim*, pres. *ušqammam*, OB also *išqammam*; stat. *šuqammum*) of persons, population; country (side); building etc.; trans. of enemy "render silent" city; > *šaqummu*, *šaqummiš*; *šaqum=matu*; *šuqammumu* I

šūqāqu → *sūqāqû*

šūqātu mng. uncert. jB om., of shepherd

šuqdānu (a plant) jB med.

šuqdu → *šiqdu*; *šukdu*

šuqlum I, OA also *šuqulum* f. "packet, load" (of 60-75 minas weight) OA, OB; < *šaqālu*

šuqlu II, *šuqulu* "marsh" jB, also (a marsh plant)?

šuqru → *šukru*

šūqu I "height" j/NB; astr. [NIM] of moon, planet "(greatest) positive distance (above the ecliptic)" (→ *šuplu*); < *šaqû* II

šūqu II ~ "plenty" jB lex.

šūqu III mng. unkn. jB lex.

šūqu → also *sūqu*

šuqullālu (an ornament, phps.) ~ "pendant" Ug. of gold; < *šuqallulu*

šuqultu(m) "weight" [KI.LÁ; KI.LÁ.BI] of textiles, metal objects; *š. šārti* "a hair's weight"; "stone weight"; < *šaqālu*

šuqulu(m) → *šuqlum* I.II

šuqummatu → *šaqummatu*

šūquriš mng. uncl. jB; < *šūquru*

šūquru(m) "very valuable" Bab. silver, stones; gifts; persons; deeds, words, rites; < *waqārum*

šuquttu → *šukuttu* II

šurampašḫu (a compensation) Nuzi in silver; < Hurr.

šurāmum (a large container) OB, Mari

šurāniš "like a cat" jB; < *šurānu* I

šurānu(m) I "cat" [SA.A] of Meluḫḫa; go like a *š.*; med. *lipî š.* "fat from cat"; also as PN; > *šurāniš*

šurānum II mng. unkn. Mari

šurārum (a ceremony) Mari

šurāšu (desig. of cloth) Nuzi

šurathu (a tree; a dye) Nuzi, jB; < Hurr.

šurāṭum "strip of cloth" OB; < *šarāṭu*

šurbatu → *šuribatu*

šurbu "cold" jB lex.; → *šurīpu*

šurbû(m); f. *šurbūtu*, NB also *šurbītu* "very great" Bab.(lit.) of deity, king; royal command, weapons; sheep; < *rabû* II; > *šurbûtu*

šurbu'ītum; pl. *šurbu'iātum* f. adj. (desig. of wool) OA, phps. "fourfold" yarn; < *erbe*

šurbûtu(m) "greatness, exaltedness" O/jB of deities; < *šurbû*

šurdu(m) (part of a waggon wheel) OB, NA

šurdû "allowed to flow, leaking" jB of canal breach; "leaking, overflowing" box; < *redû* I Š; > *šurdûtu*

šurdunû, *šardunû*, *šadurnû* (a plant) jB [Ú/ŠIM.SI.SÁ] med. root, seed of *š.*

šurdûtu "inundation" jB; < *šurdû*

šurgû (a type of door) jB lex.

šurḫatu (a word for chariot) jB comm.

šurḫullu, OAkk *šerḫullum*, OB also *šulḫullum* **1.** OAkk (a gold or silver bead) **2.** OB, Bogh. (a necklace)

šurḫungû 'appeasement of anger' (an ailment) jB [ŠÚR.ḪUN.GÁ]; < Sum.

šūri'ā'u (desig. of hunting net)? Nuzi

šur(i)batu, *šurubatu* "terror"? jB weapons, power; desert

šurīnum I, *šurinnu*, MB also *šunniru* "(divine) emblem" Bab., M/NA [(d)ŠU.NIR]; *š.* of DN; *ša ilātim* "of the goddesses"; *š. kāribum* "a praying emblem" (transf. of *nadītum*); MB(Alal.) *š. narkabti* "chariot emblem"; ext. *kakku u š.*; of silver, wood; *tarbāṣ š.* "courtyard of the emblems"; < Sum.

šurīnum II mng. unkn. OAkk in *qēm š.* "flour of *š.*"

šur'īnu → *šurmēnu*

šurīpiš "like ice" jB; < *šurīpu*

šurīpu(m) m. & f.; OB pl. f. *šurīpētum* "ice, frost" O/jB, Mari, Bogh., NA collected and transported; "snow/ice" etc. on ways, mountains; *bīt š.* "icehouse" Mari; > *šurīpiš*; → *šarbu* II; *šurbu*; *šuruppû*

šurira mng. unkn. Nuzi in desig. of sheepskins

šuristu (or *šuriṣtu*) (an object) MA rdg. uncert., of ivory and ebony

šurisûm, *šursûm* (part of a waggon) Mari
šurišṭu → *šuristu*
šūrišam adv.? mng. unkn. jB
šur'ītu → *šūru* I
***šurkubu**, NB *šuškubu* "mounted"? NB of arrow; < *rakābu* Š
šurmēnu(m), *šurmīnu(m)*, *šur'īnu*, Nuzi also *šurmīru* "cypress" [(GIŠ.)ŠUR.MÌN; GIŠ.ŠU.ÚR. MÌN; OAkk (GIŠ.)ŠU.ÚR.ME] as tree, timber; burnt as aromatic; *šaman š.* "cypress oil"; *qēm š.* "cypress powder"? jB med.
šurmû(tu) "image" jB lex.
šurnû (a medicinal plant) jB
šurpašamma adv.? mng. unkn. Nuzi
šurpītu(m), *šurpūtu* "burning thirst"? O/jB lex.; < *šurpu*
šurpu(m) "burning, incineration" O/jB, NA of wood; in mag. rit.; also "firewood; combustibles"; < *šarāpu*; → *šarpu* I
šurpû → *šuruppû*
šurpūtu → *šurpītu*
šurqiš "secretly, by stealth" jB; < *šurqu*
šurqu(m), *šurraqu* **1.** "theft"; *šuruq ilim u šarrim* "theft from god and king"; jB *ina šurqi* "by theft" **2.** "stolen goods"; < *šarāqu* I
šurra → *šūru* V
šurrâm "at first, initially" Mari; < *šurrû* I
šurraqu → *šurqu*
šurrâtu(m) "start, beginning" Ass.; < *šurrû* II
šurru(m) D "to bow o.s. down, bend forwards" O/jB of bird from roof; beams over door; of demons "peer in at" window; transf. of king, god "pay attention to"; also trans. "make s.o. bend forward" over fumigants jB med. **Dtn** iter. of D (*uš/ltanār*) of demon, cat, snake; > *mušērtu*
šurrû(m) I "start, beginning" O/jB, NA; NA *š. eqli* "start of field (harvest)"; MB(Ass.) *š. kussî šarrūtiya* "beginning of my reign"; *rēš š.* "very beginning"; < *šurrû* II; *šurrâm*
šurrû(m) II, Ass. *šarrû(m)* **D** trans. "to begin, start; inaugurate" [TAB; SAR] "make a start"; "start" s.th., work, battle, brazier; M/NA "inaugurate" palace; also intrans. "begin" of rain, thunder, eclipses, earthquakes etc.; "start, grow" of illness, scar; > *šurrû* I, *šurrâtu*; *tašrītu*
šurrû III jB, NA **D** "to fast, stop eating" **Dt** ~ D
šurrûm IV OB **D** mng. uncert.
šurrû V adj.? mng. unkn. jB lex.
šurruḫu I "very proud, splendid" M/NB of gods, kings; offerings, drinks; "overweening, insolent" of actions; < *šarāḫu* I D
šurruḫu II **D** "to drool, dribble" of baby, sheep's blood jB
šurrumma, *šarrumma* "indeed, certainly, forthwith" O/jB, Am., Nuzi, Ug.
šurruṭu "torn up" jB lex. of garments; < *šarāṭu* D
šursûm → *šurisûm*
šursudu → *šuršudu*
šuršaktu mng. unkn. jB lex.
šuršašmu, *šuršašnu* "pomegranate" jB lex.
šuršiš "to/by the roots" jB of uprooting crops; Tiāmat shuddering; foundations; < *šuršu*
šuršu(m) "root" (lit.) [OAkk SUḪUŠ (→ *išdu*)] of trees, plants; "foundations" of mountains, building, city; transf. of enemies, *(*in PNs*)* persons; > *šuršiš*
šuršudu, *šursudu*, *šunšudu*, *šulsudu* "firmly founded" M/NB of buildings; throne, boundary; "well-equipped"? of boat, troops, god; < *rašādu* Š
šuršummu, occas. *šurušūmu* "sediment, dregs" M/NB of beer, used in med.; also "lees" of wine, vinegar etc.
šuršummum → also *turšummum*
šuršurrātu pl. tant. "chain" MA in metal; < *šeršerratu*
šuršurrum I (part of a knife) OAkk(Ur III) of copper
šuršurru II (a fruit) jB
šūru(m) I, *šuḫru*, *šur'u*; f. *šur'ītu* (a colour)? OA, Nuzi of textiles, often as subst.; also of hides; jB om. "dark"? of face
šūru(m) II "reed bundle" Bab. [GI.ŠU.KIN] cut, gathered, transported; *iṣṣūr š.* "reed bird"; basket (*quppu*) of *š.*
šūru(m) III "bull" O/jB; *š. šamā'ī* "bull of heaven"; OAkk in PNs
šūru(m) IV "(a type of) ditch"? O/jB lex., Mari, Nuzi; < Sum.
šūru V, *šurra* (an object) MB(Alal.) of boxwood, ivory
šūru VI "guarantor"? Nuzi
šūru → also *šur'u* I.II; *šu'ru*
šūrû I **Š** ~ "to teach, instruct"? jB
šūrû II (a metal agricultural implement) NB
šur'u I, *šūru* (a part of the face or head) M/jB [ŠUR]; → *šu'ru*
šur'u II, *šūru*, *šu'ru* "reins" jB; also desig. of stars in Taurus
šur'u → also *šūru* I
šu'ru(m), *šūru*, also *šuḫru* "eyebrow" O/jB [ŠUR] esp. in *š. īni/ī* [SIG₇.IGI]; also "eyebrow

inlay" of lapis lazuli, gold for figurines; → *šu''uru* I

šu'ru → also *šur'u* II

šurubatu → *šuribatu*

šūrubtu(m) "bringing in, paying in" Bab. [MU.IR$_{10}$; MU.UN.IR$_{10}$] *š.* of harvest, dates, grain etc.; "dues" paid to temple etc.; Mari also "present"; < *erēbu* I Š

šuruḫtu (an ornament) Am.

šuruppû(m), *šurpû* "frost; cold fit" O/jB [A.ZA.AD; AŠ.RU] of cold weather; med., mag. of illness; → *šurīpu*

šuruptu(m), NA also *šaruptu* "burning, combustion; fuel"; (wood or reed for) "fuel"; NA (funeral) "cremation"; < *šarāpu*

šurušūmu → *šuršummu*

šusapinnu → *susapinnu*

šusḫurtu 1. (gramm. term) "non-indicative" jB lex. [NÍGIN; NÍG.KÚŠ; ÈM.KÚŠ] of Sum. vb. forms **2.** "encircling"? jB mag. figures (*ṣalmāni*) *ša š.*; < *saḫāru* Š

susḫuru (a dyed textile) jB; < *saḫāru* Š

šusikillu → *šamaškillu*

šusikkum, *šušikkum* (official responsible for disposal of animal carcases) OAkk, OB [(LÚ.)SU.SI(.IG), ŠU.SI.IG]; < Sum.

šusippu → *šušippum*

šussullu → *sussullu*

šussumu → *šūsumu*

šusubbum mng. unkn. OB

šusummû(m), *šušummû(m)* "gift, delivery" O/jB lex.; < Sum.

šūsumu, NB *šussumu* "very fitting" j/NB gold; shrine; person, stature; < *wasāmum*

šusuppu → *šušippum*

šuṣbuttu ~ "allocation, provisioning" NB sheep, dates; of the king; < *ṣabātu* Š

šuṣrupu "dyed, steeped"? NB of mats; < *ṣarāpu* I Š

šuṣu (an inferior quality of dates) jB [ŠÀ.SUD]

šūṣû(m); f. *šūṣūtu(m)* O/jB **1.** "made to leave" of wife; man **2.** ext. ~ "protruding"?; < *waṣûm* Š

šūṣubtum "addition, increment"? OB lex.; < *waṣābum* Š

šūṣūtum "lease" OB of fields; < *waṣûm* Š

šūš(a) → *šūši*

šušalšum, *šušalšam* adv. "threefold" OA; also *šīm šušalti* ?; < *šalāš*

šušannu → *šušānu*

šušannūtu → *šušānūtu*

šušānu, *šušannu*, Ass. *susānu* **1.** "horse-trainer, groom" M/NA, NB [Ass. LÚ.GIŠ.GIGIR ?]; NB official of king, of *šatammu* **2.** NB (a class of state dependants) [LÚ.KI.ZA.ZA]; < Indo-Iran.; > *šušānūtu*

šušānūtu, *šušannūtu* "status of *šušānu*" NB [LÚ.KI.ZA.ZA-]; < *šušānu*

šūšâtu ~ "chaos, disruption" jB lex.; < *ešû* IV

šušerû ~ "chill, frost" jB lex.

šūši, *šūš*, *šūša*, *šuššu* "sixty" [NB 60-*šu*; jB UŠ] *elep šūši* "sixty(-gur) ship"; (as linear measure) [UŠ] for 60 *nindan* (= 360 metres); > *šuššār*; *šūšu'û*

šūšī- in *1 šūšīšu* "60 times" OB

šušikkum → *šusikkum*

šušinnu (a garment) Am.

šušippum, *šusippu(m)*, *šus/šuppu*, NA *sasuppu*; pl. m. & f. "towel" O/jB, NA [ŠU.SU.UB] of wool, linen; dirty, clean; Nuzi, in pairs; *š. qātim* "hand towel"; < Sum.

šuškallu(m), *šušqallu(m)*, *šaškallum* f. & m. "battle-net" O/jB of gods; in similes, envelop *kīma š.* "like a net"; also jB "fishnet"; OB lex. *ša š.* "person making or using a *š.* net"; < Sum.; → *muškallu*

šuškubu → *šurkubu*

šušlušu "trebled" jB; "of triple strand" string, rope etc.; "triple" of beer-drinking tube; < *šalāšu* Š

šušmarûm ~ "basin" Mari, of metal; < Sum.

šušpulu "very low, mean" jB; < *šapālu* Š

šušqallu → *šuškallu*

šušqûm; f. *šušqūtum* "very exalted" OB; < *šaqû* II

šušqûtu(m) "exaltation" O/jB of a deity; < *šaqû* II Š

šušrātu, *uššurātu* f. pl. tant. "(a type of) leek" jB lex.

šušrû (a variety of grape) jB lex.

šušruḫu "glorified" jB of deity; < *šarāḫu* I Š

šušrūtu → *šušurūtu*

šušša = *šum-ša* (→ *šumu*)

šuššāma → *tuša*

šuššān → *šuššu* I du.

šuššār "216,000" O/jB [ŠÁR×DIŠ] (=360×600); < *šūši* + *šār*

šuššārum → *šaššāru*

šuššu(m) I "one-sixth" O/jB [IGI.6.GÁL]; du. *šuššān*, lex. also *šulšān* "two-sixths" (i.e. one-third) [ŠUŠANA (= *šalšu* 2, *šulšu* ?)]; < *šediš*

šuššu II mng. unkn. Mari

šuššu → also *šūši*; also = *šum-šu/a*

šuššû mng. unkn. NB, an offering ?

šuššūg/qu → *šaššūgu*

šuššurinnu (a barley product) Nuzi

šušû mng. uncert. Mari of metal, jB lex. of reed

šūšu(m), NA *sūsu* "liquorice" O/jB, NA [GIŠ.ŠE.DÙ.A; GIŠ.ZA.MÚŠ.ŠÉŠ] in om., med. *išid/šuruš š.* "liquorice root"; leaves, seed

šūšubtu **1.** "seat, stool" jB lex. **2.** pl. "ambush" jB [KI.TUŠ.MEŠ]; < *wašābum* Š

šūšubu "pot stand" jB lex.; < *wašābum* Š

šušummû → *šusummû*

šušuppu → *šušippum*

šūšuriš "in order, correctly" OB; < *šūšuru*

šūšuru(m) **1.** "in order, correct" O/jB of persons; *lā š.* "misguided"; ext. of features, "normal, correct, straight"; "in good condition" of sheep, house **2.** f. *šūšurtu* "straightness" jB ext. **3.** f. pl. *šūšurātu* "sweepings, domestic debris" jB; *š. bīti, ēkalli*; < *ešēru* Š

šūšuru → also *suššuru*

šuš'uru Š "to make dirty"? jB, statue; → *šu''uru* II ?

šuš(u)rūtu mng. unkn. jB lex.

šūšûtu → *šūdûtu*

šūšu'û "one-sixtieth" NB [60-*šu*-] of fractions of days for prebends; < *šūši*

šūt I, OAkk gen. *šūti* "who(m), those who(m)" (m. pl. nom., acc.) OAkk, Bab. (mostly → *ša*) **1.** before gen.: "those of ..."; persons *šūt PN*; stars *šūt Ani* "of Anu"; decisions *šūt šamê* "of heaven" etc.; (later also) for sg., NB *šarru šūt maḫri* "previous king"; *šūt abnim/ī* "the stone things"? (Gilg.) **2.** introducing rel. clause: "who, whom"; → *šu*

šūt II "he, it; that, this same" O/MA, MB(Alal.), Am., Nuzi, Bogh., Ug., Emar for → *šū* (NA → *šūtu* I) **1.** "he, it" to give emphasis *šūt(ma)* ... "it is he who ..."; pred. ... *šūt(ma)* "... it/he is" **2.** "that, this same", OA *ṭuppum šūt* "that tablet", MA *a'ilu šūt* "that man"

šūt III prep. "because of, concerning" NA(roy. inscr.)

šutabalku(t)tu, *šutablakku(t)tu* (a type of bag) jB lex.; astr. "cycle" of months; < *nabalkutu* II Štn

šutābultu(m) **1.** mng. uncert. OB of excavated earth **2.** "(omen) interpretation"? jB *š. uṣurāti* "the i. of the signs"; < *wabālu* Št

šutābulu "mixed" jB lex.; < *wabālu* Št

šutāḫû(m) "paired (off), arranged in pairs" O/jB "identical, matching", of triplets, of column, door-leaves; < *aḫû* II Št

šutakṣuru "readied" jB of weapons; < *kaṣāru* Št

šūtān → *šūtānu*

šūtānānu, *sūtānānu* "south(-east) (of)" Nuzi ina *š./s. dimti, eqli* "s.(-e.) of farm, field" etc.; < *šūtānu*

šutanīdû "antiphonal hymn" jB *š. šumeru* "Sumerian *š.*"; < *nâdu* Št

šūtān(u), *sūtān(u)*, *sūtannu* "south(-east) (of)" Nuzi *ina pāni, ištu š./s.* "to the s.(-e.)", *ina š./s. kirî, eqli* "s.(-e.) of orchard, field" etc.; < *šūtu* II; > *šūtānānu*

šutappû → *šutāpu*

šutaptu/ûm mng. unkn. OB in desig. of amount of grain

šutāpu(m), *šutappû*, *šuzāpu* "associate, partner" OAkk, Bab. [OAkk ŠU.TAB] gener. in commercial & agric. context; > *šutāpūtu*, *šutattupu*

šutāpūtu "partnership, joint venture" M/NB, Nuzi fields *ana š.* "for joint exploitation"; < *šutāpu*

šutarkubu "layered, of superimposed layers" jB astr. of moon's corona (*agû*); < *rakābu* Št

šutarruḫūtu "glorification, adulation" jB(Ass.); < *šarāḫu* I Dt(n)

šutārsûm → *šutērsû*

šutašnû "doubled" jB lex.; < *šanû* III Št

šutašubbûm mng. unkn. OB lex. (liter. 'fallen from the hand'); < Sum.

šutattupu **Dt** "to form a partnership" jB; < *šutāpu* denom.

šutātû(m) "positioned opposite one another" O/jB of archit. features; tines of fork; < *watûm* Št

šuta''ûm Št "to trifle, treat lightly" OB in letters; absol.; with *ana* or acc.; > *mušta''û*; *mušta''ûtu*

šutebrûm "long lasting, persisting" OB lex. of day; < *bitrû* II Št

šutēburum, (or *šutēpuru*) **Št** "to act precipitately, be hasty" OB, Mari, jB

šutelū'u Št ~ "to make lick up" jB of god "making" dog "lap up" enemy land like milk; → *alā'u*

šutēmudu "superimposed (on one another)" jB of beams; "consecutive" days; < *emēdu* Št

šutēpuru → *šutēburum*

šutērsû(m), *šutārsûm* **Št** "to make ready, prepare" OA, O/jB house; troops; cart etc.; < *ersû* denom.; → *tērsītu*

šuteṣlipu "criss-crossed" jB of eyes, with veinlets; < *ṣalāpu* Št

šutēšuru "(kept) in order" jB; < *ešēru* Št

šūti → *šūt* I

šutlumu(m) Š "to grant, bestow generously" (lit. "fill both hands"?) usu. of god to king, mortal(s); weapons; cities, lands; persons; prey; long life, kingship, wisdom etc.; < *atulimānu* denom.?

šuṭqu(m) (part of the intestines)? O/jB lex., ext.

šuttatu(m) "(hunter's) pitfall" O/jB for animals; *š. ša lā naplusi* "invisible trap"; *ana š. nadû*, *ina š. maqātu* "to cast, fall into trap"; in transf. sense "pitfall"; jB lex. also "grave"; → *šuttu* II

šu(t)tinnu(m), *su(t)tinnu* "bat; flying fox" O/jB [SU.TIN.MUŠEN] *kīma š. šuqallulu* "to hang like a bat"; med. *qaqqad š.* "bat's head"; also part of a chariot or plough [GIŠ.SU.TIN]

šuttu(m) I, poet. also *šunatu(m)*; pl. *šunātu(m)* "dream" [MÁŠ.GE$_6$; also MA.MÚ] *š. naṭālu*, *amāru* etc. "to have a dream, to dream"; *š. pašāru* "to interpret d." → *mupašširum*; good, bad, frightening etc.; < *šittu* I

šuttu II "pit" jB lex.; → *šuttatu*

šuttum → also *šû* I

šuttun → *šû* I

šuttuqum "cracked, split" OB of warts etc.; < *šatāqu* D

šuttūtu(m); pl. *šuttuwātum* "woven stuff, textile" Early Mari, jB lex. wool for *š.*; < *šatû* III D

šutû(m) I, occas. *sutû* "woven material, warp" OA, O/jB [(SÍG.)ŠID.MA] of wool; *paršīg š.* "headcloth"; < *šatû* III

šutû II; pl. *šutuātu* (part of a waggon) Nuzi

šutû III (desig. of a metal vessel) Nuzi; jB lex.

šutû IV "drinking" Am.; < *šatû* II

šūtu I "he" (3 m. sg. nom.) NA, occas. Ug. for *šū*; for emphasis *šūtuma* ... "it is he who ..."; as pred. *aḫūšu šūtu* "he is his brother"; → *šūt* II

šūtu(m) II, *sūtu* "south, south wind" Bab., NA [IM.U$_{18}$.LU; later IM.1] **1.** "south wind", *š. illik*, *ittalak* "south wind blew"; wing (*kappu*) of *š.* (Adapa) **2.** "south, the south", *meḫret š.* "facing south" etc.; *bīt š.* "south wing" of a building; > *šūtānu*, *šūtānānu*

šūtu → also *sūtu* I

šutuḫḫātum f. pl. mng. unkn. OAkk

šutukku(m) **1.** "reed-hut, reed shelter" O/jB rit. [GI.ŠUTUG(.UD)] for *bīt rimki* ritual; *š. nadû* "to put up a reed shelter"; also *bīt š.* **2.** "reed bundle"? jB mag.; < Sum.

šutummu(m), OA *šatummum* "storehouse" freq. *bīt š.* [É.ŠU.TÙM(.MEŠ); É.GI.NA.AB.DU$_7$; OAkk É.ŠU.TUM] for copper, precious items; grain, dates etc., NB esp. *š. šarri* "the royal storehouse, treasury"; also used for detention; < Sum.

šūtuqtu subst. "averting"? jB in *amāt šūtuqti*; < *etēqu* Š

šūtuqu(m) "surpassing, outstanding" O/jB of deity, above others; < *etēqu*

šūtuqūtu "despatch, forwarding" NB of documents (*unqātu*); < *etēqu* Š

šutur(u) (a ceremonial garment) jB lex.; < Sum.

šūturu(m) "very great, supreme" O/jB epith. of gods; animal, palace; royal power; conquest; incantation; < *watārum*

šu'u, *šû*; Hurr. pl. *šuena* "chick-pea"? M/NA, Nuzi, j/NB, usu. wr. with det. ŠE, often with *abšu*

šu'u → also *šûm* III; *šumu*

šu'û → *šuḫûm* I; *šuwā'um*

šu''û → *šuḫḫû* III

šu''udu D (*ušale''id*, *ulte''id*, M/NB also *uš'id*) "to appeal to, complain to" s.o. (= acc.) M/NB, NA

šu''uru(m) I, OB *šuḫḫurum* "hairy" O/jB; "unshorn" of sheep; (desig. of a vegetable)?; → *šārtu*

***šu''uru** II, OB *šuḫḫurum*, NA *š/sa''uru* "dirty, soiled"; of towels; → *šuš'uru*; *še'ru*

šu'ūtu mng. unkn. jB lex.

šuwāta/i → *šuāti*

šuwā'um, *šu'û* "lord, master" OAkk, jB; > *šuātum*

šuwā'um → also *šû* I

šuwēlam → *šumēla*

Šuwerum → *Šumeru*

šuwûm mng. unkn. OB lex.

šuwû → also *šumû* I

šuwwurum D "to encircle" Mari; **DRtn**; < *šawirum* denom.

šuzāpu → *šutāpu*

šuziqa'um, *šuziqû* (part of a vase) Mari, MB lex.; < Sum.

šūzubtu(m) **1.** O/jB (a gift) **2.** OB mng. uncert. of labourers; < *ezēbu* Š

šūzubu "saved, rescued" jB as PN; MB(Alal.) a category of persons; < *ezēbu* Š

šuzuta mng. uncert. Am. of jewellery

šūzuzu "very fierce" MB(Ass.) of flame, statue; < *ezēzu*; → *šēzuzu*

T

ta'alšu → *tal'ašu*

ta''artu → *tayyartu*

ta''āru → *tayyāru* I

tabākattam "in layers"? OA; < *tabāku*

tabāku(m), *tapāku* "to pour (out); lay flat" **G** (*a/u*, OA pret. also *asbuk*) [DUB] liquids; grain, straw etc.; "lay" bricks; "lay down" weapons; "lay out" corpses, enemy; (in illness) parts of body; transf. "shed" life, "expunge" sins, illness, debts; "infuse" fear, silence etc.; "flood" field, with water **Gtn** iter. **D** ~ G "pour out much" liquids; med. "excrete"; transf. fear, death; people **Dt** pass. of D **Š** caus. "make (enemy) lay down" weapons; "spew out, spill" slaver, life **N** "be poured out, laid down" of liquids, stream; of grain, weapons; of brickwork "be eroded"; of sick limbs; of sin "be expunged"; of fear "be dispensed" **Ntn** of demons, persons (mng.?); of birds "repeatedly swoop on"?; ext. of feature of lung; > *tabku*; *tibku*; *tubku*; *tubbuku*; *tubukkû*; *natbāku*, *natbaktu*; *tatbīku*; *tabākattam*

tab(ā)lānu "thief" NB; < *tabālu*

tabalātum (or *tapalātum*) (a good quality of beer) OA

tabāliš allow "to take away" OB; < *tabālu*

tabālu(m) "to take away, carry off" **G** (*a/a*) [TÙM; jB also IR] things, animals, people; health; sins, troubles; "appropriate" land, throne; of flood "carry off"; OA "fetch" (a price); of stars "remove (glow), disappear" **D** "take away much" **Š** "cause to take away" (→ *wabālu* Št) **N** "be taken away"; < *wabālu* Gt; > *tablu*; *tabālānu*; *tabāliš*

tābalu "dry land" M/NB; < *abālu*

tābalu → also *tāpalu*

tabāqu ~ "greenery, vegetation" jB lex.

tabarru, Nuzi, MA also *tab/warriw/ba*, *tabarrianni* etc., NA *tabrib/pu* "red wool" M/NA, M/NB [SÍK.ḪÉ.ME.DA; (SÍK.)ḪÉ.MED; Am. also ḪÉ.ME.TA]

tabarû → *tabriu*

tabāštānu(m) "excrement" O/jB; < *ba'āšu*

tabatum → *tapatum*

tabā'u → *tebû*

tabbanītu → *tabnītu* I

tabbānu mng. unkn. jB lex.

tabbatu mng. unkn. jB

tabbilu (an object) NA of bronze

tabbītum "lamentation" OB; < *nabû* II D

tabiltu(m) (a pottery vessel) OAkk, O/jB, MA

tābīlu(m); NB pl. *tābīlānu* liter. "drying out"; "(spicy) powder" Bab., MA as condiment; as drug; med. (dry phlegm?); (a secretion of eyes); < *abālu* D

tabīnu; pl. f. "shelter, stall" M/NB for shepherds and sheep; NB "(market) stall"; transf. of divine protection, esp. in PNs

tabīnû in *Tabīnītu* MB fPN; < *tabīnu*

tabīru/a "coppersmith" M/NA [TIBIRA] in name of city gate of Aššur; < Sum.

tābiu "lifted, loose"? NA of building materials; < *tebû* ?

tabku(m) "poured out, stored" Bab., NA **1.** as adj. "poured out, spilt"; (an illness) of parts of body **2.** as subst. "(grain) store"; < *tabāku*

tablānu → *tabālānu*

tabliltum "smearing (with oil), caulking" OB of plough, boat; < *balālu* D

tablittum "sustenance, victuals, fodder" OB for humans, animals; < *balāṭu* II D

tablu "taken away" jB, NA in *t. tabālu* "to purloin"; < *tabālu*

tabnītu(m) I, NB also *tabbanītu* 'beautification' Bab., of offering table; pl. *tabnāti* "table cover"; < *banû* II D

tabnītu II "creation" jB; < *banû* IV

tabra (or *tapra*) mng. unkn. OB

tabrâtu → *tabrītu*

tabribu → *tabarru*

tabrīmu "coloured cloth" NA for head; < *barāmu* I D

tabripu → *tabarru*

tabrītu(m), *tebrītu(m)* "appearance, sighting" OAkk, Bab., Mari "(notification of) arrival" jB "appearance, apparition"; pl. "(astonished) gaze" esp. in j/NB *ana tabrâti* "to the wonderment" (of people, land etc.); *rē'û t.* (a royal title); < *barû* I

tabriu(m), *tabrû(m)*, Ug. lex. *tabarû* ~ "fodder crop" OAkk, O/jB, M/NA esp. Nuzi *eqel t.*; NA pl. *tabriāte* (type of real estate)

tabsertum "bringing of good news" OB; < *bussuru*

tabsūtu → *šabsūtu*

tabsûtum "function of midwife" OB; < *šabsūtu*

tabšītu, *tabšûtu* "creation"? jB; < *bašû* ?

tabšu (or *tapšu*) mng. unkn. jB lex.

tabšûtu → *tabšītu*

tabû → *tebû*

tadānu(m) Ass. base for **G** infin., stat. and M/NA ptcp. of *nadānu* II "to give" [SUM]; phps. occas. also Bab.; > *tidintu*; *tādinānu*

taddītum **1.** OB math. "layer, course" of bricks (= number of bricks on 1 *mušār*) **2.** Mari (a textile) **3.** jB (a leather object); < *nadû* III

tadduntu "gift" jB lex.; < *nadānu* II

tādinānu "the seller" MA; < *tadānu*; → *nādinānu*

tādirtu "'darkening of mood', depression" M/jB, NA; < *adāru* I D; → *tādīru*

tādīru ~ *tādirtu* Bogh.

tadlultum ~ "(hymn of) praise" OAkk in PN; < *dalālu* II

tadmiqtum "friendly action, favour" = interest-free loan OA [SIG$_5$]; OB for business trip; < *damāqu* D

tadmīqu(m) "good quality dates" O/jB; < *damāqu* D

tadnintum "strengthening" OB, of an additional allowance of grain ?; < *danānu* II D

tā'ertum → *têrtu*

tagabarušḫe (or *takabarušḫe*) (piece of furniture)? Alal.; < Hurr.

tagabītu → *takpītum*

tagānu → *taqānu*

taggertum "denunciation" OB; < *nagāru* II D

ta(g)gītum mng. unkn. OB

tagmertu "completion" jB **1.** in *t. libbi* "loyalty" **2.** astr. mng. uncl.; < *gamāru* II D

tagrītum "litigation" OB; < *gerû* D (or *takrītum* "abbreviation"?; < *karû* II ?)

tāgultu → *tākultu*

taḫabaštum (or *taḫapaštum*) (object of reed) OAkk

taḫabâtu → *taḫbâtu*

taḫabbatu → *taḫarbatu*

taḫāḫu "to pour (over)"? MA, jB **G** lex. **D** "drench" s.th. with drugs, milk, oil; MA as punishment

taḫaltu (edible item)? NB

taḫamu (or *taḫašše*?) mng. unkn. Nuzi of ox- and cow-hide

taḫanātu "help" M/NB; lex.

taḫapaštum → *taḫabaštum*

taḫapšu "felt; (felt-)rug" M/NA, M/NB [TÚG.LÍL.LÁ] for horses, furniture; < Hurr.?

taḫapšuḫuli "felt-maker" Alal.; < Hurr.

taḫarbatu, *taḫabbatu* "standing platform (of chariot)" M/jB; < Kass.?

taḫaṣu (or *taḫazu*) (a plant) jB lex.

taḫašše → *taḫamu*

taḫāṭu → *šaḫāṭu* I G

tāḫāziš "in battle" jB; < *tāḫāzu*

taḫazu → *taḫaṣu*

tāḫāzu(m); pl. f. "battle; combat" [MÈ; OAkk KAS×?] *t. ṣēri* "pitched battle" jB; < *aḫāzu* Gt

tāḫāzû(m) (a kind of door)? jB lex.

taḫbāṣu mng. unkn. Am. (among gifts); < *ḫabāṣu* I or II ?

taḫbâtu, *taḫabâtu* (a wrapping)? M/jB desig. of shoes, textiles; "casing" of bull's horn; < *ḫabû* IV

taḫbīšu(m) mng. unkn. MB, also Early Mari ?

taḫdītu "greeting" (liter. "gladdening") jB; < *ḫadû* III D

taḫê → *taḫû* III

taḫḫašimma → *taḫšīmum*

taḫḫiltu, taḫḫisu → *taḫsistu*

taḫḫittu(m) mng. uncl. Mari, an administrative term; jB lex., desig. of field; < *naḫātu* D ?; → *ta''ittu*

taḫḫi(t)tu → also *taḫsistu*

taḫḫum "substitute" OB [TAḪ(.ḪA)] **1.** of soldier, cook etc.; OAkk as PN ? **2.** (an additional song)? **3.** lex. desig. of wool; < Sum.; > *taḫḫūtum*

taḫḫû → *taḫû* II

taḫḫūmu → *taḫūmu*

taḫḫūtum "replacement, substitution" OB; < *taḫḫum*

taḫīqtum "admixture" Mari; < *ḫiāqum* D

taḫīrtum mng. uncl. OB; < *ḫiāru* D ?

taḫīttu "weight check" jB; < *ḫiāṭu*; → *ta''ittu*

tāḫīzu "teaching, instruction" jB; < *aḫāzu* D

taḫla(p)pānu "goat's tallow"? jB lex.; < *ḫalāpu* I

taḫlaptu NB var. of *taḫluptu* ?; lex., var. of *naḫlaptu*

taḫlīpu "armouring, defensive covering" MB(Ass.), NA in GIŠ.GIGIR *taḫ-líp* "armoured chariot"; < *ḫalāpu* I D

taḫluptu "covering" j/NB military "armour"; archit. "cladding"; copper "overlay" for door; < *ḫalāpu* I D; → *taḫlaptu*

taḫluqtu → *šaḫluqtu*

taḫpušḫu (object of wood or bronze) Nuzi; < Hurr.

taḫrīšu mng. unkn. jB in *t. sābî* "*t.* of the brewer"; < *ḫarāšu* II D ?

taḫrumma in *t. epēšu* "to retain"? Nuzi; < Hurr.

taḫsāti pl. ~ "ambush"? NA

taḫsistu(m), MB *taḫsiltu*, Nuzi also *taḫḫi(l)tu*, *tasḫiltu* etc., NB also *taḫsittu*, *taḫḫittu*, *taḫḫisu* "reminder" OA, M/NB esp. "(written) memorandum"; Nuzi *ṭuppi t.*; lit. "remembrance, memory"; < *ḫasāsu* D

taḫṣību "breaking off, rupture"? jB med.; < *ḫaṣābu* I D

taḫšīmum, Bogh. *taḫḫa(š)šimma* (a bakemeat)? OA, Bogh.

taḫta "under" Am. in *taḫtamu* "under them"; < W.Sem.

taḫtamum, *tātamum* (an assembly) Mari; < W.Sem.

taḫtiptu "presentation of sacrifice" NB; < *ḫatāpu* D

taḫtû "defeat" jB [BAD$_5$.BAD$_5$(=IGI.IGI) (→ *abiktu*)] usu. in *t. šakānu* "to accomplish defeat (of)"; < *ḫatû* II D

taḫû I (a quality of wool) jB lex.

taḫû II (or *taḫḫû* ?) "young animal" M/jB; < Sum.?

taḫû III ~ "side"? j/NB, *taḫê* "beside"? as prep.; → *ittaḫu*

tāḫu "interior"? jB lex.

taḫūmu, *taḫḫūmu*, *tuḫūmu* "boundary, territory" M/NA, Elam, Ug., j/NB(Ass.)

ta'īṣtum "diminution, loss" OB; < *wiāṣum* D

tā'iš → *tā'um*

ta''ittu(m) "information, report" OA, O/jB; < *na'ādu* D

tā'ītum "false mark, falsification" OB; < *wu''ûm*

tā'ītum → also *tāwītum*

takabarušḫe → *tagabarušḫe*

takāku(m) "to (op)press" O/jB **G** stat. "is in suffering" **D** uncert. (→ *ekēku* Dt); → *tukku* II

takallimu → *taklīmu*

takaltu "trust" Bogh. lex. for → *tukultu*

takaltum → also *takiltu* I

tākaltu(m) (or *takāltu* ?) "bag; stomach" Bab. [(UZU.)TÙN] **1.** "bag" of doctor, scribe, on seed-plough; for weapon **2.** as part of body "stomach", med. of humans, ext. of sheep; < *akālu* or *kullu* III ?

takālu(m) "to trust" (in = *ana*, *-iš*, dat.) **G** (*a/a*, jB, NA also *i/i*; imper. *tikal*) [NIR.GÁL; in col. also GI] "trust in" esp. in PNs; "rely on"; stat. "is reliable" of god, man, animal **Gt** ~ G **D** "inspire trust, encourage"; "make reliable, check" work, fact; "make firm promise to" s.o. **Dtn** iter. of D **N** "put o.'s trust in" person, god, self, protection; > *taklu*; *tiklu*, *tikiltu*; *tuklu*, *tukultu*, *tuklatānu*; *tukkulu*, *tukkultum*; *muttaklu*; → *wakālum*

takantum → *takiltu* I

takāpu(m) "to prick, puncture" Bab., NA **G** (*i/i*) med., ext.; "stitch, sew"; stat. also "is dotted" with (coloured) spots; "impress" cuneiform wedge **D** ~ G; > *tikpu*; *takkapu*?; *takkāpu*; *tākipu*; *tikiptum*

takāṣu "slaughtering block"? M/jB; < *kâṣu* ?

takašu mng. unkn. jB lex.

takbāru, *takbarru* "fattened sheep" M/NA [UDU.ŠE ?]; < *kabāru* D

takba'u "reed leaves"? jB lex.; < *kaba'u*

takbittu "honour, honorific ceremony" OA, jB(Ass.); < *kabātu* D

takdaku → *taktaku*

takdanānu (a bush) jB med.

takdīru mng. unkn. jB; < *kadāru* II ?

takiltu I, OAkk *takal/ntum* ? "purple (wool)" OAkk(Ur III)?, M/NB, NA [SÍK.ZA.GÌN.KUR.RA; SÍK.ZA.GÌN.MI ?]

takiltum II (an algebraic square) OB math.; < *kullu* III

takiltu → also *tikiltu*

tākipu "a stitcher" NB; < *takāpu*

takirtum mng. uncl. OB; < *ḫiāru*

takittum I "confirmation" OA, OB; < *kânu* D
takittu II (a vessel) Bogh. of bronze
takkalātu f. pl. "clever, ingenious behaviour" jB; < *nakālu*
takkapu(m) "hole, window" O/jB [AB.LÀL] "window, peephole"; also to underworld; < *takāpu* ?
takkāpu(m) "stitcher" OB, Nuzi; < *takāpu*
takkassu(m) (or *dakkassu(m)*) "(small) block of stone" Bab., NA [DAG.GAZ]; usu. semi-precious stone; < Sum.?
takkasû, *takkašû* (a bakemeat for cult)? M/NB
takkīlū pl. tant. ~ "insidious, dishonest talk" OA; < *nakālu* D
takkiptu "onslaught" NB of flood waves; < *nakāpu* D
takkīrum **1.** OAkk; NB pl. f. (a garment) **2.** Bab. "diversion (canal)", also as name of canal; < *nakāru* D
takku "tablet" NB; < Aram.
takkussatta "like a reed-stem" jB
takkussu, *sakkuttu*; pl. m. & f. "reed-stem; tube" M/NB, NA [GI.SAG.KUD] med. "pipette"
takkustu "reed-stem" jB; < *takkussu*
taklimtu(m), NA also *taklittu* "revelation, instruction; display" O/jB, NA "teaching, instruction"; "display" of body? in funerary rites; < *kullumu*
taklīmu(m), NA also *takallimu* ~ "demonstration" Bab., NA term for a type of offering; < *kullumu*
taklittu → *taklimtu*
taklu(m) "reliable, trusty" O/jB, M/NA "delegate(d)", of goods "of dependable quality"; < *takālu*
takmīsu (a slaughtered sheep) M/jB, M/NA; < *kamāsu* I ?
takmu(m) (or *taqmu(m)*) mng. unkn. OB, Bogh.
takmussû (a garment) Am.
taknītu → *teknītu*
taknû → *teknûm*
takpertu(m), NB also *takpištu* "purification (ceremony)" Bab., M/NA; < *kapāru* II D
takpītum, *tukpītu*, Ug. *tagabītu* (a kidney-shaped gem) O/jB, NA [NA_4.BIR]
takpu (or *taqpu*) (a carrying basket) NA, NB
takpurtu, *takpuštu*, *takputtu* "clearance allocation, payment to equalize" NB silver, land etc.; < *kapāru* I; → *takpūru*
takpūru "clearance allocation" NB as *takpurtu*; < *kapāru* I
takpuštu, *takputtu* → *takpurtu*
takrīṣu subst. "gnawing away" jB of dog; < *karāṣu* D
takrītum → *tagrītum*
takṣâtu, NA *takṣiātu* ~ "cold weather, frost"; < *kaṣû* III D
takṣīru; pl. *takṣīrī*, *takṣīrānu* "attachment" jB med. of stone, drugs; < *kaṣāru* D
takṣiṣītu (a type of bird) jB lex.; < *kaṣāṣu* I ?
takšīru(m) "repair" OAkk, O/jB esp. of architecture; < *kašāru* D
takšītu(m) ~ "profit" OA, O/jB; < *kašû* II D
takšium, *takšû(m)*, Mari *šakšum*; pl. f. (leather container) OAkk, O/jB for valuables; < Sum.
takšû, *taškû* "triplets" j/NB of humans, animals; *takšâti/u* (a star); < *kašû* II
takšû → also *takšium*
taktaku, lex. also *takdaku* (part of a waggon) M/jB
taktīmu(m) "(textile) cover, cloak" O/jB, NA [TÚG.AN.TA.DUL]; < *katāmu* D
takulatḫu (an object) Nuzi of wood, copper, silver; < Hurr.
tākultu(m), OB also *šākultum*, NA once *tāgultu* "(cultic) meal" OAkk?, O/jB, M/NA **1.** "feeding" of troops **2.** ceremonial "meal" for king, in temple cult; < *akālu*
takulû ~ "suffering"? jB rdg. uncert.
takurassu (a functionary, official) Nuzi; < Hurr.
takuru mng. unkn. jB lex.
takuštā'um, *takuštûm* (a fabric, textile) OA; < PlN ?
takušu ? (part of a chariot) Nuzi
takwûm (or *taqwûm*) mng. unkn. OB lex.; < *kawûm* I or II ?
tal'abum mng. unkn. OB lex.; < *la'ābu* ?
talālu(m) ~ "to stretch out" O/jB, NA **G** (*a/u*) stat. of physical features; "stick out" tongue; "stretch (i.e. string)" bow; Mari stat. "is allied" **D** Mari uncl.; > *tālilum*; → *tullulu*
talammu **1.** Bab. "rump"? of human, animal **2.** NB (a beer container)
talamšukru → *tallamšukru*
tal'ašu, occas. *ta'alšu* "grain pest, weevil" jB
tal'azu (a bird) jB lex.
talbīšum "cladding, overlay" Mari, in wool; < *labāšu* D
talbuštu, *talbultu* "clothing, costume" j/NB; < *labāšu*
taldīru → *tasdīru*
talgab (part of irrigation equipment) MB; < Kass.
talgiddû (a vessel) jB [TAL.GÍD.DA]; < Sum.

talḫadīum "from Ta/ilḫad" OA desig. of garments etc.; < PlN

talḫu (a vessel) Alal. of silver

tāli(l)lu (a tree) jB lex.

tālilum "archer" Mari; < *talālu*

talīmānu → *atulīmānu*

talīmātu ~ "help"? jB lex.

talimmu → *talīmu*

talīmtu(m) ~ "favourite sister" O/jB esp. of sister of Šamaš; < *talīmu*

talīmu(m), occas. *talimmu* ~ "favourite brother" OAkk, Bab., NA [TAM.MA]; also as PN; > *talīmtu*; *atulīmānu*

tālittu(m), NB *tamlittu* "offspring of animals" Bab., M/NA [Ù.TU]; < *walādum*

tal'ītu "ointment dressing" NA; < *lu''û* II

tallakku 1. NA (a wooden object, phps.) "cart" **2.** jB, NA "way (of life), career"; < *alāku*

tallaktu(m) "walkway; way (of life); cart" Bab., M/NA [GIN.GIN] **1.** "walkway; path" **2.** abstr. "way (of life), haunts, route, traffic, passing"; MA "procedure" **3.** NA, NB "cart"; < *alāku*

ta(l)lamšukru (part of a chariot) Nuzi; < Hurr.

tallu(m) I ~ "dividing line, beam"? OAkk, Bab., NA [DAL]; math. "transverse line"; ext. of feature in entrails; "door-beam"; "carrying-pole" of sedan chair; → *gištallu*

tallu(m) II (vessel for oil etc.) Bab., MA [DUG.DAL] usu. of metal; < Sum.; > *taltallu*?; → *talmāḫu*

tallultu, NB *tullultu* "trappings" (of horse, cows) NA, NB; < *tullulu*

tallulu "equipped", "laid" of altar tables NA; < *tullulu*

tallulu → also *tullulu*

talmāḫu (or *dalmāḫu*) "prime *tallu*-vessel" jB lex.; < Sum.

talmīdu(m), *talmēdum*; f. *talmittu* **1.** O/jB, M/NA "apprentice" **2.** jB lex. (a type of plough); < *lamādu* D

talmītu (a reed object) jB lex.; < *lawûm* II

talmu "big" MA, Nuzi of animals, persons; < Hurr.

talpittu(m) "application, coating" O/MB with bitumen, colour; Ass. mng. uncl. (→ *ripītu*); < *lapātu* D

taltallu (a wooden vessel)? NA; < *tallu* II ?

taltallû "pollen, stamen" of date palm jB; < Sum.

tālu(m) "young date palm" Bab. [GIŠ.GIŠIMMAR.TUR(.TUR)]

tâlu(m) (a tree) jB lex. (= *tiālu* ?)

taluḫlu, *taluḫlītu*, *taluḫulla* (a class of person) Nuzi; < Hurr.

tāluku(m); pl. m. & f. "gait, progression, course" Bab., NA of army "advance, stage"; religious "procession" (NB pl. f.); "course" of river, astr. of heavenly body; OB math.; < *alāku*

talupadi (a plant) jB comm.

tamāḫu(m), occas. *tamāku* "to grasp" Bab.(lit.) **G** (*a/u*) objects, people, part of body; "control" natural forces, ordinances **D** ~ G **Š** caus. of G

tamalākum (a sealable container) OA for tablets, textiles

tamāmītum → *tammāmītum*

tamāmum mng. unkn. OB lex.

tamāmû → *tammāmû*

tamartu → *tawwertum*

tāmartu(m), *tāmurtu* "view(ing); audience-gift" Bab., NA [IGI.DU$_8$(.A); IGI.LÁ/LÁL] "view, viewing, inspection; observation"; "appearance, apparition" of gods, heavenly bodies; "audience-gift"; *ša t.* ~ "mirror" or "lens"?; < *amāru* I; → *nāmurtu*

tamāru → *temēru*

tamarzu mng. unkn. NA

tâmatu → *tiāmtu*

tamā'u → *tamû* II

tambukku, lex. also *tebukku* "cucumber fly" M/jB [NIM.ÚKUŠ]

tambūtu → *tibbuttum*

tâmdu → *tiāmtu*

tamertu → *tawwertum*

tamgertum "reconciliation payment, hush-money"? OA; < *magāru* D

tamgītu(m) "rejoicing song" O/jB; < *nagû* II

tamgurtu(m) "agreement, agreed payment" O/jB; Nuzi *ṭuppi t.*; < *magāru*

tamgussu → *tangussu*

tamḫāriš "to the battle" jB; < *tamḫāru*

tamḫartu "square" NB math.; < *maḫāru* Gt

tamḫāru(m) "battle, combat" OAkk, O/jB; < *maḫāru* Gt

tamḫātu ? (kind of gem) MB

tamḫâtu → *tamḫītu*

tamḫiam "in the evening(s)" OB lex.; < *tamḫû*

tamḫīru(m) "presentation" O/jB **1.** "presentation, offering" **2.** in MN *(w)araḫ T.*, at Susa, Mari, N.Mes. etc.; < *maḫāru* D

tamḫīṣu ~ "overlay, veneer"? jB; < *maḫāṣu* D

tamḫītu "evening" jB freq. pl. *tamḫâti*; < *tamḫû*

tamḫû(m) "evening" OAkk, O/jB; > *tamḫiam*; *tamḫītu*; *meḫûm* II

tamḫuṣu "battle, combat" jB; < *maḫāṣu* Gt

tamīmu "complete, perfect" NB of sacrificial animal; < Aram.

tamirtu → *tawwertum*

tamītu "oath" jB, NA (var. of *māmītu*); < *tamû* II

tāmītu → *tāwītum*

tamkārānû "like a merchant, mercantile" jB; < *tamkāru*

tamkārašše (a charge, fee) Nuzi; < *tamkāru* + Hurr. *-ašše*

tamkarḫu (a colour) Nuzi; < Hurr.

tamkāru(m), *damk/gāru* "merchant, businessman" [(LÚ.)DAM.GÀR; NA also TAM. GÀR; NB also LÚ.DAM]; *rab t.*; *wakil t.*; < *makāru* II

tamkārūtu(m), Ass. *tamkāruttu(m)*, MB *tankārūtu* "merchanthood; business, commerce" OA, O/MB [DAM.GÀR-]; < *tamkāru*

tamkīru "irrigated land" MB(Ass.); < *makāru* I D

tamlāku(m) "adviser" O/jB; < *malāku* II

tamlîš (desig. for kind of drug) M/jB rdg. uncl. (wr. UD-*liš*)

tamlittu → *tālittu*

tamlītu(m) "filling" Ass., OB; "completion" of time, number, "replenishment" of conscripts; M/NA "inlay" of stones etc.; math. "infilling", of volume; < *malû* IV D

tamlīu(m), *tamlû(m)* "filling" **1.** Bab., M/NA "terrace" **2.** "inlay" (decorative); < *malû* IV D

tammakkû (an official) Nuzi; < Hurr.?

ta(m)māmītum "oath-swearing"? Mari; < *tamû* II

ta(m)māmû(m) "one who swears oaths" O/jB lex.; < *tamû* II

tammu mng. uncl. jB lex.

tamqītu → *taqqītum*

tamqullu "flame"? jB lex.

tamrīqātu pl. tant. (a ritual)? jB lex., also comm.; < *marāqu* D

tamrirtu ~ "practice, exercise" jB in col.; < *marāru* I D

tamrīrum (a cosmetic oil) Mari; < *marāru* I D

tamrītu(m) mng. unkn. Bab. lex. phps. textual errors

tamrû (syn. of *tarpašû*) Bab. lex. rdg. uncl. (wr. UD-*ru-ú*)

tamsûtu mng. unkn. MB in *t. umāmī*; < *mesû* II ?

tamšāru(m) "whip(-thong)" O/jB; < *mašāru*

tamšīḫu "area" jB; < *mašāḫu* I D

tamšiltu "mould" for casting NA, NB; < *mašālu* D

tamšilum (a resin) OAkk(Ur III); → *damšillu*

tamšīlu(m), *tanšīlu* **1.** "image, likeness" OAkk, Bab. "equivalent, peer"; *t. abūbi* high water "like a flood" **2.** (a drinking vessel) M/jB **3.** (a bird) jB, NA (→ *tarmazilu*); < *mašālu* D

tamšītum "oblivion"? OB; < *mašû* II D ?; → *tamlītu(m)*

tamtalku ~ "deliberate" adj. jB; < *malāku* II Gt

tamtu → *damtum* I

tâmtu → *tiāmtu*

tamṭītu(m) "diminution, scarcity" O/jB; pl. "penury"; < *maṭû* II D

tamû I "having (for)sworn; cursed, bewitched" jB; < *tamû* II

tamû II, Ass. *tamā'u(m)*, *ta'û*, NB *temû* "to swear" **G** (*a/a*; NB perf. *itteme*) leg., mag.; stat. act., also pass. "is bewitched, cursed", by = acc., *ina*, *ana*, *ina libbi* **Gtn** iter. of G **D** "swear"; "bind s.o. by oath"; "make (s.o.) swear" oath (*māmīta(m)*, *nīš DN/šarrim*) **Š** Mari "make (s.o.) swear", stat. "is sworn in" **R** *uttama(m)mû* "mutually swear" oath; > *tamû* I, *tamītu*; *tammāmû*, *tammāmītum*; *tim'um*; *tumāmītu*; → *wamā'um*

tamûm III "to be amazed"? OB stat. *tamu*

tâmû (type of apple-like tree) jB lex.; < *tiāmtu*

tāmurtu → *tāmartu*

tamzīziš (or *parzīziš* ?) "like a ..." jB in simile of stabbing corpses

tanādātu → *tanattu*

tanakušri → *natakušri*

tanattu(m); pl. *tanadātu* "praise, glory" Bab., NA; < *nâdu*

tându → *tiāmtu*

tanēḫtu(m) "pacification, mollification" OA, O/jB; < *nâḫu* D

tānēḫtu → *tānēḫu*

tanēḫu "pacification" jB; < *nâḫu* D

tānēḫu(m), *tānēḫtu* "moaning, distress" OAkk, O/jB, NA also transf. of waves "sighing"; < *anāḫu* I D

tanēštum → *tenēštu*

tangagtu (a knife)? jB lex.; < *nagāgu* ?

tangallû (a vessel for salt) NB also of precious metal

tangussu(m), *tamgussu(m)* (a cooking vessel) Bab., NA [URUDU.ŠEN.TUR] of copper, bronze

tanīdu(m) "(hymn of) praise" O/jB; < *nâdu* D

tanīḫtu → *tanēḫtu*

tānīḫu → *tānēḫu*

tānīštum "(economic) weakness", "inability to pay"? OA; < *enēšu* or OA form of *tenēštu*

tanīšu mng. unkn. MB

tanittu(m), occas. *šanittum* "(hymn of) praise" Bab.; < *nâdu* D

taniwe (an object) Nuzi; < Hurr.

tankārūtu → *tamkārūtu*

tannu(m); pl. m. & f. (a wooden bowl) Bab. [GIŠ.DÍLIM.TUR]

tanpaḫu, *tappaḫu*? mng. unkn. MA?, jB; < *napāḫu* ?

tanqītu → *taqqītum*

tanšīlu → *tamšīlu*

tānuḫiš "in trouble" OB; < *anāḫu* I

tanūḫtum (a payment) OB; < *nâḫu* ?

tanūku; pl. f. mng. unkn. jB, NA

tanūqātu(m) pl. tant. "battle cry" Bab.; < *nâqu* I

tanzilam (a connecting canal) MB; < Kass.

tanzimtum → *tazzimtu*

tapāku → *tabāku*

tapalātum → *tabalātum*

tāpalātu "heiress" jB lex.; < *apālu* II

tāpalu(m), *tābalu* "pair (of objects)" Bab. of shoes, garments, beams etc.; (a kind of musical instrument) ~ "castanets"?; < *apālu* I

tapānu (an object) jB lex.

tapāšum OB **G** unattested **D** ~ "to take into custody"? **N** of garment "be taken into custody"?

tapatum (or *tabatum*, *dab/patum*) (a textile or garment) OAkk

tapatu → also *taptu*

tapḫarum (a temple collection)? Early Mari of beer; < *paḫāru* II

tapḫīrum (a temple collection)? OA; < *paḫāru* II

tapḫu (a metal cauldron) NA, NB

tapḫurtu(m) "assembly, company" OAkk, jB; < *paḫāru* II

tapḫūrum "assembly" of supplicants OB; < *paḫāru* II

tapḫušḫu (an object) Alal.; < Hurr.

tāpiltum "payment"? OB; < *apālu* I

tapliḫtu "intimidation" jB; < *palāḫu* D

tappaḫu → *tanpaḫu*

tappaštu, *tappaltu*, NA also *dappastu* (a woollen rug) NA, NB; < *napāšu* II

tappātu(m), *tappattu* "(female) companion, partner" OA, O/jB [TAB.BA-]; also Bab. "secondary wife" [DAM.TAB.BA]; < *tappû* I

tappā'u → *tappû* I

tappā'uttum → *tappûtu*

tappilātu(m) "balancing payment" O/jB; < *napālu* II

tappinnu(m), OB also *dappinnum*, NA once *tuppinnu* (a kind of flour) OAkk, O/jB, NA [DABIN]; also lex. in desig. of *šaḫû* fish; < Sum.

tappissu (a kind of mud)? jB lex.

tappīṣu "crushed matter" jB med. in *t. buqli* "crushed malt"; < *napāṣu* D

tappištum I "extension" Mari, of bed of river; < *napāšu* I D

tappištu(m) II "plucking (of wool)" O/jB; < *napāšu* II D

tappiūtu → *tappûtu*

tappû(m) I, OAkk, O/MA *tappā'u(m)* "companion, partner" [TAB.BA] "friend"; "partner" in commerce; OA "associate" of judges; also of gods as "friend" of human, esp. in PN; < Sum.; > *tappātu*; *tappûtu*; *tappûm* II

tappûm II **D** "to join in partnership with" (+ acc.) OA; < *tappû* I denom.

tappuḫtum "rising" OB of star, transf. of person's health; < *napāḫu*

tappûtu(m), once *tappiūtu*, OA *tappā'uttum*, MA *tapputtu* "companionship, partnership" Ass., O/jB [TAB.BA; NAM.TAB.BA] esp. *t. alāku(m)* "to go to (s.o.'s) assistance"; esp. "(commercial) partnership"; < *tappû* I

tapqertu "claim, reclamation" M/NB, NA; < *baqāru* D

tapra → *tabra*

tapsimtum "veiling" OB(Alal.) in PN; < *pasāmu* D

tapsû(m), NA *tapšû* (a covering) O/jB, NA [TÚG.DU$_8$.DU$_8$] of textile, leather; < *pasû* D ?

tapša(ḫ)ḫu ~ "chariot man" Nuzi; < Hurr.

tapšaḫu "resting place" jB; < *pašāḫu*

tapšertu, *tapširtu* "(magical) release" jB; < *pašāru* D

tapšīḫu "alleviation" MB of illness; < *pašāḫu* D

tapšiqtu ~ "constriction"? NB; < *pašāqu* D

tapširtu → *tapšertu*

tapšu → *tabšu*

tapšû → *tapsû*

tapšuḫtu "rest, pacification" j/NB; < *pašāḫu*

tapšūru "sale"? NB; < *pašāru*

taptānu mng. uncert. NB in PN; < *patānu* II ?

taptētu → *teptītum*

taptu, *tapatu* (a stone vessel for oil) Nuzi, Am.

taptû "land newly brought into cultivation" MA, M/NB; < *petû* II D

tapṭartum (a container)? OB; < *paṭāru*

tapṭertu "release" j/NB of divine anger; of slave ?; < *paṭāru* D

tapṭīru "castration" NB in *alpu t.* "castrated ox"; < *paṭāru* D

tapû mng. unkn. jB lex.

tâpu, *ṭapû* ~ "to devote o.s." to s.th. jB **G** (*ū*); > *tūpu*

tāpultum "payment" OB(Susa); < *apālu* I

tapzertu "concealment" jB; < *pazāru* D

taqāmu → *taqānu*

taqānu(m), NB also *taqāmu*, jB *tagānu* "to be(come) secure, in good order" **G** (*u/u*; stat. *taqun/m*) of person, land, throne **D** "put in order, secure" [LAL] **Dtn** "keep in order" cult **N** NA pass. of D "be in good order"; > *taqnu*; *tiqnu*; *tuqnu*; *tuqqunu*; *matqanu*; *mutaqqinu*

taqbû mng. uncert. jB lex.; < *qabû* II ?

taqdīšum ~ "purification" OA; < *qadāšu* D

taqmu → *takmu*

taqnu "in order, good" jB, NA; < *taqānu*

taqpu → *takpu*

taqqītum, *tam/nqītu* "offering, libation" O/jB; < *naqû* D

taqrībatum → *teqrūbatum*

taqribtu(m), once *taqriwtum* "offering" Bab., OA [ÉR] esp. as desig. of ritual of intercession *t. šakānu(m), epēšu(m)* etc.; < *qerēbu*; → *taqrību*

taqrību(m) O/jB occas. for *taqribtu*

taqrīdu "heroic, warrior" jB lex.; < *qarādu* II D

taqrintu "piling up, accumulation" M/jB of corpses, possessions; < *qarānu* D

taqrirtu mng. unkn. jB; < *qarāru* D

taqriwtum → *taqribtu*

taqrubtu "battle, combat" M/jB(Ass.); < *qerēbu* Gt

taqtīru "fumigation" jB lex.; < *qatāru* II D

taqtītu(m) "termination, end" O/jB [TIL] of reign, year; < *qatû* II D

taqwûm → *takwûm*

tarabānu (a plant) jB med.; also in glass-making

taradû (a tree) jB lex. = (a kind of) *šakkullu*

taraḫḫu(m) "slope of an earth heap" Bab. of canals; buildings; also om. of feature on gall

taraḫu "gate" NB in *bāb t.*; < Aram.

tarāḫu "to dig up"? MA, jB **G** (*a/u*) field; of animal "grub up" the soil; Susa, stat. *tiriḫ*, of part of liver **D** lex.; > *tarīḫu*

tarāḫum → also *turāḫu*

tarāku(m) "to beat, thump; be dark" OAkk, O/jB, NA **G** (*a/u*) [GE$_6$; DÚB] of whip, weapon, wind; "thump" tail; intrans. of heart "beat"; stat. "is dark, black" of parts of body, marks on liver etc. **Gtn**? of oil **D** ~ G "beat"; stat. "is beaten flat"? **Š** caus. of G **N** "be beaten"; of oil "become dark"?; > *terku*, *teriktu*?; *turku*; *matraktu*; → *tariktu*

tarammu I, *šarammu* "grain heap" M/jB, NA [ŠE.SU$_7$]

tarammu II (a part of body) jB lex.

tarāmu(m) "beloved one" Ass., OB mostly in PN; < *râmu* II

tarānu(m) "roof, shelter" Bab., also transf.

tarapḫu (a kind of wood)? Nuzi; < Hurr.

tarāpu "to be covered with colour, be painted" jB **G** lex. and stat. **D** ~ "coat with"; stat. of part of body, wall "is coloured" green, black etc.; > *tiriptum*

tarāqu(m) "to take pity, relent" OAkk, jB **G** (*a/a*) of divine anger "relent"; demon *Lā-tarāq* "Relentless"; of storm "die down"

tarāru(m) "to tremble, shake" Bab.(lit.) **G** (*u/u*) of head, tail; mountain, buildings **D** "make tremble" **N** "start to tremble, shake"; → *arāru* III

tarāsu → *ṭarāsu*

tarāṣu(m) I "to stretch out" **G** (*a/u*) [LAL; jB NIR] "extend, point" hand, finger etc.; "erect" horn, ear; "turn" face, heart towards s.th.; "spread out" net, cloth, rope; "stretch over" roof, (transf.) protection; "set up" furniture; Ug., Nuzi, Am. leg. "establish, confirm" facts; "set out, submit" words **Gtn** [NIR.NIR] iter. "repeatedly stretch out" **D** ~ G esp. "direct" face, eyes towards, "expect, long for" **Dt** pass. of D **Š** caus. of G **N** pass. of G; also of journey "be finished"; "be confirmed" OB **Ntn** iter. of N; > *tarṣu* I, III?; *terṣu*; *turruṣum*; → *t.* II; *ṭarāsu*

tarāṣu(m) II "to be(come) in order, correct" Bab., NA (demarcation from *t.* I occas. uncert.) **G** (*u/u*, Am. also *i/i*; OB(N.Mes.) pres. *itarraṣ* ?) [LAL] "be good, satisfactory", "be, seem right" to s.o. **D** "put in order"; Am. "check" words; NB "treat correctly"?; > *tarṣu* II

tarāšum mng. unkn. OB **G**

taratara (a plant) jB lex.

tarā'um → *tarû* I

tar'azu → *šer'azum*

tarbabu (a bronze object) jB lex.

tarbaṣu(m), *tarbāṣu(m)* "animal stall; courtyard" Bab., M/NA [TÙR] ext. (a feature on liver); astr. "halo" round moon; < *rabāṣu*

tarbītu(m) 'enlargement' **1.** "upbringing" of adopted child; "adopted child"; OA "(payment for) rearing" **2.** person, animal, tree "nurtured, brought up" in locality, by s.o.; "product of" **3.** Bab. pl. "promotion" in rank **4.** Elam (a month name); < *rabû* II D

tarbû(m) "alumnus, trainee" O/jB, NA [BÙLUG]; < *rabû* II D

tarbû → also *tarbu'tu*

tarbūtu → *tarbu'tu*

tarbûtu Bab. **1.** "novice" [Á.È] **2.** "shoot, seedling" **3.** "adoptive childhood"; < *tarbû*, *tarbītu*

tarbu'(t)u(m), *turbu'/ttu*, *tur(u)bu*, *turba'u*, *tarbû*, *tarbūtu* "dust (storm)" Bab.; also lex. *šam t.* (a plant)

tardennītu, *tartennītu* **1.** M/NB "younger daughter" **2.** lex. (a kind of chair or stool); < *tardennu*

tardennu, *tartennu*, *terd/tennu* "second(ary)" M/NA, M/NB of younger brother, son; of an official, esp. Nuzi, Bogh., Ug. "crown-prince"?; Nuzi, NB of garments etc. "second class"; j/NB of cultic meal, delivery "subsidiary, minor"; < Hurr.?; also phps. folk etym. < *redû* I; > *tardennītu*, *tardennūtu*; → *tartānu*

tardennūtu, *ta/erd/tennūtu*, *-uttu* **1.** Bogh., Ug. "status of crown-prince"? **2.** Nuzi "second quality"?; < *tardennu*

tardītu → *terdītu*

tardīum → *terdû*

targagû "oath" jB lex.

targamannum → *targumannu*

targīgu "evildoer" M/jB(Ass.); < *ragāgu* I

targumannu(m), *turgumannum*, *targamannum*, Ug. *targumiānu* "interpreter, dragoman" Ass., O/jB; → *ragāmu*

tarḫātu → *terḫatu*

tarīb(t)u(m) "replacement" esp. in PN; < *riābu*

tarīḫu; pl. f. (a vessel) MA, jB; < *tarāḫu*

tariktu (a metal object) NB; < *tarāku* ?

tarīku mng. unkn. jB(lit.)

tarīmtu(m), M/NB also *tarīndu* "gift, award" Bab.; < *râmu* III

tārīmu (a door or attachment for covering door) jB lex.; < *arāmu* D

tarīndu → *tarīmtu*

tarinnu mng. unkn. Nuzi in desig. of belt; < Hurr.; → *terinnu*

tāriru (a craftsman) Ug. pl. *tārirūma*; < Ug.

tarištê (desig. of pregnant sheep)? Nuzi; < Hurr.

tārītu(m) I "nurse, nanny" O/jB, M/NA [UM.ME.DA]; also in PN; of goddess; < *tarû* II

tārītu(m) II "stripping, defoliation" Bab. of date palms; "stripped" reeds; < *arû* VI D

tāriu → *tārû*

tarizaḫ (a plant) jB lex.; < Kass.

tarkibtum "fertilization" OB of date palms; < *rakābu* D; → *tarkubtu* 1

tarkībum "layer, course" of brickwork OB math.; < *rakābu* D

tarkistum "guarantor's liability" OA; < *rakāsu* D

***tarkīsu**, NB *taškīsu* (a binding) NB of linen; gold; < *rakāsu* D

tarkubtu(m) **1.** OB var. of *tarkibtum* **2.** jB "(horse-)riding"; < *rakābu* D

tarkullu(m), *darkullu*, *t/derkullum*; pl. m. & f. "wooden post, pole" OAkk, O/jB as mast of boat; in irrigation regulator; < Sum.

tarkumassu, also *tarkumasḫu*?; pl. occas. f. (an officer)? Nuzi

tarlugallu(m), NA also *tarnugallu* "hen" Bab., NA [DAR.LUGAL.MUŠEN; astr. MUL.DAR. LUGAL(.MUŠEN)]; < Sum.; → *tirugallu*

tarmāṣu ~ "butterfly" jB lex.; < *ramāṣu* ?; → *turzu*

tarmazilu (an edible bird) jB, NA; → *tamšīlu* 3

tarmiktum "pruning(s)"? Mari, of vine; < *ramāku* D

tarmīku(m) (a tree seedling) O/jB lex.; < *ramāku* D

tarmītu "release, relaxation" M/jB from work; < *ramû* III D

tarmuš "lupin" M/jB lex., med.

tarnappakkum, *turnippakkum* (a metal vessel) Mari

tarnu "mast" Ug.; < Ug.

tarnugallu → *tarlugallu*

tarpašu "otter" M/jB

tarpašû(m), *tarpašu* "open space" Bab. in military context, also archit.; < *rapāšu*

tarpīsu (a medicinal plant) jB; < *rapāsu* ?

tarqītu "oil-processing, perfume-making" MA, jB; < *ruqqû*

tarru (a bird) M/jB [DAR.MUŠEN]; < Sum.

tarsītu "prayer" Bab. lex.

tarsītu → also *tērsītu*

tarṣiātum ~ "pleasure, enjoyment" OB; → *raṣûm*

tarṣu I "stretched out" jB; < *tarāṣu* I

tarṣu II "correct, proper" M/NA, M/NB [LAL] f. as subst. "correctness, propriety"; < *tarāṣu* II

tarṣu III "extent, duration" M/NA, M/NB [LAL] in space "extent"; *ana t.* "towards", "opposite, against"; *ina t.* "opposite"; *ištu t.* "from" a place; in time *(ša) t./ana t./ina t.* "at the time of"; *ištu t.* "since the time of"; < *tarāṣu* I ?; → *terṣu*

taršītum, *teršītum* ~ "harassment" OB; < *rašû* III D

tartāmū pl. tant. ~ "love-making" O/MB(lit.); < *râmu* II

tartānu, *turtānu*, *ta/urtannu*, once *turtennu* ~ "deputy, second in command" M/NA, Nuzi; Nuzi = *tardennu*, also an official; NA "field marshal, principal military officer"; 7th century *t.* of left, right (i.e. of north, south); also of Egypt, Elam, Urarṭu; < Hurr.

tartaraḫ → *dardaraḫ*

tartennītu → *tardennītu*

tartennu → *tardennu*

tartennuttu → *tardennūtu*

tartu, *taštu* mng. unkn. NB in PNs

tarû(m) I, OAkk, OA *tarā'um* "to lead away" OAkk, OA, O/jB **G** (*u/u*; imper. *taru*, *turu*) animals, people; < *warûm* II Gt

tarû(m) II "to lift up" O/jB **G** (*i/i*) child; tail **Gtn** iter. **N** pass. of G ?; > *tārû*, *tārītu* I

tārû, MA *tāriu* "(child) minder" MA, j/NB; < *tarû* II

târu(m), OAkk, Ass. *tuāru(m)* "to turn, return; become (again)" **G** [GUR; GI4] **1.** of animate and inanimate objects "return, turn back", vent. "come back" **2.** "become again" **3.** of deities "relent" esp. in PNs **4.** ext. of features "be bent (towards)" **5.** leg. "revert to, reopen" a case **6.** "turn back from, refuse" ordeal **7.** in hendiad. "repeat"; *t.* + *X* "do X again" **8.** "turn into, become"; "be reduced" to (= *ana*) **Gtn** iter. **D** "bring, send, give, pay back" etc. [GUR; MB also GI] "restore" rituals; *awātam t.* etc. "reply"; "cancel, undo"; *ana ašri- t.* "restore" building, also transf.; *ana idi(m) t.* "bring over to (o.'s) side"; "bring up, vomit" food; "turn, bend" part of body; "turn away" breast, i.e. "retreat", also "repulse"; "swing" doors shut; "repay" good, evil, vengeance; Bab. "take captive" soldier; chariot; "repeat, do again"; also in hendiad.; "turn s.o./s.th. into, change into" **Dtn** iter. of D [GUR.GUR] **Dt** pass. of D **Š** for D in Am., Kumidi; > *tūru*, *tūra*; *tūrtu*; *tayyartu*, *tayyāru* I.II, *tayyārûm*; *ta''uru*; *turru*, *turrūtu*; *muterru*; *mutērtu*; *tīrānu* I.II, *tīrānû*, *tīru* II

taruallinnu (a wooden object) Nuzi; < Hurr.

tārūru "trembling"? jB om.; < *arāru* III ?

tarušḫu (a bucket)? MA of bronze; < Hurr.

tarwišša mng. unkn. Nuzi (a legal procedure)?; < Hurr.

tasdīru, *taldīru* "supply of offerings"? jB; < *sadāru* D

tasgalḫu, *taskarḫu* (a kind of bed) Nuzi, jB; < Hurr.

tasḫiltu → *taḫsistu*

tasḫīr(t)u, *tašḫīr(t)u* (a twisted? reed artefact)? MA, jB; < *saḫāru* D

taskarḫu → *tasgalḫu*

taskarinnu(m), *t/diskarinnum*, lex. also *dašgarinnum*, "box tree, boxwood" [GIŠ.TASKARIN]

taskidūtum (or *taškidūtum*) mng. unkn. Mari desig. of neck band

taskû → *saskû*

taslimtu(m) "(re)conciliation" O/jB; < *salāmu* II D

taslītu ~ "denigrating talk" jB; < *salā'u* II

taslītum → also *teslītu*

tasniqtu "test, verification" jB lex. in *aban t.* "touchstone"; < *sanāqu* I D

tasqû → *saskû*

tasriḫtu "destruction" MB; < *sarāḫu* D

tasrīru, *tasrirru* "lies, falsehood"; < *sarāru* D

tassa(k)kum (an oil container)? OB

tassistu(m) "lamentation" O/jB; < *nasāsu* I D

tassītum "claim" OB; < *šasû* D

tassuḫtu "removal (of cattle)"? jB om. as unfavourable prediction; < *nasāḫu*

taṣbâtu pl. "fulfilment of wish"? jB; < *ṣabû* II or *ṣabātu* ?

taṣbubtum subst. "fluttering" OB lex.; < *ṣabābu*

taṣītu(m) (a stone tray)? O/jB; < *waṣûm* ?

taṣliltu(m), *taṣlīlu(m)* "roof(ing), cover(ing)" Bab., NA; < *ṣullulu* II

taṣlītu → *teslītu*

taṣmertu "wish, desire" jB; < *ṣamāru* D

taṣraḫu (a horse groom) Am.; < *ṣarāḫu* III D

taṣû(m) "to go away, move out" O/jB (imper. *taṣi*); < *waṣûm* Gt

taš → *tašpiltu*

***tašābu(m)** "to sit down" Bab., OA only imper. *ta/išab*; < *wašābum* Gt

tašā'iu "ninth" MA; < *tiše*

taša(l)lu (an object) Alal.

tašapšu(m) (a cloth cover) O/jB

tašbītum "satisfaction, complete payment" (of goods etc.) OA; < *šebû* I D

tāšertum ~ "control, checking" OB; < *ašāru*

tašgertu(m) "defamation, deception" O/jB; < *šugguru*

tašḫīr(t)u → *tasḫirtu*

tašīḫu(m) (a kind of vegetation) OB, in desig. of field; jB lex.; < *šiāḫum* I ?

tašīltu(m) "(ceremony of) celebration" Bab., M/NA [GIR17.ZAL] in secular or religious contexts; also OB (a bird) [GIR17.ZAL.MUŠEN]?; < *šâlu* II

tašīmtu(m), NB also *tašīmdu* "discernment, sagacity" of deities, humans; OA pl. uncl.; < *šummu* II

taškidūtum → *taskidūtum*
taškīsu → *tarkīsu*
taškû → *saskû*; *takšû*
taškuttu mng. unkn. NB; < *šakānu* ?
tašlamtu, *tašlandu* (a lizard) jB
tašlimtu(m), *tašlindu* "completed handover, final payment" Bab., NA; < *šalāmu* II D
tašliqtu (a battle insult)? jB lex.; < *šalāqu* D
tašlīšu, NB also *taššalīšu*; NB pl. *tašallišā(n)nu* "third man on chariot" NA, NB [LÚ.3-*šú*; LÚ.3.U$_5$ etc.]; < *šalāš*
tašlītu → *teslītu*
tašlu mng. unkn. Am. in list of precious items; < Hurr.?
Tašmētu(m), OAkk *Tašma'tum*, Nuzi also *Tešmētu* "listening, attention" NB in PN, OAkk as fPN; goddess *Tašmētum* [^{d}KURNUN]; < *šemû*
tašmû → *tešmû*
tašna, *tašni* "double, twofold" OB; < *tašnû* (→ GAG §71c)
tašnintu(m), *tašnuntu* "battle, combat" Bab.(lit.); < *šanānu*
tašnīnu "strife" jB, in pl.; < *šanānu*
tašnīqu (internal disease) jB
tašnītu(m) "repetition" OAkk, O/jB esp. in names of repeated months; < *šanû* III D
tašnû(m) "repetition" O/jB; < *šanû* III D
tašnuntu → *tašnintu*
tašpartu "messenger"? Ug.; < *šapāru*
tašpiltu "lowering; difference" NB astr., also abbr. *taš*; < *šapālu* D
tašpītum "'hush-money', pay-off" OB; < *šapû* III D
tašqītum (a seed furrow)? OB lex.; < *šaqû* II D ?
tašqû → *saskû*
tašriḫtu(m) "glorification, boastfulness" Bab. (lit.); < *šarāḫu* I D
tašrīḫū pl. tant. "glorification" jB; < *šarāḫu* I D
tašrītu(m) "beginning; inauguration" Bab., NA also "inauguration feast"; (name of 7th Bab. month) [ITI.DU$_6$/DUL(.KÙ)]; < *šurrû* II
taššalīšu → *tašlīšu*
taššiātum pl. tant. "transport costs" OA; < *našû* II
taššītu(m) ~ "insult" O/jB; < *našû* II or *tuššu* ?
taššu → *daššu*
taštu → *tartu*
tāšūš → *idāšūš*
tātamum → *taḫtamum*
tatbīku "coating"? Am. in *t. ša ḫurāṣu* "c. of gold"; < *tabāku* D

tatīdu, *tatītu* (a tree) jB; → *tatidūtu*
tatidūtu (a kind of partridge)? MA, jB; < hypocorist. from *tatīdu* ?
tatītu → *tatīdu*
Tatium (a month) OB(Susa)
tattaru (a bronze object) M/jB
tattiktu, *tattīku* subst. "dripping, leakage" M/jB lex., med.; < *natāku* D
ta(t)turru(m) (a kind of leek) Bab. [SUM.ŠIR (or = *turû* ?)]; > *tatturrû*
tatturru → also *tattūru*
ta(t)turrû (a metal object) jB lex.; < *tatturru*
tattūru(m), *tatturru* "superfluity, profit" O/jB; < *watārum* ?
ta'û(m) "to eat; graze" O/jB **G** lex. **Gtn** ptcp. *muta''û* of sheep **Gt** "eat together" of snake and eagle? **D** "support, sustain"; > *tîtum*, *tī'u* II, *ti'ûtu*
ta'û → also *tamû* II
tā'um "inner room" OAkk, OB esp. term.-adv. *tā'iš*
ta''umu "double, twinned" NA of doors etc.; < *tū'amu*; NB → *tu''umu* I
ta''umu → also *tu''umu* II
ta''uru "turned" MA in f. pl. *ta''urāte* mng. unkn.; < *târu* D
tawa → *tawi*
tawarriwa etc. → *tabarru*
tâwatu → *tiāmtu*
tāwi/a in *nib tāwi* "lord of both lands" Bogh.; < Eg.
tāwītum, *tāmītu*, *tā'ītum* ~ "response" Bab. esp. to omen query; "wording" of inscription; < *awûm* Gt
tawûm mng. unkn. Mari **G** (prec. *lutwi*); > *tiwītum*
tawwertum, *tame/irtu*, occas. *tamartu* "(a type of) meadow" Bab., NA [GARIM(=LAGAB× KÙ)]; Ass.(roy. inscr.) esp. "(cultivated) environs" of city; < *nawāru* D ?
tayyartu(m), *ta''artu*; NA pl. *têrātu* "return; forgiveness" Bab., NA "return journey, march"; astr. "repetition"; "relentment" of divine anger; pl. "(tokens of) forgiveness"; ext. (feature on gall); Bogh. (an object); < *târu*
tayyāru(m) I, *ta''āru*, *tiyāru* adj. "returning; relenting" OA, O/jB **1.** for G ptcp. "turning back" of road, travellers in *lā t.* "without return, not returning" **2.** of deities "relenting, merciful"; < *târu*
ta(y)yāru II **1.** M/NB, NA "mercy, relentment", esp. in *t. rašû* "to have mercy" **2.** NA "amount recovered", "return" from offerings; < *târu*

ta(y)yāru III "measure" Nuzi, for fields; < Hurr.

tayyārûm "merciful" OB in fPN *Tayyārītum*; < *tayyāru* II

tazbiltu(m) "delay, retardation" O/jB; < *zabālu* D

tazkītu(m) "clearance" OAkk, OB, MA; OAkk (in PN) "manumission" of slaves; OB "settlement" of mutual claims; MA "clearance (document)", "clarification" of liquid; < *zakû* II D

tazzimtu(m), *tanzimtum, tazzintu, tezzimtu* ? "complaint" Bab., OA [I.^{d}UTU]; < *nazāmu* D

tazzīqum "vexation, anxiety" OB; < *nazāqu*

teammu → *timmu*

tebbar (syn. of *mukku*)? jB lex.

tebbukku → *tambukku*

tēbibtu(m) "purification" Bab.; usu. in rit.; Mari "census"; < *ebēbu* D

Tēbiltu (name of a canal by Nineveh) NA

tēbītu → *tēbû*

teb'ītum "investigation, search" OB for slave; < *bu''û* II

tebrītu → *tabrītu*

tebû(m) OAkk, Ass. *tabā'u(m)*, NB *tabû* "to get up, arise, set out" **G** (*i/i*) [ZI(.GA); also KUR] "get up" from ground, sleep, chair; "arise" from sick-bed; of animals, aggressively, sexually; "get up, start up" to go, in procession, in lawcourt, battle, rebellion; of ecstatic; "rise" of wind, water, plague etc.; of feature in exta "stick up" **Gtn** iter of G [ZI.ZI]; of veins "pulse, throb" **D** only Ug. for G "start legal proceedings" **Š** caus. of G "set in motion" statue, troops, weapons, wind etc.; "remove" judge, evil, curse; math. "deduct" **Štn** iter. of Š **Ntn** for Gtn; > *tēbû, tābiu*?; *tību, tibûtu*; *netbītum*

tēbu → *tību*

tēbû(m), *tību* "arising; insurgent" Bab. [ZI(.GA)] of animal "lively, active"; "ready (for battle)"; of flood "rising"; of vein "pulsing"; of demon, wound *ina lā t.* "persistent"; "rebellious"; < *tebû*; → *tābiu*

têbum (or *têpum*) ~ "to distrust"? OB om. **G**

tebukku → *tambukku*

tebûtu → *tibûtu*

tēdīqu(m), *tīdīqu* "dress, costume" Bab.(lit.) of deity, king; < *edēqu* D

tēdištu, NB occas. *tēdirtu* "renewal" M/NB of divine statues, buildings; also astr.; < *edēšu* D

tegibu (or *tegipu*) (desig. of bronze) Nuzi

tegi(l)lû → *tigillû*

tēgimtu "rage, anger" jB; < *agāmu*

tegipu → *tegibu*

tēgirtu ~ "negotiation"? NA; < *egēru* ?

tegītu → *tigû* II

tegû → *tigû* I

tēgû ~ "toil, effort" jB lex.; < *egû* III ?

teḫampašḫu (desig. of silver) Nuzi; < Hurr.

tēḫirtu "residue, amount left over" NB; < *aḫāru* D

teḫuššu (a textile or garment) Nuzi; < Hurr.

teḫuššurannu (desig. of chariot horses) Nuzi; < Hurr.

te'iqtu, *têl/îqtu* ~ "insult, injury" NB; < Aram.

te'ītu → *tîtum*

tēkītu(m), *tīkītu(m)*, NB also *tēkûtu* "complaint, grumbling" Bab, NA esp. *t. rašûm* "to complain" about (= *ana*) s.o.; < *ekû* II ?

teknītu(m), *tiknītum, taknītu*, NB also *tikanītu* "loving care; one lovingly cared for" Bab.(lit.) of goddesses; desig. of objects; < *teknûm*

teknûm, *taknû* ~ "loving care" Bab.(lit.), also *zamar t.* "hymn of blandishment"; "hospitality"; bed of "comfort"; < *kanû* D

tēkuptum ~ "(time) pressure"? OB; < *ekēpu*

tēkûtu → *tēkītu*

telannu (an object) Am., in pairs

teldātum mng. unkn. OB lex.

tele'ā'u → *tele'û*

telentu → *tilimatu*

telētu → *telītu* I

tele'û, occas. *tele'ā'u* "very competent" j/NB of gods, kings; < *le'û*; > *telītu* I; *telūtu*?

tēliltu(m), *tīliltu(m)*, NA *tēlissu* "purification" Bab., M/NA; < *elēlu* II D

têlišam "syllable by syllable"? OB; < *têlu*

tēlittu → *tēlītu*

telītu(m) I, *telētu(m), teliyatu* "(the) very competent (one)" Bab. [AN.ZÍB] epith. of goddesses esp. Ištar; < *tele'û*

telītu(m) II (a musical instrument) O/jB lex.

tēlītu(m), NB also *tēlittu* "produce, harvest (tax)" Bab., M/NA, esp. *t. adri* "yield of threshing-floor"; < *elû* III D

teliyatu → *telītu* I

tēltu(m) "saying, proverb; pronunciation" Bab. [KA.KA.SI.GA] "syllabic writing" (of Sum.); lex. esp. in *ša t.* ~ "only syllabic value of sign"; < *têlu*

telû → *tulû*

tēlu "pronounced" jB in *šumu t.* "syllabic sign"; < *têlu*

tēlu → also *tīlu* I

têlu(m) ~ "to pronounce (exactly)" O/jB **G** lex. **D** ~ "mark exactly"? OB; > *tēlu, tēltu*; *têlišam*

telūtu MB for *etellūtu* or abstr. noun from *tele'û* ?

temdum mng. unkn. OB lex.

temennu → *temmēnu*

tēmēqu → *tēmīqu*

temēru(m), *tamāru* "to cover (in earth), bury" Bab., NA **G** (*i/i*) boundary-stone; figurine; ext. "cover" part of liver **D** ~ G **Š** caus. of G; > *temrum*; *timru*; *timertum*; *tumurtu*?; *netmertu*; → *umāru*; *tumru*

temēšu, *timēšu* "forgiving" jB; < *mêšu*

tēmīqu(m), *tēmēqu(m)*; pl. m. & f. "(deep) prayer" Bab.; also OB(Susa) (a rental payment); < *emēqu* I

temkûm "neglect, abandonment" OB; < *mekû* V

temmēnu(m), *timmēnu(m)*, *te/i(m)mennu* "foundation; foundation document" Bab., M/NA [TEMEN] "base, foundation" of wall; also transf. of deity; word; OB (inscribed peg)?; "foundation document" (pl. before 800 BC); < Sum.

temrum, *timru* (a cultic meal)? Mari, of Dumuzi; jB lex. in *nūn t.* (a baked fish); < *temēru*

têmtum → *tiāmtu*

temû → *tamû* II

tēnânû ~ "seeking change" jB of dissident; < *enû* III

tenēštu(m), OA *tanēštum* ?; pl. *tenēšētu(m)*, NA *tanēšētu* "people" Bab., NA sg. "personnel"; pl. "human kind"; < *nêšu*; → *tānīštum*; *tenīšu*

teniḫu/û (a bed) jB lex.

tēnintu, *tēnindu* "weeping, lamentation" jB; < *utnēnu* II

tēnīnu(m), *tīnīnu(m)* "weeping, lamentation" O/jB; < *utnēnu* II

tēnīqu(m) "suckling" O/jB "act of suckling" a child; "payment (to nurse) for suckling"; "child being suckled"; < *enēqu*

tenīšu Bogh. for *tenēštu*

tēnītum "relief, replacement" Mari of troops; < *enû* III G(t)

tenšû; Aram. pl. *tenšīyā* (precious metal dress-ornament) NB

tēnû(m), NB also *te'nû* "substitute" Bab., NA of clothes etc. "change, spare"; of men, animals "substitute", "replacement for"; < *enû* III Gt

tenūru → *tinūru*

tepper ~ "supreme judge" OB(Susa), NB/NA?, in Elam; < Elam.

teptītum, *taptētu(m)* "opening up (land), (field in) new cultivation" O/jB *eqel t.*; "contract for cultivation of new land"; < *petû* II D

têpum → *têbum*

tēqītu(m) "ointment, anointing" Bab., M/NA [MAR] for eyes; "paste" for inlay work etc.; < *eqû* D

teqnu → *tiqnu*

teqqûtu → *tiqqûtu*

teqrūbatum, Mari *ta/eqrībatum* "escort" OB; < *qerēbu*

têqtu → *te'iqtu*

teqûtu → *tiqqûtu*

terānu (a stone) NB

tērānû → *tīrānû*

têrātu → *tayyartu*; *têrtu*

terdennu → *tardennu*

terdennuttu, *terdennūtu* → *tardennūtu*

terdītu(m), *tardītu* "addition" Bab., NA of additional, supplementary allocation, water allowance, animal, offering, labour etc.; < *redû* I D

terdû(m), OA *tardīum* "addition(al)" OA of textiles; OB (of) "younger son"; < *redû* I D

terḫatu(m), *tirḫatu(m)*, Bogh. once *tarḫātu* "bride payment" OAkk, O/jB, MA [Alal. NÍG.MUNUS.ÚS.A/SÁ]

terḫu(m) (a beer vase) O/jB used in libations

terḫutu "crack" NB in wall; < Aram.

terigû (desig. of a door) jB lex.

teriktu, *tiriktu* (kind of reed or a corner)? jB lex.; < *tarāku* ?

terinkunnu → *tirinkunnu*

terinnu, *tirinnu*, OA phps. *tarinnum*; pl. mostly f., also *terunnātu* "cone" (of conifer) O/MA, M/NB [GIŠ.ŠE.Ù.SUḪ$_5$; mag., med. NUMUN] ext. of part of liver; of ornament in stone or metal

terīqtu(m), *tirīqtu(m)* "uncultivated, cleared land" O/jB [KANKAL]; also *eqel t.*; < *riāqu* D

Terītum (a month) OB(Terqa)

terku(m), *tirku(m)* "blow; (dark) spot" OAkk, O/jB, NA [GE$_6$] **1.** "blow" of weapon, on drum **2.** Early Mari, of part of shoe **3.** "dark marking" on face, body; "darkness" of nightfall on mountain; < *tarāku*

terkullu (desig. of animals)? jB lex.

terkullum → also *tarkullu*

terru I (or *tirru*) "forest, wood" jB lex.; < Sum.

terru II mng. unkn. Elam of sheep; < Elam.

tērsītu, *tarsītu* "preparation" M/jB "equipment" of horses, grave; for work; "prepared amount" of substance; NB astr. "ready reckoner"; < *ersû*

terṣu(m) "stretching out, extension" Bab. of finger, hand etc.; "presentation" of offering, as desig. of sheep; bread, flour; (a burial garment);

in *ina t.* for *tarṣu* III "opposite, at the time of"; < *tarāṣu* I

teršītum → *taršītum*

tertennu → *tardennu*

tertennuttu, tertennūtu → *tardennūtu*

terterru (a bird) jB lex.; < Sum.?

tertītu "joint" MB of spoke to wheel; < *retû* II D

tertum "surplus, superfluity" OB; < *watārum*

têrtu(m), *tīrtum*, OAkk *tā'ertum* "instruction" [(UZU.)UR5(.ÚŠ); (UZU.)KIN] also pl.; "commission", *bēl t.* "delegate, official"; "administrative post"; Mari *bīt t.*; of gods "directive", "omen"; Mari "oracle"; *t. epēšum, šūpušum* "to take, have taken omens"; "liver" of animal; < *wârum* D

tēru(m), *tīru(m)*; pl. f. *tē/īrāni, tē/īrātē* (an archit. term) Early Mari, O/jB

tēru → also *tīru* I

ter'u (a plant) jB lex.

tērubtu(m) "entry, entrance" O/jB, MA to city; "entry" into temple; MA "bringing in" of tablet; < *erēbu* I

terunnātu → *terinnu*

tērušum "cultivation" OB lex. (with seed plough)?; < *erēšu* I

teslītu(m), OA *taslītum*, j/NB also *ta/eṣlītu*, *ta/ešlītu* "appeal, prayer" [A.RA.ZU] to man, king, deity; < *sullû* I, *ṣullû*

tespītu(m) "prayer" O/jB; < *suppû* II

teṣētu(m) ~ "suspension of work"? Ass.; < *ṣê'u*

tēṣētu, *tēṣītu* "quarrel, contest" jB; → *waṣûm* Št

tēṣītum "lease" OB(Susa) with *eqlum* ("field"); → *waṣûm* Š

tēṣītu → also *tēṣētu*

teṣû(m), *tezû(m)* "to defecate" O/jB **G** (*i/i*) **Gtn** iter.; > *tēṣû*; → *ezûm* I

tēṣû, *tēzû* "liable to diarrhoea" jB lex.; < *teṣû*

tēṣubū, *tēṣupū* pl. tant. "addition(al payment)" OA; < *waṣābum*; → *tiṣābu*

tešê → *tešiā*

tešēnu, *tušēnu* (kind of buffalo)? M/NA; → *tišānum*

tēšertu, *tēširtu* ~ "supplement(ary payment)" M/NB usu. of silver, gold; < *ešēru* ?

***tešiā**, Mari *tešê* "ninety"; < *tiše*

tēširtu → *tēšertu*

tešît(um) → *tiše*

teškītu (or *tešqītu*) mng. unkn. NB in *kurummāti ša t.*

tešlītu → *teslītu*

Tešmētu → *Tašmētu*

tešmû(m), *tašmû* "attention, listening" OAkk, O/jB usu. of deity to prayer; < *šemû*

tešqītu → *teškītu*

tešû → *tišû*

tēšû(m) "confusion, chaos" Bab. [SÙḪ] of political disruption; battle; < *ešû* IV

tēšû → also *šēšû*

tetēlum mng. unkn. Mari, in basket of *t.*

tetennu → *titennu* I

tetentu "island"? jB lex.

tetlu ~ "a notable"? jB lex. (error ?)

tē'u "covered, gummed up" jB of eyes; < *tê'u*

tē'u → also *tī'u* I

tê'u, Susa *te'û(m)* "to cover (up)" O/jB **G** (pret. *itē'*) usu. unfavourable action; eyes; of demons, mountain "cover over, smother" person **Gtn** iter. of G **D** OB(Susa) ~ "oppress"; > *tē'u*

te'uššu "eagle" or "vulture" jB lex.; < Sum.

te'ûtu → *ti'ûtu*

tezû → *teṣû*

tēzû → *tēṣû*

tēzubtum "leave, time off" OB; < *ezēbu*

tezzimtu → *tazzimtu*

tiālu(m), *ti'ālu(m), ti(')āru(m), liāru* (a tree and its wood) 'white cedar' [GIŠ.EREN.BABBAR]; → *tâlu*

tiāmtu(m), *tâmtu(m)*, Mari etc. also *têmtum*, *tâm/ndu, tâw/matu*; jB pl. also *timiāti* "sea; lake" [A.AB.BA; OB also AB]; M/NB, NA also *Māt-t.* "Sea-land"; as DN *Tiāmat* etc.; → *tâmû*

ti(')āru → *tiālu*

tiat → *tīyatu*

tiban "deben" Am.; Eg. weight of 910 grams; < Eg.

tibbuttum, *timbuttu/ūtu, ti(b)buttu/ūtu*, jB also *tambūtu*?, *timbu'u, tibu'u* (a musical instrument, phps.) "drum" OAkk, O/jB; MB (an ornament); *t. eqli* 'field-drum' (a plant)

tibku(m), Ass. also *tikpu* "outpouring, deposit" of water, grain; "detritus" of mountain; "layer, course" of brickwork; < *tabāku*

tibnu(m) "straw, chaff" [(ŠE.)IN.NU(.DA); MB also IN; NA also ŠE.IN.NI]; in *šāt t.* (a sparrow)

tibûm mng. unkn. OB lex.

tību(m), *tēbu(m)* "arousal, attack" Bab. [ZI(.GA); Susa KUR] "onslaught" in battle; "uprising" against state; "attack" of animal; "onset" of wind, storm; *t. šēr(t)i* "dawn"; *t. iltāni, šūti* "place from which the north, south wind rises"; *t. šaddû* "rising of north-east wind" (a feature of liver); "appearance, occurrence" of good, evil; "jerk, twitch" of part of body; "projection" on liver; < *tebû*

tību → *tēbû*

tibulû(m) "lute" jB lex.; < Sum.

tibūtu → *tibbuttum*

tibûtu(m), *tebûtu(m)* "rise, attack" [ZI-; ZI.GA; Susa KUR] of wind, troops, weapons; "call up, levy" of troops; "uprising" of usurper etc.; sexual "arousal"; "swarm(ing)" of locusts, fish etc.; < *tebû*

tibu'u → *tibbuttum*

tidennu → *titennu*

tidennūtu → *titennūtu*

tidintu, *tidittu* "gift" NA; < *tadānu*

tīdīqu → *tēdīqu*

tidirtum mng. unkn. OB

tidittu → *tidintu*

tidūku(m) "combat, strife" O/jB; < *dâku* Gt (→ GAG §36a)

tiggû → *tigû* I

tigidû (a libation vessel) jB lex; < Sum.

tigi(l)lû/u, *tegi(l)lû*; pl. f. ~ "colocynth" M/jB [(Ú.)ÚKUŠ.TI.GI.LI/GÍL.LA/GI.LA and var.] as drug; phps. also a bird [TI.GI.(IL.)LA.MUŠEN and var.]; < Sum.?

tig(i)rillu(m) (an obstetric anomaly) O/jB

tigītu → *tigû* II

tigrillu → *tigirillu*

tigû(m) I, *tiggû*, *tegû* "(a kind of) drum" O/jB [possibly URUDU.NÍG.KALA.GA]; also a kind of Sum. song; < Sum.; > *tigû* II

tigû II; f. *ti/egītu(m)* "drummer" O/jB; < *tigû* I + *-ī*

ti'iltu mng. unkn. jB lex.

ti'ittu → *tittu*

ti'ītu (part of a building)? NB

tikanītu → *teknītu*

tikiltu(m), *takiltu* "reliability" O/jB; < *takālu*

tikiptum "spot(ting), blemish" OB ext.; < *takāpu*

tīkītu → *tēkītu*

tikku(m); pl. f. "neck" OAkk?, Bab., of human, animal; pl. also of single individual; liter. and transf.; *(ša) t.* "neck ornament"; Nuzi "neck armour"; NB "neck(-load)"? of grain etc.; of part of object; Nuzi "bank" of watercourse

tikku → also *tīku*

tiklātu mng. unkn. Nuzi in *ša tiklāti*, of persons, chairs

tiklu "help, support" M/jB(Ass.), Ug.; esp. in pl. of gods as "helpers"; < *takālu*

tikmēnu → *ṭikmēnu*

tiknītum → *teknītu*

tikpu "spot, patch" M/NA, j/NB on animal; stone; liver; moon; *t. santakki* "cuneiform wedge mark"; < *takāpu*

tikpu → also *tibku*

tiktu → *diktu*

tīku(m), *tikku* "(rain)drop, shower" Bab. [BI.IZ; also ÚTU]; *t. šamê* "rain"; also of hail; < *natāku*

tīlāniš, *tillāniš* "into ruin mounds" j/NB [DUL-*niš*]; < *tīlu* I

til'etu → *be'tu*

tilgūtu mng. unkn. j/NB lex.; < Aram.?

tīliltu → *tēliltu*

tilim(a)tu, Bogh. occas. *telentu* (a drinking vessel) M/jB [(DUG.)TI.LIM.DÀ]

tīlišam "into ruin mounds" OB; < *tīlu* I

tillakurdu → *tillaqurdu*

tillāniš → *tilāniš*

tillaqurdu, *tillakurdu* (a medicinal plant) jB

tillatu(m) I "help; reinforcement" O/jB [ILLAT] of deities "support", esp. in PN; military "assistance, reinforcement(s); allies"; in *qān t.*, *t. eleppi* (a piece of boat equipment); > *tillūtu*

tillatu II "vine" jB, NA; also of tamarisk(-shoot?)

tillenû mng. unkn. jB(Ass.)

tillu, *tillû(m)* "appendage, trappings" Bab., M/NA "attachments" to ceremonial clothing?; to weapons, horses, chariots; to figurines; also NA (a kind of wool)

tillu → also *tīlu* I

tillû → *tillu*

tillūtu(m) "assistance" O/jB [Bogh. ILLAT]; < *tillatu* I

tilmu (syn. of *talīmu*) jB lex.

tilmunnû "of Tilmun" O/jB of a type of date palm; of copper; of ship faring to Tilmun; < PlN Tilmun

tilmuttum (a musical instrument) Mari; < PlN Tilmun?

tilpānu(m) f. "bow" Bab. [GEŠPU] as weapon; lit. divine weapon; math. as shape, also in similes; jB (a kind of bread)

tilti → *tiše*

tilû → *tulû*

tīlu(m) I, *tillu*, *tēlu*; pl. Nuzi, jB, NA *ti(l)lānu/i* "(ruin) mound" [DU$_6$]; also "mound, heap" of grain; > *tilāniš*, *tīlišam*

tīlu II (a fish) Ug., jB, lex.

timāli, *timālu*, Am. *tumāl* "yesterday" Ass., O/jB; > *timāliattam*; → *amšāli*

timāliattam "on previous day" OB lex.; < *timāli*

timālu → *timāli*

timbuttu, timbūtu → *tibbuttum*

timertum, *timirtum* "secret, buried deposit" Mari; < *temēru*

timēšu → *temēšu*

timiraš (desig. of a horse) MB; < Kass.

timirtum → *timertum*

timītu → *tiāmtu* pl.

timmēnu → *temmēnu*

timmu, *dimmu*, Nuzi lex. *teammu* "post, pillar" M/NA, Nuzi, j/NB "pole, rod"; "stake" for impalements; archit. "column"; < Sum.

timmuššatu → *dimmuššatu*

timru "buried (figurine)" NA; < *temēru*

timru → also *temrum*

tim'um "oath" OA in *t. tamā'um*; < *tamû* II

tīnānu/û 'fig-like' (a kind of apple tree) jB lex.; < *tittu*

tīnātu → *tittu*

tindû (a lyre)? jB lex.; → *tintu*

tīnīnu → *tēnīnu*

tinnar (an object) jB lex.; < Elam.

tinnû, tinnûtu → *dinnû*

tintu jB lex. = *tittu* or *tindû* ?

tīnu (a fruiting shrub) jB lex.; → *tittu*

tinūru(m), *tenūru* "oven, tannour" Bab., M/NA [IM.ŠU.RIN.NA; DILINA; DÍLINA; NINDU] domestic cooking "oven"; craftsman's; astr. (a star/planet, constellation)

tipiššu "barn, straw-store" Nuzi; < Hurr.

tippallennu, *tuppallennu* (an official) Alal., Ug.; < Hurr.

tiqnu(m), *teqnu*; pl. m. & f. ~ "proper equipment, ornament" OA, M/NB; < *taqānu*

ti(q)qû(m) ~ "flashing"? O/jB of eyes; > *tiqqûtu*

ti(q)qûtu, *te(q)qûtu* ~ "flashing eyes" jB; < *tiqqû*

tîqtu → *te'iqtu*

tiqû → *tiqqû*

tīrānu I pl. tant. "coils" O/jB [ŠÀ.NIGIN] of intestine; "curls" of hair; MB "braid" on textile; < *tīru* II

tīrānu II "mercy" jB; < *târu*

tīrānû, *tērānû* "merciful" jB; < *tīrānu* II

tirḫatu → *terḫatu*

tiridānum (a burdened man)? OB lex.

tiriktu → *teriktu*

tirimtu, *tirindu* (a drinking vessel)? jB, NA

tirinkunnu, *terinkunnu* (a usage, application) Nuzi; < Hurr.

tirinnu → *terinnu*

tiriptum "discoloration" OA; < *tarāpu*

tirīqtu → *terīqtu*

tirišu (a saddle)? jB

tirku → *terku*

tirratu → *dirratu*

tirru → *terru* I

tîrtum → *têrtu*

tīru(m) I, *tēru(m)* (a courtier) OAkk, Bab. [LÚ.TIRUM]

tīru II "coil" NA (sg. of *tīrānu* I), of intestine; of gold; < *târu*

tīru III (a covering) j/NB of precious metal "overlay"

Tīrum IV (a month) OB, phps. also OAkk

tīru → also *šīru*; *tēru*

tirugallu (a bird) NB; → *tarlugallu*

tisappum (a textile)? OA

tisa(r)ru, once *tiserru* (a topog. term) M/NA

tisḫu → *tišḫu*

tisi(s)sum (a wooden object) OB

tisīsu → *šisītu* II

tisītu → *šisītu* I.II

tiskar → *tiskur*

tiskarinnum → *taskarinnu*

tiskur, *tiskar*, *tišku/ar*, *šiškur*, *tuškar* (a plant) Nuzi, jB

tīsu → *šīsu*

tiṣābu ~ NA "addition(al amount)"?; < *waṣābum*; → *tēṣubū*

tiṣburu → *ṣabāru* I Gt

tiṣbuttum **1.** OB, Susa "combat, quarrel" **2.** jB [DAB.DAB-] "interlocking, knot"; < *ṣabātu* Gt

tiṣbutu "clasping one another" Am., of gold rings; < *ṣabātu* Gt

tiṣītu → *šisītu* II

tiṣmuru → *ṣamāru* Gt

tiṣṣulu mng. unkn. jB lex.; < *eṣēlu* ?

tišānum; f. *tišānītum* (a wild animal) OB; → *tešēnu*

tīšāriš "into a steppe" NB(lit.); < *tūšaru* 1

tišaru Ug. lex. (var. of *tūšaru* ?)

tīšārum → *tūšaru*

tišât "a ninth (part)" OB; < *tiše*

tišattalu → *šitaddaru*

tīšā'u → *dīšā'u*

tiše; f. *ti/ešē/ît(um)*, jB also *tilti* "nine"; > *tišīšu*, *tišû*, *tišât*; *tušu'a*, *tušu'û*; *tešiā*; *tašā'iu*

tišettena pl. (desig. of clothing) Alal.; < Hurr.

tišḫu (or *tisḫu*, *diš/sḫu*) (a cut of meat) NA in pl. *t/diš/sḫāni*

tišīšu "nine times" OB and elsewhere wr. 9-*šu*; < *tiše*

tišît(um) → *tiše*

tišīu → *tišû*

tiškar → *tiskur*

tiškû (or *diškû*) (a kind of table) jB lex.

tiškur → *tiskur*

tišnu (a metal vessel) Alal., Nuzi (Hurr. pl. *tišnuḫḫena*); < Hurr.?

tišqāru → *tizqāru*

tišša'e mng. unkn. Nuzi in *abul t.*

tišû(m), *tešû*, MA *tiš(ā)īu* **1.** "ninth" (in order) [9.KAM] **2.** "a ninth" (part) [IGI.9.GÁL]; < *tiše*

titāpū pl. tant ~ "beer mash" O/jB, NA [TITAB(=BARAG.MUNU$_4$)]; < Sum.

titarru → *titūrum*

tit'āru → *šit'āru*

titassû → *šasû* Gtn

titennu I, *tetennu* "hay fork" M/jB, also transf. of king *t. ša nakirē* "h. of foes"

titennu II, *tidennu* ~ "(substitute as) pledge" Nuzi; < Hurr.

titennūtu, *tidennūtu*, *dit/dennūtu* "indenture, (status of) pledge"; Nuzi of persons, also animals; fields; < Hurr.

titipu (a fruit, its tree) NA

titirru → *titūrum*

tîtiš → *tîtum*

titkurru (a bird) jB

tittu(m), *ti'(it)tu*; pl. *tīnātu(m)* "fig (tree)" [GIŠ.PÈŠ]; OA also in MN *waraḫ tīnātim*; > *tīnānu*; → *tintu*; *tīnu*; *tī'u* I

tîtum, *te'ītum* "nourishment (food)" O/jB; *tîtiš (ilī)* "for the gods' food"; < *ta'û*

ti'tu → *tittu*

titūrum, *titurru*, Ug. *tita/irru* f. "bridge"; jB *t. qablītim*, *t. išartim* (intervals between lyre strings); part of ornament; feature on liver

tityāru → *šit'āru*

tium (or *dium* ?) uncert. OAkk, OB

tī'u I, occas. *tē'u* "fig" Qatna, jB; → *tittu*

tī'u II, *tû* "nourishment, sustenance"? jB; < *ta'û*

ti'ûtu, *te'ûtu* "nourishment, sustenance" M/jB for humans, animals; MB "appurtenance"? of chariot; < *ta'û*

tiwītum (a song) OB; < *tawûm*

tiyāru → *tayyāru* I

tīyatu, occas. *tiat* (a medicinal plant) M/NB, NA

tizqāru(m), *tišqāru* "exalted, prominent" Bab. as epith. of deities, king; in PN; < *zaqāru*

tû(m) I "incantation(-formula)" O/jB [TU$_6$]; < Sum.

tû II "garment" jB lex; < Sum.

tû → also *di'u* II; *tī'u* II

tū'a, *tūya* "spider" jB lex.

tū(')amtu(m), *tū'imtum*, NB *tūmamtu*, NA *tū'intu* "twin, twinned (item)" O/jB, NA **1.** "twin sister" **2.** "double door" [OB GIŠ.IG MAŠ.TAB.BA] **3.** lex., Mari "double vessel" **4.** "double pouch, saddle bags?" **5.** also of garments, plants ?; < *tū'amu*

tū(')amu(m), *tu'īmum*, NB also *tūm(=w)amu*, NA *tu'û* "twin" [MAŠ.TAB.BA] of men, deities; animals; plants; vessels, parts of building; parts of liver; astr. (a constellation → *māšu*); > *tū'amtu*; *ta''umu*; *tu''umu* I

tuānu (desig. of horse) NA

tuāru → *târu*

tuballaṣ-qinnassa 'she ...s her rump' jB lex,, bird-name, syn. of *ballūṣītu* 1; < *balāṣu* II

tubalû(m) "belt (for climbing palm trees)" Bab.; also jB "support" for brickwork

tubāqu, NA also *du(b)bāqu* ~ "trap, snare" jB, NA; esp. *iṣṣūr t.* (a species of bird)

tubāru(m) (a textile)? O/jB, Mari

tubašinnu → *dabašinnu*

tubbuku(m) **1.** OB lex. (desig. of lame person) **2.** OAkk "deposited" of grain **3.** jB of textile mng. unkn.; < *tabāku* D

tubku "(ruin) heap" M/jB; < *tabāku*

tubku → also *tubuḫtu*

tublu, *dublu* ~ "foundation trench" jB; → *dubur*

tubqinnu; pl. f. "hole, hollow" M/jB, NA of unpleasant place; < *tubqu* ?

tubqu(m); pl. *tub(u)qātu(m)* "corner, recess" OAkk, Bab. [UB]; > *tubqû*; *tubuqtu*; *tubqinnu*?

tubqû "born in the corner" NB in fPN *Tubqītu*; < *tubqu*

tubru(m) (or *tupru(m)*) (an object)? O/jB, MA

tubuḫtu, *tubku* (a kind of leather)? MB, Nuzi

tubukkû (an offering of grain) M/jB; < *tabāku*

tubuqqu mng. unkn. jB comm.

tubuqtu "corner" jB lex., Nuzi?; < *tubqu*

tuddû, Nippur *šuddû* **D** "to make known, acknowledge" NB stat.; < *uddû* secondary formation (→ *wadûm* D)

tudellu (a bird) jB lex.; < Sum.

tudittu(m), *dudittu(m)*; pl. *t/dudinā/ētu(m)* (a dress-pin) on woman's breast

tuduqqû "spoken formula" jB [TU$_6$.DUG$_4$.GA] in incantation; < Sum.

tugāgu ~ "animals, animal life" jB lex.

tugānû, *šugānû*, *utugānû* ~ "spray, bunch" of fruit NA

tugānu(m), *dugānu(m)* (an illness) O/jB

tugāru(m), *tuqāru* "deposited material, deposition"? O/jB

tugunu → *tuqnu*

tuḫallu(m); pl. m. & f. "palm-leaf basket" Bab., MA

tuḫarum, *duḫarum* mng. unkn. OB, desig. of carnelian ?

tuḫḫanzunu mng. unkn. Nuzi

tuḫḫu(m) usu. pl. "residue, waste product" OAkk, Bab., OA [DUḪ] in food and beer processing; < Sum.; → *dišiptuḫḫu*

tuḫlu, occas. *tu'lu* (a medicinal plant) jB

tuḫlulu "(a species of) juniper" jB lex.

tuḫnu → *duḫnu*

tuḫpu (or *duḫpu*); pl. f. (an object) NB

tuḫpur (or *duḫpur*) (a plant) jB lex.

tuḫru → *šaḫūrum* II

tuḫšiwe (a kind of wool) Nuzi; < prob. Hurr. form of *dušû* I

tuḫtuḫānum (a festival)? OA, as date

tuḫūmu → *taḫūmu*

tu'iltu → *tûltu*

tu'imme(u)zubalû (a meat sauce) jB lex.; < Sum.

tū'imtum → *tū'amtu*

tu'īmum → *tū'amu*

tū'intu → *tū'amtu*

tu'issu → *tûltu*

tukantibalā'um (a leather bag) OB(Susa) lex.; < Sum.

tukerru, *tukarru* (textile remnant)? jB lex.

tu(k)kannu(m) f. "(leather) bag, pouch" O/jB [KUŠ.DÙG.GAN] for precious items, diviner's equipment; transf. *tukkann(āt) iškī* "scrotum"; < Sum.

tukku(m) I; pl. f. "alarm, warning" Bab.; with *šemû(m)* ("to hear"), *nadû(m)* ("to convey"); > *tukumma*?

tukku II; pl. *tukkāti*, *tukkāni/u* "(act of) oppression" NA, NB; < W.Sem.?; → *takāku*

tukkultum "encouragement" OB; < *takālu* D

tukkulu "encouraged" NB(Nippur) as PN; < *takālu* D

tuklātānu "trustworthy" jB; < *tukultu*

tuklu "help" MA, M/NB esp. in PNs; < *takālu*

tukpītu → *takpītum*

tukrišû(m), Qatna *tukrašḫu* "of Tukriš(-style)" O/MB of metal items, wool; < PlN Tukriš

tukšu(m) "(leather) shield" Bab.

tuktû pl. tant. "requital, vengeance" j/NB, NA *t. turru*, *râbu* "to exact vengeance"

tuktukku mng. unkn. jB; < Sum.?

tukultu(m) "trust" [GISKIM; NIR; GIŠ.TUKUL-; NB in PN once BÀD.MAḪ] "reliance (on), trust (in)" deity; "object of trust, support"; "supporting troops"; of food supply, watercourse "sustenance"; *āl tuklāte* "supply city"; *t. qinnati* (part of buttocks); < *takālu*; → *takaltu*

tukumma "come on, then" jB; < *tukku* I ?

tuldu, *tultu* (a medicinal plant) jB lex.

tulēmu, *tuli/e'u* (part of a chariot) MB of wood, gold

tulḫu (a medicinal plant) jB

tulīmātu → *atulīmānu*

tulīmu → *tulēmu*; *ṭulīmu*

tuli'u → *tulēmu*

tullal 'you purify' (a soap plant) jB; < *elēlu* II D

tullû I "encrusted, inlaid" Am. of ivory; < *tullû* II

tullû II **D** "to accoutre, bedeck (with)" Nuzi?, jB with jewellery, quiver; stat. of deity with aura; Nuzi of well, uncert.; > *tullû* I

tullugu mng. unkn. j/NB lex.

tullukum D mng. unkn. OB lex.

tullultu → *tallultu*

tullulu D "to harness, equip" jB, NA; > *tallultu*, *tallulu*; → *talālu*

tullumum D mng. unkn. OB lex.

tulmittum (a garden tool) OB(Susa)

tultu "cistern" jB lex. also NA, mng. uncert.

tultu → also *tuldu*; *tulūlu*

tûltu(m), MB *tu'iltu*, NA *tu'issu* "worm" O/jB, NA; as cause of toothache; "worm(-shaped)" objects; of wool, jewellery; (a constellation)

tulû(m), later also *ti/elû* "breast" Bab., NA of human (male and female); *appi t.* "nipple"; of sheep; (a kind of bowl), also "hub-cap" of waggon, (part of oar)

tūlu → *tulūlu*

tu'lu → *tuḫlu*

tulūlu, also *utullu* ?, *tul(t)u* ? "raincloud" jB lex.

tūma, *tūmu* mng. unkn. jB lex.

tumāgu (a kind of flour) jB lex.

tumaḫḫu/û (a ceremonial garment) M/jB [TÚG.MAḪ]; < Sum.

tumāl → *timāli*

tumāmītu(m) "oath(-taking)" O/jB; < *tamû* II

tumāmu, *tumātu* (a kind of tamarisk) jB lex.

tumāmu → also *dumāmu* I

tūmamu → *tū'amu*

tumānu "wooden beam" jB lex.; > *tumānû*?

tumānû (an animal) jB (rodent frequenting beams ?); < *tumānu* ?

tumātu → *tumāmu*

tumbû mng. unkn. NB

tumbunātu (or *dumbunātu*) (a fatty pasty) jB lex.

tummāmu → *dumāmu* I

tummu "1/4 shekel" Nuzi; < Hurr.

tumnarpu "four-year-old" Nuzi of animals; < Hurr.

tumnatala "four-legged" Alal. of chair; < Hurr.

tumnātu "four-wheeled? chariot" Nuzi; < Hurr.

tumru(m), NB also *tūru* "(glowing) charcoal, ashes" O/jB [NE.MUR.RA] esp. *akal t.* "charcoal baked loaf"

tumšā[...] mng. unkn. jB lex.

tūmu mng. unkn. jB lex.; < Sum.?

tūmu → also *tūma*

tūmulu ~ "advantage"? NA

tumunsallu "quarter-shekel" Am.; < Hurr.

tumurtu "ant's eggs" jB; < *temēru* ?

tumušše "four-..." Qatna, of gold vessel; < Hurr.

tunaniptuḫlu (an official) Nuzi; < PlN Tunana/ip- + *-uḫlu*

tungallu (a stringed instrument) jB lex.; < Sum.

tuniqānu (a shorn sheep) jB lex.

tunšu, *tuššu*, *tunzu* (a ceremonial garment) M/NB *ēpiš t.* "*t.* maker"; < phps. = *tūzu* ?

tupninnu(m) "box, casket" O/jB, NA of wood, ivory; < Hurr.?

tuppaḫḫurāti mng. unkn. Nuzi in *eqel t.*

tuppallennu → *tippallennu*

tuppānu mng. unkn. jB lex.; < Sum.?

tuppanūri (Hitt. royal official) Ug.

tuppinnu → *tappinnu*

tuppisannu (wooden container) jB

tuppu "mark on skin, mole" jB, Susa

tuppu → also *ṭuppu*

tuppussû → *duppussû*

tupru → *tubru*

tupšarratu → *ṭupšarratu*

tupšarru → *ṭupšarru*

tupšarrūtu → *ṭupšarrūtu*

tupšikkānum in *ṣāb tupšikkānim* "earth-moving troops" Mari

tupšikku(m), *šupšikkum*, *dupšikku*; pl. f. "brick-carrying frame; earth basket" OAkk, Bab., NA [GI/GIŠ.DUSU]; "forced labour, corvée"; OB *(ṣābum) nāš(i) t.* [UN.ÍL ?] "earth-carrying troops"; *ilku (u) t.* "military and civilian service"

tupšīmātu → *ṭupšīmātu*

tupšinnu (a tablet container) jB; < Sum.; → *ṭuppu*

tuptu(m) "footstool"? O/jB

tuptû mng. unkn. jB lex. in *šam t.* (a plant)

tūpu mng. unkn. jB lex.; < *tâpu*

tuputupu (a game) MB

tuqāru → *tugāru*

tuqmatum → *tuqumtu*

tuqnu(m), *tuq/gunu* **1.** Bab. (a headband)? pl.f. **2.** NA "good order", esp. in PNs; < *taqānu*

tuqqunu "laid out in order" NB of wool; < *taqānu* D

tuqumtu(m), *tuquntu*, *tuquttu*, *tuqmatum* "battle" Bab.(lit.) [GIŠ.LAL]

tuqunu → *tuqnu*

tūra "again" NA, NB liter. "come back!" imper. vent.; < *târu*

turāḫu(m), occas. *tarāḫum* "wild goat, mountain goat" [DÀRA]; also as figurines; in PNs

turānu "bearded man"? jB lex.

turaqu mng. unkn. jB comm.

turāšu(m), *turēzu*, *turazzu* "harvest" O/MA, Nuzi; OA "harvested crop"; "harvest time"

turā'u (a kind of wool) Nuzi; < Hurr.?

tur'azu → *šer'azum*

turazzu → *turāšu*

turba(l)lû "bare ground" jB lex., comm.

turba'u, turbu, turbu'/ttu → *tarbu'tu*

turdirayu (a class of person) NB

turēzu → *turāšu*

turgumannum → *targumannu*

turinnum (or *durinnum*) (a space, room) OA

turišḫi "west" Nuzi; < Hurr.

turku "dark marking" jB on liver; < *tarāku*

turminabandû (a type of mottled stone) "breccia" M/NB, NA [NA4.DÚR.MI.NA.BÀN.DA] for building, amulets; < Sum.

turminû "breccia, mottled stone" M/NB [NA4.DÚR.MI.NA] for buildings, amulets; < Sum.

turmu(m) (a granary) OB, Nuzi

turnippakkum → *tarnappakkum*

turqu (a plant) jB

turru 'turned' **1.** JB lex. of day *ūmu t.* "midday"? **2.** NB astr. of month of 29 (not 30) days ? **3.** jB lex. desig. of person; < *târu* D

turru → also *ṭurru*

turruṣum "directed" OB of face; < *tarāṣu* I D ?

turrūtu "turning, reversion" NA; < *turru*

turšummum, *šuršummum* (a prebend)? OB

turtannu, turtānu, turtennu → *tartānu*

tūrtu(m) "turning, reversion" Bab., M/NA med. of eyes; MA leg. "abrogation"?; mag. "requital, reversion" of evil to s.o.; NB "reply"; < *târu* D

turturrû → *tutturru*

turû "(a kind of) garlic" M/jB with one bulb [SUM.(SAR.)ŠIR.AŠ (→ *tatturru*)]

tūru(m) "return, retreat" OAkk, Bab., MA; in PNs "refuge"?; < *târu*

tūru → also *tumru*

turubla (or *turupla*) (a plant) jB lex.

turubu → *tarbu'tu*

turuḫtānum (a container for beer) OA

turunnu I "hen, cock"? Bogh. lex.; → *durummu*

turu(n)nu II (a setting) Qatna, in gold, for precious stones; < Hurr.?

turu'u (a cry) jB

turupla → *turubla*

turzu "butterfly" jB lex.; → *tarmāṣu*

tusiggû (a kind of soup)? jB lex.; < Sum.

tusinnum → *dusinnum*

tuskû, *tuškû* (a mineral) jB as ingredient of glass; as drug

tūṣâtu "sprout, shoot"? jB lex.; < *waṣûm*

tuṣinnum → *dusinnum*

tuṣirtum (or *tuzirtum*) (part of a house) OB

tuša, *tušām(a)*, *t/šuššāma*, lex. also *tuššāmaki* (ptcl. expressing unreality or potentiality) "it could have been that", "it was as though"; < *tuššu* ?

tušaru ~ (a pouch) jB lex.; also "cocoon" of caterpillar

tūšaru, *tūšāru*, *tīšārum* O/jB, NA **1.** "plain, flat land", Ass. *mitḫuṣ* (etc.) *t.* "pitched battle" **2.** gesture of "prostration" in prayer; < *wašārum*; > *tīšāriš*; → *tišaru*

tušēnu → *tešēnu*

tuškar → *tiskur*

tuškû → *tuskû*

tušru (a plant) jB comm.; → *kušru* I

tuššāma(ki) → *tuša*

tuššu(m); pl. f. "hostile, malicious talk" O/jB; > *taššītu*?; *tuša*?

tuššu → also *tunšu*

tušu'a "ninefold" OB; also loc.-adv. *tušûm*; < *tiše*

tušu'û adv. "on the ninth day" jB; < *tiše*

tutiwe (a piece of armour) Nuzi, in bronze; < Hurr.

tuttu "mulberry (tree)" NB; < Aram.

tuttubu(m); pl. f. (a woollen fabric)? O/jB, MA; < Hurr.?

tuttu(r)ru(m), *turturrû* ~ "leaf"? O/jB in jewellery; ~ "patch" of oil on water

tutumšu mng. unkn. jB lex.

tu'u → *di'u* II

tu'û → *tū'amu*

tu''umu I "double, twin" NB of building part; < *tū'amu*; NA → *ta''umu*

tu''umu II, NA *ta''umu* **D** "to reconsider, ponder"? jB, NA; NB(Achaem.) ~ "govern"; > *mute''imu*

tūwamtu → *tū'amtu*

tūwamu → *tū'amu*

tuwaršinnum (a cereal) Mari; < Hurr.?

tūya → *tū'a*

tuzaḫannu (a kind of soup) jB lex.; < Sum.

tuzirtum → *tuṣirtum*

tuziznakku (a fish sauce) jB lex.; < Sum.

tūzu, *tuzzu* (a ceremonial garment) jB lex.; = *tunšu* ?

tûzubalû (a meat sauce) jB lex.; < Sum.

tuzzu → *tūzu*

Ṭ

ṭabāḫu(m) "to slaughter" **G** (*a/u*) animal; human **D** ~ G **Dtn** iter. **N** "be slaughtered"; > *ṭabḫu*; *ṭābiḫu*, *ṭābiḫūtu*, *ṭabbiḫu*; *naṭbaḫu*; *ṭibḫu*?

ṭābātu(m) "vinegar" O/jB [A.GEŠTIN.NA; BIL.LÁ] also as drink; < *ṭābu*

ṭabā'u → *ṭebû*

ṭabbiḫu "butcher" MB for *ṭābiḫu*

ṭabbi'u (a diving fowl) jB lex.; < *ṭebû*

ṭabḫu(m) "slaughtered" O/jB of sheep; < *ṭabāḫu*

ṭābiḫu(m) "slaughterer, butcher" Bab., NA [(LÚ.)GÍR.LÁ; M/jB also ÚKUR(=GAL.ŠUBUR)] of animals; also as epith. of DN; < *ṭabāḫu*; → *ṭabbiḫu*

ṭābiḫūtu "office of (temple-)butcher" NB mostly as prebend [GÍR.LÁ]; < *ṭābiḫu*

ṭābiš "well, friendlily" Bab. [DÙG(.GA)-]; < *ṭābu*

ṭabnû → *dabnû*

ṭābtānu "doer of good" NA; < *ṭābtu*

ṭabtiš "like salt" jB; < *ṭabtu*

ṭabtu(m) "salt" [MUN; also occas. DU_{10}-] culinary; for conserving meat, fish etc.; *ṭ. šadî* "rock salt"; on saline land; > *ṭabtiš*

ṭābtu(m); late pl. also *ṭābtātu* "goodness, goodwill, good deed(s)" Bab., NA [MUN; DÙG.GA] *bēl ṭ.* "benefactor, friend"; "peace"; also *lā ṭ.* "ill-will, ill feeling"; < *ṭābu*; > *ṭābtānu*, *ṭābtūtu*

ṭābtūtu "goodwill" NB in *bēl ṭ.*; < *ṭābtu*

ṭābu(m) "good; sweet" [DÙG(.GA)] "good, sweet" of water, wine, food, incense etc.; of terrain, wind, shade; of mental or physical condition; "friendly, well-meaning" of words, attitude; "favourable" of time; Am., Bogh., Ug. *kī ṭābi* "well" (for → *ṭābiš*); *lā ṭ.* "bad; unfavourable; hostile; unhealthy"; < *ṭiābu*; > *ṭābiš*; *ṭābtu*, *ṭābūtu*

ṭâbu → *ṭiābu*

ṭābūtu, also *ṭābuttu* "friendship" MB [DÙG.GA]; < *ṭābu*

ṭāḫ → *ṭāḫu*

ṭaḫādu(m) "to flourish, be(come) luxuriant" Bab., NA **G** (*u/u*) transf. ~ "gloat over" **D** with 2 acc. "make" person, temple, house "rich in" honey, oil etc.; "supply copiously" with offerings **Dt** ~ "burst out"?, of boil; > *ṭaḫdu*; *ṭuḫdu*; *ṭuḫḫudu*

ṭaḫā'u → *ṭeḫû* I

ṭaḫdu(m); f. *ṭaḫittu(m)*, *ṭaḫuttu* "luxuriant" O/jB, NA of rain, flood, offerings; < *ṭaḫādu*

ṭaḫû → *ṭeḫû* I.II

ṭāḫ(u) "adjacent to" NB [DA; ÚS.SA.DU]; < *ṭeḫû* I; → *ṭēḫu*

ṭalṭaltu "homeless person"? jB; < Aram.?

ṭāmītu, Alal. *ṭēmītu* "(female) spinner" M/jB; < *ṭawûm*

ṭamû, Am. *ṭemû* "spun, plaited" Am., jB [NU.NU]; < *ṭawûm*

ṭamû → also *ṭawûm*

ṭāmu "clever"? jB lex.; < *ṭēmu* ?

ṭamûtu ~ "twisted cloth"? jB lex.; < *ṭawûm* ?

ṭāmûtu "spinner's work" MB; < *ṭāmītu*

ṭanāpu "to be(come) dirty" j/NB, NA **G** (*u/u*) **D** "make dirty, besmirch"; > *ṭanīpu*

ṭanīpu "rotten dates" jB lex.; < *ṭanāpu*

ṭapālu(m) "to slander, insult" O/jB **G** (*a/u*, jB *i/i*) **D** ~ G, also "disdain" oath **Dtn** iter. **Š** "disseminate slanders"; "put to shame" **N** OA "be insulted"?; > *ṭaplu*, *ṭapultu*; *ṭiplu*; *ṭuplu*; *ṭupullû*; *ṭupultum*; *ṭappilu*; *ṭupālu*?; *mušaṭpilu*

ṭapāpiš "for satiation"? jB of beer; < *ṭapāpu*

ṭapāpu ~ "to be very full, satisfied" MA, jB **G** (*u/u*); > *ṭappum*?; *ṭuppi*; *ṭapāpiš*

ṭapāru(m) ~ "to press towards" O/jB **G** (*i/i*) **D** "drive away" people, demons, animals; "remove, clear away" buildings, cloud; evil **Dtn** iter. of D **Dt** pass. of D "be driven away; removed"; → *duppuru* I

ṭapāšu(m) I ~ "broad part" of liver O/jB; < *ṭapāšu* II infin.

ṭapāšu II ~ "to be fat" jB **G** stat.; > *ṭapāšu* I; *ṭapšum*; *ṭupšu*, *ṭupuštu*; *ṭuppušu*

ṭapā'um → *ṭepû*

ṭapīḫum (a drinking vessel)? Mari

ṭapiltu → *ṭapultu*

ṭāpi'u → *dāpi'u*

ṭaplu(m) "slandered" O/jB; < *ṭapālu*

ṭapnû → *dabnû*

ṭappilu(m) "slanderous" jB lex., of person; Mari f. pl. "insults"; < *ṭapālu*

ṭappum mng. unkn. OB lex.; < *ṭapāpu* ?

ṭapšum ~ "fat"? OA desig. of tin; OB as PN; < *ṭapāšu* II

ṭapṭappum (or *dapdappum*) mng. unkn. OB

ṭapû → *tapû*; *ṭepû*

ṭâpu(m) "to twist, wind (thread)"? jB **G**

ṭap'um "spread out" Early Mari, desig. of a kind of shoe; < *ṭepû*

ṭapultu(m), *ṭapiltu* "slander, denigration" O/jB esp. *ṭ. dabābu(m)*, *qabû(m)* etc. "to speak slander"; < *ṭapālu*

ṭarādu(m) "to send off, despatch; send away" **G** (*a/u*) [SAR] person, vehicle, ship; "drive away" person, enemy, demon, illness etc. **Gtn** iter. of G **D** "drive, chase away" men, animals, demons **Dt** pass. of D OAkk **N** pass. of G; > *ṭardu*, *ṭardiš*, *ṭardūtu*; *ṭarīdum*, *ṭarīdūtu*; *ṭerdu*; *ṭārittu*; *muṭṭarridum*; → *ṭarāsu*

ṭarāru "to be bearded" jB **G** stat.; > *ṭarru*, *ṭarīru*, *ṭarrūtum*

ṭarāsu (or *ṭ/tarās/ṣu*) "to send" (person) Ug. **G** (pret. *aṭrus*); for *ṭarādu* or *tarāṣu* I ?

ṭarāšu mng. unkn. jB lex. **G**

ṭarā'u → *ṭerû*

ṭardiš "in rout"? MB; < *ṭardu*

ṭardu(m) "driven off, in flight" Bab. of person, animal; < *ṭarādu*

ṭardūtu → *ṭarīdūtu*

ṭarīdum "fugitive" OB esp. as PN; < *ṭarādu*

ṭarīdūtu(m), Susa also *ṭardūtu* "condition of fugitive" O/jB esp. *ṭ. alāku(m)* "to become a fugitive"; < *ṭarīdum*; → *ṭardūtu*

ṭarīru (a bearded person) jB lex.; < *ṭarāru*

ṭārittu 'driver away' jB desig. of an evil (plague ?); < *ṭarādu*

ṭarpa'u (a tamarisk) M/NA, Nuzi, jB

ṭarru(m) "bearded" O/jB of men; < *ṭarāru*; > *ṭarrūtum*

ṭarrû "beater" NB desig. of person; < *ṭerû*

ṭarrūtum "beardedness" OB lex.; < *ṭarru*

ṭātu(m), *ṭa'tu*, OA, OB? *dātum* "bribe, baksheesh" Bab., OA "voluntary gift" to king; OA (customs payment), *šāqil dāti(m)* (member of an influential group of persons)

ṭa'tūtu "(political) gift" jB(Ass.); < *ṭātu*

ṭa'û → *da'û*

ṭawûm, *ṭamû*, *ṭemû* "to spin, plait" Bab. **G** (*i/i*) [NU.NU] textiles, threads; > *ṭamû*, *ṭamûtu*?; *ṭīmu*, *ṭimītu*; *ṭumânu*; *ṭāmītu*, *ṭāmûtu*

ṭeāmum → *ṭêmu*

ṭeānu → *ṭênu*

Ṭebētu(m) (10th Bab. month) [ITI.AB(.BA.È); O/MB ITI.AB.È; Alal., j/NB ITI.AB (NA → *kinūnu*)]

ṭebû(m), Ass. *ṭabā'u(m)* "to sink, submerge" **G** (*u/u*) [SUD] intrans. of boat, objects "sink"; of persons, field, part of liver "be submerged"; "drown" **Gtn** iter. of G **D** [SUD] trans. "sink, submerge" ship, person, field etc.; jB transf. of facial expression "be depressed"; OA "suppress" tablet, affair; M/jB(Ass.) "sink" building into ground **Dt** pass. of G; > *ṭību*; *ṭubû*?; *ṭēbû*; *ṭabbi'u*; *ṭubbû*

ṭēbû(m); f. *ṭēbītu* **1.** OB (an underwater construction worker)? **2.** jB lex. *ṭēbītu(m)* (a ship with (deep) draught); < *ṭebû*

ṭēḫātu → *ṭēḫu*

ṭēḫēya → *ṭēḫû*

ṭeḫḫu → *ṭēḫu*

ṭeḫḫû(m), *ṭēḫû(m)* ~ "client, associate" O/jB; < *ṭeḫû* I

ṭēḫītum (a delegation, embassy)? Mari; < *ṭeḫû* I

ṭeḫû(m) I, *ṭaḫû*, Ass. *ṭaḫā'u(m)* "to be(come) near to, approach" **G** (*e/e*) [TE; DA] of person, animal; for sexual intercourse; disease, evil; ship, arrow, stair, feature in exta; OA, OB leg. "approach with request, claim"; OB of harvest "approach" **Gtn** iter. of G; astr. of stars **D** "bring close"; "introduce, bring before" s.o.; OA stat. "has claim against" s.o.; "include" s.th. with s.th.; "present" offerings; "bring" boat to land; "allow" evil etc. "to affect"; stat. "is placed next to" **Dt** pass. of D **Š** "bring near" jB; > *ṭēḫu*, *ṭāḫu*; *ṭeḫḫû*, *ṭēḫītum*; *ṭeḫûtu*; *ṭuḫḫû*

ṭeḫû II, *ṭaḫû* (desig. of an activity in bread-making) j/NB **G**; < Aram.; > *ṭēḫû*

ṭēḫu(m), *ṭīḫu(m)*, *ṭeḫḫu* (NB → *ṭāḫu*) "immediate vicinity, adjacent (place)" [DA; M/NA pseudo-log. "SUḪUR" in land and house descr.]; rit. "proximity" of patient; "side-wall"? of ship, building (pl. f.); < *ṭeḫû* I

ṭēḫû; Aram. pl. *ṭēḫēya* "spreader of bread dough"? NB; < *ṭeḫû* II

ṭēḫû → aso *ṭeḫḫû*

ṭeḫûtu(m) **1.** O/jB "clientele, associates" **2.** O/jB ~ "(built) access-road"? **3.** MB (attachment to clothing)? **4.** astr. "conjunction"? [TE- ?]; < *ṭeḫû* I

ṭē'intum → *ṭē'ittu*

ṭē'inu(m) "grinder" O/jB [phps. LÚ.ÀR.ÀR (→ *ararru*)]; < *ṭênu*

ṭē'inūtu "grinder's work" MA; < *ṭē'inu* or *ṭē'ittu*

ṭē'ittu(m), *ṭē'intum* "female grinder" OA, OB, Nuzi [phps. MUNUS.ÀR.ÀR (→ *ararratu*)]; < *ṭē'inu*

ṭēmānu "wise, reasonable" jB, NA; < *ṭēmu*

ṭēmītum ~ "wise" OAkk in fPN; < *ṭēmu*

ṭēmītu → also *ṭāmītu*

ṭemû → *ṭamû*; *ṭawûm*

ṭēmu(m); pl. m. & f. "(fore)thought, plan(ning); understanding; instruction" [UMUŠ; Susa UR] **1.** of gods, men "reason, rational thought"; "opinion, judgement" **2.** "plan, intention"; "decision" of god(s), *ṭ. ṣabātu* "to take a decision"; MB "disposal, disposition" of s.o. **3.** "instruction", *ṭ. šakānu(m)* "to convey an instruction, give order", "govern"; → *šakin ṭēmi* **4.** "report, information", *bēl ṭ.* "person making report", *ṭ. turrum* "to deliver a report", learn, hear, see "news" of **5.** Am., Bogh. "agreement, good relations"; > *ṭêmu*?; *ṭēmītum*, *ṭēmānu*, *ṭēmūtu*, *ṭāmu*?; → *muṭa''imu*; *šakin ṭēmi*, *šakin ṭēmūtu*

ṭêmu(m), OA *ṭeāmum* ~ "to look after, take care of" Bab., OA **G** (pres. *iṭêm*) of god, king "look after" person **N** OB mng. uncl.; < *ṭēmu* denom.?

ṭēmūtu → *šakin ṭēmūtu*

ṭēnu(m), *ṭe'nu* "ground, milled" OA, M/NB [ÀRA; ÀR.RA] flour; *saḫlû*; < *ṭênu*

ṭênu(m), M/NA *ṭeānu* "to grind" **G** [ÀRA; ÀR.ÀR] grain; flour etc.; children (in curse); transf. "pulverize" opponent **Gtn** iter. of G OB **Š** "have s.o. grind" **N** MA "be ground"; > *ṭēnu*; *ṭē'inu*, *ṭē'inūtu*, *ṭē'ittu*; *meṭēnu*

ṭe'nu → *ṭēnu*

ṭepītum "extension" OB; < *ṭepû*

ṭepû(m), *ṭapû*, OAkk *ṭapā'um* "to extend, apply, add" OAkk, Bab. **G** (*i/i*) [TAB] "add" ingredient; NB *ṭ. itti* "incorporate" addition "with", math., astr. also *ṭ. ana (muḫḫi)* "add to" s.th. **Gtn** iter. of G **D** ~ G, also med. "apply" drugs as plaster, "plaster" **N** "be added" to recipe **Ntn** transf. of words "be superimposed continually"?; > *ṭap'um*, *ṭepītum*; *ṭīpu*

ṭēpu → *ṭīpu*

ṭerdu, *ṭirdu* **1.** MB(Susa) "a driving" of cattle **2.** MB DN ^{d}*Ṭerid* (an underworld deity) **3.** NB ~ "investigation" (< Aram.?); < *ṭarādu*

ṭerītu(m) I, *ṭerûtu(m)*, *ṭirī/ûtu(m)* "mud, silt" O/jB; < *ṭēru*

ṭerītu II (or *dirītu*) (a mathematical term)? NB

ṭerru → *ṭēru*

ṭerû(m), Ass. *ṭarā'u(m)* "to penetrate, rub into; beat" **G** (*i/i*) [SUR; TE ?] OA "stamp, impress" (metal; → *ṭīru* II); stat. "penetrates" ground, heaven and earth, eye; M/jB med. "rub in" ointment; j/NB "beat (up)" as Aram. lw. **N** pass. of G NB "be beaten"; > *ṭīru* II, *ṭīrûtu*; *ṭarrû*; *maṭrû*

ṭēru(m), *ṭīru(m)*, Susa *ṭerru* "mud, silt" O/jB; > *ṭerītu* I

ṭerûtu → *ṭerītu* I

ṭiābu(m), *ṭâbu* "to be(come) good" **G** (stat. *ṭāb*) [DÙG(.GA)] "be good; sweet; in good condition"; *libbu* (of s.o.) *ṭāb* "(s.o.) is satisfied"; "favourable, suitable"; "please, be acceptable" to (= *eli*, also *ana*, dat.) s.o.; "become good, friendly" **D** "do (s.th.) well"; "improve, repair"; "heal"; *šīr X ṭ.* "give well-being to X"; "satisfy" s.o.; esp. *libbam ṭ.*; "make s.th. acceptable" to (= *eli*, dat.) s.o. **Dtn** OAkk iter. of D, in PN **Š** ~ D "make good, pleasant, friendly, acceptable"; "satisfy" heart etc.; > *ṭābu*, *ṭābiš*, *ṭābtu*, *ṭābtānu*, *ṭābūtu*, *ṭābtūtu*; *ṭūbu*, *ṭūbātu*, *ṭūbātiš*, *ṭūbtu*; *muṭībtu*

ṭibḫu (or *dibḫu*) (object on wheel) jB, NA; < *ṭabāḫu* ?

ṭību(m) "submersion" O/jB in blood; in well; of ship, bucket; < *ṭebû*

ṭību → also *ṭīmu*

ṭiddiš → *ṭīdiš*

ṭiddu → *ṭīdu*

ṭīdiš, *ṭidd/ṭṭiš* "into clay" O/jB with *ew/mû(m)*, *târu* "to become clay"; < *ṭīdu*

ṭīdu(m), *ṭīṭu*, *ṭidd/ṭṭu(m)* "clay, mud" [IM] for bricks, mortar, plaster; figur(in)es; for creation of humans; underworld food; med. substance in body; NA *šikār ṭ.* (a kind of beer); > *ṭīdiš*

ṭigīmu, *ṭiḫme(n)nu* → *ṭikmēnu*

ṭīḫu → *ṭēḫu*

ṭikmēnu (or *dikmēnu*), *ṭ/dikmennu*, *ṭ/diḫme(n)nu*, MB, Bogh. *tikmēnu*, jB also *ṭ/dig/kīmu*, MB also *dikēnu* "ashes" M/jB, NA [DÈ] NA *ṭ. ša uḫūlu* "potash"; jB *ṭ. ša diqāri* "ceramic slag"?; jB also (a plant)

ṭimītu "yarn, twine" M/NB [NU.NU] of wool, linen; < *ṭawûm*

ṭīmu, NA *ṭību* "yarn, twine" NA, NB of wool, linen; < *ṭawûm*

ṭiplu "slander" jB; < *ṭapālu*

ṭīpu(m), *ṭēpu* "addition, application" Bab. med. "poultice, wrapping"; NB "supplement, addition" esp. with *ṭepû*; < *ṭepû*

ṭirdu → *ṭerdu*

ṭirītu → *ṭerītu* I

ṭirru → *ṭīru* II

ṭīru I (kind of tree or shrub) jB lex.

ṭīru(m) II, *ṭirru* ~ "impression, stamp" O/MA on metals; MA *ṭ. aban bīt āli*; < *ṭerû*

ṭīru → also *ṭēru*; *ṭūru*

ṭirûtu → *ṭerītu* I

ṭirûtu "beating up" NB; < *ṭerû* (Aram.?)

ṭišṭišu (kind of sediment) MA

ṭiṭṭiš → *ṭīdiš*

ṭiṭṭu, *ṭīṭu* → *ṭīdu*

ṭu'ânu → *ṭumânu*

ṭūbātiš, *ṭubbātiš* "comfortably"; < *ṭūbātu*

ṭūbātu(m), *ṭubbātu(m)* f. pl. "happiness; friendliness" Bab. [DÙG(.GA)-] "goodwill", leg. *ina ṭ.* "freely, voluntarily"; < *ṭūbu*; > *ṭūbātiš*

ṭubbātiš → *ṭūbātiš*

ṭubbātu → *ṭūbātu*

ṭubbû "soaked" jB of ingredients; < *ṭebû* D

ṭūbtu **1.** M/NB "peace" **2.** jB med. "sedative"; < *ṭūbu*

ṭubû (a kind of reed) j/NB; < *ṭebû* ?

ṭūbu(m), *ṭubbu* "goodness; happiness, prosperity; free will" Bab., M/NA [DÙG(.GA)] esp. pl. "good times, prosperity"; "good relations, peace"; "contentedness, satisfaction"; *ṭ. libbi*, *ṭ. šīri* "mental, physical well-being", also *ṭ. kabatti*; < *ṭiābu*; > *ṭūbātu*, *ṭūbtu*

ṭubūsu (or *ṭupūsu*) (a window)? jB

ṭūdānu "of, from the road" j/NB desig. of tree; PN; < *ṭūdu*

ṭūdu(m), *ṭuddu* f. & m. "way, path" Bab.(lit.), NA? *ṭ. ṣabātu* "to take a road"; also transf. *ṭ. mīšari* "ways of righteousness"; NA in *šalṭu*, *qulle ṭ.* mng. unkn.; > *ṭūdānu*

ṭuḫdu(m), NA also *ṭuḫudu* "plenty, abundance" Bab., M/NA; "climax" of illness; < *ṭaḫādu*

ṭuḫḫû "brought near, presented" j/NB of offerings etc.; < *ṭeḫû* D

ṭuḫḫudu "very plentiful" j/NB; < *ṭaḫādu* D

ṭuḫudu → *ṭuḫdu*

ṭulīmu(m), *tulīmu* "spleen" O/jB [BI.RI] of human, animal; used as drug

ṭullummā'u ~ "perpetrator of violence" NA, NB; < Aram.

ṭullumum D "to do injustice"? OB

ṭumânu, *ṭumannu*, NA *ṭu'ânu* (a linen cloth) NA, NB usu. weighed; < *ṭawûm*

ṭummumiš "into a deaf person" jB; < *ṭummumu* I

ṭummumu(m) I "deaf" O/jB lex.

ṭummumu II **D** "to block (ears), make deaf" jB **Dt** pass., of ears; > *ṭummumu* I, *ṭummumiš*

ṭupālu mng. unkn. jB lex.; < *ṭapālu* ?

ṭuplu "slander(ing)" Ug., jB; < *ṭapālu*

ṭuppi (adv. or acc. pl.?), *ṭuppu* ~ "(within) time-span of" M/NB, NA; esp. NB *adi ṭ.* "(within) agreed time", also reduplicated *ṭ. ṭ.*, *ṭ. ana ṭ.* etc.; < *ṭapāpu* ?

ṭuppu(m), *tuppu(m)* m. & f.; pl. *-ātu(m)*, *-ū*, later also *-ānu* "(clay) tablet, document, letter" [DUB; IM; IM.DUB; O/MA also DUB.BI] *ṭ. šaṭāru* "to write", *ṭ. amāru*, *šasû*, *šemû* "read a tablet"; of wood, metal, stone, wax; Nuzi (part of chariot)?; < Sum.; → *dubgallu*; *ṭupšarru* etc.; *ṭupšīmātu*; *tupšinnu*; *qan ṭuppi*

ṭuppu → also *ṭuppi*

ṭuppušu "very plump" NB as (f)PN; < *ṭapāšu* II

ṭupru "(cattle) hoof" NB for *ṣupru*; < Aram.

ṭupšar-bītūtu "post of temple scribe" NB [LÚ.DUB.SAR-É-]; < *ṭupšarru* + *bītu*

ṭupšarratu(m), *tupšarratu(m)* "female scribe" O/jB [MUNUS.DUB.SAR] also as epith. of goddess; < *ṭupšarru*

ṭupšarru(m), *tupšarru(m)* "scribe; scholar" [(LÚ.)DUB.SAR; LÚ.UMBISAG; NA (LÚ.)A.BA; LÚ.ÚMBISAG; lit. in col. LÚ.GI.BÙR] also M/NB as epith. of Nabû; *rab ṭ.* "chief scribe"; "scribe" of king, city etc.; Assyrian, Aramaean, Egyptian "scribe"; *ṭ. Enūma Anu Ellil* "astronomer, astrologer" etc.; < Sum.; > *ṭupšarratu*; *ṭupšarrūtu*, *ṭupšar-bītūtu*; → *dubsarmaḫḫu*

ṭupšarrūtu(m), *tupšarrūtu(m)*, Ass. *-uttu(m)* "scribal art, scholarship; scribal practice; scribal corpus" [DUB.SAR-]; < *ṭupšarru*

ṭupšīmātu, *tupšīmātu* "tablet of destinies" jB [DUB.NAM.(TAR.)MEŠ]; < *ṭuppu* + *šīmtu*

ṭupšu "plenty, abundance" jB of grain; < *ṭapāšu* II

ṭupu mng. unkn. jB med. in desig. of plant

ṭupullû(m) "slander, suspicion" O/jB; < *ṭapālu*

ṭupultum "abuse" Mari; < *ṭapālu*

ṭupūsu → *ṭubūsu*

ṭupuštu "fatty layer"? jB on tongue; < *ṭupšu*

ṭurpu "forcible removal, seizure" MB

ṭurru(m), *turru(m)* "binding, knot" Bab., M/NA [DUR] in cloth, gold, reed; med. "bandage"; om. (feature on liver, lung); "band" on doors; "string (of stones)"; also astr. and cosmic; < Sum.

ṭūru, *ṭurû*, *ṭīru* (medicinal plant, phps.) "opopanax" j/NB [ŠIM.ḪAB]

U

u "and, but, also" **1.** between subst.s and pron.s "and", if several usu. between last two only, *X Y u Z* (→ *ū* 1); Am. *u* ... *u* ... "both ... and ..."; like prep. before gen., OB *anāku u kâti/a* (→ GAG §114i) **2.** between clauses, with nuance "moreover"; occas. Am., NB *u* ... *u* ... "both ... and ..."; Alal., Nuzi, Bogh. etc. after condit./subord. clause; occas. MA, M/jB "but"; → *ula*; *umā*; *wa*

ū "or" **1.** between subst.s, OB *še'am kaspam ū bīšam* "grain, silver or goods" (→ *u* 1) **2.** between clauses, OA *batiq ū wattur* "be it cheap or dear"; "(whether) ... or ..." *kī(ma)/ū* ... *ū* ..., e.g. *ū sāmtum ul īde ū uqnûm ul īde* "I do not know whether it be carnelian, or lapis lazuli"; with *lū* → *lū* C; → *ūl*; *ūla*; *ūlū*

û(m) "nourishment"? O/jB lex.; OB acc. *(')âm* [ŠE]; < Sum.; → *še'u*

ū'a, *ū'i*, *ūya*, *wā(ya)* "woe!; alas!" as interj.; *ina ū'a* "in woe"; "lamentation" jB *ū'a ū'a* (a bird cry)

uanta mng. unkn. Nuzi; < Hurr.

uatnannu, MA *utnānu* ~ "carriage"? MA, Nuzi; < Hurr.; → *atnannu*; *uatnannuḫli*

uatnannuḫlu ~ "carriage driver"? Nuzi; < Hurr.; → *atnannuḫlu*; *uatnannu*

ubālu → *wabālu*

ubānu(m), occas. *upānu* f. "finger, toe" [ŠU.SI; jB also U] **1.** "finger" of human, *u. qablītu(m)/ṣeḫertu(m)/šanītu* "middle/little/index f."; *u. rabītu(m)* "thumb"; *appi/ṣupur u.* "fingertip/nail" (→ *karšu*); *u. damiqti/lemutti tarāṣu* "to point finger of good/evil" **2.** "finger's breadth"; Am., Ug., jB? st. abs. *ubān* "by a whisker, all but"; as linear measure 1/30 cubit (NB 1/24); NB as surface measure; astr. as measure of sky **3.** "toe" of human, bird, lizard etc., esp. *u. šēpē* **4.** transf. (part of shoe, wooden implement); ext. (part of liver) "processus pyramidalis", *u. ḫašî(m)* (part of lung); (a small cucumber); jB/NA "(mountain) peak", *u. šadê*, *ḫuršāni*

ubartu(m) ~ "(resident) alien (f.)" OAkk, OA, O/jB; Bogh. (desig. of a foreign princess); as fPN; < *ubāru*

ubartum → also *wabartum*

ubāru(m) ~ "(resident) alien" [U.BAR]; Am., Bogh., Nuzi (corps of foreign soldiers), pl. *ubārūtu*; as PN; jB (desig. of exotic bird); > *ubartu*; → *wabrum*

ubāru → also *abāru* II

ubātum, *upātum* "fat (cow)" OB, i.e. pregnant ?; < *ebû* II

ubbubu(m) "cleansed" OB, Bogh. lex.; < *ebēbu* D

ubbulu(m) "dried (out)" O/jB, of man's skin, flour; < *abālu* D

ubbunu (or *uppunu*) jB lex. **1.** (an overgarment)? **2.** f. *ubbuntu* (a vessel)

ubbusu → *uppusu* I.II

ubbuṭu I "swollen" jB lex. of feet; < *ebēṭu* I D

ubbuṭu II "starvation, famine" M/jB esp. in om.; < *ebēṭu* I D

ubbuṭu(m) III ~ "encumbered by debt"? O/MB; esp. Nuzi, of a class of person; OB lex., MB as PN ?; < *ebēṭu* II; → *u.* IV

ubbuṭu IV **D** "to take as pledge, distrain"? NB, sheep etc.; = *ebēṭu* II D ?; → *u.* III

ubilu "bearer"? Am.; < *wabālu*

ubi(n)zar, ubinzer → *upinzer*

ubru → *wabrum*
ubsaḫarrakku (a cultic location) j/NB [UB.SAḪAR.RA; UB.SA.ḪA.RI]; < Sum.
ubsātu → *abūsu*
ubšukkinnakku, *ubšukkannakku* "court of assembly" j/NB [UB.ŠU.UKKIN.NA] of gods in heaven; NB (an inner courtyard of temple); < Sum.
ubû(m), *upû* "half iku" Bab. [UBU], as surface measure; jB as capacity measure ?; < Sum.
ūbu "thickness" jB of door; < *ebû* II
ubuḫšinnu → *abaḫšinnu*
uburtu "female stranger"? jB; also (a bird); Nuzi, NA in fPNs; < *wabrum*
ubūšū (or *upūšū*) pl. mng. unkn. Early Mari in *akal u.*
udā'ē → *udû* I
udā'u → *wadûm*
uddam "today" OB (but phps. error for *ūmam* ?)
uddagiddû(m) "omitted day" O/jB [UD.DA.GÍD.DA] at end of month of fewer than 30 days; < Sum.
uddakam, NB occas. *uddakku* "all day; for ever" Bab.(lit.); < Sum.
uddalû, *uttalû* (a vessel) Bogh., Nuzi; in gold, bronze
u(d)dasiggû (a meal-time) jB lex.; < Sum.
uddazallû(m) "date, day of the month" O/jB [UD.DA.ZAL(.LA/LÁ)] **1.** OB "date in month" **2.** jB "intercalary day" **3.** jB desig. of math.-astr. constant, ~ "timing"; < Sum.
uddeš, *ūdiš* "in distress" jB; < *ūdu*
uddi → *wuddi*
uddīni, uddinna → *udīni*
uddu (a log, beam) jB; < Sum.?
uddu → also *ūdu*
uddû I "to impregnate" NB; < Aram.
uddû II ~ "exuberance" jB lex.
uddû → also *ūdu*; *wadûm* D
uddupu(m) "blown (up)" O/jB; of ill sheep "distended"; of sky "wind-swept"; < *edēpu* D
udduru(m) "darkened" O/jB lex., of person's countenance ?; < *adāru* I D
udī-, *udē-* "alone" M/NA, *udīya/šu/šunu* etc. "on my/his/their own"; < *wēdum*; → *wēdī-*
udigallu (a priest) jB lex.; < Sum.
udīni, *qudīni*, NA also *udīna*, *uddīni*, *uddinna* "up till now, so far" M/NA; NA only before *lā* + pres. "not yet"; → *adīni*; *udī-*
udīnu (a mountain bird) NA
ūdiš → *uddeš*
udittu ~ "(growth of) rushes" jB; < *edēdu*
udru, *uduru*; pl. m. & f. "(Bactrian) camel" M/NA
udû(m) I, NA also *udā'ē* pl. tant.? "tools, equipment" of craftsman, for journey etc.; NA, NB esp. metal vessels, tools
udû II mng. uncl. jB lex.; < *edû* II ?
ūdu, *uddu*, *uddû*, *udû* ~ "distress, affliction" j/NB [UD.DA] *ū. šūtuqu* "to have troubles pass"; "ill effects" of scorpion, snake etc.; > *uddeš*
u'du, *u'udu*, *yādu* (a group of corvée workers) NB(Nippur)
udugu, *edigu* "(wooden) stick" jB lex., for beating etc.
udukalû (a kind of sacrifical sheep) jB rit.; < Sum.
udukianakku "sheep for funerary sacrifice" jB lex.; < Sum.
udukišāḫû (a kind of sacrificial sheep) jB lex.; < Sum.
udukiutukku (a kind of sacrificial sheep) jB lex.; < Sum.
udūmu "(kind of) ape" NA (or error for *uqūpu* ?)
udunmāḫu "(kind of) brick-kiln" jB lex.; < Sum.; → *utūnu*
uduru → *udru*
udurû → *adurû*
udutilû "live sheep" jB [UDU.TI.LA] for offering; < Sum.
ugallu "big weather-demon" jB [U4.GAL(.LA)] myth., mag.; < Sum.
ugārišam "meadow by meadow" OB; < *ugāru*
ugāršu "towards the meadow" jB [A.GÀR-*šú*]; < *ugāru*
ugāru(m) m. & f. "(communally controlled) meadow" [A.GÀR]; OB *mār(ū) u.* "member(s) of the meadow(-consortium)"; MA *u. āli* "city meadow", Nuzi *u. ša PlN* "meadow of village PlN"; Mari (a dry capacity measure = 4 gur); < Sum.; > *ugārišam*, *ugāršu*
ugbabtu(m), occas. *ugbantum*; pl. *ugbakkātum*; Ass. usu. *gubabtu(m)* "(kind of) priestess" OA, O/jB [NIN.DINGIR(.RA)] st. abs. OB *ugbabat* "she is a priestess"; Mari *bīt u.*; > *ugbabūtum*
ugbabūtum "status as priestess" OB; < *ugbabtu*
ugbakkātum, ugbantum → *ugbabtu*
uggatu "rage, fury" M/NB of human, deity; freq. *u. libbi*; < *agāgu*
uggu(m) "rage, fury" O/jB; < *agāgu*
uggugum "very furious" OB lex.; < *agāgu*
uggulu mng. unkn. jB, of reed-thicket
ugu I ~ "death"? jB lex.; < Sum.

ugu II "power, strength" jB lex.
ugu III (or *ugû*) "mother" jB lex.; < Sum.
ugu → also *uqqu*
ugû → *ugu* III
ugubbum → *uguppum*
ugudillû, *ugudillu* "single, solitary" jB; of day; of warts etc. [UGU.DILI]; of lion, bird; < Sum.
ugulamartûm "Amorite-supervisor" OB [UGULA.MAR.TU]; < Sum.
ugummu(m) mng. unkn. Bab.
uguppum (or *ugubbum*) mng. unkn. OB lex.
ugurtu (a kind of document)? MA; <*egēru* II
uḫaltu → *uḫultu*
uḫātu; pl. *uḫātāti* (a leather item) Am.
uḫe(n)nu → *uḫinnu*
uḫḫaḫ → *ulḫaḫ*
uḫḫu "phlegm, sputum" jB; lex. also "(copper) slag"; < Sum.
uḫḫul, *uḫḫulul* (an artefact) NB, pledged
uḫḫultu → *uḫultu*
uḫḫulu → *uḫūlu*
uḫḫulul → *uḫḫul*
uḫḫunu → *uḫūlu*
uḫḫurtu, NB *uḫḫuštu* j/NB **1.** "rear bar" under chariot **2.** (a Sum. vb. form); < *uḫḫuru*
uḫḫuru(m) "late, remaining" OAkk, O/jB of persons, math. of figures; of night-watch; "late fruiting" of palm tree; < *aḫāru*
uḫḫuštu → *uḫḫurtu*
uḫḫuzu(m) "plated with, set in (metal)" Ass., O/jB [GAR.RA] of furniture, ornaments; *ḫurāṣa u.* "inlaid, plated with gold"; < *aḫāzu* D
uḫinnu(m), *uḫe(n)nu*, OAkk *uḫuinnum* "fresh date(s)" [U$_4$/Ú.ḪI.IN] also $^{(na_4)}$*u.* "date(-shaped) bead", in stone, gold etc.
uḫīru "weed" jB, in desig. of cucumber
uḫnu (or *aḫnu*) mng. unkn. Alal. in *u./a. ša amēli*
uḫrû(m), *uḫru* "rearmost" O/jB; "ninth string" of lyre; < *aḫāru*
uḫrušḫu → *eḫrušḫu*
uḫuinnum → *uḫinnu*
uḫulgallu "unfavourable day" jB [U$_4$.ḪUL. GÁL(.E)]; < Sum.
uḫultu(m), Bogh. also *uḫḫultu*, *uḫaltu*, NA *aḫussu* (an alkaline salt) "soda" OA, M/jB, NA; Bogh. *u. irammuk* "he bathes in soda"; < *uḫūlu*
uḫūlu(m), NB also *uḫḫulu*, Ug. occas. *uḫḫunu* m. & f. (an alkali-rich plant) "potash" Bab. [(Ú.)NAGA]; as mineral; for soap; in glass recipe; esp. *u. qarnāti/qarnānu* [(Ú.)NAGA.SI] "*Salicornia*", and similar plants for glass, drug, *u. q. qalâti* "burnt *S.*"; > *uḫultu*
uḫulunašše (a wooden object) Alal.; < Hurr.
uḫummiš "like a cliff" j/NB
uḫummu; pl. m. & f. "cliff" jB; > *uḫummiš*
uḫurrā'um "remainder" OAkk; < *aḫāru*
uḫušgallu "terrible storm" jB mag.; < Sum.
ū'i → *ū'a*
u'illu(m) "bearer, porter" O/jB [LÚ.Ú.ÍL] in temple; < Sum.
u'iltu (a kind of cuneiform tablet) j/NB, NA **1.** Bab. "(legal) contract-tablet" [pseudo-log. Ú.ÌL.TÌ]; *šāṭer u.* "writer of the tablet", of scribe; *bēl u.* "creditor" **2.** Ass. (a lit. excerpt tablet), also astr., *u. ša antalî* "eclipse tablet"; < *e'ēlu*
uizza "wedjet-eye" Am.; Eg. amulet; < Eg.
ūka mng. uncl. Mari, introducing speech
Ukaduḫḫa, *Kadduḫḫa* (name of a constellation, phps.) "Cygnus" Bab. [MUL.U$_4$.KA.DUḪ.A (or = *nimru* I ?)]; < Sum.; → *kaduḫḫû*
ukalātu → *ukultu*
ukallûm (desig. of a person) OB
ukam[uššu] (a kind of cumin) jB lex.
ukāpu(m) "pack-saddle" OA, M/NB; Nuzi, of sheepskin
ukkinnu, *unkennu* "assembly (of the gods)" jB; < Sum.
ukkum I mng. unkn. OB lex.; < *ekēku* ?
ukku II (an object) Ug., of ivory; NA?
ukkudu(m) (physically handicapped) O/jB lex.; as PN; < *ekēdu* D; → *mukkidu* ?
ukkuliš "very dark(ly)" jB in *u. ew/mû* Š "to darken"; < *ukkulu*
ukkulu "very dark" jB; of day, face; < *ekēlu*; > *ukkuliš*
ukkumu "predatory" jB as name of a dog of Marduk, also ^{d}*U.*; < *ekēmu*
ukkupiš "very near" jB, of place, of time; < *ukkupu*
ukkupu mng. uncl. jB lex. D adj. or infin.; < *ekēpu*
ukkušu "driven off"? jB lex. D adj. (or infin.); < *akāšu*
uklu(m) I "darkness" O/jB; < *ekēlu*
uklu(m) II "food, nourishment" Ass., OB; for servant; OB *ukul pîya* "my victuals"; < *akālu*
uklu → also *waklum*
ukû (part of loom, phps.) "shuttle" M/jB
ukullû(m) I, MA *ukullā'u*, NA *akullû* "provisions, subsistence" Bab., M/NA [ŠÀ. GAL]; O/MB "fodder" for cattle, less freq. humans; Ass., j/NB usu. for humans, "food

allowance"; OB math. "degree of slope"; < *akālu*

ukullûm II "overseer" Mari; < Akk. lw. in Sum.; → *waklum*

ukultu(m), NA *akussu*; NA pl. *ukalāti*? "food; consumption" OA, O/jB, NA [NÍG.GU7; GU7-] **1.** "food" for human, animal, OA also "(allowance for) food"; NA (a kind of soup or sauce)? **2.** "consumption", of lion, *u. alpē* etc. "consumption of oxen etc."; of plague *u. ili/DN* "devouring of (= by) god/DN"; ext. (condition of liver); < *akālu*; → *akussu*

ukunurû "previous day" jB lex.; < Sum.

ukurbalû (a vinegar jar) jB lex.; < Sum.

ukurgiddû (a clay vessel) jB lex.; < Sum.

ukurigû (a vinegar jar) jB lex.; < Sum.

ukurrum I "(a kind of) brick" OAkk, OB

uku(r)ru II "body" Nuzi, of statue, in wood; < Hurr.

ukuššû (a gem) Ug. lex., of lapis lazuli; < Sum.

ul, OB occas. *uli* "not" Bab., to negate main clause [NB NU]; usu. immediately before vb./pred.; before other word for emphasis, MB *ul kī eqel burkūti nadnaššu* "given him not as a hereditary field"; in condit. clause after *šumma*, rarely instead of *lā*; *ul* ... *ul* ... "neither ... nor ...", with subst.s and vb.s; < *ula*; → *lā*

ūl "or" OA; *ūl* ... *ūl* ... "either ... or ...", "whether ... or ..."; *šumma* ... *ūl* ... "whether ... or ..."; < *ūla*

ula "not" OAkk, OA, arch. O/jB, to negate main clause; OA alternates with *lā*; OB, Mari *ulāman* "were it not so", "otherwise"; < *u* + *lā*; > *ul*, *ulla* I, *ullu* I

ūla, *ūlā* "or" OA, NA; OA between subst.s, vb.s, *ūla* ... *ūla* ... "either ... or ..."; NA usu. between vb.s, *ūlamā* "or else ..."; < *ū* + *lā*; > *ūl*; *ūlašūma*

ulādu "child"? OB; < *walādum*

ulādu → also *walādum*

ulaltu "helpless woman" jB; < *ulālu*

ulālu(m) "weak, helpless (person)" O/jB; > *ulaltu*, *ulālūtu*

ulālūtu, once *ilalūtu* "helplessness" jB, in *u. alāku* "to become helpless"; < *ulālu*

ūlamā → *ūla*

ulāman → *ula*

ulāpu "rag" M/jB; esp. *u. lupputti* "soiled rag" [TÚG.NÍG.DÁRA.ŠU.LÁL] med., om.; *ulāp sūni* "sanitary towel"

ul'ari → *ulmuari*

ūlašūma "or else, or on the other hand" OB(N.Mes.), Mari; < *ūla*

ulbum (a vessel) OB(Susa), Mari

ulgirītu mng. unkn. jB mag.

ulḫaḫ, *uḫḫaḫ* (a thorn-bush) M/jB lex.

ulḫi (a room or building) jB lex.

uli → *ul*

ulībum (or *ulīpum*) (a sauce) OB lex.

ulillu mng. unkn. jB lex.; < Sum.

uliltu "dried fig" j/NB [GIŠ.PÈŠ.ḪÁD.A]

ulinnu "coloured twine" M/jB [Ú.LI.IN] mag., *ina u. rakāsu*, *u. lamû* "to bind with, wind in *u.*"

ulīpum → *ulībum*

ulirkun "young male animal"? jB lex.; < Elam.

ulla I, j/NB also *ullu* "no!" Bab.; OB before imper.; jB *ulla/u mannu iqabbi* "who says no?"; < *ula* etc.; > *ullāman*

ulla II, *ullâ*, NB also *ullu* "at some time" Bab.; jB *u.* ... *u.* ... "on one occasion ..., on another ..."; *adi u.* "for ever", also *ana u.*; *ištu/ultu u.* "since earliest times", before pret. "long ago"; < *ullû* I; > *ullânu*

ullalla "anyone" jB lex.; < *ullû* I; > *ullalliassu*; *ullallû*

ullalliassu, jB *ullil[lassu]* "at some later time"? O/jB lex.; < *ullalla*

ullallû "anyone of those"? Ug.; < *ullalla*

ullāman ~ "otherwise" Mari; < *ulla* I + *-man*

ullân "apart from, except for" Mari; < *ullânu*

ullânu(m) Bab. **1.** adv., of place "there, thence" **2.** adv., of time "there and then; from the start", esp. *u.-ma*; *(ultu) u.(-ma)* "thereupon, at that very moment" **3.** conj. (+ subjunct.) "immediately after, as soon as" **4.** prep. "apart from, other than", *ullânūya ul ibašši* "there is no-one other than I"; "without (permission/ collaboration of)" **5.** prep. "before, previous to", *ullânū'a* "before me"; < *ulla* II + *-ānum*; > *ullân*; → *ellān*

ullâtu → *ullû* II

ullikī'am, Mari *ullikêm*, Bogh. *ullikâ* "there" O/MB; < *ullû* I + *kī'am*

ullillassu → *ullalliassu*

ullimettam "in his time" Mari; < *ullû* I

ullîš "later, thereafter" O/jB; lit. also as prep. "before"?; < *ullû* I; → *ullītiš*

ullîšam "thither" OB, Bogh.; < *ullû* I

ullītiš, jB occas. *ullûtiš* "the day after tomorrow" O/jB; Nuzi also for *ullîš*; < *ullû* I; Ass. → *allītiš*; *līdiš*

ullītu → *ullû* I

ullu(m) I "negative answer, refusal" Bab.; *u. apālu(m)* "to answer no, refuse"; jB *u. kīnu* "a true no"; < *ula* etc.

ullu II (a bull) OB(Bogh.), of silver

ullu → also *ḫullu*; *ulla* I.II

ullû(m) I; f. *ullītu(m)* "that; distant" Bab. **1.** "that", pl. "those" (opp. to *annû* I); as subst. "that/those one(s)", OB *ullūtīni* "those of us"; NB *ultu u.* "from there"? **2.** "distant (in time)", *ūmē ullûti* "days of yore"; > *ulla* II, *ullumma*, *ullânu*, *ullân*; *ullîš*, *ullītiš*, *ullîšam*; *ullûtu*; *ullikī'am*; *ullalla* etc.; *ullimettam*; *aḫullâ*; → *allû* I

ullû(m) II; f. *ullû/âtu(m)* "exalted" O/jB; of goddess; < *elû* III D

ullû III (a garment)? Am.

ulluḫum "tufted" OB of snake, in *ulluḫam šārātim* "with tufts of hair"; < *elēḫu* D

ullulu(m) I "cleansed" O/jB; < *elēlu* II D

ullulu II (kind of body armour) jB lex.

ullum(ma), OAkk also *allum* "thereupon" OAkk, OB; also in fPN *Ullum-eršet*; < *ulla* II loc.-adv.

ullupu (a plant) Ug. lex.

ullūru(m) (an object) OA, Mari, Am.

ulluṣu "swollen" jB, of flesh; < *elēṣu*

ullûtiš → *ullītiš*

ullūtu "garrison"? NA; < *elû* III D

ullûtu "distant time" O/jB in *ūm u.* "day(s) of old"; < *ullû* I

ulmu; pl. m. & f. (a weapon, phps.) "axe" M/NA, M/jB, of iron; Ug. for a ship

ulmuari, *ul'ari* (a plant) jB lex.

ulnu "or else"? jB lex.; < W.Sem.?

ulpānu (a leather coat) jB lex.

ulṣāniš, *ulṣiš* "joyfully" j/NB; < *ulṣu*

ulṣu(m) "pleasure; rejoicing" Bab., NA *u. epēšu* "to enjoy oneself"; *u. libbi(m)* "delight", *u. malû(m)* "to be endowed with attractiveness"; < *elēṣu*; > *ulṣāniš*

ulšānum "first-class oil" OB; < Sum.

ultu → *ištu*

ulû(m) in *ulu šamni/ḫimētim* "the best oil/butter" Bab.; < Sum.?

ūlū, *ū lū* "or" O/MA, O/jB between subst.s and clauses, OB *ūlūma* "or else"; *ū.(-ma)* ... *ū.(-ma)* ... "either ... or ..."; < *ū* + *lū*

uluḫḫu "sceptre" Ug., jB [GIŠ.Ù.LUḪ]; *u. šarrūti* "s. of kingship"; < Sum.

Ulūlu → *Elūnum*

ulušennu → *ulušinnu*

ulušinmaḫḫu "first-class emmer-beer" jB lex.; < *ulušinnu*

ulušinnu(m), *ulušennu* "date-sweetened emmer-beer" Bab. [KAŠ.ULUŠIN/ÚLUŠIN]; < Sum.

-um loc.-adv. suffix → GAG §66

umā "now" NA; < *u* + *mā*

ūma(m) "today, on this day; for a day" **1.** O/MA, O/jB "today", *kīma ša ūmam* "like today" **2.** jB "on this day"; *ū.* ... *ū.* ... "on one day ..., on another ..." **3.** OB "for the length of a day"; < *ūmu* I; → *uddam*

ūmakkal, *ūmuakkal* "for one day, for the length of one day" OA, O/jB [UD.1.KAM] OA esp. with *biātum* ("to stay"); OB *ina ū.*; *ḫarrān ū.* "a one-day journey"; < *ūmam* + *kal(a)*

ūmakkalûm adj. "one day's" OB of troops, men "assigned for one day"; < *ūmakkal*

umamtu, *umāmatu* "female animal" MA, jB lex.; in art; < *umāmu*

umāmu(m), *emammu(m)*, *emāmu* "animal; (coll.) beasts" Bab., M/NA; esp. wild animals, M/jB *u. ṣēri* "beasts of the wild", *lū ša tābali lū ša nāri* "of dry land or river", *ša tâmti* "of the sea"; jB *umāmānu ša Tiāmat* "Tiāmat's monsters"; "animal figure" in temple, on carpet etc.; MA, jB occas. "domestic animals"; > *umamtu*

umandu (part of human insides) jB

umarzanapāta "city-ruler" NB; < OPers.

umasupitrû "son of the (royal) house" NB, in *bīt u.* desig. of crown prince's estate; < OPers.

umaštu ~ "hook" jB; < *umāšu*

umāšu(m), *ḫumā/ūšum*, *emāšu* ~ "grappling-hook (for wrestlers); strength" Bab., NA [GÉŠPU]; *wakil nāši u.* "overseer of the wrestlers"; *ša (ḫ)u.* [LÚ.GÉŠPU] "wrestler", in cult, figurine, in mag.; transf. j/NB "strength" of person; > *umaštu*

umātu (a wooden object) jB lex.

ūmātu → *ūmu* I

umbūbu Ug. desig. of a harp string (for Bab. *šer'ān embūbi*); → *ebbūbu*

***umdu**; pl. *undī* (a skin complaint) NA; < *emēdu* ?

ūmiš M/NB **1.** "like day(light)"; < *ūmu* I **2.** "like a storm"; < *ūmu* II

ūmišam, *ūmiša* "daily, day by day" OAkk, Bab. freq. *ū.-ma*; < *ūmu* I + *-išam*

ūmītu "born on the day" MA, as fPN; < *ūmu* I + *-ī*

umma, MB also *ummā*, j/NB occas. *ummu* "saying:", ptcl. introducing dir. speech OAkk(Ur III), Bab., O/MA; *umma PN-/šarrum-/šī-ma* etc. "thus says PN/the king/she" etc.; OB freq. *ummāmi*; → *enma*

Ummān-manda, OB also *Ummān-m/badda* ~ "barbarian horde" Bab. [ÉRIN(.ḪI.A)-*m.*]; esp. in om.; NA, NB(roy. inscr.) = "Medes"; → *ummānu*

ummannu → *ummānu*; *ummiānu*

ummannuḫum (a kind of drinking vessel) Mari

ummānu(m), *ummannu* f.; pl. rarely m. "army, troops" [ÉRIN(.ḪI.A(.MEŠ)/ḪI.MEŠ); Bogh., Ug. also UGNIM] sg. and pl., for war, also state labour; occas. "crowd; common people"; → *Ummān-manda*

ummânu → *ummiānu*

ummânūtu, Mari *ummênūtum* "craftsmanship, scholarship" O/jB, NA; *ummênūtam quttû* "perfect in skill", *šipir u.* "a work of c."; jB, NA "(scribal) craft, learning"; < *ummiānu*

ummaru(m) ~ "soup, broth" O/jB [TU7; jB also KÁM ?]

ummatu(m) "main body, bulk" Bab. **1.** of army; *ṣāb ummatim* "the main body of troops", *ummat Ḫana* "main Hanaean force"; transf. of animals **2.** OB om. "main body" of oil [Bogh. ÚMUN] **3.** jB ext. *u. tīrāni* "complete intestine"; *u. ḫašî* "complete lung"? **4.** *u. erî* "lower grindstone" **5.** jB lex. *u. eqli* (a thorny plant) **6.** misc.: OB(Susa) (a basin)?; MB(Nippur) (a wool payment)?; jB ~ "descendants" in *ummat* DN; < *ummu* I

ummātu → *ummu* I.II

ummedu(m), *ummidu(m)* (a fever)? O/jB

ummênum → *ummiānu*

ummênūtum → *ummânūtu*

ummiānītum; pl. *ummiānêtum* "sum(s) owed to creditors"? OB; < *ummiānu*

ummiānu(m), Mari *ummênum*, *ummânu*, *ummannu*; pl. m. & f. [(LÚ.)UM.MI/ME.A] **1.** "craftsman, specialist" OB usu. *mār u.*; OAkk, Mari (field-surveyor); Bogh. (work overseer in temples), pl. *ummiā/ēnūtum*; j/NB, NA "craftsman, expert" in gener., in army **2.** NA, NB "scholar, scribal expert", (royal) "(chief) scribe" **3.** NB "expert", of trained plough-animal **4.** OA, O/MB, occas. jB "money-lender; creditor"; < Sum. ummia + *-ān*; > *ummiānītum*; *ummânūtu*

ummidu → *ummedu*

ummisallu "Emesal-composition"? jB; [EME.SAL ? (→ *mēsallu*)]; < Sum.

ummu(m) I f. "mother" [AMA] **1.** of humans, *u. ālittu* "natural mother"; *ummi ummi* "grandmother"; transf. OA *ummī attī* "you are (as) my mother", Bab. of goddess *u. bānītī* "the mother who created me" etc. **2.** of animals; *u. mê* (a dragonfly) **3.** transf., of source or origin, OA *u. ṭuppim* "original document"?; OB *ṭuppi ummātim* "document of original (fields)"?; NB *u.* A.ŠÀ.MEŠ "original deed of property"; NA, NB (accounting term, phps.) "total credits"?; of river *u. nārāti* **4.** misc.: (part of plough); lex. "quiver"; "stock" of tree, vine; NA in topog. descr. (mng. unkn.); > *ummatu*; *ummūtum*

ummu(m) II; pl. f. "heat; fever" Bab. **1.** med. "fever" [KÚM] **2.** usu. pl. "(summer) heat" [É.MEŠ; jB also AMA.MEŠ !], freq. + *umšu(m)*; < *emēmu*

ummu(m) III (a reed or rush rope) O/jB lex.; < Sum.

ummu IV (a bird) jB lex.

ummu → also *umma*

ummuliš "sparklingly" jB, of Mars; < *ummulu* I

ummulu I jB **1.** "twinkling" of star, planet **2.** lex. (desig. of a bed) **3.** of manliness ~ "stifled, suppressed"; < *wamālum*

ummulu II ~ "stifling, oppression" jB lex., of illness; < *wamālum* D infin.

ummuqu(m) O/jB ~ "deep-thinking" of person; "well thought-through" of action; < *emēqu* I

ummuru (a kind of bronze) jB lex.

ummuštu (a priestess) jB lex.

ummūtum "motherhood" OB, Emar; < *ummu* I

umnīnu, *umninnu, unnīnu(m)* II; pl. f. "chest, case" OB?, M/NA, Nuzi, for clothing, weapons, precious vessels etc.; → *tupninnu*

umsum → *umṣum* II

umṣatu(m) I ~ "mole, birthmark"? O/jB [DUB (.BU); SAMAG; SÀMAG] *u. malû* "to be covered in moles"; transf. "bumps, knobs" on basket, on vessel

umṣatu II (a tough grass) jB lex.

umṣitum (part of a door)? OB

umṣu I, *unṣu* "hunger" j/NB; < *emēṣu* II

umṣum II (or *umsum*) (an object) OA

umšarḫum, *umzarḫu*, *umzaḫḫu*, NA *unza/erḫu*, *unzaḫḫu* (a class of person) Mari, M/NA; MA man, woman *u. ša (f)PN*; NA *u. ša šarri* "freedman? of king"; also of field?, animal mng. uncl.

umšu(m), *uššu* "heat, summer" O/jB; *ina u. u. dannu ibašši* "there will be great heat in summer"; *u. kuṣṣu* "heat (and) cold"; jB also pl. *umšē rabûti* "severe heatwaves"; < *amāšu*

ūmšu(m) "till this day" OAkk, OA, OB; < *ūmu* I + *-šum*

ūmtum, M/NB *undu* "(one specific) day" Bab., OA; OB *in-ūmti* "on the day when" + subjunct.; NB/NA *ina muḫḫi*, *bāsi undi*; < *ūmu* I nom. unit.

ūmu(m) I; pl. m. & f. "day" [UD; astr. → 1] **1.** "daytime" as opp. to night [astr. ME]; is bright, cloudy etc.; *ū. kurû/arku* "short/long day" of winter/summer; times/parts of day →

e.g. *mašlu*, *mišlu*, *qablu* I 3, *šērtu* II, *šēru* II; *kal(a) ūmi* "all day" **2.** "(whole) day" (= 24 hours); as date [UD.X.KAM = "Xth day", but also "X days"]; favourable, unfavourable; MA UD-*um* "per day"; MA, jB *u/araḫ ūmāte* "a whole month"; OA *adi ū. annîm* "till today", jB *ištu ūmimma* "from today"; NA, NB *ūmu (...) ūmu* "day by day; one day ... the other"; st. abs. O/jB *ūm mašil*, *mašil ūm* "half a day" **3.** special days: for rituals, festivals → e.g. *akītu*, *isinnu*, *tēliltu*; *ūm(u) ili* "(personal?) god's day"; of death, fate etc. → *bibbulu* 2, *mūtu*, *šīmtu*, *ištēn ū.* etc. "in one day", i.e. quickly **4.** pl. "days" as period of time, of past, future; of s.o.'s lifetime; of allotted period in law, commerce, *umū/ātu* + *malû* "time is up"; of season, weather, harvest, OB *ūmāt šamaššammī* "sesame time"; *ina lā ūmišu* "at the wrong time" **5.** in temporal expressions: *(ina) ū.* "at the time of"; *adi/ultu ū.* "until/since"; *in(a) ūmišu(ma)* "at his time, then", + pres. "at the stipulated time"; > *ūm*; *ūma*; *ūmiš* 1; *ūmišam*, *ūmussu*; *ūmšu*; *ūmītu*; *ūmtum*; *ūmakkal*, *ūmakkalûm*; *anūmīšu*; *inūmē*, *inūmīšu*; *šalšūmi*; → *ū.* II

ūmu(m) II "storm(-demon); mythical lion" Bab. [UD]; *ū. meḫê* "storm"; of person, raging *kī(ma) ū.* "like a storm"; desig. of demons, of (figurines of) seven sages (*apkallī*); lex. (a mythical lion), also as wooden figure; < Sum.?; > *ūmiš* 2; → *ū.* I

ūmuakkal → *ūmakkal*

umumma in *u. epēšu* ~ "to collect" Nuzi; < Hurr.

umunnedukku "letter, missive" jB lex.; < Sum.; → *unnedukkum*

umunnû "vein(s)" jB; < Sum.

umurru (an illness) jB med.

ūmussu "daily" j/NB, NA; < *ūmu* I

umzaḫḫu, *umzarḫu* → *umšarḫum*

unâtu → *unūtu*

undī → *umdu*

undu I, Byblos *i/endu* "when; then" Am., Nuzi, Bogh., Ug. **1.** as conj. "when", Bogh. also "for as long as"; Nuzi occas. before indic. **2.** Ug. "then, at that time"

undu II (a workman)? Ug.

undu → also *ūmtum*; *umdu*

uniātum → *unūtu*

uninātu(m) mng. uncl. OB, NA

unīqu(m) f. "female kid" OAkk, Bab., M/NA [MUNUS.EŠGAR; MUNUS.ÉŠ.GÀR]; rit. *u. lā petītu* "virgin kid"; < *enēqu*; → *munīqu*

unītum (a stone) OB lex.

unkennu → *ukkinnu*

unnanniši (a composite beast)? jB; also ${}^{d}U.$

unnānu → *unnīnu*

unnatu, *unnātu* ~ "land" jB

unnedukkum, occas. *i(n)nedukku(m)* f. "letter, missive" OB; *ūm u.-ki tammarū* "when you see your letter"; *unnedukkātūka lillikānim* "mind you keep writing!"; < Sum.; → *umunnedukku*

unnīnu(m), *unnēnu(m)*, *unninnu*, NA *unnānu* "supplication, petition" OAkk, Bab., NA [in PNs ÉR] *u. leqû(m)* of deity, king etc. "to receive" s.o.'s "petition"; jB *ṣalam unnīni* "image" of king "in prayer"; O/jB "(granting of) petition"; → *utnēnu* I

unnīnu → also *umnīnu*

unnubu(m) "fructified; very fruitful" O/jB, esp. as (f)PN *Unnubu*, *Unnub(a)tum*; < *enēbu*

unnunu(m) mng. unkn. O/jB, desig. of person, also as PN; f. (an illness); < *enēnu* II ?

unnušu "weakened" jB, of teeth; < *enēšu* D

unnušūtu "weakened state" jB lex.; < *unnušu*

unnutu ~ "faint" jB of star; < *enētu*

unqu(m) I, NA also *uqqu* f. "ring; (stamp-)seal" Bab., M/NA [ŠU.GUR] **1.** as ornament, of gold, silver etc.; *kīma u.* "(shaped) like a ring" **2.** NA/NB "signet-ring, stamp-seal" **3.** NA/NB "sealed document", NA *u. šarri* "royal edict"; NB *bīt unqātu* "chancery"; OA → *annuqum*

unqu II "neck" NB, ${}^{uzu}u.$ of sheep as cut of meat; < Aram.

unṣu → *umṣu* I

unšinakku (an edible item)? jB, eaten in dream

unšu "weakness" jB of condition of populace; < *enēšu*

unû (a kind of meat) jB lex.

unumma → *anumma*

unummīum → *annimmû*

unuššu (state service) Ug.; < Hurr.?; → *unuššuḫuli*

unuššuḫuli (land-holder with state-service obligations) Alal.; < Hurr.; → *unuššu*

unūtu(m), Mari etc. *enūtu(m)*, NA *anūtu*; pl. OAkk *unuātum*, OB *uniātum*, *unêtum*, *unâtu(m)*, *enâtum* "tools, equipment, household utensils" [NÍG.GÚ.NA; Á.KÁR] of house, palace; of oxen, donkeys, plough, ship, journey, battle; of potter, carpenter etc.; of copper, gold etc.; *u. libbi* "internal organs", i.e. liver etc.

unuzānû (a wooden implement) jB lex.

unzaḫḫu, *unza/erḫu* → *umšarḫum*

upānu → *ubānu*

upatinnum (a vassal)? OA; < Hitt.?

upātum → *ubātum*

upāṭu(m) "(nasal) mucus" Bab., usu. pl.; of human, sheep; transf. of exudation from earth (a kind of bitumen)?, from plant *u. ašāgi*

upellû(m), *upillû(m)* Bab. **1.** "charcoal" **2.** "charcoal-burner" [Ú.BIL]; < Sum.

upinzer, *upi(n)zar* (or *ubi(n)ze/ar*) ~ (a caterpillar) jB lex.

upīšū, *epīšū* pl. tant.? "(magical) procedures, rites" jB, Bogh.; of Asalluḫi, of demon, of human; < *epēšu* II

upītum "ship of Opis"?; < *upûm* II

upizar → *upinzer*

uplētum ~ "late crop" OB, *še'(um) u.* "late barley"; < *apālu* II

uplu(m) "head-louse" O/jB; > *uppulu* II

upnu(m) "(cupped) hand" Bab., M/NA; *u. petû* "to open palm(s)" to pray (→ *pūtu* II); for receipt of e.g. grain, also transf. of suffering, blood; "handful" as measure, Bogh., NB, also pl. f.

uppadētu, *u/appa/udētu* (an overseer) NB; < Iran.

uppašannu, *uppasannu* (leather component of chariot) Alal., Nuzi; < Hurr.?; → *abšānu*

uppattu, *upputtu* "mole-cricket"? jB, NA [UB.PAD]; in med.; < Sum.

u(p)piātu, *uppayātu* (a source of royal income) NB; < OPers.

uppītu (an object) jB lex.

uppu(m) I "tube, socket etc." Bab., NA [(GIŠ.)MUD] "socket" for door-bolt, pick-handle; "tube, pipette" of metal, for liquids; *u. aḫi(m)* "armpit"; (part of intestines)?

uppu(m) II, *ḫuppu* "(a type of) drum" OAkk?, Bab. [ÙB]; of leather, j/NB of silver, bronze; < Sum.

uppu III (a surface)? jB lex., and in *u. šadî* mng. uncl.

uppu → also *ḫuppu* II

uppû → *upû* I; *wapûm* D; *erpu*

uppudētu → *uppadētu*

uppultu(m), Ass. *appultu* O/jB, NA **1.** "late crop" of cereals [SIG] **2.** "late-born" lex., of sheep; in PNs, of child; < *apālu* II

uppulu(m) I "late" Bab., NA [SIG] of cereal crop *še'u u.*, also *u.* alone as subst.; of animal "born late in season"; of child; of rain, flood, agricultural labour; < *apālu* II

uppulu(m) II D "to delouse" O/jB lex.; < *uplu* denom.

uppuntu → *upumtum*

uppunu → *ubbunu*

uppuqu ~ "solid" O/jB; Am. of gold artefacts; < *epēqu* or *upqu* I ?

uppusu I (or *ubbusu*) (an outer garment) M/jB; lex. *u. qāti*; < *uppusu* II

uppusu II (or *ubbusu*) **D** ~ "to fringe (with wool)"? MB; > *uppusu* I

uppusu → also *ubbusu*

uppuštu(m) **1.** OB ~ "calculated amount" of silver ? **2.** jB lex. (woman with special hair-style)?; < *epēšu* II D

uppušu ~ "well looked-after"? jB lex. of date palm; < *epēšu* II D

upputtu "blind (snake)" j/NB [MUŠ.IGI.NU.TUKU]; < *uppuṭu*

upputtu → also *uppattu*

uppuṭu "blind" jB; > *upputtu*; → *ḫuppudum* II

upqu(m) I "block; stump (of tree)" O/jB; < *epēqu* ?; → *uppuqu*

upqum II "pack(-ass)" OA; < *epēqu*

upru I (a cloth headdress) jB [TÚG.BALLA] for men, women; lex. (term for dregs, lees)?; < *apāru*; > *upurtu*; → *uprû*

upru II "dust" Am.; < W.Sem.

uprû (a headdress) MB; < *apāru*; → *upru* I

upšaššû(m) "(magical) procedure(s); sorceries" Bab., usu. pl. [NÍG.AK.A] by deity (Asalluḫi), king; usu. of malevolent spells, rites; < *epēšu* II

uptu (or *artu*) mng. unkn. NA rit.

upû(m) I, occas. *uppû* "cloud" O/jB [DUNGU]; Adad *šākin u.* "who makes clouds"; *kīma Šamaš ina u.* "like the sun from a cloud"; transf. of eyes *upê malâ* "clouded over"; < *apû* III

upûm II "of Opis" OB, of paint; < PlN; > *upītum*

upû → also *ubû*

upumtum, *upuntu*, occas. *uppuntu*; Susa pl. *upunāti* "(a type of) flour" Bab. [ZÌ.MAD.GÁ ?] jB of emmer, for offerings

upura'ena (a kind of emmer)? Nuzi; < Hurr.

upurtu(m), Mari *ḫupurtum* (a form of wig or headgear) O/jB, for woman; for statue; < *upru* I

upūšū → *ubūšū*

uqāru → *waqārum*

uqniātum, *uqnâtu* pl. tant. "blue(-green) wool" Bab., NA [SÍK.ZA.GÌN(.NA)]; j/NB *šammi u.* "woad" [Ú.ZA.GÌN.NA]; < *uqnû*

uqnītum "blue"? OB as fPN; < *uqnû*

uqnû(m), Ug. *uqunu*, NA also *iqnû* "lapis lazuli; turquoise?" [NA4.ZA.GÌN] as material for seal, jewellery etc.; pure, valuable *kīma u.* "as lapis lazuli"; as penalty to temple; *šadî u.* "mountain of l.", NB, from Sogdiana; ${}^{íd}U.$, the river

Karun; *u. kūri* "kiln l." i.e. blue glass/glaze, also of other colours; *agurri u.* "blue-glazed brick"; > *uqniātum, uqnītum, qunû; qununnītu;* → *qunātā*

uqqu, *ugu* (a paralysis) jB lex., med.; < *eqēqu*

uqqu → also *unqu* I

uqqû I "painted" jB of pot, door; < *equ* D

uqqû(m) II **D** "to incise" OAkk, O/jB; also (thereby) "to inscribe, prescribe"

uqqû → also *waqûm* D

uqqubum (or *uqqupum*) (a handicapped person) OB lex.

uqququ "tongue-tied, dumb" jB lex.; < *eqēqu*

uqqurtum → *waqqurtum*

uqquru(m) (a handicapped person) OB lex.

uqru → *waqrum*

uqu "people, populace; troops" NB [ÉRIN]

ūqu mng. unkn. jB

uqunu → *uqnû*

uqūpu, *i/aqūpu* "ape" j/NB; *šušān u.* "ape trainer"; also as PN; < Sanskr.; → *udūmu*

uqūru(m) "palm-heart" O/jB [GIŠ.ŠÀ. GIŠIMMAR] core leaves of date palm; (a kind of reed); "palm-milk"?

urādu → *warādum*

Uraḫum (a month) Mari

urāku(m) (a long implement, phps.) "rod" OAkk, Bab., OA of metal [SUD.A ?], stone; used in glass-making; NB (an engraver's chisel)?; lex. (a clay rod); < *arāku*

urannu → *uriyānu*

urantu "fennel plant" Ug. lex.; < *uriyānu*

urânu → *uriyānu*

ūrānu "puppy" jB lex.

urāsu, NB *urāšu* (a foreman) M/NA, Nuzi, NB; of state labourers, Ass. esp. in building work; > *urāsūtu, urāsuḫlu*

urāsuḫlu ~ "foreman" Nuzi; < *urāsu* + Hurr. *-uḫlu*

urāsūtu "rôle of foreman" NA, of weavers; < *urāsu*

urāṣum → *urīṣu*

urāšu(m) I (a plot of land) Bab., belonging to s.o., to PN; NB ~ "(state) dues on *u.* land"

urāšu II (s.th. dirty) jB; "a dirty cloth"; med. "septic wound, lesion"; < *warāšum*

urāšu → also *urāsu*

urâtu → *urû* I.II

ūrātu (a garment) Ug.; = *ūru* II f. pl.?

urā'u → *warûm* II

urbabillu → *ḫurbabillu*

urballu, *uruballu* "quail"? jB [ŠEN.ŠEN.BAL. MUŠEN]

urbānu, *urbannu* "papyrus" j/NB, NA; for writing; to make boats, stylus; → *urbatu* I

urbatānum "overgrown with rushes" OB, of field; also as PN; < *urbatu* I

urbatiš "like rushes" jB; < *urbatu* I; → *urubā'iš*

urbatu(m) I "rush" O/jB [Ú.NÚMUN] for boats, as fuel; as drug, also *zēr/išid u.* "seed/root of rush"; > *urbatiš, urubā'iš, urbatānum;* → *urbānu*

urbatu II, *rubatu* (a kind of worm) jB [MAR. GAL]; *u. sāmtu* "red worm"; as illness, *urbatu maruṣ* "suffers from worm(s)"

urbatu → also *urpatu* II

urbātu → *urubātu* I.II

urbītum (a stone) OB lex.

urbu(m) I "inflow" OA, NB; of goods etc.; NB for → *erbu* I; < *erēbu* I

urbu II (a work gang)? jB/NA

urdānūtu "servitude" NA [ÌR-]; < *wardum*

urdimmu → *uridimmu*

urdu → *wardum*

urduttu → *wardūtum*

urgulû j/NB, NA **1.** (a lion) [UR.GU.LA]; *šārat u.* "lion-skin"; also as figurine and illness **2.** "(the constellation) Leo" [MUL.UR.GU.LA; also MUL.UR.A ?]; < Sum.

urḫiniwe mng. unkn. Nuzi, in *bīt u.*; < Hurr.

urḫiš → *arḫiš*

urḫu(m) I, Ass., Bogh. also *arḫu* f. & m. "way, path" [occas. ITU !] difficult, distant, unopened etc.; *ālik urḫi(m)* "traveller"; *u. šadî* "mountain path", astr. *u. šamê* "heavenly path"; transf. "way of life"; > *Araḫtu*?

urḫu II (a bronze object) Nuzi

urḫu → also *warḫum*

uriānu → *uriyānu*

uribḫu, *uribšu* ~ "(kind of) plum"? jB lex.

uribittu, *uributtu* (a plant)? MB

uribšu → *uribḫu*

uributtu → *uribittu*

uriddu → *urīdum*

uridimmu, *urdimmu* "Wild Dog" jB, a myth. beast [UR.IDIM] with Tiāmat; as figurine; astr. (a constellation incl.) Lupus ?; < Sum.

urīdum, *uriddu* (a drinking vessel) O/jB; Mari, in gold

urigallu "standard, symbol; hut with standard" M/NB, NA [gi/dÙRI.GAL] *u. zuqqupu* "to erect a standard", d*u. ālik pānīya* "the standards which precede me"; "ritual hut"; "(represent ation of) standard", in gypsum, on wall; < Sum.

uriḫaše (a precious stone) Qatna; < Hurr.?

uriḫu (a thorny plant) jB lex.

uriḫul(lu) "reimbursement for work not performed" Nuzi; < Hurr.

urindu → *erimtu* II

urinnu I "eagle" M/jB; also desig. of demon; astr. [$^{mul/d}$U$_5$.RÍ.IN] (a constellation); lex. (a kind of rope)?

urinnu II "standard" j/NB; NB *bīt u.* (a treasury); as desig. of DN, of Erra *urinnāku* "I am a standard" on march; < Sum.

urīnu → *erēnu* I

uriqtu "jaundice"? jB; < *warāqum*

urīṣu(m), Mari *urāṣum* "male goat" [MÁŠ; MÁŠ.GAL; OB MÁŠ.ÙZ ?] *u. šadî* "mountain goat"

uritannu ~ "selvage, edge of textile" Nuzi; < Hurr.

urītu (a ring)? jB lex.

uriṭû → *urṭû*

uriyaḫḫu → *yaraḫḫu*

uriyanni (a functionary) Bogh., Ug.; < Hitt.?

uriyānu(m), *uriānu(m)*, *urânu(m)*, *urannu* "fennel"? OAkk, O/jB, NA [Ú.TÁL.TÁL] as vegetable, in field; as drug; *zēr/išid u.* "seed/ root of fennel"; > *urantu*

urīzu (a stone) jB; = *ḫurīzu* II ?

urkānu → *warkānum*

urkanuḫli (a retainer)? Nuzi; < Hurr.

urkat → *warkat*

urkatam → *warkatam*

urkatu → *warkatum*

urkātu, *uškātu* (a kind of meat) NB; < *warkatum* ?

urkēt → *warkītam*

urki → *warki*

urkidānum (or *urkitānum*) (a kind of timber)? OAkk

urkiš, NA occas. *urkišši* "later" M/NA "in future, at a later date"; jB → *arkiš*

urkītā, *urkītam* → *warkītam*

urkitānum → *urkidānum*

urkīte → *warkītam*

urkittu → *Urkītum*; *warkītum*

Urkītum, NA *Urkittu*, NB *Arkayītu*, *Arkattu*, *Aška'/yītu* f. "(Ištar) of Uruk"; < PlN

urkītum → also *warkītum*

urkīu → *warkûm*

urku(m) "length" OAkk, Ass.; < *arāku*

urkû → *warkûm*

urmaḫḫu "lion (statue etc.)" jB(Ass.) [UR. MAḪ]; < Sum.

urmaḫlilu, *urmaḫlullû* "lion-man" j/NB [UR. MAḪ.LÚ.U$_{18/19}$.LU] representations in mag. etc.; < Sum.

urmazillum "tree-stump"? OB

urnakku (a sanctuary)? jB lex.

urnatu I (a garment) NA

urnatu II ~ "strong, manly" jB lex.

urnibu (a plant) jB lex.

urnīgu, *urningu*, *urnīqu* "crane"? j/NB; also (a plant)?

urnu I (a snake)? jB

urnu(m) II "(small) cedar" OAkk, Bab.; < W.Sem.; → *erēnu* I

urnû, *ḫurnûm* "mint"? O/jB; *zēr/ār u.* "seed/ sprig of mint"; *u. ša šadê* "mountain m."; → *qurnû*

urnuqqu (a plant) jB lex., med.

urpāniš "as though with clouds" jB; < *urpu*

urparinnu "butcher, slaughterer" Nuzi; < Hurr.

urpatu I; pl. *urpā/ētu* "cloud" Bogh., jB [DUNGU] *u. ṣalimtu* "black cloud"; transf., of displeasure, *u. nekelmûk* "your frown is a cloud"; < *erēpu*

urpatu(m) II, occas. *urbatu* "bedroom" O/jB

urpu(m) m. & f. "cloud(s)" Bab., NA [DUNGU]; NA *u. dannat* "cloud-cover is heavy"; du. *urpēn* ~ "at sunset"?; transf. OB *urpīya akaṣṣar* "I gather my clouds" (obscure metaphor); < *erēpu*

urpumma in *u. epēšu* "to slaughter" Nuzi; < Hurr.

urqatta mng. uncl. NB; < *warāqum* ?

urqītu "vegetation, greenery" M/NB, NA(lit.) [Ú.ŠIM]; *u. ṣēri* "v. of desert"; *u. bašû(m)/ šubšu(m)*, *(w)aṣû(m)/šūṣû(m)* "to (make) v. happen, (make) v. come up"; < *warāqum*

urqu → *warqum*; *wurqum*

urra(m) **1.** OA, O/jB "tomorrow"; *urra(m) šēra(m)* "in the future, one day" **2.** jB "in the daytime"; < *urru*

urradudû (a merchant)? jB lex.; < Sum.

urrāku "sculptor" jB lex.

urrākūtu "sculptor's craft" jB(Ass.) in *šipir u.* "sculptors' work"; < *urrāku*

urrānu → *murrānu*

urrāšena pl. ~ "desiderata" Am.; < Hurr.

urrīqu → *wurrīqum*

urru(m) "daytime" OAkk, Bab., NA [Am. U$_4$.KAM ?] **1.** "day" opp. to night, *u. u mūša*, *mūša u u.*; *7 urrī u 7 mūšāti* **2.** "early morning, day(break)" (→ *šāt urri*) **3.** "tomorrow, the morn", *ina urri warḫim* "on 2nd day of month; > *urra*

urru → also *ūru* I

urrû I "trimmed, pruned" jB lex., of palm tree; < *arû* VI

urrû II mng. uncl. jB lex.
urrû → also *arû* VI D; *urû* I.II
urruḫiš "very quickly, hastily" M/jB; < *arāḫu* I
urrumbum, urruppu → *ḫurḫuppu*
urrupu "clouded" jB of sky; < *erēpu*
urruṣu mng. unkn. M/jB lex.
urrušu → *wurrušum*
urrûtu → *erûtu* II
ursānu → *uršānu* II
ursû mng. unkn. jB lex.
ursunu ~ "warrior" jB lex.; → *uršānu* I
ursuppu → *urṣuppu*
ursūtu (a storeroom, deposit)? NA
urṣītu (a plant) jB lex.
urṣu(m) I, Ug. also *erṣu* f. "mortar (for spices)" O/jB [NA4.NA.ZÀ.ḪI.LI(.A)]; *elīt u.* "pestle"
urṣu II in *kalab u.* 'dog of the earth ?', "badger" jB [UR.KI]; → *erṣetu*
urṣuppu, *ursuppu* (a vessel with knobs)? jB lex.
uršānatu(m) "heroine" O/jB(lit.); goddess *u. ilī* "heroine of the gods"; < *uršānu* I
uršānu(m) I, *uršannu* "warrior, hero" OAkk, O/jB(lit.); also as PN; < Sum.; > *uršānūtu*; *uršānatu*; → *ursunu*
uršānu(m) II, *ursānu* "wild dove" O/jB [IR7.SAG.MUŠEN; UR.SAG.MUŠEN]; < Sum.; = *amursānu* ?
uršānūtu "heroism" jB, of deity; < *uršānu* I
uršašillu (a small viper)? jB lex.
uršu(m) I "bedroom" O/jB; OB loc.-adv. *uršumma* "in the bedroom"; Ug. *bīt u.*, of prince; jB *uruš kallūti* "bridal chamber"; → *eršu* IV
uršu(m) II "desire" O/jB; < *erēšu* II
uršu III "blemish, dark spot" jB med.; < *warāšum*
uršu → also *ḫuršu*
ûrtu → *wu''urtum*
urṭû, *erṭû*, *uriṭû*, Nuzi *urṭā'iu* (a plant; a colour) M/jB, NA **1.** (a resinous bush) lex., med. **2.** (a dye, dyed wool) **3.** (part of date palm, phps.) "fibre" **4.** Bogh. (a dove); < PlN
urû(m) I, *urrû*; pl. f. **1.** MB "stallion" **2.** "stable, stall" Bab., M/NA, for sheep, oxen, esp. horses; NB also *bīt urê*; *rab urê* MB, NB as family name **3.** NA, NB "team" of horses, mules; *rab urâti* "overseer of teams"
urû(m) II "cut branch, palm frond" Bab. [GIŠ.PA.KUD] NB *Ša-urêšu* "Frond-supplier" as family name; < *arû* VI
urû IV (a bowl) Nuzi, jB [DUG.GAN.SAR]; of bronze, wood; jB med., for drug
urû V pl. tant. "aromatics" jB lex., coll. term
urû VI "fish spawn" jB lex.; < *arû* IV
urû VII; f. *urītu(m)* "of Ur" O/jB lex., of sheep, bed, ship; also as (f)PN; < PlN
urû → also *ūru* II
ūru(m) I, NB also *urru*; pl. f. "roof" [ÙR] of house, palace, temple; OAkk *iṣ ūrim* "roof-beam"; *Bēl-ūri(m)* (a demon); *bāb ū.* "door to roof"; transf. "protection" in PNs; < Sum.
ūru(m) II, *urû* "(nakedness, i.e.) pudenda" OAkk, O/jB [GAL4.LA] of man, woman; "(re-presentation of) pubic triangle" OB, in gold; < *erû* III; → *ūrātu*
ūru(m) III, *ḫūru* "limb, shaft" O/jB of human; transf. of tool, in silver; < Sum.
ūru IV "city" jB lex.; < Sum.
urubā'iš "like rushes" jB var. of *urbatiš*; < *urbatu* I
uruballu → *urballu*
urubānu "guarantor" Ug.; < Ug.
urubātu I, *urbātu* pl. tant. "keystone(s)" Nuzi, jB [SIG4.TAB.BA.KU4.RA]; *u. šakānu* "to install the k."; < *erēbu* I
urubātu II, occas. *urbātu* pl. tant. ~ "lamentation" Mari, jB
urudû "(a kind of) copper" jB, *pitiq u.* "copper casting"; < Sum.
ur'udu(m), *ḫurḫudum* "windpipe, throat" Bab. [UZU.GÚ.MUR] of human, animal, bird
uruḫḫu(m) "hair (of head)" O/jB [DÌLIB (=SAG×ŠID)] *u. qaqqadišu, nakkaptišu* "hair of his head, forehead"
uruḫlu → *eruḫlu*
urukmannu (part of a shield) Am., Nuzi; of metal; < Hurr.?
urullu I, jB also *arullu*; usu. f. pl. "foreskin" M/jB; *mūṣu ša libbi urullātišu* "discharge from his f."; → *u.* II
urullu(m) II, jB also *arullu* (a kind of reed) O/jB; = *u.* I ?
urultannu (a functionary) Nuzi; < Hurr.
urummu mng. unkn. jB lex.
urūmu (a tree) MB(Ass.) in mountains
uruntu → *uruttu* II
urunzannu (a kind of table) Nuzi; < Hurr.
uruppum "armpit" of horse OB(Susa); → *aruppu*
uruššu **1.** MB (a wooden object) **2.** jB (a bush)?
uruštum (an object) Mari
urūšu ? "dirtiness" jB; < *warāšum*
uruthū, NA *aruthū* pl. tant. (a pair of implements) M/NA, Alal., Ug. of bronze, iron
uruti (a plant) jB lex.
uruttu(m) I (a stone) O/jB

uruttu II, occas. *uruntu* (name for middle Euphrates) jB lex.

uruttu → also *erûtu* II

urutu ~ "observation"? NB ref. to military surveillance

urûtu → *erûtu* II

urzababītu(m), *urzabītum* (a lyre)? Mari, O/jB lex.; < (king) Ur-Zababa

urzīnu(m), *ḫurzīnum*, *urzinnu* (a tree) O/jB, NA

usābu(m) **1.** OB (a bird); also as PN **2.** jB (a tortoise, turtle); < PlN Adab ?

usaddû → *usandû*

usaḫum (a bird) OB lex.; = *usigu* ?

usāmu → *wasāmum*

usandû(m), *ušandû*, occas. *usaddû*, *sandû* "bird-catcher" [LÚ.MUŠEN.DÙ]; < Sum.?; > *sandâniš*

usangu ? "early crop" jB lex.; < Sum.

usāru subst. mng. unkn. NA

usātānu "generous" jB; < *usātu*

usātu(m), Ass. *usutu(m)* "help, assistance"; in gener. and financial, commercial aid; freq. in PNs; > *usātānu*

usertu, *usištu* "exaction" of payment, debt NB; < *esēru* III

usḫamu, *ušḫamu* (a pole for boats) jB lex.

usigu (a bird) jB lex.; → *usaḫum*

usikillu → *sikillu*

usištu → *usertu*

uskāru(m), *usqāru(m)*, *as/šk/qāru(m)* "crescent (moon)" Bab. [U4.SAKAR] **1.** "crescent moon", on first quarter **2.** (as epith. of Sîn) **3.** "crescent (-shaped) symbol, object" of metal, stone etc.; NB astr. (an instrument) **4.** math. (segment of a circle); < Sum.

usmītu → *usmû*

usmu → *wusmum*

usmû, *usumû*, *usumia*; f. *usmītu* "two-faced being" jB; ^{d}*U.* as deity; as monstrous birth

uspaḫḫu, *ušpaḫḫu* (a garment) Nuzi; < Hurr.

usqāru → *uskāru*

ussangû "lead goat" jB lex.; < Sum.

ussu → *ūsu* I

ussudu mng. unkn. **Dt** jB

ussuḫtu (desig. of a plant) jB lex.

ussuḫum "assigned"? OB; < *esēḫu* D

ussuktu "assignment, commission"? NA; < *esēḫu*

ussuku(m) mng. uncl. O/jB, NA; epith. of warts; of plough; < *esēḫu* or *esēqu* ?

ussulu(m), *uṣṣulu(m)* "crippled" O/jB lex.; < *eṣēlu*

ussurre(ma) → *assurri*

ustarbari, *ustar(a/i)bari/a/u* (a Persian official) NB(Nippur); < OPers.

ūsu(m) I, *ussu* "usage, custom, good practice" Bab.; *kī ū.* "according to tradition"; "correct procedure" for seed-plough; *ū. šūḫuzu(m)* "to teach good practices"; < Sum.

ūsu(m) II, OA *us'um*; pl. m. & f. "goose" Ass., O/jB [UZ.MUŠEN]; for food; representations in art, *qaqqad ū.* "goose-head" of stone; jB ^{na_4}*ū.* (a stone); < Sum.

ūsû (a street)? jB lex.

us'um → *ūsu* II

usukannu (a plant) jB lex. equated with *musukkannu*

usukānum (a bird) OB lex.

usukkatu → *musukku*

usukku(m), *sukku* Bab. **1.** "temple, upper cheek" [TE; ÚNU; jB occas. TE+MÚRU]; tears *ina u.*; also du. *usukkāya* "my cheeks" **2.** (lining wall of irrigation channel)

usukku → also *musukku*

usuktu ~ "side-piece" of furniture ? MA

usumia → *usmû*

usumittu → *asumittu*

usumû → *usmû*

usurtu(m) "encirclement (of enemy)" O/jB; < *esēru* II

usutu → *usātu*

uṣābu → *waṣābum*

uṣārum, *aṣārum* "animal pen" OAkk, OB in PlN; → *ḫaṣāru*

uṣā'u → *waṣûm*

uṣertu j/NB mng. uncl.; = *uṣurtu* ?

uṣpu → *waṣpum*

uṣṣu → *ūṣu*

uṣṣû → *wuṣṣûm*

uṣṣudu (a handicapped person) jB lex.

uṣṣulu → *ussulu*

uṣṣuru I "drawn, decorated" j/NB of pattern on lizard etc.; < *eṣēru* D

uṣṣurum II **D** "to listen attentively"? OB(poet.)

uṣṣuru III **D** "to cut through" jB; neck, of sword

uṣṣuṣu → *wuṣṣuṣum*

uṣû(m) (a textile or cloth) O/jB [NÍG.DÁRA]

uṣû → also *waṣûm*

ūṣu(m), *uṣṣu* "arrow(head)" O/jB, NA [(GIŠ.)GAG.TI; GIŠ.GAG]

uṣultu "(a kind of) knife" Am., jB, NA [GÍR.TUR], for offering; of iron

uṣurtu(m), occas. *ṣurtu* "drawing, plan" Bab., NA [GIŠ.ḪUR] **1.** "line drawing, plan" on tablet, figurine; "building plan, layout" on ground; "lines, patterns" on hand, face, liver etc.; astr. (a cruciform halo); *kakkab uṣurti* mng. uncl. **2.** transf. usu. pl. "designs, plans, ordinances" of gods; *u. ša lā etēqi* "inviolable prescription"; *ina adan lā ṣurti* "at a moment not preordained"; DN *bēl šīmāti u uṣurāti* "lord of destinies and (divine) plans"; < *eṣēru*; → *iṣratu*; *iṣurtu*; *uṣertu*

ušābu → *wašābum*

ušalliš "like river-flats" jB; < *ušallu*

ušallu(m) "(fields) along valley-bottom, river-flats" Bab., NA; *u. nāri* "river meadows"; < Sum.; > *ušalliš*, *ušallû*

ušallû "of the river-flats" jB lex., of trees

ušamītu, *ušamūtu* (an edible bird) NA

ušandû → *usandû*

ušartu → *išartu*

ušaru → *išaru* II

ušaštu, *ušāšum* "bird's nest" O/jB

ušbu "lair, hide"? jB; < *wašābum*

ušbum → also *wašbum*

ušburrudû "ritual to dispel sorcery" jB, NA [UŠ$_{11}$.BÚR.RU.DA]; NA *u. epāšu* "to carry out r.", *šumerāni ša ušburrudâni* "the Sumerian (texts) of the rituals"; < Sum.

ušdu → *išdu*

ušeštum, *ušēšum* mng. uncl. OB lex.

ušgidûm ~ (a narrow chamber) OB [É.UŠ. GÍD.DA] as storage chamber, hallway; < Sum.

ušḫamu → *usḫamu*

uškātu → *urkātu*

uškû I "later" NB adj.; also as adv. "on a later occasion"; → *warkûm*

uškû II "youth, servant" j/NB; < Sum.; → *wušgû*; *u.* I

uškûtu "service as *uškû*" NB; esp. *pūt u. X PN naši* "PN is liable for the service of X"; < *uškû* II

ušmadû ~ "side-plank" of a boat ? jB lex.

ušmannu f. "(military) camp" M/NA, jB(Ass.); *u. kaṣāru/šakānu* "to pitch camp"

ušmedû (a kind of meat)? jB lex.

ušmittu → *asumittu*

ušmûm (a functionary) Mari

ušnaru "(a kind of) lyre" jB lex.

ušpaḫḫu → *uspaḫḫu*

ušpapītu → *šubabītu*

ušpartu → *išpartu*

ušparu (a ruler's staff) j/NB [GIŠ.UŠ.BAR]; < Sum.?

ušparu → also *išparu*

ušpu (an oil container) Nuzi

ušqu → *wurqum*

ušrātum, *ušrētu* → *ešrētu*

ušriyānu "crown prince"? Ug.; < Ug.

uššābu → *waššābum*

uššatu(m) "anxiety, distress" O/jB; < *ašāšu* III

uššer → *wašārum* D 5

uššu(m) I usu. pl. "foundation(s)" OAkk, M/NA, M/NB [URU$_4$; SUḪ] OAkk *uššī bītim* "house foundations"; *u. nadû* (NA *karāru*) "to lay the foundations"; *ultu u. adi gabadibbī* "from foundation to parapet"; < Sum.?

uššu(m) II; pl. f. (a copper vessel) OAkk, for flour; jB lex.; < Sum.

uššu(m) III liter. "dead reed" O/jB [GI.ÚŠ]; < Sum.

uššu → also *umšu*

uššubu "productive" of lament, prayer ? jB; < *ešēbu*

uššuḫḫu (an object) Nuzi, of bronze; < Hurr.

uššultu (a plant) jB lex. equated with *aššultu*, *šulutu*

uššurātu → *šušrātu*

uššurtu → *wuššurtum*

uššuru → *wašārum* D; *wuššurum*

uššušiš "in much distress" jB; < *uššušu* I

uššušu(m) I "very distressed" Bab.; < *ašāšu* III; > *uššušiš*

uššušu(m) II (part of a reed) jB lex.

uššušu(m) III **D** "to renew" OB(Susa), j/NB, NA; "restore" building; *kubussâm u.* "renew land survey"; < *eššu* I denom.

uššuṭu (desig. of kind of horse) MB; < *wašāṭum*

ušta'ammu, *ušti'ammu* (a financial official) NB; < OPers.

uštabari (a Persian functionary) NB; < OPers.

ušti'ammu → *ušta'ammu*

uštu occas. OB, Susa, Nuzi for → *ištu*; > *ultu*

ušû(m), *ešium*, Nuzi *išiu*, MA *ašû* **1.** (a hard stone, phps.) "diorite, dolerite" [NA$_4$.ESI]; OAkk du. f. *ešītīn* **2.** (a hard wood, phps.) "ebony (*Dalbergia melanoxylon*)" [GIŠ.ESI] for furniture etc.; as timber, among booty; < Sum.; → *ašium*

ušuā'um mng. unkn. OAkk

ušukullatu (a reed artefact) NB

ušultu(m) I "vein" O/jB [ÚŠ]; *u. ša dāmim* "v. of blood"; demon drinks *ušlāti*

ušultu II "(lump of) mud"? jB [IM.LAGAB]; from river; in intestine

ušumgallatu 'female dragon', i.e. "monarch" MB, of Ištar; < *ušumgallu*

ušumgallu(m), *šum/ngallu* Bab., NA [UŠUMGAL] **1.** "great dragon, snake", in myth; "(image of) dragon", *šungallē ša DN ina muḫḫi izzazzūni* "d.s on which DN stands"

2. "monarch, sole ruler", epith. of deities, king; < Sum.; > *ušumgallatu*

ušummu(m), *šummu* ~ "dormouse" Bab. [PÉŠ. GIŠ.GI] eaten, offered

ušurā, *ušurû* "10 each" Nuzi, NA; < *ešer*

ušurrum "colleague" OAkk, OB(poet.); < Sum.

ušurtum "group of 10" OB [(NAM.)10] *wakil u.* "decurion"; (^{na_4})*u.* (an object, phps. a weight); < *ešer*

ušurû → *ušurā*

ušussû → *ušuzzāyu*

ušuššû (a stone item) Ug. lex.

ušuzzatta → *uzuzzatta*

ušuzzāyu, *ušussû* "standing, permanent" NB in *qaštu ušuzzāyītu*, of military land tenure; < *izuzzum*

ušuzzu → *izuzzum*

uta → *uti*

utabru (an animal)? MA, representations in art

utaqqû → *waqûm*

utara/i → *uti*

utāru → *watārum*

utatiti (a kind of wood)? Nuzi; < Hurr.

utâtu → *itûtu* I

utemenakku (a wooden object) jB lex.; < Sum.

utena → *uti*

uteqqû → *waqûm*

utḫurum (a breed of sheep)? OA

uti, *uta*, *utara/i*; pl. *utena* "(additional) payment" Nuzi, on occasion of exchange, in barley, sheep etc.; < Hurr.

Utitḫe (a month) Alal.; < Hurr.

utkû → *itkû*

utlellû(m) "to rise up, raise up" O/jB(lit.) [GALAM] math. "be higher, exceed" in number; of deity, king "be exalted"; trans. "exalt" s.o.; < *elû* III Rt; > *mutlellû*

utlu(m) "lap" OAkk, O/jB (sexually) of man, woman; of god(dess), esp. in PNs; transf. of tamarisk; of night, i.e. sleep; OB(poet.) *u. šamê* "lap (= interior) of heaven"

utnānu → *uatnannu*

utnennu → *utnēnu* I.II

utnēnu(m) I, *utnennu* "supplication, prayer" OAkk, j/NB(lit.) to deity, king; < *utnēnu* II infin.; → *unnīnu*

utnēnu(m) II, *utnennu(m)* "to pray" Bab.(lit.) "**G**" (pres. *utnên*, pret. *utnēn*, *utnīn*) to deity, person **Gtn**? (*utenennen*, pret. *utennēn*) OB; > *utnēnu* I; *mutnennû*; *tēnīnu*, *tēnintu*; → *enēnu* IV

utru "excess, profit" NB, commercially etc.; astr. *u. u muṭṭê* "excess and shortfall"; < *watārum*

utru → also *watrum*

uttalû → *uddalû*

uttartu → *attartu*

uttāru ~ "superfluous, extra"? NA of stones, (offering-)tables; < *watārum*

uttū- → *attū-*

uttû I mng. unkn. jB lex. (rdg. uncert.)

uttû II mng. unkn. MB in *nād u.* "waterskin of *u.*"

uttuku I "bent" jB, of palm tree; < *atāku* D

uttuku II, *utukku* (calculating device, phps.) "abacus" jB; < Sum.

uttulu mng. unkn. jB lex.

utturu "exaggerated, boastful" jB of speech; < *watārum*

uttūtu (or *uttûtu*) "terror"? jB lex.

uttūtum → also *ettūtu*

uttûtu → *uttūtu*

uttuzilûm "good land" OB, left untilled; < Sum.

utû "(Sum. weaving goddess) Uttu" jB lex.; → *ettūtu*

utû → also *atû* II

utugānû → *tugānû*

utuḫḫum (a kind of bread) Early Mari

utukku(m) (an evil demon) [UDUG]; *u. ṣēri, šadî, tâmti, qabri* "desert, mountain, sea, tomb demon"; also "ghost" of dead; *utukkiš* "like a demon"; < Sum.

utukku → also *uttuku* II

utulgallu "chief herdsman" jB, desig. of Ennugi; < Sum.; → *utullu*

utullu(m); pl. f. "chief herdsman" O/jB, MA [Ú.TÚL; UTUL] of cows, sheep; transf., desig. of deity, king; > *utullūtu*; → *utulgallu*

utullu → also *tulūlu*

utullūtu, Ass. *utulluttu* "post of chief herdsman" MB, Bogh. lex.; < *utullu*

utūlu → *itūlu*

utūnu(m), *itūnum*, *atūnu* f. "kiln" Bab. [UDUN] for bricks, pottery; throw slave *ana u.*; MB for gold; NB *rab u.* "kiln supervisor"; < Sum.; → *udunmāḫu*

utuplu(m) ~ "scarf, shawl"? O/jB [(TÚG.)Ú. TUP.LU] of wool

utuppu (an ornament)? Am.

utuptum (or *uṭuptum*) ~ "utensils, furnishings"? OA

uturrā'ū pl. tant. "excess" OA, of copper etc.; < *watārum*

uturtu(m) O/jB **1.** lex., math. "excess" **2.** lex. (a wooden clamp, bracket)?; < *watārum*

utūtum → *atūtum* II

utûtu → *atûtu*; *itûtu* I

utu'ūtu → *atûtu*

ūṭānum '$^1/_2$-cubiter', a wrestler ? OB lex.; < *ūṭu*; → *ūṭûm*

uṭṭatu(m), *uṭṭetu(m)* "grain, barley" [ŠE.BAR; ŠE; KU.KU (= *uṭṭātu*)] **1.** "barley"; OB, MB phps. "cereals" in gener. **2.** pl. "grains, seeds" of plants, trees etc. **3.** st. abs. *uṭṭet*, *uṭṭat* "1 grain"; as unit of weight = $^1/_{180}$ shekel, also as surface measure; linear measure $^1/_6$ *ubānu* **4.** (a kind of wart) on human, sheep

uṭṭû (a priest) jB lex.; < Sum.

ūṭu(m), OA occas. *īṭum* "span, half-cubit" [$^1/_2$ KÙŠ]; stat. abs. *ūṭ*; *ammat u ūṭu* "1 $^1/_2$ cubits"; > *ūṭānum*, *ūṭûm*; NA → *rūṭu*

ūṭûm OB lex. = *ūṭānum*

uṭuptum → *utuptum*

u'udu → *u'du*

u''urtu → *wu''urtum*

uwane, *uwene* mng. uncl. Alal.; < Hurr.?

Uwarum (or *Uwurum*) (a festival)? Mari, also as MN

uwene → *uwane*

Uwurum → *Uwarum*

ūya → *ū'a*

uyāḫu, *uyūḫu* (an exclamation)? jB lex., desig. of a kind of caterpillar or sim.

uzaglalû mng. unkn. jB lex.; < Sum.

uzalāqu "$^1/_4$ *ikû*" jB lex., surface area = 25 *mūšar*; < Sum.

uzālatum → *ḫuzālu*

uzallû(m) "third watch of the night" O/jB; < Sum.

uzāltum, uzālu → *ḫuzālu*

uzāru (cloth for cult statues)? NB, of wool; < W.Sem.?

uzbarra (a type of crown land) NB, *u. ša šarri*; < Iran.?

uzibbûm → *uzubbû*

uzību "abandoned (baby), foundling" jB lex.; < *ezēbu*

uznānātu 'eary (plant)' phps. "plantain"? jB lex., med.; < *uznu*

uznānu(m) "big-ears" O/MB, NA as PN; < *uznu*

uznu(m) f. "ear; wisdom, understanding" [GEŠTU; GÉŠTU; GÈŠTU] **1.** "ear" of human, animal; for ornaments; cut off, wounded, esp. as punishment; med., blocked, deaf etc.; NB animal's ear (as meat) **2.** transf. "awareness, attention"; *u. petû(m)* "to enlighten" s.o., OA "inform" s.o.; *u. šakānu(m)* "to pay attention", *u. ibašši* "attention is given" to s.o., s.th. **3.** "wisdom", DN *mudû gimir u.* "knowing all wisdom"; "memory, recollection", *ina u.-šunu ibši* "they were mindful of" **4.** transf. of objects, "handle, lug" of vessel; *uzun lalê* "kid's ear" (a plant, phps.) "plantain" [Ú.UR/ÚR.TÁL.TÁL]; *u. qanê* "reed's ear" (a bird, phps.) "crane"; > *uzuntu*, *uznānu*, *uznānātu*; *wazzunum*

uzubbatu "reprieve" NB in PN *U.-ili*; < *ezēbu*

uzubbû(m), occas. *uzibbûm* "divorce(-payment)" O/jB; *(kasap) u.* "divorce money"; < *ezēbu*

uzuntu, *uzuttum* **1.** ~ "ring" or attachment on implements **2.** jB, NA [NÍG.GEŠTU] (part of the entrails); < *uznu*

uzuru mng. uncl. Nuzi, desig. of horse

uzuttabara (a functionary) NB; < OPers.

uzuttum → *uzuntu*

uzuzzatta, *ušuzzatta* adv. "standing up" jB of human posture; < *izuzzum*

uzuzzu → *izuzzum*

uzzapnannu (a gold item) Am.; < Hurr.?

uzzatu(m) "anger, rage" O/jB; < *ezēzu*

uzzu(m) "anger, rage" Bab.; *u. ili ana amēli* "divine wrath towards man"; transf. *u. qabli* "heat of battle"; moon wears *agê u.* "crown of wrath"; < *ezēzu*

uzzubu(m) ~ "neglected, degenerate" O/jB lex., of human, of domestic animal; < *ezēbu*

uzzulikarû, *uzzulikirû* (desig. of women, of furniture) Nuzi; phps. "young" or "in good condition"?; < Hurr.

uzzuqu ~ "sling-stone"? jB lex.

W

wa “and” OA occas. for *u*

wā → *ū'a*

wa'ārum → *wârum*

wabādum → *wabātum*

wabālu(m), jB also *abālu*, M/NA *ubālu* (→ also *babālu*) “to carry, bring” **G** (pret. *ubil*, pl. *ublū*, also *ūbi(l)lū*; perf. *ittabal*, early OB *itbal*, NA *ittūbil*; stat. *babil*; ptcp. *(w)ābilu(m)*, O/jB also *bābilu(m)*) [TÙM; OB math. TÚM] **1.** “bring” things, animals, people; life, prosperity; message, dream **2.** “fetch” a price, “be worth” **3.** “spend” day, night **4.** of wind, of water “carry off, sweep away” crops etc. **5.** “carry” unborn child, penalty, yoke, burden of work **6.** math. “multiply” **7.** “bring” s.o. to do s.th. **8.** of heart (*libbu*, *kabattu*) “desire” **9.** of mouth (*pû*) “demand, utter” **10.** of fate (*šīmtu*) “carry off” **11.** *pānī w.* “forbear, forgive”; *bābil p.* “merciful” **12.** *qāta/ī w.* “lay hand(s) on, touch” **Gtn 1.** iter. of G **2.** “look after, maintain, serve” **3.** “control, steer”, “administer” cosmos etc. **4.** of demon, limbs “be active” (**D** → *babālu* D) **Dtn** for Gtn Am. only **Š 1.** “send, deliver” thing, animal, (subordinate) person **2.** caus. of G 4 **ŠR** Mari **Štn** iter. of Š OA, Mari **Št**^{1} pass. of Š **Št**^{2} [ḪI.ḪI] **1.** “stir” ingredients **2.** “move back and forth” lips, tongue etc. **3.** “consider thoroughly, deliberate”; “understand, interpret” omen etc. **4.** “calculate, multiply” **5.** stat. of omen “is balanced, equivocal” **N** (pret. *ibbabil*, pres. *ibbabbal*) pass. of G, esp. G 11 *pānūka/kunu ul ibbabbalū* “you will not be forgiven”; > *biltu*; *wābilum*; *muštēbilum*, *muštābiltu*; *muttabbilu*, *muttabbiltu*; *šēbultu*, *šūbultu*; *šutābulu*, *šutābultu*; *ubilu*; → *babālu*; *tabālu*

wabartum, *ubartum* (a small Ass. trading colony) OA; < *wabrum*

wabātum (or *wab/pāt/ṭ/dum*) mng. unkn. OAkk, stat. in PNs

(w)abā'u(m) ~ “to weed” O/jB **G** (*i/i*) field; > *wabûtum*

waberē → *wabrum*

wābilum “carrier” OA; < *wabālu*

wabrum, *ubru(m)*; OA obl. pl. *waberē* “stranger, foreign resident” Ass., Ug., Bogh.; OB lex. [NA in PNs SUḪUŠ]; > *wabartum*; *uburtu*; *wabrūtum*; → *ubāru*

wabrūtum “status as *wabrum*” OA; < *wabrum*

wabûtum “weeding” OB, of field; < *wabā'um*

wadā'um (or *watā'um*) (a bronze object) OAkk

waddi → *wuddi*

wadium (or *watium*) (desig. of skins and textiles) OA (or → *wēdīum* ?)

***wadûm**, M/NA *udā'u* “to know” [ZU] **G** (pres. *udda/i* or *ūda/i*) M/NA “know” (Bab., OA → *edû* II) **D** Bab., OA **1.** “identify, recognize” **2.** “make known, communicate, reveal; make intelligible” **3.** “assign, allocate” s.th., “appoint” s.o. **4.** “define, prescribe” **Dt** Bab., pass. of D **1.** “be identified, recognized” **2.** “receive as allocation” **3.** “be appointed, assigned” **ŠD** OB, as D 3 “allocate, assign”; > *wuddi*; *tuddû*

wakālum OB **G** of god, stat. “is trusted”?, in PN **D** “to appoint as overseer”; → *takālu*; *waklum*

wakāmu(m) (**G** → *akāmu* II) **D** Mari “to notice, observe” s.o.; OAkk mng. uncl.

wakiltum “(female) overseer” OB [MUNUS.UGULA]; < *waklum*

(w)aklu(m), M/NA **uklu* "overseer, inspector" [(LÚ.)UGULA] of workers, priestesses, *w. tamkārī* "chief merchant", *w. 5/10* etc. "overseer of 5/10 men" etc.; of building; Ass. (as royal title); > *wakiltum, waklūtum*; → *wakālum*

waklūtum "inspectorship, supervision" Mari; < *waklum*

wakṣum → *akṣu*

(w)alādu(m), M/NA *ulādu*, NB also *malādu* "to give birth (to)" [Ù.TU; occas. TU] **G** (*a/i*) **1.** of woman, cow etc. "give birth to" **2.** less freq. of male "beget, engender" **3.** transf. "produce, create" **Gtn** iter. of G [Ù.TU.MEŠ] **D 1.** "give birth to, beget" esp. with pl. obj. **2.** "produce, create" **3.** "act as midwife" for mother, child **Dt** pass. of D "be begotten" **Š** caus. of G **N** pass. of G children *mala waldū u iwwalladū* "as many as are or shall be born"; > *līdu, līdānu, littu* I; *lillidu*; *nuldānum, nuldānūtum*; *waldum*; *wildum, ilittu*; *wālidum, ālidānu, wālittum, ālittiš, ālidūtu*; *mušālittu*; *tālittu*; *ulādu*

waldum, *(m)aldu* "born" OA, OB, M/jB; < *walādum*

(w)ālidu(m); NA f. also *āli(s)su* "one who begets/begot; progenitor" Bab. esp. *abu(m) w.* of biological father; jB *lā ālidu* "sterile"; < *walādum*; > *ālidūtu*; *wālittum*

(w)ālittu(m), j/NB also *mālittu* "one who gives/has given/is about to give birth" Bab. [Ù.TU; TU] **1.** of woman, animal, bird etc.; "fertile"? of reeds **2.** "(mother) who bore" e.g. *ālittani* "(the mother) who bore us" **3.** *lā ālittu* "barren woman"; < *wālidum*; > *ālittiš*

(w)amālu(m) ~ "to be veiled, covered" O/jB **G** (*i/i*) of eyes "mist over", of mood "become gloomy" **D** "veil; darken, eclipse", esp. stat. of star "is obscured" **Dt** pass. of D; > *mamlu*?, *mamlūtu*?; *ummulu* I.II, *ummuliš*; *mummilu*

wamā'um "to swear" **G** (pres. *umma*) OAkk; > *māmītu*; → *tamû* II

wanā'um ~ "to put under pressure, threaten with (= acc.)"? **G** (pret. *ūni*) OA; > *wānium*

wānium ~ "stubborn"? OA, of donkey; < *wanā'um*

wapādum → *wabātum*

(w)apāšu(m) "to insult" **G** OB **D** jB lex. *pištu uppušu* "cast abuse"; > *pištu*

wapāt/ṭum → *wabātum*

(w)apû(m), OAkk *wapā'um* "to be(come) visible, appear" **G** (pret. *īpi*) "appear, become visible" M/jB **D 1.** "make visible" **2.** MA stat. "is (legally) publicized"? **Š** "make manifest, appear", "produce, create"; "make clear, display"; "make glorious" kingship, name, deeds etc. **Štn** iter. of Š **Št** pass. of Š; > *šūpû, šūpîš*

(w)aqāru(m), M/NA *uqāru*, OAkk, MB also *baqāru(m)*, NB also *maqāru* "to be(come) rare, precious" **G** (*i/i*; stat. *(w)aqar*, also *b/maqar*, M/NA *uqa/ur*) [KAL] of commodities "become rare", of life "become precious"; esp. stat. "is rare", "is expensive, valuable" **D 1.** fact. of G **2.** "ignore" order OB **Š** "make rare, scarce"; "esteem, respect, honour" god, person, name; OA "attach importance to, overvalue" s.th. **Štn** iter. of Š **Št** refl. of Š ?; > *waqrum*; *waqqaru*; *waqqurtum, šūquru, šūquriš*

waqā'um → *waqûm*

(w)aqqaru "very precious" j/NB; < *waqārum*

waqqurtum, *uqqurtu(m)* (a priestess and/or fPN) OA; NA as fPN; < *waqārum* D

(w)aqru(m), M/NA *uqru*; f. *(w)aqartu(m)*, OAkk occas. *baqartum*, M/NB also *maqartu* "rare; valuable" [KAL]; esp. *abnu aqartu* "precious stone"; of person, freq. in PNs; < *waqārum*

waqrum → also *baqru*

(w)aqû(m), OA *waqā'um* "to wait (for)" **G** (imper. *qi*) OA, OB; jB lex. **D** "wait, await" **Dt** (*uta/eqqû*) "wait, await", "expect"; "wait attentively on s.o., attend to" (= *ana*, dat.); → *qu''û*

(w)arādu(m), NB also *erēdu*, M/NA *urādu* "to go down" **G** (*a/i*; perf. *ittarad*, NA *ittūrid*) [E11] **1.** "go down, descend" **2.** of parts of the body, clothing "hang down, droop" **3.** of numbers, price "decrease, drop" **Gtn** iter. of G **Gt** "go away down" **Š** caus. of G [E11] "send, take, bring down"; > *āridu*; *wārittum*; *mūraddu, mūridum*; *mušāridum*?, *mušēridum*; *muttarrittum*

warāḫum → *arāḫu* I

(w)arāqu(m) "to be(come) green-yellow; pale" **G** (*i/i*; stat. *(w)aruq*, occas. *uruq*) [SIG7] "become green, yellow; pale" of face, invalid; of fluids, fruit, glass, star **Gtn** iter. of G [SIG7.SIG7; SIG7.MEŠ] **D** (OB lex. imper. *burriq*) fact. of G **Dt** pass. of D ? **Š** "gild" NA **N** "become yellow"; > *warqum, arqūtu*; *wurqum, urqītu, marqītu* II, *urqatta*?; *uriqtu*; *wurrīqum*; *arraqu*; *wurruqum*; *awurriqānum*

***warāšum**, *arāšu, marāšu* "to be(come) dirty" jB **G** stat., of face **D** fact. of G "besmirch, defile"; > *waršum*; *rūšu* I; *uršu* III; *urāšu* II; *urūšu*; *wurrušum*; *warrāšûm*

warā'um → *warûm* II

warbum → *arbu*

(w)ardatu(m) "girl, young woman" OAkk, Ass., O/jB [(MUNUS.)KI.SIKIL]; *ardat lilî* (a demoness) (→ *lilium*); < *wardum*

(w)ardu(m), Ass. also *urdu(m)*, occas. *aradu* "slave, servant" [ÌR(-); IR$_{11}$(-); SAG.ÌR(-); OA IR(-)]; > *arādu*, *wardatum*, *wardūtum*, *urdānūtu*, *arad-ēkallūtu*, *arad-šarrūtu*

(w)ardūtu(m), Ass. *warduttum*, *urduttu*, Mari also *wurdūtum* "slavery" [ÌR-; SAG.ÌR-; OA IR-] "status as slave"; Mari and later "vassalage, (political) servitude"; < *wardum*

(w)arḫālum (an object) OA

warḫaṣu → *marḫaṣu*

warḫiš → *arḫiš*

(w)arḫišam(ma) "monthly, every month" [ITI-]; < *warḫum*

(w)arḫītum "monthly instalment" OB; < *warḫum*

(w)arḫu(m), Ass. mostly *urḫu(m)*, OB also *barḫum* [ITI; also ITI.1.KAM; OA ITI.KAM; NB astr. ÁB] **1.** "the moon" **2.** *ūm w.* "(day of new) moon, first day of month" **3.** "month", *(w)a. ana (w)a.* "monthly"; > *warḫišamma*; *warḫī= tum*; *arḫānû*; *arḫā*; *arḫussu*; *Araḫsamna*

(w)ārittu(m) 'descending' Bab. **1.** OB math. "perpendicular" **2.** (of slave girl) "brought downstream", i.e. imported **3.** "journey downstream" **4.** NB "branch canal" **5.** "diminishing return"?; < *warādum*

(w)arka, M/NB also *arki/u* [EGIR] adv. **1.** of time "afterwards, later" **2.** of place "behind"; > *arkāniš*; *warkānum*; → *warkatum*

warka → also *warki*

(w)arkānu(m), Ass. mostly *urkānu(m)*, Bogh. also *arkāna* "later, afterwards" [EGIR]; Ug. *arkānašu* "thereafter"; < *warka*

(w)arkat, OA also *urkat* "after" Bab., OA **1.** prep. "behind; after" s.o.('s departure), a date; freq. + poss. suff., e.g. *warkatka*; also *ina w.* **2.** OB conj. + subjunct. "after" **3.** jB adv. *ana a.* "backwards"; < *warkatum* st. constr.

warkatam, OA also *urkatam* adv. "later, soon afterwards; at the rear" OA, OB; < *warkatum*

(w)arkatu(m), Ass. mostly *urkatu(m)* "rear" [EGIR; A.GA] **1.** "backside"; also du. "buttocks" of human, animal; NB also ^{uzu}*a.* as joint of meat **2.** "rear part, rear side" of weapon, ship etc.; of part of body; of house, piece of land **3.** "rear guard" of army, "later instalment" of consignment **4.** "estate, legacy" **5.** "arrears" **6.** *warkatam parāsum*, *ša'ālum*, *ḫiāṭum* "to determine, examine the background (facts)"; > *urkātu*?; *warkat*, *warkatam*; → *warka*, *warki*, *warkum*, *warkûm*

warkâtum → *warkītum*

(w)arki, OB also *warka*, j/NB also *arku/a*, Ass. mostly *urki* "after, behind" [EGIR] **1.** prep. of place and time, freq. + poss. suff. e.g. *warkišu* "behind him; after him, after his departure, death; later, thereafter"; OB *arki alpī* "oxdriver" **2.** Bab. conj. "after" + subjunct.; > *arkīši*; → *arkīnišu*; *warka*; *warkatum*

warkiātum → *warkītum*

(w)arkīta(m), OA also *urkītam*, NA *urkīte/ā*, *urkēt* "later, afterwards" OA, NA, occas. Bab.; < *warkītum*

(w)arkītu(m), Ass. *urkītum*, *urkittu* **A.** sg. **1.** O/MB "posterity, descendant(s)"; NA in PN **2.** MB "remainder" **3.** astr. ~ "secondary position" of planet **4.** O/MA *ina warkītim/ urkitte* "later, afterwards"; OB *ana w.*, *ana w. ūmim* "for the future, always" **5.** Am. *ina arkītiya* "behind me" **B.** pl. *warkīātum*, *(w)arkâtu(m)* [EGIR(.MEŠ)] **1.** "future" esp. *(w)arkīāt ūmī* "future time"; *a.-ili/ī* in M/NA, M/NB PNs "future (favour) of the god/s" **2.** *w. šattim* "latter part of the year" **3.** OA *ina w.* "later, afterwards" **4.** *ana w.* "for the future, always"; < *warkûm*; > *warkītam*

warkīum → *warkûm*

warkum "afterwards" OB; < *wark* + *-um*; > *arkiš*; → *urkiš*

(w)arkû(m), *warkīum*, Ass. mostly *urkīu(m)*, *urkû* (NB → *uškû* I) "rear, later" [EGIR] **A.** of place **1.** "rear, hindmost"; "second-ranking, secondary, lesser (in worth)" **2.** NA leg. "guarantor" **3.** Mari "reserve"? in army, M/jB(Ass.) "soldier in rearguard" **B.** of time **1.** "later, subsequent" delivery, letter, extispicy etc.; wife, child; of month "intercalary" **2.** "future" king, people; > *arkâ*?; *namarkû*?; *warkītum*; → *warkatum*

(w)arqu(m), Ass. also *urqu(m)*, *erqu(m)*; f. *(w)aruqtu(m)* **1.** "yellow, green" [SIG$_7$(.SIG$_7$)] of textiles, gold, stone, animal; of tree, plant, fruit; "sallow" of discoloured skin, body **2.** as subst. "greenery"; in pl. *(w)arqū*, *erqū*, *urqū*, NB *mašqū* "greens, vegetables" [(Ú.)SAR (.MEŠ)]; < *warāqum*; > *arqūtu*

warrāšûm "very grimy" OB lex., of person; < *warāšum*

(w)aršu(m), *maršu*, occas. *arašu*; f. *aruštu*, *maruštu* "dirty" OA, M/NB of clothing, person; f. sg. and pl. as subst. "dirt"; < *warāšum*

warûm I (a headdress)? OAkk; = *erru* II 2 ?

warûm II, *arû*, OAkk, OA *warā'um*, M/NA *urā'u* "to lead" **G** (*u/u*; imper. *ru*, jB *uru*, OB occas. *ri*) "lead, conduct" person; vent. "fetch, bring" **Gtn** "guide, steer, administer", "bring up, manage" children **Gt** "lead away (for good)" (→ *tarû* I) **Š** caus. of G "conduct, direct" person, animal, boat; > *irītu*?; *muttarrûm*, *muttarrītu*; *riātu*

(w)âru(m), *(m)a'āru*, *mâru*, Mari *wêrum* "to go (up to)" OAkk, Bab., OA **G** (pres. jB *i'/yâr*, pl. *i'irrū*; pret. OB *iwīr*, M/jB *i'īr*, also *imēr*; imper. *i'ir*) "go; go up to, approach; go against, confront" s.o. (= acc. or *ana*); jB *ašar lā a'āri* "inaccessible place" **Gtn** iter. of G **D** "instruct; govern" [KIN] **1.** "commission, give orders" to do s.th. (= acc. infin.); "charge, entrust" with s.th. (= acc.) **2.** "appoint" (to a position = *ana*) **3.** "send, despatch" person, "convey" decision **4.** "govern", "exercise power over, control", "command" troops **Dtn** iter. of D; > *muttāru*; *mu'erru*, *mu'errūtu*, *mu'ertum*; *muma''eru*, *muma''erūtu*; *wu''urtum*; *têrtu*

waruḫḫu → *wuruḫḫu*

warundu → *wurundu*

warupatḫam → *wurupatḫam*

waruqtum → *warqum*

(w)asāmu(m), NA *usāmu* "to be(come) fitting, suitable; seasonable" **G** stat. "is appropriate" **D** fact. of G, esp. in PNs; "adorn" building **Š** caus. of G, esp. stat.; > *wasmum*, *asmiš*; *simtu*; *simānu* I; *wusmum*; *wussumum*; *šūsumu*

(w)asmu(m) "fitting, suitable" Bab., OA; "seasonable" of vegetation; < *wasāmum*; > *asmiš*

(w)aspu → *(w)aṣpu*

wassumum → *wussumum*

waṣābum, *aṣāb/pu*, Ass. also *uṣābu(m)* "to add, increase" **G** (*a/i*) [TAḪ] size, number; "add on" interest **Gtn** OA iter. of G **D** intens. of G [TAḪ] "give in addition"; "add to"; "multiply" **Dt** pass. of D "be added" **N** pass. of G; > *ṣibtu* II; *šūṣubtum*; *tēṣubū*, *tiṣābu*

waṣā'um → *waṣûm*

(w)āṣītu(m) liter. 'that which goes out' [È-] **1.** OA, NA, NB? (an export duty) **2.** O/jB "expeditionary force" **3.** NB "drainage canal" **4.** "projection" from buildings, apparatus, parts of the body etc.; OB math. ~ (an added strip) **5.** OB desig. of a wayward woman, also as fPN **6.** OB, jB lex. "young shoot" of date palm **7.** jB lex. "growth" of vegetation ? **8.** lex. "future, (days) to come"; NA pl. *aṣâtu* in *a. ūmē*, *ūmē* *a.* (→ *ṣiātu*) **9.** a garment (with sleeves ?) **10.** OB lex. *ša wāṣâtim* (an occupation); < *wāṣûm*

wāṣium → *wāṣûm*

(w)aṣpu(m) (or *(w)aspu*), NA *uṣ/spu* "sling, catapult" O/jB, NA

(w)aṣû(m), OAkk, OA *waṣā'um*, Ass. *uṣā'u(m)*, NA *uṣû* "to go out", + vent. "come out" (from = *ina*, *ištu*, acc.) **G** (perf. *ittaṣi*, NA *ittūṣi*) [È; MB in PNs also UD] **1.** "go out, depart" **2.** "get out, escape" **3.** of sun, stars etc. "rise" **4.** of vegetation, parts of the body etc. "grow (out)", stat. "sticks out, is protruding" **5.** O/jB "be leased, rented" **6.** j/NB *ana qāti a.* "escape attention" **7.** *ina qāti a.* "leave o.'s possession" **Gtn** iter. of G [È.MEŠ] **Gt** separative of G "go away (for good)" **Š** caus. of G "make/let go out" [È] **1.** "send/take out", + vent. "bring out" **2.** "set free; dismiss, expel" **3.** "let go, release" liquid, wind **4.** "make grow, sprout, erupt" **5.** "give out, deliver" **6.** "reveal, disclose" secret, "make known, publicize" **7.** "obtain" (by payment), "arrange delivery" **8.** OAkk, O/jB "rent, hire" field, house **9.** *napišta š.* "save/spare life" **ŠR** Mari **Štn** iter. of Š [È.MEŠ] **ŠRtn** Mari **Št¹** pass. of Š **Št²** "quarrel, pick a fight"; > *wāṣûm*, *wāṣītum*, *wāṣûtum*; *ṣī šamši*, *ṣiātiš*, *ṣiātu*, *ṣītān*, *ṣītiš*, *ṣītu*; *mūṣû*; *mūṣium* I; *šūṣû*, *šūṣûtum*; *mušēṣû*, *mušēṣītum*; *tēṣētu*, *tēṣītum*; *tūṣâtu*; *taṣû*; *taṣītu*?

(w)āṣû(m), *wāṣium* liter. 'going out' **1.** "departing, outward bound" people, esp. troops OB, messengers OA; merchandise NB; desig. of wayward husband OB lex.; "solo" cultic singer jB lex.; of time "out-going", i.e. the month, day etc. just gone [È] **2.** "having an exit" Bab., esp. neg. *lā ā.*, *lâṣu* of cul-de-sac [ZAG.È; occas. SAG.GI4 ?], also NB of unremitting illness, demon; jB *ēribu ā.* "coming (and) going" of intermittent disease **3.** jB "prominent" part of body, "tall" person, mountain, pillar **4.** Nuzi desig. of (milch ?) goat, Hurr. pl. *aṣâtena* **5.** OB math. ~ (additional strip); < *waṣûm*; > *wāṣûtum*, *wāṣītum*

(w)āṣûtu(m) (or *(w)aṣûtu(m)*) "departure" O/jB in *w. alākum* "to sally forth" of enemy, of wayward wife, son; NB *ā. aṣû* "to depart"; < *wāṣûm*

(w)ašābu(m), Ass. mostly *ušābu(m)* "to sit (down); dwell" **G** (Bab. *a/i*; imper. *tišab*, OA *šib*; OA stat. *wašab*, M/NA *usbāku* etc.; NA perf. *ittūšib*) [TUŠ; occas. TUŠ.A] **1.** "sit (down)" of gods, persons, animals **2.** "dwell, live, stay" in a place; "occupy, reside in" a house **3.** "exist, be (currently) present" at a place, on a journey, esp. stat. **4.** O/jB of populations "live, be" in certain conditions esp. *šubta(m) nēḫta(m) w.* "live a quiet life" **5.** O/jB pass. mng. "be(come) inhabited, populated" of house, city, land **6.** M/jB, NA intrans. "settle (down)" of liquids, food **7.** Nuzi stat. of goods owed, *ina (muḫḫi) PN ašib* "is on PN's account" **Gtn** iter. of G [TUŠ.TUŠ] (**Gt** → *tašābu*) **D** OB "settle" inhabitants; NB ~ "insert" s.th. (corrupt ?) **Š** caus. of G [TUŠ] **1.** "cause to sit, dwell" **2.** "settle" people in a place, country; Ass. "colonize" a land **3.** "install" s.o. in a job, position; "place" s.th. in position **4.** Mari "settle" a matter; > *wašbum, wašbūtum; ušbu; wāšibum; šubtu* I, *šubbutu; waššābum, waššabtu, waššābūtum; mūšabu, mūšabtu; šūšubu, šūšubtu; tašābu*

wašāmum mng. unkn. OB lex.

(w)ašāpu(m) "to exorcise" **G** not attested **D** "cure" by exorcism O/jB; > *šiptu; wāšipum, āšiptu, āšipūtu; muššipu*

(w)ašāru(m) ~ "to sink down" **G** stat. and infin. only; OA "hangs down, is let down" of hair; OB "be lowered" of bar of lock; O/jB "be submissive, obedient" to deity, judgement **D** (*wuššurum*, Mari also *waššurum*, M/NB mostly *muššuru*, in West also *(w)uššuru*, M/NA *uššuru*) "release, set free" [BAR] **1.** "release, let go" persons, "set free" captives, slaves **2.** "let go of" s.th., e.g. hem Mari, Alal.; of demon, disease, affliction "let go of, leave" s.o. jB **3.** "free, release" fields, districts; Mari "liberate" towns **4.** "hand over, relinquish" tablets, merchandise, animals etc. OA; j/NB "leave" s.th. to s.o. **5.** "abandon, leave behind/ aside, give up" position, palace, city, land; person, e.g. child, brother, cripple; plan; MA imper. *uššer* "ignore, except for" s.th. **6.** MB "stop" doing s.th.; NB "leave undone, neglect" work, rites etc.; Ug. "break" treaty, Bogh. oath **7.** jB "loose, send forth" storms, rain, rays; MB in West "send" troops, ships; tablet, words **8.** jB "let fall/hang loose" hair; OA, jB "let flow" liquids, jB "void" excrement; stat. jB *uššur* "is loose" esp. ext.; OB "be undone" of sin **9.** Am. transf. "stretch out" hand; "hand over" cities to fire; Mit. "lead into" friendship **Dtn** OA iter. of D **Dt** pass. of D; Am. *yušaru* "be sent"; > *wašrum, ašriš* I; *wuššurum, wuššurtum; tūšaru, tīšāriš*

wašaššiwe mng. unkn. Nuzi; < Hurr.

(w)ašāṭu(m) "to be(come) stiff, difficult" Bab., OA **G** (stat. *(w)ašaṭ*) **1.** jB of part of body "is stiff" **2.** "is hard, difficult" of calculations OA; of mountain pass jB; *ana* + infin. *w.* "be difficult to do" **3.** of persons, animals, demons "be hard, obdurate" O/jB, Bogh. **Gtn** only jB ptcp. stat. *mūtaššiṭ* "is repeatedly constipated"? **D** "stiffen" jB lex., NB; > *wašṭum; aštūtu; uššuṭu; muttaššiṭu*

wašā'um, jB *ašû* ~ "to need"? OA, jB lex.

(w)ašbu(m), OA also *ušbum* "inhabited; resident, present" Bab., OA [TUŠ] **1.** of village, city etc. "occupied, inhabited" **2.** of person "present" OA; "resident, dwelling" in a house, place; "seated" on a chair; < *wašābum*

wašbūtum in *lā w.* "absence" OB; < *wašbum*

(w)āšibu(m) "sitting, dwelling; inhabitant" OAkk, Bab., NA [TUŠ] esp. in *(w)āšib(ūt) āli(m)* "resident(s) of a city, citizen(s)"; Mari, desig. of an official; < *wašābum*

wašibum → *yašibum*

(w)āšipu(m) "sorcerer, magician; incantation priest, exorcist" Bab., M/NA [LÚ.MU7.MU7; KA.PIRIG/PÌRIG; (LÚ.)MAŠ.MAŠ; LÚ.KA.INIM. MA; LÚ.ME(.ME)] **1.** of persons, esp. prof. exorcists **2.** of gods, esp. Asalluḫi; < *wašāpum*; > *āšiptu, āšipūtu*; → *mašmaššu*

wašranna mng. unkn. Alal.

(w)ašru(m) "submissive; humble, obedient" Bab.; < *wašārum*; > *ašriš* I

waššabtu(m) "female tenant" OB; < *waššābum*

(w)aššābu(m), Ass. *uššābu(m)* "tenant" **1.** of house, property OA, O/jB **2.** "foreign resident, metic" M/NB, Nuzi, NA?; jB of deity "resident" in city; < *wašābum*

(w)aššābūtu(m) "tenancy" Bab.; < *waššābum*

waššurtum → *wuššurtum*

waššurum → *wašārum* D; *wuššurum*

waštena Hurr. pl. mng. unkn. Alal., desig. of birds

(w)ašṭu(m), *alṭu* "stiff, difficult" Bab. **1.** of parts of body "stiff" **2.** of walls, roads etc. "hard, difficult" **3.** of persons, esp. the enemy "obdurate, headstrong"; of god, divine onslaught, flood, wind "unyielding"; < *wašāṭum*; > *ašṭūtu*

wašû → *mašû* II

watār, *matār* in *lā w./m.* "no further, that's enough!"; "really, no exaggeration" OA, O/jB; < *watārum* st. abs.

(w)atartu(m) "excess" Bab., OA [DIRI-] **1.** OA, OB "surplus" in accounting **2.** O/MB "extra piece" of land, work **3.** jB "excrescence" on liver **4.** desig. of Sum. gramm. feature **5.** OB,

MB(Ass.), j/NB *ana/kī(ma) a.* "besides, in addition; extra" **6.** OA, OB "exaggeration", also in *ša atrāti* "one who exaggerates" Bogh. lex. **7.** jB lex. (a kind of waggon wheel; → *attartu*); < *watrum*

(w)atāru(m), Ass. mostly *utāru*, jB also *matāru* "to be(come) outsize, surplus" **G** (*i/i*; OB (Susa) pres. *iwattir*, stat. *(w)atar*, Ass. *utar*) [DIRI] **1.** "increase, accumulate" freq. opp. to *maṭû* II; of land, property; of grain, silver etc. "be surplus, in excess" **2.** in hendiad., e.g. *damqū watrū* "they are exceedingly fine" OA, jB **3.** "exceed, be(come) greater" than (= *ana*, *eli*, NB also *ina muḫḫi*, *alla*, *elat*), of measurements, fields; of persons, gods; parts of body **4.** "be outsize, huge", of part of body; of debt jB; "be overlong" of day, night jB; of statement "be exaggerated" OB **5.** "be exceedingly important" of gods and their attributes etc., esp. in PNs OAkk, O/jB, NA **D** (*utta/er*, less often *uwatta/er*) "increase, enlarge; have an advantage" [DIRI] **1.** "increase, augment" property, riches, yield; strength, life; troops **2.** "enlarge" building etc., freq. + *eli*; "make outsize, huge; excessive"; "exaggerate" O/jB **3.** in hendiad., to do s.th. "extra, more" than (= *eli*) **4.** "exceed" MA **5.** intrans. "have, gain advantage; prosper" O/jB **6.** "give in great measure" Am. **Dtn** (Am. **Dtt**) iter. of D **Dt** of cattle "multiply greatly" jB **Š** "make outsize, surpassing; make excel" mostly lit. **1.** of god "make" king "surpassing"; stat. "is excellent" of god, king; power, position; name, counsel; rites; of form "is huge"; of sin "is excessive" **2.** "make" building, city "much bigger" than (= *eli*); "make" offerings "plentiful" M/NB; "exaggerate" jB; "give too much" NA, NB **3.** in hendiad. "do" s.th. "to excess" (trans. and intrans. vb.s), e.g. *š. šakānu* "to impose much more" tribute etc., *š. elû* "to rise excessively high" **Št** pass. of Š "be made more numerous" than ?; > *watrum*, *watār*, *watartum*, *atriš*, *watriššu*, *watrûm*; *tertum*; *utru*; *uturtu*, *uturrā'ū*; *itertum*; *uttāru*, *attartu*, *wattarum*; *watturum*, *utturu*; *šūturu*; *tattūru*?

watā'um → *wadā'um*; *watûm*

watiḫuru ~ "stable-boy" Nuzi; < Hurr.

watirītu (or *witirītu*) (an object) Nuzi, in pairs; < Hurr.

watium → *wadium*

watlu (a fabric) jB lex.

(w)atmanu(m); pl. f. "cella, inner sanctum; temple"

(w)atmu(m), occas. *watnu*, *atamu* "hatchling" O/jB [AMAR(.MUŠEN)] **1.** young of bird, snake, turtle **2.** transf. of human offspring; OB as PN

watnu → *watmum*

watriššu "superfluously" OB; < *watrum*

(w)atru(m), Ass. freq. *utru(m)*, Nuzi also *mat(a)ru*, NB also *ataru*; f. *(w)atartu(m)*, *utartu(m)* "huge; excellent; surplus" [DIRI] **1.** of quality "superior, excellent" OA, OB of metals, wool **2.** of degree, e.g. *Atram-ḫasīs*, jB *Atar-ḫasīs* "Exceedingly wise"; OA esp. in *damqum w.* "very fine" **3.** (in adj. and nominal use) of quantity "surplus, additional" [also SI], of silver, objects, goods, animals etc., "extra" tribute, offerings, tablets, persons, houses; days, months **4.** "too much" work OB; of part of body "extra, superfluous"?; of speech "extravagant" OB **5.** "additional" fee (a tax) NB **6.** OB *ina watrim*, Nuzi *ana atri*, *ana matrimma* etc. "in addition, over and above"; < *watārum*; > *atriš*, *watriššu*, *watrûm*, *watartum*

watrûm "exaggerator, braggart" OB lex.; < *watrum*

(w)attaru(m) "substitute, replacement" Bab. **1.** of persons [LÚ.DIRI.GA; also ÉRIN.DIRI] OB, of soldiers, slavegirl; Susa, of shepherds etc. **2.** jB lex., OB "reserve ox" [GU4.DIRI ?] **3.** M/NB (a waggon)? (→ *attartu*); < *watārum*

watturum "expensive" OA; < *watārum* D

(w)atû(m), OAkk, OA *watā'um* "to find, discover" **G** (*a/a*, later *u/u*) **1.** "find" s.th. lost, "discover" person, brother (esp. in PNs), purse, path; also abstr. obj., e.g. life, wealth, favour, counsel, inner thoughts etc. **2.** stat. "is found", "is present"; "appears (as s.th.)" **Gtn** MB iter. of G **D** ~ G **1.** "(re)discover" **2.** of god "select, choose" from (= *ina*), esp. kings **Št 1.** of persons "meet (one another)", "meet" with (= *itti*) s.o., esp. sexually; "converge" of parts of body **2.** OB "combine" amounts of sesame **3.** "be in opposition", of heavenly bodies, esp. sun and moon; > *itûtu* I; *šutātû*

wāya → *ū'a*

wazwazum (a bird) OB

wazzunum D "to listen, give ear" OA; < *uznu* denom.

we'āšum → *wêšum*

wēdēnûm → *ēdēnû*

wēdī- + poss. suff. "(he/you etc.) alone" OA; < *wēdum*; → *udī-*; *wuddi*

(w)ēdiššī-, jB also *īdiššī-* + *-šu/ka* etc. "he/you (etc.) alone" Bab. (→ GAG §67f); < *wēdum*

wēdīum → *wadium*; *wēdûm*

(w)ēdu(m); f. *ettu(m)* "single, sole; alone" [DILI] **1.** of person "single, solitary", esp. in PNs "only (child)"; as subst. "a single (person)"; OA desig. of chief of *kārum* **2.** of god "unique" **3.** of things, objects e.g. "a single" line, reed, potstand, NB "free-standing" palm tree **4.** stat. e.g. *wedēlāku* "I am alone" OA, OB **5.** *ēdukku* "you alone" jB **6.** ~ "*Asa foetida*" (a medicinal plant) [Ú.AŠ], also *šammu ēdu* M/NB **7.** (a star in Hercules) [MUL/MÚL.DILI] NB; > *ēdūtu*, *ēdiš*, *ēdāniš*; *ēdēnu*, *ēdēnû*; *ēdumānu*; *wēdī-*, *udī-*; *wēdiššī-*; *wēdûm*; → *ašarēdu*

(w)ēdû(m) "prominent, high-placed" O/jB [OB DIDLI; jB SIG] **1.** of persons of high rank, e.g. soldier, priest, envoy; OB esp. subst. "person of senior rank" **2.** ext., of city "important"; < *wēdum*

werium → *werûm*

(w)erru(m) ~ "mighty (one)" O/jB

(w)erû(m), *werium*, Ass. freq. *eriu(m)*, OA also *eru'um* "copper" [URUDU(.MEŠ/ḪI.A); also NA4.URUDU] "copper (ore)", *šad* $^{(na_4)}$*e*. "copper mountain" jB

wêrum → *wârum*

wêšum, OA *we'āšum* ~ "to relinquish"? OA, OB; stat. "is left to oneself"?

wiāṣum, *êṣum*, j/NB *mâṣu*, MA *e'āṣu* "to be(come) too little, small" **G 1.** "become few, insufficient" of people, plants, offerings etc.; "be(come) too small" of buildings, places; "decrease (in size)" of parts of the body; "be powerless" of king **2.** stat. of people, soldiers, days "are few"; of area, water, part of body "is too small, little"; of material, animal, ext. of good/bad conditions "are scarce, rare"; of treaty, work "is inadequate" **Š** caus. of G Am. only; > *wīṣum*, *ēṣiš*; *mīṣūtamma*; *ta'īṣtum*

(w)ildu(m), *mildu* "offspring, young" Bab. [Ù.TU] **1.** of human "child" **2.** esp. OB *(w)ilid bīti(m)* "house-born (slave)"; also *ilid PlN* "native of PlN" MB **3.** "young" of animals, esp. sheep and goats; < *walādum*

wirrarikkunni (desig. of horses) Nuzi; < Hurr.

wirratušḫu (a building) Nuzi; < Hurr.

wismawir[ri] mng. unkn. Alal.; < Hurr.

wissaena → *wizzaena*

wīṣum, OB usu. *īṣum*, *īṣu*, M/NB also *mīṣu*, Ass. *ēṣu(m)* "few"; of days; of people "small" in number, of body of troops; in quantity, of money, goods; esp. *ī. ū mādu(m)* "(whether) little or much"; < *wiāṣum*; > *ēṣiš*, *īṣūtu*; *mīṣūtamma*

wišmatum → *pišmatum*

witirītu → *watirītu*

wizzaena (or *wissaena*) Hurr. pl. mng. unkn. Alal.

wuddi, OA *waddi*, *uddi* "certainly, probably" OA, OB(mostly Mari); < *wadûm* D imper.

wurdūtum → *wardūtum*

wurni (an object) Alal.; < Hurr.

(w)urqu(m), jB also *murqu*, Susa *ušqu*? "yellow-green colour" O/jB [SIG7]; also "yellow-green spot, patch" med., ext.; < *warāqum*

(w)urrīqu(m) **1.** OB (a gold alloy)? **2.** M/jB (a yellow stone) [(NA4.)SIG7.SIG7]; < *warāqum*

wurruqum "very yellow" OB as PN; < *warāqum*

(w)urrušu(m) "very dirty, defiled" O/jB; < *warāšum*

wûrtum → *wu''urtum*

wuruḫ[ḫu] (or *waruḫḫu*) (a wooden object) Nuzi; < Hurr.

wuruḫli, *buruḫli* "south" Nuzi; < Hurr.

wurundu (or *warundu*) mng. unkn. Nuzi

wurupatḫam (or *warupatḫam*) "debt imprisonment" Nuzi

(w)usmu(m) "appropriateness, s.o./s.th. worthy" O/jB **1.** of kings, e.g. *wusum šarrūtim* "one worthy of kingship" **2.** of gods, esp. *usum šamê* "one suited to heaven" **3.** of door "worthy ornament" for shrine; < *wasāmum*

wussûm, *mussû*, *muššû* **D** "to identify; distinguish" OAkk, Bab. **1.** "identify" people, animals, star **2.** "discriminate, distinguish" good and evil; "ascertain, find out" truth; NB "clarify, verify" law case **3.** M/jB(Ass.) "(re)locate, identify" site of building, city **Dt** pass. of D "be told apart"; > *muwassûm*; → *messûtu*

wussumum, OA *wassumum* "especially suitable" OAkk, OB in PN; OA of package; < *wasāmum* D

(w)uṣṣû(m), jB freq. *muṣṣû* **D** "to spread out, open wide" Bab. **1.** "pull aside/apart, remove" clothing, covering **2.** "spread out" various objects, garden produce; bodies of fallen enemy; "present" s.th. as dedicatory offering; "lay out" gold as foundation deposit; "distribute" dismembered piglet over patient's body; > *muṣû*?

wuṣṣurum → *eṣēru* D; *wuzzurum*

(w)uṣṣuṣu(m) **D** "to interrogate, investigate" Bab., NA; esp. in hendiad. with *ša'ālu* j/NB(Ass.), NA **Dt** pass. jB

wušgû (or *wuškû*) mng. unkn. Nuzi; → *uškû* II ?

wušru mng. unkn. Am.

(w)uššurtu(m), OA *waššurtum* "release, exemption" Bab., OA [ŠU.BAR.RA]; < *wuššurum*

(w)uššuru(m), M/NB freq. *muššuru*, Mari *waššurum* "exempt; released, loosened" Bab. [ŠU.BAR(.RA); BAR] **1.** of persons "released, exempt" **2.** of parts of the body "loose, limp"; of hair "hanging loose/down"; of thread, lentil etc. "loosened, freed" **3.** of sheep "(grazing) free" NB **4.** as PN MA, MB, also fPN *Uššurtum*; < *wašārum*

wu''ûm D "to falsify"? OB tablet, sealing; > *tā'ītum*

(w)u''urtu(m), *(w)ûrtu(m)*, also *mûrtu* "commission, command" Bab. of god, king, master; esp. in *w. wu''urum*, *nadānum* "to commission, charge" s.o. to do s.th.; also *w. leqûm*, *šemûm* "to accept, hear an order"; *w. ša'ālum* "to ascertain an order"; < *wârum* D

wuzzurum (or *wuṣṣurum*) **D** mng. uncl. Mari

Y

ya → *ai* I
-ya "my" (1 sg. pron. suff.) (→ GAG §42g-k); → *-ī*
ya'alu → *ayyalu* I
ya'an → *yānu*
ya'aru → *ayyaru* I
yabāmum "father-in-law" OB(N.Mes.); < W.Sem.
yabbītu → *ayyabbītu*
yābiltum (a supply canal) Mari
yābilu "ram" NA lex. [UDU.NÍTA]; < W.Sem.
yābinu → *yānibu*
yābiš → *ayyābiš*
yābu → *ayyābakala*; *ayyābu*
yabuṭu (or *yapuṭu*) (a plant) jB lex.; < Aram.
yādinu (desig. of sheep) jB lex.
yādu → *u'du*
yagâtum "complaints" Mari; < W.Sem.
yaḫili (desig. of garment) NA lex.
yaḫudû(m) "simple, daft" O/jB
yaka → *ayyaka*
yakītu (a throwing-spear)? Am. of iron, bronze
yāku → *ayyakku*
yalu → *ayyalu* I
yalūtum "alliance" Mari; < *ayyalu* II
yamattu, NA *yamuttu* "each, any one" M/NA
yamḫadûm "of Yamḫad" (land of Aleppo) Mari of garment, vessel; < PlN Yamḫad
yammin(a) "who?; which one?" jB; or "seven" (< Sum.)?
yamnuqu (a garment) NA lex.
yāmu → *kusa*
yamuttu → *yamattu*
ya'na, *yāni* → *yānu*

yānibu, *nibu*, *ainibu*, occas. *yābinu* (a stone) jB lex., rit.
yannussu mng. unkn. NA
yānu, *ya'nu/a*, Bogh. *yānummâ*, NB also *yāni*, *ya'an* "(there) is not" M/NB **1.** *yānu mê* "there is no water", also after subst.; MB freq. *yānumma*, *yānummi*, NB also *yānu'amma*; with pron. suff. *yānuššu* "he is not"; *kī ibašši ū kī y.* "whether there is or not" **2.** interrog. *yānū* etc. "is there not?", "is it not so, n'est-ce pas?"; NB also "(if) there is not, otherwise" **3.** Ug. *yānummā … yānummā* "whether … or"; for pos. usage → *ayyānu*
yānummâ → *yānu*
yānummiš "anywhere"? NA in *ana y.* "to anywhere"?; < *ayyānu*
yanūqu "lamb"? NA; < Aram.
yanzu (a plant) jB lex.
yapu "beautiful" Am.; < W.Sem.
yapuṭu → *yabuṭu*
yaquqānu (a garden plant) NB
yaraḫḫu, *yaruḫḫu*, *uriyaḫḫu* jB **1.** (a kind of good quality grain) [ŠE.LUGAL; ŠE.SAG] **2.** (a brownish precious stone)
Yaratu (a month) Nuzi
yarburānu (a plant used in the preparation of perfume) NA; < *ayyaru* I + *būru* I ?
yarḫu I "pond, pool" M/NA, jB
yarḫum II adj. mng. uncl. OB
yarītu "rosette(-ornamented clothing)"? NA; < *ayyarû*
yāritu "heir" NB; < Aram.
yāritūtu "inheritance" NB; < *yāritu*
yarqānu (a garden plant) NB; < Aram.

yarru(m) "pond" Bab.; OB as watering-place; NB *y. marti* "salt pan"?

yartu → *ayyartu*

yaru → *ayyaru* I

yaruḫḫu → *yaraḫḫu*

yarūru, *(y)arūratu*; pl. f. "lament" jB lex.; < Sum.; > *yarūrūtu*

yarūrūtu, *a(yya)rūrūtu* "lamentation" jB, NA; < *yarūru*

yāruttu (a bush) MA, M/NB; also aromatic substance from it

yarzibnu (an aromatic plant) MA; < *ayyaru* I + *zibnu* ?

yāṣiru; pl. *yāṣiruma* "potter" Ug.; < Ug.

yāṣu → *ayyāṣu*

yâši etc. → *yâšim*

yašibum, *wašibum* ?, later *yašubu*, *aši/ubu*, *šub/pû* "battering-ram" (OB first syll. freq. wr. WA) Bab., NA [GIŠ.GU$_4$.SI.AŠ]

yâšim, *ayyâši(m)*, *yâši*, Am. also *yâšia*, NB also *yâša/u* "to, for me" (1 sg. dat. pron.) Bab., NA; MB and later also used for acc.

yâšinu "to, for us" (1 pl. dat. pron.) Am. for *niāši*

yašpû, *ašpû* "jasper" M/NB, NA

yaštu → *ayyartu*

yâšu → *yâšim*

yašubu → *yašibum*

yâti, *iyâti*, NB also *yâtu*, Am. also *yâtia* "me" (1 sg. acc. pron.); OA, j/NB "to me" (1 sg. dat. pron.); also gen., OA *(ša) kīma y.* "my representative(s)"

yâtinu "us" (1 pl. acc. pron.) Am. for *niāti*

yattu → *yā'u*

yâtu → *yâti*

ya'u, *e'u*, *e'a*, *ae'u* (a door strap) jB lex.; < Sum.

ya'u → also *ayyu*

yā'u(m), *yāwum*, *yû(m)*; f. *yattu(m/n)*, Bab. also *yuttu(n)*; pl. m. *yā'ūtum/n*; f. *yâtu(m)*, *yâttu(n)* "my, mine"

ya''uku (or *yûkû* ?) adj. mng. unkn. NA in words (*dibbē*) IA-*ú-ku-u-te*

ya'umma → *ayyumma*

yā'uru → *ayyaru* I

yā'ūtum/n, *yāwum* → *yā'u*

yiš → *ayyiš*

yû → *yā'u*

yûkû → *ya''uku*

yuttu → *yā'u*

yūyū (a cry of pain) jB med.

Z

zā, *zaḫ* mng. unkn. Am.; < Eg.

za'ānu(m), *zânu* "to be adorned" Bab.(lit.) **G** stat. only of gods, cultic items "are decorated with" precious stones etc.; terror, charm etc. **D** [TAG.TAG] "adorn (with = acc.), decorate" gods, king; garment; building **N** "be adorned"; > *zīnu*?; *zu''unu*

zabālu(m), occas. *s/ṣabālu(m)*, NB *zebēlu* "to carry, deliver" **G** (*i/i*) of humans, animals "carry, deliver" goods; "bear" tools, earth-basket; news; penalty, misfortune **Gtn** iter. [(ḪÉ.)ÍL.ÍL] **D** "keep (s.o.) waiting"; of disease, patient "linger"; also intens. of G **Dt** of message "be carried" **Š** caus. of G **N** pass. of G; > *zabiltu*; *zabbilu*; *zabūlātu*; *zubullûm*; *nazbalum*, *nazbaltum*; *šazbussu*; *tazbiltu*; *ziblu*?, *zibillu*?

zabardabbatum (a female official) OB [MUNUS.ZABAR.DAB(.BA)]

zabardabbu(m), once *zamardabbum*, later *zabardabbû* (an official, liter.) "bronze(-bowl) holder" OAkk, Bab. [(LÚ.)ZABAR.DAB/DAB$_5$ (.BA)]; < Sum.

zabardabbūtu(m), *zamardabbūtu(m)* "post of *zabardabbu*" Bab.

zabaru mng. unkn. jB lex.; < Sum.

zabbatu(m) (a female ecstatic)? O/jB; < *zabbu*

zabbillu → *zabbīlu*

zabbilu(m), *zābilum*, *zanbilum* "(used to) bearing; bearer" Bab. [LÚ.ŠE.ÍL(.ÍL)] adj. "bearing", of hand, woman; subst. "bearer"; < *zabālu*

zabbīlu(m), *zabbillu* "basket" j/NB; < Aram.

zabbu(m) (an ecstatic) Bab. [IM.ZU.UB]; > *zabbatu*; *zabbūtu*

zabbūtu "ecstaticism" jB; < *zabbu*

zabi (a medicinal plant) jB

zabibânu → *zibibiānum*

zabību → *ṣabību*

zabiltu(m) "betrayal (of secrets)" O/jB; < *zabālu*

zābilum → *zabbilu*

zabnakû (a metal vessel) Am.; < Eg.

zabšiš → *ṣapšiš*

zabšu → *ṣapšu*

zâbu(m), OA *zuābum* "to dissolve, flow (away)" OA, O/jB **G** intrans., of clay, wax, blood, transf. of people **D** trans. lex.; > *zā'ibu*; *zību* IV; *muzibbu*, *muzībtu*

zabūlātu in *imēru ša z.* "pack-ass" j/NB; < *zabālu*

zabzabgû (a glaze) jB

zadimgallu "master lapidary" jB; < Sum.

zadimmu(m) "lapidary" O/jB [ZA.DÍM]; < Sum.

zadrā'u (a kind of sheep) jB lex.

zad(u)rû(m) (a clay object) O/jB lex.; < Sum.

zā'eru(m), *zā'iru(m)*, MB also *zē'iru*; j/NB pl. *zā'i/erāni* "hostile; enemy" Bab.; < *zêru*

zā'erūtu "enmity" MB; < *zā'eru*

zaggu (a sacred chamber) jB lex.; < Sum.

zagid(du)rû(m), *zagindurû* **1.** Bab., OA "(a kind of) lapis lazuli" [NA$_4$.ZA.GÌN.DURU$_5$] **2.** jB "coloured glaze"; < Sum.

zagin → *zaginnu*

zagindurû → *zagiddurû*

zagingišdilû → *gišdilû*

zagingutumakû "(a kind of pale) lapis lazuli" jB lex.; < Sum.

zagin(nu) "lapis lazuli" jB lex.; < Sum.

zagmukku(m), *zammukku* "New Year (festival)" Bab. [ZAG.MUK]; < Sum.

zaguduarû (a cut of mutton) jB lex.; < Sum.

zagzagātu pl. "shrine" jB lex.; < Sum.?

zaḫ → *zā*

zaḫalû (a precious metal, phps.) "silver alloy" j/NB

zaḫamḫu (or *saḫamḫu*) mng. unkn. Nuzi; < Hurr.

zaḫan(nu) (a garden plant) jB lex.; < Sum.?

zaḫānum (or *saḫānum*) "beam, rafter"? OAkk

Zaḫarātum → *Saḫarātum*

zaḫaṭû(m) "battle-axe" O/jB [ZA.ḪA.DA]; < Sum.

zaḫḫu → *zalḫu*

zaḫimu (epith. of god) jB comm.

zaḫû (a garment)? jB lex.

zāḫu → *ṣāḫu*

zaḫulumma mng. unkn. Nuzi in *z. epēšu*; < Hurr.

zaḫumma mng. unkn. Nuzi in *z. epēšu*; < Hurr.

zā'ibu(m) (a watercourse); name of river (= Zāb) O/jB; < *zâbu*

zā'irānu → *zā'eru*; *zē'irānu*

za'irinnu → *zarinnu*

zā'iru → *zā'eru*

zā'itu "olive" NB; < Aram.

zā'izānu (an overseer of legal divisions) Nuzi; < *zâzu*

zā'iztum "dividing" OB in river name *Nār-z.*; < *zâzu*

zakādum → *zaqādum*

zakakātu → *zakukītum*

zakanum → *zakkanum*

zakāpu → *sakāpu* I; *zaqāpu*

zakāru(m), *saqāru(m)*, *zaqāru* "to speak, say; name; talk; swear" **G** (*a/u*) [MU] "name" (s.o.); freq. *šuma(m) z.* "mention" s.o.'s "name", usu. benevolently; *zakār šumi* "(good) reputation", ext. "invocation" of deity; Ass. "order" s.th.; *nīš ... z.* "swear on the life" of god, king; also ellipt., without *nīš*; Am. "remember" (< W. Sem.) **Gtn** iter. of G **Gt** ~ G, lit. [MU] imper. *tizk/qar* "speak" **D** ~ G "name, speak, pronounce" **DRt** Mari "swear to one another" **Š** caus. of G **N** pass. of G [MU; PÀD] **Nt** ~ Gt, also "decree"; > *zakru*; *zikru*; *zākirum*; *zukurrû*?; *zukkurūtu*; *mušazkirum*

zakā'u → *zakû* II

zakigû "toothache" Ug.; < Sum.?

zākirum, *sāqirum*, occas. *sāḫirum* '(name) speaker' OB, performer of ancestral rites; < *zakāru*; → *sāḫiru* 9

zakītu (woman) "freed, exempted" for temple service NB(Uruk); < *zakû* II; → *zakû* I

zakiu → *zakû* I

za(k)kanum (a building) Mari

zakkāru(m), *zakrum* "man, male" Ass. [NITA]; < *zikaru*

zakkû "(official) freed, exempted" (from corvée duty) NA, NB(Ass.); < *zakû* II D; → *zukkû*

zakru "named, mentioned" M/jB, NA; < *zakāru*

zakrum → also *zakkāru*

zakû(m) I, Ass. occas. *zakiu(m)*; f. *zakūtu(m)* (NB → *zakītu*) **1.** "pure, clear" of liquid, metal; sky, weather; "clean", of grain "dehusked", of land "free of weeds"?; of person, goods "free" (from claim, guilt); of information "clear, definite" **2.** OAkk, OB (a quality of oil, wool)? (or *sa(k)kum*); < *zakû* II

zakû(m) II, Ass. *zakā'u(m)* "to be(come) clear, pure" **G** (*u/u*, later also *i/i*) [LUḪ] of water, the sky "be(come) clear"; "be(come) clean"; of eclipsed moon etc. "become bright again"; Ug. of sun "be bright"; of grain "be(come) dehusked"; "be(come) free" (from claim, work, obligation etc.); OA of goods "be(come) free" (for sale) **D** fact. of G; "free, exempt" (from obligation, tax etc.); OA, OB "get ready" for despatch; NA "mobilize" (troops) **Dt** NA, NB pass. of D; > *zakû* I, *zakītu*, *zakûtu*; *zikûtu*; *zūku* I; *zukūtum*; *zukû*; *zukkû*, *zakkû*; *mazkûtu*; *muzakkûm*; *tazkītu*

zâku → *sâku*

zakukītum, *zakakātu*, *zakukūtu* "glaze, glass" Mari, jB

zakûtu, NA *zakuttu* "cleansing, exemption" Alal., M/NB, NA from obligation, tax, guilt; M/jB "dehusked condition" of grain; < *zakû* I

zakzakku → *zazakku*

zalaqtu in *z. ēni* "bright-eyed" Bogh. lex.; < Sum.

zalāqu (a shiny stone) M/NB, NA [NA$_4$.ZÁLAG]; < Sum.

zalḫu, *zaḫḫu* "gold" Nuzi, jB lex.

zali (an object) Alal.

zallewe (or *sallewe*) "(part of a) sword"? Am., Nuzi; < Hurr.?

zalule (or *salule*) mng. unkn. Nuzi

zāmânu → *zāwiānum*

zāmânû "hostile; enemy" j/NB; < *zāwiānum*

zamar (or *ṣamar*) "quickly, hurriedly, immediately" j/NB *z. ... z. ...* "now ..., now ..."; *z. z.* "of a sudden repeatedly"; > *zamarānu*; *zamariš*

zamarānu "suddenly" jB; < *zamar* + *-ānu*

zamardabbum → *zabardabbu*

zamardabbūtu → *zabardabbūtu*

zamariš "quickly" jB comm.; < *zamar*

zamartum, *za/umurtum* (a kind of sheep) Mari, pl.

zamāru(m) I "song" Bab.(lit.), NA; < *zamāru* II infin.

zamāru(m) II "to sing (of)" **G** (*u/u*, OB also *a/u*) [ŠÌR; DU12] **Gtn** iter. of G; also "repeatedly play" musical instrument **D** OB "sing of, about" **Š** caus. of G; "teach to sing" **N** pass. "be sung (of)"; > *zimru*; *zamāru* I, *zumāru*; *zammāru*, *zammeru*, *zammertu*, *zammerānû*

zamārum → also *samārum*

zambūru "thyme" NB; < Aram.

zamirītum (a household utensil)? OAkk; < PlN

zamītu mng. unkn. jB lex.

zammāru "singer, musician" M/NA, NB [NA (LÚ.)NAR ?]; < *zamāru* II

zammerānû ~ "songful" jB; < *zammeru*

zammertu "female singer, musician" O/jB; < *zammeru*

zammeru "singer, musician" O/jB; < *zamāru* II

zammukku → *zagmukku*

zamru → *azamru*

zamû, *azamû* "outer corner; corner pillar"? jB of building; of tablet

zamurtum → *zamartum*

zanādu mng. unkn. NB; < Aram.

zanānu(m) I "to rain" **G** (*u/u*, OB also *a/u*) [ŠUR] also of hail, snow; demons, fire; "rain down" plenty, distress, weapons **Gtn** iter. **Š** [ŠÈG] caus.; > *zunnu* I; *zinnu*

zanānu(m) II "to provision, provide (for, with)" Bab. **G** (*a/u*) people, temples, cities **D** ~ G, intens.? **Š** caus. **Št** pass. of Š **N** mng. uncl.; > *zannu* I; *zinnātu*; *zunnu* II; *zanānūtu*; *zununnû*; *zāninu*, *zāninānu*, *zāninūtu*; → *Sāninu*

zanānūtu "provisioning" j/NB; < *zanānu* II

zanā'u → *zenû* II

zanbilum → *zabbilu*

zāninānu "provider, provisioner" NB; < *zanānu* II

zaninu → *zannu* I

zāninu(m) "provisioner" Bab.; < *zanānu* II

zāninūtu(m) "rôle of provisioner" Bab.(lit.) esp. *z. epēšu* "to exercise rôle of provisioner"; < *zanānu* II

zannaru(m) (a lyre) O/jB also deified [dGIŠ.ZA.MÙŠ]

zannu I, *zaninu* "provided (with)" NB; < *zanānu* II

zannu II (a preparation of barley) Nuzi, jB

zanûm → *zenû* II

zānu → *azannu*

zânu → *za'ānu*

zanzaliqqu (a tree, phps.) "Persian lilac" jB, NA

zanzar, *zarzar* (or *ṣan/rṣar*) (a kind of spice)? OB; → *zassaru*

zanzīru "starling" NB; < Aram.

zapāru "to become rotten"? OB **G** (*a/a*) of a ship; > *zapru*; *zupru* I; *muzzapru*?

zapītu → *ṣapītu*

zappu(m), *sappu*, *azappu* **1.** Ass., O/jB "tuft of hair; bristle" **2.** O/jB "comb" **3.** O/jB "Pleiades" [MUL.MUL; MÚL.MÚL]

zapru(m) "bad, evil" O/jB; f. *zapurtu* "wickedness"; < *zapāru*

zapumma in *z. epēšu* "to steal" Nuzi; < Hurr.

zaqādum (or *z/saq/kādum*) mng. unkn. Mari; → *ziqdum*

zaqa(n)nu(m) (variety of *muššāru*-stone) O/jB, NA

zaqānu(m) "to wear a beard, be bearded" OAkk, OA, Bab. **G** [SU6] only infin. and stat., of men, goats, birds **D** stat. ~ G stat. OAkk, OA; < *ziqnu* denom.; > *zaqnu*; *zaqqinum*

zaqāpu(m), *saqāpu*, also *zakāpu* ? "to fix upright, plant, impale" **G** (*a/u*, pret. often *a/išqup*) [(GIŠ.)GUB] **1.** "erect" bed, door; stele, statue, standard; cult vessel; stat. of needle, potsherd, mountain, eyes, hair, breast, vein, penis "is upright" **2.** transf. "set up, strengthen" the weak **3.** "impale" on stake **4.** "plant" date-grove, trees, field **5.** NB leg. "pay an indemnity for" **6.** jB, NA also intrans. "rise up, attack, appear" of enemy, witness, snake **Gtn** iter. of G [GIŠ.GUB.MEŠ] **D** ~ G [GUB] "erect" objects; "lift up, make protrude" parts of body; "impale" **Dtn** iter. of D **Š** "cause to plant" **N** "rise up, be set up" **Ntn** iter. of N; > *zaqpu*, *zaqiptu*; *ziqpu*, *ziqpa*; *ziqipta*; *zaqīpu*; *zāqipānu*, *zāqipūtu*, *zāqipānūtu*; *muzaqqipu*; *zuqiqīpu*, *zuqiqīpānu*, *zuqaqīpāniš*

zaqāru(m), *saqāru* "to project, stick up; build high" OAkk, Bab. **G** (*i/i*, *a/a*, *a/u*) stat. of parts of body, features in exta "protrude"; of waves etc. "are high"; trans. "build high" **D** fact. of G; "boil up" liquid; "build (very) high" **Dt(n)**, **DRtn** metath. *tuza(qa)qquru* jB lex. **Št** OAkk(Susa) mng. unkn. **Ntn** iter. of G; > *zaqru*; *zuqāru*?; *ziqqurratu*; *zuqqurtu*; *tizqāru*

zaqāru → also *zakāru*

zaqātu(m) I "to sting" Bab. **G** (*a/u*, pres. also *izaqqit*) [RA] of scorpion, insect "sting, bite"; of parts of body "sting with pain" **D** ~ G

[TÁB.TÁB] fact. of G; "cause stinging pain to" **Dtn** iter. of D; > *ziqtu* I; *zaqqitu*

zaqātu(m) II "to be pointed" Bab. **G** only stat. and infin. of horns, teeth, weapons; of bow of a boat, parts of body "come to a point" **D** stat. "is very pointed"; > *zaqtu, zaqtiš; zuqtu; zuqqutu*

zaqību → *zaqīpu*

zāqipannūtu → *zāqipānūtu*

zāqipānu ~ "orchard worker" NB; < *zaqāpu*

zāqipānūtu, *zāqipannūtu* ~ "orchard work" NB; < *zāqipānu*

zaqiptu NB **1.** "vertical" **2.** (a standard); also deified; < *zaqpu*

zaqīpu, NA also *zaqību, ziqīp/bu* "stake" j/NB, NA for impaling victims; lex. "(palm) shoot"; < *zaqāpu*

zāqipūtu ~ "orchard work" NB; < *zaqāpu*

zāqīqiš → *zīqīqiš*

zāqīqu → *zīqīqu*

zaqnu "bearded" jB; < *zaqānu*

zaqpu "erect(ed); planted" Bab., NA [OB (GIŠ.)GUB.BA]; also NA "(person) who has arisen"; < *zaqāpu*

zaqqinum "heavily bearded" OB as PN; < *zaqānu*

zaqqipu mng. unkn. OB as PN

zaqqiqu "wind" jB lex.; < *ziāqu*; → *zīqīqu*

zaqqitu "mosquito" jB lex.; < *zaqātu* I

zaqru "high, tall" j/NB of physique; mountains, walls etc.; < *zaqāru*

zaqtiš "sharply pointed" jB; < *zaqtu*

zaqtu(m), once *saqtu* "pointed, coming to a point" O/jB of weapons; *z. ēni* "with staring eyes"; < *zaqātu* II

zāqu ~ "arm, strength"? jB lex.; < Sum.

zâqu → *ziāqu*

zaqzaqum mng. unkn. OB as PN

zarâ (or *ṣarâ*) ~ "divided into sections" jB(Ass.) [SUR.NE] of hymn, texts; → *zirâ* ?

zarābu → *zarāpu*

zarae (a desig. of barley) Nuzi; < Hurr.?

zārānū → *zērānū*

zarapḫu (a barley-bread)? Alal.; < Hurr.

zarāpu, *zarābu* "to purchase, acquire" NA **G** (*i/i*) leg.

zarāqu(m) "to sprinkle, strew" OAkk, O/jB, NA **G** (*a/u, i/i*) liquids; also dry matter; > *zerqu* II, *zerqūtu*?; *zarīqu, zirīqu*; *zāriqu*; *zurīqātu*?; *zuruqqu*; → *sarāqu*

zāratu "tent, awning" M/NA, M/NB

zarā'u → *zarû* II

zarbābu(m) Bab. **1.** (a drinking vessel) **2.** (a word for beer)

zardû (part of a waggon)? jB lex.; < Sum.

Zargatu (a month) jB lex.

zargû (a tool for turning corn-sheaves)? jB lex.; < Sum.

zarinnu(m), *za'irinnu* ~ "coarsely cleaned material" O/jB of bronze, wool

zarīnu (or *ṣarīnu*) (a stand for precious objects)? NB

zarīqu (a plant) jB lex.; < *zarāqu*

zāriqu; f. *zāriqtu* (a palace employee) M/NA; < *zarāqu*

zāriqu → also *zarriqu*

zarkidum → *zarqidum*

zarnānu (a precious stone) OB

zarnum → *sarnum*

Zarpānītu(m) (or *Ṣarpānītu(m)*) (a goddess, wife of Marduk) Bab., NA; < PlN Z/Ṣarpan or *ṣarpu* ?; → *Zēr-bānītu*

zarqidum (or *z/sark/qidum*) mng. unkn. OB lex.

zarrartu → *sarrartu*

zarriqu(m), *zāriqu, sarriqu(m)* ~ "iridescent" OAkk, Bab. of the eye; "(with) iridescent (eyes)"; also as PN, DN

zarriqūtu ~ "iridescence" j/NB

zarriš "like a swath" jB; < *sarru* II

zarru → *sarru* II.III

zarû(m) I "shaft, pole" O/jB of waggon; astr. in Ursa Major; < Sum.

zarû(m) II, *sarûm*, Ass. *zarā'u* "to winnow; scatter" Bab., M/NA **G** (*u/u*) [MAR] "winnow"; "sow"; "scatter" earth, salt, grain etc.; stat., of hair "is sparse"; > *zārû*; *zarûtu*; *mazrūtu*

zāru → *sarru* II

zārû(m), *zērû* Bab. **1.** "scattering", of trees "seeding", of hand "distributing" largesse **2.** "winnower" **3.** "begetter, progenitor"; < *zarû* II; → *zēru*

zâru, Ass. *zuāru(m)* "to twist, turn (round)" O/MA, jB **G** (*ū*) (of) parts of body, features of liver **D** ~ G **Dtn** iter. of D; > *zīru* I; *mazūru*

zâru → also *zêru*

zar'um → *zēru* II

zaruggu → *zuruqqu*

zarûtu "sowing, cultivation" jB(Ass.); < *zarû* II

zarzar → *zanzar*

zassaru(m) (a vegetable)? Mari?, NB; → *zanzar*

zaškum (or *zašqum*) (topog. term) OB

zataru → *sataru*

zateru → *sataru*

zātum (or *sātum, z/sattum* ?) (a type of flour) OAkk

za'tu → *ša'tu*

za'um (a bird) OB
za'û(m), *zā'u* "(aromatic) resin" Bab.; > *zu'û*?
zā'u → *ṣāḫu*
zâ'u → *ze'û*
za''uzu → *zu''uzu*
zāwiānum, *zāmânu* "enemy" Bab.(lit.); > *zāmânû*
zāyirānu → *zē'irānu*
zayyāru "foe, enemy" M/NB; < *zêru*
zayyārūtu "enmity" jB lex.; < *zayyāru*
zazabtu ? (a textile) NA
zazakku(m), *zakzakku* (a registry official) Bab., NA [DUB.SAR.ZAG.GA; NB DUB.ZAG; Mari DUB.SAR.ZA.GA-] also as PN
zâzu(m), OAkk, Ass. *zuāzu(m)* "to divide; get a share" **G** (pret. *izūz*) [BAR; BA; jB stat. also BA.ḪAL] leg. property, estate etc.; parts of the body, water, smoke etc.; lands, people etc.; intrans. "become separate" **D** "distribute, divide" **Dt** pass. of D **N** [BAR] pass. of G; < *zīzum* I, *zīzānu*, *zīzūtum*, *zittu*, *zīztu*; *zūzu* I, *zūzam*, *zūzâ*; *zā'izānu*, *zā'iztum*; *zu''uzu*, *zu''uztu*; *muza''iztu*
ze'ārum → *zêru*
zebēlu → *zabālu*
zēbu → *zībum* III
ze'ēru → *zēru* I; *zêru*
zē'irānu/û, NA *zā'/yirānu* "enemy; hostile" NA, NB; < *zā'eru*
ze'īru → *zēru* I
zē'iru → *zā'eru*
zemû "to be angry" **G** Ug. var. of *zenû* II
zenênû "angry" Bogh. lex.; < *zenû* I
zennē'ûm "malevolent" OB lex.; < *zenû* II
zenû(m) I; f. *zenītu(m)* "angry, offended" Bab., NA; < *zenû* II
zenû(m) II, *zanûm*, Ass. *zanā'u(m)* (Ug. → *zemû*) "to be angry" **G** (*i/i*) "be angry, offended" (with = *itti*) **Gtn** iter. **Gt** "be displeased with one another" **D** "make" s.o., heart "angry" with (= *itti*) s.o. **Š** "cause to be(come) angry"; > *zenû* I, *zenûtu*; *zenênû*; *zennē'ûm*
zenûtu "anger" M/jB; < *zenû* I
zērānū, *zārānū* pl. tant. "seed(-corn)"? O/jB; < *zēru* II
zērātu(m), *zīrātu(m)*, Mari *zērētum* pl. "hostilities" O/jB esp. with *apālu*, *šapāru*, "hostile messages"; < *zēru* I
Zēr-bānītu 'seed-producing' Bab., NA etym. of fDN *Zarpānītu*; < *zēru* II + *banû* IV
zērētum → *zērātu*
zerḫu "sunrise" jB lex.
zēriqu (or *zēriku*) "grain fodder" Nuzi
zērīu "seed(-corn)" Nuzi; < *zēru* II or Hurr.?
zerkuppu → *sarkuppu*
zermandu (or *kulmandu*?), *zermattu* ~ "small animals, vermin" jB
zermu (or *sermu*) (a copper vessel) OB
zerpu (a casket)? jB lex., comm.
zerqatu → *zerqu* I
zerqātu → *zerqu* II
zerqu I; f. *zerqatu* **1.** jB [SA.A.GAL] "desert lynx, caracal"? **2.** M/NA. (desig. of a sheep)
zerqu II; pl. f. jB **1.** "litter, strewn plants" for domestic animals **2.** (desig. of snake's faeces)?; < *zarāqu*
zerqūtu (a head covering) jB lex.; < *zarāqu* ?
zerramannu → *serramannu*
zerretu(m) (an ornamental chain) OB, Qatna, NA
zerru I (a reed fence) jB lex.; → *būnzerru*
zerru II (a type of clay) jB lex.; < Sum.
zerru III (or *serru*) (desig. of an ass)? Nuzi
zertu (a stone object) MB
zēru(m) I, *zīru(m)*, NB also *ze'ē/īru* "hated; loathsome" Bab.; < *zêru*
zēru(m) II, *zīru*, OA *zar'um* "seed(s)" [(ŠE.)NUMUN] **1.** of plants, trees etc. **2.** "sown land, arable" **3.** human "semen", "offspring, descendant(s)"; > *zērānū*, *zērīu*?; → *Zēr-bānītu*; *zarû* II
zēru → also *zīru* III
zērû → *zārû*
zêru(m), OB occas., OA *ze'ārum*, M/jB also *ze'ēru*, *zâru* "to dislike, hate; reject" **G** (pres. *izêr*, Ass. *ize''ar*) **Gt** "hate each other" **N** "be hated"; > *zēru* I, *zērātu*, *zērūtu*; *zīru* III; *zā'eru*, *zā'erūtu*, *zē'irānu*; *zayyāru*, *zayyārūtu*; *muzzirrū*
zērūtu(m), *zīrūtu(m)* "hatred" O/jB; < *zēru* I
zerze(r)ru, occas. *zerzīru*, *zeruzeru*, *zizru* "very small" M/jB **1.** (a reed) **2.** (a locust); < *zīru* II
ze'û (or *zê'u*, *zâ'u* ?) mng. unkn. **G** NB **D** NA
zēzenu (a disease) jB
zēzu → *zīzum* I
ziānātu → *siānātu*
ziāqu(m), *zâqu* "to blow, waft, gust" O/jB, M/NA **G** [RI-] of wind; demon, illness; of scent, laughter "waft"; of assault "rush on" **Gtn** iter. of G; > *zīqu* I; *zīqīqu*, *zīqīqiš*; *ziqziqqu*, *ziqziqqiš*; *zaqqiqu*
zibānītu(m) "weighing scales" [GIŠ.ÉRIN; ZI.BA.AN.NA]; astr. "(constellation) Libra" [MUL.GIŠ.ÉRIN; MUL.ZI.BA.AN.NA]
zibānu "Libra" NB [MUL.GIŠ.ÉRIN]

zibbānu (a fat-tailed sheep) jB lex.; < *zibbatu*

zibbatu(m), *sibbatu(m)*, *z/simbatu*; du. *zibbā* "tail" [KUN] of animal etc.; transf. "tail-end" of army, canal etc.; astr. "tail" of heavenly body, pl. "Pisces"; OB lex. *ša z.* (a prof.)?; > *zibbānu*; *zīpu*?

zibbu → *zīpu*

zibbūtu → *ṣippūtu*

zibiānu (or *sipiānu*) (an object) Qatna

zibibiānum, OAkk also *zizibiānum*, jB *zi/abibânu*, *šibibânu*, MA *s/šib/pib/piānu*, NA *sabubânu*, Nuzi *zibibiannu*, also *kizibiannu* (a spice, phps.) "black cumin" OAkk, O/jB, M/NA; MA also (an ornament); → *sabūbu*; *zībum* III

zibibītum (a spice plant) O/jB lex.; = *zibītum* I ?

zibillu mng. unkn. NB; < *zabālu* ?

zibingû (a cup) jB lex.

zibītum I (a kind of spice seed)? OAkk, early OB; = *zibibītum* ?; → *z.* II

zibītu(m) II (a stone) jB; = *z.* I ?

ziblu "waste matter, refuse, debris" M/NB, NA; < *zabālu* ?

zibnatu(m) (a spice plant)? MB(Alal.) lex.; OB as PlN; < *zibnu* ?; → *yarzibnu*

zibnu(m); pl. f. *zibnātu(m)* **1.** O/jB, MA (a reed mat) **2.** OAkk, OB(Ešn.) (a month name); also in PN; > *zibnatu*?

zibtu(m) (a stone) OAkk ?, O/jB

zibtum → also *ṣibtum* IV

zibû → *zību* II.III

zību(m) I "food offering" O/jB, NA

zību II, *zibû* jB **1.** "jackal" **2.** "vulture" [NU.UM. MA.MUŠEN]; > *zībû*

zībum III, *zibû(m)*, *zēbu*, MA also *zīpu* "black cumin" OAkk, Bab., MA [(Ú.)GAMUN.GE$_6$ (.SAR)] freq. in (grind)stone for *z.*; → *zibibiānum*

zību(m) IV (a blister)? O/jB; < *zâbu*

zību → also *zīpu*

zībû "jackal-like" jB (desig. of locust); < *zību* II

zidubdubbû pl. tant. (a small heap of flour) jB mag. [ZÌ.DUB.DUB(.BA/BU)]; < Sum.

zigarrû (a type of bed) jB lex.; < Sum.

zigiduḫḫum (a confection of flour) OAkk; < Sum.

zigû(m) (a piece of cloth)? O/MB; < Sum.?

ziḫḫum (a mark on the liver) OB (jB mostly → *dīḫu*) [MI.IB.ḪI ?; Susa ZA.ZÁḪ ?]; < Sum.?

zīḫu → *sīḫu* III

zi'īru → *zīru* III

zikartu "manhood" jB in *kalīt z.* "kidney of m." = "testicle"; < *zikaru*

zikaru(m), *zikru*, *zikkaru* "male, virile" [NITA; NÍTA] stat. "is manly"; of humans, animals, plants etc.; as desig. of stones, clouds (mng. uncert.); > *zikartu*; *zikrūtu*; *zakkāru*; *zukrum*

zikarūtu → *zikrūtu*

zikkaru → *zikaru*

zikru(m), *si/eqru*; jB st. constr. *siqar* "utterance; name" Bab., NA [MU; occas. NITA] "utterance, speech; command"; "name, naming"; in *z. šumi(m)* "mention of the name; reputation", OB idiomatic ~ "(a type of) gift"; in PNs *Z.-DN* "(By) command of DN"; < *zakāru*

zikru → also *zikaru*

zikrūtu(m), *zikarūtu* "manliness, virility" Bab.(lit.) [NÍTA-]; also "male sexual activity"; < *zikaru*

zikšu → *sikšu* I

zikuḫum (a part of the bridle)? OA

zikulittu (desig. of chairs, beds) Nuzi

ziku(r)rudû liter. "cutting of life" Bogh., jB, NA [ZI.KU$_5$.RU.DA/DÈ; occas. ZI.KU.RU.DA, ZI$^{!?}$. GUR.RU.DA] mag. (a type of evil spell); < Sum.

zikûtu "cleansing" NB of garments; "freeing" of slave; < *zakû* II

zillaḫta (or *ṣillaḫta*) (a bowl) Am.; < W.Sem.

zillānu "small" jB lex.

zillaru (or *sillaru*) (a gold object) Qatna

zilukannu (or *silukannu*), *zulukannu* (desig. of horses etc.) Alal., Nuzi; < Hurr.

zilullîš "like a vagrant" jB

zilullû, *sulilû*, *silullû* "vagrant, tramp" jB, M/NB; < Sum.?

zilullûtu "condition of vagrant" jB lex.

zimbānu ~ "feudal tenure" NB; < Iran.?

zimbatu → *zibbatu*

zimbuḫaru → *zinbuḫaru*

ziminzu → *zimizzu*

zimiu mng. unkn. Am.; < Eg.?

zimizzu(m), *ziminzu* (bead of specific shape)? OA, O/jB

zimmatu "lamentation" OB lex., var. of *dimmatu*, *zinnatu*

zimru, occas. *zimmeru* "song" MA, j/NB; < *zamāru* II

zīmu(m) "face, appearance" Bab., NA [(UZU.)MÚŠ] mostly pl.; "face, features" of person; "appearance" of temple, stars etc.; of metal; *z. pānī* (a piece of military equipment, phps.) "face(-guard)"?; OB, Mari in *ana zīm(i)* "corresponding, according to; according as"; OB lex. *bēl z.* "person in disguise"?

zimzeḫena (a fabric or garment) OAkk; < Hurr.

zimzimmu, NA *zinzimmu* (a red onion) j/NB, NA

zinbuḫaru, *zimbuḫaru* (a leather object) jB lex.

zingurrum → *singurru*

zinḫanaše (a class of person) Ug.; < Hurr.

zinibtu → *sinibtu*

zinnānu → *zinnu*

zinnatu (a lament) jB; → *zimmatu*

zinnātu(m) pl. tant. "support, sustenance" OB, Bogh.? of person; NB "provisioning" of temple; < *zanānu* II

zinnu(m), *zīnu*; MB pl. also *zinnānu* "rain" O/jB, NA freq. pl.; *bāb z.* "rainwater drain"; < *zanānu* I

zinû(m), *sinûm* "rib of palm-frond" O/jB [(GIŠ.)ZÍ/ZI.NA(.GIŠIMMAR)] *dalat z.* "door made of palm-rib"; < Sum.

zīnu(m) (a gem) Mari, Qatna; < *za'ānu* ?

zīnu → also *zinnu*

zinûtu → *zenûtu*

zinzaru'u (a medicament, phps.) "ginger" NA; < Hurr.?

zinzilku (a kind of oil)? Nuzi; < Hurr.?

zinzimmu → *zimzimmu*

zipadû "incantation formula" jB; < Sum.

zipinu (or *šazipīnu*) mng. unkn. NA

ziptu "pitch, bitumen" NB; < Aram.

ziptum → also *ṣibtum* IV

zīpu (or *zību*, *zibbu*) (desig. of sheep, phps.) "fat-tailed" (i.e. < *zibbatu*) MA

zīpu → also *zībum* III; *zi'pu*

zi'pu, *zīpu* j/NB **1.** "mould" for casting bronze; "impression" cast in clay; a cast coin **2.** (a skin disease)

ziqātum → *ziqtum* II

zīqātu → *zīqtu*

ziqbu → *ziqpu*

ziqdum, *ziqdūtum* mng. unkn. Mari; → *zaqādum*

ziqību → *zaqīpu*

ziqipta "vertically" NA; < *zaqāpu*

ziqīpu → *zaqīpu*

zīqīqiš, jB *zāqīqiš* "into (the) wind" M/jB esp. (to count) "as nothing"; < *zīqīqu*

zīqīqu(m), *zāqīqu* "wind, breeze" Bab.; also ~ "nothingness"; "phantom"; *(bīt) z.* "haunted place"; "dream"; (d)Z. [AN.ZÀ.GAR(.RA); AN.ZA.GÀR] god of dreams; < *ziāqu*; → *zaqqiqu*

ziqittu ~ "young cattle" jB

ziqnānu "bearded" jB of man; (a type of fish); < *ziqnu*

ziqnu(m) f. "beard" [SU$_6$] of man; *ša ziqni* "bearded man" (i.e. non-eunuch); of goat, bird; in names of plants; of light; (a kind of precious stone); > *zaqānu*; *ziqnānu*

ziqpa "vertically, upright" M/jB; also "(sexually) erect"; < *ziqpu*

ziqpu(m), MA also *ziqbu* Bab., M/NA [ŠE.DÙ] **1.** "shoot, sapling" **2.** "pole, shaft" **3.** Alal. "measuring-rod" (as a unit of measurement) **4.** MB math., NA "carrying-pole" for sesame, birds etc. **5.** "blade" of tool, weapon **6.** NA "(mountain) peak" **7.** OB math. "perpendicular; height" **8.** j/NB, NA astr. "culmination, zenith" of star **9.** jB lex. *ša z.* (a vessel)?; < *zaqāpu*

ziqqatātu mng. unkn. NB family name

ziqqatu → *sikkatu* I

ziqqatû (a small fish) j/NB [NUN.BAR.ḪUŠ.KU$_6$]

ziqqu(m) I **1.** OB (a pillar)? **2.** MA (an ornament) **3.** jB in *z. šinnī* "eye-tooth"?; < Sum.

ziqqu II (a woven fabric) M/NB

ziqqu III, *zīqu*; pl. m. & f. "wineskin" NA [KUŠ.SAL ?]; < Aram.

ziqqu IV (a kind of flour)? Ug. lex.; < Sum.?

ziqqu V (an alkaline plant) jB lex.

ziqqu → also *zīqu* I

ziqqurratu(m), Ass. *siqqurrutu*, j/NB also *ziqratu* "ziggurrat, temple tower" [U$_6$.NIR], jB transf. "peak" of mountain; also deified; MA "(cake in shape of a) *z.*"; < *zaqāru*; → *zuqāru*

ziqtu(m) I "sting, sharp point" Bab. [TAB] **1.** "sting" of scorpion, insect; "point" of arrow, goad etc. **2.** "sting-mark, pimple" on entrails, face; (a disease) **3.** (a spiny fish); < *zaqātu* I

ziqtum II in *ša ziqātim* mng. unkn. OB lex.

zīqtu "torch" NA, NB; < *zīqu* II

zīqu(m) I, *sīqu*, *ziqqu* "draught, breeze" Bab., NA, also "breath" of person; *bāb z.* "ventilation hole"; < *ziāqu*

zīqu II f. "torch" MA; > *zīqtu*

zīqu → also *ziqqu* III

ziqziqqiš "like a gale" jB; < *ziqziqqu*

ziqziqqu(m), *siqsiqqu* "gale, storm-wind" O/jB; OB as PN; < *zīqu* I

zirâ mng. unkn. j/NB comm.; → *zarâ* ?

zīrātu → *zērātu*

ziriānum (or *s/ṣiriānum*) (a food)? OB

zirīqu(m) (an irrigation device, prob.) "shaduf" OAkk, O/jB [GIŠ.ZI.RÍ.QUM/QÙM]; med. "pipette, dropper"?; < *zarāqu*; → *zuruqqu*

zirqu → *sirku*

zirru (or *zīru*) (desig. of *entu* priestess of Sîn) jB

zirru → also *zīru* II

zīru I "twisted" jB lex. of garlic; < *zâru*

zīru II, *zirru* "small" jB lex. of reed, locust, fish; > *zerzerru*

zīru III, *zēru, zi'īru* "hate" j/NB esp. in mag. [ḪUL.GIG]; < *zêru*

zīru → also *sīru* II; *zēru* I.II; *zirru*

zirua mng. unkn. Nuzi

zirušŝu (a reed fence)? NB

zirūtu (s.th. in the body) jB

zīrūtu → *zērūtu*

ziruwena pl. (wooden objects) Nuzi; < Hurr.

zisurrû "magic circle" M/jB [ZÌ.SUR.RA] of flour, whitewash; < Sum.

zišagallu ~ "divine encouragement" M/jB; < Sum.

zitlunīum (desig. of sheep breed) OA; < PlN ?

zittu(m) usu. f.; pl. *zīzātu(m)*, NB also *zinātu* "share" [ḪA.LA; also OB ḪA.LA.BA; OA ḪA.LÁ] "share, portion" of estate, other assets; "division, total to be divided"; "dividing line" between pairs of organs etc.; Ug. "due, proper deserts"; Bab. *bēl z.*, NA also *ša z.* "shareholder, partner"; < *zâzu*; → *zīztu*

zitūrum (a pot or container) OAkk, OB ?

zizānu, once *sisānu* (a cricket)? jB; OAkk, OB as PN ?

zīzānu ~ (s.th. divided in half) jB lex.; < *zâzu*

zīzātu → *zittu*

zizbannum → *šizbānu*

zizibiānum → *zibibiānum*

zizibu → *šizbu*

ziznu "small" jB lex., also of fish; < Sum.

zizru → *zerzerru*

zīztu "division" Nuzi; < *zâzu*; → *zittu*

zīzum I, MA *zēzu* "divided" OB, MA, esp. in *lā z.* "not (yet) divided" of assets, heirs; also math., mng. uncert.; < *zâzu*

zīzu(m) II "emmer" OB(Mari etc.), NA [ZÍZ]; NA *bēl zīzi* (a festival)?; < Sum.

zīzu III "teat" NA

zīzūtum "division" OB(Susa); < *zīzum* I

zizziktu → *sissiktu*

zizzum, *ṣiṣṣu* "hiss" O/jB of snake, bird

zû(m) I "excrement" O/jB [ŠE$_{10}$(=KU)] "faeces", "dung" of animal; *zê Nisaba* "chaff" [IN.BUBBU.AN.NA]; "waste product" (of ear; of potting, milling, matting etc.); in plant names *zê malāḫi, summati* "sailor's, dove's dung"; → *ezûm* I; *muqappil zê*

zû(m) II, *sû* "date-palm fibre" Bab. [GIŠ.ZÚ.GIŠIMMAR]; < Sum.

zû → also *ṣû*

zuābum → *zâbu*

zuāru → *zâru*

zuāzu → *zâzu*

zubbu(m), *zumbu, subbum*, NA *zunbu* "fly" Bab., NA [NIM] "flying insect"; (a gem in fly shape); as PN; *ša z.* "fly whisk" jB(Ass.); assoc. with animals, e.g. *z. kalbi* 'dog-fly'

zūbum "bent stick, crook" OB lex.; < Sum.

zubullûm, Ass. *zubullā'u* "marriage gift" OB, M/NA; < *zabālu*

zubultum "princess" Mari; < W.Sem.

zubuttû jB lex. **1.** (a club) **2.** (a fish); < Sum.

zugulûm "man with big teeth" OB lex.; < Sum.

zuguzi (or *sukusi*) (a measure of capacity) Alal.

zuḫarru ~ "sparkling"? MB(Ass.) of the eyes

zuḫru → *šaḫūrum* II

zuḫum → *ṣuḫum*

zuka/iqīpu → *zuqiqīpu*

zukkatu, *zukkutu* (a physical disability)? jB lex.

zukkû(m) "purified, cleansed" O/jB; < *zakû* II; Ass. → *zakkû*

zukkurūtu mng. unkn. jB lex.; < *zakāru*

zukkutu → *zukkatu*

zukrum "male personnel" Mari; < *zikaru*

zuku (or *suku*) (objects of copper)? Early Mari

zukû (a kind of frit or glass) M/jB; < *zakû* II

zūku I "clarity" jB, of river water; < *zakû* II

zūku II "infantry" NA esp. *z. šēpē*

zukurrû mng. unkn. jB lex.; < *zakāru* ?

zukūtum ~ "clear instruction" OA; < *zakû* II

zulāmātu → *ṣulāmātu*

zuluḫḫû → *sulumḫû*

zulukannu → *zilukannu*

zulumḫû → *sulumḫû*

zumāru ~ "refrain of a song"? NA; < *zamāru* II

zumbu → *zubbu*

zumītum → *sumītum*

zummû I "(one) deprived, who must do without" jB; < *zummû* II

zummû(m) II **D** Bab., NA(lit.) "to be deprived of, lack, miss"; later trans. "deprive (of = acc.)" **Š** OB "deprive"; > *zummû* I

zummunu (or *ṣummunu*) **D** mng. unkn. jB lex.

zumru(m), *zurru*, occas. *zu'ru* "body; person" Bab. [SU] of human, god, animal etc.; OB st. abs. *zumur(ma)* "in person"; transf. "body" of troops, "interior" of building, city, land; OB *ina zumur* "within" a timespan

zumurtum → *zamartum*

zunbu → *zubbu*

zunnu(m) I "rain" Bab., NA [(IM.)ŠÈG] freq. pl.; < *zanānu* I

zunnu II in *z. ramāni* "(o.'s) own resources"? jB; < *zanānu* II

zunnuqu mng. unkn. jB lex.

zuntu (a door in a city-gate)? jB lex.

zunu in *aban z.* mng. unkn. jB

zunukru (or *sunukru*) (part of a whip) Nuzi; < Hurr.?

zununnû "marriage gift" MB from father-in-law to bridegroom; < *zanānu* II

zunzi (a wooden object) Nuzi

zunzunnatu (a shoe) jB

zunzunu (a locust) jB lex.

zunzuraḫḫu (a military groom)? NA; < Hurr.?

zupku (or *z/supk/qu*) mng. unkn. Nuzi

zuprinnu (a bristle)? NB; < Aram.

zupru I in *zupur pānī* ~ "scowl"? O/jB lex.; < *zapāru*

zupru II (a metal object) Nuzi

zūpu "hyssop" or "marjoram"? NB; < Aram.

zupumma in *z. epēšu* "to give back"? Nuzi; < Hurr.

zuqaqīpāniš "like a scorpion" jB; < *zuqiqīpu*

zuqaqīpānu → *zuqiqīpānu*

zuqa(q)qīpu → *zuqiqīpu*

zuqāru mng. unkn. (= *ziqqurratu* ?) NA; < *zaqāru* ?

zuqiqīpānu, *zuqaqīpānu* "scorpion plant" jB; < *zuqiqīpu*

zuqiqīpu(m), *zuqa(q)qīpu*, *zuka/iqīpu* "scorpion" [GÍR.TAB]; also *aban z.* (desig. of stone); astr. "Scorpius"; < *zaqāpu*; > *zuqiqīpānu*, *zuqaqīpāniš*

zuqqurtu "elevation" jB comm.; < *zaqāru*

zuqqutu(m) "pointed, coming to a point"; < *zaqātu* II

zuqtu "mountain peak" jB(Ass.); < *zaqātu* II

zuqtu → also *suqtu*

zuqû mng. unkn. NB

zūqutu; pl. *zūqāte* (a small metal dish) NA

zurāyum, *zurā'um* (or *su...*); pl. *zurāyātu* (a temple festival)? Mari

zurīqātu mng. unkn. jB comm.; < *zarāqu* ?

zurmaḫâtum (desig. of wooden beams) Mari; < PlN

zurru → *zumru*

zurû (or *ṣurû*) mng. unkn. jB lex.

zu'ru → *zumru*

zuruḫ "arm" Am.; < W.Sem.

zuruqqu(m), Ass. *zaru(g)gu* (a wooden device, phps.) "shaduf" Bab., M/NA; < *zarāqu*; → *zirīqu*

zurzu(m) "sack" Ass., M/jB; esp. OA a small double packsack made of goat-hair

zūtu(m), *zu'tu*, *izūtu* "sweat; exudation" Bab., M/NA [IR] of humans, horses

zu'û D "to perfume"? lex. **Š** jB caus. "make smell sweet"; < *za'û* denom.?

zu''unu(m) "decorated" O/jB; also OB as fPN *Zu'untum*; < *za'ānu* D

zu''upu (or *ṣu''upu*) **D** mng. unkn. jB lex.

zu''uztu, *zûztu* "division" NB of property; "allocation" of field; < *zâzu* D

zu''uzu, NA *za''uzu* "divided" NA, NB, of fields "allocated"; NA also as subst. "distribution"; < *zâzu* D

zuwar → *suwar*

zūzâ ~ "from time to time" M/jB in *ana z.*, *azzūzâ*; < *zâzu*

zūzam "half-league" O/jB; < *zūzu* I

zuzi(l)lu (a prayer)? jB lex.; → *aršuzuzil*

zûztu → *zu''uztu*

zuzû mng. unkn. jB comm.

zūzu I "half unit" M/jB [BAR] **1.** of the shekel **2.** of the *qû* **3.** of the league (→ *zūzam*); < *zâzu*

zūzu II "gold" jB lex.

zuzukannu (desig. of oxen) Alal.; < Hurr.?

zuzzulaḫḫu → *sussulaḫḫu*